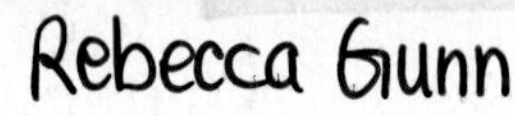

educational
PSYCHOLOGY
Constructing Learning

To Alexandra and Laura
We love you deeply as you experience the rites of passage to adulthood.
We learn from you every day about life, love, joy, sadness and pain.
Our lives are far richer because of both of you.
Dennis and Valentina

educational PSYCHOLOGY

Constructing Learning

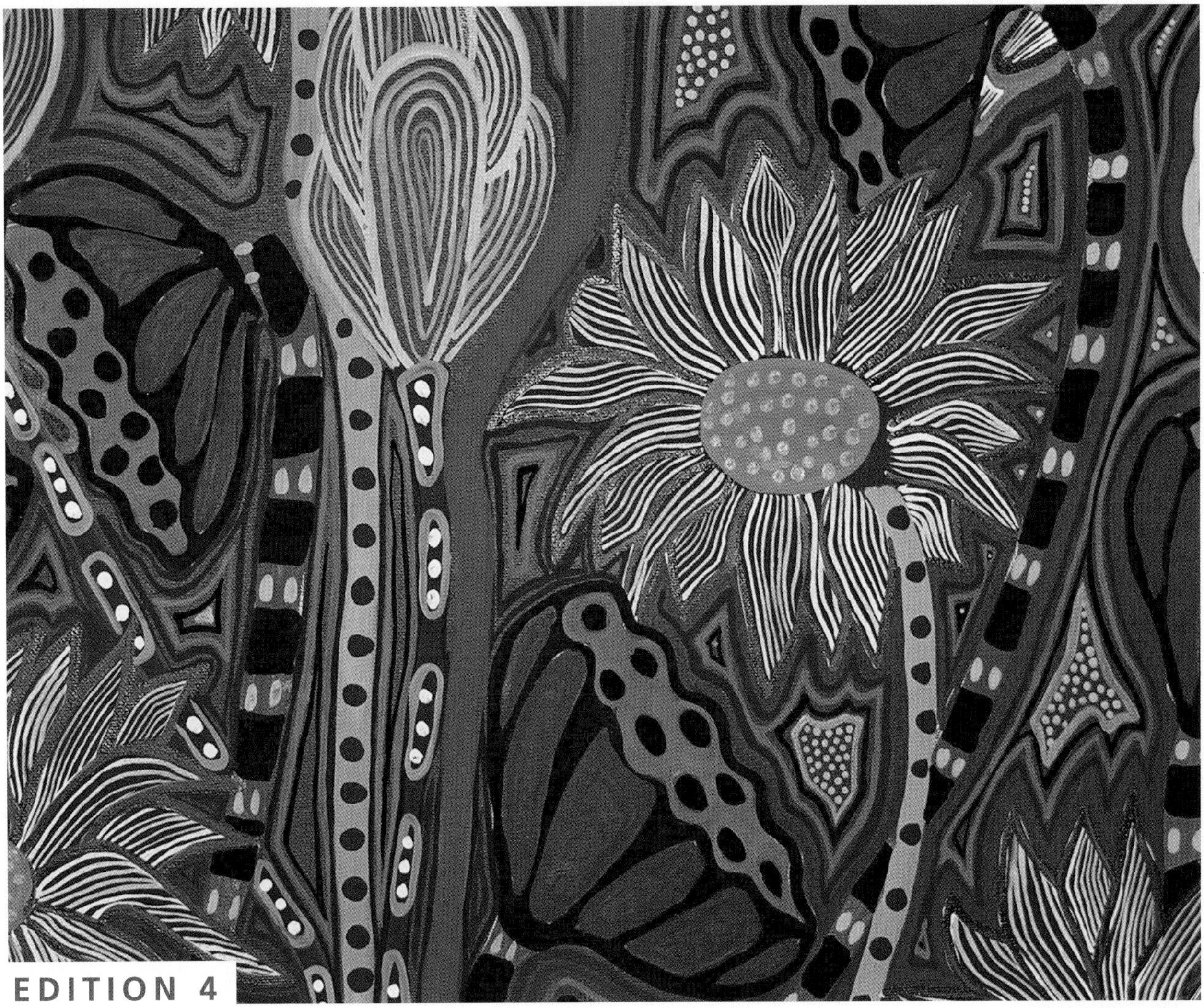

EDITION 4

Dennis M. McInerney & Valentina McInerney

PEARSON
Prentice Hall

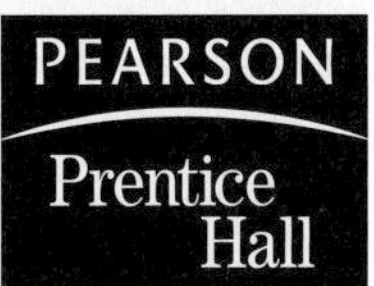

Pearson Education Australia
Unit 4, Level 3
14 Aquatic Drive
Frenchs Forest NSW 2086

www.pearsoned.com.au

Senior Editor and Development Manager: Alison Green
Senior Project Editor: Rebecca Pomponio
Editorial Coordinator: Jill Gillies
Copy Editor and Proofreader: Robyn Flemming
Permissions Coordinator: Louise Burke
Cover and internal design by DiZign
Cover painting 'Lotus in Bloom' by Patricia Marrfurra/Merrepen Arts Centre
Typeset by Midland Typesetters, Australia

Printed in China (GCC)

1 2 3 4 5 10 09 08 07 06
National Library of Australia
Cataloguing-in-Publication Data

Educational psychology : constructing learning.

4th ed.
Bibliography.
Includes index.
For tertiary students.
ISBN 0 7339 7399 X.

1. Educational psychology – Textbooks. I. McInerney, V.
II. Title.

370.15

An imprint of Pearson Education Australia (a division of Pearson Australia Group Pty Ltd)

Brief contents

Contents

PART 2 MANAGING EFFECTIVE LEARNING

CHAPTER 7
Motivation for effective learning: Cognitive perspectives *206*

CHAPTER 8
Classroom management and cooperative group work for effective learning *256*

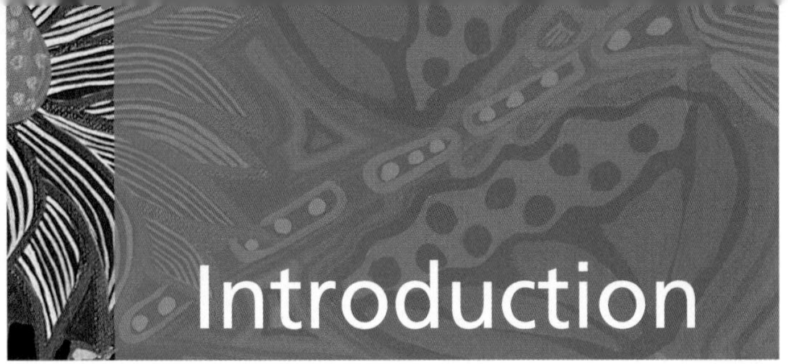

Introduction

Welcome to the fourth edition of *Educational Psychology: Constructing Learning*. We are delighted that users have found the book very useful over the more than ten years it has now been in print. It was a significant challenge to make the book fresh and alive for contemporary courses in educational and developmental psychology where there are so many exciting developments of interest and use to educators. We enjoyed the challenge and hope that our book fulfils its mission of providing educators with the most up-to-date information available to inform their educational practices.

We have updated the content and references to reflect what research and scholarly journals over the last four years have treated as 'hot topics'. The recommended readings at the end of each chapter have also been updated to present the most recent articles related to topics of interest in each chapter.

We have retained the structure of the third edition, as we know that many users are familiar with and like this format. We have also kept a number of features that have proven popular with our users, such as the Overview, Learner-centred Psychological Principles, Teacher's Case Book, What Would You Do?, Action Stations, Question Points and Essentials Tables.

Thematic parts

The text is divided into three main parts: stimulating effective learning, managing effective learning, and understanding developmental needs of children and effective teaching and learning.

We have also included a brief overview that sets the scene for the material to be covered.

Text website

To support the text we have extended and enhanced our website. The website includes a wealth of extra material to enhance your use of the text and to stimulate further inquiry. Our www modules include the following—chapter overview and objectives, lecture suggestions, multiple choice questions, test your knowledge, essays, activities, essentials of, key terms, web destinations and activities, video clips and recommended reading. The information technology chapters from the previous edition have been updated and consolidated into one chapter that is now available electronically on the website.

The website is at
www.pearsoned.com.au/mcinerney

Overview

We have also included a brief overview that sets the scene for the material to be covered.

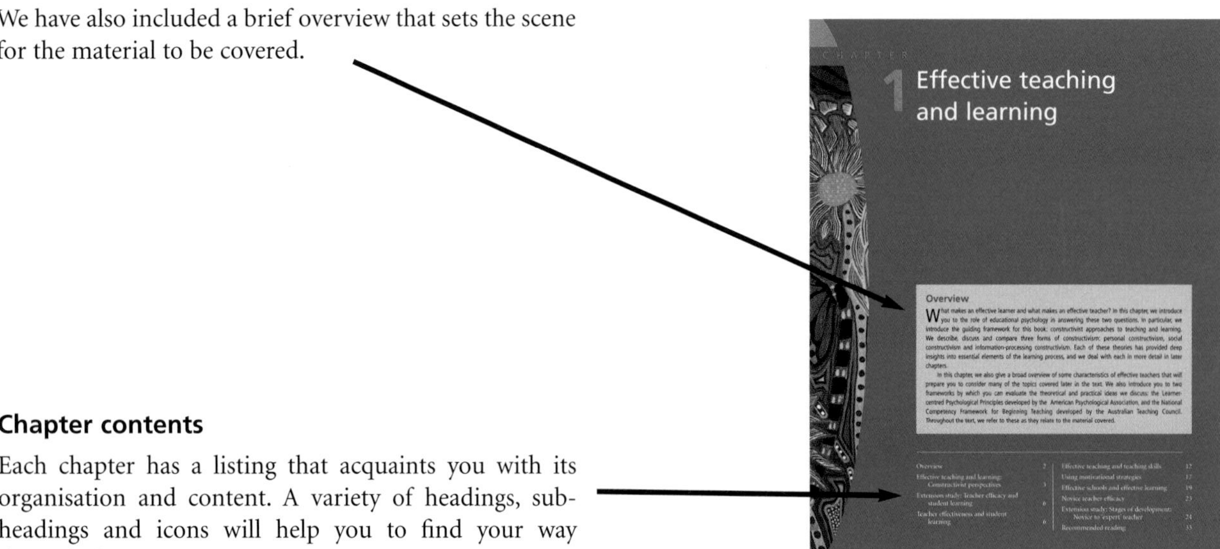

Chapter contents

Each chapter has a listing that acquaints you with its organisation and content. A variety of headings, subheadings and icons will help you to find your way through the text.

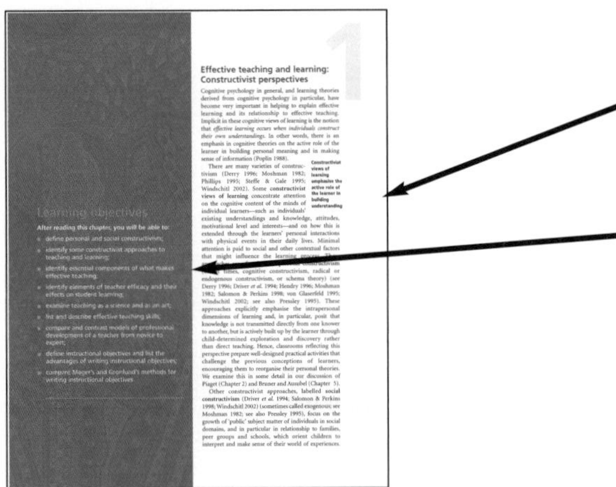
Effective teaching and learning: Constructivist perspectives

Learning objectives

Margin notes

These assist students by highlighting important concepts within the section.

Learning Objectives

Each chapter begins with a comprehensive list of learning objectives to guide the learner and instructor. These objectives may be used to gauge the level of mastery of the content covered in each chapter.

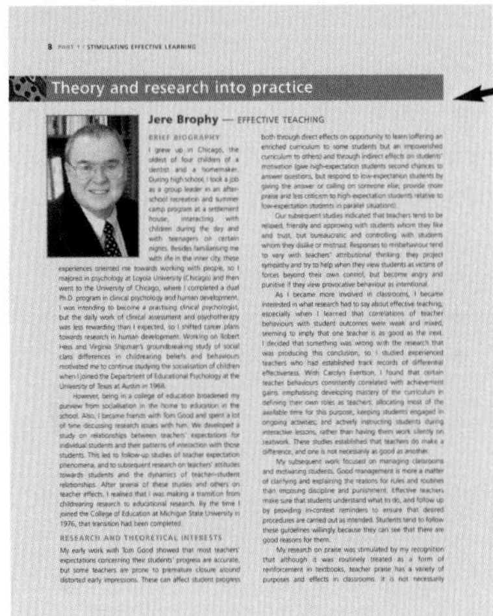
Theory and research into practice

Jere Brophy — EFFECTIVE TEACHING

Theory and Research into Practice

Twenty-six pre-eminent researchers from Australia, the United States and New Zealand have contributed significant sections related to their research interests and the applied value of their research to educational settings. These sections are very stimulating and present cutting-edge information on a range of essential topics for educators. Each Theory and Research into Practice section concludes with a number of recommended readings as well as several activities to engage students actively. These Theory and Research into Practice sections may be used to extend students' knowledge, and as exercises for assessment.

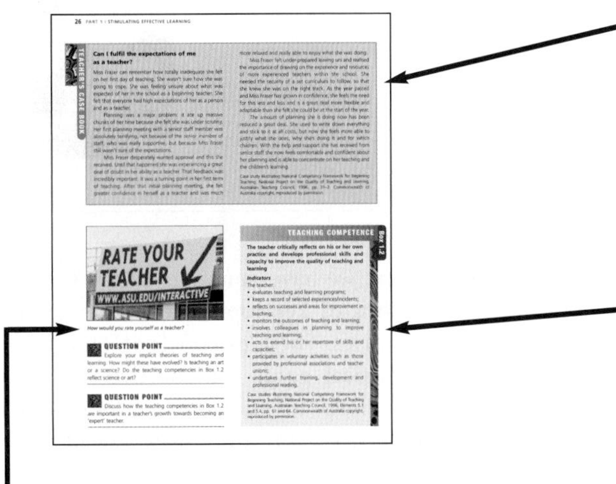

Can I fulfil the expectations of me as a teacher?

TEACHING COMPETENCE

QUESTION POINT

Teacher's case book

Selected case studies, drawn from the National Competency Framework for Beginning Teaching and produced by the Australian Teaching Council, provide a bird's-eye view of teacher–student interaction in real educational settings. An associated case study activity provides an opportunity to explore teachers' common knowledge and theory.

Teaching competence boxes

These present the basic teaching competencies for beginning teaching drawn from the National Competency Framework for Beginning Teaching produced by the Australian Teaching Council. Throughout we illustrate how material covered in the text addresses these competencies and provides the reader with suggestions on how to demonstrate these competencies through the relevant indicators.

Photo captions

The photographs have been chosen to stimulate thought and discussion on the topics illustrated. Many photographs have question-focused captions for you to consider

Extension Study

Each chapter includes one or more extension studies. These sections are selected to extend students' knowledge beyond the basic, and to challenge them to search further for information to guide their teaching. Instructors may elect to set particular extension studies for students desiring to complete higher levels of work for assessment purposes or for group activities.

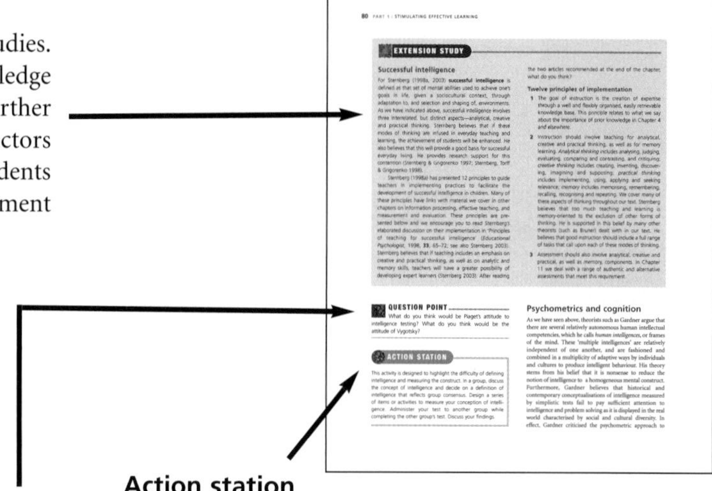

80 PART 1 | STIMULATING EFFECTIVE LEARNING

EXTENSION STUDY

Successful intelligence

For Sternberg (1998a, 2003) **successful intelligence** is defined as that set of mental abilities used to achieve one's goals in life, given a sociocultural context, through adaptation to, and selection and shaping of, environments. As we have indicated above, successful intelligence involves three interrelated, but distinct aspects—analytical, creative and practical thinking. Sternberg believes that if these modes of thinking are infused in everyday teaching and learning, the achievement of students will be enhanced. He also believes that this will provide a good basis for successful everyday living. He provides research support for this contention (Sternberg & Grigorenko 1997; Sternberg, Torff & Grigorenko 1998).

Sternberg (1998a) has presented 12 principles to guide teachers in implementing practices to facilitate the development of successful intelligence in children. Many of these principles have links with material we cover in other chapters on information processing, effective teaching, and measurement and evaluation. These principles are presented below and we encourage you to read Sternberg's elaborated discussion on their implementation in 'Principles of teaching for successful intelligence' (*Educational Psychologist*, 1998, **33**, 65–72; see also Sternberg 2003). Sternberg believes that if teaching includes an emphasis on creative and practical thinking, as well as on analytic and memory skills, teachers will have a greater possibility of developing expert learners (Sternberg 2003). After reading the two articles recommended at the end of the chapter, what do you think?

Twelve principles of implementation

1 The goal of instruction is the creation of expertise through a well and flexibly organised, easily retrievable knowledge base. This principle relates to what we say about the importance of prior knowledge in Chapter 4 and elsewhere.

2 Instruction should involve teaching for analytical, creative and practical thinking, as well as for memory learning. *Analytical thinking* includes analysing, judging, evaluating, comparing and contrasting, and critiquing; *creative thinking* includes creating, inventing, discovering, imagining and supposing; *practical thinking* includes implementing, using, applying and seeking relevance; *memory* includes memorising, remembering, recalling, recognising and repeating. We cover many of these aspects of thinking throughout our text. Sternberg believes that too much teaching and learning is memory-oriented to the exclusion of other forms of thinking. He is supported in this belief by many other theorists (such as Bruner) dealt with in our text. He believes that good instruction should include a full range of tasks that call upon each of these modes of thinking.

3 Assessment should also involve analytical, creative and practical, as well as memory, components. In Chapter 11 we deal with a range of authentic and alternative assessments that meet this requirement.

QUESTION POINT

What do you think would be Piaget's attitude to intelligence testing? What do you think would be the attitude of Vygotsky?

ACTION STATION

This activity is designed to highlight the difficulty of defining intelligence and measuring the construct. In a group, discuss the concept of intelligence and decide on a definition of intelligence that reflects group consensus. Design a series of items or activities to measure your conception of intelligence. Administer your test to another group while completing the other group's test. Discuss your findings.

Psychometrics and cognition

As we have seen above, theorists such as Gardner argue that there are several relatively autonomous human intellectual competencies, which he calls *human intelligences*, or frames of the mind. These 'multiple intelligences' are relatively independent of one another, and are fashioned and combined in a multiplicity of adaptive ways by individuals and cultures to produce intelligent behaviour. His theory stems from his belief that it is nonsense to reduce the notion of intelligence to a homogeneous mental construct. Furthermore, Gardner believes that historical and contemporary conceptualisations of intelligence measured by simplistic tests fail to pay sufficient attention to intelligence and problem solving as it is displayed in the real world characterised by social and cultural diversity. In effect, Gardner criticised the psychometric approach to

Question point

Each chapter has a range of questions distributed throughout the text to stimulate further study or group discussion.

Action station

We often learn most effectively when theory is put into practice. Included in each chapter are interesting practical exercises to challenge you. In many cases, they provide the opportunity to investigate, first hand, the use of theory in practice.

Learner-centred Psychological Principles

These boxes present key psychological principles drawn from research that should guide effective teaching and learning. Throughout the text we elaborate on, and provide applied examples of, these principles.

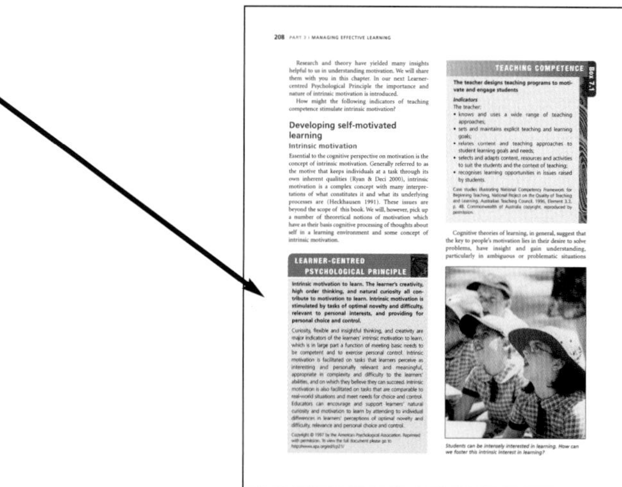

208 PART 3 | MANAGING EFFECTIVE LEARNING

Research and theory have yielded many insights helpful to us in understanding motivation. We will share them with you in this chapter. In our next Learner-centred Psychological Principle the importance and nature of intrinsic motivation is introduced.

How might the following indicators of teaching competence stimulate intrinsic motivation?

Developing self-motivated learning

Intrinsic motivation

Essential to the cognitive perspective on motivation is the concept of intrinsic motivation. Generally referred to as the motive that keeps individuals at a task through its own inherent qualities (Ryan & Deci 2000), intrinsic motivation is a complex concept with many interpretations of what constitutes it and what its underlying processes are (Heckhausen 1991). These issues are beyond the scope of this book. We will, however, pick up a number of theoretical notions of motivation which have as their basis cognitive processing of thoughts about self in a learning environment and some concept of intrinsic motivation.

LEARNER-CENTRED PSYCHOLOGICAL PRINCIPLE

Intrinsic motivation to learn. The learner's creativity, high order thinking, and natural curiosity all contribute to motivation to learn. Intrinsic motivation is stimulated by tasks of optimal novelty and difficulty, relevant to personal interests, and providing for personal choice and control.

Curiosity, flexible and insightful thinking, and creativity are major indicators of the learners' intrinsic motivation to learn, which is in large part a function of meeting basic needs to be competent and to exercise personal control. Intrinsic motivation is facilitated on tasks that learners perceive as interesting and personally relevant and meaningful, appropriate in complexity and difficulty to the learners' abilities, and on which they believe they can succeed. Intrinsic motivation is also facilitated on tasks that are comparable to real-world situations and meet needs for choice and control. Educators can encourage and support learners' natural curiosity and motivation to learn by attending to individual differences in learners' perceptions of optimal novelty and difficulty, relevance and personal choice and control.

Copyright © 1997 by the American Psychological Association. Reprinted with permission. To view the full document please go to http://www.apa.org/ed/lcp2/

TEACHING COMPETENCE Box 7.1

The teacher designs teaching programs to motivate and engage students

Indicators

The teacher:

- knows and uses a wide range of teaching approaches;
- sets and maintains explicit teaching and learning goals;
- relates content and teaching approaches to student learning goals and needs;
- selects and adapts content, resources and activities to suit the students and the context of teaching;
- recognises learning opportunities in issues raised by students.

Case studies illustrating National Competency Framework for Beginning Teaching, National Project on the Quality of Teaching and Learning, Australian Teaching Council, 1996, Element 3.3, p. 48. Commonwealth of Australia copyright, reproduced by permission.

Cognitive theories of learning, in general, suggest that the key to people's motivation lies in their desire to solve problems, have insight and gain understanding, particularly in ambiguous or problematic situations

Students can be intensely interested in learning. How can we foster this intrinsic interest in learning?

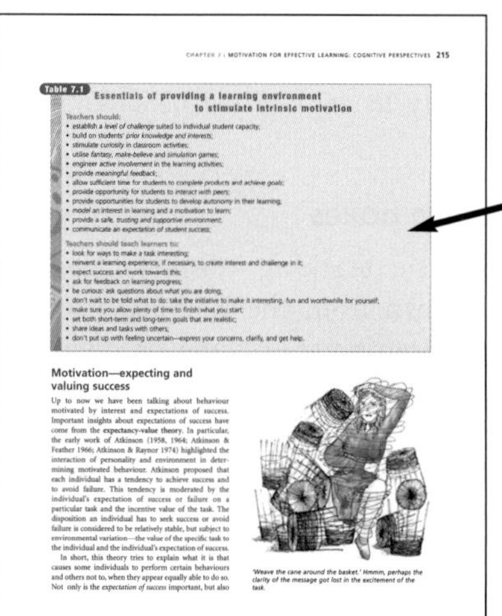

CHAPTER 7 | MOTIVATION FOR EFFECTIVE LEARNING: COGNITIVE PERSPECTIVES 215

Table 7.1 **Essentials of providing a learning environment to stimulate intrinsic motivation**

Teachers should:

- establish a *level of challenge* suited to individual student capacity;
- build on students' *prior knowledge and interests*;
- stimulate *curiosity* in classroom activities;
- utilise *fantasy*, *make-believe* and *simulation games*;
- engineer *active involvement* in the learning activities;
- provide *meaningful feedback*;
- allow sufficient time for students to *complete products and achieve goals*;
- provide opportunity for students to *interact with peers*;
- provide opportunities for students to develop *autonomy* in their learning;
- *model* an interest in learning and a motivation to learn;
- provide a safe, *trusting and supportive environment*;
- communicate *an expectation of student success*;

Teachers should teach learners to:

- look for ways to make a task interesting;
- reinvent a learning experience, if necessary, to create interest and challenge in it;
- expect success and work towards this;
- ask for feedback on learning progress;
- be curious: ask questions about what you are doing;
- don't wait to be told what to do: take the initiative to make it interesting, fun and worthwhile for yourself;
- make sure you allow plenty of time to finish what you start;
- set both short-term and long-term goals that are realistic;
- share ideas and tasks with others;
- don't put up with feeling uncertain—express your concerns, clarify, and get help.

Motivation—expecting and valuing success

Up to now we have been talking about behaviour motivated by interest and expectations of success. Important insights about expectations of success have come from the **expectancy-value theory**. In particular, the early work of Atkinson (1958, 1964; Atkinson & Feather 1966; Atkinson & Raynor 1974) highlighted the interaction of personality and environment in determining motivated behaviour. Atkinson proposed that each individual has a tendency to achieve success and to avoid failure. This tendency is moderated by the individual's expectation of success or failure on a particular task and the incentive value of the task. The disposition an individual has to seek success or avoid failure is considered to be relatively stable, but subject to environmental variation—the value of the specific task to the individual and the individual's expectation of success.

In short, this theory tries to explain what it is that causes some individuals to perform certain behaviours and others not to, when they appear equally able to do so. Not only is the *expectation of success* important, but also

'Weave the cane around the basket.' Hmmm, perhaps the clarity of the message got lost in the excitement of the task.

Essentials of . . .

Throughout the text we have summarised the essential practical implications of key topics from both teacher and learner perspectives. These 'essentials of' tables serve not only as a practical guide for effective classroom practices, but also help to clarify the relevance and importance of theory. We introduce these 'essentials of' tables with the comments 'teachers should' and 'teachers should get learners to'. The intention behind this is to have you, as an educator in training, implement effective practices to facilitate learning in your students and to encourage them also to practise the 'learners should' skills to enhance their own learning.

What would you do?

Additional case studies, also drawn from the National Competency Framework for Beginning Teaching, present an opportunity to test your solutions to real problem situations against the solutions of actual teachers. Again, this provides a great opportunity to put theory into practice.

Key Terms

These are highlighted where they appear in the text and listed at the end of each chapter for revision.

These key terms define essential concepts covered in each chapter and act as a 'ready reckoner' of mastery of content in each chapter. All terms are listed with definitions at the end of the book in the glossary.

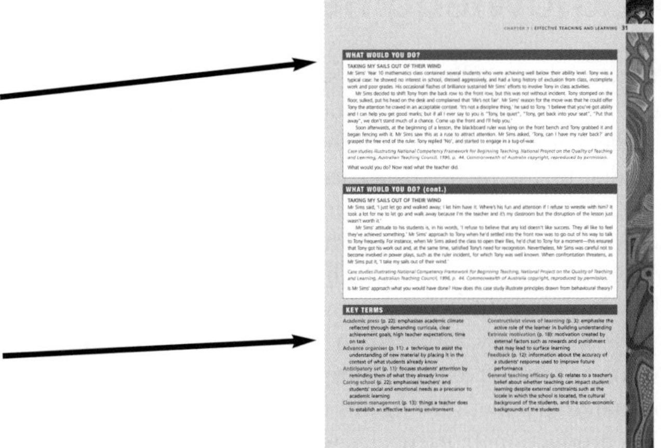

CHAPTER 1 : EFFECTIVE TEACHING AND LEARNING 31

WHAT WOULD YOU DO?

TAKING MY SAILS OUT OF THEIR WIND

Mr Sims' Year 10 mathematics class contained several students who were achieving well below their ability level. Tony was a typical case: he showed no interest in school, dressed aggressively, and had a long history of exclusion from class, incomplete work and poor grades. His occasional flashes of brilliance sustained Mr Sims' efforts to involve Tony in class activities.

Mr Sims decided to shift Tony from the back row to the front row, but this was not without incident. Tony stomped on the floor, sulked, put his head on the desk and complained that 'life's not fair'. Mr Sims' reason for the move was that he could offer Tony the attention he craved in an acceptable context. 'It's not a discipline thing,' he said to Tony. 'I believe that you've got ability and I can help you get good marks; but if all I ever say to you is "Tony, be quiet", "Tony, get back into your seat", "Put that away", we don't stand much of a chance. Come up the front and I'll help you.'

Soon afterwards, at the beginning of a lesson, the blackboard ruler was lying on the front bench and Tony grabbed it and began fencing with it. Mr Sims saw this as a ruse to attract attention. Mr Sims asked, 'Tony, can I have my ruler back?' and grasped the free end of the ruler. Tony replied 'No', and started to engage in a tug-of-war.

Case studies illustrating National Competency Framework for Beginning Teaching, National Project on the Quality of Teaching and Learning, Australian Teaching Council, 1996, p. 44. Commonwealth of Australia copyright, reproduced by permission.

What would you do? Now read what the teacher did.

WHAT WOULD YOU DO? (cont.)

TAKING MY SAILS OUT OF THEIR WIND

Mr Sims said, 'I just let go and walked away; I let him have it. Where's his fun and attention if I refuse to wrestle with him? It took a lot for me to let go and walk away because I'm the teacher and it's my classroom but the disruption of the lesson just wasn't worth it.'

Mr Sims' attitude to his students is, in his words, 'I refuse to believe that any kid doesn't like success. They all like to feel they've achieved something.' Mr Sims' approach to Tony when he'd settled into the front row was to go out of his way to talk to Tony frequently. For instance, when Mr Sims asked the class to open their files, he'd chat to Tony for a moment—this ensured that Tony got his work out and, at the same time, satisfied Tony's need for recognition. Nevertheless, Mr Sims was careful not to become involved in power plays, such as the ruler incident, for which Tony was well known. When confrontation threatens, as Mr Sims put it, 'I take my sails out of their wind.'

Case studies illustrating National Competency Framework for Beginning Teaching, National Project on the Quality of Teaching and Learning, Australian Teaching Council, 1996, p. 44. Commonwealth of Australia copyright, reproduced by permission.

Is Mr Sims' approach what you would have done? How does this case study illustrate principles drawn from behavioural theory?

KEY TERMS

Academic press (p. 22): emphasises academic climate reflected through demanding curricula, clear achievement goals, high teacher expectations, time on task

Advance organiser (p. 11): a technique to assist the understanding of new material by placing it in the context of what students already know

Anticipatory set (p. 11): focuses students' attention by reminding them of what they already know

Caring school (p. 22): emphasises teachers' and students' social and emotional needs as a precursor to academic learning

Classroom management (p. 13): things a teacher does to establish an effective learning environment

Constructivist views of learning (p. 3): emphasise the active role of the learner in building understanding

Extrinsic motivation (p. 18): motivation created by external factors such as rewards and punishment that may lead to surface learning

Feedback (p. 12): information about the accuracy of a students' response used to improve future performance

General teaching efficacy (p. 6): relates to a teacher's belief about whether teaching can impact student learning despite external constraints such as the locale in which the school is located, the cultural background of the students, and the socio-economic backgrounds of the students

On-line Learning

Today much learning is not book-based but Internet-based. Indeed, many courses depend largely on searching the Web for information on a variety of topics. One of the reasons for this is that some material on the Web is assumed to be more up to date than what is in textbooks. To combine the best of both worlds, we encourage instructors and students to use the Web to seek extension information on topics covered in our textbook. To facilitate this, we have included at the end of each chapter a number of activities to be completed utilising websites. Once you get used to this approach, you will find that the relevant websites 'explode' to many interesting issues. Our companion website at **http://www.pearsoned.com.au/mcinerney** provides direct links to all the sites listed in each chapter.

Recommended reading

At the end of each chapter we suggest a range of articles and texts that will further develop your understanding of the topics discussed. We have updated and extended this list for all chapters.

To these familiar pedagogic features we have introduced a number of exciting new features to support the pedagogical strengths of the book. These new features are Learning Objectives, Theory and Research into Practice, Extension Study, Key Terms, On-line Learning and Web Destinations.

Web Destinations

As well as on-line learning sites, we have provided at the end of each chapter a list of Web destinations that will assist you in learning more about each of the topics covered. Again, once you get used to this, you will see the usefulness of the Web in supplementing information covered in the text. However, we don't think Web sources will replace the value of a good textbook. We strongly believe that our text will help you to structure your search for useful information on the Web. Not all websites are equally useful, so you need to be astute in evaluating them.

Acknowledgments

Art work always enlivens a text, so our special thanks go to John Wiley, Lee-Anne Bethel and Stan Farbman for their excellent graphics throughout the text. Our sincere thanks are due to the many researchers and friends who provided the stimulating Theory and Research into Practice sections. Our thanks also go to those who provided photographs and tabular material. All photographs other than those with a credit were taken by the authors.

We are deeply indebted to our editors at Pearson, Alison Green and Rebecca Pomponio, who have done an outstanding job of turning this manuscript into a world-class production. In particular, we wish to thank them for going 'full colour', which we believe enhances the book enormously. We also thank the many people behind the scenes at Pearson who helped to bring the fourth edition into reality. In particular, we would like to thank the sales and marketing team who made sure the third edition was out there and sold well enough for us to be given the opportunity to write a fourth!

In the process of producing this text, we have also depended heavily on the expertise and advice of our copy editor, Robyn Flemming, who took a very complicated manuscript with many special features and made sure that it worked as a whole. Thank you, Robyn! We would also like to thank Ailleen Kim of DiZign for her outstanding book design, which we believe is as good as it gets.

Finally, we would like to extend our sincere thanks to all the students, teachers and others who permitted us to photograph them for the book. In particular, we thank students and teachers at Batchelor Area School, Northern Territory and Navajo Preparatory College, New Mexico. We are sure that you will agree that these photos enhance the text enormously.

Dennis M. McInerney and Valentina McInerney

The publisher and authors would also like to thank the following reviewers for their valuable contributions:

- Susan Beltman, Murdoch University
- Jennifer Campbell, Queensland University of Technology
- Annemaree Carroll, University of Queensland
- Debra Edwards, La Trobe University
- William Foster, Australian Catholic University
- Anne-Marie Havlat Lancaster, University of Tasmania
- Beverley Lambert, Charles Sturt University
- Graeme Lock, Edith Cowan University
- Joyce Martin, Australian Catholic University
- John Maurer, University of New England
- Debbie Neal, La Trobe University
- Fiona Spencer, Queensland University of Technology
- Elizabeth Stamopoulos, Edith Cowan University
- Harry Thompson, Griffith University
- Wilma Vialle, University of Wollongong

PART 1

Stimulating effective learning

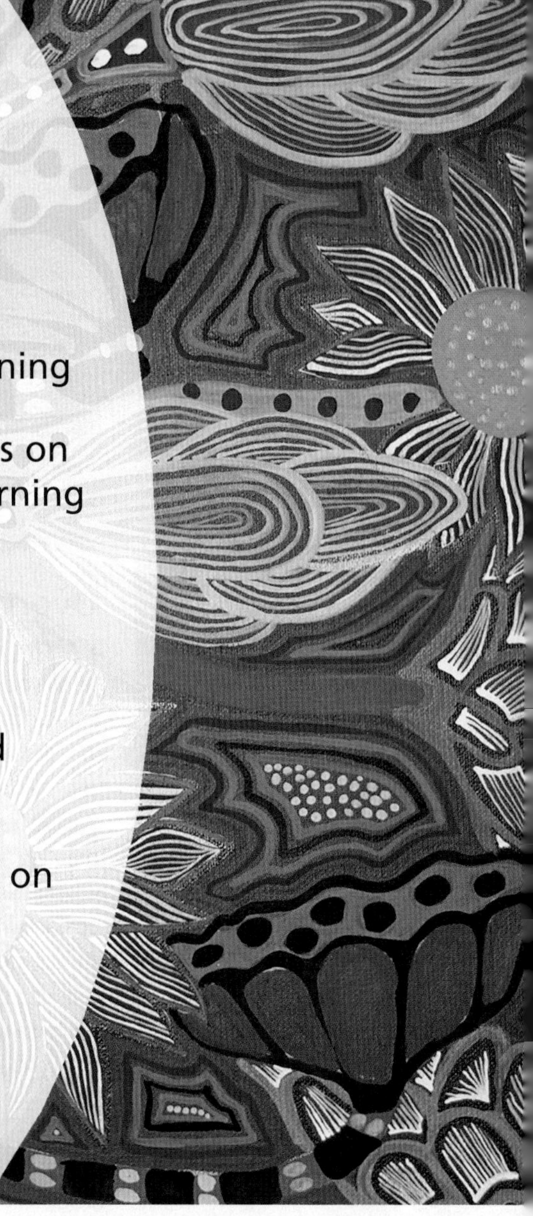

CHAPTER

1 Effective teaching and learning

Overview

What makes an effective learner and what makes an effective teacher? In this chapter, we introduce you to the role of educational psychology in answering these two questions. In particular, we introduce the guiding framework for this book: constructivist approaches to teaching and learning. We describe, discuss and compare three forms of constructivism: personal constructivism, social constructivism and information processing constructivism. Each of these theories has provided deep insights into essential elements of the learning process, and we deal with each in more detail in later chapters.

In this chapter, we also give a broad overview of some characteristics of effective teachers that will prepare you to consider many of the topics covered later in the text. We also introduce you to two frameworks by which you can evaluate the theoretical and practical ideas we discuss: the Learner-centred Psychological Principles developed by the American Psychological Association, and the National Competency Framework for Beginning Teaching developed by the Australian Teaching Council. Throughout the text, we refer to these as they relate to the material covered.

Learning objectives

After reading this chapter, you will be able to:

- define personal and social constructivism;
- identify some constructivist approaches to teaching and learning;
- identify essential components of what makes effective teaching;
- identify elements of teacher efficacy and their effects on student learning;
- examine teaching as a science and as an art;
- list and describe effective teaching skills;
- compare and contrast models of professional development of a teacher from novice to expert;
- define instructional objectives and list the advantages of writing instructional objectives;
- compare Mager's and Gronlund's methods for writing instructional objectives.

1

Effective teaching and learning: Constructivist perspectives

Cognitive psychology in general, and learning theories derived from cognitive psychology in particular, have become very important in helping to explain effective learning and its relationship to effective teaching. Implicit in these cognitive views of learning is the notion that *effective learning occurs when individuals construct their own understandings.* In other words, there is an emphasis in cognitive theories on the active role of the learner in building personal meaning and in making sense of information (Poplin 1988).

Constructivist views of learning emphasise the active role of the learner in building understanding

There are many varieties of constructivism (Derry 1996; Moshman 1982; Phillips 1995; Steffe & Gale 1995; Windschitl 2002). Some **constructivist views of learning** concentrate attention on the cognitive content of the minds of individual learners—such as individuals' existing understandings and knowledge, attitudes, motivational level and interests—and on how this is extended through the learners' personal interactions with physical events in their daily lives. Minimal attention is paid to social and other contextual factors that might influence the learning process. These approaches are often labelled **personal constructivism** (or, at times, cognitive constructivism, radical or endogenous constructivism, or schema theory) (see Derry 1996; Driver *et al.* 1994; Hendry 1996; Moshman 1982; Salomon & Perkins 1998; von Glaserfeld 1995; Windschitl 2002; see also Pressley 1995). These approaches explicitly emphasise the intrapersonal dimensions of learning and, in particular, posit that knowledge is not transmitted directly from one knower to another, but is actively built up by the learner through child-determined exploration and discovery rather than direct teaching. Hence, classrooms reflecting this perspective prepare well-designed practical activities that challenge the previous conceptions of learners, encouraging them to reorganise their personal theories. We examine this in some detail in our discussion of Piaget (Chapter 2) and Bruner and Ausubel (Chapter 5).

Other constructivist approaches, labelled **social constructivism** (Driver *et al.* 1994; Salomon & Perkins 1998; Windschitl 2002) (sometimes called exogenous; see Moshman 1982; see also Pressley 1995), focus on the growth of 'public' subject matter of individuals in social domains, and in particular in relationship to families, peer groups and schools, which orient children to interpret and make sense of their world of experiences.

This process of knowledge construction comes about as learners become encultured into the knowledge and symbols of their society. This view moves away from the position that children learn best when they self-discover to a position that advocates collaborative inquiry through which individuals appropriate information in terms of their own understanding of, and involvement in, the activity. In cases where children are having difficulty or are being challenged to extend their understanding, teachers and others provide the prompts, scaffolding and guidance needed. This form of social constructivism emphasises the importance of the continuing interaction between the child and its social environment to facilitate meaningful learning (Anderson, Reder & Simon 1997; Greeno 1997; Sfard 1998; see also Sawyer 2004). We examine this approach in our discussion of Piaget and Vygotsky (Chapter 2), social cognitive theory (Chapter 6) and cognitive apprenticeships and reciprocal teaching (Chapter 5). An extension of social constructivism is **sociocultural constructivism**, where the focus is on the larger social, cultural and historical environments in which learning is embedded (Marshall 1996; John-Steiner & Mahn 1996). We consider sociocultural approaches in Chapters 2 and 10.

A third type of constructivism, **information processing constructivism**, explains thinking and the development of knowledge in terms of interactions between environmental influences and deliberate, reflective mental constructions (see Derry 1996; Mayer 1996). In this view the learner actively selects, organises and integrates incoming experience with existing knowledge to create new knowledge and understanding.

An essential element in the constructivist view of learning is that there is an active involvement of the learner. How might these students be actively involved?

We consider information processing in detail in Chapter 4.

- **Personal constructivism:** Focuses on the learner's internal mental state and transformations of understanding that occur within the individual.
- **Social constructivism:** Focuses on the learner's construction of knowledge in a social context, with the individual making personal meaning from socially shared perceptions.
- **Information processing constructivism:** Focuses on the learner actively selecting, organising and integrating incoming experience with existing knowledge to create understanding.

We return to these classifications when considering a number of features of effective teaching and learning throughout the text.

An essential element in the constructivist view of learning is that there is an active involvement of the learner, and a shift in focus from what the teacher may do to influence learning to what the learner does as an active agent in the learning process. And for the **radical constructivists**, there is also a de-emphasis on knowledge as being simple, uni-dimensional, certain and constant. Rather than seeing knowledge as a body of understandings with an end point and shared meanings across individuals, the acquisition of knowledge is viewed as a journey with no end point, with understanding constructed, deconstructed and reconstructed in social contexts (see Putnam & Borko 2000). In contrast, social constructivism is more inclined to view knowledge as the shared resource of the group to which new learners are socialised. In the socialisation of new learners there is a reciprocal relationship between gaining/sharing knowledge and contributing to the growth of that knowledge so that the boundaries of knowledge are extended for the community of learners (see Salomon & Perkins 1998).

None of the various theories of constructivism necessarily entails specific teaching practices; rather, each provides a general orienting framework within which to address teaching issues and to develop instructional approaches (Cobb 1994a, 1994b; see also Sawyer 2004). Furthermore, there are common elements across the theories that have had an impact on teaching practice, and there is an increasing move towards merging and combining the theories so that they may provide us with an even deeper understanding of human cognitive development and the role to be played by educational environments in this development (see, for example, the special issue of *Educational Psychologist*, 31(4), 1996 and O'Connor 1998; Windschitl 2002).

We should also note that the constructivist maxim that students construct their own knowledge can be taken to imply that students can construct their *own* ways of knowing in even the most teacher-directed instructional situations (see Cobb 1994a, 1994b). For this reason, we also deal with alternative views of effective teaching derived from non-cognitive theories of learning. Through this we hope to establish a bridge that spans the supposed dichotomy between instructional approaches overtly based on student construction of knowledge and those instructional approaches that are based on transmission of knowledge.

It is also important to note that constructivism is really a philosophical position and metaphor regarding the nature of knowledge and its acquisition. There are competing philosophies, psychologies and metaphors of learning, and where appropriate we will discuss these (see, for example, Popkewitz 1998). However, we have chosen *cognitive* constructivism as our main framework as it offers us the opportunity to examine systematically theories of learning, motivation and development from the child's perspective.

'Oh! Why, thank you, Brutus. An early Christmas present. And here I was thinking of you as a murderous thug.'

ACTION STATION

Graham Hendry (1996) lists seven constructivist principles and their classroom applications. Consider these in the light of the discussion below of what makes an effective teacher. Refer to them again as we describe the many faces of constructivism throughout this text. Do they all apply to each approach? Would you add other principles? Would you delete some principles?

Principle 1 Knowledge exists only in the minds of people. In the classroom, knowledge exists in the minds of students and the teacher, not on the blackboard, in books, on floppy disks, in teacher or student talk, or in the activities that teachers and students devise.

Principle 2 The meanings or interpretations that people give to things depend on their knowledge. Teachers and students give meaning to instructional materials according to their existing knowledge and may, therefore, generate different meanings for the same materials and experiences.

Principle 3 Knowledge is constructed from within the person in interrelation with the world. Teachers or teaching methods *per se* do not change students' ideas; rather, change or construction occurs from within, through students' interrelation with the world of which teachers are a part. Students do not simply absorb transmitted knowledge.

Principle 4 Knowledge can never be certain. There are no absolutely right or wrong answers or ideas, only ones that are more or less useful and sustainable. Thus, all knowledge can be reconstructed and should be continually open to re-examination.

Principle 5 Common knowledge derives from a common brain and body, which are part of the same universe. Children share the same brain processes and body characteristics and inhabit the same world, and can construct common knowledge through their discussion of solutions to the same problems. Despite the individual nature of the construction of knowledge, this knowledge construction is based upon common biological processes (such as perception) across humans. This knowledge will reflect the biological and experiential maturity of the individuals.

Principle 6 Knowledge is constructed through perception and action. In particular, learning is facilitated by active involvement in problem solving and conflict resolution.

Principle 7 Construction of knowledge requires energy and time. Individuals are most motivated to construct knowledge in non-threatening, supportive and challenging learning environments. The construction of knowledge is promoted by encouraging students to discuss, explain and evaluate their thoughts within a social context.

EXTENSION STUDY

Teacher efficacy and student learning

Teacher efficacy refers to a teacher's perceived personal power to influence student learning, as well as their confidence that they have the teaching competence actually to make a difference. Research typically shows that there are two forms of efficacy: **personal teaching efficacy**, which relates to the teacher's belief that they have personal qualities to positively impact students' learning; and **general teaching efficacy**, which relates to a teacher's belief about whether teaching can impact student learning despite external constraints such as the locale in which the school is located, and the cultural and socioeconomic backgrounds of the students (Fives & Alexander 2004; Henson 2002).

The notion of teacher efficacy is closely related to another idea, that of *personal self-efficacy* (Bandura 1997; see also Ashton & Webb 1986; Henson 2002; van den Berg 2002), which we explore in some detail in Chapter 6. Teacher efficacy has been related to a whole host of effective personal teaching behaviours and positive student **learning outcomes**. It has been related to teacher enthusiasm and how much effort teachers put into teaching, the goals they set and the level of aspiration for themselves and their students, how innovative they are, how they structure learning activities, their control orientations and behaviour, and their response to students who are difficult to teach. Teachers with a strong sense of efficacy experiment more to meet the needs of their students. They also plan and organise well, are more tolerant of student mistakes, work longer with students having difficulties, and are less inclined to refer difficult students to special education. Teachers high in efficacy are also more resilient to difficulties, appear more committed to teaching, have greater job satisfaction, and are more likely to stay in teaching (Caprara, Barbaranelli, Borgogni & Steca 2003; Evers, Brouwers & Tomic 2002; Fives & Alexander 2004; Gordon & Debus 2002; Henson 2002; Tschannen-Moran, Woolfolk Hoy & Hoy 1998; van den Berg 2002). These positive effects are also reflected at the school level in the positive nature of the school climate. Teacher efficacy is, therefore, strongly related to being an effective teacher (Dunkin & Precians 1993; Fives & Alexander 2004). Brophy and Evertson (1976), for example, found that there was a marked difference between how effective and ineffective teachers described their roles. Ineffective teachers saw teaching as a dull job in which they did not take personal responsibility for student learning: they did not feel that they made a difference and believed that 'problems' such as poor behaviour and low ability were insoluble. On the other hand, effective teachers saw themselves as having control over problems that could be resolved. Successful teachers had higher expectations for students and saw themselves primarily as instructors whose task it was to help students learn (Gibson & Dembo 1984). Teacher efficacy can be both context and subject specific. In other words, a teacher might feel more or less efficacious in a particular setting, such as

Teacher effectiveness and student learning

Research (Westwood 1995; see also Hogan, Rabinowitz & Craven, 2003) suggests that effective teachers:

- have well-managed classrooms where students have the maximum opportunity to learn;
- maintain an academic focus;
- have high, rather than low, expectations of what students can be helped to achieve;
- are businesslike and work-oriented;
- show enthusiasm;
- use strategies to keep students on task and productive;
- impose structure on the content to be covered;
- present new material in a step-by-step manner;
- employ direct (explicit) teaching procedures;
- use clear instructions and explanations;
- use a variety of teaching styles and resources;
- frequently demonstrate appropriate task-approach strategies;
- monitor closely what students are doing;
- adjust instruction to individual needs and re-teach where necessary;
- provide frequent feedback to students;
- use high rates of questioning to motivate students and to check for understanding.

In the following sections we discuss a range of teaching practices that have been related to effective teaching. We cover a number of others in subsequent chapters. In mastering these, teachers develop a sense of efficacy and feel that they can influence how well students learn. Before reading the following sections, consider the stimulating information provided by Professor Jere Brophy on effective teaching.

with elementary students, but not with high school students, or in one subject more than another (Henson 2002; van den Berg 2002). Our purpose in this book is to introduce you to a wide variety of ideas drawn from the study of educational and developmental psychology which, we hope, will lead you to develop strong personal feelings of efficacy as a teacher that will lead you to be an effective teacher.

How is teacher efficacy developed?

Tschannen-Moran *et al.* (1998; see also Goddard, Hoy & Woolfolk Hoy 2000; Henson 2002; Henson *et al.* 2000) propose an integrated model to explain the development of teacher efficacy (see Figure 1.1). The sources of efficacy information are based on the work of Bandura (1986), which we describe in more detail in Chapter 6. There are four key elements: mastery experiences, physiological and emotional cues, vicarious experiences and verbal persuasion. Simply put, a teacher's efficacy in a particular context will reflect:

- the degree to which they believe they have been successful or unsuccessful, and their beliefs about their strengths and weaknesses as a teacher (mastery experiences);
- the degree of emotionality associated with a teaching situation—for example, positive emotions are related to the anticipation of future success (physiological and emotional cues);
- the direct (other teachers) and indirect (books, teacher talk) models of teaching to which an individual is exposed (vicarious experiences) that reinforce or challenge their capabilities; and
- the messages the individual receives from others, including teachers and students, regarding the individual's competence and techniques to use in order to teach effectively (verbal persuasion).

So, teachers who have been successful and believe they have particular teaching strengths, who look forward to teaching students, learn from positive examples of other teachers, and receive positive feedback regarding their competence in particular teaching situations are likely to feel efficacious as teachers. The converse is also true. Each of these sources of information regarding an individual teacher's efficacy is interpreted by each individual according to their background experiences. In contrast to the example we have just given, it is unlikely that each component will be totally positive. It is likely that the first two, mastery experiences and emotional cues, are particularly important in influencing the development of efficacy in younger teachers. In any event, each element will be given more or less weight when the teacher analyses the teaching tasks they are to be involved in, and when they make an assessment of their personal teaching competence for these tasks. The interactions between the analysis of teaching tasks and personal feelings of competence determine the feelings of efficacy a teacher has for the particular teaching episode (Henson 2002). Even experienced teachers may lack feelings of efficacy in certain situations.

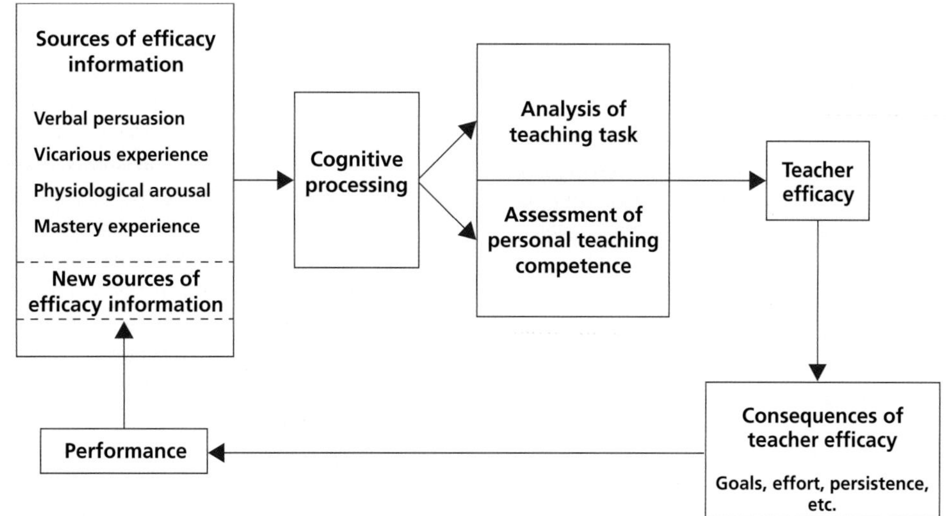

***Figure 1.1** The cyclical nature of teacher efficacy*

Source: M. Tschannen-Moran, A. Woolfolk Hoy & W. Hoy (1998) Teacher efficacy: Its meaning and measure. *Review of Educational Research*, **68**, 202–48.

Theory and research into practice

Jere Brophy — EFFECTIVE TEACHING

BRIEF BIOGRAPHY

I grew up in Chicago, the oldest of four children of a dentist and a homemaker. During high school, I took a job as a group leader in an after-school recreation and summer camp program at a settlement house, interacting with children during the day and with teenagers on certain nights. Besides familiarising me with life in the inner city, these experiences oriented me towards working with people, so I majored in psychology at Loyola University (Chicago) and then went to the University of Chicago, where I completed a dual Ph.D. program in clinical psychology and human development. I was intending to become a practising clinical psychologist, but the daily work of clinical assessment and psychotherapy was less rewarding than I expected, so I shifted career plans towards research in human development. Working on Robert Hess and Virginia Shipman's groundbreaking study of social class differences in childrearing beliefs and behaviours motivated me to continue studying the socialisation of children when I joined the Department of Educational Psychology at the University of Texas at Austin in 1968.

However, being in a college of education broadened my purview from socialisation in the home to education in the school. Also, I became friends with Tom Good and spent a lot of time discussing research issues with him. We developed a study on relationships between teachers' expectations for individual students and their patterns of interaction with those students. This led to follow-up studies of teacher expectation phenomena, and to subsequent research on teachers' attitudes towards students and the dynamics of teacher–student relationships. After several of these studies and others on teacher effects, I realised that I was making a transition from childrearing research to educational research. By the time I joined the College of Education at Michigan State University in 1976, that transition had been completed.

RESEARCH AND THEORETICAL INTERESTS

My early work with Tom Good showed that most teachers' expectations concerning their students' progress are accurate, but some teachers are prone to premature closure around distorted early impressions. These can affect student progress both through direct effects on opportunity to learn (offering an enriched curriculum to some students but an impoverished curriculum to others) and through indirect effects on students' motivation (give high-expectation students second chances to answer questions, but respond to low-expectation students by giving the answer or calling on someone else; provide more praise and less criticism to high-expectation students relative to low-expectation students in parallel situations).

Our subsequent studies indicated that teachers tend to be relaxed, friendly and approving with students whom they like and trust, but bureaucratic and controlling with students whom they dislike or mistrust. Responses to misbehaviour tend to vary with teachers' attributional thinking: they project sympathy and try to help when they view students as victims of forces beyond their own control, but become angry and punitive if they view provocative behaviour as intentional.

As I became more involved in classrooms, I became interested in what research had to say about effective teaching, especially when I learned that correlations of teacher behaviours with student outcomes were weak and mixed, seeming to imply that one teacher is as good as the next. I decided that something was wrong with the research that was producing this conclusion, so I studied experienced teachers who had established track records of differential effectiveness. With Carolyn Evertson, I found that certain teacher behaviours consistently correlated with achievement gains: emphasising developing mastery of the curriculum in defining their own roles as teachers; allocating most of the available time for this purpose; keeping students engaged in ongoing activities; and actively instructing students during interactive lessons, rather than having them work silently on seatwork. These studies established that teachers do make a difference, and one is not necessarily as good as another.

My subsequent work focused on managing classrooms and motivating students. Good management is more a matter of clarifying and explaining the reasons for rules and routines than imposing discipline and punishment. Effective teachers make sure that students understand what to do, and follow up by providing in-context reminders to ensure that desired procedures are carried out as intended. Students tend to follow these guidelines willingly because they can see that there are good reasons for them.

My research on praise was stimulated by my recognition that although it was routinely treated as a form of reinforcement in textbooks, teacher praise has a variety of purposes and effects in classrooms. It is not necessarily reinforcing, and it even can be counterproductive. Drawing from attribution theory and other sources, I developed guidelines distinguishing effective and ineffective praise.

Later I researched other aspects of student motivation, eventually writing a textbook on the topic. I emphasised three motivational aspects of learning situations: (1) the social milieu in which the learning takes place (supportive versus threatening); (2) the learner's performance attributions, expectations and self-efficacy perceptions; and (3) the degree to which the learner values the opportunity to engage in the learning activity and acquires the knowledge or skills that it develops. My own work has focused on ways in which teachers might develop motivated learning schemas with respect to the content taught at school. Suggestions include helping students to see connections between school content and their personal identities and agendas, and using modelling, coaching and feedback to scaffold their motivation along with their learning.

My most recent work has focused on primary-grade social studies. Done with Janet Alleman, the work involves two lines of research. First is studies of what K-3 children know (or think they know) about topics emphasised in the early social studies curriculum. This information is needed to identify valid prior knowledge to build on and common misconceptions to address in instruction. We also have done studies of powerful social studies teaching in the early grades, addressing such issues as how teachers might achieve an effective balance between transmission and constructivist teaching with students who are both young and limited in prior knowledge, ways to use children's literature selections for social education purposes, and ways to extend the curriculum through home assignments that engage parents and children in interactions around social studies content.

THEORY AND RESEARCH INTO PRACTICE

Teaching implications relating to my research on teacher expectation effects, teacher attitudes towards students, teacher–student interpersonal dynamics, classroom management, student motivation, and related affective aspects of teaching are spelled out in detail in my motivation text (Brophy 2004) and in the book *Looking in Classrooms* (Good & Brophy 2003). Key principles include being a positive, supportive resource person to students while simultaneously fulfilling one's instructional and managerial responsibilities; using instructional, authoritative methods for establishing the classroom as a learning community; motivating primarily by focusing the curriculum on content worth learning and developing this content in ways that enable students to appreciate its value, rather than by controlling through extrinsic rewards and punishments; phrasing praise and feedback in ways that help students to value their accomplishments and appreciate their progress, rather than in ways that emphasise competition or peer comparisons; and, in general, making sure that the things you do and expect your students to do are supportive of the long-run best interests of the students and can be appreciated by them accordingly.

A more general summary of practical implications from work by myself and others is provided in a booklet entitled *Teaching* that I wrote for the International Academy of Education. (The complete version is available on the academy's website and also on the website of the International Bureau of Education.) It offers the following 12 principles as a synthesis of what is known about effective teaching.

1. *A supportive classroom climate:* Students learn best within cohesive and caring learning communities. The teacher displays concern and affection for students, is attentive to their needs and emotions, and socialises them to display these same characteristics in their interactions with one another.
2. *Opportunity to learn:* Students learn more when most of the available time is allocated to curriculum-related activities and the classroom management system emphasises maintaining their engagement in those activities.
3. *Curricular alignment:* All components of the curriculum are aligned to create a cohesive program for accomplishing instructional purposes and goals (that is, content clusters, instructional methods, learning activities and assessment tools).
4. *Establishing learning orientations:* Teachers can prepare students for learning by providing an initial structure to clarify intended outcomes and cue desired learning strategies.
5. *Coherent content:* To facilitate meaningful learning and retention, content is explained clearly and developed with emphasis on its structure and connections. Lessons and assignments focus on developing the most important content in greater depth, structuring it around powerful ideas, explaining these ideas and the connections among them, and following up with authentic learning activities.
6. *Thoughtful discourse:* Questions are planned to engage students in sustained discourse structured around powerful ideas. Students are invited to develop explanations, make predictions, debate alternative approaches to problems, or otherwise consider the content's implications or applications.
7. *Practice and application activities:* Students need sufficient opportunities to practise and apply what they are learning, and to receive improvement-oriented feedback. Most practice should be embedded within application contexts. Feedback should be informative, rather than merely evaluative.
8. *Scaffolding students' task engagement:* The teacher supplies whatever assistance students need to enable them to engage in learning activities productively

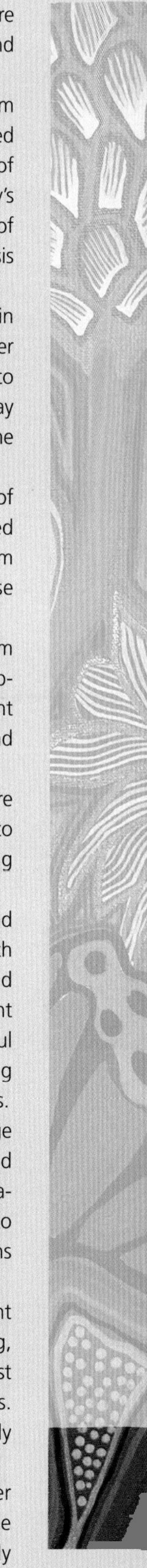

(introducing activities with emphasis on their purposes, circulating to monitor progress and provide assistance during work segments, and finishing with debriefing segments to provide general feedback and to reinforce main ideas).

9 *Strategy teaching:* The teacher models and instructs students in learning and self-regulation strategies. Much of this includes cognitive modelling in which the teacher thinks out loud to provide students with access to the thought processes that guide use of the strategy.

10 *Cooperative learning:* Students often benefit from working in pairs or small groups to construct understandings or to help one another to master skills.

11 *Goal-oriented assessment:* The teacher uses a variety of formal and informal assessment methods to monitor progress towards learning goals. Good assessment includes data from many sources besides paper-and-pencil tests, and it addresses the full range of intended outcomes.

12 *Achievement expectations:* The teacher establishes and follows through on appropriate expectations for learning outcomes.

KEY REFERENCES

Brophy, J. (2004) *Motivating Students to Learn*. Mahwah, NJ: Erlbaum.

Brophy J. & Good, T. (1974) *Teacher–Student Relationships: Causes and Consequences*. New York: Holt, Rinehart & Winston.

Good, T. & Brophy, J. (2003) *Looking in Classrooms*, 9th ed. Boston: Allyn & Bacon.

ACTIVITIES

1 Jere Brophy makes important points about how teacher expectations work, and how they might influence student behaviour and achievement. Consider and discuss these from your personal perspective as a student and teacher.

2 What are the teacher behaviours that Brophy found most correlated with achievement gains in students? Do these correspond to elements of effective teaching practice we describe in other sections of the chapter? How might these behaviours be developed in teachers?

3 Most people consider that praise is always good. Jere Brophy distinguishes between effective and ineffective praise. Do some research on the elements of effective and ineffective praise, and develop a table distinguishing between them. You might like to refer to Chapters 6, 7 and 8, which also deal, in part, with the use of praise.

4 Jere Brophy refers to three key elements of motivation. From your personal perspective, discuss the nature and importance of each of these.

5 Discuss the 12 principles of effective teaching presented by Jere Brophy. Relate these to material covered in this chapter. Debate the order of importance of these principles.

6 We strongly recommend that you read one or more of the recommended references listed by Jere Brophy. Each of these books is full of good ideas for effective teaching.

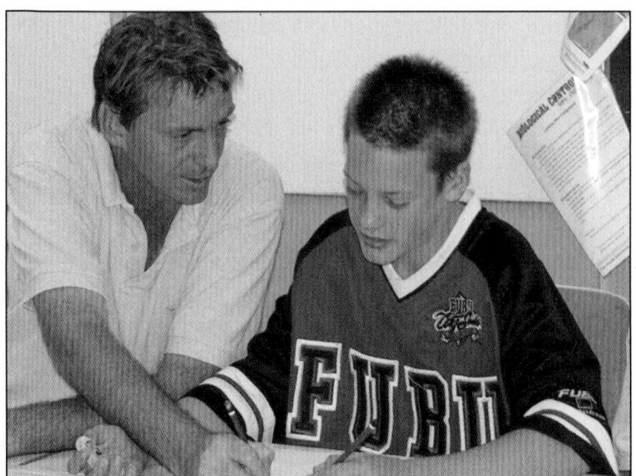

What factors influence teacher efficacy, and why is it so important to effective teaching and learning?

Planning learning experiences

Effective teachers plan learning experiences within which individually and socially constructed learning can occur (Wragg 1995; see also Sawyer 2004). Before any learning can take place, the attention and interest of the students must be gained. This is evident in the lessons of novice or student teachers, or those who cannot be bothered to put mental effort into planning the most effective ways of introducing their material. Not surprisingly, these teachers find that classroom management becomes a problem, with students going off tasks through lack of interest and motivation.

Lesson beginnings should capture the attention and interest of the student

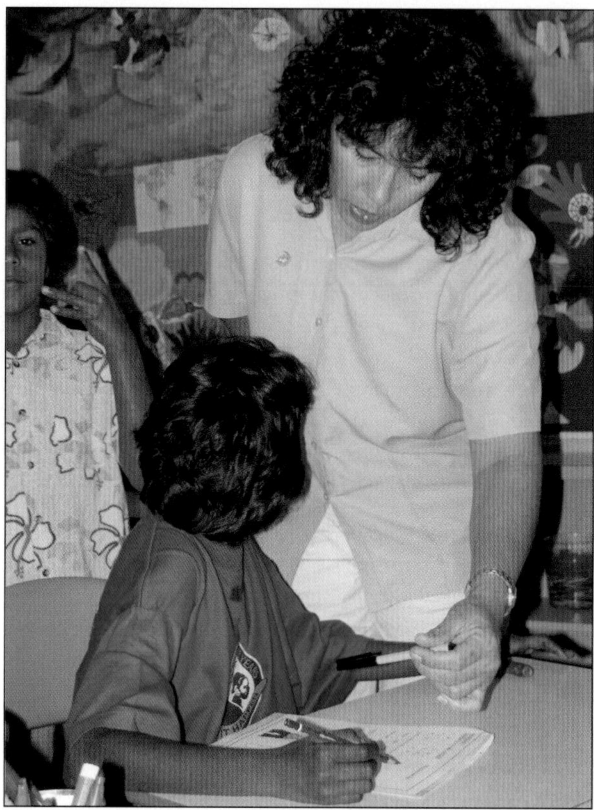

Increasingly, teachers are seen as facilitators of learning rather than as authority figures. How might this teacher be facilitating the learning of this student?

Introducing effective learning experiences

A focus for the session is vital, and this should connect the lesson to student interest and prior knowledge (see, for example, Linn *et al.* 2000). This can take the form of a sensory experience related to the content to be covered: students may be asked to listen to, look at, feel, smell or taste something.

Another technique is to use an **advance organiser** (Ausubel 1968, 1978; Corkill 1992), which places the new material in the context of what students already know. For example, when describing the human body's circulatory system an interesting advance organiser might sound something like this:

> The human body's circulatory system is like the sanitary system of a city. In both, there is a pumping station, pipelines of various sizes to carry clean water, a filtration mechanism to clean dirty water, an exchange terminal and a method of disposing of wastes. (Adapted from Eggen and Kauchak 1988)

The term *anticipatory set* is sometimes used instead of advance organiser (Hunter 1982, 1991). An **anticipatory set** focuses students' attention and reminds them of what they already know that is relevant to the topic to be covered. For example, when beginning a lesson on mass, volume and capacity, the teacher might begin with:

> What have you noticed about the level of the water when you get into a full bath and then get out again? Is it any different if someone else gets in as well?

Sometimes a **lesson review** is appropriate as an introduction to the lesson. Knowledge is constructed cumulatively, not just swallowed in separate whole chunks. Therefore, students need to have the connections with concepts and ideas covered in earlier lessons made for them through brief revision. For example:

> This week we have been learning about mammals. Let's think for a moment about what we have found so far. Jot down, or discuss with your neighbour first, three of the general characteristics that distinguish mammals from other groups of creatures such as reptiles.

Developing learning experiences

Effective teachers vary the mode of presentation according to the material and the students' skills and experiences. There are many different ways of presenting learning experiences that reflect constructivist as well as other approaches to teaching and learning: *direct teacher instruction* (reception learning), *guided discovery* (induction), *group discussion, cooperative group learning, peer* or *cross-age tutoring, individualised self-instruction* via computer or resource package (sometimes referred to as *programmed instruction*) and a host of others. We cover each of these in detail in later chapters.

Active involvement

For effective learning to occur, students need to be actively involved. Such involvement may occur through manipulating materials to explore 'what happens if . . .?'; pondering over higher cognitive-level questions which challenge their thinking and force them to apply, analyse, synthesise or evaluate what they have learned ('Why do you think . . .?' 'What would happen if . . .?' 'How might we do this differently?'); encouraging them to find applications or examples of newly learned concepts; brainstorming solutions to problems; and practising solving problems to ensure retention and transfer of new material.

Keeping students actively involved during their learning is very important

Providing effective feedback

Good and Brophy (1991; see also Crooks 1988; Kulik & Kulik 1988) point out the importance of providing students with immediate feedback on their learning, while it is emerging, to keep them on task (and thereby also preventing students from practising mistakes for too long). Effective **feedback** should specify exactly what is correct or incorrect about a student's work. Feedback should also give students corrective information about what they need to do to rectify problems (Crooks 1988). Most importantly, feedback should be communicated positively (Elawar & Corno 1985), not as one third-grade teacher was heard to remark: 'Haven't you put anything down on paper yet? For goodness sake, you'll never be a good writer the way you're going!'

Feedback should be immediate and corrective, and expressed positively

Far more conducive to improvement in both effort and product would be a comment such as: 'I can see that you're having trouble thinking of ideas for what to write. Just jot down any single words that come to mind and then have a look in your book for some pictures that might help your imagination. When you have done that, come and show me and we'll see how they can be put together into a story. I know you'll be surprised with what you come up with.'

Opportunity should also be given to children to self-evaluate and to implement alternative learning strategies as they see appropriate.

Ending learning experiences

> Well, that's it. The end. Thank you for your attention—you can go back to your seats now.

This was the closure of a measurement lesson with a group of eight children conducted by a beginning teacher trainee during a practice teaching session. It is not an uncommon conclusion to many (otherwise well-planned) lessons we have observed over the years. Student teachers often ask, 'What do you do at the end of the lesson?' The answer is to 'pull the lesson together' by reviewing with the students what has been learned, summarising the content of the lesson and arriving at a conclusion. It is akin to writing an essay: tell them what you are going to say (effective teachers tell their students what the lesson will be about and how and for what purpose they will be involved in the learning activities); say it (they then direct students through these activities, ensuring maximum student involvement in a variety of forms); and then remind them about the main message (finally, the content of the lesson is reviewed and a summary given or requested from the students: 'What did you learn today about . . .?') (see also Cole & Chan 1987; Turney *et al.* 1985b). Remember, there may well be a difference between individual 'knowing' and collective, socially negotiated 'knowledge' as transmitted through language.

For the student teacher above, the advice would be to conclude with something like:

> Today you have been estimating and measuring the length, width and perimeter of a range of large and small areas. I would like everyone in both groups to write down which measuring tools you found most useful for the particular areas you had to measure, and why they were the most suitable. [Students do so.] All right, let's hear what each group found and then we'll see what conclusions we come up with.

Additionally, students themselves should be asked to reflect on and summarise what they have learned from the experience, and to suggest what they may further need to do to extend their understanding. The lesson ending can foreshadow the next lesson (Linn *et al.* 2000).

Effective teaching and teaching skills

Naturally, in order to design and facilitate effective learning experiences, teachers need to have appropriate skills. These are detailed in Table 1.1 on p. 16. These are also skills that beginning teachers have some

TEACHING COMPETENCE — Box 1.1

The teacher plans purposeful programs to achieve specific student learning outcomes

Indicators

The teacher:

- relates learning programs to educational goals and objectives;
- establishes clear purposes for learning programs in terms of agreed student learning outcomes;
- selects and sequences learning activities to achieve planned student outcomes;
- takes account of students' goals and prior learning;
- relates assessment processes and strategies to learning objectives, content and tasks.

Case studies illustrating National Competency Framework for Beginning Teaching, National Project on the Quality of Teaching and Learning, Australian Teaching Council, 1996, Element 3.1, p. 46.

anxiety over when they start teaching (Reynolds 1992; Nathan & Petrosino 2003; Sinclair & Nicoll 1981; Veenman 1984; see also Kokkinos, Panayiotou & Davazoglou 2004). In the sections that follow we explore some of these skills of effective teaching and learning, and set the scene for their further elaboration in later chapters.

Knowledge skills

Effective teachers are *knowledgeable*, though not necessarily expert, about the material to be learned. More importantly, they must be able to communicate this knowledge to the students or demonstrate how to access it in a way that shows its utility or place in the world outside school. This knowledge will not translate into student learning unless students see that it has a purpose and is related to their world of understanding. Above all, good teachers show that education is about learning to learn and to live. The effective teacher is a professional who keeps up to date with developments in education and models to students that learning is a lifelong process.

Knowledge—possessed by teacher and able to be accessed by students

Management skills

Effective teachers are *organised*. Using general curriculum documents, programs of lessons (for a week, term or year) must be designed that are appropriate to the age and abilities of the students. In addition to content, the effective teacher plans for the strategies that will be most effective in helping students to learn this material. As we discuss in Chapter 8 (on **classroom management**), this involves organising the physical layout of the classroom, the supplies, and the rules and procedures at the start of the year. These rules and procedures are taught to students in the first weeks of school, and routines are developed to make classroom interactions more efficient. Routines maintain the activity flow in the classroom by defining appropriate behaviours for a variety of classroom activities—whether whole-class, small-group, peer tutoring or individual work (Anderson 1986). Students know, for example, what to do when they want the teacher's help, need to leave the room, have to form groups for cooperative teamwork, or forget to complete or bring their homework to school.

Effective management requires careful organisation

Questioning skills

Questioning takes a central role in the instructional process, so the use of questions should not be a hit-or-miss exercise. The issues that teachers should consider in planning for effective questioning episodes include:

How does good questioning facilitate effective learning?

how much emphasis should be placed on lower- and higher-cognitive-level questions; whether to use a recitation or discussion participant structure; how to frame questions clearly; how much wait-time to allow before eliciting a response; whether to elicit an individual or group response; how to react to students' answers; and how to adjust their questioning strategy to a particular instructional context (Gall & Artero-Boname 1995). And you thought that questioning was the easy aspect of teaching!

Good and Brophy (1990; see also Gall & Artero-Boname 1995) point out that effective teachers carefully plan sequences of questions in order to achieve particular objectives. For instance, if the objective of a lesson is for students to analyse Hamlet's relationship with his mother, initial questions might focus on knowledge, followed later by increasingly higher-order questions that would help the students to integrate the 'facts' and draw conclusions. In other words, the effective teacher does not ask questions haphazardly; there is a logic to the content and type of questions used in an instructional sequence which is closely related to the teacher's objectives or the expected learning outcomes for the students.

The quality of the questions themselves (that is, their clarity and relevance) is very important to their effective use. It is obvious that poor questions are those that are vague, ambiguous, lengthy, rhetorical, 'closed' (lead to yes/no answers), use complex language or encourage guessing.

Plan sequences of questions

What, then, are 'good' questions? Effective questions

Clarity of questions is very important

are clearly worded, and identify the aspects to which the students are expected to respond (see Barry & King 1993; Cole & Chan 1987; Groisser 1964; Turney *et al.* 1985a). For example, the question 'What do you notice about spiders?' does not give direction to students as to the information required. A better question would be 'What is the body structure of a spider?' or 'What is the shape of a spider's web?'

Effective questions have a purpose. As described earlier, questions should be sequenced in accordance with the instructional objectives. They should also be brief. A series of questions that progress a step at a time is preferable to one long one in which the focus is lost. 'What were some of the different cultural groups that have come to Australia and their reasons for settling here?' is far less effective than the following sequence: 'Name the European groups that migrated to Australia in the first 100 years after settlement. Why did each group come out?', followed by: 'Groups from the Middle East and Asia have come to Australia for different reasons in the past 20 years. Which groups are these? Why did each group leave their homeland?'

Purpose and brevity

Higher-cognitive-level questions also stimulate student interest and provide opportunities for clarifying their ideas. In this regard, an effective teacher understands that students need to learn how to answer such questions and supports the development of this skill. Students can be given time to jot down some ideas in answer to the question and then to share these with a peer before answering out loud. In other words, not only do they need to develop the skills for thinking out loud, but students need time in which to do so.

Stimulate student interest through higher-cognitive-level questions

Research has shown how very important it is for teachers to wait after they have asked a question of the whole class, and then again after nominating one student to answer (Tobin 1987). This wait-time should be no less than three seconds and has been shown to increase the amount and quality of student discussion considerably, as well as facilitating higher-cognitive-level learning by providing teachers and students with additional time to think (Swift & Gooding 1983; Tobin 1987; Turney *et al.* 1985a, 1985b). Teachers typically tend to wait no longer than half a second before they rephrase their own question or, worse still, answer it themselves (Swift & Gooding 1983). Teachers taught to monitor their wait-time by using an electronic (red light 'stop', green light after three seconds 'go') device reduced their disciplinary comments dramatically, while the amount of relevant discussion by students, the proportion of students engaged in discussion and the cognitive level of their answers were considerably raised. However, there may be little to be gained in providing students and teachers with additional time to think if recall of factual information is required. If simple recall or rote learning is the intended goal of the questioning, it may be better to use a shorter wait-time and move the activity along at a brisk pace (Tobin 1987).

Research on questioning has shown that both higher- and lower-cognitive-level questions can lead to effective learning (Gall 1984). However, much of the evidence is quite conflicting. What does emerge is that higher-level questions (that is, those that require comprehension, application, analysis, synthesis or evaluation) are not necessarily better than lower-level (factual or knowledge) questions. Students in the primary grades, those with low ability and those from lower socio-economic backgrounds benefit from questions that allow for a high proportion of correct answers, especially when learning basic skills. These are the lower-cognitive-level questions that ask for recall of knowledge; questions where there is only one right answer (Stallings & Kaskowitz 1975). Students with average to high ability, on the other hand, learn effectively from difficult questions at both lower and higher cognitive levels, especially when critical feedback is given by the teacher. Examples of effective higher-level questions are: 'Do you have any other ideas . . .?' 'Why did you come up with that conclusion?' 'How could you find out . . .?' 'What would you do if . . .?' 'Why do you think this happens?'

To this point, we have emphasised the teacher's role in questioning. Research also demonstrates that reciprocal peer questioning, and teaching students to ask questions of themselves in a guided way, facilitates student learning. We consider both these aspects of questioning later in the text. Consider the teacher's case book, 'How do I know they know?', on the value of using questions to stimulate learning and monitor students' understanding.

Using effective explanations and demonstrations

Other than for questioning, the next staples in a teacher's repertoire of skills are *explaining* and *demonstrating*, which often go in tandem. Effective teachers plan their explanations carefully so that they are precise and clear. In order to do this, teachers need to know their subject, be able to see the material from the learner's perspective, and be able to translate this into meaningful and simple terms appropriate to the learner in order to facilitate the learner's understanding. The converse—when teachers do not understand the material themselves, lack clarity in their

How do I know they know?

Ben, Sam and Rachel have just presented a movement piece they have devised, based on some music they have chosen. It is quite abstract, well controlled and focused. They have used a variety of elements such as locomotion, levels, force and speed, stillness, and so on.

At the end of drama lessons and at the conclusion of some specific activities, Mrs Hinley and her students sit and discuss elements of their work. Discussion is an important element of their work: it gives individual students the opportunity to articulate their ideas, thoughts and opinions, and it gives Mrs Hinley a chance to 'see inside their heads': 'What have they gained? What experiences have they benefited from? Was this activity worthwhile? Why? What makes it so? How will I develop, alter, redirect it to enhance the students' learning?'

Mrs Hinley now turns to the movement group. 'You were obviously engrossed in the performance today, Toby. . . . What was it about this group's work that appealed to you?' The answer to this prompting question was the focus for further questions and discussion with both the audience and the performers. Mrs Hinley considers and shapes her questions carefully. They are focused open questions which allow her to monitor the learning process that occurred. Students are asked to articulate their own learning process (for example, 'How did you arrive at the decision to start your movement piece in that particular way? The use of simple props was effective. How did that evolve?').

The students' reflection not only confirms for Mrs Hinley what they are learning, but also gives her an opportunity to plan, revise and develop her teaching.

Case studies illustrating National Competency Framework for Beginning Teaching, National Project on the Quality of Teaching and Learning, Australian Teaching Council, 1996, p. 40. Commonwealth of Australia copyright, reproduced by permission.

Case study activity

How does Mrs Hinley's strategies demonstrate effective teaching?

explanations, and use complex or convoluted terminology—only leads to student confusion. To facilitate good explanations, appropriate analogies, examples and demonstrations should be given. These can include pictures, diagrams, audio-visual material and on-line interactive material. Explanations should be constantly monitored to evaluate how effective they are by asking students relevant questions and having them comment on the explanation and ask questions of the teacher.

As with questioning, effective explaining can be accomplished by peers in collaborative and cooperative classroom structures (see Chapter 8). Giving explanations can be useful for the peer explainer, as preparing the explanation may assist in understanding and learning the material for oneself. It is also useful for the student receiving the explanation, as the level of communication between peers might be more effective in conveying meaning. Nevertheless, when peers are involved, the teacher needs to train students in the art of giving good explanations and to monitor the quality of the explanations given (see Fuchs *et al.* 1996).

Setting appropriate instructional objectives

Effective teachers plan their instruction around general and specific objectives so that there is a clear purpose to the content and activities that comprise the teacher's daily classroom interactions (see also Chapter 11). Bloom, Madaus and Hastings (1981) remind us, also, that statements of **instructional objectives** are specific descriptions of what each student should be able to do, produce or possess as a personal attribute (values, attitudes and feelings) after the instruction. The focus on instructional objectives dates back to the important work of Robert Mager (1973, 1990a, 1990b), which drew attention to the need for teachers to:

- specify the student behaviour or learning outcome that should result from the learning experience and the level at which the performance would be considered acceptable;
- describe the conditions under which the behaviour should occur and which would allow the teacher to be able to assess whether the standard had been met;
- determine the minimal level considered acceptable.

Similar to the guidelines offered by Mager, but presented as a very simple mnemonic, is the following ABCD format for writing objectives suggested by Armstrong and Savage (1983). Keep in mind:

A the *audience* (that is, each student) for whom the objectives are written;

B the *behaviour* that will indicate that learning has occurred;

C the *conditions* under which the behaviour should occur;

D the *degree* of competency required.

An example may best illustrate the way in which objectives would be written using this format:

A The *audience* are Muhammed, Paloma, Matthew and Jennifer (first-grade children who are grouped for the purpose of remedial work in basic language skills).

Muhammed and Paloma come from non-English-speaking home backgrounds; Matthew has a mild intellectual disability; and Jennifer is an Aboriginal child who has recently moved from a remote country school where access to a wide range of books was not available at home or at school.

B The *behaviour* is the ability to recognise and distinguish between the various vowel sounds and to pronounce them correctly while reading.

C The *conditions* are in the class reader *Wombat Stew* by Marcia Vaughan (1984; Ashton Scholastic, Gosford, NSW).

D The *degree* of competency required eight out of 10 vowels sounded out and pronounced correctly as part of the word (80 per cent).

Written as it might appear in a teaching program, this objective would read:

> Muhammed, Paloma, Matthew and Jennifer will be able to recognise, distinguish between and pronounce correctly 80 per cent of the vowel sounds they meet when reading *Wombat Stew*.

Norman Gronlund (1991) has argued that objectives should first be stated *generally*, using words such as 'know', 'understand', 'apply' and 'interpret'. Thus, for example, in a science course, some general objectives might be:

- Know correct laboratory procedures.
- Understand scientific facts and concepts.
- Apply scientific facts and concepts to new situations.
- Interpret data in scientific reports.

Gronlund recommends that, for effective planning of instruction, these general objectives should then be broken down into specific objectives that are, in effect, sample behaviours that demonstrate that students have achieved the general objective. For instance, in the science example above, 'Know correct laboratory procedures' would be described by such sample behaviours as choosing appropriate equipment for a procedure, assembling and operating equipment correctly, following safety rules, and cleaning and replacing equipment in the proper way.

Teaching for learning outcomes

Effective teachers communicate clear instructional objectives (broadly defined goals of instruction) as anticipated learning outcomes—that is, specific achievements that students are to show in observable ways at the end of instruction—to students so that their learning is goal directed. These teachers also introduce new material by relating it to key concepts that the students already have (advance organiser) which enables them to see a connection between previous learning and the new material. Both the advance organisers and stated learning outcomes provide students with a **learning set.** They understand the purpose of the activity to which their attention has been drawn and appreciate the anticipated academic benefits.

It will be evident by now that effective teachers are clear in their own minds about what they want students to learn. They are organised and they plan. They will have diagnosed the individual learning needs of their students and programmed the curriculum requirements stipulated by government bodies for their particular whole-class group and teaching discipline (in secondary school).

These student needs and curriculum requirements will have been used as the basis for determining the learning outcomes for that class of children, and will be expressed as specific outcome statements (for individual children and for groups with common needs) that describe what the students will be able to do at the completion of the learning tasks.

It is all very well to say that effective teachers write objectives for student learning, but how do they actually decide what these should be? We discuss sources of educational objectives and task analysis in Chapter 11. You are advised to refer to this material. The selection of tasks and associated activities is paramount in achieving effective learning outcomes. Effective teachers work hard to ensure that their approaches are appropriate, interesting, well organised and varied as the need arises.

Table 1.1 summarises the essential teaching skills for effective learning.

Table 1.1 Essential teaching skills for effective learning

Teachers should:

- demonstrate appropriate knowledge;
- utilise appropriate management skills;
- implement effective questioning techniques;
- use effective explanations and demonstrations;
- set appropriate instructional objectives;
- teach for learning outcomes;
- use motivational strategies;
- monitor and evaluate student learning;
- communicate enthusiasm, warmth and humour

Using motivational strategies

Effective teachers implement specific strategies to enhance class and individual motivation. We discuss a range of these in Chapter 7 in some detail. At this point, we wish to highlight some of the key strategies based on the work of Ames and Ames (1991)—namely, reducing social comparison, stimulating student involvement in learning, focusing on effort, promoting personal beliefs in competence, and increasing chances of student success. Table 1.2 presents these key strategies.

QUESTION POINT

Discuss how an effective teacher may reduce social comparison, increase student involvement in learning, focus on student effort, and promote student belief in their competence.

Monitoring and evaluating learning

Effective teachers monitor student progress both throughout the learning activity and at its conclusion (see Chapter 11). They do this through questioning, observation of work samples, tests and quizzes, and collection of homework assignments and projects. An important additional means of evaluation is that performed by the student. Self-evaluation is considered a vital skill in a rapidly changing society where the emphasis is on being autonomous and independent as a learner (Boud 1985; Falchikov & Boud 1989; Hall 1992; Woodward 1993). Perhaps more important than learning a whole pile of facts, which are readily available in a multitude of forms (for example, computer databases), is the opportunity for students to learn how to determine where strengths lie in their work and how to remedy weaknesses. Students should be taught how to reflect upon their learning, and evaluate their own work and that of others (sensitively). Another effective strategy to foster the development of self-evaluation is to have students maintain a folder of all work that is submitted for assessment as a means of providing them with a concrete basis for self-evaluation. It is easy, then, to sit with students periodically and go through their folders to evaluate the extent to which progress has been

Table 1.2 Essentials of effective strategies to encourage motivation

Teachers should:

Reduce social comparison by:
- avoiding social comparison and external and public evaluation;
- emphasising achievement in terms of personal best rather than comparative norms reflected through grades and marks;
- using a range of measurement, evaluation and reporting schemes;
- using evaluation that relates to the 'real' world of the student.

Stimulate student involvement in learning by:
- using variety in teaching methods (including group work, peer tutoring, games and simulations);
- allowing students choice and control over their learning in relation to method, pace and content;
- situating learning in relevant 'real life' contexts.

Focus on effort by:
- emphasising personal effort as the means for improvement;
- helping students to see that mistakes are a part of learning;
- setting realistic expectations on 'reasonable effort';
- helping students to establish realistic goals.

Promote belief in competence by:
- helping children to develop metacognitive and self-regulatory skills;
- communicating positive expectations;
- making plans with students for improvement.

Increase chances for success by:
- modelling learning approaches and motivation in the classroom;
- teaching learning skills and strategies;
- individualising instruction;
- using cooperative and peer learning situations.

(*Source:* Based on Ames & Ames 1991)

'Just say that your dog chewed it up . . . I'm sure she's never heard that one before.'

made. Asking them, 'Is this your best work?' or 'What have you learned?' can be placed in the context of their own personal best, not that of the class norm (see, for example, Paulson, Paulson & Meyer 1991; Wolf 1989). Students can be trained in the use of such metacognitive strategies as planning, monitoring and evaluating, which help them to control their own learning (see Chapter 4).

Communicating enthusiasm, warmth and humour

As an effective teacher you need to communicate genuine enthusiasm about what you are doing in the classroom, as well as being able to motivate your students. Enthusiasm is expressed in observable ways such as varied tones of voice, lively eyes that make frequent eye contact with students, use of gestures, and an energetic manner while moving around the room. Enthusiastic teachers show the emotions of surprise, joy and excitement in facial expressions and in voice. The use of appropriate and meaningful hand and arm gestures probably enhances teaching and learning, although this is an understudied area in educational psychology (Roth 2001).

No doubt we have all experienced a teacher who droned on monotonously when explaining something (without humour or colourful examples) and who tended to stand or sit in one place throughout a lesson looking only at one small group of students. This teacher's classroom was a boring place and we didn't really look forward to being there, nor did we learn very much. Not surprisingly, research has shown that both student attitude and achievement are positively affected by teacher enthusiasm (Larkins *et al.* 1985; Rosenshine 1971). The attitudes you model to your students will play a large part in determining their level of interest and enthusiasm. If you communicate lack of interest in the material—'Sorry, but I have to teach this topic. It's in the curriculum'—students are obviously not likely to be enthused either.

Can one be trained to be enthusiastic? You may be saying at this point that your personality is not naturally enthusiastic; that you are a shy person. Larkins *et al.* (1985) showed that teachers can be trained successfully in 'enthusiasm-showing behaviours' (dynamic voice and manner; teaching techniques that create suspense and build interest) with the result that students rate their teachers and the teaching more favourably. Students may not necessarily gain higher scores on achievement tests, but the classroom learning climate is improved as a result of positive student attitudes. One qualification is needed here: keep the enthusiasm to a moderate level—excessive teacher enthusiasm may create discipline problems in the primary school grades where children need clear and consistent guidelines for appropriate behaviour (McKinney *et al.* 1983).

Training in enthusiasm-showing behaviours

Enthusiasm has a lot of bearing on what psychologists talk of as motivation (see Chapter 7). Children will go to school because they are pressured to by parents and school authorities, at least until a certain age, but such **extrinsic motivation** will encourage only superficial learning or, as Biggs (1991a, 1991b; Biggs & Moore 1993) calls it, a 'surface approach to learning' wherein the student focuses on gaining rewards or avoiding failure (for fear of punishment or loss of rewards). **Intrinsic motivation** is that motivation in which students find the learning tasks genuinely interesting and relevant. The teacher's enthusiastic attitude and energy encourage a learning climate in which such interesting and personally meaningful tasks can flourish. The result is 'deep learning' (Biggs 1991a, 1991b) and a sense of purpose in classroom activities.

As with enthusiasm, warmth and humour are personal-style characteristics—rather than teaching behaviours—and are therefore difficult to define objectively. Nonetheless, research has shown that students whose teachers use humour (such as anecdotes and examples) retain more of the material they have been taught than those whose teachers use no humour (Kaplan & Pascoe 1977). Student attention and interest are improved through the use of humour, although the effects on effective learning are not as clear (Powell & Anderson 1985). As with enthusiasm, the use of humour can be

Warmth and humour facilitate learning

learned, and it is clearly related to positive student attitudes and classroom climate—important conditions for effective learning to take place. Take care, however, that humour is appropriate and in good taste (no jokes about cultural groups, for example) or your credibility will be lowered and the atmosphere soured. Excessively used, humour will reduce your ability to maintain classroom control.

What about warmth? It goes without saying that, for effective teachers, teaching is more than just a job that involves imparting information to students; these teachers care about children and genuinely like being with them. As would be expected, research in this area suggests that, in terms of influencing achievement, a friendly climate is preferable to one that is negative and critical. However, extreme friendliness—such as the over-frequent use of praise—is counterproductive. Rather, a more businesslike, or neutral, emotional climate is strongly correlated with increases in student learning, especially for primary-aged children from middle- and upper-class backgrounds (Brophy & Good 1986; Kutnick & Jules 1993; Soar 1966; Soar & Soar 1979).

ACTION STATION

What makes an effective teacher? The answer isn't simple. Techniques and approaches that work well with one class and particular children may be quite ineffective with other classes and other children. Teacher personality and school dynamics (such as **socio-economic status**, cultural background, grade levels), among other factors, all influence how effective particular teachers are with particular students. There are, of course, some general principles that apply (such as being well organised and showing a personal interest in the children) but, in practice, effective teaching is a product of a very complex set of variables. A good place to start in understanding what makes effective teaching is to ask practitioners and children what they think. Therefore, while practice teaching:

1. *Discuss* with your supervising teachers what they think makes effective teaching and relate this to the material covered in your text.
2. *Discuss* with two or three students in your class what makes an effective teacher. You may need to phrase the question appropriately (for example, 'What does a teacher do to help you learn? When do you enjoy learning? How do you know that you have learned something?').
3. *Record* your findings and relate them to what the teacher and text suggest are important elements of effective teaching.

Consult your tutor/lecturer for advice on how to conduct these interviews so that you are sensitive to the classroom teacher and students concerned.

QUESTION POINT

Are positive teacher attitudes and enthusiasm more important at some grade levels than others? Why? Are they more important in some curriculum areas than others? Why?

Effective schools and effective learning

We have been describing above some of the elements that will assist teachers in becoming effective and efficacious. During our description we have also introduced the idea that schools themselves can have a collective efficacy that is related to stude[illegible]i, Borgogni & Steca 20[illegible]d 2001, Goddard *et a*[illegible]r 2000). Considerabl[illegible]n what makes schools effective (Langer 2000; Phillips 1997; Shann 1999). The OECD has defined an effective school as 'one that promotes the progress of its students in a broad range of intellectual, social and emotional outcomes, taking into account socio-economic status, family background and prior learning' (quoted in Wyatt 1996, p. 89). Some researchers and educators believe that school effectiveness is a result of the communal organisation of the school that emphasises caring, shared values and activities, positive adult social relations, positive teacher–student relations and democratic

Good rapport is essential if we are to teach culturally different children effectively.

Theory and research into practice

Lyn Corno — TEACHING, LEARNING AND STUDENT MOTIVATION

BRIEF BIOGRAPHY

My career began in the 1970s doing educational research and development—that dry form we used to call 'instructional R&D'. I worked for a federally funded lab outside Los Angeles developing K-12 curricula thought to be 'teacher-proof'. As we have since learned, and I have documented in various forms over the years, teaching is an original enterprise that cannot be reduced to scripted formulae. The scholarship supporting this position came about when I moved on to Stanford University and pursued a doctoral degree in psychological studies in education. There I also served as an assistant professor from 1978 to 1982.

After leaving Stanford I spent the next 12 years as full-time faculty at Teachers College, Columbia University (TC), where I became a full professor with tenure. In addition to regular duties as faculty, in this stage of my career I edited two major scholarly journals, had opportunities to conduct and advise on educational research projects and grants in both the public and private sectors, served as an external reviewer for doctoral dissertations outside Columbia, continued to publish in scholarly journals and books, and held both elected and appointed offices in the American Educational Research Association and the American Psychological Association (APA). I received the honour of fellow appointments in prominent organisations such as APA, the American Psychological Society and the American Association for the Advancement of Science.

At present, I remain at TC as an adjunct professor and co-editor of *TC Record*. However, I work largely from my home office in a suburb southwest of Boston, where I moved with my young family in 1995. Although I am no longer full-time faculty at TC, I continue to advise doctoral students on dissertation research, largely using the Internet, and participate in various research initiatives through the College. I have also, for the past several years, served on the board of directors for the National Society for the Study of Education (NSSE).

RESEARCH AND THEORETICAL INTERESTS

A line of theory and empirical research formed the basis for courses I developed at Stanford and later at TC. I have focused on the juncture of teaching, learning and student motivation at the process level in a number of contexts, and these efforts have led me to model self-regulated learning as it plays out in different instructional situations. My early models addressed self-regulated learning by students in classroom settings and in computer-assisted instruction. Later, I studied homework, teacher self-regulation in professional development, and computer learning via the Internet. Supporting these topics in education is my writing and research on modern theories of volition as they apply to education. The four prominent strands can be summarised as follows:

1 **Conceptualising self-regulated learning**. Beginning in the 1980s, Stanford doctoral student Ellen Mandinach and I integrated cognitive theories of learning and motivation in relation to student engagement in academic work. Our early efforts pioneered the study of self-regulated learning in students. An increasingly prominent area of research in educational psychology, conceptions of self-regulated learning have been addressed in special issues of journals, both scholarly and practitioner-oriented books in series, and in the development of specialised forms of assessment and computer software for self-study. (See Corno & Mandinach 2004 below for full references on this topic.)

2 **Homework**. Another important focus in my career has been the quest to better understand the conditions and processes involved in doing homework at different grade levels. This work includes extensive analysis of the roles played by teachers and parents in the homework process and in developing children's homework expertise. My work on this subject began with a dean's grant I received as a new faculty member at TC in the early 1980s, through which I was able to support doctoral student Jianzhong Xu as my research assistant on several qualitative case studies. Our collaboration on the stories and truths surrounding homework continues today. (See Corno 2000 below for various research reports and other publications on this topic.)

3 **Interpreting modern theory on volition for an educational research audience**. During the past decade I have taken on what some might say is a personal crusade to clarify key constructs and applications of modern process theory on volition for educators and educational psychologists. Through special issues and key articles in scholarly journals, I have strongly advocated more research on this topic, and better direction to practitioners. The elements of productive follow-through have important implications for improving student work habits. (See

Corno *et al.* 2002 for related publications on this topic.) Towards this end, most recently I edited a special issue of *TC Record* entitled 'Work habits and work styles in education' (Fall 2004).

4 **Individual differences in learning, adaptive teaching, and aptitude-treatment interactions in classrooms**. Finally, threading through much of my work post- the era of teacher-proof curricula has been a critical analysis of early conceptions of adaptive instruction, including research methods for assessing the combinations and sequences of instructional activity that interact with student individual differences. I have come to the position that traditional investigations relating teaching and student individual differences have pointed in the wrong direction, and I have begun to lay out a research agenda to think about individual differences more like teachers do. (See Stanford Aptitude Seminar: Corno *et al.* 2002.)

THEORY AND RESEARCH INTO PRACTICE

With this combination of interests and experiences, I have been fortunate to develop a body of work in the area of self-regulated learning providing a varied array of professional opportunities. I spent several summers in the 1980s serving as a consultant to a large computer company that was heavily invested in the development of computer-based self-instructional systems. There I validated aptitude tests for systems engineers and taught instructors using computer-assisted instruction about curriculum and instructional theory and existing research on teaching.

In recent years, I have chaired the board of the NSSE—a small, century-old organisation that produces critical and historically based yearbooks on timely topics in education, broadly construed. Another board on which I served and chaired is the visiting panel for educational research at the Educational Testing Service (ETS). The panel reviews and advises ETS research scientists on many aspects of their learning and assessment projects, including measures of motivational and volitional processes.

Among the more conventional practical activities I have pursued as an educational psychologist are editing peer-reviewed academic journals, including the *American Educational Research Journal*, the *Educational Psychologist* and the *Teachers College Record*. Most of my work these days is done over the Internet, where I continue to advise doctoral students in curriculum and teaching, do on-line editing, and engage in collaborative research and writing projects. I have participated in the publishing workshops offered as mini-courses prior to national research meetings. I have chaired sessions at these meetings for journal editorial boards and councils of editors. I have served years as a graduate student mentor for students at these annual meetings.

Collaboration is a recurrent theme across my career. I strive to create a milieu for my graduate students to learn the craft of research by working as apprentices at the frontiers of their fields. From my earliest publications with students as co-authors, to chapters reviewing large bodies of research with my own dissertation sponsor, Dick Snow—including a seven-author collaboration on a book honouring Snow's legacy—to the editorship of the centennial yearbook on behalf of the NSSE, collaborative research and writing is how I do my best work.

With Judi Randi, another former student, I have written about the importance of 'collaborative innovation' in teaching as well as research—how researchers and teachers together grow in their knowledge and in reframing their points of view when they work together to examine and improve the daily practices of educating. I have never been so self-regulated as when I co-taught one summer at TC with Judi Randi, who was an experienced high school teacher. Watching Judi teach and how she plans for instruction to construct a suitably interactive curriculum, my own teaching changed altogether. I can never again look at a graduate course as an opportunity to deliver lectures. Internalising just some of the successes of Judi's experiences with high school students gave me pieces of her self-regulation for teaching that reshaped my own.

In closing, I would offer the trite observation that no career is an island. Perhaps my biggest career surprise was the response from the popular press to the first article I wrote on homework (in 1996) entitled 'Homework is a complicated thing' (see Corno 2000 for citation). The editor of the journal publishing that article was Tom Good; he asked contributors to cast aside the typical pedantic writing style of academics in favour of journalistic prose so as to appeal broadly to practitioners and policy makers. I doubt even he expected, however, that I would receive calls for interviews from writers for magazines such as *Time* and *Ladies Home Journal* who were crafting stories on homework. I gave interviews to several local news programs on the topic, as well as one with a producer of Oprah Winfrey's, and an on-camera segment with Matt Lauer on the *Today Show*. It seems there can be connections between an island and the mainland even where you do not expect them; in education, some issues resurface every September.

KEY REFERENCES

Corno, L. (2000) Looking at homework differently. *Elementary School Journal*, **100**(5), 529–48.

Corno, L. & Mandinach, E. B. (2004) What we have learned about student engagement in the past twenty years. In D. M. McInerney & S. Van Etten (eds) *Research on Sociocultural Influences on Motivation and Learning (Volume 4), Big Theories Revisited,* (pp. 299–328). Greenwich, CT: Information Age Publishing.

Stanford Aptitude Seminar: Corno, L., Cronbach, L. J., Kupermintz, H., Lohman, D. F., Mandinach, E. B., Porteus, A. W. & Talbert, J. E. (2002) *Remaking the Concept of Aptitude: Extending the Legacy of Richard E. Snow.* Mahwah, NJ: Lawrence Erlbaum Associates.

ACTIVITIES

1 Lyn Corno has been heavily involved in theory and research on teaching, learning and motivation. Four key themes have dominated her research: self-regulated learning, homework, volition in educational contexts, and individual differences. Go through later chapters in your text and other resources and outline three key findings from research on each of these areas.

2 Lyn Corno has examined the roles of teachers and parents in the homework process and in developing children's homework expertise. In a group, discuss what you think the role of parents and teachers should be, and what you think Lyn Corno means by 'homework expertise'. Prepare a set of notes for parents and teachers related to the effective use of homework for learning and motivation.

3 What do you think is meant by 'a process theory on volition in an educational context'? Give examples.

4 In Chapters 9 and 10 we deal with individual differences and education. Lyn Corno has done considerable research in this area, and in particular on adaptive teaching and aptitude-treatment interactions in classrooms. Using information in these two chapters, discuss with your group the nature of adaptive teaching and what is meant by 'aptitude-treatment interactions'.

governance. This approach to school effectiveness is often termed the **caring school.** We discuss the notion of the caring school in detail in Chapters 8 and 14. Others believe that schools are effective when they offer demanding curricula, have clear achievement-oriented goals, are efficient in their use of time for instruction, and employ teachers whose educational expectations for their students are high (Phillips 1997). This approach is often termed **academic press.** It is likely that effective schools more or less reflect both dimensions, and that both contribute to student achievement (Lee & Smith 1995; Shann 1999; Shouse 1996; Smyth 1999).

What makes schools effective is, however, quite a complex question, as there is no one global measure of school effectiveness. For example: How do we measure if a school is effective? Do we look at outcome measures such as marks and grades, and/or less tangible indicators such as school adjustment? Do schools remain effective over longer or shorter periods of time? Are they equally effective in all areas? Are they equally effective for all students? (see Wyatt 1996). Sometimes the effectiveness of schools is measured by limited criteria such as test and basic skills results; however, a broader range of values seems more appropriate (see, for example, Shann 1999). These might include helping students to (see McGaw *et al.* 1992):

- develop a positive relationship with learning;
- develop a positive self-concept;
- develop a sense of self-discipline and self-worth;
- develop living skills;
- become productive and confident members of the adult world;
- develop appropriate value systems;
- prepare for the next stage of their learning.

In our text we address each of these values. We discuss the importance of developing and maintaining warm

Teaching is a dynamic career. Making your lessons relevant to students from diverse backgrounds is a great challenge.

interpersonal relationships with students in order to facilitate their effective learning, while emphasising the importance of holding high expectations for students and establishing challenging and high standards for learning and teaching.

Learner-centred psychological principles

The scientific study of psychology in education has provided vital information on the learner and the learning process (see, for example, Wittrock 1992). In order to be an effective teacher, educators must attend to cognitive and metacognitive factors, motivational and affective factors, developmental and social factors, and, lastly, individual differences. The Learner-centred Psychological Principles developed by the American Psychological Association apply to all learners and provide a very useful framework for understanding effective learning and its relationship to effective teaching. Throughout the text we include excerpts from these psychological principles and relate them to the material covered. By considering these principles, and relating them to the material covered in our text, you will be able to make the link between theory and application more easily.

Our first Learner-centred Psychological Principle emphasises constructivism, which is a key element in the theories of Piaget and Vygotsky, which you will study in the next chapter. Later in the text we consider a number of other perspectives on learning and motivation that are reflected in this principle.

LEARNER-CENTRED PSYCHOLOGICAL PRINCIPLE

Nature of the learning process. The learning of complex subject matter is most effective when it is an intentional process of constructing meaning from information and experience.

There are different types of learning processes—for example, habit formation in motor learning; and learning that involves the generation of knowledge, or cognitive skills and learning strategies. Learning in schools emphasises the use of intentional processes that students can use to construct meaning from information, experiences, and their own thoughts and beliefs. Successful learners are active, goal directed, self-regulating, and assume personal responsibility for contributing to their own learning. The principles set forth in this document focus on this type of learning.

Novice teacher efficacy

Research that identifies effective teaching is really talking about 'particular teaching procedures and behaviours that are related to positive student learning outcomes and student attitudes to learning' in particular classrooms (Mason & Levi 1992). An important consideration to keep in mind is that what constitutes effective practice in one classroom or school setting may not be so in another. The reasons for this include differences in students (ability, background, prior knowledge and interests), parental commitment to education, and school climate (collaboration between teaching peers, and agreement on approaches to instruction, classroom management and curriculum development). As we have indicated, effective teaching involves the use of a complex set of skills to evoke effective learning—skills such as lesson design and implementation, assessment and evaluation, questioning and explanation, and motivating. However, effective teaching is not simply the ability to apply techniques and skills, but also involves the art of being reflective—thoughtful and inventive—about teaching (Peterson 1988).

Consider the case study on p. 26 of a beginning teacher and discuss her development in terms of issues covered in this chapter.

QUESTION POINT

Discuss the characteristics of two or three of the best teachers that you have come into contact with. Analyse their characteristics in terms of the points covered in this chapter.

ACTION STATION

Interview two teachers—one who has been teaching for more than 10 years and one who has started teaching relatively recently (up to five years)—about their teaching concerns. Pool your information with the rest of your class. Are there any patterns characterising the responses? Are there differences between the older and newer teachers' concerns?

QUESTION POINT

The teacher of tomorrow will no longer be the knowledgeable classroom authority on everything, but rather a flexible improviser and team player. What is your opinion?

EXTENSION STUDY

Stages of development: Novice to 'expert' teacher

Over the last few decades, there has been considerable research and theorising on the professional development of teachers (Brouwer & Korthagen 2005; Hogan, Rabinowitz & Craven 2003; van den Berg 2002), with a number of theories being developed that attempt to describe the 'stages' of professional development as a teacher progresses from novice to expert (Ingvarson & Greenway 1984; see also Nathan & Petrosino 2003). A knowledge of 'stages' may give you a framework for analysing your own professional development.

Three models that have been developed are those of Fuller (Fuller 1969; Fuller & Brown 1975; see also Oosterheert, Vermunt & Denessen 2002), Berliner (1986, 1988) and Reynolds (1992). In the Fuller model there are four stages. In the first, preteaching stage, beginning teachers tend to identify realistically with pupils but unrealistically with teachers. They really do not understand the dynamics of teaching. In the second stage, they are most concerned with survival and, in particular, with class control, content mastery and personal adequacy as a teacher. In the third stage, teachers are concerned with the limitations and frustrations of teaching situations; while in the last stage they become concerned with pupil needs (social, academic and emotional) and their ability to relate to the pupils as individuals. The model is seen as hierarchical and focuses attention on the evolution of the teacher from egocentric to pupil-centred concerns.

In Berliner's model, teachers move from the stage of novice—where the beginning teacher is consciously learning the tasks of teaching and developing strategies—through to the proficient and expert teacher, where intuition and knowledge guide classroom performance. In these latter stages, teachers operate on 'automatic pilot' without consciously being aware of what they are doing or why. Indeed, when asked to explain or reflect on their performance, expert teachers are likely to have trouble describing the processes they engaged in.

Reynolds (1992), in distinguishing between competent, experienced and beginning teachers, discusses the differences on three levels. First, experienced teachers comprehend, critique and adapt content, materials and teaching methods more effectively, and prepare plans, materials and physical space more appropriately. Reynolds calls these *preactive tasks*. Second, experienced teachers are more competent at implementing and adjusting plans during the instructional period, at organising and monitoring students, time and materials during instruction, and at evaluating the students' learning. This is referred to as skill with the *interactive tasks* of teaching. Last, on *postactive tasks*, experienced teachers reflect on their own activities and student responses in order to improve teaching, continue their professional development, and interact with colleagues more effectively than do beginning teachers.

Referring to these three models, the beginning teacher may appreciate that teaching is pre-eminently perceived as a developmental career. No beginning teacher is expected to have an expert's control of the teaching process. Nevertheless, beginning teachers can be quite competent in their own right and indeed, in many cases, can facilitate learning among children more effectively than some veterans. More recently, theorising about the development of teacher expertise has moved from sequential models such as those described above to more flexible accounts of the developmental process, and which included greater emphasis on the teachers' own beliefs and attitudes with regard to teaching practice. We recommend that you read the article by van den Berg listed in the recommended readings for further details on these developments.

Stages of development and teacher efficacy

Tschannen-Moran *et al.* (1998, see also Johnson & Birkeland 2003) also consider the development and modification of teacher efficacy beliefs as teachers move from being student teachers to being experienced teachers. As indicated earlier, efficacy beliefs are associated with a number of positive qualities. For the preservice teacher, efficacy beliefs are associated with more humane rather than custodial control of students. Preservice teachers with low efficacy take a more pessimistic view of students' motivation, and apply stricter classroom rules, extrinsic rewards and punishments to make students study, than do high-efficacy students. High-efficacy students during practicum were also rated more positively on lesson-presentation behaviour, classroom management and questioning behaviour by their supervising teachers (Tschannen-Moran *et al.* 1998). It also appears that course work and practica have differing effects on the development of efficacy beliefs (see, for example, Brouwer & Korthagen 2005). Course work appears to affect student teachers' general teaching efficacy—that is, how much they feel they are limited by external background factors such as the home or community environment and socio-economic realities of the students in doing an effective job as a teacher. On the other hand, actual teaching experiences during student teaching practica appear to impact on personal teaching efficacy—that is, how personally competent the student teacher feels in particular teaching episodes (see van den Berg 2002).

General teaching efficacy has also been shown to decline during student teaching, suggesting that the realities of the school experience may counteract the idealised picture portrayed during course work at university and challenge in a dramatic way the student teachers' feelings of competence (Weinstein 1998). As Wideen, Mayer-Smith and Moon (1998, p. 153) put it: 'The practicum is a time when student teachers see their images of teaching shattered . . ., experience the rites of passage . . ., and deal with conflicts arising from inadequate preparation for the classroom situation.' This situation occurs because practicum is seen by university supervisors and student teachers in different ways. University supervisors see practicum as a time when student teachers will examine non-traditional ways of teaching, apply pedagogical content knowledge learned on campus, reflect on their experience, take risks, and focus on the 'why' of teaching rather than the 'how'. What student teachers are most concerned with is the 'how' and with surviving. This is made more dramatic by the contrast that exists between school expectations and university expectations, with many schools' cooperating teachers emphasising the need for student teachers to teach in traditional ways and to concentrate on the 'how' of teaching (see Wideen *et al.* 1998).

Novice teachers in their first year of teaching who had a high sense of teacher efficacy found greater satisfaction in teaching, had a more positive reaction to teaching and experienced less stress (Tschannen-Moran *et al.* 1998). These teachers were also more positive about the training they had received and were more optimistic that they would remain in teaching longer.

There is little evidence about how efficacy beliefs develop over the later stages of a teaching career. It appears that efficacy beliefs among experienced teachers are quite stable, but there is little evidence about whether efficacy beliefs in general grow stronger, weaker or stay the same for cohorts as they progress through their teaching career. It would appear that, with experience, teachers develop a relatively stable set of core beliefs about their abilities. However, new challenges—such as having to teach a new grade, work in a new setting or implement a new curriculum—may elicit a re-evaluation of efficacy (Ross 1998; Tschannen-Moran *et al.* 1998). Because little is known about how efficacy develops later in a teacher's career, if at all, it is important that strong efficacy beliefs are developed early in the training of teachers.

It is also important to note that schools, as institutions, can have a collective sense of efficacy; the higher the school's collective efficacy, the more positive will be the efficacy of individual teachers within the school (Caprara, Barbaranelli, Borgogni & Steca 2003; Fives & Alexander 2004; Goddard 2001; Goddard, Hoy & Woolfolk Hoy 2000, 2004; Henson 2002; van den Berg 2002). Low school efficacy can be contagious among staff, leading to a self-defeating and demoralising cycle of failure. As we discuss in Chapter 6, low teacher efficacy can lead to low student efficacy, which in turn leads to low academic achievement. Low student achievement can then lead to a further decline in teacher and school efficacy (Bandura 1997).

TEACHER'S CASE BOOK

Can I fulfil the expectations of me as a teacher?

Miss Fraser can remember how totally inadequate she felt on her first day of teaching. She wasn't sure how she was going to cope. She was feeling unsure about what was expected of her in the school as a beginning teacher. She felt that everyone had high expectations of her as a person and as a teacher.

Planning was a major problem: it ate up massive chunks of her time because she felt she was under scrutiny. Her first planning meeting with a senior staff member was absolutely terrifying, not because of the senior member of staff, who was really supportive, but because Miss Fraser still wasn't sure of the expectations.

Miss Fraser desperately wanted approval and this she received. Until that happened she was experiencing a great deal of doubt in her ability as a teacher. That feedback was incredibly important. It was a turning point in her first term of teaching. After that initial planning meeting, she felt greater confidence in herself as a teacher and was much more relaxed and really able to enjoy what she was doing.

Miss Fraser felt under-prepared leaving uni and realised the importance of drawing on the experience and resources of more experienced teachers within the school. She needed the security of a set curriculum to follow, so that she knew she was on the right track. As the year passed and Miss Fraser has grown in confidence, she feels the need for this less and less and is a great deal more flexible and adaptable than she felt she could be at the start of the year.

The amount of planning she is doing now has been reduced a great deal. She used to write down everything and stick to it at all costs, but now she feels more able to justify what she does, why she's doing it and for which children. With the help and support she has received from senior staff she now feels comfortable and confident about her planning and is able to concentrate on her teaching and the children's learning.

Case study illustrating National Competency Framework for Beginning Teaching, National Project on the Quality of Teaching and Learning, Australian Teaching Council, 1996, pp. 31–2. Commonwealth of Australia copyright, reproduced by permission.

How would you rate yourself as a teacher?

QUESTION POINT

Explore your implicit theories of teaching and learning. How might these have evolved? Is teaching an art or a science? Do the teaching competencies in Box 1.2 reflect science or art?

QUESTION POINT

Discuss how the teaching competencies in Box 1.2 are important in a teacher's growth towards becoming an 'expert' teacher.

TEACHING COMPETENCE Box 1.2

The teacher critically reflects on his or her own practice and develops professional skills and capacity to improve the quality of teaching and learning

Indicators

The teacher:

- evaluates teaching and learning programs;
- keeps a record of selected experiences/incidents;
- reflects on successes and areas for improvement in teaching;
- monitors the outcomes of teaching and learning;
- involves colleagues in planning to improve teaching and learning;
- acts to extend his or her repertoire of skills and capacities;
- participates in voluntary activities such as those provided by professional associations and teacher unions;
- undertakes further training, development and professional reading.

Case studies illustrating National Competency Framework for Beginning Teaching, National Project on the Quality of Teaching and Learning, Australian Teaching Council, 1996, Elements 5.1 and 5.4, pp. 61 and 64. Commonwealth of Australia copyright, reproduced by permission.

ACTION STATION

Consider the following (Conners, Nettle & Placing 1990):

1. Describe the kind of teacher you would like to be.
2. Describe two significant incidents/experiences in your life that you consider have influenced your view of teaching.
3. When you think about yourself teaching, what subjects or activities would you most like to teach?
4. Are there any subjects or activities that you would *not* like to teach?

Discuss these issues in a group of four or five students and then make a full class report.

National Competency Framework for Beginning Teaching

In order to monitor the development of beginning teachers, many educational systems have implemented competency frameworks to evaluate progress towards competency. As you will have observed, one such framework—the National Competency Framework for Beginning Teaching (Australian Teaching Council 1996)—is presented throughout our text to provide benchmarks for two purposes: (1) to assess a teacher's progress in mastering essential elements of teaching for effective learning; and (2) to provide an applied set of teaching–learning principles based on theory. There are five areas of competency that we address throughout the text:

1. Using and developing professional knowledge and values.
2. Communicating, interacting and working with students and others.
3. Planning and managing the teaching and learning process.
4. Monitoring and assessing student progress and learning outcomes.
5. Reflecting on, evaluating and planning for continuous improvement as a teacher.

Each of these areas of competency is elaborated through a series of criteria referred to throughout the text.

You—the reflective teacher

Throughout this book, we hope that you not only learn about the way in which children construct their understanding of the world around them as motivated learners and thinkers, but also take the time to reflect upon yourself as a learner and thinker. Increasingly, teaching is being looked upon not as the end point of some training course but rather as a lifelong process which includes continual learning, critical reflection and growth. With a deeper understanding of your own learning, you will be in a better position to assist students to learn (see, for example, Floden & Klinzing 1990; Henderson 1992; Koop & Koop 1990; Lampert & Clark 1990; Laskey & Hallinan 1990; Peacock & Yaxley 1990; Peterson 1988).

Your reflections will call into play your background experiences as a learner (both as a child and now as a university student, in both formal and informal settings), the ideas and theories presented to you by others and the constant flow of information and judgments from classroom experiences and other sources (see, for example, Wideen *et al.* 1998; for a critical analysis of reflection in teaching, see Fendler 2003). Many of these will be considered in this text, and through our coverage we hope to help you construct increasingly valid and accurate personal theories of teaching and learning.

Theory and research into practice

Helen M. G. Watt AND Paul. W. Richardson — MOTIVATION TO TEACH

BRIEF BIOGRAPHY

I am currently a research scientist at the University of Michigan. Previously I have been faculty at Macquarie University, then at the University of Sydney, and most recently the University of Western Sydney. In my current role I am working with Professor Jacquelynne Eccles on aspects of the expectancy-value theory, and with Dr Elizabeth Moje on adolescents' literacy practices, beliefs, and motivations in and outside of school.

My undergraduate degree from the University of Sydney was a Bachelor of Education in Secondary Mathematics (Honours), for which I was awarded the university medal. I have received several international and national awards for my research. For my Ph.D. from the University of Sydney I received the American Educational Research Association doctoral award in 'Counseling and Human Development'. I completed a postdoctoral fellowship at the University of Michigan with Professor Jacquelynne Eccles. I have also received awards for the quality of my university teaching in Australia.

My expertise relates to motivation, self-concept, academic achievement, maths education, gendered occupational choices, socialisation of gender differences, motivations for teaching and teacher self-efficacy, measurement, and scale construction.

RESEARCH AND THEORETICAL INTERESTS

My interests centre on affective, cognitive and social bases for academic choices, and I have developed two large-scale longitudinal research programs on this. The first investigates (1) different achievement-related outcomes in math and English for boys and girls in Australian secondary schools; (2) key psychological predictors of those outcomes; (3) how these psychological influences interrelate through adolescent development; and (4) qualitative interview explorations for the sources of girls' underestimation of their mathematical abilities. The second is in collaboration with Dr Paul Richardson and is described below.

BRIEF BIOGRAPHY

Before taking up my position at the University of Sydney, I was a secondary school teacher of English, History and Drama for a number of years in the outer Western Suburbs and inner city of Sydney. I have worked in teacher education at the University of Sydney and at Monash University in Victoria, where my particular interests have been in English and literacy curriculum.

I completed my Ph.D. at Monash University and was awarded the Mollie Holman university medal. At Monash University I teach both undergraduate and postgraduate courses on English curriculum and literacy education as well as research methods, with a focus on learning to write academic texts. Until recently I was associate dean (teaching) in the Faculty of Education at Monash University, a position I relinquished to work as a research scientist at the University of Michigan with Professor Jacquelynne Eccles and Dr Elizabeth Moje on a major research project examining the social and cultural forces that impact on adolescent literacy development in and out of school.

RESEARCH AND THEORETICAL INTERESTS

My research focuses on two areas, both of which have grown out of my professional work in teacher education and as a university teacher and researcher: (1) the motivations of beginning teachers; and (2) the role of language and literacy in learning in academic contexts. I have a particular interest in the role that reading and writing play in learning in the disciplines in higher education, and I am investigating the development of interest and the identification individuals have within different academic disciplines.

A JOINT PROGRAM OF RESEARCH

Together we have a joint large-scale longitudinal program of research which investigates (1) motivations for selecting teaching as a career; (2) teaching self-efficacy; and (3) experiences of beginning teachers. Our research addresses problems of recruitment and retention in the current climate of teacher shortages. It will establish profiles of motivations for career choice at teaching degree entry, trace changes in perceived competencies and professional commitment from degree exit through to early professional teaching experiences, and identify factors and contexts that either encourage or discourage people to continue in the teaching profession. Our research program is interdisciplinary, involves quantitative and qualitative complementary methods, undergraduate and graduate teacher education candidates from five institutions across two nations, within a strong longitudinal design. By taking a large group of people who have enrolled in teacher education, tracking them over the course of their degree programs, and then following them into the teaching profession, we will be able to identify the complex motivational factors that influence the choice of teaching as a career and determine how those motivational factors influence career trajectories in relation to individuals' self-efficacies and specific social and cultural contexts of professional practice.

Motivations for choosing teaching as a career identified in the 1960s and 1970s, particularly in large-scale American studies, focused on the desire for social mobility, the influence of parents and extended family, the desire to work with young children and adolescents, to work in a people-oriented profession, and job-related benefits such as security, pensions and holidays. Few previous research studies have been informed by the motivation literature, which suggests important additional motivations. Prior research has also lacked an integrative theoretical framework, with individual researchers frequently investigating subsets of possible factors, and research at times proceeding in a somewhat piecemeal fashion. Additionally, while factors identified as influencing the choice of a teaching career in earlier research may have commonalities with those emerging in the 21st century, earlier explanations may no longer be adequate or relevant, due to changing definitions of the teacher's role and changes in socio-economic context.

A recent study by the European Commission's Study Group on Education and Training (1997) identified profound socio-economic and technological changes that are taking place and impacting on teachers' roles and responsibilities so that they increasingly incorporate social, behavioural, civic, economic and technological dimensions. The multidimensional character of the teachers' roles in 'new' times may well clash with their entry motivations (for example, a desire to work with children), without realising the complexity of the skills set teachers now require to be effective in the diverse and complex social and cultural contexts in which they operate as professionals. Such a mismatch between teachers' goals and features of the school environment is likely to lower their career satisfaction and commitment.

Our project is significant in that it is multidisciplinary (based on the fields of teacher education and educational psychology), multi-method (quantitative and qualitative), multi-institutional, international and longitudinal. No previous studies map relationships across time and provide for a large international sample. By involving five universities across two countries, our project is able to explore the differences and similarities between Australia and the United States—two similar yet separate career contexts. The scale of our project takes it beyond the provinces of smaller-scale studies that have followed teacher education graduates into their first years of teaching, or have sought the motives of only those teachers who have remained in the profession.

THEORY AND RESEARCH INTO PRACTICE

In many ways, our collaboration studying beginning teachers represents the nexus of our theoretical and methodological interests and expertise, fuelled by the current crisis of teacher recruitment and retention. Our project is based on three main phases: (1) at the start of teacher education, (2) completion of teacher education, and (3) two years subsequent to the award of a teaching qualification. These carefully selected time points allow us to address the reasons why people choose teaching as a career, their confidence in their teaching abilities and professional plans on completion of their teaching qualification, and their experiences and perceptions as beginning teachers on entry to the profession. Investigative methods include surveys, open responses and in-depth interviews—approaches that complement each other and strengthen breadth, rigour and depth. The practical policy applications of our findings are clear: we are able to recommend effective recruitment strategies to attract people into the teaching profession, based on those reasons we have identified for people who have chosen teaching careers. We are also able to identify the changes in teachers' beliefs about their own effectiveness on entry into the profession, the psychological and school-based processes which lead to teacher burnout, and those supports which assist beginning teachers in their career development. Such understandings will be of tremendous import in developing structures that support and scaffold teachers in their early years.

Our beginning teachers project is currently under way. Teacher graduands from both Australian and American universities are involved, with a total sample of over 2200 participants: 1661 from three Australian universities and 550 from two American universities. The study's scope means the findings will have a strong policy impact. It is essential for the social infrastructure of the country that state governments,

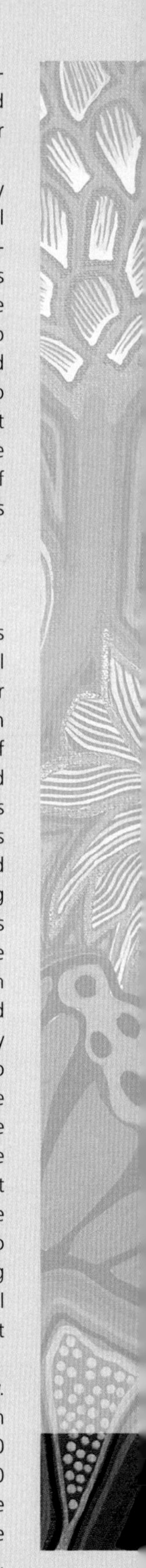

employing authorities, teacher educators, the federal government and recruitment bodies better understand the different motivational profiles of those people who are now entering teacher education, and why people are not retained in the profession, suffer burnout, or become disgruntled and less-effective teachers. It is also critical that we better understand the link between motivations, self-efficacies, and the support networks and strategies needed to sustain teachers in the profession, particularly in difficult-to-staff regions, districts and schools.

KEY REFERENCES

Freedman, A. & Richardson, P. W. (1998) Literacy and genre. In N. Hornberger & D. Corson (eds) *Encyclopedia of Language and Education. Knowledge about Language*, Chapter 17, Volume 6 (D. Corson, ed.). Dordrecht, Netherlands: Kluwer Academic Press.

Richardson, P. W. (2004) Reading and writing from introductory textbooks in higher education: A case study from Economics. *Studies in Higher Education*, **29**(4), 505–21.

Richardson, P. W. & Watt, H. M. G. (in press). 'I've decided to become a teacher': Motives for career change. *Teaching and Teacher Education*.

Watt, H. M. G. (2000). Measuring attitudinal change in mathematics and English over the first year of junior high school: A multidimensional analysis. *Journal of Experimental Education*, **68**, 331–61.

Watt, H. M. G. (2004). Development of adolescents' self perceptions, values and task perceptions according to gender and domain in 7th- through 11th-grade Australian students. *Child Development*, **75**, 1556–74.

ACTIVITIES

1 Watts and Richardson identify a number of motivations for choosing teaching as a career: desire for social mobility, the influence of parents and extended family, the desire to work with young children and adolescents, or to work in a people-oriented profession, and job-related benefits such as security, pensions and holidays. Design a survey and have teacher education students rank these as relevant personal motivators. Leave a space for some open-ended responses as well. Discuss your findings with other students. What are the main motivators today out of this list?

2 Watts and Richardson contend that the above reasons may be less adequate and relevant today. Why might this be the case, and what reasons might now be more influential in motivating individuals to take up teaching as a profession? Were any new reasons suggested in the survey above?

3 Watts and Richardson suggest that the teaching profession has become more complex owing to profound socio-economic and technological changes. Discuss with experienced teachers their perceptions of the increasing complexity of teaching in the 21st century. Discuss with your peers how your own teacher education program is preparing you to cope with these increasing complexities.

4 Watts and Richardson suggest that it is necessary to develop effective recruitment strategies to attract people into the teaching profession. They have not yet completed their research to elucidate what the elements of these strategies might be. From your perspective and in discussion with your lecturers and fellow students, devise what you consider to be an effective teacher recruitment program for the 21st century.

5 Watts and Richardson's research is longitudinal because they believe that teachers' motivations and attitudes change over time. Have your motivations and attitudes towards teaching changed over the period of time you have been training? Discuss your ideas with other students. Are there any commonalities? What are some key differences?

WHAT WOULD YOU DO?

TAKING MY SAILS OUT OF THEIR WIND

Mr Sims' Year 10 mathematics class contained several students who were achieving well below their ability level. Tony was a typical case: he showed no interest in school, dressed aggressively, and had a long history of exclusion from class, incomplete work and poor grades. His occasional flashes of brilliance sustained Mr Sims' efforts to involve Tony in class activities.

Mr Sims decided to shift Tony from the back row to the front row, but this was not without incident. Tony stomped on the floor, sulked, put his head on the desk and complained that 'life's not fair'. Mr Sims' reason for the move was that he could offer Tony the attention he craved in an acceptable context. 'It's not a discipline thing,' he said to Tony. 'I believe that you've got ability and I can help you get good marks; but if all I ever say to you is "Tony, be quiet", "Tony, get back into your seat", "Put that away", we don't stand much of a chance. Come up the front and I'll help you.'

Soon afterwards, at the beginning of a lesson, the blackboard ruler was lying on the front bench and Tony grabbed it and began fencing with it. Mr Sims saw this as a ruse to attract attention. Mr Sims asked, 'Tony, can I have my ruler back?' and grasped the free end of the ruler. Tony replied 'No', and started to engage in a tug-of-war.

Case studies illustrating National Competency Framework for Beginning Teaching, National Project on the Quality of Teaching and Learning, Australian Teaching Council, 1996, p. 44. Commonwealth of Australia copyright, reproduced by permission.

What would you do? Now read what the teacher did.

WHAT WOULD YOU DO? (cont.)

TAKING MY SAILS OUT OF THEIR WIND

Mr Sims said, 'I just let go and walked away; I let him have it. Where's his fun and attention if I refuse to wrestle with him? It took a lot for me to let go and walk away because I'm the teacher and it's my classroom but the disruption of the lesson just wasn't worth it.'

Mr Sims' attitude to his students is, in his words, 'I refuse to believe that any kid doesn't like success. They all like to feel they've achieved something.' Mr Sims' approach to Tony when he'd settled into the front row was to go out of his way to talk to Tony frequently. For instance, when Mr Sims asked the class to open their files, he'd chat to Tony for a moment—this ensured that Tony got his work out and, at the same time, satisfied Tony's need for recognition. Nevertheless, Mr Sims was careful not to become involved in power plays, such as the ruler incident, for which Tony was well known. When confrontation threatens, as Mr Sims put it, 'I take my sails out of their wind.'

Case studies illustrating National Competency Framework for Beginning Teaching, National Project on the Quality of Teaching and Learning, Australian Teaching Council, 1996, p. 44. Commonwealth of Australia copyright, reproduced by permission.

Is Mr Sims' approach what you would have done? How does this case study illustrate principles drawn from behavioural theory?

KEY TERMS

Academic press (p. 22): emphasises academic climate reflected through demanding curricula, clear achievement goals, high teacher expectations, time on task

Advance organiser (p. 11): a statement about a new topic providing structure for relating it to what students already know

Anticipatory set (p. 11): focuses students' attention by reminding them of what they already know

Caring school (p. 22): emphasises teachers' and students' social and emotional needs as a precursor to academic learning

Classroom management (p. 13): things a teacher does to establish an effective learning environment

Constructivist views of learning (p. 3): emphasise the active role of the learner in building understanding

Extrinsic motivation (p. 18): motivation created by external factors such as rewards and punishment that may lead to surface learning

Feedback (p. 12): information about the accuracy of a students' response used to improve future performance

General teaching efficacy (p. 6): relates to a teacher's belief about whether teaching can impact student learning despite external constraints such as the locale in which the school is located, the cultural background of the students, and the socio-economic backgrounds of the students

Information processing constructivism (p. 4): focuses on the learner actively selecting, organising and integrating incoming experience with existing knowledge to create understanding

Instructional objectives (p. 15): general statements of what students should be able to do as a result of instruction

Intrinsic motivation (p. 18): motivation created by internal reasons such as interest, enjoyment and relevance that may lead to deep learning

Learning outcomes (p. 6): the expected specific achievements that students are to show in observable ways at the end of instruction

Learning set (p. 16): learning expectations that condition how individuals approach a learning task

Lesson review (p. 11): making connections with concepts and ideas covered in earlier lessons

Personal constructivism/radical constructivism (p. 3): emphasises the intrapersonal dimensions of learning

Personal teaching efficacy (p. 6): relates to the teacher's belief that they have personal qualities to positively impact students' learning

Radical constructivists (p. 4): believe that individuals construct knowledge on the basis of their own experiences

Social constructivism (p. 3): emphasises the construction of shared knowledge in social contexts

Sociocultural constructivism (p. 4): emphasises the wider social, cultural and historical contexts of learning and the reciprocal interaction of these with the individual learning to construct shared knowledge

Socio-economic status (p. 19): relative standing in society based on education and income

Teacher efficacy (p. 6): the personal belief that a teacher can influence student learning

Wait-time (p. 14): the length of time between the teacher's question and the student's response

ON-LINE LEARNING

If you go to http://www.pearsoned.com.au/mcinerney, you will have hot links directly to these sites:

- **Pathways to school improvement**

This site provides useful information on effective teaching and schools. Compare the ideas and issues raised with those discussed in Chapter 1 of your text.

http://www.ncrel.org/sdrs/

- **TA Handbook**

Discuss the 12 principles of effective teaching and learning presented in the *TA Handbook*. Compare them with the principles we have introduced in Chapter 1 and reconsider them as you read other chapters in your text. Other elements in the handbook will also be of interest to you.

http://www.tss.uoguelph.ca/tahb/tah8g.html

- **Effective teaching on-line journal**

This site accesses an electronic journal dedicated to effective teaching. There are a number of interesting articles. Select an article for group or individual appraisal.

http://www.uncw.edu/cte/et/

- **Teaching learning process**

This site presents a good overview of principles of effective teaching. It provides a number of useful hot links to other sites.

http://teach.valdosta.edu/whuitt/materials/tchlrnmd.html

- **Learner-centred psychological principles**

This website should be looked up as it deals in detail with the Learner-centred Psychological Principles, which we discuss in our text. You should read and discuss the extra text presented at this website.

http://www.apa.org/ed/lcp.html

WEB DESTINATIONS

If you go to http://www.pearsoned.com.au/mcinerney, you will have hot links directly to these sites:

- **Psychcrawler**

Psychcrawler is an excellent search engine designed by the American Psychological Association to find most things related to psychology.

http://www.psychcrawler.com/

- **Psych Web**

Psych Web is an excellent site that contains lots of psychology-related information for students and teachers of psychology.

http://www.psywww.com/index.html

■ **Google**
Another excellent search engine for psychology (and matters in general).
http://www.psywww.com/index.html

■ **Encyclopedia of Psychology**
Encyclopedia of Psychology website. Type in a topic and see what you get!
http://www.psychology.org/

■ **American Psychological Association**
The American Psychological Association publishes many excellent journals in psychology. You will find a list of them at this website. It also has hot links to a number of useful psychology sites.
http://www.apa.org/

The following websites are for important associations in psychology. You should be familiar with them as they will present many resources for your study of educational and developmental psychology.

■ **American Psychological Association**
http://www.apa.org/

■ **Australian Psychological Society**
http://www.psychology.org.au/

■ **British Psychological Society**
http://www.bps.org.uk/index.cfm

■ **The American Educational Research Association (AERA)**
http://www.aera.net/

■ **Australian Association for Research in Education**
http://www.aare.edu.au/index.htm

■ **APA Style Resources**
This is a must for those writing papers in psychology.
http://www.psywww.com/resource/apacrib.htm

■ **Journal of Educational Psychology Home Page**
An important journal with which you should be familiar.
http://www.apa.org/journals/edu.html

■ **AERA special interest groups**
A site for AERA special interest groups which lists many areas that will be of particular interest to you as educators and psychologists.
http://www.aera.net/sigs/sigsites.htm

■ **Gateway to educational materials**
This is a very useful site for following up many relevant educational topics.
http://www.thegateway.org/

■ **Theory into practice**
This is a useful website for quick overviews of key theories in educational psychology.
http://tip.psychology.org/index.html

■ **Psychology journals**
This site hot-links to major journals in psychology. It is prepared by Athabasca University in Canada.
http://psych.athabascau.ca/html/aupr/journals.shtml

■ **Guidelines for effective teaching**
http://ctl.stanford.edu/TA/index.html

RECOMMENDED READING

Caprara, G. V., Barbaranelli, C., Borgogni, L. & Steca, P. (2003) Efficacy beliefs as determinants of teachers' job satisfaction. *Journal of Educational Psychology,* **95**, 821–32.

Cobb, P. (1994a) Constructivism in mathematics and science education. *Educational Researcher*, **23**, 4.

Cobb, P. (1994b) Where is the mind? Constructivist and sociocultural perspectives on mathematical development. *Educational Researcher*, **23**, 13–20.

Corno, L. & Mandinach, E. B. (2004) What we have learned about student engagement in the past 20 years. In D. M. McInerney & S. Van Etten (eds) *Research on Sociocultural Influences on Motivation and Learning (Volume 4), Big Theories Revisited.* Greenwich, CT: Information Age Publishing.

Educational Psychologist (1996) Special Issue: Recent and emerging theoretical frameworks for research on classroom learning: Contributions and limitations. *Educational Psychologist*, **31**.

Fives, H. & Alexander, P. (2004) How schools shape teacher efficacy and commitment: Another piece in the achievement puzzle. In D. M. McInerney & S. Van Etten (eds) *Research on Sociocultural Influences on Motivation and Learning (Volume 4), Big Theories Revisited.* Greenwich, CT: Information Age Publishing.

Goddard, R. D., Hoy, W. K. & Woolfolk Hoy, A. (2004) Collective efficacy beliefs: Theoretical developments, empirical evidence, and future directions. *Educational Researcher,* **33**, 3–13.

Hendry, G. D. (1996) Constructivism and educational practice. *Australian Journal of Education*, **40**, 19–45.

Henson, R. K. (2002) From adolescent angst to adulthood: Substantive implications and measurement dilemmas in the development of teacher efficacy research. *Educational Psychologist,* **37**, 137–50.

Hogan, T., Rabinowitz, M. & Craven, J. A. (2003) Representation in teaching: Inferences from research of expert and novice teachers. *Educational Psychologist,* **38**, 235–47.

Johnson, S. M. & Birkeland, S. E. (2003) Pursuing a 'sense of success': New teachers explain their career decisions. *American Educational Research Journal,* **40**, 581–617.

Nuthall, G. & Alton-Lee, A. (1990) Research on teaching and learning: Thirty years of change. *The Elementary School Journal*, **90**, 547–70.

Oosterheert, I. E., Vermunt, J. D. & Denessen, E. (2002)

Assessing orientations to learning to teach. *British Journal of Educational Psychology,* 72, 41–64.

Phillips, D. C. (1995) The good, the bad, and the ugly. The many faces of constructivism. *Educational Researcher*, **24**, 5–12.

Reynolds, A. (1992) What is competent beginning teaching? A review of the literature. *Review of Educational Research*, **62**, 1–35.

Salomon, G. & Perkins, D. N. (1998) Individual and social aspects of learning. *Review of Research in Education,* **23**, 1–24.

Sawyer, R. K. (2004) Creative teaching: Collaborative discussion as disciplined improvisation. *Educational Researcher,* **33**, 12–20.

Stipek, D. (2002) Good instruction is motivating. In A. Wigfield & J. S. Eccles (eds) *Development of Achievement Motivation.* San Diego, CA: Academic Press.

Tschannen-Moran, M., Woolfolk Hoy, A. & Hoy, W. (1998) Teacher efficacy: Its meaning and measure. *Review of Educational Research,* **68**, 202–48.

van den Berg, R. (2002) Teachers' meanings regarding educational practice. *Review of Educational Research,* 72, 577–625.

Von Glaserfeld, E. (1995) *Radical Constructivism: A Way of Knowing and Learning.* London: Falmer Press.

Wideen, M., Mayer-Smith, J. & Moon, B. (1998) A critical analysis of the research on learning to teach: Making the case for an ecological perspective on inquiry. *Review of Educational Research,* **68**, 130–78.

Windschitl, M. (2002) Framing constructivism in practice as the negotiation of dilemmas: An analysis of the conceptual, pedagogical, cultural, and political challenges facing teachers. *Review of Educational Psychology,* **72**, 131–75.

Wragg, E. C. (1995) Lesson structure. In L. W. Anderson (ed.) *International Encyclopedia of Teaching and Teacher Education*, 2nd ed. New York: Pergamon.

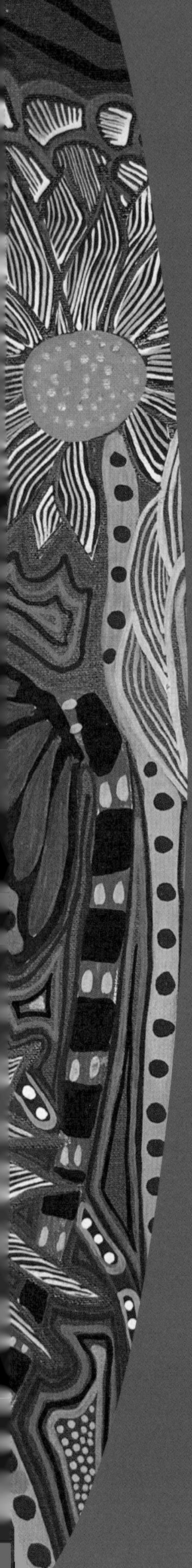

CHAPTER

2 Developmental perspectives on cognition and effective learning

Overview

As children grow older, they develop more mature cognitive processes that enable them to adapt increasingly efficiently to the world around them. In this chapter we consider two important, and contrasting, views on cognitive development, those of Jean Piaget and Lev Vygotsky. There are many similarities in the implications for learning between Vygotsky's and Piaget's theories. Both emphasise the importance of active involvement by children in learning, and the *process* of learning rather than the *product*. They both emphasise the importance of *peer interaction*, grounding learning experiences in the *real world of experiences* for children, and the need for the adult (parent or teacher) to take account of *individual differences* when structuring learning experiences for children. While each believes that learning is an intentional process of constructing meaning from experience, the means by which this knowledge construction occurs is considered differently by Piaget and Vygotsky. Three questions are raised in this chapter:

1 What is the best way to characterise children's intellectual functioning at various key points in their growth?
2 What is the best way to characterise the process by which children progress from one of these points to the next?
3 How can the developmental process be optimised?

We consider both personal constructivism, which is most connected with Piaget, and social constructivism, which is most connected with Vygotsky. Contrasts are drawn between Piaget and Vygotsky regarding the nature and function of discovery in learning, the role of social interaction in learning, and the relationship between language and learning.

2

Piaget's theory of cognitive development

Learning objectives

After reading this chapter, you will be able to:

- describe Piaget's theory of cognitive development;
- define structuralism and constructivism;
- identify and describe the stages of cognitive development outlined in Piaget's theory;
- discuss the implications of Piaget's constructivist theory for the classroom;
- discuss the implications of Piaget's structuralist theory for the classroom;
- describe Vygotsky's theory of social constructivism;
- define and apply the concept of the zone of proximal development;
- define and apply the concept of scaffolded instruction;
- discuss the implications of a Vygotskian social constructivist perspective for education;
- compare and contrast the theoretical perspectives of Piaget and Vygotsky;
- discuss the importance of play to cognitive development.

One day when our daughter Laura was three, she was staring mesmerised at a bug flying around our living room light when she spontaneously said: 'It's clever to fly. I wish I could fly, but I can't.' On another occasion, while watching her father hack away at the jungle we called a back yard, Laura asked: 'Are we at the bottom of the sky?' As a much more grown-up eight-year-old she amazed her father with: 'Can I ask you a question that has been bothering me for a long time? Why am I here? What's the purpose of me being born?' And several years later, after the death of her grandmother, 'What is death? Why did Nanna have to die?' Young children are forever learning about the world around them. Concepts such as number, time, weight, measurement, space and existence are the everyday subjects being mastered by children through their world of experiences.

The theory of psychologist Jean Piaget (1896–1980) has had a profound impact on the way teachers and other professionals think about cognitive development and learning. His theory has dual and complementary perspectives that may be termed *constructivism* and *structuralism* (Cellerier 1987; Inhelder & de Caprona 1987). First, Piaget argued that children construct their own understanding through interaction with their environment—that is, through their actions on objects in the world (what we call **constructivism**). In effect, Piaget viewed the child as a young scientist, constructing ever more powerful theories of the world as a result of applying a set of logical mental structures in increasing generality and power (Case 1992). Second, Piaget believed that intellectual development occurs through a series of stages characterised by qualitatively discrete cognitive structures (what we call **structuralism**).

While the structuralist aspects of his theory are having less impact on educational practice today, the constructivist aspects are strongly influencing current practice. In the next sections we describe elements of constructivism and structuralism, and then show how relevant a knowledge of these is to the teaching and learning processes.

Piaget and personal constructivism

A major aspect of Piagetian theory is his belief that children construct their own tools for understanding and discovering the world (Bidell & Fischer 1992; Carey 1987; Inhelder & de Caprona 1987; Sigel & Cocking 1977).

Piaget's constructivism is based on three interrelated conceptions:

1 the relation between action and thought;
2 the construction of cognitive structure;
3 the role of self-regulation or, more abstractly, **equilibration** in the development of thought. (Chapman 1988, cited in Bidell & Fischer 1992)

Piaget's basic position was that knowledge is primarily constructed from our own actions in the process of regulating our interactions with the world. By actively coordinating actions from different situations or contexts, an individual stores or internalises actions that can be reused as representations to anticipate action in other contexts. Representation in the form of internalised action provides our most fundamental knowledge about how the world works because it tells us what we can *do* with the world (Bidell & Fischer 1992).

It is significant that Piaget emphasises that actions should not be limited to the concrete; rather, they should be developed and schematised into mental **operations**. This is achieved by encouraging the child to rely on progressively less direct support from externals—for example, moving from the physical through to pictorial representations, then to cognitive representations of operations not actually being performed at that moment.

Table 2.1 summarises the essentials for education of a Piagetian personal constructivist perspective.

Piaget and structuralism: Assimilation and accommodation

Piaget's theory is complex. Our description of the structuralist elements highlights some important aspects, but is also simplified. (More detailed treatments may be found in Forman 1980; Ginsburg & Opper 1988; Wadsworth 1989.) As a biologist, Piaget was impressed with the way in which all species systematise and organise their processes into coherent biological systems and are able to **adapt**, as necessary, to the environment. He brought his eye as a biologist to the task of explaining the development of cognitive processes in children and maintained that the growth of intelligence is regulated by the same processes that determine the growth of morphology and changes in the physiology of all living systems (Forman 1980).

Biological model of cognitive development

Table 2.1

Essentials of a Piagetian personal constructivist perspective for education

Teachers should:

- hold a belief that learning is an active restructuring of thought, rather than an increase in content, and that reconstruction (recall) will reflect the particular schema of the learner;
- hold an appreciation that, as each person constructs learning in terms of his or her own schemes, no two people will derive the same meaning or benefit from a given experience;
- hold a high regard for self-regulated learning;
- use cognitive conflict to promote the consolidation of concepts;
- provide activities that provoke thought about change and the relative nature of any 'fact', rather than activities that teach the child to see discrete, static stimuli or absolute facts;
- provide a wide variety of experiences that appeal to children's interests to engage their purposes and to maximise cognitive development;
- use wrong answers in helping students to analyse their thinking in order to retain the correct elements and revise misconceptions;
- use social interaction to promote increases in both interest and comprehension in learning;
- promote peer friendship and cooperation, including conflict resolution;
- cultivate a feeling of community and the construction of collective values;
- commit to spending many hours observing children.

Teachers should teach learners to:

- exhibit active physical and mental involvement;
- manipulate concrete objects directly and ideas indirectly;
- pose questions and seek their own answers;
- reconcile what is found at one time with what is found at another;
- compare findings with those of other children.

Source: Based on DeVries (1997); Forman (1980).

Sensorimotor learning is very important for developing a sense of cause and effect.

Piaget believed that infants have relatively few functioning cognitive systems (for example, reflexes and some rudimentary thought processes) for handling the world of experiences, but great potential to develop increasingly complex thought. He believed the infant is an active agent whose mind reconstructs and reinterprets the environment to make it fit in with its own existing mental framework (Flavell 1985). These ways of dealing with experiences Piaget termed **schemes**, and the schemes are organised as cognitive structure. As novel experiences occur, such as learning to drink juice rather than milk from a teat, the child adapts by relating this new experience to familiar ones (such as, juice tastes different, yet is similar to milk, being a liquid, but the means of drinking via a teat is the same). We have all seen young children screw up their faces as they drink juice for the first time. Once they are used to the taste, they drink it happily. This process is called **assimilation**. At other times, however, the novel experience requires a more radical adaptation on the part of the child to cope with something quite new; for example, when the child learns to drink from a cup rather than from a teat. This process is called **accommodation**. Often there is quite an adaptation needed as the child tries to manipulate the liquid into his or her mouth. Children show quite a deal of pleasure when they accomplish this task. This adaptation leads to the development of a new scheme for drinking into which various new drinking vessels can be assimilated. At times the process is modified, so there is a progression. For example, some parents start off by giving children a drink in a plastic cup with a lid that is somewhat similar to a teat, and then remove the lid. The period of adjustment is called a period of *cognitive conflict* and successful adaptation leads to what is termed *equilibrium*—that is, a state of psychological and biological peace. We see this when the child goes from a state of distress (**disequilibrium**) caused by not knowing how to handle the new situation, to comfort from drinking by using a cup. The tension that exists between the demands of accommodation and assimilation, when the child adapts to or learns about novel situations, is the power that impels the child to develop new understandings and a new equilibrium (Flavell 1985). No doubt you too can think of ways in which you still learn about the world by these mutual processes of assimilation and accommodation.

In summary, assimilation and accommodation are mutual processes that lead to cognitive growth. When a child is confronted with new situations, he or she either assimilates or experiences cognitive conflict (disequilibrium) through which accommodation to existing understanding may occur, bringing about a sense of equilibrium. For Piaget, therefore, cognitive development involves an interaction between assimilating new facts to old knowledge and accommodating old knowledge to new facts and the maintenance of structural equilibration (Halford 1989). Furthermore, as children mature they develop a series of operations or thought processes that become increasingly able to handle inferential thinking. While the young infant is limited to thinking about problems and experiences in concrete terms (termed **figurative knowledge**), the adolescent is capable of thinking about problems using more sophisticated operational schemes (**operative knowledge**).

Piaget's stages of intellectual development

We now turn our attention to the structuralist elements of Piaget's theory. Operations and their groupings are the main objects of Piaget's developmental approach to concept formation. On the basis of his many experimental observations and clinical interviews with children of all ages, Piaget believed that there are four main stages in cognitive development through which the vast majority of children pass—sensorimotor, preoperational, concrete-operational and formal-operational—each characterised by qualitatively different cognitive structures. The approximate ages for each of the stages are:

- sensorimotor stage (birth to 2 years);
- preoperational stage (2–7 years);
- concrete-operational stage (7–12 years);
- formal-operational (12 to adult).

Piaget believed that in each of the stages there is a characteristic way in which children think about the world and solve problems. We must warn here that these age limits are only guidelines and there are many inconsistencies. At each stage, children develop increasingly sophisticated mental processes, leading to the acquisition of fully logical cognitive operations. While later researchers have confirmed the sequence of stages as Piaget described them, there is sufficient evidence to show that Piaget underestimated the degree of competence and organisation of very young children's thinking.

Sensorimotor stage

Piaget believed that during the first two years of life, children learn about the world primarily through motor activity. By gradually reorganising their **sensorimotor** actions, infants construct a basic understanding of their environment (Bidell & Fischer 1992). Through grasping, sucking, looking, throwing, and generally moving themselves and objects about, children begin to recognise that they are separate from their surrounding world and learn about the **permanence of objects** and certain regularities in the physical world. They develop an elementary understanding of causality, and of shape and size constancy. By two years of age, children can solve most sensorimotor problems—for example, they can obtain desired objects, use objects in combination, and mentally 'invent' means that will permit them to do the things they want. In Piagetian terms, children by two years of age have acquired a much larger and more sophisticated set of cognitive schemes than at birth as a result of sensorimotor interaction with the environment and, in particular, the ongoing processes of assimilation and accommodation which enable children to handle the world more effectively.

Representational thinking, which is the basis for anticipating actions mentally, is the outcome of sensorimotor constructions (Bidell & Fischer 1992). By gradually reorganising their sensorimotor actions, infants construct a basic understanding of the permanence of objects in space and a rudimentary ability to represent people and objects not immediately present.

Preoperational stage

During the preoperational period, between about two and seven years, children begin to know things not only through their physical actions but symbolically as well. Naturally, with the acquisition of language there is a great leap forward in the ability of children to reason about the world around them and to solve problems. Symbolic games (such as talking on the toy telephone or pretending to be imaginary characters) play an important role in the development of children's intellectual abilities.

Nevertheless, according to Piaget, children at this stage do not use logical mental operations to solve problems or to interpret experiences in the physical world—hence the term *preoperational*. Preoperations are internalised actions that have not yet been integrated into complete systems and as such are not yet true mental operations.

In a number of his books (Piaget 1954, 1971, 1974; see also Elkind 1974), Piaget describes some features of young children's mental characteristics that give rise to their 'cute' expressions and behaviours. For example, young children have a tendency to project their anger or fear impulses on to inanimate objects. Having hurt herself by running into a chair or slipping down some stairs, our daughter Alexandra was often heard to say 'Naughty chair!' or 'Silly stairs'. Such attribution of lifelike qualities to inanimate objects has been termed **physiognomic perception**. We are not convinced that it disappears as individuals grow older. The author has been heard to mutter 'Blasted hammer!' after hitting his finger, and it is amazing how many students kick and swear at the computer for 'bombs' which may be directly attributable to their own inadequacies.

Young children also show a strong tendency to regard events that happen together as having caused one another; for example, children often think that raising the blind brings out the sun or that rain comes to stop them going out to play. This type of thinking is labelled **phenomenalistic causality**. Adults often inadvertently reinforce the development of this form of thinking when, for example, they say, 'The sun has gone to sleep, so it's time for bed.' Another aspect of preoperational thinking is the young child's ready belief in magic and ritual, which is tied in with phenomenalistic causality. For young children it is perfectly reasonable that magic things can happen. As children grow older and gain a stronger grasp of causality, they begin to debunk magic—or at least try to understand the underlying processes involved in it.

As with physiognomic perception, this characteristic does not disappear entirely as the child gets older, and accounts for the superstitions we observe in older children and even in adults. For example, do you have any preparation rituals for exams? We know students who get particularly unsettled if they don't have their favourite pen for an exam or are prevented from sitting in a favourite position.

Young children also invest words and language with a power far beyond that allowed by the arbitrariness of language. This characteristic is termed **nominal realism**. For example, names of things are often sacrosanct, and the quality of the object (for example, heat or light) is thought to reside intrinsically in the name of the object, such as sun or moon. Because of this, very young children won't rename objects. Furthermore, words are very powerful. A child hates to be called stupid, because, they believe, being *called* stupid may *make* one stupid.

Throughout the preoperational period, the development of children's cognitive abilities is reflected in the growth of their powers of perception, language, reasoning and problem-solving abilities. Children's perception becomes increasingly freed from the limits of the physical appearance of objects and takes into account a range of aspects of objects, integrating this information into a more holistic understanding. Because attention becomes less centred on perceptual clues, and children are able to reorganise and integrate information coming from a range of sources, they become more flexible and adaptive thinkers.

Development of powers of perception, language, reasoning and problem solving

Perception and cognitive development during the preoperational stage

Let us look closely at the function of perception as a vital force behind the nurturance of accurate concept development, which enables children to detect and interpret relevant environmental information.

Our daughter Laura was looking at the sky when she spotted a plane. 'There's a little plane,' she exclaimed. We explained to her that it was actually a jumbo jet, but a long way away. The idea that an object is the same size whether it is far away or close, and that shapes are constant no matter from what perspective they are viewed, develops with time. Many early preschool and kindergarten activities, such as stacking objects, labelling positions, looking at things from different angles and so on, are designed to develop children's perceptual concepts such as *big* and *small*, *close* and *far*. Understanding spatial relationships is especially important for a child's accurate interpretation of the environment. So, concepts such as *left* and *right*, *short* and *long*, *near* and *far*, are developed through appropriate experiences.

Developing spatial relationships

Classifying objects into sets appears to be very difficult for young children. They also experience difficulties in understanding the relationship that exists between classes and subclasses. For example, if we present children with four red plastic flowers and two blue plastic flowers and ask them to tell us whether there are more red or more blue plastic flowers, they answer the question easily. However, there is confusion between wholes and parts if we ask them whether there are more red flowers or more plastic flowers. Often children will answer that there are more red flowers. As children grow older, they classify classes and subclasses effectively which is the precursor of much sophisticated thinking.

Classifying objects into sets

Preschool children frequently seem to make quantity judgments on the basis of perception alone; they appear to be unable to make accurate quantity discriminations logically, independent of misleading perceptual cues. Children will fight over who has the larger glass of cordial based on appearance (for example, comparing tall and thin with short and wide glasses) irrespective of the quantity equivalence. A residue of this way of thinking remains with adults. If we want our mother to think she is being fed a lot when she visits, we put the food on a relatively small plate. If she complains that we give her too much to eat, we put the same amount of food on a large plate. Advertisers make use of this technique with their deceptive packaging of material so that it looks as if buyers are getting more than they actually are. As clever shoppers, we all know that we must take careful notice of the perceptual cues given to us by packaging and discount much of the visual information. Because of the power of visual cues, and the fact that there is quite a subjective element in interpreting them (for example, when a man wears a slightly shrunken shirt everyone asks whether he is putting on weight; when he wears an oversize shirt everyone comments on how thin he is looking), concepts such as *larger*, *smaller*, *less*, *few*, *some* and *many* are frequently bewildering for young children. As they grow older, children become quite adept at using these concepts in many different ways.

Perception and judgments of quantity

There is usually a significant gap between preschoolers' counting abilities and their ability to understand conceptually what is being counted. Abstract concepts of measurement, simple addition and fractional amounts develop with time. When mathematical processes are couched in real examples, such as dividing lollies among children, preschoolers show a surprising command of counting principles. Gelman (cited in Flavell 1985) distinguishes between young children's number abstraction and their numerical reasoning principles (see Dingfelder 2005 for an interesting cross-cultural discussion of this issue). Prominent among the number abstraction abilities is the preschooler's developing command of five counting principles (see box).

FIVE COUNTING PRINCIPLES

1. Assign one, and only one, number to each and every item to be counted (*one–one principle*).
2. When counting, always recite the numbers in the same order (*stable order principle*).
3. The final number uttered at the end of a counting sequence denotes the total number of items counted (*combinatorial principle*).
4. Any sort of entity may be counted (*abstraction principle*).
5. It does not matter in what order you enumerate the objects (*order-irrelevance principle*).

One of the numerical reasoning principles that children acquire is the number conservation rule—that merely spreading out a set of objects does not change the number of objects in the set.

Children in the early years of preschool and school also have an undeveloped sense of time. They ask many time-related questions, such as: 'Is it morning now?', 'When will it be tomorrow?', 'Is it Wednesday or Saturday?' and so on, indicating an interest in time. By the time they are four years old, many children measure out their week in days at preschool, days with Grandma, days with Mum and Dad, and weekends, and have a developing sense of time. Young children also have a limited grasp of the past and the future. However, as they get older they have a growing interest in the concepts of past and future and a growing control of the elements of time. Obviously, concepts of history and the future develop slowly, which has implications for the introduction of historical and other time-related studies into the school curricula. An interesting discussion of the development of time, space and number concepts is also found in Siegler (1991), where some alternative findings and explanations are given. You should read this reference.

Importance of language to cognitive development

While language was not overly emphasised in Piaget's theory as a key element driving conceptual and logical understandings (as it is in Vygotsky's theory, discussed later in the chapter), language is very important. As children acquire increasing ability to solve problems in a systematic way by using processes of discrimination and coordination of concepts and generalisations and, most importantly, by beginning to work through problems in their heads rather than with physical objects, language is central to this development. Children's growing command of language is at once a part of, and a sign of, the development of mental capacities. For many theorists, language enables the developing child to explore the world of thoughts, and acts as a mediating process for the analysis of information received through the senses.

How do we distinguish preoperational thinking from later levels?

The usual method for distinguishing preoperational thinking from later levels is by 'testing' children on a number of problems that require logical thought, and on the operations discussed earlier in the chapter (Cowan 1978; Ginsburg & Opper 1988; Wadsworth 1989). Basically, preoperational children are unable to conserve and make deductive inferences. The following 'tests' illustrate characteristic elements in the preoperational child's thinking. You might like to look at the pictures in Figure 2.1 while we describe these tests.

After observing one of two equal lumps of clay being squashed, the preoperational child will typically suggest that one lump will have more or less clay than the other in terms of the physical appearance of the two lumps. After witnessing one of two jars of water of equal quantity being poured into a third jar of different size, the child will typically suggest that the amount of water in the new jar (usually a flat, shallow container) is less than the amount of water in the other full jar. If confronted with two pencils of equal length next to each other on a table, with one point protruding past the end of the other pencil, the child will typically argue that one or other of the pencils is longer. When asked to count two equal rows of coins, one spread out more than the other, the child will typically say that one row has more coins than the other, despite having 'accurately' counted the two rows and, indeed, even having seen the two rows of coins lined up equally.

Tests of conservation

In each of these cases, the preoperational child appears to be illustrating a preoccupation with visual perception. This is called **centration** when only one feature of the problem is attended to. Furthermore, the child does not appear to attend to the **transformation** from one state to another; for example, not understanding that, in pouring the water from one container to another, the quantity of water hasn't been altered although the final state may appear different. A simple demonstration of this is to ask a child to draw the successive points through which a vertical pencil will move to assume the horizontal

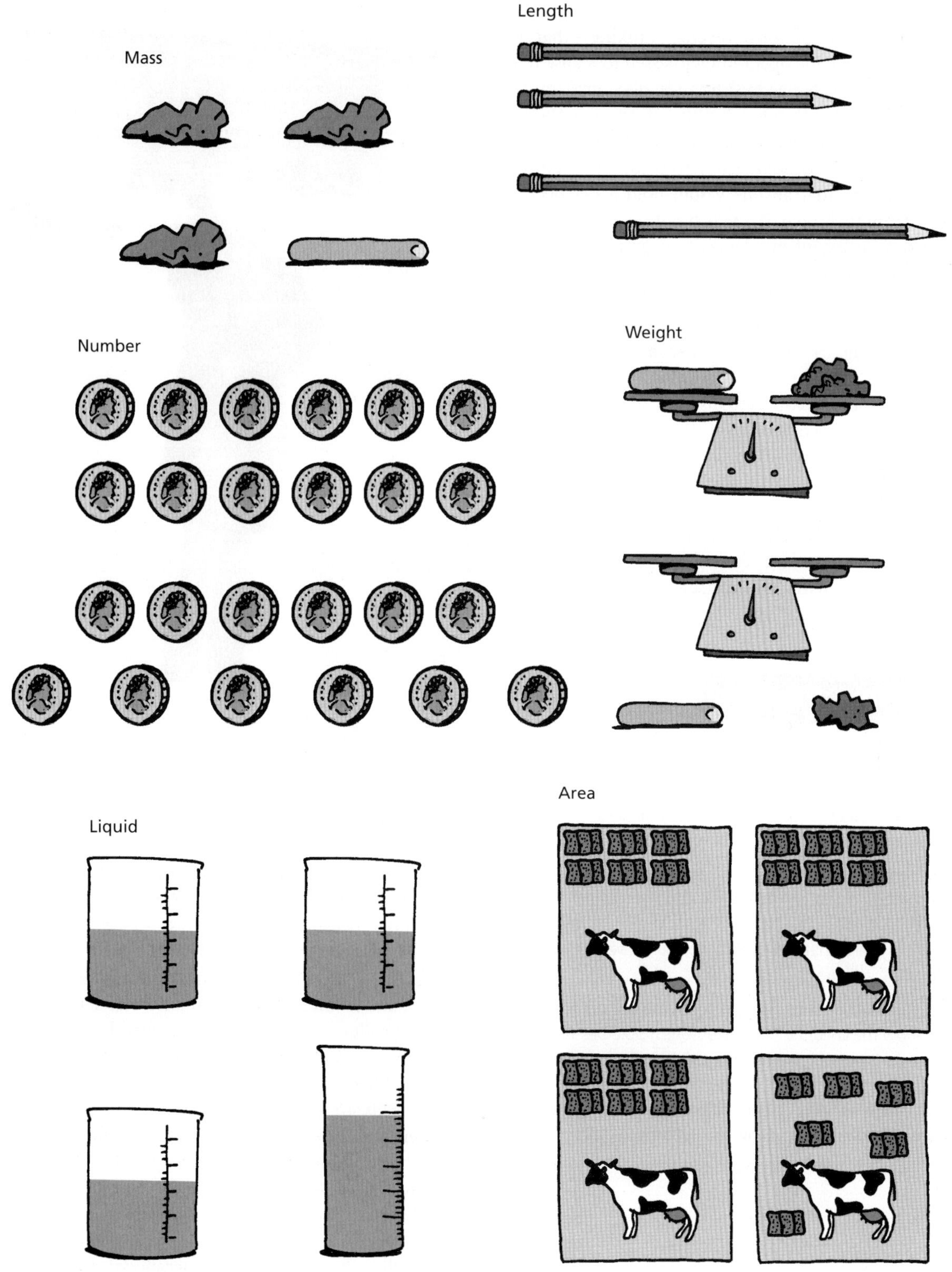

Figure 2.1 *Piagetian conservation tasks*

position: the preoperational child cannot effectively do this. Piaget believes these experiments demonstrate the child's inability to perform **reverse thinking**—that is, mentally to reverse the operation witnessed to realise that there has been no change in substance, only appearance. Compounding this limited ability of preoperational children to perceive several dimensions of a problem at once is the child's **egocentricity**, whereby children are blithely unaware that anyone would hold a perspective different from their own. It is worth noting here that such 'egocentrism' is meant in relation to cognition and does not imply that the young child is selfish or ungenerous.

According to Piaget, the characteristics of preoperational thought described above function as obstacles to logical thinking in an adult sense and derive from limitations in the ability to understand conservation. **Conservation** is the conceptualisation that the amount or quantity of particular matter stays the same regardless of any changes in shape or position of the matter. Researchers have been particularly interested in when children acquire the capacity to conserve, and whether this is consistent across a number of domains such as number, area and volume. There does appear to be a sequence, with the conservation of number, substance, area, weight and volume being achieved in that order.

ACTION STATION

This activity is designed to give you some insight into a young child's conception of the world.

Select three children of four, five and six years old. Give the following instructions to each child separately:

'We are going to play a game. I am going to ask some questions and I'd like you to tell me what you think. What do you think it means to be alive? Is a cat alive? Why? Tell me something else that's alive. How do you know it's alive (or not alive)?'

Repeat this, substituting for 'cat' each object on the list below. Show the child the first five objects if possible. Record verbatim the answers given by the children. Summarise the reasons given by each child for each object. Are there any common patterns? Any distinct differences? What conclusions can you draw about young children's thinking?

stone	river	bird
pencil	clouds	fire
broken button	tree	dog
watch	sun	grass
chipped cup	wind	bug
bike	car	flower

Concrete experiences are essential for all learners. What concrete experience is this child having?

Concrete-operational stage

While preoperational children's thinking appears to be characterised by centring on one perceptual aspect of a stimulus, concrete-operational children seem to take into account all salient features of the stimulus and thought becomes **decentred**. In contrast to the preoperational child, the concrete-operational child can attend to successive stages in the transformation of an object from one state to another and mentally reverse the operations that produce an outcome. One good example of the ability to reverse thought is shown by an experiment with three different coloured balls and a non-transparent tube. The balls are put into the tube in the order red, blue, green, and the child is asked to indicate the order in which they will come out the other end. The child predicts correctly red, blue, green. On the next test the balls are added in the same order, but the tube is rotated through 180°. Again the child is asked to predict the order in which the balls will come out. A preoperational child predicts the order red, blue, green, while a concrete-operational child predicts the right order, green, blue, red. Why?

For Piaget the clearest indication that children have reached the concrete level of reasoning is the presence of conservation. When asked whether the two lumps of clay mentioned earlier are the same or different, concrete-operational children will quickly respond 'the same'. When asked why, children might answer with a range of logical reasons: invariance, compensation or reversibility. For example, they might answer: 'You didn't add anything or take anything away, you simply changed the shape' (*invariant quantity*) or 'While the pancake is thinner than the ball, it is also wider' (*compensation*) or 'See, I can roll it back up into a ball again' (*reversibility*). In fact, older children become irritated when you ask them the reason for their answer—'It's so obvious!' they say. Preoperational characteristics of children's thinking disappear as they acquire a firm grasp of physical causality.

Among other logical operations achieved during the period of concrete operations is the ability to organise the elements of a series in either ascending or descending order of size, called **seriation**, and the ability to construct classes and subclasses of objects, called **classification**. We gave an example of classification earlier with our discussion of red and blue flowers. Concrete operational children will always say that the most inclusive classification is always larger than the subclasses.

It is obvious, therefore, that concrete-operational children are capable of using a variety of logical operations to reason about the world and to solve problems; however, these operations are restricted to concrete experiences. In other words, the content of the operations are real, not hypothetical, objects or situations.

How does make-believe play help children to learn about their world?

Water play helps children to develop quantity concepts. What other play activities may be helpful in developing shape, size and class concepts?

ACTION STATION

Consider the preoperational and concrete-operational stages of early and middle childhood as described by Piaget and brainstorm ways in which the teacher can act to foster cognitive development through play. Observe a group of children at play, and note the opportunities for teacher interaction that would not interrupt the play process but support learning.

QUESTION POINT

Many schools and curricula reflect a Piagetian approach to programming and teaching in which learning experiences are presented at what are deemed developmentally appropriate times. Consider the strengths of this approach. What are some potential weaknesses?

EXTENSION STUDY

Piaget, play and cognitive development

Before looking at play from a Piagetian perspective, we need to define what is meant by *play* (see also Chapter 14). For behaviour to be defined as 'play', a number of qualities need to be evident in combination. The behaviour will (Dockett & Lambert 1996):

- be intrinsically motivated—that is, spontaneous and self-initiated;
- be relatively free from externally imposed rules (if there *are* rules, they are imposed by the players, not by adults);
- be carried out as if the activity were 'for real' (by the use of pretence, children are demonstrating the ability to distinguish reality from fantasy);
- focus on the process of playing, rather than on any product produced;
- be dominated by the players;
- require the players to be actively (mentally or physically) involved.

In relation to cognitive development, Piaget described three types of play: practice play, symbolic play and games with rules. The first of these, **practice play**, relates to the sensorimotor stage of development after about six months of age, and describes the intentional repetition of particular actions and use of objects by infants in their exploration of their immediate world of physical objects. For instance, anyone who has had the opportunity to observe an infant over a period of time would notice the rapid transition from initially random movements such as arm waving, which might have caused a toy suspended overhead to swing, to progressively more deliberate efforts to recreate this interesting experience.

Symbolic play begins to emerge as the infant's ability to use mental representations of objects and events develops, especially the ability to imitate, both while the model is present and at a later time. Piaget describes an example of deferred imitation when his daughter of about 16 months exhibited a temper tantrum in her playpen one afternoon, identical in vocalisations and mannerisms to that performed in front of her by a child the same age on the previous day. Symbolic play—which includes pretending, fantasy and sociodramatic play (when two or more children are involved in playing imaginary roles together)—is characteristic of preoperational children and begins at two or three years, continuing until about six or seven years.

At the end of the preoperational stage, children begin to show less interest in games of pretence and engage frequently in games with prescribed rules, such as hide-and-seek, hand clapping, marbles or board games. This development follows the shift from preoperational to concrete-operational thinking, or an extension of sensorimotor and constructive activities with the added element of externally defined rules (Smilansky 1990). Constructive play emerges out of sensorimotor activities when the child has begun to form symbolic representations of experiences and objects: what appears, therefore, as 'playing with blocks' will be represented mentally by the child in constructive play as 'building a house'.

How do children construct knowledge through play?

Children's play is full of physical and social activity, conversation and pictures, both real and imaginary. These are the essential elements through which children construct their cognitive, social and emotional worlds. The role of the carer–educator requires a recognition that young children learn through play, rather than through structured activities in which they receive information about the world and directives on how to behave. Good teachers provide rich

Formal-operational stage

During the period of formal operations there emerges the ability to think abstractly and in a scientific way. The formal-operational individual possesses a unified logical mental system with which to explore systematically hypothetical situations and abstract relations independent of content. *Formal thought* refers to the ability individuals have to set up and test hypotheses, referred to as **hypothetical reasoning** or hypothetico-deductive reasoning, to think **propositionally**, and to take into account all possible combinations or aspects of a problem without reference to physical reality, referred to as **combinatorial logic**. As with the earlier stages, a number of 'tests' have been constructed to illustrate the presence of formal thinking in adolescents and adults.

To test whether children are able to use formal-operational logic—that is, whether they can set up, test, and confirm or deny hypotheses—they are given problems where they must handle several variables at the same time. A common problem is the colourless liquid opportunities for play, with plentiful resources and time without adult interruption unless there is a need to refocus because of potentially disruptive behaviour (Jones & Reynolds 1992).

What is the role of the adult in children's play?

During practice play, exploration of the self, others and the immediate world is what absorbs the young child. For the adult–carer to support this exploration, an environment with a wide range of sensorimotor experiences and modelling of oral language is necessary, along with protection from the physical danger that exploration can bring.

At the stage of symbolic play, the sensitive teacher understands that children come to 'know' by doing; personal experiences and spontaneous actions teach them about the world and about others. The important role for the teacher here is to provide the tools and symbols for representing personal reconstructions of experience: models of language (spoken and written) to describe experiences, and a range of media for building, making objects and creating images. Thus, the preoperational child has available pencils, crayons and markers with which to 'write' shopping lists and signs; play dough (wet sand or even mud!) for creating objects or just for experimenting with; construction materials such as wood or paper scraps and glue, blocks or toys such as Lego and tools; and costumes for dramatic play with character enactment.

In the concrete-operational stage, where the child is now in formal schooling, the teacher's role is to provide opportunities for the integration of play skills developed in the previous stage into tasks required in the primary school. For example, as children learn to use written symbols to record their stories, they should be encouraged to talk out loud and draw as well (Jones & Reynolds 1992). 'Writing evolves as children discover that people draw not only things, but speech' (Dyson 1989, p. 7). Teacher-designed concrete experiences should provide intellectual challenges for children to discover important concepts while they 'play'. These should be balanced with self-chosen, spontaneous activities in which children can investigate and think critically about their own discoveries. From a Piagetian perspective, such activities allow for the assimilation of new concepts or the experience of cognitive conflict through which accommodation to existing understanding may occur, bringing about a sense of cognitive equilibrium.

As they begin to focus on games with rules during this stage, children of primary school age also need to learn how to use problem-solving skills independently in conflict situations. This should be done through the teacher modelling thinking processes, language and behaviour.

The role of information technology as a tool for symbolic representation and exploration, and for the development of higher-order mental processes through play, should not be overlooked. With computers today, it is possible to play alone, play cooperatively with others, or play with a virtual community in interactions between children at separate locations and the technology. We look further at the role of information technology in cognitive development and play on the book's website.

What is the role of the social context in cognitive development through play?

Not only does there need to be a stimulating environment in which children can investigate and resolve cognitive conflict, but also the encouragement, guidance and active involvement of older children and adults in supporting children's pretend play has been shown to be very important (Haight & Miller 1993). For example, Farver and Wimbarti (1995) have shown that older Indonesian children, who often participate in pretend play with their younger siblings more than mothers, act as guides and 'expert partners' (Smolucha 1992) in stimulating make-believe play by challenging the thinking of their younger siblings and suggesting ideas for making the play more elaborate.

problem, in which children are presented with five bottles of colourless liquid and must decide which combination of three liquids produces a yellow colour. Concrete-operational children will simply try various pairs of liquids or combine all five liquids to no avail, and eventually give up. Formal-operational children establish a systematic procedure for testing the liquids in various combinations in order to arrive at the solution. They can also verbalise the logic they used to solve the problem.

With propositional thinking, formal-operational children can work through statements of an argument in their mind. For example, the formal-operational child uses deductive logic to answer the following syllogism:

All Bs are As.
All Cs are Bs.
Then all As are ______.

Or:

Bob is fairer than John.
John is darker than Bruce.
Then Bruce is ______ than Bob.

Given the above syllogism, students will say that, from the information given, Bruce could be lighter or darker

During the stage of formal operations, children can solve problems through logical operations.

than Bob, showing that they have reasoned correctly. These types of syllogism appear to be beyond concrete-operational children.

Formal-operational children are able to apply the concept of ratio and proportion to solve problems. A common problem consists of giving children two cards on which stick figures are drawn, one being two-thirds the height of the other. These stick figures are constructed so that they measure four and six paper clips high, respectively. The child is then asked to measure both of the stick figures with eight connected paper clips and to record the heights in paper clips. The paper clips are then replaced with smaller paper clips and the child is asked to measure only the large stick figure with the smaller paper clips. The child is then asked to decide how high the small stick figure is in small paper clips without measuring directly. In other words the child has to apply **proportional reasoning** to solve the problem. Perhaps you would like to try this problem yourself.

We know that topics for debates are often based on hypothetical situations. For example, an intriguing debate could be had on the topic: 'That this world would be better if water were pink.' Concrete-operational children would have difficulty mounting a logical argument that followed from the premise that water could be pink, as water is colourless in reality. Adolescents in the formal-operational stage can abstract the structure of the argument from its content and argue hypothetically. While debates in the primary school are related to the real world, debates in the secondary school can be related to purely hypothetical issues. A popular television show, *Hypotheticals*, illustrates some adults' capacity to reason hypothetically. It also illustrates the incapacity of some adults to reason hypothetically!

Studies indicate that simply arriving at the age appropriate to formal thinking does not ensure that an individual will practise formal thought (Renner *et al.* 1976). It appears that two things are necessary: level of cognitive maturity and domain-specific opportunities to practise formal thinking. If individuals are not confronted with the necessity to reason formally (that is, if concrete modes of thinking appear more adaptable) then formal thought will not be used. Indeed, most people probably go through most of their days reasoning at a concrete or preoperational level. Furthermore, even when individuals are quite adept at formal thinking, it is often domain specific. For example, while the author can hypothesise and manipulate data related to psychology, he depends on concrete (and perhaps, more often than not, sensorimotor) reasoning when he is working out carpentry problems. Conversely, most carpenters can work out solutions to tricky and involved building problems symbolically. Consequently, we cannot presume as teachers that all adolescent children think formally. The theory holds that, while they have the capacity, relevant experiences may be necessary to 'stimulate' its use.

QUESTION POINT

Science teaching should promote formal thought, but it cannot do so if concrete-operational thinkers are asked to interact with science on a purely verbal level and their teachers teach them as though they think formally. Concrete-operational learners must interact with science at the concrete level—they cannot do otherwise (see Cowan 1978, p. 278).

What are the implications for science and maths programs in secondary schools?

The underlying logical structure that is at the base of logical thinking is what Piaget calls the **structure of 'groupings'**. The child's ability to group is the requisite for conservational thought and for reasoning out problems of classification, seriation, number and space. The six conditions of grouping, which form a logico-mathematical scheme, are:

1 *Composition:* Any two units can be combined to produce a new unit.
2 *Reversibility:* Two units combined may be separated again.
3 *Associativity:* The same results may be obtained by combining units in different ways.
4 *Identity:* Combining an element with its inverse annuls it.

5 *Tautology:* A classification or relation that is repeated is not changed.

6 *Iteration:* A number combined with itself gives a new number.

While these groupings appear somewhat abstruse, they can be explained simply with examples. Any two numbers combined must give a third number—for example, 3 + 5 = 8. We can reverse this operation—for example, 8 − 3 = 5. We can achieve the same result by different number associations—for example, (2 + 1) + (3 + 2) = (6 + 2). If we take an identity from itself we end up with 0; or, all animals less all animals equals no animals. If we *repeat* a classification, a relation or a proposition, it is unchanged—such as, all men plus all men = all men (tautology). If we combine a number with itself, the result is a new number (iteration) (see Case 1985b; McNally 1977). Each of these logical processes gradually develops through the stages described above.

ACTION STATION

This activity is designed to allow you to try your hand at administering and interpreting some Piagetian tasks.

You will need two balls of modelling clay or play dough, each about the size of a golf ball. Administer the conservation of substance task individually to four children between the ages of four and 10. There are three forms in which the task is given: ball versus sausage, ball versus two smaller balls and ball versus pancake.

1. Show the child two equal-sized balls of clay and say: 'In this game we will play with clay. This will be your clay, and this will be mine. Do you have just as much clay as I do?'

   If necessary, adjust the amounts of clay in the two balls until the child agrees that he has just as much clay as you have. Then say to the child: 'I am going to roll my clay into a sausage.' Roll your clay into a sausage. Then ask: 'Now, do you still have just as much clay as I have, or do you have more, or do I have more?'

   After the child responds, say: 'Tell me why.' Record the child's responses.

2. Begin with the same sequence of questions as above. Then divide your ball into two pieces out of which you form two smaller balls. Ask the same sequence of questions as above and record the responses.

3. Begin with the same sequence of questions as above. Then divide your ball into two pieces, one of which you flatten into a pancake. Ask the same sequence of questions as above and record the responses.

You might like to try administering the conservation of liquids test as well.

Using your data, consider the concept of conservation and the arguments children use to justify their responses.

Implications of Piaget's structuralist theory for the classroom

In the following sections we describe some implications of Piagetian theory for the classroom. Piaget's theory has been a great catalyst for the development of educational curricula, methods and evaluation techniques within our classrooms (Gallagher & Easley 1978). Rather than applying Piaget's structuralist perspective literally to education, as some curriculum developers have done, DeVries (1997) believes that two more general, philosophical approaches to education emerge from Piaget's constructivism. First, the emphasis shifts from trying to foster directly the characteristics of a future stage of development to maximising children's opportunities to create and coordinate the many relationships of which they are currently capable. Second, there is an emphasis on providing children with opportunities to construct meaning out of the experiences with which they are presented. Learning is essentially considered a constructive process. Ultimately, elements of Piaget's theory, such as the types of experience presented to children, the nature of active learning and the importance of interest, autonomy and peer interaction, are related to this important notion that children construct their learning from this world of experience. Table 2.2 presents the essentials of Piaget's structuralist theory for education.

Cooperative interaction and concrete experience are essential elements in children's construction of learning.

PIAGET AT SCHOOL

- Developmentally appropriate education
- Social interaction and cognitive development
- First-hand experience with the 'real world'
- Spiral curriculum and curriculum integration
- Motivation and discipline
- Acceleration of stage development

Developmentally appropriate education

Piaget emphasises that children should be actively engaged in the content to be learned. There should be an optimal match between the developmental stage of the child and the logical properties of the material to be learned. This approach has been labelled *developmentally appropriate practice in education* (Dockett 1996; Van Horn & Ramey 2003).

To assist with this, Piaget and his followers have written books on how primary and secondary school students learn number concepts, concepts of time, movement and speed, geometry, chance and probability, logic and causality (Forman 1980). Many of the materials used to teach maths and science at school have been based on Piagetian theory. Indeed, a number of curricula and teaching materials used in our schools have been based on Piaget's stage theory, and indicate the sequence in which material should be taught and the experiences the children should have in order to maximise their learning. In some cases, Piagetian theory is also used to justify why some experiences are considered unsuitable for young children. What might some of these experiences be?

Social interaction and cognitive development

Interaction with peers through group work and discussion in the classroom, while a necessary part of socialisation, is also of considerable importance in liberating children from their egocentrism in order to facilitate cognitive growth (see, for example, DeVries 1997). Children's exposure to different points of view forces them to defend, justify, modify, concede or relinquish their position, all of which actions oblige them to modify thoughts—that is, to accommodate and assimilate. With peer interaction, the mismatch between those operating at slightly higher and lower levels is likely to be optimal, to challenge each individual to progress in their understanding. This is one of the reasons why group work and excited busy noise is so important in today's classrooms. Stanbak and Sinclair (quoted in DeVries 1997, p. 12) make the following point:

> [S]ocial interaction and especially peer interaction thus seem, at a far earlier age than is generally supposed, to prepare the principal characteristics of the main reasoning principles brought to light by Piaget with reference to the ages of 6 or 7 . . . The negotiations, justifications, and proposals of compromise observed show that at the age of our subjects the correspondences and reciprocities that, according to Piaget . . . 'constitute the most important grouping' are being constructed during the interactions.

First-hand experience with the 'real world'

Teachers should give children first-hand experiences with the natural world in order to help them form concepts of *living* and *non-living*, of *identity* and *causality*. They

Table 2.2 Essentials of a Piagetian structuralist perspective for education

Teachers should:

- have an awareness of the stage characteristics of the students' thought processes;
- have an awareness that children of a particular age are not necessarily functioning at a particular cognitive level; for example, reaching adolescence or adulthood does not guarantee the ability to perform formal operations;
- avoid efforts to 'push' a child to the next higher stage;
- individualise learning experiences so that each student is working at a level that presents an optimal mismatch between what the student knows and the new knowledge to be acquired. Moderate novelty will foster motivation (disequilibrium);
- provide concrete experiences necessary for the development of concepts prior to their use in language;
- individualise evaluation of students with the goal of improving their personal performance;
- use materials that encourage creative thought and avoid those that discourage it.

Source: Based on Webb (1980), pp. 96–7.

should let them interact with each other and encourage them to talk and think about their experiences in order to stimulate the growth of logical thinking and the development of language to express their thoughts. Creative play in the classroom should also be encouraged, because play, according to Piaget, is an assimilation of reality into the self. What do you think Piaget meant by this?

Spiral curriculum and curriculum integration

Important aspects of the curriculum should be revisited at different stages and the child required to think and act at different levels of thought and action. This can be achieved by posing questions at a range of levels to stimulate disequilibrium.

From a Piagetian perspective, there is considerable merit in developing themes in which a number of different content areas are combined and integrated. Teachers should thus try to identify structural similarities in different content areas. In the 'old days', this was called *doing an integrated project*. For example, a thematic approach to 'shapes' could encompass shape in a musical composition, in a poem or story, in mathematical and geometric constructs, in a painting, in social relationships such as 'the shape of my family', and in the natural world.

Cohesion of knowledge shown through integrated projects

Motivation and discipline

There is no place in Piaget's theory for competition, grades and places in class relative to others. Rather, motivation is derived from 'real' interest—that is, when the challenge is neither too easy nor too difficult for an individual's current cognitive structures. Moderately novel learning tasks are considered to be very motivational. Furthermore, the self-selection of learning activities is more likely to provide for genuine interest and progress at the child's own rate. Mundane rote learning of facts is hardly likely to provide the motivation to challenge thought.

Discipline problems typically emerge in the stage of late concrete operations/early formal operations and reflect the child's developing peer orientation and ability to analyse and criticise adult control. Teachers could provide means for debate, small-group discussion and social interaction, and opportunities for children to determine for themselves the class rules. In particular, the opportunity for adolescents to engage in shared reflections on issues of personal concern recognises their new cognitive egocentrism in which they focus on what they imagine others are thinking of them, and how they might 'change the world'.

Acceleration of stage development

In general, Piaget was not impressed with the notion of trying to accelerate the development of children through the cognitive stages nor, in particular, accelerating their mastery of conservation. Some acceleration may be possible if procedures involve setting up a disequilibrium in children between their cognitive level and the new concept, thus forcing them to 'accommodate'. However, research on acceleration indicates that it is probably not worth the effort, as children regress when the supporting educational structures are absent. Furthermore, the gains in levels of reasoning are not substantial relative to those of non-'trained' peers.

Acceleration is most likely to occur when children are already on the verge of acquiring the concept being taught. Research also shows that certain kinds of training in conservation are more effective than others. Field (1981) showed that three- and four-year-olds, who were given verbal rules to explain why objects did not appear the same when they really were, were most likely to conserve when they used the identity rule rather than the reversibility or compensation rule. Children who 'mentally' returned the material to its original state or appearance (*reversibility rule*) or made allowances for different dimensions (*compensation rule*) conserved better than children who didn't add anything or take anything away (*identity rule*). Furthermore, the four-year-olds benefited more from the training than the three-year-olds, suggesting that children benefit most when intellectual structures are well enough developed to handle the principle of conservation.

You can see why first-hand experience with the real world helps to construct knowledge.

Summary

For Piaget, intellectual development occurs progressively as the growing child moves through a series of stages—characterised by qualitatively different cognitive processes—and is confronted with new experiences that must be related to the existing mental schemes of the child. Through the processes of assimilation and accommodation, the child either incorporates new experiences into existing schemes or constructs or alters schemes to make them more useful. As the child develops, these intellectual schemes become more sophisticated, so that by the formal stage the child is capable of the full range of logical operations characteristic of adult thought. At each stage of development the child is confronted with situations that cannot be easily resolved by resorting to existing schemes and so conflict occurs, causing disequilibrium. The child, for example, may be faced with a conservation-like problem such as being given a certain size glass to drink from that appears to hold less than other children's glasses. The child may complain that she hasn't been given as much as the others. The parent explains otherwise, the other children at the table argue otherwise, and demonstrations of the equality of quantities are given. Such cognitive conflict! While the child may not initially understand the equivalence, a repetition of this and similar situations over a period of time 'causes' the child to adapt and develop schemes for discounting perceptual cues along only one dimension, while taking into account a number of salient cues. Through this process the ability to conserve is developed and, in each resolution of conflict, with the development of more adequate cognitive schemes, equilibrium is achieved. The resolution of cognitive conflict drives cognitive growth.

Current status of Piaget's theory

Piaget's theory has attracted voluminous research. Some researchers have been intent on providing a wider research base for the theory than Piaget's original limited clinical method, while others have conducted research to test elements of the theory (Halford 1989). In particular, research has addressed the following questions: Are the stages that Piaget described really universal? Do they cut across domains of knowledge? Do the various cognitive abilities associated with the stages emerge at the ages Piaget predicted? Are the developmental stages he described invariant across individuals and cultures (Bidell & Fischer 1992; Rogoff & Chavajay 1995)? Probably most research has been conducted in the area of conservation and, in particular, whether the acquisition of conservation is invariant across groups and whether it can be accelerated through various educational programs (Brainerd 1978; Modgil & Modgil 1976, 1982).

Problems with Piaget's theory

Among the problems noted with Piaget's theory are the following:

- the limited success of many short-term training studies on Piagetian tasks—that is, successes that exerted an impact on one class of task without affecting any other task that was supposed to be 'structurally related';
- the apparent 'unevenness' of children's intellectual development when measured across different tasks, contexts or domains;
- individual differences in the order of task acquisition, which gave rise to low correlations among tasks that were supposedly dependent on the same underlying structure (Case 1992).

In addition to these difficulties, some researchers think the theory lacks explicitness, neglects individual differences, and fails to consider affect or perception as factors influencing intellectual development.

Unfortunately, the research in this area is too voluminous, convoluted and equivocal in its findings to deal with in detail here. Suffice to say that for every experimental design constructed to demonstrate the 'fallibility of the theoretical framework', other experimental designs have been constructed that support the general tenets of the theory (see Bidell & Fischer 1992; Halford 1989).

Criticisms of the Piagetian tests

The Piagetian tests have also been subjected to considerable critical review, with many researchers considering the form of the tests (particularly the language used, relevance of the questions to background experiences, and the requirement that children justify their 'correct' answers in the 'correct' way) inadequate (for example, Rogoff & Chavajay 1995).

Michael Siegal (1991) has written a particularly interesting critique of the language framework used in the test of conservation and argues that younger children's apparent inability to conserve and decentre can be explained in terms of a clash between the conversational worlds of adults and children. In particular, Siegal believes that the framework for the Piagetian questions breaks conversational rules that children implicitly hold. While these conventions may be broken for a specific purpose in adult speech, young children, in general, abide by them. Specifically, Siegal believes that problems arise because Piagetian experimenters pose questions where the answer is obvious or repeat questions when an answer has already been given. Young children may not recognise that the purpose underlying these departures from conversational rules is to establish their understanding of concepts. Instead, they may assume that, for example, repeated questioning (characteristic of the Piagetian test) implies an invitation to switch the second time around because the first answer was incorrect. For example, in the conservation of liquids test, children who answer that the two flasks of water are equal may switch their answers after one flask has been poured into a different container, despite believing the volumes are still the same. They may do this because they want to please the experimenter and give the answer they think is expected. Siegal believes that, when given the appropriate verbal cues that take into account the relative immaturity of their language skills, young children disclose what they know. An impressive research base supports his belief.

Developmentally appropriate education revisited

As parents, we are pretty sure that classical Piagetian theory underestimates young children's reasoning capacity. We have no doubt that our daughters, at three, had notions of causality and a conception of time, were able to classify elementary groupings, and were often able to take the perspective of others, showing great concern and understanding of feelings, and modifying their attitudes and behaviour accordingly. This discrepancy between what classic Piagetian theory tells us should be the case and what we observe may be because we have exceptionally bright children (all parents think their children are exceptionally bright!) or it might be that the original Piagetian methodology did not allow the full capacities of children to be explored. More advanced research techniques (such as video cameras and audio recorders) are now available for observing infants and children and for determining what they can or cannot do (Flavell 1985). In general, research using alternative methodologies and new techniques has established that Piaget underestimated the cognitive capacity of children (for example, Gelman & Baillargeon 1983; Halford 1989; Siegler 1991). Such discrepancies between the theory and what we now know children are really capable of call into question the usefulness of what has been termed 'developmentally appropriate practice in education' (Dockett 1996; Van Horn & Ramey 2003), reflected in many curricula and teaching materials. Perhaps developmentally appropriate education sells students short in terms of what they could actually learn. What do you think?

ACTION STATION

Design a range of activities for children in organised settings in which they can reflect on their own thinking in a range of situations, and on that of others. Plan some role-taking situations for children to participate in.

Obtain a copy of an infants, primary and lower secondary curriculum in mathematics (or science). Compare the programmed activities with the supposed conceptual abilities of children at these levels. If possible, obtain a copy of a teacher's program for these classes and analyse its consistency with current thought on the conceptual abilities of children.

Neo-Piagetian theories

As a reaction to the perceived limitations in Piaget's theory, there have been three developments. First, there has been a reformulation by a number of theorists to address the limitations, while preserving those features of the theory that appear to have withstood the rigours of contemporary debate and experimentation. These approaches are generally termed *neo-Piagetian* (Biggs & Collis 1982; Case 1985a, 1985b; Demetriou 1987; Halford 1982; Pascuale-Leone 1969). Neo-Piagetian theories make an important contribution to our understanding of children's intellectual development. However, as they are many and complex, it is beyond the scope of this book to describe them. Readers are referred to Case (1985a, 1985b), Demetriou (1987), Flavell (1985) and Halford (1993). In general, neo-Piagetian views form the basis of radical constructivist views of learning discussed briefly in Chapter 1 (see Derry 1996).

A second development has occurred within the Piagetian camp, where Piagetians now re-emphasise components of the theory that deal with constructivism rather than the part that deals with structuralism (Bidell & Fischer 1992; Carey 1987; Inhelder & de Caprona 1987; Sigel & Cocking 1977). Structuralism and constructivism are discussed earlier in this chapter.

A third development is a re-emphasis on the social elements of Piaget's theory in which cooperative social interactions function to promote cognitive, affective and moral development (DeVries 1997). We have seen in this chapter the importance of providing a socially interactive classroom and fostering social exchanges of a cooperative

Theory and research into practice

Daniel T. Hickey — CONSTRUCTIVIST, COGNITIVIST AND BEHAVIOURIST APPROACHES TO LEARNING

BRIEF BIOGRAPHY

I grew up in suburban Los Angeles. As an undergraduate at San Diego State University, I devoted much of my attention to music, political activism and working at the college radio station. An interdisciplinary program let me use graduate courses in the Educational Technology department to combine my interests in telecommunications and computers. I originally planned to be a technical writer, but an Educational Technology faculty member, Brock Allen, offered me my first research position in 1982. We studied the instructional potential of new interactive cable television systems. Before graduating, I began working with Thomas Sticht on a project funded by the Ford Foundation. We refined and applied the groundbreaking 'functional context' methods that emerged in military training research in the 1970s. After a brief and rather disheartening job writing industrial training manuals, I got back into research working at the Human Resources Research Organization (HumRRO) where I worked with Ellen Gagné on studies of workplace literacy.

I began my graduate training with James Pellegrino at the University of California, Santa Barbara. I followed him to Nashville to join John Bransford and the 'Cognition and Technology Group at Vanderbilt'. A NASA Space Grant Fellowship gave me the freedom to explore the complex tensions being raised by the emergence of 'sociocultural' instructional perspectives for instruction and assessment. My dissertation was a large-scale study of *The Adventures of Jasper Woodbury* math problem-solving software. Results showed targeted, dramatic impact on high-stakes achievement, but only in classrooms whose existing math instruction was consistent with constructivist perspectives. The impact of *Jasper* on goal orientation was mixed, and I was left with doubts about prevailing models of motivation for understanding or further improving these new approaches to instruction. While at Vanderbilt, I also met my wife Ana Maria Brannan. She completed her Ph.D. at Vanderbilt and is currently a faculty member there where she studies and evaluates children's mental health services.

I completed postdoctoral training at the Center for Performance Assessment at Educational Testing Service. There I worked with Ann Kindfield to help evaluate the *GenScope* introductory genetics software developed by Paul Horwitz of the Concord Consortium. This project followed me to my Educational Psychology faculty position at Georgia State University. In 2000, I joined the Educational Psychology faculty at the University of Georgia and became a research scientist in the Learning and Performance Support Laboratory, where I coordinate funded research in assessment and evaluation.

RESEARCH AND THEORETICAL INTERESTS

My early efforts with Thomas Sticht integrated basic skills instruction into content area instruction. This helped me to appreciate how cognitive psychology could help address challenges that limited learning for all students and caused grave injustices for some. Our innovative curriculum was designed to help displaced workers seeking training in electronics and computing. Many of them (particularly women and minorities) were turned away or shunted to dead-end electronic assembly jobs because they could not pass difficult mathematics and language tests and were unable to spend a year or more completing the prerequisite basic skills courses. By meaningfully integrating instruction in basic skills in the context of electronics, we were able to improve attainment of both sets of goals.

Much of my research can be characterised as an effort to reconcile conventionally individually oriented models of motivation and assessment with the sociocultural models of learning and instruction that began emerging in the 1990s. I am particularly interested in doing so in learning environments that employ cutting-edge computing technologies. My dissertation studies around *Jasper Woodbury* made me realise how challenging it was to obtain *and* document increased scores on high-stakes tests with these kinds of innovations, and to do so in a wide range of classrooms. The study pointed me towards the value of formative assessment for enhancing these types of instructional innovations. But the study also left me wondering about the value of the prevailing models of motivation for doing the same.

During my postdoctoral training at the Center for Performance Assessment, my efforts to simultaneously tmaximise *and* document learning were reshaped by the 'comparative' approach outlined in a chapter by Greeno, Collins and Resnick in the 1996 *Handbook of Educational Psychology.* This provided the theoretical framework for the multi-level model of formative and summative assessment that emerged in refinements of the GenScope curriculum and our current assessment model. This also revealed how a uniquely sociocultural view of engagement might advance the debate over incentives, offering a new way to harness the motivational potential of assessment.

A grant from the US National Science Foundation in 2000 allowed Ann Kruger, Laura Fredrick and me to further refine the formative assessment practices and study the motivational issues that emerged in the first GenScope study. We contrasted two different approaches to integrating individually oriented and socially oriented models of cognition; this helped further to define a uniquely sociocultural model of engagement. The study also yielded a comprehensive model of assessment practice that involves three increasingly distal levels of outcomes, whose functions are iteratively refined across three increasingly formal design cycles. This model is being implemented in studies of science curriculum with Steven McGee of the NASA-funded *Classroom of the Future,* and studies of the *Quest Atlantis* multi-user virtual environment developed by Sasha Barab of Indiana University. In other projects and writings, my colleagues, students and I are exploring the potential of these core ideas in achievement motivation, classroom management, vocational education and educational evaluation.

I am particularly interested in advancing newer 'design-based' approaches to educational research. These methods emphasise the development of useful new knowledge within iterative refinements of educational practices. Our recent studies have shown how design-based refinement of formative and summative assessment practices can accomplish the seemingly conflicting goals of enhancing classroom discourse and student understanding while also maximising scores on external achievement tests. These studies are highlighting the limitations of the conventional distinction between 'basic' research focused on building fundamental theories of learning and 'applied' research aimed at solving problems of practice. Following the inspiration of scientists such as Pasteur, design-based methods support 'use-inspired basic research' that many leading scholars view as the most promising direction for educational research.

I am also very interested in the challenge of integrating different theories of knowing and learning in education practice and research. Integrating across 'behavioural', 'cognitive' and 'sociocultural' perspectives makes it difficult to use a coherent set of scientific methods. This is because each perspective represents a different scientific 'worldview'. This is most obvious in the tensions between educational policies that are increasingly behavioural, placing them in conflict with practices that reflect modern cognitive perspectives. A good deal of the current innovation in instruction reflects a 'hybrid' approach that integrates cognitive and sociocultural perspectives. These approaches use an 'aggregative' integration that characterises social functioning using aggregated assumptions about individual activity. Despite its apparent popularity, this approach is still vulnerable to comparisons with more behavioural approaches. It may also impede true scientific advance, by leading researchers to use methods in ways other than they were intended. I have been working hard to define an alternative 'dialectical' integration that starts with a sociocultural focus on collective activity. This allows one to reconcile the strengths and weakness of behavioural and cognitive perspectives by treating all activity of individuals as 'special cases' of sociocultural activity.

RESEARCH AND THEORY INTO PRACTICE

This research has very direct implications for teaching practice. Our 'multi-level' assessment model helps teachers to move beyond the simplistic distinction between 'formative' classroom assessment and 'summative' external assessment. Showing that all forms of assessment have both formative and summative functions helps the teacher to see how the summative functions can often undermine formative intent. In particular, it helps them to see that formal classroom assessments used for grading, remediation and curricular revision are usually quite summative from the perspective of the student. Our 'semi-formal' classroom assessments and 'learner-oriented' formative feedback rubrics provide useful feedback for maximising classroom discourse, student understanding and the enactment of specific curricular routines. They provide teachers with a more effective alternative to the drill and practice 'test-prep' programs. Teachers can also use them quite readily to ensure mastery of standards-based content using more open-ended and inquiry-oriented curricula.

This work also promises to provide a more coherent way for teachers to think about the consequences of extrinsic incentives. This includes the ubiquitous things like grades and praise and controversial things like pizzas and prizes for reading books. Most teacher education programs discourage the use of common forms of incentives, but many find themselves choosing to or being expected to use them in their practice. Rather than forcing teachers to accept one of the two very antithetical views about incentives, we suggest directly considering the impact of incentives on collective participation in domain knowledge practices (that is, sociocultural characterisation of classroom discourse).

This appears to be particularly useful for helping teachers to minimise the harm caused by punitive accountability policies that are based on achievement tests and behavioural indices of student conduct.

KEY REFERENCES

Hickey, D. T. (1997) Motivation and contemporary socio-constructivist instructional perspectives. *Educational Psychologist*, **32**, 175–93.

Hickey, D. T. (2003) Engaged participation vs. marginal non-participation: A stridently sociocultural model of achievement motivation. *Elementary School Journal*, **103**(4), 401–29.

Hickey, D. T. & Granade, J. (2004) The influence of sociocultural theory on our theories of engagement and motivation. In D. M. McInerney & S. Van Etten (eds) *Research on Socio-cultural Influences on Motivation and Learning (Volume 4), Big Theories Revisited,* (pp. 223–47). Greenwich, CT: Information Age Publishing.

Hickey, D. T. & McCaslin, M. (2001). Comparative and sociocultural analyses of context and motivation. In S. Volet & S. Järvelä (eds) *Motivation in Learning Contexts: Theoretical and Methodological Implications* (pp. 33–56). Amsterdam: Pergamon/Elsevier.

ACTIVITIES

1 Dan Hickey refers to constructivist perspectives on learning. Using some of the definitions given in this chapter, what do you understand by the term *constructivism*?

2 Dan Hickey refers to his efforts to reconcile conventional individually oriented models of motivation and assessment with sociocultural models of learning. Refer to Chapters 3, 4 and 5 to review the characteristics of some of what might be termed individually oriented models of motivation and assessment (behavioural and cognitive). What is meant by sociocultural models of learning, and how do these differ from the individually oriented models of learning and motivation?

3 Dan Hickey refers to the motivational value of sociocultural models of learning. Discuss with fellow students what the motivational benefits of sociocultural models of learning may be and, in particular, how these relate to assessment practices.

4 Dan Hickey refers to design-based approaches to educational research. What is meant by this term, and why is it a useful approach to educational research? You might like to refer to Chapter 11 for some additional insights.

5 Dan Hickey refers to the challenge of integrating across behavioural, cognitive, and sociocultural perspectives on knowing and learning in education practice and research. A number of our chapters deal with elements of each of these approaches. Do you think it is possible to integrate across these different streams of theorising, research and practice, and if so, what might the elements of this integration be? Compare your answers with those of other students to compile a common pool of ideas.

6 Dan Hickey believes that although much current educational practice is a product of a mix of cognitive and sociocultural approaches, these approaches are still vulnerable to comparisons with more behavioural approaches. Why is this? You will need to read more widely in the text to answer this question.

type in order to promote operational development. In later chapters we will also examine the importance of social interaction to affective and moral development (see Chapters 8 and 14).

Theories of mind

'Theories of mind' claims that a largely implicit conceptual framework allows children to understand, explain, and predict their own and others' behaviour and mental states (Bosacki 2000). As noted in our earlier discussion of constructivism (Chapter 1), children learn through making sense of their world of experiences. Young children explain their world through what might be termed naïve physical, biological and psychological 'theories' (see Dockett 1994, 1995a, 1996; Gopnik & Wellman 1992; Wellman & Gelman 1992). In other words, children make sense of physical events (for example, the sun rising), biological events (for example, growing) and psychological events (for example, interactions with others) in non-scientific ways, but in ways that prepare them to understand with greater sophistication physical, biological and psychological experiences as they develop and are exposed to more complex explanations. 'Theories of mind' relates to children's ability to impute mental states to oneself and others, and involves appreciating the distinction between these mental states and external reality, as well as understanding the causal relationships that exist between the two (Bosacki 2000; Davis & Pratt 1995). Recent research has explored 'theories of mind' as a means of defining more precisely what children are capable of understanding and learning (see, for example, Flavell, Green & Flavell 2000; Keenan, Olson & Marini 1998; Kuhn & Pearsall 2000). In particular, this approach seeks to examine how children use mental representation to interpret and reflect upon their physical, biological and psychological world. In general, the results of this work indicate that children are more capable of sophisticated thinking than was earlier thought. This suggests that educators should do two things: encourage children's reflection on their thinking and that of others, and challenge the notion of developmentally appropriate practice in educational settings.

The following Learner-centred Psychological Principle introduces our next section on Vygotsky. At the end of the section, revisit this principle and discuss its relevance to Vygotsky's notion of the zone of proximal development (ZPD) and scaffolding of learning.

Vygotsky and social constructivism

Piaget made a very important contribution to our understanding of the way in which children develop. However, Piagetian theory left many issues still to be addressed—in particular, the sociocultural aspect of learning and the role of human mediators in children's learning (see Kozulin & Presseisen 1995). Lev Vygotsky (1896–1934) was a contemporary of Piaget. For Vygotsky, the learning process was not a solitary exploration by a child of the environment, as suggested by Piaget's personal constructivist theory, but rather a process of appropriation by the child of culturally relevant behaviour (Kozulin & Presseisen 1995).

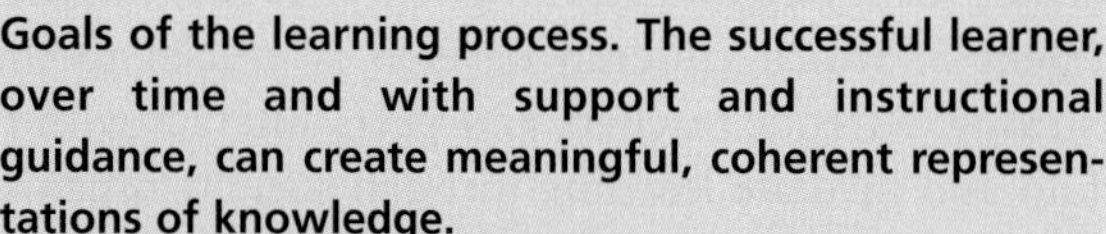

Goals of the learning process. The successful learner, over time and with support and instructional guidance, can create meaningful, coherent representations of knowledge.

The strategic nature of learning requires students to be goal directed. To construct useful representations of knowledge and to acquire the thinking and learning strategies necessary for continued learning success across the life span, students must generate and pursue personally relevant goals. Initially, students' short-term goals and learning may be sketchy in an area, but over time their understanding can be refined by filling gaps, resolving inconsistencies, and deepening their understanding of the subject matter so that they can reach longer-term goals. Educators can assist learners in creating meaningful learning goals that are consistent with both personal and educational aspirations and interests.

Cultural-historical theory

A central theme in Vygotsky's social constructivist theory (also referred to as **cultural-historical theory** or *socio-cultural theory*) is that cognitive development can be understood as the transformation of basic, biologically determined processes into higher psychological functions. According to the theory, children are born with a wide range of perceptual, attentional and memory capacities which are substantially transformed in the context of socialisation and education, particularly through the use of cultural inventions such as **tools**, social structures and language, to constitute the higher psychological functions or the unique forms of human cognition (Diaz, Neal & Amaya-Williams 1990; Smagorinsky 2001; Vygotsky 1978). In a sense, children are wrapped around by their culture (represented by these tools, social structures and language) and this directs the form and extent that cognitive development takes. On one level we have the continuing evolution of the cultural group through the collective activity of its members, and on the other we have the development of the individual as part of this collective. Individuals are therefore both part of, and the product of, this collective culture.

Tools of learning

Tools may consist of the pen, paintbrush, notepad, computer, calculator and various symbol systems. Tools, or cultural artefacts as they are sometimes called (Salomon & Perkins 1998), play a double role in learning. First, they provide the means with which to act upon the world. In other words, the learner does something with the tool that extends the learner's capacity in a particular way. Second, tools act as cognitive scaffolds that facilitate extension of knowledge into related areas (Salomon & Perkins 1998). Tools not only enrich by developing new capacities in the learner, but also can transform the learner and the learning situation. For example, memory is transformed once an individual acquires reading and writing (language tools). Classroom and learning processes can be radically altered by the common use of computers.

Also implicated in learning are the social structures and language systems of the learner. Family, social,

EXTENSION STUDY

Cross-cultural perspectives on Piaget's theory

Piaget's theory has attracted considerable attention from cross-cultural psychologists keen to demonstrate the applicability or otherwise of the theory to non-Western cultural groups such as the Australian Aborigine and the New Zealand Maori (Dasen 1972a, 1972b, 1974, 1975; Dasen & Heron 1981; Irvine & Berry 1988; Keats & Keats 1988).

As we have seen, much of Piaget's theory of cognitive development is based on the organising principles of perception and the processes of adaptation and assimilation. There is abundant evidence from cross-cultural and anthropological research that the manner in which individuals perceive, structure, interpret and relate to their world is very much a function of what the physical and social environment has influenced (Deregowski 1980; Pick 1980). (Indeed, Piaget, as a biologist, would have accepted this notion of variability.) Hence, there is an innate danger in setting up rules or stages of cognitive development on the basis of information drawn from one cultural group and applying the derived principles to other cultural groups. The power of perception in modifying individuals' methods of relating to the world is well captured in this story taken from Feuerstein (1991, pp. 23–4):

> I remember working with children who came to Israel directly from Yemen on the operation of 'Flying Carpet'. There was no illiteracy in that group and a great desire to read. Since they did not have enough books, it was not uncommon that 15–20 students shared the same book and read it simultaneously, looking at the page from different angles. They even had to learn how to read upside down. I remember one Israeli mother, who adopted a Yemenite child, and came to me for advice because she suspected that the child was not normal: 'he reads from the other side!' She thought that something was wrong with his perception!

Piaget's theoretical framework and methodology spawned a vast amount of research in cross-cultural contexts (Irvine & Berry 1988). In the early research there was little questioning of the relevance of the constructs or

political, and religious groups and organisations represent social structures. Among language systems that are important are systems of counting, mnemonic techniques, and algebraic, mathematical and musical notation (John-Steiner & Mahn 1996; Salomon & Perkins 1998).

Learning is a process through which we become one with the collective through carrying out personal activity in collaboration with other people (for example, Davydov 1995). As the tools, inventions and language of one culture may be significantly different from those of another culture, education must place learning within the appropriate social and cultural contexts. For Vygotsky, therefore, cognitive development is not so much the unfolding of mental schemes within the individual, as it is with Piaget, so much as the unfolding of cognitive understandings of social beings within social contexts. In a sense we become part of the community, and the community becomes part of us in the sharing of knowledge. In this way, social constructivism varies considerably from personal constructivism with its emphasis on the cognitive processes within the minds of individual students (see Marshall 1996). Throughout this text, we emphasise this cultural/social dimension of learning and teaching.

The zone of proximal development

For Vygotsky, who focused on the importance of sociocultural dimensions and language as characteristics of formal schooling and learning (Moll 1990), the social system in which children develop is crucial to their learning. Parents, teachers and peers interact with the child and mediate learning through socially organised instruction. Vygotsky believed that the task of teaching children is particularly complex because, in order to be effective, teachers need to know each individual student very well, be familiar with the social dynamics of each child's social setting, and have a good understanding of their own teaching skills so that these may be used effectively to facilitate the learning of students.

One of the main elements of Vygotsky's theory, derived from this belief that learning occurs in social contexts, is his notion of a **zone of proximal development** (ZPD). This is typically thought of as each person's range of potential for learning (Smagorinsky 1995). For Vygotsky, teaching is only good when it 'awakens and rouses to life those functions which are in a stage of maturing, which lie in the zone of proximal the methodology (the clinical interview and Piagetian tasks) with the major cross-cultural concession being in the use of interpreters. Early research reported by Dasen and Heron (1981), for example, suggested that in a number of cultural groups, including Australian Aborigines, up to 50 per cent of their mature adult population were unable to conserve quantity, weight or volume, as measured by standard Piagetian tests. One could argue that such findings call into question the universal nature of cognitive development as proposed by Piaget. On the other hand, it could be said that they may reflect limitations in the methodology: for example, the limited number of tests used which may not have been adequate to demonstrate the existence or otherwise of conservation and formal thinking; the subjects may not have been familiar with the materials of the test; and inadequate or incomplete communication between tester and testee. In other words, the interpretation of the answers and their significance, particularly when expressed through a translator, may not have been recognised as demonstrating conservation when in fact, with further elaboration or probing, or a change in the content of the tasks, conservation may have been clearly demonstrated (Irvine & Berry 1988; Pick 1980).

A number of other studies indicated a 'lag' in the development of conservation for members of some cultures in comparison with others (Dasen 1974; de Lemos 1969; Goldschmid *et al.* 1973; Heron & Dowel 1973). However, some researchers believe that this 'lag' can be explained in terms of level of education and familiarity with the tasks (Pick 1980). It is generally accepted today that the requirements of a culturally different environment, such as that of the Aboriginal or Maori, lead to different types of spatial orientation. Hence, tests devised to assess conservation must take this into account.

More recent criticism of this earlier research has led to a growing trend among educators and researchers to reject the notion of inherent intellectual inferiority among culturally different groups and to accept the universality of cognitive functioning. In other words, all groups are perceived equally capable of the diverse ways of thinking and processing information that characterise learning in a modern environment, and no group is inherently inferior. Whatever differences there may be reflect experience and opportunity. Educators develop programs on the basis of this belief. We deal extensively with this issue in Chapters 9 and 10.

development' (quoted in Gallimore & Tharp 1990, p. 200). Vygotsky defines the zone of proximal development as the distance between the actual developmental level of a child as determined by independent problem solving and the level of potential development as determined through problem solving under adult guidance or in collaboration with more capable peers (Vygotsky 1978). Learners ultimately make their own the knowledge engaged with through assistance of teachers, parents and peers.

To place learning in the zone of proximal development, an appropriate level of difficulty needs to be established. This level must be challenging but not too difficult. The educator then needs to provide for assisted performance. This is referred to as **scaffolded instruction**. The adult provides guided practice to the child with a clear sense of the goal or outcome of the child's performance. As with scaffolding around a building, it is gradually removed so that the child can perform the task independently. There has been a development in notions of effective scaffolding over the last years from a concern with the interactions between a tutor and a student to the design of tools to support student learning in project-based and design-based classrooms. The notion of scaffolding is increasingly being used these days to describe various forms of support provided by software tools, curricula, and other resources that have been designed to help students learn successfully in the classroom (Puntambekar & Hübscher 2005). What scaffolding have you used to facilitate your learning?

Evaluate performance

If the learning experience has been carefully structured and situated within the child's zone of proximal development, the child should be able to perform the task independently. In order to assess the success of the learning experience, therefore, the educator should evaluate the independent performance of the child on the task.

Three key principles underline the effective use of the zone of proximal development to facilitate the cognitive development of children: education must be holistic; it must be situated in a social context that mediates the learning; and it must allow for change and development in the child.

Holistic learning

For learning to be holistic, the unit of study should be the most meaningful unit, rather than the smallest or simplest. For Vygotsky, the division of potentially meaningful material into small skills and subskills to facilitate learning is actually counterproductive, as its essential meaningfulness is lost. The 'whole language' approach to teaching reading, which emphasises that reading comprehension and written expression must be developed through functional, relevant and meaningful uses of language rather than through the discrete learning of subskills (such as phonic decoding), illustrates this idea.

Social interaction and mediated learning

The importance of social interaction between adults and children, and, in particular, the role played by adults in guiding and mediating learning for children, is paramount for Vygotsky. Central to this interaction is instruction that develops in children an increasing mastery of the language of learning and instruction so that they acquire conscious awareness and voluntary control of knowledge (Moll 1990). An example of a teaching method based on this principle is the reciprocal teaching approach developed by Brown and Palincsar (1989) and considered later in this book (Chapter 5) (see John-Steiner & Mahn 1996) and The Early Literacy Project (Trent, Artiles & Englert 1998). Also reflecting **mediated learning** are the notions of distributed learning, collaborative learning and learning communities, which we discuss in Chapters 6, 7, 8 and 14.

Formal and everyday learning

Vygotsky also believed that formal learning (such as that characterised by learning scientific information) and everyday learning (such as that characterised by learning in the home) are interconnected and interdependent. Vygotsky believed that it is through the use of everyday concepts that children make sense of the definitions and explanations of scientific concepts (or schooled concepts). However, everyday concepts are also shaped and moulded by exposure to scientific concepts and, because of this, children become more aware, and in control, of their everyday worlds (Moll 1990). Hence, an effective relationship must exist between the everyday world and the 'schooled world' for learning to be significant, effective and of practical value.

To facilitate the development of learning embedded in the everyday world, teachers, students and peers must interact, share ideas and experiences, solve problems and be interdependent. This interdependence in social contexts is central to a Vygotskian analysis of instruction (John-Steiner & Mahn 1996; Moll 1990).

The teacher must also be aware that what children are able to do with assistance and collaboration today, they will be able to do independently tomorrow (Vygotsky 1978). Consequently, learning needs to be structured so that there is an expanding zone challenging children to move forward. An interesting implication of Vygotsky's approach, which stands in contrast to some of the implications that may be drawn from Piaget's theory, is that children should be challenged to be engaged in activities that appear to be beyond their current level of development. Children can often complete activities with the collaboration of teachers and peers that they could not complete on their own. In time, with this assistance and verbal mediation, the needed skills are gradually internalised and the children learn to perform them independently.

ZPD and change and development in children

Teaching and the zone of proximal development

Tharp and Gallimore (1988) give the following definition of teaching based upon Vygotskian ideas: 'Teaching consists of assisting performance through the Zone of Proximal Development. Teaching can be said to occur when assistance is offered at points in the ZPD at which performance requires assistance.' In the following boxed section we describe four states in the zone of proximal development.

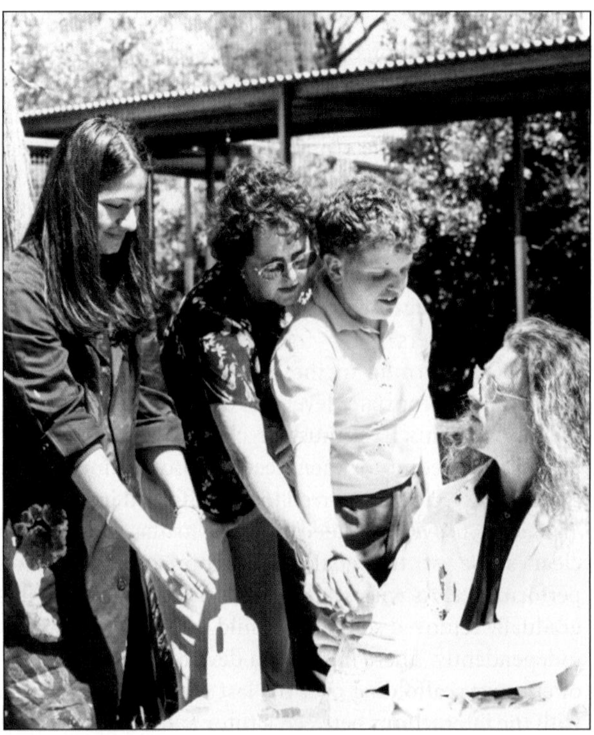

Scaffolded instruction for this blind learner involves special dimensions. Can you suggest some of these?

STAGES OF PROXIMAL DEVELOPMENT

According to Gallimore and Tharp (1990), there are four stages in the zone of proximal development that a child goes through:

1 **Assistance:** In the first stage, the performance is assisted by more capable others such as parents, teachers and peers.
2 **Growing independence:** In the second stage, there is less dependence on external assistance and the performance begins to become internalised. The children help themselves by using self-directed speech. In other words, children (and adults, too) talk to themselves about what they are doing and so begin to assume responsibility for self-guidance and self-regulation of the learning.
3 **Automation of response:** In the third stage, the performance is developed, automated and internalised. At this time, assistance from others and self-directed speech is unnecessary and, indeed, may be irritating.
4 **De-automatisation and recursion:** In the fourth stage, if the knowledge has not been used 'de-automatisation' of performance may occur, which leads the individual to re-enter the zone of proximal development. For example, at times even well-learned responses are 'forgotten' or become 'rusty'. At these times the individual re-enters the zone of proximal development and consciously talks through the matter internally or seeks external assistance. To this extent, there is a continual movement in and out of the zone of proximal development—what Gallimore and Tharp (1990) term **recursion.**

Consider each of these four stages and relate them to your own learning.

The nature of the assistance to be given by teachers (and parents and peers) to support cognitive growth was not spelled out by Vygotsky. Contemporary authors have described a range of strategies that fit within a Vygotskian perspective. Gallimore and Tharp (1990) discuss modelling, contingency management, feedback, questioning and cognitive structuring from a Vygotskian perspective. Tudge (1990) discusses the usefulness of peer collaboration and Diaz *et al.* (1990) examines self-regulated learning. All of these teaching approaches are covered elsewhere in the text. Look for examples of these as you read.

Language and learning

Vygotsky (1962, 1978) emphasises language as a major means by which cognitive development occurs. Piaget, in contrast, believes that cognitive development occurs independently of language development, and facilitates the acquisition of language. Indeed, Piaget and Vygotsky interpret children's early self-talk (that is, talk not directed to others) in quite different ways. For Piaget it illustrates children's cognitive egocentrism, which they grow out of with the acquisition of more mature schemes of social behaviour and social speech. Vygotsky, on the other hand, interprets this self-talk as **private speech** which reflects a developmental phase between that of purely social speech and that of inner speech, or thought. Initially, children are subjected to public speech, which guides their behaviour (for example, the instructions given to them by their parents to perform particular behaviour). As children develop, they become more able to use their own speech (rather than the speech of others) to guide their behaviour and solve problems. This speech is used publicly, but not socially. They instruct themselves about what they should do. In its initial stages, these instructions are aloud. As the child develops, this speech becomes increasingly quieter and subvocalised, until eventually it is internalised and silent. At this stage, the child is using thought to control actions. For Vygotsky, language remains important throughout life for the higher mental processes such as planning, evaluating, remembering and reasoning (Berndt 1992). Indeed, adults are often heard to use private speech to help structure cognitive activity when they are trying to solve complex problems. The reason for this, according to Vygotsky, is that language is a sequential way of representing the holistic experience of thought (Vygotsky 1987). How often do you use private speech?

Private speech

Table 2.3 lists the essentials for education of a Vygotskian social constructivist perspective.

ACTION STATION

This activity is designed so that you may appreciate the influence that parents have in stimulating their children in a variety of ways that are important to the children's perceptual and cognitive development.

Locate a mother or father with a young infant (birth to three years). Observe the interaction between the parent and child in one or more play situations. Particularly note visual, auditory and tactile stimulation. Compile a detailed record of the interaction observed, and relate your observations to principles of cognitive development discussed in this chapter.

Table 2.3 Essentials of a Vygotskian social constructivist perspective for education

Teachers should:

- hold a belief that education is to develop students' personality;
- hold a belief that education is to facilitate the development of the creative potential of students;
- hold a belief that effective learning requires the active involvement of the learner;
- hold a belief that teachers direct and guide the individual activity of the students but they do not dictate or force their own will on them. Authentic teaching and learning come through a collaboration between adults and students;
- hold a belief that the most valuable methods for students' teaching and learning correspond to their developmental and individual characteristics, and therefore these methods cannot be uniform;
- hold a belief that schools should provide the tools that learners need to internalise the ways of thinking central to participation in the cultural world around them.

Source: Based on Davydov (1995), p. 13; Smagorinsky (1995).

ACTION STATION

Much can be learned from closely observing an infant's interaction with the physical world. Locate an infant up to two years of age. Over an extended period, observe the child's interaction with their environment. Make detailed notes on the child's activities. What learning do you think is taking place? Discuss your observations from the perspective of Vygotsky's zone of proximal development.

Vygotsky and Piaget: A comparison

Cognitive theories originally had as their focus the individual and their construction of understanding. Piaget's theory is an example of this approach. Many theorists have widened this focus to include the individual's construction of knowledge in their social context and the reciprocal nature of this development (see John-Steiner & Mahn 1996). These constructivist theories have been labelled *social constructivist* or *sociocultural*. Vygotsky's theory is an example of this approach. Sociocultural theories tend to suggest that there is no individual knowledge, only that which is commonly constructed by individuals through interactions with the tools, language and groups in their cultural context, and that there are no broad principles of learning and teaching that can be applied across curriculum areas (Nuthall 1996). Hence, teaching and learning in mathematics will be different from that in science, and so on. Social constructivism and personal constructivism also differ in the role to be played by the teacher. From a Piagetian perspective, direct teacher involvement with a learner may actually inhibit a child's understanding if instruction gets in the way of the child's own exploration (Newman *et al.*, quoted in Smagorinsky 1995, p. 197). This contrasts with Vygotsky's notions of scaffolding and guided discovery, and his belief in the importance of continuing interaction between the child and its environment to facilitate the child's understanding of the world about them.

Guidance and assisted discovery

Piaget suggests that developmental maturity must exist in order for children to benefit from particular learning experiences, and focuses on the importance of unstructured experiences and self-initiated discovery for children's cognitive development. Vygotsky emphasises the need for guidance and assisted discovery to lead development (Blanck 1990; Tharp & Gallimore 1988). Teachers need to design instruction that lies within the range of possibilities represented by the child's real level of development and their potential for development (the zone of proximal development) (Blanck 1990).

Higher mental processes

In contrast to Piagetian theory, which holds that 'higher' mental processes are characterised by formal and specific operations, Vygotskian theory holds that there are no specific operations that characterise higher mental processes but that these are shaped by the sociocultural situation in which an individual is located. Indeed, mental processes from a Vygotskian perspective are both elastic and unbounded. In other words, cognitive growth is elastic in that it may take many different directions preparing the individual for survival within their sociocultural context. We take up this idea when we discuss the cultural dimensions of learning

TEACHER'S CASE BOOK

Learning centres

Every Thursday Anna sets up a number of learning centres for the children in her composite 1/2 class. These centres change regularly. For example, a mathematical centre catered for the interests and abilities of Troy, a gifted child who loves to be challenged. The children had been working on a space topic. Using a calculator, Troy was able to estimate the distance between planets. This task, involving very high numbers and vast differences, absorbed and extended Troy.

Tim likes to tinker with things, so Anna set up a centre where children could discover how things work. It included a broken sewing machine, a typewriter and an old bar heater. Tim made himself a skateboard from the heater!

Hilly is a Down's syndrome child who loves art. Anna planned for classical music to accompany the fingerpainting activity.

Others prefer to use blocks. 'A lot of the younger children are into game making at the moment, so they'll do that,' says Anna. 'The learning centres can give the children a chance to consolidate something. For example, Katy might sometimes go to her handwriting and sit there and practise for a while. It also gives the chance to children who want to, to extend themselves.' Anna finds it works well.

Case studies illustrating National Competency Framework for Beginning Teaching, National Project on the Quality of Teaching and Learning, Australian Teaching Council, 1996, p. 24. Commonwealth of Australia copyright, reproduced by permission.

Case study activity
Consider the usefulness of such learning centres from both the Piagetian and Vygotskian perspectives. Why do you think they work well?

later in the book. Cognitive growth is unbounded because learning occurs in the zone of proximal development and this, for any individual, is continually in a state of evolution.

A final historical note

Piaget and Vygotsky wrote most of their work earlier last century. They did not explicitly write for teachers and educators and, by and large, did not operationalise their theories in terms of classroom curricula and practices. Furthermore, their theories were embedded in, and reflected, their contemporary social, historical, scientific, religious and political times. Their theoretical models of cognitive development and learning were not part of mainstream theorising in Western nations until much more recently. As a consequence, the elements of their theories are, in a very real sense, interpreted by theorists and practitioners embedded in quite different social, historical, scientific, religious and political times (see, for example, John-Steiner & Mahn 1996; Marshall 1996; Popkewitz 1998). Consequently, we can never really know whether our contemporary understandings and applications, particularly as they relate to constructivism, reflect what Piaget and Vygotsky believed—or indeed whether they would hold the same beliefs if they were miraculously transformed to our time and place. Indeed, there is often controversy regarding what might be the 'correct' interpretations of their theories. You might, for example, like to consider the two articles, one by Glassman (2001) and one by Gredler and Shields (2004), listed in the recommended readings at the end of the chapter, where there is a clear difference of opinion on how tenets of Vygotsky's theory should be interpreted. Irrespective of this, both theories have challenged modern thinking about effective teaching and learning in profound ways, and both continue to have a profound effect.

Theory and research into practice

Mary McCaslin (PKA Mary McCaslin Rohrkemper)

— VYGOTSKIAN PERSPECTIVES

BRIEF BIOGRAPHY

I graduated from Michigan State University (MSU)—three times. As an undergraduate I majored in psychology and completed the Russian and Eastern European Studies Program. I graduated with membership in Phi Beta Kappa and high honours in 1974. My graduate work was in educational psychology. I completed the Master of Arts in 1976 and the doctorate in 1981 with a major in learning and cognition and a minor in psychology. My dissertation, 'Classroom perspectives study: An investigation of differential perceptions of classroom events', received the first Outstanding Dissertation Award from the College of Education in 1981.

Throughout my education at MSU I had the opportunity to be involved in research. As a work-study undergraduate, I was fortunate to have been hired by Dr Gary Stollak, Professor of Child and Clinical Psychology, to assist in various research projects on child–adult interactions and children's perceptions and understanding of their interpersonal worlds. These early research experiences exposed me to the adrenaline—the worry and the thrill—of research and new learning that remains an integral part of my academic life. Dr Robert Slusser, Professor of History, who specialised in Russian and Soviet studies, Dr Frank Ingram, Professor of Russian, and Dr Hiram Fitzgerald, Professor of Human Development and specialist in Russian psychology, provided me with the opportunity to study Russian history, culture and psychology, which has remained a major influence on my understanding of sociocultural theory and its relevance to educational psychology.

As a graduate student I was fortunate to have been among the first wave of interns in the Institute for Research on Teaching (IRT), a research centre funded by the National Institute of Education. Part of the research mission of IRT was the preparation of the next generation of educational researchers, which included apprenticeship opportunities for graduate students. This enabled me to extend my research interests to include teacher–student interactions and student perceptions of their schooling experiences. I continue to conceptualise students as social beings who coordinate multiple roles and expectations (for example, child, student) that are not necessarily compatible.

Upon graduation, I immediately entered the world of the assistant professor, juggling the various expectations of tenure-line appointments. My most satisfying position as an assistant professor was at Bryn Mawr College, one of the 'Seven Sisters' liberal arts colleges for women, that emphasises teaching and mentoring students. I was fortunate to be named a post-doctoral fellow by the Spencer Foundation during that period. This enabled me, along with support from the Junior Leave program of Bryn Mawr, to conduct sustained research in classrooms. When I was tenured and promoted to associate professor at Bryn Mawr I had learned so much through working with students, both in my classroom and in the public schools where I conducted my research, I felt I had earned another degree—only this time I was paid to do it! Currently, I am professor of educational psychology at the University of Arizona, which, like MSU, is a land-grant institution but without the snow. In this context, programmatic research and graduate-level teaching and mentoring are my primary responsibilities. My educational experience was and is hugely important in my development as a human being; I take my role as teacher and mentor very seriously as I try to provide others with the opportunities and support extended to me.

RESEARCH AND THEORETICAL INTERESTS

My academic life has been spent trying to better understand student motivation and learning, and the societal conditions within which they emerge. I have advanced this commitment at the elementary and junior high school levels through my research and scholarship; in undergraduate education through teaching, advising and university service; and in graduate education through teaching and mentoring in research. In each case, I have understood that my primary goal for students is the promotion of 'adaptive learning'; I believe the processes that promote that learning are 'co-regulated'.

Theoretical framework

The theoretical foundation of my research is sociocultural—the work of Russian psychologist Lev S. Vygotsky, in particular. Consistent with the general Vygotskian position on the social origins of higher psychological processes, I study what I term the 'co-regulation' of 'adaptive learning'. 'Co-regulation' refers to the dynamic relationships among opportunities and participants within students' zone of proximal development (ZPD). Meaningful learning, by definition, occurs within the learners' ZPD; however, the ZPD is not by definition healthy or helpful to the learner. Co-regulation in the ZPD can enhance or impede student adaptive learning. 'Adaptive learning' represents optimised emergent capabilities of the learner. It involves the internalisation of goals; the motivation to commit, challenge or reform them; and the competence to enact and evaluate those commitments. Adaptive learning involves a certain hardiness based upon a healthy integration of the affective and the intellectual. In classrooms, adaptive learning in one instance may be about taking charge of frustration due to difficulty or obstacles; in another it may involve coping with the tedium of boredom due to repetitive or non-challenging tasks; in yet another instance, adaptive learning may be about seeking another's assistance or deciding it is time to quit. Obviously, not all co-regulated learning is healthy or adaptive; however, a primary theme in my work is to better understand what kinds of opportunities and relationships afford adaptive activity, which in turn informs a healthy and realistic identity that renders individuals more attuned to participation in their social worlds and, thus, enabled to make a meaningful contribution to that world.

A research example

My research efforts are commonly structured by (1) defining an opportunity, (2) capturing emergent activity, and (3) exploring identity formation. It often turns out that what I 'defined' as opportunity is understood quite differently than I intended. For example, in research I conducted to assess the effects of problem difficulty (the opportunity) on student problem solving (the activity) and beliefs about oneself as a learner (identity formation), I learned that students experience objectively moderately difficult problems—the ones they recognise as having done before and believe they should know—as the *most* difficult problems. Moderately difficult problems also were unique opportunities that afforded the integration of the affective and the intellectual in students' reported 'inner speech'. Inner speech in the Vygotskian perspective involves those talks-to-the-self that regulate thinking, motivation and emotion in non-automatic situations. Inner speech self-directs the individual, but it, too, is social in origin. Language serves two functions in the Vygotskian perspective: initially, communication with others; and subsequently, both communication and self-direction. My research on task difficulty revealed the differences between inner speech that is adaptive (for example, 'I need to do this a different way'), inner speech that was not (for example, 'I can't believe how dumb I am—why don't I know this?'), and the types of tasks and relationships at home and school that afford the integration and refinement of inner speech that promotes adaptive learning.

THEORY AND RESEARCH INTO PRACTICE

All my research has been designed with implications for practice in sight. Consistent with a Vygotskian perspective, the ultimate goal of human development is the desire and capability to make a meaningful contribution to the common good. Towards that goal, my research interests have included the adults, teachers and students in children's lives. I have studied approaches to classroom management and home parenting and their potential support of students' opportunity to learn responsibility and make commitments. I also have studied how students co-regulate one another in the development of normative beliefs about learning and motivation and what it means to be a member of a classroom.

Most recently, I am studying how students of poverty who attend schools that 'need improvement' understand and engage the opportunities available to them. This is perhaps the most theoretically challenging and practically frustrating of the research projects I have engaged thus far. For example, to date I have learned that the prerequisite skill hierarchy of behaviourally defined learning objectives that researchers worry leads to student beliefs that knowledge is 'simple and sure' and citizens worry is 'teaching to the test' is neither. Students mediate instruction that follows a 'simple and sure' format and can transform it into 'rigid and right' accountability: a potentially disabling spiral belief about learning and motivation in non-automatic cognition. Similarly, citizens can rest assured that most teachers likely could not or would not teach to the tests that students are required to take in the current era of testing accountability in the United States. Classroom instruction and grading have little in common with tests that intentionally seek to seduce students with an attractive wrong answer, stress speed over thoroughness, and filling in bubbles rather than showing your work. What citizens may want to worry about is how to *better* align the conditions of teaching and testing so that student learning can be known.

In short, my application of a Vygotskian perspective is all about the integration of research on practice and its potential for improvement. In this perspective, teachers and tasks are essential features of students' ZPD. Through mutual co-regulation, schooling can provide the opportunity for students to develop as adaptive learners who are able and want to make a meaningful contribution as members of their culture.

KEY REFERENCES

McCaslin, M. (2004) Co-regulation of opportunity, activity, and identity in student motivation: Elaborations on Vygotskian themes. In D. M. McInerney and S. Van Etten (eds) *Research on Sociocultural Influences on Motivation and Learning (Volume 4), Big Theories Revisited*, (pp. 249–74). Greenwich, CT: Information Age Publishing.

McCaslin, M. & Good, T. (1992) Compliant cognition: The misalliance of management and instructional goals in current school reform. *Educational Researcher*, **21**, 4–17.

Rohrkemper, M. & Corno, L. (1988). Success and failure on classroom tasks: Adaptive learning and classroom teaching. *Elementary School Journal*, **88**, 297–312.

ACTIVITIES

1 Mary McCaslin refers to adaptive learning and co-regulated learning. What is meant by these two terms? Give some class-based examples of them. Demonstrate how both of these elements of learning relate to Vygotskian theory.

2 Mary McCaslin makes the point that co-regulation within a student's ZPD can either enhance or impede their adaptive learning. Give examples of how co-regulation might enhance and impede a student's learning.

3 What is the importance of inner speech to learning, and what is the difference between adaptive and non-adaptive inner speech? What type of inner speech do you use when you are learning a new topic or revising an old one? What determines for you when you use adaptive and non-adaptive inner speech?

4 Consider one of the key references and critique it in the light of material in this chapter.

TEACHER'S CASE BOOK

Weights and pulleys

When I looked at last year's lesson plan on pulleys in the Year 8 physics unit, it revived vivid memories of a multitude of tangled ropes and pulleys which kept slipping off the ropes. The students kept pulling over the retort stands so that the weights and pulleys went crashing to the floor.

This year I decided that I would just demonstrate the pulley systems which were set up by the laboratory technician, rather than have the students construct their own. Also, this would leave half the lesson to review the work covered so far. I was not entirely happy with this method, but I could not think of a better alternative.

We had just finished investigating the pulleys when Sarah raised her hand.

'Yes, Sarah?'

'I think there is a crane at the chapel site with a pulley,' she said.

At present, a chapel is being built at the front of the school. Another student remarked that she thought she had seen pulleys on the weight machines in the school gymnasium. I thought for a moment. We could review our work tomorrow. I made a spontaneous decision to dispense with the lesson plan. 'Well,' I said. 'Why don't we all go down to the chapel site?'

When we arrived there was a crane and also a hoist which was used to lift the sandstone blocks to the top of the walls. The workman at the site agreed to operate the hoist so that the students could see the pulley system in action. Then we went to the gymnasium. The students had a great time using the weight machines and rowing machines. They competed to see who could lift the heaviest weight. When I asked, I found that several students were able to explain how the pulley systems worked on the different machines.

After all my careful lesson planning, I realised that these students already understood what I was trying to teach them. Next year I plan to book the gymnasium and let students work out for themselves how pulleys work.

Case studies illustrating National Competency Framework for Beginning Teaching, National Project on the Quality of Teaching and Learning, Australian Teaching Council, 1996, p. 50.

Case study activity

Analyse this case study from both the Piagetian and Vygotskian perspectives. What does it say about effective teaching and learning?

Discuss your analyses with other students.

WHAT WOULD YOU DO?

REBIRTH OF A GRADE 8 CLASSROOM

At Mr Daniels' school it is a customary policy for teachers to view how another teacher is developing students' reading, writing, speaking, listening and critical thinking skills. The school is a district high school and it was decided that a primary teacher would work with a secondary teacher. This structured collaborative program continued for four weeks.

Mr Daniels felt there were so many things that he could learn from the primary area that he continued to visit the Prep/1 class at the end of the four-week structured program. Each time he went there, he was struck by the stimulating and aesthetically pleasing environment, and reminded of the sterility of his own room. So, with the cooperation of the Prep/1 teacher, a deal was struck!

Case studies illustrating National Framework for Beginning Teaching, National Project on the Quality of Teaching and Learning, Australian Teaching Council, 1996, p. 11. Commonwealth of Australia copyright, reproduced by permission.

What do you think the deal was, and how would Mr Daniels' secondary classroom be affected? Read below what actually happened.

WHAT WOULD YOU DO? (cont.)

REBIRTH OF A GRADE 8 CLASSROOM

Mr Daniels would do English/social science work with Mrs Wilson's children, and she would assist him in the overhaul of his box-like room. It took them six weeks, but now the changes include a large work board to celebrate outstanding student work; a reading corner containing numerous texts (students can borrow these); copious amounts of student work displayed around the room; a games area with educational work and thinking games for early finishers or as a reward; a knowledge area where students are kept informed about world issues—that is, writing letters to the President of Bosnia condemning the mass rape of women by soldiers; and learning centres or independent working areas, with activities related to core work.

Mr Daniels believes that his teaching and the students' learning have changed in quite significant ways. He now has a stimulating, informative environment that enhances the quality of his teaching. The efforts put into the classroom environment are recognised by the students. He feels that the new organisation of his classroom makes a strong statement about quality learning and about the value he places on this learning place. The students feel comfortable in the classroom, and they take pride in its appearance for they feel a sense of ownership. Mr Daniels is able to employ a diverse range of teaching methodologies. Students are immersed in written language every time they enter his classroom, and reluctant learners are motivated to pick up things to view and read.

Case studies illustrating National Competency Framework for Beginning Teaching, National Project on the Quality of Teaching and Learning, Australian Teaching Council, 1996, p. 11. Commonwealth of Australia copyright, reproduced with permission.

How many of the features of Mr Daniels' reborn classroom illustrate principles of constructivism? What elements represent personal constructivism (Piaget), and which illustrate social constructivism (Vygotsky)?

KEY TERMS

Accommodation (p. 39): altering existing schemes or creating new ones in response to new experiences

Adaptation (p. 38): adjustment to the environment

Assimilation (p. 39): relating new experiences to existing schemes of knowledge

Centration (p. 42): preoccupation with visual perception

Classification (p. 45): constructing classes of objects

Combinatorial logic (p. 46): using systematic analysis to solve problems

Concrete operations (p. 44): Piaget's third stage characterised by individuals operating logically with concrete, visual materials, and by classifying and ordering serially

Conservation (p. 44): characteristics of an object remain the same despite changes in appearance

Constructivism (p. 37): Piaget's view that children construct their own understanding through interaction with their environment

Cultural-historical theory (p. 57): cognitive development is the transformation of basic, biologically determined processes into higher psychological functions through socialisation and education

Decentering (p. 44): focusing on a range of perceptual clues

Developmentally appropriate education (p. 50): optimal match between the developmental stage of the child and logical properties of the material to be learned

Disequilibrium (p. 39): a state of distress when confronted by a new situation until successful adaptation occurs

Egocentricity (p. 44): assuming that others experience the world as we do

Equilibration (p. 38): search for mental balance between cognitive schemes and information from the environment

Figurative knowledge (p. 39): thinking about problems in concrete terms

Formal operations (p. 46): Piaget's fourth stage characterised by the ability to solve problems abstractly and to think combinatorially—processes characteristic of scientific thinking

Hypothetical reasoning (p. 46): reasoning based on assumptions

Mediated learning (p. 60): learning through socially organised instruction

Nominal realism (p. 41): words have a power in and of themselves

Object permanence (p. 40): the understanding that objects have a separate, permanent existence

Operations (p. 38): thought processes

Operative knowledge (p. 39): thinking about problems theoretically

Phenomenalistic causality (p. 40): regarding things happening together as causally related

Physiognomic perception (p. 40): attributing lifelike qualities to inanimate objects

Practice play (p. 46): use of objects to explore the world

Preoperational stage (p. 40): Piaget's second stage before children acquire logical operations

Private speech (p. 61): in Vygotsky's theory, children's self-talk guides their thinking and actions—these verbalisations eventually become internalised as inner speech

Proportional reasoning (p. 48): applying ratio to solve problems

Propositional thinking (p. 46): working logically through an argument

Recursion (p. 61): in Vygotsky's theory, moving in and out of the zone of proximal development

Representational thinking (p. 40): basis for anticipating actions mentally

Reverse thinking (p. 44): mentally reversing operations

Scaffolded instruction (p. 59): in Vygotsky's theory, providing structured guidance in learning episodes that allows the learner to progress through the zone of proximal development

Schemes (p. 39): cognitive structures to organise perception and experience

Sensorimotor stage (p. 40): Piaget's first stage of development when children acquire goal-directed behaviour and object permanence through the senses and motor activity

Seriation (p. 45): organising elements by size

Spiral curriculum (p. 51): concepts presented at higher levels of abstraction as learning develops

Structuralism (p. 37): Piaget's belief that intellectual development occurs through a series of stages characterised by qualitatively discrete structures

Structure of groupings (p. 48): underlying logical structure of thinking

Symbolic play (p. 46): using mental representation of objects to imitate the real world

Theories of mind (p. 56): children's ability to impute mental states to oneself and others

Tools of learning (p. 57): in Vygotsky's theory, tools such as symbol systems (numbers and language) and technology (print and computers) that allow people in society to communicate, think, solve problems, and create knowledge

Transformation (p. 42): attending to changes in states

Zone of proximal development (p. 58): the stage at which a child's skills can be developed with the assistance of others

ON-LINE LEARNING

If you go to http://www.pearsoned.com.au/mcinerney, you will have hot links directly to these sites:

■ **Constructivist learning index page**

This site is useful for looking at ways in which constructivism is implemented in educational environments. Consider and discuss a number of the examples and relate them to the material covered in this and later chapters.

http://www.prainbow.com/cld/

■ **Cultural-historical psychology**

This site presents information on Vygotsky, including on-line articles. With advice from your instructor select an article for class discussion.

http://arts.uwaterloo.ca/~acheyne/chp.html

■ **Classroom compass**
This site presents a good overview of constructivist approaches to teaching. It also gives curriculum examples of constructivism in mathematics and geometry. Critique the information presented. How has the information provided influenced your approach to teaching other curriculum material?
http://www.sedl.org/scimath/compass/v01n03/welcome.html

■ **Radical constructivism**
This site is very useful for learning more about what is termed 'radical constructivism'. How is the notion of radical constructivism different from Piagetian and Vygotskian constructivism?
http://www.univie.ac.at/constructivism/people.html

WEB DESTINATIONS

If you go to http://www.pearsoned.com.au/mcinerney, you will have hot links directly to these sites:

■ **The Jean Piaget Society**
This website introduces you to the world of Jean Piaget and provides a springboard to other sites.
http://www.piaget.org/

■ **Vygotsky**
This site will introduce you to the world of Vygotsky and provide a springboard to many other useful sites.
http://www.igs.net/~cmorris/vygotsky.html

■ **Sociocultural theory**
This site will also introduce you to the world of sociocultural theory and Vygotsky and provide a springboard to many other useful sites.
http://carbon.cudenver.edu/~mryder/itc_data/soc_cult.html#vygotsky

■ **Theory into practice**
This website is very useful as it gives a quick overview of many of the key theories in educational psychology.
http://tip.psychology.org/index.html

■ **Constructivism**
These two websites present good information to further your knowledge of constructivism.
http://www.ibiblio.org/edweb/constructivism.html and **http://www.emtech.net/links/construc.htm**

RECOMMENDED READING

Becker, J. & Varelas, M. (2001) Piaget's early theory of the role of language in intellectual development: A comment on De Vries' account of Piaget's social theory. *Educational Researcher*, **30**, 22–3.

Bosacki, S. L. (2000) Theory of mind and self-concept in preadolescents. Links with gender and language. *Journal of Educational Psychology*, **92**, 709–17.

Case, R. (1992) Neo-Piagetian theories of child development. In R. J. Sternberg & C. A. Berg (eds) *Intellectual Development*. New York: Cambridge University Press.

Davydov, V. (1995) The influence of L. S. Vygotsky on education theory, research, and practice (trans. by S. T. Kerr). *Educational Researcher*, **24**, 12–21.

De Vries, R. (1997) Piaget's social theory. *Educational Researcher*, **26**, 4–17.

Glassman, M. (2001) Dewey and Vygotsky: Society, experience, and inquiry in educational practice. *Educational Researcher*, **30**, 3–14.

Gredler, M. & Shields, C. (2004) Does no one read Vygotsky's words! Commentary on Glassman. *Educational Researcher*, **33**, 21–5.

Halford, G. S. (1989) Reflections on 25 years of Piagetian cognitive developmental psychology, 1963–1988. *Human Development*, **32**, 325–57.

John-Steiner, V. & Mahn, H. (1996) Sociocultural approaches to learning and development: A Vygotskian framework. *Educational Psychologist*, **31**, 191–206.

Kozulin, A. & Presseisen, B. Z. (1995) Mediated learning experience and psychological tools: Vygotsky's and Feuerstein's perspectives in a study of student learning. *Educational Psychologist*, **30**, 67–75.

Moll, L. C. (1990) *Vygotsky and Education*. Cambridge: Cambridge University Press.

Moyles, J. R. (ed.) (1995) *The Excellence of Play*. Buckingham: Open University Press.

Puntambekar, S. & Hübscher, R. (2005) Tools for scaffolding students in a complex learning environment: What have we gained and what have we missed? *Educational Psychologist*, **40**, 1–12.

Siegal, M. (1991) *Knowing Children: Experiments in Conversation and Cognition*. Hillsdale, NJ: Lawrence Erlbaum.

Smagorinsky, P. (2001) If meaning is constructed, what is it made from? Toward a cultural theory of reading. *Review of Educational Research*, **71**, 133–69.

Van Horn, M. L. & Ramey, S. L. (2003) The effects of developmentally appropriate practices on academic outcomes among former head start students and classmates. *American Educational Research Journal*, **40**, 961–90.

Vygotsky, L. S. (1987) *Thinking and Speech* (ed. & trans. by N. Minick). New York: Plenum Press.

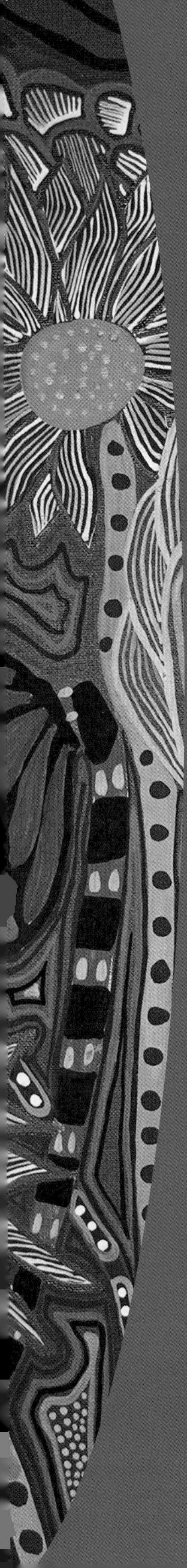

CHAPTER

3 Alternative perspectives on cognition, intelligence and effective learning

Overview

In this chapter, we look at alternative views on intelligence and cognition. We highlight theories that describe intelligence as multifaceted and defined by such qualities as flexibility of thought, efficient working memory, adaptability, creative productivity, insight skills, social skills and effective use of domain knowledge. In particular, we explore Gardner's theory of multiple intelligences and Sternberg's triarchic theory of intelligence. In both of these approaches, one's culture and specific contexts are considered to be important determinants of intelligent behaviour, as individuals interact with their external world.

We then discuss traditional psychometric views of intelligence. Intelligence testing is dealt with in some detail and we introduce the notions of mental age, intelligence quotient, and individual and group tests of intelligence. Limitations of the psychometric approach to intelligence testing are also described, especially problems emanating from cultural differences.

We also discuss heredity and environment in the context of intelligence testing and ability grouping, and introduce behavioural genetics. Throughout we draw out the relevance of each of the approaches to understanding effective learning.

Learning objectives

After reading this chapter, you will be able to:

- describe Gardner's theory of multiple intelligences;
- apply the essentials of a multiple intelligence perspective for education;
- describe Sternberg's triarchic theory of intelligence;
- define componential, experiential and contextual intelligence;
- apply the essentials of a triarchic intelligence perspective for education;
- describe the psychometric view of intelligence;
- analyse assumptions underlying individual and group tests of intelligence;
- outline the limitations of verbal tests of intelligence;
- understand the motivational variables influencing measured intelligence;
- consider the relative importance of heredity and environment on development, as well as issues related to streaming and ability grouping versus mainstreaming and integration.

3

Gardner's multiple intelligences

> Individuals differ from one another in their ability to understand complex ideas, to adapt effectively to the environment, to learn from experience, to engage in various forms of reasoning, to overcome obstacles by taking thought. Although these individual differences can be substantial, they are never entirely consistent: A given person's intellectual performance will vary on different occasions, in different domains, as judged by different criteria. Concepts of 'intelligence' are attempts to clarify and organize this complex set of phenomena. (Neisser *et al.* 1996)

Howard Gardner believes that all definitions of **intelligence** are shaped by the time, place and culture in which they evolve (Kornhaber, Krechevsky & Gardner 1990). The developmental theories of both Piaget and Vygotsky, discussed in Chapter 2, certainly bear the imprint of their historico-cultural times. Three factors appear to influence what is considered to be important in the **cognitive** development of individuals:

1. The *domains of knowledge* necessary for survival of the culture, such as farming, literacy or the arts.
2. The *values* embedded in the culture, such as respect for elders, scholarly traditions or pragmatic leanings.
3. The *educational system* that instructs and nurtures individuals' various competencies. (Kornhaber *et al.* 1990)

The cognitive skills needed to survive in a farming or herding society may be quite different from those required for survival in a technological society. Therefore, conceptions of what is *intelligent behaviour* may also vary accordingly. For example, in a farming subsistence society intelligent behaviour may be related to the production of food and skill in interpersonal relations to maintain the community's social ties. In a non-farming modern society, it might be related to technological expertise and independence. Increasingly, in modern societies, intelligent behaviour has become identified with successful performance at school—in mathematics and language, in particular. For Gardner, this is a very limited perspective on intelligence (see also Sternberg & Grigorenko 1997).

Gardner (1983; Gardner & Hatch 1989; McKenzie 2001) proposes a theory of **multiple intelligences**. The eight intelligences are logical-mathematical, linguistic, musical, spatial, bodily kinaesthetic, interpersonal and intrapersonal, and naturalist (see Figure 3.1). Gardner (1999, 2004) and others are currently investigating a ninth intelligence—existentialist intelligence. Each is characterised by core components such as sensitivity to

Figure 3.1 Howard Gardner's theory of multiple intelligences

the sounds, rhythms and meanings of words (linguistic), and capacities to discern and respond appropriately to the moods, temperaments, motivations and desires of other people (interpersonal). Although few occupations rely entirely on a single intelligence, an individual with a highly developed intelligence in one of these areas may become a composer (musical), a dancer (bodily kinaesthetic) or a therapist (interpersonal). Other occupations might require a blend of intelligences (see, for example, Chan 2003). Gardner and Hatch give the example of a surgeon who needs both the acuity of spatial intelligence to guide the scalpel and the dexterity of the bodily kinaesthetic intelligence to handle it.

Gardner's theory of multiple intelligences

Intelligence	*Core component*	*Career focus*
Logical-mathematical	An ability for numbers, reasoning and problem solving	Scientist Mathematician
Linguistic	An ability for language, arts, speaking, writing, reading and listening	Poet Journalist
Musical	An ability for songs, rhythms, instruments and musical expression	Composer Musician
Spatial	An ability for learning visually and organising things spatially	Sculptor Architect
Bodily kinaesthetic	An ability for physical activity	Dancer Athlete
Interpersonal	An ability for responding to the emotional states of others and being people-oriented	Counsellor Salesperson

Intrapersonal	An ability for understanding and monitoring one's own emotional and physical states	Sundry careers
Naturalist	An ability for understanding and relating to the plant and animal world	Botanist Farmer
Existentialist	An ability for reflective thought and philosophising	Philosopher Priest

Developmental patterns in multiple intelligences

According to Gardner, each intelligence has a developmental pattern that is relatively independent of the others. For example, linguistic intelligence is acquired by most individuals with little tutoring relatively early in life, whereas speed and extent of musical intelligence development vary widely from person to person. It is also important to note that the relative strengths of the eight intelligences vary within and between individuals (see Kornhaber *et al.* 1990) and are believed to be biologically determined (Gardner 1993). The development of these intelligences depends on the interaction of children with adults, as the great majority of what is learned after the age of two is socially constructed.

The educational implications of Gardner's multiple intelligences

At the very least, Gardner's view challenges our notion of what is intelligent behaviour. In particular, he challenges the emphasis placed in schools on the development of verbal and mathematical abilities of children to the exclusion of a broader range of intelligent behaviours. Furthermore, this approach to viewing intelligent behaviour and its development suggests a range of educational and assessment practices to encourage effective learning (see, for example Campbell, Campbell & Dickinson 1999; Vialle 1994).

Social context is a powerful influence on the development of multiple intelligences

1 Because of the importance of the social framework in which intelligent behaviour develops, educational practices such as mentoring and apprenticeships—where expert members of society are involved in tutoring individuals—are strongly endorsed. In particular, such teaching approaches, together with the cooperative involvement of parents and others in the surrounding community, are seen to strengthen the cognitive outcomes of the community's school-children (see Kornhaber *et al.* 1990).
2 In order for learning to be meaningful, material to be learned should be presented in authentic environments rather than in decontextualised settings.
3 To encourage children to develop competence in the various intelligences, an interdisciplinary curriculum should be developed, and equal time should be given to each area of development.
4 Education should be firmly grounded in the institutions and practices of society, such as art and science museums, gymnasiums, factories, technology institutions and so on.

In essence, Gardner's theory makes it clear that intelligence in its many facets reflects potentials that must be fostered in the environment. They will not develop fully without stimulation, encouragement and extensive practice.

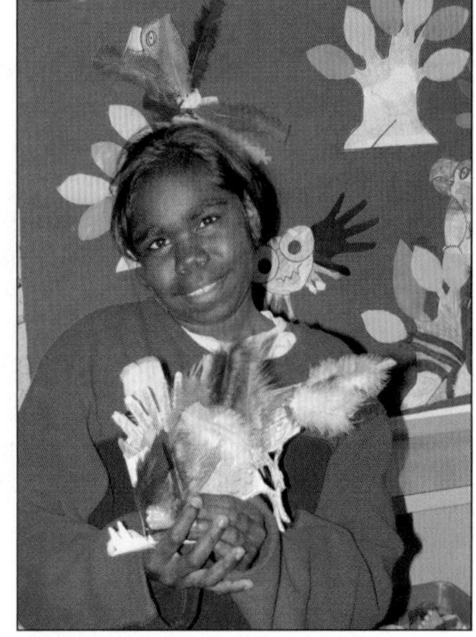

Music, art and drama should play an important role in any school curriculum

Assessment of learning across the multiple intelligences should integrate curriculum and assessment, and be flexible to allow individuals to demonstrate their various competencies in authentic settings that relate directly to the specific task being measured (see Campbell *et al.* 1999). Assessments should be intrinsically interesting, and tests for specific intelligences should be appropriate to that intelligence. Hence, assessments such as work samples, child observations and portfolios are encouraged. See Chapter 11 for further discussion of these issues. Table 3.1 shows the essentials of a multiple intelligence perspective.

Some schools have designed their curriculum around multiple intelligences, whereby children are given the opportunity to discover their areas of strength and to develop the full range of intelligences (Vialle 1991, 1993). We believe that consideration of a broader range of talents within schools will give an opportunity for many children, who may previously have been considered unexceptional or even at risk of school failure, to excel. What do you think?

The following Learner-centred Psychological Principle introduces us to the importance of goals, expectations and feelings to motivation. Consider this principle while reading the next sections of the text.

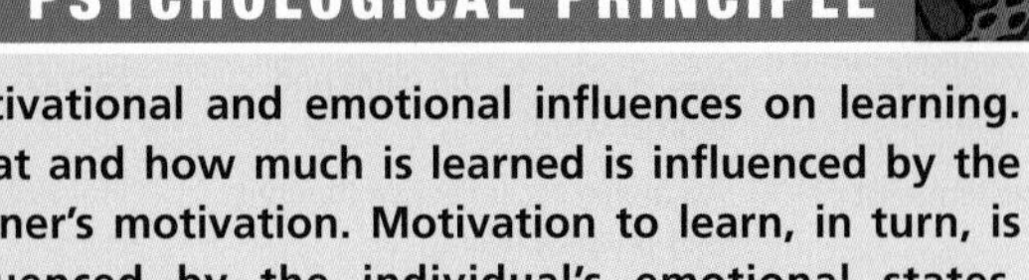

Motivational and emotional influences on learning. What and how much is learned is influenced by the learner's motivation. Motivation to learn, in turn, is influenced by the individual's emotional states, beliefs, interests and goals, and habits of thinking.

The rich internal world of thoughts, beliefs, goals, and expectations for success or failure can enhance or interfere with the learner's quality of thinking and information processing. Students' beliefs about themselves as learners and the nature of learning have a marked influence on motivation. Motivational and emotional factors also influence both the quality of thinking and information processing as well as an individual's motivation to learn. Positive emotions, such as curiosity, generally enhance motivation and facilitate learning and performance. Mild anxiety can also enhance learning and performance by focusing the learner's attention on a particular task. However, intense negative emotions (e.g., anxiety, panic, rage, insecurity) and related thought (e.g., worrying about competence, ruminating about failure, fearing punishment, ridicule, or stigmatising labels) generally detract from motivation, interfere with learning, and contribute to low performance.

Emotional intelligence

Somewhat similar to Gardner's intrapersonal and interpersonal intelligences is emotional intelligence. While the notion of emotional intelligence has been around for some time, it received a considerable boost with the publication of two articles in 1990 (Mayer, DiPaolo & Salovey 1990; Mayer, Salovey & Caruso 2000; Salovey & Mayer 1990; see also Furnham & Petrides 2004). From this time on, emotional intelligence became

Table 3.1 Essentials of a multiple intelligence perspective for education

Teachers should:

- present material to be learned in authentic environments;
- encourage all children to develop competencies across all intelligences;
- utilise mentoring and apprenticeships with experts in the area of development;
- develop an interdisciplinary curriculum to facilitate the interconnections between the intelligences;
- encourage the cooperation of parents and community in students' education;
- ground education in the cultural institutions and practices of society.

Implications for assessment

- Integrate curriculum and assessment.
- Be flexible in assessment practices to allow individuals to demonstrate their various competencies.
- Develop authentic assessments.
- Develop alternative assessments such as portfolios and work samples.
- Develop intrinsically interesting assessments.
- Set fair assessments that don't depend on other competencies as intermediaries.

popularised through a number of mass presses such as *Time* magazine (see Goleman 1995), and has had an impact on educational policy development in the United States, in particular (see Bodine & Crawford 1999). However, virtually since its inception it has generated much controversy among the scientific community and the popular media (Zeidner, Roberts & Matthews 2002) about its definition, measurement and application independent of other measures of ability, personality and motivation. **Emotional intelligence** may be defined as the capacity to process emotional information accurately and efficiently, including the capacity to perceive, assimilate, understand and manage emotion. *Perceiving emotions* involves attending to and recognising feelings; *integrating emotion in thought* involves using personal emotions in thought and communication; *understanding emotions* involves reasoning with feelings; and *managing emotions* involves coordinating with the other elements to produce behaviour that is balanced (Mayer & Cobb 2000). Emotional intelligence also has links to socio-emotional learning, which we deal with in Chapter 13, and character education, which we deal with briefly in Chapter 14. Research on emotional intelligence is in its infancy and, despite the fact that there has been considerable hype about the relationship between emotional intelligence and personal success in life, there is little empirical evidence to support the claims (Mayer & Cobb 2000; Zeidner, Roberts & Matthews 2002). It is also somewhat problematic distinguishing features of emotional intelligence such as altruism, warmth and empathy from other personality characteristics. There is currently an effort to design psychometric instruments that clearly identify emotional intelligence as a separate personality quality that might be correlated with various indices of effective behaviour, including school achievement behaviour. One interesting Australian study (Perry, Ball & Stacey 2004) attempts to design a measure of emotional intelligence for beginning teachers, and reports on some of its characteristics. You might like to read this article and consider the usefulness of designing an instrument for measuring emotional intelligence among teachers.

Emotional education

A number of socio-emotional intervention programs have been developed for schools and labelled generally *social and emotional (SEL) programs*. These deal with the knowledge, skills and competencies that children acquire through social and emotional education and instruction. Emotional education may be provided through a variety of means, including classroom instruction, extra-curricular activities, a supportive school climate, and the involvement of students, teachers and parents in community activities (Zeidner *et al.* 2002). The range of programs, and what particular social or emotional issues they address, are vast and beyond the scope of this book to address. The existence of these programs attests to the importance of educators paying attention to students' social and emotional development and learning in school. We deal with this issue further in Chapter 14.

Not all educators agree with incorporating emotional and social curricula in schools. Their objection is sometimes based on the idea that schools are mainly there for academics and there is not enough time or space to introduce these peripheral concerns. At other times the objection is based on the dubious nature of the emotional learning programs and the lack of theoretical and research support, as well as the unproven link between these programs and improved school behaviour. Zeidner *et al.* (2002) consider the area of emotional intelligence to be very unclear, so you might like to read their account in the article 'Can emotional intelligence be schooled?', listed at the end of the chapter in the recommended reading.

Sternberg's triarchic theory of intelligence

Gardner's view has given us much food for thought about intellectual functioning and has sensitised educators to the importance of stimulating students' cognitive development over a range of skill areas. But is expertise (or lack of it) in one or more of these areas necessarily a reflection of intelligence (or its lack)? For example, one can be tone deaf, physically clumsy and socially inept, yet still function effectively as a human being. What are the essential intellectual capacities that are needed for individuals to manage everyday life—what might be called *successful intelligence*? Sternberg (1985, 1986) addresses this question by considering intelligence as a kind of mental self-management consisting of three basic elements: **componential intelligence** (also referred to as analytic intelligence), **experiential intelligence** (also known as creative intelligence), and **contextual intelligence** (or practical intelligence). Each of the three intelligences refers to different aspects of intelligent behaviour. As these three intelligences govern intelligent behaviour, the theory has been called a **triarchic theory**.

1 *Componential intelligence:* At the heart of Sternberg's theory are metacomponents such as higher-order executive processes (involved in planning, monitoring and decision making) in task performance, performance components (used in the execution of the task), and knowledge-acquisition components (used in gaining new knowledge). These elements comprise componential intelligence, which relates to

Theory and research into practice

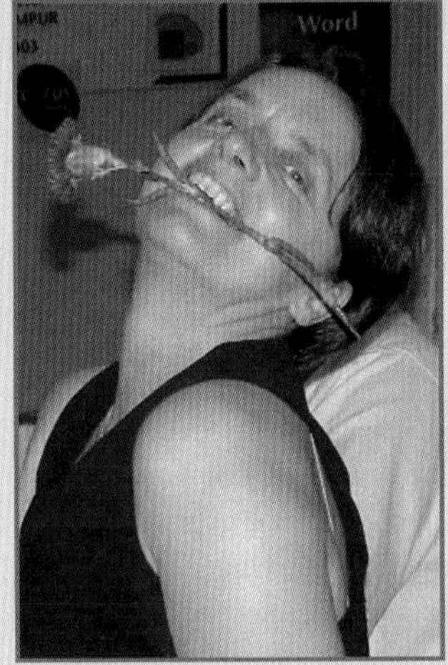

Wilma Vialle — MULTIPLE INTELLIGENCES

BRIEF BIOGRAPHY

I was born and raised in Tasmania and, after my first dream of being a famous ballet dancer was quashed by my ballet teacher, I dedicated myself to my studies. Retaining a theatrical bent throughout high school, I decided to train as an English, speech and drama teacher. After graduation, I taught initially at Penguin High School, which was a brand-new, rural, open-plan school with a small enrolment. From this experience, I moved on to Devonport High School, which was a large city high school (by Tasmanian standards) and completed my Master's degree at weekends and in the school holidays. During this time, I also worked extensively on designing the state syllabuses in speech and drama in line with a shift from norm-based assessment to criterion-based assessments. I also was a member of the state's Gifted and Talented Student committee. I moved to the United States for three years and completed my Ph.D. at the University of South Florida. After a year back in Tasmania, teaching full-time at an all-girls' school in Hobart, consulting for schools on behaviour management, and teaching part-time at the University of Tasmania, I secured a full-time lecturing position at the University of Wollongong. Eleven years have flown by and I now find that I've been here longer than I've been anywhere else.

Apart from my work, I enjoy Scrabble (I've directed four international events, including the World Scrabble Championships in 1999 and 2003) and being a devoted slave to my two cats, Rasputin (a Russian Blue) and Tucson (named after one of my favourite US cities). I'm also an avid reader; my favourite author is Margaret Atwood and I have a particular love of feminist detective fiction. My retirement plans (in the distant future) include writing a best-seller novel and learning to play the saxophone (my favourite musical instrument).

RESEARCH AND THEORETICAL INTERESTS

I believe that research is a critical element of the work I do in training teachers and that the best research is fuelled by passion. For me, that passion is related to ensuring that kids at school are given the best opportunities to think, learn and discover. Therefore, my research interests all fall under the umbrella of gifted education. In particular, I have always been interested in issues of social justice, so much of my work in gifted education is framed in that context. A major strand in my research has been concerned with the identification of, and provision for, gifted students who are culturally diverse. This cultural diversity has included a study of Deaf people who identify themselves as a cultural group rather than a disability group.

As a result of my interest in giftedness and cultural diversity, I was drawn to Howard Gardner's multiple intelligences (MI) theory because it seemed to offer a viable alternative framework for identifying giftedness in culturally diverse students who may not perform well on a traditional IQ test. My Ph.D. study utilised MI theory in a study of African-American preschoolers living in poverty and demonstrated that it was an effective framework for these students. I have continued this line of research over the last decade through collaborative research relationships with a number of Australian schools whose clientele are culturally diverse. The research, in these instances, has looked at how teachers and schools can change the focus of their teaching to appreciate the varied ways in which children think and learn.

An important question to emerge from my Ph.D. study is related to spiritual intelligence, and I have been working on this line of research for the past year. Gardner has now termed this way of thinking as 'existential intelligence' in an effort to remove the religious connotations of the word 'spiritual'. However, I am still using the latter term because it fits better with my research in classrooms. I am particularly interested in how children develop spiritual understanding, and in what contexts their spirituality is expressed. I am collecting data in government and Catholic primary schools through classroom observations and focus group activities with students from Kindergarten, Years 2, 4 and 6.

Another line of research I am pursuing is the investigation of the qualities that gifted students look for in their teachers. I really wanted to know, among other things, whether effective teachers of the gifted needed to be gifted themselves, and whether gifted students appreciated different qualities in teachers compared to their non-gifted peers. This research is now an international study of secondary school students' perceptions of the qualities that are essential in effective teachers with cohorts from Australia, the US, Austria and Indonesia. Cohorts in Germany, Hong Kong, India, Singapore and Canada are currently being included in the study. The key finding to emerge thus far is that gifted students worldwide tend to prefer the personal qualities over the intellectual qualities of their teachers. However, their judgment of the teachers' personal qualities is often inextricably linked with the teachers' intellectual qualities and their pedagogical approaches.

Finally, I am involved in a large longitudinal study with colleagues from the Department of Psychology at the University of Wollongong. The study focuses on the antecedents of emotional well-being and academic success in approximately 1000 adolescents whom we are tracking through to the end of Year 12. The kinds of things we are looking at include personality factors, attitudes to school, attributional styles, perceptions of parenting styles, ability, school grades, and so on. We hope to be able to identify the combination of factors that most accurately predicts the students' emotional and academic outcomes. Part of the study will involve an intervention with underachieving gifted students that will target emotional intelligence.

THEORY AND RESEARCH INTO PRACTICE

My research is driven by a desire to improve educational practices; it is not surprising, therefore, that there is a close connection between my research and teaching practices. As research on multiple intelligences theory is the most comprehensive area of my work, I will focus on its application in school settings.

From my research, teaching and professional development work, I feel confident in stating that Gardner's MI theory has had a significant impact on teaching in Australia. This is because, in teachers' views, it works. Good teachers have always recognised the differences among their students and have sought the means to nurture and value that diversity. MI provides a framework for teachers that helps them to look for the differing strengths in their students and offers a structure to develop their full range of intelligences. Teachers at all levels, from preschools through to university, have embraced the principles of MI and have adapted many of their teaching and learning activities accordingly. Implementation of the theory, though, is more widespread in preschools and primary schools, where teachers are more concerned with the development of the *whole* child. In contrast, high school teachers tend to have responsibility for teaching one or two subjects and limit their teaching approaches to a more narrow spectrum of intelligences. In high schools where there has been an attempt to incorporate MI principles, the usual procedure has been to set aside a period of time outside the regular scheduled subjects.

A number of teachers working in the field of special education have also welcomed MI theory. Historically, special education practices have been dominated by a remedial approach where deficits are assumed and become the driving force for the students' programs. MI theory has allowed teachers to recognise that intellectual strengths can coexist with learning problems. Rather than limiting their curricula to remediation techniques, special educators have been encouraged to seek the strengths in students and to build on those while working on areas of weakness. There is also increasing interest in MI theory in the field of gifted education that is consistent with a shift to more inclusive and broadened notions of giftedness. My research has demonstrated that MI is an effective framework for identifying giftedness in disadvantaged groups.

In a climate of diminishing resources for education and increasing demands on teachers to restructure, MI reminds teachers of the importance of the teacher–student–parent relationship. Additionally, the approach is compatible with the recent educational directives such as the NSW Quality Teaching Framework. These documents emphasise the diversity of the school population and the importance of extending all students. MI is not a universal panacea, however. The best teachers, in my experience, are those who incorporate MI as part of a total, coherent educational philosophy rather than as a simplistic recipe for designing classroom activities. For many teachers, this has meant combining the approach with other theoretical beliefs and approaches.

There have been criticisms of Gardner's theory and, to date, the research base for implementation of the theory has not been extensive. My own research seeks to address this issue. It is important to remember that no theory can be readily translated into educational practice, and Gardner, himself, would concur that educators are in a better position to translate his ideas into practice than he is. Much of my research in MI has been concerned with helping teachers to do that and evaluating the results of those efforts.

Finally, drawing on my research data, I will allow one teacher's words to sum up the impact of MI theory in Australian educational practice: 'It makes me aware of what I'm doing. It makes me a better teacher and my students better learners. It's just a different way of thinking about teaching and learning.'

KEY REFERENCES

Vialle, W. (1994) Profiles of intelligence. *Australian Journal of Early Childhood*, **19**(4), 30–4.

Vialle, W. (1995) Giftedness in culturally diverse groups: The MI perspective. *Australasian Journal of Gifted Education*, **4**(1), 5–11.

Vialle, W. (1997) Multiple intelligences in multiple settings. *Educational Leadership,* **55**(1), 65–9.

ACTIVITIES

1 Wilma Vialle discusses spiritual intelligence, which Gardner has referred to as existential intelligence. How relevant and useful is a concept such as spiritual intelligence? What part should schools play in developing spiritual intelligence? How would one evaluate and assess an individual's level of spiritual intelligence?

2 Do you think a teacher needs to be gifted and talented to teach gifted and talented students?

3 What do you think of the concept of emotional intelligence? We suggest that there is quite a deal of controversy over whether such a notion is useful, and difficulties in defining and measuring it. Do some Internet searching on the topic and write a brief report on your personal views on emotional intelligence supported by evidence obtained through your search.

4 Write a critique of one of the key references in the context of what you have read of multiple intelligences in this chapter.

an individual's capacity to acquire knowledge, think and plan, monitor their own cognitive processes and act in accordance with these.

2 *Experiential intelligence:* Experiential intelligence refers to how an individual uses experience, insight and creativity to solve new problems, and how quickly these novel solutions can be turned into routine processes to solve later related problems. This latter characteristic is labelled *automaticity*.

3 *Contextual intelligence:* Contextual intelligence refers to how individuals adapt to contexts to make the most positive use of them. Adaptations may consist of selecting environments in which one can function optimally, shaping or changing the environment to suit one's purpose better, or moving out of one environment to another one that is more compatible.

THREE INTELLIGENCES

The three intelligences can be summarised as follows:

- *Componential intelligence:* ability to acquire knowledge, think and plan, monitor cognitive processes and determine what is to be done.
- *Experiential intelligence:* ability to formulate new ideas to solve problems.
- *Contextual intelligence:* ability to adapt to contexts to optimise opportunities.

See Table 3.2 for a list of the essentials of a triarchic intelligence perspective.

What elements of Sternberg's triarchic intelligence theory can you see here?

Table 3.2 Essentials of a triarchic intelligence perspective for education

Teachers should:

- model reflective processes during learning activities;
- have students keep a reflective learning diary;
- teach learning skills and metacognitive strategies;
- encourage use of problem-solving strategies;
- provide varied contexts for problem-solving skills learned in relation to one domain to transfer to others;
- teach students to use brainstorming as a tool for generating ideas;
- incorporate cooperative learning activities that involve group investigation;
- use debates to develop creative solutions to problems;
- use role play and sociodramatic play with young children;
- provide opportunities for students to work in a variety of environments and contexts;
- encourage and model adaptable behaviour;
- provide opportunities for students to analyse, create and apply knowledge;
- provide assessment that reflects analytical, creative and application processes;
- provide opportunities for students to adapt to, shape and select educational experiences.

Teachers often make their own *ad hoc* assessments of intelligence. This activity is designed to explore the kinds of student behaviour a teacher uses to estimate a student's intelligence.

Ask a sample of teachers what kinds of behaviour they use to gain an estimate of a student's intelligence. List these behaviours. Ask several other teachers to rank them on a 5-point scale (5 = very important, 1 = unimportant) in terms of how much these factors influence their judgment of a child's intelligence.

Then ask each teacher to think of one pupil they consider as being very bright and one who is slow. Have each teacher go through your list and indicate those behaviours in which the chosen students deviate markedly, positively or negatively, from the norm. Do not let the teachers see their previous ranking of importance.

If the teachers are consistent, behaviour scaled 4 or 5 should be marked by + or –. If this is the case, then the teachers are consistent in their observations. If not, ask the teachers what other kinds of student behaviours they use in their assessments.

QUESTION POINT

How would you define and measure intelligence?

TEACHER'S CASE BOOK

Multiple intelligences and school settings

Cook Primary School, ACT, is a suburban, traditional, single-classroom school with a high degree of community involvement in policy and decision making. There is a wide range of socio-economic backgrounds and about 10 per cent of students are NESB (non-English-speaking-background) students.

Multiple intelligence theory is seen at Cook Primary to be an ideal framework to ensure good teaching and therefore improved outcomes for students. At Cook an agreed aim was to develop each child to reach her or his greatest potential, and this theory made provision to catch those children who might slip through the net.

Each classroom teacher was asked to analyse a 'typical week' from their daily planner and to total the time or the number of occasions each week they had devoted to each of the seven MI areas. This was a private analysis; however, teachers were pleased to share with other staff members their 'learnings' and omissions. They were asked to address any imbalances and report to future weekly staff meetings.

Each classroom and support teacher was asked to rank every child they taught in the seven MI areas. There were three rankings: 'white' meant highly developed; 'pink' was showing some glimmer; and 'red' meant the teacher did not know, or the child showed a deficit in that area. Numerical rankings were avoided to reduce the temptation to average out a score. Teachers noted that there were some children about whom they knew little other than in the linguistic and logical-mathematical areas. Other teachers noted that they knew very little about a lot of children in a particular MI area. They resolved to address this.

When it was believed that there was sufficient understanding, a pilot project was set up: the children were put into homogeneous groups, junior and senior, and seven teachers were elected to be an expert in one of the seven areas. Their task was to come to a real 'understanding' of their area and to locate resources in the school and the wider community that could be used to develop their area of intelligence. Each teacher had to prepare a bank of exercises related to their area and lead the groups through them. The set of experiences was offered seven times to the homogeneous groups who rotated through each teacher one morning a week for seven weeks. Teachers were asked to report at each weekly meeting about their findings. This provided professional development for other teachers who would eventually incorporate that perspective into their daily practice.

After the children had rotated through the seven groups, they were asked to assess themselves. Grade 3 and above were given a paper medallion entitled 'I am 100% intelligent' and they had to construct a pie chart of seven segments to total the sum of their intelligence. They were also asked to write, draw/talk about themselves and their strengths in each area. This was a positive and affirming exercise, not a defect-detecting exercise. Teachers filled out a rating sheet on each child three times a year, the object of which was to ensure that the teacher viewed each child from various frames of mind.

Case study provided by Judy Perry, Principal, Cook Primary School, ACT.

Case study activity

How might a multiple intelligence approach be applied to other schools? Could such a system be applied within one classroom? How would you go about this?

EXTENSION STUDY

Successful intelligence

For Sternberg (1998a, 2003) **successful intelligence** is defined as that set of mental abilities used to achieve one's goals in life, given a sociocultural context, through adaptation to, and selection and shaping of, environments. As we have indicated above, successful intelligence involves three interrelated, but distinct aspects—analytical, creative and practical thinking. Sternberg believes that if these modes of thinking are infused in everyday teaching and learning, the achievement of students will be enhanced. He also believes that this will provide a good basis for successful everyday living. He provides research support for this contention (Sternberg & Grigorenko 1997; Sternberg, Torff & Grigorenko 1998).

Sternberg (1998a) has presented 12 principles to guide teachers in implementing practices to facilitate the development of successful intelligence in children. Many of these principles have links with material we cover in other chapters on information processing, effective teaching, and measurement and evaluation. These principles are presented below and we encourage you to read Sternberg's elaborated discussion on their implementation in 'Principles of teaching for successful intelligence' (*Educational Psychologist*, 1998, **33**, 65–72; see also Sternberg 2003). Sternberg believes that if teaching includes an emphasis on creative and practical thinking, as well as on analytic and memory skills, teachers will have a greater possibility of developing expert learners (Sternberg 2003). After reading the two articles recommended at the end of the chapter, what do you think?

Twelve principles of implementation

1 The goal of instruction is the creation of expertise through a well and flexibly organised, easily retrievable knowledge base. This principle relates to what we say about the importance of prior knowledge in Chapter 4 and elsewhere.

2 Instruction should involve teaching for analytical, creative and practical thinking, as well as for memory learning. *Analytical thinking* includes analysing, judging, evaluating, comparing and contrasting, and critiquing; *creative thinking* includes creating, inventing, discovering, imagining and supposing; *practical thinking* includes implementing, using, applying and seeking relevance; *memory* includes memorising, remembering, recalling, recognising and repeating. We cover many of these aspects of thinking throughout our text. Sternberg believes that too much teaching and learning is memory-oriented to the exclusion of other forms of thinking. He is supported in this belief by many other theorists (such as Bruner) dealt with in our text. He believes that good instruction should include a full range of tasks that call upon each of these modes of thinking.

3 Assessment should also involve analytical, creative and practical, as well as memory, components. In Chapter 11 we deal with a range of authentic and alternative assessments that meet this requirement.

QUESTION POINT

What do you think would be Piaget's attitude to intelligence testing? What do you think would be the attitude of Vygotsky?

ACTION STATION

This activity is designed to highlight the difficulty of defining intelligence and measuring the construct. In a group, discuss the concept of intelligence and decide on a definition of intelligence that reflects group consensus. Design a series of items or activities to measure your conception of intelligence. Administer your test to another group while completing the other group's test. Discuss your findings.

Psychometrics and cognition

As we have seen above, theorists such as Gardner argue that there are several relatively autonomous human intellectual competencies, which he calls *human intelligences*, or frames of the mind. These 'multiple intelligences' are relatively independent of one another, and are fashioned and combined in a multiplicity of adaptive ways by individuals and cultures to produce intelligent behaviour. His theory stems from his belief that it is nonsense to reduce the notion of intelligence to a homogeneous mental construct. Furthermore, Gardner believes that historical and contemporary conceptualisations of intelligence measured by simplistic tests fail to pay sufficient attention to intelligence and problem solving as it is displayed in the real world characterised by social and cultural diversity. In effect, Gardner criticised the psychometric approach to

4 Instruction and assessment should enable students to identify and capitalise on their strengths. In effect, with this principle and principle 5, Sternberg is emphasising the need for adaptive education that takes into account the specific learning needs and styles of students. We deal with this issue at length in Chapters 9 and 10.

5 Instruction and assessment should enable students to identify, correct and, as necessary, compensate for weaknesses.

6 Instruction and assessment should involve utilisation, at various times, of all seven metacomponents of the problem-solving cycle—namely, identification, definition, formulation of strategies, formulation of mental and external representations, allocation of time and resources, monitoring and evaluation. Each of these elements is described in greater length in the article, but in essence they represent strategies for effective problem solving that can be taught to students.

7 Instruction should involve utilisation, at various times, of at least six performance components, including encoding of information, inference, mapping, application, comparing of alternatives and response. We deal with related issues in Chapter 4 when we describe learning strategies and their effectiveness.

8 Instruction should involve utilisation, at various times, of at least three knowledge-acquisition components, including selective encoding, selective comparison and selective combination. In effect, these components are very similar to elements of information processing we describe in Chapter 4.

9 Instruction and assessment should take into account individual differences in preferred mental representations, including verbal, quantitative and figures, as well as modalities for input (visual, auditory) and output (written, oral). Again, the emphasis here is on providing adaptive education to suit the specific learning needs and styles of students.

10 Optimal instruction is in the zones of relative novelty and of automatisation for the individual. This principle is very similar to principles espoused by Piaget, Vygotsky, Bruner and others, stating that there needs to be a moderate level of novelty in learning experiences to challenge and motivate students. We deal with the issue of automatisation in Chapter 4.

11 Instruction should help students to adapt to, shape and select environments. In Chapters 1 and 7, we discuss the importance of students having some control over and choice in their learning. Sternberg's principle relates to this, in that, while it is important for students to be shown how to adapt to the educational environment (for example, knowing the ropes about doing homework and tests, being on time, and so on), it is also important for students to be given opportunities for choice in order for them to shape and select environments that match their needs. This might be as simple as allowing students input into the nature of their assigned work or in selecting electives for study. These processes are important for the development of students' practical intellectual skills.

12 Good instruction and assessment integrate, rather than separate, all of the elements of intelligence.

intelligence definition and measurement. We now direct our attention to this view of intelligence.

The psychometric approach to cognitive development and its measurement has, in fact, inspired the most research and is the most widely used in practical settings. It seeks to define and quantify dimensions of intelligence, primarily through the collection of data on individual differences and through the construction of reliable and valid mental tests (Embretson & Schmidt McCollam 2000; Gardner & Clark 1992; Petrill & Wilkerson 2000). The questions that are a focus of the psychometric approach are (Siegler & Richards 1982):

- How can cognitive development be quantified?
- How can such measurements be used to predict later intellectual performance?
- How can the intelligence of individual children be meaningfully compared?
- What factors make up intelligence, and do these factors change with age?

Mental age

The pychometric approach to intelligence, and the concept of '**mental age**' in particular, stems from the work of Alfred Binet and Theophile Simon in France early in the 20th century, when they were given the task of devising a means of measuring children's ability to succeed at school (Kaufman 2000). One of Binet's basic assumptions, which became the basis of many tests, was that people are thought of as normal if they can do the things people of their age normally do; retarded if performance corresponds with the performance of people who are younger; and accelerated if the performance exceeds that of people in the subject's own age group. This assumption led to the concept of *mental* *age*—that is, that we can take a measure of a person's intellectual development in much the same way that we can assess chronological or physical age. Mental age is based on the number of intelligence test items an individual answers correctly relative to the number of items an average individual at various ages answers correctly. Thus, if a six-year-old child has a mental age of seven, he is performing as well as the average child whose actual chronological age is seven. Later, William Stern, a German psychologist, conceived of the **intelligence quotient** (IQ), which is the ratio of mental age to chronological age multiplied by 100:

$$\text{intelligence quotient} = \frac{\text{mental age}}{\text{chronological age}} \times 100$$

It can be seen that, if a child has an IQ of 100, their performance is average for a child of their age. As the IQ rises above 100, the child is considered increasingly superior to other children at that age and, as it drops below 100, the child is doing relatively less well than their peers. An adjustment was later made to convert the units to standard scores so that IQs across various age groups were comparable in meaning.

IQ scores are often poorly understood by parents, children and teachers alike. A joke goes that one parent, on hearing of his child's IQ score, was absolutely delighted. It was the first time that his child had scored 100 out of 100!

Assumptions underlying the Binet intelligence test

Three general assumptions underlie Binet's approach to assessing intelligence:

1 General intelligence is a trait that develops with age.
2 Performance in the form of skills is assessing an underlying capacity to learn.
3 What has been learned is a measure of what could be learned in the future.

The intention in the Binet–Simon test was to measure general intelligence at work by sampling various types of mental activities such as comprehension, vocabulary knowledge, logical reasoning through analogies, knowledge of opposites, similarities and differences, ability to complete verbal and pictorial compositions, identifying absurdities, drawing designs, and memory for meaningful material and for digits. The test was individually administered and consisted of a series of questions and activities chosen because they were representative of levels of knowledge and abilities at particular ages. The Binet–Simon test became known as the Stanford–Binet after it was revised a number of times at Stanford University. The latest revision was completed in 1986 (Thorndike, Hagen & Sattler 1986). The Binet–Simon test was the forerunner of a whole range of individual and group tests designed to measure intelligence (see, for example, Petrill & Wilkerson 2000). Unfortunately, because of this the notion of intelligence and intelligent behaviour became identified with those individual attributes that appear most obviously related to academic achievement, are readily able to be measured, and are able to distinguish between children's ability to learn effectively in the school setting. In much recent literature, a number of these tests are referred to as ability tests (see, for example, Sternberg 1998b). Have you ever done an intelligence test or an ability test? What did you do it for? What was it like, and how did you go on the test?

Tests similar to those in the various Wechsler intelligence scales. These questions are examples of six verbal subtests.

1 *General information:* These questions relate to a range of information—for example, 'How many hands do you have?' and 'How many cents make up a dollar?'
2 *Comprehension:* These questions test practical information and the ability to evaluate past experience—for example, 'What do you do when you cut your foot?' and 'Why do we keep money in the bank?'
3 *Mathematics:* These questions test arithmetical reasoning—for example, place eight blocks in a row before the subject and ask them to 'count these blocks with your finger' and 'If 14 apples weigh 4 kg, how much do 21 weigh?'
4 *Similarities:* These questions ask in what way certain objects or concepts are similar; measures abstract thinking—for example, 'What is the relation between a piano and a violin?'
5 *Vocabulary:* These questions test word knowledge—for example, 'What is the meaning of knife, table, . . . dilatory?'
6 *Digit span:* These questions test attention and rote memory by presenting a series of digits auditorily which the individual has to repeat either forwards or backwards.

There is also a performance scale that consists of a variety of manipulative tasks that require the individual to complete patterns, arrange pictures, assemble objects and relate numbers to marks.

Wechsler intelligence tests

David Wechsler worked with children and adults afflicted with various forms of mental illness. He was impressed by the fact that many mentally ill people perform very well on standard intelligence tests, which measure academic ability, but are relatively incompetent in everyday problem solving and social interaction. Considering tests such as the Binet test inadequate because they are verbally and academically biased, Wechsler set about constructing a test that took more account of intellectual potential in relation to experience, motivation and personality factors. This was based on the rationale that emotional factors may heighten attention, persistence and adaptability, or they may impair ability to mobilise intellectual resources. While the Wechsler scales were initially intended to assess the intellectual skills of older adolescents and adults, there have been two downward extensions of the original scale (the Wechsler Adult Intelligence Scale: WAIS-III): these are the Wechsler Intelligence Scale for Children (WISC-III, the third edition) and the Wechsler Preschool and Primary Scale of Intelligence (WPPSI-R, the revised edition). The tests are produced by and available from Psychological Corporation (Gardner & Clark 1992).

The Wechsler tests have considerable clinical value. They also show up patterns presented by certain psychotic groups and some patterns of brain damage. These tests have been used in Australia and New Zealand with small changes to a few items.

Group tests of intelligence

Individual intelligence tests such as the Stanford–Binet and the Wechsler are time consuming, expensive, and require expert administration and analysis. Because of this they are most often used in clinical situations. Group tests of intelligence, often called *pen and paper tests*, were developed to make testing speedy and cheap, while retaining accuracy and predictive validity. One of the initial reasons for the development of group tests was to select men for the US Army during the First World War. These army tests were used to select individuals for various levels of army training, or to exclude them altogether if they were considered unsuitable for any training (Aiken 2003). After the appearance of these initial group tests, there was an explosion in the development of paper and pen tests. Among common group tests used in Australia and New Zealand are the ACER Junior A Test, ACER Intermediate Test A and ACER Intermediate D, ACER Advanced Test B40 and ACER Advanced Test N, ACER Test of Reasoning Abilities, the Otis Higher Test and the Slosson Intelligence Test. The ACER Australian tests are based on norms derived from Australian samples. However, the format and style of the tests and the psychometric techniques of item construction and validation are strongly influenced by overseas models, in particular the work of the Educational Testing Service (ETS) in the United States (Keats & Keats 1988).

Paper and pen tests

These group tests of intelligence have been used extensively in the past to stream children into different levels of schooling, with the purpose of providing special opportunities for the very bright, as well as for those with intellectual disabilities.

Group tests used for academic streaming

Since the 1980s, there has been a movement away from using group tests for streaming purposes towards individual assessment for the purpose of integrating children with intellectual disabilities into the mainstream classes (Doherty 1982) (see Chapters 9 and 10). To a certain extent, this movement against mass tests has been the product of lobbying by immigrant and minority communities concerned that the language component in general ability tests may militate against the fair assessment of children of migrant and non-English-speaking-background origins. The Australian Teachers Federation, together with various teachers' groups, has also been influential in the partial demise of group tests. These groups are concerned with the possibility of inherent biases in the tests. In particular, it is thought that children from advantaged socio-economic and racial groups would be better prepared to answer the questions because of their greater access to information (Keats & Keats 1988). Increasingly, psychological tests—such as intelligence and personality tests—are being made available through the Internet, with many paper and pencil tests being adapted to completion on computer (Naglieri *et al.* 2004). This move has introduced a number of new issues that need to be considered so that this type of testing is valid, reliable and ethical. Many of these issues are dealt with in the article 'Psychological testing on the Internet' in the recommended readings section at the end of the chapter (see also Hannan 2005).

QUESTION POINT

Do you think it is more useful to consider intelligence quantitatively or qualitatively? Give reasons for your answer.

The limitations of intelligence tests

What the original Binet–Simon intelligence test (and other tests following in its footsteps) measured was *actual acquired learning*, which has been referred to as

Many talents illustrate intelligence. Why have schools defined intelligence only in terms of academic work?

crystallised intelligence. This crystallised intelligence was then used as an index to what might be expected from individuals in the future. As such, these tests have always correlated very highly with each other and with academic performance at school, and have been reliable guides as to what individuals might achieve at school if—and this is important—schools emphasise as their primary goal an individual's acquisition of knowledge in the form of facts and figures, and the development of particular reasoning skills.

Alternative notions of intelligence

However, as you can probably see, the psychometric notion of what constitutes intelligence is limited to what the test developers define as intelligent behaviour. It excludes other very valuable forms of expressing intelligent behaviour through creativity, social skills and excellence in physical performance. (Refer to the earlier section on multiple intelligences and to Sternberg & Grigorenko 1997.) Furthermore, it takes little account of individuals who have had atypical or different experiences, poorly preparing them to achieve in such tests. Examples of this, of course, are the application of such tests to non-English-speaking-background individuals, individuals from cultural backgrounds other than the one in which the test is developed, individuals who have not received appropriate, or extended, schooling, or individuals who suffer endemic health problems (Sternberg & Grigorenko 1997; Rogoff & Chavajay 1995). Indeed, some people think intelligence testing is a way of excluding many individuals, particularly from disadvantaged groups that are labelled as

EXAMPLES OF GROUP TESTS OF INTELLIGENCE

Group tests of intelligence are often designed to measure individuals' general intelligence as revealed by their performance on verbal and numerical questions. Items are generally arranged in ascending order of difficulty and may include analogies, classifications, synonyms, number and letter series, and questions involving arithmetical and verbal reasoning. These tests are usually timed. Typically these tests say:

> *This is a test to see how well you can think. It contains questions of different kinds. Some examples and practice questions will be given to show you how to answer the questions.*

This is then followed by instructions which might say:

> *Try each question as you come to it but if you find any question too hard, leave it out and come back later if you have time. Do not spend too much time on any one question. Try to get as many right as possible.*

Questions are then asked similar to the following:

1 Foot is to man as claw is to (?)
1 dog 2 horse 3 lion 4 cat 5 bird ( )

2 Book is to library as animal is to (?)
1 beach 2 boat 3 house 4 zoo ( )

3 What is the next number in this series (?)
2, 4, 6, 8, 10 ( )

4 What is the next number in this series (?)
1, 5, 2, 5, 3, 5, 4, 5 ( )

5 What group of letters comes next in this series (?)
AA, BB, CC, DD ( )

6 What group of letters come next in this series (?)
AC, BD, CE, DF ( )

7 Four of the following words are alike—what is the other word?
1 coat 2 shirt 3 singlet 4 sweater 5 socks ( )

8 Four of the following words are alike. What is the other word?
1 laugh 2 giggle 3 chuckle 4 smirk 5 cry ( )

9 Large means:
1 cold 2 big 3 short 4 funny 5 small ( )

intellectually disabled, from participating in mainstream society (Davidson 1984; Goodnow 1988; Smith 1999). This is because essential to the concept of intelligence testing is the purpose of ranking and categorising people. Ranking implies that people have more or less access to advantages according to their rank. **This is an important point. What do you think?**

Table 3.3 summarises the limitations of verbal intelligence tests.

Table 3.3 Limitations of verbal intelligence tests

1. Measure academic (school) learning only.
2. Do not measure creativity, social skills or excellence in physical performance.
3. Biased against those from different backgrounds in relation to school performance (for example, language, experiential background).
4. Measure speed but not necessarily diligence and attention to detail.

Non-verbal intelligence tests

It is a moot point whether there can ever be a genuinely unbiased and **culture-free test** (see, for example, Gipps 1999). In most cases, tests are designed so that there is no obvious bias. For example, in designing pen and paper tests, questions are either rejected by the writers if too many males or too many females get the question right, or selected so that there is a balance between items that are more relevant to males and females. However, despite this, it is not surprising, given the differences in the daily lives of males and females, that there are questions that will be answered correctly more often by one sex or another (Halpern & LaMay 2000). Males might more easily be able to answer questions about directions and geography, while females might be more able to answer questions about health and relationships. To alleviate the potential bias inherent in verbal tests, a number of non-verbal tests have been designed that measure intelligence through activities such as pattern completion (Raven Progressive Matrices), pictures and diagrams (ACER Junior Non-verbal Test; Jenkins Intermediate Non-verbal Test; Peabody Picture Vocabulary Test—PPVT; Tests of General Ability—TOGA) and drawing (Goodenough–Harris Drawing Test) (see Figure 3.2). Test writers have also given their attention to developing culture-fair tests, with the Raven Progressive Matrices and the Culture Fair Intelligence Test as examples of these. Details on these tests, and others, may be found in Aiken (2003). The score obtained by these non-verbal,

Non-verbal tests use pattern completion, pictures, diagrams and free drawings

Pattern completion exercises

Non-verbal tests of intelligence often consist of pattern completion exercises. They may begin with a statement such as:

> This test consists of a series of patterns in which the bottom right square has been left blank. Complete the pattern by drawing in the design you think should be there.

These tests may be timed or untimed. Usually there is a cut-off point where the test is terminated if the individual fails to answer correctly a sequence of pattern completions. Try your hand at the following.

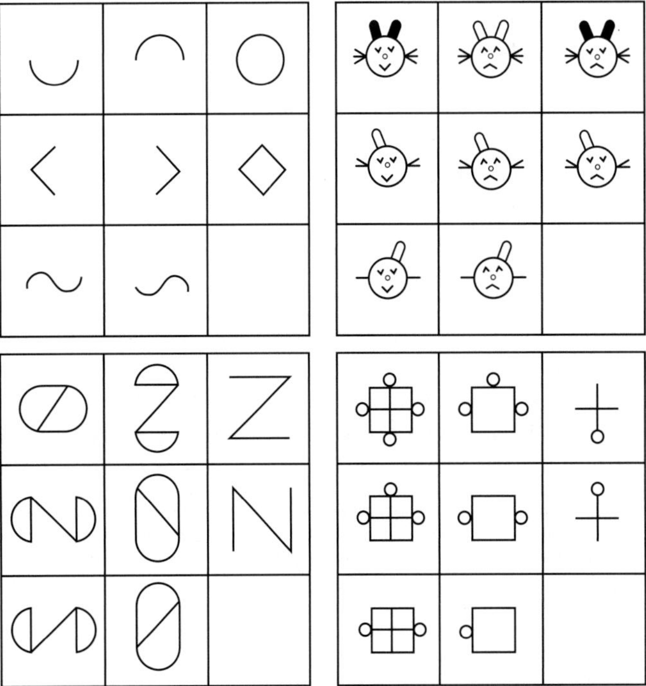

Figure 3.2 *Examples of non-verbal tests*

culture-free and 'unbiased' tests is often referred to as an index of **fluid intelligence**—that is, a measure of capacity rather than a measure of what a person already knows (crystallised intelligence). However, evidence suggests that even non-verbal tests are not independent of culture and that they are also biased in favour of individuals from the dominant culture who designed the tests (Gipps 1999). You can therefore see how complex the issue of intelligence testing is.

Variables influencing measured IQ scores

People can be more or less expert in taking intelligence tests. Taking tests in verbal or figural analogies or mathematical reasoning might involve the following skills (Sternberg 1998b):

- puzzling out what someone else wants (in this case, the test writer);
- command of English;
- reading comprehension;
- allocation of time;
- sustained concentration;
- abstract reasoning;
- quick thinking;
- symbol manipulation;
- suppression of anxiety and other emotions that can interfere with test performance.

Some of the variables that may influence measured IQ scores are presented in Tables 3.4 and 3.5. As you can see, they are quite extensive. An IQ score, therefore, may not so much record an individual's intellectual capacity as the combined effect of all the factors operating on the child at the time of the testing, and the extent to which individuals are consciously acquainted with the rules and procedures of test taking. (This is particularly important if the test is being given to groups not used to taking such tests, such as traditional Aboriginal, Maori, Native American and Islander groups.) In the long term, any marked changes in an individual's physical or emotional environment—such as moving from the country to the city, losing a parent through death or divorce, and periods of ill health—may result in a change in intellectual performance. IQ scores, to be of much use, should be continually updated, and results from a range of tests should be taken into account.

Because of these potential influences, it is dangerous to assume that a child with a high IQ will necessarily perform well, and that a child with a low IQ will perform poorly. IQ scores should be used as a *guide only*. Teachers should consider primarily the individual's ability as demonstrated in the classroom, rather than what the IQ score leads them to expect (see Sternberg & Grigorenko 1997).

Table 3.4 Test variables influencing measured intelligence

1. **The actual test administered**
   Different tests measure different attributes—verbal, motor, perceptual, abstract reasoning, and so on. Intelligence tests seldom tap interpersonal skills, athletic abilities, creativity, and a variety of other desirable human attributes.
2. **Cultural differences**
   There may be cultural and social factors operating that influence a person's performance in IQ tests.
3. **Inappropriate norms**
   Norms for tests quickly become dated and unreliable. Tests are not frequently updated.
4. **Test-taking experience**
   Competence in taking tests comes with training and practice.

Table 3.5 Motivational variables influencing measured intelligence

1. *Parental pressure* (you must do well to get into the selective high school).
2. *Positive or negative school experiences* (this is a 'daggy' school and I'll show them what I think by not bothering about the test).
3. *Peer affiliations* (it's not good to be seen doing too well at school).
4. *Rapport with teachers and testers* (I'll try my hardest for my teacher because I like her).
5. *The educational policy of the school* (some schools emphasise competition, grading, ability grouping, promotion).
6. *Personality of the child* (levels of general anxiety, impulsiveness, persistence, conformity, alertness).
7. *Health* (I've got a headache and it's a hot day, so I won't bother).
8. *Enculturation into a culture that values IQ tests.*

Practical use of intelligence tests

The practical use of intelligence tests and IQ scores depends on their validity, reliability and stability (Hannan 2005). Technical issues of validity and reliability in test construction are considered in Chapter 11. IQ scores, in general, appear valid and predict fairly accurately a child's performance in *academic work*, but they do not predict performance in non-academic areas. The reason these tests predict academic achievement so well is that the underlying abilities and skills utilised in these tests are very similar to those used in academic tasks (Sternberg 1998b). Sternberg argues that while verbal analogies tests and mathematical problem-solving tests are used as predictors of school performance, school performance could just as easily be used to predict the former. This is a very important point, as it is often erroneously believed that there is a causal link between measured intelligence scores and the later achievement scores. The scores are simply correlated, for the reasons outlined above, and it is dangerous to believe that the intelligence measure is prior to, and in some sense, causes or controls academic achievement. It might be that students who have had poor educational experiences lack the skills to perform well in the intelligence tests. The problem is that once students have been categorised as having low intelligence, their educational experiences may be further limited. This then denies them further growth opportunities and makes it impossible for them to improve their intellectual performance on ability tests. We discuss this issue in another context when we consider the self-fulfilling prophecy in Chapter 7.

Intelligence test scores are fairly stable as children grow older—the average change in IQ score between the ages of 12 and 17 is about 7.1 IQ points, with a variation of up to 18 points for some individuals (see Neisser *et al.* 1996). It is important to note here that, while IQ scores remain stable, this does not indicate that the performance of individuals is the same over this time. Individuals gain in knowledge, reasoning skills and vocabulary. However, what does not change is the individual's score relative to others of the same age.

It is also important that IQ scores are reliable for individuals if they are to have any value in terms of the programs that teachers develop for students on the basis of their scores. In fact, IQ scores can be subject to a variation of up to 20 points on successive testings as they can be influenced by many non-intellectual factors at the time of testing (see, for example, Gipps 1999). We should look therefore at individual scores within a broad range of possible scores. Furthermore, it is important to note that the boundaries of what is normal intellectual capacity are very wide, and encompass most children in our schools. Hence, there is little justification for streaming on the basis of intelligence scores (except perhaps for the extremely talented, and the uneducable). The **normal distribution** of IQ scores is represented in Figure 3.3.

QUESTION POINT

Research shows that intelligence tests predict school performance fairly well, and also predict scores on school achievement tests that are designed to measure knowledge of the curriculum. However, academic performance is not explained by intelligence alone. Successful school learning depends on many personal characteristics other than intelligence. List a number of personal characteristics that might affect school learning. What other factors might also influence school learning and achievement?

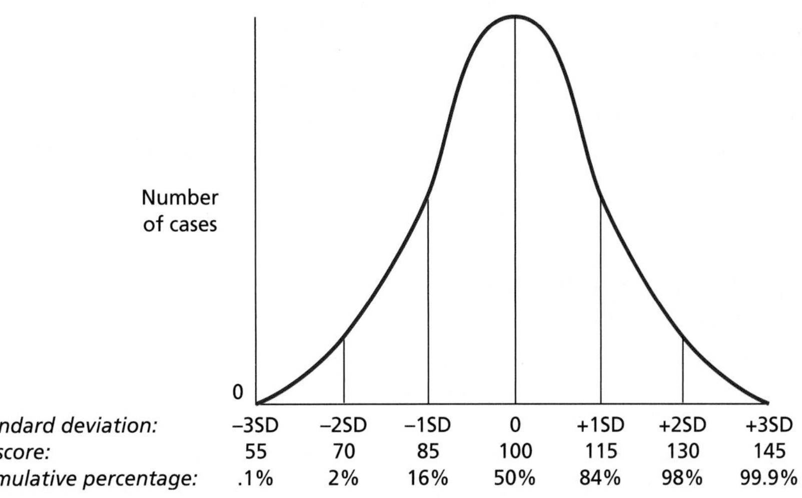

Figure 3.3 *Normal distribution of IQ scores*

Heredity, environment and behavioural genetics

The topic of heredity and environment, and their relative impacts on physical and psychological development, is vast and complex, and beyond the scope of this text (see Papalia & Olds 1989; Turner & Helms 1991). However, we wish to highlight a number of points for you to consider in the context of this chapter and later chapters on individual development.

Development: Heredity versus environment

It is clear that all genetically programmed effects on the development of an individual are potentially modifiable by the environment (even those that are hard to observe and may be biochemical in nature). It is also clear that all environmental effects on the development of physical and psychological characteristics involve genetic structures. The essence of the heredity and environment issue lies in the relative importance of each of these to human development, and how environmental factors (and interpersonal and cultural factors, especially) may facilitate the development of genetic potential, inhibit its development, or compensate for the inadequate inherited potential of an individual. Two extreme positions are possible. On the one hand, it is argued that individual potential is very malleable and, provided the environment is healthy and stimulating, individuals may develop many different physical and psychological skills and talents, irrespective of supposed limitations from their genetic inheritance. This is referred to as the **environmentalist** position. On the other hand, it is argued that individual development reflects genetic potential and that no amount of environmental engineering can alter the course of development of the individual. This is referred to as the **hereditarian** position. If we hold the position that the behaviours of the young—whether physical, emotional, social or intellectual—are the result of maturation alone, then all we need to do to develop their full potential is let the children grow by themselves.

In many areas of human development, the hereditarian position appears to have considerable strength. It is virtually impossible to change environmentally the development of height, eye and hair colour, and the acquisition of various motor skills such as toilet training and walking (although, of course, an impoverished environment or ill health may retard natural growth). However, when we consider the vast array of behaviours that characterise human beings, it becomes problematic to argue that genetic potential alone is the primary cause of development. In accounting for intelligence, personality characteristics, creativity, physical skills, interpersonal skills and so on, we are confronted with the strong probability that the development of such skills is highly influenced by the environment.

Behavioural genetics

Educators generally aspire to the view that both environmental and hereditary potential are important and interacting during the development of individuals (see, for example, Petrill & Wilkerson 2000; Sternberg & Grigorenko 1997). This interrelationship explains the marked variations in the patterns of development of different children. If human development were due to maturation alone, as in some animal species, there would be no such thing as individuality. A specialised area of psychology, **behavioural genetics**, explores the interaction of environment and heredity (see, for example, special issue of the *Australian Journal of Psychology*, 2004, 56). For behavioural geneticists, the question is not whether genes or environments are operating, but how much impact genes and environments have on intelligence and achievement. These researchers have designed complex research using identical and fraternal twins and unrelated people to examine this. There is also research examining DNA sequences to identify

Psychometric view of intelligence and developmental change

Piaget and Vygotsky attempted to explain developmental changes in intellectual functioning. While psychometric theories of intelligence were developed mainly with adolescents and adults in mind, there are ways in which these theories can accommodate developmental change. For example:

- *Changes in the number of dimensions characterising intelligent thought:* As children grow older, the number of psychometric dimensions that can be meaningfully measured increases. In other words, there appears to be an increasing differentiation in mental functioning.
- *Changes in the relevance or weights of dimensions with age:* As children grow older, dimensions measured by

the genes that are associated with cognitive ability and achievement. There is no doubt that genes influence intelligence and other personality characteristics such as emotional stability, with estimates of gene influence averaging around 50 per cent when combined across all available twin and adoption studies (Petrill & Wilkerson 2000; Wortman & Loftus 1992). Nevertheless, there is considerable evidence that environmental influences play a significant role as well. The patterns of relationships between heredity and environment that characterise intelligence also apply to academic achievement but, as we have seen earlier, there is a strong correlation between the measures of intelligence and academic achievement, so these findings are not surprising.

Some theorists have developed models to explain how the interaction between genes and environment might occur in influencing intelligence and achievement. Scarr and McCartney (quoted in Petrill & Wilkerson 2000; see also Bates *et al.* 2004) outline three types of gene–environment interactions. The first of these is *passive interaction*, where both genes and environments derive from the same source, the parents. In this case, if parents are cognitively able—that is, in common language, 'bright' or 'intelligent'—they might provide their children with more books than other children normally receive. Hence, because the parents provide both the genes and the books, the child's environment is indirectly correlated with their genes. In the second model, genes directly influence the type of environment the child experiences. This is called *reactive interaction*. For example, if a child expresses an interest in reading as a result of their genotype (traits passed on through genes), then the parents may alter the environment as a result and read to the child more, thus increasing the child's competence and interest in reading. This is best tested out with adopted children, where the behaviour of non-biological parents is shaped by the genetically influenced behaviour of the child. Finally, a third model posits *active interaction*, when a child's genes make them more likely to seek out certain environments. In this case, it may be that more academically oriented children seek out more academically enriched environments and hence increase their performance as a result. The point behind this analysis is to indicate that genes may be influential in mediating the extent to which children seek out academically related environments or have more or less enriched environments provided for them. However, as with many areas of inquiry, this is still in its infancy.

Streaming and ability grouping

Both the environmentalist perspective and the hereditarian perspective have, at various times, influenced educational practice. When educators believe that the development of children reflects genetic potential, there is an emphasis on testing for potential and streaming children accordingly, so that individual development is maximised (within the constraints set by that genetic potential). Consequently, educational environments based on such a belief stream children into classes of different abilities and talents, and restrict activities to those thought most appropriate for the children within a particular ability grouping. Special schools are established to cater for the very talented and the physically, mentally or socially disabled children. The emphasis in such settings is on the individual development of the child in the context of assessed potential to benefit from particular educational programs.

When educators believe that the environment is particularly powerful in shaping human development, there is an emphasis on having children experience a range of environments to maximise individual development. Educational environments based on this belief have parallel classrooms, and children with assessed developmental or learning difficulties are mainstreamed so that they may benefit from the enriched environment of the regular classroom (see Chapter 9). Progression and exposure to a variety of enrichment or special programs is in terms of presumed ability of individuals to benefit from such programs.

tests become more or less important in discriminating between individuals. For example, infants may be most distinguished by perceptual-motor factors and older children by verbal-symbol manipulation factors.

Other elements of psychometric analysis that indicate developmental change are beyond the scope of this text but may be followed up in Sternberg and Powell (1983).

Are we becoming more intelligent?

An intriguing aspect of the measurement of intelligence by psychometric tests is that, across successive generations, intelligence levels appear to be increasing by about three IQ points per decade, despite the fact that tests are renormed periodically to adjust for increasing test sophistication (Flynn 1996; see also Kanaya, Scullin & Ceci 2003; Neisser *et al.* 1996). This is known as the

Flynn effect, after James Flynn who documented this rise over the years. What is particularly interesting is that the gains appear greatest on tests that were designed to be free of cultural bias, such as the Raven Progressive Matrices. A further interesting aspect of this phenomenon is the lack of relationship between increasing levels of intelligence as measured by intelligence tests and actual school or academic performance, which has not, in general, improved.

What are the explanations for increased measured intelligence levels? Three explanations have been given to account for this effect. The first of these relates to the increased complexity of most people's daily lives through exposure to much more information. The many forms of mass media and technology, extended and more sophisticated schooling, and the array of new and ever changing experiences to which people are exposed may have produced corresponding changes in complexity of mind and in certain psychometric abilities.

A second explanation attributes gains to improvements in nutrition. Most people are aware that children, on average, are growing taller and larger as a result of dietary changes. (This is particularly noticeable in certain Asian countries, such as Japan.) Perhaps brain size is also increasing and affecting intellectual functioning.

Exposure to mass media improved diet

Lastly, some argue that intelligence as such has not risen but, rather, one aspect of thinking is improving, that of abstract problem solving. This improvement in abstract thinking may be the result of greater exposure of individuals to opportunities to use abstract thought in their everyday lives. As abstract thinking is a major component of IQ testing, it is plausible that people will increasingly perform better on this dimension of thinking.

Abstract problem solving

QUESTION POINT

These are interesting hypotheses explaining increases in measured intelligence. What do you think of each?

ACTION STATION

Consider a range of intelligence tests (such as the Stanford–Binet, ACER tests, WPPSI, Goodenough–Harris Draw-a-Person, Kaufman Assessment Battery for Children and Raven Progressive Matrices). Consider the tests critically in the context of the theory of psychometric testing of intelligence. Indicate clearly:

1 the nature of each test;
2 the underlying constructs each test is attempting to measure;
3 the strengths of each test;
4 the weaknesses of each test.

Discuss your conclusions within a group.

Children are growing taller, larger and hungrier today. Is this contributing to their increased intelligence?

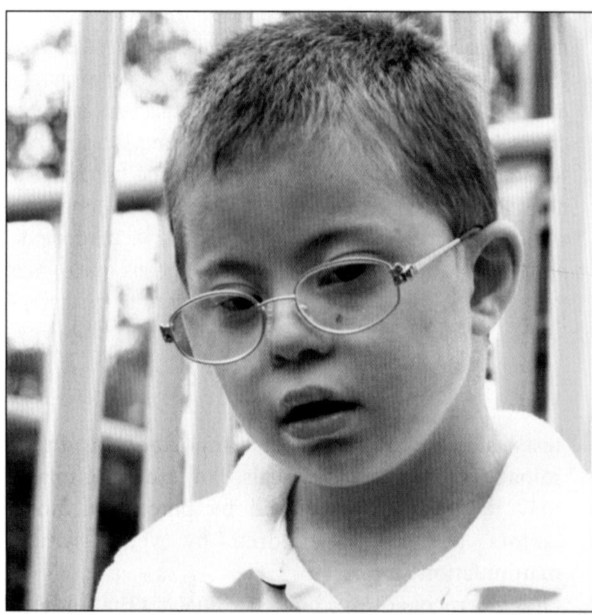

What are the developmental horizons for this modern-day Down syndrome child?

WHAT WOULD YOU DO?

PHYSICAL REARRANGING OF THE LETTERS HELPS HIM LEARN

Billy, in Miss Clifford's class, struggles with his work in all areas. He has a lot of trouble picking up on new ideas that are presented in a written or verbal way. Through observation and working intensively with him, Miss Clifford discovered that the easiest way for him to learn was to use concrete tactile aids and to provide him with many practical experiences.

One example of this was when she was working with him on spelling. They were looking at a particular word family and Billy was having trouble recalling what he was doing. Miss Clifford started working with letter tiles with the individual letters on them and played a variety of games that involved arranging the letters to form different letter patterns. This physical rearranging of the letters really seemed to help Billy clarify his understanding of what they were doing.

Case studies illustrating National Competency Framework for Beginning Teaching, National Project on the Quality of Teaching and Learning, Australian Teaching Council, 1996, p. 9. Commonwealth of Australia copyright, reproduced by permission.

What other modifications could be made to the teaching program to enhance Billy's learning? Consider the teacher's reasons for making modifications to her program set out below.

WHAT WOULD YOU DO? (cont.)

PHYSICAL REARRANGING OF THE LETTERS HELPS HIM LEARN

The content that Miss Clifford plans for Billy is different from the rest of the class because he is a delayed learner and she has to match the content of her teaching program specifically to him to accommodate his learning needs. Making ongoing observations has allowed Miss Clifford to track Billy's development over the year and to continually modify her approach to his needs as they have arisen. This has involved making many new resources, and trying to focus on his interests in order to increase his motivation towards learning.

Case studies illustrating National Competency Framework for Beginning Teaching, National Project on the Quality of Teaching and Learning, Australian Teaching Council, 1996, p. 9. Commonwealth of Australia copyright, reproduced by permission.

What solutions did you come up with? How does this case study illustrate the importance of considering individual differences in learning? How does it relate to the educational principles derived from Gardner's and Sternberg's theories of intelligence?

KEY TERMS

Behavioural genetics (p. 88): the study of the relative contributions of environmental and hereditary factors to differences in human thought and behaviour

Cognition (p. 71): the use of thinking processes such as attention and perception

Componential intelligence (p. 75): in Sternberg's theory, ability to acquire knowledge, think and plan, monitor cognitive processes and determine what is to be done

Contextual intelligence (p. 75): in Sternberg's theory, ability to adapt to contexts to optimise opportunites

Crystallised intelligence (p. 84): acquired learning

Culture-free test (p. 85): a test without cultural basis

Emotional intelligence (p. 75): the capacity to process emotional information accurately and efficiently, including the capacity to perceive, assimilate, understand and manage emotion

Environment (p. 88): genetically programmed development of individuals is influenced by external forces such as climate, food and family background, and by our internal, non-genetic environment such as toxins, bacteria and viruses

Experiential intelligence (p. 75): in Sternberg's theory, ability to formulate new ideas to solve problems

Fluid intelligence (p. 86): the capacity of a person to learn

Flynn effect (p. 90): the systematic rise in IQ scores over time necessitating the renorming of IQ tests periodically

Heredity (p. 88): genetically programmed development of individuals

Intelligence (p. 71): ability to acquire knowledge, think and plan, monitor cognitive processes and to determine what is to be done

Intelligence quotient (p. 82): intelligence test score comparing chronological and mental age

Mental age (p. 81): in intelligence testing, a score based on average abilities for a particular age group

Multiple intelligences (p. 71): in Gardner's theory of intelligence, a person's eight separate abilities—

logical-mathematical, linguistic, musical, spatial, bodily kinaesthetic, interpersonal, intrapersonal, naturalist

Normal distribution (p. 87): measurement scores distributed evenly around the mean

Successful intelligence (p. 80): in Sternberg's theory, that set of mental abilities used to achieve one's goals in life, given a sociocultural context, through adaptation to, and selection and shaping of environments

Triarchic theory of intelligence (p. 75): in Sternberg's theory, the three intellectual capacities (componential, experiential and contextual) that lead to more or less intelligent behaviour

ON-LINE LEARNING

If you go to http://www.pearsoned.com.au/mcinerney, you will have hot links directly to these sites:

■ **Learning network multiple intelligences**

Map your way through this site and consider the presentation of multiple intelligences presented. In particular, critique the manner in which multiple intelligences are measured.

http://www.familyeducation.com/article/0,1120,21-12850,00.html

■ **Intelligence testing**

This is a PowerPoint presentation that may be interesting.

http://spruce.flint.umich.edu/~debrae/ln8/

■ **Emotional intelligence**

This site, a commercial one, deals with emotional intelligence. View the site and develop a critique on its usefulness or otherwise.

http://www.eqhelp.com/selfimp2.htm

■ **Culture-free intelligence tests**

Discuss the article 'The illusion of culture-free intelligence testing' by Michael Cole.

http://communication.ucsd.edu/MCA/Paper/Cole/iq.html

WEB DESTINATIONS

If you go to http://www.pearsoned.com.au/mcinerney, you will have hot links directly to these sites:

■ **Theory into Practice TIP**

Don't forget to use the other search engines we suggested in Chapter 1. Also remember to use some key sites such as Theory into Practice TIP. This site will give you much useful information on the three key topics in this chapter: multiple intelligences, the triarchic theory of intelligence, and the psychometric view of intelligence and intelligence testing.

http://tip.psychology.org/index.html

■ **US Department of Education**

This site contains links to educational research and information sites with a topic index that allows you to search by name the issue of concern, such as classroom management or cooperative learning.

http://www.ed.gov/index.jhtml

■ **The Multiple Intelligences of Howard Gardner**

This site provides further information on multiple intelligences, as well as hot links to other sites.

http://www.igs.net/~cmorris/talk.html

■ **Theories of learning index**

This site, developed by an instructor in the United States, contains useful information on Gardner for you to explore.

http://www.uwsp.edu/education/lwilson/LEARNING/index.htm

■ **Triarchic theory of intelligence**

A site useful for learning more about the triarchic theory of intelligence.

http://tip.psychology.org/stern.html

Many universities have sites that present lecture notes and slide presentations on the topics covered in this text. Probably one of the best search engines for locating information on material covered in this chapter is through www.google.com.

RECOMMENDED READING

Campbell, L., Campbell, B. & Dickinson, D. (1999) *Teaching and Learning Through Multiple Intelligences*, 2nd ed. Boston: Allyn & Bacon.

Gardner, H. (1993) *Multiple Intelligences: The Theory in Practice. A Reader.* New York: Basic Books.

Gardner, M. K. & Clark, E. (1992) The psychometric perspective on intellectual development in childhood and adolescence. In R. J. Sternberg & C. A. Berg (eds) *Intellectual Development.* New York: Cambridge University Press.

Mayer, J. D. & Cobb, C. D. (2000) Educational policy on emotional intelligence: Does it make sense? *Educational Psychology Review*, **12**, 163–83.

Naglieri, J. A., Drasgow, F., Schmit, M., Handler, L., Prifitera, A., Margolis, A. & Velasquez, R. (2004) Psychological testing on the Internet. *American Psychologist*, **59**, 150–62.

Neisser, U. *et al.* (1996) Intelligence: Knowns and unknowns. *American Psychologist*, **51**, 77–101.

Petrill, S. A. & Wilkerson, B. (2000) Intelligence and achievement: A behavioral genetic perspective. *Educational Psychology Review*, **12**, 185–99.

Rogoff, B. & Chavajay, P. (1995) What's become of research on the cultural basis of cognitive development? *American Psychologist*, **50**, 859–77.

Sternberg, R. (1998a) Principles of teaching for successful intelligence. *Educational Psychologist*, **33**, 65–72.

Sternberg, R. (1998b) Teaching triarchically improves school achievement. *Journal of Educational Psychology*, **33**, 374–84.

Sternberg, R. J. (2000) *Handbook of Intelligence.* New York: Cambridge University Press.

Sternberg, R. J. (2003) What is an 'expert student?' *Educational Researcher*, **32**, 5–9.

Sternberg, R. J. & Grigorenko, E. L. (eds) (1997) *Intelligence, Heredity and Environment.* New York: Cambridge University Press.

Zeidner, M., Roberts, R. D. & Matthews, G. (2002) Can emotional intelligence be schooled? A critical review. *Educational Psychologist*, **37**, 215–31.

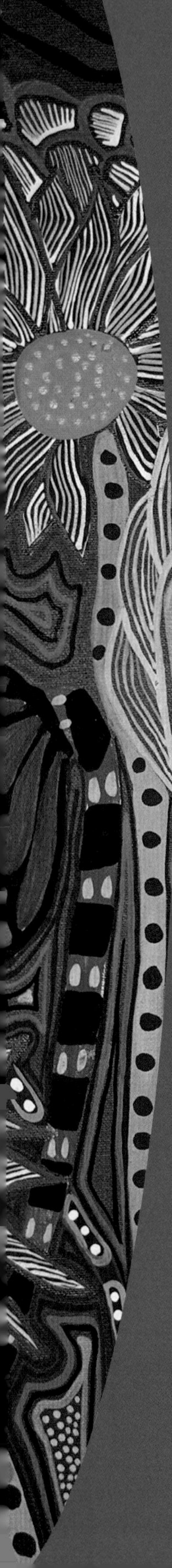

CHAPTER 4

Information processing and effective learning

Overview

In this chapter, we focus on information processing as a model for explaining human learning. We explore in detail the computer as an analogy for the learning process by examining the way in which information is attended to, encoded, processed, stored and retrieved.

Information processing research suggests that there are limits to the amount of information that learners can attend to and process effectively. If we overload our processing system, the working memory is unable to cope with the demands and processing becomes inefficient.

Information processing research demonstrates the need for the learner to be actively engaged in processing the information in order to transfer it from the working memory to the long-term memory. We refer to this as learning for retention.

Information processing research also demonstrates that learned material should be encoded in such a way as to facilitate recall and facilitate transfer to new but related situations.

Throughout this chapter, we discuss learning strategies to enhance the encoding, storing and retrieval of information, and the teacher's role in these processes.

4

Learning objectives

After reading this chapter, you will be able to:

- describe information processing as a form of constructivism;
- identify the components of human information processing;
- identify and describe cognitive strategies to enhance learning;
- explain the importance of prior knowledge to effective learning;
- explain the importance of learning strategies;
- discuss how learning strategies may be taught;
- describe transfer of learning and how it might be facilitated;
- define declarative and procedural knowledge;
- apply principles drawn from information processing to educational settings.

The next Learner-centred Psychological Principle and the Teaching Competence box prepare the scene for our discussion of information processing. At the end of your reading of this chapter, reconsider the relevance of these for teachers intent on facilitating effective learning.

LEARNER-CENTRED PSYCHOLOGICAL PRINCIPLE

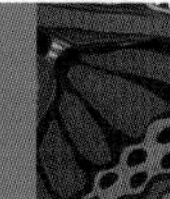

Construction of knowledge. The successful learner can link new information with existing knowledge in meaningful ways.

Knowledge widens and deepens as students continue to build links between new information and experience and their existing knowledge base. The nature of these links can take a variety of forms, such as adding to, modifying or reorganising existing knowledge or skills. How these links are made or develop may vary in different subject areas, and among students with varying talents, interests and abilities. However, unless new knowledge becomes integrated with the learner's prior knowledge and understanding, this new knowledge remains isolated, cannot be used most effectively in new tasks, and does not transfer readily to new situations. Educators can assist learners in acquiring and integrating knowledge by a number of strategies that have been shown to be effective with learners of varying abilities, such as concept mapping and thematic organisation or categorising.

TEACHING COMPETENCE

Box 4.1

The teacher engages the student actively in developing knowledge

Indicators

The teacher:

- makes explicit connections between content and students' prior learning, contexts and interests;
- presents content with confidence;
- encourages students to acquire and organise knowledge and to convey it to others appropriately.

Case studies illustrating National Competency Framework for Beginning Teaching, National Project on the Quality of Teaching and Learning, Australian Teaching Council, 1996, Element 3.8, p. 53. Commonwealth of Australia copyright, reproduced by permission.

Information processing and constructivism

Currently, information processing is probably the leading conceptual framework for the study of cognitive development and learning (Kail & Bisanz 1992; Kantowitz & Roediger 1980; Lohman 1989, 2000; Siegler 1991; Wessells 1982; Winne 1995a). Prior to the 1970s the dominant psychology of learning in Western countries was behaviourism. We discuss behaviourism in detail in Chapter 6. In essence, behaviourism, particularly operant theory, is founded upon a belief that the association between a stimulus and a reinforced response leads to the learning of new behaviour. This model is not at all concerned with what happens within the mind of the learner, considering this irrelevant and, indeed, inaccessible to investigation. **Information processing**, as a theory of learning, attempts to 'look inside' the minds of learners to explore what happens when learning occurs. In its earliest forms, information processing was relatively mechanistic, being based upon a computer analogy, which we describe below. The main focus of attention in these early conceptualisations was an examination of inputs, the mental processing of these inputs and the consequent outputs or outcomes, in terms of learned behaviours. More recent information processing models are also concerned with exploring the active involvement of the learner in these processes: how the learner selects, organises and integrates incoming experience with existing knowledge, and the functioning of meta-mental processes in this (see, for example, Mayer 1996). Because of its emphasis on the cognitive mechanisms by which information is processed—that is, the active role of the learner and the importance of personally meaningful elaborations—information processing is a constructivist approach to learning. Because of its emphasis on the way in which teachers can manipulate and teach cognitive strategies to facilitate student learning, while also de-emphasising the idiosyncratic personal characteristics of the learner, such as interest and motivation, and interpersonal dimensions such as peer interaction, educational practices based on this model are most accurately classified as representing a form of **information processing constructivism** (see Winne 1995a).

The information processing approach has challenged some of the fundamental premises of the Piagetian approach, particularly in regard to the mechanics of processing information by younger and older people (Flavell 1985). We examine the above components in this chapter.

BENEFITS OF INFORMATION PROCESSING AS A WAY OF CONCEPTUALISING LEARNING

- It provides a conceptualisation of learning that enables psychology to move away from behaviourist conceptions of learning by focusing attention on mental representations.
- It provides a unified framework for examining and describing learning.
- It provides stimulus for the study of learning and thinking strategies, the teaching of cognitive strategies, and the assessment of cognitive strategies in the context of performance on academic tasks.
- It provides stimulus for studying learning in the natural environments where learning occurs.

Source: Based on Mayer (1996).

The origins of information processing theories

Information processing theories had their origins in cybernetics, game theory, communication theory and information theory, and reached their fruition with the development of computer hardware and computer programs. The mind is considered a processing system in which knowledge is represented in the form of symbols, and processing is fundamentally symbol manipulation according to a set of rules. A variety of frameworks are used to characterise cognition and cognitive processing. These take the form of:

- a computer language with a precisely defined syntax and set of procedures;
- graphic models (such as flow designs and decision trees) that represent the temporal course of processing information and embody particular assumptions or theories as to the organisation of knowledge in memory;
- higher-order concepts such as plans, scripts, schemata and frames that embody larger units of cognitive organisation.

Researchers use the information processing model of learning and memory to study how individuals learn, remember, and use the verbal and mathematical symbol systems necessary for communication. It is very important for teachers to understand how information is encoded, processed, stored and retrieved, because it is their job to help students acquire the facts, concepts, principles and skills considered important in our culture.

How has information processing theory been derived from computer models?

Basically, information processing psychologists seek to explain the relations between observable stimuli (input) and observable responses (output) by describing activities that intervene between input and output.

According to Kail and Bisanz (1992), a complete model of cognition for a certain task should incorporate the specific mechanisms for all cognitive activities that underlie performance, including perceptual mechanisms for encoding information, processes for manipulating and storing information, processes for selecting and retrieving stored information, and processes that decide between alternative actions. Also important in a complete model would be specification of the ways in which information is organised, sequenced and represented internally. The computer is an appropriate model, therefore, to illustrate the integrated components of the information processing model, through which a parallel is drawn between the functional components of the computer and psychological structures (Beilin 1987; Flavell 1985; Kail & Bisanz 1992; Lohman 1989). Flavell states that in this approach the human mind is conceived of as a complex cognitive system analogous in some ways to a digital computer. Like a computer, the system manipulates or processes information coming in from the environment or already stored within the system. It processes the information in a variety of ways: encoding, recoding or decoding it; comparing or combining it with other information; storing it in memory or retrieving it from memory; bringing it into or out of focal attention or conscious awareness, and so on.

Computer analogy

Computer simulation is also used by some information processing psychologists to model their view of how human information processing occurs. In artificial intelligence research, for example, the effectiveness with which elements of an artificial intelligence program captures elements of human information processing is evaluated. If the match is high, researchers argue that they have captured in a physical model what they theorised was occurring with human mental processing (Kail & Bisanz 1992; Schank & Towle 2000).

Input of information

Each of the components of a computer has a specific function to perform, and if any one component is faulty the computer will be functioning less than optimally. Indeed, if a major fault is present in any component the computer will not be able to function at all. We once had a keyboard for our personal computer that had been given such a hard time over the years that the letter 'e' literally dropped off. You hav* no id*a how oft*n you us* th* l*tt*r wh*n you ar* typing. Imagine what would happen if you also lost the letter 'a'. C*n you im*gin* how difficult th* t*sk of typing would b*com*? Of course, if we lost three or more letters the keyboard and computer would be virtually useless.

Processing information

The ability of a computer to manipulate and process the input depends on the quality of the computer software program and the processing size of the central processing unit (CPU). The CPU for most microcomputers enables users to analyse large data sets with complex statistical methods, to use electronic mail, and to word process with only several dozen basic instructions.

Storing information

In order to retain a permanent record of our work on the computer, we need to save the file. This file may be stored in a variety of forms (for example, hard disk, floppy disk) and the quantity that can be stored depends on the capacity of the disks, and these are getting larger by the day! It is essential to save and store the information in a retrievable form. Lots of us have had disastrous experiences such as a sudden electrical surge, a clumsy foot dislodging the power cord, the wrong cut-and-paste procedure or a system fault, only to see our hard work lost before we could make a permanent copy.

Retrieving information

Finally, having successfully processed the material and stored it, we need to be able to retrieve the file for printing. Some of us have had the unlucky experience of safely storing our work on a hard or floppy disk, only to forget the name of the file under which the material was stored. Of course, the material is useless unless it can be retrieved in some form. We once had the experience of being able to call up a file on screen only to be given the message that no such file existed when we put in a command for that particular file to be printed. On other occasions we were told that the software package couldn't read the file and so we couldn't access the information we had so laboriously stored earlier. No doubt you have had a similar experience!

The components of the human information processing system

Forming perceptions

As you can see, the computer is an integrated system, and if any one component is malfunctioning or inefficient the system will be less effective. Well, you might ask, what has this to do with human thinking and learning? The computer analogy is actually quite a neat model of one view of what happens conceptually when a person learns. In Figure 4.1 on page 98 the computer components are

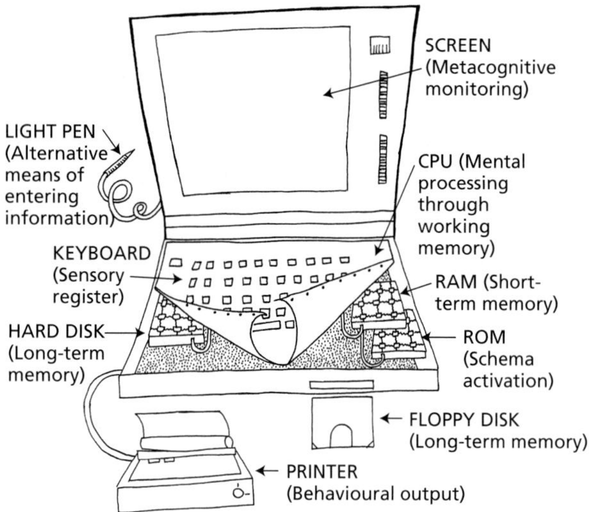

Figure 4.1 *Computer components as cognitive components*

shown paralleled with the components of the information processing model. Each of the components of the human system in the diagram are also integrated, and must function effectively for the system as a whole to be effective.

Sensory receptors, working memory and long-term memory

In Figure 4.2 we present the components of the human information processing system. We describe each of these components briefly and then address the information processing model in more detail. The sensory receptors (such as our eyes, ears, touch, smell and taste) are the senses through which we perceive stimuli. Depending on an individual's orientation, particular stimuli are selected for attention through the sensory register or CPU. The working memory is that part of the person's mind that processes information. Some researchers consider that the working memory consists of three components: the central executive, the visuospatial sketchpad and the phonological loop. According to these researchers, the central executive is responsible for the management of data within the **working memory**, the retrieval of information from the long-term memory, and the computation and storage of information being processed (Abu-Rabia 2003; see also Yeigh 2002; Kalyuga, Ayres, Chandler & Sweller 2003). Only limited chunks of information can be worked on, and the information can only be stored for a brief period. In a sense, the working memory is the 'workpad' or 'jotter' of the mind (Abu-Rabia 2003; Kumar 1971; Taylor 1980), the place where the construction process occurs—that is, the place where incoming information makes contact with prior knowledge and the interaction between the two produces an interpretation of the

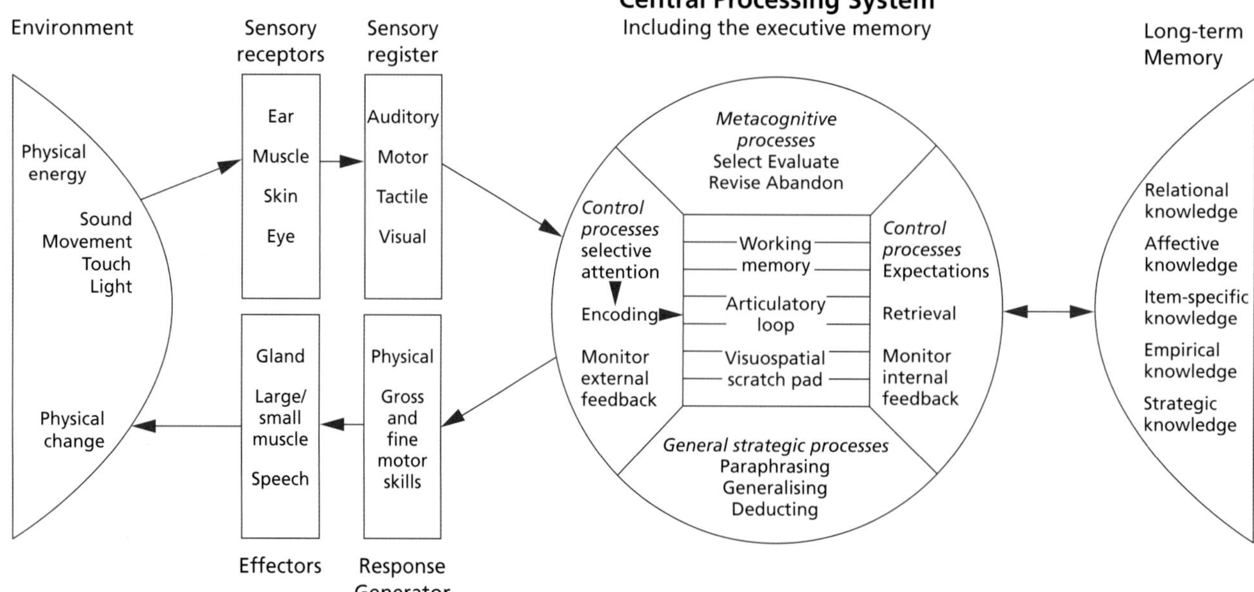

Figure 4.2 *Components of the human information processing system*
Source: Reprinted with permission of Marchant (1985).

incoming information (Royer 1986). As such, the working memory functions very much like the RAM (Random Access Memory) in a computer system. Long-term memory is the repository of stored information (Royer 1986) and is very much like the floppy disk or a hard disk. The long-term memory is a permanent store of information and appears to be unlimited in capacity (unlike computer storage systems). As we have suggested, the long-term memory contains huge amounts of information but the most important thing is that this information is organised into knowledge structures (or schemas) that allow us to work with and categorise new information, thus enhancing the capacity of the working memory (Kalyuga, Ayres, Chandler & Sweller 2003). Unfortunately, most of us use only a limited amount of our capacity, and a lot of what is stored is irretrievable. At the end of processing, action is performed by the person's muscle systems on instruction from the working memory which calls up information from the long-term memory for enacting behaviour (akin to making a computer printout).

ACTION STATION

Consider the elements of the human processing system above. How well do these components help you to understand your own learning processes? Select one new learning activity and draw a chart that illustrates how each of the components listed above is called into action to lead to effective learning, retention and recall. Compare your chart with those designed by other students.

Implications for teachers

When we consider each of these components in turn, we will see how the information processing model is very useful in helping teachers to analyse tasks presented to learners so that they are most easily perceived with attention, actively memorised, effectively stored and retrieved for future action.

Importance of attention to sensory input

For **sensory input** to be effective, the senses must be fully operational. Just as a faulty keyboard will prevent the effective input of information to the computer, so the learner who cannot see or hear properly or who is poorly oriented to attend to appropriate stimuli will not be in a position to input information effectively into the working memory. Where sensory problems are evident, the teacher needs to take remedial action. This action may be as simple as moving students who cannot see or hear properly to the front of the room, or more intrusive interventions—such as the use of hearing aids and eyeglasses—may be needed. With the mainstreaming of special needs students into regular classrooms, it is even more critical for teachers to pay attention to how well individual students can perceive and receive the sensory stimulation of the classroom (refer to Chapter 9). Very often, however, poor attention (or poorly focused attention) is the root cause of faulty input, and so the teacher must always be aware of the need to orient students to attend to appropriate stimuli. The means of doing this are covered in other places in the text.

Obviously we must make salient features of the stimuli prominent so that students can attend to the correct cues. Here we introduce two further terms, *figure* and *ground*. When interpreting information in the environment, we are continually distinguishing main figures from the background in order to perceive patterns accurately. When figure and ground are ambiguous or not easily distinguishable, problems in interpretation occur. Examine Figure 4.3(a). What do you see? Some people instantly see two white profiles; others instantly see a black vase. If you focus on the white, the white is the figure and the black the ground. If you focus on the black, it is the figure. You cannot focus on both figure and ground at once, although you can fluctuate between making the white the figure and then the ground. If you were teaching about the profiles, and your students were perceiving the vase, then there would obviously be a lack of communication of considerable importance. In fact, some people are so fixated on black as ground that they find it inordinately difficult to see the vase.

Now examine Figure 4.3(b). What do you see? In the first part you might see a young lady, in the last an old lady, but the middle figure might be confusing. Some readers might see an old lady, while some see a young one. Again, the reason for this is that the perceptual cues for the middle figure are ambiguous; depending on your frame of reference for interpreting the figure, you will see either an old lady or a young lady. You can't see both at once, and in some cases you might see one but not the other.

Finally, examine Figure 4.3(c). Focus on the black. What do you see? Focus on the white. What do you see? It might help you to draw a line across the top and bottom of the diagram. When we do this, the pattern becomes instantly meaningful as we have been able to distinguish figure and ground effectively. Visual illusions such as these are informative about fundamental perceptual processes involved in learning (Gordon & Earle 1992; Wenderoth 1992). Figure and ground can also be thought of as auditory concepts. There are implications here for reading, mathematics and other subjects. In

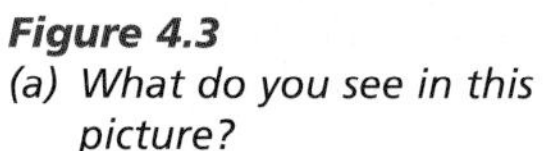

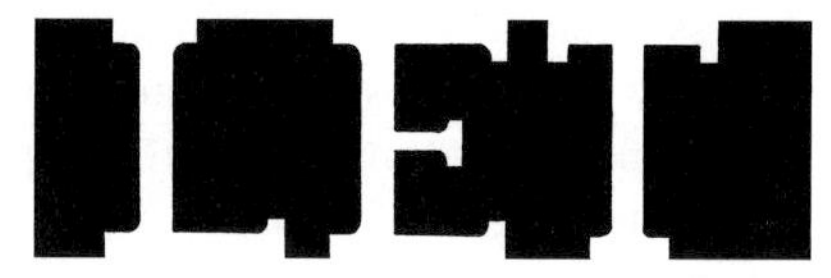

Figure 4.3
(a) What do you see in this picture?
(b) Compare these three drawings. One is ambiguous. Why?
(c) Focus on the black. What do you see? Focus on the white. What do you see?

reading, for example, if students focus on the white page as the figure and the black marks as background, they will have great difficulty in reading. For most students their teacher's lectures and questions are the main figures of their attention, and background noise stays in the background. However, if a student perceives the buzz of fluorescent lights, the hum of the heater or air conditioner, or the shuffling of feet and papers as the figure, and the teacher's voice as background, learning will suffer. This often happens when the teacher is boring or dealing with overly difficult material.

QUESTION POINT

Constructivists believe that cognitive processes such as perception and memory involve interpretation. Do you agree? In what ways are interpretative processes involved in perception and memory?

TEACHER'S CASE BOOK

Butter menthols or fruit tingles?

'I'd like you to think about blood. Try to remember what we've discussed so far. Can anyone tell me what blood is made of? Put your hands up, remember. Don't call out. What is blood made of?' Mrs Fraser waited 10–15 seconds until over half the class had their hands up and then asked Frank, who answered, 'It's got cells . . . and liquid?'

'Yes, Frank, that's right. Cells and liquid. Today I want to talk to you about the cells, specifically one type of cell. Who can tell me the name of the most common type of blood cell? Wait, Jenny, just put your hand up. Think carefully, what is the most common blood cell?' Again Mrs Fraser waited until there were plenty of hands up before selecting a student.

'White cells . . .?' was Gina's response.

'No, Gina, there are white cells, but they're not the most common type. Can someone else tell me what is the most common blood cell?' Mrs Fraser chose another student.

'Yes, Brendan?'

'Red blood cells . . . I think . . . they're called.'

'Thanks, Brendan. Yes, they're red blood cells and they're called erythrocytes. I'll write it on the board for you—they're called erythrocytes, or red blood cells.

'There are millions of erythrocytes in even a small drop of blood, but it's the shape of the red blood cell that I want you to take note of. They're round . . . and they're flat . . . can anyone remember? It's a bit like a butter menthol or you say it's a bit like a doughnut. Not so much a doughnut, more a butter menthol. You know what I mean by a butter menthol? They're round, and they dip in the middle on either side, but it's not like a lifesaver where the hole goes right the way through, it's just got a dip in it. Now that's significant for all sorts of reasons but I'm not going into that. Let's say this diagram here on the blackboard represents a red blood cell . . .'

Jamie's hand was up. When Mrs Fraser asked for his comment, he upset this idea: 'But butter menthols aren't shaped like that, they're square. They come in square packets.'

The realisation hit Mrs Fraser. Someone had changed the shape of her butter menthols! Mrs Fraser's mental image was of a round lolly but the students were seeing a square butter menthol and wondering how on earth that could be like a round, red blood cell. Mrs Fraser stopped and with the class worked out a better analogy, one they were all happy with. The students and Mrs Fraser came to the conclusion that, to use her words, 'Fruit tingles were a better example of red blood cells because they're more the right shape—they're solid but with a concave on both sides.'

Case study activity

How is the importance of perception to learning demonstrated in this case study?

Perception and effective learning

We cannot presume that what we, as teachers, perceive is what students also perceive, or that it is grounded in the same experiences. Merely because someone familiar with the topic (a teacher or expert) may see an organising structure with many interrelationships between the various parts (or other stimuli) does not mean that the novice learner can make sense out of them (Shuell 1990). The case study above illustrates the point very well.

Mismatch between teacher and student perception

Research by Tasker (1981) presents a good example of the mismatch that may exist between teachers' perceptions and students' perceptions, leading to significant learning problems. Of central interest to Tasker is the finding from a number of Australian and New Zealand studies that secondary (and, indeed, university) students tend to retain their intuitive understanding of scientific concepts despite significant exposure to scientific models (Osborne 1980; Osborne & Gilbert 1980). In his explanation of this, Tasker highlights the gap that exists between the teacher's perception of the learning episode and that of the students. Lessons are perceived by students as isolated events, while to the teacher they are parts of a related series of experiences. Tasker comments (1981, p. 34):

> This narrow focus of some pupils is of significance for teachers who draw heavily on previous classroom experiences when setting the scene for a task at hand. Links which a teacher perceives as strong and obvious, especially if they relate to the scientific ideas taught in previous lessons rather than to what pupils did or what happened, may be far from obvious to pupils whose concern is with what they will have to do today. Another aspect of this problem is that as teachers we often refer to these past experiences in terms of our own perceptions and unfortunately . . . these perceptions are often not those of our pupils.

There can also be a mismatch between the perceived purpose of the task for the teacher and for the student, with pupils constructing the purpose of the task to be either following the set instructions or getting the right answer. Students' perceptions of the nature of a task may not include those critical features that teachers assume they are aware of. Furthermore, the knowledge structures that teachers assume students use while investigating scientific concepts, for example, may not be the ones actually used by students, usually because students lack the assumed prerequisite knowledge or are unable to grasp the mental set required. As if this were not enough, at the output level the students' perceptions relating to the significance of the task outcomes achieved may not be those the teacher assumes are perceived!

Intuitive understanding and the learning of science

Reading requires a lot of information processing. Can you suggest the cognitive skills required for effective reading?

How does information get into long-term memory and how is it retrieved?

The next three elements of the model are best looked at in terms of two key questions: How do we get information from the working memory into the long-term memory? And, perhaps more importantly, how do we retrieve the information for use? To answer these questions, we consider: the means by which we gather and represent information mentally—a process we call **encoding**; the means by which material is retained in the memory for later retrieval—**retention**; and the means by which we get information from long-term memory when it is needed—in other words, the **retrieval** system used. In the old days it seemed a lot simpler: all we learned about was how people remembered and why they forgot!

Just as the CPU of a computer processes a large amount of information with a combination of relatively few basic instructions, so information processing psychologists assume that the number of fundamental processes underlying human cognition is relatively small and attempt to identify these. They also seek to discover how higher-order intellectual functions are formed from more elementary cognitive processes. In the following sections we outline some of the elements considered important for effective encoding of new information (see also Siegler 1991).

Why is some information easier to process?

A friend regularly drives an hour to work on a major highway, mostly by farms and fields. On several occasions he feared he had missed his turning because he saw a building or sign that he had never noticed before. This fear subsided when he saw a familiar landmark, or when a check of his watch reassured him that he could not possibly be too far off track. Experiences like this inform us that simple repetition of information or an event may not lead to effective processing. Probably the most important aspect of the material being presented is its **meaningfulness**.

Meaningful material is encoded and stored more efficiently than non-meaningful material. But what do we mean by meaningful material? Remember the computer analogy? All computers require a software program of some kind in order to recognise material being fed into the computer. With the Macintosh, a friendly smiling face greets you when it accepts a disk that can be read by its system program. On the other hand, if you put in a disk that is unfamiliar to the system, you get a frown! In other words, the computer has an existing framework for recognising and incorporating commands. In information processing terms, your **short-term memory** operates as a system that processes new information more readily when it is related to information already held in the long-term memory. So, in effect, meaningful material really means material that can be related to already existing schemes of knowledge in the long-term memory. The new material is recognised in terms of prior knowledge and concepts already understood. When adults are given a mental task to perform in an area in which they have little knowledge, they often process the information less efficiently than children who have knowledge in that area (Flavell 1985).

Consider the following lines of text. Try to memorise each one in turn and note the number of trials taken.

He clasps the crag with crooked hands
Close to the sun in lonely lands
Ringed with the azure world he stands.

Puisque sept pèches de nos yeux
Ferment la barrière des cieux, Reverend Père,
Je vous jure de les abhorren en tout point.

Hap ock laba tch
Crtch mit fer tch laf
Mag tenkt pate bork fizt tchnt.

Which of the three passages was the easiest to learn? As fluent speakers of English, the first passage is most meaningful to us because the language is familiar and it is patterned in a logical way. Indeed, it might become even easier if you are told before memorising the lines that they are taken from a short poem by Tennyson called 'The Eagle'. If we were French-speaking we would probably find the second passage easier to learn, and if we were Martian, the third! For most of us, however, the third passage is very difficult because it is neither familiar nor patterned, and therefore gives us fewest associations to help understand and remember it.

Compare the first quotation above, from 'The Eagle', with the following:

Clasps he hands the crooked crag with
Lands to sun in close the lonely
The stands with world azure he ringed.

Makes it harder, doesn't it? The words are familiar, but they are not patterned in a familiar way. We should not presume that material that is inherently meaningful to us as teachers is meaningful to the students. We conduct a little experiment when lecturing on the topic of meaningfulness, using the following three lines of words.

1 *sleck ploge sengs bligo lange prack reldi roeda celnt talma*
2 *xtspi ltspi axpti lxtvo ntvmq stvaz ztvso tsvnp tlpsa mptst*
3 *hcnul tsaot sknis riahc elbat efink repap orcim etalp noops*

We introduce the task by saying that we have three lists containing 10 five-letter combinations and we want to ascertain how quickly, and by what means, students learn the lists. We uncover the first row and ask students to memorise it from left to right for two minutes and then recall as many words as possible. We then present the second list and ask the students to repeat the procedure. We then present the third list, giving the students the same two minutes, and a recall time. We then ask the students to rate the lists in terms of difficulty.

Why don't you do the task before we tell you how the students rate the lists?

Nine minutes later. In most cases, the students rank the second list as the hardest. (There is no accounting for the small number of students who regularly rank one of the other lists as harder!) In about two-thirds of the cases, the first list is ranked the easiest and the third list that of middle difficulty. (How did you rank them?) We then discuss why the second list is the hardest and the means students use to try to simplify the encoding. Usually students refer to the non-meaningful nature of the material, its length and complexity, the fact that it is hard to chunk syllables without vowels, and so on. Indeed, some of the techniques used to remember the material are quite ingenious—the similarity of the material to car number plates and the use of rhythm and rhyme. When questioned about the first list, many students indicate that they find it relatively easy because they can make the nonsense words into real words; for example, 'sleck' is like slack and 'seng' like song. When asked why they found the third list harder, the usual comment is that the words are less like real words and so techniques such as imagery and rhythm and rhyme don't work so well.

We then turn our attention to the one-third of students who ranked the third list as the easiest and ask why? Of course, it's because the third list consists of *real words* spelt backwards, and, what's more, they are all words relating to the kitchen. So for those who crack the code the list is meaningful, and items on the list are able to be chunked around kitchen items. In fact, some students make up a story containing the words, and then simply retell the story to recall the words later. Has the penny dropped for you?

Two important issues arise from this example. First, it is not always obvious to the learner that material is meaningful. Often we, as teachers, need to indicate to students the patterns that exist in the material that will make it easier for them to relate it to their existing schemes. For example, if we had told the groups before starting that one of the lists contained words spelt backwards, the task would have become immeasurably easier.

Second, at times we can be given a **learning set** that creates the wrong expectations so that we end up making a task harder than it really needs to be. In this case, most students were led to believe that the three lists consisted of nonsense syllables and looked no further for meaningful patterns. Often we generate expectations for students that work will be difficult or that a particular procedure must be used to solve a problem. There are studies showing that when students have been led to believe that a long and rather tedious approach will be needed to solve particular maths problems, they become blind to the simpler solutions that could be applied in particular instances.

In the structure of our lessons, and the sequence of presentation of material, we can set up many wrong expectations and cause learners greater difficulty in encoding the material presented than is necessary. The converse is also true. The demonstration of meaningful patterns to learners in order to facilitate learning is of fundamental importance in the teaching of reading, mathematics and science.

Demonstrates meaningful patterns

One final note on the experiment described above. Even after pointing out the patterns that exist in the third list, some students remain convinced that list one is the easiest. Why? Because they cannot read right to left, and find the task of reverse reading cognitively very difficult. What would you do in cases like this?

The importance of prior knowledge to effective learning

The importance of material being meaningful and relevant to the learner is not new, and indeed is the cornerstone of all cognitive approaches to learning (see Alexander, Kulikowich & Jetton 1994; Ausubel 1963, 1977; Bruner 1961, 1966, 1974; Nuthall 2000). The most powerful and positive learning outcomes occur in those contexts where students' knowledge and interests are well matched to the nature of the learning task (Alexander *et al.* 1994). Research has shown that the development of an integrated and generative knowledge base rests upon a learner's prior knowledge (Dochy, Segers & Buehl 1999; see also Wood *et al.* 2003). The activation of prior knowledge about a topic before presenting new material is therefore very important, as it can act as a springboard for further learning. The assessment of the learner's prior knowledge by the educator (or, indeed, the learner) can offer valuable information regarding the direction instruction should take by identifying inaccuracies and misconceptions that can be detrimental to learning, as we discuss below. Prior knowledge, in a general sense, is 'the knowledge, skills, or ability that students bring to the learning process' (Jonassen & Gabrowski, quoted in Dochy *et al.* 1999). However, Dochy *et al.* (1999) define it more precisely, stating that it is a person's actual knowledge that is available before a certain learning task, is structured in schemata, is declarative and procedural (see our section on Anderson on pp. 126–7), is partly explicit and partly tacit, and is dynamic in nature and stored in the knowledge base. You will see how this definition effectively reflects many of the ideas we have discussed in this and previous chapters. However, the assessment of prior knowledge is difficult, as any one measure might not give a full indication of knowledge conceptions and misconceptions. For example, in class a teacher might use a multiple choice test or an essay to evaluate level of prior knowledge of students before beginning a new topic. The technique used may only give a limited slice of information. Hence, it is always advisable to use multiple forms of assessment in order to be confident. We deal with this issue in considerable detail in our chapter on measurement and evaluation (Chapter 11) where we consider the formative value of assessment (what we are really talking about here), which is used to shape further learning activities, and summative assessment, which is used to evaluate what has been learned.

Activating prior knowledge

Research indicates that the activation of prior knowledge assists in the learning of new knowledge. This can be student induced or teacher facilitated. Earlier in the text we discussed several strategies, such as advance organisers, for activating prior knowledge and we consider others throughout (such as explicit teaching). Furthermore, when students are asked to participate in learning tasks for which they are ill prepared and which they perceive as irrelevant to their personal goals or aspirations, effective learning is made very difficult. How many times have you been asked to learn material that you perceive as irrelevant or too difficult given your present level of understanding or expertise?

It is not certain how prior knowledge facilitates the learning of new material (see Dochy *et al.*, 1999; Nuthall 2000). Certainly, as we have indicated earlier in this chapter, the structure and accessibility of knowledge stored in the long-term memory influences how effectively it can be used for learning new material. We have already discussed some methods that might assist in knowledge being well structured and accessible to the working memory. Prior knowledge also interacts with a number of other key components of the learning episode, such as the structure and content of the information to be learned, the learning materials used, the learning strategies used, the activities involved, level of motivation and interest, and so on. Research is currently being conducted in these areas to examine the relationship of prior learning to these factors in order to derive further principles that might guide educators in establishing effective learning environments.

Can the activation of prior knowledge cause learning problems?

At times we wish to teach students new material (such as some scientific laws or processes) that conflicts with their pre-established intuitive understandings or stereotypes. In this case, the new material may be non-meaningful in terms of the learners' pre-existing schema. The informal knowledge that students bring to the learning situation can influence effective learning and can be quite resistant to change (see, for example, Chinn & Malholtra 2002; Wood *et al.* 2003). There are two points we wish to make here. First, teachers should make a conscious effort to find out what students' informal knowledge is before teaching new concepts. Second, where this informal knowledge is likely to conflict with teaching, attempts need to be made to have the students alter their misconceptions so that an adequate knowledge base is developed. Doing this is not easy, and involves helping the learners to see the limitations in their understandings and convincing them of the merits of the alternative (see Chinn & Malhotra 2002; Chinn & Brewer 1993; Prawat 1989). Chinn and Maholtra (2002) comment that while children are often viewed as highly resistant to changing beliefs in response to evidence or even unable to distinguish between beliefs and evidence, they are actually fair minded in their observations of data about empirical regularities in science and are willing and able to change their beliefs in response to their observations. However, when they are resistant to changing their ideas, it is usually because they have difficulties making the correct observations. Chinn and Maholtra suggest, therefore, that instructional efforts directed to promoting conceptual change about empirical regularities in response to data should focus on sharpening the students' observation skills.

ACTION STATION

The activation of prior knowledge is an important component of the effective learning of new information. Select an area in which you would like to learn some new knowledge or skill. What prior knowledge do you think is important? In what form is the prior knowledge? What strategies would you use to activate this prior knowledge? Construct a flow chart illustrating the sequence and components of the relevant prior knowledge, and the strategies you would use to activate this prior knowledge in order to facilitate your learning of the new information or skill. Construct a second flow chart of a learning episode containing the same elements in a lesson of your choice.

Students' informal knowledge and learning

At times the students' knowledge base is not inaccurate but nevertheless interferes with the retention of new information because it is incongruent. Lipson (1983) reports a study in which Grade 4, Grade 5 and Grade 6 students who were enrolled in either Catholic or Hebrew parochial schools were given three passages to read and recall. One passage was culturally neutral (dealing with Japan), the second was about a bar mitzvah and the third about first communion. As was expected, there was a greater exact recall and greater recall of correct inferences concerning material that was congruent with the children's religious background. In contrast to this, there were more distortions in recall of the incongruent passages. In particular, the students tended to distort the information presented in the incongruent text to make it consistent with their own knowledge of religious ceremonies. To handle this kind of situation, teachers need to help students to identify information that is inconsistent with their prior beliefs and then to teach them to process such information so that they remember the accurate text rather than a version distorted by incompatible prior knowledge (Pressley *et al.* 1989).

Incongruent knowledge

The following Learner-centred Psychological Principle emphasises the importance of thinking and reasoning strategies to effective learning. We deal with a number of these throughout this chapter.

LEARNER-CENTRED PSYCHOLOGICAL PRINCIPLE

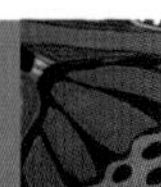

Strategic thinking. The successful learner can create and use a repertoire of thinking and reasoning strategies to achieve complex learning goals.

Successful learners use strategic thinking in their approach to learning, reasoning, problem solving and concept learning. They understand and can use a variety of strategies to help them reach learning and performance goals, and to apply their knowledge in novel situations. They also continue to expand their repertoire of strategies by reflecting on the methods they use to see which work well for them, by receiving guided instruction and feedback, and by observing or interacting with appropriate models. Learning outcomes can be enhanced if educators assist learners in developing, applying and assessing their strategic learning skills.

Strategies to help learning

Chunking

Even potentially meaningful material is at times difficult to encode because of its complexity, length or mode of presentation. A simple demonstration will illustrate this. Have a look at the following letters:

Chunking long and complex material into more meaningful units

EVLEWTSIEMITEHT

Such a combination of letters is particularly hard to encode. However, the following arrangement is easier:

THETIMEISTWELVE

particularly when it is broken into these units:

THE TIME IS TWELVE

In this example, it is easy to encode the material and remember it because there are fewer units to learn and they are now more meaningful. One of us remembers teaching a Year 5 class about long division. I began with one method, and was very happy that everyone in the class appeared to have 'cottoned on'. I thought, 'Great, now I'll explain another approach.' I was pleased when it seemed as if a fair number of the class had also followed this second approach. I then launched into the third, different explanation. I was devastated at the end when I found that no one was able to follow what I was talking about, and had also forgotten or confused the first two approaches. Many teachers attempt to teach students too much at one time. We can only absorb so much. After a certain amount of information has been presented, it may be a waste of time presenting more because people just cannot absorb more. The time would be better used consolidating the information already encoded. Learning tasks that are too long or too complex for the learner not only fail to teach the extra facts presented, but also interfere with earlier material that could easily have been learned.

Story-grammar training

Two strategies that have been found useful for facilitating encoding of textual material are story-grammar training and question-generation strategies. Story-grammar training consists of teaching students to ask themselves five questions as they read stories:

1 Who is the main character?
2 When and where did the story take place?
3 What did the main characters do?
4 How did the story end?
5 How did the main character feel?

In posing and answering these questions while reading, children are more actively involved in mentally processing the elements of the story so that encoding, retention and recall are facilitated (Pressley *et al.* 1989).

Self-questioning

With question generation, students are taught how to generate integrative questions concerning text that capture large units of meaning. This facilitates encoding, because readers become more active and, in particular, monitor

Question generation

their own reading, so that problems in their comprehension become more apparent. For example, elaborative interrogation is a 'why' questioning strategy that promotes memory by encouraging learners to connect new to-be-learned information to existing knowledge (Pressley *et al.* 1987; Wood *et al.* 2003). This technique has been found useful for the acquisition of factual information and other learning across a wide range of instructional contexts.

As part of the training in one study (Davey & McBride 1986), students were instructed specifically about the need for integrative questions, were taught to evaluate whether their questions covered important information, whether their questions were integrative and whether they could answer the questions. Students were given practice in developing these types of questions and received feedback from the teacher.

One way of using questions is to turn text headings into questions and then to read the text material with answering the question in mind. Reading to answer a question was a prominent feature in the SQ3R (Survey, Question, Read, Recite, Review) approach (Robinson 1970) and the **PQ4R** (Preview, Question, Read, Reflect, Recite, Review) variation (Thomas & Robinson 1972). With the PQ4R, the reader *previews* the material to be read, generates questions from the headings, *reads* the material for the main ideas and supporting details, *reflects* on connections between the new information and what was previously known, *recites* the answers to the questions, and *reviews* what is known and still left unanswered. Try it for yourself while you are reading this chapter.

SQ3R and PQ4R

Summarisation

A final strategy that could be mentioned here is the use of summarisation. The active generation of summaries has been found to facilitate the comprehension and retention of textual learned material (Mayer *et al.* 1996; Wittrock & Alesandrini 1990). There are many techniques suggested for using summaries (Pressley *et al.* 1989; Snowman 1986) that are too extensive to develop in this text. No doubt you are familiar with some of them (for example, marginal notes, underlining topic sentences, highlighting key ideas). Many of these techniques are quite structured and methodical. For students to use them successfully, they need to be actively taught the strategies. However, the usefulness of summarisation training for children younger than about 10 years of age is not conclusive. One technique (Berkowitz 1986) is elaborated upon.

Berkowitz taught Grade 6 students to construct maps of passages. The title of the passage was written in the centre of a plain sheet of paper, and students were instructed to survey the passage for four to six main ideas, which were to be written in their own words and arranged in a circle around the title. Students were then asked to find two to four important details in the passage that were associated with each of the main ideas. These were summarised briefly and written under the main idea. To make the presentation more visually graphic, boxes were drawn around each main idea and its supporting details. Students were then taught to use this graphic summary to self-test until they could recite the main ideas in order together with their supporting details. Overall recall of the passages was improved by the use of this graphic summarising technique.

Learning non-meaningful material

Not all material to be learned is inherently meaningful—for example, lists of dates, telephone numbers, the names of a class, algebraic formulae, spelling words, periodic tables (perhaps even multiplication tables?). To the degree that the material to be learned is not meaningful, it puts an extra burden on the processing unit to encode the material. There are a number of strategies—such as chunking, mental imagery and mnemonic imagery—that will improve the encoding, and retention, of this type of material, as we have indicated earlier. These same techniques are also useful for remembering meaningful material that is long and complex. Research also shows that training in memory skills may assist in incidental word learning, which consists of deriving the meaning of an unknown word from a text and storing this in memory. This incidental learning partly explains the spontaneous growth in children's reading vocabulary (Swanborn & de Glopper 1999).

Chunking

Our short-term memory is limited in the number of units of information we can process at one time. This is usually estimated to be between three and seven, depending on age, although some people appear to be able to process more. The units are *chunks*, rather than a number of physical units. A letter, a number, a word, or a familiar phrase can function as a single chunk because each is a single unit of meaning. Thus it is as easy to remember a set of three unrelated words with nine letters (for example, hit, red, toe) as it is to remember three unrelated letters (for example, q, f, r) (Miller 1956; Siegler 1991). **Chunking** is a mental strategy by which we break long and complex series into smaller chunks to facilitate learning and recall. Have a look at the following words:

TSNUKEBIERHCSZRUK
KURZSCHREIBEKUNST

You would probably find the second word easier to encode, as you can chunk it into *kurz schrei bekunst* (especially if you have any knowledge of German). Long spelling words, long stanzas of poetry and telephone numbers can all be chunked and, as chunks, become easier to encode.

In these instances, teachers need to present the material in a way that facilitates the chunking.

Using mental imagery

There are two different types of image that can be constructed to assist with retention and recall of verbal material. The first, called *representational images*, exactly represents the content of the prose to be learned. For example, 'The dog barked when the cat ran near him' can be directly represented, as we can form an image of each element in the prose that will facilitate recall. There is consistent research evidence that active construction of representational images—that is, creating visual images of what one is reading or hearing—facilitates children's learning of text (at least from the age when children begin to process concrete stories).

Representational images represent content to be learned

Mnemonic images

Sometimes it is more difficult to imagine elements of prose, and in these cases proxies may be used to stand for elements to be remembered. These proxies are called mnemonic images (Pressley *et al.* 1989). Mnemonic imagery is useful when we are trying to learn information about totally unfamiliar concepts, such as the accomplishment of unfamiliar people or information about unknown countries. It seems especially useful when there are many previously unknown concepts that must be acquired in a relatively short time. There are simple mnemonic devices—such as rhymes, acrostics and acronyms—and more complicated forms such as the keyword method.

We use **mnemonics** when we deliberately impose some sort of order on the material we want to learn. For example, if we want to remember the definitions of *sine*, *cosine* and *tangent*—and, especially, which is opposite or adjacent to the hypotenuse—we may use the mnemonic SOHCAHTOA:

Sine Opposite Hypotenuse
Cosine Adjacent Hypotenuse
Tangent Opposite Adjacent Angle

We are all familiar with rhymes such as 'Thirty days has September, April, June and November' and 'All good boys deserve fruit' which help us to remember lists of items. Again, the principle is to reduce the amount that has to be encoded into a form that is easily retrievable later. (This is a crucial point.) Red, orange, yellow, green, blue, indigo and violet becomes reduced to three units ROY G. BIV. In this latter case, an acrostic is used to help encode the information. An **acrostic** is a sentence made up of words that begin with the first letter of each item to be learned. Even simple **acronyms**, where only the first letters are used, are useful as shorthand for remembering long names. Be careful, however—we know one librarian who can rattle off thousands of library acronyms, but when asked what they stand for hasn't got the foggiest! Acronyms tend to acquire a life of their own (and breed as well).

With the **keyword method**, a word is keyed to the prose so that it triggers off a rich set of associations that recall the prose (Carney, Levin & Morrison 1988; J. R. Levin 1985). Levin, Shriberg and Berry (1983) report on a study in which some students were given the keyword 'frost' to stand for a story about a fictitious town of Fostoria which was noted for abundant natural resources, advances in technology, wealth and growing population. The students were then shown a picture in which the attributes of the town were covered with frost. At a later time, when presented with the name Fostoria, students were able to recall the frost and what it covered. Children who were not exposed to the keyword mnemonic recalled fewer of the town's attributes. In this case, it was important to select a mnemonic that related to the name of the town.

Keyword mnemonics

Other strategies that students find useful are *peg-type mnemonics*, where particular concepts to be remembered are located in some space (such as a living room) and identified with common objects (for example, in the living room). This is called a **method of loci** peg-type mnemonic and has been used for centuries. Greek and Roman orators advised their students to remember the points in a speech they were to make by forming images of the points and locating them at successive places along a familiar path. When they were to give the speech, they could retrieve the points they wished to make by mentally walking down the path and 'looking' to see images of the different points (Kantowitz & Roediger 1980). Imagine you have a 15-item shopping list (which you are not in a position to write down) consisting of the following: milk, eggs, flour, peas, carrots, bread, washing powder, detergent, meat, toilet paper, tissues, fly spray, cheese, ice cream and a can of sardines. To employ the loci method as a mnemonic, you would locate these items in various parts of your house and then mentally take a walk through your house

Peg-type mnemonics

Theory and research into practice

Graeme Sydney Halford — CONCEPTUAL COMPLEXITY

BRIEF BIOGRAPHY

I obtained my Ph.D. from the University of Newcastle in 1969. I have held the positions of lecturer, then senior lecturer at the University of Newcastle, associate professor at Queens University, Canada, and a senior lecturer, then reader at the University of Queensland. I was awarded a personal chair at the University of Queensland in 1989. I have published approximately 100 technical works, including *The Development of Thought* (Erlbaum 1982), and *Children's Understanding: The Development of Mental Models* (Erlbaum 1993), *Mathematics Education: Models and Processes* (with L. English, Erlbaum 1995) and *Developing Cognitive Competence: New Approaches to Process Modeling* (edited with Tony Simon, Erlbaum 1995), as well as articles in *Cognitive Psychology*, *Child Development* and *Behavioral and Brain Sciences*. I am a Fellow of the American Psychological Society, the Australian Psychological Society and the Academy of the Social Sciences in Australia. I have been a member of the National Committee for Psychology of the Australian Academy of Science, and a consulting editor of the *Psychological Review*. In 2003 I became a professor emeritus in Psychology at the University of Queensland and an adjunct professor at Griffith University. My main recreations are yachting and kayaking, but I also enjoy theatre and ballet and am interested in the graphic arts.

RESEARCH AND THEORETICAL INTERESTS

My research interests are in cognition and cognitive development, with a cognitive science approach. The rationale is that to make genuine progress with cognitive development, it is first necessary to understand some basic processes in cognition, including processing capacity and complexity, learning and induction, and reasoning mechanisms. My main contributions have been under the following headings.

Conceptual complexity

With my colleagues, Associate Professor William H. Wilson (University of New South Wales) and Dr Steven Phillips (National Institute of Advanced Industrial Science and Technology, Japan) I have developed a conceptual complexity metric based on dimensionality, which corresponds to the number of interacting variables that need to be processed in parallel. Developmental norms for levels of relational complexity have been determined (with Dr Glenda Andrews, Griffith University). A paradigm has also been developed for assessing the number of variables that adults can process (with Dr Rosemary Baker, Dr Julie McCredden and Professor John Bain). I am currently reviewing the cognitive development literature to assess the extent to which attainments of younger children can be explained by lower structural complexity. This acknowledges the validity and importance of early cognitive attainments, but also takes account of development, and provides for a more orderly interpretation of the cognitive development literature. It also leads to prediction of previously unrecognised capabilities. For example, the theory predicts that two- to three-year-olds can discriminate weights or distances, but not both, on the balance scale, subsequently confirmed empirically. The relational complexity metric is receiving increasingly wide application, including in brain imaging studies. The research team has developed techniques for precise manipulation of cognitive complexity with other factors controlled.

Three levels of cognition

This is possibly the most ambitious project by the research team, and it aims to define the fundamental properties of symbolic cognition, and to distinguish it from subsymbolic and associative processing (with Dr Phillips and Associate Professor Wilson). The formulation defines three levels of cognition: *non-structured* (including elemental associative), *functionally structured* (with computed internal representation but no system for operating on symbols) and *symbolically structured* (relational). The three levels are distinguished formally by empirical criteria, and by the types of neural nets required to implement them. The formulation therefore goes some way to define the phenomena to which multi-layered (sometimes called eliminative) connectionist models are applicable, by contrast with symbolic connectionist models. A major review has shown that the formulation provides a more orderly interpretation of the literature, and generated many predictions (for example, that conditional discrimination should be possible at six months, as distinct from approximately five years, as reported in the literature so far). The representation of relations in neural nets potentially explains the basis of capacity limitations, and shows why they affect higher cognitive processes more. Complexity of cognitive processes at the symbolically structured level can be determined by the relational complexity metric. When combined with the non-structured and functionally structured levels, this yields seven levels distinguished by representational rank, defined as the number of identifiable components bound into a structured representation, such that the components satisfy the constraints imposed by the structure. This provides a general cognitive complexity metric.

Analogical reasoning

It was also realised that because analogy is at the core of human reasoning, an analogical reasoning model with realistic processing capacity limitations would have the potential to explain many of the difficulties children have with cognitive tasks. This resulted in the STAR (Structured Tensor Analogical Reasoning) model (with Associate Professor Wilson and others). This is a symbolic connectionist model, and has been expanded to integrate analogy and categorisation (with Dr Brett Gray and others).

Acquisition of structured knowledge

We have developed the relational schema induction paradigm for acquisition of structured knowledge without specific training in the structure (with Professor John Bain, Dr Murray Maybery and Dr Glenda Andrews). This work was recently extended in collaboration with Janie Busby.

A self-modifying production system model of strategy development in transitive inference has been developed. It was used to simulate acquisition of cognitive skills and strategies.

THEORY AND RESEARCH INTO PRACTICE

The research has been applied to mathematics education (for example, English & Halford 1995), to Aboriginal cognition, to human understanding of global change, and to analysis of complexity in industrial situations, including air traffic control.

The largest area of application has been to analysis of cognitive complexity. Complexity has become a major factor in both work and personal activities in the 21st century. Human operators and decision makers often experience overload in the amount of information that needs to be attended to at one time. The approach developed by the research team has been applied to many areas of cognitive psychology, cognitive development and to education, as well as to industrial contexts including air traffic control and to the work environment in a major organisation. General principles are being formulated to enable complexity analyses to be performed objectively in a manner that is consistent across all contexts. The core of our analysis is that the limiting factor is the complexity of relations that humans can process at any one time. Humans are generally limited to recognising relations between four variables in parallel. The processing load, which corresponds subjectively to effort experienced, increases with the number of variables that have to be related. It is more when processing four variables in parallel than when processing three, and so on. The limitation is normally overcome by either segmentation or chunking. Segmentation means breaking a task down into components each of which is small enough not to exceed processing capacity, then processing each component in turn. Conceptual chunking entails 'collapsing' variables into a single dimension. An example occurs when we simplify the relation between speed, time and distance by calculating distance over time, yielding a single variable, speed. Experts in a task develop highly effective strategies for processing large amounts of information without overloading their capacity. However, difficulties can arise in unusual circumstances for which strategies are not fully efficient. Such strategies are often developed by trial and error, without real insights into the causes of the problem. Not only is this process likely to be slow, but it may have more serious disadvantages, particularly in safety-critical industries, or those where error is costly.

KEY REFERENCES

Andrews, G. & Halford, G. S. (2002) A cognitive complexity metric applied to cognitive development. *Cognitive Psychology*, **45**, 153–219.

English, L. D. & Halford, G. S. (1995) *Mathematics Education: Models and Processes*. Hillsdale, NJ: Erlbaum.

Halford, G. S., Baker R., McCredden , J. E. and Bain, J. D. (in press, 2005) How many variables can humans process?, *Psychological Science*.

ACTIVITIES

1. Graeme Halford is very interested in the number of pieces of information individuals can process at one time. Why is this important in a school setting? Does the age of a student influence the nature (complexity) and number of pieces of information that can be processed at the same time? If so, how should teachers use this information in structuring their learning experiences for students?
2. Discuss the importance of analogical reasoning to cognitive development. See also the section by Patricia Alexander on pp. 124–5.
3. The theoretical propositions outlined by Graeme Halford are complex. Consider his applications to practice. How important is the information he presents for structuring appropriate learning experiences for students? Relate his discussion to elements of effective information processing that we have covered in this chapter.
4. Read and critique one of the key references listed.

when at the shop. Association with a particular room should more easily recall each item.

A **pegword mnemonic** associates an item with a rhyme, such as in *one-bun, two-shoe, three-tree* and so on. With a shopping list, each item would be associated with the rhyming pair so that the recall of the pair should trigger off the image of the required item. For example, the carton of eggs may be imagined as sitting on a bun, a milk carton stuffed into a shoe, peas hanging from a tree, and so on. At the cue 'tree', you should remember the incongruous image of peas hanging from the tree. Another device, the *link method*, simply constructs an overall image in which the items to be remembered form component and interacting parts. You could visualise each of the items on the shopping list interacting in some way, such as a milk carton balancing on an egg surrounded by flour, and so on. Alternatively, you could construct a sculpture of your shopping list, as shown in Figure 4.4. While walking through the shop you simply have to remember your sculpture and the items should also be recalled. Of course, a shopping list would be easier, but sometimes we are not able to carry a written record of what is to be remembered, such as a role in a play or points for an examination. In such cases, mnemonics are invaluable. Certainly, some great feats of memory are the result of well-applied mnemonics (see Lorayne & Lucas 1974; Wollen, Weber & Lowry 1972; Yates 1966).

My shopping sculpture

Figure 4.4 *Mnemonic devices: The link method*

Why do mnemonics work?

The usefulness of a variety of mnemonic devices is currently being researched, but the general results indicate that the use of well-constructed mnemonic devices in encoding enhances retrieval and the transfer of knowledge and skills to related or similar situations (Carney & Levin 2000; Snowman 1986). It appears that

TEACHER'S CASE BOOK

Green for up bows

Rebecca is a Year 4 student who has been learning the violin for two years. She practises regularly but has problems getting her bow direction right.

Over the last few weeks she had played *Musette* with any old bowing, usually a different direction each time. Janette, her teacher, had colour-coded the bows on the music in her book and made a teaching tape for her practice, all to no avail. Each week she came back performing it incorrectly. In desperation, Janette rewrote the song on large staff lines and coloured the notes in green and pink highlighter—green for up bows and pink for down bows. During the lesson she went over and over the tricky bowing, and the colour coding seemed to work.

When Rebecca arrived for the next lesson she had a secretive little smile on her face.

Rebecca: You are going to be surprised today.
Janette: Oh, good. Why?
Rebecca: Because my bows are right this week. Shall I play *Musette*?
Janette: Yes, please. Go ahead.

With a furtive glance to see Janette's reaction, Rebecca played with almost perfect bowing.

Case studies illustrating National Competency Framework for Beginning Teaching, National Project on the Quality of Teaching and Learning, Australian Teaching Council, 1996, p. 17. Commonwealth of Australia copyright, reproduced by permission.

Case study activity

Why did the colour coding help?

many people use these skills spontaneously (Carney *et al.* 1988). Indeed, the spontaneous use of mnemonics is so pervasive that it is difficult to set up a controlled experiment to test the effect of subjects' use of trained mnemonic devices because members of the control group (those not trained in the use of the particular mnemonic) also engage in constructing spontaneous mnemonics to cope with the learning task—hence the differences between controls and experimental subjects are minimised!

Mnemonics seem to assist with encoding because they provide meaning through associations with more familiar, meaningful information. Forming images of the material to be learned greatly aids later recall. Mnemonics also assist the learner to organise unrelated and often abstract material. Importantly, mnemonics associate the material to be learned with retrieval cues—for example, with the peg method we have only to remember one bun and the incongruous image will be triggered. Mnemonics should be easy to learn, interesting and fun, and as such they should enhance the motivation of students to learn. Indeed, some of the strongest evidence favouring the teaching of mnemonic imagery skills is that students appear to be impressed by how effective these strategies are when they use them and tend to incorporate them into their learning styles (see Pressley *et al.* 1989).

However, strategies such as the ones described above have some hidden dangers. For example, we may become quite inflexible in our recall, or if an element of the mnemonic is missing we may not be able to retrieve the rest. Most of us have to recite the little poem on the months of the year to remember the number of days in each. When flexibility of recall is important, the encoding should not be tied too tightly to a rigid mnemonic, and of course the most useful devices of encoding are those that are inherently meaningful in themselves.

Hidden dangers in using mnemonics

How does coding and classifying help learning?

For many cognitive psychologists, it is the linkages and relationships seen between pieces of information that are the hallmark of understanding and effective learning (Prawat 1989). The adequacy of the organisational structure connecting elements of the knowledge to be retained determines the accessibility or availability of the information at a later time. Some quite elaborate coding systems have been devised to assist students to see the connectedness of information and to facilitate the encoding and retention of quite difficult material. Coding is particularly useful for structuring both meaningful and non-meaningful material so that it is more easily learned and recalled later. Often all one has to do is to remember the structure, and the elements will also be remembered. Imagine that you have to remember the following list and the characteristics of the elements comprising the list:

platinum	silver	gold
aluminium	copper	lead
bronze	steel	brass
sapphire	emerald	ruby
limestone	granite	slate

Quite a job! However, if we organise the material into a **coding frame**, or **classification table** as it is sometimes called, starting with the general and working to the specific in a hierarchical form, the task is simplified.

MINERALS				
METALS			STONES	
RARE	COMMON	ALLOYS	PRECIOUS	MASONRY
platinum	aluminium	bronze	sapphire	limestone
silver	copper	steel	emerald	granite
gold	lead	brass	ruby	slate

The organisation of this material into a form of hierarchical tree makes it more meaningful, and therefore encoding, retention and retrieval should be enhanced (see Anderson 1990; Bower *et al.* 1969).

Concept mapping

Concept mapping (Danserau, O'Donnell & Lambiotte 1988; Novak 1981; Pines & Leith 1981; see also Chmielewski & Dansereau 1998; Graff 2005), a more elaborate form of coding, is a useful strategy for teaching students about concepts. Concept mapping allows the student to combine elements into meaningful statements or propositions. This linking helps students to see the relationships between concepts and to build on their conceptual framework.

A **concept map** is a two-dimensional diagram representing the conceptual structure of subject matter. To construct a concept map, we first identify the concepts and principles to be taught. Then the content elements are arranged in a hierarchical order from general to detailed, top to bottom. Finally, a line is drawn between each two related elements to show the linkage (Van Patten, Chao & Reigeluth 1986). For example, students are asked to identify the relevant concepts in a section of their textbook. A good way to begin is to pass out small paper rectangles and have students write all the key concepts that appear in the study material on these rectangles. The students are then asked to organise these concepts into a hierarchy, with the most general, most inclusive concepts at the top and the more specific concepts in two or more 'levels' below this. After a concept hierarchy is built, the students use narrower paper rectangles to write the relevant proposition to 'link' the concepts. A sample concept map constructed by a student in a Year 7 science class is shown in Figure 4.5. You can see from this example how the concepts 'plants' and 'energy' are linked by the word 'need' to form the proposition 'plants need energy'. Figure 4.6 represents a concept map with several levels in the hierarchy, such as types of dog, caring for dogs, what dogs do and so on. These types of concept maps not only help students to understand the material and to see the links between various pieces of information, but also to remember it more effectively.

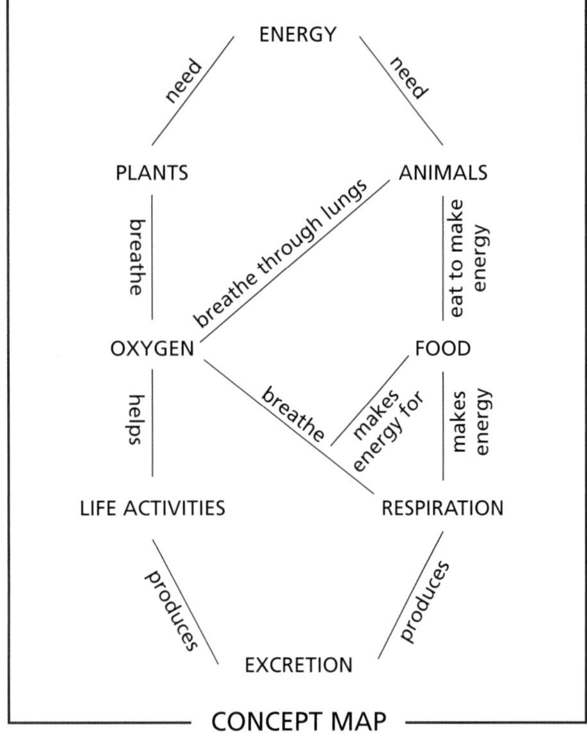

Figure 4.5 *Map showing concepts and linking propositions*

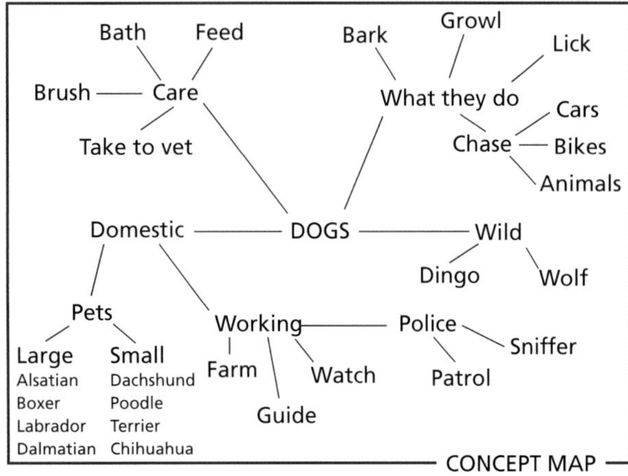

Figure 4.6 *Concept map with several levels in the hierarchy*

In some instances, teachers find it useful to have students develop a prediction map which helps to integrate their understanding. A prediction map is shown in Figure 4.7. What do you think of it?

Often students are asked to discuss their concept maps in class. This helps them to assess what they know and to clarify their understanding of concepts. Concept mapping, once learned, becomes a very valuable evaluation tool. Are there criteria for what makes an effective cognitive map? In the following box we suggest three criteria that may be used by teachers to evaluate the quality of cognitive maps designed by their students.

THREE CRITERIA OF EFFECTIVE CONCEPT MAPS

1 Does the map show a good hierarchy? There is no best hierarchy, but consider whether the concepts and propositions shown represent an acceptable order in terms of moving from a more general, more inclusive concept to a less general, less inclusive concept as related to the particular study material.

2 Are the propositions shown valid and 'correct'? Are all concepts 'connected' into propositions?

3 Are there cross-linkages between segments of the map?

Source: Based on Novak (1981).

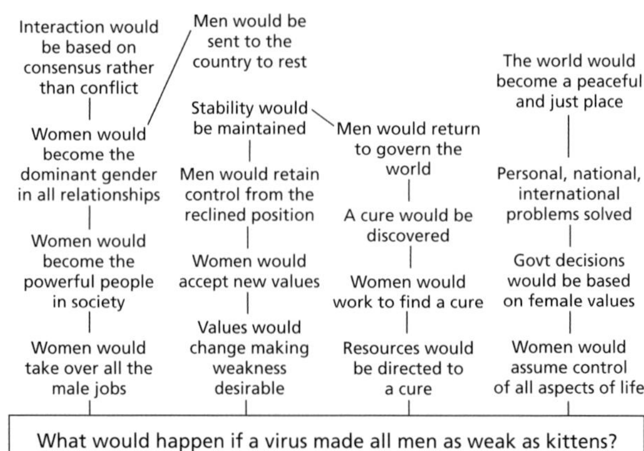

Figure 4.7 *A prediction map*

Networking

Another form of concept mapping is networking. Networking requires students to identify the important concepts or ideas in the text and to describe the interrelationships between these ideas in the form of a network diagram using nodes and links. Dansereau (1985) asserts that students' application of this networking technique will result in their improved comprehension and retention of the material since the network diagram provides a visual, spatial organisation of the information and helps the student to see an overall picture of the material. A teacher-made network can be used as an advance organiser (Ausubel 1963, 1978), and incomplete or inaccurate networks completed by students can be used by the teacher to assess the students' level of comprehension and any misconceptions they might have.

Making good use of networking and concept maps is not without difficulties (Van Patten *et al.* 1986). First, students have to be trained for hours before they can use the techniques proficiently. Second, many types of relationships (conceptual, propositional, procedural, cause–effect, factual) are present simultaneously and linked by intertwined lines and words, which may make it difficult for students to use the map effectively. Because of the complexity of much learning, concept maps and networking may oversimplify relationships so that much important information is left out. Nevertheless, we believe that this approach is beneficial in facilitating learning and recall, and also helps learners to make clear to themselves what similarities there are between concepts, thereby improving generalisations of learning (Anderson, Reder & Simon 1996).

QUESTION POINT

Consider how a teacher could facilitate the development of memory skills in children by referring to the techniques that are discussed in this chapter.

Table 4.1 summarises the essentials for encouraging strategy development and use, while Table 4.2 presents a number of key principles of information processing constructivism with which you should be very familiar.

Table 4.3 presents a taxonomy of learning strategies which you can use to guide your use of these strategies.

Remembering

Our computer analogy highlighted the importance of disk storage space and procedures for making permanent records of our data processing. In this section, we consider procedures that facilitate or inhibit the effective retention of human information processing. Much of the material presented to our senses each day is not remembered because we do not attend specifically to the stimuli. For example, who can recall the portraits on our currency? We remember on several occasions giving a listening exercise to a class, which then had to answer comprehension questions, only to be unable to answer the questions ourselves. Despite 'mouthing the words', our attention was obviously elsewhere.

Factors that affect remembering in educational settings

Research into remembering and forgetting in educational settings indicates that students actually retain quite a lot of what is taught in the classroom (Semb & Ellis 1994).

Table 4.1 Essentials for encouraging strategy development and use

Teachers should:

- describe strategies;
- start with one or two strategies;
- indicate why and when to use the strategies;
- model strategy use with 'think-alouds';
- give guided practice in strategy use in varied situations;
- give feedback on strategy use;
- give autonomous practice in a variety of contexts;
- motivate students to use strategies;
- encourage positive self-beliefs by showing students how good strategy use prepares them better for everyday life and gives them an opportunity for self-advancement.

Source: Based on Pressley & Woloshyn (1995).

EXTENSION STUDY

How should learning strategies be taught?

Strategic learners

As we have suggested above, cognitive strategies enhance learning (see, for example, Dahl, Bals, & Turi 2005; Derry 1989; Escribe & Huet 2005; Swanson & Hoskyn 1998). The appropriate use of strategies depends on how familiar the learner is with the material to be learned, and is also domain specific (Garner 1990; see also Lucangeli *et al.* 2003). The aim of strategy use is to minimise the demands on the working memory, and to make learning and responses as automatic as possible (Sweller 1993). When students already know a great deal about a topic, they really don't need to use strategic routines for acquiring new concepts. Effective learners know when they need to be strategic and when they do not. Furthermore, strategies that are appropriate in one domain may be inappropriate in another. For example, it may be important to give extra attention to numerals in mathematics and history, but it would be unimportant in most language studies. Rehearsing information with attention to temporal or serial order may be useful in some domains (such as history) but inappropriate in others. Attention to the subjective content of some material may be essential (such as in literature), but in other areas it could interfere with processing information (such as physics). Weak strategies in particular domains may be strong strategies in others (Garner 1990).

In general, students (and adults, too) are not strategic learners. There are a number of explanations for this:

- Students don't monitor their own learning and therefore don't really know when they are being ineffective.
- Students resort to well-practised routines that get the job done even when these routines do not really enhance learning.
- Students' meagre knowledge base about task demands blocks the appropriate use of strategies.
- Students' inappropriate attributions (to ability, rather than effort) and school/classroom goals, such as performance-based goals that do not support strategy use and greater involvement in deep, rather than surface, learning (Garner 1990).

Because many students are not strategic learners, they should be taught to monitor their use of strategies and their effectiveness. In line with this, students should be taught when and where to use particular strategies and to be flexible—that is, if a particular approach is unsuited to a specific learning task, they should adopt another strategy (Garner 1990; Paris, Lipson & Wixson 1983; see also

Table 4.2 Essentials of information processing constructivism for education

Teachers should:

- focus on the child constructing knowledge in interaction with a more competent adult or peer;
- instruct in groups, with students providing input and feedback to each other;
- monitor the child's progress in determining future input;
- implement non-scripted dialogues between teachers and students, characterised by meaningful adult reactions to student attempts to write, speak or solve problems, followed by student reaction to feedback;
- provide continual teacher encouragement of students to apply their knowledge to new situations;
- have an acceptance of individual differences in the degree of assistance required and of rates of progress;
- provide modelling and explanations (teachers and peers) that allow students to progress to greater competence through the creative transformation of teacher- and peer-modelled skills by students;
- emphasise learning through understanding.

Teachers should teach learners to:

- practise applying strategies to new situations or learning domains;
- think 'deeply', rather than superficially, about what they read;
- consciously make connections to what they already understand or are familiar with;
- monitor performance of strategy use in a variety of tasks, some similar and some different.

Source: Based on Pressley *et al.* (1992); Pressley & Woloshyn (1995).

Weinstein & Hume 1998). It is also important to teach strategies within the context of real learning events such as mathematics, language and social science. Pressley *et al.* (1989) suggest the following points to guide the explicit teaching of a strategy. First, they suggest the teacher should describe the strategy to students and model its use. This modelling should include think-aloud statements about how to execute the procedure. These 'think-alouds' should also include important information on *why* and *when* the strategy could be used. Teacher-guided practice with the strategy should be given to students, followed by detailed feedback by the teacher on how individuals might improve strategy use. The practice–feedback loop continues until students can use the strategy efficiently. To facilitate acquisition, practice may begin with easier material and progress to harder tasks. To train for transfer of the strategy, the practice examples should be drawn from different content areas, and the strategy can be employed at various times during a day's instruction and as part of homework exercises. As you can see from this description, teaching effective strategy use to students should be explicit, intensive and extensive. The goal is for students to use the learned strategies autonomously, skilfully and appropriately.

It is probably best to teach only a few strategies at a time, and to teach them well. Ultimately, the type of strategies employed by learners should be related to the amount of prior knowledge they possess, the nature of the material to be learned and the kind of outcome the learner is trying to achieve (Garner 1990; Prawat 1989). At times, simple mnemonics will be appropriate; at other times, concept maps will be more suitable.

Is strategy instruction a form of constructivism?

The teaching of cognitive strategies to students should emphasise that the learner must construct meaning from the material, otherwise strategies may become harmful and simply be used by students to commit facts and definitions to memory without any real meaning or applied value for the individual (Iran-Nejad 1990; see also Pressley, Harris & Marks 1992). Strategy instruction has been criticised as non-constructivist. Pressley *et al.* believe that, while good strategy instruction incorporates features of behavioural and direct instruction approaches to teaching (see Chapter 6), which are considered by constructivist educators as mechanistic, good strategy instruction is anything but mechanical. They believe that strategy instruction is an extremely student-sensitive form of teaching designed to stimulate students to construct effective and personalised ways of tackling academic problems. In their article, 'But good strategy instructors are constructivists!', they explore the constructivist principles that can be incorporated into strategy instruction.

Why is it important to pay attention for effective information processing?

The long-term retention of school learning is quite complex and influenced by many factors. Among very important factors are the degree of organisation and structure of the material being learned. In particular, if this structure relates to students' prior knowledge, retention should be enhanced. Practice, relearning, advanced training and continued exposure to the content being learned also facilitate retention because they increase the degree of original learning. Instructional techniques also have an effect. In particular, research indicates that mastery learning approaches, which are highly structured around achievement goals and provide opportunities for practice, recall, feedback and review, produce superior academic performance. (We discuss mastery approaches to instruction in Chapter 11.) Instructional techniques that require the active involvement of the learner also facilitate remembering and recall. Finally, remembering is also affected by the nature of the assessment tasks. Tasks that call on recognition appear to stimulate remembering better than tasks that rely on recall. This is probably because the prompts for

Table 4.3 A taxonomy of learning strategies

Cognitive strategies	Basic tasks (e.g. memory for lists)	Complex tasks (e.g. test learning)
Rehearsal strategies	Reciting list	Shadowing Copy material Verbatim note taking Underlining test
Elaboration strategies	Keyword method Imagery Method of loci Generative note taking Question answering	Paraphrasing Summarising Creating analogies
Organisational strategies	Clustering Mnemonics	Selecting main idea Outlining Networking Diagramming
Metacognitive strategies	**All tasks**	
Planning strategies	Setting goals Skimming Generating questions	
Monitoring strategies	Self-testing Attention-focus Test-taking strategies	
Regulating strategies	Adjusting reading rate Re-reading Reviewing Test-taking strategies	
Resource management strategies	**All tasks**	
Time management	Scheduling Goal setting	
Study environment management	Defined area Quiet area Organised area	
Effort management	Attributions to effort Mood Self-talk Persistence Self-reinforcement	
Support of others	Seeking help from teacher Seeking help from peers Peer/group learning Tutoring	

Source: Based on Paul R. Pintrich's research on motivation and learning strategies.

recognition are more explicit. Individual differences in ability also play a role in retention (Semb & Ellis 1994).

Research indicates that things to be recalled need to be consolidated in the long-term memory, and that a period of time is necessary for learning to become established. The actual physiological processes involved in this have attracted considerable attention from psychologists and physiologists but are beyond the scope of this text (for example, see Kantowitz & Roediger 1980). We will concentrate on the mechanics of learning for retention.

There are a number of techniques that may be used to enhance retention: whole and part learning, repetition and drill, overlearning and automaticity, and distributed practice.

Whole and part learning

Whole and part learning refers to the nature of the unit chosen for learning and memorising (Conklin 1976; Kingsley & Garry 1957; Seagoe 1972; van Merrienboer, Kirschner & Kester 2003). With the **whole learning** approach the integrity of the block of material to be remembered is maintained and encoded as a unit. With the **part learning** method, a large block is broken into smaller subsections and then put together again at the end. The most effective method is determined by the nature of the material to be learned and the age and ability of the learner. Sometimes complex tasks with many interconnections between distinct parts or constituent skills can't be broken into smaller parts effectively. Other tasks may be broken into smaller units. The purpose of breaking the task into smaller units is to reduce the cognitive load demands on the working memory (van Merrienboer, Kirschner & Kester 2003; see also, Nadolski, Kirshner & van Merriënboer 2005). Whole and part learning approaches have implications for a range of learning activities such as learning the piano (should we learn to play with one hand and then the other, or both together?), poetry (stanza by stanza?), music (the whole piece or phrase by phrase?).

One of the authors recalls having to learn the whole of *The Rime of the Ancient Mariner* by heart. The whole class was expected to know it, word perfect, and each morning we were lined up around the wall to recite, in turn, stanza after stanza. Needless to say, with a poem this size, the part method was used and if the previous stanza was correct, the following student was prompted to make the correct response. Woe betide anyone who made an error! Not only did this cause a problem for the forgetful student, but following students also became confused.

On the other hand, when faced with learning a speech from Shakespeare, the whole method often works better. There are no hard and fast rules, but there are some important principles when adopting one or other approach. The whole method binds material together at the outset into a meaningful whole; however, learning may seem slower. Part learning supplies immediate goals, shows more rapid learning and is therefore more satisfying. But part learning does not necessarily transfer to the whole, and too complete a learning of individual parts may inhibit later learning of the whole. Table 4.4 lists essential guidelines for using whole or part methods of learning.

Repetition and drill

Repetition and drill are time-honoured practices among teachers and are directed towards maximising the retention of learned material. Repetition, in itself, does not lead to greater retention; the important criterion for the usefulness of this as a technique is that it must be based on attention and understanding. The belief that if students do it often enough they will catch on, is quite erroneous. Students can write out a list of spelling words many times without learning them; a student can practise some aspect of writing skills without improving in penmanship; and a student may do a series of exercises by following the steps indicated in the example without mastering the principles involved. Basically, repetition is useful if it has the interest, attention and purpose of the learner and is associated with meaningful learning; it is most useful in refining and improving the retention and recall of material already learned.

Overlearning and automaticity

Continuing repetition of the material past the point of first mastery, called **overlearning**, is also beneficial in facilitating retention and recall. This repetition is also necessary for the development of automaticity. **Automaticity** refers to the status of a skill or behaviour that has been repeated to the point of being 'automatic'. That is to say, the skill or behaviour can function with little mental effort while other thinking occurs. Another characteristic of automaticity is that skills requiring several steps of behaviour are 'chunked' into a single unit.

Table 4.4

Essentials for using whole or part methods of learning effectively

- When information to be learned is highly unified and independent of other units, it is better for students to learn it as a whole.
- When information consists of many loosely related parts, which are in themselves unified, the part approach is perhaps better.
- Work from the whole to the part in cases such as these: when teaching a poem, read through the poem several times as a whole before memorising individual stanzas; with vocabulary building, locate the words in a context before memorising a definition, and have children hear many stories before they are asked to write small sentences.
- Many exercises that are often taught partly can be taught wholly; for example, vocabulary, language and writing practice can be covered in the one exercise.
- Be flexible in approach.
- Give guidance in the use of the appropriate method as students do not always choose the best method.

Consider a young man learning to play a musical instrument for the first time. He has to discern where the musical note is on the staff, what note it is, what position the hands must be in to create that note, and then execute the playing of the note. Early on, this process can fill the limited space in the working memory. Notes are produced slowly, deliberately and, occasionally, incorrectly. Repeated practice can lead to automaticity, which connects all the steps necessary to produce the note into one process, thereby taking up less space in the working memory. This allows the musician to think about future notes to be played and the emotion that should be conveyed in the musical piece.

Another demonstration of automaticity can be seen in the efforts of a person learning to drive a car with a manual transmission. The driver, faced with two feet, two hands, three pedals, five gears, mirror, steering wheel and congested highways has her hands and feet, and working memory, full. In the early stages of learning to drive, the car can lurch, the clutch is forgotten and the gears grind: every bit of attention is necessary. After repeated experience, however, the driving process becomes automatic. The shifting process occurs smoothly, effortlessly and almost without thought. Robert Sternberg (1986) regards the ability to automatise as an element of intelligence (see Chapter 3). In his triarchic theory of intelligence, he describes the ability to deal with novel situations and to automatise familiar experiences as one aspect of intelligence.

Distributed practice

Practice, like medicine, may be presented in small or large doses. It may be concentrated into relatively long, unbroken periods or spread over several short sessions. When practice is concentrated in long periods it is called **massed.** When it is spread over time, it is called **distributed.**

When to use distributed practice

Almost without exception, the studies concerned with the relative effectiveness of distributed and massed practice, whether it is with motor skills (such as writing) or verbal learning (such as reading), show that practice should be spaced for the best results (for example, Dempster 1988; Semb & Ellis 1994). A few words in spelling each day for a week will be mastered better than a large number bunched in one lesson.

It appears that when the amount of work involved in a task is great, and when the task is complex or not particularly meaningful, there should be regular practice periods separated by rest periods to allow for the consolidation of the material. This also applies to situations where a high level of attention or energy is required (such as learning to use complex machinery) and where the possibility of errors increases as individuals become fatigued. It also appears that the length of the rest period is not so crucial. A five-minute 'breather' or 'smoko' (as they used to call it before the days of smoking bans) may be all that is necessary to allow the consolidation of information to take place, and to alleviate potential fatigue effects.

Massed practice periods are nevertheless very useful for tasks that are meaningful or already partially learned. They are also useful for revising material or bringing the individual or group to a peak level of mastery on the material (Kingsley & Garry 1957; Seagoe 1972).

When to use massed practice

One of the authors remembers rehearsals for a major drama production she was directing. Individual actors were given both extensive and short, focused practice sessions in their roles. Musicians also practised difficult sections of their scores individually. As the performance night drew closer, the pieces were fitted together and a whole-day dress rehearsal was held to 'get rid of the bugs'. That night, the final performance was held and, after all that massed and distributed practice, it was a great show, even if somewhat exhausting.

Serial position effect

It is an interesting fact that when faced with learning a list of things such as the alphabet, mathematical tables, spelling lists, historical dates, a long poem or a song, the material presented early is most easily remembered; material near the end is remembered relatively easily; but we often have great difficulty remembering the middle sections of the material. Students tend to make spelling errors in the middle of words and in the middle of spelling lists; they get up to 4 × 6 easily in their tables but forget the next in the sequence until they sigh with relief at 4 × 10, 11 and 12. Students forget the middle of songs or poems, and pronunciation errors are made in the middle of words (for example, 'chimbley'). This fall-off in retention in the middle of the sequence is known as the **serial position effect**. It doesn't apply only to lists of things. Students have a tendency to listen to the beginning of the lesson, fall asleep in the middle and wake up for the conclusion. It has been known to happen to students in lectures at university as well (Greene 1986; Rundus & Atkinson 1970; Stigler 1978).

This ability to retain and recall the first and last elements of a list more easily than the middle section is referred to as the *primacy* and *recency effects*, respectively. It appears that the serial position effect may be explained by a fall-off in attention in the middle, so encoding is therefore less effective and retention and recall are lessened.

Primacy and recency effects

In itself, this is no problem if precautions are taken to alleviate the effect. Important material should be presented at the beginning or end of the list. Less important or more easily remembered material could be included in the middle. If all material is of equal importance, then the position in the list should be varied over a number of trials so that no item is located in the middle consistently. For example, spelling lists could be presented over three nights with a variation in word position each night. Alternatively, parts of the same list could be presented over three nights, with several words repeated in each until all the words are included.

Structure lessons to alleviate the serial position effect

At times the sequence cannot be altered (as with a long soliloquy or a long song). However, we can effectively make the middle the start of a new learning episode by saying 'We are going to pay particular attention to stanza two today' or 'Let's go over the middle phrase of the song a couple more times'.

Simply drawing attention to middle items by saying 'I want you to pay special attention to this' can be effective, as is using variety throughout the learning episode. Students can also be taught to take extra care with particular aspects of learning tasks so that there is less variation in attention, for example: 'You might make mistakes in the middle section, so watch this carefully.'

Another problem with learning material in serial order for retention and recall is that the order in which we learn the material determines the order of easiest recall. In general, if we have slavishly learned material in a serial form, it is very hard to recall items without resorting to the whole list. For example, how many people have to go through a large part of the alphabet in order to recall a letter's position or right through a multiplication table to locate a particular sequence? If we require flexibility of recall, items should not be learned in a serial fashion.

Why do we have difficulty remembering some things?

Earlier we illustrated problems that can occur in accessing and retrieving information from computer files. Retrieval of information stored mentally also depends upon the effectiveness with which the information was encoded and the utility of the retrieval cues associated with the stored information. In this section we discuss some techniques to enhance memory retrieval.

We have seen that information in the working memory may disappear unless it is consolidated, and we discussed above some of the techniques for encoding and retaining material that should facilitate long-term memory and retrieval. Some researchers have suggested that the amount of effort put into encoding a memory may affect how long it lasts and how easily we can retrieve it. What are some of the reasons for why we might forget things? The boxed information below gives four basic reasons. We wonder how many of these have applied to you in the past?

Reasons for forgetting

FOUR BASIC REASONS WHY WE FORGET

1. The information in the working memory was never effectively transferred to the long-term memory.
2. The information is not used over a long period, and so the memory appears to fade.
3. We cannot retrieve the cues for information that is in the long-term memory.
4. Our retrieval of specific information is interfered with by similar information, causing confusion.

Obviously, in the first case, lack of attention or appropriate consolidation procedures, such as those discussed above, would prevent the effective encoding of information for retention and recall. We have all been pleased with ourselves for having remembered the names of people at a party while we are at the party, only to be embarrassed the next day by forgetting a name when we meet one of the party-goers at a local shop.

Some research indicates that our memories are encoded chemically in the brain, and if not reactivated periodically the memory traces simply fade with time. The third and fourth explanations are of more immediate interest to us. In our description of the encoding and retention processes, we have emphasised the importance of encoding material in such a way that particular cues can be used to recall the information. Indeed, successful mnemonics depend upon cues that are easy to remember, acting as the trigger for remembering more difficult material. The effectiveness of retrieval cues depends on their relation to the nature of the stored material. For example, if you are given the word *violet* to remember, and it follows the words *daisy*, *tulip* and *zinnia* in a list, you are likely to encode it as a flower. Later, you are more likely to recall *violet* if you are given the retrieval cue *flowers* than if you were simply left on your own to remember the word. If you were given the word *violet* among a list of girls' names, such as *Bridie*, *Agnes* and *Beatrice*, and you were given the retrieval cue *girls' names*, you would probably also remember the word *violet* as belonging to the list. On the other hand, if the word was included in a list of girls' names and you were given the retrieval cue *flowers*, you may very well have difficulty retrieving the word (Kantowitz & Roediger 1980).

Two further causes should be considered. First, much apparent loss of memory is simply the result of an individual's not associating the material with cues that can serve as triggers for the retrieval of the memory. This is a memory skill that can be taught.

Second, apparent loss of memory may also be the result of the wrong retrieval cue being used. Some teachers go to considerable lengths to teach material to students in one context, only to require them to recall it in a context that does not present the relevant retrieval cues. For example, if students are taught a mathematical process such as multiple addition through drill and practice, but are examined for their recall of the procedures through a test where the procedures are buried in verbal problems, the students could very well appear to have forgotten how to do the procedure. In fact, what is happening is that the appropriate cue for recall is missing.

Interference effects

Some argue that the basic reason we forget is not that we have lost the available information from memory, but that the memory is blocked from retrieval because of competing responses. In other words, events occurring before or after events that are to be remembered interfere with recall of the to-be-remembered events. One phenomenon that all teachers are familiar with is memory loss for student names at the beginning of a new term. We can remember all of the students' names in our class in a particular year. At the beginning of a new year we have considerable difficulty learning the names of those in our new class but recall the names of those in our old class reasonably well. However, some time into the new term we consolidate the names of those in our new class, only to be embarrassed when we can't then recall the names of those in our last class. This effect on retention is known as the **interference effect** and, depending on the direction of the interference, we have either proactive interference or retroactive interference.

Proactive interference occurs when earlier learning interferes with new learning; for example, a teacher learning the names of students in his new class may have difficulty because he confuses the names with those of an earlier class. In general, when we find it difficult to respond to new situations because of our established ways of responding, we have proactive interference. There are many examples of this effect—driving on the other side of the road in Europe, learning to touch type, correcting a well-established spelling error, driving an automatic car after a manual car. Recently a teacher relayed to us the difficulty that children from a Lebanese background have in learning our number system. It appears that, while the Western world borrowed many of the orthographic features of the Arabic number system, the numerical value, placement and way of reading them (right to left, rather than left to right) were not retained. Can you imagine the trouble experienced by children who have an established Arabic number system which is similar to, but confusingly different from, the system in use in our schools? This is a very good example of proactive interference.

When new learning impedes the retention of the old learning, we have an example of **retroactive interference**. When we first started word processing on a computer, we used the Macintosh format and became very adept at it. At a certain point we were provided with IBM machines for work. We found it inordinately difficult converting from the Macintosh to the DOS IBM, a good example of proactive interference. However, as we had no alternative we persevered and became quite adept at using the IBMs. Now, when we return to the Macintosh we find it hard remembering exactly what to do, an equally good example of retroactive interference!

For educators the main implication of interference effects is to sequence learning experiences so that present learning does not inhibit the retention and recall of earlier or subsequent learning. For example, if we were to give students a spelling list that contained 'ie' words, such as *achieve* and *piece*, any subsequent list should not contain 'ei' words, such as *conceive* and *receive*, until the earlier material is consolidated. We all use the rhyme 'i before e except after c' to try to sort this out. The problems most of us still have with 'ie/ei' words indicates the power of the interference effects.

Proactive facilitation

It should also be noted that learning one thing can often help a person to learn similar material. For example, learning Spanish first may help a student to learn Italian, a similar language (see, for example, Cunningham & Graham 2000). This is known as **proactive facilitation**. If we are teaching children how to spell 'ie' words and we follow up the initial learning with further lists containing 'ie' words, the earlier learning should be consolidated. This is known as **retroactive facilitation**. It is argued that the more similar the mother tongue is to English for ESL students, the greater the help the mother tongue can give in acquiring the second language (Corder 1983, cited in Ringbom 1987). The difficulties in learning to understand any foreign language, for example, may be the result of the lack of cross-linguistic and orthographic similarities to the native language upon which the learner can draw. Many people find it helpful to recall the Latin roots of a somewhat obscure word to help decode its meaning. Facilitation and inhibition effects are related to transfer of learning, which we discuss below.

There are a number of general principles regarding interference effects that will help you to understand how they operate and suggest techniques for maximising facilitation while minimising interference:

- A task that is closely related to an earlier one, so that it is confusing, may interfere with the recall of the previous task; for example, a spelling list with 'ie' words followed by one with 'ei' words would lead to confusion and neither list would be easily remembered or recalled.
- A task that is closely related to an earlier one, but reinforcing it, may facilitate recall—for example, learning to drive a car, then a tractor; learning a list with silent p's and then one with other words with silent p's.
- A task unrelated to an original task may have no effect on the recall of the original task—for example, following a maths lesson with an art lesson.
- A task that is extensive in nature may interfere with the consolidation and recall of an earlier task because of the fatigue induced.

QUESTION POINT

Define and differentiate between retroactive interference and proactive interference. Discuss classroom examples. How can teachers use proactive facilitation to increase learning?

In Table 4.5 we consider some of the essential pedagogical techniques teachers should use to enhance students' remembering of material covered in class.

What elements are essential for the development of expertise by novices?

Table 4.5

Essentials of enhancing remembering

Teachers should:

- provide opportunities for the active involvement of the learner;
- provide multiple and varied learning opportunities;
- provide opportunities for students to engage the material at higher cognitive levels to stimulate schema building and deep processing;
- provide coherent and well-organised material relevant to students' prior knowledge;
- provide corrective feedback;
- provide recognition tasks to evaluate learning.

Teachers should teach learners to:

- indicate whether understanding of new material has taken place ('Do I understand this?');
- think of examples similar to the new material or procedure ('How is this similar to/different from what I already know about?');
- try to relate the new information to prior understanding ('How does this connect to what I already know?').

EXTENSION STUDY

How do experts differ from novices in information processing?

Expertise in human learning is something that teachers aspire to develop in their students. Early studies on differences between experts and novices in learning sprung from artificial intelligence and information processing theory. The primary goal was to determine the characteristics and actions of experts so that these features could be programmed into 'intelligent' machines, or trained into non-experts (Alexander 2003). Considerable research relates to examining what distinguishes experts from novices in various learning tasks and domain areas (see, for example the special issue of *Educational Researcher*, 32, 2003). Much of this research relates to models of expert learning that draw from other areas, such as domain learning and triarchic intelligence. In this chapter, we consider differences between experts and novices from an information processing perspective.

In general, we consider adults more cognitively mature and capable of more sophisticated information processing than children. However, as illustrated earlier, when adults are given a mental task to perform in an area in which they have little knowledge, they often process the information less efficiently than children who have more knowledge in that area. This raises the question of the relationship between the amount of knowledge possessed and its impact on cognitive processing.

Increasingly, therefore, attention is being paid by researchers to the different cognitive characteristics of experts and novices in particular performance domains to find out how they differ in what they know and the

Transfer of learning

While at times learners master particular skills and knowledge that are naturally restricted in application to specific and limited contexts, there is a whole range of things that we learn that should have application far beyond the boundaries of the contexts in which they are learned. A key concern of education is to provide students with skills and knowledge that they can transfer broadly to other situations (see, for example, Bransford & Schwartz 1999). This is what is meant by **transfer of learning.** In other words, mathematics that we learn in the classroom should help us with our shopping, English should help us with writing business letters, keyboard and computing skills should transfer to a range of other electronic equipment, and so on. Learning one language should assist in learning another (Cunningham & Graham 2000). This elementary and simple notion of transfer of learning is, however, not so simple and has spawned an enormous amount of research examining the issue over the last 100 years (see, for example, Beach 1999; Bransford & Schwartz 1999; Cox 1997; Dyson 1989; Gentner, Loewenstein & Thompson 2003). The reason for this is that the rules we think should apply to transfer do not seem to work that well. It is a common occurrence that individuals do not transfer skills and knowledge across contexts, and the further one context is from another the less likely transfer is to occur. So, for example, students who are taught mathematical solutions for particular problems may transfer these to similar problems (what we might call specific or direct transfer), but are less likely to transfer them to different but related problems—for example, in physics (what we might call general transfer). Even if the principles behind the solutions are relevant, as the context becomes less similar students become less likely to transfer them to the new context. This is, of course, a great problem, and it is the reason why so much research and theorising has gone into studying transfer of learning. We would like to be more certain as educators that what we teach in one context will broadly transfer to similar and related contexts.

In a sense, each of the theories of learning we examine in our text has embedded in it notions of transfer. For example, when we discuss Gestalt psychology in the next chapter, we will see that notions of transfer lie in the conceptualisation of insightful learning and the perception of meaningful patterns intrinsic to the perceptual field. The active recognition of meaningful patterns facilitates transfer (Cox 1997). When we discuss behaviourism in Chapter 6, we will see that transfer is thought to lie in stimulus–response generalisations. With regard to sociocultural theories of learning (discussed in Chapter 2 and elsewhere), transfer is facilitated through the embeddedness of the learner in the social context and the reciprocal relationship established between the individual and their situation (Beach 1999). Information processing theory suggests that transfer is facilitated through the learning of cognitive skills such as rehearsal, processes they use for performing a sequence of cognitive actions on the content (Chi, Glaser & Rees 1982; Shuell 1990; Sweller 1990, 1993). The findings from this research are thrown into strong relief when the experts are children and the novices adults.

Not surprisingly, the evidence shows that the expert knows more domain-specific concepts than the novice does, and that these concepts are more differentiated and interrelated, with each of the expert's concepts closely connected in long-term memory with many other concepts. Hence, encoding, storage and retrieval are facilitated. Experts also appear to be more likely to use **cognitive strategies** such as planning and analysis before processing information. In many cases, this simplifies the processing procedure as the experts call to mind appropriate templates for cognitive action from their rich 'bank' of stored experiences and memories. In other words, the expert's response can be more automatic, unconscious and effortless (Shuell 1990; Sweller 1990, 1993; see also Alexander 2003). Nevertheless, if both adults and children are equally unfamiliar with the problem to be solved or the material to be learned, adults generally may be expected to perform better because of their larger repertoire of experience-based learning, which will facilitate the solving of novel problems. It may also be that they have a greater store of strategies for learning new material than children.

By and large, the development of expertise in a domain area depends on experience and practice; but of course what individuals choose to, or have the opportunity to, invest time and practice in is subject to a wide number of environmental circumstances. One would expect that formal education at least makes all children expert in basic skills, with some measure of high-level, developmentally mature-looking cognitive performance (see Flavell 1985).

overlearning, automaticity and metacognitive skills discussed above (Cox 1997).

Most research on transfer has been concerned with examining the transfer of elements of learning to other particular situations, what might be termed the *direct application* of principles, skills and knowledge to new situations. There is another way of looking at transfer, and this is to consider it as preparation for future learning (Bransford & Schwartz 1999). In this case, transfer is not demonstrated by the direct application of specific skills and knowledge to new situations so much as by the broad application of skills and knowledge in new situations. Bransford and Schwartz (1999, p. 68) give the following relevant example:

> . . . [I]magine elementary education majors who graduate and become classroom teachers for the first time. By the standard DA [direct application] definition of transfer, the test of transfer would be whether the beginning teachers, without coaching, can apply to the classroom the methods they learned in school. As noted earlier, this is an important concern, yet it is only one part of the larger story. The larger story involves whether the novice teachers have been prepared to learn from their new experiences, including their abilities to structure their environments in ways that lead to successful learning (e.g. arrange for peer coaching). There is no preliminary education or training that can make these people experts; it can only place them on a trajectory toward expertise.

Bransford and Schwartz believe that this view of transfer is more in keeping with how the world of learning actually operates. Our aim as educators is, of course, to facilitate transfer and there are some broad principles (based on Bransford & Schwartz 1999; Cox 1997) that should be applied.

- Effective transfer requires a sufficient degree of original learning.
- Practising through to automaticity of cognitive and metacognitive skills in a range of related areas facilitates transfer.
- The degree to which learning has made the retrieval of relevant knowledge 'effortful' or relatively 'effortless' affects transfer.
- Developing abstractions and principles to apply in future situations facilitates transfer.
- Embedding learning in a community of shared knowledge, and demonstrating the links between components of knowledge rather than emphasising discrete components facilitates transfer.
- Emphasising meaningfulness and understanding facilitates transfer.
- Using appropriate prompts and guides to show the links between existing knowledge and skills and new applications of these facilitates transfer.
- Emphasising understanding and active involvement of the learner facilitates transfer.
- Using concrete examples facilitates transfer.
- Learning in multiple contexts facilitates transfer.

Theory and research into practice

Patricia A. Alexander — NOVICE TO EXPERT LEARNERS AND DOMAIN LEARNING

BRIEF BIOGRAPHY

After years as a middle-school teacher, I received my Master's degree as a reading specialist from James Madison University in the United States in 1979. I then pursued a doctoral degree in reading from the University of Maryland. After receiving my doctorate in 1981, I took a position at Texas A&M University, where my primary responsibilities were to teach courses in reading, gifted education and educational psychology. I remained at Texas A&M University until 1995, where I rose to the rank of professor and research fellow and was honoured by the university for my research and teaching. In 1995, I returned to the University of Maryland where I joined the faculty in the Department of Human Development. Currently I hold the title of 'professor and distinguished scholar-teacher', and head the educational psychology specialisation while teaching courses in educational psychology and learning theory.

I have published over 170 articles, books or chapters, and have presented over 160 papers or invited addresses at national and international conferences. Currently, I serve as the editor of *Contemporary Educational Psychology* and *Instructional Science* and am on the editorial boards for nine leading journals in the fields of learning and instruction, educational psychology and literacy.

Among memberships of many organisations, I am a fellow of the American Psychological Association, and was a Spencer fellow of the National Academy of Education. I have served as president of Division 15 (Educational Psychology) of the American Psychological Association, and vice-president of Division C (Learning and Instruction) of the American Educational Research Association. Recently, I was named one of the 10 most productive scholars in educational psychology, and I was the 2001 recipient of the Oscar S. Causey Award for outstanding contributions to literacy research from the National Reading Conference.

RESEARCH AND THEORETICAL INTERESTS

So much of who I am as a researcher traces back to those years of teaching middle-school students, and the invaluable lessons they taught me. During my last three years as a public school teacher, I had my own lab (really an old cannery converted into a classroom). There I worked with students who needed more than teachers could provide them in the regular classroom. My students—who included highly gifted learners, as well as those who struggled with physical, cognitive and emotional problems—helped me realise the importance of learning from text in academic success. For that reason, I set out to pursue my doctorate in reading at the University of Maryland, because I wanted to help other students realise their full academic potential.

My mentor at Maryland was a scholar named Ruth Garner, who was known for her research in strategies and in metacognition (that is, the monitoring and regulation of one's own thinking and learning). I soon realised that all students would benefit from becoming more strategic and self-regulating readers. Much of my early research in the 1980s centred around strategies and on teaching students to be more strategic readers. This concern for strategies and problem solving remains a central thrust in my teaching and research.

Interestingly, the deeper I got into the study of strategies, the more I came to appreciate that students' knowledge of the content played a major role in their ability to use strategies efficiently and effectively. Therefore, I became immersed in the relation between strategies and knowledge. In fact, the interplay between knowledge and strategies became the centrepiece of my work in the 1980s and early 1990s.

Over time, I became sensitive to the fact that knowledge and strategies, while essential for academic success, did not ensure that students learned well in school. I recognised that students' investment in their learning and their will to succeed (that is, *will*), combined with their interests or passions for learning (that is, *thrill*) mattered greatly in what they achieved academically. Thus, the integration of skill, will and thrill became a hallmark of my research.

As I engaged in teaching and research, I kept thinking back to my middle-school students and the changes I witnessed in them over the years. During the 1990s, I became increasingly concerned that educational research, my own included, was not answering the most fundamental question about formal education: What systematic changes should we see in the knowledge, strategic processing and motivations of our students if they are becoming more competent in the subjects we teach? This question led me to frame the Model of Domain Learning, or MDL. The MDL is a theory of academic development. It describes the systematic changes that should occur in students' knowledge, interest and strategic processing as they move from being acclimated or naïve in a field of study (for example, history or reading) to being competent and even expert in that domain. I have devoted much of my work in the past decade to testing the MDL and learning more about academic development. This pursuit has also led me to ask related questions about teaching and learning, such as: What do students believe about knowledge, and how do those beliefs affect their learning? What does it take to change students' pre-existing knowledge and beliefs? What can teachers do to be more persuasive in the classroom?

I am confident that these various questions about teaching and learning will keep me quite busy for the next several decades. But I am committed to paying homage to those middle-school students who set me on this career path so many years ago by learning all I can about the educational process so that all students have a chance to succeed academically to their full potential.

THEORY AND RESEARCH INTO PRACTICE

Because my research grew directly out of my experiences as a classroom teacher, I feel that its practical value is strong, although each phase of my research career has made its own unique contributions to teaching and learning. For instance, my early work on strategies served to identify particular strategies that would facilitate students' learning from text and resulted in the construction of lessons that could be directly and effectively applied in elementary, high-school and even college classes. Along with Stephen White, I developed the Test of Analogical Reasoning in Young Children, or TARC, that could be used to measure even preschoolers' ability to reason analogically (for example, cat : dog :: meow : ?). Analogical reasoning has been found to be a powerful tool in student learning and in the ability to transfer what is learned to new tasks or new contexts. The processes at the core of the TARC also became the basis for a classroom-based intervention that proved successful in teaching students of varying ages and abilities to reason analogically.

One of the contributions of the research on interest has been the realisation that some actions taken to spark students' interest, such as inserting personally interesting but tangentially important information in texts, can actually interfere with the learning of important information. This research on the 'seductive detail effect' was the brainchild of my mentor, Ruth Garner, and reminds us that not all the motivational tools we ply have the desired effects on students. Nonetheless, the research on interest reminds us how powerful student interests can be in promoting learning if used wisely.

More recently, I have been working with P. Karen Murphy and Helenrose Fives to understand teaching as a persuasive process. From decades of research on conceptual change and persuasion, we know that changing students' knowledge and beliefs can be extremely difficult. Yet, students cannot become well educated or more competent in a domain unless they can abandon naïve understandings or perceptions in favour of more sophisticated ones. Further, in the persuasion literature, it is recognised that our knowledge and beliefs shape how we engage in learning and what we come to learn as a consequence. By teaching persuasively, teachers learn how to recognise and incorporate students' pre-existing knowledge and beliefs into instruction, and how to make their own instruction more interesting and convincing to their students. The persuasive lessons we have constructed have resulted in much deeper learning for participating students.

In terms of the MDL, I believe that there are values to be realised not only for students, but also for teachers, parents and the general public. For instance, I believe that models like the MDL make us aware that we still know too little about the systematic changes that students *should* experience, if they are gaining from the educational experience. It also cautions policy makers that efforts to hold students, teachers and schools accountable for learning must be based on an understanding of what it really means to become educated. Testing factual knowledge or basic skills in a domain is only one piece of academic development. If such content and processes become the singular or primary focus of education, we risk hampering the full development of students, whose deeper knowledge, strategic abilities and motivations are not given adequate attention in the classroom.

At a minimum, the research I have done these past decades reminds us that there is much we can do to help students acquire the knowledge, strategies and interests that are essential to the educated mind.

KEY REFERENCES

Alexander, P. A. (1997) Mapping the multidimensional nature of domain learning: The interplay of cognitive, motivational, and strategic forces. In M. L. Maehr & P. R. Pintrich (eds) *Advances in Motivation and Achievement*, Volume 10 (pp. 213–50). Greenwich, CT: JAI Press.

Alexander, P. A. & Jetton, T. L. (2000) Learning from text: A multi-dimensional and developmental perspective. In M. L. Kamil, P. B. Mosenthal, P. D. Pearson & R. Barr (eds), *Handbook of Reading Research*, Volume III (pp. 285–310). Mahwah, NJ: Lawrence Erlbaum Associates.

Alexander, P. A. & Judy, J. E. (1988) The interaction of domain-specific and strategic knowledge in academic performance. *Review of Educational Research*, **58**, 375–404.

ACTIVITIES

1 Patricia Alexander believes that all students benefit from becoming more strategic and self-regulated. What are the elements of being a strategic and self-regulated learner, and how may teachers facilitate this?

2 Patricia Alexander briefly describes her Model of Domain Learning, which describes systematic changes that should occur in students' knowledge, interest and strategic processing as they move from being novice to expert learners. Complete an Internet search on MDL and describe in detail its elements.

3 Patricia Alexander asks three questions: What do students believe about knowledge, and how do those beliefs affect their learning? What does it take to change students' pre-existing knowledge and beliefs? What can teachers do to be more persuasive in the classroom? Provide answers to these questions and discuss your answers with fellow students.

4 Analyse the *seductive detail effect*. Why do you think it might interfere with student learning?

5 Patricia Alexander talks of the need to change students' naïve understandings to more sophisticated and accurate ones through persuasion. What are the elements of persuasive teaching that are appropriate for teachers to use?

6 Read and critique one of the key references and relate the content to material covered in this chapter.

Cognitive load theory

Closely connected with information processing and transfer is cognitive load theory (CLT). **Cognitive load theory** is concerned with the design of instructional methods that efficiently use people's limited cognitive processing capacity to apply acquired knowledge and skills to new situations (Paas, Tuovinen, Tabbers & Van Gerven 2003; Kester, Kirshner & van Merriënboer 2005). There is a considerable research base underlying principles derived from cognitive load theory (Paas, Renkl & Sweller 2003). However, it is beyond the scope of an introductory text to deal with this in detail. You are recommended to consider the Research and Theory into Practice treatment of John Sweller's research, and to read *Educational Psychologist*, 38(1), which is dedicated to cognitive load theory.

QUESTION POINT

Discuss the information processing model of learning. What classroom implications can be drawn from this learning theory? How is the information processing model of learning a constructivist one?

ACTION STATION

Reflect on your own knowledge of study skills. What knowledge do you have about the best ways for you to study for an exam? What strategies do you employ to maximise your attention, concentration and memory recall when studying for an exam? Make a brief list of these and highlight those most frequently used.

In groups of three or four students, compare your study skills knowledge and behaviour. Then discuss the following questions:

EXTENSION STUDY

How is knowledge organised and structured?

Anderson's ACT*

A theoretical information processing model of the learning process that has attracted a lot of attention from cognitive psychologists is John Anderson's Adaptive Control of Thought (ACT*) system, which uses a computer program to mimic human cognition and problem solving (Anderson 1982, 1983, 1990; Lohman 1989; Shuell 1986). The system is too complex to describe in detail here, but a few general points might give you an idea of how ACT* operates.

At its simplest, the model posits that the acquisition of new knowledge is related to three processes: the expansion of declarative knowledge, which deals with facts; the development of procedural knowledge, which deals with how to produce knowledge; and the transaction between the two.

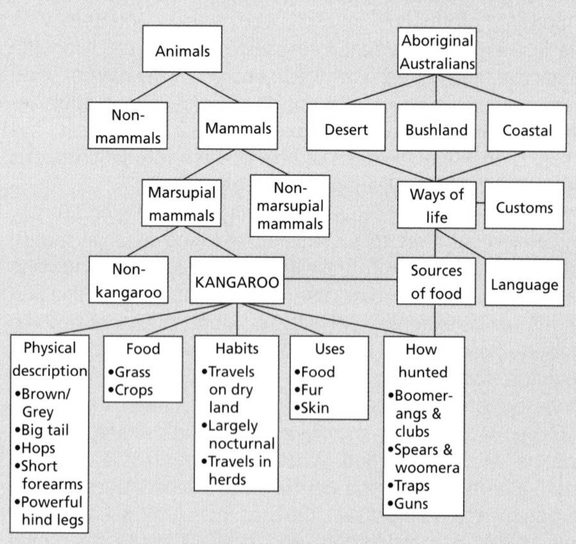

Declarative knowledge: A schema for the word 'kangaroo'

Declarative knowledge

Declarative knowledge is knowledge about things (for example, mathematical knowledge such as 7 + 3 = 10). This knowledge is hypothesised to be structured as an interrelated network of facts that exist as propositions. In other words, we don't know 'kangaroo' as a static concept; rather, we know about the concept 'kangaroo' because of its relationship to a number of other concepts such as animals, grass, hides, meat, farming and so on. Any one concept is networked with any number of other concepts, and it is this networking that ultimately gives the concept meaning and enables us to remember it. Furthermore, it is the richness of the networking that makes particular

1 Do you have a well-developed knowledge of study skills behaviours? Do you regularly use these skills? Why or why not?

2 How did you acquire your study skills behaviours and knowledge?

3 The efficient and effective use of study skills requires considerable practice and effort. Do you consider this practice and effort to be worthwhile?

4 What encourages you to use particular strategies and discourages you from using others?

Developmental implications of information processing theory

As with all models of learning, information processing has limitations. For example, the model implies that thinking and learning occur in a serial (linear) processing form, whereas we know that thinking and learning are more complex than this. (It is a recursive process.) Furthermore, the model fails to take into account motivation, affect and social interaction as elements affecting learning processes (Mageean 1991; Mayer 1996). Other essential elements of a full model of learning, such as social interaction and motivation, are examined elsewhere in the text.

Nevertheless, the model gives us many useful starters as teachers for considering how we might structure information in order to facilitate learning. In any event, to the present, no theory has successfully combined all the possible components of learning into an integrated and holistic theory. It is our job as teachers to construct this integrated theory within the context of our classrooms from the information we have available.

Apart from the general description of key components of the model of information processing, a number of information processing theories of development have

concepts more potent—that is, more easily retrievable from our long-term memory. Networks of connected ideas or relationships are referred to as **schemata** (a somewhat similar construct to that used by Piaget). We have presented in the illustration a schema for the word 'kangaroo' to illustrate declarative knowledge.

Procedural knowledge

Procedural knowledge is knowing how to perform various cognitive activities, such as how to do addition sums and solve verbal problems. In this case, there is a transaction between the declarative knowledge and the actions performed upon it (procedural knowledge—which in ACT* theory is called a production system; you can see how this model of thinking originated in the development of computerised, artificial intelligence).

When new information is encountered it is coded into a network of existing propositions or ideas (a schema). New information that fits into a well-developed and well-practised schema is retained far more readily than information that does not fit into a schema.

From this point the declarative knowledge is compiled into higher-order procedures (called *productions*) that apply the knowledge to solve problems. These productions are made in the following format: if a certain condition holds, then perform a certain action. For example, children acquire declarative knowledge about the number system through expository teaching. By linking the information they are receiving to already existing nodes, they develop a rather static understanding of mathematical concepts. Through a series of demonstrations by the teacher, the students learn to manipulate the number system in the IF–THEN form. For example, IF the goal is to do an addition problem, THEN add the numbers in the right-hand column. This sequence is called a **production**.

Productions are built up on one another; for example, a second production might be that IF the goal is to do an addition problem and the right-hand column has been added, THEN add the numbers in the second column. More and more sophisticated systems of productions are developed through processes of generalisation and discrimination so that increasingly difficult addition problems may be solved smoothly and efficiently (Shuell 1986). Depending on the positive and negative feedback that particular productions receive, better rules (higher-order processes) are strengthened and poorer rules are weakened.

The theory is useful for examining the differences in cognitive processing that characterise novices and experts in particular areas. The declarative knowledge of both groups may be equivalent, but the procedural knowledge of the expert is more efficient. The theory is also useful for thinking about the ways in which children should be introduced to problem solving, and the relationship that exists between knowledge and procedures for operating upon this knowledge.

Theory and research into practice

John Sweller — COGNITIVE LOAD THEORY

BRIEF BIOGRAPHY

I began conducting research on the psychology of learning in 1969 during the final honours year of my Bachelor degree in the Department of Psychology at the University of Adelaide under the supervision of Dr Tony Winefield. My intention was to progress to a Ph.D. but while my thesis went well, the associated coursework did not. After a somewhat mediocre result, I received my letter from the University of Adelaide regretfully informing me that I had failed to obtain the Ph.D. scholarship for which I had applied. A few months later, I received a second letter that, with no mention of the first, congratulated me on my successful scholarship application. I didn't argue and my research career commenced in 1970. Tony Winefield had been a great supervisor, so I chose to work with him again.

It was a period between eras. Behaviourism was dying and the cognitive revolution was starting. I commenced work on cognition but, in deference to behaviourism, used rats, the favoured species of behaviourists. After 18 months, the pendulum had swung sufficiently from behaviourism for even the densest Ph.D. student to realise that this route might not be a good career move. I switched to human problem solving and completed my thesis 18 months later.

From Adelaide I moved to Launceston in 1973 to take up a lectureship in education at what was then the Tasmanian College of Advanced Education. I liked the College and while Launceston is a very attractive small town, I like large cities, especially Sydney where I particularly wanted to live. At that time the Whitlam Labor government was in power and was vastly expanding teacher education. Good universities were having difficulty finding staff for the huge number of available positions. The situation was dire and I felt a Sydney institution might hire me out of desperation. Halfway through my first year in Launceston, an application for a lectureship in the School of Education at the University of New South Wales succeeded. I began in 1974 and am still there as a professor of education.

RESEARCH AND THEORETICAL INTERESTS

My research into problem solving continued at UNSW. In the late 1970s, while collecting data for one of my experiments, I noticed a strange effect. I was presenting sets of puzzle problems to my experimental participants who were first-year UNSW educational psychology students. The problems required the students to find a series of moves leading from the problem start to the goal. The correct series of moves could be described by a simple rule that was identical for each problem. Finding this series of moves was moderately difficult but curiously, while most of the students were able to find the correct moves, they seemed to learn almost nothing from the exercise. When presented with similar problems, they had no idea that all the problems had the same rule-based solution and that they had followed that rule in solving each problem.

What causes problem solvers to successfully solve a problem but remain oblivious to its essential structure? The reason, I suggested, lies embedded in some basic features of human cognitive architecture. We use working memory to deal with novel information, and working memory is severely limited in both capacity and duration when processing unfamiliar material. When solving a novel problem, we cannot make use of information in long-term memory and so must rely on working memory. Because working memory is limited, its resources are likely to be devoted entirely to finding a problem solution. Solving a problem and learning important structural features of the problem are largely unrelated activities. If working memory resources are devoted to problem solving, few resources are available to learn important structural features such as rule-based relations between moves. My problem solvers were using working memory to find a problem solution, not to learn how to solve the same problem subsequently. Learning, which would allow problem solvers to recognise a problem as belonging to a category of problems requiring particular moves for solution, was not occurring. In other words, because working memory was overloaded, there were minimal changes to long-term memory. If nothing changes in long-term memory, nothing has been learned.

Cognitive load theory was born from these findings and the theoretical constructs used to explain them. Subsequent work established that, as was the case for puzzle problems, minimal learning occurred when students solved school-based mathematics or science problems. For instance, students learned more and so performed better on subsequent problem-solving tests by studying worked examples rather than solving the equivalent problems.

The two decades following this initial work saw cognitive load theory both develop as a theory and generate an increasing number of applications concerned with how to present information and how to organise the activities of learners to maximise learning. Initially, most of the relevant work was carried out by my research students and me. For some years, that work was either ignored or generated a degree of hostility. The times were against us and we had considerable difficulty convincing a sceptical field. Despite a near complete lack of empirical evidence, most of the field seemed convinced that problem solving was the best way to learn and that conviction resulted in the near total rejection of not only our original work on problem solving, but also our subsequent work on more general instructional design. Gradually, under the weight of evidence, views have changed. Today, cognitive load theory is widely accepted and most work on the theory is carried out by a large number of researchers from around the globe.

THEORY AND RESEARCH INTO PRACTICE

Cognitive load theory has generated many applications beyond the original work demonstrating that problem solving could interfere with learning and that learners would gain more from alternative activities such as studying worked examples. Only some of that work can be described here.

In the mid-1980s, we demonstrated that studying algebra worked examples was superior to solving the equivalent problems, resulting in the worked example effect. While we could readily obtain the effect using algebra transformation problems (for example, $(a + b)/c = d$, solve for a), when we attempted to obtain the same effect using geometry or physics, we consistently failed. It took several years to realise why. A geometry worked example usually consists of a diagram and its associated statements. Little can be learned from either in isolation. To understand a geometry worked example, we must simultaneously consider both the diagram and the set of statements and search for references between them. That activity requires working memory resources that consequently become unavailable for learning. The difficulty is eliminated by physically integrating the diagram and its statements. The advantage of physically integrated instruction over split-source instruction led to the split-attention effect.

It took another few years to realise that physically integrating all split-source information such as diagrams and text was not a good idea! If a diagram and text are unintelligible in isolation, they must be integrated, either physically or mentally, before they can be understood. Often, diagrams and text can be easily understood in isolation because they contain exactly the same information presented in a different form. Such material should not be physically integrated. Rather, the redundant material should be eliminated. Similarly, presenting the same information in both auditory and visual form, a common occurrence in today's power-point environment, decreases rather than increases learning compared with having an audience just listening or reading. Experiments demonstrating that the elimination of redundant information facilitated learning led to the redundancy effect.

The next instructional effect we studied was the modality effect. Working memory includes both an auditory processor for speech and a visual processor for two- or three-dimensional objects. The size of working memory can be somewhat increased by using both processors. Assume split-attention conditions where a diagram and text cannot be understood in isolation. Rather than integrating the verbal material into a single, visual entity, some of the verbal information can be off-loaded to the auditory processor by presenting the verbal material in spoken rather than written form. The superiority of this form of audio-visual presentation led to the modality effect.

All of these instructional advantages, and others, are obtainable using novice learners who have just begun learning a new area. As learners gain experience in an area, the effects gradually disappear. With additional experience, the effects reverse. Instructional procedures that are relatively advantageous with novices become relatively less effective than their alternatives. This effect is the expertise reversal effect, which is caused by redundancy. To give one instance, a set of worked examples may be beneficial for novices but once learning has progressed, studying worked examples may be less beneficial than practising solving problems. Worked examples are redundant and increase, rather than decrease, cognitive load for more experienced learners.

Cognitive load theory is continuing to generate instructional applications. For example, we are now studying the effects of asking learners to imagine a procedure or concept rather than studying. Imagining is effective if the material has been sufficiently well-learned to allow it to be manipulated in working memory; otherwise, studying the material is superior—another example of the expertise reversal effect. These and other effects suggest that new instructional procedures generated by the theory are far from being exhausted. Furthermore, the theory has not just generated applications; currently, it is being used to throw light on human cognitive architecture and its evolutionary origins. The logic that underlies evolution by natural selection may be identical to the logic that underlies human cognition. This work, along with work on applications, provides a pointer to possible future directions for the theory.

KEY REFERENCES

Sweller, J. (1999) *Instructional Design in Technical Areas.* Melbourne: ACER Press.

Sweller, J. (2003) Evolution of human cognitive architecture. In B. Ross (ed.), *The Psychology of Learning and Motivation*, Volume 43 (pp. 215–66). San Diego: Academic Press.

Sweller, J., van Merriënboer, J. J. G. & Paas, F. G. W. C. (1998) Cognitive architecture and instructional design. *Educational Psychology Review*, **10**, 251–96.

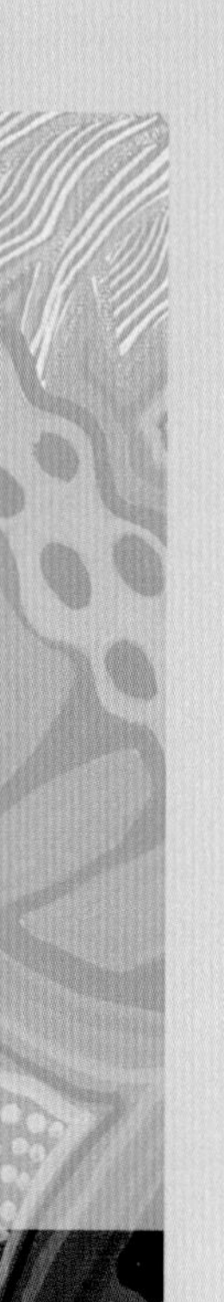

ACTIVITIES

1. John Sweller discovered the intriguing fact that problem solvers don't seem to generalise solutions across related problems. Why is this, and why is this information of importance to teachers?
2. What are the strengths and weaknesses of working memory?
3. Why are solving a problem and learning important structural features of a problem largely unrelated activities? How can we assist learners to see structural similarities in problems and save this information in long-term memory so that it is accessible to recognise and solve related problems in the future?
4. Traditionally teachers believed that solving problems was the way to teach students to be problem solvers. The work of John Sweller and others suggests that this is not necessarily the case and that studying worked examples could lead to better solving of new but related problems. How does cognitive load theory explain this phenomenon? What examples does John Sweller give to support his argument that worked examples are an effective method for teaching problem solving? What complexities did he and his co-researchers have to address in order to ensure that worked examples 'worked'?
5. John Sweller makes the interesting point that power-point presentations that have text supported by identical verbal presentation may be quite ineffective. Why is this so? What should we do to make these presentations more effective? In particular, examine his concept of the modality effect and split attention and how these might be used most effectively to facilitate attention and learning.
6. Discuss the expertise reversal effect. How would our knowledge of this effect influence the instructional design of our lessons?
7. We strongly recommend that you read one or more of the key references listed above.

been constructed (Case 1985a; Klahr & Wallace 1976; Siegler 1991; Sternberg 1985). It is beyond the scope of this text to describe these in detail. Table 4.6 summarises key elements of the theories, and readers are recommended to read Siegler (1991) for further information.

As children grow older there is an increase in short-term memory capacity and processing and encoding skills, an improvement in retrieval from long-term memory, and increasing development and use of cognitive strategies and self-monitoring metacognitive skills to enhance encoding, retention and retrieval. These developments occur as children are exposed to novel learning experiences, particularly modelling by parents, teachers and peers. At present it is not possible to say whether these changes reflect structural changes in the child's information processing capacity (akin to Piaget's changes across stages) or whether they are functional capacity changes as the child becomes more expert in cognitive strategy use (Flavell 1985).

Table 4.6 Overview of information processing theories of development

Theorist	Goal of theory	Main developmental mechanisms	Formative influences
Sternberg	To provide an information processing analysis of the development of intelligence.	Strategy construction based on the use of knowledge acquisition components, metacomponents and performance components. Also encoding and automatisation.	Information processing theories' emphasis on encoding, time, course of processing, and dividing thinking into components. Intelligence-testing emphasis on individual differences in intellectual ability.
Case	To unite Piagetian and information processing theories of development.	Automatisation and biologically based increases in working memory, both of which increase processing capacity. Also strategy construction.	Piaget's emphasis on stages of reasoning and on between-concept unities in reasoning. information processing theories' emphasis on short-term memory limits automatisation and problem-solving strategies.
Klahr & Wallace	To formulate a computer simulation model of cognitive development.	Generalisation based on the workings of regularity detection, redundancy elimination and the time line. Also encoding and strategy construction.	Piaget's emphasis on self-modification and on assimilation. information processing theories' emphasis on encoding and on computer simulation as a means for characterising thinking.
Siegler	To understand the adaptive character of cognitive development.	Choices among existing strategies and construction of new strategies. Also generalisation.	Piaget's emphasis on self-modification and equilibration. information processing theories' emphasis on adaptation to the task environment and on computer simulation.

Source: Reprinted with permission from R. S. Siegler (1991) *Children's Thinking*, 2nd ed. p. 68, © Pearson Education, Inc., Upper Saddle River, NJ.

WHAT WOULD YOU DO?

HE'LL SPEAK TO HIS BRAIN

Andrew was a very slow writer. He constantly stared into space and was easily distracted and yet didn't admit he had a problem. Miss O'Brien believed that a lot of Andrew's behaviour was linked to being afraid of getting it 'wrong' and she had her suspicions that pressure came from home. She developed a strong relationship with Andrew and he eventually admitted to her that he had a problem with his writing.

One day when Miss O'Brien was working with Andrew, she asked him why he couldn't write what was in his head. He said, 'When I get up to five things in my head they burst like a bubble—it's like trying to pick up a bubble; when you touch it, it bursts.' It was a real insight into Andrew. He had just shown her how able he was at using and controlling language to capture his thoughts and feelings. He had identified his short-term memory problems. After that Andrew really unburdened himself, saying that he was anxious that Mum and Dad might realise he had a problem and that he believed himself that he couldn't write. Together Miss O'Brien and Andrew devised three ways to help.

Case studies illustrating National Competency Framework for Beginning Teaching, National Project on the Quality of Teaching and Learning, Australian Teaching Council, 1996, p. 10. Commonwealth of Australia copyright, reproduced by permission.

What three ways would you suggest? See the teacher's solution below.

WHAT WOULD YOU DO? (cont.)

HE'LL SPEAK TO HIS BRAIN

Together Miss O'Brien and Andrew devised three ways to help.

First, they had a book of ideas which Andrew could carry around, and when he saw or did something interesting he could make a note of it. Second, he would 'speak to his brain' on a daily basis to explain to his brain that he was a writer. Third, they would celebrate his writing together and in front of the class.

Two days after this discussion, Andrew came to Miss O'Brien and asked her if he could write a story on an idea that had come to him from the book they were reading in class.

Case studies illustrating National Competency Framework for Beginning Teaching, National Project on the Quality of Teaching and Learning, Australian Teaching Council, 1996, p. 10. Commonwealth of Australia copyright, reproduced by permission.

What do you think of these solutions? Are they similar to any suggestions you made? How does this case study illustrate principles of information processing?

KEY TERMS

Acrostics and acronyms (p. 107): memory devices using first letters of concepts to facilitate recall

Automaticity (p. 117): a process that occurs when information or operations are overlearned and can be retrieved and used with little mental effort

Chunking (p. 106): a mental strategy by which we break long and complex series into smaller chunks to facilitate learning and recall

Classification table (p. 111): the grouping of objects that are alike into categories according to common characteristics

Coding frame (p. 111): (cognitive) a hierarchy of ideas and concepts to organise knowledge

Cognitive load theory (p. 126): concerned with the design of instructional methods that efficiently use people's limited cognitive processing capacity to apply acquired knowledge and skills to new situations

Cognitive strategies (p. 123): cognitive approaches that enable the learner to attack a problem more effectively

Concept map (p. 111): a two-dimensional diagram representing the conceptual structure of subject matter

Declarative knowledge (p. 126): knowledge about memory and facts, definitions, generalisations and rules

Distributed practice (p. 118): practice spread over time with rest intervals

Encoding (p. 101): the process by which we represent information mentally

Information processing (p. 96): the human mind's activity of receiving, storing and retrieving information

Information processing constructivism (p. 96): focuses on the learner actively selecting, organising and integrating incoming experience with existing knowledge to create understanding

Interference effect (p. 120): the process that occurs when remembering certain information is hampered by the presence of other information

Keyword method (p. 107): mnemonic associating new words or concepts with similar-sounding cue words and images

Learning set (p. 103): learning expectations

Learning strategies (p. 114): plans for approaching learning tasks

Massed practice (p. 118): practice concentrated in long periods

Meaningfulness (p. 102): connecting new ideas with ideas already stored in long-term memory

Method of loci (p. 107): a mnemonic device involving the association of items to be remembered with a series of places, or loci, that are already fixed in memory

Mnemonics (p. 107): memory devices that aid retrieval

Overlearning (p. 117): practising past the point of mastery

Part learning (p. 117): unit of learning broken down into subunits for learning

Pegword mnemonics (p. 110): a mnenomic device that involves associating items to be learned with appropriate keywords that are easily visualised

Perception (p. 101): interpretation of sensory information

PQ4R (p. 106): a system for reading for understanding involving previewing, asking questions, reading, reflecting, reciting and reviewing

Proactive facilitation (p. 120): earlier learning assists later learning of new material

Proactive interference (p. 120): earlier learning interferes with new learning

Procedural knowledge (p. 127): knowledge of how to perform various cognitive activities

Productions (p. 127): higher-order procedures that apply knowledge to solve problems

Retention (p. 101): the transfer to memory of material for later retrieval

Retrieval (p. 101): the process of accessing information from long-term memory

Retroactive facilitation (p. 120): later learning consolidates earlier learning

Retroactive interference (p. 120): new learning impedes the retrieval of old learning

Schemata (p. 127): networks of connected ideas or relationships

Sensory input (p. 99): receiving stimuli through the senses

Serial position effect (p. 118): remembering the beginning and end of lists while forgetting the middle

Short-term memory (p. 102): working memory, holding a limited amount of information briefly

Transfer of learning (p. 122): the application of knowledge learned in one context to another related context

Whole learning (p. 116): focusing on the full unit of learning and binding it together into a meaningful whole

Working memory (p. 98): a store for the performance of mental operations

ON-LINE LEARNING

If you go to http://www.pearsoned.com.au/mcinerney, you will have hot links directly to these sites:

- **Personality papers**

Read the article entitled 'One intelligence or many' and discuss the issues raised in the context of the material covered in this chapter. You can scroll through the first site (where you will see many interesting papers and their responses) or use the second web address to go straight to the article.

http://wps.prenhall.com/mcinerney_au/0,7245,72915-,00.html; http://www.personalityresearch.org/papers/paik.html

- **Application and misapplications of cognitive psychology**

Read the article by Anderson, Reder and Simon, and discuss the issues raised in the context of this and other relevant chapters.

http://act-r.psy.cmu.edu/papers/misapplied.html

WEB DESTINATIONS

If you go to http://www.pearsoned.com.au/mcinerney, you will have hot links directly to these sites:

■ Theory into practice

This site will give a brief introduction to information processing.

http://tip.psychology.org/index.html

■ The information processing approach

This is a good site for exploring elements of information processing as a theory of learning. Don't forget to use the hot links in this site.

http://teach.valdosta.edu/whuitt/col/cogsys/infoproc.html

■ Mind tools memory

This link is part of the extensive Mind Tools site that covers many of the topics discussed in this chapter.

http://www.mindtools.com/memory.html

■ Mind tools information skills

This link is part of the extensive Mind Tools site that covers many of the topics discussed in this chapter.

http://www.mindtools.com/page3.html

■ Mind tools problem solving

This is an interesting site that covers many of the topics discussed in this chapter.

http://www.mindtools.com/page2.html

■ Learning to learn

Learning to Learn is a useful site that discusses a whole range of cognitive skills, including mnemonics.

http://www.ldrc.ca/projects/projects.php?id=26

RECOMMENDED READING

Alexander, P. A., Kulikowich, J. M. & Jetton, T. L. (1994) The role of subject-matter knowledge and interest in the processing of linear and nonlinear texts. *Review of Educational Research*, **64**, 210–52.

Anderson, J. R., Reder, L. M. & Simon, H. (1996) Situated learning and education. *Educational Researcher*, **25**, 5–11.

Cox, B. D. (1997) The rediscovery of the active learner in adaptive contexts: A developmental-historical analysis of transfer of training. *Educational Psychologist*, **32**, 41–55.

Dochy, F., Segers, M. & Buehl, M. (1999) The relation between assessment practices and outcomes of studies: The case of research on prior knowledge. *Review of Educational Research*, **69**, 145–86.

Garner, R. (1990) When children and adults do not use learning strategies: Toward a theory of settings. *Review of Educational Research*, **60**, 517–29.

Halford, G. S. (1993) *Children's Understanding: The Development of Mental Models*. London: Lawrence Erlbaum.

Kail, R. & Bisanz, J. (1992) The information-processing perspective on cognitive development in childhood and adolescence. In R. J. Sternberg & C. A. Berg (eds) *Intellectual Development*. New York: Cambridge University Press.

Mayer, R. E. (1996) Learners as information processors: Legacies and limitations of educational psychology's second metaphor. *Educational Psychologist*, **31**, 151–61.

Pressley, M., Harris, K. R. & Marks, M. B. (1992) But good strategy instructors are constructivists! *Educational Psychology Review*, **4**, 3–31.

Pressley, M., Johnson, C. J., Symons, S., McGoldrick, J. A. & Kurita, J. A. (1989) Strategies that improve children's memory and comprehension of text. *The Elementary School Journal*, **90**, 3–32.

Pressley, M. & Woloshyn, V. (1995) *Cognitive Strategy Instruction that Really Improves Children's Academic Performance*. Cambridge, MA: Brookline.

Semb, G. B. & Ellis, J. A. (1994) Knowledge taught in school: What is remembered? *Review of Educational Research*, **64**, 253–86.

Shuell, T. J. (1986) Cognitive conceptions of learning. *Review of Educational Research*, **56**, 411–36.

Shuell, T. J. (1990) Phases of meaningful learning. *Review of Educational Research*, **60**, 531–47.

Weinstein, C. E. & Hume, L. M. (1998) *Study Strategies for Lifelong Learning*. Washington DC: American Psychological Association.

Winne, P. H. (1995) Information-processing theories of learning. In L. W. Anderson (ed.) *International Encyclopedia of Teaching and Teacher Education*, 2nd ed. Tarrytown, NY: Pergamon.

Wood, E. *et al.* (2003) Can gender stereotypes facilitate memory when elaborative strategies are used? *Educational Psychology*, **23**, 169–80.

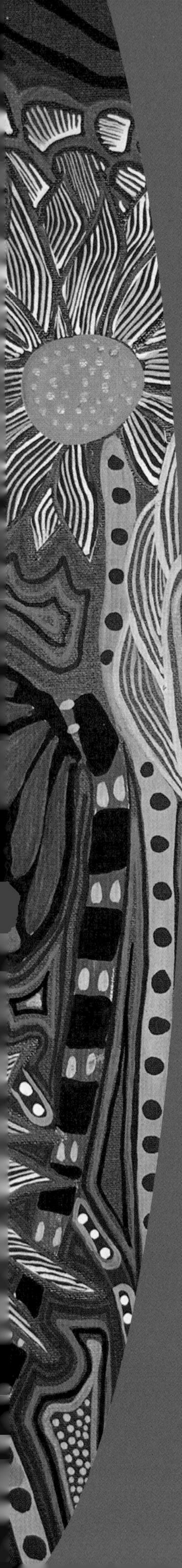

CHAPTER

5 Alternative cognitive views on effective learning

Overview

Teaching practices based on cognitive views of learning vary widely. In this chapter, the perspective shifts from a cognitive constructivist view that emphasises the reproduction of knowledge in the form in which it was presented (the information processing approach) to a constructivist view that emphasises the construction and reconstruction of knowledge as interpreted by an individual. Discovering personal understanding becomes a very significant part of the learning process. In this context we discuss Gestalt psychology and Bruner's theory, as examples of personal constructivism, and consider their teaching implications.

We then compare Bruner's approach with that of Ausubel, an example of information processing constructivism. Classroom practices based on Ausubel's theory are discussed and compared with those of Bruner.

We also consider some important recent developments in cognitive psychology—namely, metacognition, learning strategies and self-regulated learning. Finally, we consider situated cognition and distributed cognition, examples of social constructivism being applied in theory and practice.

5

Learning objectives

After reading this chapter, you will be able to:

- describe the nature of cognitive psychology and how it has influenced the interpretation of the learning process;
- discuss the importance of meaningfulness to effective learning;
- describe Gestalt psychology and its relationship to personal constructivism;
- describe Bruner's theory of intellectual development and its relationship to personal constructivism;
- define discovery learning and discuss its strengths and weaknesses as a pedagogical method;
- describe Ausubel's theory of reception learning and its relationship to information processing constructivism and personal constructivism;
- discuss the strengths and weaknesses of reception learning as a pedagogical method;
- compare and contrast teaching approaches derived from the theories of Bruner and Ausubel, and argue for the relevance of each for particular learning episodes;
- define and describe metacognition as an element of constructivism;
- list essentials of learning environments to encourage students' use of metacognitive strategies;
- define self-regulated learning and discuss its relationship to metacognition and constructivism;
- define and discuss examples of social constructivism exemplified by situated cognition and distributed cognition.

This chapter deals with alternative views on effective learning. At the end of this chapter you should be able to illustrate, with examples, the competencies outlined in our Teaching Competence Box 5.1.

Gestalt psychology and personal constructivism

Cognitive psychology has influenced learning theory and classroom practice in several significant ways. **Cognitive theories of learning** place emphasis on the way knowledge is represented and structured in memory. Teachers influenced by cognitive theory view learning as an active, constructive process that involves higher-level procedures. Furthermore, cognitively oriented teachers believe that learning is cumulative and that the prior knowledge of the learner plays a fundamental role in the acquisition of new knowledge. Cognitively oriented teachers analyse learning tasks and performance in terms of the cognitive processes involved, and select content and instructional procedures to engage the psychological processes and knowledge structures appropriate for the students to achieve the desired learning outcomes. Meaningful learning occurs when individuals are able to discover knowledge for themselves, perceive relations between old and new knowledge, apply their knowledge to solve new problems, communicate their knowledge to others and have continuing motivation for learning. Our first example of how this works deals with Gestalt psychology.

Gestalt psychology contributes to our understanding of how individuals personally construct meaning. Wertheimer, the founder of the Gestalt movement in

TEACHING COMPETENCE **Box 5.1**

The teacher structures learning tasks effectively

Indicators

The teacher:

- manages and paces teaching time to meet student learning goals;
- provides for individual differences in rates and styles of learning;
- links new content and processes with prior learning, contexts and interests;
- uses purposefully a range of material, human and technological resources.

Case studies illustrating National Competency Framework for Beginning Teaching, National Project on the Quality of Teaching and Learning, Australian Teaching Council, 1996, Element 3.4, p. 49. Commonwealth of Australia copyright, reproduced by permission.

What'll we do?

Germany (Gillam 1992; Wertheimer 1980), was impressed by the fact that humans do not usually perceive events as individual or disparate elements, but as whole, unified patterns, rather like how the units of a motion picture (the individual photographs) are perceived as moving images when played at a particular speed. He believed that, because of the capacity of our perception, we always have a tendency to structure our world into meaningful patterns (the word *Gestalt* means pattern), and that when we structure disparate elements into a whole the whole is greater than its parts. We are familiar with this principle whenever we listen to a musical composition composed of discrete notes, view a work of art composed of discrete colours, or view a digital photograph made up of hundreds of thousands of pixels.

Human insight

Gestalt organising principles

Koffka (1935; Wertheimer 1980) also did much to popularise Gestalt ideas and experimented with the organising tendencies of perception. These organising tendencies were grouped together as a series of 'laws', the most general of which was ***pragnanz***—which refers to the tendency we all have to organise unorganised stimuli into patterns that make some sense to us. In other words, when faced with a problem we attempt to organise the features of the problem so that we have some insight into it. At a simple level this may be illustrated by our solving a jigsaw puzzle. In the first instance, we may gather similar items together (for example, all the pieces that have blue on them). This is referred to as the *law of similarity*. At other times, two or three connecting pieces may fortuitously lie together on the table and we perceive this and join them. This is referred to as the *law of proximity*. As we complete more of the puzzle we perceive spaces that may be completed by particular pieces with the appropriate shape or colour. This is called *closure*. And finally, we organise pieces with flat edges along the outside. This is called the *law of continuation*. Using these perceptual processes helps us to solve the jigsaw puzzle.

Similarity
Proximity
Closure
Continuation

Gestaltists believe that we use these same processes naturally every day (although usually unconsciously) in our interaction with the world around us, and that they are the means by which we learn much about the world. At the moment of forming the complete pattern or realising the solution to the problem (for example, in a crossword) we are said to experience an insight, colloquially referred to as the 'ah ha' experience. We hope that at least on some occasions while reading this text you will also have some 'ah ha' experiences.

As you have probably gathered, Gestalt psychologists view learning as a purposive, exploratory, imaginative and creative enterprise. For Gestaltists, learning is a change of insight. These theorists are concerned with important cognitive processes such as problem solving, decision making and perception. When faced with problematic situations, people bring an analytic ability to bear which enables them first to structure the problem and then to solve it through cognitive processes.

Learning viewed as purposive, exploratory, imaginative and creative

Classroom applications of Gestalt psychology

The Gestalt approach has had a great impact on the world of education generally, with teachers implementing the principles shown in Table 5.1, which are drawn from this theoretical approach.

QUESTION POINT

Constructivists believe that cognitive processes such as perception and memory involve interpretation. Do you agree? In what ways are interpretative processes involved in perception and memory?

Gestalt psychology was a forerunner of a number of other cognitive theories that have had a significant impact on classroom materials and procedures. In the following sections we describe two key theories, and draw out those elements that have most clearly impacted upon classroom practices and the development of materials for learning and teaching.

Table 5.1

Essentials of a Gestalt approach for education

Teachers should:

- provide for *insightful learning*, which is the key to effective meaningful learning;
- structure the learning environment with materials necessary for *discoveries* to be made, such as in learning centres;
- motivate learners through their *intrinsic interest* in solving problems;
- deal with *principles* rather than specifics;
- provide *imaginative* and *exciting curricula*;
- demonstrate how *abstract principles* can be drawn from *specific concrete examples*.

Teachers should teach learners to:

- actively *search for patterns* in apparently unconnected materials;
- brainstorm, then *draw together ideas* into similar or dissimilar concepts;
- *create puzzles* for others to solve.

Teaching Competence Box 5.2 points out the importance of teachers selecting educational processes appropriate to the curriculum and field of inquiry. In our next sections, we consider the educational processes proposed by Bruner and Ausubel. Try to imagine how you would demonstrate the competency indicators while reading this material.

Box 5.2

TEACHING COMPETENCE

The teacher understands the relationship between processes of inquiry and content knowledge and uses educational processes appropriate to the curriculum and the field of inquiry

Indicators

The teacher:

- demonstrates the relationship between subject matter and appropriate modes of inquiry;
- encourages students to pursue processes of inquiry appropriate to curriculum content;
- utilises approaches to learning which explore the breadth of modes of inquiry;
- builds a repertoire of teaching approaches to facilitate and enhance students' knowledge and understanding;
- implements learning programs that enable students to learn from experience;
- uses resources to facilitate students' understanding.

Case studies illustrating National Competency Framework for Beginning Teaching, National Project on the Quality of Teaching and Learning, Australian Teaching Council, 1996, Element 1-2, p. 30. Commonwealth of Australia copyright, reproduced by permission.

Bruner's theory of cognitive development and learning

Bruner's stages of intellectual development

Bruner theorised that children go through three main stages of intellectual development. In the first stage children learn about the world around them by acting on objects. In a sense, an object is what you can do with it. A glass is used to drink from, a bed is to lie in, clothing is to wear, and so on. This stage is referred to as the **enactive** stage. Children progress from this stage to the **iconic** stage, where experiences and objects are represented as concrete images. Children no longer need to manipulate objects in order to learn about them, but can learn through models, demonstrations and pictures. Children can operate mentally with pictures. Lastly, children enter the **symbolic** stage when they develop the capacity to think abstractly with symbols. In this stage, individuals go beyond the present and concrete experiences to create hypotheses. For Bruner, it followed that instruction of children should also be sequenced. In other words, for learning to occur best, children should first experience it, then react to it concretely, and finally symbolise it. While progression is believed to be in order through these stages, more mature learners who are already at the symbolic stage often function best when two or more of the modalities are called upon when learning about something new.

If you wanted to learn how to use a new camera, you could simply have the operations explained to you (*symbolic explanation*). Under this circumstance, you would probably find it difficult to absorb the information and use it effectively. You might, alternatively, be shown a diagrammatic representation of the

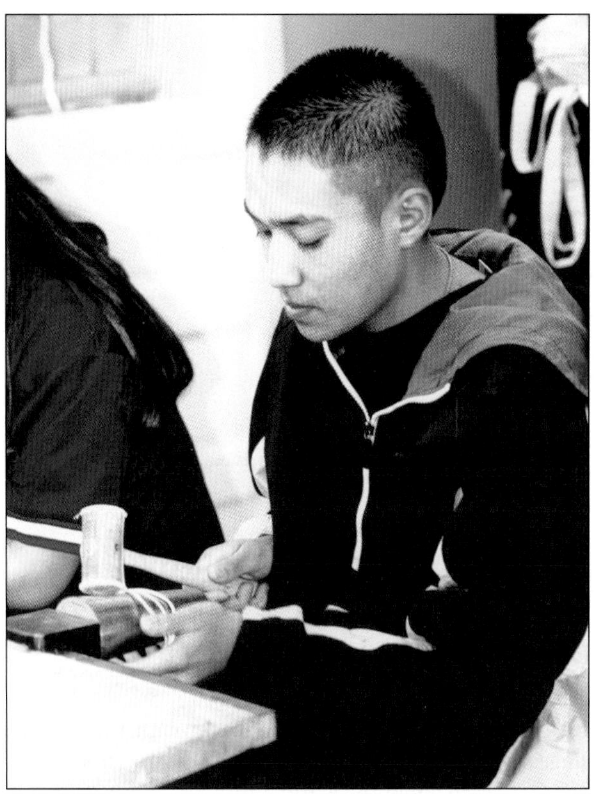

Learning by doing is important in Bruner's theory. This Navajo student is learning to make jewellery.

camera while being given the explanation (*iconic explanation*). In this case, your understanding would be enhanced. However, you would probably feel most at ease and learn most efficiently if an explanation were given to you while you were handling the camera (*enactive explanation*). At a later time, you might simply refer to the verbal instructions or pictures to refresh your memory about what you had been taught. Bruner's principle is that, at any age, teachers will get a better result with learners if they combine concrete, pictorial and symbolic presentations of the material. It should also be apparent that material that can be presented only in symbolic form should not be taught until children have acquired this mode of operation. A key to successful teaching is giving learners the opportunity to operate on material at appropriate levels of abstraction.

Personal constructivism and learning

Bruner's theory reflects many of the tenets of *personal constructivism*. Bruner believes that discovery of connections and patterns is central to meaningful learning, and he emphasises the importance of imagination and discovery to effective learning. We look at each of these in more detail below.

Bruner believes that schools should structure learning experiences so that they are appropriate to each student's level of development. Schools should also facilitate the development of flexible thinking in children by encouraging intuitive thinking as well as analytic thinking. *Analytic thinking* characteristically proceeds step by step and the learner is, in general, aware of the information and operations involved. This is the type of thinking commonly encouraged in schools, and is most often used in mathematics and science. **Intuitive thinking** is characterised by hunches and solutions not based on formal processes of reasoning. Intuitive thought is based on a feeling one has for a particular subject in its wholeness. As a consequence, it does not necessarily advance in carefully defined steps but tends to involve spurts and leaps reflecting the individual's perception of the total problem. Bruner believes that schools should establish an intuitive understanding of materials in children before exposing them to more traditional methods of deduction and proof.

The need to develop flexible thinking

Bruner believes that the basic ideas of science, mathematics and literature are as simple as they are powerful, and are capable of being translated to any level of experience. For this reason, he advocates the use of a **spiral curriculum** for developing concepts at increasingly higher levels of abstraction. If teachers of young children, for example, begin teaching the foundations of subjects in a manner appropriate for the pupil's intellectual development, the groundwork for later development is effectively laid. It is important that later teaching builds on earlier reactions and understandings, and that it seeks to create an ever more explicit and mature understanding of particular concepts. For example, understanding great human tragedy as reflected in the works of Shakespeare can be built on a young child's understanding of the concepts of happy and sad, developed through exposure to stories in kindergarten and primary classes, and extended through later grades in moral dilemmas, re-creations through role play or dramatisations, and story writing. Understanding of complex mathematical concepts can be based on work carried out with Dienes blocks. While the general principle of building on children's prior knowledge is a characteristic of most curriculum programs, few schools have implemented a fully integrated spiral curriculum. What would this involve?

Discovery learning

We have suggested in a number of places that the construction and reconstruction of knowledge may be personal and idiosyncratic. Indeed, from this perspective,

Science discovery enhances learning. What might these students be learning? What difficulties might they be experiencing?

effective learning occurs when individuals are able to incorporate knowledge (both mental processes and content) for themselves into their cognitive structures. A number of principles may be deduced from the work of Bruner for application in constructivist-based classroom settings that relate to students discovering knowledge for themselves, which would seem to be a good reflection of constructivist theory. Bruner believes that learning should progress from specific examples to general principles by way of induction. One way to achieve this is through the use of **discovery learning**, which refers to the learning of new information as a result of the learner's own efforts (Tamir 1995; see also De Jong & Van Joolingen 1998; Mayer 2004). The subject matter is not presented to the child in its final form, but rather the child, through their own manipulation of the materials, discovers relationships, solutions and patterns. In the past, discovery learning reflected a personal constructivist approach; however, more recently, it has become associated with group work and so reflects a social constructivist perspective. Advocates of discovery learning believe that the following advantages characterise this approach:

- Discovery learning is more meaningful and hence results in better retention. Principles that emerge from discovery are significant because they come from the student's own work.
- Discovery learning enhances motivation, interest and satisfaction.
- Discovery learning enhances the development of intellectual capacities, information and problem-solving skills. Students learn how to discover, how to learn, and how to organise what they have learned.
- Discovery learning encourages transfer of skills to solve problems in new contexts.

Classrooms using discovery learning need to be resource-rich. Teachers need to abandon their role as purveyors of knowledge and become facilitators of children's learning. To perform this function well, teachers need to be well prepared and competent in their understanding of the basic underlying principles of their discipline. This is particularly important in handling the range of 'discoveries' and personal interests that may characterise any one group of children in the classroom. Teachers must also be willing and able to try a variety of approaches to accommodate the varying needs of children and their modes of cognitive reasoning (enactive, iconic and symbolic).

Far from being easy for the teacher, discovery learning approaches are demanding of organisation and management skills. Novice teachers will need to anticipate thoroughly the sorts of needs the children will have in terms of movement around the learning space, noise and activity levels, resources, and guidance about the purpose of the learning activity. The quality of learning needs to be carefully monitored throughout, and interventions made to focus student attention on salient issues emerging from their discovery. 'Chalk and talk' approaches often appear far easier to manage and to ensure that concepts the teacher feels are important are imparted in their entirety. What do you think?

Beware—students may need considerable guidance

Teaching through discovery is demanding on the teacher

in their discoveries, because they have a developing knowledge base and are inexperienced in drawing 'scientific' conclusions on the basis of random pieces of evidence in the same way as adults do. Think back to Bruner's spiral curriculum and consider how you might structure development of important concepts in children over a period of time.

Pure versus guided discovery learning

There has been a debate for a long period of time over whether discovery learning episodes should be relatively unstructured, what might be termed 'pure' discovery methods, or discovery guided by the teacher through prompts, direction, coaching, feedback and modelling in order to keep the student on track (Mayer 2004). The reasoning of proponents of guided discovery is that pure discovery is not cost–effort-effective, does not necessarily lead to better understandings and the incorporation of new information with an appropriate knowledge base, and, in many circumstances may lead to inaccurate or useless discoveries. That this debate is still 'hot' is attested to by the article by Richard Mayer (2004) listed in the recommended readings. Read the article and weigh the pros and cons for guided discovery.

Summarised in the following box are some of the problems that have been associated with implementing effective discovery learning environments (see De Jong & Van Joolingen 1998; Tamir 1995).

PROBLEMS IN IMPLEMENTING EFFECTIVE DISCOVERY LEARNING ENVIRONMENTS

- Lack of skills by teachers.
- Lack of appropriate resources.
- Time pressure to complete the mandated curriculum.
- Difficulties encountered by students, especially slower learners.
- Failure by teachers to recognise the need to give individual assistance and guidance according to the abilities of the children.
- Generation of anxiety in students, with teachers being unsure of how to proceed.
- The challenge of discovery learning—especially in science, where hypothesis generation, design of experiments, interpretation of data and regulation of learning may be too high and lead to failure and dissatisfaction.

Table 5.2 lists the essentials for education of Bruner's discovery learning approach.

QUESTION POINT

Discuss the advantages and disadvantages of discovery learning. Compare this with Vygotsky's notion of assisted discovery.

Table 5.2 Essentials of Bruner's discovery learning approach for education

Teachers should:

- redefine the teaching role as *facilitator* rather than transmitter of knowledge;
- stimulate learning and inquiry by setting *challenging problems* for students to solve;
- provide *resource-rich* learning environments;
- provide opportunities for students to *interact with material* enactively, iconically and symbolically;
- allow for *individual differences* in ability, interest and prior experience;
- monitor the *quality of learning* taking place in terms of students' ability, interest and experience;
- revisit material at *increasingly higher levels of abstraction*.

Teachers should teach learners to:

- *participate actively* in learning experiences—do not sit idle;
- *ask questions* while investigating: 'What does this mean?', 'How is this similar to . . ./different from . . .?';
- touch; draw pictures and diagrams; write summaries and descriptions of experiences.

Ausubel and reception learning

As we have stated throughout this and other chapters, cognitive learning theorists have one central concern, and that is to make learning meaningful rather than encouraging rote methods of learning. However, the range of beliefs as to how this is best achieved is vast. As evidenced above, Bruner believes that the most effective way is for learners to discover or induce principles from examples through the process of discovery learning. For Ausubel (1963, 1966a, 1966b, 1968, 1977), however, concepts should be presented more directly as principles embedded in meaningful examples related to what children already know. In Ausubel's theory, effective learning occurs when learning is meaningful and students acquire personal understandings. However, Ausubel believes that personal meanings can be achieved through the transmission of information from the teacher to the learner. It is what the learner does with the information that is important. Ausubel's approach has become known as *reception learning*.

How might the use of an advance organiser have helped this student focus on the lesson?

How does reception learning operate in the classroom?

In **reception learning** the material to be learned is presented to learners in a relatively complete and organised form. We have noted that in discovery learning, learners are expected to discover much of the material for themselves and to organise it in their own way. Ausubel maintains that in most classrooms learning is through reception, and that discovery learning is inefficient and not necessary in most circumstances. The focus of attention should be on how to make reception learning most effective.

To this end, the teacher uses expository methods such as *demonstration*, *explanation* and *narration*. Practising skills in varied circumstances and revision are also important. Equally importantly, Ausubel warns against abuses of teaching techniques that may lead to meaningless learning. A number of these methods are presented in the box below.

Demonstration
Explanation
Narration

TEACHING TECHNIQUES THAT LEAD TO MEANINGLESS LEARNING

- premature use of verbal approaches with cognitively immature learners;
- arbitrary presentation of unrelated facts without any organising or explanatory principles;
- failure to integrate new learning tasks with previously presented materials;
- use of evaluation procedures that merely measure ability to recognise discrete facts or to reproduce ideas in the same words or in the identical context as originally encountered.

Source: Ausubel (1968), p. 18.

To help children learn verbal material, Ausubel recommends what he calls **expository teaching** in which material is organised in a deductive sequence—that is, from the most inclusive to the most specific—and is presented to students in a relatively finished form through expository methods. To prepare students for the material, Ausubel (1966b, 1978) also advocates the use of advance organisers. As mentioned earlier, an **advance organiser** is a set of ideas or concepts that is given to the learner *before* the material to be learned. It is meant to provide the stable cognitive structure to which new learning can be anchored. Organisers can also be used to facilitate recall.

Two types of organiser are suggested by Ausubel. The first is the **expository organiser**, which is to be used with new material and presents an overview of the relevant concepts to attend to. For example, the teacher might say, 'Today we are going to learn about rats. I want you to notice the following aspects of . . .' The second type, the **comparative organiser**, is used with material that is somewhat familiar. This type of organiser is likely to make use of similarities and differences between new material and existing cognitive structure. For example, the teacher might say, 'Today we are going to learn about green apples. Remember, yesterday we learned that red apples had . . .'

Considerable research (Corkill 1992; Mayer 1989; Van Patten *et al.* 1986) has also taken place into the effectiveness of advance organisers, showing they are an effective teaching strategy when:

- they are presented as written analogies in paragraph form as diagrams and models;
- they are used with older students;
- there is sufficient time and help to use the organiser to make connections with previous understanding.

Table 5.3 summarises the essentials for education of Ausubel's reception learning model.

Much ink has been used in debating the relative effectiveness of discovery versus meaningful reception learning. You will address some of the issues in activities related to this chapter.

QUESTION POINT

Consider Ausubel's notion of meaningful reception learning. Does the provision of guiding principles and analogies by the teacher reflect principles of constructivist learning?

Metacognition and constructivism

The ability to plan, monitor and regulate our cognitive processes while constructing knowledge is considered by many to be essential to effective learning. The following Learner-centred Psychological Principle introduces the very important topic of metacognition: Why might the students' awareness of metacognitive processes—and, in particular, their ability to plan, monitor and regulate their cognitive processes—promote more effective learning?

LEARNER-CENTRED PSYCHOLOGICAL PRINCIPLE

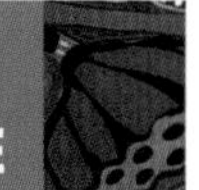

Thinking about thinking. Higher-order strategies for selecting and monitoring mental operations facilitate creative and critical thinking.

Successful learners can reflect on how they think and learn, set reasonable learning or performance goals, select potentially appropriate learning strategies or methods, and monitor their progress towards these goals. In addition, successful learners know what to do if a problem occurs or if they are not making sufficient or time progress towards a goal. They can generate alternative methods to reach their goal (or reassess the appropriateness and utility of the goal). Instructional methods that focus on helping learners develop these higher-order (metacognitive) strategies can enhance student learning and personal responsibility for learning.

Table 5.3 Essentials of Ausubel's reception learning model

Teachers should:

- logically *organise material*;
- *link material* to what children already know;
- relate material directly to the *learner's existing concepts*;
- use *effective expository teaching methods*—in particular, explanation, narration and demonstration;
- present *advance organisers* (expository and comparative) to the learner before the material to be learned is presented;
- present material to be learned in a *variety of contexts*;
- *review material* presented and learned and *provide effective feedback*;
- apply acquired learnings in *novel situations* to demonstrate transferability.

Teachers should teach learners to:

- think about how the new information *fits in with what is already known*;
- *ask questions* (of teachers and peers) to clarify understanding;
- *think of examples* of principles given.

What is metacognition?

One of the key principles of constructivism is that students are self-directed in their learning. Not only are educators interested in learners acquiring the facts and figures of knowledge, but they are also interested in their acquiring the skills, strategies and resources needed to perform learning tasks effectively. Just as important is the ability to know when and how to use particular learning strategies. In other words, students need knowledge about how to monitor their cognitive resources (what we call **metacognition**) and how they learn (called *metalearning*) in order to learn more effectively (Brandt 1986; Costa 1984; Derry & Murphy 1986; Flavell 1976, 1979, 1985; McKeachie, Pintrich & Lin 1985; Marzano & Arredondo 1986a, 1986b; Shuell 1988; Thomas & Rohwer 1986; Weinstein & Mayer 1986). Many teachers, as part of their routine teaching, try to encourage the development of metacognitive skills in their students. Other teachers, however, emphasise content acquisition at the expense of learning skills acquisition and give very little attention to student needs in this area. Some simple techniques used by teachers to promote the development of metacognitive skills have been discussed by Anderson and Hidi (1989), Costa (1984), Costa and Marzano (1987), Dart and Clarke (1990), Derry (1989), Marzano and Arredondo (1986a, 1986b), Pressley *et al.* (1989), and Weinstein and Mayer (1986). These involve the teacher encouraging the students to:

- ask questions about processes;
- reflect on their learning;
- problem solve by thinking aloud;
- be flexible in their approach to learning;
- develop learning plans;
- learn to summarise.

One very obvious feature of all classrooms is that some students seem to learn particular concepts and processes very easily, while others make heavy work of the learning. Effective learners appear to have more knowledge about their own memory and are more likely than poor learners to use what they do know. This is sometimes referred to as **declarative knowledge**. Effective learners also have knowledge of a range of cognitive skills, using them strategically and automatically. This is referred to as **procedural knowledge**. Such students plan ahead, define goals and develop a strategy for reaching them. They monitor their performance while using that strategy, correcting errors and then checking at the finish to see that they have completed what they set out to do. Finally, effective learners know when and why to apply various cognitive skills. This is referred to as **conditional knowledge** (see Biggs 1987a, 1987c; Schraw & Moshman 1995; Shuell 1988; Thomas 1988).

It is believed that metacognitive knowledge appears early and continues to develop at least throughout adolescence. Adults, because of their greater experience, tend to have more knowledge about their own cognition than younger people, and are also better able to describe it. However, children as young as six can reflect with accuracy on their own thinking, especially when asked to do it with familiar material (Schraw & Moshman 1995).

Reflect on your own study skills knowledge and behaviour. What knowledge do you have about the best ways for you to learn? What techniques and strategies do you employ to maximise your attention, concentration and memory recall when studying for an exam? Make a brief list of these techniques and strategies. How effective are they? Compare with others in your group.

Self-regulated learning and metacognition

In earlier sections we discussed the components of metacognition. However, research indicates that young children often find it difficult to use their knowledge about memory and learning strategies to regulate their cognition (Flavell, Miller & Miller 1993; Schraw & Moshman 1995). A reason for this is that children have not integrated their metacognitive knowledge and regulatory skills. As a consequence, many of the skills that might be used remain unused and difficult to apply. As we have suggested earlier, it is probably very useful to teach even young children metacognitive and learning strategies (see, for example, Perry 1998; Wood, Motz & Willoughby 1998).

Closely allied to metacognition is the process of self-regulation, which some see as the motivational equivalent of metacognition (Prawat 1998). Educators agree unanimously that the most effective learners are also self-regulating. Self-regulated learners set goals for learning, decide on appropriate strategies, monitor their learning by seeking feedback (both self-generated and external) on their performance, and make appropriate adjustments for future learning activities. Self-regulated learners are thus aware of the qualities of their own knowledge, beliefs and motivation, and cognitive processing, and adjust their strategies and goals to make progress (Butler & Winne 1995; Winne 1995b). Butler (1998) conceives of strategic learning in terms of a model of self-regulation. She believes self-regulated learners begin by analysing

Theory and research into practice

Douglas J. Hacker — METACOGNITION AND SELF-REGULATION

BRIEF BIOGRAPHY

In a short essay about the importance of the relationship between students and teachers, Alan Lightman asks a critical question, 'Yet without a good teacher, a young student of science could read a row of textbooks stretching from here to the moon and not learn how to practice the trade. Exactly what is it, in this age of massive information storage and retrieval, that you can't learn from a book?' (Lightman, 1996, p. 30). When I first read this question, my immediate answer was the *practice* of science as learned through a mentor. My mentor at the University of Washington was the late Earl Butterfield, who distinguished himself in several areas but most prominently in the area of transfer. He was also an impeccable research methodologist.

Under the tutelage of Dr Butterfield, I was introduced to several areas of research, including metacognition, writing processes, and of course, transfer. But more importantly, regardless of the content area, what I learned was the practice of science: how to theorise in a specific domain, how to develop testable hypotheses, how to develop rigorous methodology to test those hypotheses, and how to interpret the findings. Since my graduation in 1994 as an educational psychologist, during my five years at the University of Memphis, and currently in my tenure at the University of Utah, I have tried to practise science in the way my mentor lived science. Perhaps the most important point that I had learned from his example was that there is always a better way to investigate a research question. Later in the same essay written by Lightman, he provides an answer to his own question, 'Perhaps in the end, our own imperfection is the most vital thing we learn from teachers' (p. 38). Realising the imperfections in my own research, accepting those imperfections, and developing better ways to investigate my questions has kept me active in science, and my mentor is in no small way responsible for this.

RESEARCH AND THEORETICAL INTERESTS

Most of my work has been directed to two areas of research: metacognitive processing, and the connections between reading and writing processes. In the metacognitive area, I have concentrated primarily on calibration accuracy—that is, the degree to which people's judgments of performance match actual performance. The specific types of judgments that I have been examining are predictions and postdictions. *Predictions* are judgments made before performance and involve psychological processes in which a person *assesses* both task-centred and person-centred variables. The former variables include such things as the kind of test, the particular domain to be tested, or how 'tricky' the instructor tends to be; and the latter include what a person knows about the particular domain that is to be tested, how much effort was put forth towards studying, how proficient he or she is at taking tests, and a variety of affective beliefs, including how 'good' one feels on the particular day of the test, or for some, how lucky they feel. *Postdictions*, although related to predictions, are judgments made after performance and involve primarily *evaluative* processes that require a person to evaluate which questions were known, which were probably known, and which were definitely not known.

As one would expect, postdictive judgments tend to be more accurate than predictive judgments, but the majority of calibration research has shown that even though judgments of performance are better than chance, people, in general, do not show high levels of predictive or postdictive accuracy. Higher-performing students tend to be more accurate but slightly underconfident in their predictions and postdictions as compared to lower-performing students, who tend to be less accurate and overconfident, with the lowest-performing students showing gross inaccuracy and overconfidence. In addition, people tend not to show improvements in their calibration, even under conditions in which treatments to improve accuracy are administered.

There have been numerous investigations into the reasons for poor calibration that have focused on methodological problems, statistical analyses, and on identifying other variables that could contribute to calibration accuracy. My recent research in this area has focused on the last of these alternatives. Psychological processes that have been mostly overlooked in calibration research involve social–cognitive factors. I have identified several social–cognitive variables and am currently investigating their correlations with the accuracy of students' predictive and postdictive judgments. The social–cognitive variables I have concentrated on so far are explanatory style variables (also known as attributional style) and social variables. The explanatory style variables (that is, how people explain discrepancies between anticipated outcomes and actual outcomes) focus on task-centred and person-centred explanations, and the social variables focus on the influence of 'others' on metacognitive judgments.

Preliminary results have shown significant correlations between accuracy of judgments and all three of these social–cognitive factors. However, because accuracy appears to vary with test performance, I have developed mediation models using academic achievement as a mediator between these variables and the accuracy of predictive and postdictive judgments. What these models suggest is that the social–cognitive factors do play a role in a person's metacognitive judgments, but the amount of knowledge a person has about a particular subject mediates this role. That is, the use of external attributions and negative academic self-appraisals to explain discrepancies between metacognitive judgments and performance is associated with lower performance, and lower performance is associated with less accurate judgments. Conversely, the lack of external attributions and the presence of positive academic self-appraisals are associated with higher performance and more accurate judgments.

In sum, based on my preliminary findings and on findings from other areas of metacognitive research, it appears likely that people do not simply make objective judgments on what they know or do not know. Rather, their judgments are being shaped, in part, by personal attributes, such as internal and external locus of control, social influences and academic self-appraisals. Because calibration accuracy may be influenced by a global self-concept of ability in addition to actual performance, this may be one reason why calibration accuracy is so resistant to change. Self-appraisals are, in general, very durable. However, this particular line of research has only just begun and these interpretations await further empirical confirmation.

My second research direction focuses on how the psychological processes of reading and writing are combined to result in learning. In these investigations, I have been using a multiple methods approach. In addition to using conventional measures of comprehension and knowledge growth, I have been using eye-tracking technology to track the fine-grained course of cognition as students acquire knowledge from text and then use that knowledge to write. Although eye tracking has been used for at least the last 20 years in reading research, to my knowledge, this is the first use of the technology in the analysis of writing.

There are numerous measures of reading behaviour made available through eye-tracking technology, but because there are problems with using only one of these, researchers have adopted a strategy in which several of the measures are used concurrently to converge on a particular interpretation. The measures that I have been using include: fixation duration (the amount of time the eyes fixate at a particular point in a text); second pass reading time (the amount of time spent rereading a portion of text); gaze duration (the total amount of time of all fixations made on a text segment prior to a forward saccade to another segment); and regressions (saccades in which the reader looks back at previously read parts of the text).

The use of eye-tracking technology to track eye movements during a writing task allows me to track the fine-grained level of the links between how readers comprehend text, how they write about their comprehension, and how they go back to the text or their writing to reread or rewrite. Using this technology, I am able to track each word as it is written, revised or deleted, where and when written ideas take form in relation to text that is read, how entire sections of written text are edited, and how people navigate between reading and writing, to name but a few.

Preliminary results have shown that the kind of reading and writing that leads to learning consists of regular and frequent checking back to the text and the written text, sequences of short segments of writing followed by long periods of editing, high frequency of text words used in the written text, and that, with greater frequency of navigations between written and read texts, writers become more strategic in their reading. There may be other characterisations of reading and writing that lead to learning, depending on the nature of the writing task; however, it appears that high interactivity between reading and writing, high levels of revision and strategic reading, and long periods of reflection between the generation of new ideas are critical elements of reading/writing-to-learn.

THEORY AND RESEARCH INTO PRACTICE

The primary goal of my research has been to inform and advance educational practice. In the area of calibration research, I have been motivated, in part, by the current educational atmosphere of high-stakes testing and accountability. The responsibility of adequately preparing students for testing rests with many, but of course, much of this responsibility must rest squarely on the students' shoulders. If students are to become effective self-regulated learners, it is essential that they are deeply involved in their own preparation for and performance on tests.

An important ingredient in their preparation and performance is the ability to assess prior to testing how well they will perform (predictive accuracy), and subsequent to the testing, evaluate how well they did perform (postdictive accuracy). Therefore, knowing the psychological processes involved in these self-judgments is essential to helping students maximise the effectiveness of their self-regulated learning.

My goal to inform and advance educational practice also has motivated my research in the area of reading and writing processes. As nearly everyone has experienced for themselves, the use of reading and writing is nearly ubiquitous in schools from the early primary grades to higher education. With such prevalence in the use of reading and writing tasks to facilitate learning, the overall impression is that there is little doubt that this combination of processes leads to learning and that there is no doubt that reading and writing should be in all classrooms. Yet surprisingly, the empirical base supporting the effectiveness of reading and writing processes to promote learning is weak, and theoretical conceptualisations of writing-to-learn are nearly nonexistent.

My goal in this line of research, therefore, is to provide researchers and educators with the empirical and theoretical bases to effectively design reading/writing-to-learn tasks that make use of cognitive and metacognitive strategies that can enhance students' learning. Instruction in these areas has too often been directed by intuition and anecdotal evidence, and research has not been tremendously helpful for teachers. Knowing the psychological processes of combining reading with writing and developing instruction that can better guide and drive those processes hopefully can do much to improve learning. Over the past 30 years, writing researchers have provided teachers with good theoretical bases on which to base instruction. My belief is that it is time to make the next steps in the expansion of theory using new tools to develop more effective instruction that is more usable by teachers.

KEY REFERENCES

Hacker, D. J. & Dunlosky, J. (2003) Not all metacognition is created equal. Problem-based learning for the information age. *New Directions for Teaching and Learning*, **95**, 73–80.

Hacker, D. J., Bol, L., Horgan, D. & Rakow, E. A. (2000) Test prediction and performance in a classroom context. *Journal of Educational Psychology*, **92**, 160–70.

Hacker, D. J. (1998) Metacognition: Definitions and empirical foundations. In D. J. Hacker, J. Dunlosky & A. C. Graesser (eds) *Metacognition in Educational Theory and Practice*. Mahwah, NJ: Erlbaum.

Further reference

Lightman, A. (1996) *Dance for Two*. Students and teachers (pp. 29–38). New York: Pantheon Books.

ACTIVITIES

1. Doug Hacker refers to calibration accuracy—that is, the degree to which students can accurately predict their performance on a task, or explain or evaluate their completed performance in terms of their prior learning and abilities. He suggests that most people are quite inaccurate. Why is it important for students to be able to accurately predict and explain their performance? What reasons does he give for lack of calibration accuracy among students? What solutions does he offer? And how is this information of use to teachers?
2. Why do you think lower-performing students are less accurate and more overconfident in both their predictive and postdictive judgements? Relate your answer to what you know of metacognitive processing.
3. Doug Hacker discusses the importance of social–cognitive variables in predictive and postdictive judgments. What are these social–cognitive variables, and why are they potentially influential?
4. Doug Hacker utilises eye-tracking to analyse the reading–writing process and its relationship to effective learning. What new insights have been gained through this approach to research?
5. What is the relationship between metacognition and self-regulation as outlined by Doug Hacker?

tasks and interpreting requirements in terms of their existing knowledge and beliefs. They then set task-specific goals, which they use as a basis for selecting, adapting and even inventing appropriate strategies to accomplish their objectives. Self-regulated learners monitor their progress towards these goals, evaluating the success of their efforts. They adjust their learning approaches on the basis of their perceived progress. Finally, self-regulated learners adaptively use motivation and will-power to keep themselves on task when they become discouraged or meet an obstacle. We have covered a number of specific learning strategies in Chapter 4 and you should review these in the context of our discussion of self-regulated learning.

Feedback is very important in stimulating self-regulation and metacognitive behaviour. Information from self-generated and external feedback, particularly in terms of how one thinks progress is going relative to existing goals and strategies, orients the student's future choice of goals, and the strategies to achieve them. To be most effective, feedback should not only provide information about the mastery of material but also

Concentration and reflection are important components of metacognitive awareness

information for guiding the use of strategies for processing the information effectively—what we might term *cognitive feedback* (see Butler & Winne 1995). We discuss self-regulated learning in more detail in Chapter 6. However, consider the material prepared by Doug Hacker on the relationship between metacognition and self-regulated learning presented on pp. 146–8.

Importance of feedback

Reciprocal teaching and guided peer questioning

Effective teachers promote learning by providing their students with strategies for monitoring and improving their own learning efforts as well as with structured opportunities for independent learning activities (Porter & Brophy 1988). As we have seen, students can be trained in the use of such metacognitive strategies as planning, monitoring and evaluating, which help them to control their own learning. One approach to such training is **reciprocal teaching**, developed by Palincsar and Brown (1984; see also Hacker & Tenent 2002; Hart & Speece 1998; Wright & Jacobs 2003). This is a cooperative teaching method in which students are shown the processes involved in reading comprehension through teacher modelling, and then progressively trained in their use. For students with difficulty in reading comprehension, research has shown that this approach has significant benefits (Alfassi 1998; Moore 1991; Hart & Speece 1998; Wright & Jacobs 2003). In reciprocal teaching the teacher, as expert, first models the strategies of:

- *summarising* a reading passage ('What is this passage about?');
- *predicting* ('What is going to follow?');
- *clarifying* ('What don't I understand?'); and
- *asking questions* about the main message of the passage ('What do I think this means?').

Students then practise these strategies aloud as the teacher monitors, providing feedback on the purpose of each strategy and the student's developing use of it, and gives encouragement (*scaffolding*—see our earlier material on Vygotsky and social constructivism) until they demonstrate they have mastered the strategies. This teacher support is gradually withdrawn as the students transfer to cooperative peer groups in which they take on greater responsibility for using the skills with each other. Such active involvement by students in their own learning provides the motivation needed for the 'deep learning' of higher-order cognitive processes (Biggs 1991a).

This cooperative technique also provides students with a metacognitive strategy that develops their problem-solving skills. Alison King (1991; see also King 1992a, 1992b, 1994; King, Staffieri & Adelgais 1998;

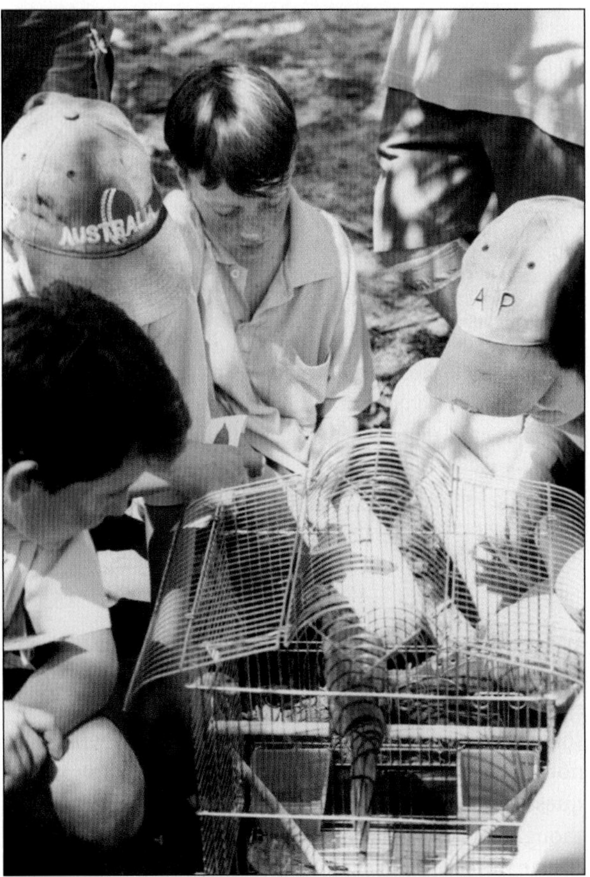

Reciprocal teaching has been shown to encourage the development of metacognitive strategies

EXTENSION STUDY

Does metacognitive training improve student learning?

Considerable research has been directed towards understanding metacognitive and metalearning processes in the classroom and how these processes may enhance learning (Anderson & Walker 1990; Bakopanos & White 1990; Biggs 1987a; Dart & Clarke 1990; Mageean 1991; Pressley & Woloshyn 1995; Swan & White 1990; Watkins & Hattie 1981; White & Gunstone 1989; Winne 1997; Wright & Jacobs 2003). Students develop some metacognitive and self-regulating strategies as a normal part of their own learning and observing others learn, in lieu of explicit instruction (see, for example, Winne 1997). However, while these strategies may be effective, they may also be limited and faulty. Consequently, explicit instruction in strategy use with appropriate feedback will, in most cases, enhance student learning and also enable students to develop further their repertoire of strategies. There are a number of programs designed to teach students to be self-regulated and metacognitive learners. Three programs are the *Project for the Enhancement of Effective Learning (PEEL)* (Loughran, Mitchell, Neale & Toussaint 2001), the *Study Habits Evaluation and Instruction Kit (SHEIK)* (Jackson, Reid & Croft 1980; White & Baird 1991) and the *Strategic Content Learning Approach* (Butler 1998).

The Strategic Content Learning Approach is a tutoring package that can be used one-to-one with an instructor, within a peer tutoring framework or within a group-based study skills program. There are five key instructional components (Butler 1998). First, instructors help students to engage in a complete range of cognitive processes central to self-regulation. This involves effective feedback to the students so that they can appreciate the usefulness of specific strategies. Second, help is provided in the context of meaningful tasks. This is facilitated by providing choice to students so that they work on tasks that are important to them. Third, social interaction is encouraged through interactive discussions as students and teachers collaboratively work on tasks. Fourth, explicit and structured strategy instruction is provided. This involves: focusing discussion on the cognitive processes required to self-regulate learning; requiring students to talk about their emerging understandings about the tasks, criteria for performance, strategic approaches and the outcomes of monitoring; and asking students to keep records of strategies that work for them. Fifth, instructional activities are designed to promote students' construction of productive metacognitive knowledge and beliefs. In other words, students are encouraged to think about the learning process itself, and to focus on the relationship between using strategies and performance improvements. In this way, students can be taught to control their own learning. Butler (1998) believes that utilising these five principles helps students to learn effectively. In particular, embedding instruction within meaningful tasks may help students to recognise the usefulness of strategies. Students are also likely to feel ownership over strategies that are personally meaningful, and are therefore more likely to transfer these to other learning situations. Helping students to see the relationship between effort, the use of strategies and improved task performance should also increase self-efficacy and positive attributions for success, which should further enhance motivation for future tasks. Helping students to construct metacognitive knowledge about strategic processing based on concrete task experiences should help them to develop general principles of strategy use that can be applied in a variety of circumstances. Finally, giving appropriate feedback and support, and encouraging students to think about their learning and to monitor their strategy

Wright & Jacobs 2003) has demonstrated that training pairs of children in **guided peer questioning** or the use of strategic questions (see below) improved their problem-solving ability, compared with those children who were not given any structure for discussion. In this guided questioning approach, students are trained to ask thought-provoking questions and to generate elaborated explanatory responses. In the sequence of questioning, students asked and answered questions in a reciprocal manner so that the thought-provoking question by one elicited an explanatory response by the other, leading to a gradual building of knowledge. King *et al.* (1998) believe that this approach is successful because it ensures that partners carry out specific cognitive activities known to promote learning, such as rehearsing orally, accessing prior knowledge, making connections between ideas, elaborating ideas, assessing accuracy of responses and monitoring metacognitively. It is apparent that providing some structure for peer tutoring is important so that students don't simply interact on the basic knowledge-implementation, should enable them to become reflective learners, which should assist them during subsequent learning activities. Research indicates that students taught using the Strategic Content Learning Approach developed better metacognitive knowledge about key self-regulated processes and constructed more positive perceptions of task-specific self-efficacy. Evidence also suggests that students' attributional patterns become more positive, and they become actively involved in developing personalised and focused strategies, transferring strategies across contexts and flexibly adapting strategic approaches across tasks. Task performance is also enhanced.

The Project for the Enhancement of Effective Learning (PEEL) is also concerned with encouraging students to be more metacognitive through the development and use of teaching procedures that emphasise the need for students to think about their own thinking, rather than to passively follow procedures and routines that concentrate simply on completing tasks. A main focus of PEEL classrooms is, therefore, an emphasis on having students question what they are doing and why, while they are learning (Loughran, Mitchell, Neale & Toussant 2001). In particular, this will include students actively processing, synthesising, analysing, and applying knowledge and skills. PEEL also emphasises a range of what it calls good learning behaviours to foster effective learning. These good learning behaviours are outlined below:

- seeking assistance;
- checking progress;
- planning work;
- reflecting on work;
- linking ideas to each other;
- developing a view.

Australian studies using the PEEL show that students can improve in metalearning as a result of direct teaching of metacognitive skills. A study with 19 16-year-olds from Essendon Grammar School, Victoria, who were given training in reflective thinking, showed that those with such instruction increased the quality of their learning as evidenced by the depth of their questions at the end of the study (Bakopanos & White 1990; Loughran, Mitchell, Neale & Toussant 2001).

Another study (Swan & White 1990) investigated whether students could be trained to become more conscious, purposeful learners through writing statements about their learning processes in class. Students of a Year 3 class were given an exercise book which they labelled 'Thinking Book'. The training involved a cycle in which:

- the children reflected on their learning each day and wrote in their thinking books;
- the teacher reflected on their entries and wrote a response in each book;
- the next day the child read the teacher's response and thought about it in making the next entry.

The two main objectives of the teacher in writing the responses were for the children:

- to increase links between what they were learning, what they already knew and their out-of-school experience;
- to become more active in learning through questioning things they did not understand, the purposes of classroom activities and the effectiveness of their work habits.

The results indicated that the children increased markedly in their formation of links with prior knowledge and their own past experiences. It also showed that the students asked questions to find out more about the things that interested or puzzled them.

Both these studies illustrate the potential benefits to be achieved from training students in metacognitive skills. Both cases also illustrate, however, that interventions to increase metalearning may have to alter the ingrained habits of years and cannot be brief. As such, they have to be part of the normal program, not taught as separate lessons (Swan & White 1990).

retelling level. (We even find that this happens at the graduate level unless some stimulating structure is provided.) On the other hand, too much structure might constrain discussion and thinking. A fine line needs to be walked and it is probably through experience that a teacher finds out what works best. One approach to structuring peer tutoring interactions has been designed by Alison King and has the catchy title 'ASK Your Partner to Think' (King *et al.* 1998). This approach tries to provide structure that facilitates high-level complex learning while at the same time being realistically able to be used by same-age peers to scaffold each others' learning. More detail on this program is given in King *et al.* (1998). This approach is certainly worth your consideration.

ASK Your Partner to Think . . . strategic questioning

In the guided questioning approach, students are given the following types of questions (adapted from King 1991) as prompts for discussion during problem-solving activities:

- *Planning*
  What's the problem?
  What do we know about it so far?
  What's our plan?
  How else can we do this?
  What should we do next?
- *Monitoring*
  Are we using our strategy properly?
  Is it time for a new one?
  Has our goal changed?
  What is it now?
  Are we on the right track to our goal?
- *Evaluating*
  What worked and what didn't?
  How would we do it next time?

Effective teachers can help their students to become more effective learners by teaching them the strategy of **reciprocal peer questioning** (Rosenshine, Meister & Chapman 1996). In this technique, students are taught to use open-ended, generic question stems to create their own content-specific questions about expository material presented in classroom lectures. They then take turns asking these questions and responding to each other's questions in small cooperative groups, to help each other learn the material (King 1990, 1994, 1997). The level of questions used should differ according to whether the students are learning factual material for recall or are expected to construct new knowledge. In the former case learning can be accomplished through verbal interaction that consists of asking for and providing information. When knowledge construction is the aim, higher-order questions requiring analysis and synthesis are required. As such, these question sequences might include the mutual exchange of ideas, explanations, justifications, speculations, inferences, hypotheses, conclusions and other high-level interactions (King *et al.* 1998). Higher-order interactions seem to facilitate better quality learning.

Examples of generic question stems that can be used in mutual peer tutoring are:

- How are . . . and . . . similar?
- What is the difference between . . . and . . .?
- What do you think would happen if . . .?
- What is a new example of . . .?
- Explain why . . ..
- What conclusions can you draw about . . .?
- How would you use . . .?
- What are the strengths and weaknesses of . . .?
- How is . . . related to . . . that we studied earlier?

Using this technique, students are truly cognitively active in their own learning. They have to make mental connections between ideas and link this with previous knowledge. When students have to explain, elaborate or defend a point of view, their learning is greatly improved. This is because of the active need to *construct* the material cognitively for themselves, and then to reconstruct it in a way that is relevant and meaningful to another person. Much research has shown that, in peer tutoring and small-group work, those students who do the explaining or summarising learn the most compared with those who listen to explanations or check for errors (Brown & Campione 1986; Dansereau 1988; Webb 1989; Webb & Farivar 1994). For older learners, cooperative group work in which generic question stems are used to assist revision of new material enhances achievement, self-concept and sense of mastery (McInerney & McInerney 1996b; McInerney, McInerney & Marsh 1997). This approach represents a social constructivist approach to learning, because the interaction between the students facilitates their learning. We deal with peer tutoring again and cooperative learning in Chapter 8.

It is apparent, and we have all probably experienced this, that when members of a group or pair provide explanations of material to be learned, their own learning is enhanced. Why do you think this happens? King *et al.* (1998) suggest that explaining something to someone else probably improves understanding for the individual doing the explaining because it forces the explainer to clarify concepts, evaluate and conceptually reorganise material, recognise and reconcile inconsistencies, and probably change the individual's own way of thinking about the material. The cognitive benefits of such tutoring are reciprocated when students act as partners in alternating tutor–tutee roles (King 1997).

ACTION STATION

In groups of three or four, compare your knowledge and practice of effective learning strategies. Then discuss the following questions:

1. Do you have a well-developed knowledge of learning strategies? Do you regularly use them? Why or why not?
2. How did you acquire your knowledge of these learning strategies?
3. The efficient and effective use of learning strategies requires considerable practice and effort. How can the teacher ensure that students have this practice and make the necessary effort?

QUESTION POINT

Should classroom teaching and learning be based on metacognitive principles? How might such classrooms operate? What might be the role of the teacher in a metacognitively oriented classroom?

QUESTION POINT

What is metacognition? What are the generally accepted components of metacognition?

QUESTION POINT

How do Vygotskian theorists explain the development of metacognitive processes? How does this view differ from the Piagetian view? (Refer to Chapter 2.)

Table 5.4 lists the essentials of learning environments to encourage students to use metacognitive strategies.

Can students change their approach to learning?

It is clear from research that both adults and children use learning strategies inadequately. For example, both adults and children often fail to monitor their cognitions. Such faulty monitoring is evidenced when children fail to listen to instructions and when adults' minds wander while they are reading. Perhaps this is happening to you at this very moment! How often do you stop and ask the question 'Am I understanding this?' It is also apparent that students don't utilise a range of cognitive strategies, such as summarising and reviewing, that could make learning more efficient and effective (Garner & Alexander 1989).

Teaching learning strategies

There is considerable evidence, however, that learning strategies can be taught and generalised beyond the original instructional context, and that study skills enhancement courses are successful in elevating student

Table 5.4 **Essentials of learning environments to encourage student use of metacognitive strategies**

Teachers should:

- provide an explicit *statement of goals, expectations and standards*;
- provide an *appropriate level of cognitive challenge* in tasks;
- provide encouragement and support for *active engagement* of the learner in processing and cognitive monitoring of material;
- provide latitude for *self-direction* in learning;
- *reduce emphasis on performance-oriented tasks* and competitive grading;
- provide support for the development of *self-efficacy* in students;
- *think aloud* while demonstrating and have children talk their way through problem solutions.

Teachers should teach learners to:

- develop appropriate content knowledge and *activate relevant knowledge*;
- develop a realistic *assessment of capabilities*;
- *plan* ahead by being aware of the purposes of the activity and the end-goals;
- *monitor* progress or lack of progress in order to orient future activity;
- *evaluate* alternative ways of handling the task and identify the ways that are likely to work best in the context;
- know when and why to use various cognitive functions and *automate* these;
- *predict outcomes* of stories;
- *summarise* progressively the content of a lesson;
- use colour to *highlight key points*;
- *draw flow charts* to identify connections of ideas;
- practise *self-questioning* while working through new problems;
- practise *self-evaluation*: 'How could I complete this task differently?' 'How could this work be improved?';
- *set goals* through the use of a learning diary of personal contracts;
- utilise *learning strategies*—for example, in literacy: 'How can I make sense of this new material?'

Source: Based on Biggs (1987a); Schraw & Moshman (1995); Thomas (1988).

Teaching learning strategies

These students are monitoring their own work. What are the elements of this, and why is self-monitoring important?

performance (Anderson & Hidi 1989; Anderson & Walker 1990; Dansereau 1985; Derry 1989; Derry & Murphy 1986; Idol, Jones & Mayer 1991; Kulik, Kulik & Schwalb 1983; McKeachie *et al.* 1985; Pressley & Woloshyn 1995; Thomas & Rohwer 1986; Weinstein & Underwood 1985; Winne 1997).

In a study conducted with two Hunter Valley Year 11 classes (Edwards, cited in Biggs 1987a), using the Study Habits Evaluation and Instruction Kit (SHEIK) (Jackson *et al.* 1980), and a control class that continued with normal lessons, the experimental classes completed an evaluation of their learning processes using the Learning Process Questionnaire (Biggs 1987b) which gave students feedback on how they were going about their study in comparison with others. Students then individually discussed the possible need for change in their learning strategies and ways of achieving this.

The students' approaches to learning were assessed on the Learning Process Questionnaire before and after intervention, and later the Higher School Certificate performance of both groups was followed up. It was found that the SHEIK groups improved their deep approaches to learning and that their final examination performance was an average of 34 aggregate marks higher than the control group (Biggs 1987a; Biggs & Telfer 1987b).

This raises the issue of the usefulness of teaching learning and thinking strategies and whether there is a 'best' way of doing this. Many authors have turned their minds to developing effective means of teaching learning strategies (Butler 1998; Ashman & Conway 1993; Jones 1981; Nickerson, Perkins & Smith 1985; Rowe 1988a, 1988b, 1988c, 1989a; Ruffels 1986; Sofo 1988; Splitter 1988; Weinstein & Hume 1998). In the next section we consider a number of the issues.

Thinking skills or content information first?

Authors package their thinking skills courses in many different ways. Idol *et al.* (1991) present a very thorough analysis of model programs and approaches to teaching thinking skills which includes the Instrument Enrichment Program (Feuerstein 1978), Tactics for Thinking (Marzano & Arredondo 1986a, 1986b) and Reciprocal Teaching (Palincsar & Brown 1984) programs. (See also Ashman and Conway (1993), for a description of their Australian Process-Based Instruction in the Classroom Kit.) Reciprocal teaching is discussed earlier in this chapter, together with reciprocal questioning strategies for enhancing the development of self-regulated learning and metacognitive skills in students.

Two basic approaches are possible. Proponents of the strategy/skill approach argue that it is difficult for most students, and especially for low-achieving students, to learn complex content and skills at the same time. Hence this approach provides explicit instruction of strategies and skills as an adjunct course with some attempt to transfer learning to content areas.

On the other hand, others argue that there should be a dual focus on content and skills. The primary focus should be content objectives, taught by the content teacher, but supported by a repertoire of specific strategies that will help students to learn the new content (Idol *et al.* 1991; see also Wright & Jacobs 2003). From our perspective, the second approach seems more appropriate for use in the regular classroom.

Some authors argue that, as research indicates that most children are able to theorise about their own cognition by the age of four, and are able to use these theories to regulate their performance, it is reasonable to place some degree of emphasis on metacognitive training from the time children enter school, regardless of their basic skills level (Schraw & Moshman 1995). From this point of view, schools should actively promote the development of metacognitive skills among all students.

The following model (Rowe 1989a) illustrates the second approach and covers the main principles that underlie the practices and methods developed to teach thinking and learning skills. This model is a useful starting point for teachers and can be incorporated into the teaching of specific content.

Rowe's model of thinking and learning skills

How might teachers promote awareness of learning processes and strategies in regular learning settings? Teachers can encourage students to keep a daily learning diary in which students record their reflections on and reactions to academic activities. Such diaries can help students to identify points of confusion, to formulate questions for further clarification or investigation, and to recognise important insights in their thinking. The diary shifts the focus of attention from getting the right answers from learning to using the right processes in learning.

Learning diary

Teachers can also promote awareness of learning processes and strategies by the use of teacher and peer modelling. 'Thinking aloud' about processes and sharing different processes through peer interaction can be particularly effective. Rowe suggests that, after an assignment has been given, class discussion can focus on processes such as estimating task difficulty, identifying goals, choosing strategies, identifying a sequence of steps and planning for evaluation.

Thinking aloud

Finally, it is important for the teacher to encourage students to self-disclose what they know, and the processes they use to think and learn, so that teaching method and content can be adapted to the students' cognitive needs. Because children have not been encouraged or taught how to disclose in this way in the past, they may be hesitant or incompetent at describing where they are coming from. In these circumstances, Rowe describes a number of direct and indirect techniques that can be used, such as questionnaires, interviews and verbal reports obtained by the thinking aloud method, teacher observation of spontaneous private verbalisations, and the use of rating scales, performance and behaviour analyses, and task analyses.

Self-disclosure

Facilitating conscious monitoring of work

To promote conscious monitoring of their work, students must be given effective feedback. This feedback may come from teachers, peers or the material itself. Reciprocal teaching, where students take turns in adopting the role of the teacher and apply their knowledge to teach skills and strategies to others, can provide opportunities for students to receive feedback about their understanding.

Effective feedback and reciprocal teaching

Rather than encouraging students to complete their work as soon as possible, teachers can stimulate more active involvement with the task by training students in self-questioning and monitoring. Questions such as 'What am I asked to do here?' or 'Do I understand this?' or 'How else could I have gone about this task?' encourage students to take more personal control of and responsibility for their learning. Strategies such as rereading, looking back for examples of similar questions and assignments, studying the examples provided and going back to assignment instructions for clues should become automatic.

Self-questioning and monitoring

Students should also be shown the effectiveness of summaries (as a form of self-testing) to analyse the state of their own understanding and determine what steps must be taken to improve this understanding. In particular, students must be encouraged to attempt to identify the reason (if one exists) for their difficulty in understanding. It might be an unfamiliar area, a new word in the text or the unavailability of a rule. Difficulties may be caused by the manner in which the material was presented and/or organised.

Summaries

Once the source of the problem is identified, the teacher can guide the student in their consideration of remedial activities.

Teachers can assist in decisions about how to handle new learning by directing their students to consider: the nature of the material to be learned or the problem to be solved; the learner's current skills and knowledge relevant to the task; the strategies required from the student; and the criterion tasks or tests used to evaluate the degree of learning or correctness of the solution. Rowe suggests that the following four questions provide a useful approach:

Encourage a deliberate and systematic approach

1 What am I supposed to do?
2 What do I already know about this subject?
3 How could I start and how can I proceed?
4 How will I be evaluated?

Answers to these questions will lead to a plan for handling the task.

Finally, an overall plan for the study activity should be implemented. Before commencing, the student should have identified the purposes for doing it, with appropriate activities including browsing, skimming and posing questions that might be answered later. During the task the learner should consistently self-question about the processes involved, and after the task the learner should review the processes used and question whether the goal(s) were achieved. Rowe believes that asking themselves these types of questions increases students' self-control, process and strategy awareness, executive control and independence in learning.

Develop an overall plan for study activity

Table 5.5 summarises the essentials of learning strategy instruction to encourage effective learning.

QUESTION POINT

Is teaching students how to learn in a particular content area a constructivist approach? How can it be a powerful means of enabling students to construct their own effective ways of learning?

Consider how the teaching competence indicators shown in Box 5.3 might be achieved by teaching learning strategies.

TEACHING COMPETENCE

Box 5.3

The teacher fosters independent and cooperative learning

Indicators

The teacher:

- encourages students to take responsibility for achieving learning goals;
- encourages students to develop problem-solving and inquiry skills;
- develops student strategies in using learning resources and technology.

Case studies illustrating National Competency Framework for Beginning Teaching, National Project on the Quality of Teaching and Learning, Australian Teaching Council, 1996, Element 3.7, p. 52. Commonwealth of Australia copyright, reproduced by permission.

Table 5.5

Essentials of learning strategy instruction to encourage effective learning

Teachers should:

- model the effective use of *learning strategies*, particularly by means of 'think-alouds';
- complete *task analyses* of the content to be taught, in particular learning contexts, so that 'think-alouds' are based on a thorough understanding of the nature and demands of the task;
- apply strategies in a *variety of contexts* so that students learn to generalise their application;
- commit *extensive time* to teaching the strategies, and *integrate strategy instruction* across the curriculum;
- provide students with opportunities to practise the strategies they have been taught so that these eventually *become automatic*;
- provide *guided practice and feedback* to students on their effective use of strategies;
- let *students teach other students* how best to go about reading, problem solving, learning and other cognitive processes;
- provide *motivation* for the use of the strategies and show the links between strategy use and learning outcomes;
- situate strategy instruction and use within a *mastery* rather than *performance* context.

Source: Based on Garner & Alexander (1989); Rowe (1989a).

Many educators believe that situated learning is most meaningful. This student is learning to use a lathe. Do you think this is an example of situated learning? Why?

QUESTION POINT

What opportunities do school learning environments give for developing distributed cognition, and is it important? How would you set up your classroom so that there was a balance between cognitive approaches and situated approaches to learning?

ACTION STATION

Can we teach children how to learn? It appears from research that one key to successful learning is a child's understanding of the learning process. In other words, successful learners are able to step back from their learning and monitor what they are doing. They appear to be strategic and can call upon a number of cognitive skills (such as story grammars and mnemonics) to assist with their learning. As it is clear that metacognitive skills are learned, greater attention is being paid by teachers today to the teaching of learning skills.

1. Discuss with teacher(s) how they teach children how to learn. In particular, make a list of techniques used. (These may be quite formal, such as SQ4R, or informal, such as the use of mnemonics or underlining.)
2. Interview two children while they are learning new material (which could be in mathematics, science or language) and ask them to describe in what ways they are trying to learn or solve a problem. Make verbatim notes and try your hand at interpreting each child's use of metacognitive skills (assuming they are using any!).

TEACHER'S CASE BOOK

Got it, Miss!

Bronwyn Letts' kindergarten class is involved in process writing. Steven raises his hand. 'How do you spell *walking*, Miss Letts?'

'What do you think goes on the end of it?' Bronwyn replies.

Steven answers 'ing'.

'Yes,' says Bronwyn. 'Now you need to find what goes on the front. Maybe you could find the word in a book. Maybe *At the Park*.' Bronwyn indicates the bookshelf near Steven's desk.

Steven goes to the bookshelf and looks through the book, searching for the word. 'It's not in *At the Park*,' he tells Bronwyn. She does not hear him as she is engaged in conversation with another child.

Steven continues his search and triumphantly finds the word he is looking for on the cover of the book *Rosie's Walk*. He takes it to his desk where he copies *walk* on to his page and then adds *ing*.

'Got it, Miss!' he beams.

Case studies illustrating National Competency Framework for Beginning Teaching, National Project on the Quality of Teaching and Learning, Australian Teaching Council, 1996, p. 8.

Case study activity

How does this case study illustrate the fostering of self-regulated learning by the teacher?

EXTENSION STUDY

Cognitive and situated learning

In much of our discussion above we have been concentrating on a cognitive model of learning that, in a sense, separates the skills of learning and cognitive processes from their content and situation, and emphasises the individual construction of learning. As such, these approaches provide us with information regarding the ways in which knowledge is structured and about the structures of knowledge in learners' minds that support task performance and transfer to new situations. Cognitive approaches also provide us with information regarding the kinds of learning experience that will lead best to the acquisition of new knowledge and skills (Anderson *et al.* 2000).

An alternative cognitive approach is referred to as *situated learning* (or *situated cognition*). Proponents of **situated learning** emphasise that much of what we learn is social in nature, context-bound and tied to the specific situation in which it is learned (Greeno 1997; Putnam & Borko 2000; Rogoff 1995). It is common to find examples of individuals using skills and knowledge to solve specific real-life situations, while being unable to use the same operations in classroom-based contexts. For example, research has shown that street vendors can use quite complex maths to work out sums while showing little formal knowledge of mathematics. For this reason, some researchers suggest that learning is most effective when it is in a situated context, and that 'real' learning is a form of apprenticeship in which new members become enculturated into the language, customs and beliefs of a learning community (Greeno 1997). An important aspect of situated learning is, therefore, that learning activities in the classroom should be authentic—that is, similar to what real-world practitioners do—or at least develop thinking and problem-solving skills that will be useful in out-of-school activities (see Putnam & Borko 2000). At this point you should refresh your understanding of **social constructivism** (see Chapter 1), as situated learning is a good example of this.

There are some extreme views on situated learning which hold that all learning is bound to the specific context in which it occurs, making transfer virtually impossible. (We dealt with transfer of learning in Chapter 4.) A number of debates have raged over this issue (see, for example, the discussions by Anderson *et al.* 2000; Anderson, Reder & Simon 1996; Cobb & Bowers 1999; Kirshner & Whitson 1998) and the issue is far from resolved. What is clear, and strongly argued by a number of educators and research from both camps, is that, in order to prepare students for successful participation in society, schools must achieve a balance between those activities that stress the development of individual competence and how to be good learners in school settings and those activities that incorporate the development of situated and distributed cognition, which will help students to become good out-of-school learners (see Putnam & Borko 2000). There is not necessarily a conflict between the cognitive and situative approaches in practice. Both approaches represent an attempt to shed light on important and different aspects of effective learning. In summary, both approaches agree that individual and social perspectives on learning are fundamentally important in education, and both agree that learning can be general and abstractions can be useful (as argued more by the cognitive approach than the situated approach); however, sometimes generalities and abstractions are not useful (Anderson *et al.* 2000).

Distributed cognition

Evolving from the idea of situated cognition is the notion of **distributed cognition**. As we have noted above, the situated learning approach moves away from a belief that learning and thinking is largely an individual process to considering it as a process embedded in social interaction. Hence, situative theorists believe that cognition is distributed or 'stretched over' the individual, other persons and various artefacts such as physical and symbolic tools (Putnam & Borko 2000). We discussed elements of this in our presentation of social constructivism in Chapter 1. There are many real-life situations where it is obvious that cognition (or knowledge) is distributed throughout the group so that the group can function effectively. Hutchins (1990, cited in Putnam & Borko 2000) gives the example of navigating a US Navy ship where the knowledge necessary for successfully piloting the ship is distributed among many different people. The distribution of cognition across people and tools (for example, computers) made it possible for the crew to accomplish cognitive tasks beyond the capabilities of any individual crew member. You could also describe similar examples of distributed cognition.

WHAT WOULD YOU DO?

TAKING THE CLASSROOM OUTSIDE

Miss Black took her Prep/1 class on an excursion. She included three parents and the school principal in her plan for the day. The children were divided into four groups, and the parents and principal each selected to lead one of the planned learning experiences. Miss Black had planned learning activities in the historical building of the national park where the children were required to look, listen to a commentary, touch various objects and talk about these experiences. Another group was to walk along a path in the bush, identifying favourite plant species and sketching them, and identifying the animals that also used the path by searching for droppings and footprints. A third group was to imagine that they were environmentalists and find a list of objects (for example, something that was once alive, something impossible to photograph, and so on); and the fourth group played environmental games (for example, 'hug a tree' and 'mini parks').

Case studies illustrating National Competency Framework for Beginning Teaching, National Project on the Quality of Teaching and Learning, Australian Teaching Council, 1996, p. 8. Commonwealth of Australia copyright, reproduced by permission.

What types of learning might be expected from this excursion?

WHAT WOULD YOU DO? (cont.)

TAKING THE CLASSROOM OUTSIDE

The children (and parents) were fascinated by the number of living things they had never before noticed in a small area of grass; at how much evidence of animal presence they could find without seeing the animals; by the notion that someone lived alone among the mountains and had to walk for days to talk to another person; and at how aspects of the environment are interdependent. They also learned more about cooperating with each other and the responsibilities of bushwalkers and visitors. Miss Black moved between groups asking questions and guiding discoveries. She was able to view her class outside the school environment and learn more about their personalities—one child who was quite dependent in the classroom surprised her by being able to locate and guide other children to public toilets and assume responsibility for garbage collection. She was also made aware of further things the children wanted to know, which they would research when back in the classroom.

Case studies illustrating National Competency Framework for Beginning Teaching, National Project on the Quality of Teaching and Learning, Australian Teaching Council, 1996, p. 8. Commonwealth of Australia copyright, reproduced by permission.

How do the types of learning that the children experience relate to the theory of constructivism and especially to Bruner's theory of effective learning through discovery?

WHAT WOULD YOU DO?

FINDING THE BALANCE POINT

On Friday, period 6 (last period of the day), I was introducing students to levers and the terms *fulcrum*, *effort* and *load*. The question arose as to whether the fulcrum was always exactly in the middle of a first-class lever. I asked the class what they thought. I was surprised when the entire class insisted that the fulcrum or balance point is always in the middle of a lever or rod.

I went to the storeroom and obtained a metre ruler and three different brooms. I used a common method where you move your hands in from both ends to find the balance point. As expected, with the metre ruler the balance point or fulcrum was at the centre. Then I tested the broom. As I expected, the balance point was now closer to the broom head. The students did not believe me. They thought I was playing a trick on them. They were convinced the balance point would always be in the middle. The students' intuitive understanding of how things work was an impediment to their learning. I knew that misconceptions were common in science and very resistant to change. I asked a volunteer to run her hands along the broom until she found the balance point. She did so, but the rest of the class were still unconvinced. I encouraged students to try it with their pens. Unfortunately, some pens did have a balance point in the centre which they took as confirmation of their views.

Case studies illustrating National Competency Framework for Beginning Teaching, National Project on the Quality of Teaching and Learning, Australian Teaching Council, 1996, p. 41. Commonwealth of Australia copyright, reproduced by permission.

How would you change student misconceptions?

WHAT WOULD YOU DO? (cont.)

FINDING THE BALANCE POINT

I understood that each student would need to try the broom, so I abandoned my planned lesson and let them all experiment with the brooms, metre rulers and pens. During the last 10 minutes we discussed our results and agreed that some rods do have a balance point at the centre, but not all. I described an example of a seesaw with a heavy handle at one end. If the seesaw is to balance, then the fulcrum must be moved towards the heavy handle. This same situation occurs when a heavy person moves towards the fulcrum when a light person is on the other end.

Even though the activity was not planned, I was pleased to see students actively engaged in experimenting, reflecting on and modifying their intuitive understanding.

Case studies illustrating National Competency Framework for Beginning Teaching, National Project on the Quality of Teaching and Learning, Australian Teaching Council, 1996, p. 41. Commonwealth of Australia copyright, reproduced by permission.

Do you agree with this approach? How does it represent a discovery approach to learning? What might be some remaining problems with the students' understanding? What else might the teacher have done? In particular, consider how the teacher might have presented the material using effective expository teaching.

KEY TERMS

Advance organiser (p. 143): a statement about a new topic providing structure for relating it to what students already know

Cognitive learning theories (p. 137): explanations of learning that focus on the internal mental processes individuals use in their effort to make sense of the world

Comparative organiser (p. 144): makes use of similarities and differences between new material and existing cognitive structure

Conditional knowledge (p. 145): knowledge of when and why to apply various cognitive skills

Declarative knowledge (p. 145): knowledge about memory and facts, definitions, generalisations and rules

Discovery learning (p. 141): material is not presented to the learner in its final form but rather the learner discovers relationships, solutions and patterns

Distributed cognition (p. 158): knowledge is distributed throughout a group so the group can function effectively

Enactive (p. 139): learning through actions on objects

Expository organiser (p. 143): presents an overview of the relevant concepts for students to attend to

Expository teaching (p. 143): the teacher presents information to students in a relatively finished form

Gestalt (p. 137): a meaningful pattern that the brain constructs from sensory information

Guided peer questioning (p. 150): peers are trained to ask thought-provoking questions and to generate elaborated responses

Iconic (p. 139): learning through seeing images

Intuitive thinking (p. 140): making imaginative leaps to correct perceptions or workable solutions, not based on formal processes of reasoning

Metacognition (p. 145): knowing about how one thinks and the ability to regulate it

Pragnanz (p. 138): organising unorganised stimuli into patterns that make sense

Procedural knowledge (p. 145): knowledge of how to perform various cognitive activities

Reception learning (p. 143): material to be learned is presented to learners in a relatively complete and organised form by the teacher

Reciprocal peer questioning (p. 152): small groups ask and answer each other's questions about lessons

Reciprocal teaching (p. 149): a method to teach reading comprehension strategies based on modelling

Situated learning (p. 158): learning is context bound and tied to the specific situation in which it is learned, making transfer difficult

Social constructivism (p. 158): emphasises the construction of shared knowledge in social contexts

Spiral curriculum (p. 140): concepts presented at higher levels of abstraction as learning develops

Symbolic (p. 139): learning through abstract symbols such as words

ON-LINE LEARNING

If you go to http://www.pearsoned.com.au/mcinerney, you will have hot links directly to these sites:

■ **Constructivist Learning Design 1**

Consider the guidelines for teaching in a constructivist manner presented at this website in the context of the material covered in this chapter. How do elements in the guidelines reflect principles of learning advocated by Bruner, Ausubel and the metacognitive approaches discussed in this chapter, and other constructivist approaches? Design a lesson using this approach.
http://www.prainbow.com/cld/cldp.html

■ **Bruner**

Go to the following websites and learn more about Jerome Bruner and his principles of effective learning.
http://www.infed.org/thinkers/bruner.htm and
http://www.psy.pdx.edu/PsiCafe/KeyTheorists/Bruner.htm

■ **Concept maps**

Review the material covered at this website on concept maps. How do concept maps represent a form of reception learning? You might like to review material you covered in Chapter 4 on concept maps.
http://cmap.coginst.uwf.edu/info/printer.html

■ **Learning effectively**

Consider the hints based upon metacognition given at this website in the context of what you have read in this chapter. Are the strategies suggested likely to be effective?
http://www.studygs.net/metacognition.htm

■ **Reading and reciprocal teaching**

The following website gives instructions for teaching reading using the four strategies of reciprocal teaching (summarising, questioning, clarifying and predicting). Structure a series of lessons using reciprocal teaching as suggested in the notes of this website. Don't forget you have to teach the strategies first.
http://curry.edschool.virginia.edu/go/readquest/strat/rt.html

WEB DESTINATIONS

If you go to http://www.pearsoned.com.au/mcinerney, you will have hot links directly to these sites:

■ **Learning to learn**

Leaning to Learn is a useful site that discusses a whole range of cognitive skills, including metacognition.
http://www.ldrc.ca/projects/projects.php?id=26

■ **Metacognition**

This site from the Learning to Learn site contains useful information on metacognition. Don't forget to use the hot links, particularly for other resources.
http://www.ldrc.ca/projects/projects.php?id=26

■ **Metacognition2**

You will find further information on metacognition at the following website.
http://www.gse.buffalo.edu/fas/shuell/cep564/Metacog.htm

■ **Reciprocal teaching**

Learn more about reciprocal teaching at the following website.
http://www.ncrel.org/sdrs/areas/issues/students/atrisk/at6lk38.htm

RECOMMENDED READING

Anderson, J. R., Greeno, J. G., Reder, L. M. & Simon, H. A. (2000) Perspectives on learning, thinking, and activity. *Educational Researcher*, **29**, 11–13.

Bruner, J. S. (1974) *Beyond the Information Given*. London: Allen & Unwin.

Butler, D. L. & Winne, P. H. (1995) Feedback and self-regulated learning: A theoretical synthesis. *Review of Educational Research*, **65**, 245–81.

Corkill, A. J. (1992) Advance organisers: Facilitators of recall. *Educational Psychology Review*, **4**, 33–67.

De Jong, T. & Van Joolingen, W. R. (1998) Scientific discovery learning with computer simulations of conceptual domains. *Review of Educational Research*, **68**, 179–201.

Derry, S. J. & Murphy, D. A. (1986) Designing systems that train learning ability: From theory to practice. *Review of Educational Research*, **56**, 1–39.

Garner, R. (1990) When children and adults do not use learning strategies: Toward a theory of settings. *Review of Educational Research*, **60**, 517–29.

Hacker, D. J. & Tenent, A. (2002) Implementing reciprocal teaching in the classroom: Overcoming obstacles and making modifications. *Journal of Educational Psychology*, **94**, 699–718.

King, A. (1994) Questioning and knowledge generation. *American Educational Research Journal*, **31**, 338–68.

King, A. (1997) ASK TO THINK—TEL WHY: A model of transactive peer tutoring for scaffolding higher level complex learning. *Educational Psychologist*, **32**, 221–35.

King, A. (1999) Discourse patterns for mediating peer learning. In A. O'Donnell & A. King (eds) *Cognitive Perspectives on Peer Learning*. Mahwah, NJ: Lawrence Erlbaum.

King, A., Staffieri, A. & Adelgais, A. (1998) Mutual peer tutoring: Effects of structuring tutorial interaction to scaffold peer learning. *Journal of Educational Psychology*, **90**, 134–52.

Mayer, R. E. (2004, January) Should there be a three-strikes rule against pure discovery learning? The case for guided methods of instruction. *American Psychologist*, **59**, 14–19.

Pressley, M., Harris, K. R. & Marks, M. B. (1992) But good strategy instructors are constructivists! *Educational Psychology Review*, **4**, 3–31.

Pressley, M., Johnson, C. J., Symons, S., McGoldrick, J. A. & Kurita, J. A. (1989) Strategies that improve children's memory and comprehension of text. *The Elementary School Journal*, **90**, 3–32.

Putnam, R. T. & Borko, H. (2000) What do new views of knowledge and thinking have to say about research on teacher learning? *Educational Researcher*, **29**, 4–15.

Rosenshine, B., Meister, C. & Chapman, S. (1996) Teaching students to generate questions: A review of the intervention studies. *Review of Educational Research*, **66**, 181–221.

Schraw, G. M. & Moshman, D. (1995) Metacognitive theories. *Educational Psychology Review*, **7**, 351–71.

Shuell, T. J. (1990) Phases of meaningful learning. *Review of Educational Research*, **60**, 531–47.

Tamir, P. (1995) Discovery learning and teaching. In L. W. Anderson (ed.) *International Encyclopedia of Teaching and Teacher Education*, 2nd ed. Tarrytown, NY: Pergamon.

Weinstein, C. & Hume, L. M. (1998) *Study Strategies for Lifelong Learning*. Washington DC: American Psychological Association.

Wright, J. & Jacobs, B. (2003) Teaching phonological awareness and metacognitive strategies to children with reading difficulties: A comparison of two instructional methods. *Educational Psychology*, **23**, 17–47.

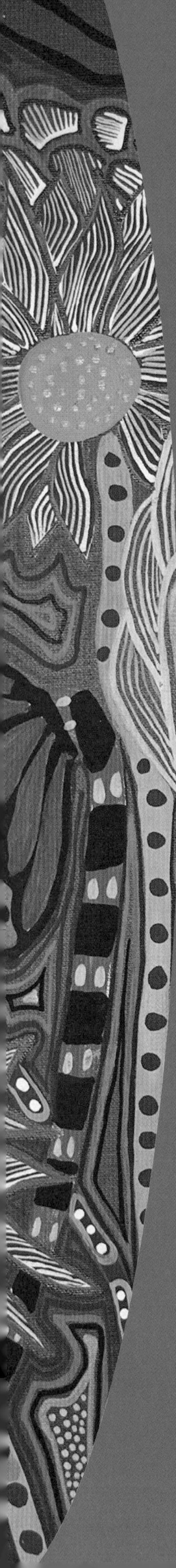

CHAPTER

6 Behavioural and social cognitive perspectives on effective learning

Overview

In this chapter, we look at two forms of teacher-controlled instruction that can lead to active and successful learning. We first look at behaviourism and its implications for effective teaching and learning. Our main attention is given to operant conditioning and the work of Skinner. In particular, we explore the classroom applications of behaviourism by discussing the use of behavioural goals, reinforcement in the classroom, applied behaviour management and direct instruction. Rosenshine's explicit teaching model is presented as a contemporary example of direct teaching and illustrates a movement that is occurring within the behavioural camp to include some cognitive elements in its approach.

Our second form of teacher-controlled instruction is social cognitive theory. Key elements of social cognitive theory—modelling, inhibition, disinhibition, elicitation and facilitation—are explored. The four processes involved in social learning—attention, retention, reproduction and motivation—are described with examples. The emphasis that social cognitive theory places on self-efficacy and self-regulated learning is also discussed.

Learning objectives

After reading this chapter, you will be able to:

- contrast behavioural and cognitive views of learning;
- describe behavioural views of effective learning;
- distinguish between classical conditioning and operant conditioning;
- define and apply in educational settings key concepts derived from behavioural theory such as conditioning, shaping, reinforcement, fading;
- compare and contrast punishment with reinforcement;
- discuss the advantages and disadvantages of using punishment in educational settings;
- describe the elements of applied behaviour analysis;
- consider direct instruction as a behavioural strategy;
- consider whether behavioural approaches to teaching and learning can be constructivist;
- describe social cognitive theory;
- list and apply classroom applications of social cognitive theory;
- define self-regulated learning, and describe its use in educational settings and its relationship to constructivism;
- describe and outline the importance of self-efficacy in learning;
- outline the relationship between self-efficacy and constructivism;
- describe defensive and self-handicapping approaches to learning and the means of correcting these.

6

Behavioural views of effective learning

Some years ago we had a long-haired Persian cat called Tiffany. Tiffany was a wonderful cat, although her long hairs had a tendency to get attached to our noses and cause sneezing fits. Tiffany had the habit of rushing to the kitchen whenever there were sounds of chopping on a board or whirring noises from an electric can opener. While we were busily cutting up tomatoes or opening tins of soup, the cat would be purring and meowing, pawing at the cupboards and becoming more agitated the longer we ignored her.

Why was Tiffany doing this? We remembered a time when we had been cutting up liver on the board and threw her the scraps. She was excited by the liver, and on subsequent occasions we also gave her scraps while cutting up other meat. Over time, just the sound of cutting on the board was enough to elicit the same desperate meowing. In effect, Tiffany had been taught new behaviour through conditioning.

Classical conditioning and simple learning

The early years of the 20th century saw a growth of research interest in trying to explain how **learning** takes place by investigating the observable mechanisms of learning. This new scientific, physiologically based interest in learning contrasted with earlier mentalistic models of the learning process and concurrent cognitive models of learning represented by the European Gestalt school (Wertheimer 1980), Piaget and Vygotsky. Focus was directed on observable forms of behaviour, which included not only bodily movement as seen by an observer watching a subject but also the internal physical

Tiffany trained us through behavioural conditioning.

processes related to overt bodily movement, and how these could be modified. Ultimately, this model of learning developed into a theory of learning called **behaviourism.** Three early behavioural scientists were Pavlov (1849–1936), Watson (1878–1958) and Thorndike (1874–1949).

Pavlov demonstrated the simple relationship between **stimulus** and **response** in teaching (**conditioning**) an organism to modify its behaviour. Using the simple paradigm below, Pavlov conditioned a dog to salivate to the sound of a bell by linking a neutral stimulus to an unconditioned stimulus, meat powder.

Unconditioned stimulus US (meat)	→	Unconditioned response (saliva)
Conditioning stimulus (bell) + US	→	Unconditioned response (saliva)
Conditioned stimulus (bell)	→	Conditioned response (saliva)

By pairing the neutral stimulus (bell) on repeated occasions with the meat powder (which automatically produced saliva in the dog), the bell became the new **conditioned stimulus** for the salivation (the **conditioned response**). In general terms, this early research demonstrated that any stimulus that readily leads to a response can be paired with a neutral stimulus (one that does not lead to a response) in order to bring about the type of learning described. It is important to note that the learner is typically unaware of this growing association.

Relationship between stimulus, response and learning

Table 6.1 lists the essentials of the classical conditioning process.

Many years ago one of us taught an educational psychology course in which we used to give students lecture notes on white paper. We also used to conduct occasional psychological exercises with the students, such as learning nonsense syllables, learning under various levels of distraction, mastering techniques to enhance learning, and so on. These exercises were usually presented on yellow paper. On one occasion the lecturer ran out of white paper and printed the lecture notes on yellow paper instead. When entering the room the lecturer noted a degree of disquiet. The lecturer hadn't made a comment. A neutral stimulus, yellow paper, had become associated with an unconditioned stimulus, psychological testing, and with the unpleasant feelings associated with this. Yellow paper had acquired the capacity to elicit negative feelings. To this day, we surmise that some former students still have problems referring to the *Yellow Pages*!

Figure 6.1 *Pavlov's apparatus for classical conditioning of a dog's salivation*

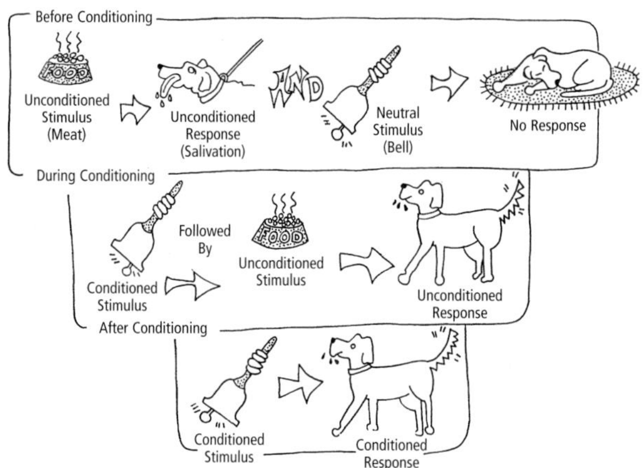

Figure 6.2 *The classical conditioning paradigm*

There are a number of ways of demonstrating the power of classical conditioning with humans. Two that

Table 6.1 Essentials of classical conditioning

Conditioning (C)	a process of learning
Stimulus (S)	any change in the physical world eliciting a response
Response (R)	the response to the stimulus—can be organic, muscular, glandular or psychic
Unconditioned stimulus (US)	a stimulus that produces a reflex or unlearned response
Conditioned stimulus (CS)	a stimulus paired with an unconditioned stimulus that becomes capable of producing a response
Conditioned response (CR)	a learned response resulting from pairing US and CS

we have conducted in the past with students are conditioning the patellar reflex (knee jerk) and the eye blink. In the former case, the 'teacher' rings a bell while lightly tapping the tendon. (Don't hit it too hard. You don't want to bruise the subject!) After a number of trials the bell alone is sufficient to elicit the knee jerk. On one occasion, we had a student so well conditioned that other students would sneak up behind him and ring a bell, screaming with delight when his leg jerked out involuntarily. Luckily for the hapless individual, the conditioning fades with time if it is not periodically reassociated with the unconditioned stimulus—on this occasion, the tap on the knee. The eye blink is exceptionally sensitive to conditioning; unfortunately, on most occasions when we demonstrated conditioning of the blink by pairing a bell with a light puff of air to the eye, students ended up with conjunctivitis, so we abandoned this demonstration.

Patellar reflex and eye blink

Early behavioural views of learning

J. B. Watson (1913, 1916, 1930) further developed the concept of classical conditioning and was the person who coined the term *behaviourism* to denote this approach to exploring and describing learning. Watson drew heavily on Pavlov's work and became convinced that learning was a process of building conditioned reflexes through the substitution of one stimulus for another. Watson defined the human in mechanistic, behavioural terms and totally rejected any mentalistic notion of learning (Bigge 1971). His work was particularly concerned with the acquisition of affective responses such as fear.

Thorndike (1913, 1931) made a very significant contribution to behavioural theory in exploring the effect of consequences of behaviour on subsequent behaviour. His findings were generalised as the **law of effect**, which *proposes that a response is strengthened if it is followed by pleasure, and weakened if followed by displeasure (or pain)*. This principle has become a keystone of behavioural theory and is known now as **reinforcement**.

While early behavioural theorists such as Watson and Thorndike hoped that their explanations of learning would be useful in understanding the human learning process generally, their models fell far short of explaining the complex nature of learned human behaviour. However, within the classroom context, classical conditioning does help to explain why children behave the way they do in particular circumstances. For example, some children learn to dislike poetry or mathematics, not because of the nature of the subject *per se*, but because the subject has been paired with fear-producing stimuli such as belligerent teachers. In other words, an unfortunate event accompanying an otherwise pleasant or neutral event can so alter the associations for an individual that the person avoids similar situations in the future at all costs. This process is known as **stimulus generalisation**.

Of course, classical conditioning can also be used positively. Having children work on difficult assignments under pleasant conditions will enhance their positive attitudes. For example, many teachers play music while children complete assigned work. Classical conditioning can similarly be used to **countercondition** anxieties, fear responses and phobias. For example, children who are afraid of dogs may be counterconditioned through a carefully worked-out procedure not to fear dogs, and children who fear particular school activities, such as performing forward rolls, can be counterconditioned not to be anxious. In these cases, the repeated association of non-threatening or pleasant experiences with the fearful object or experience serves to reduce the anxiety over time.

Positive use of classical conditioning

Operant conditioning and learning

B. F. Skinner (1948, 1954, 1968, 1971, 1986; see also Catania 1980) has had a powerful impact on the world of education. Skinner's work is now commonly considered an extension of Thorndike's law of effect (Iversen 1992). Extrapolating from techniques that he found very successful in training animals, Skinner (1951) maintained that these same techniques should be highly effective when used with children. In general, Skinner believed that all animals, including humans, learn things by having certain aspects of their behaviour reinforced while other aspects are not. Reinforcement occurs when something, such as a reward, is added to the situation that makes the performance of the behaviour more likely in the future.

Oh, oh! Looks like Ivan left the bell ringing all night again.

Early studies on the effectiveness of operant conditioning were conducted with animals. To train an animal such as a rat or a pigeon, Skinner devised an apparatus now called a *Skinner box*. The **Skinner box** enables the animal's behaviour to be observed and controlled so that particular behaviours called **operants** are more likely to occur. When the researcher wants to shape or strengthen these behavioural units, they are reinforced immediately they are performed by the application of a reward such as food. By progressively reinforcing operants that come closer to a goal behaviour, such as a bird pecking twice and turning around—a process called **shaping**, the animal is gradually taught to perform quite complex behaviour. Hence, in the initial stages of conditioning an animal to press a lever or peck a button, the animal is reinforced each time it turns in the direction of the lever or button. This is called *continuous reinforcement*. Subsequently, reinforcement is only administered when the animal adds to the response (for example, by moving closer to the lever or button). Over a number of trials the animal progressively acquires the desired behaviour (for example, pressing a lever). At this point, reinforcement is moved to an intermittent schedule, and secondary reinforcers (such as lights and buzzers) may be introduced to facilitate behaviour when primary reinforcers are no longer effective. (Even rats and pigeons become satiated with food pellets!) **Intermittent reinforcement** may be presented in a **fixed ratio**—that is, after a specific number of responses; at a **fixed interval**—that is, a specific period of time after a response occurs; or at a **variable interval**—that is, at any time subsequent to a correct response. In general, continuous reinforcement is necessary to establish responses. Once the response is established, *an intermittent schedule enhances the retention of behaviour* (Iversen 1992). If a response is not intermittently reinforced, it will gradually fade. Indeed, **fading** behaviour is an important counterpoint to shaping behaviour, as we discuss later.

Similar results of training may be achieved using **negative reinforcement**—that is, reinforcement that strengthens a response because the response removes some painful or unpleasant stimulus or enables the individual to avoid it. For example, the floor of the Skinner box may be mildly electrified. On the performance of the appropriate operant, the current is turned off. A bright rat would very quickly learn to sit on the lever! In general, **positive reinforcement** is found to be more effective than negative reinforcement, and avoids deleterious side effects.

Behaviour established through conditioning can be very difficult to change. We were once the proud parents of a new Schnauzer puppy. For the first couple of months we kept him on a large balcony outside our living room. As the balcony had slatted wood decking overhanging another balcony it was essential to train Lochie, our dog, to do his toilet in a particular area that was covered with paper. To do this we practised all the appropriate operant conditioning techniques and soon we had a house- and balcony-trained pup. Some time after this we moved Lochie out into our yard, which is paved. We again wanted the dog to do his toilet in a limited area of the yard where we spread paper. However, we found for a period of time it was very hard to train Lochie to go to the toilet in the yard. Instead the dog would rush through the house to the balcony and relieve himself! Indeed, even today, when he is conditioned to go to the toilet in the yard, he will still revert and occasionally go on the balcony but, thankfully, nowhere else. There is one further twist to the complications of operantly conditioning a dog to go to the toilet. We can take Lochie on very long walks, and the poor dog holds on the whole way and then rushes to the paper in the yard and does the biggest wee you have ever seen with a great look of relief on his face!

The complex behaviour of dolphins at Sea World is not conditioned in one go but is the result of many hours of laborious training. And the behaviour of getting Lochie to go to the toilet on paper on command is also the result of many hours of laborious training (believe me). Therefore, it is important that the goal behaviour to be acquired is analysed into those components that can be sequenced and successively reinforced. Toilet behaviour is relatively simple to analyse into tasks! The behaviour of dolphins at Sea World is not, and so it is even more important to analyse the final behaviour into its component parts.

Goal-directed task analysis

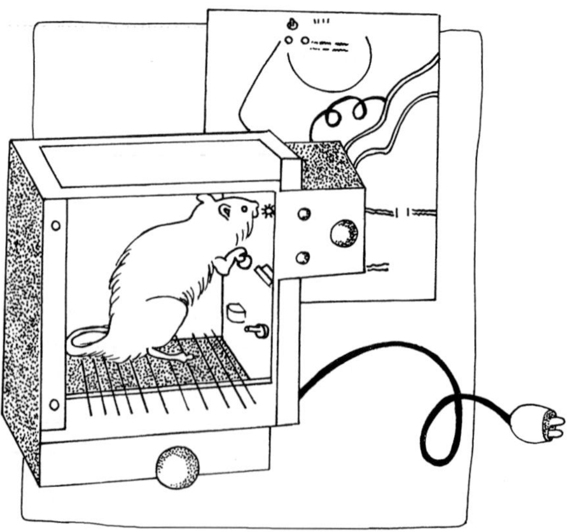

Figure 6.3 *A rat in a Skinner box*

Furthermore, unless the acquired responses are reinforced intermittently, the behaviour will fade and ultimately be extinguished. Why do you think an intermittent schedule of reinforcement would enhance the retention of learned behaviour? What would be some problems in applying only continuous reinforcement?

Table 6.2 summarises the essentials of operant conditioning.

Skinner, behaviourism and education

Each of the principles of behaviourism—reinforcement, shaping and fading—can be applied effectively in human learning environments (Cairns 1995; Sladeczek & Kratochwill 1995; Sulzer-Azaroff 1995). Skinner (1965, 1984; see also Merrett & Wheldall 1990; Sulzer-Azaroff 1995 and Wheldall & Merrett 1990) believed that learning in traditional classrooms is dominated by children trying to avoid unpleasant situations (such as punishment and negative reinforcement) rather than working for pleasant rewards. He also believed that there was too great a lapse of time between the performance of particular behaviour and its reinforcement. In fact, Skinner believed that reinforcement of desired behaviour occurred much too infrequently and erratically. Furthermore, learning episodes were not sufficiently goal directed in the sense that teachers did not adequately define the terminal behaviour desired as goals, or establish the steps that children needed to progress through in order to achieve these goals.

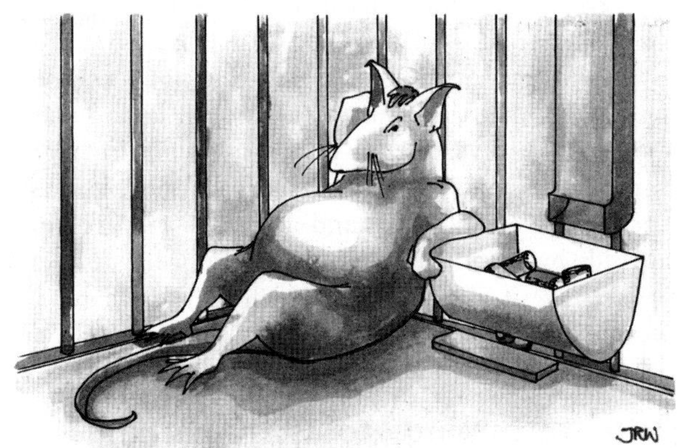

'I find that if I keep my performances intermittent, my staff are more motivated to control their tendency to overfeed.'

Behavioural goals

In applying Skinner's approach to a learning environment, teachers need to establish the goal of a particular lesson in terms of behavioural outcomes and design a set of experiences that are tightly sequenced in hierarchical steps to achieve this goal. Furthermore, students should be placed in a context where particular forms of behaviour (operants) are more likely to occur. For example, if a teacher wishes to teach mathematics, then students should be put in a situation where mathematical behaviour is more likely to occur. If the teacher wishes to teach swimming, then the logical classroom would be the local pool. Many teachers run into the difficulty of trying to teach behaviour in contexts where inappropriate behaviour (operants) may be stimulated. Hence, there is a strong argument for specialised resource rooms.

Reinforcement in the classroom

As we have noted, a key to the success of operant conditioning lies in the application of reinforcement and punishment. For children, **reinforcers** may be: *material*, such as toys or some enjoyable activity; *token*, such as stamps and gold stars; or *social*, such as the goodwill and recognition of the teacher or competition. Often this

Table 6.2 Essentials of operant conditioning

Operants	the label used by Skinner to describe a behaviour not elicited by any known or obvious stimulus
Shaping	the continuous reinforcement of operants that become increasingly closer approximations of the desired behaviour
Fading	the eradication of a response through the withdrawal of reinforcement
Positive reinforcement	a stimulus that increases the probability of an operant recurring as a result of its being added to a situation after the performance of the behaviour. It usually takes the form of something pleasant
Negative reinforcement	a stimulus that increases the probability of an operant recurring when it is removed from the situation. It usually takes the form of something unpleasant
Punishment	the addition of an unpleasant stimulus to a situation as a consequence of behaviour that has occurred. The aim is to suppress behaviour rather than to establish new behaviour
Reinforcement schedule	the application of positive or negative reinforcement, continuously or intermittently, by time or ratio of responses

Children are often proud of themselves when they receive extrinsic reinforcers. What are the strengths of extrinsic reinforcers? What are some of the dangers?

Material, token and social reinforcers

style of reinforcement is called **extrinsic reinforcement** as it is externally applied, usually by the teacher. The teacher needs to decide what reinforcers are appropriate and available. The important point here is not what the teacher thinks is rewarding (or punishing), so much as the effect it has on later behaviour.

Reinforcement for a job well done.

A number of studies show that pupils' opinions about rewards and punishments vary a lot from those of their teachers. There are many examples of things that teachers believe are positive reinforcers but which actually turn out to be negatively reinforcing or punishing, and examples of things that teachers believe are punishing but which are actually acting as reinforcers and thus establishing behaviour (Merrett & Tang 1994). Among some of the controlling or punishing strategies that teachers use are nagging, scolding and grumbling. But to the extent that teachers use these constantly and persistently they may become ineffective, and may in fact be shaping undesirable student behaviour. How do you think this occurs? Could you think of some examples?

Positive reinforcement is considered more effective than negative reinforcement. One could construct a classroom so that all the seats of the desks are connected to a mild electric current. When the children perform an appropriate behaviour, such as putting up their hands, the current would be switched off. No doubt the children would 'learn' the behaviour very quickly, but perhaps the cost in terms of parental complaints (and escalating electricity bills as the few wayward children persisted in not performing the appropriate behaviour) would not make it a viable approach. However, the use of negative reinforcement is common, if not quite as extreme. For example, some teachers have children stand up until they respond correctly by putting up their hands, after which they are allowed to sit down. Often children work hard not because of the inherent interest they have in the task, but to turn off the teacher's nagging!

Use of negative reinforcement

Using technology to assist learning

How many of us have sat in classrooms where our good behaviour or good work has gone unnoticed or ignored by the teacher? How many students have decided that it really isn't worth the effort if they are not getting appropriate feedback or reinforcement? Skinner wished to avoid such problems—caused by the erratic application of reinforcement by teachers—by the use of technology to assist learning. As we have noted, reinforcement in the classroom must be given immediately upon the performance of the desired behaviour, especially in the early stages of learning new behaviour. To ensure that reinforcement was immediate and contingent upon the correct response, Skinner advocated the use of **programmed instruction** in the form of 'teaching machines'. These delivered small amounts of information and exercises to which students would respond and for which they would receive prompt feedback (reinforcement) on their accuracy. Of course, today the notion of teaching machines and students winding information through frames appears quaint. Technology has far outstripped these clumsy methods of programmed instruction. Today there is so much sophisticated computer software available to teach through programmed instruction that the mind boggles. Not only do we have the opportunity for endless pathways for learning through programmed instruction, but also 'virtual reality', which raises the whole area of instruction to a new dimension.

QUESTION POINT

Discuss the use of teacher attention and praise as reinforcement; include, especially, examples of when it is valuable, reasons why teachers find it difficult to use, the components of effective praise, and the mistakes that teachers often make in its use.

Students benefit from positive reinforcement. Consider exciting, innovative and fun ideas for rewarding everyone—individuals or the entire class. Draft a pamphlet that presents your ideas on the use of creative reinforcement.

ACTION STATION

Make a list of potential motivators that seem appropriate for very young children, those in infants and primary school, high school students and young adults. List both tangible and non-tangible rewards and motivators. Some people find it easier to generate reinforcers for certain ages than others. Which group was the most difficult? Why?

Problems in the use of extrinsic reinforcement

The use of extrinsic reinforcers at school (and at home) is widespread although, often, very poorly used from a theoretical point of view. Walters and Grusec (1977, p. 124) state:

> We have good reason to suspect that agents of socialisation may well have diminished the effectiveness of social and material reinforcement by being too prodigal in its use, or at least by often administering it independent of the behavior engaged in.

Often, teacher education students have the feeling that the application of extrinsic reinforcement is not very different from bribery. Of course, from a theoretical perspective it can't be bribery because the knowledge of the reward is incidental to its effect. We see this clearly in the case of training animals and very young children. However, the knowledge of the reward does seem to 'contaminate' the effect of extrinsic reinforcement with older students. Under certain circumstances, extrinsic reinforcement can be detrimental to motivation and performance. Students begin to think distracting thoughts, such as: 'Am I being given enough stickers?'; 'Why did Johnny get two stickers while I only got one?'; 'Boy! the teacher is going to give us a chocolate bar for finishing this exercise—it must be more difficult than I thought'; 'I'm never going to get the reward, so why try?'; 'This must be a boring exercise because the teacher has to give us a reward for doing it'; 'Is that all I'm going to be given for all this work?' and so on. One child was heard to say with reference to a popular fitness program sponsored by a pizza company: 'If you don't get the reward, the whole thing is a waste of time.' No doubt you can remember yourself saying these exact things.

A number of interesting research programs addressing

I'm glad you're watching now

The junior education support class sat closely around the concept keyboard, engaged in a reading task. Each child was taking turns at pressing the keyboard and carrying out the instruction, matching a drawing of an animal with the written work. After a short period of time, Miss Wild noticed that Brett's attention was wandering and he began to fidget.

Miss Wild then said to Troy, who was sitting beside Brett, and paying attention, 'Troy, I love the way you're watching what we're doing. You must want the next turn.'

Troy proceeded to have his turn. This caught Brett's attention and he immediately turned around and focused on the task.

Miss Wild was then quick to comment, 'Brett, I'm glad you're watching now. You'll be able to have the next turn.'

Case studies illustrating National Competency Framework for Beginning Teaching, National Project on the Quality of Teaching and Learning, Australian Teaching Council, 1996, p. 28.

Case study activity

Why do you think Brett refocused on the task? What elements of reinforcement are illustrated in this case study?

this issue are presented in an appropriately titled text, *The Hidden Cost of Reward* (Lepper & Greene 1978). Reviews (Boggiano & Barrett 1992; Butler 1988; Deci, Koestner & Ryan 2001; Kohn 1996a; Lepper & Hodell 1989; Ryan, Connell & Deci 1985) re-emphasise the key findings of the earlier research but widen their analysis to include the effects of external evaluation and performance feedback, social control, task design and task structure on the student's *continuing motivation* for the task, problem-solving ability and creativity. They strongly suggest that extrinsic controls frequently have a negative effect on continuing motivation.

Counter views are expressed by a number of authors who believe that, in settings such as classrooms, verbal rewards (praise and positive feedback) can be used to enhance intrinsic motivation. When tangible rewards, such as gold stars or money, are offered contingent on performance of a task, or are delivered unexpectedly, intrinsic motivation may be maintained. Rewards can be offered for work completed, for solving problems successfully, or for maintaining a predetermined level of performance without undermining intrinsic motivation (Cameron & Pierce 1994, 1996). A problem occurs when the rewards are offered without regard to the level of performance of the student. In this case, when rewards are withdrawn, students demonstrate diminished continuing motivation in the task. Another major problem with the application of such rewards is that, once children are removed from the particular circumstance under which the token system was used, there may be no transfer to a new situation. Many classes work well for their regular teacher but misbehave for the relief teacher because they do not use the same extrinsic reward (and punishment) systems for specific behaviour.

As you can see, the argument about the usefulness or otherwise of extrinsic rewards has not been resolved (Cameron & Pierce 1994, 1996; Deci, Koestner & Ryan 2001; Kohn 1996a; Lepper, Keavney & Drake 1996; Ryan & Deci 1996).

Weiner (1990) believes that the simple theoretical notion that a reward automatically increases the probability of an immediately prior response occurring again does not stand up when applied to human motivation. Weiner (1990, p. 618) summarises this in the following way:

> . . . if reward is perceived as controlling, then it undermines future effort, whereas reward perceived as positive feedback is motivating . . .. Furthermore, reward for successful completion of an easy task is a cue to the receiver of this feedback that he or she is low in ability, a belief that inhibits activity, whereas reward for successful completion of a difficult task indicates that hard work was expended in conjunction with high ability, a belief that augments motivation. In addition, reward in a competitive setting is based on social comparison information, signaling that one has high ability and is better than others, whereas reward in a cooperative context signals that one has bettered oneself and has tried hard. Hence, it became recognized that reward has quite a variety of meanings and that each connotation can have different motivational implications.

The following Learner-centred Psychological Principle refers to factors that may impact on motivation. How do these factors relate to the theories of learning covered in this chapter?

LEARNER-CENTRED PSYCHOLOGICAL PRINCIPLE

Effects of motivation on effort. Acquisition of complex knowledge and skills requires extended learner effort and guided practice. Without learners' motivation to learn, the willingness to exert this effort is unlikely without coercion.

Effort is another major indicator of motivation to learn. The acquisition of complex knowledge and skills demands the investment of considerable learner energy and strategic effort, along with persistence over time. Educators need to be concerned with facilitating motivation by strategies that enhance learner effort and commitment to learning and to achieving high standards of comprehension and understanding. Effective strategies include purposeful learning activities, guided by practices that enhance positive emotions and intrinsic motivation to learn, and methods that increase learners' perceptions that a task is interesting and personally relevant.

Appropriate uses of extrinsic rewards

As we have seen, the misuse of extrinsic rewards and sanctions can have a variety of detrimental effects on children's intrinsic motivation, task performance and learning. Under appropriate conditions, however, extrinsic rewards such as stamps and stars can enhance motivation and promote learning. Extrinsic rewards may be used to get children interested in tasks for which they have little interest or aptitude. Indeed, there may well be some tasks for which everyone needs a little prodding. (How many of you learned the mathematical tables with great intrinsic interest?)

Extrinsic token rewards are often used appropriately to indicate to children how well they have performed individually in comparison with others. As such, these rewards state something about the competence of the child, and may function as an effective motivator for further task involvement and striving for excellence in their work. Indeed, children may become 'turned on' to the task and not really require further token reinforcement once they have experienced some level of success. Among appropriate rewards for younger children are sweets, small presents, free time, teacher praise, house points, badges, stars, certificates, or a letter home to parents and child saying how well the student has done. For older students, rewards that have been found to be effective are free time and a positive letter home. It appears that involving parents is very important in determining how effective rewards and punishments are at school (Merrett & Tang 1994; see also Miller, Ferguson & Moore 2002). However, for the children who don't receive rewards such a system can lead to a reduction in their sense of competence and a subsequent loss of interest in the task.

Involving parents is important in determining the effect of reinforcement

Extrinsic rewards are often used by teachers (and parents) to distinguish between valued activities and less valued activities (Lepper & Hodell 1989). For example, prizes may be awarded for mathematics and reading but not for art or PE. Unfortunately, valued activities are often not academic ones. We are concerned that at some schools the football team gets more rewards in the form of special uniforms, responsibilities and privileges than the school intelligentsia!

Extrinsic rewards and valued activities

We believe that extrinsic reward systems must be used with great care and not as a matter of course. At the very least the teacher must consider the potential impact of such rewards for the individual involved in specific activities. Sadly, it appears that, despite the research evidence that the use of extrinsic motivation systems is fraught with dangers, they are still widely used indiscriminately in classrooms.

Punishment and learning

Reward and punishment, and their relationship to the process of learning behaviour, have long been the subject of much folklore. We have proverbs enshrining society's attitudes to these control devices:

Spare the rod, spoil the child.
You win more bees with honey than vinegar.

Western society has vacillated in its attitude towards reward and punishment. Through the early stages of mass education, good discipline and motivation were associated with severe punishment techniques—belting, starving, stuffing children's mouths with paper, pulling children's hair, shaking, ear pulling, detentions, loss of privileges and extra assignments (Maurer 1974). Many of these excesses continued into the second half of the 20th century. The older author remembers vividly the leather strap that formed part of the essential accoutrement of his teachers at both primary and secondary schools. A good day was when you and your friends avoided getting a belting.

A more 'enlightened' time saw the demise of some of the more extreme punishment techniques and the rise of the belief that reward is more effective in establishing desirable behaviour in children. Punishment was criticised as ineffective, productive of undesirable behavioural traits, immoral and inhuman. Baby books and psychology textbooks emphasised the use of rewards rather than punishments as the key to effective behaviour change. This change was supported by early Freudian, behavioural and social learning theories.

The relative effectiveness of reinforcement and punishment has been subjected to research. **Punishment** is defined in research as the application of something unpleasant to a situation to suppress behaviour (such as a sudden clip across the ear for talking out of turn), or the removal of something pleasant to suppress behaviour (such as a favourite activity—'you have been grounded'). A large body of research, all of it carried out with children, suggests that punishment for incorrect behaviour leads to faster learning than does reinforcement for correct behaviour, and a combination of reinforcement and punishment is no better than punishment alone (Constantini & Hoving 1973; Penney 1967; Walters & Grusec 1977; Witte & Grossman 1971). A possible explanation for this effect may be that reward is generally non-specific, pervasive and indiscriminate (associated with a general pleasantness of the teacher to children) while punishment is used most often for specific acts. The behaviour (or non-behaviour, such as non-completion of an exercise) responsible for the punishment is clearly associated with the punishment, and more specific information is communicated to the child by punishment than by reinforcement. One problem, however, with research such as this is the nature of the punishing stimulus that has been used. Typically, the use of punishment has not been like that used in real classrooms and may not necessarily reflect the true impact of punishment (see Haviland 1979).

Response cost

Response cost refers to the loss of positive reinforcers when particular behaviours are not performed. For example, teachers sometimes allocate individuals or groups 30 minutes of free time per day for their own chosen activities. Each time an individual or member of a group misbehaves, a minute is lost. As such, response cost acts as a punishment. One study of the effects of response cost (Constantini & Hoving 1973) found that the motivational effect of children losing marbles was greater than that of receiving them, even when the number of marbles retained or received by the students was the same! It appears from this study that the withdrawal of positive reinforcers as a method of controlling behaviour is effective for at least three reasons:

1 It generates a weaker emotional effect than does the presentation of something unpleasant and tends to foster and maintain the subject's orientation towards the agents who control the positive reinforcers.
2 There is less recovery of the punished response when the contingency is removed.
3 It is more frequently used in naturalistic settings than punishment.

Parents often use response cost when they tell their children that they will lose particular privileges if they don't behave. This is often found to be more successful than smacking them when they are naughty. Some parents also believe that it is better than giving rewards to children for behaving and finishing their chores, for these behaviours are expectations and should not be rewarded. What do you think?

Are there appropriate forms of punishment?

It appears that punishment can be an effective motivational agent for children in particular contexts (see an interesting discussion of this in Reyna & Weiner 2001). Punishment is, however, often criticised for producing too many unpleasant side effects to be useful in the classroom. For example, punishment communicates more about what *not* to do than what to *do*; punishment may affect the attitude of the child to the teacher; and, in some cases, punished behaviour, such as thumbsucking, bedwetting and out-of-seat behaviour, becomes more resistant to change. The following forms of punishment may nevertheless be valuable aids to socialisation and learning:

- verbal rebuke and social disapproval that do not attack a person's worth;
- withdrawal of privileges and material objects;
- occasional use of mild physical punishment contingent on specific behaviour.

Punishments at the secondary level that students think effective are an unfavourable note sent home to parents complaining about their child's behaviour, being put on report and detention, and being sent to the head teacher (Merrett & Tang 1994; Miller, Ferguson & Moore 2002). Private interviews with teachers (while not necessarily seen as punishment) are also considered very effective. Punishments that students consider less effective are 'being told off' and being sent to another teacher.

Student views on effective punishment

Research indicates that it is important for the child to be given an explanation for why a particular behaviour is being punished. There should also be consistency in applying the punishment. If the person administering the punishment is perceived by the child to be a nurturant person, there is less likelihood of negative consequences as a result of the punishment. Punishment that is extremely severe, administered randomly so that the relationship between the action and its consequences is not clear, or administered by a hostile and rejecting caretaker is to be avoided (Walters & Grusec 1977).

Importance of explanation for punishment

Despite the apparent value of some forms of punishment, however, the evidence against the use of corporal punishment is very strong (Edwards & Edwards 1987). We must be careful not to return to the bad old days when barbaric forms of retribution were used on children. An early article (Maurer 1974), 'Corporal punishment', shows how many thousands of children were subjected to cruelty under laws that were defended, at least in part, by research evidence that punishment can change behaviour. One apparent and unfortunate side effect of the use of corporal punishment in schools is that children subjected to it appear to become more tolerant and supportive of its use—surely not a good sign for socialising individuals as caring and loving parents, teachers and colleagues in the future (see Ritchie 1983).

Teaching strategies based on behaviourism

Skinner's approach is reflected in many teaching strategies, from the use of programmed instruction materials such as DISTAR (Direct Instruction System for the Teaching of Arithmetic and Reading), SRA reading laboratory materials and computer-assisted instruction, through to the use of complete classroom and school procedures based on behavioural principles such as positive teaching, applied behaviour analysis (sometimes called **behaviour modification**), direct instruction, precision teaching and the personalised system of instruction (Merrett & Wheldall 1990; Sulzer-Azaroff 1995; Wheldall 1987). Consider the indicators of teaching competence in the following box and relate them to the behavioural principles presented in this chapter.

Box 6.1

TEACHING COMPETENCE

The teacher encourages positive student behaviour

Indicators

The teacher:

- acknowledges appropriate student behaviour and fosters self-discipline among students;
- uses an approach that emphasises consequences for inappropriate behaviour;
- applies a variety of behaviour management strategies—for example, negotiating rules, applying effective sanctions;
- develops clear routines for managing student behaviour consistent with school policy;
- takes appropriate action promptly, firmly, fairly and consistently.

Case studies illustrating National Competency Framework for Beginning Teaching, National Project on the Quality of Teaching and Learning, Australian Teaching Council, 1996, Element 2.4, p. 40. Commonwealth of Australia copyright, reproduced by permission.

In the following Theory and Research into Practice section, Kevin Wheldall discusses applied behaviour analysis. In Table 6.3 we present essential elements of applied behaviour analysis.

Direct instruction as a behavioural strategy

Direct instruction is a general term that has acquired a number of different meanings referring to somewhat different instructional practices (Rosenshine & Meister 1995). What they all have in common, however, is a teacher-centred control of presentation and evaluation of learning material; specifically, delivery, scheduled practice and feedback. Australian teachers appear to have positive attitudes towards direct instruction as an effective teaching technique (see, for example, Demant & Yates 2003).

One form of direct instruction, based on behavioural principles, is a systematic, tasks-analysed teaching procedure (Maggs *et al.* 1980). Three examples of this approach to direct instruction have been used in Australia and New Zealand: the Direct Instruction System for the Teaching of Arithmetic and Reading (**DISTAR**); morphographic spelling; and corrective reading. Research here and overseas indicates that these direct methods of instruction can be quite effective with a broad range of children (Maggs *et al.* 1980). However, the approach generates as much heat as light in Australia and New Zealand, where academics and teachers argue over the merits of a system that appears to guarantee student success, but is extremely teacher and content dominated. Key elements of this approach are listed in Table 6.4 on p. 178.

How might the indicators of teaching competence outlined in Box 6.2 on p. 179 facilitate the management of student behaviour as well as learning? Relate these indicators to the elements of direct instruction discussed here.

Direct instruction as a cognitive strategy

More recently, views of direct instruction have moved from the rather narrow definition of tightly sequenced instruction with constant feedback, to definitions that emphasise the development of cognitive strategies. Key elements of this approach are:

- explicit strategy or skills instruction—teacher explanations of *what* the strategy is and *when*, *where* and *how* to use it, as well as *why* it should be used;
- the gradual transfer of responsibility for learning from the teacher to the student;
- a focus on constructing meaning and problem solving;

Table 6.3

Essentials of applied behaviour analysis

Teachers should:

- specify the nature of the behaviour desired in behavioural terms—for example, the child will spend more work time at their desk;
- set a level of behaviour that will be the goal for the behaviour—for example, the child will work for 20 minutes at a time without leaving their desk;
- instigate an effective reward-keeping procedure and assess the behaviour through direct observation, such as counting how often it occurs. This form of teaching is often called *precision teaching* and involves the use of stopwatches, graphs and charts;
- work out appropriate reinforcing strategies—for example, tokens will be awarded for the performance of the appropriate behaviour, and on the cumulation of 20 tokens a reward (a lolly or free activity) may be traded for the tokens.

Theory and research into practice

Kevin Wheldall — POSITIVE USES OF BEHAVIOURISM

BRIEF BIOGRAPHY

I was born in Derby in the UK in 1949. In 1970 I graduated from the University of Manchester with an honours degree in psychology, having spent the previous three years wondering whether I should become a rock star or a poet. Almost immediately after graduation, I began working as a research associate for Professor Peter Mittler at his newly established Hester Adrian Research Centre (HARC) 'for the study of learning processes in the mentally handicapped'. It was at HARC in the early 1970s that I first became seriously interested in behavioural psychology, under the influence of James Hogg and Peter Evans. (Anything to do with operant conditioning had been virtually banned from my undergraduate course in psychology.) I completed my doctoral research at HARC on receptive language development, which was subsequently awarded the Education Section Prize of the British Psychological Society.

In 1974, I was appointed to a lectureship in education at the University of Birmingham, where I continued to research in language comprehension, including a novel way of assessing the Piagetian notion of conservation using operant conditioning. But I soon became much more interested in using behavioural psychology to help teachers to manage classroom behaviour more effectively, working with my doctoral student and subsequently research partner, Frank Merrett.

In 1980, I jointly founded the journal *Educational Psychology* (published by Taylor and Francis), with my colleague Richard Riding, in an attempt to encourage more experimental research in the psychological study of education. Then in 1981 and 1982, respectively, I was elected honorary general secretary of the British Psychological Society (BPS) and appointed director of the Centre for Child Study at the University of Birmingham. Prior to moving to a chair in education at Macquarie University in Sydney in 1990, I was elected a fellow of both the British Psychological Society and of the College of Preceptors and also chaired the BPS Education Section and the Association for Behavioural Approaches with Children.

Since 1990, I have been director of Macquarie University Special Education Centre and in 2004 was also appointed associate dean (research) of the Australian Centre for Educational Studies at Macquarie.

RESEARCH AND THEORETICAL INTERESTS

I have researched and written extensively in the area of learning and behaviour difficulties, with particular emphasis on classroom behaviour management and helping older low-progress readers, and have published over 150 books, chapters and journal articles in the field of special education and educational and child psychology. I have also acted as an adviser to both state and federal government education bodies and ministers on matters relating to special education generally and on behaviour and reading, in particular.

My research and theoretical interests fall (very) roughly into three main areas:

- language comprehension;
- classroom behaviour management;
- effective instruction for low-progress readers.

I have researched many other topics that do not fall within these three areas (such as the development of very low-birthweight babies and vocal pitch in 'motherese'), but I shall concentrate on these three.

My early research focused on receptive language development, particularly sentence comprehension, which was a hot topic in the 1970s. My work included studies examining the factors influencing sentence comprehension in young children both with and without disabilities. For example, we looked at whether intonational emphasis helped children to understand sentences presented to them. This line of inquiry also led to the development and subsequent publication of the Sentence Comprehension Test (Wheldall, Mittler & Hobsbaum 1979).

It was this concern with children's ability to understand spoken language that led to my subsequent research attempting to develop a non-verbal means of assessing the Piagetian notion of conservation. In one of those rare moments of lucid insight, it occurred to me that my developing interest in operant conditioning might provide the answer to the problems of asking young children complicated questions. By systematically training young children to press a button when they perceived two glasses of water as holding the same quantity of liquid, we were then able to observe their responses when we subsequently poured one of the glasses of water into a different shaped container. In brief, we found that many more young children could indeed conserve liquid quantity when asked to make their judgments non-verbally—that is, when they were not confused by complicated questions (Wheldall & Poborca 1980).

This fascination with operant conditioning also manifested itself in the program of research completed in the late 1970s and 1980s with my colleague Dr Frank Merrett on classroom behaviour management. In brief, we found that while teachers continually complained about the amount of time they wasted reprimanding children for 'talking out of turn' or disturbing others, they (typically) hardly ever praised children for behaving well. In various studies we demonstrated that by 'catching them being good', teachers could greatly increase the amount of time students spent behaving well. Another line of inquiry repeatedly showed that children spent far more time getting on with their work when seated in the traditional rows format than when seated in table groups, which had become the norm in most primary classes. We subsequently developed these ideas into the Positive Teaching Package, a course for teachers in how to manage classroom behaviour (Wheldall 1987; Wheldall & Merrett 1989; Merrett & Wheldall 1990).

During this period, I also became interested in the behavioural tutoring of reading using the 'Pause, Prompt and Praise' remedial tutoring method developed by Ted Glynn and his colleagues. Helping older low-progress readers became the focus of much of my work in the 1990s after I had moved to Macquarie University Special Education Centre. After completing a controversial evaluation of Reading Recovery (Center, Wheldall, Freeman, Outhred & McNaught 1995), I initiated the Making Up Lost Time In Literacy, or MULTILIT, research and development initiative (see www.multilit.com). We developed a highly effective program for teaching reading and related skills to older low-progress readers (Wheldall & Beaman 2000). This aspect of my work has also included the development of the Wheldall Assessment of Reading Passages (WARP) (Wheldall & Madelaine 2000).

THEORY AND RESEARCH INTO PRACTICE

In my research career, spanning nearly 35 years now, I have had little time for so-called pure research. I have had my more esoteric moments (researching eye widening and eyebrow raising in response to surprise in nursery school children, for example!) but they have been rare. There has simply been too much to be done on a practical level. I believe firmly in evidence-based practice and see experimental and behaviourally based educational psychology as the main means by which we can address the problems confronting education. I tire very quickly when faced with post-modern speculation and so-called critical theory.

This is not to say that I have no interest in theory or that I have not attempted to contribute to the development of psychological models. Hans Eysenck used to say that there is nothing so practical as a good theory. I agree with this, but also believe that practice undoubtedly influences theory. In considering the influence that my research may have had on practice, I shall focus on two areas: classroom behaviour management and reading instruction, since it is a source of continual amazement to me that we teach neither of them well in education faculties.

My work has clearly identified (and this has been replicated many times) that classroom behaviour of most concern to teachers is not violence and aggression (as the media would have us believe) but rather the relatively trivial but persistent and time-wasting behaviours such as 'talking out of turn' (TOOT) and 'hindering other children' (HOC). TOOT and HOC account for the vast majority of teacher complaints about student behaviour and lead to low levels of student on-task behaviour. Being on-task (paying attention to the teacher and getting on with your work) is a necessary (but not, of course, sufficient) condition for learning to take place in the classroom. Our observational studies have repeatedly shown that while teachers typically praise students for good academic product, they almost never praise them for behaving well in class. But by using methods based on positive teaching (rather than continual reprimanding), teachers can be readily trained in how to use positive reinforcement to increase levels of on-task behaviour in their classroom. We have repeatedly demonstrated this to be the case.

The other necessary condition for learning to take place is effective instruction, but we hardly ever seem to employ it in schools! This is particularly evident in the teaching of reading. In spite of the failure of so-called whole language in teaching reading, this is the approach that most teachers identify with and which dominates practice in our schools. Even when young children fail to learn to read, we tend to give them more of the same in the form of Reading Recovery. Our experimental research clearly showed that Reading Recovery is, at best, effective for only one child in three exposed to it. But it is only now, 10 years after we showed this, that Reading Recovery is beginning to be questioned.

This frustration with ineffective instruction in reading and related skills led to our development of MULTILIT. By employing a rigorous, intensive, systematic, skills-based program of instruction, we have demonstrated that low-progress readers can make extraordinary progress. By incorporating what we have learned about how reading works from international research over the past 30 years and coupling it with what we know to be the most effective methods of instruction, we now have a program that makes it possible for most non-readers or low-progress older readers to reach, at least, functional literacy. Moreover, by using curriculum-based measures of reading such as the WARP, we can track the progress students are making over successive weeks and modify their instruction accordingly.

KEY REFERENCES

Center, Y., Wheldall, K., Freeman, L., Outhred, L. & McNaught, M. (1995) An evaluation of Reading Recovery. *Reading Research Quarterly*, **30**, 240–63.

Wheldall, K. & Beaman, R. (2000) *An evaluation of MULTILIT: 'Making Up Lost Time In Literacy'*. Canberra: Department of Education, Training and Youth Affairs.

Wheldall, K. & Glynn, T. (1989) *Effective Classroom Learning: A Behavioural Interactionist Approach to Teaching*. London: Basil Blackwell.

Further references

Merrett, F. & Wheldall, K. (1990) *Positive Teaching in the Primary School*. London: Paul Chapman.

Wheldall, K. (ed.) (1987) *The Behaviourist in the Classroom*. London: Allen & Unwin.

Wheldall, K. & Madelaine, A. (2000) A curriculum-based passage reading test for monitoring the performance of low-progress readers: The development of the WARP. *International Journal of Disability, Development and Education*, **47**, 371–82.

Wheldall, K. & Merrett, F. (1989) *Positive Teaching in the Secondary School*. London: Paul Chapman.

Wheldall, K., Mittler, P. & Hobsbaum, A. (1979, 1987) *Sentence Comprehension Test*. Windsor: National Foundation for Educational Research.

Wheldall, K. & Poborca, B. (1980) Conservation without conversation? An alternative non-verbal paradigm for assessing conservation of liquid quantity. *British Journal of Psychology*, **71**, 117–34.

ACTIVITIES

1. Kevin Wheldall states that anything to do with operant conditioning had been virtually banned from his undergraduate course in psychology. Referring to material in earlier chapters, consider why this might have been the case. Why do you think behaviourism has survived and still contributes to a range of educational approaches to learning and teaching?
2. Kevin Wheldall describes a behavioural approach to testing for conservation in young children. His findings suggest that many more young children are able to conserve than appear to be able to do so using conventional tests. Compare this with comments we made in Chapter 2 on Piagetian tests. Why do you think his results were different?
3. A strong application of behavioural approaches is in classroom management, and in particular positive teaching. Consider the comments made by Kevin Wheldall. Why do you think positive teaching works?
4. Kevin Wheldall makes the comment that having children sitting in traditional rows leads to more time on task and better learning than having children sit around tables in groups. Should we revert to traditional classroom organisations to facilitate learning?
5. Kevin Wheldall makes the controversial statement that he has little time for pure research and tires quickly when faced with post-modern speculation and so-called 'critical theory'. What is your opinion of the relative importance and value of pure and applied research? How might pure research contribute to progress in the art and science of teaching and learning?
6. Read one of the key references provided above.

Table 6.4 Essentials of direct instruction as a behavioural strategy

Teachers should:

- develop an explicit step-by-step strategy;
- ensure mastery at each step in the process;
- provide specific corrections for student errors;
- gradually fade teacher-directed activities towards independent student work;
- provide adequate and systematic practice through a range of examples of the task;
- provide for a cumulative review of newly learned concepts.

Source: Based on Rosenshine & Meister (1995).

Box 6.2

TEACHING COMPETENCE

The teacher plans purposeful programs to achieve specific student learning outcomes

Indicators

The teacher:

- relates learning programs to educational goals and objectives;
- establishes clear purposes for learning programs in terms of agreed student learning outcomes;
- selects and sequences learning activities to achieve planned student outcomes;
- takes account of students' goals and prior learning;
- relates assessment processes and strategies to learning objectives, content and tasks.

Case studies illustrating National Competency Framework for Beginning Teaching, National Project on the Quality of Teaching and Learning, Australian Teaching Council, 1996, Element 3.1, p. 46. Commonwealth of Australia copyright, reproduced by permission.

- both cognitive and metacognitive instruction are involved. (Idol, Jones & Mayer 1991)

In short, while appearing teacher-centred, the emphasis is on the student's needs and responses, with teacher awareness of student understanding a priority. The essentials of direct instruction as a cognitive strategy are given in Table 6.5.

Do these approaches have elements in common? One element in common across these approaches to direct instruction is that students experience a *high level of success* after each step of the learning activity during both guided and independent practice. The amount of material presented, the extent of teacher-guided practice, and the length of time spent on independent practice should be determined by the age of the students and their previous knowledge of the content. Other features in common are:

- presenting new material in small steps;
- modelling learning;
- guided practice;
- 'think-alouds' by teachers and students;
- regulating the level of difficulty in the task;
- cueing learning;
- providing systematic corrections and feedback;
- supporting student corrections;
- providing for independent practice.

Remember that these are the teaching functions that have been found to be most effective. However, they do not have to be followed as a series of prescribed steps: feedback to students, correction of errors, and misunderstanding and reteaching must occur as necessary.

For unstructured material where skills do not have to be sequenced, or where there is no general rule to be learned that has to be applied, such as in problem-solving activities, writing essays, analysing literature or creative expression, explicit teaching is obviously less appropriate and less effective. For this type of material, indirect approaches such as brainstorming, guided questioning and cooperative group work are more appropriate.

Why is direct instruction successful?

Research demonstrates that direct instruction is a very effective instructional technique for both regular and learning-disabled students (Swanson & Hoskyn 1998). Among the reasons for its success are the following:

- The teacher's classroom management is structured, leading to a low rate of student interruptive behaviours.
- The teacher maintains a strong academic focus and uses available instructional time intensively to initiate and facilitate students' learning activities.

Table 6.5

Essentials of direct instruction as a cognitive strategy

Teachers should:

- begin the lesson with a short review of previous learning and a short statement of goals;
- present new material in small steps, providing for student practice after each step;
- give clear and detailed instructions and explanations;
- provide a high level of practice for all students;
- ask a large number of questions, check for student understanding and obtain responses from all students;
- guide students during initial learning phases;
- provide systematic feedback and corrections;
- provide explicit instruction and practice for seatwork exercises and, where necessary, monitor students during seatwork.

Source: Based on Rosenshine & Meister (1995).

EXTENSION STUDY

Positive teaching

The basis of **positive teaching** is for teachers to identify what children find rewarding and then to structure the teaching environment so as to make such rewards dependent on both the social and academic behaviour that they want to encourage (Merrett & Tang 1994; see also Chapter 8). As we stated earlier, teachers have a great deal of control over many of the consequences they provide for their pupils, but few use them consistently and well. Positive teaching shows teachers how to use behavioural techniques such as shaping, fading and reinforcement consistently and effectively.

Applied behaviour analysis

The conditioning of socially appropriate behaviour through the use of reinforcement and punishment has been used successfully in the modification of human behaviour, particularly in cases where the behaviour is atypical and resistant to other forms of modification—for example, aggression in the class, day-dreaming and non-attention, out-of-seat behaviour and antisocial behaviour (such as spitting and verbal abuse) (Cairns 1995; Greenwood *et al.* 1992; Wheldall 1987; Wheldall & Merrett 1990). This approach has been labelled *applied behaviour analysis*.

- The teacher ensures that as many students as possible achieve good learning progress by carefully choosing appropriate tasks, clearly presenting subject matter, information and solution strategies, continually diagnosing each student's learning progress and learning difficulties, and providing them with effective help through remedial instruction (Weinert & Helmke 1995).

Constructivism and behavioural approaches to teaching and learning

The emphasis of behavioural theorists on observable behaviour has led to many educational practices that focus on producing and evaluating specific kinds of overt behaviour, rather than other indicators of learning such as affect and insight. As we have seen, constructivism emphasises developing students' understandings. Within a behavioural teaching context, 'understanding' may be less emphasised than performance. Because of this, students may be able to perform particular academic activities without really understanding the meaning behind them. It is not unusual to see students skilfully doing mathematical calculations without understanding place value, and teachers having to re-explain it with the introduction of each new operation because students never understood it in the first place (Fosnot 1992). Many students can recite the multiplication tables without any idea of how tables are constructed (multiple addition). Students can perform chemical experiments and write up reports without understanding the basic science involved. These 'empty' learnings are not necessarily a by-product of behavioural teaching, but it is something that needs to be guarded against. In fact, if care is taken by the teacher to be aware of what students already know and monitor their progressive development of knowledge, understanding should take place.

For constructivist educators, tasks themselves should be intrinsically interesting, thus obviating the need for extrinsic motivators. Because the instructional sequence is of primary concern in a behavioural approach, teachers (and program designers) may take little care to develop programs that are also stimulating and interesting. Some behaviourally based teaching programs are so crushingly boring that the only recourse for the teacher to keep students motivated is the application of extrinsic reinforcers (such as moving up colour levels, achieving prizes, and so on). These reinforcers are often built into the programs themselves. We discussed earlier in the chapter the potential limitations of applying rewards to ensure that students engage in learning.

Constructivist programs emphasise individual initiative and creative thinking in learning. In many behaviourally based programs there is little, if any, scope for individual initiative as students are locked into preprogrammed material to which they have to make a controlled (predictable) response. In saying this, we also need to emphasise that good behavioural programs are individualised.

Can behavioural approaches incorporate cognitive constructivist elements?

In classical behavioural theory, the centre of attention is clearly the teacher and the materials, with the student being a passive recipient of teacher management and behaviourally manipulated through the use of reinforce-

As with all behavioural approaches, **applied behaviour analysis** must be a carefully planned program designed to lead students to a predetermined goal through the use of rewards. The teacher needs to set up a situation that allows students to experience good behaviour, discriminate between acceptable and unacceptable behaviour, and associate their appropriate behaviour with a reward. The teacher also needs to praise students, telling them how well they are doing, when the agreed-upon reward is presented. Particularly important is the need to help students to become progressively less dependent on the extrinsic reward and to function appropriately in the regular classroom as well as in other settings.

Timeout from reinforcement is used to reduce unwanted behaviour. This means that all reinforcement is removed. In **timeout**, students may be removed to a room (or part of the classroom) where they cannot participate in the ongoing activities or be distracted by occurrences around them. The theory is that the withdrawal of positive consequences will encourage the child to choose to behave in order to be returned to the more rewarding environment of the classroom.

ment. Little opportunity is given for students to construct their own learning (Mageean 1991). Nevertheless, neo-behavioural theorists believe that a cognitive element can be incorporated into their model and, increasingly, efforts are being made to demonstrate this (Wheldall 1987). We see the application of cognitive elements to behavioural interpretations of learning in the next section, on social cognitive theory.

Social cognitive theory and effective learning

The original theory, called *social learning theory*, was based on a framework derived from operant theory. It has its roots in the early work of Bandura and Walters (1963) but is most closely associated with the work of Albert Bandura (1962, 1969, 1977a, 1977b). **Social cognitive theory**, as it is now called, has grown beyond its roots to provide a view of learning that has much to offer educators. Bandura's learning theory (1986) differs from the traditional behaviouristic theories in that it emphasises symbolic representation and self-regulatory procedures (Holland & Kobasigawa 1980) in addition to operant learning. As such, it reflects a number of important constructivist principles. In this theory the functioning of operant conditioning in a social context is examined, as well as the role of cognition in processing information.

Social learning experiences and modelling

Modelling has been shown to aid in the development of many social behaviours, such as moral judgments, altruistic behaviour, resisting and yielding to temptation, aggression and violence, self-reward and social interaction (see, for example, Bushman & Anderson 2001; Ford 2004; Unsworth & Ward 2001).

How might play-acting illustrate the modelling effect?

As an example of the acquisition of behaviour through modelling, consider the growth of assertive and aggressive behaviour in males and females. Gender differences in the development of aggression can be related to the different social learning experiences of males and females (Sanson *et al.* 1993; see also Conrade & Ho 2001; Ford

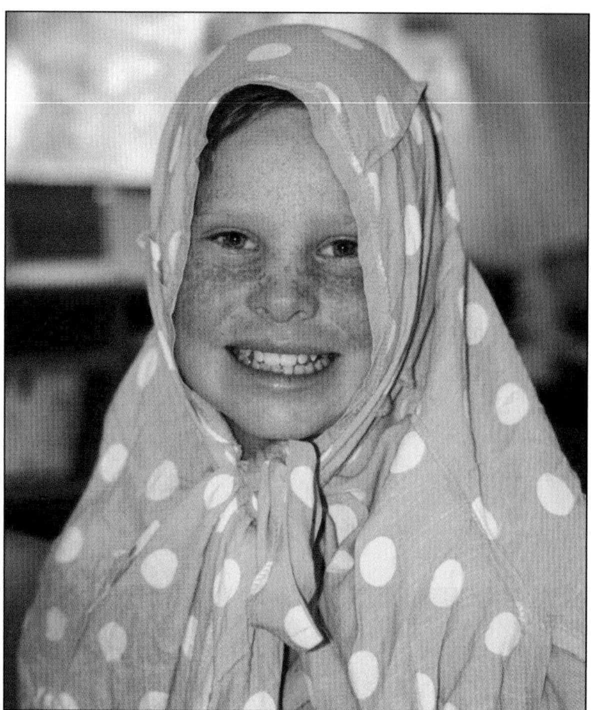

How might opposite-sex role playing be useful?

2004). A key element in this is the nature of the social role stereotypes that males and females experience. In Australia the predominant male stereotype continues to be the 'macho' image. This is reinforced through the aggressive sporting pursuits promoted for males and the many aggressive toys and TV, video and DVD games and programs designed for males. All these factors serve to promote and reinforce the idea that male aggressive behaviour is appropriate, effective and rewarded. This may be coupled with a father model who demonstrates dominance and aggression within the home (see, for example, Conrade & Ho 2001).

This social experience of males stands in marked contrast to the experience of females, who tend to receive reinforcement for exhibiting sympathetic, cooperative and nurturant behaviour, and are expected to be helpful and to take responsibility for the well-being of the family (Sanson *et al.* 1993). The increasing level of assertive behaviour among females, which for some spills over into aggression and violence, has been attributed to the effect of the broader range of models to which females are now exposed, and their increasing involvement in sports and activities that have stereotypically been viewed as male. Films such as the *Aliens* trilogy, *Terminator 2*, *Kill Bill* and *Barb Wire*, and certain types of rap music, present females in violent roles. Many people believe that media violence encourages the development of violence in children and adolescents apparently through some type of modelling effect. Others do not believe that it has this effect. What do you think? (See Anderson & Bushman 2002; Bloom 2002; Bushman & Anderson 2001; Ferguson 2002; Hennigan *et al.* 1982; Smith 1979; Talkington & Altman 1973; Unsworth & Ward 2001.)

Eliciting behaviour

We are all aware that we know how to perform particular actions as a result of observation even if we never actually perform them. Observed learned behaviour does not have to be performed by the learner and, indeed, may never be performed if environmental circumstances don't elicit it. For example, by observing violence, we learn how to be violent; by observing loving behaviour, we learn how to be loving; by observing the way people dress and speak, we learn various ways of dressing and speaking. Sometimes we choose to imitate and practise particular behaviour as a result of our observations; at other times we don't. The theory states that this is because we develop various outcome expectations about the behaviour. The functional value of behaviour, whether it results in success or failure, reward or punishment, exerts strong motivational effects on observer modelling called the **disinhibitory effect**. Modelled behaviours are more likely to be performed if they previously led to rewarding outcomes than if they resulted in punishment. This is regardless of whether individuals experienced the consequences directly or vicariously (Schunk 1987). For example, in the sporting context, youngsters note if aggressive play helps athletes to achieve their goals and whether this is met with approval or disapproval. Behaviour that is rewarded is more likely to be imitated than behaviour that is punished. However, despite this, the youngsters learn the disapproved behaviours but avoid enacting them if parents and others are present, but may perform the behaviours if the people who can potentially punish are absent (see Ford 2004; Wann, Melnick, Russell & Pease 2001). There has been a considerable move over the last years to 'clean up' violence in sport by the imposition of more severe penalties for sports people transgressing. Part of this is to make sport safer, while some of the new punishments are to act as deterrents so that sports people do not act as negative models. Rewards may be extrinsic (such as positive praise from parents or a token such as pocket money) or intrinsic (the satisfaction of performing the action as well as the model). These reinforcers elicit the performance of the modelled behaviour.

When we inhibit the performance of behaviour because we anticipate that its performance will lead to negative consequences and punishment, we see the inhibitory effect of perceived consequences of the act. For example, children learn to smoke and drink alcohol by observing others smoking and drinking (see, for example, Byrne, Byrne & Reinhart 1993, Byrne & Reinhart 1998; Ho 1994; McClellan 1989). On most occasions children do not do either, because they are worried that parents or teachers will catch them at it; hence the behaviour is inhibited through fear of punishment. This is called the **inhibitory effect.** However, many children have smoked behind the toilet block when it was believed that the act was hidden, or raided their parents' liquor cabinet while their parents were out. Adolescents are more likely to smoke and drink if the social climate allows these behaviours and they wish to emulate the behaviour of influential models who smoke and drink (see, for example, Byrne & Reinhart 1998). This is called the *disinhibitory effect.* The incidence of looting, arson and violent behaviour during periods of civil unrest or national disaster can be well explained by the disinhibitory effect.

Four principles governing social cognitive learning

According to social cognitive theory, learning through observation is governed by four processes:

- attention;
- retention;
- reproduction;
- motivation.

People cannot learn effectively unless they *observe, attend to* and *perceive accurately* the significant features of the modelled behaviour. **Observational learning** is the process through which information is obtained from watching models' actions, hearing their descriptions and discerning their consequences (Zimmerman & Kitsantas 2002). Among the factors that influence attention are model characteristics, observer characteristics and features of the modelled behaviour.

Each of these characteristics can be illustrated effectively by many everyday examples. Film stars, sportspeople, teachers, parents and peers have a combination of model characteristics that at times make them very powerful models for young children—and also for not so young people!

Model characteristics influencing attention are:

- *attractiveness* (physical and emotional);
- *social power* (over reward and punishment);
- *status* (perceived importance of the model);
- *competence* (specifically in the area of interest);
- *nurturance* (perceived concern for the observer);
- *interaction level with observer* (degree of contact, energy of contact);
- *similarity* (characteristics in common—such as sex, age, interests—between observer and model).

Also found to be important is whether the model is perceived to be a *mastery* or *coping* model. **Mastery models** demonstrate rapid learning and make no errors while performing a particular task. In contrast, **coping models** show their hesitations and errors, but gradually improve their performance and gain self-confidence. Coping models illustrate how determined effort and positive self-reflections may overcome difficulties (Braaksma, Rijlaarsdam & van den Bergh 2002). Coping models are found to be particularly effective in many circumstances, probably because they don't intimidate the observer with their skills and show how one overcomes difficulties.

Personal observer characteristics also have considerable impact on the attention brought to the model. For example, the perceived competence of a student in a particular activity, referred to as **self-efficacy**, and the activity's importance influence student's attention. Students attend to models of activities at which they feel competent, rather than activities at which they feel less competent.

Observer characteristics influencing attention are:

- level of dependency;
- socio-economic status;

Smoking is modelled behaviour. Despite campaigns to dissuade adolescents from smoking, more girls than ever are beginning to smoke. Why do you think this is?

- race and sex;
- individual's perception of competence in the specific area;
- relevance of incentives.

Features of the modelled behaviour

The modelled behaviour itself must also be capable of attracting attention. In any learning situation the material to be modelled must be characterised by variety and distinctiveness. Material that is bland, presented too quickly or too slowly, or is overly complex will not attract attention, and may lead to downright boredom or frustration, so potential for learning from such models is minimised. Those of you who are preparing to be teachers will be paying particular attention to these aspects in your lesson preparation.

Encoding modelled behaviour to facilitate retention

Learning is most effective when the modelled behaviour is encoded symbolically in images and verbal codes. This basically means that individuals think about what they are doing and rehearse the behaviour mentally before performing it overtly. *At this level, the theory becomes explicitly constructivist in the sense that individuals interpret the modelled behaviour in terms of their existing mental schema.* Among techniques that have been found useful to facilitate retention are talking about the activity to oneself, labelling elements of the performance, or using vivid imagery to imagine the performance of the activity before the event. Many of you will have practised giving a speech in front of a mirror or rehearsed a lesson mentally (and physically) before entering the classroom. Our daughter Laura often says to her father, 'Daddy, what are you saying?' when he is talking to himself rehearsing a lecture.

Retention facilitated through using images and verbal codes

Facilitating reproduction

The third component of modelling is to convert these symbolic representations into appropriate **motor reproductions**. When these actions are accompanied by *immediate corrective feedback* from the model or other source, they become more accurate. Obviously, effective performance depends on appropriate motor skills being available to the individual. Where these are deficient, corrective adjustments must be made. For example, individuals with physical coordination problems will have difficulty writing neatly even if they have learned the modelled behaviour cognitively.

Motivation and social cognitive theory

According to social cognitive theory, motivation is a function of personal expectations and goals and self-evaluative processes (Bandura 1986, 1991; Schunk 1996). As people work to achieve goals, they evaluate their progress. If the evaluation is positive, personal feelings of self-efficacy are enhanced, which sustains motivation. Social and contextual factors affect motivation through their influence on expectations, goals and self-evaluations of progress (Schunk 1989, 1996; see also Vrugt, Oort & Zeeberg 2002). Among the factors that have an impact are social comparisons, goals, rewards and reinforcement, classroom organisation and types of feedback. Aspects of classroom processes that enhance student self-efficacy (such as perceived similarity to the model, discussed earlier) can foster further motivation.

As with operant theory, social cognitive theory holds that observers are more likely to attend to the model's actions (thereby improving the potential for learning) and to adopt the modelled behaviour if the behaviour results in outcomes they value or averts punishment. Observing consequences to the model (that is, **vicarious reinforcement** or punishment) similarly influences the learner's motivation. How many children have resisted the temptation to try a cigarette after witnessing an older sibling being reprimanded by irate parents for smoking?

Social cognitive theory emphasises that reinforcement may facilitate but is not a necessary condition for observational learning to occur. In contrast to operant theory, anticipated rewards are thought to strengthen retention of what has been learned observationally by motivating observers to encode and rehearse the behaviour they value. In this way, reinforcement is believed to be most effective when used as an incentive rather than a reward. In other words, informing observers in advance about the benefits of adopting modelled behaviour is considered to be more effective than waiting until they imitate a model and then rewarding them.

The importance of anticipated rewards to motivation

QUESTION POINT

Discuss the potential strengths and weaknesses of using reinforcement as a reward for, or a facilitator of, behaviour in and out of the classroom.

QUESTION POINT

Discuss, with examples, the four processes—attention, retention, reproduction and motivation—in the context of a classroom lesson. Illustrate how these processes may reflect constructivism.

ACTION STATION

Select a boy or a girl for observation over a period of time, preferably a younger member of your own family. Consider the behaviour of that individual in various situations, at home and with friends. In particular, note participation, sharing, leadership, deference to others, defiance, and so on. Analyse specific aspects of the child's behaviour in objective terms using the following criteria:

1 What are the social influences operating on the child, and how are they influencing the child's behaviour?
2 What appears to be reinforcing the behaviour, where does the reinforcement come from, and how frequently?
3 Which behaviours appear to be shaped by observational learning? How can you tell?
4 What behaviours appear to be modelled? What behaviours appear to be elicited? Have you seen any evidence of the inhibitory/disinhibitory effect?

ACTION STATION

Choose five or six television programs, some catering for adults and some specifically designed for children. Note their titles, type (comedy, drama, nature, and so on), origin and duration. Make the following observations:

1 What types of models are presented?
2 What kinds of vicarious experiences are offered to young children?
3 Are there differences in the models that are presented to girls and boys, and to female and male adults?
4 What kinds of vicarious reinforcers and punishers are presented?
5 Suggest some positive and negative aspects of television as a social influence on children.

Classroom applications of social cognitive theory

Social cognitive theory can be applied directly to the classroom (Yates & Yates 1978). The theory draws our attention to the power of models in the classroom and to the effects of vicarious reward and punishment on the performance of behaviour. There is a rich research base that illustrates the power of modelling in shaping student academic, emotional and affective behaviour (Copeland & Weissbrod 1980; D. Deutsch 1979; Gresham 1981; King, Ollendick & Gullone 1990; Schunk 1987; Stoneman & Brody 1981).

Vicarious effects of reward and punishment

Social cognitive theory gives strong support for the use of peer modelling. Reinforcement given to one child may 'spill over' and serve as a cue to other peers that their own behaviour could attract the teacher's attention (Kazdin 1973). For example, when a teacher's attention is focused on the inattentive behaviour of one student, nearby peers actually increase their attentive behaviour. In other words, direct reinforcement or punishment of target students may have a vicarious effect on peers watching them. Observing others' successes, failures, rewards and punishments creates outcome expectations in observers that they are likely to experience similar outcomes for performing the same behaviours (Schunk 1987). However, a target student's reactions to the praise or punishment may serve to strengthen or weaken the intended effect of vicarious consequences. For example, a student ridiculed for asking 'stupid' questions becomes a negative model for his equally naïve, though now inhibited, classmates. Students who revel in the attention of annoyed and angry teachers, or disparage the positive attention of teachers, act as negative models and undermine the intended effect of the vicarious reward or vicarious punishment (Yates & Yates 1978).

Spill-over effect

It is important to ensure that students who do perform appropriate modelled behaviour after witnessing vicarious consequences are themselves directly rewarded, at least intermittently, otherwise these behaviours will not be performed, even though learned.

Peer models, self-efficacy and motivation

Peers may be effectively used to demonstrate classroom procedures. A teacher may call upon students in his class to demonstrate how to do a forward roll, draw a bushfire or complete a mathematical exercise. University students

Peer demonstration

may be asked to demonstrate aspects of good teaching practice to their peers. These motivational effects are hypothesised to depend, in part, on perceptions of self-efficacy, or personal beliefs about one's capabilities to perform the desired behaviours to the same level of proficiency as demonstrated (Bandura 1986; Schunk 1987, 1996).

One important aspect of peer models is therefore that they can supply a realistic gauge of what is potentially possible for children who lack a sense of self-efficacy. Adult models may be perceived as possessing a level of competence that children are unlikely to attain, whereas peer models may be seen as more similar and hence able to be copied. Same-sex models do not appear to be any more successful than different-sex models except in those behaviours that relate to gender-appropriate behaviour. Sex of model seems less important in general learning contexts.

Factors influencing the impact of the model

Students are inclined to model equally the behaviour of peers and adults, depending on two criteria: first, the modelled behaviour must appear to be instrumental in achieving goals; second, the model must appear competent. Where peers are viewed as being as competent as adults, the behaviours of both are likely to be modelled. When children question the competence of peers, they tend to model the behaviour of adults. When same-age peers are viewed as less competent than younger peers, children pattern their behaviour after the competent but younger children rather than age-mates of lower competence than themselves (Schunk 1987).

Apart from academic areas, teachers use peer modelling for a variety of purposes. One common use is to illustrate that activities shouldn't be sex stereotyped: thus we have girls and boys alike emptying the school bins, learning bush dancing, and doing cross-stitch and embroidery. Teachers use symbolic models such as literature, pictures and posters, or video to illustrate and emphasise the models. Observational learning principles and, in particular, peer modelling are used with children who experience various forms of social anxiety such as social withdrawal and isolation. Typically, the isolate child is required to observe peers engage in the requisite behaviours. This modelling process may be achieved through the use of live or video models. In one experiment, young isolate children viewed a film depicting several peer models engaging in a variety of social activities. In contrast to a control group of children who viewed a film about dolphins, these children showed substantial increases in peer interactions after viewing the film (King *et al.* 1990).

Teachers as models

Student attitudes towards school

Teachers are highly influential models in establishing and maintaining students' attitudes towards their studies. Teachers' expressed attitudes towards dress, television, morals and so on can have a significant influence on students. Students can also learn attitudes towards school: cheerfulness, enthusiasm, patience, fairness, consistency and optimism. If teachers fail to display these qualities, they are unlikely to see them in their students (Yates & Yates 1978).

Teacher demonstrations

In order to function as effective models of academic skills, teachers should make use of effective demonstrations. Table 6.6 illustrates some features of effective demonstrations from a social cognitive perspective.

Modelling thought processes and constructivism

Modelling of thought processes does not mean explaining how something is done. **Modelling** is thinking aloud to express the thoughts, feelings and attitudes of teachers as they figure something out, with all the stops and starts, puzzlements, revisions and on-line processing of thinking that occur in reality (Idol *et al.* 1991). Modelling of thinking aloud is particularly important in teaching students how to construct meaning (especially because of the non-linear aspect of thinking), how to monitor one's thinking, and how to answer a question through reasoning. Modelling also demonstrates how people may construct somewhat different meanings because they have different prior knowledge and perspectives about a specific topic (Idol *et al.* 1991).

How might peer group modelling be a powerful influence on children?

TABLE 6.6

Essentials of a social cognitive approach in education

Teachers should:

- *focus attention* on a specific area or task and ensure that all students are paying attention;
- give a *general orientation* or overview—explain what is to happen;
- *label* verbally and visually any new concepts or objects, and have students repeat these;
- *verbalise thought processes* involved in problem solving or performing behaviours;
- *model methods of gathering information* through questioning so that students can learn these cognitive strategies themselves;
- *proceed step by step*—break each complex behaviour into smaller operations and demonstrate processes by thinking aloud;
- perform actions with appropriate pace to *maintain attention*;
- provide student opportunity for *guided practice*—for example, through teacher mentoring or peer tutoring—so that corrective feedback can be given by the teacher;
- provide opportunity for *independent practice*;
- *not emphasise mistakes*—redemonstrate and encourage another attempt;
- *provide antecedent reinforcement* for efforts and achievements;
- *use valued models* to demonstrate behaviours, skills and attitudes.

Teachers should teach learners to:

- pay attention;
- check to see if they understand what is to be done: ask questions if they are unclear;
- draw or write a description of a new idea or procedure to show that they understand what to do;
- talk out loud/describe what they are doing or thinking while working out a solution or doing an activity;
- copy the teacher or other students who show them good ways to find information;
- practise what they have been shown and try again if they make a mistake;
- think about how they can break down a large piece of work into a series of small tasks;
- observe what happens to other students when they do a task or solve problems. Do they get rewards or feel good about themselves?
- think about what might encourage them to work hard on a task.

Scaffolded instruction and mentoring for apprentices

New learners in a particular area are often referred to as apprentices. The learning of apprentices can be facilitated by mentoring and scaffolding. Both mentoring and scaffolding of apprentices involve observation of models, guided practice by the model, and feedback on the efforts of the apprentice that is progressively reduced. For Idol *et al.* (1991, p. 80), the hallmarks of successful models of teaching thinking skills are presented in Table 6.7.

Social cognitive theory and self-regulated learning

From Bandura's social cognitive theory has developed the self-regulated learning model (Corno 1992; Martin 2004; Zimmerman 1990, 1998; Zimmerman & Schunk 1989). The study of self-regulation is one of the major topics in educational psychology today (see, for example, Perry 2002, and whole issue; Pintrich & Zusho 2002, Zimmerman 2004). **Self-regulation** can be defined as

Table 6.7

Essentials of modelling effective thinking skills

Teachers should:

- model, especially thinking aloud about how to apply strategies or skills;
- coach, which involves diagnosing problems, prescribing corrections and providing feedback;
- articulate, getting students to articulate their knowledge and thinking process;
- reflect about the process of thinking;
- explore—that is, push students to extend their learning.

Source: Based on Idol *et al.* (1991).

self-generated thoughts, feelings and actions for attaining academic goals (Zimmerman 1998, 2004). Self-regulated learners view learning as a systematic and controllable process and accept responsibility for their achievement outcomes. Self-regulated learners approach tasks with confidence, diligence and resourcefulness, and proactively seek out information when needed, attempting to take the necessary steps to master it. Self-regulated students are metacognitively, motivationally and behaviourally active participants in their own learning (Winne 1995b; Zimmerman 1990, 1994, 2004; see also Wolters 2003a, 2003b). In terms of metacognitive processes, self-regulated learners plan, set goals, organise, self-monitor and self-evaluate at various points during the learning process. Because of this they are self-aware, knowledgeable, and decisive in their approach to learning. Self-regulated learners appear to be self-motivated and report high self-efficacy (that is, a belief in themselves as learners) and self-attribution (that is, they accept responsibility for successes and failures); they value the importance of effort and intrinsic task interest (Pintrich & De Groot 1990; see also Bråten, Samuelstuen & Strømsø 2004). Self-regulatory behaviour may not be applied equally in all situations. Whether a learner self-regulates can depend on the domain and situation (for example, curriculum area, specific activity); the social and learning environment (and, in particular, the degree of student initiative allowed relative to teacher regulation); and the nature of the learning outcomes desired by the learner (Alexander 1995; Boekaerts 1995; Butler 1998; Cordingley *et al.* 1998; Zimmerman 1998).

The way in which learners self-regulate is also a function of a number of important cognitive processes regarding their knowledge and beliefs (Butler 1998; Butler & Winne 1995). These processes include their interpretation of the tasks and goals they set themselves, which may be influenced by: their understanding of typical task demands; their beliefs about factors responsible for successful and unsuccessful performance (which we call attributional beliefs); and task-specific perceptions of their self-efficacy. Learners' understanding and mastery of learning strategies may also influence the degree and manner in which they self-regulate. We cover these points in greater detail in the next section on self-efficacy, and in our chapter on motivation.

The nature and dynamics of self-regulation may also vary across cultures, with particular types of behaviour being more associated with self-regulation in one culture than in another (see, for example, Boekaerts 1998; Purdie, Hattie & Douglas 1996; Purdie & Hattie 1996). We consider this cross-cultural issue further in Chapter 10. Psychological dimensions implicated in whether a student self-regulates or not (at least in Western educational settings) are the individual's degree of self-motivation for the task (involving goal setting and self-efficacy), the opportunity to choose learning approaches and manage time limits (involving task strategies, self-instruction and time management), some control over the physical and social environment (involving environmental restructuring to make it more conducive to learning, and selective help seeking from peers, teachers and others), level of control over selecting appropriate outcome behaviour (involving self-monitoring, self-evaluation and self-consequences), and the balance between teacher- and student-perceived control over classroom learning (Eshel & Kohavi 2003; Perry 1998; Zimmerman 1998).

Self-managed reinforcement

Some self-regulated learning strategies thought to regulate students' personal functioning, academic behavioural performance and learning environments are given below (Purdie *et al.* 1996; Zimmerman & Martinez-Pons 1990). How many of these do you use in your learning?

SELF-REGULATED LEARNING STRATEGIES

1 *Self-evaluation*—'I check over my work to make sure I did it right.'
2 *Organisation and transformation*—'I make an outline before I write a paper.'
3 *Goal setting and planning*—'I commence revision a number of weeks before the test.'
4 *Information seeking*—'I read as widely as possible on the subject.'
5 *Record keeping and self-monitoring*—'I pick out the unknown words and make cards.'
6 *Environmental structuring*—'I make my desk clean and tidy and put all the books I need nearby.'
7 *Giving self-consequences*—'I give myself rewards during study breaks, such as watching TV.'
8 *Rehearsing and memorising*—'I write out all the important points many times so that I can remember them.'
9 *Seeking social assistance (from peers, teachers and other adults)*—'I discuss the assignment with my friend on the way home in the train.'
10 *Reviewing (notes, books or tests)*—'I go over my notes on the topic.'

TEACHER'S CASE BOOK

That was fun. Let's do it again.

Nicole teaches Japanese to Year 8 students at a metropolitan high school. In their eighth Japanese lesson, Nicole was teaching the students to respond appropriately to simple classroom instructions given in Japanese. She used a series of games to help her students overcome their resistance to speaking a new language in front of their peers. The lesson was started with students listening to the instructions and mimicking the teacher's actions.

Tatte kudasai (Stand up). Suwatte kudasai (Sit down).

As practice time continued, the teacher stopped doing the actions herself and allowed the students to determine the responses. At this stage some students merely copied the responses of others. They were shy and reluctant to participate.

The next stage was to play a game of 'Simon Says' in Japanese. Students who were 'out' helped to judge who was slowest or who did the action incorrectly. At this stage, unwilling students were still not fully involved as they copied others and were quickly eliminated from the game.

Saimon wa tatte kudasai, to iimashita (Simon says 'stand up').

The class was then divided into four teams for a new game. One member from each team came to the front of the class. The teacher then gave an instruction to the four students at the front.

Mite kudasai (Please look). Kiite kudasai (Please listen).

The first person to respond won a point for their team. All students were encouraged by their team-mates and were participating in the class. When students were given a quiz at the end of the lesson, most of the class gained 100 per cent and, as one of the students said as he left the room, 'That was fun. Let's play again.'

Case studies illustrating National Competency Framework for Beginning Teaching, National Project on the Quality of Teaching and Learning, Australian Teaching Council, 1996, p. 50.

Case study activity

In what ways does this case study exemplify social cognitive theory?

Self-regulation, motivation and achievement

Self-regulated learning is related to academic motivation and academic achievement. Research indicates that students who are academic high achievers practise a greater range of self-regulatory strategies, and more often, than low achievers (Ablard & Lipschultz 1998; Cordingley *et al.* 1998; Purdie & Hattie 1996; Zimmerman & Martinez-Pons 1990). In particular, high-achieving students report greater use of organising and transforming, reviewing notes and seeking assistance from adults (Zimmerman & Martinez-Pons 1990). They may also make greater use of the full range of strategies such as self-evaluating, goal setting and planning, keeping records, and monitoring and reviewing texts (Ablard & Lipschults 1998). However, some high-achieving students, when asked how they approach learning tasks, do not report the use of self-regulating strategies and it is possible that this is because they use alternative cognitive strategies or have automated the self-regulating strategies so that they are no longer aware of them (Ablard & Lipschults 1998). There is also some evidence for gender differences in the use of self-regulating strategies, with high-achieving females using more record keeping and monitoring, structuring the environment, and goal setting and planning than high-achieving males. The reasons and implications for this are not yet clear and this issue is currently under research.

Developing self-regulation

The skills of self-regulation detailed above don't occur naturally or spontaneously in learners. Indeed, the development of such skills is complex and long term. Teaching episodes need to be developed to encourage learners to develop these skills across a range of subjects so that, in the long term, self-regulating becomes a generalised capacity (see Butler 1998; Pressley 1995; Zimmerman 1998).

Even within a behaviourally oriented classroom, children may still practise self-regulatory strategies and be involved in goal setting, monitoring their own work, keeping progress records and evaluating their work. They may also be involved in selecting their own rewards and punishments and administering them. Obviously, the developmental level of the children has much to do with the successful implementation of such a plan. The ability of students to set goals is very important to self-management and motivation. Students who successfully set goals and can communicate them to others (such as the teacher) perform better than those who have vague goals (Hayes *et al.* 1985). With appropriate training, students can monitor their own work and keep progress records, which should also foster their motivation to learn. Some suggest that they can also be taught to evaluate their own work adequately (Rhode, Morgan & Young 1983; Paris & Oka 1986), although monitoring by the teacher is important to validate the accuracy of the evaluation. Self-reinforcement is the final step. Bandura

Theory and research into practice

Barry Zimmerman — SELF-REGULATION AND EFFECTIVE LEARNING

BRIEF BIOGRAPHY

I was born and raised in the American state of Wisconsin. I received my B.A. degree in 1965 and my Ph.D. in Educational Psychology in 1969 from the University of Arizona. Upon graduation, I joined the faculty at Arizona as an assistant professor. In 1974, I accepted a faculty position as an associate professor at the City University of New York, and in 1978, I was promoted to professorial status. In that same year, my colleague Ted Rosenthal and I published *Social Learning and Cognition*, which summarised our and others' research on instructional modelling. During the 1980s, I shifted my focus to studying students' development of self-regulatory competence to learn. I co-edited a book with Dale Schunk in 1989 entitled *Self-Regulated Learning and Academic Achievement*, which focused on various theoretical perspectives on this emerging topic. Dale and I co-edited a second book in 1994 that summarised the results of the first wave of research on students' self-regulatory processes. In that same year, I received the Senior Scientist Award of the American Psychological Association for outstanding contributions to school psychology. In 1996, I was elected president of the educational psychology division of the American Psychological Association. In that same year, I was appointed as distinguished professor at the City University of New York. Dale Schunk and I co-edited a third book in 1998, entitled *Self-Regulated Learning: From Teaching to Self-Reflection,* which focused on teaching self-regulation. In 1999, I received the Sylvia Scribner Award of the American Educational Research Association for exemplary research in Learning and Instruction. Dale and I co-edited a second edition of *Self-Regulated Learning and Academic Achievement* in 2001, which updated the various theories of self-regulation in light of a decade of research. I currently serve as head of the Learning, Development, and Instruction concentration at the City University of New York.

RESEARCH AND THEORETICAL INTERESTS

When I began my research career in the early 1970s, social modelling was not viewed as a teaching technique that could convey abstract cognitive skills to novice learners, such as young children. Critics charged that modelling could produce only imitations of pre-existing overt behaviour and that such learning would not be transferred or sustained over time. In a series of studies, Ted Rosenthal and I demonstrated that even young children could be taught a wide variety of cognitive skills precociously using modelling, and that these responses were transferred to new tasks and maintained. These conceptual skills included learning strategies, Piagetian concepts, moral rules, problem-solving strategies, linguistic knowledge, and even creative ideas. Based on this research and that of others, in a 1974 *Psychological Bulletin* article Ted and I challenged developmental stage theories as underestimating children's ability to learn.

During the 1980s, I shifted my research focus to a learner's self-regulatory competence. I questioned conceptions of education that merely sought to provide students with passive knowledge and skill, and suggested instead that educators should develop youngsters' capability to take charge of their own development of competence, a phenomenon I labelled 'self-regulated learning'. I hypothesised that mature learners feel a sense of control of and responsibility for their learning, and as a result, they find a way to adapt when they encounter difficult conditions. My studies with my student, Manuel Martinez-Pons, demonstrated that students' self-regulated learning processes could be measured reliably and were highly predictive of the achievement and perceived self-efficacy. These self-efficacy findings were significant because they revealed increased student motivation to continue learning in a self-directed manner. To introduce these issues to the field, I edited and contributed to special journal issues of *Contemporary Educational Psychology* (1986) and *Educational Psychologist* (1990) on self-regulation of academic learning, and authored an article in the *Journal of Educational Psychology* (1989) that provided a comprehensive social cognitive perspective on this topic. My conceptualisations of self-regulated learning influenced not only academic researchers but also researchers in other applied fields, such as health and disease management.

During 1991, I was a visiting scholar at Stanford University where I worked with Albert Bandura pioneering path analytic studies of the role of self-efficacy in students' academic functioning. These studies demonstrated that students' self-efficacy beliefs were not only predictive of their use of self-regulatory processes, such as goal setting and self-evaluation, but were also predictive of their academic achievement. In these studies, students' self-efficacy beliefs and self-regulatory processes enhanced predictions of their subsequent achievement by more than 30 per cent compared to prior achievement indices.

During the latter part of the 1990s, I developed a model of self-regulation that integrated students' use of a wide variety of self-regulatory processes and self-motivational beliefs in three cyclical phases: forethought, performance and self-reflection. My colleagues and I demonstrated that poor learners did not engage in effective forethought, and this led to poorly self-regulated efforts to learn and to unproductive self-reflective processes, which undermined future efforts to learn. I also developed a model of academic skill development that began with modelling and led to self-regulation. My students and I demonstrated that learners who were first exposed to exemplary models of self-regulated learning were able to gradually emulate the model's learning techniques and then practise the modelled skill effectively on their own. Students who were taught according to this sequence not only displayed higher levels of achievement, but also higher levels of motivational beliefs associated with sustained efforts to continue learning. These two models were validated in a series of studies that were published in the *Journal of Educational Psychology* and *Journal of Applied Sport Psychology*.

THEORY AND RESEARCH INTO PRACTICE

My modelling research was used in collaboration with Ronald Henderson and Rosemary Swanson (1975) to create instructional videotapes to teach Piagetian conservation concepts to young rural Native American children. These youngsters represented a demanding test for this modelling instructional methodology because they came from a poor, culturally isolated subgroup. The videotapes utilised hand puppet models to depict mythical creatures from tribal folklore. Prior experimental research had demonstrated that instructional modelling effects were enhanced by self-verbalised rule statements by the model, and these verbalisations were integrated into the narrative via the puppets' explanations for their conserving judgments. Transfer was designed by having multiple puppet models respond to a series of conservation tasks involving different materials, such as clay, containers of water, and plastic chips. Significant learning and transfer was subsequently found with these academically at-risk children who showed little evidence of Piaget's concrete operations phase before training.

A second issue involves whether teachers typically utilise modelling as part of their instructional techniques. My student Cheryl Fuss Kleefeld and I (1977) asked elementary school teachers to teach the Piagetian skill of seriation to a young child. Very few teachers spontaneously used modelling to demonstrate how to perform this skill on a series of problems, even though such materials were readily available. Instead, the teachers tended to use a questioning approach designed to help the students to understand the task better. These untrained teachers were ineffective in conveying the seriation skill to preschool children, whereas teachers who were trained to use instructional modelling not only conveyed the skill effectively to the children but did so in 40 per cent less time. Clearly, modelling is a powerful but underused instructional technique!

During my initial efforts to assess students' self-regulation, Manuel Martinez-Pons and I (1986) developed a structured interview for individually assessing students' self-regulatory reactions to hypothetical academic problems, such as writing an essay or motivating oneself to complete one's homework when tired. This instrument proved to be a reliable measure of student differences in self-regulation and was highly predictive of their academic achievement. We were curious to discover whether teachers were aware of a student's degree of self-regulation, so we developed a questionnaire for teachers to report visible signs of each student's self-regulation in class, such as whether a student completes his or her homework assignments on time or whether the student knows how well he or she did on a test before it is graded by the teacher. We discovered that teachers' ratings of their students' use of self-regulated learning processes were highly correlated with the students' self-reports. Thus, these teachers were very aware of their students' level of self-regulatory discipline.

My students Sebastian Bonner and Robert Kovach and I authored a teachers' manual for enhancing students' self-regulation and self-efficacy entitled *Development of Self-Regulated Learners: From Achievement to Self-Efficacy* in 1996. This book described how middle- and high-school students could be empowered to learn more effectively by improving five essential academic skills: (a) planning and using study time more effectively; (b) understanding and summarising text material better; (c) improving methods of note taking; (d) anticipating and preparing better for examinations; and (e) writing more effectively. Each skill was learned as part of typical homework exercises by prompting students to use four self-regulatory processes: (a) self-observing and self-evaluating one's initial level of skill; (b) choosing a strategy and setting a goal for improving one's effectiveness; (c) implementing the strategy; and (d) judging its personal effectiveness in reaching the goal.

In recent years, I have studied the role of self-regulatory processes and their enhancement in diverse fields, including music, sports and health, as well as academic functioning.

KEY REFERENCES

Schunk, D. H. & Zimmerman, B. J. (eds) (1998) *Self-Regulated Learning: From Teaching to Self-Reflective Practice*. New York: Guilford Press.

Zimmerman, B. J. (1998) Academic studying and the development of personal skill: A self-regulatory perspective. *Educational Psychologist*, **33**, 73–86.

Zimmerman, B. J., Bonner, S. & Kovach, R. (1996) *Developing Self-Regulated Learners: Beyond Achievement to Self-Efficacy*. Washington, DC: American Psychological Association.

ACTIVITIES

1 Barry Zimmerman argues that modelling can be used to teach a wide variety of cognitive skills and hence bridge the gap between radical behaviourism (in which cognition is ignored) and radical cognitive theories (in which overt behaviour plays little part). How do you think modelling may be used to teach cognitive skills?

2 Why is self-regulation an important component of effective learning? What are the essential elements of self-regulation?

3 What self-regulatory skills do you use? Compare your answers with those of other students. Which skills did you learn? Which skills came 'naturally'? If they came naturally, can you explain how and why? On the basis of this discussion, develop a comprehensive list of self-regulatory skills used by efficient learners and suggestions on how they might be fostered.

4 Barry Zimmerman makes the point that modelling is a powerful but underused instructional technique. Why do you think this is the case? Have you observed teachers using modelling effectively in the classroom? Discuss your experiences with other students. Based on your combined experiences, what do you think are the elements of effective modelling in classrooms?

5 Read and critique the article by Barry Zimmerman in *Educational Psychologist* (1998).

How can peer models enhance feelings of self-efficacy in other children?

(1986) argues that giving oneself rewards on the basis of good performance enhances future performance, although other psychologists maintain it is unnecessary (Bandura 1986; Hayes *et al.* 1985; Rhode *et al.* 1983; Schunk 1990, 1991; Zimmerman 1990, 1994).

Obviously it is important for teachers to create learning environments that encourage a shift from strong external regulation from the teacher to some forms of shared control if students are to develop effective self-regulated learning processes. Many schools and educational environments do not encourage their students to take a proactive role in learning.

Self-reinforcement is very important. Here a group is congratulating itself on a job well done.

Defensive and self-handicapping learning

Self-regulated learning contrasts with an approach to learning that has been called defensive (Paris & Newman 1990) and self-handicapping (Covington 1992). Students who are defensive and self-handicapping typically have low efficacy for learning and avoid failure and damage to self-esteem by seeking easy tasks, procrastinating or avoiding work altogether (Perry 1998).

Instructional designs and theories

We began our discussion of effective learning by asking a basic question: How do people learn? In our analysis of this we have covered a broad range of theoretical perspectives. Among other questions we have addressed are the following:

- What are the influences that determine teaching practice?
- Are some teaching practices more effective than others? Why?
- Are some teaching practices more suited to particular activities?
- Are some teaching practices more suited to particular students?

Perhaps Bruner's insights (1985, pp. 5–7) on the best way to foster learning will give you food for thought:

> Any model of learning is right or wrong for a given set of stipulated conditions, including the nature of the tasks one has in mind, the form of the intention one creates in the learner, the generality or specificity of the learning to be accomplished, and the semiotics of the learning situation itself, what it means to the learner . . .
>
> It was a vanity of a preceding generation to think that the battle over learning theories would eventuate in one winning over all the others. Any learner has a host of learning strategies at command. The salvation is in learning how to go about learning before getting to the point of no return. We would do well to equip learners with a menu of their possibilities and, in the course of their education, to arm them with procedures and sensibilities that would make it possible for them to use the menu wisely.

The current status of learning theories

What is the current status of these theories, and what evidence is there that models derived from them are effective? Each of the theories covered in Chapters 4, 5

Seeking help from others is an important aspect of self-regulated learning. How may teachers most encourage the development of self-efficacy in students?

and 6 has generated a vast amount of research. A review of some aspects of this research conducted since 1977 yields impressive evidence for the effectiveness of a variety of innovative teaching practices drawn from *cognitive*, *behavioural* and *social cognitive* theories (Joyce, Showers & Rolheiser-Bennett 1987). With regard to social cognitive theory, cooperative learning approaches which represent social models of teaching appear effective in producing positive outcomes in higher-order thinking, problem solving, social skills and attitudes. The use of advance organisers (derived from Ausubel's theory) and other cognitive tools for learning (such as mnemonics), on the other hand, can help students to remember learned material with long-lasting effects. Research on DISTAR, an example of the behavioural family of models, is similarly associated with increased achievement and influences aptitude to learn.

As mentioned previously, when these models and the strategies derived from them are combined, they have even greater potential for improving student learning. We should use a variety of models because: certain models are more appropriate to particular pupil needs; certain models are more appropriate to particular subjects; models can be adapted and combined to increase effectiveness; the multiplicity of school and classroom objectives requires a variety of models; and the effective use of a variety of models enhances flexibility and the professional competence of the teacher (Brady 1985).

Table 6.8 on p. 199 presents a comparison of the four main learning theories covered in the text.

QUESTION POINT

Using the information contained in this and earlier chapters, discuss how particular pupil needs may best be met by a particular teaching model or combination of models.

QUESTION POINT

Discuss how the demands of particular school subjects may make one teaching model more suitable than another.

ACTION STATION

Observe a teacher over a period of a day (or several days). Make notes on the teacher's use of instructional designs for teaching. For what purposes were they used? When were they used? How were the designs combined? In what ways did learner characteristics influence the choice of instructional approach?

Prepare a timetable of the teacher's day and indicate the material or topic being taught, the time and length of the session, and which particular design or combination of designs was used by the teacher.

ACTION STATION

Select a topic from a curriculum area in which you are specialising. Write three separate lesson plans for the presentation of this material, one reflecting a behavioural approach, one a cognitive approach and one a social cognitive approach. You will need to describe the age and ability levels of the children for whom the lesson is being prepared. Compare and contrast the different approaches. You might like to trial each approach during practice teaching.

Social cognitive theory and self-efficacy

In social cognitive theory there is an emphasis on self-efficacy. *Self-efficacy* refers to individuals' belief that they can exercise control over their own level of functioning and over events that affect their lives. Efficacy beliefs influence how people feel, think, motivate themselves and behave. Albert Bandura believes that *students' beliefs in their efficacy* to regulate their own learning and to master academic activities determine their aspirations, level of motivation and academic achievements. *Teachers' beliefs in their personal efficacy* to motivate and promote learning affect the types of learning environments they create and the level of academic progress their students achieve (see Chapter 1). Bandura also believes that whole-school beliefs in their collective instructional efficacy contribute significantly to the schools' level of academic achievement (Bandura 1986, 1993; Fives & Alexander 2004; Goddard 2001; Goddard, Hoy & Woolfolk Hoy 2000, 2004; Schunk 1991). This area of collective efficacy beliefs is receiving considerable attention today and we dealt with this and other efficacy beliefs in more detail in Chapter 1. Our own research (McInerney 1993; McInerney, Roche, McInerney & Marsh, 1997; McInerney & Swisher 1995; see also Pajares, Miller & Johnson 1999) suggests that self-efficacy for the task of school learning is one of the most important determinants of school motivation and achievement across a wide range of cultural groups. Self-efficacy has to do with self-perception of competence rather than actual level of competence. Some individuals may display a lot of skill in an area and yet evaluate themselves negatively because of the high personal standards they have set themselves (Tschannen-Moran, Woolfolk Hoy & Hoy 1998; see also Pajares *et al.* 1999).

Bandura believes that the higher individuals' perceived self-efficacy, the higher the goal challenges they set for themselves and the firmer their commitment to them. It is believed that students base their appraisals of ability on a wide range of sources, including their actual performance, feedback from others, and vicarious (observational) experiences such as seeing others performing in a like manner being praised, ignored or ridiculed. High self-efficacy (or perceived ability) for a particular activity does not in itself necessarily lead to motivated behaviour. The perceived value of the activity and outcome expectations also influence level of motivation. However, without a sense of self-efficacy it is unlikely that children will engage in activities, irrespective of whether they are perceived as important or not.

Help seeking and self-efficacy

As we have seen above, seeking help from peers, teachers and others is an important aspect of self-regulated learning. Research suggests that students who are low in self-efficacy for learning avoid seeking help because it implies that they are less able than other students. On the other hand, students who are high in self-efficacy seek help more often (Ryan, Gheen & Midgley 1998; see also Karabenick 1998; Newman 2002). This contrast is exacerbated depending on the nature of the motivational goals established in the classroom. For example, if classrooms emphasise relative performance on tasks through competition and ranking, then students low in self-efficacy are even more likely to avoid seeking help. No doubt the irony of the situation has struck you. Students who most need help don't seek it, while students less in need of help do! Hence, students low in self-efficacy put themselves at a greater disadvantage for learning and achievement. This danger is reduced in classrooms that emphasise personal improvement, understanding, mastery and the intrinsic value of learning. The difference in help-seeking behaviours between high- and low-efficacy students is also reduced in classrooms that emphasise good interpersonal relationships and provide a warm and supportive environment (Ryan *et al.* 1998). We discuss the issue of motivational orientations and goals further in Chapter 7.

Helping students to develop self-efficacy

Bandura (1997) postulates four sources of efficacy beliefs: (a) mastery experiences, (b) physiological and emotional states, (c) vicarious experiences, and (d) social persuasion. The perception that one has been successful at an activity raises efficacy beliefs and therefore raises expectations that future performances will also be successful. The opposite also applies, with perceptions that one has not been successful leading to decreased efficacy beliefs and perceptions for future success. Physiological and emotional states add to the feelings of mastery or failure, thereby heightening future beliefs about success or failure. In other words, an activity in which one has been highly engaged will have a greater impact than one in which one was less engaged. Vicarious experiences also influence efficacy beliefs through the impact of a model's success or failure and their subsequent efficacy beliefs. Finally, social persuasion can also influence one's feelings of efficacy. In other words, valued friends, family and teachers can heighten our feelings of self-efficacy by telling us 'You can do it!', provided the individual trusts the persuader.

How can we help students to develop self-efficacy? There are a number of important ways of helping to develop and maintain self-efficacy among students, including teaching goal setting and information-processing strategies, using models, and providing attributional feedback and rewards (Schunk 1991; see also Schunk & Pajares 2004).

The setting of challenging but attainable goals and the achievement of these goals enhances self-efficacy and motivation (Schunk 1990; Zimmerman, Bandura & Martinez-Pons 1992). Teachers need to assist students to set both *proximal* or (short-term) goals and *distal* (or long-term) goals. Among techniques suggested by Schunk are setting upper and lower limits on students' goals and removing them when students understand the nature of the task and their immediate capabilities, using games (such as shooting for goals in basketball), and goal-setting conferences where students learn to assess goal difficulty and their present level of skill in collaboration with the teacher. As students become more self-regulated they will be more adept at setting their own goals. Short-term goals are important, particularly for younger or novice learners, as progress is more noticeable. However, the achievement of long-term goals is ultimately more important for the development of self-efficacy, as it offers more information about developed capabilities. Associated with this point is the notion that, if students feel they have control over their goal setting and learning, self-efficacy is enhanced.

If students are taught information-processing strategies (that is, their **metacognitive** and *metalearning* skills are developed), they are more likely to feel competent in a range of learning situations and therefore more motivated to continue in these activities. We have discussed the importance of teaching thinking skills and ways of achieving this in Chapter 4. Classroom models (both teachers and peers) may also be used to demonstrate that particular tasks lie within the range of ability of particular students. Observing others succeed can convey to observers that they too are capable, and can motivate them to attempt the task. We have also dealt with the importance of modelling in our discussion of social cognitive theory.

We need to provide appropriate attributional feedback so that students see the relationship between *ability, effort* and *success*, and in particular to encourage them to attribute their failures to factors over which they have some control (see Chapter 7). When a student feels in control, motivation is enhanced. In this context, it is worth remembering that this sense of control as a function of effort may come from mastering strategies for learning and problem solving. Indeed, even in the face of failure, effort attributions, for example, can encourage a student to try again. At other times, attributing success to ability enhances self-efficacy and motivation. This has important implications for students with learning disabilities who may develop a sense of helplessness about their lack of ability relative to others and therefore not try.

To enhance self-efficacy, feedback should also emphasise goals achieved or gains made, rather than shortfalls in performance. For example, we can tell students that they have achieved 75 per cent, emphasising progress, or we can highlight the 25 per cent shortfall in their performance. Accenting the gains enhances perceived self-efficacy, while highlighting deficiencies undermines self-regulative influences with resulting deterioration in student performance (Bandura 1993).

Probably the most important source of feedback for younger children is the teacher. As children become more self-regulated, they will self-evaluate their performance in terms of their perceived ability and effort and the appropriateness of particular goals, and will modify their involvement accordingly. Under these circumstances, motivation is channelled into achieving goals that are perceived as attainable and worthwhile.

Finally, rewards may be used to indicate that a goal has been achieved, and hence enhance self-efficacy and motivation. The strengths and weaknesses of reward use have been discussed earlier.

Theory and research into practice

Dale H. Schunk — SELF-EFFICACY AND EFFECTIVE LEARNING

BRIEF BIOGRAPHY

I was born and grew up in Chicago, Illinois, in the United States. After completing my undergraduate degree in psychology at the University of Illinois at Urbana I served six years in the US Air Force as an education and training officer. For four of those years I was stationed in Italy, where I completed my Master's degree in education.

After leaving the Air Force I enrolled at Stanford University to pursue my doctorate in educational psychology. I took a personality course from Albert Bandura and became fascinated with his clinical research on self-efficacy. I wanted to apply self-efficacy to school learning and motivation. He was very interested in this and became my dissertation adviser. I also worked as his research assistant. This research showed that self-efficacy significantly predicted children's learning and motivation and that forms of instruction differentially affected self-efficacy.

After graduating from Stanford in 1979 I took my first faculty position at the University of Houston (Texas), and subsequently moved to the University of North Carolina at Chapel Hill. At both sites I conducted research to determine the process whereby students acquired information about their academic self-efficacy. I also became interested in the role of self-efficacy in self-regulation. While in Chapel Hill I published the first edition of the text *Learning Theories: An Educational Perspective* which is now in its 4th edition.

In 1993 I moved to Purdue University (Indiana) as chair of the Department of Educational Studies. While at Purdue, Paul Pintrich and I published the first edition of the text *Motivation in Education: Theory, Research, and Applications.* In 2001 I came to the University of North Carolina at Greensboro as dean of the School of Education. I have been able to maintain my writing while serving in these administrative roles (albeit on a lesser scale), and I enjoy working with faculty and students on research issues. I continue my research and writing on aspects of learning, motivation and self-regulation.

RESEARCH AND THEORETICAL INTERESTS

Not surprisingly after studying with Albert Bandura I became a proponent of social cognitive theory. There are several features of this theory that appeal to me. One is its emphasis on reciprocal effects among cognitions, behaviours and environmental features. What we think affects how we behave, which affects feedback and responses from our environments, which affects what we think, and so forth. I never felt, as the behaviourists contended, that our actions were controlled by environmental events.

Another strong point is social cognitive theory's emphasis on observational learning through modelling. Prior to Bandura's seminal research studies, researchers had a limited view of modelling as imitation of actions. Bandura showed that new skills, strategies and behaviours could be acquired by observing models. Observational learning is especially relevant to education.

Third, social cognitive theory contends that, assuming students possess the requisite skills and that environmental conditions are favourable, self-efficacy influences choices of activities, effort and persistence, and overall achievement. This focus is important because much research shows that students' abilities, as measured by standardised tests, cannot fully account for their school performances. Clearly, other factors are involved. Despite objective measures showing that they possess the ability to learn, students who doubt their capabilities are apt not to feel motivated to learn and their achievement will suffer. Conversely, those who feel self-efficacious are likely to demonstrate enhanced motivation and expend effort and persist to overcome difficulties.

In my research I have investigated how different conditions associated with schooling affect students' self-efficacy. My research has identified the following conditions as having beneficial effects on students' self-efficacy:

- learning goals that are specific, short-term and moderately difficult;
- goals indicating progress in learning rather than completion of work;
- verbal feedback informing students of their progress in learning;
- social comparative information indicating that students are performing well relative to their peers;
- social models whom students perceive as similar to themselves in learning capabilities;
- rewards linked to progress in skill acquisition;
- feedback linking students' progress to their effort (during the early stages of learning) and to their enhanced abilities (during the later stages of learning);
- strategy instruction and information on how strategy use improves performance.

Based on this research, I concluded that although these conditions differ in many ways, they affect students' self-efficacy through the common mechanism of *informing them that they are making progress in learning.* When the same conditions (for example, goals, feedback, rewards) do not provide information on learning progress, they do not raise self-efficacy to the same extent. Bandura identified four sources of self-efficacy information: (a) performance attainments, (b) vicarious influences, (c) social persuasion, and (d) physiological indicators. The conditions that I have explored fit into one of these categories.

I also have conducted research on the role of self-efficacy in self-regulated learning. Consistent with the predictions of social cognitive theory, students who feel self-efficacious about learning are more apt to use adaptive learning strategies, monitor and evaluate their performances, adjust strategies as needed, and set new goals upon attaining their present ones. Further, students can become better self-regulators by receiving instruction and practice on the various subcomponents of self-regulation, such as learning strategies, self-monitoring, self-evaluation and goal setting. In the area of self-regulation I have been highly influenced by the theory and research of Barry Zimmerman, who has developed and tested a social cognitive model of self-regulated learning.

I also have been influenced by the work of Paul Pintrich on the role of motivation in self-regulation. As students develop and advance in school their cognitive capabilities increase and their academic lives demand greater self-regulation, but a common research finding is that motivation often declines. How to sustain adolescents' motivation and improve their self-regulated learning is a central interest of mine at present.

THEORY AND RESEARCH INTO PRACTICE

Over the years I have been very concerned about what my research findings would suggest to parents and educators about ways to help improve students' self-efficacy, motivation, self-regulation and learning. I think there are several key implications for educational practices.

One is that everything we ask children to do, all of the models in their environments, and the feedback we give them, can affect their self-efficacy, so we should consider what those effects might be. Even when we do things that are well intentioned, they may not have desirable effects on self-efficacy. Consider giving students help. Help is called for when students are confused and do not know what to do or when they need corrective instruction. But too much help is a problem. Students who perform well only when they receive help from others are apt to attribute their successes to the helper, which does not build their self-efficacy. Bandura made it clear that independent mastery is the best way to build strong self-efficacy.

Use of models is another area. A common instructional practice is for teachers to ask high-achieving students to tutor low-achieving children. This practice may result in instructional benefits, but it may not be the best way to build the low-achieving children's self-efficacy. The low achievers may perceive themselves as too dissimilar to their tutors and think that just because the tutors understand the material does not mean that they will be able to. Better models are children whom the lower achievers perceive as more similar to themselves—for example, other lower achievers who have mastered the skills. This type of situation is more likely to lead to the thought, 'If he/she can do it, so can I.'

A third implication concerns the use of effort feedback. Teachers and parents commonly stress effort to children with statements such as, 'Keep trying', or 'Work hard'. Such statements may build self-efficacy if students believe that they will perform better with harder work, but a key issue is whether harder work leads to success. There is nothing more demoralising than working as hard as you can and still failing! Harder work followed by failure lowers self-efficacy. It is imperative to ensure that students possess the needed skills, because no amount of effort will produce success in the absence of skills.

Fourth, we must keep in mind that although self-efficacy is a key influence on learning, motivation and self-regulation, it is not the only one. Students who perceive no value or importance of learning may be unmotivated to learn despite feeling self-efficacious about learning. Outcome expectations, or beliefs about the probable outcomes of actions, also are important. Students may be unmotivated to perform well if they believe that success will bring no positive outcomes, or possibly result in negative ones. The latter situation might occur among higher achievers who believe that if they perform too well in school they may be socially shunned. In short, self-efficacy is important, but it must be considered in the light of skills, values, outcome expectations and other variables (for example, attitudes) in determining its potential effects on achievement.

Finally, self-regulatory skills do not simply emerge but must be developed. Parents and teachers should teach students self-regulatory skills such as planning, organising, monitoring and assessing progress, and strategies for learning, and then allow them to practise. Self-regulation skills are keys to lifelong learning, and we must help to prepare students while they are in school.

KEY REFERENCES

Schunk, D. H. & Pajares, F. (2004) Self-efficacy in education revisited: Empirical and applied evidence. In D. M. McInerney & S. Van Etten (eds) *Research on Sociocultural Influences on Motivation and Learning (Volume 4), Big Theories Revisited* (pp. 115–38). Greenwich, CT: Information Age Publishing.

Schunk, D. H. (2001) Social cognitive theory and self-regulated learning. In B. J. Zimmerman & D. H. Schunk (eds)

Self-Regulated Learning and Academic Achievement: Theoretical Perspectives, 2nd ed. (pp. 125–51). Mahwah, NJ: Erlbaum.

Schunk, D. H. & Ertmer, P. A. (1999) Self-regulatory processes during computer skill acquisition: Goal and self-evaluative influences. *Journal of Educational Psychology*, **91**, 251–60.

ACTIVITIES

1 Dale Schunk gives a number of reasons for researching within a social cognitive framework. Discuss with others each of these in light of your knowledge of behavioural and cognitive theories covered in your text. What are the links between social cognitive theory, behavioural theories and cognitive theories of learning?

2 Why is self-efficacy important to effective learning? Review the conditions associated with schooling presented by Dale Schunk that might affect self-efficacy, and suggest how your teaching behaviours might be structured to enhance student self-efficacy.

3 Dale Schunk states that there are four sources of self-efficacy information: (a) performance attainments, (b) vicarious influences, (c) social persuasion, and (c) physiological indicators. Allocate the conditions listed above to one of these four sources and discuss your allocation with other students.

4 Consider and discuss the links between self-regulation, self-efficacy and motivation. What are some key implications from research for educational practice to enhance student self-regulation, self-efficacy and motivation?

5 We strongly recommend that you read one or more of the key references above to further your knowledge of self-efficacy and self-regulation.

Table 6.8

A comparison of four major learning theories

	Behaviourist	Humanist	Social cognitive	Cognitive
Means of introducing material	1 Limiting stimuli to those strictly relevant to task (Skinner box). 2 'Engineer' initial operants appropriate to task. 3 Presentation of structured materials (e.g. DISTAR). 4 Teacher-centred. 5 Specification of ends of exercise (behavioural objectives).	1 Part of ongoing self-selected work (e.g. projects). Student-centred. 2 Relation of material to some event or experience of interest in children's lives. 3 Student self-selection of time and materials to work with (perhaps in consultation with teacher). 4 Supply large range of interesting materials. Focus attention on what is happening here and now by creating moderate novelty.	1 Display of models, e.g. teacher demonstration, audiovisuals, peer performance, guest speakers. Material should be relevant and interesting to children if the model is to gain attention. 2 Child-centred. Directed at gaining and maintaining attention.	1 Advance organisers and problem setting. 2 Integration of new material with pre-existing knowledge. 3 Establish procedures to assist encoding, retention and retrieval of material presented.
Activities/ Methodology	1 Individualisation of task assignment, of rewards and discipline. 2 Detailed methods to develop skills, and use of technology. 3 Linear progression in teaching content and skills—emphasis on mastery. 4 Emphasis on content rather than process of learning.	1 Based on needs and individuality of each child. 2 Integrated approach—emphasis on 'real' experience related to child's personal needs. 3 Emphasis on insight learning and understanding (not mere acquisition of skills). 4 Emphasis on the process of learning rather than content of learning. 5 Emphasis on effective interpersonal skills.	1 Detailed method—step-by-step following of model. (Model methods of working process.) 2 Explanations and verbal cues given. 3 Instructional material well structured and of interest to children. 4 Opportunity for children to code and rehearse material.	1 Hierarchical order of concepts and skills emphasised. 2 Emphasis on 'insight' learning and understanding (not mere acquisition of skills). 3 Emphasis on process of learning rather than content of learning. 4 Development of metalearning and metacognitive skills.
Motivation and goals	1 Extrinsic, through reinforcement, consequent on act being performed. 2 Mastery of specific skills—competence.	1 Intrinsic, satisfaction of needs, self-fulfilment and understanding. 2 Social and personal development, communication skills, sensitivity to group and individual needs. 3 Acquisition of self-learning skills and responsibility (self-reliance). 4 Development of affective attitudes. 5 Self-evaluation.	1 Reinforcement—antecedent to task being performed (anticipated reward). 2 Intrinsic and vicarious reinforcement emphasised. 3 Acquisition of modelled behaviour and its transfer to new situations.	1 Intrinsic—task involvement, solving problems. 2 Learning through discovery. 3 Mastery of processes.
Evaluation	1 Constant formative evaluation. 2 Formal summative evaluation (perhaps a pre-test/post-test arrangement). 3 Completion of set task at a specified level of mastery (e.g. the students will complete 10 sums correctly).	1 Observation checklists; interest shown in task. 2 Self-chosen enrichment work. 3 Completion of contract work. 4 Conferences with teacher, skill checklists, record folders, diary accounts, etc. 5 Peer acceptance and classroom adjustment. 6 Effective adult interaction.	1 Constant formative evaluation—immediate and positive corrective feedback. 2 Satisfactory motor reproduction of acquired behaviour. 3 Use of acquired skills in new but similar situations (transfer). 4 Effective peer and adult interactions.	1 Self-evaluation. 2 Mastery of process and quality of insights. 3 Ability to transfer learning. 4 Use of higher-order cognitive strategies. 5 Understanding of 'how to learn'.

WHAT WOULD YOU DO?

A TICK FOR CHRIS

Chris had been disruptive during class on a few occasions and had already been in Timeout twice during the past two weeks. On this particular afternoon, the children were writing out their favourite recipes to make a class cookbook. Chris was slow in starting his work, spending his time talking loudly to the neighbouring children at his group table. Meredith, his new teacher, gave him one warning about the rule he was breaking but he did not change his behaviour. She was concerned about putting him in Timeout again because he seemed to be experiencing only failure lately, so she took him aside for a talk.

Case studies illustrating National Competency Framework for Beginning Teaching, National Project on the Quality of Teaching and Learning, Australian Teaching Council, 1996, p. 18. Commonwealth of Australia copyright, reproduced by permission.

What do you think the talk consisted of? What actions do you think resulted, and can you predict their consequences? See below to read what Meredith said.

WHAT WOULD YOU DO? (cont.)

A TICK FOR CHRIS

First, Meredith ensured that Chris understood the rule he was breaking. Next, she set him the task of taking responsibility for his behaviour by asking him how he could avoid distractions. He opted for moving away from the group he was working with and sitting alone on the floor in front of the chair. Meredith praised him for his solution and challenged him to complete his work by the end of the session, so that he could get his recipe into the book. She added that if he could do this task, he would be awarded a 'tick' on his merit chart. This reward system is part of the school's discipline code.

Chris worked diligently for the remainder of the session and handed over his completed recipe at the end. His smile conveyed the message that he was satisfied with his work so Meredith honoured their agreement and put a tick on his chart. Then she verbally praised him for his work once again before home time. The next day, Meredith had no cause to warn him about being disruptive.

Initially, Meredith was concerned about offering external rewards for work. However, she felt that if she could ensure his success in some way, then internal motivation might follow.

Case studies illustrating National Competency Framework for Beginning Teaching, National Project on the Quality of Teaching and Learning, Australian Teaching Council, 1996, p. 18. Commonwealth of Australia copyright, reproduced by permission.

Did you predict the teacher's action and its consequences? What other alternatives might solve this and similar problems in the classroom?

KEY TERMS

Applied behaviour analysis (p. 181): the application of behavioural learning principles to understand and change behaviour

Behaviour modification (p. 174): systematic application of operat conditioning to change behaviour

Behaviourism (p. 166): a theory of learning that focuses on external events as the cause of changes in observable behaviours

Conditioned response (p. 166): a response to a previous neutral stimulus learned through association in the process of conditioning

Conditioned stimulus (p. 166): the stimulus that elicits a new response as a result of the conditioning process

Conditioning (p. 166): a process of behavioural learning

Coping models (p. 183): show their hesitations and errors while performing a task, but gradually improve their performance and gain self-confidence. Coping models illustrate how determined effort and positive self-reflections may overcome difficulties

Countercondition (p. 167): reduction or elimination of a classically conditioned response

Direct instruction (p. 175): a highly structured, goal-oriented approach to teaching, characterised by teacher presentation, teacher modelling and student practice with feedback

Disinhibitory effect (p. 182): outcome expectations and functional value of behaviour increases likelihood of observed behaviour being performed

DISTAR (p. 175): Direct Instruction System for the Teaching of Arithmetic and Reading

Elicitation (p. 182): performing behaviour similar to but not identical to modelled behaviour

Extrinsic reinforcement (p. 170): the application of

rewards by the teacher or parent that influences behaviour

Fading (behaviourism) (p. 168): The eradication of operantly conditioned behaviour through the withdrawal of reinforcement

Fixed interval reinforcement (p. 168): reinforcement presented after a set period of time

Fixed ratio reinforcement (p. 168): reinforcement presented after a set number of responses

Inhibitory effect (p. 183): inhibiting behaviour to avoid negative consequences

Intermittent reinforcement (p. 168): presenting reinforcement after only some appropriate responses, not after every response

Law of effect (p. 167): any action producing a pleasant effect will be repeated in similar circumstances

Learning (p. 165): process through which experience causes permanent change in knowledge or behaviour

Mastery models (p. 183): demonstrate rapid learning and make no errors while performing a particular task

Metacognition (p. 195): knowing about how one thinks and the ability to regulate it

Modelling (p. 186): learning as a result of observing a model

Motor reproduction (p. 184): in social cognitive theory, converting symbolic representations into motor movements

Negative reinforcement (p. 168): reinforcement that strengthens a response because the response removes some painful or unpleasant stimulus or enables the individual to avoid it

Observational learning (p. 183): learning by observation and imitation of others

Operant conditioning (p. 167): learning in which voluntary behaviour is strengthened or weakened by consequences or antecedents

Operants (p. 168): voluntary behaviours emitted by a person or animal

Positive reinforcement (p. 168): a stimulus that increases the probability of an operant (behaviour) recurring as a result of its being added to a situation after the performance of the behaviour. It usually takes the form of something pleasant

Positive teaching (p. 180): identifying rewards relevant to students and making these rewards contingent on appropriate social and academic behaviour

Programmed instruction (p. 170): instruction that emphasises reinforcement by providing the student with immediate feedback for every response. Information is provided sequentially in small units and the learner does not proceed to a new unit until mastery of the present one is demonstrated

Punishment (p. 173): the addition of an unpleasant stimulus to a situation as a consequence of behaviour that has occurred. The aim is to suppress behaviour rather than establish new behaviour

Reinforcement (p. 167): consequences used to shape behaviour

Reinforcer (p. 169): any event that strengthens a response

Response (p. 166): observable reaction to stimulus

Response cost (p. 173): removal of positive reinforcers as a punishment

Self-efficacy (p. 183): one's perceptions of one's ability to succeed on valued tasks

Self-regulation (p. 187): responsibility for learning outcomes assumed by the learner including self-generated thoughts, feelings and actions for attaining academic goals

Shaping (p. 168): reinforcing progressive steps towards a desired goal or behaviour

Skinner box (p. 168): experimental box designed to isolate stimulus-response connections

Social cognitive theory (p. 181): a theory of learning that emphasises learning through observation of others

Stimulus (p. 166): cue that activates behaviour

Stimulus generalisation (p. 167): the performance of a learned response in the presence of similar stimuli

Timeout (p. 181): the removal of reinforcement, in practice isolating the student from classroom activities for a brief period

Variable interval reinforcement (p. 168): reinforcement presented variably after appropriate response

Vicarious reinforcement (p. 184): observing reinforcing consequences to others

ON-LINE LEARNING

If you go to http://www.pearsoned.com.au/mcinerney, you will have hot links directly to these sites:

■ **Advances in classical conditioning**
Read this article on classical and operant conditioning and discuss the applications, strengths and weaknesses of both in educational settings. You will find some further applications of classical and operant conditioning on
http://clawww.lmu.edu/Faculty/LSwenson/Learning511/L9CCAPP.html
http://clawww.lmu.edu/Faculty/LSwenson/Learning511/L11RAPP.html
http://clawww.lmu.edu/faculty/lswenson/Learning511/L8CLCON.html

■ **Learning theories**
This site compares constructivism and behaviourism. Consider the material presented and answer the question: Can behaviourism be constructivist? Make sure you look up the hot links attached to this site.
http://www.ucalgary.ca/~gnjantzi/learning_theories.htm

WEB DESTINATIONS

If you go to http://www.pearsoned.com.au/mcinerney, you will have hot links directly to these sites:

■ **Behaviour analysis list**
This list of websites from Athabasca University in Canada is very useful for searching for information on behavioural psychology.
http://psych.athabascau.ca/html/aupr/ba.shtml

■ **Glossary of behavioural terms**
A useful site to find that definition you need.
http://web.utk.edu/~wverplan/gt57/glayout.html

■ **Learning**
This is a very interesting site with lots to tempt you to think! See if you can figure out how to navigate through the site and locate the information relevant to this and other chapters in the text. In the next two sites we draw on this learning site—but you will probably locate these yourself.
http://www.brembs.net/

■ **Learning 1**
This site provides a quick view of elements of the learning process that you will find interesting.
http://www.brembs.net/learning/

■ **Operant conditioning**
This site gives a comprehensive overview of key elements of operant conditioning.
http://www.brembs.net/operant/

■ **Personalised system of instruction (PSI)**
A site dedicated to one application of behavioural theory. See also the following site:
http://ww2.lafayette.edu/~allanr/gallup.html
http://ww2.lafayette.edu/~allanr/psi.html

■ **Direct instruction**
A site dedicated to another application of behavioural theory.
http://www.adihome.org/phpshop/members.php

■ **Social cognitive theory**
This site provides some more information on social cognitive theory.
http://psych.athabascau.ca/html/aupr/ba.shtml

■ **Self-efficacy**
This is an excellent site for further information on social cognitive theory and self-efficacy (and a number of other very useful topics).
http://psych.athabascau.ca/html/aupr/ba.shtml

■ **Bandura**
This site, provided by Emory University, provides further detail on Bandura and self-efficacy.
http://www.emory.edu/EDUCATION/mfp/self-efficacy.html

■ **E-Psychlopedia**
Has information related to a number of topics in this chapter.
http://www.epsychlopedia.net/exitGR.php?GID=0

■ **Journal of Applied Behavior Analysis**
This site is worth visiting as it has a number of recent articles dealing with applied behaviour analysis on-line. It also provides links to a number of other useful sites.
http://www.envmed.rochester.edu/wwwrap/behavior/jaba/jabahome.htm

■ **Applied behaviour analysis**
This site provides some more detailed information on applied behaviour analysis.
http://www.iaba.com

RECOMMENDED READING

Bandura, A. (1986) *Social Foundations of Thought and Action.* Englewood Cliffs, NJ: Prentice Hall.

Bandura, A. (1991) Self-regulation of motivation through anticipatory and self-regulatory mechanisms. In R. A. Dienstbier (ed.) *Perspectives on Motivation: Nebraska Symposium on Motivation,* Volume 38. Lincoln, NE: University of Nebraska Press.

Bandura, A. (1993) Perceived self-efficacy in cognitive development and functioning. *Educational Psychologist,* **28**, 117–48.

Bushman, B. J. & Anderson, C. A. (2001) Media violence and the American public. *American Psychologist,* **56**, 477–89.

Cameron, J. & Pierce, W. D. (1996) The debate about rewards and intrinsic motivation: Protests and accusations do not alter the results. *Review of Educational Research,* **66**, 39–51.

Chiu, C., Salili, F. & Hong, Y. (2001) *Multiple Competencies and Self-regulated Learning: Implications for Multicultural Education.* Greenwich, CT: Information Age Publishing.

Deci, E. L., Koestner, R. & Ryan, R. M. (2001) Extrinsic rewards and intrinsic motivation in education: Reconsidered once again. *Review of Educational Research,* **71**, 1–27.

Demant, M. S. & Yates, G. C. R. (2003) Primary teachers' attitudes toward the direct instruction construct. *Educational Psychology,* **23**, 483–98.

Karabenick, S. A. (1998) *Strategic Help Seeking. Implications for Learning and Teaching.* Mahway, NJ: Lawrence Erlbaum.

Merrett, F. & Wheldall, K. (1990) *Positive Teaching in the Primary School.* London: Paul Chapman.

Newman, R. S. (2002) What do I need to do to succeed . . . when I don't understand what I'm doing!?: Developmental influences on students' adaptive help seeking. In A. Wigfield & J. S. Eccles (eds) *Development of Achievement Motivation.* San Diego, CA: Academic Press.

Pintrich, P. R. & Zusho, A. (2002) The development of academic self-regulation: The role of cognitive and motivational factors. In A. Wigfield & J. S. Eccles (eds) *Development of Achievement Motivation.* San Diego, CA: Academic Press

Pressley, M. (1995) More about the development of self-regulation. Complex, long-term, and thoroughly social. *Educational Psychologist,* **30**, 207–12.

Rosenshine, B. V. (1986) Synthesis of research on explicit teaching. *Educational Leadership,* **43**, 60–9.

Rosenshine, B. & Meister, C. (1995) Direct instruction. In L. W. Anderson (ed.) *International Encyclopedia of Teaching and Teacher Education,* 2nd ed. Tarrytown, NY: Pergamon.

Ryan, R. M. & Deci, E. L. (1996) When paradigms clash: Comment on Cameron and Pierce's claim that rewards do not undermine intrinsic motivation. *Review of Educational Research,* **66**, 33–8.

Schunk, D. H. (1987) Peer models and children's behavioral change. *Review of Research in Education,* **57**, 149–74.

Schunk, D. H. & Pajares, F. (2004) Self-efficacy in education revisited: Empirical and applied evidence. In D. M. McInerney & S. Van Etten (eds) *Research on Sociocultural Influences on Motivation and Learning (Volume 4), Big Theories Revisited.* Greenwich, CT: Information Age Publishing.

Sladeczek, I. E. & Kratochwill, T. R. (1995) Reinforcement. In L. W. Anderson (ed.) *International Encyclopedia of Teaching and Teacher Education,* 2nd ed. Tarrytown, NY: Pergamon.

Sulzer-Azaroff, B. (1995) Behavioristic theories of teaching. In L. W. Anderson (ed.) *International Encylopedia of Teaching and Teacher Education,* 2nd ed. Tarrytown, NY: Pergamon.

Unsworth, G. & Ward, T. (2001) Video games and aggressive behaviour. *Australian Psychologist,* **36**, 184–92.

Wheldall, K. (ed.) (1987) *The Behaviourist in the Classroom.* London: Allen & Unwin.

Winne, P. H. (1995) Inherent details in self-regulated learning. *Educational Psychologist,* **30**, 173–87.

Zimmerman, B. J. (1994) Dimensions of academic self-regulation: A conceptual framework for education. In D. H. Schunk & B. J. Zimmerman (eds) *Self-Regulation of Learning and Performance: Issues and Educational Applications.* Hillsdale, NJ: Lawrence Erlbaum.

Zimmerman, B. J. (1995) Self-regulation involves more than metacognition: A social cognitive perspective. *Educational Psychologist,* **30**, 217–21.

Zimmerman, B. J. (1998) Academic studying and self-regulation. *Educational Psychologist,* **33**, 73–86.

Zimmerman, B. J. (2004) Sociocultural influence and students' development of academic self-regulation: A social-cognitive approach. In D. M. McInerney & S. Van Etten (eds) *Research on Sociocultural Influences on Motivation and Learning (Volume 4), Big Theories Revisited.* Greenwich, CT: Information Age Publishing.

PART 2

Managing effective learning

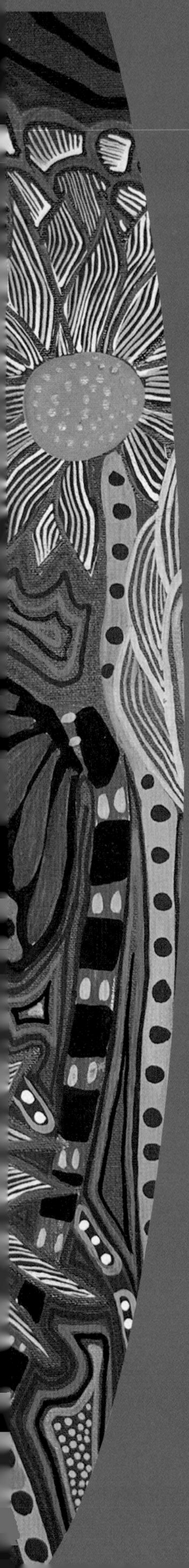

CHAPTER

7 Motivation for effective learning: Cognitive perspectives

Overview

In this chapter we consider theories that attempt to explain why people are motivated to do some things but not to do others. We have selected cognitive theories that have particular relevance to educational settings.

An increasingly important theme in the literature on motivation is the role played by thoughts and perceptions in guiding and directing behaviour. In particular, cognitive psychologists believe that any theory of motivation must consider the psychological processes involved in our decisions about which activities to invest our energies in. This chapter explores cognitive views of motivation and draws out their implications for classroom practice. In particular, we consider intrinsic motivation, achievement motivation, expectancy-value theory, attribution theory and goal theory. We also have a close look at the reasons why motivation appears to decline as students progress through school, and whether there are special characteristics of adolescence that need to be considered when designing educational programs to maximise learning and motivation.

Using a model of motivation drawn from goal theory (TARGET), we consider ways in which a school's psychological environment may be changed so that it facilitates the motivation and achievement of all students. We also consider the nature and importance of teacher expectations for student motivation and achievement.

7

Learning objectives

After reading this chapter, you will be able to:

- describe, compare and contrast major cognitive theories of motivation;
- define and contrast motivation in learning settings from behavioural, social cognitive and cognitive perspectives;
- consider the strengths and weaknesses of intrinsic and extrinsic motivation;
- consider special issues related to motivating adolescents in school settings;
- describe and give examples of the teacher expectation effect;
- discuss the relationship between motivation and constructivism.

What is motivation?

Motivation is an internal state that instigates, directs and maintains behaviour. All teachers are familiar with highly motivated classes and individuals. There is a zing in the air. No work seems too hard, or too much or too boring. Teacher and students work harmoniously and energetically. Students are alert, and attention is focused. Highly motivated individuals and classes persist at the task, desire high levels of performance, and come back to the task time and time again voluntarily. Perhaps you have experienced such a class as a student or as a teacher. Or perhaps you have been in classes where the absence of such motivation was evident.

Within any class there is great variation between individuals in the level of motivation for particular tasks (and this applies equally to students and teachers). Sometimes this variation appears to reflect interests and values, ability and effort. Sometimes the variation seems to relate to sex differences (for example, girls appear more motivated in language activities and boys in construction activities); sometimes the variation appears to reflect ethnic differences (for example, Aboriginal and Maori children appear less motivated for academic work than Chinese or Eastern European children) (see, for example, Dandy & Nettelbeck 2000; Yee 1992); and sometimes the variation seems to be connected with socio-economic and family background variables. As such, motivation is a very complex and multifaceted phenomenon with deep roots that stretch back into the whole world of the child. Students come to school with a complex history that includes family, culture, health, physical, social, emotional and prior learning experiences. These experiences orient the individual in new learning situations, sometimes positively and sometimes negatively. We cannot hope to understand the full complexity of these forces, but we can come to understand better some elementary dynamics that are more or less likely to facilitate or impede an individual's interest in learning in the classroom.

One of our main concerns as educators is why so many students who have such a zest for learning before beginning school appear to lose motivation for learning while attending school (Anderman, Maehr & Midgley 1999; Lepper & Hodell 1989; Meece & Miller 1996; Obach 2003; Wigfield, Eccles & Rodriguez 1998). What is it that schools and teachers do, or don't do, that seems to demotivate so many students? Why is it that some students maintain motivation even in difficult circumstances, while others give up?

Research and theory have yielded many insights helpful to us in understanding motivation. We will share them with you in this chapter. In our next Learner-centred Psychological Principle the importance and nature of intrinsic motivation is introduced.

How might the following indicators of teaching competence stimulate intrinsic motivation?

TEACHING COMPETENCE — **Box 7.1**

The teacher designs teaching programs to motivate and engage students

Indicators

The teacher:

- knows and uses a wide range of teaching approaches;
- sets and maintains explicit teaching and learning goals;
- relates content and teaching approaches to student learning goals and needs;
- selects and adapts content, resources and activities to suit the students and the context of teaching;
- recognises learning opportunities in issues raised by students.

Case studies illustrating National Competency Framework for Beginning Teaching, National Project on the Quality of Teaching and Learning, Australian Teaching Council, 1996, Element 3.3, p. 48. Commonwealth of Australia copyright, reproduced by permission.

Developing self-motivated learning

Intrinsic motivation

Essential to the cognitive perspective on motivation is the concept of intrinsic motivation. Generally referred to as the motive that keeps individuals at a task through its own inherent qualities (Ryan & Deci 2000), intrinsic motivation is a complex concept with many interpretations of what constitutes it and what its underlying processes are (Heckhausen 1991). These issues are beyond the scope of this book. We will, however, pick up a number of theoretical notions of motivation which have as their basis cognitive processing of thoughts about self in a learning environment and some concept of intrinsic motivation.

LEARNER-CENTRED PSYCHOLOGICAL PRINCIPLE

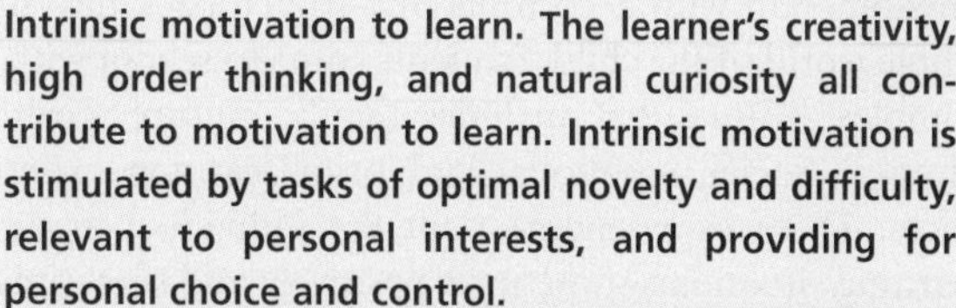

Intrinsic motivation to learn. The learner's creativity, high order thinking, and natural curiosity all contribute to motivation to learn. Intrinsic motivation is stimulated by tasks of optimal novelty and difficulty, relevant to personal interests, and providing for personal choice and control.

Curiosity, flexible and insightful thinking, and creativity are major indicators of the learners' intrinsic motivation to learn, which is in large part a function of meeting basic needs to be competent and to exercise personal control. Intrinsic motivation is facilitated on tasks that learners perceive as interesting and personally relevant and meaningful, appropriate in complexity and difficulty to the learners' abilities, and on which they believe they can succeed. Intrinsic motivation is also facilitated on tasks that are comparable to real-world situations and meet needs for choice and control. Educators can encourage and support learners' natural curiosity and motivation to learn by attending to individual differences in learners' perceptions of optimal novelty and difficulty, relevance and personal choice and control.

Cognitive theories of learning, in general, suggest that the key to people's motivation lies in their desire to solve problems, have insight and gain understanding, particularly in ambiguous or problematic situations

Students can be intensely interested in learning. How can we foster this intrinsic interest in learning?

These learners are obviously enjoying their work—in the words of Csikszentmihalyi, joyous absorption in the activity. What might be encouraging this?

(Andre 1986). Elements of intrinsic motivation include enthusiastic task involvement, desire to experience adventure and novelty, striving for excellence in one's work, trying to understand something and wishing to improve, and goal direction (that is, seeing a purpose in what one is doing). For Piaget, intrinsic motivation involved the feelings of satisfaction at resolving cognitive incongruities; for de Charms (1968), feelings of personal causation were important for motivation; for Heckhausen (1991), valuing of the activity for its own sake was particularly important. For Deci and Ryan (1991), intrinsically motivated behaviours are undertaken out of interest. In this regard, interest and intrinsic motivation are virtually synonymous (Deci & Ryan 1991; Tobias 1994). One definition that we particularly like is that **intrinsic motivation** is the joyous absorption in the activity which characterises truly motivated persons (Csikszentmihalyi 1975; Csikszentmihalyi & Nakamura 1989). The nexus between intrinsic motivation and cognitive theories of learning is neatly highlighted by the definition offered by Corno and Rohrkemper (1985): 'a facility for learning that sustains the desire to learn through the development of particular cognitive skills'.

Elements of intrinsic motivation:
task involvement
adventure and novelty
striving for excellence
goal orientation

The contrast between intrinsic and extrinsic approaches to understanding motivation is neatly put by Csikszentmihalyi and Nakamura (1989, p. 69):

> If we conceive of human behaviour mechanistically and explain phenomena in mechanistic terms, we stand to treat people accordingly. On the other hand, if we conceive of humans as intentional agents, who sometimes choose to act for the sake of intrinsic enjoyment alone, we might be able to facilitate people's enjoyment of the activities in which they engage.

Students who are intrinsically motivated—that is, who think a task is useful, interesting and important—are more likely to persist with it and be more willing to try different strategies to achieve their goals (Covington 2002a, 2002b; Pokay & Blumenfeld 1990). Recent research indicates that both *intrinsic motivation* and *extrinsic motivation* can be experienced simultaneously, depending on the nature of the task. We deal with extrinsic motivation extensively in Chapter 6 and you should review this material. Can you think of occasions where intrinsic and extrinsic motivation were both important to your motivation? What about a time when you were motivated intrinsically with no extrinsic motivator being present? What was it like when you worked only for the intrinsic reward?

How can we engage the interest of the learner intrinsically?

Research indicates that the features of activities and learning environments discussed below are most likely to engage the interest of the learner intrinsically (see Brophy

Is receiving a diploma an extrinsic reward? May it also be intrinsic? Why?

Even adult learners enjoy role play. How might role plays enhance motivation?

1987; Covington 2002a, 2002b; Dweck 1985; Ryan & Deci 2000; Lepper & Hodell 1989; Renninger & Hidi 2002; Ryan *et al.* 1985; see also Fredrichs, Blumenfeld & Paris 2004).

For individuals to be motivated in a particular task, the task must involve a *level of challenge* that is suited to their perceived capacity so that their skills are put to an appropriate test. This level of challenge needs to increase as the individual becomes more proficient. Teachers should therefore help students to set realistic and challenging goals.

Level of challenge

Curiosity is also a major element of intrinsic motivation. Curiosity is stimulated by situations that are surprising, incongruous, or out of keeping with a student's existing beliefs and ideas. An enthralling display was given by a student teacher motivating a class to write a creative composition. He had a large black box of furry, feathery, squishy, squashy, hard, long and thick objects. Each child had to put their hand through a small hole, feel an object and then go back and write a short story on what they had felt. The pupils were spellbound and couldn't wait to have their turn and write their story. On another occasion the same student teacher had a large treasure chest in which there was an assortment of items. He drew out one item at a time while telling a pirate story. Each item was part of the story. Interest was very high as the students were asked to predict what would come next out of the chest.

Curiosity and motivation

Students are proud of their achievements. How might this enhance motivation for further activities?

Also important is a child's feeling of having a *choice* in and *control* of an activity (Deci, Vallerand, Pelletier & Ryan 1991; Ryan & Deci 2000; Wigfield *et al.* 1998). When learners experience feelings of competence and autonomy, intrinsic motivation is maintained and achievement enhanced. It is a truism that we work best at things we are interested in and have some control over (consider also Assor, Kaplan & Roth 2002; Schraw, Flowerday & Reisetter 1998; Reeve, Nix, & Hamm 2003; Stefanou, Perencevich, DiCintio & Turner 2004).

Sense of autonomy

Three types of autonomy support are often referred to: (1) *organisational autonomy*, such as allowing students some decision making in terms of classroom management issues such as who to work with; (2) *procedural autonomy*, such as offering students choices about the use of different materials in class projects; and (3) *cognitive autonomy*, such as giving students opportunities to evaluate work from a self-referent standard and to adopt multiple approaches and strategies to thinking and learning. Stefanou *et al.* (2004) consider that providing organisational autonomy support may encourage in students a sense of well-being and comfort with the way the classroom operates, while procedural autonomy support may encourage initial engagement with learning activities. Cognitive autonomy support may foster a deeper approach to learning. What do you think from your own learning experiences? Consider our Theory and Research into Practice section by Ed Deci on self-determination theory.

Fantasy, *make-believe* and *simulation games* can also help students to become intrinsically interested in learning (Lepper & Hodell 1989; Parker & Lepper 1992).

The success of the ABC television program *Play School* illustrates this. Young children spend a lot of time reciting nursery rhymes and singing songs heard on *Play School*, their only reward being the joy of singing and knowing that they are learning new things. Often classrooms are set up as shops to teach about money, or students prepare a class newspaper to learn about journalism. Many of the computer software programs now available capitalise on fantasy and simulation to captivate the interest, attention and motivation of the user. Curiosity, fantasy and simulations elicit what has been termed *situational interest* in the task, which facilitates motivation (Tobias 1994; see also Ainley, Hidi & Berndorff 2002). We discuss simulations at other places in the book where we deal with situated cognition (see Chapters 5 and 10). Children's play is a clear opportunity to observe intrinsic motivation at its best. In fact, if the teacher structures the play by telling children what to do or what resources to use, it may no longer be intrinsically motivated and, therefore, no longer 'play' (see Lillemyr, McInerney, Sobstad 2004).

Fantasy, make-believe and simulation games

Other classroom practices that have been associated with developing students' intrinsic motivation include giving students the opportunity to be actively involved in the lesson through manipulation of objects, cooperative group work and presentations; providing immediate positive feedback to students on their work so that they see how well they are going; allowing students time to complete their work and achieve goals; and providing students with the opportunity to interact with peers in a variety of learning situations such as role plays, dramas, debates and simulations. The busy, productive work of children in groups working on projects is a measure of their intrinsic interest.

Active involvement, immediate feedback, finished products, peer interaction

Teachers should model an *interest in learning* and a *motivation to learn* by being enthusiastic, interested in the tasks being presented and curious. They should also show interest (and, dare we say it, excitement) at what children initiate, and indicate to children that they expect them both to enjoy their learning and to be successful. Students' natural motivation to learn will also be enhanced if teachers provide a safe, trusting and supportive environment. This environment would be characterised by quality relationships in the classroom, learning and instructional supports that are tailored to individual needs, and opportunities for students to take risks without fear of failure (McCombs & Pope 1994; A. Martin 2003a, 2003b).

Teachers as model

QUESTION POINT

How realistic is it to tell students that they should not be working for marks? Can a school subject ever be made interesting for its own sake?

Cautions about the use of intrinsic motivation

It is important to note that the use of highly motivating techniques should not be at the expense of the substance of learning. In other words, a lot of razzmatazz may be highly interesting and motivating, but unless it is used to support meaningful learning activities it is educationally valueless. Furthermore, techniques used to enhance the presentation of a learning activity should not be so distracting as to conflict with the purpose of learning. For example, when a teacher sets up a competition to stimulate interest, some children become more concerned with the competition and scoring points for their work than with the quality of work they are completing. Often children enjoy participating in an educational game without trying to derive any academic benefit from it (Blumenfeld 1992; Brophy 1983, 1987; Corno & Rohrkemper 1985). Many multimedia computer software programs are very entertaining but provide little in the way of 'educational content'. It is important, therefore, that situational interest generated by such techniques be converted to topic or task interest that will be relatively enduring for the students. In particular, this is related to the acquisition of knowledge.

You're trying to contact who?

Theory and research into practice

Ed Deci — SELF-DETERMINATION THEORY

BRIEF BIOGRAPHY

I graduated from Hamilton College, in the United States, in 1964 with a major in mathematics. Unclear about what to do for a career, I travelled in Europe for a year, one semester of which I spent in London studying art history and behavioural science. When I returned to the United States I did an MBA at the University of Pennsylvania. Those two years were very important for me. I taught statistics to undergraduates, and I worked as a research assistant running a laboratory experiment. I loved doing both, so becoming a university professor seemed very appealing. Then, I took a course in organisational psychology, and suddenly I realised that psychology, which I had loved as an undergraduate but thought of as an avocation, could in fact be a vocation. I entered the social psychology program at Carnegie-Mellon University and received a Ph.D. in 1970. Motivation had nearly died as an area of psychology at that time, but it was my primary interest and my adviser, Victor Vroom, encouraged me to pursue my interests. So, I began immediately to focus on human motivation.

The years I was at C-MU were ones of social unrest in the United States, and part of what I took away from that experience was a belief in the importance of using psychology to improve the human condition. Still, I was committed to basic science and to the development of theory, so I have continually moved back and forth between the psychology lab (where I try to isolate basic principles of motivation) and the field (where I examine their relevance to life's domains). After C-MU, I was an interdisciplinary post-doctoral fellow at Stanford University, where I wrote my first book, *Intrinsic Motivation*. I have spent my entire professional career based in the Psychology Department at the University of Rochester.

RESEARCH AND THEORETICAL INTERESTS

While I was at C-MU I began to wonder about the interrelation of intrinsic and extrinsic motivation—whether they were additive, synergistic or, perhaps, negatively interactive. My initial experiments examined the effects of extrinsic rewards on intrinsic motivation—some used monetary rewards and others used positive feedback, which is sometimes referred to as verbal rewards. The studies showed that monetary rewards undermined intrinsic motivation, whereas positive feedback enhanced it. I postulated that the tangible rewards diminished people's feelings of autonomy or self-determination, whereas the positive feedback enhanced people's feelings of competence, resulting in the observed effects on intrinsic motivation.

The finding that tangible rewards decrease intrinsic motivation was very controversial, and some psychologists still argue that rewards are not detrimental. Nonetheless, a 1999 meta-analysis of 128 experiments confirmed that tangible rewards do indeed undermine intrinsic motivation, whereas positive feedback tends to enhance it. The meta-analysis also specified limiting conditions to the phenomena.

During the 1970s I did experiments on intrinsic motivation leading to the formulation of cognitive evaluation theory (CET). In the late 1970s I began a collaboration with Richard M. Ryan that continues to this day. Together we have formulated self-determination theory (SDT), which now incorporates CET along with three other mini-theories—organismic integration theory, causality orientations theory and basic psychological needs theory.

Although tangible rewards tend to undermine intrinsic motivation, implying that people are not self-determined when pursuing rewards, we suggested that it is possible to be self-determined when extrinsically motivated. Specifically, we proposed that people can internalise extrinsic motivation for behaviour and thus be self-determined when enacting that behaviour. However, we differentiated the concept of internalisation, suggesting that people can internalise motivation more or less fully and thus be more or less autonomous in the relevant behaviours. Some internalised motivation is experienced as internal pressure based on ego-involvements and self-esteem contingencies. Although a powerful motivator, this does not represent self-determination, and it tends to be associated with anxiety and ill-being. In contrast, fully internalised extrinsic motivation is not only a powerful motivational force but is also associated with the experience of choice and well-being outcomes.

We have postulated that people need to feel competent, autonomous and related to others. Considerable research has now confirmed that the more people experience these feelings while engaging in an extrinsically motivated activity, the more likely they are to fully internalise the motivation for that activity, thus being able to engage it in a self-determined way. Conversely, if these three needs are not satisfied while doing the behaviour, people will tend to partially internalise it and enact the behaviour with the experience of pressure and tension. The work on internalisation is outlined in organismic integration theory.

Some research has focused on relatively enduring individual differences in the way people orient towards the social environment and the regulation of their behaviour across domains. The strengths of their autonomous orientation, controlled orientation and impersonal orientation have been effective in predicting other aspects of personality as well as behaviour and well-being.

Because SDT posits that people have basic psychological needs for competence, relatedness and autonomy, we have empirically linked satisfaction of these needs to optimal development, effective performance and psychological health. These needs are hypothesised to be universal, so studies have confirmed that they are essential for well-being in countries as disparate as Korea, Russia, Turkey, Japan, Bulgaria and the United States. That is, people in varied countries, whether orientated towards collectivism or individualism, need to experience satisfaction of all three needs in order to be psychologically healthy.

These topics represent but a sampling of the work that Richard Ryan and I, along with many colleagues, have done throughout our careers as we have worked to expand, refine and continue to test self-determination theory.

THEORY AND RESEARCH INTO PRACTICE

Our first classroom studies were published in the *Journal of Educational Psychology* in 1981. Since then we have studied intrinsic and extrinsic motivation not only in elementary and secondary schools, but also in college classes and medical school rotations. All of the work has been guided by SDT.

We posited that the climate in classrooms can vary in the degree to which it tends to control students' behaviour versus support their autonomy and initiative. In the first study, we found that students in elementary school classrooms where teachers were more oriented towards supporting students' autonomy became more intrinsically motivated and reported higher self-esteem relative to those in classrooms where the teachers were more oriented towards controlling the students' behaviour.

Subsequent research in elementary schools indicated that autonomy-supportive classrooms also led students to more fully internalise extrinsic motivation for doing well in school. Greater internalisation in turn led to better performance in school and to better adjustment. Research in Japan has also shown the relevance and importance of the motivational differentiation provided by SDT as a basis for understanding students' motivation in the classroom.

The same general finding has emerged from research in universities. In organic chemistry classes, students who perceived their instructors as more autonomy supportive became more autonomously motivated over the semester and got better grades in the course (assessed independent of the instructors) than did students who found their instructors to be more controlling. Similarly, experiments have shown that presenting material to students in ways that facilitate their active engagement leads to greater learning, particularly with regard to conceptual understanding.

In studies of medical education, research has shown that when instructors are more autonomy supportive, students are more likely to internalise the values embodied in the training and to behave in accord with those values months later. Further, studies showed that during students' rotations to various specialities such as surgery, psychiatry and pediatrics, the more autonomy supportive the instructor in a rotation, the more likely the students were to choose that speciality for their residencies.

In these studies the focus has tended to be on the relationships between teachers and students. When teachers relate to students in ways that allow students to satisfy their basic psychological needs for competence, autonomy and relatedness, the students tend to be more intrinsically motivated and more autonomously extrinsically motivated, and this results in better learning and adjustment.

It is particularly interesting that similar findings have been obtained in other life domains as well. For example, when parents are more autonomy supportive, their children are likely to be more intrinsically motivated and to internalise motivation for activities that are uninteresting but important, and this leads the children to perform better on the activities and to feel better about themselves. Further, when physicians are more autonomy supportive of their patients, the patients are more likely to internalise motivation to behave in healthier ways—for example, to stop smoking, eat healthier diets and take prescribed medications. Similarly, managers who are more autonomy supportive have subordinates who are more trusting of the organisation and more satisfied working in it. They also tend to perform better.

Substantial information about self-determination theory and its relevance to education and other life domains can be found at http://selfdeterminationtheory.org.

KEY REFERENCES

Deci, E. L., Koestner, R. & Ryan, R. M. (1999) A meta-analytic review of experiments examining the effects of extrinsic rewards on intrinsic motivation. *Psychological Bulletin*, **125**, 627–68.

Deci, E. L. & Ryan, R. M. (2000) The 'what' and 'why' of goal pursuits: Human needs and the self-determination of behavior. *Psychological Inquiry*, **11**, 227–68.

Ryan, R. M. & Deci, E. L. (2000) Intrinsic and extrinsic motivations: Classic definitions and new directions. *Contemporary Educational Psychology*, **25**, 54–67.

ACTIVITIES

1 Ed Deci investigated the interrelation of intrinsic and extrinsic motivation and whether they were additive, synergistic or negatively interactive. We have discussed this issue in this chapter, and provided a number of recommended readings addressing the issue. After reading Ed Deci's views and counter-views of others, what do you think the interrelation is, and how would you therefore use intrinsic and extrinsic motivation to maximal positive effect in your classroom?

2 A major contribution of Ed Deci and his colleagues to theory and research is self-determination theory. What are the elements of this theory, and what can we learn, as teachers, from the theory to maximise our effectiveness in motivating students?

3 It appears that the involvement of the learner's ego through comparison with others can be detrimental to motivation and learning. This is particularly the case with extrinsic reinforcement. How does self-determination theory explain this effect? How does this explanation concur with or differ from other theoretical perspectives?

4 Ed Deci believes that learners need to feel competent, autonomous and related to others in order to be effective learners. Discuss with your colleagues strategies to enhance competence, autonomy and relatedness among your students.

5 Select one or more of the key references to clarify issues raised in this section and to critique the issue of the relative effects of intrinsic and extrinsic motivation.

ACTION STATION

Of central importance to motivation is interest in the learning exercise. Interest may be generated in a number of ways. For example, relating new material to a student's needs and existing capabilities often fosters interest. Moderate levels of challenge, relating learning experiences to the 'real world', and the perceived importance and relevance of the learning to the individual also facilitate interest.

Observe and discuss with a classroom teacher the ways in which interest is gained and maintained in the classroom. Record your observations.

ACTION STATION

Observe a range of television programs aimed specifically at children and adolescents (such as *The Simpsons*, *The Science Show*, *Neighbours*). Also observe a range of commercials directed at the same age groups.

List the elements of motivation you see demonstrated in these programs.

What principles of motivation seem to be used most often in these programs to engage, maintain and increase interest and attention? Do these vary according to the age group targeted? Illustrate how these same principles may be used effectively in the classroom.

Table 7.1 summarises the essentials of providing a learning environment stimulating intrinsic motivation.

How might the following indicators of teaching competence foster student motivation to learn?

TEACHING COMPETENCE

Box 7.2

The teacher matches content, teaching approaches and student development and learning in planning

Indicators

The teacher:

- balances the curriculum and process goals of teaching and learning;
- selects or devises content and activities appropriate to student learning needs, strengths and interests;
- caters for individual differences within the group in terms of teaching approaches and learning materials;
- anticipates and prepares for situations that may arise incidentally;
- organises resources (human, material and technological) that facilitate achievement of learning goals.

Case studies illustrating National Competency Framework for Beginning Teaching, National Project on the Quality of Teaching and Learning, Australian Teaching Council, 1996, Element 3.2, p. 47.

Table 7.1

Essentials of providing a learning environment to stimulate intrinsic motivation

Teachers should:

- establish a *level of challenge* suited to individual student capacity;
- build on students' *prior knowledge and interests*;
- stimulate *curiosity* in classroom activities;
- utilise *fantasy, make-believe* and *simulation games*;
- engineer *active involvement* in the learning activities;
- provide *meaningful feedback*;
- allow sufficient time for students to *complete products* and *achieve goals*;
- provide opportunity for students to *interact with peers*;
- provide opportunities for students to develop *autonomy* in their learning;
- *model* an interest in learning and a motivation to learn;
- provide a *safe, trusting and supportive environment*;
- communicate *an expectation of student success*;

Teachers should teach learners to:

- look for ways to make a task interesting;
- reinvent a learning experience, if necessary, to create interest and challenge in it;
- expect success and work towards this;
- ask for feedback on learning progress;
- be curious: ask questions about what you are doing;
- don't wait to be told what to do: take the initiative to make it interesting, fun and worthwhile for yourself;
- make sure you allow plenty of time to finish what you start;
- set both short-term and long-term goals that are realistic;
- share ideas and tasks with others;
- don't put up with feeling uncertain—express your concerns, clarify, and get help.

Motivation—expecting and valuing success

Up to now we have been talking about behaviour motivated by interest and expectations of success. Important insights about expectations of success have come from the **expectancy-value theory**. In particular, the early work of Atkinson (1958, 1964; Atkinson & Feather 1966; Atkinson & Raynor 1974) highlighted the interaction of personality and environment in determining motivated behaviour. Atkinson proposed that each individual has a tendency to achieve success and to avoid failure. This tendency is moderated by the individual's expectation of success or failure on a particular task and the incentive value of the task. The disposition an individual has to seek success or avoid failure is considered to be relatively stable, but subject to environmental variation—the value of the specific task to the individual and the individual's expectation of success.

In short, this theory tries to explain what it is that causes some individuals to perform certain behaviours and others not to, when they appear equally able to do so. Not only is the *expectation of success* important, but also

'Weave the cane around the basket.' Hmmm, perhaps the clarity of the message got lost in the excitement of the task.

the *value of that success* in terms of anticipated rewards or punishments. For example, we probably all know of someone who has tried to give up smoking. The motivation to persist at this difficult task over a period of time is very much influenced by how successful they feel they will be and how personally valuable that success will be in terms of its rewards—pleasant breath, greater social acceptability and less risk of serious health problems—versus its negative consequences—unpleasant withdrawal side effects, increased hunger and potential weight gain, and the sense of bowing to social pressure.

Atkinson proposed two theoretical personality types: the person for whom the need to achieve is greater than the fear of failure; and the person for whom the fear of failure is greater than the need to achieve. The first group is labelled **high-need achievers** and the second **low-need achievers**. For the *high-need achievers*, situations of intermediate challenge are most motivating. However, for the *low-need achievers*, tasks of intermediate challenge appear most threatening. Figure 7.1 depicts the situations.

According to this theory, the individual's subjective experience of success or failure will vary according to the person's level of need achievement and will further influence later goal-setting behaviour. For example, a high-need achiever who perceives a task as easy, but fails at it, is likely the next time around to reassess the task as more difficult than at first anticipated and to persist with it. On the other hand, a low-need achiever who perceives a task as easy and fails at it will reassess it as moderately difficult and withdraw from it completely. Even when low-need achievers succeed with a task perceived as very difficult, they are still likely to withdraw from it, judging that in the future failure is highly likely. In other words, best to stop while ahead.

Attainment value, intrinsic value and utility value of success

Expectancy-value theory has been developed from its original conception by Eccles and Wigfield (Eccles 1983; Wigfield 1994; Wigfield & Eccles 2000, 2002b). In their model, expectancies and values are assumed directly to influence achievement choices, as well as performance, effort and persistence. Expectancies and values are assumed to be influenced by task-specific beliefs such as

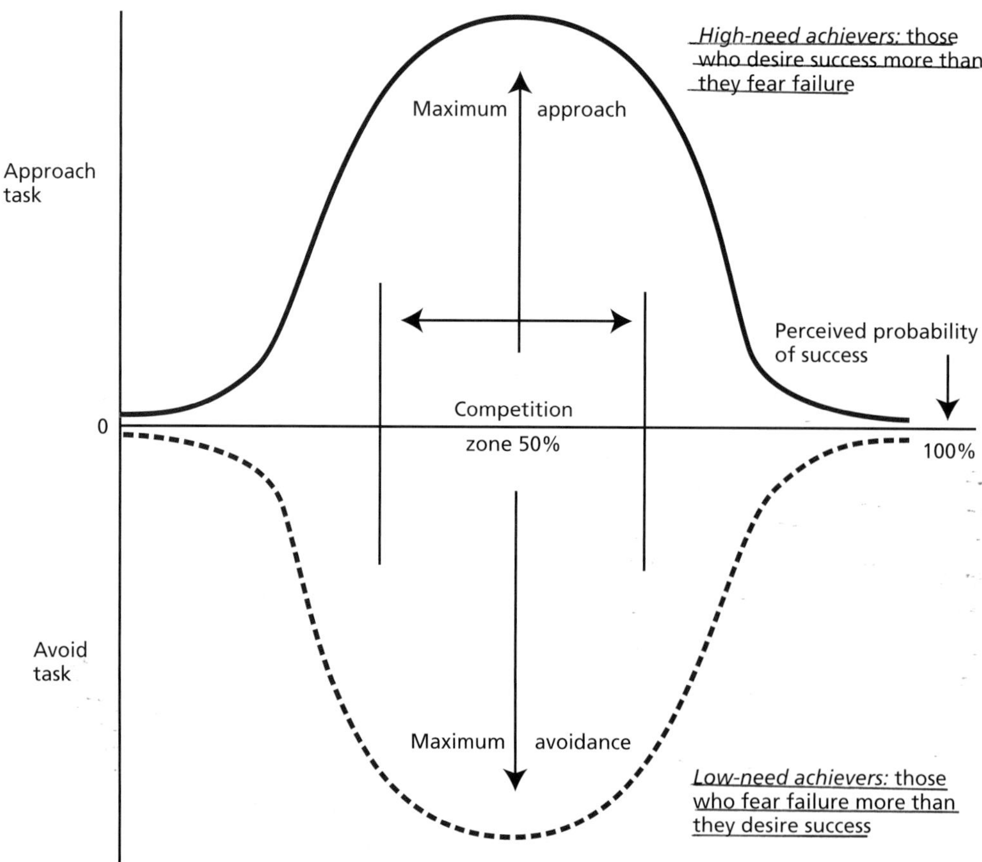

Figure 7.1 *Probability of success, motive predominance and task involvement*

Some of us get 'fired-up' to achieve.

ability beliefs (the individual's perception of their current competence for a given activity), the perceived difficulty of the task, and the individual's goals, sense of self and affective memories for similar tasks. These social cognitive variables are influenced by an individual's perceptions of their previous experiences and a variety of wider socialisation influences (Wigfield & Eccles 2000, 2002b; Wigfield, Tonks & Eccles 2004). Eccles and Wigfield have explored four components of the value of a task: **attainment value**—that is, the importance of doing well on the task; **intrinsic value**—that is, the inherent, immediate enjoyment one derives from the task; **utility value**—that is, the perceived importance of the activity to a future goal such as advancing one's career prospects; and **cost**—that is, how the decision to engage in one activity (for example, doing schoolwork) limits access to other activities (for example, calling friends), assessments of how much effort will be taken to accomplish the activity, and its emotional cost (such as performance anxiety and fear of failure) (Wigfield & Eccles 2000, 2000b; Wigfield, Tonks & Eccles 2004; Wigfield *et al.* 1998). Research has shown that the while value of a task is positively related to achievement when expectancy for success and value of the activity are used to predict success, it is a person's expectancy beliefs that are significant predictors, not the value of the task. It appears, therefore, that while valuing a task may be important in the initial choice of activity (we don't usually get involved in activities that have little value or interest), expectancy of success is more important to motivation than valuing after that.

As we have noted above, expectancies for success are assumed to be influenced by ability beliefs. Eccles and Wigfield have failed to measure ability and expectancies as separate constructs, and hence the impact of ability on the development of expectancies has not been effectively examined (Wigfield & Eccles 2000, 2002b; Wigfield, Tonks & Eccles 2004). However, they have examined developmental patterns in ability beliefs and found that students' ability-related beliefs for a variety of subjects declined across primary school and through into high school. Students' subjective values (attainment, intrinsic and utility) also declined, but these declines vary across different domains which means that it is important to examine the separate aspects of students' subjective valuing of different activities. The general pattern is for students to have optimistic beliefs and values in the early grades which decline across the school years. Wigfield and Eccles give two reasons for these negative changes. The first explanation is that students become much better at understanding and interpreting the evaluative feedback they receive and engage in more social comparison with their peers. As a result, many students become more accurate or realistic in their self-assessments, so that their beliefs become relatively more negative. The second reason is that evaluation becomes more salient as students move through the school environment, and relative performance a criterion of success, hence lowering some students' achievement beliefs.

QUESTION POINT

Discuss the potential effects on students of each of the following classroom procedures. In particular, discuss the effects on high- and low-need achievers of:

(a) streaming
(b) open classrooms
(c) mastery learning
(d) competitions.

Classroom applications of the expectancy-value theory

One of our functions as teachers is to assist students to set realistic and challenging goals and to ensure that they experience success at least a lot of the time. In terms of expectancy-value theory, this will reinforce the

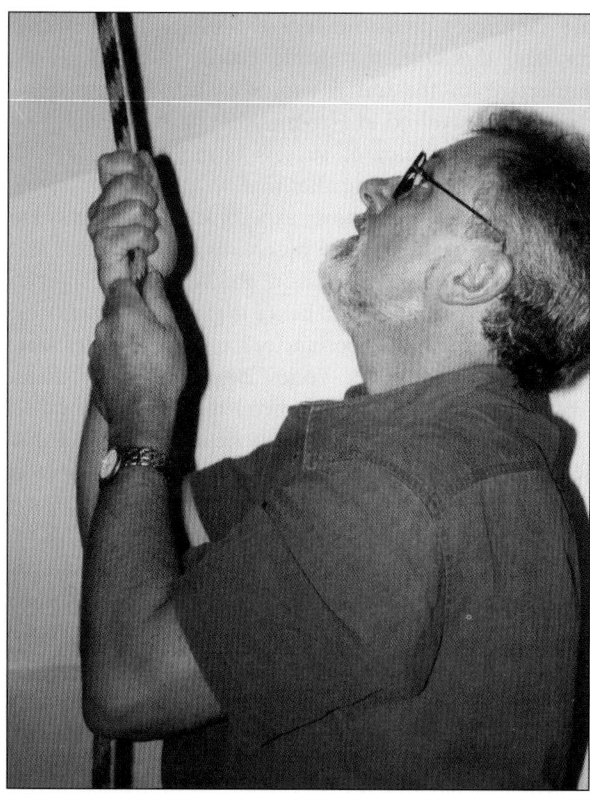

Do I really want to climb this rope, and can I? Authors also have expectancy-value dilemmas!

student's perception that success for effort can occur, even if tasks may appear difficult. Of course, there needs to be appropriate incentives for the student to make the effort: these should be negotiated with the student and may be designed as individual contracts.

It is worth keeping in mind that students with a low expectancy of academic success often defy classroom and school rules, because the value of academic achievement is also low relative to the value of status among their peers. For such students, threats of detention, suspension or even expulsion from school are not a disincentive: it is more motivating to have the (negative) attention of teachers and schoolmates than to try to achieve academically and fail publicly. Table 7.3 suggests effective strategies teachers can use drawn from expectancy-value theory.

Coping strategies

Children with a low need for achievement, faced with possible failure, may adopt a range of **coping strategies** to minimise the effect of failure on their self-esteem; this is considered by Covington (1984, 1992, 2002a, 2002b, 2004; Harari & Covington 1981) as either *failure-avoiding* behaviour or *success-guaranteeing* behaviour. These self-protecting mechanisms have been divided into three related categories: self-worth protection, self-handicapping strategies and defensive pessimism (Covington 2000; A. Martin 2003b). **Self-worth protection** describes a general strategy by which students withhold effort when risking failure. In the event of failure, the causes are ambiguous and can be attributed to the lack of effort rather than lack of ability. **Self-handicapping strategies** involve creating some impediment to performance so that the individual has a ready excuse for potential failure (Urdan, Midgley & Anderman 1998; Wolters 2003b, 2004). These impediments may be real or imagined. Among the strategies students use are procrastination and setting unrealistically high achievement goals. Not having enough time to study (the result of procrastination) provides a ready excuse for failure. If one fails to meet very high goals, then this does not reflect on ability as it is unlikely that anyone else would have met these goals. Finally, with **defensive pessimism** individuals maintain unrealistically low expectations for ever succeeding, or discount the importance of the work in an effort to minimise feelings of anxiety over potential failure. In Table 7.2 we have

Table 7.2 Failure-avoiding and success-guaranteeing strategies

Failure-avoiding behaviour
• *non-attendance*—just don't turn up; • *non-participation*—'nothing ventured, nothing failed'; • *false effort*—apparent effort such that the student will get praise for busy work or effort, and at least avoid substantial reproof for failure; • *irrationally high goals*—'no one can be blamed if the task is obviously too difficult'; • *lack of effort*—'if I'd tried harder I could have done it'; avoids personal criticism of the student's ability, and also avoids any real test of ability.
Success-guaranteeing strategies
• *low goal setting*—the selection of simple tasks so that success is certain: 'anyone can pass this easy task'; • *academic cheating*—success is guaranteed through cheating. This presents a great problem for the student: how to maintain the success when the possibility for cheating is removed. The student may go to great efforts to conceal the cheating, often using quite extravagant subterfuges; • *overstriving*—expenditure of extravagant effort to achieve success and avoid failure.

listed some coping strategies used by students. See if you can categorise these as self-worth protection, self-handicapping strategies or defensive pessimism. Are there other strategies that might be listed?

Coping strategies are used to preserve our sense of self-worth in competitive situations. They are commonly used by students in our classrooms, particularly in classrooms that emphasise relative ability and performance goals (Urdan *et al.* 1998; Wolters 2003b, 2004). However, while the use of coping strategies may give temporary relief from anxiety over failure, they are dangerous if used habitually. If used habitually, an individual's sense of self becomes degraded and overall achievement is diminished, leading to even greater levels of anxiety and withdrawal from school (Covington 2002a, 2000b; Midgley, Arunkumar & Urdan 1996). In order to avoid this happening, we should show students the value of learning ways of dealing with difficulty and temporary failure. The author recalls one student, who was able but not brilliant, preparing for the final high school exams. Over the months leading up to the exams he became seriously fatigued. On talking to him the author discovered that the student was getting only about three hours' sleep a night. The rest of the time was spent in putting in an extravagant effort to ensure that he would not fail in the levels he had chosen to do for the examinations. With considerate advice and parental consultation, the student reshaped his expectations and work schedules so that he could cope with the task of preparing for the tests in a more healthy fashion. This meant a reassessment of the need for success and the fear of failure for that individual—not an easy personal readjustment in a competitive academic climate such as final exams.

Consider your own motivation and performance levels in particular activities and relate this to the high- and low-need achievement profiles described in the text. How adequate is the expectancy model as an explanation of your personal motivational level?

Motivation—attributing success and failure to the right causes

It is implied in expectancy-value theory that individuals must feel some ownership of and control over their successes if they are to be motivated. The motivational importance of such perceived causal control over one's successes and failures has been made a focus of the work of Bernard Weiner (Weiner 1972, 1979, 1984, 2004) in relation to attribution theory. The hub of **attribution**

Table 7.3 **What teachers can do to influence student motivation: Insights from expectancy theory**

Expectancy: ***'If I try hard, what are my chances of success?'***

Teachers should:

- help students to identify the behaviours associated with successful learning; for example, asking questions, searching for answers from knowledgeable sources, and reflecting on learning progress (that is, understanding);
- teach strategies for learning and metacognition; bolster expectation of success as a result of personal actions;
- provide support if learner will benefit; tutor individually or use alternative materials (for example, computer based).

Utility value: ***'To what extent will I get something I want, or avoid something I don't like, if I do this?'***

Teachers should:

- help to clarify with students the relationship between actions and consequences;
- provide appropriate rewards and recognition for effort and achievement in a number of areas;
- provide rewards equitably across the class;
- counsel students on the long-term consequences of effort and academic achievement;
- support students in long-term goals in situations where parental support may be lacking.

Attainment value: ***'If I work hard and reach the desired standard, do I really care?'***

Teachers should:

- diagnose the values that students place on academic achievement;
- relate this knowledge to the effort expended by students;
- reinforce students' self-awareness of negative consequences for not making efforts in learning;
- model positive consequences for effort and achievement; reward with desirable reinforcers.

(Source: Based on Hancock 1995)

Theory and research into practice

Norm T. Feather — THOUGHTS ON MOTIVATION THEORY AND RESEARCH

BRIEF BIOGRAPHY

My undergraduate training began in 1947 at the New England University College in Armidale, New South Wales. The college was administered by the University of Sydney who awarded the degrees. After majoring in psychology and mathematics, I graduated with a B.A. (Hons.) in psychology in 1951, followed by a Dip.Ed. in 1952. I taught mathematics for a brief period at Lismore High School in northern New South Wales before being recalled to New England in 1952 to fill a vacancy caused by an absent staff member. The New England University College later became the University of New England (UNE) and I was on the academic staff for 15 years. During that time I completed an M.A. (Hons.) degree that was awarded in 1958. As I see it now, this degree was really the equivalent of a Ph.D.

I was awarded a Fulbright scholarship in 1958 and took leave from UNE until mid-1960 when I attended the University of Michigan, completing a Ph.D. under the supervision of John (Jack) Atkinson. My interests meshed with his. In my Masters research I had developed ideas about expectancy-value theory, and about committed versus wishful choice between alternatives. These ideas were critical of traditional decision theory in which the utilities of outcomes were assumed to be independent of the subjective probabilities of attaining them. My focus in the Masters research was on the context of achievement, and I proposed that the attractiveness of success and the aversiveness of failure were related to a person's expectations or subjective probabilities of success and failure. Papers stemming from this research were published in leading journals during my time as a graduate student at Michigan. Atkinson had been developing similar ideas in his theory of achievement motivation. My Ph.D. dissertation on persistence in achievement situations elaborated on this theory and it was the first to be awarded the Donald G. Marquis prize for the best doctoral dissertation in that year.

I returned to UNE and was awarded a second Fulbright award in 1967. In 1968 I left UNE to take up the Foundation Chair of Psychology at the Flinders University of South Australia and have remained there ever since, helping to establish it as a major centre for social psychology in Australia.

I was elected a fellow of the Academy of Social Sciences in Australia in 1970. I am also a fellow of the Australian Psychological Society (APS) and was its president in 1978–9. In 1998 I received the Distinguished Scientific Contribution Award from the APS and the Distinguished Alumni Award from UNE. I retired from Flinders University in 2000 and the university gave me the title of emeritus professor. I continue to maintain an active research program in my retirement.

RESEARCH AND THEORETICAL INTERESTS

I have conducted research in a number of different areas. In the area of human motivation I focused on expectancy-value theory, a basic approach that analyses choice, persistence and performance in relation to a person's expectations, the subjective values or valences that are assigned to possible outcomes, and how these variables combine with individual difference variables (needs and values) to influence motivated behaviour. My 1966 edited book with Jack Atkinson, *A Theory of Achievement Motivation*, described the early research in relation to success or failure in achievement situations. In 1982, I edited *Expectations and Actions: Expectancy-Value Theories in Psychology*, a book that examined expectancy-value theory more generally and that continues to be cited. My later theorising developed expectancy-value theory further so as to include the effects of a person's values on the valences (perceived attractiveness or aversiveness) of possible outcomes, thereby bridging the gap between values and actions (Feather 1990).

Another major research interest over many years has been the psychology of values—mapping the values that people hold and their effects on thought and action. I reviewed research on values and described results from my research program in my 1975 book, *Values in Education and Society*, a pioneer work that built on the seminal work of Milton Rokeach, extending it both empirically and conceptually (Feather 1975). I continue to conduct research on values, believing that the concept of value is one of the central concepts in the social sciences.

Other research interests include attribution theory, cognitive balance and consistency, gender roles, the psychological impact of unemployment, Type A behaviour, cross-cultural psychology, and social attitudes and values such as 'tall poppy' attitudes and the so-called cultural cringe in Australia.

My book, *The Psychological Impact of Unemployment*,

was published in 1990. In addition to reviewing the literature of unemployment effects, this book described an extensive program of research on unemployment that I conducted with my colleagues during the 1980s. In that book I reviewed theories and research on unemployment. Following the research strategy advocated by the influential social psychologist, Kurt Lewin, I am a firm believer in developing theory and then testing it in both laboratory and real-life contexts.

My research on social attitudes and values in Australia began with studies that investigated 'tall poppies', or people holding positions of high status, and the variables that influence a wish to see tall poppies cut down to size. I found that whether or not people wanted to see tall poppies fall depended on a number of variables, an important one being whether the tall poppies were perceived as deserving or undeserving of their high status. The further analysis of deservingness resulted in a structural model that incorporated the value dimension as well as perceived responsibility, ingroup/outgroup relations, and like/dislike relations between people. This model was influenced by the theoretical contributions of Fritz Heider, and it was applied to the analysis of deserved or undeserved success or failure in achievement situations and to other situations where justice-related beliefs were important considerations.

My book, *Values, Achievement, and Justice: Studies in the Psychology of Deservingness* (Feather 1999), reviewed the literature on deservingness, including the contributions of legal theorists, and presented the deservingness model and the results of an extensive research program that included not only the tall poppy studies but also research on retributive justice and reactions to penalties for crimes.

I have continued investigating deservingness and entitlement in recent years and I have extended the analysis to the consideration of emotions such as resentment, *schadenfreude* (or pleasure about another's misfortune) and sympathy. Over the years I have authored or edited six books and over 200 articles in national and international journals in the research areas that I have mentioned.

THEORY AND RESEARCH INTO PRACTICE

Much of this research is directly relevant to education. For example, my early research on values examined value differences in relation to students attending different types of schools, such as single-sex and coeducational schools, and state and independent schools. The research also investigated children's attitudes towards school, testing the hypothesis that students would be happier at school when their own value priorities were more in tune with the value priorities they perceived their school to have. Other research has examined how values and expectations of success influence course enrolment at university, testing the hypothesis that choosing to enrol in arts versus science courses will be influenced by a student's values and expectations of success relating to self-concept of ability (Feather 1988). The values research has also provided information about gender differences in value priorities among students at school and university, generational differences in values, and the values of immigrant groups and students from different cultures. A recent study examined the effects of parents, teachers and schools on student values (Astill, Feather & Keeves 2002).

My studies of tall poppies at school investigated how students react to the fall of a high-achieving student and an average-performing student who each obtained a lower mark than one would expect in an important final exam. This research showed that students did not report feeling happy about the student's fall, but they were least unhappy when the high achiever fell to the middle or average position in class and most unhappy when the average performer fell to near the bottom of the class. These results suggested that egalitarian values influenced the students' judgments. Another study showed more negative reactions to a high-achieving student who was found cheating when compared to an average performer. These studies open up research into achievement status within the classroom and how this status affects students' reactions to another's success or failure.

Finally, more recent studies testing the deservingness model have begun to clarify the conditions under which students report resentment or pleasure about another person's success, and *schadenfreude* (pleasure) or sympathy about another person's failure. They build on the earlier tall poppy studies and include both status and degree of effort that a student puts into study and preparation as important variables that influence perceived deservingness and emotional reactions. These studies bring considerations of justice into the analysis of social perceptions within the classroom, and they show the effects of variables such as deservingness and resentment on how students feel about another student's success or failure.

Over many years my research interests have reflected several common themes: achievement, human motivation, values, cognitive consistency, social attitudes, gender and cultural differences, causal attributions, deservingness, justice, emotions, and applications to social issues. I believe that theory and research in social psychology has a lot to offer educational psychology and that many bridges remain to be built.

KEY REFERENCES

Astill, B. R., Feather, N. T. & Keeves, J. P. (2002) A multilevel analysis of the effects of parents, teachers and schools on student values. *Social Psychology of Education*, **5**, 345–63.

Feather, N. T. (1975) *Values in Education and Society.* New York: Free Press.

Feather, N. T. (1988) Values, valences, and course enrolment: Testing the role of personal values within an expectancy-valence framework. *Journal of Educational Psychology,* **80**, 381–91.

Feather, N. T. (1990) Bridging the gap between values and actions: Recent applications of the expectancy-value model. In E. T. Higgins & R. M. Sorrentino (eds) *Handbook of Motivation and Cognition: Foundations of Social Behavior (Volume 2)* (pp. 151–92). New York: Guilford Press.

Feather, N. T. (1999) *Values, Achievement, and Justice: Studies in the Psychology of Deservingness.* New York: Kluwer Academic/Plenum.

ACTIVITIES

1 Norm Feather was one of the earliest theoreticians and researchers interested in expectancy-value theory of motivation. His work was further developed by Jacque Eccles, Alan Wigfield and others. Read some of the earlier theoretical work and compare it with the theory as developed by Eccles, Wigfield and others over the last 20 years. What modifications have been made to the theory?

2 Norm Feather considers that the concept of value is one of the central concepts in the social sciences. Do a search of the values literature as related to social sciences, and in particular social psychology, to understand its nature and why Norm Feather considers it so important.

3 Over his career the research interests of Norm Feather have been quite extensive. Select one or more areas of interest—such as attribution theory, gender, social attitudes and values, relationships—and do further reading and research in these areas. Why are these relevant to education, and what have you learned from these areas that is of use to you as a teacher?

theory is that individuals seek to explain and interpret (what we call 'attribute') their successes and failures in activities in terms of causes. In other words, individuals ask questions such as 'Why did I fail the exam?' or 'Why did my team lose?' or 'Why did I achieve so well?'. It is, however, more likely that these types of questions are asked after failure, rather than after success. In answering these questions, people attribute their successes and failures to various causes, some of which can be personally controlled while others lie outside personal control. Depending on the nature of the attribution made, motivation may be more or less enhanced (Heckhausen 1991; Maehr 1989; see also Seegers, van Putten & de Brabander 2002).

Basic assumptions of attribution theory

Attribution theory rests on three basic assumptions. First, it assumes that people attempt to determine the causes of their own behaviour and that of others. In other words, people are motivated to seek out information that helps them to make attributions about cause and effect, particularly in situations where the outcome is unexpected or negative. Second, attribution theory assumes that the reasons people give to explain their behaviour govern their behaviour in predictable ways from one situation to the next. The final assumption is that causes attributed to a particular behaviour will influence subsequent emotional and cognitive behaviour.

Weiner originally postulated four causes that are perceived as most responsible for success and failure in achievement-related contexts:

- ability;
- effort;
- task difficulty; and
- luck.

Ability refers to a person's perceived performance capacity in a particular activity; for example, some people feel they are good at tennis, others at mathematics, others at drama, and so on. *Effort* refers to the energy expended on a task (whether that effort is general and typical, or specific to the task). We have all experienced times when we put a lot of effort into completing a task or achieving a goal. We have also experienced times when we really put little effort into our work. *Task difficulty* refers to the parameters of the task. Tasks that most people can perform are labelled easy, while tasks that few can master are labelled difficult. *Luck* refers to the variables that lie outside personal control that may affect the behaviour (other than the first three mentioned). Things like being unwell, or suffering a flat tyre on the way to an exam, could affect performance.

Dimensions of causes:
internal/external
stable/unstable
controllable/
uncontrollable
globality

Each of these 'causes' of success and failure can be further categorised along the following locus of control dimensions: *internal/external* (referring to the degree of personal influence involved); *stable/*

unstable (referring to the perceived constancy of the factors over time); *controllability/uncontrollability* (referring to the perceived element of personal responsibility and intentionality involved); and *globality* (referring to the general feelings of success or failure the person experiences, over a range of events—that is, some people are generally success- or failure-oriented, while others are oriented more by specific tasks).

Each of these dimensions is presumed to influence a person's interpretation of the significance of success and failure. The stability dimension affects the individual's expectancies for future success or failure on a given task, while the internal/external dimension affects their feelings of self-esteem. We feel more guilty if we fail for reasons within our own control. Table 7.4 illustrates how the attribution model may be used to analyse the impact of success and failure on an individual's motivation for future tasks. Consider some of your own success and failure experiences in this context.

Importance of attributions to future motivation

The first element in the mental processing of success or failure on a particular task for the individual is an *affective* one. When we are told we have succeeded or failed at something, we are generally flooded with emotions—feelings of joy or disappointment, happiness or frustration, and perhaps a range of other emotions (Hareli & Weiner 2002). Many of these emotions are social in nature and relate to considerations of other people and social norms, such as what did other people expect of me and what is their reaction to my success or failure relative to others? These affective reactions to the outcome gradually become moderated or intensified as we begin to attribute the failure to external or internal causes that are either stable or unstable. In other words, there may be a change in emotions depending on the attributions made. The individual who fails in a mathematics test may attribute the failure to lack of preparation. In this instance, the effect on future motivation will be considerably different from the individual who attributes their failure to lack of ability. If the failure is attributed to bad luck (such as illness), future motivation may not be affected; however, if the failure is attributed to task difficulty, the individual may withdraw from involvement in the task in the future.

Affective reaction to success or failure

This process of attribution can also be illustrated with a success example. While a student will initially feel pleased that she has successfully passed a test or performed an activity, further affective feelings and motivation will be influenced by whether the success is attributable to ability, effort, task difficulty or luck. Whether the task was perceived as easy or difficult, or whether the student was lucky, will have a considerable impact on how she feels and on later motivation. The student might consider that her success was not really in her control (not related to her effort), so motivation would drop. If, on the other hand, the student felt that the task was easy because she had put a lot of effort into preparation, then her motivation would remain high because of pride in her achievement.

Antecedents of student attributions

What factors are known to influence attributions for performance? The *performance of others relative to our own* is one important factor. For example, if students perform much the same as others, they are more likely to attribute their success or failure to external causes (such as task difficulty). On the other hand, if a student's performance varies from others, and is significantly better or worse, the individual is likely to attribute it to internal factors (such as ability or effort).

A person's *history of performance* also affects attributions as it is associated with the stability dimension. Outcomes that are consistent with previous performances are likely to be attributed to stable causes ('I always fail in reading'). Outcomes that run counter to previous patterns are likely to be attributed to unstable causes (such as effort or luck).

Beliefs about competence also influence causal attributions. Individuals who believe they are competent, and also perform well, have this competence confirmed and are likely, therefore, to attribute their success to stable causes (such as ability). Students who believe they are competent, but fail, are likely to identify their failure in terms of unstable causes (such as effort or luck). Conversely, students who believe they lack competence are likely to attribute their successes to unstable causes (such as luck), which is consistent with their perception of themselves as incompetent. *Teacher feedback* is also important and we consider this later in this chapter. Table 7.4 shows the attributions as a function of stable and unstable, external and internal causes.

Characteristics of good attributions

In achievement tasks it is important that individuals attribute the success or failure in previous performance to causes that will positively motivate future performance, and not to dysfunctional ones that will discourage further involvement. It has been found through a number of research programs (Dweck & Repucci 1973; Kukla 1972; Nolen & Nicholls 1993; Weiner 1972; Weiner

Table 7.4

Attributions as a function of stable and unstable/external and internal causes

Type of cause	Locus of control	Failure experience Outcome attributed to		Success experience Outcome attributed to	
UNSTABLE		**1. Bad LUCK**		**5. Good LUCK**	
	EXTERNAL (uncontrollable)	AFFECTIVE REACTION	Disappointment, annoyance, little shame	AFFECTIVE REACTION	Pleasure, surprise, thankfulness, relief, decreased pride
		MOTIVATIONAL IMPACT	Possible change in future performance, but not highly motivational	MOTIVATIONAL IMPACT	Possible change in future performance, but not highly motivational
		2. Insufficient EFFORT		**6. Sufficient EFFORT**	
	INTERNAL (controllable)	AFFECTIVE REACTION	Disappointment, regret, guilt, some shame	AFFECTIVE REACTION	Pleasure, relief, satisfaction, augmented pride
		MOTIVATIONAL IMPACT	Expectation of possible change in future performance with increased effort. Probable increase in achievement behaviour	MOTIVATIONAL IMPACT	Possible change in future effort Maintenance of, or increased probability of, achievement behaviour
STABLE		**3. Difficult TASK**		**7. Easy TASK**	
	EXTERNAL (uncontrollable)	AFFECTIVE REACTION	Disappointment, little shame, possible frustration	AFFECTIVE REACTION	Little pride, reduced pleasure and satisfaction
		MOTIVATIONAL IMPACT	Withdrawal from task with expectations of similar performance outcome in future	MOTIVATIONAL IMPACT	Little motivational impact
		4. Low ABILITY		**8. High ABILITY**	
	INTERNAL (uncontrollable)	AFFECTIVE REACTION	Disappointment, increased shame, anxiety, embarrassment	AFFECTIVE REACTION	Pleasure, confidence, satisfaction, competence, pride
		MOTIVATIONAL IMPACT	Avoidance of task in future with expectations of similar performance outcomes	MOTIVATIONAL IMPACT	Increased probability of achievement behaviour

(Source: Based on Bar-Tal 1978; Biggs & Telfer 1987a; Weiner 1972, 1979, 1984, 1994)

& Kukla 1970) that individuals high in **achievement motivation** generally attribute their successes to ability and effort (internal causes) and failures to lack of effort or external factors, while those low in *achievement motivation* generally attribute their successes to external causes (such as the ease of the task or luck) and thereby discount the extent to which their ability and effort are responsible for their success. Hence, this group has less pride in their successful performance. These students also attribute their failures to lack of ability rather than to external factors or to lack of effort (Bar-Tal 1978). Weiner suggests that the main differences between individuals high and low in achievement needs are that individuals in the former group are more likely to *initiate* achievement activities, work with greater *intensity*, *persist* longer in the face of failure, and *choose* more tasks of intermediate difficulty than persons low in achievement needs (Weiner 1972, 1979, 1984). Among variables that have been found to influence achievement motivation and attributions are sex differences, ethnic differences, achievement needs, self-esteem, emotional state, reinforcement schedules and internal/external control perceptions (Bar-Tal 1978; Biggs & Telfer 1987a). The nature of the attributions made might also reflect the age and grade level of the students (Obach 2003).

Differences between high- and low-need achievers

If I try my hardest, I'm sure I'll do well!

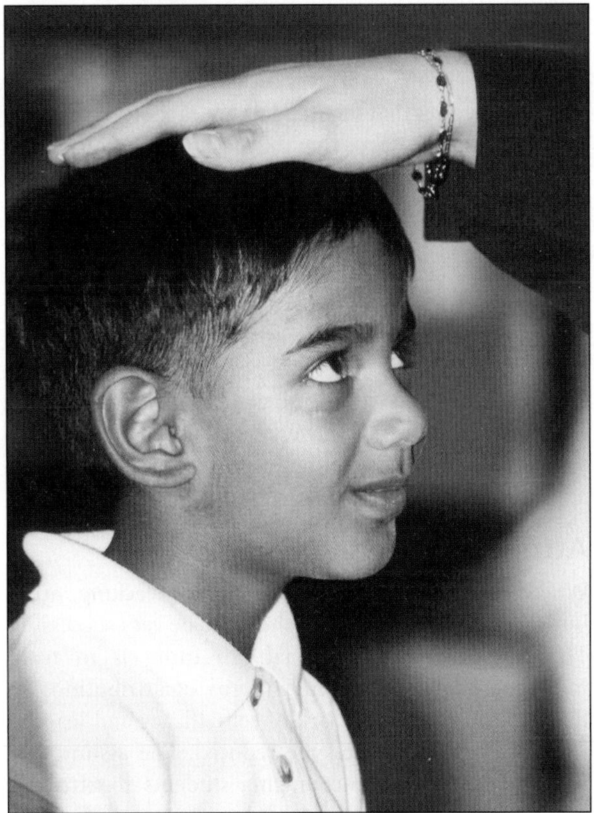

Affirmations of one's effort are very important for future motivation.

How might teacher attributional beliefs influence student motivation?

The primary focus in attribution theory is on the individual's reaction to success or failure in terms of the personal attributions made. As discussed above, when an individual's failure is attributed to lack of ability, which is *uncontrollable*, shame and embarrassment may lead to a decrease in performance. On the other hand, failure attributed to lack of effort, which is *controllable*, may provoke guilt feelings in the individual and lead to an increase in performance. However, Weiner (1994; Reyna & Weiner 2001; Weiner 2004; see also Graham 1988) points out that the reaction of the teacher to a child whose failure is perceived to be the result of either lack of ability or lack of effort has significant implications for the child's future motivation for the task.

Research indicates that when teachers believe that students' failures are due to lack of ability, they often express sympathy and offer no punishment. On the other hand, when teachers believe that students' failures are due to lack of effort, they often express anger and punish the student (for example, through verbal reprimands). Weiner believes that, in the first instance, expressed sympathy and lack of punishment will lead students to believe that the teacher ascribes their failure to uncontrollable causes (for example, low ability), increasing those students' personal beliefs about lack of controllability and non-responsibility. Shame and reduced future performance will be the result. On the other hand, when teachers express anger towards students for exerting insufficient effort, and that anger is accepted by the students, then there should be increased inferences of self-responsibility which raise guilt and lead to improved future performance of these students.

Research certainly tends to support these notions. For example, it appears that teachers give negative feedback to failing students whom they perceive have ability but have not put in sufficient effort, yet give little or sympathetic feedback to students whose ability they doubt. One study (Graham 1988) showed that when teachers communicated anger to children following their failure, children tended to ascribe their poor performance to lack of effort. This was subsequently related to high expectancy of success and increased performance.

It would appear from this information that communications of anger and punishment for failure will prove more effective in stimulating further motivation to improve performance than sympathetic feedback and the absence of reprimand. This is certainly the case when the teacher perceives that the students are capable of the task. However, Weiner warns that this principle should not be accepted without considering qualifying conditions and mitigating circumstances. In particular, as teachers we must be very certain that increased effort will, in fact, lead to improved performance. As Weiner points out, persistence in the face of failure in some instances may not be the best approach to achieve long-term success, and it would be beneficial for the student to alter the direction of their energies. In this case, being sympathetic and withholding punishment may be the appropriate methods of producing achievement change.

Relationship of anger and punishment to motivation

Attributional retraining

Where motivation to achieve is severely lacking, **attributional retraining** has been shown to be very successful. The essence of attributional retraining is to train individuals to change their patterns of attributions so that lack of motivation, lack of self-efficacy and learned helplessness are reduced. The assumption is that encouraging students to attribute their poor performance to temporary causes over which they have control, such as lack of effort or inappropriate strategy use, should increase their expectations of future performance, reduce anxiety and feelings of helplessness, and lead to better motivation and task performance in later activities (Ho & McMurtrie 1991; Obach 2003; Weiner 1994). Furthermore, particularly for failure-oriented students, it is important to teach them to accept credit for success rather than to concentrate only on training them to substitute lack of effort attribution following failure in place of inability attribution (Thompson 1993).

Goal structures and self-worth

In one American study (Ho & McMurtrie 1991), 45 junior high school students who were identified as underachieving received training in organisational skills, editing and planning strategies. During this training they periodically received either effort attributional feedback, ability plus effort feedback, or no attributional feedback. Children in both feedback groups successfully substituted adaptive causal attributions for those that were dysfunctional. In other words, they learned to reattribute their success and failure more to their effort (or lack of it) and less to the causal factor of luck. As well, both effort and ability plus effort feedback conditions were found to be equally effective in raising the children's success expectations. The results clearly indicate the importance of emphasising effort as a source of success for underachieving children, as the effort plus ability feedback was no more effective (see also Forsterling 1985). In this case, success perceived as a function of effort can exert motivational effects on future achievement behaviour. For children who are not underachievers, effort and ability feedback might lead to greater feelings of *self-efficacy* and, as a consequence, to enhanced motivation (Ho & McMurtrie 1991). (See Chapter 6 for a discussion of self-efficacy.)

It is important that teachers acknowledge positive effort rather than emphasising lack of effort, which can be counterproductive. For example, it is useful for teachers to comment, when appropriate, that they can see that certain students are putting a lot of effort into their work, and to associate this effort with the better achievement resulting from this. Teachers can also comment, with good effect, on the attitude of students—for example, by commenting on their thoughtfulness and the interest they are showing in their work (Nolen & Nicholls 1994).

Attributional retraining can also be used to change emotional and affective behaviour such as anger and peer-directed aggression based upon faulty attributions (Graham 1997). For example, if a student's work is damaged by another student a malicious motive might be imputed to the offender, rather than it being seen as an accident. In this case the student whose work was damaged might be aggressive towards the offender because of the faulty attribution made. In one study (Graham 1997), aggressive behaviour of African American students was first analysed within an attributional framework. Then a school-based attributional intervention to alter the internal attributions of children labelled as aggressive was developed. The intervention was a six-week, 12-session program designed for children in the later primary grades. Through a variety of activities, children were given training in how to detect accurately intentionality from social cues and to assume non-malicious intent in situations of ambiguous causality. The program was successful in altering the judgments of the boys in the training group, who were less angry and hostile and less likely to impute malicious intent to others. In another study (reported in Graham 1997), teachers reported that students who had undergone the attributional retraining were rated as less aggressive, less angry and less verbally aggressive than students who had not undergone the treatment.

Classroom applications of attribution theory

Research into attribution theory indicates that the attributions an individual makes influence task choice, need for and type of feedback sought, persistence and performance outcomes (Heckhausen 1991; Weiner 1979, 1984, 2004). Success-motivated individuals strive for information about their proficiency and prefer moderately difficult tasks, while failure-avoidant individuals try to avoid such feedback and therefore choose tasks that are too easy or too difficult.

It is important that students attribute their successes and failures to factors that will enhance further motivation. If students attribute failures to stable causes, whether internal or external (ability or task difficulty), there is little perceived point in trying again at the task. Indeed, such future efforts will simply confirm the situation and reduce the individual's self-esteem. Generally, teachers should encourage and teach children (particularly low-achieving children) to attribute their successes and failures to the factors over which they have most control—that is, personal effort or strategy use. In particular, it is important for teachers to modify children's dysfunctional attribution patterns for failure and success. Among techniques that have been found valuable are persuasion, providing opportunities for meaningful success experiences, exercises and demonstrations through role models, and training in appropriate strategy use (Forsterling 1985, 1986).

Enhance motivation through the use of attributions

We must caution here about ascribing inappropriate attributions with the intention of improving student motivation. For example, the attribution to effort can be a double-edged sword (see Covington & Omelich 1979, 1984a). Imagine that Josh has a perceptual motor problem and his writing is very untidy. He receives feedback from his teacher that he needs to improve, and that the best way to do this is by increasing his effort. Well, Josh puts in more effort . . . and more effort . . . and more effort, to no avail. The teacher says his writing is still very sloppy and he needs to put in more effort and practice. What can Josh do? He will probably withdraw from the task and become alienated from writing. In Josh's case, the poor writing should have been attributed to a motor skill deficiency and the problem addressed through a restructuring of the task or special remedial programs, rather than insisting on more effort.

Avoid inappropriate attributions

Teachers also inappropriately ascribe poor performance to a student's supposed lack of ability. For example, teachers may ascribe low ability to a student in mathematics when, with a restructuring of tasks so that they are appropriate to the student's capability, along with increased effort on the part of the student, success will be achieved. In many cases, situations need to be restructured so that individuals see the link between effort and success. The experience of success alone may be sufficient to effect positive changes to learning motives and strategies, and be the most salient factor in promoting positive emotive responses. These feelings may, in their turn, result in alterations to behaviours designed to increase the probability of further success. What do you think?

Restructure learning situations to guarantee success

Research indicates one interesting crossover effect of ability and effort relating to self-esteem (Covington 1984; Nicholls 1976). Younger children generally equate ability and effort. In other words, they believe bright kids work hard, dumb kids loaf. Adolescents, however, are likely to maintain that, if students are putting in a lot of effort, they are probably not so bright. In their view, students with a lot of ability appear to achieve success effortlessly. Many adolescents go to a great deal of trouble to cover up the effort they put into achieving success. It is not unusual even for university students to be dismissive of any effort they have put into exam preparation. Perhaps you have heard students bemoaning their lack of preparation for an upcoming test, while in reality they have secretly studied very hard (see Covington 1984). Mind you, this might also be an example of a failure-avoiding strategy.

Developmental relationship between ability and effort attributions

Learned helplessness

What is **learned helplessness**? In much of what we have stated above, we have suggested that students should be guided by teachers towards a belief in themselves as constructive forces influencing their own successes and failures in the classroom. De Charms (1968, see also 1972, 1976, 1984; Dweck 2002) introduced the notion of origins and pawns when describing individuals' perceived level of control in particular challenging situations. Children who seize the initiative, perceive the relationship between success and effort, restructure situations to maximise their chances for success, as far as circumstances permit, and have a realistic view of their abilities are **origins**. To the extent that students believe their successes and failures are subject to external forces (such as the teacher setting easy or hard tasks), or are a matter of luck, they are acting like **pawns**, as in a game of chess (de Charms 1968). In other words, they feel powerless and ineffective in particular circumstances. If this feeling of powerlessness generalises to a range of behaviours, children may demonstrate learned helplessness (Diener & Dweck 1978; Johnson 1981; Thomas 1979; Tiggemann & Crowley 1993; Zuroff 1980). In other words, they lose the capacity

Student accountability
Success and failure
Origins and pawns

Theory and research into practice

Bernard Weiner — ATTRIBUTION THEORY: IS CRITICISM FOR POOR PERFORMANCE GOOD OR BAD?

BRIEF BIOGRAPHY

I am the third son of poor Russian immigrants, born in Chicago, Illinois on 28 September 1935. I was an undergraduate student at the University of Chicago, walking distance from my grammar school. University Chancellor Maynard Hutchins had established an innovative program where only the Great Books were assigned and all students received a Bachelor's degree in liberal arts. Following this experience, I received a Master's degree in business administration, also from the University of Chicago, majoring in industrial relations. A course in industrial psychology from Professor Harold Leavitt, a student of Kurt Lewin, and a subsequent research assistantship with Leavitt, shifted my life direction towards psychology. Following two years as a private in the US Army, I enrolled for the Ph.D. at the University of Michigan. There I came under the influence of Dr John W. Atkinson, a leading motivational psychologist. I completed the Ph.D. in 1963, with my dissertation examining persisting motivation after failure. A two-year postdoctoral period in the Center for Personality Research at the University of Minnesota followed. I then left cold Minnesota for sunny California and remain active at the University of California, Los Angeles (UCLA; 1965–). My research interests continued in motivation, initially focusing on achievement strivings but later veering towards social phenomena and social justice, including reactions to the stigmatised, help giving, impression formation, punishment and moral emotions. I also contributed to the development of attribution theory. I have been fortunate in receiving some honours for my work; the awards I most cherish are honorary doctorate degrees from the University of Bielefeld, Germany and the University of Turku, Finland, and the Outstanding Teacher Award at UCLA. I live in Los Angeles with my wife and school-aged daughter and have a son who is a professor of legal history.

RESEARCH AND THEORETICAL INTERESTS

My primary interest as a psychologist is theoretical—the development of a general theory of motivation. I have formulated two related theories of motivation, one for intrapersonal behaviour (such as striving for success) and the other for interpersonal behaviour (such as evaluating others who have failed). Both have causal attributions as their foundation—that is, people's perceptions of the causes of events. For example, considering the interpersonal theory, individuals who do not put forth effort and fail in achievement situations are especially reprimanded by others, such as teachers and parents. Imagine your reaction towards a person on your team who is not trying and the team loses. In a similar manner, persons with perceived behaviour-originated stigmas—such as drug and alcohol abuse, obesity and AIDS—tend to elicit negative reactions and are admonished. In addition, individuals asking to borrow money because they 'do not feel like working' often are denied help. Theoretically, these quite disparate observations are linked because the causes of the untoward events are perceived as subject to volitional control (try harder given achievement failure, just say 'no' in the case of drugs, and remain on the job), so the person is held responsible. This moral judgment gives rise to anger and reprimand. On the other hand, those failing because of lack of aptitude, those with a biologically originated stigma such as Alzheimer's disease, and those needing money because their firm closed generate pro-social responses. Imagine your reactions to the mentally handicapped person who cannot complete a math problem or the physically handicapped person who cannot compete in sports. These persons are not held responsible for their plights and elicit sympathy. Thus, disparate phenomena in different psychological domains (achievement evaluation, stigmatisation and help giving) are subject to the same psychological law.

My underlying belief is that motivation is characterised as a thinking–feeling–doing sequence (causal attributions–responsibility judgments–linked emotions–interpersonal behaviour) and this approach explains a wide array of behaviours (but certainly not everything). My own research in the interpersonal domain has focused on a variety of topics that fit within this attribution framework, including achievement evaluation, reactions to the stigmatised, help giving, aggression, compliance, impression management, punishment and moral emotions. The phenomena are of importance both within and out of the classroom. This research often manipulates information about causality and involves judgments about others.

Educational psychologists may be more directly interested in my attribution approach to achievement strivings, or what I label intrapersonal behaviour. Here I consider the student's perceived causes of achievement success and failure, the fundamental properties of causes (including their locus in the person or the world, perceived endurance and controllability), causal linkages to emotions and expectancy of success, and achievement performance. For example, lack of aptitude is perceived as an internal, stable and uncontrollable cause of failure. Being internal to the person, this attribution for failure reduces self-esteem; since it is unchangeable, expectancy of future success is low; and because it is uncontrollable, feelings of shame are evoked. Low esteem, low expectancy and shame give rise to poor performance. This contrasts with lack of effort as the perceived cause of failure, which is changeable (thereby not reducing expectancy), and controllable (evoking guilt, a motivator, rather than shame, an inhibitor). Here again there is a proposed motivation sequence, initiated by causal thoughts and involving emotions. In pertinent research, I vary the perceived causes of failure and assess their effects on expectancy, affect and subsequent performance.

In sum, my research interests are primarily conceptual and the research context is chosen because it provides a good testing site for the theory. The research is undertaken to explore, test and refine my attribution framework, but in so doing it also sheds light on the phenomenon under study.

THEORY AND RESEARCH INTO PRACTICE

I restrict the discussion of practical applications of my work to the intrapersonal theory and specifically to the achievement domain, as this is likely to be of most relevance to readers. Two topics are examined: (1) attribution change programs, and (2) contributions to teacher training.

Attribution change programs

There are a number of programs that attempt to increase achievement strivings by changing attributions, and certainly different approaches are needed depending on the source of the problem. For an attribution theorist, one promising method for achievement change is to alter attributions of the achiever (student, employee) so they are more adaptive. Ascription of failure to lack of ability (aptitude) is particularly dysfunctional and demotivating (as discussed previously). Hence, often attribution change programs are designed to alter personal attributions for failure from low ability to lack of effort and/or poor strategy, which are less stable and controllable by the person. One useful procedure is to show failing individuals filmed interviews of other students reporting how they overcame failure through extra effort or by changing study methods. Other procedures provide students with effort feedback during experimental training as they work on tasks. And still another method that has been used successfully focuses on changing attributions for failure from stable or enduring to unstable, so that expectancy of future success is maintained. For example, in one program failing students are merely informed that the grading policy of the school is less harsh as one progresses into more advanced classes, so they should not drop out because life becomes easier! Hence, perception of task difficulty as the cause of failure is shifted from stable to unstable. All these procedures have met with some success.

Teaching training programs

Attribution theory provides a number of insights for teachers to use in their daily classroom lives, and thus attributional knowledge is useful to incorporate in teaching training. Here I examine two related topics that provide useful hints regarding good motivational practices. They concern low-ability cues and the meaning of emotional communications.

Often individuals communicate to others that they 'cannot', which inhibits achievement striving, although the communicators' (teacher, employer) intentions are positive and the desire is to increase motivation. For example, providing positive reinforcement for success at a very easy task, or the absence of negative reinforcement given failure at an easy task, convey to the achiever that he or she is low in ability. In the latter case, not punishing failure at an easy task conveys that the person tried hard, inasmuch as punishment is linked with lack of effort. If the person tried hard and failed at an easy task, then according to attribution logic regarding causal rules there must be an absence of ability. Note the complex attribution reasoning that the naïve person uses (or is assumed to use)—from lack of punishment to an inference about the presence of effort, and from effort beliefs to an inference regarding the absence of ability. In a similar manner, unsolicited help often evokes beliefs by the student that he or she lacks ability. Furthermore, communication of sympathy following failure can be a cue for the absence of ability. Sympathy is given to individuals who 'cannot'; we sympathise with those having Alzheimer's disease or with the very aged. Just as uncontrollable plights elicit sympathy, the communication of sympathy conveys that one 'cannot'. In sum, positive social acts (withholding punishment, unsolicited help and conveying sympathy) can have unintended negative motivational consequences.

On the other hand, giving punishment for failure at an easy task, not providing unneeded help, and expressing anger for failure communicate that the cause of non-attainment of a goal is lack of effort (rather than an absence of ability). As already indicated, effort is both unstable and controllable by the achiever, so it is an adaptive causal ascription. When and under what conditions lack of ability is an adaptive cue for failure—that is, what role should 'reality' play in causal beliefs—is a debated and unresolved issue. These topics illustrate some of the usefulness of an attributional analysis in the classroom.

KEY REFERENCES

Weiner, B. (1985) An attributional theory of achievement motivation and emotion. *Psychological Review*, **92**, 548–73.

Weiner, B. (1992) *Human Motivation: Metaphors, Theory, and Research*. Newbury Park, CA: Sage.

Weiner, B. (1995) *Judgments of Responsibility: A Foundation for a Theory of Social Conduct.* New York: Guilford.

ACTIVITIES

1 Bernard Weiner describes two theories of motivation: one for intrapersonal behaviour and one for interpersonal behaviour. Underpinning both are the causal attributions the self and others make about one's success or failure that either stimulate motivation or undermine it. Examine the elements of each theory and discuss with fellow students personal experiences that support or refute Weiner's arguments.

2 Bernard Weiner states that 'My underlying belief is that motivation is characterised as a thinking–feeling–doing sequence', which explains a wide variety of behaviour. Consider your personal experiences. Does this sequence of thinking–feeling–doing explain your motivation or de-motivation for particular activities?

3 Bernard Weiner contrasts the effects of attributions to internal, stable and uncontrollable causes of failure and the effects of changeable and controllable causes. How is this information useful for teachers?

4 Consider Bernard Weiner's arguments in support of attributional change programs to elevate achievement strivings. How would you use this information in structuring class activities and in your feedback to your students?

5 Bernard Weiner believes that positive social acts such as withholding punishment, unsolicited help and conveying sympathy can have unintended negative motivational consequences. Why is this so, and what difference does this information potentially make to the type of feedback you will give your students?

6 We strongly recommend that you read the key references listed above, as they will deepen your understanding of attribution theory and motivation theory in general.

to be accountable for their own behaviour and performance, and learn to be helpless.

The two dimensions, origins and pawns, lie along a continuum, and individuals are neither one nor the other exclusively. In certain situations, children may be origins while in others they may be pawns. Some children, for example, are very much pawns in the classroom, but origins on the sporting field.

Children are not born as origins or pawns. They develop these characteristics through socialisation in various circumstances. Teachers can act as effective agents in developing origin characteristics in children.

QUESTION POINT

Define motivation, and differentiate between behavioural, cognitive and social learning approaches to its interpretation.

QUESTION POINT

Success and failure are both important motivating agents. How can teachers use these to maximise motivation in the classroom? What might be the effects of repeated success and repeated failure on level of aspiration and self-concept?

QUESTION POINT

Some teachers rationalise, 'Why should I break my neck to teach children who just don't want to learn?' How might the impasse be resolved? Do some teachers operate under misconceptions of their role?

The goals of schooling

How do the goals of schooling affect motivation? The theories covered so far emphasise the importance of learners' beliefs about themselves as constructive, active agents. Mention has also been made of the importance to motivated learning of valuing the task. Students ask the question, 'Why am I doing this task?', and the answer to this question influences their motivation to continue. The measures of achievement used in schools communicate to students the value placed on particular tasks and are represented as *goals of schooling*. The goals stressed by schools have dramatic consequences for whether children

TEACHER'S CASE BOOK

How did it go?

Children in Sylvia's family-grouped class of five-to-eight-year-olds have been working in groups making a timeline of Australia. Each group has worked independently, organising materials and sharing ideas. Sylvia has been circulating the room assisting if needed, questioning, encouraging and extending the children's experience. At the conclusion of the activity, she brought the children together.

Sylvia: I was really impressed with how you worked in the group and the work you produced. I would like some feedback on how your group worked.

Charles: I liked how none of my group wandered off and did other things. They did look at other things, but they came back.

Sam: I think our group worked well. Everyone had something to do.

Daisy: Our group was sensible. They didn't muck up.

Sylvia: That's fantastic.

Case study activity

How would cooperative group work motivate students? What special precautions should the teacher take to ensure that the group work is well done?

develop a sense of efficacy and a willingness to try hard and take on challenges, or whether they avoid challenging tasks, giving up when faced with failure (see Ames 1984, 1992; Covington 1992, 2000; Elliott & Dweck 1988; Maehr 1989; Maehr & Midgley 1991; Wigfield *et al.* 1998; Wolters 2004). This perspective is referred to as **goal theory.**

Mastery, performance, work avoidance and morality-based goals

Goals represent the purposes that students have in different achievement situations, and are presumed to guide students' behaviour, cognition and affect as they become involved in academic work (Ames 1992; Anderman, Austin & Johnson 2002; Covington 2000; Pintrich, Marx & Boyle 1993). Two academic goal structures have received considerable attention from researchers: **mastery goals** (also called learning goals) and **performance goals** (sometimes called ego goals). Central to a mastery goal is the belief that effort leads to success: the focus of attention is the *intrinsic value of learning*. With a mastery goal, individuals are oriented towards developing new skills, trying to understand their work, improving their level of competence or achieving a sense of mastery. In other words, students feel successful if they believe they have personally improved or have come to understand something. Their performance relative to others is irrelevant; of greater importance to them is the task.

In contrast, central to a performance goal is a *focus on one's ability and sense of self-worth*. Ability is shown by doing better than others, by surpassing norms or by achieving success with little effort. Public recognition for doing better than others is an important element of a performance-goal orientation. Performance goals and achievement are 'referenced' against the performance of others or against external standards such as marks and grades. Consequently, 'self-worth' is determined by one's perception of ability to perform relative to others. Hence, when students try hard without being completely successful (in terms of the established norms), their sense of self-worth may be threatened (Ames 1992; Covington 1992, 2000; Dweck 1986; Nicholls 1989). There appear to be two forms of performance motivation, **performance-approach** and **performance-avoidance** (Elliot 1997, 1999; Harackiewicz, Barron, Pintrich, Elliot & Thrash 2002; McGregor & Elliot 2002; Smith, Duda, Allen & Hull 2002; Urdan 1997; Wolters 2004). Students who hold a performance-approach goal orientation want to do better than their classmates so that they will be recognised as competent by their peers, teachers and parents. Students who hold a performance-avoidance goal orientation do their academic work primarily because they fear appearing incompetent (Elliot 1999; Pajares & Valiante 2000).

The research evidence on mastery motivation appears relatively clear and suggests that students, in adopting a mastery orientation, focus on learning, understanding and mastering the task, and appear to use deeper processing strategies such as elaboration, as well as more metacognitive and self-regulatory strategies (Covington 2000; Elliot, McGregor & Gable 1999; Fuchs *et al.* 1997; Harackiewicz, Barron, Tauer & Elliot 2002; Nolen 1988; Obach 2003; Wolters 2004) (see Chapters 4 and 5). It also appears that mastery-oriented students can retrieve information more effectively from long-term memory (Graham & Golan 1991). Research has further shown that mastery goals increase the amount of time students spend on learning tasks and their persistence in the face of difficulty, as well as being related to reduced levels of student disruptive behaviour (Kaplan, Gheen & Midgley 2002). In summary, mastery goals appear very adaptive to school achievement (Covington 2000).

The research evidence on performance motivation is not so clear (Covington 2000; Harackiewicz, Barron & Elliot 1998; Wolters 2003b, 2004). In many ways, performance-approach goals seem to have a positive effect on valued educational outcomes (such as higher grades) and particularly when they are combined with mastery goals, which, as we have said above, are generally related to a whole host of good educational traits and outcomes (Harackiewicz, Barron, Pintrich, Elliot & Thrash 2002; Harackiewicz, Barron, Tauer & Elliot 2002; see also Midgley, Kaplan & Middleton 2001). There is evidence, however, that individuals who are performance-avoidance oriented appear more likely to use surface-level strategies such as rote memorisation and rehearsal (see Chapter 4 and Watkins, McInerney, Lee, Akande & Regmi *et al.* 2002; Watkins, McInerney, Akande & Lee 2003). Furthermore, because this approach is linked with social comparison, it has been associated with both avoidance of challenging tasks (particularly with those students who have a low self-concept of ability) and withdrawal from tasks after an initial failure (why continue if one lacks ability?) (Covington 2000). Performance orientation, particularly performance-avoidance, also appears to diminish intrinsic motivation for learning (Rawsthorne & Elliot 1999) and be related to academic self-handicapping. **Academic self-handicapping** refers to students creating impediments to successful performance on tasks that the individual considers important in order to provide an excuse other than lack of ability for poor performance should it occur. Performance-avoidance is related to academic self-handicapping such as low task engagement, low self-determination while studying, distraction, procrastination and an unwillingness to seek help with schoolwork, fear of evaluation and elevated levels of student disruptive behaviour (Elliot 1999; Elliot *et al.* 1999; Kaplan, Gheen & Midgley 2002; Urdan 2004; Wolters 2003b; see also Pintrich 2000).

Setting goals is important to motivation. What mastery and performance goals may be motivating this youngster?

A third type of goal orientation, **work avoidance**, has received less attention by researchers but appears to be quite important in influencing students' attitudes towards their school work (Ainley 1993; Blumenfeld 1992; Elliot 1999; Dowson & McInerney 2001; Lee & Anderson 1993; Meece & Holt 1993; Nicholls *et al.* 1989; Nicholls, Patashnick & Nolen 1985; Wolters 2003b). Work-avoidance (or work-avoidant) goals represent a type of goal orientation where students deliberately avoid engaging in academic tasks and/or attempt to minimise the effort required to complete academic tasks. This orientation, although distinct from both performance and mastery orientations (Meece & Holt 1993), may nevertheless combine with these orientations to affect students' cognitive engagement and academic achievement (Ainley 1993). Among the work-avoidant strategies used by students are copying, asking teachers to complete their problems, asking teachers for help on relatively easy tasks, engaging in off-task behaviour, such as talking to friends, organising and reorganising materials such as pens, paper and rulers, trying to negotiate less demanding alternatives to assessment, tuning out on all but the simplest or most urgent classroom tasks, and feigning incompetence or misunderstanding, even when understanding or competence on a given task had been demonstrated. It is also associated with surface learning (Meece & Miller 1996). We wonder if any of these have applied to you! We think work-avoidant tactics are used by most students sometimes. Work-avoidant orientations appear to be associated with feelings of laziness, boredom, inertia and, at times, anger. These feelings distract students from engaging and sustaining effective involvement in academic work (Dowson & McInerney 2001), and are associated with behaviour directed at minimising the effort required to complete tasks. As you can see from this description, work-avoidance goals are inimical to effective learning. Unfortunately, it appears that while intrinsic motivation declines over the school years, work-avoidance motivation increases (Meece & Miller 1996). It is possible that the increase in work-avoidance goals is associated with declining competency beliefs as children progress through schooling (see, for example, Bouffard 2000; Meece & Miller 1996). We discuss some reasons for this decline in competency beliefs in another section.

In addition to academic goal structures, individuals can also have **morality-based goals.** By this we mean a motivational system in which the goal is to help others in a cooperative group work situation in the hope of increasing the group's achievement (Ames 1984).

When the focus of attention is effort, as with mastery-oriented and morality-based learning, and perhaps also performance-approach orientation (see, for example, Rawsthorne & Elliot 1999), pride and satisfaction are associated with successful effort and guilt with inadequate effort. As the relationship between ability and outcome is not an issue, the student is encouraged to expend greater effort to improve performance next time round. In this sense the utility of the mastery-goal approach fits within the attributional framework discussed earlier in the chapter. Mastery-oriented students are more likely to be tolerant of failure (Ames 1992) and see it as a necessary condition for further effort in learning. Similarly, with morality-based motivation, individual effort is seen in terms of contribution to a group product and helping others, as in cooperative teamwork. The *intention* of group members to help or expend effort takes priority over their actual ability to do so, irrespective of group success or failure (Abrami *et al.* 1992, 1995). Some behavioural and affective characteristics of mastery and performance goals that teachers might note are listed in Table 7.5.

The importance of effort

Academic cheating

Performance goals (with their emphasis on ability and social comparison) also seem to be related to academic cheating, which is a form of coping mechanism quite prevalent during adolescence (Anderman, Griesinger & Westerfield 1998; Blackburn & Miller 2000). The reason for this is that, as schools emphasise ability and performance more—and in particular, social comparison, some students will be induced to resort to cheating as a means of coping with an environment that is perceived as threatening to their sense of self by ensuring that they are successful on particular tasks. Blackburn and Miller (2000) explore the relationships between cheating, performance and mastery motivation, ability and importance of future consequences, and reveal that the antecedents of cheating behaviour are very complex indeed. For example, they found that students who had

Table 7.5 Behavioural and affective components of mastery and performance goals

Behavioural components of mastery goals
Students motivated by mastery goals: • take extra effort in class even when there are no marks for it; • seek challenging work for the sake of it; • ask for additional work; • ask more than the usual number of questions about their work; • make applications of school knowledge to the real world.
Affective components of mastery goals
Students motivated by mastery goals: • are pleased when they find the solution to a problem; • enjoy challenging work even though it is more difficult; • are pleased when extra effort leads to a good result; • want to understand things even if it requires extra effort or explanation from the teacher.
Behavioural components of performance goals
Students motivated by performance goals: • ask questions often about the teacher's expectations related to assignments; • ask questions about the structure of assignments, especially how many marks are awarded to each section; • do work beyond the usual expectations to get more marks; • question the distribution of exam and assignment marks.
Affective components of performance goals
Students motivated by performance goals: • get upset when their academic results are not as good as expected; • are never satisfied with anything less than their very best; • are constantly concerned about relative performance.
(Source: Based on Dowson & McInerney 1996a, 1997, 2001, 2003)

high perceived ability were more likely to cheat when future consequences were less important and less likely to cheat when future consequences were important. In contrast, students who had low perceived ability cheated less on less important future consequences and more when future consequences were high. Cheating, of course, becomes quite difficult to maintain and so only provides a short-term 'solution'.

Some students, however, who are performance-approach oriented and who focus on getting a good mark or doing better than other students, may have enhanced intrinsic motivation and academic achievement. This is particularly the case if they focus on the possibility of a positive outcome, are not anxious about their public performance, don't fear failure, and put in the extra effort to ensure that they do well (Harackiewicz *et al.* 1998). In many cases, performance approach and mastery orientation go hand-in-hand (Pintrich 2000; Rawsthorne & Elliot 1999). It would appear, therefore, that performance-approach goals can function adaptively in educational settings. This is particularly the case if the educational setting is perceived as nurturing and caring. Conversely, the evidence appears clear that, by and large, performance-avoidance goals are detrimental to motivation and achievement, and educational settings should be structured to minimise this type of goal orientation. (However, see Barker, Dowson & McInerney 2002.)

How do schools communicate achievement goals?

There is considerable research directed at examining ways in which schools and teachers implicitly and explicitly communicate various achievement goals.

There are many ways in which schools communicate achievement goals to students: through the *tasks* that are set, the *assessment* and *evaluation* policies implemented, and the *distribution of authority* within the school and classrooms (Ames 1992; Blumenfeld 1992).

The nature of the tasks set

Clearly, the nature of the tasks set for students will influence whether they are likely to become intrinsically interested or strive for extrinsic goals (such as grades and marks). Among key aspects of tasks that have been found to be related to interest and intrinsic motivation are *variety*, *diversity*, *challenge*, *control* and *meaningfulness*. We have made many suggestions throughout this and other chapters about how student interest in learning tasks may be enhanced by developing these task dimensions. When motivation is intrinsic, social comparison and other performance criteria become less salient to the student.

The way in which schools and teachers evaluate and

EXTENSION STUDY

Expanding goal theory to other dimensions of importance

Recent theorising and research suggest that performance and mastery goals are not opposites and that individuals may hold both, varying in importance, depending on the nature of the task, the school environment, and the broader social and educational context of the school (see, for example, Blumenfeld 1992; McInerney 1991b; McInerney & Sinclair 1992; Pintrich & Garcia 1991; Urdan & Maehr 1995; Wentzel 1991a, 1991b). Furthermore, students may hold multiple goals such as a desire to please their parents and teachers, to be important in the peer group (especially for girls, in some cultures) and to preserve their cultural identity, each of which may impact upon their level of motivation for particular tasks in school settings. Indeed, these multiple goals interact, providing a complex framework of motivational determinants of action (see, for example, Wentzel 1996). A child from a minority group, for example, may feel strong conflicting pressures between maintaining cultural values that may not foster academic achievement and achieving in a school context, which is valued by teachers. Meanwhile, yet another pressure is operating, that of being accepted and liked by one's peers, which may further influence whether doing well at school is seen as appropriate or not.

Personal investment in achieving goals

Schooling does not consist solely of learning academic material. Indeed, the social dimension of schooling (including the influence of parents, teachers and peers) may be equally important, and extremely influential in affecting children's attitudes towards schooling in general and learning in particular (Wigfield *et al.* 1998; Wentzel 2002). A goal model of motivation that considers other relevant and interacting goals has been used in a number of studies of student motivation. This approach is called the *personal investment theory of motivation* (Maehr & McInerney 2004). This model is helpful in conceptualising motivation as it highlights, first, the fact that students may hold multiple goals, each of which may impact upon their level of motivation for particular tasks and, second, that there is a recognise student performance also establishes both overt and covert goal structures. For example, if teachers structure learning episodes so that students engage in intrinsically motivated learning and they are then evaluated through non-competitive means (such as portfolios), students are likely to be mastery-oriented. On the other hand, if teachers structure learning episodes so that students experience intrinsically motivated learning and then evaluate them through formal normative testing, students are likely to be performance-oriented. In this case, the covert goal established through the assessment process is performance-based. Whenever evaluation is based on social comparison, performance goals are established: the overt mastery goals established through the structure of the learning episodes are thereby undermined. We deal with this issue in some detail in Chapter 11.

The type of evaluation conducted

As discussed earlier, the use of extrinsic reward systems may also undermine mastery orientation under certain conditions (see Chapter 6).

Another powerful factor that will influence whether children perceive the classroom as mastery- or performance-oriented relates to who holds the power to make decisions in the classroom. The extent to which children perceive that they genuinely share authority and have significant levels of autonomy in making choices appears to be a significant factor in their engagement in learning and the quality of their effort (see, for example, Fredrichs, Blumenfeld & Paris 2004; Grolnick, Gurland, Jacob & Decourcey 2002; Reeve, Deci & Ryan 2004; Stefanou, Perencevich, DiCintio & Turner 2004). Indeed autonomy, along with competence and relatedness, form core elements of self-determination theory (see the Theory and Research into Practice section by Ed Deci). To the extent that external controls are reduced and children have some meaningful level of control over the selection of tasks, materials, method of learning, product, pace and assessment, they are more likely to be mastery-oriented than performance-oriented. Again, this issue is dealt with in a number of chapters. Table 7.6 presents behavioural and affective characteristics of social goals with which teachers should be familiar.

Distribution of shared authority

QUESTION POINT

Competition is a powerful incentive since it brings the full force of group pressure to bear upon the learner. On the other hand, it can be dangerous and should be used judiciously. How might competition be used judiciously and effectively?

potential interaction between a variety of important goals for students in school-related areas (Dowson & McInerney 2001, 2003).

In the personal investment model, the goal structures are described as task, ego, social solidarity and extrinsic rewards. *Task goals* emphasise the intrinsic interest of the learning exercise where the goal of learning is to gain understanding, insight or skill. Learning in itself is valued, and the attainment of mastery is seen as dependent on one's effort. *Ego goals* and *extrinsic goals* emphasise individual comparison and competition, and achievement is seen as the means of obtaining external rewards. *Social solidarity goals* emphasise the cooperative and affiliative dimensions of learning. Among social goals that have been found influential in determining a student's motivation at school are approval, responsibility, welfare, affiliation and survival (Dowson & McInerney 2003).

Each of the goal structures described in the personal investment model potentially impacts upon an individual's sense of competence, sense of autonomy and sense of purpose in learning, and contributes to the motivational orientation of the individual. Our own research indicates that classrooms and schools should emphasise task and social solidarity goals. Unfortunately, many schools emphasise ego and extrinsic goals through competition and social comparison, ability grouping and tracking, and public evaluation of performance and conduct based on normative standards of performance. Such schools give students little opportunity to cooperate and interact with other students, and little opportunity to choose the tasks that are of most interest and relevance to them. There are, of course, classrooms and schools that emphasise task and social solidarity orientations and give opportunities for peer interaction and cooperation; they group students according to interest and needs, allow flexibility in choice of activities and opportunities for student initiative and responsibility, define success in terms of effort, progress and improvement, and put emphasis on the value and interest of learning. Students in these classrooms are likely to be highly motivated, to set themselves meaningful and challenging goals of achievement, and to persist at school for the perceived benefits that will accrue to them.

We consider personal investment theory in more detail when we discuss motivation in a cross-cultural context in Chapter 10.

Table 7.6 Behavioural and affective components of social goals

Students motivated by social goals may:

- ask about marks and grades on behalf of parents;
- work hard at school to please parents;
- make opportunities to talk to teachers;
- work hard at school to please teachers;
- become involved in charity/fundraising activities;
- volunteer for activities that help the class to run well, such as book and lunch monitoring;
- pass notes in class;
- stake out an area in the playground;
- want to work only with particular people;
- interact with peers beyond the immediate school situation;
- be upset when friends are reprimanded;
- become involved in peer tutoring;
- voluntarily help special needs students in the class/playground;
- volunteer to be a buddy or peer adviser;
- promote the social development/interaction of less accepted peers;
- make other students aware of school rules and conventions.

(Source: Based on Dowson & McInerney 1996a, 1997, 2001, 2003)

EXTENSION STUDY

Classroom goal structures

Another perspective on motivational goals has been termed classroom goal structures. There are three classroom goal structures: individualised, competitive and cooperative (Ames 1984; Johnson, Maruyama, Johnson, Nelson & Skon 1981). Individualised structures occur when students are judged on their own performance irrespective of the performance of other students. Under this type of structure all students can be successful if they work appropriately, and the performance of one student does not affect the evaluation given to another student. In contrast to this, in competitive structures students' performance is judged on the basis of relative performance with other students, and the attainment of rewards is only possible if other students don't attain them. This is typically the case when ranking and grading occurs in classroom activities. In competitive structures, social comparison and judgment of ability are particularly significant. Cooperative structures reflect group work where group members share rewards and punishments on the basis of the overall performance. We deal with various models of cooperative structures in Chapter 8.

You might surmise from this that competitive goal structures are potentially more likely to generate negative attitudes towards learning, and to threaten a student's self-esteem. In general, research does support the view that competitive goal structures can be inimical to good motivation and learning (see, for example, Covington 1992). This is because, under this type of structure, students focus on their perceptions of their ability, with winners' perceptions being enhanced while losers' perceptions are diminished. Consistently we have found that students, in general, do not like competitive goal structures. At the least, many find competition irrelevant—that is, they believe that they should work to better their own achievement, not to better someone else's. At the worst, competition can alienate many students who believe that in competitive situations they are bound to be the loser (McInerney & McInerney 2000). In a study with Navajo students at Window Rock (McInerney, McInerney, Ardington & De Rachewiltz 1997) students gave the following reasons for the lack of salience of competition for them:

- It is inappropriate to set oneself above others and for only some people to be winners. In other words, group allegiance makes personal competition inappropriate and difficult.
- Competition can generate poor social interactions.
- Interpersonal competition is not necessary as people should compete against their own best, and work at their own pace.
- Competition is selfish.

These reasons would apply to most students from a variety of cultural and social groups. On the other hand, there were some positive reasons given by this group of students for competition. Among these were:

- Competition is all right in sport but not in academics.
- It is necessary to compete in the wider society in order to survive.

QUESTION POINT

What is the importance of goal structure in influencing motivation and relationships with others? Differentiate between and give examples of individualistic, competitive and cooperative goal structures.

Peer group influences on student motivation

In the extensive research (Dowson & McInerney 2001; McInerney & McInerney 2000; McInerney, Roche, McInerney & Marsh 1997; McInerney *et al.* 1998) conducted into student motivation across a range of cultural groups it has become quite apparent, and is somewhat surprising, that peer group influence on student motivation and learning is perceived by students as important and, by and large, positive. While teachers have often viewed peer group influences primarily in negative terms (for example, Ashman & Gillies 1997), having friends has been related positively to grades and test scores as well as to involvement in school-related activities (Wentzel, Barry & Caldwell 2004). Students in our studies describe peer group influence largely in positive terms with respect to school learning; that is, holding a social affiliation orientation to one's peers promotes positive approaches to learning rather than the opposite. Hence, social affiliation with the peer group is seen primarily in adaptive terms, facilitating both effective engagement in learning and positive feelings towards learning. Moreover, students hold these views despite the fact that they also identify the potentially detrimental effects that the peer group may have on their ongoing motivation and achievement: 'I really want to

- It is necessary to show other people that individuals and the Navajo people generally can be successful.

What do you think of these reasons for the usefulness of competition at school? Can you think of any other reasons?

In contrast to this, **individualistic goal structures** are more likely to heighten mastery goals because the focus is on improving one's own skills. In this case, there is an emphasis on personal effort and there is little worry over the performance of others (**competitive goal structures**) as the measure of achievement is one's own performance, irrespective of others' performance. **Cooperative goal structures** enhance shared effort and interdependence. Hence, cooperative goal structures probably have a positive effect on motivation and achievement. In some sense, the focus is taken off the individual, and so individual ability becomes less salient. We discuss in some detail the merits of cooperative group learning and different forms of cooperative learning in Chapter 8.

It would appear, therefore, that while many schools and classrooms still emphasise competitive goal structures, they would do better to emphasise individualistic and cooperative goal structures. What do you think?

Another recent way of conceptualising classroom goal structures relates to our discussion earlier of mastery- and performance-oriented personal motivational goals. In this way of looking at goal structures, a mastery goal structure describes a classroom or school environment in which the instructional practices, policies and norms convey to students that learning is important for its own sake, and that effort is related to achievement over and above ability. A performance goal structure describes an environment that communicates to students that being successful means getting rewards, demonstrating high ability, and doing better than others. As with individual goal orientations, these school and classroom goal structures can emphasise approach or avoidance dimensions (Linnenbrink & Pintrich 2002; Urdan 2004; Wolters 2004). Generally, research indicates that schools and classrooms that emphasise mastery structures have students that are more personally mastery-oriented; with all the positive aspects this entails (greater persistence, higher achievement, the use of learning strategies and metacognitive skills), while these students engage in less self-handicapping behaviour. Classrooms and schools that have more performance-oriented structures appear to have students that are more performance-oriented (Wolters 2004). The results for performance-approach and performance-avoidance goal structures on student academic engagement and achievement are less clear than for mastery orientation, but there is some evidence that performance-approach goal structures are related, in some instances, to positive qualities such as the use of learning strategies and higher achievement. There is also evidence that performance-avoidance classroom and school goal structures are related to negative behaviours such as academic self-handicapping, as well as poorer performance. However, much more research needs to be conducted on the effects of performance-approach and performance-avoidance class structures before definitive conclusions can be made about their effects on motivation, learning and achievement (Urdan 2004; Wolters 2004; see also Midgley, Kaplan & Middleton 2001).

work with my friends, and sometimes we get lots done, but sometimes we just muck around and don't get anything done at all. Then I feel like I haven't really tried and it makes it harder to get started on it [work] again' (Dowson & McInerney 2001). Our findings are certainly in line with other research which indicates that socially supported and well-liked students do better in school and have more positive motivation (Wigfield *et al.* 1998).

Students, by and large, seek out membership of a peer group. What is important is not so much belonging to a peer group, which appears to be very important for social adjustment, but whether the peer group one belongs to is positively or negatively oriented to learning. High-achieving students more often than not seek out other high-achieving students and, as a consequence, have their own motivation to achieve enhanced and reinforced. On the other hand, low-achieving students may join low-achieving groups with work-avoidance goals. In this case, there may be a further diminishing of their motivation and achievement. Often these low-achieving groups will engage in activities that are not conducive to good learning and indeed can devalue academic achievement relative to other goals and activities. Most authors agree that the power of peer group influences becomes strongest during the adolescent years when peer group acceptance becomes so important, and when social activities become more important and enjoyable than most other activities (Wigfield *et al.* 1998, 2002b; see also Chapter 14). Classrooms can exacerbate this effect by setting up ability groups for work activities. In this case, often the able work with the able, and the less able with the less able. It is no wonder, then, that some groups are more motivated and produce better work than others. In contrast, work groups can be organised so that high-achieving and low-achieving students can become co-learners. In this situation, the motivation of the low-achieving student may be enhanced. We discuss this in our section on peer learning in Chapter 8.

Social goals and communities of learners

Apart from the affiliative need to belong to a group, which is important for students, there are a number of other **social goals** that are highly influential in orienting student motivation. These pro-social goals, such as social responsibility and social concern, can help to organise, direct and empower individuals to achieve more fully (Covington 2000; Wentzel 1999, 2002).

Social responsibility

Social responsibility is seen primarily by students in adaptive terms, with it facilitating effective engagement in learning and associated extracurricular activities, as well as generating feelings of pride, self-worth, satisfaction and excitement through fulfilling responsibilities and satisfying communal role expectations. A feature of the social responsibility orientation is that while it includes references to those in authority over students, it also includes substantial references to peers. Thus, students feel a responsibility towards each other, as well as to their parents and teachers, to achieve in academic situations. As one student put it, 'I want to do well for my friends' sake too, because we all feel like we've done the right thing if the school is going well [academically]' (Dowson & McInerney 2001).

Social concern

Another important social goal is social concern for one's peers at school. Ford (1992), Wentzel (1991a) and McInerney, McInerney, Ardington & De Rachewiltz. (1997) have recognised that students may act in academic situations in order to enhance the welfare of other students. That students may see their own academic achievement as a means of assisting others is a new perspective on social concern orientation. In other words, there is a relationship between social concern, responsibility and cognition; that is, being responsible and concerned is perceived by many students as enhancing their use of cognitive strategies. Helping other students to learn helps oneself to learn better. Previously, studies have focused on academic achievement as an outcome of what Wentzel calls 'pro-social' behaviour. However, academic achievement may be viewed from within a social concern orientation as a means of displaying pro-social behaviour. Thus, academic achievement may be conceptualised as both an outcome and an antecedent of pro-social behaviour. This perspective is consistent with some goal theory studies, especially those in cross-cultural settings which, similarly, see academic achievement as both a product and precursor of pro-social, concern-oriented behaviour (McInerney *et al.* 1998).

Both social responsibility and social concern are important aspects of students' motivation. Many schools are recognising this more effectively by providing students with opportunities to work together cooperatively as communities of learners. In these communities, peers and teachers are co-learners. Doing learning in a social context is fun and can provide the opportunity to help others and to obtain support and help from others. In this way all students can focus more clearly on mastery than on performance. The role of the teacher is very important in establishing a climate in which social responsibility and social concern among students can flourish. The willingness of students to work cooperatively towards learning goals and to help each other is related to whether they consider that teachers care about them as persons and students. When students perceive teachers as having failed to provide support, they feel no obligation to behave in socially responsible ways, nor do they enjoy school (Covington 2000). We provide many examples throughout the text of how communities of learners may be established. (See, for example, our sections on peer tutoring, cooperative group work and peer assessment in Chapter 8.)

Communities of learners

Adolescence and school motivation: Are there special issues?

It is a common experience of teachers that it is easier to motivate younger children academically than adolescents. There is clear evidence that there is a decline in school motivation for many students as they move from primary grades to high school (Anderman & Maehr 1994; Anderman *et al.* 1999; Mac Iver, Young & Washburn 2002; Midgley & Edelin 1998; Roderick & Camburn 1999; Wigfield *et al.* 1998). Research tends to support the view that motivation is a serious issue during adolescence, and that whether adolescent students are motivated academically may have major consequences for later life choices.

What are the causes of this decline in school motivation? Studies suggest that declines in motivation during adolescence are associated with contextual/environmental factors and are not simply the result of pubertal changes (Anderman & Maehr 1994; Anderman *et al.* 1999; Eccles & Midgley 1989; Lohaus, Elben, Ball & Klein-Hessling 2004; Midgley & Edelin 1998; Roderick & Camburn 1999). There is a direct link between changes in classroom learning environments as children move from primary into secondary schools and the decline in motivation, with a number of researchers suggesting that the instructional practices and educational policies of secondary schools may be inappropriate for maintaining student motivation.

Contextual and environmental factors

Secondary schools, for example, emphasise comparative student performance through exams and assignments much more than primary schools. As children grow older they become more convinced that ability is relatively fixed and that expenditure of effort, particularly in an activity in which they are not very successful, demonstrates their lack of competence to others. Consequently, many individuals avoid putting in effort simply to avoid being labelled 'dumb'. Through their assessment and evaluation policies and practices, many secondary schools do not encourage adolescents to become academic 'risk-takers'.

As students move into high school they experience major changes in authority relationships. High schools are often characterised by less personal and positive teacher–student relationships. As we have discussed on many occasions, positive teacher–student relationships are associated with student achievement. Adolescents seek opportunities for developing a sense of self-efficacy and autonomy. We see this commonly demonstrated by the way in which adult power is constantly challenged by adolescents. Secondary schools, by and large, are very regimented places in which the power hierarchy is quite explicit, both within and outside the classroom. There is greater emphasis on teacher control and discipline, and fewer opportunities for student decision making, choice and self-management (Anderman *et al.* 1999; Wigfield *et al.* 1998). With little opportunity to take charge of their own learning and motivation in such a context, many adolescent students simply oppose or withdraw from engagement (see, for example, Eccles & Midgley 1989; Eccles *et al.* 1993).

Self-efficacy and autonomy

On a social level, peer networks are often disrupted when students change schools at the end of primary school. This can be because children go to different schools or take different academic courses in high school. New social networks take time to establish, and this can take precedence over learning in the classroom with many adolescents being more preoccupied with this than with anything else that goes on at school.

Many primary classrooms emphasise the fun of learning and thus captivate students intrinsically in activities. Who said that adolescents no longer want or need to be captivated? Yet many secondary classrooms are crushingly dull places in which to learn. It is still common to hear of teachers who engage their students in monotonous rote recall activities such as copying notes off the whiteboard. With little real stimulation in many classrooms, students will engage in a diverse range of more stimulating, non-academic activities. It is not a case of adolescents lacking motivation but, rather, of them investing their motivational energy in the wrong activities for the lack of something better at school.

QUESTION POINT

Discuss the reasons given for the decline in adolescent motivation at school. Were these reasons relevant to you and your peers?

Course failure

As we have indicated above, the transition from one level of school to another often leads to a fall-off in motivation and achievement. School performance, involvement and perception of their school environments decline significantly for many students as they move into secondary schools (Roderick & Camburn 1999). For many students this ultimately leads to school failure and dropping-out (Murdock 1999). The reasons for failure are relatively simple—students who fail do not attend class, do not complete required work or do not pass examinations (Roderick & Camburn 1999). However, the causes of these reasons are far more complex and include the level of skill the students have (such as study skills), level and type of motivation (mastery, performance, social and work avoidance), peer influences (both positive and negative), parental encouragement and support, perceived instrumental importance of education, school processes (such as the distribution of authority and goal structures supported) and teaching effectiveness. We deal with all of these issues at various points throughout the text. The thing to note here is that the importance of each of these becomes greater as students progress through school. It is also important to note that many of these factors influencing school failure are factors over which the school has some control. In the next section we address the question of how schools can more effectively fit the needs of students so that motivation is enhanced and school failure minimised.

Changing a school's psychological environment to enhance student motivation

It is clear that to enhance students' motivation we must improve school and classroom practices. Maehr and others have called this changing the school's 'psychological environment' (Anderman & Maehr 1994; Anderman *et al.* 1999; Maehr & Buck 1993; Maehr, Midgley & Urdan 1992; Midgley & Edelin 1998; Wigfield *et al.* 1998). Maehr believes there is a need to change a lot of the messages that classrooms and schools communicate to children about the purposes of schooling—messages that are communicated through policies and practices related to rewards, praise and recognition, the nature of school tasks, grouping and evaluation practices, and resource allocation. A number of these topics have been covered in earlier sections of this chapter. Our research, and that of an increasingly large group of educators, has shown that the personal engagement of children in learning seems to be most affected by the sense of self that students have in the school context. The expectations that students hold for themselves as they generalise from past experiences and incorporate the more immediate expectations of parents, teachers and peers profoundly affect motivation and performance level. Children's sense of self, reflected through a **sense of competence** and of the purpose of schooling, is critical to their motivation, academic achievement and retention at school.

Sense of competence relates to students' self-concept for the task of learning: how they assess their capacity to learn. A sense of competence is a major determinant of children's school confidence, how much they like school, their level of attendance, and the goals they set for themselves while at school and later. Our research has shown that children who feel incompetent dislike school, and have limited occupational aspirations, high absenteeism and lower classroom grades (McInerney 1993; McInerney & Swisher 1995).

Students who have a strong sense of the purpose of schooling value school more, intend to complete school, perform better academically at school and desire more prestigious occupations after leaving school than those who do not see a purpose in schooling. Clearly, those students who set academic goals and see a purpose in schooling are more likely to be successful in that context.

In all the studies conducted by the authors, level of intrinsic motivation, such as striving for excellence in one's work and desiring improvement against personal standards, strongly predicted a student's commitment to learning. In contrast, competition and extrinsic rewards were either unimportant or contrary to the best interests of the children. For example, in our Australian study extrinsic rewards only appeared to be important to children already determined to leave school! In a Navajo study we conducted, the extrinsic dimension was excluded from the final profile for these students as it appeared to be

The culture of caring and academic dimensions of school improvement

It is important that two dimensions receive special focus if schools are to serve the needs of students better. The first of these is the relationship dimension and the second the academic dimension (Midgley & Edelin 1998). Throughout our text we discuss the importance of schools establishing a caring and responsive school environment in order to enhance interpersonal relationships so that students do not become alienated from school, and feel secure and happy within the school environment. This is often referred to as a culture of caring (Noddings 1992, 1995; Osterman 2000; Shann 1999; Wentzel 1997). In other words, it is important that students have good interpersonal relationships with people who might help them do well at school. This support can come from teachers, friends, parents and the neighbourhood of the school (Lee & Smith 1999; see also Murdock 1999 and Fredrichs, Blumefeld & Paris 2004), and might consist of positive modelling, expectations based on individual differences, provision for autonomous decision making and democratic interactions, and nurturance (Wentzel 1997, 1998, 1999). Students with more support should learn more as a result (Shann 1999; Wentzel 1997, 1998, 1999). School and the relationships made at school take on increasing importance as students enter adolescence. However, research suggests that students who attend schools with strong social support but a weak press for academic achievement do not do as well as students who attend schools where there is strong

culturally irrelevant! With regard to competition, all groups appear to be competitive to some degree, but competitiveness does not seem to be related to school motivation and achievement.

Diagnosing current school practice

As we have suggested, many schools and classrooms do not implement policies and practices that are in the best interests of motivating students, and in some cases school practices actually run counter to effective motivation strategies within classroom settings. For example, a teacher may work very hard to encourage students' intrinsic interest in reading only to have the school executive decide to implement a commercial program, such as that presented by a particular pizza company, where rewards and incentives become a goal. Or a teacher may decide to grade according to improvement, only to have this undermined by a normed assessment program across grades. Teachers may provide recognition on the basis of progress, improvement and effort, while the school rewards relative ability. Obviously, best practice must be introduced consistently, across classrooms and across the school as a whole.

Borrowing an acronym (TARGET) from Epstein (1989), Maehr (Anderman *et al.* 1999; Buck & Green 1993; Maehr & Anderman 1993; Maehr & Midgley 1991; see also Maehr, Kan, Kaplan & Peng 1999) has developed a framework that can be used to guide the development of a school-wide emphasis on task goals in learning rather than ego goals (see Table 7.7). TARGET is a process for effectively assessing current practices within a school, and planning future directions in order to integrate and implement the findings, discussed above, on what practices are most likely to engage the intrinsic motivation of children in learning (Ames 1990). The acronym stands for:

Task	**G**rouping
Authority	**E**valuation
Recognition	**T**ime

Within each of the TARGET areas, teachers and administrators can use strategies that either focus on task and social solidarity goals or on ego and extrinsic goals. Tasks that are diverse, interesting and challenging, and that students have a reasonable chance of completing successfully, encourage students to be task-oriented. Sharing authority so that students have opportunities to make decisions and take responsibility fosters task-oriented goals. Giving *all* students recognition, and recognising effort as well as ability, also fosters task-oriented goals. Cooperative group work rather than ability grouping and evaluating students' progress and mastery rather than only their outcomes, while providing opportunities for students to improve, fosters the development of task goals. Finally, allowing students time to complete their work and helping them to plan their own work schedules fosters task orientation (Anderman *et al.* 1999; Wigfield *et al.* 1998). We have mentioned each of these principles in other contexts throughout our book. You should refer to Table 7.7, which gives a general framework for redesigning aspects of school programs so that schools emphasise task goals in learning.

Table 7.7

General framework employed in the development of a school-wide emphasis on task goals in learning

Target Area	Focus	Goals	Strategies
Task	Intrinsic value of learning	• Reduce the reliance on extrinsic incentives • Design programs that challenge all students • Stress goals and purposes in learning • Stress the fun of learning	• Encourage programs that take advantage of students' backgrounds and experience • Avoid payment (monetary or other) for attendance, grades or achievement • Foster programs that stress goal setting and self-regulation/management • Foster programs that make use of school learning in a variety of non-school settings (e.g. internships, field experiences and cocurricular activities)
Authority	Student participation in learning/school decision making	• Provide opportunities to develop responsibility, independence and leadership skills • Develop skills in self-regulation	• Give optimal choice in instructional settings • Foster participation in cocurricular and extracurricular settings • Foster opportunities to learn metacognitive strategies for self-regulation
Recognition	The nature and use of recognition and reward in the school setting	• Provide opportunities for all students to be recognised • Recognise progress in goal attainment • Recognise efforts in a broad array of learning activities	• Foster 'personal best' awards • Foster policy in which all students and their achievements can be recognised • Recognise and publicise wide range of school-related activities of students
Grouping	Student interaction, social skills and values	• Build an environment of acceptance and appreciation of all students • Broaden range of social interaction, particularly of at-risk students • Enhance social skill development • Encourage humane values • Build an environment in which all can see themselves as capable of making significant contributions	• Provide opportunities for group learning, problem solving and decision making • Allow time and opportunity for peer interaction to occur • Foster the development of subgroups (teams, schools within schools, etc.) within which significant interaction can occur • Encourage multiple group membership to increase range of peer interaction
Evaluation	The nature and use of evaluation and assessment procedures	• Increase students' sense of competence and self-efficacy • Increase students' awareness of progress in developing skills and understanding • Increase students' appreciation of their unique set of talents • Increase students' acceptance of failure as a natural part of learning and life	• Reduce emphasis on social comparisons of achievement by minimising public reference to normative evaluation standards (e.g. grades and test scores) • Establish policies and procedures that give students opportunities to improve their performance (e.g. study skills and classes) • Create opportunities for students to assess progress towards goals they have set
Time	The management of time to carry out plans and reach goals	• Improve rate of work completion • Improve skills in planning and organising • Improve self-management ability • Allow the learning task and student needs to dictate scheduling	• Provide experience in personal goal setting and in monitoring progress in carrying out plans for goal achievement • Foster opportunities to develop time management skills • Allow students to progress at their own rate whenever possible • Encourage flexibility in the scheduling of learning experiences

(Source: Reprinted with permission from Maehr & Midgley 1991)

social support as well as a strong press for academic achievement (Lee & Smith 1999). In other words, social support is particularly effective when students attend schools that set genuinely high expectations for academic achievement.

It is important, therefore, for schools to establish high academic standards, but ones that are appropriate for all students' abilities and needs and in which all students feel they can be successful (Lee & Smith 1999; Phillips 1997; Shouse 1996).We deal with this latter issue in more detail

This teacher works in a tough school but is highly regarded by his students. What might he be doing right?

in our next two chapters on special needs education. However, students who attend schools that emphasise academic standards but who do not have appropriate social support may not do well academically. In other words it would appear that emphasising one or other of these dimensions alone will not lead to as effective school improvement as emphasising both conjointly (Lee & Smith 1999; Shann 1999). How do you think schools should improve the relationship and academic dimensions of schooling?

QUESTION POINT

Do you know what the interests of the learners in your class are? How might you find out what their interests are? How would you use this knowledge in planning your teaching/learning activities?

Teacher expectations and effective motivation

How do teacher expectations influence motivation and achievement?

Positive expectations are important to the success of all children.

The self-fulfilling prophecy effect

Implicit in much of what has been written so far is the notion that the beliefs that students hold about themselves and the expectations they have for their academic performance are strong influences on their school motivation. Where do these beliefs and expectations come from? One source, of course, is the classroom teacher. Significant research has been conducted into teacher expectations and their effects on learning, attitudes, beliefs, attributions, expectations, motivation and classroom conduct (see Brophy 1983, 1985a, 1985b for a review, and also Weinstein 1989, Weinstein, Marshall, Sharp & Botkin 1987). In an early study, 'Pygmalion in the Classroom', Rosenthal and Jacobson (1968; also see Rosenthal 1973) demonstrated the effects of what has become known as the **self-fulfilling prophecy**, in which initially false expectations held by teachers set in motion a chain of events that cause the expectations to come true (Brophy 1985a, 1985b, 1986; Good 1995).

Pygmalion effect

Four factors are believed to produce the Pygmalion effect (Rosenthal 1973): climate, feedback, input and output. Teachers who have been led to expect good things from their students appear to do the following:

A model of how expectations become self-fulfilling

1. *Climate:* they create a warmer social/emotional mood around their 'special' students.
2. *Feedback:* they give more feedback to these students about their performance.
3. *Input:* they teach more material and more difficult material to their special students.
4. *Output:* they give their special students more opportunities to respond and question.

Good and Brophy (1990, p. 445; see also Good 1995) propose the following model to explain how teacher expectations become self-fulfilling:

- The teacher expects specific behaviour and achievement from particular students.
- Because of these expectations, the teacher behaves differently towards different students.
- This treatment by the teacher tells each student what behaviour and achievement the teacher expects, and it affects the student's self-concept, achievement motivation and level of aspiration.
- If the teacher's treatment is consistent over time, and if the student does not actively resist or change it in some way, it will shape the student's achievement and behaviour. High-expectation students will be led to achieve at high levels, but the achievement of low-expectation students will decline.
- With time, the student's achievement and behaviour will conform more and more closely to that expected by the teacher.

In both of these models the student appears to be a relatively passive element in the process, and teachers appear to be relatively inflexible once they have embarked on an expectation-'driven' course of action. Much research since the original Rosenthal and Jacobson study has indicated that the process is far more complicated than this (see Brattesani, Weinstein & Marshall 1984; Brophy 1983; Goldenberg 1992; Good 1987). Good talks of both the *self-fulfilling prophecy effect,* in which an originally *erroneous* expectation leads to behaviour that causes the expectation to become true, and the **sustaining expectation effect,** in which teachers expect students to sustain previously developed behaviour patterns, to the point that teachers take these behaviour patterns for granted and fail to see and capitalise on changes in student potential. There are many examples of this latter effect, such as the class clown always being typecast and the uninterested mathematics student not being actively encouraged to be involved despite his renewed interest. Good suggests that the sustaining expectation effect may be more pervasive than the self-fulfilling effect.

'My dad says the way Sir treats us kids is like something out of Shakespeare—whatever that *means!'*

The sources of teacher expectations

Some common sources of erroneous expectations that may influence teachers are stereotypes based on: *socio-economic status* (children from public housing don't have the same ambitions as children from affluent suburbs, or children from professional homes are more motivated to achieve at school than children from working-class homes); *sex differences* (girls are less interested and able in mathematics than boys, girls are better behaved than boys, boys are better at mechanical activities than girls); *physical appearance* (good-looking children are more motivated and better behaved than unattractive children); and *racial grouping* (Maori children are lazy, while Asian children are very studious; Aboriginal children are less academically motivated and able than non-Aboriginal children). Among other sources of expectations are *student profiles* passed on from teacher to teacher, the individual's demonstrated *personality* (for example, introvert, extrovert), apparent *achievement orientation* and *prior behaviour patterns* (Braun 1976).

An extensive literature review (Dusek & Joseph 1983) examined whether or not expectations based on some of the above assumptions were, in fact, related to various indices of student academic performance and social/personality behaviours. *Physical attractiveness* (usually measured by facial attractiveness) was found to be a determinant of teacher expectations for both academic performance and social/personality attributes. However, while expectations may initially be based on physical features in lieu of any other information, as other more academically pertinent information becomes available these expectations are modified by teachers. Despite research evidence suggesting that teachers interact differently with girls and boys in the classroom, this review concluded that student gender is not a basis of teacher expectations for general academic performance. However, student gender was related to expectations for classroom behaviour.

Information, such as *cumulative record files* and more informal sources of information (such as corridor talk), was found to be strongly related to teacher expectations. It is important to note here that teachers apparently distinguish between reliable and unreliable information, and that more reliable information is used as a basis for developing programs for the individual. In this context the expectations may be highly valid and useful. Social class and racial stereotypes were also examined, and both were found to be significantly related to the formation of teacher expectations—for example, students from a lower social class were expected to perform more poorly than students from a higher social class, and students who were black or Mexican were expected to perform less well than white students.

Other possible sources of expectations studied were whether teachers held expectations of siblings after experience with an older brother or sister, and whether expectations were based on family profiles, such as single parenting. In the first case there is some evidence that an older sibling's previous performance (with the same teacher) is related to the formation of the teacher's expectations, while family situation does not appear to be systematically related to the development of expectations. No doubt some of you can recall anecdotal stories of these expectations in operation. Table 7.8 summarises the findings from the Dusek and Joseph study.

Sibling and family profiles

Expectations, even erroneous ones, are only likely to have an effect when the teacher holds them consistently and implements practices in line with these expectations that are not challenged by changes in student behaviour or other environmental events. Most of us have been guilty of expecting poor assignments and test results from particular students because they are inattentive or appear non-involved in our particularly interesting lessons, only to be surprised when the student performs exceptionally well in a particular task. It is amazing how we look upon the student in a new light! Students who are perceived as disruptive will at times be 'little angels'; 'rude' students bring the teacher a Christmas present; students from low-income areas have professional parents; students we think of as academically hopeless are highly thought of by other teachers, and so on. These types of disconfirmation of expectations happen all the time in the classroom. Furthermore, particularly in high school, students have a variety of teachers over a school day, and so the impact of any one teacher is lessened. It should also be noted that many of the expectations that teachers have of students are based upon good understanding of the individual, are accurate, and are used to facilitate the effective development of the student. Indeed, one of the tasks we have set ourselves in this text is to give prospective teachers the information needed to make informed decisions about the likely needs of individual students, and to act appropriately to set up the best possible educational environment for them.

Disconfirmations of teacher expectations

So, perhaps the impact of inappropriate and inaccurate expectations of students is not as destructive as the theory of the self-fulfilling and self-sustaining prophecy would suggest. However, we must emphasise that the

Table 7.8 Summary of bases of teacher expectations

Student characteristics related to teacher expectations
• attractiveness • student classroom conduct • cumulative record folder • race • social class
Student characteristics not related to teacher expectations
• gender • one-parent family situation
Student characteristics on which there is questionable evidence
• older sibling's previous performance (with same teacher) • sex-role behaviour • name stereotypes

effect of expectations on student motivation and performance is quite pervasive. At times, expectations become detrimental to the effective learning of many students perceived by teachers to be low in motivation or low in ability because the expectations themselves become associated with *poor teaching*. Expectations can affect the type of groups that teachers establish, the type of questions asked and the wait-time given for pupils to respond, the type of reinforcement and feedback given, the different activities that students are allowed to be involved in and the general quality of interaction (Braun 1976; Good 1995). In general, high-expectation students are taught more effectively. They receive more positive and warm contact from the teacher. They are given more opportunities to learn new and more difficult material, and are given more clues and wait-time than low-expectation students. High-expectation students receive more praise and recognition for correct responses and less criticism for incorrect responses than low-expectation students (Brophy 1983; Good 1995). However, what really matters for student achievement is what teachers do or don't do, despite their expectations. In other words, if a teacher holds low expectations of a student but nevertheless takes strong corrective action to enhance the student's performance, the chances of student success increase, despite low expectations. Conversely, if a teacher fails to teach effectively, even students for whom high expectations are held may perform poorly (Goldenberg 1992).

Classroom implications of teacher expectations

While teacher expectations may affect a range of behaviours, our particular focus in this chapter is motivation. It would seem likely that when teachers expect learners to be interested in their work, productive and capable, and demonstrate this in their own preparation for teaching, they are more likely to find that learners make efforts to be so than if they expect the reverse. Several studies have shown the beneficial effects of such positive expectations on children (Andrews & Debus 1978; Dweck 1975; Schunk 1982, 1983).

Teachers and positive expectations

While teachers should hold positive expectations that students will want to learn, enjoy learning and be successful at learning, these positive expectations need to be tempered by a sense of reality. Teachers should seek to communicate a confidence that accurately reflects the students' actual ability and potential. Students need to be taught to monitor their own learning and achievements towards desired learning goals as well. Positive teacher and student expectations need to be buttressed by effective teaching. Even low-achieving students in such contexts improve their academic performance (Good 1995).

QUESTION POINT

Researchers have examined the effects of teacher expectancies on three factors: kinds of questions asked, quality of interaction, and reinforcement. Discuss the findings, indicating how high achievers and low achievers would be differentially treated in each area.

QUESTION POINT

What unfounded assumptions are often held of students at school that might affect their self-concept and performance at school? What action should be taken to alleviate the negative effects of such assumptions?

Teachers' common knowledge and theory about motivation

We have covered a range of potential sources of classroom motivation and have suggested that motivators that arise from a student's inherent interest in the task and desire to master new information are probably more potent and effective than those derived from external influences such as a teacher's application of rewards and punishments, or social comparison. But what do teachers actually believe as part of their common knowledge, and what do they actually do?

It appears that teachers have a good knowledge of, and preference for, strategies to stimulate and maintain motivation that are not dissimilar to those proposed by research as useful (Nolen & Nicholls 1994). The most preferred strategies for enhancing motivation are showing interest, giving responsibility, attributing thoughtfulness and improvement, promoting cooperation, selecting stimulating tasks and giving choice of tasks. Among strategies rejected by teachers as less useful are attributing failure to low effort alone and publicising superior performance. Teachers are divided on the value of extrinsic rewards, although more appear to consider them harmful than useful (Nolen & Nicholls 1994).

What motivators do teachers use?

What strategies do teachers actually use? It appears that teachers restrict their use of motivational strategies to a limited range that includes strategies not considered the most desirable (Newby 1991; Nolen & Nicholls 1993, 1994). One study investigated the quantity of motivational strategies used, the types most frequently used, and the relationship between strategy use and student behaviour in the classrooms of 30 beginning elementary teachers in the United States. The findings indicate that these teachers directed a lot of effort into motivating their students and used a range of strategies reflecting those covered in this text. For example, teachers used attention-focusing strategies such as dividing the class into four work groups and switching them to a new location and task on the sound of a bell (representing arousal techniques); relevance strategies such as using familiar past experiences to introduce a subject (representing cognitive approaches); confidence-building strategies such as minimising the feelings of failure, and demonstrating and modelling performance (representing social cognitive and attributional approaches); and, lastly, satisfaction strategies such as giving verbal reinforcement, tangible rewards or taking away privileges (representing a behavioural approach). *The majority of strategies used, however, were based on supplying or restricting extrinsic reinforcers!* Although not as frequently used as satisfaction, the attention-focusing strategies were used to a much greater degree than the relevance and confidence-building strategies.

The extensive use of extrinsic reinforcers and attention-focusing strategies by these teachers may reflect the age of the students taught and the perceived need for frequent changes of activity. However, the small percentage of confidence and relevance strategies used may be an indication of:

- the limited knowledge these teachers had about implementing such strategies;
- the difficulty they found in building students' confidence or in making the instruction relevant to the students;
- the attitude that such motivation should be the responsibility of the student, not that of the instruction or the teacher; and
- increased individualisation that is required for such strategies, which may be inhibitory on the teacher's time or which may require more experience to implement effectively (Newby 1991).

The most important finding from this research was that there was a significant positive relationship between the teachers' use of relevance strategies and the observed on-task behaviour of the students. Those classrooms in which there was a higher incidence of giving reasons for the importance of the task or in which students were encouraged to relate the task to their personal experiences showed a higher rate of on-task behaviour (see also Marshall 1987). Students in classrooms in which higher levels of either rewards or punishments were delivered were observed to have lower levels of on-task behaviours. This latter case could illustrate that the reinforcers and punishments were losing their effect, or that the teachers involved perceived that students were getting off-task and increased the rewards or punishments in an attempt to get the class back on-task. In both cases, the motivational outcome is unsatisfactory.

A further study (Nolen & Nicholls 1994) also found a discrepancy between what teachers believed were effective strategies and what they actually practised. Among the reasons suggested for this situation are the coercive influences of mandated curricula and accountability constraints, which induce teachers to use strategies that ensure output irrespective of whether they encourage intrinsic motivation.

There are a number of messages coming from this research. What do you think are the implications for teachers, students and administrators?

QUESTION POINT

Teachers who fail to ensure the frequent and continued success of their pupils should be regarded as negligent. Discuss.

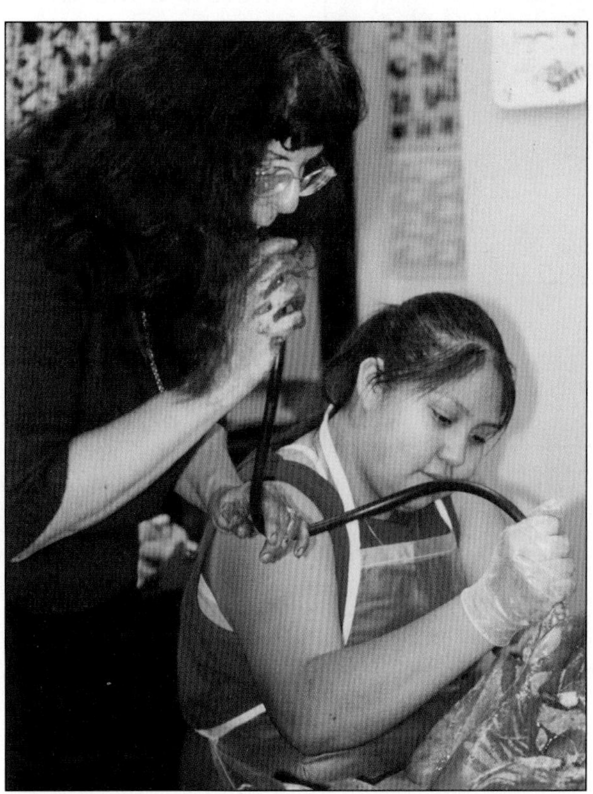

This teacher is blowing up a sheep's lung in this biology lesson. What aspects of good motivation are being demonstrated?

The relationship between motivation and constructivism

When looking back over the content of this chapter, what elements appear to reflect a constructivist approach? Clearly, whenever the focus shifts to what the student does to interpret and become engaged in learning experiences (that is, motivated to learn) we have elements of constructivism. So, when teachers foster intrinsic motivation, autonomy, self-regulation and self-management, and stress meaningful learning, prior knowledge, real-world problems, authentic tasks, and student engagement in problem solving as sources of motivation, we have evidence of a personal constructivist approach. We have also suggested that motivation is facilitated in social contexts. The social constructivist or sociocultural view of learning and motivation emphasises the role of culturally organised, socially mediated practices in children's development. From this perspective, motivation shifts from being seen as a component of an individual's behaviour to being seen as derived from interaction with and within the larger sociocultural context of the learner (Rueda *et al.* 2001). This insight is particularly important when we consider the motivation of students from non-traditional and diverse backgrounds (see Chapters 9 and 10). In this context, we have discussed the influence of the peer group and the idea of communities of learners with their emphases on collaborative, cooperative learning. Our discussion of mastery, performance and social goals separated these out for conceptual clarity and emphasised the individual focus of these. However, realistically each of these is likely to operate simultaneously for each student for any given activity (see Dowson & McInerney 2001) and the importance of one over another will reflect, to a large extent, the broader social context of the learning activity.

THE STUDENT MOTIVATION AND ENGAGEMENT WHEEL

Andrew J. Martin

Self-concept Enhancement and Learning Facilitation (SELF) Research Centre, University of Western Sydney

What is motivation and engagement?

I define motivation as students' energy and drive to learn, work effectively, and achieve to their potential at school. I define engagement as the thoughts, emotions and behaviours that follow from this energy and drive. Motivation and engagement play a large part in students' interest in and enjoyment of school and study. Motivation and engagement also underpin their achievement.

The Student Motivation and Engagement Wheel

I have developed the Student Motivation and Engagement Wheel, which comprises constructs central to motivation and engagement, and the Student Motivation and Engagement Scale (www.ajmartinresearch.com) to measure each facet of the wheel. The wheel (and the scale) separates motivation into factors that reflect enhanced motivation and engagement, those that reflect impeded motivation and engagement, and those that reflect reduced motivation and engagement. These are called adaptive cognitions/thoughts (or 'booster thoughts'), adaptive behaviours (or 'booster behaviours), impeding dimensions (or 'mufflers'), and maladaptive dimensions ('guzzlers').

The strength of the wheel is that it can be easily communicated by teachers to students and following from this, is readily understandable by students. The teacher and student can easily separate the 'helpful' (boosters) motivation and engagement from the 'unhelpful' (mufflers and guzzlers). Thus, this model is an easy way for students to understand their motivation and engagement and an easy way for teachers to explain it to them. When students understand motivation and engagement and the dimensions that comprise them, intervention is more meaningful, and as a consequence, is likely to be more successful.

Adaptive dimensions of the wheel ('booster thoughts' and 'booster behaviours')

Each adaptive dimension falls into one of two groups: thoughts (cognitions) and behaviours. Adaptive thoughts ('booster thoughts') include self-efficacy, mastery orientation and valuing of school. Adaptive behaviours ('booster behaviours') include persistence, planning and study management. Below is a brief description of each of these adaptive dimensions.

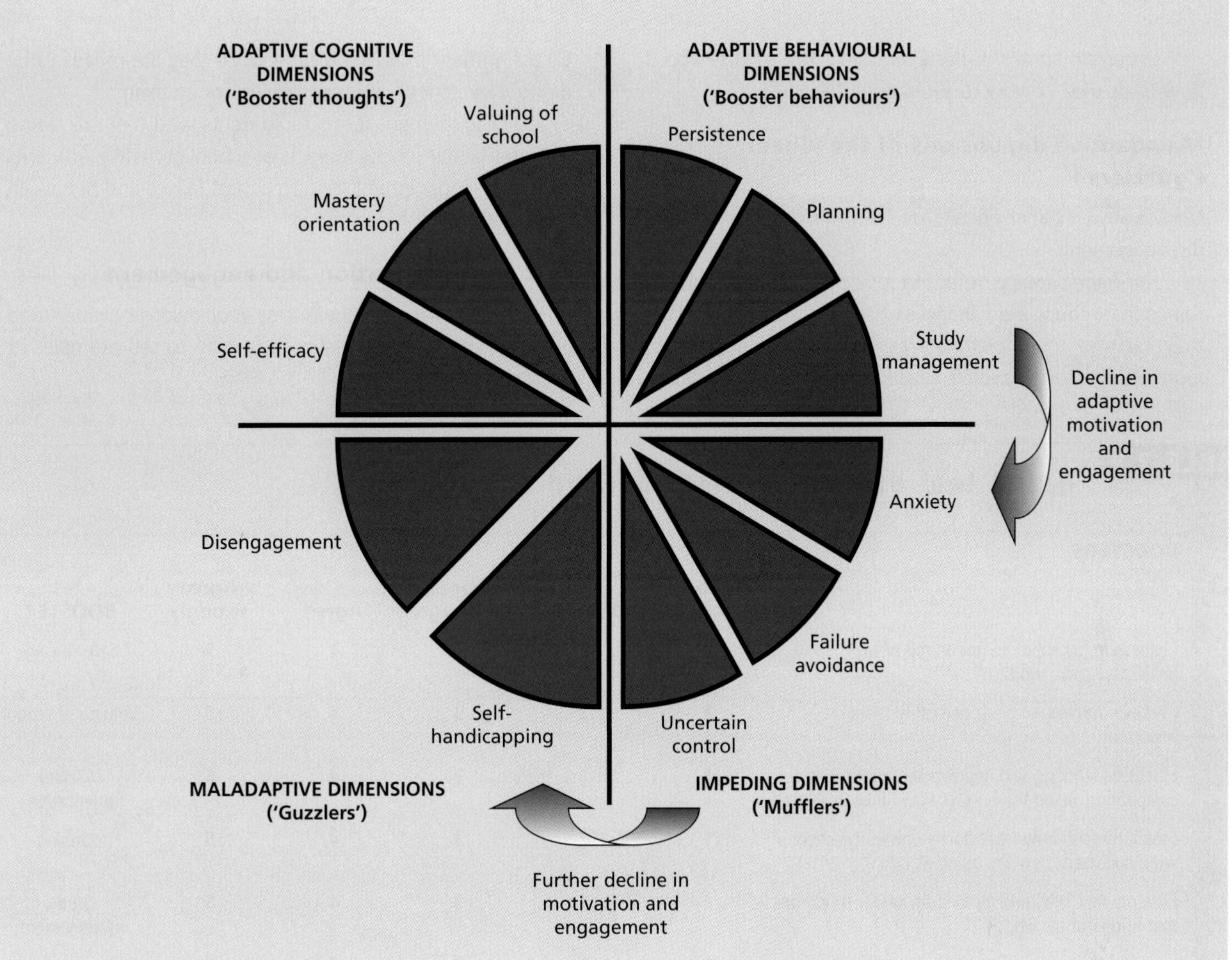

Figure 7.2 *The Student Motivation and Engagement Wheel*
(Source: Adapted with permission from A. Martin 2003b)

Self-efficacy is students' belief and confidence in their ability to understand or to do well in their schoolwork, to meet challenges they face, and to perform to the best of their ability.

Valuing of school is how much students believe what they learn at school is useful, important, and relevant to them or to the world in general.

Mastery orientation is being focused on learning, solving problems, and developing skills, more than being focused on competition, ability and comparisons with others.

Planning is how much students plan their schoolwork, assignments and study, and how much they keep track of their progress as they are doing them.

Study management refers to the way students use their study time, organise their study timetable, and choose and arrange where they study.

Persistence is how much students keep trying to work out an answer or to understand a problem even when that problem is difficult or challenging.

Impeding dimensions of the wheel ('mufflers')

Impeding dimensions of motivation and engagement are anxiety, failure avoidance and uncertain control.

Anxiety has two parts: feeling nervous and worrying. Feeling nervous is the uneasy or sick feeling students get when they think about their schoolwork, assignments or exams. Worrying is their fear of the performance situation and fear about not doing very well in their schoolwork, assignments or exams.

Failure avoidance refers to students' tendency to do their schoolwork for the primary purpose of avoiding doing poorly or avoiding being seen to do poorly.

Uncertain control reflects students' uncertainty about how to do well or how to avoid doing poorly.

Maladaptive dimensions of the wheel ('guzzlers')

Maladaptive dimensions are self-handicapping and disengagement.

Self-handicapping refers to students' tendency to do things that reduce their chances of success at school so that they can use these obstacles as excuses if they perform more poorly than expected. Examples are putting off doing an assignment or wasting time while they are meant to be doing their schoolwork or studying for an exam.

Disengagement refers to students who feel like giving up in particular school subjects or school generally. Students high in disengagement tend to accept failure and behave in ways that reflect helplessness.

Test your motivation and engagement

In Table 7.9, you can briefly test your own motivation and engagement. It is also a chance for you to see examples of each part of the wheel.

TABLE 7.9 Quick test of your motivation and engagement

BOOSTERS

	Disagree strongly	Disagree	Neither agree nor disagree	Agree	Agree strongly	BOOSTER
I believe in my ability to get on top of my university/school work	1	2	3	4	5	Self-efficacy
I believe that what I do at university/school is important	1	2	3	4	5	Valuing of school
I focus on learning and improvement more than competition, being the best, or how I'll be evaluated	1	2	3	4	5	Mastery orientation
I think through how I will do my university/school work and check how I'm going as I do it	1	2	3	4	5	Planning
I use my time well and try to study under conditions that bring out my best	1	2	3	4	5	Study management
I persist even when my studies are challenging or difficult	1	2	3	4	5	Persistence

- Your highest score is a strength
- Your lowest score is an area where you can improve

MUFFLERS AND GUZZLERS

	Disagree strongly	Disagree	Neither agree nor disagree	Agree	Agree strongly	MUFFLER and GUZZLER
I'm quite anxious about my university/school work	1	2	3	4	5	Anxiety
I mainly do my study to avoid failure or disapproval, rather than to aim for success	1	2	3	4	5	Failure avoidance
I do not think I have much control over how I perform at university/school	1	2	3	4	5	Uncertain control
I seem to limit my chances of success (e.g. waste time, disrupt others, procrastinate, etc.) at university/school	1	2	3	4	5	Self-handicapping
I often feel like giving up or quitting at university/school	1	2	3	4	5	Disengagement

- Your lowest score is a strength
- Your highest score is an area where you can improve

Educational resilience and the 4Cs

The wheel also provides insight into students' educational resilience. I define educational resilience as students' ability to deal effectively with academic setbacks, challenge, stress and study pressure. I argue that educational resilience is relevant to all students. This is because at some stage in every student's school life, he or she will experience some level of poor performance, setback, or stress or pressure. This immediately renders educational resilience relevant to every student, and it is proposed that there is a need to better understand the factors that underpin it. Identifying specific factors that underpin educational resilience holds important implications for psychological practice and teaching, because targeted intervention and support is likely to be more effective than global support directed at educational resilience as a global construct.

This is where the Student Motivation and Engagement Wheel is a useful research tool. Through it we are able to identify which facets of the wheel are most predictive of students' educational resilience. In doing this, there is clear direction as to which facets of the wheel are important in intervention work seeking to enhance students' educational resilience. In research among high school students, I have found that four facets in particular are significant predictors of educational resilience: self-efficacy, persistence, control and low anxiety—or the 4Cs: confidence, commitment, control and composure. In further research, I have also found positive teacher–student relationships and involvement in school are significant predictors of students' educational resilience.

To sum up

The Student Motivation and Engagement Wheel is a model of motivation and engagement that can be readily located in the classroom, is easily used by educators, psychologists and counsellors, and is understandable to students. It is also an important tool in better understanding educational resilience, students' ability to effectively deal with setback, challenge and adversity. Taken together, the wheel is a helpful framework for researchers studying motivation, engagement and educational resilience, but is also relevant to teachers, psychologists and counsellors working in contexts in which students require assistance to sustain motivational strengths and address areas of motivation and engagement that may be of some concern.

Further reading

Martin, A. J. (2001) The Student Motivation Scale: A tool for measuring and enhancing motivation. *Australian Journal of Guidance and Counselling*, **11**, 1–20.

Martin, A. J. (2002) Motivation and academic resilience: Developing a model of student enhancement. *Australian Journal of Education*. **14**, 34–49.

Martin, A. J. (2003a) *How to Motivate Your Child for School and Beyond*. Sydney: Bantam.

Martin, A. J. (2003b). The Student Motivation Scale: Further testing of an instrument that measures school students' motivation. *Australian Journal of Education,* **47**, 88–106.

Martin, A. J., & Marsh, H. W. (2003) *Academic Resilience and the Four Cs: Capacity, control, composure, and commitment*. Presented at Joint AARE/NZARE Conference. Auckland, New Zealand.

Martin, A. J. & Marsh, H. W. (2004) *Academic Resilience: Analysis of predictors using a longitudinal approach.* Paper presented at 3rd SELF Research Centre Biennial International Conference. Max Planck Institute, Berlin, Germany.

WHAT WOULD YOU DO?

THEY'RE JUST NOT WRITING

Christine teaches Years 1 and 2 at a remote community school. It is not her first year teaching in an Aboriginal community, but it is her first year at this school.

Comparing this year's Year 2 students with the students in her last school, she was very concerned. What was happening? What had gone wrong? 'I'd put a piece of paper in front of them and they wouldn't do it. They wouldn't touch it.'

Case studies illustrating National Competency Framework for Beginning Teaching, National Project on the Quality of Teaching and Learning, Australian Teaching Council, 1996, p. 32. Commonwealth of Australia copyright, reproduced by permission.

What would you do? Find out what the teacher did.

WHAT WOULD YOU DO? (cont.)

THEY'RE JUST NOT WRITING

Christine spoke to the principal, Paul, complaining that 'they're just not writing'. His response was to ask her to focus on what the Year 2s *could* do, not what they *couldn't* do. They might not be ready for formal writing, but were they ready to role play writing at a writing table?

So Christine set up a big writing table with paper, crayons, textas, magazines, telephone books, telephones, a blackboard and a shop. For half an hour each morning, Christine's students had free time at the writing table. They played and drew pictures, and Christine used the writing materials for her own telephone messages and shopping lists.

It was just amazing. They weren't afraid to write because it was so informal. It wasn't, 'Here's a piece of paper. Off you go.'

Case studies illustrating National Competency Framework for Beginning Teaching, National Project on the Quality of Teaching and Learning, Australian Teaching Council, 1996, p. 32. Commonwealth of Australia copyright, reproduced by permission.

Did you suggest this solution? If not, what solution did you suggest?

WHAT WOULD YOU DO?

WE'VE LOST THE PLOT

Mrs Chalmers found that teaching the novel *The Shiralee* to Grade 8 students as a recommended text proved to be one of those classroom experiences that caused her to wonder about her teaching and the appropriateness of the choice of text. During class the students were very clearly uninterested. They were reluctant to listen, discuss or participate in any written activities. Was it her teaching? Was it her reading? She thought it was a great novel, but it wasn't until they were some way through the story that it occurred to her that the problem wasn't necessarily the way she was teaching but, rather, the language of the text. It came from a different era and, as far as the kids were concerned, it might as well have been written in Russian. The structure was too complex and the idiom, although Australian, was unfamiliar. It was beyond their experience and age level.

Case studies illustrating National Competency Framework for Beginning Teaching, National Project on the Quality of Teaching and Learning, Australian Teaching Council, 1996, p. 44. Commonwealth of Australia copyright, reproduced by permission.

What would you do? Read the teacher's solution.

WHAT WOULD YOU DO? (cont.)

WE'VE LOST THE PLOT

Mrs Chalmers decided to discuss with the class why they were responding to the novel in this particular way. Through discussion and reflection they were able to come to an understanding of what was causing the difficulties.

The class watched a video of the novel and Mrs Chalmers found it very interesting to notice how attentive the students were when they were viewing as compared to when they were reading. When she discussed why this happened, it seemed to be that they could more easily make links between the language and the action and plot with a visual medium. They found it difficult to visualise anything when reading the novel because of the language and the complexity of the time-frame structure of the novel.

They had been so busy deciphering the language that they had lost the plot and then simply lost interest. Mrs Chalmers found this to be a good learning experience for her. She had misjudged both the referential and structural reading experience of the class. They needed to be led through other reading experiences before being presented with *The Shiralee*. Abandoning the reading of the novel at this stage seemed to be the best course of action.

Case studies illustrating National Competency Framework for Beginning Teaching, National Project on the Quality of Teaching and Learning, Australian Teaching Council, 1996, p. 44. Commonwealth of Australia copyright, reproduced by permission.

Do you agree with this solution?

KEY TERMS

Academic self-handicapping (p. 232): students create impediments to successful performance on tasks in order to provide an excuse other than lack of ability for poor performance should it occur

Achievement motivation (p. 224): a desire to excel at learning tasks which is related to pride in accomplishments

Attainment value (p. 217): the importance of doing well on a task

Attributional retraining (p. 226): training individuals to change their patterns of attributions to enhance motivation

Attribution theory (p. 219): individuals' reasons for success and failure influence their future motivation

Competitive goal structure (p. 237): students' performance is judged on the basis of relative performance with other students, and the attainment of rewards is only possible if other students don't attain them

Cooperative goal structure (p. 237): group members share rewards and punishments on the basis of the overall cooperative group performance

Coping strategies (p. 218): strategies used to guarantee success and avoid failure

Cost (p. 217): in expectancy-value theory, the physical and emotional resource implications

Defensive pessimism (p. 218): unrealistically low expectations for ever succeeding or discounting the importance of the work in an effort to minimise feelings of anxiety over potential failure

Expectancy-value theory (p. 215): motivation as a result of expecting and valuing success in an activity

Goal theory (p. 231): students' purposes in learning influence the nature and quality of their motivation and engagement in learning

High-need achievers (p. 216): individuals for whom the need to achieve is greater than the fear of failure

Individualised goal structure (p. 237): students are judged and rewarded on the basis of their own performance irrespective of the performance of other students

Intrinsic motivation (p. 209): motive that keeps individuals at tasks through its own inherent qualities

Intrinsic value (p. 217): the enjoyment one gets from a task

Learned helplessness (p. 227): the expectation of continued failure of an individual based on previous experiences

Low-need achievers (p. 216): individuals for whom the fear of failure is greater than the need to achieve

Mastery goal (p. 231): individuals are oriented towards developing new skills, trying to understand their work, improving their level of competence or achieving a sense of mastery

Morality-based goals (p. 233): a motivational system based on helping others

Motivation (p. 207): internal state that instigates, directs and maintains behaviour

Origins and pawns (p. 227): terms used to describe students' perceived level of control in learning situations

Performance-approach goal (p. 231): students want to do better than their classmates so that they will be recognised as competent by their peers, teachers and parents

Performance-avoidance goal (p. 231): students do their academic work primarily because they fear appearing incompetent

Self-fulfilling prophecy (p. 243): an erroneous teacher expectation that becomes confirmed

Self-handicapping strategies (p. 218): creating some impediment to performance so that the individual has a ready excuse for potential failure

Self-worth protection (p. 218): a general strategy by which students withhold effort when risking failure

Sense of competence (p. 240): beliefs about personal competence in a particular task

Social goals (p. 238): a wide variety of needs and motives to be connected to others or part of a group

Sustaining expectation effect (p. 244): teachers expect students to maintain behaviour patterns and don't recognise improvements

Utility value (p. 217): the perceived importance of the activity to meeting one's goals

Work-avoidance goals (p. 232): students deliberately avoid engaging in academic tasks and/or attempt to minimise the effort required to complete academic tasks

ON-LINE LEARNING

If you go to http://www.pearsoned.com.au/mcinerney, you will have hot links directly to these sites:

■ **Attribution theory**

Read and discuss this article on attribution theory provided by Athabasca University in Canada.

http://www.as.wvu.edu/~sbb/comm221/chapters/attrib.htm

■ **Teacher expectations**

This site prepared by McREL provides a discussion of ways to increase positive classroom relationships through understanding the communication of teacher expectations embedded in classroom interactions, variables that influence expectations as a result of unexamined beliefs and behaviours, and action steps for improving the quality of teacher and student interactions for increased learning and achievement. Discuss the suggestions made.

http://www.mcrel.org/topics/noteworthy.asp

WEB DESTINATIONS

If you go to http://www.pearsoned.com.au/mcinerney, you will have hot links directly to these sites:

■ **Psychlopedia**

This is a very useful site for further information on the topic of motivation and other topics covered in your text.

http://www.epsychlopedia.net/exitGR.php?GID=0

■ **Self-efficacy**

This site, established by Professor Frank Pajares at Emory University, will provide you with almost everything you need to know about self-efficacy!

http://www.emory.edu/EDUCATION/mfp/self-efficacy.html

■ **Learned helplessness**

This site provides a wealth of further information on learned helplessness.

http://psych.upenn.edu/~fresco/helplessness.html

■ **Self-help**

This site presents information on a number of topics related to learning and motivation. Check the site out for information that might be of use to you.

http://mentalhelp.net/psyhelp/

■ **Arousal and memory**

An important component of motivation is arousal. Indeed, earlier theories of motivation were concerned with examining the relationship between arousal level, motivated behaviour and learning. Consider the information provided at this site, as it will extend your understanding of this component of motivation. Also refer to the material on test anxiety provided in Chapter 11.

http://pmc.psych.nwu.edu/revelle/publications/rl91/rev_loft_ToC.html

RECOMMENDED READING

Anderman, E. M., Austin, C. C. & Johnson, D. M. (2002) The development of goal orientation. In A. Wigfield & J. S. Eccles (eds) *Development of Achievement Motivation*. San Diego, CA: Academic Press.

Assor, A., Kaplan, H. & Roth, G. (2002) Choice is good, but relevance is excellent: Autonomy-enhancing and suppressing teacher behaviours predicting students' engagement in schoolwork. *British Journal of Educational Psychology*, 72, 261–78.

Bandura, A. (1993) Perceived self-efficacy in cognitive development and functioning. *Educational Psychologist*, 28, 117–48.

Covington, M. V. (2000) Goal theory, motivation, and school achievement: An integrative review. *Annual Review of Psychology*, 51, 171–200.

Covington, M. V. (2002a) Rewards and intrinsic motivation: A needs-based developmental perspective. In T. Urdan & F. Pajares (eds) *Motivation of Adolescents*. New York: Academic Press.

Covington, M. V. (2004) Self-worth theory goes to college: Or do our motivation theories motivate? In D. M. McInerney & S. Van Etten (eds) *Research on Sociocultural Influences on Motivation and Learning (Volume 4), Big Theories Revisited*. Greenwich, CT: Information Age Publishing.

Dowson, M. & McInerney, D. M. (2003) What do students say about their motivational goals? Towards a more complex and dynamic perspective on student motivation. *Contemporary Educational Psychology*, **28**, 91–113.

Fredrichs, J. A., Blumenfeld, P. C. & Paris, A. H. (2004) School engagement: Potential of the concept, state of the evidence. *Review of Educational Research*, **74**, 59–109.

Good, T. L. (1995) Teacher expectations. In L. W. Anderson (ed.) *International Encyclopedia of Teaching and Teacher Education*, 2nd ed. Tarrytown, NY: Pergamon.

Maehr, M. L. & Anderman, E. M. (1993) Reinventing schools for early adolescents: Emphasizing task goals. *The Elementary School Journal*, **93**, 593–610.

Maehr, M. L. & McInerney, D. M. (2004) Motivation as personal investment. In D. M. McInerney & S. Van Etten (eds) *Research on Sociocultural Influences on Motivation and Learning (Volume 4), Big Theories Revisited*. Greenwich, CT: Information Age Publishing.

Martin, A. J. (2003) *How to Motivate Your Child for School and Beyond*. Sydney: Bantam.

Nolen, S. B. & Nicholls, J. G. (1994) A place to begin (again) in research on student motivation: Teachers' beliefs. *Teaching and Teacher Education*, **10**, 57–69.

Perry, N. & Winne, P. (2004) Motivational messages from home and school: How do they influence young children's engagement in learning? In D. M. McInerney & S. Van Etten (eds) *Research on Sociocultural Influences on Motivation and Learning (Volume 4), Big Theories Revisited*. Greenwich, CT: Information Age Publishing

Schunk, D. H. (1991) Self-efficacy and academic motivation. *Educational Psychologist*, **26**, 207–31.

Stefanou, C. R., Perencevich, K. C., DiCintio, M. & Turner, J. C. (2004) Supporting autonomy in the classroom: Ways teachers encourage student decision making and ownership. *Educational Psychologist*, **39**, 97–110.

Urdan, T. C. & Maehr, M. L. (1995) Beyond a two-goal theory of motivation and achievement: A case for social goals. *Review of Educational Research*, **65**, 213–43.

Weiner, B. (1994) Integrating social and personal theories of achievement striving. *Review of Educational Research*, **64**, 557–73.

Weiner, B. (2004) Attribution theory revisited: Transforming cultural plurality into theoretical unity. In D. M. McInerney & S. Van Etten (eds) *Research on Sociocultural Influences on Motivation and Learning (Volume 4), Big Theories Revisited*. Greenwich, CT: Information Age Publishing.

Wigfield, A. (1994) Expectancy-value theory of achievement motivation: A developmental perspective. *Educational Psychology Review*, **6**, 49–78.

Wigfield, A., Eccles, J. S. & Rodriguez, D. (1998) The development of children's motivation in school contexts. *Review of Research in Education*, **23**, 73–118.

Wigfield, A., Tonks, S. & Eccles, J. S. (2004) Expectancy value theory in cross-cultural perspective. In D. M. McInerney & S. Van Etten (eds) *Research on Sociocultural Influences on Motivation and Learning (Volume 4), Big Theories Revisited*. Greenwich, CT: Information Age Publishing

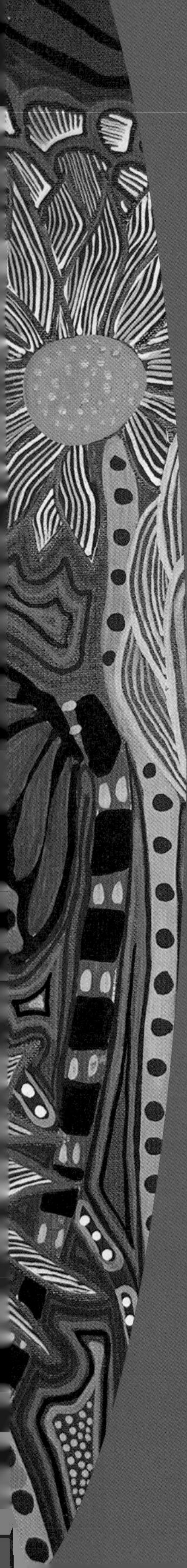

CHAPTER

8 Classroom management and cooperative group work for effective learning

Overview

In this chapter we provide an overview of a number of well-established theoretical perspectives on management and discipline and, from these, suggest some practical ideas for managing instructional activities and preventing discipline problems, as well as some means of dealing with misbehaviour when it occurs. You will read in this chapter about a range of approaches that lie along the continuum of control in the classroom, from teacher-centred through to student-centred. We also present many ideas on effective management in multicultural classroom settings.

The different views on management and discipline should not be seen as being in opposition. Ideas from a number of approaches can be combined over any one school year, depending on the age of the students and their readiness for taking ownership of their own behaviour and learning. In this context, we outline for you the approach to behaviour management of Bill Rogers in which he integrates many of the powerful strategies from a number of models.

In addition, the effectiveness of a number of highly regarded cooperative learning models will be highlighted as effective teaching techniques and related to principles of classroom management.

8

Social responsibility, caring and achievement: Discipline strategies in democratic classrooms

Learning objectives

After reading this chapter, you will be able to:

- relate good teaching to effective management and discipline;
- distinguish between effective management and effective discipline;
- discuss the role of the teacher as classroom leader;
- describe, compare and contrast six models of discipline;
- describe, compare and contrast individualistic, competitive and cooperative classroom goal structures;
- describe issues related to effective management in multicultural classroom settings;
- describe four models of cooperative learning;
- implement four general approaches to learning in cooperative groups;
- identify difficulties in using cooperative learning strategies.

Schools and classrooms in the Western world have always been perceived as places characterised by rules and regulations about behaviour. On a superficial level, such rules are put in place to keep children 'in line' so that schools and classrooms are orderly, well-disciplined and characterised by harmonious interpersonal relationships. This is argued as being the most effective way to ensure that academic learning time can be maximised to the benefit of students in terms of their achievement, and to the benefit of teachers in terms of their sanity! However, there are other important reasons for the implementation of rules and regulations and codes of behaviour. In this chapter, we examine the many issues around how schools and educators in traditional learning settings should prepare students to take their place in society as self-disciplined, independent and lifelong learners. These issues involve questions about the relative strengths and limitations of teacher-centred and student-centred approaches to classroom management and discipline. They also raise very important questions about the extent to which students' cultural backgrounds may clash with the expectations for behaviour of the dominant school culture. To what extent, for example, should educators vary their expectations for student behaviour in order to accommodate culturally and socio-economically different understandings about authority, group and individual responsibility, gender roles and communication styles? In this chapter, we will consider mainstream approaches to classroom and behaviour management based on current Western theorising which may vary in their applicability to classrooms characterised by diversity. The sociocultural differences of individual children need always to be borne in mind, however, as we discuss at some length in the extension section, 'A cross-cultural perspective on classroom management and discipline'.

Schools and social values

Schools in the Western world are, among other things, institutions for the socialisation of children into their society and for passing on the mores of social behaviour from one generation to the next. Ideally, they are structured so that progression through a school exposes children to a range of personal and social rules, norms and roles that characterise caring interpersonal communication and activity in the wider society. Because the development of social responsibility and moral character is a matter of great concern to parents, teachers and students themselves, most school systems formulate behaviour and civics policies that define the manner in which they should foster the adaptation and integration of children into social settings. Hence, rules are developed to reflect cooperation, respect for others and positive forms of group interaction, as well as those that relate to facilitating academic learning and performance. Producing socially responsible students is seen as a valuable outcome in its own right, irrespective of achievement (Doyle 1986).

Developing pro-social behaviours

Undoubtedly, **pro-social behaviour** and academic achievement are related. Behaving in a responsible way may also be a critical student characteristic that directly contributes to learning and academic performance (Wentzel 1991a, 1991b). Correlational studies in the United States have shown a relationship between intellectual outcomes in elementary school with pro-social behaviour, classroom conduct and compliance (Entwisle *et al.* 1986; Feshbach & Feshbach 1987). A study with high school students, for example, showed that students have a better chance of achieving success in high school if they (and their parents and peers) believe in the value of 'good' behaviour (Hanson & Ginsburg 1988).

How does behaving in a socially responsible way contribute to achievement at school? Wentzel (1991a, 1991b) suggests three reasons. First, a socially responsible student would adhere to student role requirements such as paying attention, keeping to the task and completing work, qualities that are related to academic achievement.

Second, socially responsible behaviour can play a role in facilitating positive social interactions with teachers and peers, which may enhance the learning process. It appears that teachers may give less attention to students who misbehave and don't adhere to agreed upon standards for responsible behaviour. Hence, these students do more poorly academically. It also appears that peer groups can influence classroom performance and learning outcomes in positive ways (see McInerney 1991b), and that they can complement teacher behaviour in ways that support the instructional process (Wentzel 1991a, 1991b). Consequently, strong peer group ties, particularly with peers who value education, enhance the individual's motivation and achievement (Hanson & Ginsburg 1988).

Third, the motivation underlying socially responsible classroom behaviour may influence the degree to which students become engaged in academic work. This is particularly the case if learning and social responsibility goals are pursued at the same time. The question, however, about which causes the other remains. Does social responsibility affect learning and achievement in the sense that socially responsible children feel guilty if they are not working hard at school and achieving as well as they can? Or does being successful at school subjects promote socially responsible behaviour? Clearly, the two interact. If a person is performing poorly academically, then the chances of misbehaviour are increased and social rejection is more likely.

Relationship between academic achievement and responsible behaviour

Nell Noddings: Teaching themes of care in the classroom within a school culture of caring

Few would disagree that there is more to education than merely average to high scores on standardised achievement tests. Some would go further to say that there is even more needed in our schools and classroom than fostering pro-social behaviour. Given the violence within schools and on the streets that pervades much of the Western world today, we strongly agree with Nell Noddings (1995) in her call for teaching *themes of care* in all classrooms, irrespective of grade level. As she argues (Noddings 1995, p. 48):

> ... caring is not just a warm fuzzy feeling that makes people kind and likeable. Caring implies a continuous search for competence. When we care, we want to do our very best for the objects of our care. To have as our educational goal the production of caring, competent, loving, and lovable people is not anti-intellectual. Rather, it demonstrates respect for the full range of human talents. Not all human beings are good at or interested in mathematics, science, or British literature. But all humans can be helped to lead lives of deep concern for others, for the natural world and its creatures, and for the preservation of the human-made world. They can be led to develop the skills and knowledge necessary to make positive contributions regardless of the occupation they may choose.

We urge you to take some time to reflect on the ideas that Noddings (1995) proposes. How might you be able to (re)design your curriculum and classroom management strategies to include themes of care such as: 'caring for oneself'; 'caring for intimate others, strangers and global others'; 'caring for the man-made world and its technologies'; 'caring for the natural world and its inhabitants'? Think about how you could creatively integrate such themes through team planning and teaching across various disciplines, and over a period of time. In such classrooms there will be undoubtedly issues of morality and ethics raised that may prove to be confronting to both students and teachers—these will come from the

Supportive environment of mutual trust

real-world experiences of many of the students. Exploring these sensitive issues in a supportive environment of mutual trust (perhaps a family-like grouping across several grades at school) will do much to alleviate the tensions that adolescents especially bring to the classroom, and that often precipitate misbehaviour of varying degrees of severity.

A special responsibility lies with those charged with the education and care of young children who can be helped in their early lives to develop pro-social and caring behaviours. In this context, Honig and Wittmer (1996) describe a wealth of strategies and techniques for families, classrooms, schools and whole communities to implement. Some of the suggestions they make for educational settings are the following:

- conflict resolution and cooperative games;
- children's literature, videos and video games that have pro-social themes and provide caring and altruistic models;
- guided social interaction between children following norms for development and those with special needs;
- in-school buddy systems;
- visitors who can talk about their roles as moral mentors in their own lives;
- parent resource lending library;
- 'maternal teaching' (morning meetings, singing, warm greetings) in schools where children lack compassion for others.

The importance of developing and maintaining an atmosphere of caring is brought home powerfully by suggestions for violence prevention given by the very students who are in high schools where severe violence prevails (shooting, stabbing, rape, assault). These suggestions could best be summarised by the word 'care'. As Astor, Meyer and Behre (1999, p. 34) report:

> Not surprisingly, a teacher's willingness to intervene (in violent situations) was a significant part of the students' definition of a caring teacher. There was consensus among the students that caring teachers saw their role as transcending the walls of the classroom to all areas of the school and, for that matter, into the surrounding community and the children's home lives. These teachers knew about the children's home circumstances, after school activities, and their long-term hopes.

This approach is in keeping with the works of Barbara Coloroso (1994) and Alfie Kohn (1996b), who discuss the need for educators and administrators to develop students' inner discipline and involve them as partners in solving problems responsibly within whole school communities. What do you think about this notion of care in relation to your role as an educator of the future?

Student-centred classrooms and management

Recent research has shown that high academic achievement and pro-social behaviour are positively related in schools where students perceive that their teachers both care for and are committed to them, and are collegial with each other and the principal (Shann 1999). The implications of such research are that if students are to be expected to behave well and achieve their best academically, the school climate needs to be a nurturing one that fosters cooperation among students and affiliation among teachers (Prillaman, Eaker & Kendrick 1994).

This cooperation is a sign of a mutual respect and trust between teachers and students, and between teachers themselves, each of whom feels part of a learning community. In such a community everyone's efforts towards learning and relating to one another are their best, and their contributions are valued and publicly recognised (Emmer *et al.* 2000). Ideally, of course, in such a learning community competing for grades has no place, as the focus is on intrinsic reasons for learning, appreciation of the subject matter and the process by which knowledge is gained (Covington 1999). This is not to say that grades cannot be awarded if deemed necessary, as long as these are explained to students as indicators of their current learning, and a chance for improvement is given following corrective feedback. By creating a positive and caring learning environment that is student-centred, therefore, managing student behaviour that is not conducive to learning becomes an opportunity for teaching students how to take ownership of their academic and social goals and to develop a healthy identity and an internalised moral structure (Martin 1997). Through the development of problem-solving strategies, students acquire a sense of self-direction in relation to their behaviour, motivation and learning (McCaslin & Good 1998). At this point, it would be worth looking at the previous chapter on motivation, where the notions of attributions, self-worth and self-determination are considered in some detail.

We would also strongly recommend that you think about how you might apply the essentials of developing a classroom environment that is student-centred with regard to learning and behaviour (see Table 8.1).

Good teaching minimises misbehaviour

In our experience, misbehaviour just doesn't seem to occur in schools where students are engaged in activities that they find absorbing and meaningful. What is

Table 8.1

Essentials of linking instruction and management in a student-centred classroom

Teachers should:

- develop a sense of belonging to the learning community of the classroom by fostering mutual trust and respect;
- find ways of helping every student feel a sense of worth and belonging in the class;
- use class meetings to foster a sense of group cohesion and mutual responsibility for learning and behaviour;
- involve students in developing the norms for classroom conduct, their supporting explanations and consequences for non-compliance;
- use misbehaviour as opportunities to develop problem-solving skills for planning more appropriate behaviour;
- preserve the dignity of the individual despite instances of misconduct or poor achievement;
- ensure that motivation to learn is not a casualty of discipline techniques;
- provide learning activities that are varied, interesting and allow for student choice;
- design learning activities that require structured cooperative interaction in order to develop interpersonal and social skills along with cognitive skills;
- teach that students are responsible for their own behaviour: 'Others might influence us, but no one can actually "control" anyone except him/herself';
- position the teacher's desk to the side of the room rather than centre front. This communicates that the teacher is only one part of the student learning community, not the pivotal point: each student is responsible for doing their own work.

(Source: Based on Charles 1999; Martin 1997; O'Donnell & King 1999)

'meaningful' to children is what they feel excited about learning, discovering or experimenting with, and feel they can master. Learning activities must be seen as purposeful, and the procedures and expectations for completing them must be clearly understood by all students (Jones & Jones 1995). If schools are boring places, out of touch with young people's interests, their challenges and the pace of the rest of the world outside school, then the classroom will be a place for dissension and disorder, quelled only by an authoritarian regime.

Schools can no longer guarantee students a successful future and a job as a reward for compliance with whatever policies and curricula they impose. Difficult economic times and a rapidly changing technological society have shown that this is not the case. The onus on teachers today is to ensure that learning is enjoyable and perceived to be valuable for its own sake. Furthermore, the design of effective learning experiences in which *all* children can experience success within a caring environment is at the heart of managing student behaviour well in educational settings. We suggest that you refer to Chapter 1, where we discuss the many elements of effective teaching.

What potential classroom management problems are illustrated in this picture?

It is worth noting at this point that despite its irritating quality for teachers, *nearly all classroom misbehaviour is of a minor nature* (Little 2005). The sorts of 'discipline problems' that we face daily as teachers should be kept in perspective as merely nuisance behaviour, often annoyingly repetitive and certainly not conducive to either student learning or the teacher's peace of mind. However, there is a real danger of the teacher over-reacting to such minor misbehaviour out of frustration and weariness, of labelling children as having 'behaviour problems' and, as frequently happens, of taking the easier course of ignoring the offenders and excluding them from class activities. Why is this not a good approach?

In some situations, of course, teachers may find themselves faced occasionally with more serious student misbehaviour which may be aggressive, violently defiant, immoral or disruptive. In these cases, more than just an individual teacher's one-off response will do; instances such as these will necessitate a collegial approach to behaviour management that involves the whole school—students, teachers and administrators alike. Sad to say, it has become necessary in some high schools in the United States to install metal detectors to prevent weapons from being brought in (Charles 1999), to have security guards patrol the school premises (Johnson & Johnson 1995) and to have electronic monitoring of whole schools (Astor *et al.* 1999).

Clearly the way in which the teacher manages classrooms and misbehaviour in potentially violent settings where students have little motivation to achieve academic success will be quite different from those settings where students are keen to learn and respectful of themselves and others: it becomes a matter for the whole community, school and wider.

The good news is that much of what causes disruption to learning in classrooms *can be avoided*. In this chapter, a range of approaches will be presented that will help you to prevent a large number of discipline problems, as well as show you how to deal with them once they have erupted. A range of discipline models, from preventive approaches through supportive to corrective ones, will be considered. You might wonder in what ways these methods are different. We can characterise discipline as **preventive discipline** when we implement verbal and non-verbal strategies to prevent misbehaviour occurring; **supportive discipline** when we prevent misbehaviour developing any further; and **corrective discipline** when we implement strategies to stop misbehaviour when it has occurred and redirect behaviour into positive channels. The eclectic approach of Bill Rogers (1995) integrates elements of all these models and presents *positive behaviour management* as an integrated set of practical strategies for beginning and experienced teachers alike, grounded in a philosophy of respect for human dignity. Other scholars such as Barbara Coloroso

TEACHING COMPETENCE — Box 8.1

The teacher establishes clear, challenging and achievable expectations for students

Indicators

The teacher:

- establishes a positive learning environment oriented towards achieving learning objectives;
- maintains a secure environment in which expectations for student learning and behaviour are clearly understood and reinforced;
- develops routine procedures to manage recurring tasks;
- fosters and positively reinforces responsible student behaviour.

Case studies illustrating National Competency Framework for Beginning Teaching, National Project on the Quality of Teaching and Learning, Australian Teaching Council, 1996, Element 3.6, p. 51.

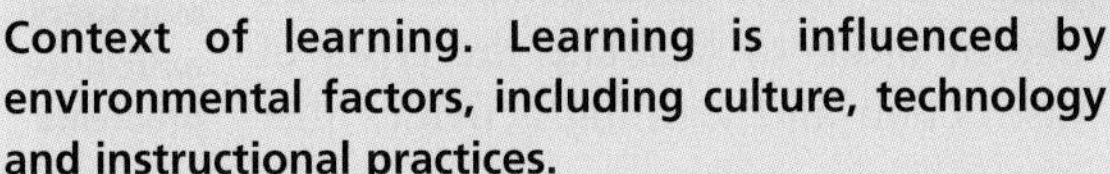

LEARNER-CENTRED PSYCHOLOGICAL PRINCIPLE

Context of learning. Learning is influenced by environmental factors, including culture, technology and instructional practices.

Learning does not occur in a vacuum. Teachers play a major interactive role with both the learner and the learning environment. Cultural or group influences on students can impact many educationally relevant variables, such as motivation, orientation towards learning, and ways of thinking. Technologies and instructional practices must be appropriate for learners' level of prior knowledge, cognitive abilities, and their learning and thinking strategies. The classroom environment, particularly the degree to which it is nurturing or not, can also have significant impacts on student learning.

 To view the full document please go to http://www.apa.org/ed/lcp2/

TEACHING COMPETENCE — Box 8.2

The teacher encourages positive student behaviour

Indicators

The teacher:

- acknowledges appropriate student behaviour and fosters self-discipline among students;
- uses an approach that emphasises consequences for inappropriate behaviour;
- applies a variety of behaviour management strategies—for example, negotiating rules, applying effective sanctions;
- develops clear routines for managing student behaviour consistent with school policy;
- takes appropriate action promptly, firmly, fairly and consistently.

Case studies illustrating National Competency Framework for Beginning Teaching, National Project on the Quality of Teaching and Learning, Australian Teaching Council, 1996, Element 2.4, p. 40.

(1994) and Alfie Kohn (1996b) go one step further in encouraging educators to teach students to take control over their own academic lives through the regular use of classroom meetings, and to develop students' sense of a caring community in the classroom, respectively.

Classroom management: The teacher as classroom leader

At this point it would be useful to distinguish between classroom management and **discipline**. *Classroom management* is a broad term that refers to everything that teachers do to establish and maintain an environment in which effective learning takes place (Copeland 1987). *Discipline*, therefore, is only one aspect of classroom management, and relates specifically to methods adopted to manage student behaviour and involvement in school-based activities. It is an important aspect of teacher leadership in that the teacher leads students towards particular positive goals.

Goals of discipline

We strongly agree with the goals of discipline that Bill Rogers (1998) proposes (see Table 8.2).

Prevention is better than cure

No longer is the classroom a place where the teacher, armed with chalk, duster and cane or strap, dispenses knowledge like an interactive textbook. Today's classrooms are places where the teacher serves as a highly knowledgeable guide who leads students to sources of factual information, but who also encourages shared problem solving and reasoning through talk and group work. Children are encouraged to express opinions, to clarify values and to critically think through problems. Media models of assertive, even defiant, behaviour by young people, uncertain economic and employment futures, universal recognition of the rights of the individual—child, disabled or minority group member—along with the abolition of corporal punishment in schools in Australia in the 1980s have encouraged children to be more outspoken and far less submissive to adult authority.

Nowhere is it more obvious than in a classroom 'out of control' that preventing the occurrence or development of misbehaviours is preferable to trying to regain order from pandemonium. It should be strongly emphasised at the outset that no classroom management strategies will prevent discipline problems if effective teaching is not taking place. When children are motivated because what they are learning is interesting, exciting and relevant; when they feel respected and cared for by their teacher even if they are not always able to get all the answers right; and when they feel they have a legitimate place in *our classroom*—then inattentive, problem behaviour is most unlikely to occur. This is not to say that children won't have 'off days' when they don't feel like complying or getting involved in learning activities; after all, there is much more to their world than just academic learning—a fight with a best friend or parent; an impending attack of influenza; a hormone-led growth spurt with consequential embarrassment and touchiness; parental marital friction—any number of factors may be responsible. An effective teacher will have a repertoire of strategies on which to call. Let's have a look at these now.

Effective teaching and classroom management

Planning for good classroom management

Teachers who successfully prevent misbehaviour and foster learning have an effective management system that consists of three phases:

1. *Planning* before the school year starts what their room arrangement will be like in order to facilitate the types of instruction and learning activities that

Effective classroom managers anticipate problems

Table 8.2 Essentials of developing socially responsible goals of discipline

Teachers should:

- develop self-discipline and self-control;
- enhance self-esteem;
- encourage accountability for behaviour;
- recognise and respect the rights of others;
- affirm cooperation along with responsible independence in learning;
- enable on-task class behaviour;
- promote values of fairness and honesty;
- enable rational conflict resolution.

(Source: Based on Rogers 1998)

they will be using, as well as the necessary rules and procedures (guidelines for behaviour) to maintain effective learning.

Along with the cane, the chalkboard eraser was a marvellous management tool!

2. *Developing* during the first few weeks of school the students' understanding of these guidelines for behaviour and reinforcing their adherence.
3. *Maintaining* the momentum of the first few weeks throughout the year by preventive measures with regard to lesson management and facilitating the development of students' self-regulation of their learning and behaviour.

The planning stage involves deciding on preventive measures that will *minimise potential problems*. Organising the physical space of the classroom is an important place to start in planning for a new school year. Will the children sit individually, in pairs or groups? Where will the teacher's desk be best placed to allow for easy student access and monitoring? How will classroom supplies be stored and distributed? Table 8.3 presents a number of the most important aspects of the physical working environment that an effective teacher would prepare for before teaching begins.

Organising the physical setting of the classroom

Other important management decisions involve planning an integrated set of rules and procedures to be taught to the new class in the development stage of the year. Behaviour problems due to boredom or a lack of purpose can often be prevented by careful planning. A simple example would be the preparation of lesson starters that students routinely undertake until the

Table 8.3

Essentials of effective planning of the classroom environment

Teachers should ensure that:

- the main instructional purposes of the learning space have been considered in order to plan the most appropriate layout of student seating, storage, equipment and materials;
- high-traffic areas are free of congestion. Wherever possible, make sure that students do not have to crowd or negotiate other students' desks in order to leave or enter the room, consult the teacher, or gain access to equipment, resources or their belongings;
- students and teacher are able to see each other easily. Check that students can be monitored at all times from any location in the classroom at which the teacher will be teaching and interacting with students;
- frequently used teaching materials and student supplies are readily accessible. Use shelves to store and display books, storage trays to hold and distribute materials, hooks to keep bags and coats tidy and accessible, and trolleys to move overhead projectors and computers around the room;
- students are able to see/hear instructional presentations and displays easily. Check that all students will be able to participate in whole-group instructional activities without having to move their furniture or themselves excessively. If students have to strain to see or hear, or have to turn around or leave their seats, the opportunity for inattention and disruption increases;
- students are able to move quickly into small-group activities without disturbing others. Ensure that furniture can be easily and quietly moved on wheels or carpet;
- adequate seating is provided for the age and size of the students;
- optimal physical conditions exist for learning: classroom lighting, ventilation and heating.

(Source: Based on Cooper 1999; Emmer *et al.* 2000; Evertson *et al.* 2000)

Craft activities can be very exciting. Why is it essential to teach the procedures for such activities to students?

teacher begins the lesson formally, promptly and energetically—students are quick to sense and respond to teachers' lassitude and poor organisation.

Developing appropriate behaviours during the first few weeks

The first few weeks of school are a time of uncertainty for all students as to what the teacher's expectations for behaviour and class work will be. Considerable research has demonstrated that effective teachers have a framework of appropriate classroom behaviours (rights, responsibilities, rules and routines) and devote the beginning of the school year to ensuring that there is no ambiguity about their expectations (Doyle 1986). Consequences associated with these behaviours are also planned for in advance. This 'establishment phase' (Rogers 1994, 1995), with its preventive focus, is crucial to effective teaching and learning later in the year (Kyriacou 1986, 1991). With younger children, it has been shown that teachers who have little difficulty throughout the year in managing their classroom *actually teach* rules and procedures to the class on the first day of school and during the next few weeks, rather than merely explaining them in words or listing them on the wall (Evertson, Emmer & Worsham 2000). As with any effective teaching, there are three important steps here: describing and demonstrating the desired behaviour, rehearsal and feedback. *Describe* in specific terms what you expect and *demonstrate* with actions (or allow students to do so) what behaviours are desirable. Don't assume that students know precisely what you want them to do or that they can actually perform the procedures correctly. Rules such as 'Students may whisper during group work', 'Enter and leave the classroom in an orderly fashion' and 'Get on with something quiet when you've finished your set work or you are waiting for the teacher' should be clearly demonstrated and then rehearsed. *Practising* the desired behaviours ensures that rules and procedures are understood. *Feedback* to students on their performance is very important in shaping future behaviour. For example, 'I am very pleased that you all lined up outside the classroom door as soon as the bell rang, but I was not happy about the talking' gives clear guidelines as to what is considered appropriate behaviour and what is not.

Describe and demonstrate desired behaviours

Provide for rule rehearsal and feedback

For secondary school students it is preferable to explain rules, procedures and consequences (sometimes referred to as 'expectations' with senior students) in a positive way and to discuss their necessity. Rules and procedures that are presented as a means of ensuring a fair and productive classroom learning environment for all students, rather than as idiosyncrasies of the teacher, will be accepted more readily. Such an approach is supported by the research of Lewis and Lovegrove (1984), who found that secondary school students prefer teachers to establish clear and reasonable rules that are based on the teacher's desire to ensure that effective learning takes place, rather than on the teacher's authority. Table 8.4

Explain rationale for rules

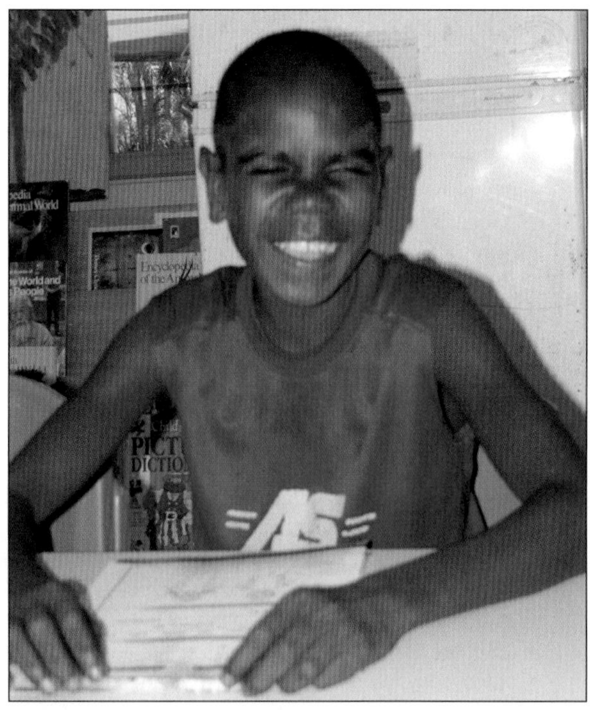

This child is looking forward to the positive consequences of finishing work and packing up—an 'early mark'.

Table 8.4

Essentials of establishing good classroom management

Teachers should:

- be prepared at the beginning of the year. Have name tags made and ready to wear (as well as extra labels for unexpected students). Label students' desks for at least the first few days in the earlier grades. Older students may be left to choose their own seats;
- greet each student as they enter the room (and take the younger ones to their seats);
- introduce themselves briefly and have the students do so as well, perhaps with a few words about themselves ('My favourite hobby is . . . ');
- use an 'ice-breaker' activity to reduce inhibitions and establish the classroom as a warm, cooperative environment. One such activity we have had success with at all age levels is 'Tangles' (or 'Human Chain'). You need to divide the class into groups of about six to eight people and have each group cluster together with both hands stretched up. Each person takes the hand of another person with their left hand and of another person with their right hand. The aim is to form a circle after untangling the chain without breaking hands. There is usually much laughter, the beginnings of cooperative group work and evidence of potential group dynamics—those who are 'leaders' will give directions to the others;
- present and discuss rules, procedures and consequences along with the reasons for each of these in terms of establishing a positive learning atmosphere;
- be available to all students: move around checking on student progress and avoid sitting at your desk for the first few days. Make it obvious that you are *interested, aware and in charge*.

(Source: Based on Evertson *et al.* 2000)

lists some procedures that will provide a sense of order and calm at the start of a new year when nerves are likely to be strained.

The four Rs: Rules and routines expressed as rights and responsibilities

The next aspect of an effective management plan is to decide what sorts of behaviour the teacher requires to ensure a smoothly functioning classroom that is conducive to learning: movement around the room, talking to the teacher and peers, marking of work, requesting help and treatment of others. Can you think of other areas where you would want to establish your standards and expectations of students at the start of the year? Such guidelines can be imposed top down by the teacher or negotiated with the students. They will be expressed as **rules** and **routines** (along with their corresponding consequences) which will vary as a function of teacher personality (for example, some teachers tolerate more student noise and movement than others), student age and school policy. Just a brief pause for definitions here. *Rules* define general standards for behaviour and often indicate what constitutes unacceptable or prohibited behaviour—for example, students must stay in their seats unless they have the teacher's permission to move around. A positive classroom climate will be fostered more by rules that are positively worded than those that prohibit behaviours (McDaniel 1983). *Routines* refer to behaviours that relate to specific activities or situations. For example, how will students enter and leave the classroom? What are students to do when the teacher is called from the room or when someone becomes ill? If, in line with the current philosophy of democratic classroom management, students are encouraged to design their own classroom rules and routines, a sense of ownership of learning and of 'their' classroom will be engendered.

In contrast, we can all probably remember our school days when rules were presented as dictates from higher authority and included some of the following:

- Don't speak in class.
- Don't get out of your seat until the bell goes.
- Don't talk in lines or in the corridors.
- Wear your school uniform in its entirety at all times to and from school.
- Don't play in the 'out of bounds' areas in the playground.

From punishment to rights and responsibilities—'the fair rule'

These so-called rules said nothing about rights or responsibilities, let alone about effective learning. Let us consider this recent transition in thinking about discipline a little more closely.

As pointed out by Bill Rogers in his book *You Know the Fair Rule* (1998), classroom and school-wide rules should not be imposed arbitrarily from above, but should evolve from commonly held values. These community values are expressed as *rights*, which have associated *responsibilities* that protect them. Rules that are equitable are derived from these rights, and indicate the due responsibilities of students, teachers and parents, or education systems where appropriate. Rogers refers to this approach as *collaborative democracy* and argues that the four Rs focus (rights, responsibilities, rules and routines) is not only an effective basis for determining equitable classroom management policies, but also prepares children to participate in, and enjoy the benefits of, being part of a social group.

Collaborative democracy

Let us illustrate this process with an example. A fundamental value of Western democracy—and, many would argue, of humanity in general—is that of equality and fairness of treatment. Thus, irrespective of background, ethnicity, colour, gender or disability, all children should be treated equally and have equal access to educational opportunities. This value is expressed as *the right of children to learn in a warm, supportive and encouraging environment.* Similarly, *the teacher has the right to teach in a positive environment, and one that is physically and emotionally safe.* Both parties, therefore, have the responsibility of being considerate and supportive. Student responsibility includes being cooperative and completing work as requested, while teachers must provide support and guidance to students at all stages of learning, encouraging effort and being fair in discipline. Parents must also support both children and their teachers in fulfilling their responsibilities. Box 8.3 presents an illustration of a list of classroom rights and responsibilities designed by a Year 6 class.

The right to learn

If you adopt the rights and responsibilities approach to classroom management, then rules will emerge as logical ways of protecting the rights of the participants in the education process, and will be seen as an acceptable means of enforcing the responsibilities that accompany them. Clearly, positive and negative consequences follow naturally from choices made to observe the rules or not.

Rules outline one's responsibilities and allow the enjoyment of rights

Rules are, therefore, preventive measures, logically derived from agreed upon rights of both teacher and students, and are most effective if they are:

- *Expressed positively:* 'Hands up before you speak', rather than 'Don't call out'; or 'Walking in corridors' rather than 'Don't run'.
- *Kept to a minimum number:* No more than five to eight rules should be needed for defining acceptable student behaviour. In fact, any more than this can be difficult for younger children to remember, and appear very authoritarian to older students.
- *Unambiguous:* Specify, clearly, exactly *what* students are to do and *when*. 'Respect other people's property' or 'Don't steal' may be worthwhile principles to teach but do not tell students, especially young ones, precisely what behaviour you expect in your classroom. A better rule is: 'Ask first before you use another person's things.' Similarly, 'Be polite', 'Don't run', 'Don't call out', are neither positive directions for how to behave nor specific to particular situations. Do children know what being polite means? Are they *never* to run or call out in school time?

How many, and which, rules?

Here are some commonly used rules:

- Raise your hand before speaking to the teacher.
- Listen quietly while others are speaking.

Box 8.3

CLASSROOM RIGHTS AND RESPONSIBILITIES

Rights	Responsibilities
To discuss openly with teachers any aspect of class management that we feel is unfair or a problem	To abide by the decisions made by the parties involved
To be treated with dignity and respect always	To treat others with dignity always
To work in the canteen	To be honest and accurate when giving change
To use things in the classroom	To take care of things and put them back in their proper place
To help and show small children the right thing to do in the playground	To set a good example and not to yell or scare them
To be able to eat at our desk on cold days	Not to make a mess, and to put rubbish in the bin
To write on the whiteboard	To use the pens carefully and only for school-related things
To have a neat, clean classroom	To clean up after ourselves; to cooperate with each other and finish the job
Not to have weekend homework	To finish off all other work during the week
To sit next to who we like	To work well together

- Walk (don't run) in the classroom.
- Leave toys and games in schoolbags for lunchtime play.
- Discuss problems after the bell goes.

In your explanation of this last rule you might specify the exact procedure: disputes are negotiated between the participants in the first instance, and then with the teacher if necessary.

The 'golden rule'

With older age groups, the 'golden rule' may be the only one you need: '*Do unto others as you would have them do unto you*' or '*Treat others as you would like to be treated*'.

Some teachers like to involve students in designing rules, believing that personal 'ownership' will help develop a positive classroom climate and that peer encouragement to uphold them is preferable to teacher enforcement alone. Rogers (1990, 1995), for example, suggests that children from Grade 3 or 4 should be encouraged to write out classroom rules in their own words. He also advocates the use of general labels for easy reference to rules as the occasion arises, especially for younger children. For instance, you might have these categories:

Involving students in designing rules

- communication or 'talking rule';
- fair treatment rule;
- conflict or 'problem-fixing rule';
- movement rule;
- safety rule; and
- learning rule.

Much better than drafting general rules in 'neutral language' is wording class rules in 'inclusive' language (Rogers 1995) such as: 'In *our* class, we . . .'; '*Our* rule for . . . is'. A useful strategy, therefore, in the establishment phase is to have a general rule reminder before on-task activity begins: 'Before we begin our work/our discussion, I want you to remember our communication rule. Hands up, thanks.'

In cases of misbehaviour, therefore, such as an argument over who 'stole' whose ruler, the question can be asked, 'Monica and Tom, what's our problem-fixing rule?' Answer: 'We talk about it after the bell goes, and then come to you if we can't sort it out.' The teacher can reply: 'Thank you. Now would you both go on quietly with your work, please, and wait behind at recess?'

It should be pointed out here that research on effective management shows that it is not always necessary to have younger students negotiate class rules. It is more important that the teacher presents the few rules needed for creating an environment conducive to learning clearly and concisely with reasons for their need, and then allows for student discussion (Evertson *et al.* 2000). It is perhaps more important for older students, whom we are training for civic responsibility, to be involved in writing and negotiating class rules with each other and with the teacher (see Eccles & Midgley 1989; Ericson & Ellett 1990). What do you think?

Consequences for rules and procedures

In the context of classroom management, consequences for behaviour emerge from classroom rules that are established to protect the rights of individuals in that class. As well as defining rules and procedures, therefore, teachers must plan the consequences for following or neglecting to follow them. These should be 'logical'—that is, they should relate as closely to the behaviour as possible so that students can see a connection between them (Dreikurs & Cassel 1975, 1995; Dreikurs, Grunwald & Pepper 1982). In this way, students are taught to foresee the outcome of their behaviour (Rogers 1994) and to develop an ownership of it. For consequences to be effective, it is important for them to be understood and agreed to by the students. **Logical consequences** are not punishments; they are not imposed by the teacher as authority but are a conscious 'choice' made by the student about how to behave, thus encouraging the development of responsible self-discipline: bad choices of behaviour *always* result in unpleasant, but just, consequences. Without doubt, it is important that consequences are applied calmly and never in anger. Most theorists also advise that in a democratic classroom the same consequence should be used for every student. On this point, however, those who adopt a student-oriented approach would add an important qualification of appropriateness.

Include positive and negative consequences

Some examples of positive and negative logical consequences are:

Consequences should always be logical, applied calmly, and be appropriate to the student

- Students who work quietly without disturbing others may work with a group of friends.
- Students who damage school property must repair or replace it.
- Students who constantly leave their seats should be made to do without one until they decide that they need one, and will stay in it!
- Students who regularly hand in their work on time may be allowed extra time to submit one assignment of their choice.
- Students who talk loudly or call out during reading and free time forfeit their opportunity to bring a favourite piece of music to share with the class during these times.
- Students who keep their work area clean may bring

something to beautify their desk (pot plant, favourite ornament).
- Students who hurt someone on purpose—for example, by kicking or name calling—are to do two things for the hurt child to make them feel better (write an apology; make something for them) (Rogers 1995).

Table 8.5 suggests how poorly expressed rules and consequences may be reworded positively and logically.

Maintaining effective management throughout the year: Kounin's approach

Once a system of rules and procedures is in place, teachers should monitor the behaviour and work habits of students by using the strategies discussed below (Kounin's preventive measures): 'withitness', overlapping and group focus. It is equally important to monitor the impact of teaching styles and work demands on individual students, as it is more likely that students who are having difficulty coping with lesson content or meeting teacher expectations for achievement will be predisposed to misbehave. Such difficulties need to be diagnosed for what they are: learning ones. Perhaps peer and cross-age tutoring, an individualised program of work, enlisting parental support for extra practice at home, or a contract negotiated with the student that sets out short-term mastery goals are preferable alternatives to dismissing such students as 'behaviour problems' and inflicting penalties on them.

Kounin's preventive measures

Obviously, dealing with misbehaviour or unproductive work habits is the final component of maintaining

Table 8.5 Improving rules and consequences

Poor (vague)	Negative rule	Positive rule	Contrived punishment	Logical positive and negative consequences
1 Respect each other	Don't hit classmates	Settle arguments by discussion	Detention	Timeout from reinforcement (to make a plan or contract). 'Peacemaker' award
2 Be cooperative	Don't call out	Put up your hand when you wish to speak	Lines: 'I shall not call out in class'	Teacher ignores calling-out behaviour. Teacher praises and responds to students with raised hands
3 Be prompt to class	Don't be late	Come to lessons on time	Detention	Make up missed work at recess, lunchtime or after school. Privilege such as 'early mark' before the bell
4 Work hard	Don't leave homework unfinished	Complete all homework	Teacher lecture or nagging	Finish homework in recreation time at school. Letter sent to parents. Exemption from a particular piece of homework. Letter of praise sent home
5 Be honest	Don't cheat	Do your own homework	Teacher lecture or sent to the principal	Work redone in class recreation time. 'Honour' award

TEACHER'S CASE BOOK

Timeout

It's last period on Friday afternoon and Peter Firth's Year 9 model-making class has been busily painting, gluing and wiring models for about 20 minutes. Suddenly, over the top of the low hum of industry, someone calls out: 'Hey, Graeme, chuck us that blue tube, will you?' Peter looks up just as Graeme's misdirected paint tube whizzes past and smacks Michael Travers' unsuspecting ear.

There is a tense pause. A golden rule of the practical arts centre about throwing objects has been broken. Peter, a high-profile local basketball player, stands, motions to Graeme and calls 'foul', using a basketball umpire's familiar hand signal.

'How many's that you've got?' someone asks Graeme.

'Four.'

A buzz goes round the room. Five fouls in a week means temporary suspension from the game. The team checks out each other's foul count. Time to settle down.

Case study activity

How effective is this teacher's management policy in terms of fostering student responsibility and accountability in this educational setting? What approach would you use?

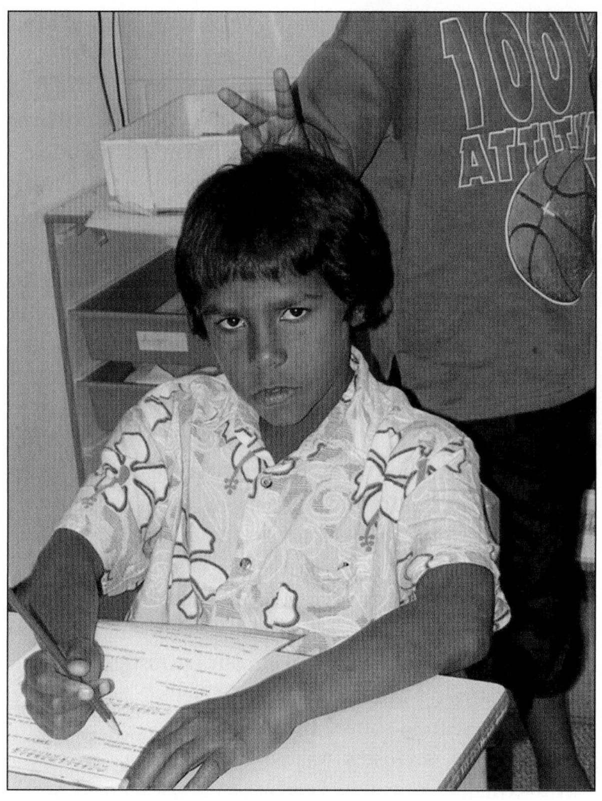

Attentive or bored? The 'withit' teacher scans the classroom in order to monitor student engagement in the lesson.

'Miss Jones, I thought you were supposed to have eyes in the back of your head!'

effective classroom control. A number of powerful means of doing this will be considered in detail later in this chapter. For now, it would be valuable to look at one other approach to preventing discipline problems, that of lesson management.

Jacob Kounin's (1970, 1977; Copeland 1987) research on group management, based on analysis of thousands of hours of videotaped classroom interactions, has provided teachers for two decades now with insights into powerful strategies for preventing misbehaviour. The central focus of Kounin's research findings is that good classroom behaviour depends on effective lesson management. Especially important are appropriate reactions to misbehaviour, maintaining activity flow in lessons, smooth transitions between activities, group (whole-class) alerting and individual student accountability. Some of Kounin's key concepts will be examined in greater detail.

Teachers should be aware of what is going on in all areas of the classroom at all times. The term Kounin uses to describe such awareness is 'withitness' and it is like the popular expression 'having eyes in the back of the head'. The **'withit'** teacher is always **visually scanning** the room even when working with an individual child or small group of students and will act promptly (timing is very important) to prevent any potentially disruptive behaviour from developing. An important proviso for 'withitness' is that the action taken does not interrupt the flow of the learning activity for the rest of the class.

Let us illustrate this technique with an example. The scene is an art lesson where the teacher is outlining the procedure for blending primary colours to create secondary ones before letting the class experiment for themselves. During the explanation, the teacher sees two children snatching at the same box of craft equipment in order to have the first pick of the paint pots. Without stopping the lesson, the 'withit' teacher moves towards the offenders and either makes stern eye contact with both of them or taps one on the shoulder while gesturing to stop the misbehaviour. The 'non-withit' teacher, on the other hand, would stop the lesson saying, 'Would both of you stop fooling with the craft box until you are told what to do, otherwise you will be doing your maths homework while the rest of the class paints! Now what was I saying before?' Needless to say, the other students have now become uninvolved with the lesson content and there is potential for new misbehaviour.

Remember also that a 'withit' teacher does not wait too long before taking action; children may interpret your hesitation as weakness and take advantage of your apparent lack of awareness. Behaviourists might recommend the technique of *tactically ignoring* behaviours in order to avoid reinforcing them. (See Chapter 6 for an

Why is it important for a 'withit' teacher to have effective group management skills for whole-class activities?

explanation of behavioural theory.) Experience has shown us that such a choice by the teacher depends heavily on the nature of the situation—some obvious but 'mild' form of attention-seeking behaviour, such as calling out, pouting and refusing to speak or clowning, may be consciously ignored as long as the child is reinforced for on-task behaviour as soon as it occurs. Of course, any serious or potentially dangerous off-task behaviour—fighting, swearing, rude calling out—cannot be ignored. The strategy of ignoring is discussed in greater detail in the section on models of discipline later in the chapter.

Two additional, important features of 'withitness' need to be highlighted. The first is that of making sure that the right culprit is chosen for the disciplinary action: a teacher's credibility can be rapidly diminished if an 'un-withit' accusation of misbehaviour is made. Negative student attitudes to teacher and to schoolwork are related to incorrect targeting, either by choosing the wrong student or by blaming the wrongdoings of one individual on a group (Lewis & Lovegrove 1984, 1987). The second feature to remember is to attend to the more serious misbehaviour when two problems occur at the same time. Thus, intervening swiftly in a potential fight in the playground takes precedence over reprimanding children for dropping their lunch scraps.

Choose the right culprit

Attend to more serious behaviour

Skilful classroom managers are expert at dealing with two issues arising at the same time. For example, while working with a small group of readers, the teacher looks up to see two children bobbing under their desks to look at a 'forbidden' comic. A number of **overlapping responses** are possible: 'Keep reading, John, that's fine. Julia and Mario, put the comic away (or on my desk) and get back to your work.' Another method would be to encourage the reading group to continue while moving silently towards the offending children. With a light tap on one of the children's shoulders, or stern eye contact, remove the comic and gesture to the culprits to resume their work.

A teacher who stops a learning activity to berate naughty children causes a loss of momentum which is hard to restore, and which can encourage restlessness and boredom among other class members. Kounin's research shows that student misbehaviour is closely related to the way in which lessons flow (momentum and smoothness). **Momentum** refers to pacing and is evident in lessons that move briskly. *Slowdowns*, which encourage students to lose interest in the main idea of an activity, are frequently caused by teachers giving directions in a laborious, detailed way, nagging when correcting students, and having students wait for each other before moving from one activity to the next. For example, during a science lesson a teacher may slow down a lesson by saying, 'Students in the first row may come up and collect their equipment. Now those in the second row. Those in the third row may come up next.' With better planning, this teacher could prevent student boredom and inattention by not fragmenting the lesson into unnecessary steps—for example, each member of a group could have a role such as collecting the paper for the group.

Smoothness and slowdowns

Where teachers are able to move smoothly from one activity to the next, student attention is maintained. For instance, a teacher who is giving a mathematics lesson glances at her watch and realises that she has forgotten to collect permission notes and money for the class excursion, which must be sent to the office for filing and banking before the lunch bell. She will be guilty of poor **movement management** ('jerkiness') if she interrupts the lesson and says, 'How many of you are coming on the excursion? I had better finalise numbers as soon as I have finished explaining this problem.' Even worse, in Kounin's estimation, would be the abrupt cessation of the lesson in order to attend to the administrative matter immediately.

A skilful classroom manager must be able to direct the activities of the whole class while ensuring that its individual members are all engaged in the lesson. Kounin suggests two main techniques for achieving this **group focus**: group alerting and individual accountability.

It is of paramount importance to have the attention of all students at the start of any learning activity. Always *wait* for full student attention while visually scanning the room and making direct eye contact with each student. This **group alerting** communicates to the students both that you are in control and that you are sufficiently interested in them to wish to teach effectively. After gaining the full attention of the class, there are a number of effective ways of keeping all students attentive. These are listed in Table 8.6.

Group alerting is reduced by calling on a particular student before asking a question or discussing an answer at length with only one student. Let's have a look at a situation where group focus is lacking. Having just read a story with the class the teacher says, 'Max, why do you think that the character . . .?' Max says, 'Because he . . .' The teacher continues: 'What did the writer say that gives you that idea, Max?' Meanwhile, what do you imagine is happening to the involvement of the rest of the class? How could the teacher have maintained group focus more effectively?

Following the reading the teacher could say, 'Think about why the main character . . .' Now the teacher pauses to allow for *wait-time*: students need at least three seconds to be able to formulate a simple verbal response from their thoughts, and from eight to 10 seconds for difficult or thought-provoking questions. Then, 'All right, we should be ready now to hear what you think. Why did the main character . . .?' Pause. 'Max, what do you think?' Following the answer, the teacher keeps the group's attention by asking, 'What did the writer say that gave Max that idea? Sandra?' Sandra responds, and so on.

Students will be kept accountable for their learning if the teacher communicates that their participation will be monitored and their performance evaluated in some way. This can be achieved by (adapted from Charles 1999):

- asking all students to write their answers on a card and hold them up;
- asking students to turn their thumbs up or down depending on their answer;
- having the students write their answer to a question in a special notebook which is checked while the teacher circulates;
- asking all students to work out a solution to a problem in their books at the same time as one student is asked to solve it on the board; answers are then compared;
- asking students to write a summary of what they have just been doing;
- having students record reflections in a diary or journal;
- having pairs of students show or tell each other their responses, and then calling on them to share their partner's answers aloud;
- posing a question to the whole class and then randomly selecting respondents.

In cases of misbehaviour, asking a student to answer a question is a sure way of regaining their attention. This is provided that it is done in such a way as to avoid embarrassing the student or creating an opportunity for argument—that is, by phrasing the question in such a way that the inattentive student can once again participate: 'Jane, Sam says that cars contribute to the destruction of the ozone layer . . . what do you think?', rather than 'Jane, tell me what Sam just said.'

ACTION STATION

Discuss the range of strategies that you could adopt in situations of minor student misbehaviour where you keep the intervention private and minimise disrupting the lesson as much as possible.

Table 8.6

Essentials of maintaining student attention

Teachers should:

- pause (for at least three seconds) after asking a question to allow students thinking time, then name a student to answer;
- call on students at random;
- create suspense by saying things such as 'I wonder if anyone will have heard of this?' or 'This is going to be a tricky one';
- ask students to listen carefully because they might be asked to contribute something to another student's answer;
- look at other students at the same time as calling on one student to answer a question;
- teach active listening.

Theory and research into practice

Ramon Lewis — EFFECTIVE DISCIPLINE

BRIEF BIOGRAPHY

After I started my career as a teacher of maths and physics in the early 1970s, I continued to study part-time at Monash University in Melbourne. I managed to complete a B.Ed. and Ph.D. by 1976 and spent that year at the Australian Council for Educational Research as part of a team of researchers investigating numeracy and literacy in Australian schools. I have been on staff at Latrobe University since then. I generally convene a diploma in education course of between 30 and 60 students and teach in the graduate program. My teaching areas cover classroom pedagogy, statistics and research methodology. I have also had the pleasure of supervising over 40 Ph.D. or Master's students. Together with my colleagues, Drs Malcolm Lovegrove (dec.) and Eva Burman, I conducted many research projects focusing on a range of issues related to classroom discipline. Over more than 20 years I have published five books and many articles in this area of research. During a sabbatical in 1987 I returned to teach full-time as a maths and science teacher, and taught part-time for the following seven years, while at Latrobe. After that I began consulting with schools in a bid to help teachers discipline students in a way consistent with their view of best practice. Generally this meant helping them to remain calm when dealing with students' inappropriate behaviour, to recognise students' appropriate behaviour, and to involve them in the process of ensuring responsible student behaviour in classrooms. Most recently, I have been working with a number of primary and secondary schools (some for six years) to help them develop a culture where teachers are supported to work calmly and professionally with more difficult students, rather than send them to others to 'get fixed'.

RESEARCH AND THEORETICAL INTERESTS

Since 1980 I have been steadily developing the academic area of classroom discipline. This research program has involved surveys of, and interviews with, students, teachers and parents. It has also involved examining the discipline policies of over 300 schools. The aim has been to investigate a comprehensive series of research questions in the area of classroom discipline. These include: *What classroom discipline techniques do teachers use? What effect do teachers' disciplinary techniques have on students? What techniques do teachers, parents and students prefer? What rationales do students, teachers and parents provide for their preferences? In all of the preceding questions are the differences associated with age or gender? How consistent with government policy is current classroom disciplinary practice and the preferences of the main players? How often are teachers aggressive towards students who misbehave? Why are teachers more aggressive towards difficult students? Why don't teachers provide more recognition for the appropriate behaviour of difficult students? Why don't teachers have more discussions with more difficult students? How can teachers be assisted to act more in accordance with their own (or others') ideas of best practice?*

Since 2001 I have been involved with academics in China and Israel who are attempting to replicate some of my research. The most important findings of my recent research concern the empirical relationship between student responsibility and discipline. The results for these analyses are consistent for both primary and secondary levels of schooling in Australia, and are also similar in China and Israel. More responsible classes are associated with teachers who are less abusive and punishment-oriented and who are seen as more likely to discuss misbehaviour with their students, involve students in decision making, hint when students misbehave and recognise appropriate student behaviour.

Consequently, it might be argued that the more frequent use of strategies such as *discussion*, *recognition*, *hinting* and *involvement* results in less student misbehaviour and more responsibility. It may also be argued that teachers who use more punishment, more aggressive techniques such as yelling in anger, class detentions, and fewer inclusive techniques promote more misbehaviour and less responsibility in their students.

Alternatively, it may not be the teachers' behaviour that is influencing student responsibility, but vice versa. This could occur in two distinct ways. First, teachers may be choosing discipline techniques suitable for their clientele. That is, when their students have more self-discipline, teachers use more hinting, discussion and involvement to provide them a voice, since that voice can be trusted. They are also more likely to recognise their students' behaviour, because more responsible students do more praiseworthy things. Further, there is little recourse to aggression as more responsible students do not confront teachers' authority.

A second rationale may explain why teachers' disciplinary strategies are influenced by the level of responsibility displayed by their students. When students act less responsibly in class, it is possible that teachers may become frustrated. They may feel confronted by their inability to ensure that all students are respectful of rights. They may even become angry and hostile towards less responsible students. Angry or upset teachers may not be interested in being reasonable towards unreasonable and disrespectful students. They therefore may find it unpalatable to recognise difficult students when they act appropriately. Rewarding 'Neanderthals' for being normal may not come naturally. Similarly, they may find it unpleasant and unproductive to spend time letting such students tell their side of events, in a bid to try and get them to acknowledge that their behaviour is unfair and needs to change.

Regardless of which of the explanations applies to these findings, my research shows that teacher aggression and, to a lesser extent, punishment are ineffective in fostering student responsibility, whereas hinting, discussion, recognition and involvement may be helpful in this regard. That being the case, it is problematic to note that teachers who are teaching less responsible students are not more likely to be utilising productive techniques (such as hinting, discussing, recognising and involving). It is equally problematic to see an increased use of aggression and punishment, given that they are at best of limited usefulness, and at worst counterproductive.

THEORY AND RESEARCH INTO PRACTICE

In interpreting the findings of my research it is useful to refer briefly to a theory of power developed by French and Raven (1960). This analysis of power in relationships continues to provide a valuable framework for those examining classroom discipline (Tauber, 1999). In dealing with the misbehaviour of students, teachers may knowingly or unknowingly draw upon five kinds of power (Tauber, 1999). The first is *coercive power*. It is the power a teacher has over a student that comes from the student's desire to avoid punishment associated with inappropriate classroom behaviour. The second is *reward power*. Teachers who provide desired recognitions and rewards for appropriate behaviour have such power. The third, *legitimate power*, is the power that is inherent in the role occupied by teachers. It is bestowed upon them by society, coming with the position they occupy. The fourth is *referent* or *relationship power*. This is the power that students give to teachers whose relationships they value. It stems from respect for, or liking of, the teacher. Teachers with referent power are trusted by students, as friends are trusted. The fifth and final power, *expert power*, has least to do with the following analysis of teachers' disciplinary behaviour. It stems from students' belief that the teacher has the ability to pass on important knowledge and skills.

According to my research findings, students appear to attribute legitimate power to teachers, in that they expect them to take charge of student behaviour. The presence of clear, fully explained 'rules', which form the basis for teachers to make demands and follow through if students fail to comply, supports such an argument. Teachers are to utilise coercive power in the form of logical or reasonable consequences. Students also support the isolation of students who misbehave but want to minimise the likelihood of emotional discomfort. This expressed need for calm, reasonable teachers provides evidence of the relevance of referent power. Further support for referent power relates to the expressed desire by both students and teachers for students to have a voice, both individually and as a class group. It is interesting to note that compared to primary teachers, secondary teachers appear to provide less support for both referent and reward power while giving greater emphasis to legitimate and coercive power.

There are three main implications. First, it appears that teachers fail to provide sufficient recognition for appropriate behaviour, particularly to difficult students. Second, secondary teachers should provide more of a voice for students, both individually and collectively—for example, in determining expectations for appropriate behaviour in class and, to a lesser extent, choice of sanctions. Finally, to act more in accord with perceptions of best practice, teachers should reduce their use of group punishments, sarcasm and loss of temper when handling misbehaviour in classrooms. In terms of the power analysis discussed above, teacher aggression can be seen to contribute towards increasing their coercive power but reducing their referent power. To act more in accord with a conception of perceived best practice, teachers would need to increase their reward and referent power, while reducing their use of the more extreme forms of coercive power. This need is greater for more difficult students.

Encouraging teachers to build rather than destroy goodwill with students who are more provocative is a challenging request. It will not be easy and can take many years of persistent effort accompanied by considerable support. No matter how it is achieved, there is a need to support teachers to avoid becoming coercive in the face of increases in student misbehaviour and, rather, to respond calmly and assertively while rewarding good behaviour, discussing with students the impact their misbehaviour has on others, and involving them in some of the decision making surrounding rules and consequences. If teachers do not, it may mean less student time on task, less schoolwork learned and, possibly more significantly, less responsible students.

KEY REFERENCES

French, J. P. R. Jr. & Raven, B. (1960) The basis of social power. In D. Cartwright & A. Zander (eds), *Group Dynamics*. New York: Harper & Row.

Lewis, R. (1997a) Discipline in schools. In L. J. Saha (ed.) *International Encyclopedia of the Sociology in Education* (pp. 404–11). Oxford, UK: Pergamon.

Lewis, R. (1997b) *The Discipline Dilemma: Control, Management or Influence*, 2nd ed. Melbourne: The Australian Council for Educational Research.

Lewis, R. (1999a) Teachers coping with the stress of classroom discipline. *Social Psychology of Education*. **3**, 1–17.

Lewis. R. (1999b) Preparing students for democratic citizenship: Codes of conduct in Victoria's schools of the future. *Educational Research and Evaluation*, **5**(1), 41–61.

Lewis, R. (2001) Student responsibility and classroom discipline: The student's view. *Teaching and Teacher Education*, **17**, 307–19.

Lewis, R. (in press) Classroom discipline in Australia. In C. Evertson and C. S. Weinstein (eds) *Handbook of Classroom Management: Research, Practice and Contemporary Issues.* Hillsdale, NJ: Lawrence Erlbaum Associates.

Lewis, R., Romi, S., Xing, Q. & Katz, Y. (in press) *A comparison of teachers' classroom discipline in Australia, China and Israel.* Teaching and Teacher Education.

Tauber, R. T. (1999) *Classroom Management: Sound Theory and Effective Practice*. 3rd ed. Westport, CT: Bergin & Garvey.

ACTIVITIES

1 In your experience, what do you think are teachers' beliefs about best practice in classroom discipline and management? Compare your ideas with those of fellow students and compile a list of the common ones. How do these teacher beliefs relate to the issues Ramon Lewis raises, and to issues raised in other parts of this chapter?

2 Ramon Lewis lists a series of questions that are quite important for understanding the nature and use of classroom discipline. With a group of peers, consider each of these questions. You might need to do further Internet searches to find information on government policies and related studies that shed light on the issues.

3 According to Ramon Lewis, what are the characteristics of more responsible classrooms? Consider how you might include in your classroom management regime discussion, recognition, hinting and involvement. Would the nature of these processes differ according to the grade level you are teaching?

4 How are the behaviours of teachers and students reciprocal, and how may this impact on discipline strategies applied by teachers?

5 Ramon Lewis describes five kinds of power structure that may characterise classrooms. In a group, discuss each of these and role play positive and negative examples of each. How common do you think these 'powers' are in regular classrooms? How is knowledge of this power structure useful to you as a teacher?

6 Consider one or more of the key references above to further your understanding of this important topic.

Models of discipline

The degree to which students and teachers should share responsibility for, and have control over, discipline in the classroom has engrossed the minds of many educators, psychiatrists and psychologists over the last 50 years. In this section, we explore a range of the models of discipline that have proved valuable in many settings. First we consider the widely used student-centred approach of Thomas Gordon (discipline as self-control) and the body language approach of Jones. Next we examine approaches in which students and teachers interact in solving discipline problems: Dreikurs (democratic classrooms and mistaken goals) and Glasser (non-coercive discipline). Newer systems of discipline that have grown out of these two approaches are discussed next: Nelson, Lott and Glenn (positive discipline in the classroom) and Albert (cooperative discipline). Finally, we conclude with a consideration of one of the longest standing formalised approaches to classroom discipline that is fully teacher-centred—namely, that of the Canters (assertive discipline).

Gordon's 'discipline as self-control' approach

Thomas Gordon's humanistic approach, originally expressed in his book *Teacher Effectiveness Training* (Gordon 1974) and more recently elaborated in *Discipline that Works: Promoting Self-Discipline in Children* (Gordon 1989), encourages the creation of a warm, supportive relationship between teacher and student where the teacher is sensitive, accepting and non-critical of the student. Above all, Gordon's approach stresses that the teacher uses minimal control, seeks to *understand* the student, and involves the student in problem solving about the source of the problem and decisions about its management.

First, Gordon maintains that the teacher must give up their efforts to control student behaviour and instead help students to develop their own sense of control and judgments about what is right and wrong. (See Chapter 14 where we talk about the development of morality.) How is this done? In the first instance, teacher and

Who 'owns' the problem?

student need to clarify the source of their dispute: who 'owns' the problem, the teacher or the student? In other words, is the student having a problem that is the cause of the misbehaviour, or does the teacher own the problem because the student's behaviour is having a direct and concrete effect on them? If the problem is the student's, then the teacher's role is to listen critically in order to understand the 'real message' underlying it. This should be done in the first instance by non-verbal encouragement such as nodding or gestures (*critical listening*), followed by non-directive statements (*active listening*) which summarise and repeat or mirror what the student is saying to confirm that the student's real message and feelings are being clearly understood.

Let us look at an example of this approach in practice. The problem is one of a student who is pushing others and defiantly refusing to join the rest of the class in gymnastics.

Teacher: Abdul, I would like you to line up with that group at the floor mats, please. We will be doing some tumbling.
Student: I'm not going to!

At this stage, the teacher has to decide whether the problem is the student's and should be worked out without any influence from the teacher, or whether the teacher is having a problem with the student's behaviour and, therefore, 'owns' the problem. The following dialogue illustrates Gordon's approach.

Teacher: Abdul, when you refuse to join in, I get annoyed that I have to spend extra time with you when other students need my help. I'm also worried that someone might get hurt because I'm not watching them.
Student: I hate gym . . . I can't do all the things you want.
Teacher: Uh, huh (*nodding while listening critically*). You don't like gym because you feel that you can't do it? (*active listening*)
Student: Yeah.
Teacher: Why? (*door opener*)
Student: All the other kids laugh at me because I can't do the cartwheels and tumbles properly.
Teacher: You feel that the other kids will laugh at you if you can't do everything in gym, and that's why you don't want to join in?
Student: Uh, huh. They all say I'm hopeless.

Here it is clear that the student and teacher both own the problem and it is up to the teacher to help Abdul explore some solutions to the problem.

Teacher: Abdul, I need to be able to concentrate on helping everyone in the gym, or accidents will happen. I want you to join in the activities willingly, but you're not happy to because kids tease you. What do you think you can do about it?
Student: I suppose I could practise a bit more.
Teacher: Mmm. What else?
Student: Maybe I could get Zac (*a more proficient friend*) to show me how to do some of the gym.
Teacher: Any other ideas?
Student: Not really.
Teacher: Okay, I'm sure your ideas would help. I could also give you some coaching at lunchtime when none of the class was there, if you would like. Maybe Zac could come too? What do you think?
Student: I'd like you to show me what to do by myself first, and then Zac and I could go to the gym later to practise until I get good at it.
Teacher: Sounds like we've got a plan to work with, Abdul. Next week, we'll see how much the practice and extra coaching has helped. Okay?

If the teacher owns the problem, they give a **directive 'I-message'**, which has three components: (1) a description of the student's behaviour which does not judge or blame the student; (2) the negative effect the behaviour is having on the teacher; and (3) how the teacher feels about the behaviour. These three aspects of an effective I-message are seen in the following example: 'When you forget to bring your homework in, I can't check all the work at the same time to see if everyone is ready for me to teach the next topic. This makes me feel very frustrated at the waste of time.'

Directive 'I-messages'

The I-message thus allows the teacher to prompt appropriate behaviour without negative evaluation of the student or issuing a direct command (Weinstein & Mignano 1993). Of course, the responsibility for changing the behaviour rests with the student. However, there is a greater likelihood of this happening than if an accusatory 'you-message' is given ('You are being very inconsiderate when you don't hand in your homework on time').

At times, active listening and I-messages are not enough to solve problems between teacher and student. When both own the problem, Gordon advocates the use of a **no-lose approach** to conflict resolution where neither teacher nor student is winner or loser, but rather both are winners. In other words, the emphasis is on cooperation, not power. How is this done? In the earlier example of Abdul, the teacher adopts a problem-solving strategy that follows these steps:

No-lose approach to conflict resolution

1 Define the problem.
2 Brainstorm possible solutions.
3 Evaluate the solutions.
4 Select one solution that is mutually acceptable.
5 Decide how to put the solution into practice; establish an agreement as to who will do what and when.
6 Assess how successful the solution was.

For communication with students to be effective, Gordon insists that at no stage should the teacher put up 'roadblocks' such as *moralising* ('You should know what happens if you . . .'); *judging* ('That wasn't a very smart thing to do'); *stereotyping* ('That's typical behaviour for someone like you!'); *advising* ('What you need to do is . . .'); or *sympathising* ('I always found gym difficult when I was your age, but if you really practise, you'll find it gets easier'). These responses impose teacher control and prevent students from solving the problem themselves.

As you can see, Gordon's approach will not always be easy to implement: time pressures may prevent extended conferences with students; their language development may limit how effectively they can express their thoughts and feelings; and the age and reasoning ability of children may restrict the extent to which the teacher can use logical argument. Furthermore, one needs to be patient and committed to genuinely empathising with students in order to hear their messages. Even more difficult for a teacher is the ability to admit to 'owning' a problem, rather than seeing blame as originating with the student, especially when faced with hostility or defiance. The approach requires a good rapport between teacher and students to be already in place, or some students, especially adolescents, may find it patronising rather than sincere.

The no-lose conflict resolution approach may be best used with students who have chronic behaviour or personality problems, rather than as a general classroom approach (Good & Brophy 1990, 1991). Such a student-centred approach may also be well suited to follow-up interactions with students who have been placed in detention or extended timeout. It is during this time that teachers have the opportunity to use active listening to help students formulate a solution to their unacceptable behaviour.

Self-worth and dignity

This approach is clearly compatible with Barbara Coloroso's (1994) beliefs about the importance of developing students' inner discipline through any approaches that work, while preserving both students' and teachers' feelings of self-worth and dignity.

Jones's 'positive discipline' approach

Experienced educators will tell you that the bulk of classroom misbehaviour is made up of students talking without permission, daydreaming, and being noisy or out of their seat—seemingly minor offences, but quite disruptive and wasteful of teaching–learning time (Charles 1999). They will also tell you that a large proportion of teacher communication is non-verbal.

Body language

Fredric Jones (1987a, 1987b) has developed a management system for training teachers that focuses on these two facts. The emphasis of this system is on having teachers consciously use their *body language* to help students behave responsibly and to focus on their own learning.

Teacher 'presence'
Direct eye contact

Jones maintains that teachers can effectively prevent misbehaviour, or reduce it significantly before it develops, by the use of body postures and gestures, movement around the classroom, teacher 'presence' in the form of bodily carriage, facial expressions and eye contact. Somewhat similar to Jacob Kounin, Jones would recommend that the teacher always minimise intrusion into instruction. The teacher should never stop a lesson to discipline a student for their nuisance behaviour, but should position their body closer to the student's, or pause momentarily and look directly into the student's eyes (with a frown, wink, head shake, nod, icy glare, or whatever else is appropriate and private). It is not easy to lock eyes with another individual (beginning teachers have particular difficulty with this), but the ability to do so in a classroom communicates awareness and authority: a skill well worth the practice.

See if you can find ideas among those in Table 8.7 that you can apply to your teaching environment. It is certainly worth practising some of these in a conscious effort to have a repertoire of tools that can communicate your displeasure at student misbehaviour privately (positively and negatively), without verbal comments that may embarrass or humiliate students or provoke defensive arguments.

Dreikurs' democratic classroom: A group-oriented approach

In his major works, *Psychology in the Classroom* and *Discipline without Tears*, Rudolf Dreikurs and his colleagues maintained that teachers should be involved in the ongoing process of helping students to develop *inner control of their behaviour*, rather than imposing control externally during conflict (Dreikurs 1968; Dreikurs & Cassel 1995). In a classroom where the teacher is seen as a firm but kind friend who does not patronise students

Table 8.7

Essentials of using assertive body language to manage behaviour

Teachers should:

- enter and move around the classroom with confidence: hold body erect rather than drooping or slouching; be aware that energetic movements will communicate confidence and leadership (even when tired or troubled), whereas lethargic movements will suggest anxiety, disinterest or resignation;
- maintain self-control and dignity before disciplining a student by taking several deep (silent) breaths (not audible sighs along with eyeball rolling!);
- look directly but briefly into the eyes of the 'offending' student;
- use facial expressions instead of words when possible: disapproval can be shown by tight lips, shake of the head, narrowing or flashing eyes; approval and enthusiasm can be shown by a wink, smile, wide eyes;
- move closer to the misbehaving student and stand there momentarily while continuing instruction: this will communicate teacher awareness and expectation that the student will adopt the desired behaviour (and they usually do);
- use gestures such as head nodding or shaking to show approval or disapproval; pointing to a student with palm facing upwards in a relaxed position rather than stabbing at the air palm down.

(Source: Based on Charles 1999; Rogers 1995)

and treats them with respect, discipline problems will be prevented, according to Dreikurs. In true democratic style, teachers and students should decide together on class rules and the logical consequences for keeping or breaking them. You will remember that we have already discussed such an approach earlier in the chapter (see 'The four Rs').

For Dreikurs, student behaviour is motivated by a need to be recognised and to belong, and misbehaviour is the product of efforts to achieve this recognition by satisfying four mistaken goals: *attention getting, power seeking, revenge seeking* and displaying *inadequacy*. Students choose to misbehave because socially acceptable means to achieve recognition and build their self-esteem have failed them. What help does this give the teacher in dealing with misbehaviour? If a student tries to get attention—for example, by clowning, asking incessant questions or annoying other children—the teacher should *avoid* responding in the way the student expects. In fact, Dreikurs would advise that teachers must always resist their first impulse in cases of misbehaviour, whichever mistaken goal is being expressed, as this is precisely what satisfies the student's goal.

Misbehaviour reflects a need for recognition

In Dreikurs' view, to deal effectively with misbehaviour teachers should determine which of the four goals of misbehaviour is being satisfied by their reaction. By not reacting in the expected way, the teacher can help the student begin to eliminate the destructive behaviour and substitute other means of developing a sense of belonging. In the case of a student seeking *attention* by being late, for example, the reaction should be to ignore the lateness, but to point out calmly that the missed work must be made up in the student's own time (a logical consequence). A student who seeks *power* by being defiant and argumentative should have no one to fight with; it is futile arguing if there is no response. When a student shows *revenge* by destroying property or stealing, the consequence is not retaliation by the teacher but, rather, restitution. As for the individual who is attempting to gain *recognition* by being 'inadequate', the teacher should withhold giving help constantly, as this merely serves to reinforce the helplessness. Instead, setting short-term, achievable goals for which encouragement can be given is preferable (Balson 1992; Charles 1999). Providing lots of genuine encouragement for evaluating the reasons for their inappropriate behaviour is essential.

In conclusion, it is worth remembering that when using a group-oriented approach, unless the teacher has built up a good relationship with students their efforts to teach self-discipline and choices about appropriate behaviour to students will be to little avail. It would be wise to heed Ramon Lewis's (Lewis 1997, p. 120) advice in this matter:

> If you actively seek opportunities for encouraging students without making the acceptance conditional on the students' performance, you will generate a substantial pile of goodwill. In addition, by providing students with a venue at which they feel their opinion is valued and their decisions taken seriously (classroom meetings and time-out discussions) you will further the quality of the teacher–student relationship.

Glasser's interactionist approach

Glasser's philosophy is a blend of *humanist* and *behaviourist* approaches. Although it was intended to be used with students who persistently violate rules, Glasser's approach has been adopted by a number of Australian schools as their whole-school discipline policy.

There have been two stages in the development of Glasser's theory. The focus of the first stage (Glasser 1969) was on the *power sharing* between teacher and student(s), and especially the responsibility of the group for the behaviour of its members. Glasser encouraged the use of regular *classroom meetings* to deal democratically with issues that are most relevant to the group: class rules, appropriate behaviour (of particular class members, as well as the whole class) and discipline. A brief look at how these meetings should be run may give you a better insight into whether you feel such an approach could be added to your management repertoire.

Power sharing and classroom meetings

Hmmm! Make a mental note: Review the work by Dreikurs.

Holding classroom meetings

Reality therapy

1 Teacher and students sit in a closed circle.

TEACHER'S CASE BOOK

Let's make our own rules

Miss Langridge is a Year 7 homeroom teacher. At the beginning of the year the students and Miss Langridge decided to come up with a set of class rules. They brainstormed together and the students really enjoyed having a say in how 'their' classroom should operate. Once they had finished brainstorming and come up with a set of class rules, they compared them with the school rules and discovered that they had devised rules totally consistent with the school rules.

Miss Langridge then posed the question: 'Okay, we now have some class rules which we have devised and agreed about. What do we do if one of us violates one of the rules?' They brainstormed again and some students came up with some innovative strategies, and after seeing the school discipline policy again decided that they would like to use that. However, one student suggested that this was not enough and some other means of punishment was necessary to prevent further unnecessary behaviour. Susan suggested that violation of rules should result in that person forfeiting participation in the end-of-term activity days. There were some people who opposed this suggestion, so a secret ballot was held. There was more support for Susan's suggestion than not, so her motion was carried.

Miss Langridge asked the students if they thought that a note should be written home in their diary to let parents know of a rule violation. Once again a group vote was taken and this was agreed upon. Angela asked a very good question: 'How will you know that the note has been seen by the parent?' Miss Langridge suggested that they could have it signed by a parent and there was general consensus for this suggestion.

After all these decisions had been made, Miss Langridge typed them up in the form of a contract and had each individual student sign this contract to endorse the agreed set of rules and consent to abide by their agreement. Miss Langridge has found this to be most successful in encouraging positive student behaviour and fostering personal development, for the students take responsibility for their own actions.

Case studies illustrating National Competency Framework for Beginning Teaching, National Project on the Quality of Teaching and Learning, Australian Teaching Council, 1996, p. 44. Commonwealth of Australia copyright, reproduced by permission.

Case study activity

As a group, discuss this teacher's democratic, interactionist approach to establishing a classroom management policy with high school students. Is it an approach that you would use and, if so, in what circumstances?

How do these children illustrate the important elements of Glasser's control theory?

2 The length of meeting should depend on the age of the children: for early grades, 10 to 30 minutes; for older grades, 30 to 45 minutes.
3 Problems and topics for discussion are those that emerge from the needs of the group.
4 Students should feel free to express their opinions and feelings without fear: there are no right or wrong answers.
5 The teacher leads the discussion but does not make evaluative comments; it is important for the teacher to keep the discussion focused by summarising or paraphrasing what students say.
6 The goal of the meeting is to solve the problem in a positive way and come up with a plan of action that is agreed upon by all participants—this may need a couple of meetings.
7 *Action* is important following the discussion. There should be no 'letting off the hook'. Teachers and students see that what is decided actually occurs.

Where a student has broken rules, Glasser recommends a technique called **reality therapy**. *Reality therapy* is based on the premise that each individual has a need for self-worth and that, in order to feel worthwhile, they must maintain a satisfactory standard of behaviour (Wilkins 1987). Using this approach, the teacher focuses on helping the student to evaluate their behaviour and make some efforts to improve it. When a student misbehaves, therefore, the teacher must avoid making judgments and assigning blame; instead, the teacher should use direct questioning to encourage self-evaluation and accountability in the student in the following way:

1 The student is confronted and told to stop the misbehaviour: 'Jake, sit back down in your seat.'
2 The student is then asked to *explain* the behaviour that was occurring. The teacher uses 'What' questions, not 'Why': 'What are you doing?' This prevents the student from finding excuses such as 'I had to get up because he stole my pencil' and draws attention to the *cause* of the problem (self-evaluation).
3 If the rule-breaking behaviour continues, step 2 is repeated, adding 'Is it against the rules?' Here the emphasis is on the *consequences* of the behaviour (student responsibility): 'If you continue to do this, what will happen?'
4 The teacher asks the student to make a *plan* or commitment to finding alternatives: 'What are you going to do about your behaviour?' or 'What is your plan, so that you don't break the rule again?'
5 Sometimes the student may be asked to go to the 'castle' (Glasser's term for the *isolation desk or corner in the classroom*) until the problem is worked out. This isolation is a logical consequence of breaking the class rules. This step is vital, as it places responsibility with the student for their own behaviour and for finding alternatives (accountability).
6 If the rule-breaking behaviour still persists, steps 2–5 are repeated but the teacher indicates that support will be provided: 'We have to work it out.' The teacher arranges a specific time and location in the near future to help in the development of the plan and to provide encouragement for it to work. The student is allowed to return to the class after a solution has been arrived at.
7 If the student fails to fulfil their commitment and plan, the next step is *isolation to a designated room* (principal's office or special isolation room). Steps 2–5 are repeated by the principal, grade supervisor or school counsellor, who has been notified earlier. Parents may be involved in solving the problem.
8 If the student is out of control, the parents are notified and asked to collect the student immediately. The student may return to the school when they are able to obey the rules.
9 If all else fails, the parents and student are referred to an outside agency to 'work it out'.

As for the notion of punishment, Glasser sees that the use of teacher-imposed punishment for failing to keep to a plan is counterproductive to students' development of a sense of self-control. He sees it as more beneficial for them to suffer the logical consequences of not abiding by class rules for behaviour—that is, exclusions from the class—together with the natural consequence of failing to follow their plan—that of having to start all over again on a new one.

The teacher's role in reality therapy

One of the most important features of Glasser's discipline plan is his emphasis on the need for the teacher to give positive attention to students when they are *not* breaking the rules: wish them 'Good morning' when they arrive at school, reward them for effort, simply acknowledge them in a pleasant manner when they are around. In other words, develop a positive relationship with students, letting them see you as genuinely warm, as well as firm in your resolve to have them abide by the rules. Furthermore, it is vital that you examine what *you* are doing to cope with discipline problems and how effective your methods are: do you ridicule or threaten students? Does this work, or does it merely encourage hostility and further misbehaviour?

Since 1985, Glasser has adopted a different philosophy to discipline called **control theory** (Glasser 1992). As with reality therapy, the focus in control theory is on the *causes* of misbehaviour. However, whereas reality therapy places

How do these children illustrate the important elements of Glasser's control theory?

these causes with the student, control theory maintains that it is the school's responsibility to prevent student misbehaviour. Specifically, Glasser has advocated in his new theory that discipline problems will not erupt if schools fulfil powerful student needs for belonging, power, fun and freedom. In other words, student behaviours—in fact, all our behaviours—are efforts to control our lives. His approach should be compared with that of Maslow (see Chapter 13). Certainly, in some schools the importance of fulfilling student needs has been demonstrated in the establishment of breakfast programs for primary schoolchildren. Glasser maintains that the major problems in schools are not defiance or hostility from students, which requires teacher control, but rather apathy and unwillingness to participate in learning activities through boredom. His philosophy is a *humanistic* one: motivation cannot be coerced or manipulated externally, as the *behaviourists* would argue—it comes from within the individual.

Three basic notions stand out in control theory:

1 Schools must meet the basic psychological needs of students for *belonging* (security, comfort and group membership), *power* (importance, status, being taken into account by others), *fun* (having an emotionally and intellectually good time) and *freedom* (being able to choose, to be self-directed and to have responsibility).

2 The way in which curriculum material is presented in teacher-directed methods must be replaced by 'quality' schoolwork in which skills are developed, not facts learned, and learning that has been traditionally evaluated by achievement tests alone should incorporate *student self-evaluation* as well.

3 Teachers must become 'lead-managers' who make learning interesting and help students, rather than 'boss-managers' who dictate in their teaching and discipline (Glasser 1992). Boss-managers turn students into adversaries by relying on coercion and criticism, which are not conducive to encouraging high-quality work in students. Lead-management, on the other hand, is non-coercive; it encourages cooperative learning which gives students power and, therefore, the incentive to work harder.

The teacher's role in a '**quality school**' is to use the skills of problem solving and persuasion to show students how it is in their best interests to produce high-quality work. Of course, the school environment must provide the tools (*curriculum* and *resources*) and the atmosphere (*non-coercive* and *cooperative*) for this to be feasible (Glasser 1992, 1993).

QUESTION POINT

What are your thoughts on this approach to teaching and management? To what extent are you prepared to organise your teaching and the class to meet students' psychological needs; or do you believe that students should fit in with your needs as the teacher?

Looking at the two approaches advocated by Glasser, we feel that both offer valuable insights for managing student learning and behaviour. Control theory is an ideal that may genuinely foster *intrinsic motivation* in students, thereby preventing much misbehaviour. Reality therapy gives the teacher an organised and proven method for encouraging the development of student self-management, and for dealing with problems once they erupt. *Cooperative learning strategies* (see later in this chapter) provide ideal opportunities for students to satisfy their needs and gain a sense of control at school. How is this so?

- *Belonging:* By working together in teams on learning tasks, students develop a sense of mutual interdependence and motivation to achieve.
- *Freedom and power:* Students who are academically more able gain a sense of power from helping those in their group who are less able. All students gain a sense of importance and self-worth from their contributions to the group project. Later in this chapter, we describe in greater detail how to structure cooperative tasks so that each member of a group has an equally valuable part to play.
- *Fun:* When students work cooperatively together on exciting projects, 'fun' is guaranteed.

The quality school

According to Glasser (1993), in a 'quality school' the focus should be on quality learning and teaching (see Table 8.8). This can be achieved through some key strategies that are reminiscent of many of the ideas we have already discussed in Chapter 1.

Nelson, Lott and Glenn's 'positive discipline in the classroom' approach

Nelson, Lott and Glenn's (1997) approach to discipline is based on a belief in the capacity of students to control their own behaviour and to be responsible and cooperative. The system they have developed is not one based on rewards and punishments that are imposed by an authoritarian figure. Rather, it is a democratic one in which the teacher encourages students to think about the causes of classroom problems and conflicts in an effort to find solutions to them, both individually and in class meetings. This notion of 'solutions' that help students to develop life skills is a critical one in their program and is contrasted with the 'logical consequences' which they maintain are often just disguised punishments to make students 'pay for' their mistakes. The following example illustrates the important difference (see Charles 1999).

Positive discipline in the classroom

Let's imagine that there is a problem with several students who claim they were late for class because they did not hear the recess bell. Using the positive discipline approach, the teacher would bring this problem to a class meeting at which the class would be asked first to brainstorm possible consequences for the inappropriate behaviour, and then to brainstorm a second time for possible solutions that would help to prevent the problem next time. Why don't you try this exercise yourself before you find out what the students came up with?

'Consequences' versus 'solutions'

As *consequences*, the class suggests:

- Putting names on the board.
- Staying in after school for the length of time that they were late to class.
- Losing time from the following day's recess.
- Forfeiting their recess the next day.

In contrast, their *solutions* are:

- Having a friend tap them on the shoulder when the bell goes.
- Have a buddy remind them about coming in from recess.
- Ask for the bell to be louder.
- Locate themselves closer to the bell during their play.

There is a great deal of difference between the two lists, isn't there? Through such a process, students are shown that their teacher has high expectations of their ability to solve their own problems without being told what they have done wrong and how to fix it. Nelson, Lott and Glenn consider that enduring skills of effective communication, showing respect, collaborating with others and having a positive attitude are developed progressively with this way. Many more ideas will be found in reading their work.

Albert's 'cooperative discipline' approach

The value of structuring learning activities as cooperative interactions is discussed later in this chapter. Here we outline what Linda Albert (1996a, 1996b, 1996c) has to offer in the way of cooperative approaches to discipline. The extensive range of strategies she has developed builds largely on the ideas of Dreikurs—namely, his notion that by meeting students' needs in positive ways they can be encouraged to find alternatives to unacceptable behaviour. This brief overview will highlight some of these. The reader is advised to consult Albert's extensive list of publications to gain a full appreciation of her program for educators and administrators.

What is **cooperative discipline**? Albert believes strongly that students will choose to cooperate with their teacher about their behaviour when they have a strong sense of belonging in the classroom. This sense of

Table 8.8

Essentials of quality teaching for quality learning

Teachers should:

- ensure that learning activities take place in a caring, supportive environment in which teachers show their willingness to help;
- require students to learn what they can demonstrate to be useful and valuable skills and information for students' lives;
- encourage students to put in their best effort and then have them evaluate their own work without grading it. Have students improve the work further;
- teach students to apply the acronym *SIR* until they have achieved the best quality in their work: **s**elf-evaluation, **i**mprovement and **r**epetition;
- help students to recognise that doing quality work will produce positive and pleasant feelings in them.

(Source: Based on Glasser 1993)

EXTENSION STUDY

The Canters' assertive discipline model

Lee and Marlene Canter (1976, 1992; Canter 1990) have developed a program for *corrective* classroom control known as **assertive discipline** (or positive behaviour management), which is widely used in many schools today. This behaviourist approach puts the teacher in control of student behaviour through the use of reinforcement and punishment. Many practising educators maintain that assertive discipline allows them to use class time more productively for teaching rather than disciplining students. In theory, teachers can prevent discipline problems from occurring by issuing a warning because students have a clear understanding of the consequences of keeping and breaking the rules.

We look first at the important features of the approach and then consider some of the major criticisms of it made by educational experts. Think about whether this is the approach that best suits your views of classroom management.

First, the notion of 'assertiveness' is clarified. The Canters distinguish between non-assertive, hostile and assertive teachers:

- *Non-assertive:* 'For the sixth time, boys, will you please try your best to stop talking and finish your work?' (Doesn't really convince students that the teacher expects them to change their behaviour.)
- *Hostile:* 'Okay. I've had it! The next person who opens their mouth will have the whole class staying back after school to clean up the playground!' (Communicates teacher dislike of students and establishes an atmosphere of mutual mistrust and vengeance.)
- *Assertive:* 'John, you know it's against the rules to talk when I am teaching. This is the second time: please move to the timeout desk.' (Businesslike communication of reasonable teacher expectations and disapproval followed by a clear indication of what the student is to do.)

The Canters' aim is to establish a positive discipline system that reinforces the teacher's authority to teach and to control in order to ensure an environment that is optimal for learning. They recommend that this be done in the following way.

At the outset

1. Select the behaviours expected of the students together with the positive and negative consequences.
2. Seek the principal's support for the list of rules.
3. Discuss the expected behaviours and their consequences with the students in the first class meeting.
4. Have students write the rules and consequences on paper and take it home for parents to read and sign.
5. Emphasise that the rules have been made to ensure effective learning and appropriate behaviour.
6. Teach the behaviours that you want from students in particular situations. For example, if you require students to stay seated during group work but will allow 'quiet talking', then you must explain the directions for this behaviour clearly and teach these by modelling and checking for understanding: students can demonstrate the correct behaviour by practising in an actual example. Have the students repeat orally what the rules are and their consequences.

Once introduced

1. Use positive repetition to reinforce students when they are correctly following the directions: 'Kasper put his hand up before he spoke. Thank you.'
2. Apply positive and negative consequences, which have already been defined and communicated to the students earlier, as appropriate.

You will notice that these are not 'logical' consequences, as described earlier in the chapter. In effect, the 'consequences' advocated by the Canters are rewards and punishments in the behavioural sense (Cairns 1995).

The Canters believe that positive consequences are more powerful in shaping student behaviour than negative ones. If students deliberately violate the rules, the Canters suggest that the negative consequences that result should be graded in severity, according to the number of times the offence is repeated during the lesson or day (each day starts afresh), as follows:

1. First offence—a warning (name recorded privately not publicly such as on the chalkboard, as this can either humiliate students or, in some cases, serve to feed their attention-seeking needs). This should be done without interrupting the lesson.
2. Second offence—10-minute timeout (within-class isolation).
3. Third offence—15-minute timeout.
4. Fourth offence—parents contacted.
5. Fifth offence—sent to principal.

For students who are very disruptive, the Canters approach recommends two control techniques: 'moving-in' and the 'freeze' approach. *Moving-in* involves the teacher walking up to the student, using eye contact and gesture when speaking to the student, and stating the consequences that the student has chosen with their behaviour: 'By throwing your books around the room, you have chosen to go to detention after school.' The *freeze* technique, for example, has the teacher saying 'freeze' to the offending student in an assertive tone, and then stating the rules that should be followed in this instance. Sometimes the *broken record* method is also used in cases of misbehaviour. This is merely the repetition of the rules and consequences in the face of persistent argument:

Teacher: Kate, either stop speaking or choose to do your work at lunchtime.
Kate: That's not fair, Mario and Peter were talking, too!
Teacher: You will stop speaking now or spend 15 minutes at lunchtime.
Kate: I can't stay in at lunchtime because I have drama practice.
Teacher: You have now chosen to stay in the classroom for 15 minutes at lunchtime to finish your work. If you continue to speak now, you will be choosing to stay for half an hour.

Of course, in the case of serious misbehaviour that is potentially harmful, approaching the student could be dangerous, as could be imposing consequences. If there is no fighting involved, giving verbal directions in a strong, calm and clear voice, and even waiting until the student had cooled down and following up later, is advised. In the case of fighting, physical intervention by the teacher along with verbal commands may be unavoidable. Should there be any threat by a student of using weapons, collegial assistance should be sent for urgently while using the 'broken record' technique of repeating instructions slowly to the offender in an authoritative tone (DiGiulio 1995).

Some argue that the assertive teacher (in the style of the Canters) is too dominant and harsh, and focuses more on preventing undesirable behaviour than on providing opportunities for students to develop responsibility for their own behaviour, an important social skill, particularly as students get older. Another criticism is that teachers make excessive use of rewards and punishments with the effect that motivation is externally controlled, not intrinsic to the students. In other words, students are trained to respond to anticipated positive and negative consequences, rather than being taught the value of responsible behaviour for its own sake. What are your feelings on this?

Despite the longevity of the assertive discipline approach and its claims of effectiveness by classroom teachers and administrators (McCormack 1989), some would argue that it is most appropriately used only in severe cases of inappropriate behaviour. Critics of the approach maintain that it has not been scientifically compared with other discipline approaches to see which is more effective (Render, Padilla & Krank 1989). The research evidence, however, that has been conducted in before and after implementation settings has shown that it does improve students' self-perceptions, student behaviour, time-on-task and teacher satisfaction, as well as reducing classroom disruptions (McCormack 1989).

In the final analysis, it is worth remembering that the 'success' of any student discipline policy should be measured by the extent to which it supports teaching and learning, rather than the degree of order and quiet in the classroom (Evertson 1995).

belonging can be fostered in educational settings with the '**three Cs**': teachers and parents helping students to feel *capable*, *connected* with others in the classroom, and able to make *contributions* in the class and outside. Clearly, these are ingredients for building anyone's self-esteem, aren't they? A summary of Albert's main ideas for fostering cooperation is given in Table 8.9.

QUESTION POINT

Of the approaches to classroom management and discipline that have been described up to this point, which appeal to you the most? What is your own personal philosophy on the approach that would best support your teaching and the learning of your students?

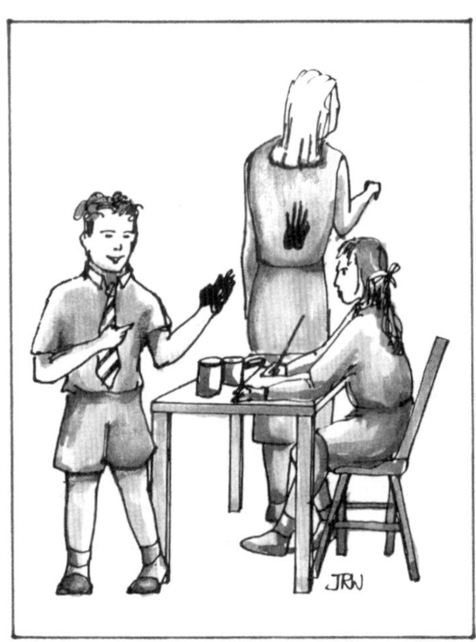

'I think it improves her dress.'

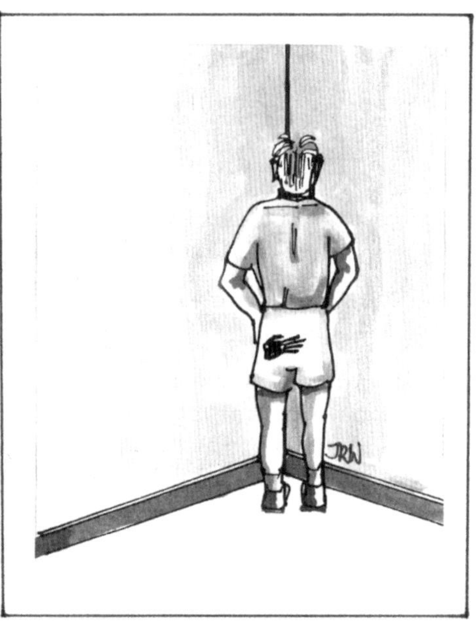

'I think it improves my behaviour!'

Table 8.9

Essentials of using cooperative discipline

Teachers should:

- teach students that their behaviour is their choice;
- help students to feel valued in the classroom;
- recognise that student misbehaviour is motivated by needs to avoid failure, feel powerful, gain attention or obtain revenge;
- realise that they can have an influence on student behaviour but cannot control it;
- remember that a democratic style of management reaps more rewards than stern control or permissiveness;
- plan their classroom interactions in line with the three Cs: help students to feel capable, able to contribute and connected;
- cooperate with students in planning their classroom code of conduct and consequences;
- maintain a dialogue with parents about their use of cooperative discipline approaches and enlist their support;
- remember to model self-control at all times;
- desist from power struggles with students—remain calm but businesslike and firm;
- encourage, encourage, encourage students in their correct choices of behaviour.

(Source: Based on Albert 1996a, 1996b; Charles 1999)

'Well, Eddie, I was speaking figuratively when I said to get out there and tear them apart.'

What elements of cooperative group learning are evident here?

Cooperative learning and classroom management

In educational circles internationally, there is a growing interest in the benefits of grouping children for learning. Classroom grouping is an important management function that has implications for effective learning and classroom behaviour. Typically, classrooms and lessons can be structured in one of three ways: individualistically, competitively or cooperatively. In *individualistic* goal structures the student is expected to do the very best that they can, alone. Achieving individually does not interfere with the achievement of others. Rewards are based on the extent to which a student's performance meets specified standards, not on how well or poorly the student performs in comparison with others. When *competitive* goal structures are used, success and rewards are determined by others' 'failure', by 'beating' other students: for there to be a winner (the scorer of the 'A' grade) there must also be a loser, or many losers. Currently, there is considerable interest in the use of *cooperative* goal structures in which students work together to achieve or complete shared or common tasks. In this context, the success of individuals depends on the success of *all* members of the group: helping each other to achieve in groups ensures both individual and group rewards.

Typically, teachers report that cooperative group work is most effective when student interaction will enhance

See what happens when individuals cooperate.

EXTENSION STUDY

A cross-cultural perspective on classroom management and discipline

It is important at this point to pause and reflect on the extent to which these management and discipline principles apply to a classroom that is not homogeneous in cultural background or is culturally different. In other words, how do you, if at all, modify your discipline approach to accommodate the ethnic composition of your class group? According to Partington and McCudden (1992, p. 159):

> The purpose of an effective management program should be to accommodate the needs of students in a supportive manner, not punish them for behaviours which are a consequence of their different upbringing and different perceptions of issues that gave rise to the disruptive behaviour.

What are some of the differences that teachers may need to be aware of?

Communication with parents

Here is an example from our own experience. It was pick-up time for young Nicholas who had just started in Grade 4 after moving to a new school. To his mother's polite inquiry about Nicholas's behaviour for the first week, his new young female teacher's response was that Nicholas had 'been a bit cheeky at lunchtime today', claiming that he didn't have to pick up a juice carton and put it in the garbage bin because it wasn't his. The next day, Nicholas arrived at class badly bruised about the body and face, having been punished at home by his migrant parents for speaking rudely to the teacher. (The bruises were the result of his insistence at home that he merely told the teacher that the carton was not his and that he had not been cheeky.)

The incident demonstrates how cultural background can contribute to discipline problems. Nicholas's socialisation had encouraged him to feel confident in his (male) right to assert a point of view, as did his two older brothers, especially in response to a directive issued by a female. (His mother is always submissive to her husband's authority.) His parents saw the incident primarily from the perspective of family dignity—in this case, it was very important for the family to be accepted in the new school community, largely upper-middle-class Anglos. (Nicholas's father was a builder and keen to make business contacts.) Doing what the teacher says was one way of earning a good reputation.

The lesson learned by the teacher? To be very careful about communications given to parents about students' misbehaviour, and to be aware of the cultural 'baggage' that students bring with them to school.

Expectations about authority

Different expectations exist with regard to teacher authority. There is a danger of government policies on classroom discipline running counter to the cultural values of a number of minority groups (Lewis 1993, personal communication). For example, Orthodox Jews, New Zealand Maoris and Arabic-speaking groups may take exception to the teacher engaging in dialogue with students about the rules for classroom control. After all, the teacher is expected to lead and control the classroom, and students are required to be obedient. Like the elders in these cultures, teachers represent authority. In these cultures the philosophy is that teachers and parents must be strict and not enter into any discussion with students over misbehaviour. Today, young people are bombarded with messages that exhort them to demand an equal hearing. Conflict is often the result of the mixture of expectations that children receive from school and home.

The role of females

In some Middle Eastern and other cultures, females are traditionally accorded lower status in society and, consequently, female teachers may not be recognised as authority figures, particularly in upper primary and high school grades. Among Orthodox Jews, the role of women in the decision-making process is quite clearly defined. Although the female has status and power in family matters, it is the male who makes and enforces laws (Lewis 1993, personal communication). Jewish parents may be very concerned, therefore, about their daughters being encouraged to be involved in making classroom rules—for example, in Glasser's (1992) democratic classroom meeting approach.

Teacher as educational expert

Some cultures expect the teacher to be the fount of all knowledge from whom students should receive constant help and regular homework. In a classroom where the teacher tries to encourage students to learn independently through guided discovery or inquiry-based approaches, students may feel confused about how to respond to the freedom, and react in a disorderly way. Because of their affiliation orientation, groups such as Aboriginal Australians may prefer collaboration to individualised work where students sit one to a desk. Teachers may regard the 'sharing of ideas' by some groups of students as plagiarism. Negative comments from parents regarding the appropriateness of various 'new' teaching strategies may also undermine teacher authority.

There may also be a clash when the teacher, perceived as an expert in a limited area (formal school curriculum), presumes to act as an expert in culturally sensitive areas. For example, while the Pitjantjatjara are willing to accept the prerogative of teachers in English and mathematics, they are very resentful of teachers attempting to teach Aboriginal languages and cultural traditions, which they believe is their prerogative. Furthermore, they ultimately believe that they have the right to authorise the content of much that is taught in the school so that it does not conflict with cultural values. The tension existing over who is the appropriate expert at particular times can flow over into classroom interactions between teacher and students, with students disparaging the teacher's efforts and expertise (Folds 1987).

On the other hand, parents of some groups such as Arabic-speaking children do not believe it is their place to question the teacher about class or school issues; in fact, they may feel quite inadequate educationally to do so. As Campbell *et al.* (1992, p. 62) comment, 'a lack of understanding of the Australian school system makes Arabic-speaking parents reluctant to be directly involved with the school'. This attitude may translate to Australian teachers as lack of interest and set the stage for poor communication.

Some students may have been socialised not to 'argue' with the teacher or to indicate that they are having difficulty. These students may not give explanations for incomplete work or show that they are confused.

'Good manners' and proper behaviour

Differences in values and the nature of interpersonal communication resulting from socialisation within particular cultural groups can lead to severe clashes between teacher and students (Malin 1990). Values such as autonomy, social equality and affiliation may be demonstrated quite differently across cultural groups. Teacher-established behavioural norms for these values may conflict with those of culturally different students. As Malin (1990, p. 318) states:

> The autonomous and affiliative orientation of many of the Aboriginal students [in her study] was evident in their responses to classroom life in quite remarkable ways. The unfortunate thing was that the teachers were largely unaware that they were witnessing culturally based expressions of a particular competence which had been valued in these children's previous four years at home. Instead some expressions of this autonomy were interpreted, by one teacher in particular, as disrespect for her, as defiance, and as a lack of acceptance of the legitimacy of her role as teacher.

Illustrating from her case study, Malin goes on to say that the autonomous orientation of many Aboriginal students means at times that they ignore teacher directives, either by delaying their response, not responding at all or walking away from teachers while they are in the process of addressing them. The children are oblivious initially to the teacher's expectations that they maintain eye contact while being addressed and then acknowledge that they have heard and understood what is being said to them. These behaviours are not meant to be disrespectful, but rather illustrate the children's need for a degree of self-regulation, and their feeling of proprietorship for their classroom. Their slowness at complying carries the assumption, brought from home, that within certain bounds adults and children hold mutual respect for each other.

The manner in which students respond to a teacher's question may also be a reflection of cultural background and this can get them into trouble. For example, in Pitjantjatjara society respect is shown to another person by inclining the head away and making infrequent eye contact (for example, see Folds 1987). Teachers, however, may regard the downcast eyes as an indication of insolence and insist that the student 'Look at me when I speak to you!' The teacher's response may compound the problem so that, in retaliation, students may engage in a highly exaggerated form of avoidance, characterised by a complete lack of eye contact or any other form of recognition (Folds 1987; Malin 1990).

Folds (1987; see also Munns 1996) highlights forms of behaviour that Aboriginal students engage in when attempting to resist culturally different expectations of behaviour—absenteeism, and classroom resistance consisting of ridicule and disruption, and the 'wall of silence'. The most pervasive form is the 'wall of silence' when students refuse to communicate with the teacher, failing to respond to the teacher's solicitations or directions to do something.

Language and effective communication

Students who come to school with little or no English can become uncooperative and troublesome if they experience ridicule for mistakes with language. It is desirable for such students to be allocated a 'buddy' who is prepared to offer friendship and who will encourage conversation that focuses on meaning rather than correctness. Teachers should take care with polite expressions they may use in the classroom which really communicate a more assertive message. For example, saying 'You might like to finish this . . . for homework' may be taken literally by some students who are less familiar with subtleties of the language.

It is important to remember that many minority group students who come in as refugees, especially the older ones, have already received a significant proportion of their education before their arrival in our schools and, in some cases, this may have been at a standard in advance of the rest of their class. It can be very demoralising and frustrating for these students to find, for example, that numerical notation or the direction of writing and reading have to be unlearned or, at least, relearned in a new form. (The division symbol in Vietnam is (:), the multiplication sign in Chile is (.) and the decimal marker in Laos is (,).)

Frustration felt by such students, aggravated by teacher impatience and student ridicule, can erupt into misbehaviour. Sometimes these students are inappropriately placed into lower-ability groups on the basis of achievement and psychological tests. It is important to make an accurate diagnosis of the 'slow learner' as distinct from the student with 'inadequate English'. Research on the factors contributing to Aboriginal and ethnic minority group disenchantment and dropping out of school has shown that incorrectly streaming minority group children into low-ability groups is one of the major contributors to their entry into the cycle of self-defeating problem behaviours in school (McInerney & McInerney 1990; see also Simkin 1991).

Taboos

Many groups have cultural *taboos*. The head is considered by a number of Asian cultures as an altar to their ancestors and the fount of the mind or soul. Thus, patting the head of a student or waving something over it would be regarded as disrespectful, as would standing over someone who is seated. Others consider the left hand the 'toilet' hand and its use in handing something to another person in class or at meal times would be seen as quite vulgar (New South Wales Department of School Education 1990).

In some cultures, such as the Muslim, females are strictly constrained and not permitted to expose their bodies in public. This creates difficulty in a number of school-related areas to do with participation in sporting activities such as swimming and those involving contact with males, as well as participation in sex education lessons and excursions (McInerney *et al.* 2000; McInerney, Dowson & Yeung 2004).

Establishing effective management in culturally mixed classrooms

Some words of qualification should be noted about the concerns expressed above. It is clear that significant cultural differences may exacerbate discipline and management problems in some classrooms. There is a danger, however, in making generalisations about groups based on stereotypes.

Some minority group students (such as Aboriginal and Maori), who may have little confidence in themselves as students in the mainstream educational system, and who see little value in education generally, may be predisposed to misbehave or drop out. In these cases, discipline based on the behaviourist model of reward and punishment will be ineffective as this focuses on the end product—the problem behaviour, or lack of it—rather than the cause of the problem.

Fostering a positive classroom climate

What is the answer to the dilemma of establishing effective discipline in culturally mixed classrooms? The teacher's task in the first instance is to foster a classroom climate that is responsive to differing student learning styles. This can be achieved by systematically varying teaching methods and activities to accommodate student differences. In this way, all students can experience cooperative grouping, individual work, peer tutoring, structured and informal discussions, and questioning in accordance with their cultural expectations (Simkin 1991). In cross-cultural classrooms, cooperative learning structures are superior to those that focus on competition and individualistic goals in fostering positive relationships between different groups (Johnson & Johnson 1989b). Where such positive attitudes and relationships flourish, discipline problems will diminish (Abrami *et al.* 1995)

There needs to be a compromise between the teacher adopting a *laissez-faire* policy which allows all forms of behaviour in the classroom and an autocratic one in which the conventions of the majority culture rule (Simkin 1991). This compromise is reached through negotiation within the classroom as to the rules that are acceptable and that will encourage harmony and effective learning. This is preferable to forcing students into behaving in ways that they see as culturally 'wrong', wherein lies the potential for tension and hostility.

Establishing mutual respect

For successful management in culturally diverse classrooms, the effective teacher must establish an environment built on genuine mutual respect where difference and similarity are equally valued. An important factor in this process is that of building self-esteem in all students, regardless of cultural background. The teacher fosters the development of positive attitudes in a variety of ways: by acting as a model for positive behaviour through avoiding ridicule and punishment; by providing opportunities for all students to demonstrate proficiency in some area that is not necessarily academic; by the use of cooperative grouping for class activities (Cohen 1994b) as well as other means of ensuring interaction between students, such as shared interests; and by establishing rules for class behaviour, ideally derived from democratic classroom decisions. The difficulties in actually implementing such an approach have been examined earlier.

Consulting with parents

It is strongly recommended that opportunities be made for consultation between school and parents about the issues of greatest concern with regard to classroom discipline. As Lewis recommends, both groups need to identify which cultural values are 'not negotiable' (the complexity of this becomes obvious when there are many minority groups within the one school). Both sides must resolve a way of accommodating such values. One option is separate schooling, which has been suggested by some Aboriginal and Maori groups as the most effective solution for their dissatisfaction with the mainstream education system (Folds 1987; Teasdale & Teasdale 1993).

It is interesting to note here that by far the majority of Arabic-speaking parents choose to send their children to single-sex schools rather than having to compromise on cultural values. This is in keeping with one interpretation of what a multicultural society is: one within which cultural groups have the right to maintain their individual identity, and not have to adopt the ideals of the majority. Another view is that a truly multicultural society is one in which 'inter-cultural' understanding and interaction takes place and, as such, all groups give some ground. When applied to the area of classroom discipline, this approach would mean that minority and majority groups alike need to expose students to all the options, even if one is more strongly endorsed. Thus, Muslim and Jewish girls may be prevented from participation in decision making if this is requested by parents; however, they should be made aware that the process of democratic decision making is the one that is endorsed by the state in the country in which their parents have chosen to settle.

learning such as in learning complex conceptual material. There is no advantage for students to use cooperative learning structures for activities that involve completing merely factual or computational tasks where the fastest worker or the one who knows the answers will 'share' with the rest of the group (Cohen 1994a, 1994b). This isn't to say that cooperative learning approaches are not effective for lower-level tasks such as recall of factual information, decoding and motor skills: they are (Slavin 1990). Probably of greater interest to us as educators, however, is the very strong research evidence that cooperative efforts at higher-level tasks such as problem solving are superior to competitive or even individualistic ones for students of all ages from preschoolers to adults (Johnson, Johnson & Stanne 2000; Qin, Johnson & Johnson 1995). Specifically, for problems expressed in words such as discussion and essay questions, mathematical problems, figures, mazes and puzzles, and creative problems requiring imagery or novel representations, cooperative groups are better able to find solutions than those who work competitively or alone.

Cognitive value

If, on the other hand, the goal is the development of harmonious interpersonal relationships, especially of an intercultural nature, the research evidence for the use of team-based approaches (such as STAD, TGT, Jigsaw and Group Investigation, described later in the chapter) also shows strong positive effects (Slavin 1990). In addition, low-achieving students find that their achievement is enhanced because they must seek to clarify any lack of understanding in order to contribute to the group goal. This is more motivating than merely performing a task because the teacher says so. Also, the low expectations held by low-status students are dissipated as group members discover similarities other than academic ones, and also find that the final product of collaboration is far richer than any one individual could produce.

Social value

Planning to use cooperative learning in the classroom

If you think you would like to try a cooperative learning approach to a learning activity, Abrami *et al.* (1995) recommend that you ask yourself the following questions first. Can this work be done better in a group than individually? That is, will the mix of different abilities, viewpoints and creative talents be an advantage? Is the task so large or complex that only a group can handle it? If the answers are 'yes', then you have a recipe for success. If, on the other hand, you have answered 'no', then it is unlikely that students will put a great deal of effort into a group project which they feel they would do better or enjoy independently. Group tasks must be carefully planned and structured by the teacher so that cooperative interaction between students is required for successful completion: students must understand what the objectives are, what their individual responsibilities are, and how these are interrelated with those of other team members. In fact, research has shown that the most effective cooperative learning techniques incorporate both group goals and individual accountability (Abrami *et al.* 1995).

QUESTION POINT

What are the types of management issues that you would need to consider when planning to make cooperative learning activities a regular part of your teaching?

Cooperative group work and classroom management

Needless to say, students who are productively engaged are unlikely to cause discipline problems. In the traditional classroom, where the teacher directs the flow of student interaction and conversation, management of behaviour is less complex than in the cooperative classroom. Ideally, in terms of enhancing student learning outcomes, cooperative techniques (carefully structured so that students *are* productively engaged) enable the teacher to spend more time giving direct instruction to specific groups as needed, as well as to act as a consultant to all groups. However, in relation to cooperative learning the following question is often raised: 'If students are allowed to argue or debate among themselves while they work on group projects, won't serious management problems develop that will be too hard to control?' We would be lying if we said that you will not find the implementation of cooperative strategies demanding in terms of management, at least until the students have become accustomed to the skills required in collaboration. Nonetheless, the evidence is clearly in favour of the benefits of consistent use of cooperative learning approaches over a period of time, especially in terms of social skills which contribute to improved classroom behaviour (Jordan 1997). In Table 8.10 we list some helpful hints that can get you started and minimise potential problems. Before that, what were some of those classroom management issues you were thinking of?

Issues that generally present themselves as problems are the following:

- noise;
- seating arrangements;
- presenting students with directions;
- accessing materials for collaborative use; and
- dealing with inappropriate behaviours that violate the norms for cooperation—not helping others, put-downs, arguments, bullying and loafing.

Establishing cooperative learning in the classroom

As indicated in the earlier part of this chapter, the establishment of clear behavioural and learning expectations by the teacher is critical for effective classroom management. The same principle applies to the use of cooperative learning approaches. The first few weeks of the year are the ideal time to begin. During this period the teacher should establish a cooperative learning atmosphere in which students develop a sense of trust in

Table 8.10 Essentials of getting started with cooperative learning in the classroom

Teachers should:

- plan well ahead: set realistic and attainable goals for the activity and communicate these to the students;
- begin with small-scale topics and group composition with which you are likely to be successful: don't be too ambitious at the start;
- use very small groups (pairs) at first and increase size to threes or fours later;
- restrict the first cooperative activity to less than 15 minutes;
- design the activity to require group processes;
- use a 'quiet signal' or 'noise meter' to help students monitor and control noise levels;
- evaluate the outcomes of the group collaboration in terms of your planning and learning objectives. Have the students do the same;
- experiment with a variety of cooperative approaches: it takes a lot of practice to master any teaching approach. Students also need to learn how to work collaboratively: it will come with the teacher modelling and mentoring appropriate behaviours and dialogue.

(Source: Based on Abrami *et al.* 1995; Cooper 1999)

and appreciation of each other. Fear of making mistakes or of not being 'the best', competitive concerns which inhibit collaborative interaction and learning, should be progressively eliminated through class-building and team-building activities such as those described by Spencer Kagan (1994) in his book *Cooperative Learning*.

Kagan also recommends that rules for cooperative behaviour, even better described as 'class norms', should be formulated by the students where appropriate rather than presented by the teacher. One way of doing this is to have the students reflect on how they feel when participating in group work themselves. What feels good? What makes it work? What spoils it? Perhaps you can also think about that now, from your own experiences? The norms can be broken down into two categories: those that relate to personal responsibility (I am responsible for these types of behaviours: . . .); and those that relate to team responsibility (We are responsible for these types of behaviours . . .).

Box 8.4 illustrates the types of class norms that are useful.

Box 8.4

CLASS NORMS FOR COOPERATIVE BEHAVIOUR

Personally, I am responsible for:

- Helping my team-mates
- Asking for help
- Putting in my best effort
- Being polite
- Encouraging and praising

As a team, we are responsible for:

- Using quiet working voices
- Figuring out our own problems
- Asking each other before the teacher
- Helping other teams

ACTION STATION

Imagine that you have a Year 9 English class of boys for the year which is composed of a number of ethnic groups who do not work collaboratively in class, and call each other names or even fight in the playground. You are going to begin a six-week unit of work on the theme of 'What it is to be an Australian' after the next school holidays and have decided to adopt a cooperative learning approach instead of the traditional lecture and group discussion method.

Your aim is to improve the interpersonal relations between the students by devising activities that will help them to recognise their similarities, understand and appreciate their differences and begin to develop a class identity. What will you do when you first begin and then progressively over the six weeks?

Working with a group, brainstorm some of the possible ways in which your goals may be fulfilled.

The benefits of cooperative group learning

What are the positive outcomes, both cognitive and non-cognitive, that have been claimed for cooperative structures? As well as being an effective method of managing students (once they have learned the skills of collaboration), cooperative learning structures have been shown to improve academic achievement for students of a range of ability levels at primary and secondary school level, irrespective of subject area and type of school (Slavin 1991a, 1995; see also Buchs, Butera & Mugny 2004). Particular achievement gains have been shown in mathematics (Davidson 1991), verbal skills in social studies, reading, language, arts and English (Winitsky 1991) and computer-based learning (Rysavy & Sales 1991).

As for non-cognitive outcomes, it has been demonstrated that cooperative learning produces positive attitudes towards learning, raises self-concept and self-esteem, improves relationships between students, increases feelings of social support, and enhances acceptance of 'difference' such as minority group membership, gender or disability (Johnson & Johnson 1989–90; Wilkinson 1988–89). In fact, the evidence in favour of adopting cooperative learning as a method of improving non-academic classroom outcomes is far more clear-cut than that for academic achievement, where the research findings are not always consistent (Good & Brophy 1991). The reason for this difference in effects lies not so much in the strategy but in the methods used to synthesise the results of the many different research studies on the effects of cooperative strategies on achievement (Abrami *et al.* 1995).

Why does cooperative learning work?

There are two broad theoretical perspectives on why cooperative learning works: cognitive and motivational. Within the *cognitive* viewpoint, there are those (followers of Piaget and Vygotsky; see also Rohrbeck, Ginsburg-Block, Fantuzzo & Miller 2003) who support a *cognitive-developmental* view in which they argue that the cognitive benefits of cooperative learning derive from peer interaction around cognitive tasks. Damon (1984), for

Cognitive-developmental perspective

example, argues that student learning increases as a consequence of the cognitive conflicts that occur when discussion takes place between students who are at slightly different levels of cognitive development. The use of language during student–student interaction is a critical factor in enhancing thinking: when children argue their point of view with other children, verify it and criticise the opinions of others, they are engaging in generating a variety of ideas from which to learn.

In addition, there are those who argue for a *cognitive-elaboration* explanation of the cognitive processes underlying small-group cooperative interaction (Dansereau 1985). They maintain that for learning to take place there must be some form of cognitive restructuring in the mind of the learner. One way in which this takes place in a group learning situation is when concepts are elaborated, such as when explaining something to others who ask for help or clarification (Webb 1989; Webb & Farivar 1994). In the cognitive-elaboration view, both the person providing the elaborated explanation and the recipient of the help benefit cognitively. You have probably experienced this yourself—teaching something to someone else helped you to learn the material even better yourself. Why do you think that might be so? Theorists maintain that in explaining their thinking through a problem and the steps they took to find a solution, individuals trigger their metacognitive awareness—that is, thinking about their own thinking (Berardi-Coletta *et al.* 1995).

Cognitive-elaboration perspective

Finally, Johnson and Johnson (1992, 1994) advocate cooperative learning as a constructivist method for fostering cognitive processes. They support this assertion with the following reasons:

Cognitive constructivist perspective

- *Rehearsal:* peer discussions help the coding of information into memory through the need to explain, elaborate and summarise to group members.
- *Mixed groups:* the mix of abilities, learning styles and viewpoints towards the learning task within groups fosters divergent thinking.
- *Varied perspectives:* the need to take different perspectives on the task results in better understanding of their ideas.
- *Feedback:* peer feedback regarding the contributions of others is regularly provided throughout a group project. This may challenge group members to consider the value of their contribution in terms of its relevance and quality.
- *Conflict:* different opinions which may erupt into controversy promote critical thinking.

The second theoretical perspective is a *motivational* one (see, for example, Rohrbeck, Ginsburg-Block, Fantuzzo & Miller 2003). This focuses on understanding why individuals within a group are motivated to work interdependently for a common goal. We look here at three motivational approaches to cooperative interaction: (1) cooperative rewards, (2) morality-based cooperation, and (3) social interdependence. Some proponents of a motivational view of cooperative group interaction maintain that rewarding the group on the basis of individual achievements is a powerful way to motivate individual learning. *Cooperative reward structures* (extrinsic rewards or recognition based on the group's performance as a sum of individual achievements) can be gained only if the entire group is successful. Slavin (1987c, 1992), for example, would argue that building group incentives into the cooperative activity will motivate students to contribute and do their best. Theoretically, individual accountability for learning is encouraged by this approach.

As discussed elsewhere in this book, there is concern about the detrimental effects of extrinsic motivators on interest and intrinsic motivation (learning for its own sake). Slavin maintains that incentives need to be used when the material to be learned would not otherwise be found interesting or be engaged in willingly by students. However, he feels that any potential harmful effects of individual competition or motivation are compensated for by the encouragement and help of team members working for group rewards.

Should rewards be built into cooperative activities?

QUESTION POINT

What do you think about learning for group rather than individual rewards? What are some of the potential difficulties that may emerge when students are not of the same ability or equally disposed to work together? What strategies need to be adopted to protect against difficulties?

As described in the chapter on motivation (Chapter 7), Ames (1984) suggests that individual effort in cooperative interaction is motivated by a wish to help the group achieve its goal and to help others in order to do so. One's ability is less important in this situation than one's genuine attempts to contribute. Research has shown that when groups do not achieve well, however, those of low ability feel that it was their lack of ability rather than effort that was to blame (Abrami *et al.* 1992). When the group is successful, on the other hand, effort is considered more important. How might you prevent feelings of failure lowering the motivation of less able students if their group performs less successfully than others?

Morality-based motivation

Abrami *et al.* (1995) suggest three ways: (1) make sure that teams are not put in competition with each other; (2) have groups reflect on the process used to set goals and to achieve them ('What worked and what didn't?'); and (3) allocate group improvement points to encourage effort and persistence in addition to individual improvement points.

Johnson and Johnson not only argue for a cognitive rationale for cooperative learning but also put forward a strong motivational perspective on why some groups are successful in terms of learning (Johnson & Johnson 1992, 1994). This approach proposes that cooperative groups who are cohesive and work well together are motivated by the understanding that the success of the group is positively related to how well they work as a *team* and help each other. This positive social interdependence is a function of trust and can be fostered through many team-building activities, such as those developed by Kagan (1994) and his colleagues. Once this interdependence is established, the Johnsons believe that motivation to learn together follows and is shown in helping and negotiation behaviours.

Positive social interdependence

Four general approaches to learning in cooperative groups

While teachers have typically grouped students informally for discussions, projects and problem-solving activities, these group structures have not necessarily been 'cooperative'. Structured cooperative learning methods, which have particular defining characteristics, have been developed as a result of research over many decades. We will consider now some of the approaches to cooperative classroom organisation that have been shown to be effective for developing cognitive and social skills.

To give you insight into the range of approaches that are available to you, together with their advantages and disadvantages, we focus on four main models of cooperative learning:

- learning together (Johnson & Johnson);
- student team learning (Slavin);
- structures (Kagan); and
- group investigation (Sharan & Sharan).

The choice of approach to cooperative group work that you adopt will depend on the purpose of the task and the degree of student familiarity with the social skills involved in cooperative interaction.

Learning together (Johnson & Johnson)

According to Johnson and Johnson (1989c, 1994), for a lesson to be described as truly 'cooperative' there are certain criteria that apply. These are:

- positive interdependence;
- face-to-face interaction;
- individual accountability;
- collaborative skills; and
- group processing.

Positive interdependence means that students must demonstrably function as a group with a shared goal; one that 'sinks or swims together'. No individual who is more able or more assertive should be able to dominate the group. Such interdependence may be expressed in a variety of ways: a common product or goal; assignment of unique roles (task specialisations) that combine to form a whole; shared resources; and shared rewards for a group effort (the motivational perspective) which provide incentives for all members of the group to help each other.

Positive interdependence

It is important that tasks be set that require group members to have *face-to-face interaction*, rather than allowing for independent completion of discrete components that are merely combined as separate pieces at the end. Students must be able to reach consensus on what the task entails and how they can best help each other achieve the group goal. They must encourage and support each other's efforts to learn.

Face-to-face interaction

Cooperative learning strategies vary in the extent to which they use rewards based on group performance. In some approaches, group rewards are given only when all members of the group achieve their individual learning goals. The onus is on each member of the group to master their own particular material (which may be at a different level from other members), and to be responsible to the group for doing so: each individual is accountable for their contribution. The essential element here is that *the individual must feel a responsibility to participate*, either through intrinsic motivation, or extrinsic individual or group rewards based on the sum of all the individual contributions made.

Individual accountability

In other methods, rewards are given on the basis of a single group product. As mentioned earlier, developmentalists would reject, outright, the notion of extrinsic rewards for group learning (Damon 1984), maintaining that peer interaction alone is enough to increase student learning. Those who take a humanistic stand argue that intrinsic motivation for the task is destroyed when rewards are used to 'bribe students to work together' (Kohn 1991). Research conducted on cooperative learning approaches that use rewards has not shown this to be the case. Cooperative strategies that intentionally avoid using rewards have been shown to be no more effective than traditional classroom structures, which are competitive and individualistic, in terms of increasing academic achievement (Solomon *et al.* 1990).

Collaborative skills

Collaborative skills are crucial to effective cooperative learning. Students need to develop the skills required for working cooperatively. Not all students know how to work and to learn collaboratively; for that matter, probably a large proportion of the adult population could benefit by being taught such skills. Increasingly, employers are looking for individuals who can work as part of a team. Students need to be trained in the necessary social skills of listening, asking and answering questions, giving and receiving explanations, sharing, helping, and treating all group members with respect (Webb 1982, 1985a, 1985b, 1987, 1989; Webb & Farivar 1994). This should be done through teacher modelling, examples and reinforcement of the behaviours that demonstrate cooperative group interaction. We give examples of some of these collaborative skill behaviours later in this chapter.

Groups need to evaluate how well they are achieving their goals, how their group is performing, and how best to maintain productive working relationships between all members of the group. Time must be made available for *group processing* or reflection to occur, and assistance should be given by the teacher, initially, in suggesting ways of giving constructive feedback to group members on their participation. Individual students should also evaluate their personal achievement and contribution.

Group processing

This model takes time for the teacher and students to master and use but is well worth the effort for learning tasks that focus on concepts and skills.

Collaborative skills are crucial to effective cooperative learning. How can these be taught?

Student team learning (Slavin)

The research focus of Robert Slavin has been on the use of cooperative learning strategies for the acquisition of basic skills. The following three types of activity are characteristics of his approach.

1 In the **Teams-Games-Tournament** (TGT), the teacher presents first to the whole class material which heterogeneous teams of four to five members then proceed to help each other master during the rest of the week, until they compete against other teams on the Friday. These competitions take the form of 'tournaments' at which three students of similar previous performance sit at tables and attempt to gain the most points for their group by answering as many questions on the material as they can from a teacher-prepared handout. Each tournament winner brings the same number of points (six) back to their team, irrespective of initial level of ability. Thus, all members have an equal chance of success and of a boost in self-esteem when they contribute to the group total. It is clearly to everyone's advantage in the group to help their team-mates learn. TGT has the advantage of being adaptable to any age group or curriculum area.

Teams-Games-Tournament

2 **Student Teams-Achievement Divisions** (STAD) is a simpler version of TGT that replaces the tournaments between students with individual quizzes. Individual quiz scores are compared with previous averages, and points are given based on how much a student meets or improves on past performance. Thus, this method de-emphasises competition between classmates and focuses instead on self-improvement. The sum of individual points is the team score, and teams compete to gain the highest total, for which they are rewarded by the teacher.

Student Teams-Achievement Divisions

3 One of the earliest approaches to cooperative learning was **Jigsaw**, developed by Aronson and his colleagues (1978). In this method, students are assigned to six-member

Jigsaw

teams of mixed ability, gender and ethnicity. The material to be learned is divided between the members of the team. Each team has the same material to learn. Individuals with the same section combine to form 'expert' groups who study their part together. They then return to their original groups to teach these parts in turn to the other team members. Finally, all students are tested on the complete material. Subsequently, Jigsaw II has been modified by Slavin (1985a) so that all students read the entire assignment and are then allocated particular topics on which to become 'experts'. As with STAD, grades are awarded on the basis of individual quizzes to assess individual improvement and then combined to give a team score.

The student team learning model is an easy one to use but requires good classroom management skills on the teacher's part and students who are well behaved or who have developed the cooperative learning ethic. According to Dalton (cited in Bellanca & Fogarty 1991), the Australian approach to integrating curricula and focusing on developing intrinsic motivation and control over their learning in students is at odds with the competitive, content-specific emphasis of this model. In this context we like to remember the acrostic for 'team' developed by one of our beginning teachers, which he taught to his students as part of their preparation for engaging in cooperative group work (personal communication with Grant Dodds, November 2000):

T-(ogether) E-(ncourage) A-(nd) M-(otivate)

The structural model (Kagan)

Spencer Kagan's (1994) structural approach has successfully translated the abstract concepts of positive interdependence and individual accountability into practical lesson plan formats for teachers. These allow the teacher freedom to use a variety of *content-free* cooperative learning 'structures' with any subject matter to help provide different ways of organising cooperative interaction between students. Kagan provides activities for six categories of structures that can be adapted to any number of content areas, according to the teacher's objectives. These are:

- thinking skills;
- communication skills;
- information sharing;
- mastery;
- class building; and
- team building.

We will take two examples of popular structures to show you how they can apply to any number of classroom situations.

Numbered Heads Together

In *Numbered Heads Together*, students form teams of four, each student with a separate number. All team members work together to answer the teacher's questions, although only one number will be called from each group to reply. These students will represent their groups but are individually accountable for their answers as there is no prior warning as to which number will be called. Such a structure can be used to check for understanding of content and review of previously learned material (Weinstein & Mignano 1993).

Think-Pair-Share

Think-Pair-Share has been designed to encourage the development of thinking skills. In this structure a problem is posed which students think about alone, initially, for a specified period. They then pair up with someone to discuss the question. At this stage, careful listening to each other is important, as students may be called on to explain their partner's answer during the final stage when all pairs come together to share their answers with the whole class. One interesting variation of this method is to substitute reporting to the whole class with joining another pair in the Think-Pair-Share structure to make a team, which can further extend the students' thinking and discussion.

The group investigation model (Sharan & Sharan)

Group investigation

Group investigation is a model for classroom organisation derived from John Dewey's view that children should have some responsibility for directing and influencing their learning, as well as a sense of belonging to social groups while retaining their individuality (Sharan & Sharan 1992). Furthermore, it encompasses a constructivist philosophy that cognitive development involves actively building understanding from personal experiences, not from information being presented by external sources.

Four critical components of group investigation

According to Sharan and Sharan, there are four critical components of group investigation:

1 *Investigation:* This refers to the way that classroom learning is organised to enable inquiry-based (project method) learning to occur. It involves changes in student attitudes as much as physical changes in classroom organisation.
2 *Interaction:* Sitting students together in small groups does not guarantee that cooperative interaction will take place. They need to be shown the ways in which to talk and work with each other for academic purposes.
3 *Interpretation:* Students will interpret both their interpersonal relationships and the information they are

EXTENSION STUDY

The difficulties in using cooperative learning strategies

Teachers face several problems when attempting to introduce cooperative goal structures into their classrooms. Cultural differences, for example, may inhibit some students from wanting to share their ideas, as competitive rather than cooperative goal structures are common in many of our students' cultures.

Teachers have also traditionally cautioned students to keep their eyes on their own work; not to speak to their neighbour while solving problems; to ask the teacher for any help needed; and to do their own work (Weinstein & Mignano 1993). Such warnings are clearly not conducive to developing a spirit of cooperation in task performance and learning.

Teachers who have themselves been taught by teacher-centred methods, or believe they are the source of all knowledge, will find it difficult to 'let go' of the control of instruction. Parents may also question the educational value of cooperative learning.

Teachers who first introduce cooperative strategies into their classrooms frequently report disappointment: students are noisy in talk and movement; arguments erupt over who will work with whom, and what responsibility each will have; some students dominate, others are ostracised; time is wasted with little accomplishment; and cooperative social behaviours are lacking.

Overcoming problems in introducing cooperative learning

Four problems most commonly associated with the use of cooperative groups are (Weinstein & Mignano 1993):

- segregation of particular groups on the basis of disability, ethnicity or gender;
- unequal participation of group members either by dominance or 'freeloading';
- lack of achievement as a result of socialisation and noise; and
- lack of cooperation because of lack of understanding of cooperative behaviour and inexperience in cooperative group work.

How can such difficulties as these be overcome? For cooperative learning activities to be successful, there are two simple things to remember: first, plan the activity, specifying exactly what is to be done, why and by whom; and, second, teach the 'rules' and procedures for cooperative interaction, publishing the guidelines in written form for each student to see. There are also several practical approaches for avoiding difficulties.

First, start with very simple, brief group activities (not necessarily cooperative ones) until students have mastered some of the important skills required. These would include: asking others for assistance; helping one another; explaining; checking for another's understanding; providing support; active listening without destructive comments; taking turns in expressing an opinion or contributing to a task; and reaching consensus (Cohen 1994).

Second, as mentioned earlier, classroom control may be difficult to maintain when students are not stimulated by the learning task. In other words, the content of their learning must be relevant and interesting to students, as well as at the appropriate level of difficulty, *before* considerations of grouping or other structures are considered. Well-chosen and strategic teacher interventions during cooperative learning can improve time on task and problem solving among students who were off-task or making little progress (Chiu 2004).

Third, for cooperative techniques to be effective the teacher must ensure that students have mastered the skills necessary to engage in academically and socially cooperative group learning. As Cohen (1986, p. 11) points out:

> There is no point to a discussion that represents collective ignorance. Furthermore, there must be some way to be sure that people will listen carefully to each other, explain to each other, and provide some corrective feedback for each other. All this is unlikely to take place by magic; the teacher has to lay the groundwork through meticulous planning.

Ways of introducing cooperative interaction

How can you introduce students to cooperative interaction and minimise classroom management problems while maximising student learning?

Johnson and Johnson (1989–90) suggest that an effective way of making cooperative behaviours clear to students is by describing what the particular behaviours look like and sound like—that is, making the behaviours explicit. This should be done as part of class discussion. Thus, a list of behaviours for taking turns, for example, might look like this (adapted from Hill & Hill 1990):

Taking turns

Looks like:

- Eyes look at eyes.
- People wait until the speaker has finished.
- Nodding head as you listen.

Sounds like:

- 'Have you finished?'
- 'Do you want to say anything else?'
- 'Can I say something now?'

Role plays that demonstrate cooperative behaviours in action can be of great value, especially when introducing the behaviours for the first time or with younger students. The *teacher acting as model* will add even more to the demonstration (Hill & Hill 1990). In fact, in terms of cooperative behaviours generally, it is recommended that the teacher explain, demonstrate and even role play what is meant by particular cooperative behaviours such as being part of a team, rather than merely describing it (Kagan 1994).

It is also important for students to gain experience in these behaviours through *regular practice*. Dalton (1985) suggests that, until cooperative skills are learned, practice should be given to a portion of the class at a time, moving gradually to include the whole class. This can best be done through work with a partner—for example, in 'listening pairs', where students first take alternate roles as listener and talker and then begin to introduce the skills of responding and questioning. With practice, these pairs can be extended to include another pair and then another until groups are formed.

Webb and Farivar (1994, 1999; see also Karabenick 2002) point out that asking for help is neither cheating nor dependency. Rather, it is instrumental to learning as seen from both a Piagetian view of resolving cognitive conflict, and a Vygotskian view of participating in social interaction with a more capable person who can scaffold one's understanding to the next level. (It would be worth looking up what we say on developing cognition in Chapter 2.) Unfortunately, most students (and adults as well) do not naturally have the skills of obtaining and giving effective help in a learning environment, and must be taught them. We strongly suggest you take a look at the extensive research in this area of Webb and Farivar (1999), some of whose suggestions are adapted in Table 8.11.

Research has shown that, particularly in mathematics, unless teachers instruct and model what constitutes *'asking for help'* and *'giving help'*, low-achieving students (often girls) will typically withdraw effort from group tasks in which they feel (or are made to feel) inadequate or too slow (Karabenick 2004; Mulryan 1996; Webb & Farivar 1999).

For cooperative group interaction to be productive, equal participation of all members needs to be ensured. An effective way to do this is through *role taking*, an important skill in itself, and one that also fosters the development of individual accountability within a group. Teachers can help students to practise different roles by assigning them at the outset of a group project and ensuring that they are rotated each new lesson. Tactfully done, it is also an important strategy to use when trying to restrain domineering students (allocating them to the role of observer, for example) or assisting shy students to have more authority within the group (as reporter of group findings, for instance) (Abrami *et al.* 1995). Graves and Graves (1990) provide details of a number of roles that children might play in cooperative group work:

- *Initiator:* gets things going.
- *Clarifier:* checks that everyone understands.
- *Contributor:* makes active contributions to the task.
- *Listener:* models active listening techniques.
- *Summariser:* sums up ideas and contributions.
- *Encourager:* encourages all team members to participate.
- *Evaluator:* checks that the team has completed the task.
- *Tension reliever:* identifies humour in situations, suggests compromises.
- *Checker:* checks for accuracy.
- *Reader:* reads problems to the group.
- *Explainer:* paraphrases contributions and explains tasks.
- *Praiser:* gives positive feedback to group members.
- *Mover/organiser:* organises furniture to enable all group members to participate.
- *Timekeeper:* makes sure the group completes the task on time.
- *Challenger:* asks group to justify decisions/actions.
- *Observer:* checks participation and roles—gives feedback to group.
- *Noise monitor:* keeps group noise level within acceptable limits.
- *Gopher:* collects all materials needed by the group.
- *Reporter:* reports group findings.

It is vital that you do not assume that students, especially young ones, will know what a particular role entails. Discuss what each student's role involves, model it or even make a chart with explanations on it. For example: 'The encourager's job is to get everyone in the group to talk and share ideas. What are some of the things the encourager might say and do?' (Dalton 1985, p. 14).

Table 8.11 Essentials of giving and getting help in cooperative learning groups

The help-receiver should:
- *realise* that they need help;
- *decide* that they will ask for help;
- *choose someone* in their group to help them;
- *request help* from them;
- *ask questions* that are clear and specific;
- *keep asking questions* until they have definitely understood.

The helper should:
- *notice* when other students need help;
- *tell other students* that they can ask them for help;
- *be a good listener* when they do ask them, and give them specific help;
- *explain how* to do the problem instead of telling them the answer;
- *watch the person* they are helping try to work it out;
- *give feedback* to this person on each step of how they solved the problem;
- *check for understanding* by asking another question;
- *congratulate them* for their effort and for doing a good job.

studying. There needs to be an opportunity for reflection by students (individually and as a group) and by the teacher.

4 *Intrinsic motivation:* This is an essential component of effective group investigation as there are no extrinsic rewards provided. Students need to be personally interested in the topic and their part in its study.

Let us see how group investigation operates. Two to six students (heterogeneous in ability and ethnicity) combine to choose a section of a topic from a general unit of work being studied by the class. They then break down this subtopic into individual activities which the members set about completing. It is important that students determine their own learning goals, what to study and how. Students carry out their individual tasks, discuss and synthesise their findings as a group, and present their final product to the entire class. In this way, all groups contribute cooperatively to a broader understanding of the original unit.

The teacher's role in the group investigation approach is very important, as students need to be guided and monitored through each stage of the inquiry process. An essential component of this approach is the *evaluation* at the end of the project by both students and teacher. Students evaluate their own learning and affective experiences, as well as the dynamics of the group's participation in the investigation.

This model is ideal if your aim is to develop *student inquiry* and *creative problem-solving* skills while exploring concepts (Kagan 1992). It is not effective for covering specific curriculum content or when students are inexperienced in communication skills such as asking questions and reaching consensus.

Content-free structures such as those described above have the advantage of enabling the teacher quickly to incorporate cooperative group work into any classroom or curriculum, and can be used across a whole school to encourage the development of problem-solving skills,

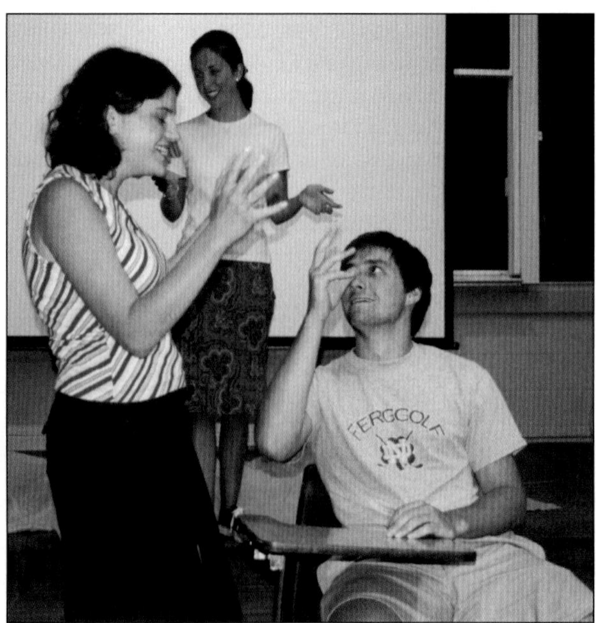

Even older students learn to cooperate through role play.

teamwork, social skills and curriculum content mastery. We are impressed with the versatility of this structural approach, which allows the teacher to set learning objectives across the range of levels in the cognitive and affective domains. Above all, the approach is truly constructivist in that the students are largely in control of both the interaction within the group and the group outcome. Just one final note: for benefits to accrue in personal, social and cognitive terms, cooperative structures should become a regular part of each week, and not relegated to 'Friday afternoon fillers' as play activities (Bellanca & Fogarty 1991).

Cooperative group work in Australia and New Zealand

Although the four models discussed above have considerable research support and are widely used in classrooms in the United States, the cooperative learning model typically adopted in Australia and New Zealand is a 'holistic' one. By this we mean that it begins from a whole-school perspective which then flows into classrooms, with all school members becoming a 'community of learners' (Graves & Graves 1990). The emphasis in Australia is on cooperation as a *social value*, with social skills being emphasised and explicitly taught (Dalton 1985, 1992), while in the United States cooperative structures are more commonly used for curriculum-based team activities, often for mastery of lower-level cognitive objectives such as knowledge or comprehension.

Deciding on group composition

You might well wonder which *method of grouping* students works best. A great deal of research has been done on finding the most successful combinations of ability, gender, status, and so on—there is no such thing as the best way. What has been shown to be successful depends on the nature of the project and the initial achievement levels of the participants in a group. We discuss later in this section some of the most recent findings that can help you to make wise decisions.

We have seen many times in our visits to classrooms teachers who are keen to try out creative, student-oriented ways of asking students to 'get themselves into groups'. Not surprisingly, students proceed to choose their friends, often without consideration of any other qualities relevant to the task. Our advice is that it is the *teacher* who should decide on group composition, for many good reasons. The first is to overcome segregation by gender, popularity, ethnicity or ability. In this context, Woolfolk Hoy & Tschannen-Moran (1999) caution that it is not wise to distribute students 'equally' to groups based especially on their gender or racial minority/majority in order to appear 'fair'. It is far better to assign them on the basis of their interests or special talents and skills, or to let students self-select their own groups once they have become used to working cooperatively on projects where common interests are important for motivation and rapport.

Allocate students to their groups

As for the merits of combining students with different achievement levels, recent research is illuminating. While you are reading about these findings, you might think about ways in which you could apply them in your planning of cooperative learning groups. The work of Webb *et al.* (1998) with middle-school children has shown that students of high ability perform best (higher-quality answers with explanations about how to solve problems, as well as higher achievement) when they are in groups with other high-ability students. On the other hand, below-ability students do best when there is a high-ability student in their group and only do well when that individual is present. The quality of performance for the high-ability students in this latter grouping is only marginally less than otherwise. In short, it is best for the academically weaker students to be placed with at least one stronger student who acts as expert resource. Although this may not appear to be best for maximising the *academic performance* of the high-ability student, it raises philosophical issues about the many purposes of education: is it only about scores on tests, or is it also about *helping and caring for others* as part of the wider learning community? Such questions need to be discussed among educators and with parents, who will want to know what you are doing for their children's learning.

Combining different ability levels

Grouping for achievement or helping and caring?

Heterogeneous grouping may seem equitable and even beneficial for the low-ability student, but there are dangers if high-ability students are dominant, impatient or even disparaging about the efforts of others. The effect on those with lower ability may be to dampen their enthusiasm for participating or asking questions (McCaslin & Good 1996).

The choice between *homogeneous* or *heterogenous* grouping will depend on the nature of the task: homogeneous high-ability students will profit from complex tasks which have a clear solution, while heterogeneous groups are suited for tasks which have no clearly correct answer and allow for multiple perspectives and competencies in the final product (Cohen 1994a, 1994b; Fuchs *et al.* 2000).

Homogeneous or heterogenous?

All small group activities benefit older learners

Interestingly, studies with older students show that any form of small-group learning (older students and adults do not distinguish between collaborative, cooperative or any other small-group procedure) is beneficial to achievement and learning-related behaviours, as well as to raising self-esteem (Springer, Stanne & Donovan 1999).

Although the evidence is strong that teachers should determine the composition of cooperative learning groups, if this is done exclusively, student resentment might be an outcome. *Random assignment* to groups is often seen as fairer by students ('Think of an animal, flower, country, food, colour, etc. and write it down. Find someone else in the room who has written down the same thing. These people will be the members of your group.'). Another quick, fun variation of this strategy for younger children is to hand out cards with pictures of animals, musical instruments, colours, and so on, on them and have all those with matching cards team up.

Free-rider effect

One final caution to be kept in mind when engaging students in cooperative groups is what Slavin (1990) calls the **'free-rider' effect.** By this, he means the tendency for some students to be allowed to 'come along for the ride' and not contribute or learn anything, either by choice or accident. This can occur when the group has a single product to present—in other words, where individual accountability is not required. Some group members who are considered less capable of a task than the rest of the group may be perceived as a liability and ignored, to the detriment of their learning. High-achieving students, on the other hand, may find the group task unstimulating and remain passively uninvolved. Of course, shy students may also prefer to be uninvolved, as this means that they are not obliged to speak in public. There are ways of encouraging all students to participate, and we consider these in Table 8.12.

Ensure equal participation

There will always be those who don't want to join in

Some students (sometimes the more able ones) just don't want to be part of a cooperative group, at least initially. Others may refuse to work with particular students or leave the group without participating. For the former, it may be helpful to discuss the academic and social benefits of group learning and the importance of acquiring teamwork skills for their future role in the workplace (Abrami *et al.* 1995). Much research has shown that those students who give help with detailed explanations (akin to teaching someone) in cooperative groups actually learn more themselves than if they give short or no answers (Webb, Trooper & Fall 1995).

For disruptive students and those who find it difficult initially to develop socially cooperative behaviours, it is most effective to use behavioural strategies of reinforcement for the desired behaviours (Graves & Graves 1990). For instance, individual and group rewards may be tied to a particular behaviour such as 'working with everyone in the group' which is group and individually monitored. Therefore, every time the student (or the others) works appropriately (or approximates it) they are able to score a point for the team or contribute to a reward that is desirable to the whole group. This strategy should be applied to all groups in the first instance, so that no one group or individual is singled out.

You may already be thinking that an obvious solution is to try to organise an activity that capitalises on the special interests or abilities of the more difficult students,

Table 8.12

Essentials of ensuring that all students participate in cooperative learning activities

Teachers should:

- explicitly train students in the skills required to work collaboratively and constructively;
- model the process, teach students about the cognitive benefits of explaining the reasoning behind their problem-solving processes to others;
- structure projects so that every group member's talents and skills will need to be called upon for its successful completion;
- assign active roles of responsibility to the uninvolved students (for example, group reader, spokesperson or scribe);
- ensure that the roles assigned to high achievers are challenging ones—that is, roles with which they may be unfamiliar, such as that of facilitator. Reward them for helping others to solve problems;
- promote for the 'free riders' individual accountability by issuing bonus points for improvement and for individual contributions to group scores and rewards;
- design problem-solving tasks for which there is no one set answer, thus requiring the creativity and negotiation of all.

(Source: Based on Graves & Graves 1990; O'Donnell & King 1999) thereby letting them feel successful. This is certainly helpful as long as it is done with subtlety—making such students feel that they are being singled out may be counterproductive in a number of ways. Can you think of reasons why?

Efforts on the part of the teacher to develop active listening skills and the use of non-aggressive 'I-messages' among *all* group members would have obvious benefits for cooperative interaction. This is especially so for disruptive students who would learn how their behaviour affects the rest of the group. (Refer to the earlier discussion of Thomas Gordon's counselling approach to discipline problems.) If there is little improvement in the behaviour of the disruptive student, it may be wise to pair them with one other student only until cooperative behaviours can be developed (Graves & Graves 1990).

A common complaint by teachers introducing cooperative learning structures into their classrooms for the first time is the increase in the level of classroom noise and apparent lack of accomplishment. It is important to differentiate between the sound of busy and exuberant interaction and the noise of students who are out of control. Young children will certainly need to have demonstrated to them what you mean by 'quiet voices' and to have an opportunity to practise speaking this way simultaneously, but so that groups cannot hear each other.

One beginning teacher we have observed actually holds a 30-centimetre ruler to his lips to demonstrate what he means by 'partner voices'—only the person sitting the length of the ruler away can hear. He then holds a metre ruler to his lips to demonstrate his 'group work voices'—those a metre away should be able to hear each other, but no further. What a great concrete way to teach an abstract concept!

A tangible signal is just as necessary for any age group. Many forms of signals have been used with success: timers, noise meters, noise monitors, coloured cards to indicate degree of noise, bells and gestures. The *'quiet signal'* (Kagan 1994) is a very useful gesture as it is non-intrusive and allows students to exercise some responsibility for controlling their noise. The teacher raises one hand and those nearby signal others until all students progressively raise their own hands, stop talking and working, and give their full attention to the teacher. Of course, the teacher will have previously introduced this signal by explaining that when groups talk to each other noise levels can rise progressively and the teacher will need to indicate that this is happening and regain order. The signal and procedure will then be modelled and practised until it is learned. Have you seen or thought of your own alternatives to the 'quiet signal'?

Quiet signal

It is important for the teacher to circulate during cooperative group work in order to monitor individual efforts and progress. Providing students with a list of expected progress markers is a useful way of keeping them on track. Another is to stop group work periodically to ask groups for progress reports. If projects are large, break them into smaller components that are checked daily (Weinstein & Mignano 1993). Equally important is to have students evaluate their contribution to the group once during the time allocated for group interaction: 'What am I doing that is helpful in achieving the group's goals?' At the conclusion of the activity, all group members should be asked to evaluate their effectiveness as a team: 'What did we do well? What could we do better next time?'

Monitor and self-evaluate individual effort and progress

A final word of warning. Despite their obvious effectiveness, cooperative learning methods should not be overused as students will find it monotonous to work in teams on all learning tasks. It goes without saying that effective classroom managers vary their teaching approaches according to the nature of the task and the students involved. Some would argue that enabling students to take responsibility for their own learning as well as for their behaviour, by substituting direct supervision with authority delegated by the teacher, is the most important aim of education. Certainly, well-designed and monitored cooperative learning activities provide students with the opportunity to gain experience in taking such responsibility.

QUESTION POINT

Individual achievement and competition is what we (educators) practise; cooperation is what we preach. How can we be teaching the social skills and values of cooperation in learning when we continue to assess children's individual academic performance and grade them accordingly? Is there a compromise?

WHAT WOULD YOU DO?

ENOUGH IS ENOUGH

Darryl was a 12-year-old student who came from a very unfortunate background. Consequently, he was a difficult and obstinate student who abused other children as well as teachers and would simply refuse to do things. During the first month of term 1, when Darryl encountered a situation that displeased him, he would pack his schoolbag, swear and go home. This was becoming a real problem and nothing Miss Jordan had been doing was working. She tried pleading with him, growling at him, joking with him, and adopting a calm and rational approach aimed at trying to get him to see the importance of remaining at school.

Case studies illustrating National Competency Framework for Beginning Teaching, National Project on the Quality of Teaching and Learning, Australian Teaching Council, 1996, p. 46. Commonwealth of Australia copyright, reproduced with permission.

WHAT WOULD YOU DO? (cont.)

ENOUGH IS ENOUGH

Finally, the turning point came one day. Things were not going Darryl's way and he stood up, swore at Miss Jordan and went to the cloakroom, packed his bag and said, 'I'm f...ing going home. You can't make me stay here.' She had had enough; she was frustrated by this child's constant interruption of the class. She managed to stay calm and said, 'Fine, Darryl, you're right, I can't make you stay and frankly I'm not even going to bother. You've been annoying me and the children, and interfering with their learning—and we'd all be better off without you. So just go and we'll see you later.' She requested politely, 'Can you please shut the door after you?' and turned back to the class and ignored him.

Out of the corner of her eye she could see that Darryl hadn't moved. He eventually put his bag down and came and sat on the mat. Darryl never threatened to go home again, and he has ceased to be such a problem. Miss Jordan is no longer playing his game. She has stated clearly what is acceptable behaviour in her classroom and has taken unmistakable control of the situation. Those who do not choose to accept these conditions will not be missed; threats will no longer be effective.

Case studies illustrating National Competency Framework for Beginning Teaching, National Project on the Quality of Teaching and Learning, Australian Teaching Council, 1996, p. 46. Commonwealth of Australia copyright, reproduced by permission.

What are some of the principles of effective classroom management that the teacher appears to have used with success here? How else might Miss Jordan have dealt with Darryl?

KEY TERMS

Assertive discipline (p. 282): protecting and restoring order in classrooms through use of reinforcement and punishment

Control theory (p. 279): based on the school's responsibility to prevent misbehaviour by fulfilling student needs

Cooperative discipline (p. 281): discipline based on meeting students' needs for belonging so that they choose to cooperate with the teacher and each other

Corrective discipline (p. 261): stopping misbehaviour through the use of authority or punishment

Culture of caring (p. 258): environment in which deep care for oneself and others, for the natural world and the human-made world is modelled and taught

Directive I-messages (p. 275): clear non-accusative statements of how something is affecting the teacher

Discipline (p. 262): methods adopted to manage student behaviour and involvement in learning

Free-rider effect (p. 300): in group work, the tendency for some students to be allowed to 'come along for the ride' and not contribute or learn anything, either by choice or accident

Group alerting (p. 271): capturing students' attention and quickly letting them know what they need to do

Group focus (p. 271): teacher's ability to keep students attentive and actively involved in learning tasks

Individual accountability (p. 293): keeping students individually responsible for their involvement in learning

Jigsaw (p. 294): a cooperative structure in which each member of a group is responsible for teaching other members one section of the material

Logical consequences (p. 267): positive or negative events that have an obvious (logical) connection

Momentum (p. 270): starting activities promptly, keeping their pace energetic and closing them decisively

Movement management (p. 270): maintaining student interest and attention by avoiding jerkiness through interruptions and managing smooth transitions between tasks

No-lose approach (p. 275): in conflict resolution, neither teacher nor student is a winner or loser
Overlapping responses (p. 270): a teacher attending to two or more matters at once in the classroom
Positive discipline (p. 276): discipline based on a belief in the capacity of students to control their own behaviour and to be responsible and cooperative
Positive interdependence (p. 293): in cooperative group work, students must demonstrably function as a group with a shared goal
Preventive discipline (p. 261): verbal and non-verbal strategies for preventing misbehaviour
Pro-social behaviour (p. 258): behaving in a socially responsible way
Quality school (p. 280): in Glasser's approach, students are encouraged to produce their best work being provided with quality teaching, evaluation, curriculum, resources and atmosphere
Reality therapy (p. 279): a discipline approach based on the premise that each individual has a need for self-worth and that, in order to feel worthwhile, they must maintain a satisfactory standard of behaviour
Routines (p. 265): behaviours that relate to specific activities or situations
Rules (p. 265): guidelines that define general standards of behaviour
Student Teams-Achievement Divisions (p. 294): cooperative learning with heterogeneous groups and elements of competition and reward
Supportive discipline (p. 261): putting a stop to misbehaviour in its early stages to prevent it escalating
Teams-Games-Tournament (p. 294): learning arrangement in which team members prepare cooperatively, then meet comparable individuals of competing teams in a tournament game to win points for their teams
'Three Cs' (p. 284): helping students to feel capable, connected and able to make contributions
'Withitness' and visual scanning (p. 269): preventive management strategy in which the teacher constantly monitors the classroom and is aware of what is happening at all times

ON-LINE LEARNING

If you go to **http://www.pearsoned.com.au/mcinerney**, you will have hot links directly to these sites

■ Cooperative discipline

You will find lots of practical ideas at this site for implementing cooperative discipline strategies in your classroom. Make a list of those ideas that apply to your teaching situation.

http://members.tripod.com/igreen/resources/id49.htm

■ How to manage

Investigate this site to find plenty of 'tips' for classroom management. Select those that have particular practical value for you as a teacher and try them out with members of your group.

http://www.teachnet.com/how-to/manage/index.html

■ Challenging behaviours—tip sheets

This site provides 'tip sheets' on positive ways of intervening when students' behaviours are challenging. You should follow the links to explore the many possible approaches for preventing, minimising and dealing with student misbehaviour.

http://ici2.umn.edu/preschoolbehavior/tip_sheets/social.htm

WEB DESTINATIONS

If you go to **http://www.pearsoned.com.au/mcinerney**, you will have hot links directly to these sites

■ TeacherTalk

In this journal for teachers you will find useful articles on classroom management, as well as many practical ideas for fostering a sense of classroom community through inclusiveness.

http://education.indiana.edu/cas/tt/tthmpg.html

■ Glasser's Choice Theory and Reality Therapy

Here you will find links to a series of articles and discussions on the work of William Glasser. Consider how you might incorporate Glasser's approaches into your classroom management with older students.

http://www.angelfire.com/ab/brightminds/

■ Ted Panitz's Cooperative Learning Site

This site has been compiled by a cooperative learning devotee. It has an enormous amount of practical information.

http://home.capecod.net/~tpanitz/

RECOMMENDED READING

Abrami, P. C., Chambers, B., Poulsen, C., de Simone, C., d'Apollonia, S. & Howden, J. (1995) *Classroom Connections: Understanding and Using Cooperative Learning*. Toronto, Ontario: Harcourt Brace.

Albert, L. (1996) *Cooperative Discipline*. Circle Pines, Minn.: American Guidance Service.

Balson, M. (1992) *Understanding Classroom Behaviour*, 3rd ed. Melbourne: ACER.

Charles, C. M. (1999) *Building Classroom Discipline*, 6th ed. White Plains, NY: Longman.

Cohen, E. G. (1994) Restructuring the classroom: Conditions for productive small groups. *Review of Educational Research*, **64**, 1–35.

Coloroso, B. (1994) *Kids are Worth It! Giving your Child the Gift of Inner Discipline*. New York: William Morrow.

Dalton, J. (1992) *Adventures in Thinking: Creative Thinking and Cooperative Talk in Small Groups*. Melbourne: Thomas Nelson.

Dreikurs, R. & Cassel, P. (1995) *Discipline without Tears*. New York: Penguin-NAL.

Emmer, E. T., Evertson, C. & Worsham, M. E. (2000) *Classroom Management for Secondary Teachers*. Boston: Allyn & Bacon.

Evertson, C. M. (1995) Classroom rules and routines. In L. W. Anderson (ed.) *International Encyclopedia of Teaching and Teacher Education*, 2nd ed. Cambridge: Pergamon.

Evertson, C. M., Emmer, E. T. & Worsham, M. E. (2000) *Classroom Management for Elementary Teachers*, 5th ed. Boston, MA: Allyn & Bacon.

Gordon, T. (1989) *Discipline that Works: Promoting Self-Discipline in Children*. New York: Random House.

Graves, N. & Graves, T. (1990) *A Part to Play*. Melbourne: Latitude Publications.

Johnson, D. W. & Johnson, R. T. (1994) *Learning Together and Alone: Cooperative, Competitive, and Individualistic Learning*, 4th ed. Boston: Allyn & Bacon.

Johnson, D. W. & Johnson, R. T. (1995) Why violence prevention programs don't work—and what does. *Educational Leadership*, **52**(5), 63–8.

Kagan, S. (1994) *Cooperative Learning*. San Juan Capistrano, CA: Kagan Cooperative Learning.

Kyriacou, C. (1991) *Essential Teaching Skills*. Oxford: Basil Blackwell.

Lewis, R. (1997) *The Discipline Dilemma*, 2nd ed. Melbourne: ACER.

McCaslin, M. & Good, T. L. (1998) Moving beyond sheer compliance: Helping students develop goal coordination strategies. *Educational Horizons*, Summer, 169–76.

Martin, N. K. (1997) Connecting instruction and management in a student-centred classroom. *Middle School Journal*, March, 3–9.

Nelson, J., Lott, L. & Glenn, H. (1997) *Positive Discipline in the Classroom*. Rocklin, CA: Prima.

Noddings, N. (1995) Teaching themes of care. *Phi Delta Kappan*, **76**, 675–9.

O'Donnell, A. M. & King, A. (eds) (1999) *Cognitive Perspectives on Peer Learning*. Mahwah, NJ: Lawrence Erlbaum.

Qin, Z., Johnson, D. W. & Johnson, R. T. (1995) Cooperative versus competitive efforts and problem solving. *Review of Educational Research*, **2**, 129–43.

Rogers, B. (1995) *Behaviour Management: A Whole-School Approach*. Gosford, NSW: Ashton Scholastic.

Rogers, B. (1997) *Cracking the Hard Class: Strategies for Managing the Harder than Average Class*. Gosford, NSW: Ashton Scholastic.

Rogers, B. (1998) *You Know the Fair Rule*. Melbourne: ACER.

Slavin, R. E. (1995) Cooperative learning. In L. W. Anderson (ed.) *International Encyclopedia of Teaching and Teacher Education*, 2nd ed. Cambridge: Pergamon.

Webb, N. M. & Farivar, S. (1999) Developing productive group interaction in middle school mathematics. In A.M. O'Donnell & A. King (eds) *Cognitive Perspectives on Peer Learning*. Mahwah, NJ: Lawrence Erlbaum.

CHAPTER

9 Special needs and effective learning

Overview

Students bring a range of personal packages—physical, behavioural, social and cultural—to the learning situation, which affect their learning and motivation in the classroom. In this chapter we focus on the individual qualities of learners that demand the attention of educators in making adaptations to the educational environment in order to facilitate their learning.

Our first focus concerns learning and cognitive styles and the links between these, academic achievement and classroom practice. We then take a detailed look at special needs education and discuss including learners with disabilities in mainstream classrooms. In this context, we examine a range of physical and intellectual disabilities and draw out the educational implications of these disabilities for educators. We also consider the educational needs of learners who might be considered gifted, talented or creative, and suggest adaptations that might be made to educational environments in order to support the development of these individuals.

Finally, we consider ways in which teachers and schools can adapt the educational environment to suit individual student needs. We discuss adaptive education and illustrate forms of micro-adaptations, which may be introduced into the classroom or school with little difficulty, and macro-adaptations, which might require greater system resources.

Learning objectives

After reading this chapter, you will be able to:

- describe cognitive styles and their relationship to effective learning;
- identify, describe and explain sex differences in learning and achievement;
- discuss the advantages and disadvantages of single sex and co-educational schooling;
- identify appropriate teaching approaches to reduce sexism in educational environments;
- identify and describe the characteristics of special needs in mainstream classrooms;
- contrast inclusion and streaming for special needs students;
- describe giftedness and talent, and discuss appropriate educational programs to facilitate the development of giftedness and talent;
- describe creativity and discuss appropriate educational programs to facilitate the development of creativity;
- describe and explain approaches to adapting educational environments to individual differences.

9

The following Learner-centred Psychological Principle and Teaching Competence Box 9.1 set the scene for this chapter. Revisit these when you have completed your reading. You should be aware of principles and practices to implement these effectively.

LEARNER-CENTRED PSYCHOLOGICAL PRINCIPLE

Individual differences in learning. Learners have different strategies, approaches and capabilities for learning that are a function of prior experience and heredity.

Individuals are born with and develop their own capabilities and talents. In addition, through learning and social acculturation, they have acquired their own preferences for how they like to learn and the pace at which they learn. However, these preferences are not always useful in helping learners reach their learning goals. Educators need to help students examine their learning preferences and expand or modify them, if necessary. The interaction between learner differences and curricular and environmental conditions is another key factor affecting learning outcomes. Educators need to be sensitive to individual differences, in general. They also need to attend to learner perceptions of the degree to which these differences are accepted and adapted to by various instructional methods and materials.

TEACHING COMPETENCE Box 9.1

The teacher recognises and responds to individual differences

Indicators

The teacher:

- identifies and fosters student learning strengths;
- uses students' social and cultural backgrounds to enrich the learning process;
- uses strategies that assist students to overcome individual learning difficulties;
- uses support services where appropriate.

Do students differ in their approach to learning?

Three learning styles

We are all different as learners. Where do these differences come from? Perhaps some of them are biological, and perhaps some are socially and culturally conditioned. One way of looking at these differences in learning is by looking at learning styles. **Learning styles** may be considered as characteristic cognitive, affective and physiological behaviours that serve as relatively stable indicators of how learners perceive, interact with and respond to the learning environment (see, for example, Cassidy 2004; Price 2004). They are demonstrated in the pattern of behaviour and performance with which individuals approach educational experiences (Beishuizen & Stoutjesdijk 1999; Butler 1986; Keefe & Ferrell 1990; Kolb 1976; McLoughlin 1999; Messick 1995; Perry 1996). Learning styles are seen as encompassing a number of components that are not mutually exclusive, and which may include perceptual modality preferences, group or individual work preferences, and environmental preferences (relating to factors such as light and heat) (O'Neil 1990). It is believed that if instruction takes into account a range of learning styles, learning will be enhanced (Rasmussen 1998; Riding & Grimley 1999).

Sources of individual difference

Three styles of learning that relate closely to learning tasks have received attention from researchers interested in the effect these styles have on learning outcomes. These three are meaning, reproducing and achieving orientations (Biggs 1987b; Messick 1995). Students with a **meaning orientation** adopt deep processing strategies to maximise personal understanding. Students with a **reproducing orientation** tend to adopt a shallow processing approach such as rote learning and memorisation. Students with an **achieving orientation** will utilise whatever approaches lead to high grades and are rewarded, so both deep and shallow processing strategies may be used. The style adopted will often reflect the achievement goals and tasks established in the classroom (see Chapters 4 and 7), and each may be useful given specific circumstances. Another way of categorising styles is as **deep** or **surface learning styles**. A person with a deep approach has an intention to understand the learning material and is motivated by an interest in the subject matter. In contrast, a surface learning approach is related to the intention of reproducing the learning material. It is associated with rote learning and fear of failure. Both of these approaches are used by students at various times; however, it is believed that a deep learning style leads to better understanding and retention of the information learned (see, for example, Barker, Dowson & McInerney 2002; Diseth & Martinsen 2003; Watkins, McInerney, Lee, Akande & Regmi 2002). Deep learning styles are usually strongly related to achievement outcomes, while surface approaches are typically negatively related to achievement outcomes.

Meaning style
Reproducing style
Achieving style

Sixteen elements of learning styles

A number of models of learning styles have been developed, including those of Kolb (1976; Cassidy 2004; Loo 2004), Gregorc (Butler 1986) and Dunn and Dunn. Dunn and Dunn (Brandt 1990; Cassidy 2004; Care 1996; Dunn & Dunn 1972, 1979; Dunn, Beaudry & Klavas 1989; Honigsfeld & Schiering 2004; Keefe & Ferrell 1990; Kidd 1996; O'Neil 1990) have listed 21 elements of learning style under five global headings (see Table 9.1).

This model outlines the environmental, emotional, sociological and physical preferences that children might have which potentially influence their learning and motivation. For example, when is the student most alert? What level of noise can the student tolerate? How does the student work best—alone, with one person or in a larger group? Where does the child work best—at home, in learning centres, in the library? What type of physical conditions suit the child best—floor, carpet, reclining, table lighting? How does the child learn most easily—visual materials, sound recording, printed material, tactile experiences, kinaesthetic activities, multimedia packages, combinations? What type of learning structure suits the student most of the time—strict, flexible, self-determined, self-starting, jointly arranged with teacher? What type of assignments suit the student best—contracts, totally self-directed projects, teacher-selected tasks (Dunn & Dunn 1972)? Dimensions such as these are assessed via observation and the use of a learning style inventory (Dunn, Dunn & Price 1985). Dunn *et al.* then advocate individualising instruction to accommodate these various needs.

Individualising instruction

Matching learning and teaching styles

Individualisation takes into account teaching styles and attempts to make the best match possible between what the teacher (and, more broadly, the educational environment) can offer and what the individual student needs (Dunn & Dunn 1979; Hendry *et al.* 2005; Rosenfeld & Rosenfeld 2004). When there is a best match between the needs of the student and what the environment provides,

Table 9.1 Elements of learning style

The immediate environment	The sociological elements
1 sound	10 working best alone
2 light	11 working best in a pair
3 temperature	12 working best with a small group
4 furniture and seating designs	13 working best as a team
The emotional elements	14 working best with an adult
5 motivation	15 working with variety rather than with routines
6 persistence	**The physical elements**
7 responsibility	16 perceptual strengths
8 conformity versus non-conformity	17 need for intake and mobility while learning
9 need for structure or opportunity to do things in one's own way	18 time of the day energy levels
	Processing inclinations
	19 global versus analytic
	20 right brain versus left brain
	21 impulsive versus reflective

learning and motivation (according to the advocates) are enhanced (Dunn *et al.* 1989; Honigsfeld & Schiering 2004). Many other instruments for measuring learning styles have also been developed (for example, Keefe & Ferrell 1990; Owens, Nolan & McKinnon 1992; see also Cassidy 2004).

However, matching learning and teaching styles may not be very effective, for the following reasons (adapted from Good & Stipek 1983; see also Loo 2004):

1 There is no single dimension of learners that unambiguously dictates an instructional prescription. Effective learning is the result of a number of variables, such as level of prior knowledge and ability.
2 There are higher levels of interaction between learner characteristics and instructional treatments such as the relationship of the teacher to the learner, the time of the year and the nature of the learning task.
3 Most students are adaptable to a variety of instructional modes, even if they are not preferred. The main concern is how well the instruction is designed to motivate the learner to attend. More important instructional qualities may be task clarity, importance of the goals, effective feedback and opportunities for practice.
4 Teachers have particular skills, and certain approaches may be more compatible with these skills than other approaches. Effective teachers use a variety of presentations to help all individuals see the material from a variety of perspectives.

Criticisms of learning styles

There is an inherent attractiveness about learning style inventories such as those proposed by Dunn and Dunn, Kolb and Gregorc, as they provide a rich resource for considering potential influences on students' learning and motivation. However, at the practical level the sheer diversity of possibilities creates great problems for the classroom teacher coping with such diversity (Desmedt & Valcke 2004; Doyle & Rutherford 1984). A major concern really has to be: What difference do the differences make? In other words, which differences between learners have consequences for the outcomes of instruction? Some educationalists believe that there are other important factors that are more likely to impact on student learning than those suggested in such inventories. Furthermore, they argue that the research evidence supporting such micro levels of adaptation to individual differences is quite equivocal (Curry 1990; Dunn 1990; Karvale & Forness 1987, 1990; Loo 2004; see also Duff 2004; Hendry *et al.* 2005). Indeed, there appears to be no empirical demonstration of a particular teaching method that is matched to a particular individual style of learning (what is technically called an aptitude–treatment–interaction effect) affecting achievement outcomes.

Probably the best strategy is to ensure that any educational setting includes a variety of approaches to teaching and learning to account for all the possible preferences in learners (Loo 2004).

QUESTION POINT

To what extent can individualisation of instruction take into account all the possible learning and cognitive styles of students?

Each of us has different learning styles. How much attention should teachers pay to the differences?

Cognitive style and effective learning

While *learning style* generally refers to that vast range of internal and external factors that may influence our learning and motivation in a given situation, **cognitive style** more specifically refers to the stable perceptual and thinking processes by which individuals within a culture comprehend their world, conceptualise meanings, learn a task, solve a problem and relate to others (Entwistle 1991; Messick 1976, 1984, 1995; Tiedemann 1989; Wolman 1989; see also Cassidy 2004; Price 2004). Cognitive styles are generally considered to be information-processing habits: individually characteristic ways of interpreting and responding to the environment (Shipman & Shipman 1985). Many cognitive styles are talked about in the literature and are often seen in terms of bi-polar dimensions: category width; cognitive complexity versus simplicity; levelling versus sharpening; scanning; automatisation versus restructuring; converging versus diverging; wholist versus analytic style; visualiser versus verbaliser (sometimes referred to as verbal versus imagery). Few have been subjected to significant empirical research. Among these are field dependence versus field independence, conceptual tempo and locus of control (Messick 1995; Tiedemann 1989), visualiser versus verbaliser (Mayer & Massa 2003), although wholist versus analytic is receiving increasing attention today (Evans 2004).

Field dependence and field independence

Witkin and his colleagues (1977; Kogan 1971; see also Cassidy 2004) focused on the dimensions of field dependence and field independence or *global* versus *analytic perceptual style*. **Field dependence** refers to a type of cognitive perceptual processing in which stimuli are perceived as parts of a whole, while **field independence** refers to a type of cognitive perceptual processing in which stimuli are differentiated and then organised on the basis of structural differences and similarities (Witkin *et al.* 1977). Witkin *et al.* conclude that while field-dependent and field-independent students don't differ in learning ability or memory, they do differ in the kinds of material they learn most easily and the strategies they use for learning. For example, it appears that field-dependent students have difficulty isolating independent elements of a problem or situation. They are easily affected by manipulations of the surrounding contexts. In contrast, field-independent individuals are able to 'dis-embed' parts of a task from its organisational framework and devise alternative organisational patterns, if necessary, to understand information and solve problems. It is thought that field-independent students learn better under intrinsic motivation and low structure (for example, open classrooms, discovery learning and problem solving), although the differences between field-independent and field-dependent learners can be altered by various interventions such as pointing out salient cues and directly teaching particular problem-solving skills to field-dependent children.

Field-dependent individuals appear to be more influenced by the social circumstances of their learning; for example, they spend more time looking at faces, pay more attention to statements with social content, are more influenced by the opinions of prestigious others, and prefer shorter physical distances between themselves and others (Shipman & Shipman 1985). As a consequence, field-dependent people appear to be more socially competent, better liked and more sociable than their field-independent peers (Shipman & Shipman 1985; Witkin *et al.* 1977).

Of course, teachers can also be categorised as field dependent or field independent, and perhaps an individual teacher's cognitive style might have an impact upon the way they structure learning experiences for children. For example, field-dependent teachers may be more concerned with structure and interpersonal relationships in the class, while field-independent teachers may be more concerned with lecturing and discovery learning (Entwistle 1991).

Teachers as field dependent/field independent

Some research has been directed to examining what happens when there is a match/mismatch between learner and teacher styles and student achievement, but as yet there are no definitive findings (Shipman &

Shipman 1985). Your training as a professional should equip you to teach using approaches that are attractive to both groups of students.

Conceptual tempo

Kagan (1965, 1966; Kagan & Kogan 1970; see also Cassidy 2004) concentrated on **conceptual tempo**, which refers to the degree to which people are cognitively *reflective* versus cognitively *impulsive* in deciding on a response when two or more alternatives are plausible. **Impulsive** learners give the first answer that occurs to them and are often inaccurate. **Reflective** learners, on the other hand, examine alternative hypotheses and attempt to validate their answers before responding. They take longer to respond but are often more accurate (Entwistle 1991; Messer 1976). Children who are classified as reflective (slow and accurate) in reading, for example, tend to be better readers than impulsive children of equal IQ (Kagan 1965, 1966; Zelniker & Jeffrey 1976).

However, we must caution here against adopting too simplistic a view of what this means in real life. For example, there are individuals who make up their minds quickly and are right, and others who make up their minds slowly and are wrong. Hence, speed of a response may indicate level of background knowledge rather than impulsivity. Furthermore, impulsive thinkers are not necessarily impulsive people generally. Kagan and Kogan (1970) suggest that reflective children may have been taught to regard absence of errors as a mark of competence, and as such become anxious over making mistakes, which slows them down. Impulsive children, on the other hand, might have learned that being quick indicates competence, and therefore become anxious about responding slowly. Other reasons for impulsivity/reflectivity in particular situations may be the degree to which an individual needs to pay attention to detail (that is, the degree of complexity of the task), the description of the task, and the degree of accuracy implied for satisfactory completion of the task.

In general, research indicates that impulsive learners perform more poorly on a variety of academic tasks. Research has been directed towards teaching such children to be less impulsive, and some techniques for this are covered in Chapter 8.

Locus of control

When individuals think that they are responsible for their success and failure and believe they have substantial control over their learning, they are said to have an **internal locus of control**. On the other hand, individuals who believe that they have little control over their own learning, and that their successes and failures are due to forces outside their control (such as teacher control), are said to have an **external locus of control**. Locus of control forms a major component of Weiner's attributional model of motivation discussed in Chapter 7.

As well as these delineations of various cognitive styles, there are numerous others discussed in the educational literature—so many, in fact, that they become quite confusing in their overlap (see, for example, Messick 1995). We have chosen just a few to indicate the diversity of constructs used to describe various forms of cognitive functioning.

Are there problems with cognitive-style approaches to student learning?

Dynamic nature of cognitive styles

Cognitive styles are not static but dynamic—that is, they might be task specific or reflective of an individual's stage of development and experience and, most importantly, they act in concert with other cognitive styles for a given person in a given situation. Therefore, the notion that we can identify an individual's cognitive style and design educational experiences based on this style is far too simplistic.

Artificial dichotomies

While each of the styles (such as locus of control) is described as a continuum from one dimension to the other (for example, internal to external), they are often seen as polarised—for example, internal versus external. Individuals are grouped as belonging to one or the other classification (Entwistle 1991). The dichotomising of cognitive styles also suggests that one pole is good and the other bad. Indeed, the terms used (such as dependent, external and impulsive) predispose us to think this way, although the terms themselves are not meant to be value laden. Within particular situations some cognitive styles may be more useful than others and it is not simply a case of one end of the continuum being more positive. Nevertheless, within a Western-oriented school system, field-independent characteristics, such as a high valuation of independence, individualism and a desire for personal rather than group achievement and success, are considered most valuable (Nedd & Gruenfeld 1976).

Culture and cognitive style

In societies as culturally diverse as Australia and New Zealand, groups that manifest the opposite qualities, such as *collectivism* and *group orientation*, are often believed to be poorly suited to a Western education system. This notion is currently being challenged by a number of authors (McInerney 1991a, 1991b; McInerney & Swisher 1995; McInerney, Roche, McInerney & Marsh 1997; Ogbu 1983, 1992; Ogbu & Matute-Bianchi 1986). Furthermore, there is a danger in assuming that there is a

Theory and research into practice

Gerry Fogarty — LEARNING STYLES, CULTURE AND METACOGNITION

BRIEF BIOGRAPHY

I am professor of psychology and founder of the Centre for Organisational Research and Evaluation at the University of Southern Queensland, a large regional university located in the city of Toowoomba, 150 kilometres west of Brisbane. I grew up in a farming community on the north coast of New South Wales before moving inland to the city of Armidale to study psychology and education at the University of New England. After graduating with an honours degree in psychology at the end of 1972 and then a diploma of education in 1973, I worked as a high school teacher in Sydney's Western Suburbs from 1974 to 1976 as part of my preparation for a career as a school counsellor. However, the call of research was too strong and in 1976, instead of continuing my training in counselling, I enrolled in the Ph.D. program in the Department of Psychology at the University of Sydney, completing my dissertation on the structure of intelligence in 1984.

A shortage of jobs in the academic sector at that time then resulted in my career once again taking an applied direction when I joined the staff at the head office of the Australian Mutual Provident Society in 1985 as a human factors specialist. While working in this commercial environment, I developed a strong interest in applied problems, such as the use of technology in training, the role of values and interests in shaping career preferences, and the many factors that influence learning outside the formal educational system.

I returned to academic work in 1988 when I accepted a position in the Department of Psychology at what is now the University of Southern Queensland. Reflecting my varied background, my areas of interest include human factors, educational psychology, sports psychology, organisational psychology, and individual differences. I have published extensively in journals such as the *Journal of Vocational Behavior*, *Intelligence*, *Journal of Business and Psychology*, *Journal of Outcome Measurement* and *Personality and Individual Differences*. I am a fellow of the Australian Psychological Society and currently chair of the society's Division of Research and Teaching. Within the university, I am deputy dean of the Faculty of Sciences and a part-time member of the Psychology Department.

RESEARCH AND THEORETICAL INTERESTS

My research interests have always centred on aspects of individual differences and organisational factors that influence learning and performance in educational and occupational settings. My early work in this area focused on the assessment of learning styles and the impact of these styles on academic achievement. There are various definitions of cognitive styles, and it is easy to confuse them with a plethora of related constructs such as learning preferences, approaches to study, cognitive styles and personality types, to name just a few. The conceptual confusion has been partly triggered by difficulties encountered trying to develop good operational definitions of these various constructs.

My interests in this area of individual differences are both theoretical and practical. I have conducted studies designed to examine issues relating to convergent and divergent validity across different measures of learning styles and I have also looked at the relationship between styles and academic performance. My research program on styles has a distinctively applied flavour, incorporating two studies in psychological skills training in golf as well as studies conducted in educational settings.

A second research stream that has long formed a part of my activities concerns the influence of culture on behaviour. This work began with a cross-cultural comparison of the individualism/collectivism value dimensions among indigenous and non-indigenous Australians and the influence of these values on academic achievement and tendency to persist in study. Results indicated that the Aboriginal group placed greater emphasis on values associated with tradition, conformity and security and significantly less emphasis on values associated with achievement, self-direction, stimulation, hedonism and benevolence. These findings are consistent with previous research on the world view of traditional Aboriginal people and suggest that even among younger, more 'Westernised', representatives of this culture, collective values are likely to be strong determinants of behaviour.

Over the past eight years, this research on values has taken an interesting applied twist with my current involvement in the role of safety culture in the aviation and health industries. At first glance, this might appear to be quite a research leap, but the notion of culture applies to all human behaviour and there is no doubt that the future of the aviation industry—or any other high-risk industry, for that matter—depends very heavily on the development of appropriate safety cultures in organisations. The collectivist/individualist dimensions have their place in this research, and it is now widely recognised that safety behaviours vary according to the value orientations of the societies in which the behaviours are studied. For example, obvious mistakes by a captain of an aircraft are more likely to go uncorrected in societies where there is a strict observance of power structures.

A third major area of study stems from my original interest in human intelligence. It concerns the higher-level intelligence construct known as metacognition. The aspect of metacognition that is of most interest to me concerns the accuracy of self-assessments. Using what is known as the calibration paradigm, participants are asked to answer items in typical aptitude or achievement tests and then to state how confident they are that their answers to these items are correct. A bias (or calibration) score can be calculated by subtracting the proportion correct score from the average confidence rating across all items in the task. The usual finding is that people tend to be overconfident on some tasks, such as tests of general information, and underconfident on others, such as tests of perceptual judgment. Individual differences are also evident, with males tending to be more overconfident than females and experts showing better calibration than non-experts.

THEORY AND RESEARCH INTO PRACTICE

Learning styles

For the most part, I have concentrated on a subset of learning styles that are derived from the so-called modality theories. The best known of these styles are the visual and verbal, but there are others, including kinaesthetic and tactile. This is an important area of research because the claim has often been advanced by educational theorists that students learn best when taught through their preferred modalities. I began by studying the various instruments used to measure styles and found that although they all claimed to be measuring the same constructs, there was little evidence of convergent validity. In other words, if an educational practitioner picked two measures of learning styles from those available from test distributors, it is likely that the two instruments would classify the students differently. Viewed in this light, the practice of tailoring educational programs to suit individual strengths and weaknesses is flawed because we are not yet in a position to make accurate assessments of these strengths and weaknesses. An enriched multi-modality training program for all students is therefore likely to be the best option for most teachers.

Culture

Apart from the development of some in-house training programs, my research on culture has no major outcomes at this stage but it is part of a literature that forms the background to a growing awareness among educators and practitioners that the concept of culture is a root cause of many patterns of inter-group differences. The collectivist orientation of the indigenous Australian students who took part in our cross-cultural studies of values triggered a realisation among university staff that the emotional cost of being separated from friends and families is not the same for all students and that close community networks need to be re-created within a university setting if students from collectivist societies are to persist and succeed in higher education. The extension of this cultural research into applied fields such as aviation further highlights the strength and importance of cultural factors. Safety training programs (for example, assertiveness training) that work in one culture have been shown to be dismal failures in others because they promote behaviours that clash with underlying cultural norms.

Metacognition

My research on metacognition and calibration has both a theoretical and an applied orientation. Reliable findings that people tend to be overconfident in some situations and underconfident in others, and that there are stable individual differences in self-monitoring ability, serve to remind us that possession of knowledge and skills should not be our only goal in education and training. Most students in a typical classroom will not be well-calibrated; they will tend to have too much confidence relative to their actual ability levels. While a little bit of overconfidence is probably a good thing, too much overconfidence suggests a basic lack of self-monitoring skills. Unfortunately, the weakest members of the class tend to exhibit the greatest overconfidence. Research indicates that this tendency can be corrected to some extent by targeted feedback. In high-risk fields such as aviation and medicine, it is equally important that people know what they know. There are too many well-documented instances of both overconfidence and underconfidence leading to catastrophic accidents. It follows from these studies that we should be devoting more effort to teaching self-monitoring skills. People will not be motivated to learn or to develop skills if they do not realise that they lack the knowledge and skills in the first place.

KEY REFERENCES

Baker, S. & Fogarty, G. (2004) Confidence in cognition and intrapersonal perception: Do we know what we think we know about our own cognitive performance and personality traits? In M. Katsikitis (ed.) *Proceedings of the 39th APS Annual Conference: Psychological Science in Action* (pp. 24–8). IBN 0-909881-25-1, 29 September–3 October 2004, Sydney: Australian Psychological Society.

Fogarty, G. & White, C. (1994) Differences between values of Australian Aboriginal and non-Aboriginal students. *Journal of Cross-cultural Psychology*, **25**(3), 394–408.

Thomas, P. R. & Fogarty, G. (1997) Psychological skills training in golf: The role of individual differences in cognitive preferences. *The Sport Psychologist*, **11**(1), 86–106.

ACTIVITIES

These activities are relevant for Chapters 9 and 10.

1 Gerry Fogarty believes that there is difficulty in applying the concept of cognitive and learning styles because of the confusing array of terms used to describe different and similar styles, and the inconsistent way in which they are measured. Consider the information in this chapter and discuss within a group the pitfalls of relying on cognitive and learning style research and measurement for guiding teaching practice. What might be an appropriate course of action for teachers to take who are convinced that learning and cognitive styles among students differ?

2 Gerry Fogarty is also interested in the impact that culture has on learning (see Chapter 10). What is the importance of the individualism/collectivism value dimensions for interpreting differences between cultural groups on approaches to learning and motivation in school settings? Look up further research on individualism and collectivism as it applies in educational settings. (A good source of research is the *Journal of Cross-cultural Psychology*.)

3 Gerry Fogarty broadly interprets the notion of culture in his study of aviation culture and makes a number of important points. In particular, he relates the issue of safety in aviation to cultural factors. Discuss other areas in which culture, broadly defined, might influence attitudes towards outcome behaviour such as safety practices, investment of energy in a task, conformity to group norms such as speeding, drinking alcohol, smoking, and so on.

4 Gerry Fogarty introduces the notion of metacognition (see also Chapter 5) as an area in which individual differences, and in particular the accuracy of self-assessments, are observable. Discuss his findings that people tend to be overconfident on some tasks, such as tests of general information, and underconfident on others, such as tests of perceptual judgment, and that males tend to be more overconfident than females and experts show better calibration than non-experts. What are the implications from this for classroom practice?

built-in relationship between being a member of a particular cultural group and a particular learning or cognitive style. Although learning style research warns against stereotyping and generalising about the cognitive styles of various groups, some teachers try to match learning styles to particular cultural groups based on stereotypes and design learning programs, such as time of day for instruction or seating arrangements that are supposed to be more conducive for particular groups, without taking into account individual differences (Gutierrez & Rogoff 2003). We take up this issue a number of times in our text.

There have been so many difficulties in cognitive style research and application that Tiedemann (1989, p. 273; see also Price 2004) was moved to say that 'the cognitive style concept has to be considered a failure on the diagnostic level and, therefore, the empirical level as well'. He recommends we abandon it as a fruitful source of information on individual differences. This is a controversial view. What do you think?

Teachers' cognitive styles

Our focus in the sections above was on students' learning and cognitive styles and the suggestion that in order for teachers to be effective in the classroom they need to take these differences in learning and cognitive styles into account while teaching. It is perfectly possible, of course, that the learning and cognitive styles of teachers themselves may have a considerable impact on the way they teach. For example, in one study (Evans 2004) comparing analytic cognitive style versus wholist cognitive style (whether an individual tends to process information in wholes or parts), teachers with an analytic cognitive style showed greater concern about subject knowledge and developing pedagogy; they also revealed more concern about the self, being more worried about being observed and assessed and developing relationships. A higher percentage of teachers with a wholist style felt that their own experiences as a learner had a greater impact on their teaching than the analytic teachers, whereas analytic teachers were more likely to stress their own ability as a factor affecting their teaching. Wholists appeared more sensitive to situational factors such as the culture of the school, support from a mentor, ability to accept criticism, and resource provision, whereas few analytic teachers had these concerns. Rather, analytics raised the issue of the demands of the subjects they were teaching as dominant concerns (Evans 2004). So, as you can see, the permutations and possibilities of considering both student and teacher learning and cognitive style are quite immense.

Are there sex differences in learning and achievement?

Sexism in the classroom

There are important school achievement differences between boys and girls in terms of key educational processes and outcomes (Ainley & Lonsdale 2000; Martin 2003a), although over the last few years the gap has been closing. Among major concerns are the disproportionate number of males that are placed in special educational settings, and the differential in achievement levels between girls and boys in language, mathematics and science (particularly the physical sciences) (Bailey 1993; Barnes & McInerney 1996; Beal 1999; Burkam, Lee & Smerdon 1997; Collins, Kenway & McCleod 2000; Halpern & LaMay 2000; Kahle *et al.* 1993; Kleinfeld 1998; Weaver-Hightower 2003). There are no differences in general intelligence as measured by standard intelligence tests such as the Stanford–Binet or the WAIS-III. Indeed, the tests are designed so that there are no average differences between males and females across the tests. Nevertheless, there are differences on many subsets of these tests that reflect the differences in achievement levels mentioned above. Much research finds that girls outperform boys on tests of verbal fluency, foreign language, fine-motor skills, speech articulation, reading and writing, and math calculation, and they typically earn higher grades in school in all or most subjects. Boys have been found to do better on tasks such as mental rotation, mechanical reasoning, math and science knowledge, and verbal analogies (Halpern 1997; Naglieri & Rojahn 2001). The most frequently cited difference between males and females is the ability to transform a visual-spatial image in working memory. In general, males perform better on these types of tasks (Halpern & LaMay 2000; see also Quaiser-Pohl & Lehmann 2002). These spatial differences between males and females appear early in life and so seem to be more genetically influenced than environmentally. Males also appear to be better in tests of mathematical and scientific ability, although females appear to do better in classrooms and grades (Beal 1999; Burkam *et al.* 1997; Pomerantz, Altermatt, & Saxon 2002). This is probably related to the visual-spatial strengths of males. It is also possible that males are more capable of retrieving mathematical facts in tests than females, but the reasons for this are as yet unclear (Beal 1999). There are a large number of other explanations for gender differences in mathematics and science, including: that girls use more concrete strategies than boys, and that this may lead to less understanding of important ideas on which further learning of mathematics and science is based (Burkam *et al.* 1997; Sowder 1998); stereotyping of mathematics and science which encourages different responses from boys, girls and their teachers (Burkam *et al.* 1997; Hyde & Jaffee 1998; Tiedemann 2000); and lack of interest and salience of mathematics and science for girls (Burkam *et al.* 1997; Noddings 1998). On the other hand, females appear to have higher levels of ability on a variety of memory tasks such as word recall. The differences between males and females appear to be strongest in the higher ranges of ability with little differences in the average range (Burkam *et al.* 1997; Halpern & LaMay 2000). Halpern and LaMay (2000) make the interesting point that many of the sex differences found in the laboratory are mirrored in the real world. For example, when males and females give directions, males are more likely to use north-south-east-west directions, and are more accurate with these relational strategies. Women, on the other hand, are more likely to use landmarks and left-right directions. What do your personal experiences suggest?

What different expectations might these three students have of their education?

Table 9.2 summarises some of the factors that may contribute to differences in achievement levels of boys and girls.

A more recent concern that is emerging is the apparent growing underachievement of boys within school settings, particularly reflected in school retention and graduation performance (Collins, Kenway & McCleod 2000; Weaver-Hightower 2003; West 1999; see also Pomerantz, Altermatt & Saxon 2002). The nature and reasons for this apparent decline in boys' achievement at school are unclear. The article by Weaver-Hightower in the recommended readings gives some interesting perspectives on this issue.

Single-sex and co-educational schooling

Because of the differences between behaviour and achievement levels of boys and girls at school and their impact on students' consequent life chances (see, for example, Collins, Kenway & McCleod 2000), there have been significant debates concerning the relative value of single-sex versus co-educational schooling (Gilmore, Patton, McCrindle & Callum 2002). Over the last three decades there has been a steady decline in the number of single-sex schools internationally, particularly in developed countries (LePore & Warren 1997). Nevertheless, there is considerable argument over the merits of single-sex education and, ironically, today there is some increase once more in single-sex schools. This is particularly the case with girls' education, and most specifically with girls from Muslim backgrounds. What are the arguments for and against single-sex schooling? The following contentions are often proposed in support of either single-sex or co-educational schooling (Mael 1998; see also LePore & Warren 1997):

1 Single-sex schooling has positive benefits for the academic achievement of both sexes.
2 Single-sex schooling is positive for females in sex-typed subject areas.
3 Single-sex schooling is beneficial for female career aspirations.
4 Single-sex schooling is beneficial for positive sex-role attitudes and self-esteem.
5 Co-educational classrooms foster gender inequities.
6 Co-educational schooling is beneficial for male discipline.
7 Co-educational physical fitness programs adversely affect both sexes.

Table 9.2

Why girls and boys may achieve differently at school

- Boys and girls are socialised in their families and communities to value different activities and form different competence beliefs (self-concept) for particular activities. These gender role stereotypes may influence later achievement (see, for example, Burkam *et al.* 1997; LePore & Warren 1997; Martin 2003a, 2003b; Quaiser-Pohl & Lehmann 2002; Tiedemann 2000; Weaver-Hightower 2003).
- Teachers often hold expectations about individual students and groups of students. These expectations, sometimes based on gender differences, may limit the opportunities that teachers present to students (Altermatt, Jovanovic & Perry 1998; Burkam *et al.* 1997; LePore & Warren 1997; Tiedemann 2000).
- Teachers treat boys and girls differently in many learning contexts: boys participate in more interactions with teachers, receive more feedback, help and praise from teachers, and are reprimanded more (thereby receiving more attention) than girls. It should be noted here that not all boys receive this attention. It is more often the case that a few 'star' male students receive the bulk of the teacher's attention to the exclusion of all other pupils, male and female (Altermatt *et al.* 1998; Bailey 1993; Burkam *et al.* 1997; LePore & Warren 1997; see also Gentry, Gable & Rizza 2002).
- Teachers initiate more low-level and high-level interactions with boys than girls—for example, calling on boys to answer word problems and to give their explanations. It is important to note that the direction of interaction is *from teacher to student.* Both boys and girls ask the teacher questions with the same frequency. However, it has been found that when boys call out answers the teacher responds more often than to girls and, in fact, girls are often reprimanded for calling out (Bailey 1993; Kahle *et al.* 1993; LePore & Warren 1997). It is often the level of interaction between the teacher and males and females that is used to explain the imbalance in student performance in science and maths (see, Jones & Dindia 2004).
- Males volunteer responses to questions and requests more often than females and teachers respond to this, thus attending more to boys. When volunteer rates are taken into account, the response rate of teachers to boys and girls is about the same (Altermatt *et al.* 1998).
- From the early grades, boys and girls develop friendship groups along gender lines. As a result, boys and girls develop different modes of operating in the educational environment. When they are put together in mixed groups it is thought that boys dominate discussion and monopolise equipment and materials, to the disadvantage of girls. In particular, girls may be 'silenced' or relegated to gender-stereotyped roles. While girls proffer assistance to boys, this is not reciprocated. So, boys 'win out' (Eccles & Blumenfeld 1985; LePore & Warren 1997).

What is the evidence in support of each of these contentions?

1 *Single-sex schooling has positive benefits for the academic achievement of both sexes.* Mael (1998) conducted a review of research literature examining the evidence. It appears that single-sex schooling does have positive benefits for the academic achievement of both sexes, though the effects appear more pronounced and less ambiguous for females than males. Some researchers still argue that this is not the case (see, for example, LePore & Warren 1997).
2 *Single-sex schooling is positive for females in sex-typed subject areas.* There is no clear evidence in support of the second contention. One major flaw in research examining the advantages for females in sex-typed subject areas (such as mathematics) in single-sex schools is that virtually no counterpart research has been done on increasing male participation in female-stereotyped disciplines in single-sex male schools.
3 *Single-sex schooling is beneficial for female career aspirations.* There is little evidence to support the idea that single-sex schooling is beneficial for female career aspirations.
4 *Single-sex schooling is beneficial for positive sex-role attitudes and self-esteem.* There is no clear evidence to support this contention. This is largely because the number and types of criteria used to assess this are extensive, and the range of methodologies used makes it difficult to make broad generalisations.
5 *Co-educational classrooms foster gender inequities.* There is support for this contention; however, it is not clear whether inequities disappear in single-sex schools (Lee, Marks & Byrd 1994; LePore & Warren 1997; Mael 1998). In this latter case, new inequities may be substituted for old (for example, through the existence of single-sex cliques) with some students still suffering.
6 *Co-educational schooling is beneficial for male discipline.* This contention has received limited support. Countering this is the evidence that delinquency and sexual harassment is higher for girls in co-educational schools and that single-sex schooling might reduce both of these for girls.
7 *Co-educational physical fitness programs adversely affect both sexes.* There is indirect support for the contention that co-educational physical fitness programs adversely affect both sexes (see, for example, McInerney *et al.* 2000).

Table 9.2 **Why girls and boys may achieve differently at school *(continued)***

- Boys appear to benefit more from competitive learning structures, while girls seem to benefit from more cooperative learning structures. Many classrooms, however, emphasise performance goals in a competitive setting that advantages boys.
- Some boys tend to 'throw their weight around', which can intimidate girls and other boys. This form of bullying can occur during classroom activities, negatively impacting on the work of other children (see, for example, Kahle *et al.* 1993; LePore & Warren 1997).
- Some curricula are gender stereotyped. For example, schools and teachers might construct gender, science and achievement in ways that define achievement and the study of science as masculine (see, for example, Beal 1999; Pomerantz, Altermatt & Saxon 2002; Quaiser-Pohl & Lehmann 2002).
- There may be differences in self-efficacy for males and females regarding specific tasks or academic areas such as mathematics and reading (see, for example, Gentry, Gable & Rizza 2002; Martin 2003a, 2003b; Pajares *et al.* 1999; Quaiser-Pohl & Lehmann 2002; Tiedemann 2000).
- Girls may be more interested in the social dimensions of learning and interpersonal relationships, while boys may be more interested in control and analysis, predisposing them to look upon science, mathematics and humanities differently (see, for example, Burkam *et al.* 1997).
- Much curricula material is specifically single-gender stereotyped. For example, many computer activities based on 'warring' analogies are of little interest to girls; and literature that deals with topics such as dancing, friendships or animals is of little interest to boys. Much material also provides sexual stereotypes of appropriate behaviour for boys and girls (such as women being 'homemakers' and men being 'breadwinners'), which further limits opportunities (see, for example Quaiser-Pohl & Lehmann 2002).
- Psychobiosocial causes suggest that prenatal hormone levels affect patterns of cognition in sex-typical ways (for example, spatial-visual abilities are better than verbal abilities for males) and that normal fluctuations in daily and monthly hormone levels in healthy adults correlate with performance on some cognitive tasks (see, for example, Halpern & LaMay 2000).
- Society as a whole reflects value systems that are embedded in **gender stereotyping**.
- Appropriate activities for girls and boys, appropriate career aspirations, and appropriate behaviour and values are often sharply delineated and reinforced by families, peer groups, and organisations such as churches and clubs. These values, which are passed on to children through socialisation (much of which occurs before children begin school), are quite resistant to change, irrespective of what the school and teachers do (Martin 2003a, 2003b; Quaiser-Pohl & Lehmann 2002; Weaver-Hightower 2003).

So, as you can see from this, the evidence, while mildly in favour of single-sex schools for females, does not give sufficient reasons to abandon co-educational education at the high school level. Indeed, there may be other ways of obtaining similar benefits while retaining the advantages of co-education, such as single-sex activities within a co-educational structure. What do you think? (See also Wallace, Boylan, Sharman & Kay 1990.)

What, then, are the implications of this research for the effective teaching and learning of females and males? Go through each of the points above and in Table 9.2 and see if you can work out strategies that might alleviate sex biases in the classroom. After doing this exercise, consider Table 9.3 which details some potential strategies.

Children with special needs in mainstream classroom settings

In this section we consider the special needs of children with disabilities. A disability refers to the functioning of a person within the environment, the expression of a physical or mental limitation in a social context, and the gap between a person's capabilities and the demands of the environment (Pledger 2003). There is a strong environmental component in assessing whether a person has a disability or not, as the environment helps to determine what an individual can or can't do. In other words, disability is not necessarily inherent but is revealed through interactions of the individual with the environment. This is important, as it means we can't label individuals as able or disabled, or determine the level of disability, without some reference to their environment.

We describe categories of disability for the sake of clarity. However, categories blend for all children and it is important to keep this in mind while reading the following sections.

Some children have sensory disabilities, motor disabilities, health impairments or emotional disorders that require special attention from parents, teachers and other professional groups involved with children. The causes and nature of these disabilities are usually well described in developmental psychology and special educational texts and will not be discussed in detail here.

Table 9.3

Essentials of a non-sexist classroom

Teachers should:

- monitor interactions with girls and boys to see that they are equivalent;
- encourage non-volunteering students of either gender to participate actively in activities;
- implement classroom practices to facilitate equal opportunity for responses—for example, greater wait-time after questions (to facilitate responses from girls and shyer boys) and deliberate turn-taking;
- organise practical activities so that all students have equal time with equipment and materials. Learning centres and rosters might help;
- model problem solving rather than giving the answer or strategy;
- emphasise divergent and independent thinking;
- stress cooperative activities more than competitive ones;
- proscribe any form of bullying or gender harassment;
- provide curricula materials that are of interest and relevance to girls and boys in all academic areas;
- provide models of women in mathematics, computing, science and politics, as well as in the humanities. Have real-life guest speakers, visits to workplaces and video library material;
- include social and real-life contexts in as many activities as possible;
- vary assessment tasks and modes;
- provide opportunities for student choice of assessment mode.

(Source: Based on Altermatt *et al.* 1998; Bailey 1993; Fennema & Peterson 1987; Munter 1993)

Teachers should teach learners to:

- be confident about asking the teacher for help with work or answering questions;
- ask for opportunities to experience a range of activities, computer software and books (irrespective of whether you are a male or female);
- offer opinions in small groups or whole-class discussions—be an active listener; ask questions; encourage others to speak;
- not allow anyone to intimidate or harass you—enlist the help of others or the teacher;
- be an active participant in cooperative activities—remember, your role is important to the whole group achieving its goal.

TEACHER'S CASE BOOK

Sexist remarks

Nancy was concerned about remarks she heard Thomas making in her second class. 'Girls can't do computers!' 'I don't have to do a project with her, she's just a girl.'

She had tried chatting quietly with him about these opinions, but had found him resistant to her point of view. Subsequently, during a parent–teacher interview, Nancy felt she needed to tell Thomas's parents that their son had a tendency to make genderist remarks to the other children. Nancy knew from a previous experience that such remarks were acceptable at home.

She explained to the parents that children, particularly girls, did not like to work with their son because of his remarks, and that because of this Thomas was beginning to miss out on some things. The parents became quiet and left shortly after.

Nancy continued to seek informal opportunities to follow up her concerns with Thomas and his family. She also started to collect magazine articles, books and photographs that showed men and women involved in and excelling in a range of sports and occupations. She planned to include them in her teaching.

Case studies illustrating National Competency Framework for Beginning Teaching, National Project on the Quality of Teaching and Learning, Australian Teaching Council, 1996, p. 13.

Case study activity

Consider Nancy's approach. How effective do you think it would be? Will classrooms and schools ever be able to alter children's values that are the product of socialisation within the home?

Our main focus is to highlight some of the more common disabilities and their implications, and some of the supports available for these children and their teachers. Further details can be found in Ashman and Elkins (2002), Butler (1990), and Cole and Chan (1990).

Among the common disabilities that children have are learning disabilities (such as attention deficit hyperactivity disorder), intellectual disabilities, autism and cerebral palsy. Others suffer from behavioural, physical, hearing and visual disabilities.

Keeping in mind that we don't advocate a categorical approach (that is, categorising children with disabilities), for the purposes of description we give a brief survey below of a few of the identifiable characteristics of a number of these disabilities.

Attention deficit hyperactivity disorder

Among the student disabilities that teachers are most likely to encounter in the regular classroom is **attention deficit hyperactivity disorder** (ADHD). The title of the disorder really sums up the symptoms—namely, children characterised by low attention to task, distractibility, poor impulse control and high physical activity levels. There are a number of subtypes of the disorder in whom one or other patterns of symptoms, such as hyperactive-impulsive or inattentive types, predominate (Hoong, Houghton & Douglas 2003). By physical activity we mean intensity level, frequency and duration of small motor behaviour such as fidgeting, body ticks, tapping of feet and hands, and excessive locomotion (Pelligrini & Horvat 1995; see also Hoong, Houghton & Douglas 2003; Purdie, Hattie & Carroll 2002). Children with high, rather than low, physical activity levels are typically low achievers at school and often experience such social problems as peer rejection and teasing. Inattention to task has obvious implications for academic achievement. When both these characteristics occur together, they can cause profound problems for the children concerned.

American data suggest that ADHD is a significant educational problem and this is also the case in Australia and New Zealand. Data from the United States indicate that about 4 per cent of the primary school population have ADHD and that, of these, about 80 per cent are boys (Pellegrini & Horvat 1995; see also Chess & Gordon 1984; Kelly 1988). In Australia, prevalence of ADHD has been found to range from 3–9 per cent to as high as 15–24 per cent (Hoong, Houghton & Douglas 2003). The onset of ADHD appears to occur in the first grade and remains relatively stable after that. Symptoms of what appears to be ADHD in a range of settings, including school, are assessed using a diagnostic manual.

No one is certain of the cause of ADHD. Biological causes are implicated, and ADHD has been related to both *minimal brain dysfunction* and *attention deficit disorder* in which inattention and impulsivity are key symptoms. However, it is very likely that, while biology might explain the initial occurrence of ADHD, later social experiences within the home and school probably contribute to its maintenance and development (Bailey 1992; Purdie, Hattie & Carroll 2002).

It is not unreasonable to speculate that children who exhibit 'problem' behaviour at both home and school may be subjected to coercive socialisation and educational practices that exacerbate the 'problem'. Pelligrini and Horvat (1995) suggest that it might be issues such as this that explain the difference in the diagnosed incidence of ADHD between boys and girls, and between older and younger children. Many of the behaviours that are considered 'normal' for younger children, such as high levels of exploratory activity and energetic, lively play and movement, are considered undesirable or even 'abnormal' in primary grades. These behaviours are actively fostered by the adult caregivers and teachers of younger children. In contrast, primary school and high school are often regimented places, which demand particular behaviours of students that are in marked contrast to their established behaviour patterns. In other words, ADHD may be compounded by the lack of fit between expected classroom routines and students' individual temperament.

For many teachers, students diagnosed as ADHD can be particularly difficult to handle, although behaviour modification programs and an increasing use of drug therapy have helped to alleviate their symptoms. Dietary changes (for example, eliminating food dyes and additives from the individual's diet) have also reduced the level of hyperactivity in some children (Pelham & Murphy 1986; Purdie, Hattie & Carroll 2002; Walden & Thompson 1981). Some would argue that it is possible that a better matching of students' temperaments to educational experiences may alleviate the problem for many students. (See Pelligrini & Horvat (1995) for a discussion of this issue.) Others believe that ADHD may be related to the unpreparedness of some students for particular learning activities and advocate further learning experiences to improve these inaptitudes. (See the section on aptitudes later in this chapter.) For example, Laszlo (1996) suggests that giving ADHD-diagnosed students extra visual-motor coordination training should enhance their school behaviour and performance.

Intellectual disability

Intellectual disability is a very broad term encompassing a wide range of disabilities within two basic categories: mild intellectual disability and moderate to severe disability. Two criteria are usually employed to classify individuals as intellectually disabled: (1) their intellectual functioning must be significantly below average; and (2) their adaptive behaviour (that is, their ability to be personally and socially independent) must be severely impaired. You will appreciate the danger inherent in classifying individuals in terms of their IQ score alone.

Increased educational opportunities for the academically disadvantaged

Research has consistently shown that either changing environmental conditions or increasing environmental stimulation for the intellectually disabled enhances development, in some cases quite dramatically (Balla & Zigler 1975; Dennis 1973; Horn 1983; Nelson, Cummings & Boltman 1991; Scarr & Weinberg 1983; Turkington 1987). Behavioural disorders, which are often manifested by intellectually disabled individuals, create further management difficulties for teachers and parents, and limit the placement of such individuals in regular school settings. However, there is sufficient evidence to indicate that intellectually disabled individuals benefit from the experiences that characterise a normal person's lifestyle, even though the stresses on the caregiver may be high.

Autism

Autism relates to an individual's extreme inability to relate to other people and a tendency to withdraw from real life and indulge in day-dreaming and bizarre fantasies (Jones 1988; Wolman 1989). Autistic individuals often display symptoms such as repetitive rocking, head banging, apathy, fear of change, insistence on preservation of sameness, lack of interest in people, severe speech disorders with frequent mutism, and extreme aloneness (Wolman 1989). The educability of these individuals depends on the severity of the symptoms as well as their level of intelligence. When severity is less and the individual has a reasonable level of intelligence,

Autism severely limits the capacity of individuals to relate to other people.

parental and educational interventions can enhance the person's development so that they become able to socialise and engage in productive work (Chess & Gordon 1984; Jones 1988).

Cerebral palsy

Cerebral palsy is a form of paralysis resulting from brain injury (Wolman 1989). In addition to the motor dysfunction caused by the paralysis, cerebral palsy may also include learning difficulties, psychological problems, sensory defects, convulsions and behavioural disorders (Bigge & Sirvis 1982; Chess & Gordon 1984). As with the other disabilities we have discussed, there is a great range in severity and manifestation. While intellectual disability may be associated with cerebral palsy, not all cerebral palsied individuals are intellectually disabled. (Indeed, some are in the higher levels of intellectual functioning.) Furthermore, it is not certain whether some who are classified as intellectually disabled really are, or whether the tests used to measure level of intellectual functioning have been inadequate to assess their true potential (Cruickshank, Hallahan & Bice 1976). Due to the neurological damage, even cerebral palsied people with normal intelligence suffer significant difficulties with perceptual and language disorders, poor manual control and visual-motor ability, distractability and lessened physical vitality. Associated emotional problems together with absenteeism related to their disability problems (Chess & Gordon 1984; Kirk & Gallagher 1983).

Visual impairment and hearing impairment

While there are clinical definitions of both visual and hearing impairment, such definitions unfortunately do not allow for the diversity in the manifestation of either condition, or indicate appropriate remedial action that will alleviate the condition and allow the mainstreamed student to benefit from education in a regular classroom. Added to this are complications arising from the time of onset of the disability and its association with other disabilities. For example, many individuals who suffer visual impairment also suffer multisystem disorders that involve other parts of the brain as well (Chess & Gordon 1984).

Visual impairment

As indicated in Chapter 2, much of the early learning of a child is sensorimotor-oriented. Children who are blind from birth may therefore have limited opportunity to test themselves out in the physical world. (Parents may be hesitant to allow the visually impaired child to explore in case they hurt themselves.) Consequently, the gross and fine motor skills, perception and perceptual-motor integration that are so important for development

Often children only need small adjustments to their environment (such as eyeglasses) to stride ahead with their learning.

will not be acquired. Furthermore, such restricted experiences ultimately limit cognitive development. Visually impaired children may also develop mannerisms such as rocking or tilting the head, which can be disturbing to parents and other people such as teachers (De Mott 1982; see also Scholl 1987).

A general term, *hearing impaired*, is often used to describe individuals with all levels of hearing loss. However, there is great diversity within this group related to the degree and nature of the hearing loss, the age of onset of the loss (for example, prelingual or later), existence of other disabilities, and the nature of the infant care and socialising experiences of the child (among a host of other things). To highlight one of the complexities here, we note that some hearing-impaired individuals might not learn to speak as a result of intellectual disability that is also manifested in hearing impairment, while in other cases they may fail to speak simply because they have never heard the spoken word.

Hearing impairment

In general, hearing-impaired individuals with no other handicap have essentially the same distribution of intelligence as hearing individuals. The use of hearing aids and knowledge of speech reading help many of these individuals to develop well (Mollick & Etra 1981). There is some debate as to whether signing should be taught or whether children should be taught speech reading exclusively. However, today the trend is to teach sign and speech reading as part of a total program that also includes gestures and facial expressions (Hallahan & Kauffman 1988).

Other disabilities

Within any classroom there are students who suffer a range of other disabilities that have an impact on their learning and motivation. For example, you will teach students who have *behaviour problems*, *speech disorders* (such as poor articulation, stuttering and delayed language development), motivation and attention problems, and psychological problems such as excessive fear and *anxiety disorders* (for example, test anxiety and school phobia). Increasingly, individuals with even severe physical impairments, such as being restricted to a wheelchair or walking with the aid of callipers, are being mainstreamed (see Butler 1990; Cole & Chan 1990; King *et al.* 1990).

Behaviour problems
Speech disorders
Motivation and attention problems

We also note here a range of other debilitating conditions, such as *asthma* and *epilepsy*, which may impede an individual's education. These health impairments should cause few problems if the teacher is fully aware of the student's condition and physical and medical requirements. Schools today request emergency contact phone numbers and procedures from all students on enrolment. Medications, if required, should be clearly labelled and stored in an accessible place. Teachers should have a *peer support system* to operate in case of emergency. Peers need to be trained in procedures involving illness or emergency. We remember one class we visited in which a child was prone to sudden and severe epileptic seizures. The third-grade children were well aware of the child's behavioural and facial changes, and had been trained to notify the teacher promptly and to clear furniture away from the child so that injury would be minimised. The sense of responsibility and care for the disabled child was very obvious.

Asthma and epilepsy

Inclusion and effective learning

The least restrictive environment

As a flow-on from the civil rights movement in the United States, educators and parents became more concerned with the rights of children with disabilities. Foremost among these was the right to an education that took into account the individual differences charac-

Increasingly, children with disabilities are being included. When effectively handled, this enriches the experiences of able and disabled children alike.

terising disabled children and which would maximise the quality of their lifestyle. As a result, a significant law called the *All Handicapped Children Act*, Public Law 94-142 (PL 94-142), was enacted by Congress in 1975 (Gallagher 1989; US Congress 1975). Now known as the *Individuals with Disabilities Education Act* 1997, this law guaranteed the right of a disabled individual to an appropriate public education in the '**least restrictive environment**'; in other words, individuals with disabilities were to be schooled along with their regular peers unless their disabling conditions were so severe as to make this undesirable or impracticable. In the latter case, special educational provisions were to be made available, such as special classes and special schools. The inclusion of individuals with disabilities within regular classrooms has been called **inclusive education** (Alper & Ryndak 1992; Frederickson, Osborne & Reed 2004; Madden & Slavin 1983; Mamlin & Harris 1998; Zigmond 1995). Initially, **inclusion** was to apply to learners with mild disabilities who had some academic proficiency. Increasingly the approach was applied to the integration of students with moderate and severe disabilities, which has been termed *full inclusion* (Brantlinger 1997). Not everyone agrees with inclusive education, and the issue of how best to serve the educational needs of disabled students is as political and ideological as it is educational (see, for example, Brantlinger 1997; Ferguson & Ferguson 1997; Frederickson, Osborne & Reed 2004; Gresham & MacMillan 1997a, 1997b; Smith 1999). In our later sections we provide some of the educational arguments for and against inclusive education. Table 9.4 provides some essential points on the least restrictive environment.

To enable the effective inclusion of disabled students, an **individualised educational plan (IEP)** was prescribed for each disabled student who was to be educated within the regular classroom and school. There were levels of restriction (referred to as the *cascade of services* model), which reflected the potential of the individual (Reynolds 1984). The following list is one form of the cascade model (Fuchs, Fuchs & Fernstrom 1993). On the successful accomplishment of tasks at one level, individuals were to be moved into the next level of least restriction.

- Regular classroom
  - Regular classroom with consultative assistance
    - Regular classroom plus part-time resource room
      - Regular classroom plus part-time special class
        - Full-time special class
          - Full-time special day school
            - Homebound instruction
              - Hospital or residential placement

The passing of PL 94-142 had a significant effect on provisions for students with disabilities in both Australia and New Zealand and internationally (Bailey 1992; Frederickson & Furnham 1998; Gow 1989; Levin 1985; Rietveld 1988). A survey by the United Nations Educational, Scientific and Cultural Organization (UNESCO) reported that mainstreaming (now referred to as *inclusion*) was a declared policy in 75 per cent of the 58 countries responding in 1988 to a survey (cited in Frederickson & Furnham 1998). There is wide consensus throughout Australia and New Zealand that individuals with disabilities have the same basic rights to a full education as all other individuals. There is also general acceptance of the notion of integration. This is reflected in goals of the national and state Departments of Education, which typically include statements on the integration of all students with disabilities into regular classroom environments whenever practicable, and the necessity of providing high-quality services that are sufficiently diverse and flexible to meet the educational needs of all students (Gow 1989). The least restrictive environment (sometimes referred to as the *most advantageous environment*) concept has been the guiding principle in the development of programs across Australia and New Zealand over the last two decades. And, as noted earlier, this model allows for the placement of people with disabilities along a continuum of services ranging from the least restrictive to the most restrictive (Gow 1992).

As a result of these initiatives in special education, students with disabilities are being integrated increasingly into regular classrooms and schools. As a teacher, you will probably face the added challenge (characterised by joys and frustrations) of teaching students with disabilities in your classroom. There are significant differences, however, between Australian states in their interpretation and implementation of inclusion. Within Australia, Victoria comes closest to the **zero reject model**, in which all individuals, irrespective of disability, are educated within the environment of the local school (Grbich & Sykes 1992; see, however, Marks 1992a, 1992b). New Zealand is also strongly committed to this model (Harvey & Green 1984) and because of its unified system of education has been more successful in applying inclusion.

Arguments for the least restrictive environment

Many educators argue that labelling and segregated schooling restrict the educational opportunities made available to individuals with disabilities, as teachers fail to appreciate the potential of these individuals and teach to

Table 9.4 Essentials of a least restrictive environment for students with disabilities

- Providing educational services in the regular classroom.
- Providing services in a more restrictive setting only when necessary and moving students to the next level when they are 'ready'.
- Meshing special and regular education services as indicated by students' needs.
- A special-needs perspective which supports the notion that curricula and instructional procedures should meet individual needs.
- Encouraging a sharing of responsibility by special and regular educators.
- Enhancing the likelihood that the student will function more appropriately in society at large.

(Source: Based on Gow 1992)

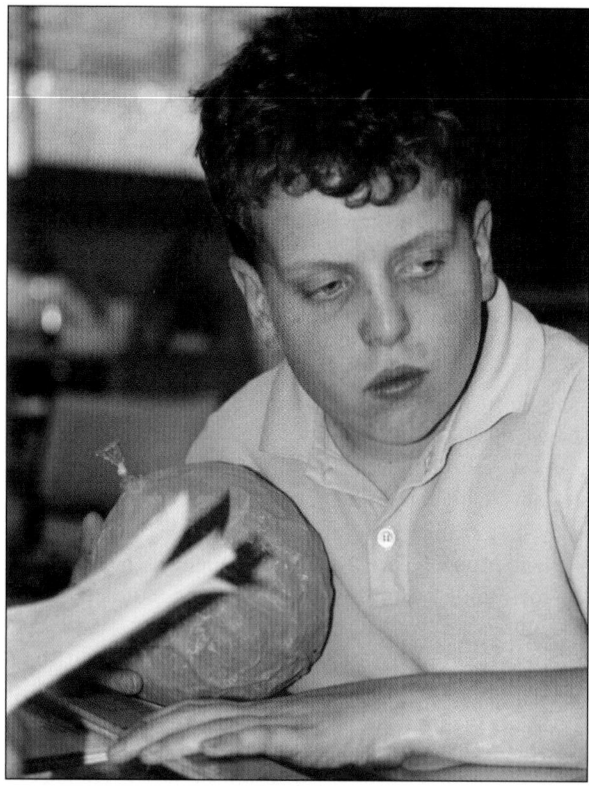

The blind learner enjoys working in the mainstream classroom. What particular advantages would the mainstream classroom provide?

limited expectations (see, for example, Smith 1999). There is also limited opportunity for students with disabilities to interact with their age peers, which reduces their opportunity to learn much normal behaviour modelled by their peers, as well as restricting the opportunity of non-disabled peers to learn from the disabled (Atkins & Lewis 1982; Casey *et al.* 1988; Grbich & Sykes 1992; Jenkins, Odom & Speltz 1989; Madden & Slavin 1983). Furthermore, the labels used to describe students with disabilities are considered to be detrimental to their sense of self as humans and learners, making it difficult for them ever to enter the mainstream (Gow 1992).

Positive effects of inclusion

There is no doubt that inclusion has been successful for many children (Center *et al.* 1989; Frederickson, Osborne & Reed 2004; Gow 1989; Jenkinson & Gow 1989; Madden & Slavin 1983). There is a general consensus that inclusion leads to either improved academic and/or social progress for learners with special needs, or at least to the same outcomes as those experienced by students who are segregated (Jenkins *et al.* 1985; Wang, Reynolds & Walberg 1988). Furthermore, well-designed inclusion also appears to benefit the non-disabled peers of disabled students. Among the benefits cited are: the opportunity for non-disabled students to learn new skills and new values and

EXTENSION STUDY

Alternative models of inclusion

Gow and others argue that we should be moving to a new model of integration, the *all-inclusive collaborative school model.* The basic notion here is that all students have special needs of one kind or another and all teachers should, in a sense, be special educators. As such, it is a matter of degree, and all students with disabilities should be accommodated in regular classrooms and schools (especially equipped to integrate the students effectively) as a matter of course, and only be restricted when it is demonstrated that such integration is not appropriate. In the all-inclusive collaborative school the arbitrary distinction between those students who receive 'special help' because they are labelled 'special' and those who don't is broken down.

Similar calls for what has been termed the **Regular Education Initiative** (REI) are being made in the United States. Advocates of REI argue that all students, whether or not they have been identified as having disabilities, should be educated together (Alper & Ryndak 1992; Fuchs *et al.* 1993; Gallagher 1990; Lipsky & Gartner 1989; Schloss 1992). This movement addresses the right of each student who lives in the catchment area of a school to be included in all aspects of life at that school. It also affirms the right of those students with disabilities to participate fully in that life alongside the non-disabled peers who attend the school.

Problems of implementing the least restrictive environment

There is opposition to full inclusion from some academics, teachers and parents who fear the burden will be too great for schools to carry, and that students who need specialised attention will not receive it adequately in a mainstreamed setting (see, for example, Brantlinger 1997; Frederickson, Osborne & Reed 2004). Bain (1992) argues that because there is no legislative equivalent of PL 94-142 determining attitudes about human differences; the opportunity for non-disabled students to develop a greater sense of responsibility and to assume new social roles; the opportunity for non-disabled students to develop valuable social, emotional and personal perspectives; and the opportunity to make friends with and learn from people who are different from themselves (Alper & Ryndak 1992).

As well as these important considerations, effective instructional methods developed for the learning disabled are equally likely to be effective with non-disabled students. All students should do better academically and socially in classrooms where the focus is on individual needs (Schloss 1992).

QUESTION POINT

Consider the potential problems with inclusion outlined above. How would you address such issues?

ACTION STATION

Consider a range of individual education programs (IEPs) in schools. Discuss, with those responsible for their development, how particular IEPs were designed. Using information provided about a particular student and classroom observation over a period of time, if possible, design an appropriate IEP.

What are some classroom implications of inclusion?

At times there will be students in your classroom with very mild forms of disabilities which may not have been identified in the home. Observant educators take note of unusual behaviour of individuals, such as holding books too close to the eyes or turning one ear in the direction of the teacher, and refer any student suspected of having a disability to a health specialist. Early attention, even at this stage, will help to avoid more severe problems developing and may have positive consequences for behavioural and learning outcomes (see, for example, Nicholson, McFarland & Oldenbury 1999).

Early identification

The early identification and treatment of problems may be hampered in a number of ways. For example, children of migrant parents who speak little or no English may have disabilities that are not diagnosed before the child begins school owing to the parents' lack of awareness and lack of information on sources of health monitoring (Masselos & Hinley 1981). When at school the problems may continue to be undetected for a period because of the child's lack of English. In other cases, isolation may be a confounding factor in the early identification and treatment of problems. For example, Aboriginal children living in remote areas may develop eye problems that

Children of migrant parents

entitlement to special education in Australia, and there is little commitment to resource inclusion effectively, the policy has the potential of returning special education to what it was like 50 years ago—that is, severely disabled students placed in highly restrictive settings, and more moderately disabled individuals placed in regular classes with minimal support from untrained personnel.

Some academics (for example, Bornholt & Cooney 1993; Chapman 1988; Marsh 1984; Marsh & Johnston 1993; see also Frederickson & Furnham 1998) argue that students' self-concepts as learners are more likely to be positive when their frame of reference for comparison is peers of like ability. Placing these students in a situation where their limitations are more obvious in comparison with others who have greater apparent skills and talents may cause a decrease in perceived competence, and a decline in academic and physical self-concept. Consequently, inclusion may have more harmful side-effects for individuals with disabilities than the labelling that occurs when they are put into special classes and schools (Marsh & Johnston 1993). (See also Cole, Vandercook & Rynders 1988; Ferguson & Ferguson 1997; Gresham & MacMillan 1997a, 1997b; and Chapter 14.)

There are also many teachers who do not feel competent to handle special needs students within the regular classroom and refer these students on for diagnosis, identification and special services in more restricted educational environments. Among the reasons given for this are lack of teacher preparation to work with at-risk students; lack of knowledge or experience with referral processes; lack of other sources of services, system or school failure to accommodate individual differences and heterogeneous populations; and the insistence often of parents and child advocates that students should be placed in more specialised educational settings (Mamlin & Harris 1998). Many teachers refer students to other levels of special education because of different kinds of social and emotional behaviour problems that teachers cannot control (Mamlin & Harris 1998). This is particularly the case where the family or guardians were not able or willing to work with the school to address these problems.

go undetected and untreated as a result of their geographic isolation.

At other times, parents may fail to acknowledge that their child has a disability, hence delaying and frustrating attempts by other caregivers to assist their child. This can be made worse if parents spend little time with their young children and don't want to acknowledge 'problems'. Such situations occur if both parents work and leave the child for long periods in the care of untrained caregivers rather than family members (Judge 1987; Masselos & Hinley 1981) or leave them by themselves. It is important to note that certified early childhood caregivers are trained to take note of developmental anomalies in young children.

When individuals with disabilities are mainstreamed, there are several implications for the schools and teachers charged with their care and education. To assist schools and class teachers, a number of resources are made available by education departments to service students' and teachers' needs. These include special facilities, support teachers, specialist advisers, special classes and placements. Each school will have a list of the relevant services that are available.

You may feel a little daunted by the prospect of having to teach students with disabilities in your classrooms and wondering how you will cope. You are not alone in these concerns. A study of students with severe intellectual disabilities who had been mainstreamed found that school personnel involved in integrating these students were concerned about: (1) their own lack of knowledge and skills necessary to modify the curricula; (2) their need for more specialist support; (3) the lack of positive evidence of academic progress for the integrated student; (4) timetable problems; and (5) lack of time and lack of resources (Grbich & Sykes 1992; see also Harvey & Green 1984; Madden & Slavin 1983). Other less frequently

EXTENSION STUDY

How do attitudes towards disability impact on motivation and learning?

An attitude is a disposition to respond favourably or unfavourably towards some person, thing, event, idea, place or situation (Wortman & Loftus 1992). These thoughts and feelings encourage us to act as if we like or dislike something. Psychologists believe that attitudes have three components: (1) what you think or believe about something (the cognitive component); (2) how you feel about it (the emotional component); and (3) how you act towards it (the behavioural component) (Wortman & Loftus 1992). Often these three components are consistent, but at other times they may be conflicting, and competing demands may produce behaviour inconsistent with thoughts and emotions. At times, individuals hold attitudes that need to be changed or modified.

Individuals with disabilities come from families that have varying attitudes to disability. While many come from supportive homes, others come from homes characterised by blame and superstition, by a belief that the disability results from curses, evil spirits or even a punishing god (Judge 1987; Smith & Smith 1991). These attitudes towards the cause of the disability and the disabled provide a less than ideal environment. Some parents want to hide their disabled child. Some remain in a state of grief and don't establish an effective relationship with the child. Others resent the attempts made by educators and health professionals to rehabilitate their children if this is seen to run counter to cultural beliefs.

A further problem for many individuals with disabilities lies in their physical appearance and perceived incompetencies, which can be disconcerting both to other peers and teachers in the regular classroom and to parents and the community in general. The spasticity and abnormal speech patterns characteristic of some disabled individuals readily set them apart and often, sadly, provoke negative attitudes and social rejection by peers and teachers. Many mainstreamed students may feel socially rejected (Frederickson & Furnham 1998). This, in turn, can cause psychosocial development problems that have little to do with the original condition (Lewandoski & Cruickshank 1980). Clearly, as teachers, we must be prepared to change our own attitudes and to assist students who hold negative attitudes to change them.

Strategies to improve and develop positive attitudes

Research over several decades has shown that teachers' attitudes are one of the most important variables in the success of inclusion schemes. In general, teachers have been found to express positive attitudes towards the inclusion of children with special needs in regular classrooms, and in some cases are more positive than parents (Hastings &

reported concerns were student resentment and teasing (by students without disabilities), and staff resentment of the presence of a student with disabilities. Among the advantages mentioned were improved social benefits for all, improved confidence, and sometimes improved academic performance for the student with disabilities.

Teacher concerns

It is important that those who work with students with disabilities see those learners as individuals first and as students with disabilities second. Throughout this text we emphasise the need for teachers to design educational programs with an eye to individual differences in the classroom, and have considered a range of topics related to this, such as team teaching, mixed ability teaching, cooperative learning, peer tutoring, teaching for diversity, individualising instruction through special programs and the use of technologies, and a variety of evaluating and reporting schemes. You will find specific suggestions to enable you to help the student with disabilities in your classroom at the end of this chapter in the section on adaptive education. The chapters on learning, motivation, classroom management, effective teaching and instructional technology will also be of considerable help. Educational programs that are effective in promoting academic achievement for students with disabilities in mainstream educational settings are effective for all students. To the extent that teachers apply good teaching practice in regular classrooms, they are already in a strong position to teach students with disabilities effectively. Further sources of information on this important topic may be found in Ashman and Elkins (2002), Butler (1990), and Cole and Chan (1990). Table 9.5 provides some essential elements of an effective school for children with disabilities.

Oakford 2003). Attitudes have been found to vary according to the nature of the disability, the level of training and previous contact with disability of the teacher, and the age group of the disabled children. In general, children with less severe special needs, and who are therefore less demanding in terms of teaching resources, are viewed more positively than those with severe disabilities. Teachers who have had non-work experience of disability are more positive than those who haven't, while teachers with more years of teaching experience are found to be more negative (Hastings & Oakford 2003). Some teachers are more positive about working with children with disabilities in younger classes, while others feel more positive about working with these children in older classes.

Not being able to 'get into the mind' of those with apparently severe disabilities, it is natural for many to feel profound sympathy for those afflicted and to want to do things for them. This can be very damaging to the self-esteem of a disabled person, who may well want to make the effort (albeit very laborious and even painful) to function as 'normally' as possible. Be prepared to feel helpless and confused as to what is acceptable, and do not hesitate to ask the disabled person what they would like you to do. Such respect is appreciated and deserved.

Part of our role as teachers of students with disabilities in regular classrooms is to educate ourselves and others (children and parents) to accept students with disabilities as individuals with strengths and talents. Furthermore, we need to educate students with disabilities to be adaptive to society, to help them develop the personal skills to cope with the good and bad that society will present and to become socially integrated (Fisher *et al.* 1989; Harvey & Green 1984; Paterson 1992; Rietveld 1988; Stephens & Stephens 1986).

How attitudes can be changed has been the subject of much research that is beyond the scope of this book. However, *persuasive communication* involving an expert source of knowledge, honesty and sincerity, importance and relevance, can be most effective. Having individuals experience unpleasant tension (sometimes called *cognitive dissonance*) by confronting incompatible thoughts (such as the belief that one doesn't want to associate with disabled individuals and the belief that disabled individuals are entitled to normal respect and treatment) can lead to a shift towards behaviour consistent with more positive attitudes.

In addition to such programs, which are designed to improve attitudes and behaviour, the following strategies are important: school authorities need to support fully the notion of integration; students with disabilities must be considered part of the normal student body; planning should be effective and include input from students, family members, teachers and others involved in the placement; there must be effective communication before and during the integration between concerned parties; and classrooms and schools should be mastery-oriented, rather than performance-oriented, to alleviate the negative effects of social comparison (Alper & Ryndak 1992; Cole *et al.* 1988; Madden & Slavin 1983).

Table 9.5 Essentials of an effective school for students with disabilities

Teachers should:

- adopt a philosophy, state it and plan for it strategically—for example, 'Every child is here to learn';
- remove labels such as 'Special Education' from doors, from students and teachers, and especially from resource rooms;
- make resource rooms open to all students and teachers; a place where all students can go for more assistance and a place where teachers can go to consult collaboratively with their colleagues;
- plan according to the needs of the individual students, not for administrative expedience;
- work as a team. Collaborate with special educators and resource teachers, parents, guidance officers and other professionals;
- use an integrated, multidisciplinary team approach. Be flexible in your use of human resources;
- create a more caring school environment where diversity is celebrated and not merely accepted. Help all students, teachers and parents feel that they belong by working to establish a school policy of caring;
- make use of the special resources in your region.

(Source: Based on Gow 1992; Mamlin & Harris 1998)

ACTION STATION

Discuss the arguments for and against the inclusion of students with disabilities. Does the type of disability make a difference?

Social constructivism and special needs education

There is a growing interest in applying principles of social constructivism to special needs education (Gindis 1995; Trent *et al.* 1998). Indeed, Vygotsky had a special interest himself in special education (see, for example, Gindis 1995). You will recall from our discussion of social constructivism in Chapters 1 and 2 that social constructivism focuses on the growth of 'public' subject matter of individuals in social domains and in particular in relationship to families, peer groups and schools which orient children to interpret and make sense of their world of experiences. This process of knowledge construction comes about as learners become encultured into the knowledge and symbols of their society. This view emphasises collaborative inquiry through which individuals appropriate information in terms of their own understandings of, and involvement in, the activity. In cases where learners are having difficulty or are being challenged to extend their understanding, teachers and others provide the prompts, scaffolding and guidance

TEACHER'S CASE BOOK

Playground insults

When I heard some of my Year 3 students using the word 'spastic' as a playground insult, I was offended. I told them the comment was completely inappropriate, and we had several class discussions about the terms 'spastic' and 'cerebral palsy'. Most of the children agreed that the word 'spastic' should not be used as a derogatory comment towards someone. However, I observed that there were still several individuals who persisted in using the word as an insult. After discussion with some colleagues during a break, it was obvious that the problem did not exist exclusively within my class, and so it was decided to invite some guest speakers from the Cerebral Palsy Association to address the students.

The two visitors, both sufferers of cerebral palsy, spoke frankly and openly to the students in each class at the middle and senior school levels. Their honest and humorous presentation was well received by the students, many of whom were keen to ask questions of the speakers throughout the sessions. I particularly observed the thoughtful questions and comments made by some of the former perpetrators from my class both during and after the talk. It was clear that the visitors had some effect on the attitudes of these students.

Case study activity

Why did the presentations by the two cerebral palsy visitors have a more positive effect than teacher admonition? Why are positive expectations of teachers towards students with disabilities so important to their success at school?

Why are positive expectations of teachers towards children with disabilities so important to their success at school?

Even small tasks can be quite an achievement for severely disabled children.

needed. This form of social constructivism emphasises the importance of continuing interaction between the learner and its social environment to facilitate meaningful learning (Anderson *et al.* 1997; Greeno 1997; Sfard 1998). As we noted in Chapter 2, for Vygotsky cognitive development is not so much the unfolding of mental schemas within the individual as the unfolding of cognitive understandings of social beings within social contexts. In a sense, we become part of the community and the community becomes part of us in the sharing of knowledge. Vygotsky believed that all learners should be challenged to be engaged in activities that appear to be beyond their current level of development. Students can often complete activities with the collaboration of teachers and peers that they could not complete on their own. Aspects of social constructivism, such as the zone of proximal development, scaffolded instruction and mediated learning through peers and adults are, therefore, particularly relevant to special needs learners. Although Vygotsky never argued that special needs students should be educated in mainstream settings (see Gindis 1995), special programs of education that isolate the special needs learner in separate classrooms or other educational settings are considered by many social constructivists to be inappropriate and inhibitory of these learners developing their full potential. Social constructivists consider that many of the 'remedial' approaches used in these settings (such as direct instruction) are not appropriate and fail to provide the holistic education essential for the development of human potential. Indeed, it is believed that such approaches characterise the individual as suffering deficits that must be remediated rather than looking for the strengths of the individual as a person developing within a heterogeneous community who both learns within and contributes to the growth of that community. For these social constructivists there is no 'normal' community from which the 'abnormal' can and should be separated, but rather one holistic heterogeneous community.

As you would have surmised, not all educators believe in the merits of social constructivism for special needs students and criticise the approach for being too vague. Many of these authorities advocate direct instruction and other approaches derived from behavioural theory as more effective. Indeed, many of these advocate teaching these students in specialised settings in order to maximise their learning. We have looked at this argument in our sections above. Two teaching approaches derived from social constructivism that have been found to be very helpful for mildly intellectually disabled students are reciprocal teaching (see Chapter 5) and the Early Literacy Project (Trent *et al.* 1998). As with most areas of teaching and learning, extremes are probably unwise and so we recommend you consider both approaches and incorporate elements of both, as appropriate.

The gifted and talented and effective learning

Ability in various academic, creative and social domains lies along a continuum. We have spent some time discussing the needs of individuals with various forms of disabilities that affect their effective learning. We now move to the other end of the continuum to consider the special needs of individuals who are gifted and talented.

Who are the gifted and talented?

Among the characteristics of gifted individuals are above-average intelligence, above-average problem-solving ability (particularly in their use of metacognitive strategies), greater intellectual curiosity, academic interest and challenge-seeking behaviour, higher preference for independent mastery, an emotive interest in their work, greater motivation and persistence than average-ability students (for example, see Dai, Moon & Feldhusen 1998; Hoge & Renzulli 1993; Reis 1989; Renzulli 1986; Shaughnessy 1993; Tannenbaum 1986). High perceived academic competence sets gifted students apart from other students, and they have higher mathematical and verbal self-efficacy (Dai *et al.* 1998). However, gifted and talented students do not form a homogeneous group. They can display many different talents and come from many different backgrounds. Individuals who are quite gifted across a number of areas may nevertheless require remediation in certain subject areas, and various talents may become evident as individuals grow older (Cropley 1993a, 1993b; New South Wales Department of School Education 1991; Reis 1989; Sternberg & Davidson 1985; Torrance 1986; Weill 1987; Yewchuk 1993). Some argue that giftedness and talent is dynamic, evolving in different sociocultural contexts and therefore varies from context to context. It is dependent on the dynamic interaction between individuals and their physical and sociocultural contexts (Barab & Plucker 2002). Barab and Plucker state:

Broader perspectives on giftedness and talent

'So there you are, Leonardo! Will you stop that infernal doodling and get yourself down to the footy field where a boy of your size belongs!'

'Whether a particular individual-environment interaction is considered talented is very much socioculturally determined. Therefore, an important part of exhibiting talented behaviour involves understanding how to act in a manner that is consistent with those ways that have been socioculturally endorsed—that is, functional for a particular group' (2002, p. 174). We examine this issue later in the chapter when we discuss minority interpretations of giftedness and talent. You can also see a link here with both Sternberg's triarchic theory of intelligence and Gardener's multiple intelligences.

The issues of the definition and measurement of giftedness and the identification of gifted and talented individuals are enormously complicated (see Dai *et al.* 1998; Hoge 1988). In the past, individuals who scored an IQ of 130 on the Binet performance test were considered gifted (Shaughnessy 1993). However, the specific attributes assessed by such a single measure often bore little relationship to the cluster of qualities more

Identifying gifted and talented individuals

All children are potentially gifted and talented. How should schools foster talent?

broadly characteristic of the gifted individual. Today, a more thorough screening process, based on a wider conceptualisation of giftedness, is used to identify gifted and talented individuals for purposes of special educational programs. Among the measures that may be used are standardised tests of creative and general ability, behavioural checklists, anecdotal records, interviews, products and performance, class grades and multi-dimensional testing (Frasier 1989; New South Wales Department of School Education 1991; Reis 1989; Sternberg & Davidson 1985). As with any assessment of students' abilities, we should consider the evidence from a number of sources.

Programs for the gifted and talented

We have maintained many times throughout this text that teachers of the regular classroom should be competent to facilitate the learning of all students in their classroom. The previous section, dealing with students with disabilities, indicates that there is some movement towards inclusive schooling and mainstreaming educational opportunity for these students. It would appear a little odd, therefore, to argue here that the gifted and talented should be educated in special schools or special classrooms isolated from the mainstream. One objection to special programs is that they neglect the important fact that all individuals can be talented and gifted to a greater or lesser degree, and well-trained teachers should endeavour to maximise the talents of all students.

The all-inclusive school

Many people argue that the gifted and talented student's educational needs are not being met adequately in the regular classroom and because of this they are a disadvantaged group (Cropley 1993a, 1993b; Horowitz & O'Brien 1986; Relich & Ward 1987; Rothman 1990; Walker & Barlow 1990). Some argue very strongly for the establishment of special classes, schools and programs for the gifted. Selective high schools and gifted classes are designed to meet the needs of the gifted student. Research generally indicates that grouping gifted students facilitates their cognitive and social development while having no impact on the achievements or attitudes of the peers remaining in the regular heterogeneous classroom (Feldhusen 1989; Urban 1993).

Special classes for the gifted

There are, nevertheless, a number of provisions that can be made to facilitate the education of these gifted students which can be provided within the context of the regular classroom and regular school (Lloyd 1999; Urban 1993). Regular classes can give enough room to improve the achievement of gifted students by reshaping teaching methods, grouping with differing levels of difficulty, encouraging creative thinking, and using well-designed and organised extracurricular activities. Indeed, we have argued strongly that schools need to be adaptable to the special needs of all learners. This is particularly important when we consider the fact that very few potentially gifted individuals will ever find themselves in a special program for the gifted. Provisions that can be made within the regular school context are shown in Table 9.6.

Classroom provisions

Many schools run camps, clubs or extension programs where courses of study are provided in one or more areas for gifted and talented students so that the students may extend their talents while working with similarly talented and focused youngsters (McKeith & Daniel 1990; Rickard 1981; Torrance 1986). Various states in Australia and schools in New Zealand have applied different policies governing these practices (Braggett 1987; Smith 1987).

Coping with giftedness

Apart from the academic issues, teachers of gifted learners need to help them cope with the special problems that might arise from their giftedness (Hoge & Renzulli 1993). Cropley (1993a, 1993b) suggests that teachers and counsellors should help gifted learners with special problems such as:

- perfectionism and fear of failure;
- ambivalence about themselves (that is, a concern over whether they are really gifted or not and whether they want to push themselves);
- arrogance or its opposite;
- self-doubt;
- deviation from family or peer norms; and
- social isolation associated with being different.

Many gifted learners develop interests and ambitions that are widely different from the expectations held by parents and peers, and this may cause them to become isolated.

Table 9.6 Classroom provisions for the gifted and talented

- *Teaching strategies* that involve the implementation of appropriate and specific strategies in the regular classroom to stimulate the development of gifted and talented students. These strategies could include self-directed and independent study, and individual education plans (IEPs) (for example, see Treffinger 1982; Urban 1993).
- *Flexible progression,* which involves the promotion of a student to a level of study beyond the usual one for their age group. This flexible progression may take one of the following forms:
  - *early enrolment*;
  - *early completion* of a stage and entry into the next stage in one or more subjects;
  - *early entry to tertiary education*;
  - *compaction of course content* (for example, see Brown 1982; Feldhusen 1989; Kulik & Kulik 1984; Rogers & Kimpston 1992; Stanley 1978, 1980; Torrance 1986; Urban 1993);
  - *vertical grouping,* which may involve grouping students by ability across age ranges or stages of development (for example, see Maxwell *et al.* 1989).
- *Enrichment,* which is a process of adaptation of the curriculum to enable gifted and talented students to pursue study of a particular topic at greater depth and breadth. It might include special tasks, projects, freely selected activities, interest clubs, resource rooms, seminars, independent study and field trips (for example, see Maker 1987; Print 1981; Urban 1993).
- *Mentor programs,* whereby gifted and talented students are matched with mentors with expertise and ability to foster the development of the students (see Urban 1993).

Cropley also suggests that educational and career guidance take on additional dimensions with gifted individuals: linking students up with out-of-school programs or mentors; finding teachers who display special sympathy or skills with gifted learners; and so on. Personal counselling is needed to help gifted learners set realistic goals, accept and live with the consequences of giftedness on social relations, come to grips with the social and emotional situation within the family, and develop a strong self-concept and identity.

The effects of teacher and parental expectations on gifted students

In general, teachers hold expectations of gifted and talented learners that facilitate their development. Good and Brophy (1990), however, appropriately caution teachers about holding expectations of gifted students that may cause problems. High-achieving students are often expected to do too much too soon, and are 'not allowed' to make mistakes, 'slacken off' or be reflective. They are expected to be deeply knowledgeable, but are often given too little opportunity to develop and deepen their understanding before being pressured to move on (see also Horowitz & O'Brien 1986).

Family pressures may create difficulties

Family pressures may also create difficulties for the gifted. Problems can be caused by overambitious parents determined to push their children to the limits, or by parents who are afraid that their children may 'get above' their station in life and therefore doom themselves to isolation from family and friends. In some cases, parents become overawed by the child's talents and expect the child to become the emotional support for the family. Accumulated pressures may lead to gifted adolescents feeling they have been robbed of their childhood (Cropley 1993a, 1993b).

Gifted and talented minority children

Sternberg and Davidson (cited in Reis 1989) state that giftedness is a concept that we invent, not something we discover. As such, it is whatever a society wants it to be, making it subject to change according to time or place. Very often we think of giftedness and talent from a limited cultural perspective. Some cultures even refuse to accept the notion of giftedness (Shaughnessy 1993). As teachers, we need to be sensitive to cultural variations in the meaning and demonstration of giftedness and talent. As a simple example, from a Western cultural perspective giftedness may be recognised in those children who are competitive and verbally fluent. Other cultural groups may not value these qualities, but rather value an individual's capacity to coordinate and lead a group while remaining in the background.

Our cultural and socio-economic group may either facilitate or inhibit access to the means of developing particular talents. For example, children with the capacity to be gifted, and talented writers, musicians and sportspeople, may be limited in their access to opportunities. Some cultural groups give little freedom to females to engage in sport or a wide range of social activities, consequently limiting the opportunity for the development of talent (Cropley 1993a, 1993b).

Minority groups, whether they are cultural, socio-economic or gender-based, are often underrepresented in special programs for the gifted and talented (Boyd 1993; Frasier 1989). We should assume that giftedness and talent are normally distributed and we must ensure, therefore, that our methods of identifying the minority gifted and talented are not biased (Brown 1983; Feldhusen 1989; Frasier 1989). The Implementation Strategies for the Education of Gifted and Talented Students (NSW Department of School Education 1991) suggest that a wide range of methods is needed to ensure that all students who are gifted and talented are identified, particularly when identification is generally difficult. There are many reasons for this. Students, for example, may be:

- from non-English-speaking backgrounds;
- Aboriginal or Maori;
- disadvantaged by gender inequity;
- socio-economically disadvantaged;
- disabled physically or in terms of sensory functions;
- diagnosed as intellectually disabled; or
- conduct-disordered.

As you can see from this list, special needs blur across categories. Further complications are introduced when we realise that some students may actively disguise their giftedness and talents to maintain peer acceptance. It is commonly believed that Aboriginal students cover up their talents so that they are not perceived to be 'better than their mates'. Some students just don't like to appear different.

QUESTION POINT

What special precautions should be taken by schools and teachers to identify the gifted and talented among minority groups and children with disabilities?

QUESTION POINT

Should there be special educational programs for the gifted and talented?

Creativity and effective learning and teaching

What is creativity?

As with intelligence, there is no agreed-upon definition of **creativity**. Indeed, the fuzziness of the term has caused problems for both research and program development in the area (Plucker, Beghetto & Dow 2004). Some definitions of creativity emphasise personality characteristics, while others focus on the process of thought. Still others emphasise the product of effort as the criterion of creativity (Feldhusen 1995; Logan & Logan 1971; Perkins 1981, 1988).

Characteristics of creative people

Torrance (1962, 1986) found that the creative children he studied had a reputation among their peers for having 'wild' or 'silly' ideas, and their work was atypical, characterised by humour, playfulness, relaxation and lack of rigidity.

MacKinnon (1962) found that more creative individuals described themselves as inventive, determined, independent, individualistic, enthusiastic and industrious, while less creative individuals described themselves as responsible, sincere, reliable, dependable, clear-thinking, tolerant and understanding.

Getzels and Jackson (1962) found that personality characteristics such as relative absence of repression, openness to experience, sensitivity, lack of self-defensiveness, and awareness of people and phenomena in the environment were related to creativity.

Research into the personal characteristics of creative people supports many of these stereotypes (Perkins 1981). A person can't be very creative without seeing things in unusual ways, accepting unconventional thoughts or exhibiting independence of judgment. Other personal characteristics, such as being highly observant

Being creative starts early! How can creativity be stimulated by parents and early childhood educators?

or tolerant of ambiguities, also seem to play clear supporting roles in creative effort. However, such personal characteristics may cause a problem for teachers who may view creative students as nonconformists and troublemakers (Plucker, Beghetto & Dow 2004).

Stages in creative thinking

Creative thinking may also be looked at as a cognitive process involving various stages of mental processing by which individuals discover something new (at least for themselves) or rearrange existing knowledge, a rearrangement that might involve an addition to knowledge (Frederiksen 1984). Many techniques have been used to uncover elements of the creative process, including retrospective self-disclosure by creative people, tracking through 'hard data' such as drafts of stories, paintings and other compositions, and psychological monitoring of the process while it is occurring (such as having people report on their thoughts during or right after a mental activity) (Perkins 1981).

Among the stages that might characterise creative thinking are the following suggested by Wallas (1926):

1 *Preparation*—intense study of the problem at hand; involves assembling all the available information and working through it so that it is clearly understood. Often the creative individual becomes so immersed that they won't even break for refreshment. We have all heard of the artist hidden away in a garret producing the definitive poem, novel or musical score.
2 *Incubation*—a period of rest and reflection, engagement in an activity not related to the work under consideration. Somehow, during this period, the mind continues its search as it seeks to uncover new relationships between the assembled facts.
3 *Illumination*—flash of insight that puts the various elements into their proper relationship. Distractions at this time can be disastrous, as they disrupt the flow of thought.
4 *Verification*—a period of intense, systematic work during which the poem is written down and polished, the theory tested or the machine built. It is at this time that the idea must be tested against the cold reality of fact. Will it work? Does the building stand up? Does the audience applaud? This stage is very irksome for many individuals who like to pass the baton on to someone else to continue with the work while they move on to other endeavours.

Do you go through these stages when you are 'being creative'?

The creative product

What makes a truly creative product? This is highly contentious, as the judgment of creativity is so subjective. Some products achieve fame because general consensus holds that they are creative. But once we move outside the area of general consensus it is extremely difficult to judge what is truly creative. One of us has been standing admiring Jackson Pollock's *Blue Poles*, only to hear passers-by comment that a class of preschoolers could have produced something as good. We are not particularly impressed by gallery collections that include crumpled garbage cans or large canvases filled with various shades of white (called *Illumination in White*). Creative products appear, nevertheless, to be characterised by competence, originality, scope and significance.

In a review of a number of creative people in a special issue of *American Psychologist* (56(4), 2001) it is obvious that the characteristics of creativity are diverse. Sternberg, editor of this special edition, summarised that highly creative people decide, among other things, to redefine problems, analyse their ideas, attempt to persuade others of the value of their ideas rather than expecting others readily to accept them, take sensible risks, seek bizarre connections between ideas that others do not seek, and realise that existing knowledge can be a hindrance as much as it is a help in generating creative ideas (2001, p. 361). Many of these ideas reflect those dealt with above.

ACTION STATION

From their review of definitions of creativity, Plucker, Beghetto and Dow (2004) derived a definition of creativity that they argue clarifies defining elements of creativity. They believe that creativity is the interaction among *aptitude, process* and *environment* by which an individual or group provides a *perceptible product* that is both *novel* and *useful* as defined *within a social context*. After completing reading of this chapter, you should illustrate with an example each component of this definition. How useful do you think this definition is for clarifying the concept of creativity?

How do we assess creativity?

Tests of creativity

Just as understanding what creativity is across many diverse domains of human activity is complex, so too is the assessment of creativity. Tests have been designed to measure the person, process and product components (Feldhusen 1995).

J. P. Guilford (1967, 1985; see also Meeker, Meeker & Roid 1985) devised a series of tests of creative thinking, based on his model of intelligence, which attempt to tie together the qualities of the creative process and the creative person. The traits that Guilford believes are related to creativity are the *ability to see problems*, *fluency of thinking* (that is, coming up with a lot of ideas), *originality* (no one else thinks of the idea), *redefinition* and *elaboration* (describing the features of the solution in detail). Guilford believes that these elements may be measured through a series of tests:

- *Word fluency*—how many words ending in 'ion' can you think of (the divergent production of symbolic units)?
- *Ideational fluency*—think of as many words as you can that refer to things soft, white and edible (the divergent production of semantic units).
- *Originality*—unusual and clever responses, such as the consequences test: What would happen if everyone in the world doubled in size? What would happen if all teachers had a strike for 12 months?
- *Spontaneous flexibility*—freedom from inertia in giving a diversity of ideas, such as in the uses test: How many uses of a house brick can you think of (the divergent production of semantic classes)?
- *Adaptive flexibility*—the tricky problems test, where solutions require ingenuity and unconventional responses. This involves lateral thinking—that is, seeing a number of possibilities and evaluating them.

The more creative the individual, the higher the score on each of these tests.

Fluency
Flexibility
Originality
Elaboration
Tests of creativity

Paul Torrance (1962, 1966, 1973, 1986; see also Plucker 1999) believes the creative process to be characterised by *fluency*, a fertility of ideas; *flexibility*, the ability to abandon old ways of thinking while initiating new ones; *originality*, the ability to produce uncommon responses and unconventional associations between ideas; and *elaboration*, the capacity to use two or more abilities for the construction of a more complex object. His thoughts have also been reflected in a series of tests. One common type of test is the circles test (see Logan & Logan 1971). For this test, individuals are given a series of empty circles (see Figure 9.1) and invited to use the circles to complete as many objects as possible in 10 minutes. By objects we mean such things as a fried egg or a pair of glasses. A circle must be a main component of each drawing and individuals are encouraged to put as many ideas into each drawing as they can think of. We have had many university students complete this test and it is very illuminating! Why don't you try it?

The 'test' is scored for the number of responses made (fluency); the number of idea changes that occur (flexibility) (some individuals have a one-track mind and simply draw lots of objects related to food, while others move rapidly across a range of objects); the amount of detail in the drawing (elaboration) (some people present just an outline of a pair of glasses, while others draw a full face with glasses, including eyebrows, hair, and so on); and, finally, originality—that is, the number of ideas that rate as unique (based on surveys of the most common responses). This last one always gets us into trouble, with individuals arguing that drawing a fried egg is highly original!

The validity of creativity tests

Guilford, Torrance and others maintain that tests of creativity measure ability for creative thinking and are predictive of later creative behaviour. However, some authors believe that, to the extent such tests have time constraints, involve some level of anxiety and are conducted in an artificial atmosphere, they really don't measure creativity as it occurs 'in the real world'. (See Plucker (1999) for a description of some of the perceived limitations of creativity tests.) These authors believe that creativity occurs only in open, stress-free situations, and basically the response made must be to a real situation (see Feldman, Csikszentmihalyi & Gardner 1994). What do you think?

Teacher and pupil ratings

Less formal means of assessing creativity may be through teachers' ratings of students and peers' ratings of each other. You will find that some students in a class will be very popular during composition time as their stories are always interesting, full of action and humour. The other students will love listening to them. Others will produce paintings and craftwork that the class really appreciates. And, of course, there are always the individuals who are great at theatrics (both wanted and unwanted!). Using this information, it is relatively easy to assess individual levels of creativity without resorting to formal tests. Torrance suggests the following clues to help a teacher decide when creative behaviour is taking place:

- intense absorption in listening, observing or doing;
- intense animation and physical involvement;
- use of analogies in speech;
- tendency to challenge ideas of authorities;
- taking a close look at things;
- eagerness to tell others about discoveries;
- continuing in creative activities after time allocated;
- showing relationships between apparently unrelated ideas;
- various manifestations of curiosity;
- spontaneous use of discovery or experiments;
- habit of guessing and testing outcomes;
- independent action, boldness of ideas; and
- manipulation of ideas and objects to obtain new ones.

CIRCLES See how many objects you can make from the circles. Add lines to complete your picture, inside, outside or both. Try to be original. Make as many objects as you can.

Figure 9.1

How can we develop creativity in the classroom?

Many of our classroom activities are concerned with developing conventional ways of doing things. Teachers really don't want students to invent new tables and spellings or new ways of doing long division. Many classrooms supply little opportunity for the development of creativity. Indeed, many of our classrooms do not appear to be creativity-fostering places for a variety of reasons, including the biases of teachers, traditional classroom organisations, assessment processes, and mandatory curricula among others (see, for example, Plucker, Beghetto & Dow 2004; Strom & Strom 2002).

Potential hindrances to the development of creativity

Torrance has listed the common educational hindrances to creative thinking, including: attempts by adults to eliminate fantasy; restriction of the individual's manipulativeness and curiosity; overemphasis or misplaced emphasis on gender roles; overemphasis on prevention, fear and timidity as control measures; misplaced emphasis on certain verbal skills; emphasis on destructive criticism; and coercive pressures from peers to conform.

Holistic approach to teaching and learning

What we envisage to address this situation is a total approach to teaching that does not divide the creative, intuitive and **divergent** from the **convergent**, deductive and logical. The responsible teacher should develop an approach that integrates all modes of thinking and, most importantly, should model these in the classroom. A number of formal programs have been developed to help teachers stimulate students' creativity. Among these are de Bono's CoRT program and the Purdue Creativity Thinking Program. Reviews of research on the effectiveness of creativity enhancement programs suggest that creativity can be taught effectively (Feldhusen 1995).

Creative self-expression is the ultimate example of constructive thinking.

What does this mean in practical terms? The acrostic in Table 9.7 presents a number of ideas for stimulating creativity in the classroom. Being creative is the ultimate in constructivism, and teaching to stimulate creativity is the ultimate in being a constructivist teacher (see, for example, Plucker, Beghetto & Dow 2004).

ACTION STATION

Consider the options for stimulating giftedness and talent presented in Table 9.6, earlier in the chapter. Arrange these in order of acceptability and practicality. What can you do personally to encourage the development of giftedness and talent in the children you teach?

Adapting schools and classrooms to individual differences—constructivism in practice

As we have seen throughout this chapter, students in any one classroom differ from one another in many ways, although there are broad similarities that make it reasonable to group them as a cohort. Providing they are not extreme, some individual differences, such as levels of physical and motor development, and behavioural and personality differences, can be adequately catered for in any well-organised classroom. Tolerance and understanding on the part of the teacher, as well as some level of individual attention and individualising of instruction, are often all that is needed for most individuals to thrive in regular classrooms.

At times there will be individuals in our classrooms whose special needs require a little more attention at either the classroom, school or system levels. There is a continuum: all individuals have special needs of one kind or another at some time or another, and all individuals have common needs of one kind or another.

Adapting teaching programs

While the thought of adapting your teaching program to suit each individual in your classroom may appear daunting, we have already covered many of the essential features of adaptive education. All the chapters in this text give perspectives on how you might function effectively as an adaptive teacher, whether in terms of presenting material programmatically for some students and through discovery learning for others, the nature of the resources you choose, or the way you evaluate. As well, you will

Theory and research into practice

Mary Ainley — STUDENT APPROACHES TO LEARNING

BRIEF BIOGRAPHY

My career has been built around both psychology and education. As a young psychology graduate with a B.A. (Hons) Dip Ed., I was appointed to the Secondary Teachers' College in Melbourne at a time when there was a desperate shortage of teachers. One of the courses designed to fill that gap required qualified psychology staff. This opportunity crystallised my academic interests into the psychology of education and development. It was in this environment that my interest in curiosity and intrinsic motivation grew.

I have been fortunate to be involved in education, learning and development across a variety of areas. Choosing to spend time with my children when they were young provided me with what could be called intensive participant observation of children's development. It was also immensely enjoyable. Important developmental experiences were happening in front of me—curiosity, play, exploring the environment, mastering language, enjoying books and early attempts at reading.

I spent a couple of years in the early 1990s as chair of the Eastern Metropolitan Council of Adult, Community and Further Education. This experience gave me an appreciation of the wide variety of ways that people in the community express their desire to learn and understand their world. Lifelong learning is alive and well.

For most of my career I have taught developmental psychology to large classes of undergraduate students, and provided supervision for postgraduate and honours research projects. I find teaching a challenging experience, as my research into curiosity, interest and other aspects of student motivation is always confronting me with what the best in learning is all about. Currently I have a senior lecturer position at the University of Melbourne Psychology Department. I also support the work of the International Conflict Resolution Centre.

RESEARCH AND THEORETICAL INTERESTS

My explorations into the nature of curiosity in my Ph.D. studies have coloured my thinking on a wide range of issues. My early investigations into the nature of curiosity taught me that most complex human behaviour depends on closely intertwined affective and cognitive processes. Some of the techniques I have been using to measure affect in learning contexts have applications for identifying affective processes that influence children's social skills.

In the early 1970s there was a landmark symposium on intrinsic motivation in Toronto and the papers were published in a volume edited by Day, Berlyne and Hunt (1972). This brought together the research on curiosity that was stimulated by Berlyne's (1966) volume, *Curiosity and Exploration* and work by researchers such as Day who were taking an individual differences approach and treating curiosity as a trait.

As a young Ph.D. student I wanted to contribute my synthesis to the debate and, following work by Langevin (1971), developed a model of curiosity that distinguished breadth-of-interest curiosity from depth-of-interest curiosity. Both involve approach to novelty, but the quality of the approach behaviour is different. Breadth-of-interest curiosity involves approach to novel experiences in order to experience the sensations, to sample the experience. On the other hand, depth-of-interest curiosity is about approach to novelty in order to understand, to find out about, to get to the bottom of the novel event. My argument was that these different forms of curiosity are similar in being approach behaviour, but they also share some affective qualities. Using Izard's differential emotions theory I was able to show that they share an emotional quality of interest-excitement but they have different combinations of supporting affects. Breadth-of-interest curiosity involves balancing fear and excitement, while depth-of-interest curiosity combines interest, enjoyment and surprise. It has not been hard for me to see links between the arguments I advanced for the importance of affective responses in curiosity and directions to be pursued in researching affective components of students' interest in learning.

Developing research interests are also about the networks that are established with other researchers. I have been lucky to be part of a very productive research relationship with Dr Suzanne Hidi from the Ontario Institute for the Study of Education, now part of the University of Toronto. Suzanne Hidi has written extensively on the nature of interest and its role in learning and development. Together we have developed a strategy for measuring how interest that might be triggered by the topic of a learning task plays out across the entire learning episode. In particular, I wanted to be able to identify the role of positive affect in maintaining the connection between student and task to allow learning to happen. Earlier with Di Bretherton and Ann Sanson, colleagues in the Psychology Department and

International Conflict Resolution Centre, we planned to develop an interactive measure of children's social problem-solving skills. Emotion icons were used to measure children's affective responses. We were a little too demanding for the technology of the time and the complex monitoring of action and reaction we wanted was just out of our reach. With the speed of technological development I have been able to make use of our earlier trials and have developed a means of having students report how they are feeling during the course of an achievement task. The technique that I have used at the upper primary and secondary levels involves emotion probes consisting of face icons. These appear on the screen at pre-set points in a learning task. A number of clicks and the student has reported feelings and the intensity of those feelings with minimal disruption to the task.

All of this comes together in the basic issue that concerns me in all my research. The person comes to a new situation, whether it is an achievement or a social interaction setting, with a certain combination of traits, dispositions and well-developed interests. It is the interaction of person and situation that is intriguing, the processes triggered by specific features of learning situations and how these processes play out for different students.

THEORY AND RESEARCH INTO PRACTICE

There are two specific areas of my research that have contributed to the broad body of knowledge of how motivational processes influence students' learning. In one of my first academic papers published in the *Journal of Educational Psychology* (Ainley 1993), I presented some findings concerning relationships between students' approaches to learning or the structure of their learning goals, and the types of strategies they use when preparing for examinations. This was one of the early papers in the student motivation literature to use cluster analysis techniques. If we take seriously the idea that motivation is multidimensional, we need to employ analytic techniques that capture some of that complexity. Identifying groups of students who share similar patterns of motivation for learning and then comparing their behaviour in a specific learning setting allows us to appreciate how students function, not just how variables operate when everything has been controlled. These two approaches to research are sometimes referred to as 'person' versus 'variable' approaches. Findings from these different research traditions are complementary rather than being in competition. Interestingly, my study was able to demonstrate that students with different motivational profiles were likely to use different learning strategies when preparing for exams. It was not so much which type of strategy was used but the balance of transformational (deep) and reproductive (surface) strategies. Students who were committed both to developing their skills and to performing well were more likely to show the balance in favour of the deep, transformational strategies. Disengaged students relied more heavily, but not exclusively, on surface or reproductive strategies. School achievement was also related to these motivational profiles.

The second area which has contributed to my work being known internationally has been my collaboration with Suzanne Hidi and our development of what could be called a micro-level approach to understanding motivational processes. Our thinking led us to consider that it is important to understand the processes that colour students' experience of learning. Work that Suzanne Hidi reviewed in 1990 clearly showed that it may be easy to trigger students' interest in learning tasks, but maintaining that interest for sufficient time to promote learning is a problem for educators at all levels. We decided first to design software that would allow recording of students' reactions while engaged on a learning task. This has been achieved with our *BTL* software (*Between the Lines,* Ainley, Hidi & Tran 1997), a research tool that can be adapted for investigation of specific research questions. The basic idea is that students are required to make choices and to respond to probes as they work through a learning activity. As researchers we then have a detailed record of targeted aspects of students' learning experiences. We have used this to investigate the processes that contribute to the influence of interest on learning. Most of our studies have involved students responding to text passages. The latest version of the software presents problem topics and information resources for students to use as they work on the problem. In this way we have a window into some of the important component processes of student motivation and examine how they relate, first, to students' prior dispositions, interests and abilities, and second, to achievement outcomes. These research interests have been challenging, sometimes frustrating, but worthwhile in their contribution to practical understanding of the complex processes that underpin students' achievements.

KEY REFERENCES

Ainley, M. (1987) The factor structure of curiosity measures: Breadth and depth of interest curiosity styles. *Australian Journal of Psychology*, **39**, 53–9.

Ainley, M. (1993) Styles of engagement with learning: A multi-dimensional assessment of their relationship with strategy use and school achievement. *Journal of Educational Psychology*, **85**, 395–405.

Ainley, M. & Hidi, S. (2002) Dynamic measures for studying interest and learning. In P. R. Pintrich & M. L. Maehr (eds) *Advances in Motivation and Achievement: New Directions in Measures and Methods (Volume 12)* (pp. 43–76). Amsterdam: JAI.

Ainley, M., Hidi, S. & Berndorff, D. (2002) Interest, learning and the psychological processes that mediate their relationship. *Journal of Educational Psychology*, **94**, 545–61.

ACTIVITIES

1 Mary Ainley believes that most complex human behaviour depends on closely intertwined affective and cognitive processes. This would imply that individuals differ quite a bit on the interaction of these in any particular context. Discuss some of the affective and cognitive processes that have oriented your behaviour in specific contexts. How do these differ from those of your peers?

2 Mary Ainley discusses the differences between breadth-of-interest curiosity and depth-of interest curiosity. Explore each of these and describe how these perspectives are important to teachers.

3 *Interest* in learning is a relatively new area of research. Students differ in interest, and teachers have different capacities to stimulate interest. Consider the points made by Ainley on the nature and importance of interest and follow up her work, and the work of her colleagues, to discover more about the role of interest in learning.

4 Mary Ainley presents much evidence for the importance of studying individual differences in learning. Outline some of the main issues she addresses and follow these up in her key readings as well as in topics covered throughout this chapter.

attempt to foster intrinsic motivation and to teach metacognitive and self-regulating skills to learners. In other words, you have knowledge that should enable you to adapt your program of teaching to the special needs of all the students in your class, and to assist individual students to adapt to particular forms of instruction.

Adaptive education refers to educational approaches aimed at effectively accommodating individual differences in students while helping each student to develop the knowledge and skills required to learn particular tasks. Adaptive education is characterised by flexibility in instructional procedures, assessment procedures, and resources so that students can take various routes to, and amounts of time for, learning (Abedi, Hofstetter & Lord 2004; Brophy 1988; Corno & Snow 1986; Pitoniak & Royer 2001; Wang & Lindvall 1984). Essentials of adaptive education are found in Table 9.8.

One of the first things you need to do as a teacher is to assess the special strengths and weaknesses of individuals in your classroom in terms of the learning outcomes to be achieved. Particular learning goals will call upon different student strengths (in a number of places these are called *aptitudes*), while particular student weaknesses (often called *inaptitudes*) will inhibit the attainment of specific goals (Corno & Snow 1986; see also special edition *Educational Psychologist*, 38(2), 2003). Aptitudes may be *cognitive* (such as intellectual abilities and prior knowledge), *conative* (such as cognitive and learning styles) or *affective* (such as academic motivation and related personality characteristics). Aptitudes interact in a complex way to facilitate or inhibit learning particular tasks (Ackerman 2003).

Student aptitudes and inaptitudes

Depending on your assessment of the relevant aptitudes of each student in your classroom, you can begin to develop programs that build on existing aptitudes or remediate or circumvent inaptitudes. In other words, you need to devise instructional alternatives that are matched to the performance and needs of the learner.

Another consideration when developing individual programs for students is whether or not the goals being set are common educational goals that are to be met by each individual in the educational system (to a greater or lesser extent) or goals that might more appropriately be individual. Teachers often confuse the two and give themselves endless problems trying to get all their students to master the same goals. For example, aspects of literacy and numeracy are common, socially desirable goals. In contrast, an ability to play the recorder may be an individual goal. When we look at the curriculum from this perspective it gives us a better sense of where our efforts should lie in helping students to learn.

Common goals and individual goals

Many adaptations can be made in the classroom, while some can be made by the school or indeed by the educational system as a whole. Adaptations that can be made in the classroom may be termed *microadaptations*, while larger school or system adaptations may be termed *macroadaptations* (Corno & Snow 1986). Table 9.9

Table 9.7

Fostering creativity in the classroom

Confidence: Instil in students a confidence in their abilities in all activities. Many students believe that they just aren't any good at writing, art, music, performance and general problem solving. Creativity can be shown across the curriculum and children must be encouraged to try their skills at everything. There are many underachievers in creative behaviour, but few overachievers. The challenge for teachers and parents is to discover ways of equalising creative potential and creative achievement. Confidence in themselves as learners and creators is an essential element of this.

Respect: Respect students for all their ideas and contributions. Show that you value creation. Encourage students to think of knowledge as incomplete, to ask questions, to look beyond given facts.

Enjoy: Learning and creating is fun! Far too many adults have lost their joy in creating. Recapture in your classrooms the energy and joy that characterises young students learning and discovering in the natural world. Abandon the distinction between work and play in the classroom. Provide opportunities for students to explore and create in a non-evaluative atmosphere.

Activity: Provide opportunity for unstructured and active involvement in learning and discovering. Excessive seatwork and formal exercises can stultify creativity.

Time: Allow time for students to reflect; this will allow ideas to incubate. Rather than expecting immediate responses and disciplined schedules of production, encourage students to research, think, rest and then come back again to the task with new insights. Show students how to use time effectively for reflection—model it yourself!

Integrate: Design learning experiences that integrate formal logical thinking with the opportunity for divergent thinking. Show how they work in tandem to produce really important knowledge. Show that information from a variety of sources can and should be used to solve problems. Show how there is mathematics in music and science in art!

Value: Reward and praise the unusual and unconventional as much as the conventional and convergent. Show that you value the creative contribution made by individuals whether it be in academic, social, interpersonal or performance areas. There should be a place where students can exhibit their art, display their stories and demonstrate their abilities. Treat students' ideas with respect, as indifference or ridicule will stifle students' creativity.

Invite: Members of your school's community have many talents. Invite them into your classroom as colleagues to motivate students to be creative.

Tolerate: Be prepared to tolerate disorder and messiness during the creative process. If you insist on neatness and everything being done in the 'right' way at the 'right' time, you will stifle creativity. At the appropriate time students should be disciplined to 'verify' their production according to the appropriate criteria for presentation. Remember that being creative is not an excuse for a sloppy final product, but a certain level of disorder is essential to the creative process. You must also be prepared to tolerate a certain level of the unexpected, whether it be in behaviour or product. When students are given the opportunity to create, they will also set out to shock.

You: Yes, *you* play a very important role in developing the creative powers of students in your care. Through your expectations, modelling, designing of appropriate educational experiences, valuing and enjoying what your students produce, you are a major player in the student's development as a creator and thinker.

Table 9.8

Essentials of an adaptive learning environment

- Instruction based on the assessed capabilities of each student.
- Materials and procedures that permit each student to progress at a pace suited to their abilities and interests.
- Periodic evaluations that inform the student about mastery.
- Student assumption of responsibility for diagnosing present needs and abilities, planning learning activities and evaluating mastery.
- Alternative activities and materials for aiding student acquisition of essential academic skills and content.
- Student choice in selecting educational goals, outcomes and activities.
- Students' assistance of one another in pursuing individual goals and cooperation in achieving group goals.

(Source: Based on Wang & Lindvall 1984)

TABLE 9.9 Adapting education to suit individual needs

MICRO ADAPTATIONS	using a variety of teaching skills; variability, questioning, reinforcement focusing on diversity and individual differences giving students the time needed to learn providing flexibility in classroom rules and organisation monitoring and processing student feedback and other environmental cues—modifying instruction as required modelling thinking and learning processes using a variety of lesson formats and resources for presenting material, e.g. programmed instruction lecture, self-directed guided learning, ICAI—Intelligent Computer Assisted Instruction, parent educators and excursions structuring lessons through the use of advance organisers, headings, reviews using a variety of styles of discourse
MICRO/MACRO	providing for individualised goals and programs, e.g. negotiated curriculum providing flexible teaching/learning spaces, e.g. individual study spaces, clustered desks, interest centres, resource centres using group work—student collaboration, cooperative learning, provisions for students to seek help and give help, peer and cross-age tutoring using task analysis and matching student characteristics (such as competence, attitudes, values) with task demands, e.g. IEPs—Individualised Education Plans teaching thinking/learning skills to provide the student with skills to adapt to the demands of the material/course to be learned implementing enrichment/remediation programs implementing intervention strategies to develop in students a positive sense of self as a learner, and self-regulatory and self-management skills providing flexibility in assessment and reporting criteria
MACRO ADAPTATIONS	providing appropriate physical (such as ramps and special equipment) and educational (a variety of teaching aids and materials) resources providing elective as well as core subjects implementing streaming by ability and needs implementing multi-age or multigrade classrooms implementing vertical grouping and semesterisation providing opportunities for accelerated promotion implementing special programs aimed at providing for students' individual differences, e.g. PLAN—Program for Learning in Accordance with Needs, PSI—Personalised System of Instruction, IPI—Individually Prescribed Instruction, TAI—Team Assisted Individualisation, IGE—Individually Guided Education, ML—Mastery Learning providing resource personnel (such as support teachers), special curriculum advisers and teacher aides providing effective guidance counselling adopting a whole-school approach, e.g. ALEM—Adaptive Learning Environment Model; establishing special schools/centres, e.g. selective high schools, hospital schools, extension programs, intensive language centres implementing bilingual and community language programs

presents ideas on some of the adaptations that may be made to individualise instruction in your classroom, and indicates how these overlap with school and system adaptations. Many of these adaptations are discussed in this text.

QUESTION POINT

How can classrooms and schools best adapt to the wide range of individual differences between children in our classrooms?

ACTION STATION

In Table 9.9 we have listed adaptations that can be made within schools and school systems to cater for the individual needs of students. Using this framework as a guide, consider ways in which adaptations for students have been made in schools with which you are familiar. Highlight adaptations that are micro, macro or a combination of each. Consider adaptations that have not been made. Why is this so? Are they potentially useful? Could they be introduced?

WHAT WOULD YOU DO?

GIRLS DON'T MAKE CARS

The Year 2 children were happily engaged in a construction project during a maths activity session when Mrs Arturo overheard Ben make a sexist remark to another student. 'You can't use those wheels, Kelly, because girls don't make cars, so give them to me,' said Ben.

This placed Mrs Arturo in a dilemma. She always tries to accept the home values of each child, but she also wants to support community standards of gender equity. Mrs Arturo stood outside the group and listened to the children's response to Ben.

'Girls do,' replied Kelly. 'I'm allowed to.'

'No, you're not,' replied Ben. 'My sister's not allowed to play with my Lego at home.'

'She can make cars,' said Michael, 'because my sister does.'

'Yes, I think she can too,' added Josh.

Case studies illustrating National Competency Framework for Beginning Teaching, National Project on the Quality of Teaching and Learning, Australian Teaching Council, 1996, p. 13. Commonwealth of Australia copyright, reproduced by permission.

How would you deal with Ben's sexism? Now read what the teacher did.

WHAT WOULD YOU DO? (cont.)

GIRL'S DON'T MAKE CARS

Mrs Arturo then joined in the discussion and it was agreed finally that anyone could make a model car and that girls were certainly capable of doing so.

Case studies illustrating National Competency Framework for Beginning Teaching, National Project on the Quality of Teaching and Learning, Australian Teaching Council, 1996, p. 13. Commonwealth of Australia copyright, reproduced by permission.

Do you think this response is adequate? What else could be done to ensure that similar sexist values are challenged? Give some further examples of family values that might run counter to broader community standards. Consider Mrs Arturo's dilemma: is it inappropriate to challenge family values within the classroom and school? What different expectations might these two students have of their education?

WHAT WOULD YOU DO?

WE'D LOVE TO HELP MICHAEL

Michael was a new student, arriving in week 9 of term 3 in Miss Ingram's Grade 5 class. Michael was 12 years old; he had extremely poor reading and writing skills and, basically, he was illiterate. Miss Ingram was really at a loss to know where to start with him. Eventually, after a shared reading and writing session, it became apparent that he did not know any sounds or letter blends—the obvious place to begin.

Because the rest of the children were progressing nicely, a lot of Miss Ingram's time was focused on Michael, which was not fair to the other students. She needed Michael to be able to continue with his work, but she didn't want to spend every minute of her day with him.

Case studies illustrating National Competency Framework for Beginning Teaching, National Project on the Quality of Teaching and Learning, Australian Teaching Council, 1996, p. 10. Commonwealth of Australia copyright, reproduced by permission.

What would you do? Now read what the teacher did.

WHAT WOULD YOU DO? (cont.)

WE'D LOVE TO HELP MICHAEL

After much experimentation, Miss Ingram came up with an individual spelling and reading program for Michael, where everything was written on cards so that he could physically manipulate any words he was attempting to make. It was a very simple system: matching sounds and blends, making words, and so on. The system was carefully explained to Michael. Miss Ingram also asked the class if anyone would be interested in becoming a peer tutor to Michael. She had heaps of volunteers. She chose five responsible students and explained how Michael's spelling and reading system worked.

The system is working well. Michael can now work more independently, his knowledge of sounds, words, blends of letters is improving all the time, and not only has it released Miss Ingram to work with other children, but she has noticed positive improvements in the learning and behaviour of the peer tutors.

Case studies illustrating National Competency Framework for Beginning Teaching, National Project on the Quality of Teaching and Learning, Australian Teaching Council, 1996, p. 10. Commonwealth of Australia copyright, reproduced by permission.

Using Michael's case study as an example, discuss the usefulness of IEPs within the regular classroom.

KEY TERMS

Achieving orientation (p. 308): students utilise whatever learning styles lead to high grades

Adaptive education (p. 340): educational approaches designed to accommodate individual differences

Attention deficit hyperactivity disorder (p. 319): disruptive behaviour disorder characterised by low attention to task and high activity levels

Autism (p. 320): extreme inability to relate to other people, characterised by withdrawal and bizarre behaviour

Cerebral palsy (p. 321): paralysis resulting from brain injury

Cognitive style (p. 310): stable perceptual and thinking processes

Conceptual tempo (p. 311): the degree to which people are cognitively reflective or impulsive

Convergent thinking (p. 337): narrowing thinking to a single answer

Creativity (p. 333): imaginative, original thinking or problem solving

Deep learning (p. 308): a student's active search for meaning, underlying principles and structures in knowledge

Divergent thinking (p. 337): coming up with many possible solutions to problems

External locus of control (p. 311): individuals who believe that they have little control over their own learning

Field dependence (p. 310): cognitive perceptual processing in which stimuli are perceived as parts of a whole

Gender stereotyping (p. 317): a view of sex roles that results in distorted or limited visions of what it means to be male or female.

Field independence (p. 310): cognitive perceptual processing in which stimuli are differentiated and then organised

IEP (p. 323): individualised educational plan

Impulsive style (p. 311): cognitive style of responding quickly but often inaccurately

Inclusive education (p. 322): teaching students with disabilities in regular classrooms

Internal locus of control (p. 311): individuals who think they have substantial control over their learning

Learning styles (p. 308): cognitive, affective and physiological behaviours influencing learning

Least restrictive environment (p. 322): placing each individual with a disability in as normal an educational environment as possible

Locus of control (p. 311): whether individuals locate the reasons for success and failure in personal or external factors

Meaning orientation (p. 308): students adopt deep processing strategies to maximise personal understanding

Reflective style (p. 311): cognitive style of responding slowly, carefully and accurately

Regular Education Initiative (p. 324): an educational movement that advocates giving regular teachers the responsibility for teaching students with disabilities

Reproducing style (p. 308): students adopt a shallow processing approach such as rote learning

Surface learning (p. 308): students learn in a superficial way often characterised by role memorisation

Zero reject model (p. 323): despite disabilities all individuals are educated in local schools

ON-LINE LEARNING

If you go to http://www.pearsoned.com.au/mcinerney, you will have hot links directly to this site:

- **Criteria of giftedness**

Using the following website, hot-link to some of the resources that describe the characteristics of gifted students. Compare these criteria with those listed in your textbook.
http://www.awesomelibrary.org/Library/Special_Education/Gifted/Gifted.html

- **Creativity web**

This site presents a lot of fun activities related to creativity. Review the site in the context of information provided in this chapter. Could you use some of the activities in your classroom?
http://members.optusnet.com.au/~charles57/creative/index2.html

WEB DESTINATIONS

If you go to http://www.pearsoned.com.au/mcinerney, you will have hot links directly to these sites:

- **Gifted students**

The following site for Advocacy for Gifted and Talented Education in New York State provides a range of useful information.
http://www.agateny.org/

- **Awesome school**

This site includes everything from lesson plans and articles to dealing with issues from teacher, student and parent points of views. It is very useful for chasing up a number of key topics related to attention deficit disorder, visual impairment, the gifted and talented, and a wealth of other topics related to special needs.
http://awesomelibrary.org/

- **Awesome school special education**

This site covers key issues relevant to special education.
http://www.awesomelibrary.org/Library/Special_Education/Special_Education.html

- **Attention deficit hyperactivity disorder**

A good site for obtaining further information on this 'modern-day' problem.
http://www.nimh.nih.gov/publicat/adhd.cfm

- **Learning Network gifted students**

This site from the Learning Network lets you explore the topic of giftedness.
http://www.familyeducation.com/topic/front/0,1156,59-10880,00.html

- **Awesome school gifted students**

This site covers key issues relevant to special education.
http://www.awesomelibrary.org/Library/Special_Education/Gifted/Gifted.html

- **Learning to Learn**

Further information on creativity for you to consider.
http://www.ldrc.ca/projects/projects.php?id=26

RECOMMENDED READING

Altermatt, E. R., Jovanovic, J. & Perry, M. (1998) Bias or responsivity? Sex and achievement-level effects on teachers' classroom questioning practices. *Journal of Educational Psychology*, **90**, 516–27.

Ashman, A. F. & Elkins, J. (2002) *Educating Children with Special Needs*. Sydney: Prentice Hall.

Bailey, S. M. (1993) The current status of gender equity research in American schools. *Educational Psychologist*, **28**, 321–39.

Brantlinger, E. (1997) Using ideology: Cases of nonrecognition of the politics of research and practice in special education. *Review of Educational Research*, **67**, 425–59.

Cassidy, S. (2004) Learning styles: An overview of theories, models, and measures. *Educational Psychology*, **24**, 419–44.

Cropley, A. J. (1993a) Creativity as an element of giftedness. *International Journal of Educational Research*, **19**, 17–30.

Feldhusen, J. F. (1995) Creativity: Teaching and assessing. In L. W. Anderson (ed.) *International Encyclopedia of Teaching and Teacher Education*, 2nd ed. Tarrytown, NY: Pergamon.

Halpern, D. F. & LaMay, M. L. (2000) The smarter sex. A critical review of sex differences in intelligence. *Educational Psychology Review*, **12**, 229–46.

Hoge, R. D. & Renzulli, J. S. (1993) Exploring the link between giftedness and self-concept. *Review of Educational Research*, **63**, 449–65.

Loo, R. (2004) Kolb's learning styles and learning preferences: Is there a linkage? *Educational Psychology*, **24**, 99–108.

Mael, F. A. (1998) Single-sex and coeducational schooling: Relationships to socioemotional and academic development. *Review of Educational Research*, **68**, 101–29.

Mamlin, N. & Harris, K. R. (1998) Elementary teachers' referral to special education in light of inclusion and prereferral: 'Every child is here to learn . . . but some of these children are in real trouble'. *Journal of Educational Psychology*, **90**, 385–96.

Messick, S. (1995) Cognitive style and learning. In L. W. Anderson (ed.) *International Encyclopedia of Teaching Education*, 2nd ed. Tarrytown, NY: Pergamon.

Pellegrini, A. D. & Horvat, M. (1995) A developmental

contextualist critique of attention deficit hyperactivity disorder. *Educational Researcher*, **24**, 13–19.

Plucker, J. A., Beghetto, R. A. & Dow, G. T. (2004) Why isn't creativity more important to educational psychologists? Potentials, pitfalls, and future directions in creativity research. *Educational Psychologist,* **39**, 83–96.

Purdie, N., Hattie, J. & Carroll, A. (2002) A review of the research on interventions for attention deficit hyperactivity disorder: What works best? *Review of Educational Research,* **72**, 61–99.

Smith, P. (1999) Drawing new maps: A radical cartography of developmental disabilities. *Review of Educational Research,* **69**, 117–44.

Trent, S. C., Artiles, A. J. & Englert, C. S. (1998) From deficit thing to social constructivism: A review of theory, research, and practice in special education. *Review of Research in Education*, **23**, 277–307.

Weaver-Hightower, M. (2003) The 'boy turn' in research on gender and education. *Review of Educational Research,* **73**, 471–98.

CHAPTER

10 Cultural dimensions of effective learning

Overview

In this chapter we highlight the importance of cultural context for effective schooling, the importance of teachers, parents and schools in developing learners' life chances, and the relevance of mainstream psychology and cross-cultural psychology in understanding the special needs of culturally different learners. The implications of these factors for educators are discussed in particular.

Among issues examined are the nature and importance of multicultural education, the importance of home language maintenance, and the roles of bilingualism and English as a second language. Special attention is given to indigenous minority education and the needs of non-traditional and traditional Aboriginal and Maori learners. Creative responses to these needs in the form of bilingual/bicultural education, two-way schools and two-way learning, and *kohanga reo* are described. We consider in detail culturally relevant teaching.

10

The material in this chapter will help you to implement the following Learner-centred Psychological Principle and the teaching competencies in Box 10.1.

LEARNER-CENTRED PSYCHOLOGICAL PRINCIPLE

Learning and diversity. Learning is most effective when differences in learners' linguistic, cultural and social backgrounds are taken into account.

The same basic principles of learning, motivation and effective instruction apply to all learners. However, language, ethnicity, race, beliefs and socio-economic status can all influence learning. Careful attention to the factors in the instructional setting enhances the possibilities for designing and implementing appropriate learning environments. When learners perceive that their individual differences in abilities, backgrounds, cultures and experiences are valued, respected, and accommodated in learning tasks and contexts, levels of motivation and achievement are enhanced.

TEACHING COMPETENCE

Box 10.1

The teacher values diversity and believes that all students can, and have the right to, learn

Indicators

The teacher:

- values and uses the gender, and cultural and linguistic backgrounds of the students;
- encourages students to value the cultural backgrounds of other students;
- designs programs that are sensitive to individual students' backgrounds;
- recognises own cultural assumptions and biases and those within the school's curriculum and practices;
- ensures that students' learning is not limited by expectations based on stereotypes and prejudices;
- acts equitably towards all students.

Case studies illustrating National Competency Framework for Beginning Teaching, National Project on the Quality of Teaching and Learning, Australian Teaching Council, 1996, Element 1.7, p. 35. Commonwealth of Australia copyright, reproduced by permission.

Learning objectives

After reading this chapter, you will be able to:

- describe key components of multicultural education in Australia and New Zealand;
- relate multiculturalism to social constructivism;
- describe the importance of second language acquisition and the maintenance of community languages for children from non-English-speaking backgrounds (NESB);
- discuss arguments for and against bilingual/bicultural education;
- apply principles of multicultural education in homogeneous educational settings and settings characterised by diversity;
- describe key elements of indigenous minority education in Australia and New Zealand;
- define culturally relevant teaching, and describe principles for implementing culturally relevant teaching in your classroom.

Social constructivism and multiculturalism

Taking into account our students' cultural backgrounds

The manner in which children respond to school and benefit from the experiences presented will reflect the cultural environment in which they are socialised. The cognitive development of children is shaped by personal and cultural histories related to gender, class, race and family, and the self-regulation of valued activities (Ferrari & Mahalingam 1998). These valued activities are set in political and cultural contexts that define what is acceptable and valued. Within these political and cultural contexts, individuals and groups seek to fulfil their self-identities by participating in activities that develop the skills and dispositions needed to excel in their cultural milieu (Ferrari & Mahalingam 1998; McInerney & Van Etten 2001). Maehr (1984, p. 12) expresses this well:

Individual respect for children's backgrounds

> Most practising educators are aware that students place different values on school tasks quite apart from their ability to perform. That this may be the critical feature in explaining cross-cultural variation in achievement patterns has recently been illustrated in a series of cross-cultural studies . . . Generally, it seems that individuals project different pictures of what they would like to become. They derive these pictures from personal experiences within their own culture . . . all have their own pictures of the nature of successful achievement. But the critical point is that, as events are interpreted as conforming to these pictures of achievement, they are associated with success. Simply a performance outcome or any information that is perceived as indicating that we are becoming what we want to become is readily defined as success . . . Of course, events, outcomes and information to the contrary eventuate in perception of failure.

What defines academic success in one cultural milieu may not be the same as what defines success in another. Cognitive development through learning is therefore a very complex process when viewed through these lenses, and any attempt to describe this complexity as it applies in diverse cultural settings must, by necessity, be an oversimplification. In our description of the elements of effective learning in multicultural contexts we run the risk of oversimplification, but we hope at least to highlight some key elements that might make your role as an educator in such environments more effective.

Race, gender and a range of other labels such as 'gifted', 'talented' and 'special needs' are being increasingly viewed not as inherent or ascribed characteristics of people but as social constructions (Riehl 2000; see also Chapter 9). In other words, personal identity appears to develop out of the tasks, social relationships and contexts within which each individual learns. As we discussed in Chapter 2, learning from this perspective is a process through which we become one with the collective through carrying out personal activity in collaboration with other people by using the tools, languages and social organisations of the group. This constructivist view of human development, and in particular its sociocultural elements, has significant implications for understanding cultural diversity and our function as educators within culturally diverse educational settings. However, as the tools, inventions and language of one culture may be significantly different from those of another culture, effective education must place learning within the appropriate social and cultural contexts. We deal with a number of these social and cultural contexts in the following sections.

Are cultural displays such as this one important for students?

Culture and the zone of proximal development

Language and conversational forms and learners' familiarity or lack of familiarity with the use of various conventions (such as questioning) and tools (such as computers) within the school context must be considered by teachers if they are to make education relevant (Smagorinsky 1995). Teachers need to build on the experiences of their students in order to advance their academic and social development. In other words, as we suggest in Chapter 2, effective education from a Vygotskian perspective must be situated within the zone of proximal development for individuals. Generally, school practices are consistent with how mainstream students have been socialised in their home culture and with the learning preferences and strengths they have developed. However, effective teaching also requires that teachers make linkages between students' home culture and classroom practices even when the students are non-members of the mainstream group (Hollins 1996).

Vygotskian perspectives have strongly influenced educators' ideas of effective learning in cultural settings. In particular, the sociocultural milieu of learning (see Chapter 2; also Rogoff & Chavajay 1995) affects the following:

- the way individuals go about learning;
- values and goals appropriate to learning;
- definitions of meaningful learning;
- definitions of intelligence and intelligent behaviour;
- the importance of individual versus group activities;
- appropriate measurement and evaluation.

In the following sections we discuss some of the features that characterise children who are socialised in cultural contexts different from that of the mainstream, and how these need to be considered by effective teachers.

Multicultural education—Australian and New Zealand perspectives

All schools in Australia and New Zealand are called upon to implement *multicultural education policies* that have been mandated by state and national governments (Alcorso & Cope 1986; Brentnall & Hodge 1984; Office of Multicultural Affairs 1990; Smolicz 1987). These policies emphasise teaching for intercultural understanding and, in schools where need demands, developing the English language competence and preserving the ethnic traditions and language of students from **non-English-speaking backgrounds (NESB)**. Multicultural education policies are also widespread internationally, particularly in societies characterised by diversity, but take many different forms. Some initiatives address curriculum reform to make curriculum less Eurocentric; others address equity pedagogy in which the focus is to develop the talents and capacities of all children irrespective of race and background. Still other initiatives address multicultural competence, and in particular the reduction of racial and cultural prejudice. Initiatives based on multicultural competence reflect the belief that individuals can become multicultural and that they need not reject their familial worldview and identity to function comfortably in another cultural milieu. Finally, some multicultural initiatives address societal equity, believing that social change is essential to bring about equitable education access, participation and achievement (Bennett 2001).

Multicultural education policies

Our multicultural classrooms bring many teaching challenges

ACTION STATION

Consider multicultural policy documents relevant to your state. Illustrate how they reflect one of more of the themes above, viz, curriculum reform, equity pedagogy, multicultural competence and societal equity.

Potential problems of children of migrants

In a survey in the Metropolitan South West Region of the New South Wales Department of School Education (McInerney 1979) teachers identified the significant problems of children of migrants at that time. It is likely that the situation is the same today. The findings are given in Table 10.1.

These perceptions of teachers give us much food for thought when we consider ethnically diverse classrooms, particularly ones in which there are large numbers of new arrivals and/or refugee children.

QUESTION POINT

Discuss the list (in Table 10.1) of adjustment difficulties faced by children from other cultures. What can we do as teachers to alleviate the potential stress caused to our NESB students by these adjustment difficulties?

The notion of multiculturalism is quite different in New Zealand. Within New Zealand, mandated multicultural policy development is largely synonymous with the development of bilingual/bicultural programs for Maori and Pakeha (European) students (Corson 1993; Irwin 1989). Other ethnic groups, such as Pacific

Table 10.1 Potential problems of children of migrants

In society as a whole, difficulties through

- Loss of close family ties. Loss of peers of the same nationality, and the difficulty of making friends outside the ethnic group.
- Inability to communicate basic emotional needs.
- Understanding the rules of the new society with the insecurity of not knowing what is acceptable behaviour.
- Conflict between parental ideas and the developing ideas of the children regarding food, dress, excursions, dates, responsibilities, and male and female roles.
- Inability or reluctance of some members of the family to change to new language and customs. The hesitancy of most parents to assimilate as quickly as their children would like them to.
- Protective ethnic grouping resulting in confrontation between groups and a consequent refusal to assimilate.
- Sudden change from a low socio-economic group to an affluent society.

Within schools, difficulties through

- The demand by schools and other institutions for children to be more responsible and independent of the family than is expected at certain ages in other cultures.
- Cutting ties with mothers who insist on bringing children to school and waiting at school for them all day.
- Adjusting to different ideas of schooling; frequently, antagonistic attitudes of teachers who do not welcome migrants.
- Being labelled 'unintelligent' throughout school years when the problem is basically one of language.
- Ostracism by Australian children and the feeling that they are never going to be like Australians.
- Parental insistence on their mother tongue at home. Parents often do not have the same opportunities for learning English as their children; consequently they often speak only the mother tongue at home which makes it difficult for migrant children to practise at home what they have learned at school.
- The reluctance of some migrant parents, particularly non-English-speaking women, to venture near the school for fear of non-acceptance or being misunderstood.

TEACHER'S CASE BOOK

The missing human element

Mr Kirkwood teaches in a district high school. The student intake is from the surrounding farming area and the people living in the area are concerned with their own lives and the local activities. Strangers are looked upon with suspicion, and students who attend the school have limited knowledge of, and little interest in, the world beyond their own community.

Last year, Mr Kirkwood was dissatisfied with the Grade 10 Social Science Asian Studies unit. The students were uninterested. What was more disconcerting was their failure (and he realised it was his failure also) to see Asian people as people. The human element was missing.

This year he was fortunate enough to work alongside an Indonesian woman. Bingo! They decided they would team-teach the grade.

Mrs Varido talked informally about her experiences and reasons for coming to live in Tasmania. Once a week for four weeks, students cooked food from China, India, etc. Primary students joined the Grade 10 lessons, giving the senior students a chance to show leadership skills. This was videotaped and photos were taken.

The students collected and posted a variety of materials to an international school in Japan. Groups of students built up folders of materials on Asian people and they added information to a class map. At the end of the unit Mr Kirkwood asked the students to write a personal opinion of the issue of Asian migrants living in Australia.

Because students had experienced this human element and had interacted with Mrs Varido, they were able to provide a more balanced, reasoned and informed view on the question. Even though a majority found it difficult to give a 'yes–no' answer, they were able to discuss advantages of having Asian migrants living in Australia.

Case studies illustrating National Competency Framework for Beginning Teaching, National Project on the Quality of Teaching and Learning, Australian Teaching Council, 1996, p. 43. Commonwealth of Australia copyright, reproduced by permission.

Case study activity

How would you handle the situation faced by Mr Kirkwood if you did not have a co-teacher of Asian origin?

TEACHER'S CASE BOOK

He just won't answer

Carl, a teacher at Railway Fields Primary School, was concerned about the progress of Mikael, one of the NESB children in his mainstream class. Mikael spoke some English, but his schooling had been in Finnish until 18 months previously. When Carl asked some of the other students about Mikael, one class member said: 'Mikael won't answer you if you talk to him. Often he understands but he just won't answer, so we walk off.'

A few days later, when Carl was visiting Mikael's ESL withdrawal class, he heard the ESL teacher asking the children to examine the processes they went through when they listened. A typical response was: 'Well, first I translate what is said into my own language, then I think of the answer in my own language, think of the English words, put the words into the right order for the English way to say it, and then I say it.'

Carl could not help but think that the mainstream students would benefit from hearing this explanation. Instead of walking off on Mikael as he was struggling to frame a response, they might learn to give him some 'wait-time'. Carl introduced his class to this idea of wait-time for translation—along with a number of other initiatives designed to heighten students' awareness of cultural and linguistic differences—and was very pleased by their response.

Comments in Carl's journal a few months later summarise the changes:

> Children seem to be more eager to listen to Mikael and to discuss differences between their cultures. The (mainstream) children seem to be displaying more interest in listening to and learning about how other people live.

Case studies illustrating National Competency Framework for Beginning Teaching, National Project on the Quality of Teaching and Learning, Australian Teaching Council, 1996, p. 52. Commonwealth of Australia copyright, reproduced by permission.

Case study activity

Discuss other potential problems between students and new arrivals. What solutions might work to alleviate these?

Island and Indo-Chinese groups (as well as more established European immigrant groups), are largely ignored in official legislation and policy.

There are important historical reasons for this, including the dominance of the Maori group within New Zealand society (Maoris make up approximately 15 per cent of New Zealand's population of 3.5 million) from early settlement days, and the Treaty of Waitangi. Because of this the Maori are accorded the most prestige in the initial development of multicultural curricula. However, it is envisioned that the Maori–Pakeha base will be the first step in the development of a full multicultural program to serve all cultural groups within New Zealand (Irwin 1989). We discuss elements of this bilingual/bicultural response to multicultural education later in this chapter.

It is interesting to note the difference in the development of multicultural policies for Aboriginal, migrant and Maori communities. Within Australia, multiculturalism is identified with immigrant settlers. The indigenous Aboriginal groups consider that it is inappropriate to have their special needs lost within curricula developed for the wider group. Instead, a separate set of policies has been mandated for Aboriginal groups that seeks to foster the development of Aboriginal identity and achievement. These policies have been introduced with considerable vigour in many Aboriginal and non-Aboriginal communities.

Applications of multicultural education

Apart from mandated educational policies, which come with a number of support documents to assist with the implementation of multicultural programs, and an extensive range of resource materials available through various educational resource centres, the following points represent school practices aimed at adapting the school and classroom environment to the needs of these children. All these practices are in place in particular schools and are found to be very helpful:

- School notes and reports written in several languages (especially important notices such as immunisation papers).
- Use of community and ethnic services (for example, interpreting and translation services).
- Meetings with migrant parents where school procedures and programs are explained via an interpreter. Interviews with parents carried out through an interpreter.
- Children encouraged to welcome their parents to the school and parent/child excursions arranged.
- Community times organised when parents teach all children crafts, cooking and dancing.
- ESL classes held for adults on school premises. Pupils and parents attend.

EXTENSION STUDY

Learning English

Australia is one of the most culturally diverse countries in the world. Cultural diversity often brings with it language diversity. In fact, approximately 15 per cent of Australian residents speak a language other than English at home (Thomas 2004). Among the most commonly spoken languages are Italian, Greek, Cantonese, Arabic, Vietnamese and Spanish. There is also a large number of Aboriginal Australians who speak an indigenous language at home. Many children are therefore brought up in homes in which English is not spoken, or spoken rarely and perhaps badly. Indeed, many may arrive at school on the first day speaking little English. It is essential that these NESB children become fluent in English if they are to have good opportunities later in life. At the most obvious level, students who arrive at school unable to understand or speak the language of instruction suffer a double jeopardy. While they are expected to master new cognitive skills, they are also expected to master a new oral and written language in which these skills are encoded (Diaz 1983; Garcia 1993; Genesee & Cloud 1998; Guthrie & Hall 1983; Snow 1992). Effective teaching of English as a second language is of utmost importance, therefore, if students are to have unrestricted access to grade-appropriate instruction in challenging academic subjects (Valdes 1998). TESOL (Teaching English to Speakers of Other Languages 1997) has established three goals for ESL (English as a Second Language) that students should achieve: (1) to be able to use English to communicate in social settings; (2) to use English to achieve academically in all content areas; and (3) to use English in socially and culturally appropriate ways. In other words, second-language learners should acquire a language that does not distinguish them from native English speakers in the full range of uses of the language. The reason for this is that language is one of the most powerful means of inclusion or exclusion from further education, employment or social position (Penneycook 1994). Most schools in English-speaking countries with NESB immigrants or groups have made provisions for these children to learn English through intensive language programs in ESL and follow-up classroom-based programs.

There is considerable debate, however, over the appropriate ways to teach children the second language (Benton 1989; Brizuela & Garcia-Sellers 1999; Cummins 1999; Garcia 1993; Lam 1992; McCroarty 1992; Olneck 2000; Snow 1992; Pease-Alvarez & Hakuta 1992; Wright, Taylor & Macarthur 2000). One argument holds that students learn best in intensive language centres where the emphasis is clearly on the acquisition of English. In this case there is a belief that the real goal of education for NESB students should be their social and economic advancement in mainstream society, not the preservation of their native language and culture (Porter 1990). The school's focus should be on equipping students with fluent English as quickly as possible, thereby empowering them with the tools to enter the mainstream—namely, the English language and mainstream curriculum (Pease-Alvarez & Hakuta 1992; see also Hollins 1996). In other contexts, such an 'immersion' approach is used to teach a foreign language. For example, in Canada, English-speaking

- Playgroups established and migrant mothers encouraged to attend with their younger children, to foster an interest in the school.
- Use of Australian parents in home tutor plans.
- Parents involved in teaching community languages.
- School staff encouraged to take an interest in ethnic functions in the district.
- Teachers visit parents personally in their homes.
- Migrant Parents and Citizens Associations.
- Ethnic aides appointed to help solve problems and to translate.
- 'Shopping centres' established where parents are guided on buying habits and currency usage in their new country.

ESL lessons are essential for new arrivals who speak no English.

students may elect to learn French in an immersion school in which all their subjects are taught in French. Research tends to suggest that these students do at least as well as, and in some cases better than, their English-speaking peers' learning in English (Cunningham & Graham 2000).

Another argument holds that English should be learned in a bilingual/bicultural context (Benton 1989; Clyne 1983, 1988). Much of this debate is philosophical/sociocultural/human rights-oriented. For example, Cummins (quoted in Pease-Alvarez & Hakuta 1992, p. 5) says:

> Educators who see their role as adding a second language and cultural affiliation to students' repertoires empower students more than those who see their role as replacing or subtracting students' primary language and culture in the process of assimilating them to the dominant culture.

In this case, the linguistic and cultural differences of the students are seen as both individual and societal resources not to be wasted (Cziko 1992; Smolicz 1991; see also Wright *et al.* 2000). Many NESB immigrant communities (as well as non-English-speaking indigenous communities) are reluctant to see their children lose their community language through immersion in intensive English courses, although individual members of particular communities may have little interest in preserving their home language.

Significant educational issues in second language teaching

Much of the language debate highlights significant educational issues, such as whether the cognitive development of a child is delayed while the child is learning a new language to label old concepts. Some people argue that it is better to keep cognitive development on track by teaching in the children's first language while gradually introducing English as the medium of instruction. If and when appropriate, English can become the dominant medium of instruction (Diaz 1983; Genesee & Cloud 1998; Smolicz 1991). Others argue that there is inhibition from one language to another, and that students faced with learning two languages and two sets of labels for new concepts at the same time are jeopardised (McCroarty 1992). Auerbach (1993) (cited in Valdes 1998) argues that the exclusive use of English in the classroom results in non-participation by students, language shock, dropping out, frustration, and inability to build on existing native-language literacy skills (cited in Valdes 1998). Others argue that learning in immersion programs where English only is used not only does not disadvantage students but actually facilitates their development (see, for example, Cunningham & Graham 2000). Of course, the fluency with which students speak their mother tongue is an important factor that impacts on whether either approach is successful.

Another aspect of this issue relates to the extent to which a learner's *sense of self* is inextricably interwoven with culturally mediated experiences. Language is considered an essential element in the development of a sense of self (see, for example, the discussion of Vygotsky in Chapter 2). This is one of the strongest arguments for bilingual education and community language programs in our schools. Furthermore, as language is one of the main vehicles for the preservation of a culture, multicultural education programs that are designed to preserve ethnic diversity should have a significant language component. If they do not, they are tokenistic (McInerney 1987a, 1987b, 1987c; Smolicz 1986, 1991; see also Genesee & Cloud 1998).

Snow (1992) answers a number of questions regarding the acquisition of a second language that are helpful for us as teachers to consider. Table 10.2 presents a summary of her answers.

Authorities argue about the merits of bilingual/bicultural education versus concentrated ESL for new NESB arrivals to our country. Conduct a debate which examines the arguments for and against these options.

Teacher attitudes to community language maintenance and bilingual education

Alongside the argument over the importance and nature of non-English-speaking-background (NESB) students learning English is an equally strong argument over the importance and best means of preserving the languages of origin of immigrant groups. The global economy, as much as any philosophical/psychological argument for the preservation of community languages, demands that this natural language resource not be squandered (Genesee & Cloud 1998; Lo Bianco 1987, 1988, 1990). Hence, many countries have introduced **community language** programs. The success of these programs,

Table 10.2 Common questions about the acquisition of a second language

- *Is there a best age to start second-language acquisition?*
  As children get older, their capacity to benefit from formal second-language teaching gradually increases. However, fluency depends on using the language in a range of social interactions. Younger learners should be exposed to the second language in relatively unstructured and unthreatening 'real-life' language situations.
- *How long does it take to learn a second language?*
  One can learn enough of a second language in a few hours to perform some tasks in it. Other tasks (including some academic and literacy-related tasks) may take years to master. Even native speakers continue to acquire fluency as they encounter new language situations (for example, the language of educational psychology).
- *How can second-language acquisition be facilitated?*
  Real-life language encounters with native speakers are most important. Positive regard for the culture of the language also helps, as do well-designed curricula and good teachers.
- *Can learners function as effectively in communicating, learning, reading and talking in a second language as in a first?*
  Learners can become better in their second language than in their first. Fluency in either or both language(s) depends on exposure to a full range of language experiences in the languages.
- *Does acquisition of a second language have any positive or negative consequences for the learner?*
  Acquiring a second language can give young learners some advantage in metalinguistic and analytic tasks, but it can also increase processing times slightly for both languages. Both of these effects are quite small, and the costs in processing speed do not outweigh the advantages of knowing two languages.
- *Why do some people have so much trouble with second-language acquisition, when it is relatively fast and easy for others?*
  Differences in aptitude, motivation, opportunities to communicate in the second language effectively and pleasantly, as well as teaching effectiveness, influence the ease with which an individual will learn the second language.
- *How should we test for language proficiencies of second-language learners?*
  There is a range of domains of language proficiencies. Tests should relate to the goals of the instruction. For example, if oral acquisition is important, then this should be assessed. Good oral language does not predict academic performance in the language. If command of academic language is the goal, this should be assessed.

particularly those mainstreamed in government schools, depends upon the commitment and expertise of the schools and teachers responsible for implementing these programs. Teachers are generally in favour of multicultural education. However, there is a widespread lack of understanding among teachers that the policy is to be applied in all schools whether or not they have significant numbers of migrant-background children. One study (McInerney 1987a) indicated that, while 84.5 per cent of 800 teachers surveyed in southwest Sydney agreed that it was important for children to retain their mother language, and 77.9 per cent thought that schools should encourage children to retain their mother language, only 23.4 per cent of the teachers believed that schools should assume responsibility for language maintenance. There was little support for ethnic languages being used as a medium of instruction for part of the day in schools with large numbers of NESB children. Indeed, 22.1 per cent of the teachers surveyed believed that NESB children should not be encouraged by the school to retain their ethnic language. Research (McInerney, McInerney, Cincotta, Totaro & Williams 2001) indicates some improvement in this situation, but there is still an ambivalent attitude on teachers' behalf as to the appropriate role schools should play in **bilingual/bicultural** education.

Ambivalent attitudes to multicultural education

Dialects and learning

Many of the issues that apply to learning English as a second language and the preservation of community languages apply also to groups who speak dialectic forms of English. Many students face problems because they speak **dialects** that do not conform to standard English. For example, many Aboriginal children speak dialects and, within the United States, many African-American children face problems because of their dialects (Ogbu 1999; Lee 2001). A study in Oakland (California) concluded that the poor school achievement of African-American students could be attributed to the differences between the students' home English and the standard English used within the school setting. Most communities, irrespective of their language background, agree that students should be fluent with standard English within the school setting in order to facilitate learning and to enhance their future prospects within the job market. However, the issue of dialects is somewhat more socio-politically complex than the issue of community languages and ESL. In the case of oppressed groups such as African-Americans and Australian Aboriginals, dialects and slang are a means of identifying with one's own group while excluding members of the dominant English-speaking group. Because of this, there is often an ambivalent attitude towards learning and using standard English. The use of

Attending to cultural needs is an important aspect of effective teaching.

Cultural background is one factor that might influence achievement at school. What are other factors?

standard English represents, for many, a capitulation to the oppressor. This issue, while very interesting and important for educators, is beyond the scope of this book. You are recommended to read Ogbu (1999), who highlights a number of important issues.

Indigenous minority education in Australia and New Zealand

Within the wider multicultural context of Australia and New Zealand, two indigenous minority groups are making significant educational progress, despite the economic and educational disadvantage they have suffered historically (see, for example, Bell 1988; Eckermann 1999). Much of the important progress with Aboriginal Australians and Maori communities is the result of creative initiatives currently being taken by the communities to develop educational programs that are culturally relevant and appropriate, but that look ahead to future possibilities.

The notion of what is culturally relevant and appropriate in the modern world is complex, however, and this is particularly the case with Aboriginal and Torres Strait Islander communities, which are characterised by great diversity. Some Aboriginal groups live very traditional lifestyles in isolated communities; some live semi-traditional lifestyles on the outskirts of country towns; others participate fully in the urban life of city communities. Clearly, one form of education cannot be culturally relevant and appropriate to all Aboriginal and Torres Strait Islander communities (see Jordan 1984). Furthermore, there is great diversity of opinion among Aboriginal and Torres Strait Islander groups as to what constitutes relevant and appropriate education for their children. For example, some urbanised Aboriginal people who do not have any language other than English vehemently support the concept of bilingual education, while there are traditionally oriented Aboriginal people who reject the need for bilingual education for their children (see Gale *et al.* 1987; Williamson 1991).

Effective education for non-traditional urbanised Aboriginal groups

In a survey of Aboriginal parents in urbanised Aboriginal communities in New South Wales (McInerney 1989b), parents clearly indicated that mainstream education is very important to their children and that it must provide a good education in the basics, a grounding in social skills and personal development (in particular, life skills such as a sense of autonomy and self-understanding), and improve employment prospects. These goals of education were very similar to those given by the non-Aboriginal parents interviewed at the same time. Some parents thought that the school difficulties experienced by Aboriginal children could be attributed to a curriculum that was not appropriate to Aboriginal needs; they also believed that schools were discriminatory and did not give enough individual attention to Aboriginal children. Doing badly at school was perceived by Aboriginal parents as radically diminishing an Aboriginal child's self-esteem within the school context, the child's motivation to continue with school and, consequently, the child's life chances.

Urban Aboriginal communities

As well as school-related reasons for the poor performance of many urbanised Aboriginal children in this survey, such as poor teaching, insensitive and uncaring teachers, inadequate curriculum, and inadequate teacher and school support (see also Eckermann 1999; Hewitt

Theory and research into practice

Rhonda Craven — SELF-CONCEPT AND ABORIGINAL EDUCATION

BRIEF BIOGRAPHY

I began my career as a primary teacher. My very first class was a composite class whereby all the bottom Year 5 and Year 6 students were placed in the one class. The latter grouping had resulted in these children being labelled as the 'dummies' in the school. As a starry-eyed beginning teacher I stayed up to all hours of the morning creating engaging learning activities. I soon learned that all the real beaut teaching strategies I had been taught were not going to help these students until I could make them feel better about themselves and their abilities. I focused on enhancing their academic self-concepts and teaching them that learning to be smart was like 'eating an elephant' – one bite at a time. As a result, my students developed their academic self-concepts and soon engaged in learning – they all also doubled their marks on the yearly examinations and became no longer the class of 'dummies'. This experience was the dawn of my realisation of the importance of enhancing self-concept as an important goal in itself and the impact this could have on multiple desirable educational outcomes. Since this time I have been actively involved in a range of self-concept research, as I believe enhancing self-concept makes a difference to people's lives.

I left teaching to become a teacher educator with the aim of making a contribution to improving teaching by helping to shape the next generation of teachers. I discovered that student teachers knew very little about Aboriginal studies and how to teach Aboriginal students, both of which I consider vital social justice issues of our time. At this time I was fortunate to meet and have the opportunity to live for a number of years with Oodgeroo Noonuccal, whom some of you may know as the late Kath Walker—one of Australia's leading Aboriginal educators and poets—and also Uncle Charles Moran—a highly respected Bundjalung Elder. During this period, we embarked on a huge task with our colleagues—the task of encouraging all teacher education institutions to teach teachers how to understand and effectively teach Aboriginal studies and Aboriginal students. This project has resulted in an important historic change in education. However, there is still a long way to go before Aboriginal students experience educational outcomes commensurate with their non-Aboriginal peers. I have also found that what I have learned about self-concept is fundamental to enhancing both the teaching of Aboriginal studies and Aboriginal students.

I am very fortunate in that I currently hold a full-time research position in the Self-concept Enhancement and Learning Facilitation (SELF) Research Centre, University of Western Sydney. I am also living proof that you can have a full-time career and young children simultaneously, given I have two gorgeous daughters, Violet (aged four) and Charlotte (aged two).

RESEARCH AND/OR THEORETICAL INTERESTS

My research focuses on large-scale quantitative self-concept research studies in educational settings. My research interests include: the structure, measurement, development and enhancement of self-concept; the relation of self-concept to desirable educational outcomes; the effective teaching of Aboriginal studies and Aboriginal students; identity research, and interventions that make a difference in educational settings such as peer support, anti-bullying, early intervention for young children, and maximising the self-concept of gifted and talented children, particularly in selective settings.

I am particularly passionate about the need for high-quality Aboriginal education research. Aboriginal students are the most disadvantaged students on all socio-economic indicators and, as such, experience severe educational dis-advantage that predicates important life opportunities. I believe this situation is unlikely to change until more researchers identify new solutions for intervention that are demonstrated empirically to have tangible effects on Aboriginal students' educational outcomes. Currently, there is a lack of research in Aboriginal education in general, and in relation to schooling in particular. This is problematic in that theory, research and practice are all intertwined, such that a flaw in any one area will have adverse effects on the others. In Aboriginal education research, this is particularly problematic given that research is currently plagued by: a-theoretical approaches, small sample sizes, purely descriptive research, and a lack of large-scale quantitative research studies. As such, there is a paucity of good-quality Aboriginal education research, as well as experienced researchers—both Aboriginal and non-Aboriginal—engaged in addressing Aboriginal educational disadvantage. I also believe that enhancing self-concept is critical to achieving socially just outcomes for Aboriginal Australians. Furthermore, teacher education in Aboriginal studies is fundamental to addressing the goal of reconciliation between Aboriginal and non-Aboriginal Australians by ensuring that all Australians are taught the truth about our shared history, and is vital for creating a socially just Australia that serves as an exemplar to the world.

To begin to address some of these issues, my research has focused on developing a model primary core teacher education subject in consultation with colleagues to teach preservice teachers how to understand and teach both Aboriginal studies and Aboriginal students effectively. I have also undertaken research to test the effect of undertaking appropriate teacher education courses on preservice and inservice teachers' self-perceptions of their ability to teach Aboriginal studies and Aboriginal students. The results of these studies have led me to conclude that the introduction of mandatory Aboriginal Studies Teacher Education courses, elective courses and perspectives permeating the teacher education curriculum is vital. My research also demonstrates the dire educational disadvantage Aboriginal students continue to experience. For example, I have found that: academic self-concept facets for Aboriginal Australians are statistically significantly lower in comparison to non-indigenous Australians; and the barriers Aboriginal Australians experience in relation to setting and achieving their aspirations in comparison to non-Aboriginal Australians is statistically significant for all barriers measured and simply unacceptable. My research also shows promise for new solutions for intervention underpinned by advances in self-concept theory, research and practice.

My self-concept research interests include: the structure, measurement, development and enhancement of self-concept; the relation of self-concept to desirable educational outcomes; the effective teaching of Aboriginal studies and Aboriginal students; and interventions that make a difference in educational settings in regard to early intervention, bullying, youth obesity, educational disadvantage, and appropriate education for gifted and talented students. For example, I am particularly interested in enhancing students' self-concepts in educational settings. I believe that enhancing students' self-concepts makes students feel good about themselves, helps them to respect and value their peers, and facilitates the attainment of multiple desirable educational and social outcomes.

THEORY AND RESEARCH INTO PRACTICE

My research in Aboriginal education has provided an impetus for a significant historic change in teacher education. When the *Teaching the Teachers Project of National Significance* was commenced, only one Australian university implemented a mandatory primary teacher education Aboriginal studies course. Currently, over 50 per cent of Australian teacher education institutions have introduced a mandatory primary Aboriginal studies teacher education course. While this is a significant change, I along with my colleagues hope to live to see the day when this figure is 100 per cent in both primary and secondary teacher education courses, and when all courses also include electives and Aboriginal perspectives permeating the teacher education curriculum. The NSW Aboriginal Education Consultative Group considers that this national project is one of the most widely consulted national projects in the field and one of the most successful projects undertaken with demonstrated tangible outcomes. I am also deeply moved when student teachers who have read the text *Why Teach Aboriginal Studies* send emails describing the effect this work has had on their commitment to teaching Aboriginal studies and Aboriginal students effectively.

My research with Aboriginal secondary students has resulted in identifying that career education for Aboriginal students needs reconceptualising, as currently strategies that are utilised are often simply inappropriate, inadequate and ineffective. This research has important implications for shaping policy and practice, and a suite of key recommendations have been developed. One key strategy for intervention identified in my Aboriginal education research is the need to foster adaptive psychological functioning displayed by Aboriginal students who continue to Year 12. Such adaptive functioning includes high academic self-concept, motivation to succeed, and resilience. These strategies, I believe, are fundamental to effective intervention. I am also hopeful that my colleagues and Ph.D. students can continue to tease out the elements of what makes a real difference in the teeth of Australia's 'black history'.

My self-concept research has resulted in advances in theory, research and practice. For example, I have developed a successful technique for enhancing self-concept and other desirable outcomes in the primary classroom. Recently my colleagues and I synthesised progress in self-concept enhancement research and created guidelines for enhancing the next generation of self-concept enhancement theory, research and practice capitalising on recent advances in the field. My self-concept research focuses on educational settings and has resulted in new solutions for addressing a number of significant educational issues, including Aboriginal disadvantage, bullying, appropriate education for gifted and talented students, and early intervention. My colleagues and I have also developed self-concept measurement instruments to measure young children's self-concepts so that advances in theory and research can be more readily extended to early intervention. I have also theorised the separation of cognitive and affective domains of self-concept and found that interventions can often impact differentially on these domains.

Underpinning and synergising my research interests are my beliefs that maximising self-concept is vital to unlocking full human potential and, as such, an important means for addressing and resolving significant educational and social issues of our time. My research program is designed to provide sound empirical research to generate new solutions to inform the development of educational interventions that directly maximise and enhance desirable educational outcomes and result in making a difference to young people's lives.

KEY REFERENCES

Craven, R. G., Marsh, H. W. & Burnett, P. (2003) Cracking the self-concept enhancement conundrum: A call and blueprint for the next generation of self-concept enhancement research. In H. W. Marsh, R. G. Craven & D. M. McInerney (eds) *International Advances in Self Research (Volume 1)* (pp. 91–126). Greenwich, CT: Information Age Publishing.

Craven, R. G., Tucker, A., Munns, G., Hinkley, J., Marsh, H. W. & Simpson, K. (in press). *Indigenous Students' Aspirations: Dreams, Perceptions and Realities*. Canberra: Department of Education, Science and Training, Commonwealth of Australia.

Marsh, H. W., Craven, R. G. & McInerney, D. M. (eds) (2003) *International Advances in Self Research (Volume 1)*. Greenwich, CT: Information Age Publishing.

ACTIVITIES

1 Rhonda Craven believes that enhancing the self-concept of underachieving students will lead to greater academic achievement. What do you think is the relationship between self-concept and achievement? You should consider the material on self-concept and self-esteem in Chapter 14.

2 Discuss with a group of your peers how you would set about enhancing the self-concept of students. Then consider a range of reading and Internet sources on self-concept enhancement programs and evaluate how effective your techniques would have been. Do you think the approaches taken to self-concept enhancement should or would vary depending on the type of classroom and students being taught?

3 Rhonda Craven has developed a policy and series of instructional materials on Aboriginal studies and teaching Aboriginal students for implementation in teacher training courses. She states that while over 50 per cent of primary teacher training courses include some form of Aboriginal curriculum, many institutions and courses do not. Consider your program of studies. If it includes Aboriginal perspectives and content, what is the nature of this, and how useful have you found it? If your course does not include such perspectives you might like to inquire as to why this is the case and whether it should be included.

4 Investigate the reasons for the poor academic achievement of Aboriginal students at school. Do these reasons vary according to whether the students come from remote and more traditional communities, relatively urbanised communities or fully urbanised communities? It might be necessary for you to read some of the recommended readings at the end of the chapter, as well as to conduct some Internet searches. Discuss your findings with members of your course group.

5 Rhonda Craven makes a number of suggestions regarding how educators might foster adaptive psychological functioning in Aboriginal students so that they might aspire to, and complete, secondary education. Consider material presented in this chapter, and others, and draw up a series of guidelines with your peers on how this might be facilitated.

Reasons for the poor achievement of many Aboriginal children

2000), the Aboriginal parents also suggested that poor parental encouragement, bad home life, and little parental understanding of the value of schooling affected the school progress of some Aboriginal students.

The students themselves also attracted some blame for being lazy and poorly motivated. It should be noted that similar reasons were also given for the poor performance of non-Aboriginal students (McInerney 2003; Dowson & McInerney 2005).

Our own research has indicated that lack of motivation or laziness is not the main influence on poor school performance. Rather, the key factors influencing Aboriginal school students' performance and motivation in mainstream school settings appear to be the students' perception of themselves as competent learners, their level of confidence in school settings, their level of intrinsic motivation, and how much they like and value school (McInerney 1991b, 1992b, 1993; McInerney & Swisher 1995). It is unlikely that the performance of

What is relevant and meaningful education for remote Aboriginal communities?

Aboriginal students will improve unless they are encouraged to believe in themselves as effective learners who can be successful within a Western education system. We develop this notion further in the chapter on motivation (Chapter 7). Aboriginal education programs, Aboriginal resource centres and Aboriginal teacher assistants are part of the initiatives that have been introduced into mainstream schools to enhance the confidence of Aboriginal students.

QUESTION POINT

Consider the special educational problems of remote and traditional Aboriginal students. What role should/could non-Aboriginal teachers play in designing a relevant education for these students?

Educational initiatives among remote and traditional Aboriginal groups

Clearly, the results of our survey apply only to a particular group. Other surveys and studies have indicated a need for education at all levels to be radically reshaped to focus on the special needs of remote and traditional groups, as well as of those communities that are re-establishing their cultural identity within the wider social milieu (for example, see Folds 1987; Jordan 1984; Sonn, Bishop & Humphries 2000). In particular, attention has been directed within many of these communities towards developing curricula and school structures that give access to Western knowledge, while rebuilding, fostering and preserving cultural values and traditions important to the identity of the people. On this level there have been some exciting developments.

Bilingual/ bicultural education for Aboriginal children

There has been a significant growth of bilingual/ bicultural Aboriginal education throughout Australia. The Northern Territory began developing these programs in 1973 (Allen 1986; Benton 1989; Folds 1987; Gale *et al.* 1987) and other states have also implemented programs. Bilingual programs have been difficult to establish because of the number of Aboriginal languages and the fact that the languages are unwritten. Hence extensive preliminary work has to take place to establish the written characteristics of each language. From this point it is necessary to develop written curriculum materials and to train bilingual teachers. Despite these extensive problems, bilingual programs are flourishing.

As an example of this development, Yipirinya School in Alice Springs uses Aboriginal culture, knowledge and language as the starting point for all learning. Aboriginal culture and language are never phased out to enable transfer to an English language and Western culturally dominated curriculum. Learning begins with the known and gradually introduces the unknown by relating Western concepts to Aboriginal concepts.

In a number of communities, Aboriginal people have established their own schools or taken control of existing facilities. Within Western Australia, for example, a network of Aboriginal schools that share a number of common features has been established (Teasdale & Teasdale 1993, 1994; Vallance & Vallance 1988):

1 They are fully controlled and administered by the local Aboriginal communities, funding being provided by a system of state and federal grants that are paid to all non-government schools in Australia.
2 Although trained non-Aboriginal teachers are employed, they are expected to work at all times under the direction of community leaders.

3 Community observations of and participation in all school activities are encouraged; community ownership of the school is stressed.
4 In general, children are taught in kin rather than age groups, taking account of mutual obligation and avoidance relationships.
5 Traditional authority structures are maintained by first presenting curriculum materials' based on Western knowledge to the older members of the community.
6 Strong emphasis is placed on maintenance of traditional languages; vernacular literacy programs are given high priority.

The concept of the two-way school (see, for example, Harris 1990) has been developed at Yirrkala, a large community in northwest Arnhem Land where the government school is staffed and administered largely by Aboriginal teachers. **Two-way schools** attempt to introduce Western knowledge while at the same time taking active steps to promote culture and language maintenance. Language is considered essential, and the mother tongue is used as a language of instruction in the early years of schooling in many of these schools (see Hewitt 2000).

The main features of two-way schools are:
1 The Aboriginal ownership of the school program is recognised.
2 Aboriginal people are taking the initiative in shaping, developing and implementing the program.
3 Clan elders come into the school to teach, thus reaffirming relationships between older and younger generation levels.
4 Children are organised by clan and family relationships, and by separating boys and girls.
5 Flexible structures allow for recognition of traditional ceremonial obligations, especially during initiation.
6 Equal respect is given to Aboriginal and Western knowledge; the exchange of knowledge is stressed.

Schools in the Kimberley region in the north of Western Australia have evolved a concept of two-way learning that underlines all curriculum planning. It emphasises the need for children to learn both Aboriginal and mainstream ways of life by sharing and exchange. Implementation involves Aboriginal decision making, integration of school and community, the strengthening of teaching–learning relationships between older and younger members of the community, and the development of flexible school structures (Teasdale & Teasdale 1993).

Two-way learning

A number of Aboriginal communities have opted out of Western education almost entirely and established homeland schools. **Homeland schools** have an element of formal structure, but there is little emphasis on learning Western knowledge or language. Some communities have opted for voluntary exclusion and have no formal schooling at all for their children. The focus of these communities is clearly on re-establishing the identity of the groups as a cultural entity (Folds 1987; Teasdale & Teasdale 1993).

Homeland schools

Educational initiatives among Maori

As with many indigenous minority groups, the Maori has typically been disadvantaged in mainstream educational settings (Cazden 1990; Fergusson, Horwood & Shannon 1982; Fergusson, Lloyd & Horwood 1991; Rubie, Townsend & Moore 2004; Sultana 1989). Ranginui Walker (cited in Irwin 1989) identifies variables that he considers are the main problems of Maori education. The first is that the teachers in New Zealand are, by and large, Pakeha (European), monocultural people who lack the skills, sensitivity and knowledge to be able to teach effectively in multi-ethnic classrooms. Because education is geared to this monocultural, Pakeha frame of reference, Maori children see little of relevance to them at school. Success is limited to those stereotyped areas that Maoris are good at, such as sport and music. Maori peoples have learned to have an ambivalent attitude towards education because success in Western schools appears to run counter to their own important cultural values, and the schools themselves do little to encourage and develop the cultural qualities that Maoris consider very important.

Others argue that the reason for the disadvantage and under-achievement lies in the socio-economic differences between Maori and Pakeha, rather than a cultural mismatch between Western schooling and Maori cultural values (Fergusson *et al.* 1991).

In contrast to Aboriginal Australians, Maori peoples form a relatively homogeneous group sharing the one language and many cultural traditions. This has facilitated, in recent years, the development of educational initiatives to preserve Maori language (*te reo Maori*) and Maori culture (*taha Maori*) within and outside the regular school system (Corson 1993; Irwin 1989, 1991, 1992, 1993).

One exciting development is the ***kohanga reo*** (language nests) movement, which began in 1982. This offers a preschool all-Maori language and culture immersion environment for children from birth to school age, aimed at developing children within a context replicating a Maori home, where only Maori language is spoken and heard. The *kohanga reo* are open to all children from all cultures and have proved to be very popular. Following on from this is the increasing provision of bilingual/bicultural education for children at the primary level, ultimately through to secondary school. There are also several Maori language and culture immersion primary schools (*kura kaupapa Maori*) (Corson 1993; Irwin 1991, 1992; Irwin & Davies 1992), and these are becoming increasingly common.

Situating schools in their cultural context

The importance of these schools lies in their attempt to situate learning in the appropriate cultural context. Corson (1993, p. 56) says:

> The new schools try to restore *mana* [*mana* means status, prestige, power] to the Maori learner in a meaningful way by creating an environment where Maori culture is the taken-for-granted background against which everything else is set. For the pupils, being Maori in *te kura kaupapa Maori* is the norm; the school and classroom environment connects with the Maori home; cultural and language values are central; Maori parents make decisions for their children unimpeded by majority culture gatekeeping devices; and the *whanau* (extended family group) assumes responsibility for the education of their children along with control and direction of the school itself. At the same time, these schools are concerned to teach a modern, up-to-date and relevant curriculum, following national guidelines set by the state, whose outcome will be the production of bilingual and bicultural graduates.

A study of Maori culture has been included in the curriculum of New Zealand state schools (Townsend, Manley & Tuck 1991). This has met with about the same level of success as the multicultural education initiatives within Australian schools. In many schools, *taha Maori* has been enthusiastically endorsed; in others the program has been poorly implemented (see, for example, Rubie, Townsend & Moore 2004). The nature of the program, as well as its method of implementation, are controversial, however, which has handicapped its effective implementation. The issue is beyond the scope of this book. Interested readers should refer to Corson (1993).

Maori cultural studies

QUESTION POINT

How important is language to identity? Discuss the merits of ESL versus bilingual/bicultural education for NESB children. In particular, consider the possible ramifications of each for cognitive development and learning. In this context also discuss the bilingual/bicultural schools established by Aboriginal and Maori communities.

Educational implications for indigenous minority education

In much of what has been discussed it is evident that Aboriginal and Maori communities are repossessing education and making it more culturally relevant and appropriate for their children. In some cases this is happening outside the regular school settings and under the control of community leaders and teachers. Regular teachers may have little input into these developments. What, then, is the role of mainstream teachers? And how does a knowledge of educational psychology prepare them for assuming this role?

Implications for mainstream teachers

First, we have argued many times throughout this text that, for education to be meaningful, it must take notice of the learner's background. This applies to all children, but in some cases the mismatch between teachers' understanding and the children's backgrounds and culture can be so vast as to impede effective schooling. Obviously, therefore, we must support wholeheartedly attempts by these, and other cultural communities, to restructure schools and teaching so that the community's culture becomes an essential basis from which to develop educational programs for the community's children. Schooling must be situated within the appropriate cultural context.

Schools and cultural context

Second, schools should be concerned with more than simply passing on information and academic skills. They should also be concerned with developing *life chances* for the children they serve (see, for example, Evans & Poole 1987). There are two basic types of life chance: those that relate to increasing social options for children (such as employment and further education), and those that relate to helping children to establish themselves within a social framework that acts as a personal network for the development of a sense of identity. On the whole, schools don't do very well on the first kind of life chance for Aboriginal, Torres Strait Islander and Maori children, and also perform poorly on the second. Many mainstream schools ignore the community element of education and fail to situate education effectively within the context of mutually respectful relationships where children can develop the social bonds and a sense of identity that bind them to each other and to their family community. Many schools also foster values (such as individualism and competitiveness) that are in conflict with community values. This has the potential to set up a personal (and often unresolvable) dualism for the children (see Folds 1987; Hohepa, Jenkins & McNaughton 1992; Jordan 1984; Malin 1990; Williamson 1991). As Folds (1987, p. 34) states:

Schools and life chances

> In practice, as *anangu* are well aware, most school activities exclude community concerns and inevitably make Pitjantjatjara youth dissatisfied with their own society and culture. What most school activities have in common is that they are precisely the opposite to the bicultural ideal. Few activities at any grade level embrace community experiences, start where the children are or reinforce a positive Pitjantjatjara self-image. Most do nothing to contribute to community feeling that the school is 'theirs'. On the contrary, they reinforce beliefs among the older generation that school remains whitefella business.

The dilemma of mainstream schools is how to enhance the options for indigenous children in the wider community (that is, giving them Western literacy and numeracy skills and work values such as competitiveness, independence, individualism, responsibility and punctuality), while also fostering values important to growing Aboriginal or Maori children (such as family ties, community bonds and cooperation) (see Teasdale & Teasdale 1993, 1994).

What can mainstream psychology contribute to our understanding?

Much mainstream psychological theorising on the importance of self-concept, identity formation, learning and cognitive styles, information processing and effective teaching (and many other factors) for effective learning can supply valuable insights in our attempt to understand the needs of these indigenous and other non-Western groups for an education that is culturally relevant yet appropriate to the modern world of which these communities are now a part. Many Western notions on effective learning are challenged by cross-cultural psychological research (see our sections on Piaget and Vygotsky for examples), and increasingly research is examining the relevance of many of our 'taken-for-granted' approaches to teaching and learning (see, for example, McInerney & Van Etten 2001). It is our view that principles of good teaching are, in the main, applicable to all students, whatever their cultural background, and that their implementation in even quite culturally diverse classrooms will enhance the learning of all students. One caveat to this is that the cultural backgrounds of the students should form a base in which these teaching/learning approaches are anchored.

In our modern theorising about the most effective ways to facilitate learning for all students, we can also learn from models characteristic of traditional Aboriginal and Maori learning styles and settings. Traditional emphases on learning through real-life performance, learning through observation and imitation, constructing knowledge holistically rather than through decontextualisation and fragmentation, and learning through cooperation and group work are not far removed from the notions of effective learning and teaching models currently being developed and fostered within Western education settings. Furthermore, the emphasis on community involvement in educational programs, a major element in Aboriginal, Torres Strait Islander and Maori schools, is being strongly encouraged in mainstream schools through the establishment of school councils (see also Townsend *et al.* 1991).

It is unlikely, in the foreseeable future, that most Aboriginal and Maori children will be educated in other than mainstream schools. Consequently, many teachers trained for mainstream schools will have the opportunity to teach Aboriginal and Maori children. How can these schools and teachers best assist these children to achieve?

Serving the needs of indigenous students

For schools to serve the needs of Maori children more adequately, Corson (1993) argues that they need to provide an atmosphere that encourages a sense of belonging, a family feeling of physical closeness where each student is given personal attention, praise, encouragement, and the daily experience of success and accomplishment. Teachers should pay attention to the preferred learning approaches of the students so that the students' self-esteem is enhanced. Because learning is a cooperative exercise, children, teachers, parents and *whanau* should all be involved. As oral communication is so important to traditional Maori education, opportunities should be given for oral language interaction; older children should be given the chance to assist and care for younger children within school, as they are expected to do in the community at large. Schools should emphasise collaboration, cooperation and group benefit, and de-emphasise competitive individualism and individual gain. Assessment and evaluation need to be designed with these collaborative goals in mind. These points also have great relevance for Aboriginal education and, in our opinion, mainstream education could equally benefit from such values.

The importance of self-esteem

As indicated above, self-esteem and confidence is an important element in orienting a learner's attitude towards school. Students' sense of confidence in the school context is influenced by their expectations of success and by their performance in key academic areas. Schools, through their policies, programs and administration, must be places where indigenous minority students can experience academic success. This success, however, should be in harmony with significant cultural values such as cooperation and affiliation. The chapters on motivation and effective teaching supply a number of suggestions on how this might be achieved.

Positive teacher support is also very important. We believe that teachers can most help these learners by giving effective feedback and recognition to students in line with their performance and by helping them to develop a sense of competence, confidence and a positive self-image within the school context. Fundamental to this is the need for teachers to have cross-cultural awareness (Bell 1986; Malin 1990).

The role of the teacher

Parental support and encouragement for their children to do well and to continue with school is perhaps one of the most important factors influencing children's attitudes towards school. Obviously, community values are of paramount importance. If children receive messages from their cultural community that it is good to do well at school, and that their life chances will be enhanced by successful schooling, they will stand a greater chance of success. Conversely, if the community's messages indicate that success at school is at best irrelevant, and at worst inimical to their cultural identity, children will not look to the school as the arena in which to demonstrate their successes (Eckermann 1999; Folds 1987; McInerney 1993; McInerney & Swisher 1995).

The role of parents

When indigenous learners are encouraged to feel that their efforts are going to be worthwhile, when they receive support from parents and teachers, and especially when they feel capable of success, their performance improves dramatically. Throughout this book we discuss many ways of restructuring educational experiences for learners so that the experiences are more sensitive to individual needs, and we emphasise the active role played by learners in constructing their knowledge of how the world works. Many of these suggestions have particular relevance for restructuring educational experiences to make them more culturally relevant and appropriate to Aboriginal, Torres Strait Islander and Maori learners.

School achievements of children from minority cultural groups

Within Australian, Canadian, New Zealand, British and American schools there are two basic groups of minorities: indigenous minorities and children of immigrants. Not all immigrant or indigenous groups perform equally well; indeed, some perform relatively better than other groups (see, for example, Pollock 2001). In the Australian context, groups with an Asian background tend to achieve better in school than groups from the Middle East (Suliman & McInerney 2005); in the US context, African-American and Latino-American children appear to do less well than some more recently arrived immigrant groups from Korea and students of Anglo-American background (see, for example, Dandy & Nettelbeck 2000; Okagaki & Frensch 1998; Lee 2002; Osborne 2000; Riehl 2000; Tucker & Herman 2002).

The reasons for these differences between groups are not at all clear. They probably involve a vast range of factors that include level of parental education and their socio-economic status, ethnicity, self-concept, language usage, youth culture and student behaviour (such as motivation and effort for learning, alcohol and illicit drug usage, crime), and school conditions and practices (such as instructional resources, teachers, courses, segregation, dropout profiles) (see Lee 2002; Tucker & Herman 2002). There may also be differences in parental expectations for children's achievement, differences in the congruence between the cultural practices of the home and the cultural practices of the school, racial stereotyping, and oppression of specific groups which might lead these groups to develop avenues for achievement that do not depend on accepting the values of the dominant group (see, for example, Brizuela & Garcia-Sellers 1999; Okagaki & Frensch 1998; Osborne 2000; Portes 1999). There are also vast intra-group differences. In other words, not all members of a particular group perform well or poorly; many individual and family factors are also involved. One potential problem is that members of particular groups may be stereotyped by teachers as poorly motivated and lacking achievement orientation. In this case, a self-fulfilling prophecy effect may come into play. Based on the information above, it is very dangerous for teachers to apply simple stereotypes to explain the under-performance of particular groups or individuals. It is essential to examine the specific situations applying to under-achieving individuals in order to address issues that might be impeding their performance in order to implement strategies to facilitate their achievement at school (see, for example, Gutiérrez & Rogoff 2003; Tucker & Herman 2002). We discuss some possible ways of doing this in both this chapter and Chapter 9.

Despite the difficulties faced by many children of immigrant parents, there is no indication that immigrant groups, in general, are disadvantaged in Australian schools. The evidence supports the belief that many students from non-English-speaking and Asian backgrounds (including recently arrived groups) are succeeding in our schools (Bullivant 1986, 1988b; Dandy & Nettelbeck 2000). Among the reasons given for this

Theory and research into practice

Simone Volet — STUDENT LEARNING AND MOTIVATION IN HIGHER EDUCATION

BRIEF BIOGRAPHY

I was born in Francophone Switzerland, in a small country town where my family had been farming the land for generations. I first graduated as a primary school teacher. After further study I obtained a 'Licence ès Sciences de l'éducation' from the University of Geneva with a dissertation entitled *Ecole, Communes, Canton: le cas du Pays de Vaud* (Schools, Cities, State: The case of the 'Pays de Vaud'). This work examined the significance for local communities of self-determination and autonomy with regard to school matters. These processes were found to be critical in maintaining the social identity of those communities. This early research fostered my interest in negotiated decision making, tolerance of diversity and social commitment that is still noticeable in my current research endeavours.

After many years as a primary then as a secondary school teacher in Switzerland, I moved to Australia in 1981 and became interested in the development of theory and research on metacognition, self-regulation and the nature of expertise, with a focus on adult cognition. I completed a Ph.D. on the significance of goals in academic study, and took a lecturing position at Murdoch University in Western Australia. My research interest in adult cognition led to the conceptualisation and development of an innovative program in tertiary and adult education at Murdoch University.

I was dean of the School of Education from 2000 to 2003. I am presently professor of educational psychology and involved in teaching, administration, research and supervision of doctoral students. I also serve as associate editor of *Learning and Instruction*, am president of the Educational, Instructional and School Psychology Division of the International Association of Applied Psychology (IAAP), and co-convenor of the Special Interest Group on Motivation and Emotion of the European Association for Research on Learning and Instruction (EARLI). I was the recipient of the inaugural Outstanding Publication Award of EARLI in 1997.

RESEARCH AND THEORETICAL INTERESTS

My current research interests are in the area of student learning and motivation in higher education with a focus on both theory development and applied endeavours. Over the years, I have been working on the development of a multi-dimensional, multilevel, interactive and dynamic conceptual framework to represent the complexity and holistic nature of learning and motivation in real-life contexts. This development is influenced by the growing importance given to the person-in-context position within cognitive theory, motivation research and cross-cultural/cultural psychology. The proposed framework combines social-cognitive and situative, sociocultural perspectives on learning and motivation. I have argued that conceptualising contexts at different levels of specificity is critical to understanding the dynamic and interactive influences of broad societal values, cultural-educational systems, classroom practices and immediate tasks on students' overall dispositions, situational tendencies and situation-specific appraisals in regard to motivation and engagement. At the core of the framework is the notion of 'experiential interface'. From a cognitive perspective, this is the most important aspect since this is where individuals' activation of prior knowledge and beliefs, situational interpretations, immediate emotions and the construction of meaning take place. From a sociocultural, situative perspective, this is also the most critical aspect since it represents individuals' engagement and participation in the community of practice. I have argued that the ideal learning situation is when there is congruence at the experiential interface. Congruence is achieved when the learning context supports students' needs and circumstances and reciprocally when students are attuned to the opportunities afforded by the learning environment. Of course, what produces congruence is expected to vary across groups and individuals, task purposes and subject matter. It is also expected to change for the same person over time and across situations, although some consistency is expected overall. An appreciation of the notion of congruence at the experiential interface is critical for teachers' development of powerful learning environments as well as for students' effective self-regulated learning.

My research also stressed that what are appropriate cognitions, motivations and behaviours is subjectively perceived. When students move across different educational settings, as is the case with international students, substantial adjustments are experienced since the norms and expectations that are prevailing in a particular context are often tacit rather than explicit. Substantial mismatch in intersubjective perceptions can occur and congruence needs to be re-established.

Studies of international university students moving from the familiar cultural-educational context of high school or college in their home country to the unfamiliar context of the host university in another country highlighted this phenomenon. Various types of subjective experiences in the transfer of learning across contexts can be identified: congruence, ambivalence, difficulty and incongruence. Congruence is re-established in the host environment if the learning practices that students bring with them travel well, and like at home, are perceived by all parties as congruent with what is valued in the new setting. Other strategies may require adjustments or may be unsuited to the demands of the new environment. Stressing the notion of transfer of learning across cultural-educational contexts that may value different learning and motivation practices provides a sound basis for questioning the deficit model and stereotyped, negative and static view of Southeast Asian students' learning held by many academics in institutions hosting international students.

On multicultural campuses, students often have to complete assignments in culturally mixed groups. Studying the socio-emotional dynamics of assignments completed in such groups has made me realise the significance of promoting reciprocal cultural understanding between staff and students, and among students from diverse backgrounds. My empirical work is revealing that students with substantial intercultural experience—most of them bi- or multilingual—have significantly more positive attitudes towards group work in general and group work in mixed groups of local and international students, than students from monocultural backgrounds. It is also highlighting the significance of cultural dimensions as inhibiting factors in the interactions of small groups of local and international students. From a self-regulation perspective, one would expect that unless the benefits of mixing are perceived as outweighing any potential drawbacks, both local and international students would continue to choose the less emotionally demanding option of forming teams of peers from the same background. This clearly defeats the major aims of internationalisation and calls for carefully designed and monitored social engineering.

I also have an interest in the development of internationalised higher education curricula that enrich the learning of all students, local and international alike. I believe that the most challenging goal for the internationalisation of universities worldwide is to foster students' appreciation of the culturally situated and non-value-free nature of knowledge, and in particular to foster their capacity to critically analyse the tensions between different agendas when applying knowledge in local and global environments. Mobilising students' critical reflection on the plurality of sources of knowledge and its distribution across groups with unequal power, for example, agrees with the basic principles and objectives of metacognitive, process-oriented forms of instruction, since critical reflection is embedded within the teaching of domain-specific knowledge. Combining the educational goals of internationalisation with socio-cognitive theories of learning makes it possible to outline a set of learning objectives and principles for designing internationalised curricula that would provide added value to student subject matter learning.

Overall, my research with university students has acknowledged the importance of examining learning as a holistic process that incorporates cognitive, motivational, volitional, emotional, social and cultural aspects as they interact in real-life situations. Recent developments have involved international collaborative research with colleagues from Finland and the United States, with a focus on theory development in self-regulation from a social perspective, the significance of personal goals in self- and co-regulation, and help-seeking in cultural context.

THEORY AND RESEARCH INTO PRACTICE

Much of my research has aimed at theory development in the field of learning and motivation in social contexts. It has also included the development of collaborative projects aimed at improving teaching and learning with colleagues from other disciplines, such as computer science, information technology, economics and management. This work has combined my colleagues' subject-matter expertise and related teaching experience with my own knowledge of learning theory to produce and test effective process-oriented, metacognitive forms of instruction. I have enjoyed the opportunities for joint research but also for collaborative writing for a range of audiences, including educational psychology journals as well as specialised subject-related educational literature. Recent collaborative work is exploring the motivational and social dynamics of student group projects and is carried out with colleagues from the field of business.

With regard to internationalisation policy, I have argued that in view of the recent explosion of initiatives for internationalising higher education curricula, it has become critical for researchers in education to develop an interest in and commitment to issues related to university teaching, learning and curriculum development in an international perspective. I believe that a commitment is necessary to ensure that the educational and cultural objectives of internationalisation are included alongside professional, customer-oriented and political agendas. My research in this area has attracted some attention in Australia and Europe. I have been privileged to discuss some critical issues with senior executives from several universities and with academic colleagues involved in the development of internationalised curricula or engaged in teaching international students.

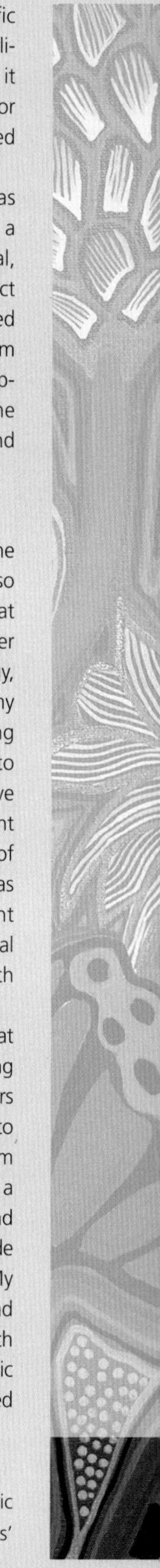

KEY REFERENCES

Volet, S. E. (1997) Cognitive and affective variables in academic learning: The significance of direction and effort in students' goals. *Learning and Instruction,* **7**(3), 235–54.

Volet, S. E. (1999) Motivation within and across cultural-educational contexts: A multi-dimensional perspective. In T. Urdan (ed.) *Advances in Motivation and Achievement (Volume 11)* (pp. 185–231). Greenwich, CT: JAI Press.

Volet, S. E. (2001) Learning and motivation in context: A multi-dimensional and multi-level, cognitive-situative perspective. In S. E. Volet & S. Järvelä (eds) *Motivation in Learning Contexts: Theoretical Advances and Methodological Implications* (pp. 57–82). London: Elsevier.

ACTIVITIES

1 Simone Volet is interested in the complexity and holistic nature of learning and motivation in real-life contexts that combine social-cognitive, situative and sociocultural perspectives. In our text we deal with these perspectives on a number of occasions. What is the nature of these perspectives, and why do you think they are important? Discuss your answers with your fellow students.

2 What special learning and motivational issues might be relevant for international students studying at schools and colleges outside their cultural contexts? How would knowledge of these special issues help educators to maximise the achievement of these students?

3 Simone Volet believes that it is important to mix students from different cultural groups in interactive activities and suggests the need for carefully designed and monitored social engineering to achieve this. What might the elements of this 'social engineering' be?

4 What do you think are the key elements of effective internationalised curricula?

5 We recommend that you read the key references above, as they will shed light on each of the issues in the earlier activities.

success are their capacity for hard work, academic motivation, self-discipline, good behaviour and reliability in class, and high-achievement orientation and aspirations, coupled outside the school with parental support and their choice to put in long hours of work. In particular, students who are backed by strong motivation from their families perform well at school and become outstanding students (Bullivant 1988b; see also McInerney 1988a, 1988b; Marjoribanks 1980).

It is also clear that many children from indigenous minority groups do not do well in Western schools. Australian Aboriginal, New Zealand Maori and Native American and Native Canadian students are over-represented among children who do not do well at school, are attending remedial classes, are held back a grade, chronically non-attend and drop out of school early. Again, the reasons for this are not at all clear and very complex, although many causes have been suggested as above (see, for example, Gray & Bereford 2002; McInerney 2003; Dowson & McInerney 2005; McInerney & Swisher 1995; Ogbu 1992, 1997). We have suggested above some educational practices designed to improve the chances of these minorities doing well at school. In our next section, dealing with culturally relevant teaching, we highlight some practices that should enhance the learning of all groups.

ACTION STATION

In groups of three or four, review a number of multicultural or bicultural education policy documents. Discuss the philosophy or rationale underlining each policy and identify the assumptions implicit in the document. Relate your findings to issues raised in this chapter.

Using this information as a basis, translate these general policy statements into specific aims suited to a school with particular characteristics (region, size, pupil/teacher characteristics to be determined by your group).

Discuss how these aims can be put into practice. This will involve a consideration of suitable content and techniques, and an evaluation of existing resources and programs.

In a study of the effects of culturally relevant teaching in the Maori context, Rubie, Townsend and Moore (2004) found that a year-long cultural intervention program designed to increase self-esteem and locus of control among Maori students actually improved their positive self-esteem and locus of control in comparison to matched groups of children who did not participate in the intervention. Parallel improvements were also made in scholastic aptitude. One of the important aspects of this study is that it shows what can be done to improve many educational characteristics of indigenous students by using culturally relevant teaching practices, and immersing children in their culture within mainstream schools. This is important, as we have indicated earlier, because whatever special schools are set up (such as *kohhanga reo* and *kura kaupapa*, or homeland schools) most indigenous children will continue to be educated within mainstream schools. We recommend you read this article, which is referenced at the end of this chapter. Table 10.3 presents essentials on classroom practices to enhance learning for children of different cultural backgrounds

QUESTION POINT

What might some essentials be from the learner's perspective?

In dealing with individuals from different cultural groups, we should show sensitivity. It is obvious in this case that the individual did not want to be photographed.

Table 10.3

Essentials of classroom practices to enhance the learning of students from different cultural backgrounds

Teachers should:

- empower students to direct their own learning;
- adopt a personalising strategy and treat all students as individuals rather than representatives of a social group;
- appreciate the cultural knowledge that students bring to school;
- hold high expectations of all students; focus on academic achievement;
- facilitate meaningful parent and community participation in decision making;
- embed learning within culturally valued knowledge and experiences (such as learning historiography through a study of one's own group or music from one's culture);
- situate learning within culturally appropriate social situations (such as teacher–student interactions that are consistent with cultural values and practices);
- establish an environment built on genuine mutual respect where difference and similarity are equally valued;
- create a caring environment and a high level of cooperation among students, teachers and families;
- foster a classroom climate that is responsive to differing student learning styles (in particular, ways of knowing, understanding, representing and expressing typically employed in a particular culture);
- include culturally appropriate curriculum content and instructional processes.

(Source: Based on Hollins 1996; Riehl 2000)

EXTENSION STUDY

Culturally relevant teaching

In the sections above, we have discussed some key aspects of teaching students from diverse cultural backgrounds. A term used to describe teaching that is responsive to the cultural backgrounds and needs of students is **culturally relevant teaching**. Teachers responsive to cultural difference 'promote learning among diverse students when they honor different ways of knowing and sources of knowledge, allow students to speak and write in their own vernacular and use culturally compatible communication styles themselves, express cultural solidarity with their students, share power with students, focus on caring for the whole child, and maintain high expectations for all' (Riehl 2000, p. 64; see also Lee 2001; Quiocho & Rios 2000). We now wish to draw together some general principles that you should consider when teaching in ethnically diverse educational settings. The following points are drawn from the work of Gloria Ladson-Billings with exemplary teachers of African-American students (Ladson-Billings 1995), but the principles are applicable in all diverse educational settings. Culturally relevant teaching should do three things:

- produce students who can achieve academically;
- produce students who demonstrate cultural competence; and
- develop students who can both understand and critique the existing social order.

In her work with exemplary teachers, Ladson-Billings found culturally responsive teachers were characterised by the conceptions of self and others they held, the manner in which social relations were structured and their conceptions of knowledge. When we present elements of these characteristics below, you will note that we deal with each of them at various points throughout our text. Please reread these sections so that you are aware of the important dimensions of being a culturally responsive teacher.

Conceptions of self and others

We have noted before that teachers who have high self-efficacy and encourage self-efficacy in their students are more effective teachers (see Chapter 6). According to Ladson-Billings. culturally responsive teachers:

- believe that all students are capable of academic success;
- see their teaching as an art;
- see themselves as members of the community the school serves;
- see teaching as a way to give back to this community; and
- believe in teaching as a process of pulling knowledge out.

Social relations

We have indicated throughout the text that good personal and interpersonal relationships within the educational setting are essential for effective learning to take place. For this reason there is considerable emphasis today on the social elements of learning (see our material on social constructivism throughout), and in particular on the implementation of cooperative learning (see Chapter 8) and various forms of heterogeneous ability groupings (see Chapter 9). Culturally responsive teachers:

- maintain fluid student–teacher relationships;
- demonstrate a connectedness with all of the students;
- develop a community of learners; and
- encourage students to learn collaboratively and to be responsible for another.

Conceptions of knowledge

We have also indicated throughout the text that effective teachers must have a firm grasp of knowledge and its acquisition and the assessment of that knowledge. Ladson-Billings (1995) found that for culturally responsive teachers:

- knowledge is not static; it is shared, recycled and constructed;
- knowledge must be viewed critically;
- there must be passion about knowledge and learning;
- scaffolding, or building bridges, to facilitate learning must occur; and
- assessment must be multifaceted, incorporating multiple forms of excellence.

As you will surmise, these are principles of effective teaching with any group. It is the case, however, that these principles are less often used within classrooms characterised by diversity, and in particular with students who are academically disadvantaged, such as indigenous minorities (Aboriginal Australians, Native Americans) and ethnic minorities (such as African-Americans and Mexican-Americans).

WHAT WOULD YOU DO?

JULIO CAN DO IT

Sixteen-year-old Julio had recently arrived from South America, where English was his second language. He was placed in Miss Miley's Grade 7 English class at the beginning of the year. Mr Cugliari, his ESL teacher, his Grade 7 English teacher and Miss Blainey, who taught the Grade 8 English class, met to discuss the possibility of Julio being placed in Grade 8 for third term.

Case studies illustrating National Competency Framework for Beginning Teaching, National Project on the Quality of Teaching and Learning, Australian Teaching Council, 1996, p. 49. Commonwealth of Australia copyright, reproduced by permission.

Imagine you are Miss Blainey. What arguments would you present for keeping Julio in Grade 7? What arguments would you use to support his move to Grade 8? Now read what happened.

WHAT WOULD YOU DO? (cont.)

JULIO CAN DO IT

Miss Blainey felt very hesitant and unsure about this proposal. Surely it was unwise, since Julio was having difficulty with English.

However, during the discussion, Miss Miley and Mr Cugliari spoke of the importance of this move for Julio's social development, of the tremendous staff support for both Julio and Miss Blainey, and of the boy's own determination to do well. Miss Blainey changed her opinion, and Julio moved to her class.

One day, a number of weeks later, Miss Blainey asked Julio to read a passage aloud from the class novel. He approached this task in a very positive fashion and read clearly and slowly. When he came upon a word that he was unsure of, he successfully worked out the correct pronunciation. Miss Blainey felt very pleased and proud of Julio's achievement. She was grateful to her fellow staff and for their insistence on giving the boy the opportunity to develop and fulfil their expectations of him.

Case studies illustrating National Competency Framework for Beginning Teaching, National Project on the Quality of Teaching and Learning, Australian Teaching Council, 1996, p. 49. Commonwealth of Australia copyright, reproduced by permission.

WHAT WOULD YOU DO?

ABORIGINES ARE AUSTRALIANS, TOO

Miss Gray always approaches parent–teacher evenings with a certain feeling of apprehension despite being reassured by other members of staff that it is worse for the parent. Her fears were justified when at the most recent parent–teacher evening a parent seriously questioned her teaching of Aboriginal studies as part of the Grade 7 social science course. 'Haven't you done enough? Why focus on the Aborigines?'

Case studies illustrating National Competency Framework for Beginning Teaching, National Project on the Quality of Teaching and Learning, Australian Teaching Council, 1996, p. 48. Commonwealth of Australia copyright, reproduced by permission.

What would you say in this situation? Now read about the teacher's reaction.

WHAT WOULD YOU DO? (cont.)

ABORIGINES ARE AUSTRALIANS, TOO

After her initial shock, Miss Gray tried to explain to the parent the importance of Aboriginal culture and heritage in students' understanding of the history of Australia. The parent was not completely convinced, although she seemed reasonably satisfied with Miss Gray's approach.

Miss Gray finished the meeting by focusing on what topics were to be covered in the following term and highlighting the fact that the course covers a broader curriculum, of which Aboriginal studies is a part.

Case studies illustrating National Competency Framework for Beginning Teaching, National Project on the Quality of Teaching and Learning, Australian Teaching Council, 1996, p. 48. Commonwealth of Australia copyright, reproduced by permission.

Is Miss Gray's response adequate? What would you have added to the discussion?

KEY TERMS

Bilingual/bicultural education (p. 356): education programs that offer instruction to non-English speakers in English and another language

Community languages (p. 355): non-English languages spoken in immigrant communities

Culturally relevant teaching (p. 370): teaching that is responsive to the cultural backgrounds and needs of students

Dialect (p. 356): a variation of standard English that is distinct in vocabulary, grammar or pronunciation

Homeland school (p. 362): school that has an element of formal structure, but where there is little emphasis on learning Western knowledge or language

Kohanga reo (p. 362): all-Maori language and culture immersion environment for preschool children

NESB (p. 355): non-English-speaking background students

Two-way schools (p. 362): an attempt to introduce Western knowledge while at the same time taking active steps to promote culture and language maintenance

ON-LINE LEARNING

If you go to http://www.pearsoned.com.au/mcinerney, you will have hot links directly to these sites:

■ **Multicultural educator**
Discuss the 10 points presented in this article. Relate them to the information covered in this chapter.
http://www.edchange.org/multicultural/resources/self_critique.html

■ **Multicultural education definition**
Consider the definition of multicultural education provided at this site. Would you modify the definition in the context of the material presented in Chapter 10?
http://www.edchange.org/multicultural/initial.html

■ **ESL**
Consider the suggestions made for teaching ESL.
http://education.indiana.edu/cas/tt/v2i2/ideas.html

WEB DESTINATIONS

If you go to http://www.pearsoned.com.au/mcinerney, you will have hot links directly to these sites:

■ **Curriculum Corporation**
Curriculum Corporation works in the education sector and is owned by all Australian ministers of education. The company develops products and services to help schools improve student learning. It is the key national organisation providing curriculum support to schools and school systems, and producing and disseminating high-quality education products and services, including books, videos, magazines, multimedia, on-line services and professional development. In addition, the corporation markets and distributes resources developed by some state and territory school systems.
http://www.curriculum.edu.au/

■ **Multicultural pavilion**
A useful site hot-linked to many other informative sites.
http://www.edchange.org/multicultural/

■ **Teacher talk multicultural education**
Another site that provides information on a range of topics including cultural diversity and ESL.
http://education.indiana.edu/cas/tt/v2i2/table.html

■ **Sociosite**
A site maintained by the University of Amsterdam that provides resources on migration, ethnicity and anti-discrimination.
http://www2.fmg.uva.nl/sociosite/

■ **Diversity digest**
This site provided by the Association of American Colleges and Universities provides ideas and resources on multicultural education especially for the university sector.
http://www.diversityweb.org/Digest/F97/contents.html

■ **Culture and learning**
This site provides an honours thesis on culture and learning by Peter Ninnes. There is a lot of very useful information provided.
http://fehps.une.edu.au/f/s/edu/pNinnes/ma/Contents.html

■ **Maori links**
As indicated in the title, this site provides links to many sites dealing with Maori education.
http://www.maori.org.nz/

RECOMMENDED READING

Bennett, C. (2001) Genres of research in multicultural education. *Review of Educational Research*, **71**, 171–217.

Corson, D. (1993) Restructing minority schooling. *Australian Journal of Education*, **37**, 46–68.

Ferrari, M. & Mahalingam, R. (1998) Personal cognitive development and its implications for teaching and learning. *Educational Psychologist*, **33**, 35–44.

Folds, R. (1987) *Whitefella School*. Sydney: Allen & Unwin.

Garcia, E. E. (1993) Language, culture, and education. *Review of Research in Education*, **19**, 51–98.

Hollins, E. R. (1996) *Culture in School Learning. Revealing the Deep Meaning*. Mahway, NJ: Lawrence Erlbaum.

Ladson-Billings, G. (1995) Toward a theory of culturally relevant pedagogy. *American Educational Research Journal*, **32**, 465–91.

McInerney, D. M. (1987) Teacher attitudes to multicultural curriculum development. *Australian Journal of Education*, **31**, 129–44.

McInerney, D. M., Roche, L., McInerney, V. & Marsh, H. W. (1997) Cultural perspectives on school motivation: The relevance and application of goal theory. *American Educational Research Journal*, **34**, 207–36.

Malin, M. (1990) The visibility and invisibility of Aboriginal students in an urban classroom. *Australian Journal of Education*, **34**, 312–29.

Ogbu, J. U. (1999) Beyond language: Ebonics, proper English, and identity in a black American speech community. *American Educational Research Journal*, **36**, 147–84.

Partington, G. & McCudden, V. (1992) *Ethnicity and Education*. Wentworth Falls, NSW: Social Science Press.

Riehl, C. J. (2000) The principal's role in creating inclusive schools for diverse students: A review of normative, empirical, and critical literature on the practice of educational administration. *Review of Educational Research*, **70**, 55–81.

Rogoff, B. & Chavajay, P. (1995) What's become of research on the cultural basis of cognitive development? *American Psychologist*, **50**, 859–77.

Rubie, C. M., Townsend, M. A. R. & Moore, D. W. (2004) Motivational and academic effects of cultural experiences for indigenous minority students in New Zealand. *Educational Psychology*, **24**, 143–60.

Smolic, J. J. (1991) Language, culture and the school in a plural society: An Australian perspective for the 1990s. *Migration Monitor*, **23/24**, 3–15.

Thomas, E. (1994) (ed.) *International Perspectives on Culture and Schooling: A Symposium Proceedings*. University of London Institute of Education: Department of International and Comparative Education.

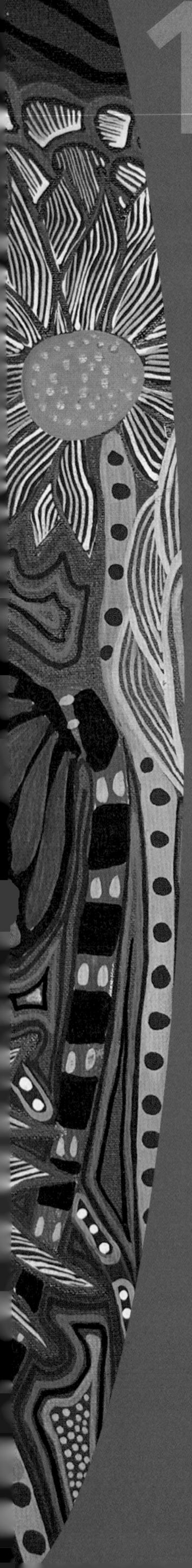

CHAPTER 11

Measurement and evaluation for effective learning

Overview

Measurement and evaluation are integral parts of the teaching and learning process. In this chapter, we address such important questions as:

- What is measurement and how does it differ from evaluation?
- Why do we measure and evaluate student learning?
- What are the available methods of measurement and evaluation, what are their strengths and weaknesses, and how do we report the results?

With increasing concern over educational standards, quality assurances and accountability, teachers and schools are obliged to implement strategies of measurement and evaluation that are based upon the best available information. We hope to present you with such information in this chapter, equipping you to choose from a wide range of sound measurement and evaluation practices. In particular, we aim to help you develop a critical and reflective attitude to measurement and evaluation.

In line with our focus on constructivism, we also present you with a number of alternatives to traditional tests and methods of measurement and evaluation such as journals and portfolios, work samples, and peer evaluation and self-evaluation. We also discuss sociocultural aspects of measurement and evaluation, and consider the relationship between school assessment, school motivation and school anxiety.

11

Learning objectives

After reading this chapter, you will be able to:

- define measurement and evaluation;
- list reasons for measuring and evaluating student performance;
- define validity and reliability and list essential features of validity and reliability in the classroom context;
- compare and contrast formative and summative measurement and evaluations;
- compare and contrast norm-referenced and criterion-referenced measurement and evaluation;
- describe learning objectives and learning outcomes;
- compare and contrast methods of writing learning objectives;
- list and describe the three domains of Bloom's taxonomy of educational objectives;
- apply rubrics to guide instruction and evaluation;
- describe and discuss the characteristics of mastery learning;
- outline and discuss the strengths and weaknesses of a range of alternative measurement strategies;
- explain the importance of feedback to student learning and describe characteristics of effective feedback;
- evaluate forms of peer and self-evaluation;
- describe features of classroom anxiety and give examples of how anxiety might be reduced;
- evaluate a range of reporting methods commonly used in schools.

Both the following Learner-centred Psychological Principle and Teaching Competence Box 11.1 emphasise the importance of assessment to good teaching and learning. At the end of this chapter, reconsider both of these in the light of what you have read.

LEARNER-CENTRED PSYCHOLOGICAL PRINCIPLE

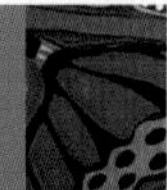

Standards and assessment. Setting appropriately high and challenging standards and assessing the learning as well as learning progress—including diagnostic, process and outcome assessment—are integral parts of the learning process.

Assessment provides important information to both the learner and teacher at all stages of the learning process. Effective learning takes place when learners feel challenged to work towards appropriately high goals; therefore, appraisal of the learner's cognitive strengths and weaknesses, as well as current knowledge and skills, is important for the selection of instructional materials of an optimal degree of difficulty. Ongoing assessment of the learner's understanding of the curricular material can provide valuable feedback to both learners and teachers about progress towards the learning goals. Standardised assessment of learner progress and outcome assessment provides one type of information about achievement levels both within and across individuals that can inform various types of programmatic decisions. Performance assessments can provide other sources of information about the attainment of learning outcomes. Self-assessments of learning progress can also impact on students' self appraisal skills and enhance motivation and self-directed learning.

Box 11.1

TEACHING COMPETENCE

The teacher knows the educational basis and role of assessment in teaching

Indicators

The teacher:

- justifies assessment processes and strategies in terms of planned student learning outcomes;
- uses assessment procedures consistent with content and process goals;
- values collaborative approaches with parents and others in assessing student progress;
- plans and conducts assessment in accordance with school policies;
- is aware of ethical and legal issues relating to the collection and use of assessment data.

Case studies illustrating National Competency Framework for Beginning Teaching, National Project on the Quality of Teaching and Learning, Australian Teaching Council, 1996, Element 4.1, p. 55. Commonwealth of Australia copyright, reproduced by permission.

In Western society, the public evaluation of learning begins early.

Measurement and evaluation—general principles

In Western societies the measurement of children begins early. From infancy onwards, caregivers and other involved people weigh, measure, poke and prod youngsters to assess whether or not they are growing and developing according to norms or other expected standards. The process of **measurement** relates to collecting specific quantitative data, which might be in centimetres, kilograms, number of erupted teeth, heart rate or visual acuity (Gronlund 1985). In the context of education, measurement usually refers to marks obtained in tests or other pieces of work set by the teacher. **Evaluation**, on the other hand, refers to the quality, value or worth of the information gathered (Gronlund 1985; Mager 1990a, 1990b). So while a child might weigh 15 kilograms (an objective measurement), they might be evaluated as being scrawny or pudgy (a subjective, 'evaluative' judgment). To make the interpretation less subjective, other criteria (such as age norms) need to be applied to make the evaluation. These evaluations are often referred to as *assessments* (see Delandshere & Petrosky 1998). Throughout most of the 20th century, educational achievement has been judged through measurement—that is, by the assignment of numbers to responses with the resulting scores used to make value judgments about the quality of performances (Delandshere & Petrosky 1998). Within a class, an individual's score of 80 in a mathematics test may indicate average, below-average or above-average performance (relative to the rest of those being tested or to some other criteria). Furthermore, the score may be interpreted in terms of the individual's perceived ability and motivation, such that the performance may be evaluated as representing good achievement or underachievement for a student who was expected either to do much better or much poorer, irrespective of class norms. In this latter case, we are talking about the evaluation based on the measurement. It is clear that it is the evaluation element that is of most importance, but this must be based on valid and reliable measurement.

What is validity in measurement?

We generally use the term **validity** in measurement to refer to whether we are indeed *measuring what we intend to measure*. More importantly, validity refers to the *appropriateness* of a measure for the specific inferences or decisions that result from the scores generated by the measure (Griffin & Nix 1991; McMillan 1992; Messick 1989; Moss 1992). If we wish to describe pupil achievement, we should be confident that our interpretations are based on a dependable measure, do not exceed the limits of the measure and are appropriate to the intentions of the measurement's use.

Various types of evidence may be accrued to support the validity of measurements (Gronlund 1985; Messick 1989; Moss 1992; Shepard 1993). Among the evidence that may be used to support the validity of a particular measurement are face, content, criterion and construct evidence.

Face validity evidence indicates that the assessment task, at least on the surface, measures what it purports to measure (Sprinthall, Schmutte & Sirois 1991). It is a relatively low-level indicator of validity, but it is, nevertheless, an important starting point. Imagine answering a test on your mathematical knowledge in which all the questions seemed to relate to issues only tangentially connected with mathematics. You would probably question the usefulness and relevance of the test in terms of its expressed aims, and perhaps not answer it seriously or carefully.

Content validity evidence is provided when measurement activities reflect the appropriate domain of study. In other words, the activity should match as closely as possible the objectives of the teaching for which it was designed. If a teacher wishes to test mathematical reasoning, the questions should be selected from the same content and examples as covered in the teaching.

Criterion validity evidence is provided when the results of specific measurement tasks converge with the results of other measurement tasks. For example, we might be interested in comparing individual performances in a particular test with other evidence of performance—completion of a practical activity, position in class, teacher rankings—to see if our test is measuring the same underlying quality. In each of these cases we are establishing a benchmark with which to assess how well our measurement techniques 'measure up' (McMillan & Schumacher 1989). If the data from our measurements are compared at the same time and lead to the same conclusions about the individual's performance, the evidence from each is called *concurrent validity*. When the data are able to predict a criterion such as school performance or job promotion, we can say that the measurement provides *predictive* evidence for its validity.

At times, educators and researchers design questionnaires to measure psychological constructs such as competitiveness, self-concept, figural intelligence, creativity or computer anxiety. When researchers wish to establish that the questions designed to measure a dimension such as self-concept do measure this underlying theoretical construct in a systematic way, they may use a statistical procedure called factor analysis. When procedures such as factor analysis are used to support the underlying dimensions being measured by a test, we speak of establishing *construct validity* evidence. Factor analysis is a statistical procedure used to discover a structure within a larger number of variables. It does this by reducing the larger set of variables to a smaller number of more basic composite variables called factors. These resulting factors summarise the essential information contained in all the original variables (Ferguson & Takane 1989; Kleinbaum, Kupper & Muller 1988).

Factor analysis is well beyond the scope of this book. For our purposes, a simpler method of establishing construct validity of assessment tasks in the classroom context might be used. For example, if we design a test to measure mechanical aptitude we should be able to use the data obtained from testing individuals to classify them as either more or less mechanically able. To the extent that our classification is supported by external evidence (such as performance in mechanical tasks), we have evidence of the construct validity of the test (Tuckman 1988).

What is reliability in measurement?

As well as being concerned with issues of validity in measurement and evaluation, teachers must also be concerned that their measurements and evaluations of students are reliable—that is, they are stable and consistent over time.

Methods of assessing reliability

There are four common methods used to assess **reliability**: measures of stability, equivalence, internal consistency and inter-marker reliability (Collis 1989; McMillan 1992; McMillan & Schumacher 1989). A coefficient of **stability** is provided by testing and retesting the same individuals after a period (so that the second results are not affected by practice). If the correlation between the two tests is high, it shows a consistent response by the individuals to the test on two separate occasions. In other words, those who scored highly on the first occasion also scored highly on the second, and so on.

When two equivalent or parallel forms of the same test are administered to a group at about the same time and the scores are related, the reliability that results is a coefficient of **equivalence**.

Internal consistency may be established by splitting the items in a test into comparable halves and correlating individuals' performances on both halves of the test. If students perform comparably on both halves of the test, then the test has high reliability. Other forms of the internal consistency measure, such as the

Kuder–Richardson techniques and the Cronbach Alpha, measure the degree to which the individual item responses correlate with the total score. The score is considered reliable if a high index is obtained, as this indicates that each item is contributing to the total score (Collis 1989).

When the scores of two markers are correlated (or the judgment of one person on the same test on two separate occasions is correlated), we have an index of **inter-marker reliability**.

Each of these forms of reliability has strengths and weaknesses that are well described in introductory educational research texts. If a test is unreliable, it cannot be valid. Can you suggest why?

Validity in the classroom context

As we have stated, teachers and educators must ensure that the measures they use are both valid and reliable. Commercially available testing instruments (such as those supplied by the Australian Council of Educational Research (ACER) and the New Zealand Council of Educational Research (NZCER)) and basic skills tests used by some education departments are usually rigorously tested for validity and reliability. Some of these tests may be administered only by qualified counsellors or psychologists. Other tests may be administered by classroom teachers. ACER and NZCER will supply a catalogue of tests to interested parties. If we choose to use one of these commercial tests, then we must ensure that we use it according to the instructions supplied and interpret the results within the constraints of the test protocols.

'Before we begin the task, Miss, the class wants to know if it comes with a guarantee.'

Many **standardised tests** have fallen into disfavour because they are perceived as invalid for particular classroom use. The real problem often lies in their inappropriate use and the inappropriate (invalid) interpretations that result (Griffin & Nix 1991; Popham 1999). Standardised tests can, however, play a useful role in student measurement and evaluation.

Teacher-made measurement tasks: Issues of validity

Teachers in Australia and New Zealand more often depend on teacher-made tests and measurement tasks to measure student learning than on commercially available ones (Stiggins 1985). Unfortunately, many teachers develop these tests and measurement tasks without giving much thought to issues of validity, and fall into the trap of relying on the face validity of their tests and measurement procedures (Stiggins 1985). Teachers should evaluate the content and, where appropriate, the criterion validity of their tasks (Griffin & Nix 1991). What does this mean in practice? Let's look first at content validity.

Measurement and context

Learning is situated in a particular context. A teacher may, for example, wish to teach the addition of two-digit and three-digit numbers. Various practice examples, such as 356 + 21, are given, with additional drill exercises completed by the students. In order to measure the students' mastery of this particular addition process the teacher may then set a number of problems of the kind: 'John was building a rectangular wall with a length of 150 metres and a width of 38 metres. How far was it around the wall?' On the face of it, the problem involves simply the addition of two-digit and three-digit numbers, the process already drilled by the students. Any poor performance of the students on this and similar problems may not reflect their lack of understanding of the addition process, but rather indicate that the test lacks instructional content validity. In effect, there are dimensions to the task in the test of the process that were not part of the original teaching procedure—dimensions such as the verbal presentation of the problem and the extra calculation required to measure the length of the perimeter. In another example, if a final test uses essay questions to assess higher-order thinking skills, then similar essay questions should have been used throughout the learning program. Imagine you have just completed 12 practical lessons on how to swim freestyle. As the final test to accredit your achievement, you are given a written theoretical test on correct strokes, breathing, kicking and mouth-to-mouth resuscitation. How valid would you consider the test?

The measurement activities must be relevant to the teacher's goals of measurement and evaluation. For example, if you wish to sort out students who can write fluently and stylishly about current affairs, it would be inappropriate to examine their knowledge of current affairs by a multiple choice test (Biggs & Moore 1993).

Teachers should also use criterion validity to evaluate their measurement activities. It should be common practice for teachers to cross-reference results on a particular activity or task with a variety of other information available on the students' performance. In other words, a particular measurement should be validated against other criteria. Criteria may include other tests and assessments already completed by the students, as well as former reports and results. Any anomalies such as a poor result in the face of generally good performances should be carefully scrutinised to evaluate whether this reflects a truly poor performance or a poorly designed measurement activity.

Teacher measurement and criterion validity

When relevant, indicators of predictive validity may also be used. For example, there should be a relationship between the school-based marks obtained by students in the final school examination and those obtained in the external examination. When there is a gross difference, one could suspect that the school-based procedures used to assess the students are not valid for the purpose. There may be occasional discrepancies when a particular individual performance is affected by sickness, nerves or (hopefully more likely) an extra spurt of motivation at the end. In general, however, there should be a considerable degree of concurrence between school-based measurement and that achieved in the external exams.

Measurement tasks and predictive validity

Reliability in the classroom context

Teacher biases and marking

We would be very concerned if we tested students one day with a particular test and, on a subsequent occasion, using the same or a similar test, found that the results were wildly different. We would also be concerned if different markers varied widely in their marking of similar pieces of work. A series of classic studies (Starch & Elliott 1912, 1913, cited in Biggs & Telfer 1987a) investigated the reliability of English, history and geometry assessment through tests. A total of 180 teachers graded two English papers per student on a 100-point scale, with 75 as a pass mark. At the low end teachers gave a paper 50 points and at the high end of the scale 97 points. Quite a range of marks on the one paper! Similar results were found in the marking of geometry and geography papers. In effect, teachers were looking for different evidence of achievement (for example, neatness, spelling, punctuation, showing calculations) and hence the measurements were quite unreliable. One of the most important findings from these studies was the discovery that subjectivity in marking was not confined to a particular subject. Individual grades tended to reflect the individual standards of the marker, and the unreliability of the scoring procedure.

Frame of reference effect and marking

In a study of the interaction between markers' handwriting clarity and the neatness of examination papers, the researchers found that markers with neat writing downgraded untidy essays heavily, while markers who were untidy writers were not influenced by the neatness of the essays (Huck & Bounds 1972). We are also aware that a *frame of reference effect* operates for markers and that the one marker can vary substantially in applying criteria of assessment, depending on the number of pieces of work being assessed and the quality of surrounding work. For example, if a piece of work is marked in the context of very good pieces of work it may be graded down; on the other hand, if the same piece of work is graded in the context of poor pieces of work it might be graded up (Hales & Tokar 1975).

Naturally, we want to have some faith in the consistency of the measures we take. If we are measuring students' learning for the purpose of academic ranking or streaming of some kind, it is essential that we take more than one measurement to ensure that the results are consistent from one test to the next (or from one marker to another). When results are consistent (within an acceptable range), we can be happy that our measurements are reliable and proceed with the ranking. On the other hand, if there are considerable differences, we must question whether we are using reliable measuring devices and continue with further measurement. Note that even when the two measurement devices produce the same results, we cannot be sure that they are valid—validity depends on other criteria. However, when measurements produce inconsistent student results, as well as being unreliable, they must also be invalid. Can you see why? Appropriate measures of reliability that can be used in the classroom are measures of stability, equivalence and inter-marker reliability.

Collaborative checks on teacher measurements

It is not unreasonable to have another teacher periodically check on our measurement of students' work in order to evaluate how reliable we are. At university we often 'double mark' student work in a team and compare our ratings on important measurement tasks. Across-the-grade marking of standardised measurement tasks can also alleviate marker subjectivity. Remember, our measurements, and the evaluations we make on the basis of them, have a profound impact on students: we owe it to them to be reliable and valid in our measurement.

Why and how do we measure and evaluate students?

By now you are familiar with some of the technical issues associated with valid and reliable measurement, but we haven't directly addressed the issue of *why* teachers need to measure and evaluate. Perhaps this seems too obvious; after all, as teachers we want to know whether we are being successful and whether the students in our care are learning. Table 11.1 outlines some of the reasons typically given for measuring and evaluating our students.

What do you think of these arguments for measurement and evaluation? Among these reasons, you will note that some people believe that grades motivate. However, some educators believe that grades have only a limited value as motivators, and are only really effective with those students who receive good grades (Yelon & Weinstein 1977; see also Airasian 1995). Low grades can be interpreted as a form of punishment or can become a source of anxiety and frustration and, as such, turn many children off school. The scramble for good grades (when only a few can achieve them) may result in unhealthy competition and cheating. Grades, as a form of extrinsic motivation, may diminish the student's desire to learn for its own sake (see Chapter 7).

Formative and summative measurement and evaluation

Measurement and evaluation may be either formative or summative (Scriven 1967). **Formative measurement and evaluation** refers to the continuous monitoring of the teaching/learning process to ensure its effectiveness, and to ascertain whether other approaches to teaching and learning should be introduced or whether there should be a change in goals (Conner 1985). Hence, the *process of learning* is of central importance, and rapid feedback is given to students to facilitate their mastery of the material to be learned, where appropriate, or scaffolding by the teacher in the case of exploratory learning. Essentially, formative evaluation asks the questions:

- How well are the students learning?
- What are they learning?
- What do they need to know?
- What can they do?
- What do they appear not to understand?

Key elements in the process are listed below:

Observe

- Are students asking and answering questions?
- Are students completing the assigned work in the set time?
- Are students showing interest and involvement in what they are doing?

Listen

- What is being said to you and other students about the learning tasks?
- What is the relevance and depth of the questions that students ask, and what is the nature of the answers they give?
- Is there a voluntary contribution of ideas, and how do these relate to what the students are doing?

Table 11.1 Reasons for measuring and evaluating students

- Measurement and evaluation help to clarify goals and objectives and can serve as a means of improving learning and instruction and as an incentive to increase student effort.
- Measurement and evaluation enable the teacher to give feedback to students, in particular about strengths and areas where further study is needed. It provides a record of achievement.
- Measurement and evaluation enable teachers to determine whether the processes of teaching and learning are effective, and whether other approaches to teaching and learning should be introduced or whether there should be a change in goals.
- Measurement and evaluation give information to parents. Teachers are accountable to parents for the quality of education their children are receiving.
- Measurement and evaluation are used to assist with the selection and certification of students for special classes and programs. They are also used to predict later scholastic and career performance.
- Measurement and evaluation are used by teachers and schools as a performance indicator to the funding and employing bodies. As such, they serve an administrative function to help determine the competency of teachers and to evaluate schools.

(Source: Based on Gipps 1999; Gronlund 1985; Natriello & Dornbusch 1984; Slavin 1989, 1991b; Withers & Cornish 1985)

Test

- Can the students do what is required?
- What shortcomings are there in students' understanding and achievement?

Questionnaires

- What do students say when they are given an opportunity to evaluate the learning experience?
- How do students rate various aspects of the instruction, such as teacher performance, materials, assessment?

Summative measurement and evaluation refers to the process of determining whether or not learners have achieved the ultimate learning objectives that have been set up in advance. As such, summative measurement will typically consist of assessment items such as a test, assignment or presentation that represents what the student has learned to that stage. At this point the emphasis is placed on the achievement of the student, rather than the process of learning and teaching that led to it. Unfortunately, many teachers overemphasise summative measurement and evaluation and fail to monitor the teaching/learning process adequately. As a consequence, opportunities to make corrective adjustments to teaching practices, which may have facilitated a better performance, are missed.

We add here that, while evaluation tends to emphasise the student learning component, formative and summative evaluation should also apply equally to the teacher's role, materials used and goals set.

Norm-referenced measurement and evaluation

At times educators may need to compare the achievement of students with other students or with established norms of achievement (see, for example, Ansley 1997; Popham 1999). This occurs, for example, when large numbers of students are ranked for specific purposes such as access to special school programs. When this is done, it is an example of **norm-referenced measurement and evaluation**. Most commercially available achievement tests are norm-referenced. During the construction of these tests, large numbers of students (similar to those on whom the tests are later to be used) are tested, and norms representing average performance by age or grade are developed so that individuals sitting for the test at a later time can be compared with these averages. Because these tests represent standards with which individuals can be compared (and the scores obtained by individuals are directly comparable to one another) they are often called *standardised tests*. Standardised tests are carefully constructed to provide accurate, meaningful information on students' levels of achievement or performance relative to the standardising group. The process of standardising such tests is beyond the scope of this text and interested readers are referred to texts such as Aiken (2004).

This teacher is giving feedback to her students as part of her formative evaluation. What are the elements of effective formative feedback?

An important element of these tests is that the distribution of performance is often constrained by statistical procedures so that it follows a *normal distribution*. Simply speaking, this means that there is a large number of students who perform in an average fashion, with decreasing numbers performing very well and very poorly. The normal distribution follows a bell-shaped curve, and a particular student's score is plotted against this curve to indicate whether they are performing below average, about average or above average. Judgments based on standardised tests are used for selection and placement of students, diagnosis of learning difficulties, evaluation of achievement and, increasingly, as indicators of school and teacher performance (a form of accountability measure). Figure 11.1 indicates the *normal* curve and the distribution of scores that are located at various standard deviations from the mean.

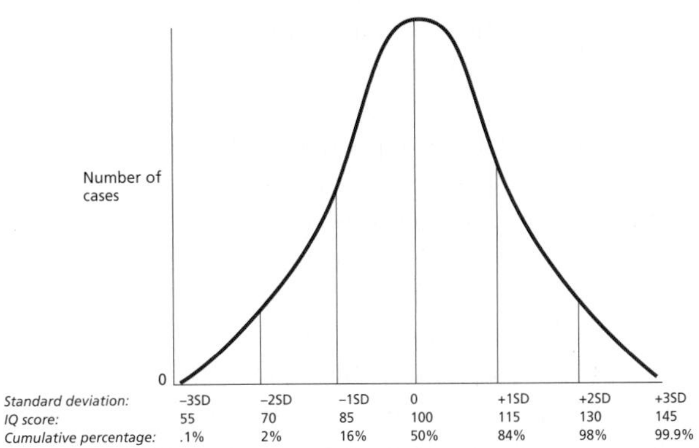

Figure 11.1 *The normal curve*

Like commercially available tests, teacher measurements may also be norm-referenced. Whenever a teacher compares an individual's score with the average score of the class on an activity, they are using a norm-referenced approach. The focus is on relative performance and, as such, the definition of a good performance or a poor performance is determined by the group's mean and standard deviation (which is a measure of the dispersal of scores around the mean). Hence, a score of 70 per cent on a mathematics test may represent a relatively good or poor score when compared with the average.

Are there problems with norm-referenced measurement and evaluation?

Standardised tests have a number of potential problems relating to their norms. First, it is important that norms be continually updated so that the measurement obtained appropriately reflects what the children know. Second, it is important that norms reflect the cultural background and social experiences of the students being tested. Unfortunately, some standardised tests are not frequently updated and therefore the interpretation of the measurement scores obtained by students must be interpreted with care. The norms in some tests are not sensitive to cultural backgrounds, so students from culturally different backgrounds may be disadvantaged. Furthermore, the manner in which these tests are conducted (for example, in English, and usually using a paper and pen format) may be inappropriate for some students (Abedi, Hofstetter & Lord 2004).

Teacher-produced norm-referenced measurement and evaluation may present a number of problems for the teacher, particularly when a procedure called **grading on the curve** is used. With this procedure, an implicit assumption is held that the distribution of grades should follow a normal distribution. For example, we are all aware that classes vary in ability from year to year, and we are also aware that so-called parallel classes are often anything but equivalent in ability. So we can have the anomalous situation of students who perform objectively no worse than other students (in previous years or in parallel grades) being graded lower because their particular reference group scores higher. Statistical procedures are available to moderate this potential problem.

In relatively homogeneous classes where there is little difference in achievement or ability between the students (they may all be high achievers or slow learners), the application of grading on the curve is not appropriate. In such cases, we may be constrained to award low grades to some students irrespective of what they have actually achieved. Very few classes are large enough or diverse enough in ability for grading on the curve to be defensible.

A further problem or limitation results from the fact that, in general, grades derived from typical norm-referenced measurement techniques (such as aggregated test marks) cannot be used to describe the specific competencies a student may or may not have. This is particularly the case when measurement procedures sample only a small area of the subject domain, and often in a haphazard fashion.

As a result of these limitations, and for a number of other reasons, the use of norm-referenced testing has declined considerably over the last 20 years, particularly at the primary level (Marzano & Costa 1988).

Criterion-referenced measurement and evaluation

An alternative to norm-referenced evaluation, increasingly popular with many teachers, is **criterion-referenced measurement and evaluation**. Here the focus is not on an individual student's comparative performance against norms established by a group of students, but rather on *the comparison of an individual's performance against achievement goals*. Very often the criteria are relative to the student's individual performance standards. In other words, goals and their timing can be individualised to take into account a range of individual characteristics including ability and motivation (Docking 1986).

In criterion-referenced measurement and evaluation, achievement goals (such as learning to spell 10 words or mastering two-digit addition) are clearly specified. The goals may be target goals for the entire class (this is appropriate when the skills are determined to be essential for all students) and the students keep at the task of learning until they have mastered the goals to a particular level of achievement (for example, spelling all 10 words correctly or completing 90 per cent of the additions correctly). At other times the goals may be individual and programs of learning devised to assist the student to achieve the target.

Clearly, criterion-referenced measurement and evaluation should be less competitive than norm-referenced evaluation. All students achieving a particular goal are graded as having satisfactorily completed the work at a particular standard. It is important here to note that the achievement of a particular grade is not determined by the distribution of grades that applies within norm-referenced measurement and evaluation. In the criterion-referenced system, all students can be given an A or, conversely, if none of the students achieves mastery to appropriate standards, they may all be graded as failing. Teachers may, however, apply a grading system to criterion-referenced evaluation, grading mastery at particular levels with As, Bs and Cs. For example, mastery of 85 per cent or more of the material may entitle the student to an A, 80 per cent to a B, and so on.

One of the complex issues in criterion-referenced measurement and evaluation is the setting of appropriate criteria. At times it may be necessary to establish that the criterion for successful mastery is 100 per cent accuracy. Can you think of examples where 100 per cent accuracy should be required? Theoretically, these criteria should be set before the learning takes place and the task completed, and students should be made fully aware of what they are. However, often the criteria are set after the task is completed and the teacher has evaluated performance. In this case, the criterion becomes less of a criterion than a norm. Why?

Why are more teachers using criterion-referenced measurement and evaluation?

There are three reasons why more teachers are using criterion-referenced measurement and evaluation (Biehler & Snowman 1990). First, educators and parents complain that norm-referenced measurement and evaluation provides little information about what students can or cannot do. The approach indicates where a student's performance lies relative to other students but, as already indicated, everyone within the group may be performing relatively strongly or weakly. Little information is communicated regarding individual strengths and weaknesses.

Second, as many educational objectives are clearly specified in performance terms, the criterion-referenced approach appears most suitable for measuring the achievement of these performance objectives. Criterion-referenced tests are constructed in such a way that individual scores yield some 'direct meaning' or are directly interpretable in terms of specified performance standards (Haertel 1985). Last, and associated with the previous point, contemporary theories of school learning claim that most, if not all, students can master most school objectives under the right circumstances. Consequently, a system that de-emphasises performance based on competition, while emphasising individual goal achievement, appears more appropriate (see Chapter 7). In effect, criterion-referenced evaluation focuses attention where it belongs: on whether or not the learner has learned what they were intended to learn (Airasian & Madaus 1972, cited in Biggs & Telfer 1987a).

In an education system in which the focus is truly on student learning, criterion-referenced evaluation gives greater opportunity for student involvement in their own assessment. This can have benefits both for the student through improved self-monitoring and for the teacher in reducing the need for constant supervision (see Docking 1984, 1986). Table 11.2 presents essential elements of norm- and criterion-referenced measurement and evaluation.

QUESTION POINT

Discuss the advantages and disadvantages of norm-referenced and criterion-referenced measurement and evaluation.

QUESTION POINT

Consider a number of learning activities such as learning to swim, learning to drive a car and learning to speak a foreign language. Discuss the relative merits of norm-referenced versus criterion-referenced evaluation in regard to the activities. What reference standards should apply?

Learning objectives and learning outcomes

The primary purpose of measurement is to monitor progress in students' learning and to measure students' achievement against learning objectives (Australian Teaching Council 1996). Teachers need to devise measurement strategies that are closely related to learning objectives, reflect the nature of students' programs of work and allow them to provide appropriate feedback on progress. An important aspect of the measurement and evaluation of learning is that it enables teachers, students and their parents to contribute to ongoing learning (Australian Teaching Council 1996).

Today it is more common to speak of desired learning outcomes than of teacher-set objectives. Nevertheless, learning objectives strongly influence learning outcomes and therefore the course of study to be evaluated. There is, of course, a need to retain a degree of flexibility in evaluation so that, at the end of a program of learning activities, teachers can look back and evaluate the learning that occurred irrespective of whether it was prescribed by objectives.

In order to measure how well particular learning outcomes or objectives have been mastered, objectives must be clear. Robert Mager (1990a) outlines three characteristics of good objectives which facilitate effective assessment and evaluation (Table 11.3). The point of these characteristics is to clarify instructional objectives so that they can be identified ('the student will recognise time'), related to a context ('when given a

Theory and research into practice

Ken Rowe — EDUCATIONAL ASSESSMENT

BRIEF BIOGRAPHY

Currently, I am the research director of the Learning Processes and Contexts research program at the Australian Council for Educational Research (ACER)—based in Melbourne. Prior to this appointment, I was principal research fellow and associate professor in the Centre for Applied Educational Research at the University of Melbourne (1993–99), senior research officer in the Department of Education, Victoria (1986–92), Commonwealth Relations Trust fellow at the University of London Institute of Education (1984–85), and teacher and principal in Victorian government schools (1967–83). Between 1968 and 1970 I worked with the Australian defence forces in Papua-New Guinea, as well as in Vietnam where I (*inter alia*) taught senior-level mathematics (in French) at Vung Tau High School. I have also had visiting research fellow appointments at the University of Twente (the Netherlands, 1995) and at the University of London (1996).

I received my undergraduate training in philosophy, psychology, sociology and statistical methods at Swinburne University and the University of Melbourne. My postgraduate training in program evaluation, quantitative/qualitative evidence-based research methodology and design, educational psychology, assessment, psychometrics and advanced statistical modelling was undertaken at the University of London, and my doctoral research at the University of Melbourne. During 1993 I was awarded an honorary fellowship of the Australian Council for Educational Leaders (FACEL).

In addition to attempts to 'keep up' with three active sons and grandchildren, my consultant paediatrician wife of 33 years (Dr Kathy Rowe, at Melbourne's Royal Children's Hospital) and I are in high demand as keynote speakers/presenters at local and international professional seminars and academic conferences, related to our separate and collaborative research. Both of us publish widely. I am also in demand as a methodological consultant and collaborator for applied research and evaluation projects across several fields of inquiry, including criminology, economics, education, epidemiology, paediatrics, political science, psychology, sociology and statistics – both locally and internationally. For example, with two other senior ACER staff members, I am a consultant to the World Bank Institute (Washington, DC, USA) and conduct training courses for senior representatives from developing countries in evaluation and performance monitoring.

RESEARCH AND THEORETICAL INTERESTS

My substantive research interests include: 'authentic' educational and psychological assessment; models of quality assurance; multilevel, 'value-added', educational and organisational performance indicators, achievement target setting and benchmarking; teacher and school effectiveness; differential gender effects of schooling in the context of teaching and learning; and the teaching and learning needs of students with learning difficulties. Moreover, together with my wife Kathy, I have longstanding research interest in the 'overlap' between education and health—especially the impact of externalising behaviour problems on students' learning outcomes in literacy and numeracy; and the educational/epidemiological implications of attention-deficit/hyperactivity disorder (AD/HD), chronic fatigue syndrome (CFS) and auditory processing for children and adolescents.

My methodological research interests and expertise are predicated on the assertion that the foundation of all responsible analysis and reporting of performance indicator (PI) data in educational, epidemiological and psychosocial inquiry is the fundamental importance of accounting for their measurement, distributional and structural properties by: (1) fitting the response data to sound measurement models that meet the requirements of measurement (that is, Rasch measurement), followed by (2) fitting multilevel explanatory models to the measured PI data. In this context, and as Australia's leading exponent of multilevel, structural equation modelling, since 1991 I have continued to be a national training consultant and instructor for the summer and winter programs conducted by the Australian Consortium for Social and Political Research Incorporated (ACSPRI), administered by the Research School of Social Sciences at the Australian National University. In particular, I conduct training workshops in advanced statistical modelling applications of multilevel and covariance structure analysis of data obtained from large-scale monitoring, evaluation and survey projects, as well as in explanatory educational, epidemiological, and psychosocial inquiry. More detailed information about ACSPRI courses is available at http://acspri.anu.edu.au/courses/. Further, several recent examples of both my substantive and methodological research interests and expertise are available for downloading (in PDF format) from my research program website at http://www.acer.edu.au/research/programs/learningprocess.html.

THEORY AND RESEARCH INTO PRACTICE

It is widely recognised that findings from my evidence-based research output over a period of more than 30 years have made significant contributions to the 'body of knowledge' in education and psychosocial inquiry. Moreover, these contributions continue to have strategic impacts on the academic community, government policy and on professional practice, via invited submissions to major government inquiries, regular demands for my participation in consultative policy committees, as well as for the conduct of specialist courses in research/evaluation methodologies and explanatory statistical modelling. These impacts are evidenced by all-too frequent requests for my comments from the popular printed and visual media, and keynote speaker presentations at local and international professional and academic conferences—especially related to practical issues surrounding teacher and school effectiveness, the education of boys, and the 'overlap' between education and health.

Among the advantages of working at the Australian Council for Educational Research (widely recognised as Australia's premier educational research organisation) is the privilege of collaborating closely with a 'critical mass' of experienced and highly competent educational and psychosocial researchers (and support staff). Much of ACER's local and international contract work derives from direct requests by government agencies and/or international organisations (for example, Asian Development Bank, IEA, OECD, World Bank Institute, UNESCO, UNICEF) for assessment, research and evaluation projects—the findings from which are designed to have direct implications for shaping theory, policy and professional practice. The products of my own research, and that of the research program I lead, are major contributors to these outcomes. Further information about ACER's research/evaluation programs, assessment services, reports publications and products, is available at http://www.acer.edu.au.

KEY REFERENCES

Rowe, K. J. (2003) Estimating interdependent effects among multilevel composite variables in psychosocial research: An example of the application of multilevel structural equation modeling. In S. P. Reise and N. Duan (eds) *Multilevel Modeling: Methodological Advances, Issues, and Applications* (Chapter 12, pp. 255–84). Mahwah, NJ: Lawrence Erlbaum Associates.

Rowe, K. J. & Rowe, K. S. (1999) Investigating the relationship between students' *attentive-inattentive* behaviors in the classroom and their literacy progress. *International Journal of Educational Research*, **31**(1–2), 1–138 (Whole Issue).

Rowe, K. J., Turner, R. & Lane, K. (2002) Performance feedback to schools of students' Year 12 assessments: The *VCE Data Project*. In A. J. Visscher and R. Coe (eds) *School Improvement Through Performance Feedback* (pp. 163–90). Lisse, The Netherlands: Swetz & Zeitlinger.

Rowe, K. S. & Rowe, K. J. (2002) Symptom patterns of children and adolescents with Chronic Fatigue Syndrome. In N. N. Singh, T. H. Ollendick & A. N. Singh (eds) *International Perspectives on Child and Adolescent Mental Health (Volume 2)* (pp. 395–421). New York: Elsevier.

ACTIVITIES

1 Ken Rowe is research director of the Learning Processes and Contexts research program at the Australian Council for Educational Research (ACER). This is a very important organisation in Australia with which all educators should be familiar. Look up http://www.acer.edu.au and investigate the range of research and measurement activities it is involved with. How do these activities help teachers, educators and related professionals generally in their everyday activities in classrooms and schools?

2 Ken Rowe refers to a large number of his measurement and evaluation interests, including authentic and psychological assessment, quality assurance, achievement target setting and benchmarking, teacher and school effectiveness, differential gender effects of schooling, and the learning needs of students with learning difficulties. We cover these topics throughout this and other chapters. Describe each of these areas, and discuss why they are important, and what research generally shows are important considerations in order to facilitate effective teaching and learning.

3 Ken Rowe refers to the overlap between education and health. Consider Chapter 9 (and other relevant chapters such as 12, 13 and 14) and list important components of the relationship between effective education and health. Compare your list with lists compiled by other students. What major issues are most likely to have relevance for classroom teachers?

4 Ken Rowe lists a number of useful websites for your attention. Review the content of these websites.

TABLE 11.2 Essentials of norm- and criterion-referenced measurement and evaluation

Norm-referenced measurement and evaluation:

- compares students against norms of performance that have been established by other groups;
- assesses the range of abilities in a large group;
- ranks and selects the best students for competitive placements;
- typically covers a large domain of learning tasks with a few items measuring each specific task.

Criterion-referenced measurement and evaluation:

- measures mastery of specific skills;
- determines whether students have the prerequisite skills to start a new unit of work;
- assesses psychomotor skills;
- groups students into relatively homogeneous groups for instruction;
- is typically used for guidance and diagnosis;
- typically focuses on a limited domain of learning tasks, with a relatively large number of items measuring each task.

Table 11.3 Essentials of good learning objectives

- A statement of what the learner will be able to do.
- A statement of the relevant conditions under which the performance is expected to occur.
- A statement of the quality or level of performance that will be considered acceptable.

(Source: Based on Mager 1990a)

clock-face with Arabic numerals') and evaluated according to an appropriate and relevant criterion ('to a criterion of 100 per cent correct responses').

Norman Gronlund (1985) takes a slightly different approach. He believes that it is best to state a general learning objective first that is broad enough to encompass a number of general learning outcomes (which direct our teaching), followed by a number of specific learning outcomes that relate to the types of learning performance we are willing to accept as evidence of the attainment of the objective. This is then followed by assessment tasks that obtain samples of pupil performance like those described in the specific learning outcomes.

The following two examples taken from Gronlund (1985, pp. 41–3) illustrate his approach.

1. *General objective*
   - understands scientific principles.

   Specific learning outcomes related to this general objective
   - describes the principle in own words;
   - identifies examples of the principle;
   - states tenable hypotheses based on the principle;
   - distinguishes between two given principles;
   - explains the relationship between two given principles.
2. *General objective*
   - demonstrates skill in critical thinking.

   Specific learning outcomes related to this general objective
   - distinguishes between fact and opinion;
   - distinguishes between relevant and irrelevant information;
   - identifies fallacious reasoning in written material;
   - identifies the limitations of given data;
   - formulates valid conclusions from given data;
   - identifies the assumptions underlying conclusions.

The Mager and Gronlund approaches both focus on learning outcomes or instructional objectives and matching measurement techniques to the types of performance specified by the intended outcomes. If you are preparing to become a teacher you will have many opportunities to practise writing instructional objectives.

Taxonomy of educational objectives

Cognitive domain

Many teachers refer to **taxonomies of educational objectives** for writing their own teaching objectives (see Bloom 1956; Krathwohl, Bloom & Masia 1956; Simpson 1972). Three basic taxonomies have been developed covering the cognitive, affective and psychomotor domains. Within each domain there is a hierarchy of categories. For example, within the **cognitive domain**, educational objectives may relate to *remembering* material (which may or may not demonstrate an understanding), to *comprehending* (which requires an ability to interpret what the material means), to *application* (which requires working over the material in new contexts), to *analysis* (which requires breaking down material into its component parts), to *synthesis* (which requires working over disparate material to combine it into an intelligible whole) and, finally, to *evaluation* (which requires judging the value of material). As you can see, there is a progression here from low-level learning outcomes to higher levels. Many teachers teach with an eye to leading children through these various levels, as appropriate to the material being taught and the ability of the children. A criticism often levelled at some teachers is that their teaching and the educational objectives they set for learners become fixed at the lower levels (knowledge and comprehension), rather than extending to the higher levels of understanding.

Affective domain

Major categories within the **affective domain** are *receiving* (that is, the individual is willing to receive or attend to particular stimuli, events or information), *responding* (referring to the active participation on the part of the student in the experience), *valuing* (referring to how much the student values the experience), *organisation* (referring to integrating values across a range of experiences into a philosophy of life) and *characterisation* (referring to the individual's behaviour that reflects value systems incorporated into a consistent lifestyle).

As you have probably guessed, the writing of objectives reflecting levels within the affective domain, and the evaluation of these, is more difficult than with the cognitive domain. Nevertheless, there are many opportunities for teachers to use dimensions drawn from the affective domain when writing objectives in such areas as literature, multicultural education and environmental education. Indeed, student growth in the affective domain—that is, in the development of attitudes and values—is a component of many syllabuses. For example, Aim 1 of the NSW Science 7–10 Syllabus (1989) is to foster the development of values that will provide a context for students to make informed and reasoned decisions about issues concerning science, technology and society. The objectives derived from this aim require students to demonstrate that they have a lively interest in natural phenomena and that they value a scientific approach to problem solving.

Psychomotor domain

The **psychomotor domain** moves through simple objectives such as *perceiving, readiness for* and *guided response to particular motor actions.* Higher levels are concerned with *establishing motor responses as habitual behaviours* that can be performed with some degree of skill and the *combining of motor movements into complex motor actions.* The higher levels are concerned with adapting well-developed skills to meet new situations and originating new motor skills based on those already learned.

None of these domains stands alone. In most learning experiences the cognitive, affective and psychomotor domains are intertwined, and each of the levels should also be intertwined. Thus, a range of assessment methods needs to be utilised appropriately.

Rubrics to guide instruction and evaluation

Bloom, Hastings and Madaus (1971) and Gronlund (1985) indicate how these domains may be used to develop a *table of specifications* or **rubrics** to guide instruction and evaluation. More recently, these tables of specifications have been termed *rubrics.* The notion is quite simple. A two-way matrix is constructed, with content forming one axis and objectives forming the other axis, as indicated in the following table of specifications matrix.

	Objectives
Content	

Table of specifications matrix

Listed under 'Objectives' are those of relevance to the particular topic. If we were concerned with the cognitive domain they would range from knowledge to evaluation. Underneath 'Content' we would list the material to be covered. In a unit for primary children on how people work we might list the following content: tools of trade, clothing, location, grouping, transport and hours. The table of specifications would then look something like Table 11.4.

Within each cell we might list one or more specific learning objectives. (Some cells may have no entries.) At a glance such a table of specifications indicates the material to be covered and the relative weighting to be given for particular objectives. This weighting should then be reflected in the number and kind of tasks used to measure how well students have mastered the material. Indeed, some teachers list within each cell the number of items to be used to test that particular objective. Such a system brings to a teacher's mind the full range of objectives possible so that simple

Table 11.4 Table of specifications (rubrics)

TOPIC **How people work**			**Objectives**			
Content	**Knowledge**	**Comprehension**	**Application**	**Analysis**	**Synthesis**	**Evaluation**
TOOLS OF TRADE	What tools are used? STATE/LIST	Describe different tools of different jobs. DESCRIBE	Explain why we have different tools for different jobs. SOLVE		Invent a new tool for a certain job. INVENT	Why do people need tools? ASSESSING/DECIDING
CLOTHING	Make a list of working clothes. LIST		Make a piece of clothing. UNDERSTAND/ DEMONSTRATE	Is the clothing practical? INVESTIGATE	Imagine you are a clothes designer and design a uniform for a specific job. DESIGN	Positive/negative characteristics of work clothes/ uniforms. JUSTIFYING
LOCATION	Survey and list the location of people's workplaces. LIST	Draw conclusions from the survey. Explain findings. EXPLAIN	Graph the findings. Plot locations on map. SHOW	Compare/contrast the location with the profession. COMPARE/CONTRAST	Construct a workplace diorama. CONSTRUCT	
GROUPING	Speaker on employment 'hierarchy': • other countries • slavery. RETELL/REMEMBER	Explain the duties within each level of personnel. EXPLAIN	Report on duties. Role play staff and duties. DEMONSTRATING/ APPLYING			Argue/debate the social structures in society and their relevance to work. ARGUE/DEBATE
TRANSPORT	Name the different types of transport used to get to work. NAME	Interview working people to find out why they choose that method of transport. EXPLAIN	Report findings of the interviews. REPORT	Analyse the information. ANALYSE		Debate the best way of getting to work. DEBATE
HOURS	List, e.g. 24 hours: • night shift • afternoon shift, etc. LIST	Explain why there are different shifts. EXPLAIN	Demonstrate concept of time-tabling, rostering. DEMONSTRATE		Design a timetable or roster for jobs. DESIGN	Evaluate the effectiveness of the timetabling. EVALUATE
TALLY	6	5	6	3	4	5

knowledge and comprehension objectives are not focused on exclusively.

QUESTION POINT

Discuss why instructional objectives are desirable from the teacher's point of view. What difficulties might arise in formulating objectives, and what are possible strategies to counteract these difficulties?

QUESTION POINT

Demonstrate your understanding of Bloom's taxonomy by listing and defining levels in each of the domains. Where are various domains and levels most likely to be appropriate?

What is mastery learning?

A number of educational innovations are based on the criterion-assessment model, perhaps the most common being Benjamin Bloom's **mastery learning** model (Bloom 1984, 1987; Guskey 1987, 1995; Guskey & Gates 1986). Within these mastery learning programs a criterion of mastery is established, and the progress of students towards the mastery of a given skill or concept is regularly assessed. There is also provision for corrective feedback and for opportunities to achieve mastery for students who are having difficulties. The expectation is that all students will achieve mastery of the given skill or concept.

Under the group-based mastery learning program designed by Bloom, a formative test is given to the students every two to three weeks, followed by feedback/corrective instruction and then a parallel formative test. The feedback/corrective process begins with the teacher noting the common errors of the majority of students and designing instructional approaches to remedy these common errors. After this, small groups of students (with or without teacher guidance) work through the items they missed in the test, referring back to the original instructional materials to see where problems occurred. Finally, students attempt a parallel test to confirm that they have mastered the material to the mastery standard. Reviews of mastery learning indicate that, in general, it can be an effective approach to ensuring that a large number of students achieve educational goals (Guskey & Gates 1986; Walberg 1984), although some debate exists over the level of its effect on student achievement, particularly when it is group-based rather than individualised (Slavin 1987b, 1989). Essentials of a mastery approach to instruction are given in Table 11.5.

In our next section we describe a range of measurement strategies. Relate these to the indicators of teaching competence outlined in Box 11.2.

TEACHING COMPETENCE — Box 11.2

The teacher uses assessment strategies that take account of the relationship between teaching, learning and assessment

Indicators

The teacher:

- knows and uses a range of assessment strategies to build a holistic picture of individual student learning;
- uses assessment procedures consistent with content and process goals;
- plans an assessment program as part of the teaching and learning program;
- uses assessment to inform future planning;
- encourages student self/peer assessment where appropriate.

Case studies illustrating National Competency Framework for Beginning Teaching, National Project on the Quality of Teaching and Learning, Australian Teaching Council, 1996, Element 4.2, p. 56. Commonwealth of Australia copyright, reproduced by permission.

Traditional measurement strategies

There is a vast array of measurement strategies, a number of which you will probably be quite familiar with. In selecting a particular approach it is important to consider the relative advantages and disadvantages of each format, as well as issues of validity and reliability. Among the common forms of measurement are essays, short-answer questions, projects, objective tests, practicals, simulated tasks and oral presentations.

Essay tests and assignments have a number of advantages. They are easy to set and they encourage written fluency, the organisation and integration of ideas, and originality. As such, they permit the student to go beyond simple rote memorisation of facts and figures while stimulating a search for information. Unfortunately, marking essay questions can be quite unreliable, the coverage of material might be inadequately sampled by a limited number of questions and, where the essay is

Table 11.5 Essentials of a mastery approach to instruction

Teachers should:

- specify what is to be learned as learning outcomes;
- motivate students to learn it;
- provide appropriate instructional materials;
- present materials at a rate appropriate for individual students;
- monitor students' progress and provide corrective feedback;
- diagnose difficulties and provide remediation;
- give praise and encouragement for good performance;
- give review and practice;
- maintain a high rate of learning over a period;
- provide challenging and rewarding extension and enrichment activities upon mastery of initial learning;
- match measurement and evaluation with the instruction and the learning outcome desired.

(Source: Based on Carroll 1971; Guskey 1995)

Why is project work a useful alternative for evaluating student achievement?

The student is building a rocket. Later the rocket is fired. What might the student learn about rocketry from this practical?

written under test conditions, there might be an undue emphasis on writing speed.

Short-answer questions, in which students are required to recall information rather than simply recognise correct responses, allow for a broader coverage of the course's content and for more reliable marking. However, there is little opportunity for students to display argument or originality, and rote learning is often encouraged, particularly when the nature of the questions is indicated in advance of the test. An advantage of many short-answer questions is the ease of marking.

Projects are commonly used at school to stimulate student interest, motivation and learning by encouraging students to read widely and research information. Because of the originality and individuality characteristic of completed projects, they are difficult to grade objectively. One important aspect of project work to be noted is the potential for it to relate to 'real life' and, as the scope can be broad or narrow, the approach allows for integration between various curriculum areas.

Objective tests (such as multiple choice, matching, completion and true–false) are frequently used at schools and universities. This form of assessment has significant advantages for the teacher. A wide range of objectives can be assessed within a broad coverage of the syllabus. The marking is objective (that is, any marker will mark the test in the same way) and precise and rapid feedback is possible (particularly if computer scoring is used). However, there are also significant limitations: objective tests are hard to set; students have to recognise rather than recall information; and there is little scope for divergent responses and higher-order thinking processes.

Practicals are particularly useful for students to demonstrate psychomotor skills such as playing the recorder, completing an experiment, handling power tools or typing. However, they can be very time consuming for the teacher. Associated with practicals are **simulated tasks** or **role plays**. This form of measurement closely approximates what the individual will be required to do 'in the real world' and the coverage of material can be quite broad. Thus it supports the application, rather than regurgitation, of knowledge. When the performance test is a simulation, it must resemble the real situation as closely as possible, and clear criteria of performance need to be spelled out in advance. **Work sample assessments** can reflect the highest degree of realism in simulations—for example, student teachers conducting a real lesson in a real classroom or a jumbo jet flight officer flying their first 747 as pilot. In this form of measurement, students perform a representative sample of behaviours under realistic conditions.

Oral presentations

Oral presentations provide the opportunity for students to tell the examiner what they know. This form of task allows for interpersonal interaction and for the examiner to elicit information as appropriate. Hence, coverage can be both broad and deep. Oral presentations are particularly useful to confirm other measurements. However, they can be highly subjective and require expert examiner skills. Oral presentations may also be given in front of a class and, as such, may induce an audience effect causing anxiety for some students.

In line with the approach we have taken in this book, we advocate that teachers use a variety of the above methods.

QUESTION POINT

Consider the strengths and weaknesses of the traditional assessment strategies discussed in this chapter. Thinking back to your school days, which assessment strategies seemed most effective at motivating you to greater effort, and which were least effective?

Alternatives to traditional measurement—reflections of constructivist approaches

Authentic measurement strategies

Increasingly today, teachers are employing **alternative assessment** strategies to supplement those discussed above (Alleman & Brophy 1997; Cambourne & Turbill 1990; Carr & Ritchie 1991; Gullickson 1985; Lester, Lambdin & Preston 1997; Linn, Baker & Dunbar 1991; Moss 1996; Sackett *et al.* 2001; Shepard 1991; Swanson, Norman & Linn 1995; Wolf *et al.* 1991; Woodward 1993). Often the term 'authentic' is used as a synonym for these alternative forms (Alleman & Brophy 1997; Newman 1997). **Authentic assessments** attempt to situate the assessment within 'real' contexts of learning and involve construction of knowledge, disciplined inquiry, and value of the achievement beyond school (Wiggins 1997, 1998). Criteria applied to evaluate successful accomplishment would be those applied in a real setting, rather than marks and scores—for example, successfully completing a specific task such as designing an architectural drawing. Authentic assessment also emphasises self-assessment and public presentation of work (see, for example, Wiggins 1989) and is used to improve performance as much as to measure it (Wiggins 1998). One of the reasons for the authentic assessment movement is the current emphasis on constructivist approaches to teaching and learning that we have emphasised in our text. Traditional modes of measurement and evaluation discussed earlier in this chapter may be appropriate when there is a one-to-one correspondence between the assignment of points and the number of correct responses made by the student, usually determined by the teacher. However, when the definition of correct response shifts in line with constructivist views of learning that value knowledge as individually and socially constructed, such methods are, perhaps, less appropriate (see, for example, Delandshere & Petrosky 1998; Gipps 1999). A number of alternative strategies have been developed that are believed to 'capture' more authentically the learning of students.

These strategies include:

- focused evaluation;
- pupil profiles;
- journals and portfolios;
- work samples; and
- peer evaluations and self-evaluations.

Focused evaluation (Edwards & Woodward 1989; Woodward 1993) allows for an intensive evaluation of a student's development over limited periods. Among common methods of assessing students' development are anecdotal records, checklists and observations. Typically, a class is divided up into small groups (five to eight), each of which becomes the focus of measurement and evaluation for a period of one to two weeks. In this way, all students in the class are focused on once every seven weeks or so. Throughout the year, different learning areas are concentrated on and all students are closely measured and evaluated a number of times in each of these areas. Opportunities are provided for parents and students to have an input. In the early stages of the program, letters are sent home explaining the nature and purpose of focused evaluation. Parents are invited to comment on their child in a particular area (for example, mathematics or reading) and to provide additional information considered useful for getting a full picture of the child (for example, the child's hobbies and leisure pursuits). Parental involvement is maintained by asking for written feedback on children's progress and by providing the opportunity for conferences. Both formative and summative evaluations are provided.

Parents find focused evaluation an informative and practical guide to their children's progress (Woodward 1993). Students enjoy being focused on, and usually look forward to taking their reports home because they feel proud of their achievements. Teachers maintain that, although it is a continuous process, the benefits gained from focused evaluation for the students, parents and themselves far exceed any other systems tried (see Table 11.6).

Pupil profiles

Pupil profiles can be based on anecdotal records as well as on more formal assessment. Evaluation in the early grades of schools (and the reports based on them) are increasingly using the anecdotal format. The following suggestions (adapted from Gronlund 1985) may be helpful for using anecdotes effectively.

- *Determine in advance what to observe, but be alert for behaviour that is not typical.* Be wary of recording only behaviour that is out of the ordinary as this will not give a true picture of the student. To guard against this, it is important to have a series of objectives for making observations. The unusual behaviour can then be recorded in this context and may give valuable insights into the development of the student.

Theory and research into practice

John Hattie — STATISTICS AND MEASUREMENT

BRIEF BIOGRAPHY

I was raised in a small town in the South Island of New Zealand. The horizons were close and my upbringing safe and secure. The highest aspiration in this town was to become a bank teller, with the aim of then working your way up the hierarchy. I worked as a painter and paper hanger and then for many years as hospital porter, kitchen hand and ward orderly. It was when I discovered that the government paid you to go to teachers' college, that I found a way out of Timaru. I went to Dunedin Teachers' College, and as I had matriculated from school with 'university entrance' was allowed to do one university course during this first year.

During my college years, I also completed two full-time years at the University of Otago. The university taught education as a discipline and provided a broad and deep grounding in all aspects of education (other than teacher education). It was a requirement to have a foreign language, and I was delighted when they redefined 'foreign language' to include 'statistics'; this began a fascination with all things statistical. I graduated with a diploma from the college, a BA and Diploma of Education, and then taught for a year at Macandrew Intermediate School in Dunedin. This year of teaching was so much fun that it was easy to take a risk and apply for another year to undertake a Master's; if it didn't work out, I could always return to teaching. During this year I did a class with Tom Maguire and Mel Swanson and they introduced me to the area of measurement and research design, which became my main field of study. I also attended sessions with Alan Musgrave and Karl Popper in philosophy of science, and met R. S. Peters, the great UK education philosopher. They left lasting effects on the importance of inquiry, the advancement of knowledge, and the need to understand the concepts being studied. After the Master's, I left for Toronto and completed a Ph.D. at OISE.

I was supervised by Rod McDonald, who is one of the preeminent factor analysts and psychometricians. He was a superb teacher, an excellent mentor, a tough but clear supervisor, and he taught me so much about psychometrics. A major message was to discover meaningful problems and attack them, not study topics. Another supervisor, Ross Traub, introduced me to item response theory (latent trait models, as it was then called), and impressed upon me that we must use these statistical models to tackle real-world problems.

RESEARCH AND THEORETICAL INTERESTS

My thesis was about unidimensionality—a fundamental assumption of test theory. If a test measures more than one attribute it is difficult to make sense of the total scores (for example, if you get 12 out of 20 and 10 of the items are spelling, and 10 arithmetic, what does the 12/20 mean?). I completed a simulation study, and as a consequence touched most of the traditional and many of the brand-new methods. It opened many doors, was one of the first studies to be published on this topic, and the papers written from the thesis are still among my most cited papers. Measurement has remained the underlying theme of my interests.

I took a job in Australia and spent 10 years in northern New South Wales. Life was easy, the university well resourced, the department exciting with many who are now senior academics throughout Australia. I lived on a 600-acre farm in a 36-room house, and my partner and I had a great life. Being in measurement and statistics meant you could dabble in almost every area of education, and I certainly did that. For example, when the new notion of meta-analysis was published, Brian Hansford encouraged me to join him and undertake a meta-analysis to learn about their benefits and problems. We chose, almost arbitrarily, the relation between self-concept and achievement, and this provided me with a field of study in which to apply many measurement notions. I published a book on self-concept in 1992 and that book included many new meta-analyses, a conceptual analysis of self-concept, and a number of measurement features. This early interest in literature reviews has led to a decade-long project to synthesise the various meta-analyses in education (Hattie, 1992, 1997) to address the issue of what makes the difference to student achievement. I am completing a book on the topic and it certainly shows how we can use the richness of prior studies to address major problems in education. It is fascinating to consider literature reviews as a discipline and I have completed reviews on ADHD, relations between research and teaching, study skills, outward bound and adventure programs, communication apprehension, alternative testing methods for creativity assessment, effectiveness of para- and professional counselling, class composition and peer effects, and attributes of excellent teachers.

I then was appointed to full professor and head of school at the University of Western Australia, at age 35. It was heady stuff.

Another excellent university and my first real senior role. Besides heading an exciting department, I continued working on topics of unidimensionality, self-concept, meta-analysis and reputation enhancement, and became more involved in working with local school districts. After 10 years in Perth, came the hard decision—to stay in the same place for the next 25 years or move. Our three boys were still young enough to make a move and we moved to North Carolina. Here I worked in a department where *all* members were measurement and evaluation people. Dick Jaeger and Lloyd Bond were in charge of the technical advisory group for the National Board for Professional Standards. This brought together the leading measurement people in the United States a few times a year, and rubbing shoulders with such talent was invigorating and informative. I became involved in the measurement of performance, the intricacies of scoring rubrics for portfolios, and the debate about how to conceive validity in new ways. I proposed and piloted a study on the validity of the National Board model, which later received full funding. This study was not only huge, but has received much attention not only because of its methods but in the exciting results. The contrasts were striking.

THEORY AND RESEARCH INTO PRACTICE

We then decided to return Down Under, partly because we wanted our now teenage boys to identify with our own heritage and to be closer to our own families. At the University of Auckland I was head of school and also ventured on building a national assessment model for New Zealand. It combined my interests in linear programming, dimensionality, item response models, standard setting and validity—and a rich reporting system. asTTle (assessment tools for teaching and learning) is a computer application that allows teachers to create tests (using linear programming), and its main benefit is a very rich reporting and interpretation engine that allows a deep understanding of the student or class performance relative to national norms (contrasts can be interactively altered by teachers to various comparison groups), a curriculum analysis of the strengths and gaps for each student and the class, and a direct connection to a series of quality resources tied directly to the student's performance. It has been welcomed by teachers and has won innovation awards, and now we are building an Internet version with additional features such as computerised performance assessment.

Hence, a major commitment is the interface between theory and practice in education: specifically, the use of excellent research design, measurement, evaluation and statistical methods to important educational questions.

KEY REFERENCES

Hattie, J. A. (1985) Methodology review: Assessing unidimensionality of tests and items. *Applied Psychological Measures*, **9**, 139–64.

Hattie, J. & Marsh, H. W. (1996) The relationship between research and teaching: A meta-analysis. *Review of Educational Research*, **66**, 507–42.

Hattie, J., Biggs, J. & Purdie, N. (1998) Effects of learning skills interventions on student learning. A meta-analysis. *Review of Educational Research*, **66**, 99–136.

Hattie, J., Krakowski, K. & Rogers, H. J. *et al.* (1996) An assessment of Stout's index of essential unidimensionality. *Applied Psychological Measurement*, **20**, 1–14.

Hattie, J. A., Jaeger, R. M. & Bond, L. (1999) Persistent methodological questions in educational testing. *Review of Research in Education*, **24**, 393–446.

Hattie, J. A., Biggs, J. & Purdie, N. (1996) Effects of learning skills intervention on student learning: A meta-analysis. *Review of Research in Education*, **66**, 99–136.

Hattie, J. A. (1992) *Self-concept*. Hillsdale, NJ: Lawrence Erlbaum.

Hattie, J. A., Brown, G. T., Keegan, P., Mackay, A. and team (2004, December). asTTle: Assessment Tools for Teaching and Learning. V4. Ministry of Education, Wellington.

ACTIVITIES

1 John Hattie started his professional life as a teacher and then developed a passion for statistics and measurement. Why is an understanding of statistics and measurement essential for any teacher?

2 John Hattie was taught to discover meaningful problems and attack them, not study topics. Do you think that this approach to learning has application within school settings? How might this approach lend itself to assessment of students' growth in learning?

3 In this chapter we have emphasised the need for teachers to use valid and reliable measurements of their students' achievement. John Hattie introduces the notion of undimensionality in measurement. Discuss with your fellow students why undimensionality is so important in measurement tasks. How do the alternative methods of measurement discussed below lend themselves to undimensional measurement?

4 What is meta-analysis? As a project, link with a number of other students and locate some meta-analyses in education and psychology that interest you. Discuss what these meta-analyses conclude about areas of interest to you as teachers. You might like to consider meta-analyses in the areas John Hattie has researched: self-concept, ADHD, relations between research and teaching, study skills, outward bound and adventure programs, communication apprehension, alternative testing methods for creativity assessment, effectiveness of para- and professional counselling, class composition and peer effects, and attributes of excellent teachers.

5 Discuss the benefits of asTTle for teachers. How would you use asTTle?

Table 11.6 Some advantages and requirements of focused evaluation

Some advantages of focused evaluation
• Teachers are able to get to know the students in the class more quickly and gain a better understanding of how students learn. • Teachers evaluate their students in normal day-to-day activities rather than in a test situation. This reduces student anxiety. • All students are evaluated, and none of the 'quiet achievers' can slip through unnoticed. • Parents are provided with a continuous record of specific achievements. • Any problems can be dealt with as they occur. Students' needs can be identified and future lessons and planning structured to cater to these needs.
Some requirements of focused evaluation
• Reports take 60–90 minutes to complete per focus group. • Teachers must be well organised. Evaluation sheets, report forms and folders must be accessible and ready for immediate use. • Teachers need to be flexible, as each focus period will have its interruptions—school development days, sports carnivals, book week, education week, and so on. • Focused evaluation requires teacher commitment.
(Source: Based on Edwards & Woodward 1989, p. 41)

- *Observe and record enough of the situation to make the behaviour meaningful.* Student behaviour can be quite ambiguous. What might be interpreted as aggression by a teacher or parent may, in fact, be perceived by both the actor and other students as good-natured fun. Consequently, it is essential to record enough of the context of the behaviour to ensure that your interpretation is accurate.
- *Make a record of the incident as soon after the observation as possible.* We have short memories for detail, so it is important to make at least brief notes on observations close to the event. These notes can then jog the memory when we come to write fuller comments at a later time.
- *Limit each anecdote to a brief description of a single incident.* Brief and concise descriptions take less time to write, less time to read and are more easily summarised. However, make sure that the report is detailed enough for you to make sense of it at a later date when you come to write summative reports.
- *Keep the factual description of the incident and your interpretation of it separate.* Be factual in your reporting and avoid coloured language. Interpretations that you make on your observation can be subjective, but they should be labelled as such and kept separate from the objective reporting of behaviour.
- *Record both positive and negative behavioural incidents.* We have emphasised repeatedly that teachers should focus on the actual learning that all students are capable of and seek evidence of this learning so that they can support it. Very often teachers focus on the evidence that little learning is taking place, and so anecdotal reports become a depressing record of lack of achievement. Keep a balance. Certainly, it is important to record difficulties and problems, but it is equally important to record successes and achievements.
- *Collect a number of anecdotes about a pupil before drawing inferences concerning typical behaviour.* We have also emphasised that multiple sources of evidence should be considered before making final judgments about students' typical performance. There are days when all teachers feel 'flat', and their teaching will reflect this. They would hate to have their teaching evaluated on those days. It would be more accurate if evidence were collected over a period of time, in a number of contexts, before judgments were made. It is only after observing a student a number of times in a variety of settings that a pattern of behaviour begins to emerge. Until that time we should suspend our judgment.
- *Obtain practice in writing anecdotal records.* Practice refines a skill. Writing good anecdotal records is a skill that must be worked on. Collaborative work in the school, where a number of teachers help each other to write and evaluate anecdotal reports, is a useful means of developing such skill.

Journals and portfolios (Alleman & Brophy 1997; Lester *et al.* 1997; Stecher & Herman 1997) are collections of student work that exhibit the student's efforts, progress and achievements in one or more areas. Paulson *et al.* (1991) present the following guidelines for portfolio development:

- Developing a portfolio offers the student an opportunity to learn about learning. Therefore, the end product must contain information showing that the student has engaged in self-reflection.

- The portfolio is something that is done *by* the student, not *to* the student.
- The portfolio is separate and different from the student's cumulative folder.
- The portfolio must convey explicitly or implicitly the student's activities.
- The portfolio may serve a different purpose during the year from the purpose it serves at the end.
- The portfolio should contain information that illustrates growth.
- Many of the skills and techniques involved in producing effective portfolios do not happen by themselves. Models are needed.

Work samples

Work samples can be assessed in **simulated environments** and real environments. A good example of this is work experience where a sample of work, such as the class management of a student teacher, can be observed in an actual classroom.

Such performance-based modes of measurement must still demonstrate validity and reliability, although the traditional forms of determining these may not apply. Considerable work is being done by measurement and evaluation experts to develop criteria for ensuring validity of these performance-based modes (Shepard 1991; Swanson *et al.* 1995). Potential limitations in the use of performance-based tasks (based on Swanson *et al.* 1995) are:

- The fact that examinees are tested in realistic performance situations does not make test design and domain sampling simple and straightforward.
- No matter how realistic a performance-based task is, it is still a simulation, and examinees do not behave the same as they would in real life.
- Scoring performance-based behaviour can be problematic because of its diversity and complexity.
- Regardless of the method used, performance in one context does not predict performance in other contexts very well.
- Correlational studies of the relationship between performance-based test scores and other measurement methods targeting different skills typically produce variable and uninterpretable results.
- Performance-based methods are often complex to administer.
- All high-stakes measurement, regardless of the method used, has an impact on teaching and learning. The nature of this impact is not necessarily predictable, and careful studies of (intended and unintended) benefits and side effects are obviously desirable but rarely done.
- Neither traditional testing nor performance-based methods of measurement and evaluation is a panacea. Selection of methods should depend on the skills to be measured and, generally, use of a blend of methods is desirable.

Dynamic assessment

This is a form of assessment whereby a child is given examiner assistance when the student is having difficulty. When a student is having difficulty, the examiner attempts to move the student from failure to success by modifying the format, providing more opportunities, providing information on successful strategies, or offering increasingly more direct cues, hints or prompts in order to improve learning and performance (Swanson & Lussier 2001).

In Table 11.7 we present some of the essential features of authentic assessment.

ACTION STATION

1 (a) State your personal philosophy of how students learn best.

(b) Take each point raised in your philosophy and show how this will affect teaching methods and 'style'.

(c) Suggest appropriate assessment strategies to fit your philosophy and teaching methods.

2 Prepare a teaching unit in a given curriculum area, ensuring that:

(a) assessment strategies are built in as part of the teaching process;

(b) both formative and summative assessment are included;

(c) indicators of student mastery of key concepts, skills, and so on are stated;

(d) details of methods and time schedules for data collection and recording are organised.

If you design a unit for a senior grade:

(e) design a test as an assessment tool;

(f) ensure that problems are written in clear, positive terms;

(g) include a mixture of test formats.

You may be able to use this unit in teaching practice. If you do, consider the effectiveness of your assessment strategy. How will you ensure that the measurement was valid and reliable?

QUESTION POINT

Within your own educational setting, discuss the use of work samples, journals and portfolios as a means of assessing your development of teaching skills. What do you personally believe their strengths and weaknesses to be? In what circumstances would you use one or other, or a combination, of these approaches in your classroom?

Peer evaluation and self-evaluation

Some time ago, when the author was a mere stripling, he studied history for the Leaving Certificate. His teacher at the time set many essays, but escaped the burden of marking them by exchanging essays between students and getting them to measure and evaluate each other's efforts. It was a bright class and each student used to rip

Table 11.7 Essentials of authentic assessment

Teachers should:

- model interest in learning and self-evaluation in real-life contexts;
- derive assessment tasks from students' everyday learning in school;
- collect diverse evidence of students' learning from multiple activities over time;
- design assessment tasks that are varied, functional, pragmatic and beneficial, to stimulate student learning;
- design assessment tasks that reflect local values and standards;
- design activities that encourage student responsibility for self-assessment, peer assessment, and for selecting learning activities and outcomes.

(Source: Based on Paris & Ayres 1994)

TEACHER'S CASE BOOK

Records of development (RODs)

Records of development are kept as an ongoing folio of children's work samples. They are begun in kindergarten and added to each year until the end of Grade 6 when children take them home. They involve collecting samples of children's work from all areas of the curriculum during the year.

At Mr Paynter's school the teachers work on two cycles of collection throughout the year.

Cycle 1
2 maths
1 art
2 writing
1 reading conference
1 other (for example, science, social studies)

Cycle 2
2 maths
1 art
1 pencil sketch
1 reading conference
1 other
2 writing (narrative)

As each piece of work is collected, teachers write observations and focus on future teaching needs for individual children.

Children in higher grades (for example, 3–6) contribute to the selection process as they are encouraged to feel ownership of the ROD. It is their personal record and document. In kindergarten, the selection of work is very individual so that teachers can select work which shows a particular breakthrough or discovery.

The comments that teachers include on children's work samples are then incorporated into their planning, so the RODs are not separate from the classroom planning. Mr Paynter tries to incorporate them continually into what he is doing in his classroom. RODs are the focus of his parent–teacher interviews which are held after cycle 1. He finds them very useful for focusing parents' attention on particular aspects of their child's development throughout the year, and most parents appreciate the depth of comments and the time and effort put into compiling them.

Originals of work samples go home at the end of each year in a profile for each child. Teachers keep a photocopy in the ROD of the last writing, maths, reading conferencing, pencil sketch and report for the future year's teacher. This enables the teachers to see at a glance exactly what stages children are at before they come to their class the following year. In this way, the RODs help to provide for a greater sense of continuity of learning throughout children's primary school years.

Case studies illustrating National Competency Framework for Beginning Teaching, National Project on the Quality of Teaching and Learning, Australian Teaching Council, 1996, p. 30. Commonwealth of Australia copyright, reproduced by permission.

Case study activity

Discuss the strengths of this approach to measuring and evaluating student progress. Are there any limitations in this approach?

Teachers can observe work habits, attitudes and skills in preparing an accurate cumulative assessment file for each student without resorting to formal testing.

into the essay written by the other student with great gusto! The author would spend hours looking up obscure references to prove that the causes of the First World War posited by his 'target' student were, in fact, codswallop, and that the real reasons were related to the cost of sugar beet on the world market! At times friendships were strained as we looked in horror at the red lines and comments scrawled over our essays by our friends and peers and waited for the opportunity (in a dark corridor) to get even with the perpetrator. We all seemed to survive the peer evaluation process, however, and in fact did quite well in our history exams.

Student involvement in the evaluation process is increasing and typically takes the form of *peer assessment* or self-assessment (Falchikov & Goldfinch 2000). For **peer evaluation** to be effective it must share the characteristics of good measurement and evaluation generally. It should be specific, descriptive, predominantly non-judgmental in tone and form, and directed towards the goals of the person receiving it. It must also be well timed. Very importantly, it must be directed at the work and not at the personality of the person who completed the work (often a hard thing to do!). (Comments such as 'You're a fool, writing such rubbish' are not very constructive or helpful.) As students are inexperienced at commenting on the work of others, considerable effort must be expended by the teacher in preparing students for this process. Students, particularly younger ones, should be given guidelines on what is being measured and how to evaluate. Older students can work this out with each other in collaboration with the teacher (Boud 1985).

Peer evaluation has particular relevance to *peer tutoring* and *cooperative learning strategies* (see Chapters 6 and 8), and can be used in combination with teacher measurement and evaluation. Sometimes, peer evaluation can be used across the whole class (when, for example, a student makes a classroom presentation and all members of the class complete an evaluation form on the presentation which is given to the presenter). This often happens in peer teaching in teacher education courses. At other times, peer evaluation may be one-to-one—for example, when two students have collaborated in a learning experience (as in *collaborative learning* or peer tutoring). This latter use is probably more valuable. Members of a group can also evaluate each other's mastery of material before a general group presentation to be evaluated by the teacher.

One opportunity we were never given in those Leaving Certificate history classes was that of **self-evaluation**, where we were challenged to set learning goals and to evaluate our achievement of these goals in terms of

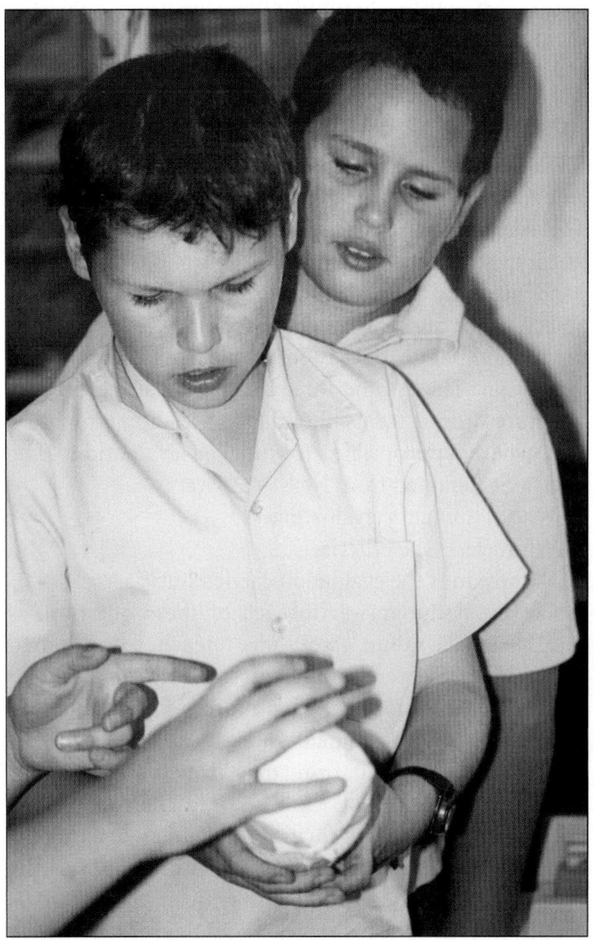

Why are peer and self-evaluation important in constructivist learning?

established criteria. We were never given the opportunity, at first hand, to evaluate the quality of our own learning. The evaluation was always filtered through the judgment of our teachers or others. Yet the ability to self-evaluate is fundamental to our effective functioning as adults. For several years now there has been growing interest in the educational goals of autonomy, independence and self-regulation in learning, and self-evaluation is an important part of this (Boud 1981, 1985; Falchikov & Boud 1989; Falchikov & Goldfinch 2000; Gipps 1999; Hall 1992; Paris & Ayres 1994; Wolf 1989). Self-evaluation has strong links with the development of metacognitive skills, covered in Chapter 4.

Given the argument that self-evaluation is an essential part of teaching students to be independent learners, the process should be introduced as a component of the regular teaching and learning activities of the classroom rather than as an element only of the formal assessment procedure. As with peer evaluation, students are not naturally inclined or prepared to evaluate their work so the teacher must put considerable effort into preparing them for this task (Gipps 1999). One way to develop this skill is to introduce a system of co-evaluation.

Co-evaluation and self-evaluation

Measurement and evaluation shared between students and teacher is often termed *co-evaluation* (Hall 1992). This seems an effective and acceptable way of balancing learning strategies—it emphasises autonomy and independence, and teaching responsibilities and accountability. Three questions may be asked as a guide to where the locus of control lies in individual measurement and evaluation. These same three questions can be used to structure various forms of evaluation leading ultimately, and where appropriate, to full self-evaluation. The questions (adapted from Hall 1992) are:

1 Who is doing the evaluating?
2 Who selects the criteria?
3 For whom is the evaluation carried out?

Clearly, if the answer to each of these questions is 'the teacher', then we have teacher-dominated evaluation. However, if we answer 'the student' to one or more of the questions, we have a form of **co-evaluation**. If the answer is 'the student' in each case, we have self-evaluation. Co-evaluation may involve a student evaluating their work on the basis of teacher-established criteria or the teacher evaluating the student on student-established criteria. Both 'doing the evaluating' and the 'selecting of criteria' can be shared so that there is collaboration at each level. The degree to which evaluations are private or public influences the nature of the evaluation in important ways. Forms of co-evaluation commonly used in educational settings are *negotiated evaluation*, *conferencing*, the *contract system*, *critiques of performance*, *journals* and *diaries* (to the extent that the criteria of material to be included and evaluated is decided by the teacher), and *individualised projects* negotiated with the teacher.

Advantages of self-evaluation

Self-evaluation should help to motivate student learning. When students evaluate their own achievement they may have new insights into their learning, and may be more able to identify specific problems they are experiencing. As self-evaluation requires honesty of students, there is great potential for a trusting relationship to be developed between students and teacher. Self-evaluation can also help to increase students' aspirations and achievements. However, we must be aware that students' perceptions of the quality of their work and the degree of their effort do not always match those of their teachers; consequently, some monitoring of self-evaluation by the teacher is always necessary to ensure that the evaluations are honest and realistic (Falchikov & Boud 1989; Griffin & Nix 1991).

Critique of authentic assessment

Not all measurement authorities agree with the authentic assessment movement (Terwilliger 1997, 1998). In particular, they emphasise that traditional measurement and evaluation are just as authentic (or inauthentic) and useful as the above alternative practices. It depends upon context and how effectively the measurement techniques are used. So-called authentic assessment can be used very badly. In particular, many anti-authentic assessment writers are concerned that authentic assessment does not emphasise sufficiently the acquisition of basic skills and their effective measurement, and pays inadequate attention to issues of validity and reliability. This position is, of course, debated, and you might like to read some of the debate in *Educational Researcher*, 17(6). Our advice, as on many other occasions in this book when there are conflicting views, is to include both forms of measurement and evaluation in your classroom. In this way, you are sure to be effective in monitoring student development. Table 11.9 presents essentials of effective measurement and evaluation.

Build a resource file of alternative assessment 'tools' for use across the curriculum. Include examples of each where practicable: for example, close passages, pupil-constructed tests, pupil self-assessment.

TEACHER'S CASE BOOK

Assessment by the students

At the completion of an English unit with a Year 9 class, Mr Blair wanted to provide each student with as much feedback as possible.

Through discussions with students, it was decided that each student would present a five-minute oral presentation once the English unit was completed. At the completion of the presentation, the student was given a sheet to write a self-evaluation. Two students from the audience were asked to write some constructive comments on the quality of the performance and the work completed by the student. Mr Blair also completed an assessment of the student's work. All this information was photocopied on to an A4 sheet and returned to the presenter.

Such a variety of feedback provides the students with a broad picture of their performance. It also provides the basis of planning for future presentations.

Case studies illustrating National Competency Framework for Beginning Teaching, National Project on the Quality of Teaching and Learning, Australian Teaching Council, 1996, p. 51.

Case study activity

What are the strengths of peer evaluation? Are there any dangers in this approach that should be guarded against? Is it an approach that can be used across grades and across subjects?

The impact of measurement and evaluation on students

For all the complexity of measurement and evaluation in the classroom, it cannot be avoided. There is one guiding principle that should be employed whenever we measure and evaluate students: we must do it with the best interests of every learner in mind. Unwanted side effects can arise from the nature of the assessment tasks, from the content and skills being tested, and from the methods of reporting. Some measurement and evaluation procedures used by teachers and schools are destructive of students' confidence in learning and motivation to learn (Deutsch 1979b; see also Gipps 1999). *Evaluations affect learners* and they affect learners in short-, medium- and long-term ways (Crooks 1988). Crooks enumerates a number of potential positive effects. His list (Table 11.8) is an effective checklist of the qualities of good evaluation.

Among the long-term goals of measurement and evaluation is to influence students' ability to retain and apply the material learned in a variety of contexts, to help develop student learning strategies and styles, and to encourage students' continuing motivation, both in particular subjects and more generally (Crooks 1988).

Table 11.8 Goals of evaluation

Goals of evaluation
Short-term goals
• Reactivating or consolidating prerequisite skills or knowledge prior to introducing new material. • Focusing attention on important aspects of the subject. • Encouraging active learning strategies. • Giving students opportunities to practise skills and consolidate learning. • Providing knowledge of results and corrective feedback. • Helping students to monitor their own progress and develop skills of self-evaluation. • Guiding the choice of further instructional or learning activities to increase mastery. • Helping students to feel a sense of accomplishment.
Medium-term goals
• Checking that students have adequate prerequisite skills and knowledge to be able to learn the material to be covered effectively. • Influencing students' motivation to study the subject and their perceptions of their capabilities in the subject. • Communicating and reinforcing the instructor's or the curriculum's broad goals for students, including the desired standards of performance. • Influencing students' choice (and development) of learning strategies and study patterns. • Describing or certifying students' achievement in the course, thus influencing their future activities.
(Source: Based on Crooks 1988)

Deep and surface learning

At times, strategies used to measure student performance, such as tests and assignments, simply encourage students to learn, in a relatively superficial way, the material required to pass a test rather than to delve more deeply into the subject matter under study. Indeed, many students become quite adept at picking out what is minimally required by the teacher to pass the test. This approach to learning has been called a *surface approach* and is typically characterised by rote learning. Surface-learning approaches are contrasted with *deep approaches*, which are characterised by the individual's active search for meaning, underlying principles and structures in knowledge (Biggs 1984, 1987a, 1987b; see also Leung & Kember 2003). If one of our teaching aims is to encourage deep learning, then we should be conscious of the potential effects of various measurement tasks and evaluations based on these measurement tasks. Students are versatile in their choice of learning approaches (Crooks 1988) but, like all of us, will take the line of least resistance, especially when there are competing demands, limited time and little intrinsic interest in the task. Teachers often labour the need for students to obtain a deep grasp of the importance and relevance of particular learning experiences, while simultaneously communicating what is 'really' important through the more hidden curriculum of the evaluation policy. Students often pay more attention to this covert or hidden curriculum than to the formal curriculum (Crooks 1988).

From time to time, both authors have been criticised by students for 'setting too high standards' in work. We believe that higher standards increase student effort and ultimately improve performance. However, if evaluation standards are unrealistically high they are likely to demotivate students (Natriello 1989; Natriello & Dornbusch 1984). Within the classroom context it would appear necessary to set standards that are attainable, which will involve some individualising of standards as needed. We strongly believe that if a teacher accepts substandard work, students will be encouraged to work at a minimal level.

Evaluation standards

Evaluation and sense of self

When teachers evaluate students' work they are saying something to them about success or failure. It is important that the manner in which this feedback is given to students encourages further motivation to continue with the task. A failure resulting from poor effort has a different impact from one resulting from lack of ability. As we saw earlier in the chapter on motivation (Chapter 7), our attributions for success and failure in a particular task are important determinants of later motivation for the task. Our own research has shown (McInerney 1991b, 1992b; McInerney & Swisher 1995; McInerney, Roche, McInerney & Marsh 1997; see also Covington 1992) that students who believe they are competent, and are told they can achieve by parents and teachers, are more likely to be motivated at school. Students who feel they cannot cope, that it is all beyond them, tend to be poorly motivated and make minimal efforts at learning. Any evaluation we give to students must emphasise their competence and potential for learning growth. This is particularly important for the less able students and requires us to point out clearly where errors are made while designing further learning tasks so that individual success is experienced. Social comparisons with others in the group should be minimised.

It is important to note here that praise as part of the evaluation does not appear to be as important as constructive and positive feedback that emphasises mastery and progress (Crooks 1988).

What is the role of feedback?

Implicit in what has been said above is the notion of feedback to students. There are three characteristics of effective feedback (Crooks 1988). First, feedback is most effective if it focuses students' attention on their progress in mastering educational tasks. Such emphasis on personal progress enhances self-efficacy, encourages effort attributions and reduces attention to social comparison. Second, feedback should take place when it is still clearly relevant. This usually means that it should be given during the task or soon after the task is completed, with an opportunity also provided for the student to demonstrate learning from the feedback. How many of us have received feedback so long after task completion that it becomes irrelevant? Furthermore, feedback without the opportunity to practise for improvement would seem to be a waste of time. Finally, feedback should be specific and related to need (see also Hattie 1992 and Kulhavy 1977).

Feedback that brings errors to students' attention in a motivationally favourable way is effective and more advantageous than spending time re-examining work well done (Elawar & Corno 1985). Teachers can ask four useful questions to guide their feedback:

1 What is the key error?
2 What is the probable reason the student made this error?
3 How can I guide the student to avoid the error in the future?
4 What did the student do well that should be noted?

The importance of monitoring student progress and providing effective feedback is reiterated in our Teaching Competence Box 11.3.

Some students become anxious in a testing situation. How might we structure tests to alleviate anxiety?

Box 11.3

TEACHING COMPETENCE

The teacher monitors student progress and provides feedback on progress

Indicators

The teacher:

- observes and responds to patterns of student learning behaviour;
- draws on a range of information sources in assessing individual student performance;
- provides consistent and timely feedback to students and parents;
- assesses to check progress, identify specific learning difficulties and indicate achievement;
- uses monitoring and assessment activities to enhance the self-esteem of students;
- maintains student achievement records in accordance with school policies.

Case studies illustrating National Competency Framework for Beginning Teaching, National Project on the Quality of Teaching and Learning, Australian Teaching Council, 1996, Element 4.3, p. 57. Commonwealth of Australia copyright, reproduced by permission.

Table 11.9

Essentials of effective measurement and evaluation

Teachers should:

- design a range of assessment tasks that promote meaningful learning;
- establish for students the purpose of the measurement and evaluation;
- establish for students that the assessment tasks used are valid and fair, and consistent with the regular curriculum and instruction provided in the classroom;
- design assessment tasks that elicit students' genuine effort, motivation and commitment to the assessment activity and situation;
- provide opportunities for all students to demonstrate what they have learned across a variety of assessment tasks;
- make explicit the criteria for evaluation;
- provide effective feedback that includes a number of dimensions (such as a mark and a comment);
- provide periodic and regular assessment rather than irregular and infrequent assessment;
- ensure that the assessment tasks are fair and equitable to all students regardless of prior achievement, gender, race, language or cultural background;
- provide opportunities to measure students' motivation, attitudes and affective reactions to the curriculum, as well as their cognitive skills, strategies and knowledge;
- design appropriate reporting mechanisms that provide clear and comprehensible information to parents and students;
- provide opportunities for parents to have an input into the measurement and evaluation process.

(Source: Based on Natriello 1989; Paris & Ayres 1994).

EXTENSION STUDY

Test anxiety

Many students experience moderate to severe **anxiety** within the school setting (Hadwin, Brogan & Stevenson 2005). Such anxiety can be general (that is, an overall feeling of unease while at school) or it can be more specifically related to particular subjects, teachers or school practices (such as testing and evaluation). It appears that general forms of anxiety increase as students move from primary into secondary grades. This has been associated with changing school environments. Secondary schools are more evaluative and social comparisons become more prevalent. Other factors that are thought to increase school anxiety are moving from a smaller to a larger school, having different teachers (and classmates) throughout the school day, experiencing ability grouping, and having fewer opportunities for decision making and less autonomy (Wigfield & Eccles 1989). One specific form of anxiety we will consider is test anxiety (see, for example, Kouzma & Kennedy 2000; Wigfield & Eccles 1989; Zohar 1998).

Test anxiety

What is test anxiety? Does it affect all students? How does test anxiety affect motivation and learning, and what can the teacher do to prevent or minimise any negative effects?

Research in the area of anxiety has differentiated between individuals who show **state anxiety** (which is experienced only in certain situations such as exams or learning to use a computer) and those for whom anxiety is a **trait** (which generally affects much of what they do in their lives). **Test anxiety** (Wigfield & Eccles 1989) is an example of state anxiety—specifically, it is a state of anxiety about not performing well when being evaluated in a test situation. The anxiety is experienced by those for whom the test situation involves a perceived threat to their self-esteem, sometimes referred to as 'ego-involvement' (Heckhausen 1991). Other authors (Zohar 1998) consider test anxiety as a situation-specific form of trait anxiety which relates to stable individual differences in levels of anxiety during test taking and other evaluative situations.

Why do some students become more test anxious than others? There are two current theories about the causes of test anxiety; let's have a closer look at them.

The first theory, **attention interference**, suggests that students find it *hard to focus attention* on the task at hand because of self-doubting and task-irrelevant thoughts generated in the evaluative situation (for example, worrying about how one is doing, rather than concentrating on the task) (Hadwin, Brogan & Stevenson 2005). It is argued that these thoughts interfere with the retrieval of learned material and that students perform poorly as a consequence (Wigfield & Eccles 1989; Wine 1971). A more recent **information-processing skills** theory regards the *ineffective information-processing skills* of some highly test anxious students as the main factor in their anxiety and poor academic performance in test situations (Hadwin, Brogan & Stevenson 2005). Naveh-Benjamin (1991), for example, demonstrated that, for highly test anxious students who had poor study habits, a training program in study skills reduced anxiety and improved performance in a test situation. Prior to such training, these students had performed poorly in both take-home tests (with no external pressure) and written (essay and short-answer) questions under test conditions. This type of evidence suggested that *initial* learning and organisation of material was ineffective, thereby making retrieval of complex learning material difficult, rather than there being a problem of blockage during recall. As Covington and Omelich (1987, p. 393) suggest: 'Simply put, learning must be present for it to be interfered with.' The cause of anxiety for these students is their *metacognitive awareness* of their inadequate knowledge (Tobias 1985a).

The evidence strongly suggests, therefore, that there are two types of test-anxious student: those who have good study habits but who suffer from interference (through negative cognitions) at the retrieval stage of information processing; and those who have poor study habits which prevent them from learning material effectively at the outset (Wigfield & Eccles 1989). (See also Chapter 4 for a thorough description of the elements of information processing.)

Naveh-Benjamin (1991) found that, for the first type of student, the most effective treatment was a program that *desensitised* the student to the anxiety-producing elements of the exam situation so that attention could be focused on the task itself. For these students, strategies that taught them how to deal with their interfering thoughts were most effective. In particular, training in *relaxation techniques* paired with *visualisation* of anxiety-producing test situations (such as entering the exam room, seeing printed exam questions and receiving grades) was beneficial.

For the second type of anxious student (with poor study skills), *improvement in study habits*, such as training in the *PQ4R technique* (Preview, Question, Read, Reflect, Recite, Review) (Thomas & Robinson 1972), improved performance in situations perceived as evaluative, because knowledge of material was increased and hence anxiety decreased because of greater metacognitive awareness of improved mastery (see Chapter 5).

Testing stereotype threat

An emerging theory that shows some promise for explaining differences in achievement across race and sex is the **testing stereotype threat** (Osborne 2000; Sackett, Hardison & Cullen 2004a; Steele & Aronson 1995, 2004; Urdan & Giancarlo 2001). The gist of this theory is that the under-performance of disadvantaged groups (which include racial minorities in particular academic areas and females in traditionally male domains) on tests is due to **stereotype threat**. Stereotype threat involves the fear and anxiety produced when a person feels they are in danger of fulfilling a negative stereotype about their group. While most students experience some anxiety when being evaluated, students who belong to groups with a negative intellectual stereotype not only risk personal embarrassment and failure, but also risk confirming the negative group stereotype. As a result, this leads to increased anxiety, which depresses performance through its effects on preparation and sitting for the evaluation (see Osborne 2000, p. 1). In a sense, this theory dovetails with the first theory of test anxiety discussed above where irrelevant thoughts and self-doubt interfere with the retrieval of learned material. In this case the self-doubts and irrelevant thoughts are triggered off by the stereotype. Hence, the argument would go that even equally able girls do more poorly than boys in mathematics tests because of the impact of the stereotype that girls do not do as well as boys in mathematics. As we discussed in Chapter 9, there is paradoxical information that girls do better than boys when doing mathematics activities in the classroom (where there is no test threat) yet do more poorly in testing situations than boys. This supports the stereotype threat hypothesis. There is also evidence that despite ability many African-Americans do more poorly than their white peers in testing situations. Again, the stereotype may apply that black Americans do not do as well academically as whites. Finally, there is also evidence that when white males are evaluated against Asian males in mathematics their performance is not as good as the Asian males. In this case, the stereotype is that Asian students do better than white students in mathematics. We must caution, however, that removing the stereotype threat does not automatically mean that differences between groups on achievement outcomes (such as girls doing as well as boys in mathematics, or minorities such as black Americans doing as well as whites) will be eradicated, as there are many other factors potentially involved in the different levels of performance, as we have indicated in this and other chapters. However, it is likely that the removal of stereotype threat will improve the performance of girls and other groups vis-à-vis what their performance might have been under stereotype threat conditions (Sackett, Hardison & Cullen 2004a, 2004b; see also Steele and Aronson 2004). What do you think of the testing stereotype threat hypothesis? Considerable research is currently engaged in examining the implications of this for classroom practice and you might want to review the Sackett, Hardison and Cullen, and Steele and Aronson articles in the recommended readings for some insights into this.

Are there effective means of alleviating test anxiety?

There will always be a number of students in your care who are anxious about evaluation. It is important that you identify and address the source of their anxiety before motivation to achieve becomes seriously affected. Knowing that for highly test anxious students grading and testing may reduce their performance or even debilitate them, you need to consider the matter of assessment carefully.

Effective reduction of anxiety involves the use of coping strategies to remove or circumvent the cause of stress and to deal with the reactions and emotions that are experienced. Coping strategies can be categorised in three ways (Zeidner 1995; see also Warren 2000):

1 *Problem-focused* coping, which tries to manage or solve the problem by dealing with the source of the stress in a positive way (for example, through planning, collecting resources, studying hard).

2 *Emotion-focused* coping, which tries to reduce the emotional symptoms associated with stress (for example, talking to friends to gain reassurance, crying, denying the importance of the situation).

3 *Avoidance-oriented* coping, which tries to avoid the stressful situation (for example, by isolating oneself from others, wasting time on irrelevant tasks, watching television excessively).

The evidence is clear that, while emotion-focused or avoidance coping might help the individual to keep an emotional balance for a short time, they may become maladaptive or even dysfunctional over time (Wills 1986). There are plenty of examples of the negative long-term effects of ventilation of emotions, mental disengagement, binge eating, and the use of tension-relieving substances such as alcohol and drugs where the maladaptive nature of such coping strategies becomes evident (Carver, Scheier & Weintraub 1989).

With important tests or exams the stressor cannot be removed. However, the perceived threat that it poses can be reduced by planning a study schedule, increasing study time, and working with a friend or parent to revise important material. Such coping strategies are adaptive in that they are problem focused and provide a sense of mastery over the stressor. This sense of personal control over the situation changes the perspective, diverting attention in a positive direction. It also helps to reduce the physiological and emotional reactions that initially build up at the anticipatory stage: 'What am I going to do to cope? There are all these demands on me.'

One method of helping students for whom the test situation is debilitating is to reduce the perceived threat of evaluation. Covington and Omelich (1987), for example, provided opportunities for students to resit an exam with unlimited time in which to complete answers. They found that, for students who were well prepared, this opportunity disinhibited anxiety and allowed original learning to be effectively retrieved. Not surprisingly, for those who were poorly prepared (although anxious) the disinhibition did not improve performance.

Bandura believes an individual's perceived coping self-efficacy regulates anxiety arousal. The stronger people's belief that they can cope, the bolder they are in taking on threatening situations (Bandura 1993). Students who have a low sense of efficacy at managing academic demands are especially vulnerable to achievement anxiety. Bandura suggests that the best way of alleviating this is to develop in students cognitive capabilities and self-regulative skills for managing academic task demands and self-debilitating thoughts.

Researchers distinguish between **failure-avoiding** and **failure-accepting** students. Students who are failure avoiding (highly anxious with good study skills) are motivated to achieve in order to maintain their sense of personal value which is judged by external performance. However, they are anxious that if they fail despite all their efforts, they will be seen as lacking in ability. On the other hand, students who fail repeatedly because of poor study skills will be anxious but failure accepting, believing that their failure is an indication of low ability. Over time, such students will become resigned to defeat, having little or no motivation to achieve, akin to learned helplessness (Abramson, Seligman & Teasdale 1978).

Researchers interested in the effects of the testing stereotype threat discussed earlier have listed some recommendations for alleviating test anxiety. These include: inoculating students against stereotype threat by emphasising improvement rather than competitive achievement; emphasising ability as a malleable rather than fixed trait; using group work; and emphasising effort rather than ability. These are all in line with the suggestions made above. Essentials of reducing student anxiety are presented in Table 11.10.

Final phase of preparation for an exam.

Sociocultural aspects of measurement and evaluation

You will recall from Chapter 3 the difficulties inherent in making intelligence testing fair, particularly when intelligence tests are used in diverse cultural and social settings. Indeed, many authorities argue that intelligence tests are inherently biased in favour of individuals from the dominant culture in which the tests were designed. Most often this means those from a white, middle-class background. The same issue applies to measurement and evaluation. Measurement and its evaluation can be inherently biased against students from minority groups, particularly for those for whom English is a second language (Abedi, Hofstetter & Lord 2004; Solano-Flores & Trumbull 2003; see also Sackett, Schmitt, Ellingson & Kabin 2001). Poor performance in achievement tests at school may be the product of a range of social and cultural background factors. These might include poverty, poor resources at home and/or at school, absenteeism due to work, domestic or social duties, mismatch between the language and culture of the home and school, gender bias and discrimination (Gipps 1999). We considered a number of these factors in Chapter 10. Despite its declared purpose to enhance student learning and life chances, measurement and evaluation may actually limit the life opportunities of minority students who perform badly in tests and assignments that are used to sort and rank and control access to further education and the professions (see, for example, Gama & Meyrelles de Jesus 2001; Gipps 1999; Sackett, Schmitt, Ellingson & Kabin 2001). Measurement and evaluation must therefore be culturally and socially sensitive if it is to perform its legitimate function, not restrict the opportunities of students from diverse backgrounds. For this reason, alternative forms of measurement and evaluation discussed above might be more appropriate in diverse settings than standardised tests and measurements (Sackett, Schmitt, Ellingson & Kabin 2001). What do you think?

Reporting student achievement

In Teaching Competence Box 11.4 the importance of recording and reporting on student progress and achievement is highlighted. In the following sections we provide you with some guidelines to assist in implementing the indicators of this competence.

Communicating information to parents on children's achievement is not easy, and no one appears to have developed the perfect system. Verbal descriptions (such as the wonderful one-liners teachers write to sum up students' performance in mathematics or language over a period of 12 months) have an obvious limitation! Simple

Table 11.10 **Essentials of reducing student anxiety**

Teachers should:

- teach effective study habits to students and review them periodically;
- teach relaxation techniques;
- utilise desensitisation strategies such as exposure to 'mock' exam situations, as appropriate;
- reduce time pressures in evaluative situations;
- de-emphasise the evaluative nature of the task in test situations. Emphasise the nature of the task and self-evaluation (relative to previous performance) rather than competition and student–student comparison;
- whenever possible, give students feedback on their performance that is task related (such as comments) rather than ego related (such as grades and praise). In this way, intrinsic motivation will be fostered and concerns about self-worth will be minimised;
- provide opportunities for overstriving (well-prepared), anxious students to meet as a group with the teacher to share concerns. Often this reassurance will reduce anxiety considerably;
- provide models of anxious individuals engaging in successful task-completion strategies;
- provide more organised instructional material for highly anxious students.

Teachers should teach learners to:

- recognise signs of anxiety such as negative self-talk ('I can't do this'; 'I'm going to fail'), fearfulness, irritability, avoidance and worry;
- practise positive self-talk ('I can do this if I try/ask for more help/work harder/manage my time better/don't allow myself to be distracted');
- learn and use relaxation techniques: deep breathing, muscle contraction and relaxation, brisk exercise, conscious 'emptying' of mind and focusing on a positive image;
- set short-term achievable goals rather than global, long-term goals;
- learn study skills (from teachers, friends, books) and reward yourself with special privileges when you practise them successfully;
- practise working to a time limit for some tasks;
- ask the teacher for feedback on their work;
- talk to others who tend to be anxious and share their worries; talk to their teacher about their concerns; listen to others' advice;
- confide in significant adults (parents or other family members) and encourage them to show interest in their work.

(Source: Based on Butler 1987; Nicholls 1984; Sarason 1972, 1975; Wigfield & Eccles 1989)

Theory and research into practice

Sid Bourke — QUALITY OF SCHOOL LIFE

BRIEF BIOGRAPHY

My first employment in education was as a secondary mathematics teacher, followed by an appointment as education officer in the Australian Army where I first learned assessment skills in my role as a training consultant. During that time I undertook a study of the effect of frequent school changes (student mobility) on student achievement—in the main there seemed to be little achievement effect, but perhaps we should have been looking more at student affect. I moved from the Army to become a chief research officer at the Australian Council for Educational Research (ACER) where I directed the first national program of literacy and numeracy assessment—the Australian Studies in School Performance. During 11 years at the ACER I also developed and conducted a national oracy skills assessment project, the second national assessment of student progress in literacy and numeracy and subsequently the Australian component of the International Classroom Environment Study (CES). The CES was concerned with identifying teaching practices that were related to high student achievement. It was during the CES that I first developed an interest in the measurement of affective outcomes of schooling, initially primary student attitudes to mathematics, and later student perceptions of the quality of their lives at school. This new interest for me initially supplemented my work on cognitive assessment, but increasingly supplanted it. I then took an academic position in the Faculty of Education at the University of Newcastle, where I have now remained for almost 20 years. Over this period I have taught research methodology at undergraduate and postgraduate levels, with a focus on quantitative methods. I have also supervised the completion of more than 20 research Master's and Ph.D. projects across a range of areas, and it is this that sustains me academically—keeping up with these interesting and talented people, most of them part-time students who simultaneously maintain a full-time school or university teaching post or other educational administrative position.

RESEARCH AND THEORETICAL INTERESTS

Quality of school life

About 25 years ago, students' perception of the quality of their school life (QSL) was identified as an increasingly important aspect of schooling—a desired outcome being that students enjoy, or at least do not dislike, their time at school. We argued that, regardless of any spin-off effects on student achievement that it might have, student QSL was an important educational and life outcome in itself. Following the development by colleagues at the ACER of a questionnaire for assessing secondary student QSL, we found it was soon also being used in primary schools. This was not appropriate, given the questionnaire's secondary focus, but it was being used because the concept was valued by many principals and teachers and there was no similar instrument designed for primary-age students. Consequently, I developed a form of the instrument specifically for primary students, assessing two general scales (general satisfaction and negative affect) and five specific aspects of school life (satisfaction with relationships with their teacher, with their achievement, opportunity, social integration within the school, and a sense of adventure in learning). An indicator of the validity of the questionnaire which was intended to distinguish between different school experiences, is that student views of their life at school are not closely related to their personal and background characteristics, but are apparently more strongly related to their actual individual, class and whole-school experiences.

Over the past 15–20 years, the QSL questionnaires have been used by researchers, research students, teachers and school administrators in several Australian states and overseas, in many cases as an additional measure of school program effectiveness—that is, additional to cognitive achievement measures. The NSW DET has developed on-line forms of the QSL questionnaires and assists schools to use, analyse and interpret the results for school reporting and other purposes, for example, evaluating the effects of student welfare programs. At the time of writing, work is being undertaken by this department to develop both the questionnaires further by adding new scales. Although they have been found to be extremely useful in a wide range of settings, the QSL instruments are now about 20 years old, and some redevelopment would seem to be appropriate.

Class size

Using data previously gathered for the Classroom Environment Study, one of my briefer research forays looked into relationships of class size with cognitive achievement for students in the upper primary school. I was concerned not simply with establishing the existence of a relationship between class size and achievement, but with how such a relationship might operate. For 63 classes ranging from 12 to 33 students, teaching practices that mediated the effects of class size on student mathematics achievement were identified. Practices related to grouping, the amount and nature of teacher–student interactions including teacher questioning behaviour (probing and wait time), homework practices and classroom noise levels tolerated. It is interesting that the benefits of smaller classes seem to be clearly established by carefully designed research, but class size has never really been satisfactorily resolved as an issue. It is also interesting that an additional analysis I did with the same data found that teaching practices associated with smaller classes had a greater impact on student liking for mathematics than they had on achievement.

Research methodology

Arising out of the QSL assessments and earlier work, Lorin Anderson and I published a text designed to assist researchers and other educators in selecting or developing questionnaires, and analysing the data obtained from them, with an emphasis on creating reliable and valid affective scales (Anderson & Bourke 2000). This publication relates to my interest in developing procedures to assist researchers and research students, who are not measurement specialists, to obtain the maximum from their quantitative data. To this end, the analyses recommended and described in this monograph are relatively simple.

Many studies and their associated analyses undertaken in education and other social sciences need to recognise the sample clustering effect of students in classes and classes in schools. Because of the applied nature of educational research, we tend to work with intact classes or other groupings (for example, teachers and students in schools), and it is rare that we select simple random samples for our studies. This should be recognised in the ways in which we analyse our data. In this respect, I have developed and taught procedures for moving scale development from simple factor analysis to check construct validity and simple regression analyses, to structural equation modelling and scale inclusion in multilevel regression analyses. It is generally accepted that there is a dearth of quantitative researchers in education—certainly in Australia. A significant part of my role as a quantitative methodologist is the training of research students at least to understand these techniques, and how to implement them appropriately when novice or even experienced researchers wish to use quantitative methods in their research.

One advantage of being a research methodologist (of whatever inclination) is the opportunity to work with research students and other researchers on a wider range of project areas than would otherwise be the case. I am currently working with one Ph.D. student on reading in the infants school, with another on possible links between student and teacher satisfaction and student achievement in the upper primary school, and with a third on managerial and leadership concomitants of effective secondary schools—but, in the last project, first we had to define and assess school effectiveness. Of course, other subject-matter experts are also directly involved with these students.

THEORY AND RESEARCH INTO PRACTICE

Although my interest in affective outcomes of schooling continues, particularly in conjunction with the projects of several of my research students, more recently I have focused my own research on the research process and its impact, and on research training. As part of a team commissioned by the Federal Education Department, I was involved in a study of the impact of educational research on schools and schooling which included universities, professional associations, postgraduate students, school principals and departmental administrators as informants (Holbrook *et al.* 2000). This study mapped the educational research being undertaken in Australian universities on a range of criteria, including content area. One finding from this study was the extent to which educational research in Australia depended on the work of research students in the universities—these students were responsible for most of the research undertaken. Another finding was the crucial nature of the role of postgraduate students as initiators and mediators of research and research applications in schools. Most postgraduates were usually part-time students while maintaining their positions as teachers or education administrators in school systems, and their mediation role was clearly recognised by school principals and departmental officials.

Continuing with the theme of research and research training, I am currently involved in a number of studies concerned with various aspects of Ph.D. candidature and examination. Team research in education particularly, and in the social sciences generally, is becoming increasingly important, because it facilitates multidisciplinary and mixed methods research which is increasingly seen as necessary in adequately addressing complex educational and social issues. In recognition of these needs, a research centre for the Study of Research Training and Impact (SORTI) was set up at the University of Newcastle in 2000. As a member of SORTI, I am one of a small team currently undertaking a national mixed-methods study of relationships of candidate, supervisor and examiner characteristics with the detailed content of examiner reports and their recommendations on theses. This study includes all discipline areas across eight universities, with information from 800 Ph.D. candidates and more than 2100 examiners who examined their theses. Thesis quality is assessed following an analysis of the text coding of the examiner reports. Although the study is not complete at the time of writing, I can say that we are obtaining interesting findings about completion times as well as thesis quality (Bourke *et al.* 2004). For example, contrary to many other claims about

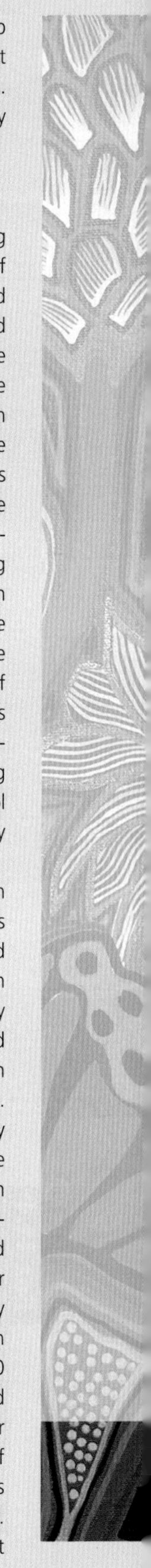

completion times, our large study indicates that, in general, 'candidacy time' as measured by actual enrolment time after adjusting for full-time and part-time candidature, does not differ substantially by discipline area. It might seem surprising that calculating a sensible measure of candidacy time is not a trivial exercise, but this has been largely lacking in research to date.

Three other ongoing SORTI studies focus on the level of and reasons for research candidate attrition, on developing and analysing the content of research candidate annual reporting to maximise information flow with a view to facilitating completion, and on the different nature of candidature and examination in fine art. Fine art, along with other creative disciplines, is distinguished from most other disciplines by the normal requirement for research degree examination to include assessment of an exhibition (or performance, and so on) in addition to a thesis or exegesis.

The ultimate aim of our work in the areas of research training and impact is to improve the quality of research training, to the benefit of the individual and the nation, and to facilitate the impact of research on the Australian social and economic scene. For further information on SORTI objectives and projects, see the web page http://www.newcastle.edu.au/centre/sorti.

KEY REFERENCES

Anderson, L. & Bourke, S. (2000) *Assessing Affective Characteristics in the Schools*, 2nd ed. Mahwah, NJ: Lawrence Erlbaum.

Bourke, S., Holbrook, A., Lovat, T. & Farley, P. (2004) Attrition, completion and completion times of Ph.D. candidates. Paper presented at the Annual Conference of the Australian Association for Research in Education, Melbourne, November–December. AARE website, www.aare.edu.au, January 2005.

Holbrook, A., Ainley, J., Bourke, S., Owen, J., McKenzie, P., Misson, S. & Johnson, T. (2000) Mapping educational research and its impact on Australian schools (pp. 15–278). In *The Impact of Educational Research*. Canberra: Department of Education, Training & Youth Affairs.

ACTIVITIES

1 In this chapter we have considered many issues related to measurement and evaluation. Among these issues, although not nearly so emphasised as other areas, is the measurement and evaluation of the affective area of learning. Sid Bourke has a considerable interest in the affective outcomes of schooling. Why is this important, and how has Sid Bourke gone about investigating the issue?

2 Sid Bourke talks about quality of school life as an important component of school effectiveness. Reflect on your experiences as a student and compare these with others. What are the essential elements of good-quality school life, and what elements may inhibit quality of school life?

3 Review the QSL questionnaires. What are their essential components? How would you use them to supplement and inform your teaching?

4 Two issues that have also occupied Sid Bourke's research interest are class size and its impact on effective learning, and improving research methodologies and training in education. Select one of these topics for further study and prepare a report outlining some of the key concerns and findings from your reading.

Box 11.4

TEACHING COMPETENCE

The teacher maintains records of student progress and reports on student progress to parents and others responsible for the care of students

Indicators

The teacher:

- designs a recording system of appropriate detail and utility;
- records assessment outcomes accurately and consistently;
- adheres to principles of confidentiality;
- provides detailed, accurate and comprehensible reports on progress;
- uses assessment and reporting procedures consistent with school policies;
- prepares information to meet certification requirements.

Case studies illustrating National Competency Framework for Beginning Teaching, National Project on the Quality of Teaching and Learning, Australian Teaching Council, 1996, Elements 4.4 and 4.5, pp. 58–9.

raw scores (such as 15 marks out of 20) communicate an element of information but fail to indicate whether this shows effective mastery of material or relative performance. Rankings indicate where a student lies relative to the rest of a group, but fail to indicate what the student's starting point was and how much individual progress characterised the student's performance.

All schools have a policy that guides their reporting on student evaluation. Reports can be **formative**, when parents and others are progressively kept up to date on their children's performance. This can be informal, such as a merit card being sent home reporting a good achievement in a project or a quick word to a parent in the playground after school. At other times formative reporting might be more formal, such as systematic reports written by the teacher in a homework book or student diary. Cumulative records, kept by teachers and students on students' work, also serve as an effective means of plotting how a student is performing at any particular time. These records are useful for writing up summative reports.

Summative reports are usually in the form of written reports and parent–teacher interviews which summarise, in a more formal way, a student's achievement. Summative reports usually occur at the end of each term or biannually. Unfortunately, no one has yet invented the

This folder gives you a comprehensive report on your child's progress in each of the six key learning areas and on his/her attitude towards school. Please read it carefully and discuss it frankly and sympathetically with your child.

Key: **Effort**	**Achievement/Grade**
O Outstanding	O Outstanding
H High	H High
S Satisfactory	S Satisfactory
L Low	L Low
M Minimal	E Experiencing Difficulty
	I Individual Program

ENGLISH: Reading Writing Listening Speaking

Comments..
....
....
....
....
....
....

☐ Effort ☐ Achievement

English	Level	Effort
Oral Reading		
Comprehension		
Spelling		
Written Communication		
Handwriting		
Talking		
Listening		

English General Comment

Mathematics		
Space		
Measurement		
Number		

Mathematics General Comment

Science		
Computers		
Social Studies		
Health & Personal Dev.		
Physical Education		
Music		
Visual Arts		
Craft		
Drama		

Comment

Level Attained Code
A - Outstanding **C** - Satisfactory
B - High **D** - Low

Assessed Effort Code
A - Outstanding **C** - Satisfactory
B - High **D** - Low

Class ____ **Year** ____ **Days Absent** ____

Social Development		**Work Habits**	
Shows consideration for the rights of others		Listens attentively	
Is polite and courteous		Follows instructions	
Mixes well with other children		Works co-operatively in a group	
Obeys class and school rules		Is reliable	
Accepts constructive criticism		Able to work independently	
Exercises self control		Participates in class activities	
Displays self confidence		Completes set tasks	
Adjusts easily to new situations		Seeks help when required	
Is punctual		Takes pride in work	
Readily accepts responsibility for tasks		Is prepared and organised	
Respects their own and others' property		Completes homework	

Code for Social Development and Work Habits
A - Consistently **B** - Sometimes **C** - Rarely

Teacher's Comment

Teacher ____

Supervisor ____

Principal ____

December 1993

NAME ....

ACHIEVEMENT/GRADE		**EFFORT**	
O	Outstanding	**O**	Outstanding
H	High	**H**	High
S	Satisfactory	**S**	Satisfactory
L	Low	**L**	Low
E	Experiencing Difficulty	**M**	Minimal
F	Follows an Individual Program		

ENGLISH **EFFORT** ❑

....

....

....

....

....

....

Achievement ❑

MATHEMATICS **EFFORT** ❑

....

....

....

....

....

....

Achievement ❑

SCIENCE & TECHNOLOGY **EFFORT** ❑

....

....

....

....

....

HUMAN SOCIETY & ITS ENVIRONMENT **EFFORT** ❑

....

....

....

....

....

CREATIVE & PRACTICAL ARTS **EFFORT** ❑

....

....

....

....

....

P.D./HEALTH/P.E. **EFFORT** ❑

....

....

....

....

....

Level Attained Code

A Outstanding Achievement

These students accomplish with ease all of the objectives of the subject that are relevant to their Year. They complete assigned tasks accurately and promptly without need of further assistance from their teacher or peers. Their work frequently shows that they can take the understandings and skills taught in class and develop them further without additional help from the teacher, and it occasionally shows a unique flair or inventiveness.

B High Achievement

These students accomplish nearly all of the objectives of the subject that are relevant to their Year. They complete most assigned tasks accurately and promptly without need of further assistance from their teacher or peers. Their work sometimes shows that they can take the understandings and skills taught in class and develop them further without any additional help from the teacher.

C Satisfactory Achievement

These students accomplish many of the objectives of the subject that are relevant to their Year. They complete many assigned tasks, though not always accurately or promptly, and they sometimes need further assistance from their teacher or peers. Their work occasionally shows that they can take the understandings and skills taught in class and develop them further without additional help from the teacher.

D Low Achievement

These students accomplish a few of the objectives of the subject that are relevant to their Year. They sometimes complete assigned tasks without assistance from their teacher or peers. Their work shows little sign that they can take the understandings and skills taught in class and develop them further without additional help from the teacher.

Effort Code

A Outstanding Application

These student attempt all set tasks and seek assistance when they encounter difficulties. They participate fully and enthusiastically in all whole and small group activities, either as leaders or as supportive followers, and they frequently suggest ideas. They assist other members of the class or school willingly and spontaneously.

B High Application

These students generally attempt the set tasks and either seek assistance, or freely accept it, when they encounter difficulties. They participate fully in all whole and small group activities, either as leaders or as supportive followers, and they often suggest ideas. They willingly assist other members of the class or school if requested.

C Satisfactory Application

These students attempt most of set tasks. They accept assistance when they encounter difficulties, and sometimes seek it. They participate in most whole and small group activities, either as leaders or as supportive followers, and they occasionally suggest ideas. They assist other members of the class or school if requested.

D Low Application

These students attempt some of the assigned tasks but they make reluctant attempts or no attempt to complete others. They rarely seek assistance when they encounter difficulties, and are unenthusiastic about accepting it when it is offered; or they make excessive demands for assistance. They participate in few whole and small group activities. They rarely suggest ideas for classroom activities and are reluctant to help others.

	JUNE				NOVEMBER			
PERSONAL DEVELOPMENT	1	2	3	4	1	2	3	4
Completes work on time								
Takes pride in work								
Participates in activities								
Works independently								
Cooperates with others								
Shows initiative								
Accepts responsibility for own actions								
Shows self control								

November: Position in Grade.

English 0 — 25 — 50 — 75 — 100

Maths 0 — 25 — 50 — 75 — 100

• Your child's position indicates X

Teacher comment: (June) ______________________________

____

____

Class Teacher........................ Supervisor ....

Parent comment: ______________________________

____

____

(November) ______________________________

____

Class Teacher........................ Supervisor ....

1 Consistently
2 Usually
3 Sometimes
4 Rarely

KEY 1 = Consistently 2 = Usually 3 = Rarely

Living Skills			
Cares for own property			
Displays self-confidence			
Mixes well with other children			
Respects property of others			
Displays tolerance			
Displays self control and self discipline			
Is courteous and well-mannered to peers			

Study Skills			
Works independently			
Co-operates in group work			
Responds positively in help and correction			
Listens and carries out instructions			
Begins work promptly			
Completes set tasks			
Takes pride in bookwork			
Is well organised			

GENERAL COMMENTS

____

____

____

DAYS ABSENT ....

INTERVIEW REQUESTED YES/NO

CLASS TEACHER ....

PRINCIPAL ....

perfect report card that effectively communicates to the appropriate audiences what the student has actually achieved. The examples shown present a sample of report cards for you to consider. What do you see as the strengths and weaknesses of each in terms of what has been discussed throughout this chapter?

'Oh, good. Your mid-year reports are in. I wonder how I rated on the Homework and Project items this term?'

Two types of written report are commonly used—one that relays normative information to parents regarding the relative performance of their child in various learning areas, and one that relates a child's performance to specific criteria of achievement.

When we were in primary school, report cards were considerably different from report cards of today. Listed on the reports were our raw score marks in each of the 'important' subjects, a rank position in that subject (such as 1st out of 40, 15th out of 40), and an overall ranking in class based on some cumulation of the raw scores within a subject and across subjects.

While the emphasis on overall place in class has diminished, parents are still very keen to find out how well their children are doing relative to the rest of the class. The most common way of presenting normative reports today is still through raw scores or percentages, which are sometimes converted to letter grades. Often grades are awarded according to a predetermined distribution that loosely reflects the normal curve. In other words, few high and low grades are awarded in comparison with a large number of 'average' grades. The primary purpose of this system of grading is to show how a particular student performs relative to their peers. Unfortunately, this system means that there are only a few who can really feel very successful, a large number who may feel adequate, and a number, who by virtue of the system, must feel failures. There is also a problem with cut-offs for the allocation of grades. Is it defensible to award an A to one student and a B or C to another when the difference between their scores may be marginal at the cut-off points? Under such circumstances we are really putting a lot of unwarranted faith in the accuracy of our measurement. No doubt some of you can recall being 'unfairly' graded on the curve.

While written comments such as 'Ned has worked well this term and is a pleasant boy to teach' may be used to cushion the effect of a low ranking, we all know that the parents' eyes home in on the significant information: 33rd out of 35 students. Norm-referenced reporting, in general, does not indicate how much a particular student has learned relative to their starting point, simply where they stand relative to the group. Indeed, some critics suggest that standardised assessments measure socio-economic status, innate ability and non-instructionally related material, and thus yield little valid information about student achievement (Abedi, Hofstetter & Lord 2004). If a pre-test and post-test format is used for the norm-based assessment, a report can include details on how well an individual has improved over the course of instruction.

The way in which some teachers cumulate raw scores from a diverse set of tasks, without regard to weighting and standardising scores, makes the whole procedure of 'norm-referencing' quite invalid. Few teachers graduate from their training with sufficient skills in measurement to implement such a system (Crooks 1988; Gullickson 1985; Stiggins 1985; Wright & Wiese 1988).

To overcome one limitation in norm-referenced reports—namely, the lack of qualitative information on the student's performance—some reports use a dual system of reporting. On one page teachers report the raw scores, percentages or letter grades for students in key learning areas, and on the opposite page they report a judgment of effort based on a teacher's estimation of the student's ability relative to achievement. There are two problems with this system. First, it is very difficult to measure ability and effort. Second, unless the achievement mark and effort (or attitude) grades coincide reasonably well, the achievement mark would carry more weight in most homes (Withers & Cornish 1985).

QUESTION POINT

Teachers often assume that grading cannot be avoided. Is there a practicable alternative to grading?

Criterion-referenced reporting systems indicate how a student has performed against specific criteria. Reports will typically have a code indicating that the student has met an objective, is on the way to meeting the objective, or has not mastered the objective. There is no attempt to average scores across assignments for the one student, or to average scores across students; indeed, there is essentially no comparison of one student with another. When grades are awarded, they are in terms of number of objectives achieved rather than relative performance. Consequently, in contrast to norm-referenced measurement and evaluation, there is no limit to the number of students who can achieve at any particular grade level.

As we have all experienced, reports are written to parents, and the main person involved—the student—is always referred to in the third person. There is a strong argument that reports should be written primarily to the students themselves (Docking 1984). Table 11.11 lists the advantages of this system. Many schools are adapting this approach with considerable success. What do you think about such a reporting system?

Should reports be written to the student?

If anything, the complexities of measurement and evaluation, as well as the potential effects on student learning and motivation, should teach us to be humble, flexible and cautious in the way we use measurement results. As a final point, considerations of privacy and accountability are increasingly being included as essential elements of the data-gathering, storing and reporting process. You must make yourself aware of all ethical principles that apply to measurement and evaluation in your educational setting.

QUESTION POINT

Consider the above information. Do you think reports should be written to students or their parents?

ACTION STATION

Review a number of school measurement and evaluation policies. Can the goals of evaluation listed in Table 11.8 be identified in the policies? If particular purposes are not readily identifiable, discuss why.

ACTION STATION

A number of models of report cards are presented on pages 409–11. As a group, design your own report card which reflects what the group believes is the current thinking on appropriate reporting. Justify your report form by referring to principles of measurement and evaluation covered in this chapter.

Table 11.11 A comparison of student-oriented and parent-oriented reports

A comparison of student-oriented and parent-oriented reports
Student-oriented reports
• Student-oriented reports make clear to the students that they are learning for their own sake, not for the benefit or pleasure of their parent(s). • Student-oriented reports make clear that the learning process is a personal interaction between the learner and the resources (including the teacher), not a public exhibition. • Student-oriented reports can be more specific and forward-looking as the feedback can relate to particular learning strengths and weaknesses with the prospect of further work to enhance performance. • Student-oriented reports are easier for teachers to write as they are writing to someone known and in terms that should be more meaningful, precise and with less chance of misunderstanding. • The child at school is often a different person from the child at home, and student-oriented reports give the child the opportunity to break free from family attitudes and constraints. • The reader of the student-oriented report is an expert who is well informed about the school, needs the feedback the most, and can do most with the information.
Parent-oriented reports
• Parent-oriented reports encourage competitiveness, since they are public and very often norm-referenced. • Parents are powerless to do anything with the information given in a parent-oriented report, whereas students can act on the information. • The parent may have language difficulties that make the report meaningless. • The information written for parents is often abused by parents, who use the material to put their children down, punish or bribe them. • Teachers sometimes misuse the report form as a threat to 'motivate' their students, warning children that they will get a bad report that will disappoint their parents, or as a bribe to get on the right side of students. Student-oriented reports can be honest and motivating without invoking fear or favouritism. • The parent-oriented report often takes on much more authority and significance than it deserves because parents take it at face value as a definitive statement of their child's progress. A student-oriented report is less likely to assume the exaggerated authority traditional reports usually acquire. • The parents can learn all they need to know from a student-oriented report and probably experience some sense of relief that the school is not laying on their shoulders responsibilities they cannot fulfil, and also a sense of pride that their child is able to be responsible for their own development.
(Source: Based on Docking 1984)

WHAT WOULD YOU DO?

IT DIDN'T SEEM LIKE A TEST

Dianne had worked very hard to capture the interest of her Year 3 charges in a topic on dinosaurs. Although this was one of the lower-ability classes in the school, Dianne was pleased to find that the students became really motivated and extended by related topics such as palaeontology, carnivores and extinction. As the topic drew to a close, Dianne was faced with the task of reporting the progress of the students to parents. She was anxious for the assessment to reflect the involvement of the students and the learning that she felt sure had taken place.

'This was one of the lower-ability classes and they worked so hard. I didn't want to make the test too difficult but really I wanted to show the parents what the children had actually done.'

Case studies illustrating National Competency Framework for Beginning Teaching, National Project on the Quality of Teaching and Learning, Australian Teaching Council, 1996, p. 29. Commonwealth of Australia copyright, reproduced by permission.

What would you do? Now read what the teacher did.

WHAT WOULD YOU DO? (cont.)

IT DIDN'T SEEM LIKE A TEST

Rather than use a designated 'test day', Dianne adopted a strategy to integrate the assessment into the actual lesson. Using the words and the terms that she had used in the class and verbal prompts for some of her poorer readers, she asked the students to respond to questions such as 'Why do you think the dinosaurs became extinct?' and 'What does a palaeontologist do?' Dianne was very pleased that the students responded with some high-standard imaginative work.

'I was worried at first about what the parents might think about asking all these difficult questions. But the answers were really terrific. The students drew these pictures of how they thought the dinosaurs became extinct with bits of dust in the air blotting out the sun. I was really impressed.'

Dianne found that her strategy of integrating the test with the classwork and backing her judgment about the students' ability had paid off.

'I found that because I had captured their interest in the first place, when I tested them it didn't seem like a test. They really got involved in the answering of the questions and I got some lovely compliments from the parents.'

Case studies illustrating National Competency Framework for Beginning Teaching, National Project on the Quality of Teaching and Learning, Australian Teaching Council, 1996, p. 29. Commonwealth of Australia copyright, reproduced by permission.

What aspects of good measurement and evaluation are demonstrated in this case study? What other assessment strategies could have been used?

KEY TERMS

Affective domain (p. 387): in learning, related to feelings, attitudes and values

Alternative assessment (p. 391): activities that attempt to situate the assessment within 'real' contexts of learning and involve construction of knowledge, disciplined enquiry and value of the achievement beyond school

Anxiety (p. 402): feelings of uneasiness and tension

Attention-interference theory (p. 402): students find it hard to focus attention on the tasks because of self-doubts and task-irrelevant thoughts

Authentic assessment (p. 391): measurement of important abilities using procedures that simulate the application of these abilities to real life

Co-evaluation (p. 398): evaluation shared between teacher and students

Cognitive domain (p. 387): in Bloom's taxonomy, dealing with thinking and knowing

Content validity evidence (p. 377): choosing assessment items from the appropriate domain

Criterion validity evidence (p. 377): comparing results with other evidence for consistency

Criterion-referenced measurement and evaluation (p. 382): comparing an individual's achievement with criteria of performance

Equivalence (p. 377): the reliability that results when two equivalent or parallel forms of the same test are administered to a group at about the same time and the scores are related

Essay tests and assignments (p. 389): a form of measurement in an extended-response format that tests ability to organise and express ideas, and to defend arguments
Evaluation (p. 376): qualitative judgments on data
Face validity evidence (p. 377): making the test look right
Failure-accepting students (p. 404): students who fail repeatedly and come to accept their failures as a sign of low ability
Failure-avoiding students (p. 404): students who are motivated to achieve in order to maintain their sense of personal value when judged by external performance
Focused evaluation (p. 391): intensive evaluation of a student's development over a selected period of time
Formative measurement and evaluation (p. 380): continuous monitoring of the teaching learning process to ensure effectiveness
Formative reports (p. 409): reporting progressively on student progress throughout a learning sequence
Grading on the curve (p. 382): grades are distributed so that they follow a normal distribution
Information-processing skills theory (p. 402): in testing situations students' anxiety is produced through ineffective information-processing skills
Inter-marker reliability (p. 378): consistency between scores obtained from two markers
Internal consistency reliability (p. 377): scores on comparable halves of the test are similar
Journals and portfolios (p. 394): collections of students' work achievements
Mastery learning (p. 388): a teaching approach where students must learn one unit and pass a test at a specified level before moving to next unit
Measurement (p. 376): the process of collecting specific quantitative data
Norm-referenced measurement and evaluation (p. 381): comparing an individual's achievement to that of other students
Objective tests (p. 390): multiple choice, matching, or true or false items; reliability of marking enhanced
Oral presentations (p. 390): provide the opportunity for students to tell the examiner what they know
Peer evaluation (p. 397): student involvement in the evaluation of the work of other students
Practicals, simulated tasks and role plays (p. 390): measurement tasks that approximate what is required in the 'real' world
Projects (p. 390): extended practical work to encourage learning
Psychomotor domain (p. 387): in Bloom's taxonomy, dealing with action and physical development
Reliability (p. 377): consistency and stability of measures over time
Rubrics (p. 387): a table of instructional specifications to guide instruction and evaluation
Self-evaluation (p. 397): students are challenged to set learning goals and to evaluate their progress towards these goals
Short-answer questions (p. 390): short-response format measure to recall information
Simulated environments (p. 395): assessment programs that enable students to perform particular activities in a lifelike manner
Stability (p. 377): similar scores obtained on separate testings
Standardised tests (p. 378): tests that have been normed on large samples—an individual's score on the test is compared with the scores of the norming group
State anxiety (p. 402): an anxiety experienced in certain situations such as exams
Stereotype threat (p. 403): learning stereotypes (such as females are not good at mathematics) produce anxiety in individuals that they may confirm the stereotype—this anxiety then impacts on the level of performance
Summative measurement and evaluation (p. 381): determines whether learners have achieved learning objectives
Summative reports (p. 409): reporting on a student's achievement at the end of a learning sequence
Taxonomy of learning objectives (p. 386): a classification system for learning objectives—cognitive, affective and psychomotor
Test anxiety (p. 402): a state of anxiety about not performing well when being evaluated in a test situation
Testing stereotype threat (p. 403): involves the fear and anxiety produced when one feels one is in danger of fulfilling a negative stereotype about one's group
Trait anxiety (p. 402): a general anxiety that pervades much of what one does in life
Validity (p. 376): appropriateness of measure
Work sample assessments (p. 390): assessment based on performance at the actual tasks

ON-LINE LEARNING

If you go to http://www.pearsoned.com.au/mcinerney, you will have hot links directly to these sites:

- **Reporting assessment results**

Consider the suggestions made at the following website and relate them to the points made throughout Chapter 11.

http://www.ncrel.org/sdrs/areas/issues/methods/assment/as600.htm

- **What does research say about assessment?**

Discuss the points made in the following essay. What impact has constructivist approaches to learning and teaching had on measurement and assessment? Complete the activities section of the essay.

http://www.ncrel.org/sdrs/areas/stw_esys/4assess.htm

WEB DESTINATIONS

If you go to http://www.pearsoned.com.au/mcinerney, you will have hot links directly to these sites:

- **North Central Regional Educational Laboratory**

This site provides links to very useful information related to measurement and evaluation.

http://www.ncrel.org/sdrs/areas/as0cont.htm

- **CRESST**

The National Center for Research on Evaluation, Standards, and Student Testing maintains this site and you will find much useful information as well many useful links to other sites.

http://cresst96.cse.ucla.edu/resources/justforteachers_set.htm

RECOMMENDED READING

Abedi, J., Hofstetter, C. H. & Lord, C. (2004) Assessment accommodations for English language learners: Implications for policy-based empirical research. *Review of Educational Research*, **74**, 1–28.

Airasian, P. W. (1995) Classroom assessment. In L. W. Anderson (ed.) *International Encyclopedia of Teaching and Teacher Education*, 2nd ed. Tarrytown, NY: Pergamon.

Bloom, B. S., Hastings, J. T. & Madaus, G. F. (1971) *Handbook on Formative and Summative Evaluation of Learning*. New York: McGraw-Hill.

Delandshere, G. & Petrosky, A. R. (1998) Assessment of complex performances: Limitations of key measurement assumptions. *Educational Researcher*, **27**, 14–24.

Docking, R. A. (1984) Writing school reports. *Unicorn*, **10**, 332–48.

Docking, R. A. (1986) Norm-referenced measurement and criterion-referenced measurement: A descriptive comparison. *Unicorn*, **12**, 40–6.

Gipps, C. (1999) Socio-cultural aspects of assessment. *Review of Research in Education*, **24**, 355–92.

Griffin, P. & Nix, P. (1991) *Educational Assessment and Reporting. A New Approach*. Sydney: Harcourt Brace Jovanovich.

Gronlund, N. E. (1991) *How to Write and Use Instructional Objectives*. New York: Macmillan.

Guskey, T. R. (1995) Mastery learning. In L. W. Anderson (ed.) *International Encyclopedia of Teaching and Teacher Education*, 2nd ed. Tarrytown, NY: Pergamon.

Kouzma, N. M. & Kennedy, G. A. (2000) Academic stress, self-efficacy, social support, and health behaviours in female Victorian Certificate of Education (VCE) students. *The Australian Educational and Developmental Psychologist*, **17**, 24–43.

Mager, R. F. (1990a) *Measuring Educational Results*, 2nd ed. London: Kogan Page.

Mager, R. F. (1990b) *Preparing Educational Objectives*, 2nd ed. London: Kogan Page.

Moss, P. A. (1996) Enlarging the dialogue in educational measurement: Voices from interpretive research traditions. *Educational Researcher*, **25**, 20–8.

Paris, S. G. & Ayres, L. R. (1994) *Becoming Reflective Students and Teachers with Portfolios and Authentic Assessment*. Washington DC: American Psychological Association.

Phye, G. D. (ed.) (1997) *Handbook of Classroom Assessment. Learning, Adjustment, and Achievement*. San Diego, CA: Academic Press.

Sackett, P. R., Schmitt, N., Ellingson, J. E. & Kabin, M. B. (2001) High-stakes testing in employment, credentialing, and higher education. Prospects in a post-affirmative-action world. *American Psychologist*, **56**, 302–18.

Sackett, P. R., Hardison, C. M. & Cullen, M. J. (2004a) On interpreting stereotype threat as accounting for African American–White differences on cognitive tests. *American Psychologist*, **59**, 7–13.

Sackett, P. R., Hardison, C. M. & Cullen, M. J. (2004b) On the value of correcting mischaracterizations of stereotype threat research. *American Psychologist*, **59**, 48–9.

Shepard, L. (1993) Evaluating test validity. *Review of Research in Education*, **19**, 405–50.

Solano-Flores, G. & Trumbull, E. (2003) Examining language in context: The need for new research and practice paradigms in the testing of English-language learners. *Educational Researcher*, **32**, 3–13.

Steele, C. M. & Aronson, J. A. (2004) Stereotype threat does not live by Steele and Aronson (1995) alone. *American Psychologist,* **59**, 47–55.

Terwilliger, J. (1997) Semantics, psychometrics, and assessment reform: A close look at 'authentic' assessments. *Educational Researcher*, **26**, 24–7.

Terwilliger, J. S. (1998) Rejoinder: Response to Wiggins and Newmann. *Educational Researcher*, **27**, 22–3.

Warren, L. J. (2000) School-related stress and coping strategies in Victorian Year 11 students. *The Australian Educational and Developmental Psychologist,* **17**, 44–57.

Wiggins, G. (1989) A true test: Toward more authentic and equitable assessment. *Phi Delta Kappan*, **20**, 703–13.

Wiggins, G. (1998) An exchange of views on 'semantics, psychometrics, and assessment reform: A close look at "authentic" assessments'. *Educational Researcher*, **27**, 20–2.

Woodward, H. (1993) *Negotiated Evaluation*. Sydney: Primary English Teachers' Association.

PART 3

Understanding developmental needs of children and effective teaching and learning

CHAPTER

12 Learning and physical/motor development

Overview

In this chapter we examine issues related to physical and motor development and, especially, those features that are of most interest to teachers and parents. We consider the importance of physical activity from the broadest perspectives: to support the normal growth of individuals, to establish good life habits, and to facilitate the development of other systems (such as cognitive, social and personal) which are intrinsically entwined with the physical development of the person.

Topics covered in the first section of the chapter relate to cycles of physical development. In the second section, we look specifically at motor development in the light of four key principles: maturation, motivation, experience and practice. Individual and sex differences in both physical growth and motor development are highlighted.

Finally, we consider briefly a range of issues related to general physical health and safety issues with which teachers need to be familiar.

An accurate picture of developmental patterns is fundamental to an understanding of children, and a knowledge of what causes variations in development is essential to an understanding of each individual.

12

Learning objectives

After reading this chapter, you will be able to:

- describe patterns of physical and motor development from infancy through to adolescence and their implications for schooling;
- identify general principles of physical and motor development;
- give definitions of cephalocaudal and proximodistal development;
- define and give examples of asynchrony in development;
- relate physical growth and self-concept;
- give examples of eating disorders in childhood and adolescence;
- describe Sheldon's typology of body type, and critically examine the relationship between body type and opportunity for learning and development;
- identify elements of good physical health and the role the school environment has in fostering this.

The following Learner-centred Psychological Principle sets the scene for the last three chapters in our text, which deal with the developmental needs of children.

LEARNER-CENTRED PSYCHOLOGICAL PRINCIPLE

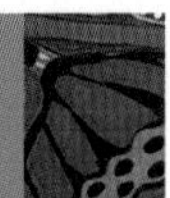

Developmental influences on learning. As individuals develop, there are different opportunities and constraints for learning. Learning is most effective when differential development within and across physical, intellectual, emotional and social domains is taken into account.

Individuals learn best when material is appropriate to their developmental level and is presented in an enjoyable and interesting way. Because individual development varies across intellectual, social, emotional and physical domains, achievement in different instructional domains may also vary. Overemphasis on one type of developmental readiness—such as reading readiness, for example—may preclude learners from demonstrating that they are more capable in other areas of performance. The cognitive, emotional and social development of individual learners and how they interpret life experiences are affected by prior schooling, home, culture and community factors. Early and continuing parental involvement in schooling, and the quality of language interactions and two-way communications between adults and children, can influence these developmental areas. Awareness and understanding of developmental differences among children with and without emotional, physical or intellectual disabilities can facilitate the creation of optimal learning contexts.

Principles of physical development

Orderly and sequential development

Physical and **motor development** from conception to adulthood is orderly and sequential. This regularity or continuity in development, impelled by genetic forces, is often referred to as **canalisation**. There are, however, particular periods of rapid growth and development (Brim & Kagan 1980; Garn 1980; Tanner 1990), as well as dramatic changes in individual growth and **maturation**

caused by the interaction between genetic and environmental forces that influence development (for example, caloric deprivation can slow growth, delay development and slow the end of adolescence) (Garn 1980; Tanner 1990). *Growth charts* (that is, graphs representing chronological norms of development for height, weight, skeletal structure, muscles, internal organs, the brain and the sexual system) are very useful for teachers, parents and other professionals involved in childcare, for four reasons (Malina & Bouchard 1991; Sinclair 1989; Tanner 1990):

1. Periods of peak human physical development can be identified. This is important information for matching diet, rest and exercise to the needs of children and adolescents at these times. Teachers dealing with children and adolescents can also be prepared for particular behavioural symptoms of rapid growth.
2. The order in which physical systems become operational can be identified. This is particularly important for scheduling curriculum activities so that they are presented at an optimal time in terms of students' development.
3. Comparisons can be made between the sexes in their growth to physical maturity. This allows questions to be answered about such issues as the appropriateness of particular physical activities for both sexes, the presentation of sex education courses, and the need for personal health and dietary information.
4. Children and adolescents can be evaluated in relation to the general developmental level of others their age and the ability and readiness to learn of the individual.

Cephalocaudal development and proximodistal development

Human growth proceeds in a cephalocaudal and proximodistal direction. *Cephalocaudal growth* refers to the development of physical and motor systems from the head down, while *proximodistal growth* refers to growth from the central axis of the body outward.

The human head (brain, sensory receptors) is one of the earliest systems to become functional. The human trunk is next in overall rate of growth, followed by the legs. Motor skills involving the use of the upper body develop before those using the lower body. Infants are capable of lifting their heads before they can lift their trunks, and then sit up and walk. This progression in physical and motor growth continues from conception to young adulthood and is called **cephalocaudal development**. Can you think of other examples?

The internal organs of the body, such as heart and lungs, develop and become operational before the development of the long limbs of the body, then fingers

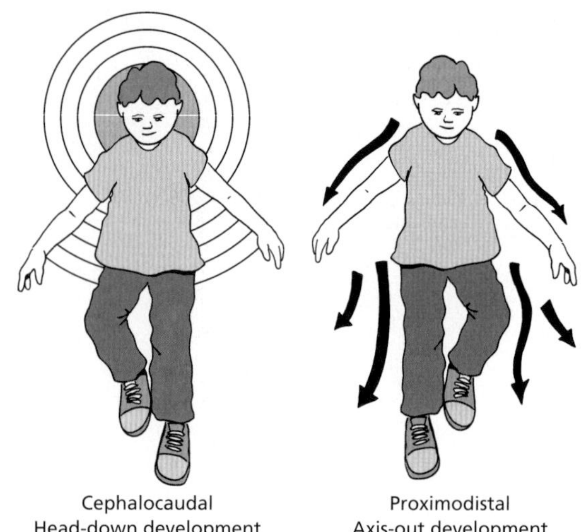

Figure 12.1

and toes, and the child's capacity to use their limbs. This is called **proximodistal development**. Infants, children and adolescents are capable of mastering skills requiring gross motor movements of the body before those requiring the use of fine, or peripheral, motor movement. Typically, we master the movement of shoulders and trunk before we master the use of hands and fingers.

QUESTION POINT

Recognising that children in educational settings (preschools and schools) are proceeding through physical changes at different rates, how might you, as a sensitive educator, take this into account when programming learning experiences?

Key characteristics of growth patterns

Growth patterns are frequently described in the following stages:

- prenatal development and the newborn;
- infancy: two months to two years;
- early childhood: two years to six years;
- middle and later childhood: seven years to puberty;
- adolescence: puberty to 18 years;
- adulthood.

These ages are only approximate. We will take a brief look at the physical and motor development that characterises each of these periods and draw out the implications for parents and teachers. We emphasise that many other developmental systems, such as the cognitive, emotional and personal developmental systems, develop hand-in-hand with the physical and motor systems. Indeed, they interact to such a degree that a separate examination of each is only useful as a schema around which to organise our ideas. A full picture of the growing person requires us to see the systems acting interactively (Brim & Kagan 1980; Brooks-Gunn & Warren 1989; Holt 1991; Malina 1990).

Prenatal development and the newborn

Early physical development

The nine months of pregnancy and the first few months of life are times of rapid growth (Bee 1992; Holt 1991; Turner & Helms 1991). During the 280-day gestation period, the child rapidly progresses from a fertilised egg engaged in cell division (often called the ovum or germinal period) to an *embryo* with organ systems developing, and then to a *foetus* which increasingly resembles a human being. The rate of growth may be appreciated when we realise that within four weeks of conception the organism has grown 10 000 times larger than the original fertilised egg, and that internal organs assume nearly adult positions by the fifth week.

The support systems necessary for life—heart, lungs, brain, nervous system and muscles—are sufficiently developed after 26 weeks (out of 40) for the foetus to survive outside the womb.

Newborn reflexes

At birth, the baby is born with a series of reflexes, such as the sucking and breathing reflexes, that are essential for the child's survival. (The newborn attaches to the mother's breast and sucks with great energy only hours after birth.) Other reflexes, such as the grasping and stepping reflexes, signal the effective operation of the child's nervous system. These reflexes are used by paediatricians at regular times to assess the physiological development of the child (Berk 1996, 1997; Holt 1991).

Birth problems that may affect development

During the prenatal and neonatal period, genetic or environmental influences may cause developmental problems for the baby which become manifest in delaying or limiting physical, motor and intellectual development. In particular, a range of *genetic diseases* (such as cystic fibrosis, phenylketonuria), *chromosomal abnormalities* (such as Down syndrome and Klinefelter syndrome), *birth complications* (such as oxygen deprivation—called *anoxia*), *drugs* taken by the mother during pregnancy (such as alcohol, nicotine, cocaine or heroin), maternal diseases passed on to the infant (such as AIDS), and malnourishment of the foetus and newborn have been shown to be related to later developmental problems. It is beyond the scope of this text to describe these in detail and you are referred to Berk (2004) for further details.

Infancy and early childhood

The first month after birth is a period during which the infant, often referred to as a *neonate*, learns to coordinate its body. The subsequent period is generally named *infancy* and lasts around two years. During infancy there is a lengthening of the lower limbs and, in general, the baby's body proportions become more adult-like. On average, the child gains about 9 kilograms in weight and 40 centimetres in height in the period between two months and two years. As a ready reckoner, by two years of age, females have achieved approximately half their adult height. By two and a half years, males have reached about half their adult height.

Major developmental tasks of infancy

One way of looking at physical and motor development is to consider a child's development against benchmarks of development. These benchmarks are often referred to as **developmental tasks**, the accomplishment of which marks a transition to a new stage of development (Havighurst 1959). Major developmental tasks of infancy relate to their rapidly developing motor skills and acquisition of early language. In particular, the infant learns to adjust to liquid and solid foods, to control the neck and shoulders, and to sit, reach and walk. There is also a development of fine muscle movement and the ability to grasp and hold with the fingers. Major social developments that occur alongside the physical and motor development are learning to talk and to form basic relationships with adults. The increasing mobility of the infant, coupled with language development, is accompanied by an increasing resentment of being babied and a growing desire to be independent. It is very important for parents to give the child frequent and sustained contact during these early years and to provide a stimulating environment that helps the child develop a feeling of having some control over what happens.

In these first two years of life, the difference between boys and girls in growth rate and body proportions is of no practical significance. As the child becomes more mobile, is able to communicate effectively and becomes more social, the age of infancy comes to an end.

The development of broad and fine muscle systems

While the rate of growth during early childhood is slower than during infancy, the considerable changes that take place are nevertheless significant. Fatty tissue, which characterised the bouncing baby, is gradually replaced by the developing muscle systems, beginning with the *broader muscle systems* and then the

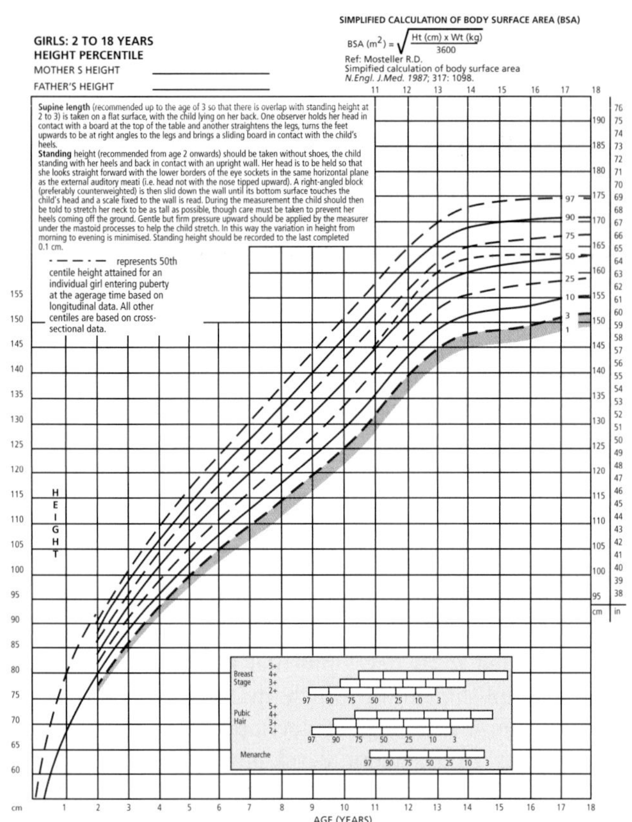

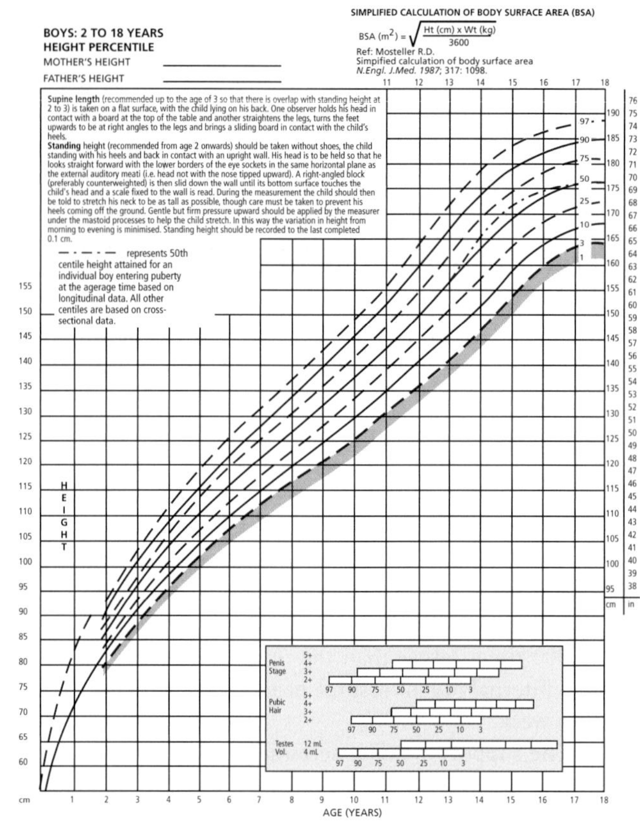

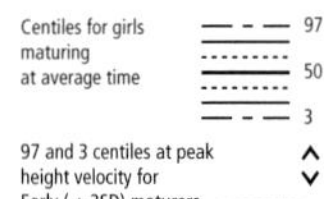

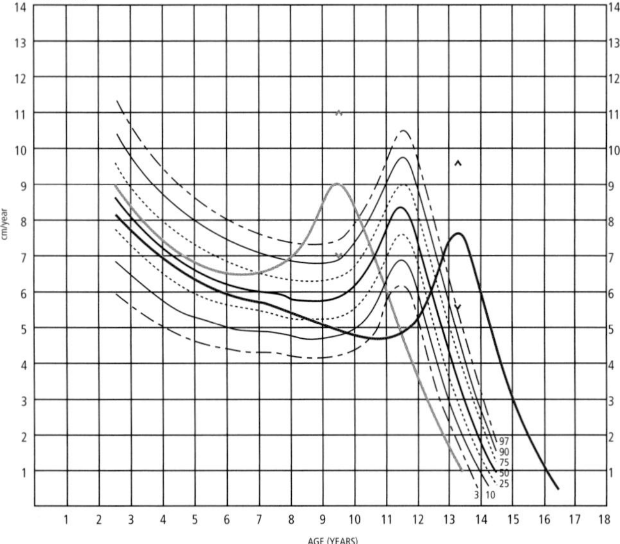

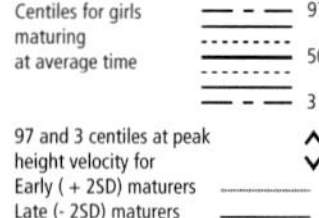

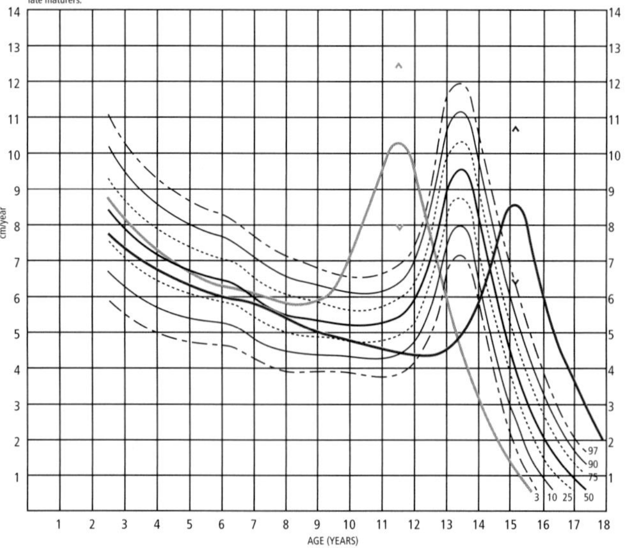

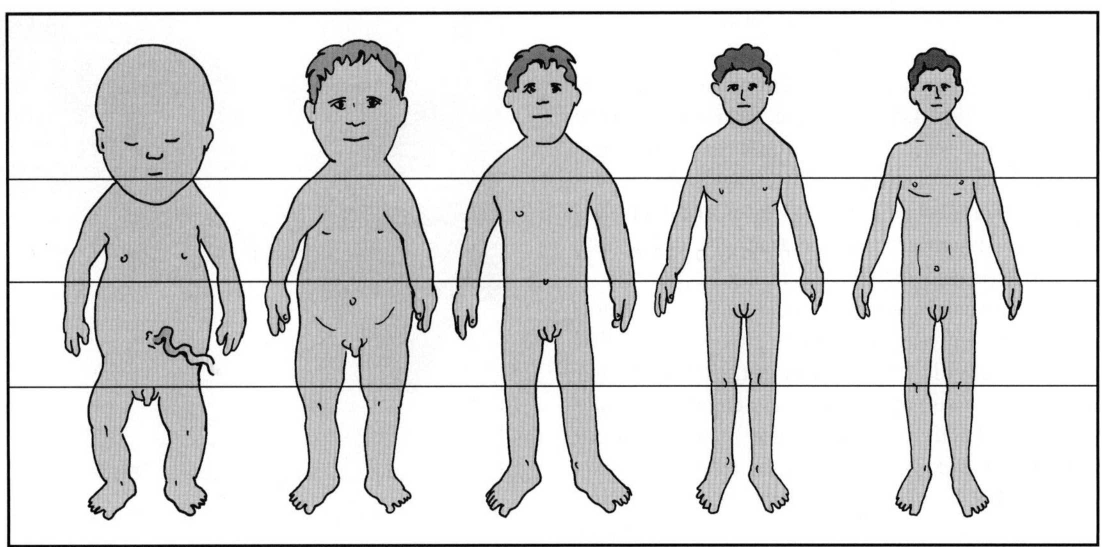

Figure 12.2 *The changing shape and proportions of the human body from birth to maturity*

finer muscle systems. The trunk and legs of the child grow rapidly and the skeletal system becomes more developed; new bone is established with the conversion of cartilage into bone and the growth of existing bones. By about three years, most children have a complete set of baby teeth. On average, children's height increases by 6 centimetres and weight increases by 2–3 kilograms each year.

Cranial growth

Cranial growth is slower during this period; however, by the age of five the brain has reached 75 per cent of its adult weight and, within another year, 90 per cent. The nervous system also develops during this time, and the sheathing of the nerve fibres in the brain is substantially completed by the end of this period (Schmidt 1975, 1982). Females, even at this early age, tend to mature faster than males.

Changing body proportions

By six years of age, children have substantially assumed the body proportions they will have as adults. Parents, particularly grandparents, often mourn the passing of the period of infancy and early childhood as children lose some of their cuddliness and become more lean and mean action machines! There is a temptation at this time for caregivers to overfeed children to compensate for their apparent loss of weight. However, as children get taller, body shape and levels of fat change naturally.

Major developmental tasks of early childhood

Major developmental tasks in early childhood are the coordination of body movements and, in particular, learning gross motor skills such as running, skipping, hopping, catching and balancing, and fine motor skills such as writing and drawing. This is also an important time when healthy children begin to form concepts of social and physical reality and are intensely curious about the world around them.

As energetic physical activity is typical of young children of this age, teachers and parents must be prepared for this in both its constructive and destructive modes. The energy needs to be channelled: children should be given the opportunity to exercise gross motor and fine motor skills in both directed and undirected settings and to be responsible for doing 'important' things—for example, kitchen chores, dressing and undressing. It is important to foster pride in doing these things, as is encouraging children to copy and be involved in adult activities. In this context, it is important that adults are reasonable in what they expect from children and avoid making comparisons between them.

Sex-typing activities

Few sex differences

There is very little difference between the size of boys and girls during early childhood, and they have very much the same body proportions. While girls tend to retain more fat than boys, boys develop more muscle tissue. There is, however, no justification for different physical education, sport or health programs for boys and girls. Their coordination skills are the same. Any apparent differences in performance are likely to be the result of differing social expectations and opportunities presented to girls and boys (Berk 1996, 1997; Corbin 1980; Gallahue 1976,

1982; Thomas & French 1985). It is not uncommon for children, from an early age, to be encouraged by parents, siblings and peers to engage in different physical activities that are sex stereotyped. For example, fathers might play ball less frequently with their daughters than with their sons in the backyard. Cricket bats and footballs are purchased for sons, while skipping ropes and jacks are purchased for daughters. As children get older, differences in motor skills between girls and boys increase, reflecting the social pressures on boys to be active and physically skilled and girls to be more passive and skilled at fine motor activities. It is important, therefore, that girls and boys are given opportunities to engage in a wide range of physical activities and are not limited to those that might be considered sex-typed. Increasingly, child-care settings and schools are encouraging young children to participate equally in physical activities such as dancing, skipping and team ball games. These are presented as a means of developing physical fitness and team cooperation that is appropriate to all.

Middle and late childhood to puberty

Middle and late childhood is a period of steady growth that ends with the dramatic arrival of **puberty**. If well nourished, children grow 4.4 to 6.6 centimetres in height and gain from 2 to

Refinement of motor skills

Each of these children is eight years old. Growth differences reflect a number of factors. What are some of these?
Photo: Debbie Blazley

Losing and gaining teeth are a sign of growing maturity. Look how proud these boys are!

2.75 kilograms a year. Some body parts grow at different rates relative to other body parts during middle to late childhood, and some awkwardness and lankiness may characterise children's appearance and coordination. The growth of the skeleton, for example, is frequently more rapid than the growth of the muscles and ligaments. **Asynchrony** is the term used to describe this differential development. During this period, children's bodies gradually approach adult dimensions. By 12 years of age, children have reached approximately 90 per cent of their adult height. Significant advances are made in gross and fine motor skills coordination.

Children in early primary grades appear to be in a state of perpetual motion. They love to run, chase and climb. As a result, they are easily susceptible to injury and fatigue. Gross motor skills are more developed than fine motor skills and hand–eye and foot–eye coordination are being developed. Many of these finer skills do not come to full maturity until adolescence. During this time the first teeth begin to fall out (or are wiggled out by a compulsive tongue) and the tooth fairy becomes very busy. Permanent teeth appear and many smiles are cutely 'marred' by toothless gaps and oversized teeth. As speech, appearance and body image are all affected by the health of teeth, sound oral hygiene and dental care must be encouraged by parents and teachers.

Oral hygiene

Children in the early grades enjoy physical activities and can be very individualistic, curious, imaginative, creative and dramatic. They display a desire to please and excel, and to assume leadership and responsibility. Nevertheless, they seek to establish this growing independence in a secure environment.

By about fourth grade, children are aware of growing up, and feel that they are too big for little ones (first graders) and too little for the big ones (sixth graders). Children at this age tend to display very distinctive individual characteristics, argue over fairness, and may become, at times, aggressive and quarrelsome across a range of activities. They are capable of longer attention spans, and are highly creative and imaginative.

By fifth grade most children are going through another period of rapid physical growth, with the further development of muscular strength and bone length paralleled by the continuing development of motor skills and coordination. Children in upper primary continue to enjoy vigorous physical activities, and are increasingly interested in competitive activities and organised games with rules and become concerned with their correct application. This attitude is generalised to an interest in ethics and values, and the desire to make fair judgments. You can see here the interaction of cognitive, social and moral development.

At this time there will be considerable differences in rates of development, and children may show increasing interest in growth patterns, comparing who is the smallest and who is the tallest. As girls tend to mature earlier than boys, the development of sexual characteristics may become noticeable.

Many children at this time begin to display independent behaviour demonstrated in some forms of rebellion against teachers and parents. It is also a period of strong peer allegiance and hero worship.

Major developmental tasks of middle childhood

Among the major developmental tasks for this period are the development and refinement of physical skills for games and academic purposes, and acquiring a healthy concept of self. Social skills in dealing with peers, appropriate social and sex roles, and aspects of personal independence also develop along with intellectual capacity. Within this context, children learn many moral and social concepts required for daily living, including conscience, morality and values.

The role of the family is very important at this time, as it is the main setting for learning appropriate sex roles, developing relationships and achieving personal independence. School is also very significant, as it is the first wide social environment of the child that facilitates the development of attitudes towards social groups and institutions, learning to get along with age-mates, and developing life skills.

QUESTION POINT

If there is little average difference between males and females in physical capacity prior to puberty, why do we get such different performance levels from them in physical education classes and in the playground? Why do some teachers have different attitudes towards males and females regarding their performance levels in such classes?

Puberty and adolescence

Physiological differences between males and females that are related to average developmental rates, disposition of muscle and fat tissue, rate of skeletal ossification, and overall strength and size are programmed genetically at conception (Brooks-Gunn & Petersen 1983; Corbin 1980; Lockhart 1980a, 1980b; Malina & Bouchard 1991; Tanner 1990). These differences are, for all intents and purposes, minor before puberty and are less significant

There is more to him than his body

Tony, the 'fat boy' in Miss Rodgers' class, suffered much teasing about his size and had very low self-esteem. Miss Rodgers ran a session where class members said things about each of the other students in the class and, excluding physical attributes, described what made each person special. The comments about Tony were not size-related, but were 'caring'; a 'good friend'; 'happy and funny'.

Two days later she found out that one of the most popular girls in the class was now his 'steady' girlfriend. When Miss Rodgers spoke to her about this, she said: 'I realised that there is lots more to Tony than his body.'

Miss Rodgers was aware of her power to influence the students' attitudes and planned to use a deliberate approach that would focus on the students' thoughts about the broad range of positive personal attributes their peers possessed.

Case studies illustrating National Competency Framework for Beginning Teaching, National Project on the Quality of Teaching and Learning, Australian Teaching Council, 1996, p. 15. Commonwealth of Australia copyright, reproduced by permission.

Case study activity

How might Miss Rodgers develop a program to focus on the students' thoughts about the broad range of positive personal attributes their peers possessed?

Puberty and adolescence brings with it dramatic body changes. Accompanying this is a desire to dress 'more adult'.

than individual differences within the sexes. In any one classroom we find slight and heavy boys and girls, and quite large differences between the tallest and shortest, heaviest and lightest children.

The onset of puberty comes with the physiological development of the sexual system, which leads into a longer period of physical development called *adolescence*. **Pubescence** (derived from the Latin 'to grow hairy'!) refers to changes that result in sexual maturity. In boys, these changes include the enlargement of the testes and penis; growth of pubic, underarm and facial hair; changes in the voice; and the production of and ability to ejaculate semen.

In girls, pubescence is characterised by rapid physical growth, particularly of the uterus, vagina and fallopian tubes. Other changes are the occurrence of the first menstrual cycle (menarche or period); a slight lowering of the voice; an enlargement and development of the breasts; rounding of the pelvic area; and growth of pubic and underarm hair (Brooks-Gunn & Petersen 1983; Daniel 1983; Faust 1983; Malina 1990; Malina & Bouchard 1991; Peterson & Taylor 1980; Tanner 1990; Warren 1983).

While the biological system (the ability to procreate) matures relatively early in this period, physical changes of quite large proportions continue for a number of years. One of the most obvious changes is the *growth spurt*, when adolescents always seem to be growing out of their shoes and clothing. Perhaps some of you remember meeting a relative for the first time after a few months and being greeted with the comment: ''Struth, what are they feeding you?!' Such unthinking reactions can be quite upsetting for the teenager trying to cope with the countless physical and mental changes that are occurring. One teenager we knew developed the habit of stooping so that he would not attract comments about his height.

Dramatic and rapid physical changes

This abrupt increase in stature begins between the ages of eight and a half and 10 and a half for the average girl and reaches its peak around 12, while for boys the growth spurt occurs between the ages of 10 and a half and 12 and a half and reaches peak rates of increase at about 14 or 15. So, in general, boys begin the pubertal growth spurt after girls, but it lasts three to four years longer than that of girls. Because of this, girls are initially taller and heavier than boys in the age range 11 to 14+, but boys surpass them and end up, on average, significantly taller and heavier than girls.

Differences in timing of growth spurt for boys and girls

The increase in muscle growth during adolescence is greater for boys than for girls, and is more marked in the arm than in the calf. Hence the adolescent male is stronger than the adolescent female.

Males usually develop larger hearts and lungs, together with a greater capacity for absorbing oxygen in the blood and for eliminating the biochemical products of exercise. Males also develop wider shoulders, while females develop a wider pelvis and store more fat in their tissues. Lastly, most men develop deeper voices than females. The overall average size and strength difference between boys and girls after puberty is due to the longer pre-adolescent growth period of males prior to the onset of puberty.

Physiological differences between sexes

At this developmental stage there is some justification for differentiated sporting and health programs for males and females. Unfortunately, this has often been interpreted in the past as support for vigorous physical activity for males and relatively sedentary physical activities for females. Consequently, beyond the age of 10 to 12 years there are rather substantial differences between the average male and female *in all areas of physical performance.* We should ensure that all males and females receive appropriate fitness and endurance training, including vigorous physical activity for girls (Wilmore 1989). As noted earlier, over the last decade schools have increasingly encouraged females to participate in a wide range of male sex-stereotyped sports, such as cricket, touch football and golf. However, the number of females engaged in such vigorous sports still lags behind the number of males.

We should note here that there are racial differences in the age of onset of puberty and the growth spurt (Malina & Bouchard 1991; Tanner 1990). Furthermore, norms for height and weight derived from Western groups may not be representative of other non-Western groups (for example, children from a number of racial groups are typically lighter and shorter than Western children at each level of development, while others are typically heavier). Care should be used, therefore, when applying norms in racially diverse societies.

Racial differences in onset of puberty

Asynchrony during adolescence

We have already mentioned the notion of asynchrony in the context of late childhood development. Asynchrony refers to the differential rate at which different body parts grow. In late childhood, individuals appear to be blissfully unaware of their gawkiness but asynchronous development seems to cause distress for some adolescents. There are two types of asynchrony: **interpersonal**, where development varies from individual to individual; and **intrapersonal**, where there is an uneven progression of development within an individual (Collins & Plahn 1988; Cramer 1980; Wright 1989).

The onset of development can vary quite markedly within any cohort of age peers, so that in any Year 6 grade there might be prepubescent, pubescent and adolescent children. This is a case of interpersonal asynchrony. For example, while most boys acquire pubic hair before the height spurt, and most girls' breasts have nearly finished growing before menarche, some individuals deviate from this sequential pattern. This can be a source of serious worry for them.

For any individual, intrapersonal asynchrony can also cause concern. The nose, for example, develops to full size very early and consequently appears disproportionately large on a youngster's face. Ears, limbs and fingers may also give an appearance of gawkiness to this age group. The sebaceous (oil-producing) glands of the skin can develop more quickly than the ducts, causing the blockages and infections known as acne for some children. Shoulders and hips may grow out of sequence for girls, giving them an overly masculine appearance or an exaggerated 'pear' shape.

'Go on! Make our day!
Early and late development can cause special problems for some children.

Both intrapersonal and interpersonal asynchrony can have an effect on boys' and girls' self-concept and self-confidence. Teachers, in particular, need to be aware of and alleviate potential problems in sensible and sensitive ways. For example, the custom of students changing clothing publicly for sport can be embarrassing for many children; consequently, alternative opportunities for students to change should be provided (see, for example, McInerney *et al.* 2000).

Early and late maturation

One form of interpersonal asynchrony is the age of onset of pubertal development. Some individuals develop early, while others develop relatively late. Research has studied the effects of early and late maturation on males and females (Faust 1983; Livson & Peskin 1980; Petersen

Characteristics of early and late maturing boys

1987; Tobin-Richards, Boxer & Petersen 1983). Among the findings are that early maturing males appeared more self-assured, more relaxed, more masculine, better groomed, and more poised and handsome than both the late and average group. Late maturers apparently stood out for their restless attention seeking, their tense manner, and their boyish eagerness and social awkwardness. Early maturers appeared more popular with their male peers than the late maturers, and they were chosen in preference to both late and average maturers in contests for leadership. The late maturers were judged by adults to be less responsible and less mature than other males their age in their relationships with females. Late maturers emerged at a disadvantage to early maturers in virtually all areas of behaviour and adjustment during adolescence. While in later life the physical differences between these groups have been shown to disappear, personality differences may persist (Mussen & Jones 1957, 1958).

What might be the cause of these differences? Early maturing males are expected by parents and teachers to be more competent than less developed peers and therefore may be given more responsibilities and opportunities to develop personality characteristics such as independence and responsibility. Any difference between early and late maturers could well be artefacts of socialisation. Furthermore, many physically underdeveloped males are sufficiently cognitively, socially and emotionally developed to benefit from these same responsibilities and opportunities, but are often denied them, which may breed resentment and poor adjustment. On the other hand, some physically advanced males may not be cognitively and emotionally prepared for the responsibilities they are expected to assume. As sensitive parents and teachers, we must look at all developmental aspects when deciding when it is appropriate to increasingly relinquish our control and give children greater responsibility.

Characteristics of early and late maturing girls

Most research on early and late maturing females finds very few differences between the two groups. The explanation might be the relatively shorter pubertal period for females, and the fact that late maturing females still compare themselves with males of the same age who are less developed physically and sexually than they are. However, early developing females sometimes experience emotional and social difficulties that may be reflected in lack of popularity, withdrawal and low self-confidence (Berk 1996). This may be because early maturers' psychological preparedness is inadequate to cope with the physical stress of menstruating or the added responsibilities that they might be expected to assume. In some cases, parents of early maturing females become more restrictive in an attempt to protect them from potential sexual dangers and consequently frustrate their attempts to become more independent. This stands in marked contrast to the way that early maturing males are treated. Finally, early maturing females may feel isolated from their peer group. (See Hill and Lynch (1983) for a discussion of gender-related role expectations during early adolescence.)

In this regard, parents and teachers must be alert to messages that children give about developmental stress, and be sympathetic, empathetic and loving in their caring for children. This will not always be easy, as children and adolescents struggle to understand why they may be different when they want to be the same as others, and may feel that adults could not possibly understand their fears and disappointments about their appearance.

Are there long-term consequences of early or late maturing?

Longitudinal research indicates that several aspects of adolescent adjustment may remain evident into middle adulthood. In one study the social skills of early maturing males were still in evidence at age 38, while the late maturing adolescents remained more impulsive and assertive over the years (Livson & Peskin 1980). It is evident, however, that there can be some interesting reversals. For example, many late maturing males and early maturing females, who initially lacked self-assurance, developed into very self-assured and caring adults. In contrast, many confident and self-assured early maturing males and late maturing females became somewhat discontented adults (Berk 1996; Peterson 1996). These findings show that earlier social experiences can have differential effects on the long-term development of early and late maturing adolescents. Perhaps as a result of the 'deviant' timing of their development, late maturing males and early maturing females encounter more adjustment problems which give them superior skills for dealing with the stresses of adult life (Peterson 1996).

Trend towards larger size and earlier maturation

During the past 100 years or so, there has been a trend towards accelerated maturation in height and weight among males and females. Similar observations have been made with respect to sexual maturation. This tendency has been termed the **secular trend** towards earlier growth (Frisch 1983; Garn 1980; Tanner 1990; Warren 1983). It has been suggested that the age for the onset of puberty has decreased by about four months per decade in Western Europe over the past 120 years. There are a number of suggested explanations for this, and you might like to discuss these with friends and parents, particularly older people. One explanation is that improved nutritional standards, together with the conquest of several major childhood illnesses, have led to the secular trend. It is also suggested that intermarriage among a wider genetic pool, the result of increased world travel and immigration, may be implicated. For example, people from warmer climates appear to mature earlier, as do certain races. Hence, when there is intermarriage between races the age of the onset of puberty moves towards the average age of the two groups. There is also a suggestion that our present Western culture's emphasis on sexuality, particularly through very accessible and ubiquitous mass media, might be hastening puberty for modern adolescents. In other words, psychological factors could be having an effect on the purely physiological process. Gives us much food for thought, doesn't it? Current research indicates that this trend ceases to have an impact when a nation's (or cultural/ social group's) health and nutritional standards reach an optimal level. This is just as well—otherwise, like the Japanese, we would all be redesigning our buildings with higher doorways!

Adolescents and 'ideal' body type

Adolescent preoccupation with looks and popularity

Peer and social pressures during adolescence dictate to a large extent appropriate sexual attitudes and behaviour for each gender. This has a strong impact on adolescents' apparent preoccupation with their looks and popularity. The 'ideal' body type for males and females, as presented through the mass media, may lead those who vary from such types to feel negative towards themselves (Cusimano & Thompson 1997; Faust 1983; Langlois & Stephan 1981; Lerner & Korn 1972; Levine & Smolak 1998; Staffieri 1972; Tobin-Richards *et al.* 1983). Two factors that are basic to the adolescent's concern with physique are the desire to meet culturally prescribed standards of beauty, and the desire to have the requisite sex-appropriate characteristics. Some adolescents experience considerable anxiety over such issues as weight, strength and attractiveness. When rating photographs of various male body types, males between the ages of 10 and 20 clearly preferred strong athletic types on dimensions such as leadership, popularity and ability to endure pain. Stereotypes associated with the other physical types, such as skinny and fat, were generally negative. Thus, adolescents who perceive their bodies as being fat or skinny probably feel bad about themselves and believe that their peer group dislikes them (Lerner 1969). For both men and women, positive self-concept is strongly correlated with the degree of satisfaction with one's own bodily characteristics (Cavior & Dokecki 1973; Cavior & Lombardi 1973; Faust 1983; Lerner 1969; Lerner & Korn 1972; Staffieri 1967, 1972; Styczynski & Langlois 1977; see also Marsh & Craven 1997).

These issues, and the general concern generated by such a period of rapid development, can introduce greater personality problems in adolescence than at any other stage of development.

QUESTION POINT

What adjustment problems may be generated by differential growth spurts of males and females in a co-educational class? What are the implications of the differential physical development in adolescent males and females for physical education and sports activities?

ACTION STATION

Above we list some possible reasons for the secular trend in maturation.

1 What do you think about these reasons?

2 Interview a number of older adults of varying ages regarding this issue and discuss in a group the various explanations given. Your interview could start: 'It appears that children today are growing bigger and maturing earlier than children 50 years ago. Have you noticed this? If so, how do you account for the increased growth and earlier maturation?'

QUESTION POINT

We have indicated a number of implications for school programs and facilities derived from our knowledge of the ways in which males and females grow. Discuss these in the context of your own school experiences. What changes would you make in the way that your school taught you?

QUESTION POINT

What role should schools play in sex education? Does the cultural mix of the school make a difference?

QUESTION POINT

Discuss eating disorders among adolescents and adults. What might the sensitive teacher do to help prevent and alleviate such problems?

Theory and research into practice

Marita P. McCabe — BODY IMAGE AND HUMAN SEXUALITY

BRIEF BIOGRAPHY

I started my working life as a high school maths and science teacher after having studied at the University of Sydney and Sydney Teachers College. Because of my love for pure mathematics, I decided to do further study in pure maths at Macquarie University in the evening. However, I needed an additional subject for the degree, so I decided to study psychology as well. I found psychology so interesting that I eventually completed my undergraduate and honours degrees in psychology, while I continued to teach Year 11 and 12 chemistry and physics. This brought me to a crossroads in my career; do I continue as a schoolteacher and become a science mistress, or do I accept a Commonwealth Postgraduate School Scholarship and complete a Ph.D. at Macquarie University? This decision was made during the Whitlam era, when universities were expanding and academic life looked very attractive. I decided to take the risk of leaving secure, well-paid employment for the life of a student. I completed my Ph.D. in three years, two of these years employed as a full-time tutor in education and then psychology at Macquarie University.

I continued my employment at Macquarie until the end of 1990 (13 years' full-time employment) and was promoted to the position of associate professor during this time. In 1991 I left Macquarie to take up a Chair at Deakin University, a position I continue to hold. During my time at Deakin I have held positions at various times as head of school of Psychology and associate dean (research) within the Faculty of Health and Behavioural Sciences. I have also been instrumental in the development of our Master of Psychology (Clinical), Doctor of Psychology (Clinical), Doctor of Psychology (Health) and Doctor of Psychology (Forensic) programs. Who knows what the future holds? I currently enjoy my academic life, and am pleased with the decision I made 27 years ago to move to academia.

RESEARCH AND THEORETICAL INTERESTS

I currently conduct research primarily in the area of body image and health risk behaviours associated with body image concerns. In particular, I have conducted (with my colleague Dr Lina Ricciardelli), a series of studies on body image, disordered eating and muscle change strategies. We have investigated relationships among these variables with preschool children, primary school children, adolescents, adults, menopausal women, people who attend gymnasiums, and people with disabilities. Our focus has been to evaluate the validity of a biopsychosocial model to understand body concerns and health risk behaviours. In particular, we have examined the role of body mass index, gender, negative and positive affect, self-esteem, and sociocultural pressures from parents, peers and the media on the attitudes and behaviours related to the body for both males and females.

Our particular focus has been on males, given that much of the previous literature had attempted to generalise a paradigm developed with females to male attitudes and behaviours. We have found that, although some of the body concerns are similar for males and females, there are also differences between the sexes. In particular, males are more likely to value a muscular body, and so engage in strategies to both lose weight and increase muscles. We have found that body image importance is a major factor in shaping body change strategies among adolescent boys, whereas for girls the major factor is body dissatisfaction. It appears that if boys are focused on their bodies, regardless of their level of satisfaction with the size and shape of their body, they will engage in strategies to change their body.

The other major area of research in which I have been involved for the last 30 years has focused on various aspects of human sexuality. This interest originated from my experience working as a high school teacher, where girls asked me about the normality or otherwise of their sexual experience. It became apparent to me that we had little understanding of the sexual attitudes and experiences of adolescent boys or girls. I was particularly interested in the psycho-affectional aspect of the dating relationship. In fact, I found that although adolescent boys were more sexually experienced than girls, there were no differences between the sexes in the level of psycho-affectional involvement—that is, the level of intimacy, affection, companionship, and so on.

I have extended this earlier sex research with adolescents to conduct a series of studies with other colleagues and postgraduate students in a broad range of areas of sexuality: aetiology and treatment of sexual dysfunction, sexual harassment, characteristics of rapists, effectiveness of intervention programs for rapists and men who engage in child sexual abuse, impact of child sexual abuse on victims, and sexuality of people with physical or intellectual disabilities. People's sexual lives and their attitudes towards sexuality have an enormous impact on other aspects of their lives. Problems in the sexual area frequently underpin feelings of depression, obsessive compulsive disorder, body image concern, and disordered eating. I have developed theoretical models to explain sexual decision making among adolescents, and aetiology of sexual dysfunction. In addition, I have developed and evaluated a series of psychological interventions to treat sexual dysfunction among both men and women.

THEORY AND RESEARCH INTO PRACTICE

The research that we have conducted on body image concerns and health risk behaviours associated with changing body size and shape has significant application, particularly among children and adolescents. Our research demonstrated a significant link between body image concerns and health risk behaviours, and self-esteem, peer relationships, physical activity and negative affect. As a result of these findings, we have developed a series of prevention and intervention programs for children and adolescents that we are in the process of evaluating.

The first of these programs, ACE Kids, is targeted at primary school-age children, and was designed to encourage children to become involved in a range of physical activities and to strengthen peer relationships. The program was also designed to take the focus off body size and shape, and to focus on other characteristics of boys and girls that make them good friends. In this way, it was expected that body image concerns and disordered eating, which normally start to increase at the end of primary school, would be prevented. We are currently in the process of analysing the data, but the results seem to suggest that the children who participated in the program evidence lower levels of health risk attitudes and behaviours than the non-intervention group.

There is a strong link between negative affect and body dissatisfaction and health risk behaviours, particularly among girls. As a result, we have developed a second prevention program for children that focuses on lowering levels of negative affect, and improving peer relationships (the Think Happy—Feel Happy Program). The program focuses on developing skills among respondents to work cooperatively together and develop problem-solving skills. We are currently implementing this in 15 schools in Victoria. We would predict that the program will lead to improved peer relationships and lower negative affect among the children who complete the program sessions.

We have also used the data we obtained from our adolescent population to develop a prevention program for young adolescent boys. This program specifically targets self-esteem, broader ways of defining oneself (other than in terms of the size and shape of one's body), and ways to resist sociocultural messages that pressure boys to achieve a body shape endorsed by society. Preliminary investigations indicate that it is particularly effective in enhancing the self-esteem and reducing body image importance among the boys in the program group.

A further application of my research has been in the development of psychological interventions for the treatment of sexual dysfunction among men and women. These programs are based on the model of the development of sexual dysfunction that I developed in the late 1980s. These programs build on Masters and Johnson's earlier treatment programs, and include a focus on general body pleasuring, development of communication and intimacy, as well as other strategies to reduce the high levels of performance anxiety that are often present among both men and women with sexual dysfunction. We have also conducted a study to better understand the role of medication for the treatment of male erectile disorder, with the view to evaluate combination therapies (oral medication combined with psychological interventions) for this disorder.

KEY REFERENCES

McCabe, M. P. (2002) Relationship functioning and sexuality among people with multiple sclerosis. *Journal of Sex Research*, **39**, 302–9.

McCabe, M. P. & Ricciardelli, L. A. (2003) A longitudinal study of body change strategies among adolescent males. *Journal of Youth and Adolescence*, **32**, 105–13.

Ricciardelli, L. A. & McCabe, M. P. (2004) A biopsychosocial model of disordered eating and the pursuit of muscularity in adolescent boys. *Psychological Bulletin*, **130**, 179–205.

ACTIVITIES

1 One of Marita McCabe's research interests is in body image and health risk behaviours associated with body image concerns. What are some body image concerns, and what are the heath risks associated with these? Are there differences between males and females? Do these concerns change as people grow older? Are there differences between social and cultural groups?

2 In examining body concerns and health risk behaviours, Marita McCabe uses a biopsychosocial model. Discuss with your fellow students what the elements of this model are and why using this model would provide valuable insights.

3 Another of Marita McCabe's research interests is the sexual attitudes and experiences of adolescent boys and girls. She particularly focuses on the psycho-affectional aspect of the dating relationship, and while she finds that boys are more sexually experienced than girls there are no differences in level of intimacy, affection and companionship. Why do you think this is the case?

4 Marita McCabe studies a wide range of other sexual issues, such as sexual dysfunction, sexual harassment, rape and rape intervention programs, and child sexual abuse and its effects. Select one of these topics for further investigation through the research literature and the Internet, and write a brief report on your findings.

5 Marita McCabe and her colleagues have developed a series of prevention and intervention programs for children related to body image such as ACE Kids and the Think Happy—Feel Happy Program. Locate further information on these programs, and discuss with your fellow students how you might implement these programs in your educational setting.

EXTENSION STUDY

Eating disorders

Offer *et al.* (1988) conducted a comprehensive cross-cultural study of adolescent self-image, and found body image in Australian females to be the lowest and in Australian males the second-lowest of the Western industrialised countries examined (see also Gregor 2004). It is believed that men's body image dissatisfaction has tripled in the previous 25 years from 15 per cent to 45 per cent of all Western men (Gregor 2004). These findings are cause for concern, as poor body image and weight loss behaviours have been associated with disordered eating among female adolescents (Attie & Brooks-Gunn 1989; Tricker & McCabe 1999).

It appears that body dissatisfaction increases with age, with the onset beginning for many children in late childhood (Davies & Furnham 1986; Levine, Smolak & Hayden 1994; Tricker & McCabe 1999; see also Gregor 2004). Recent reports indicate that girls as young as eight are dieting, some to the point of starvation, because they wish to grow up to be supermodels. As a result, these children go without morning and afternoon teas and often refuse to eat dinner in their quest to have the perfect body type. Unfortunately, children who starve themselves become lethargic, and unable to concentrate during lessons or take part in sport. Damage can also be long term.

Research in the last decade has pointed to a high prevalence of body dissatisfaction among female adolescents and increasingly with male adolescents, causing many of them to diet unwisely through crash diets and unhealthy eating habits (Gregor 2004; Paxton *et al.* 1991). At a time when the mass media (and especially television and magazine advertisements for fashion, diet foods and entertainment) seem to promote the ideal that to be attractive and popular one needs to be slim, adolescents are going through a growth spurt that leads to weight gain! It appears that many adolescent girls confuse obesity with normal weight gain that occurs with the pubertal growth of bones, muscles, breasts and hips (Peterson 1996). As a consequence of this, many adolescent girls wish they were thinner (Berger 1991). Peer and parental influence may also contribute to these unhealthy attitudes and behaviours of adolescents in regard to weight, body shape and eating (Levine *et al.* 1994; Paxton, Schutz & Muir 1996; Wertheim, Mee & Paxton 1996). Friendship cliques operate as an important subcultural environment that influences broader sociocultural pressures for thinness in adolescent girls. Girls who belong to friendship cliques that do not emphasise calorie counting and dieting are less likely to be involved in dieting (Paxton *et al.* 1996). However, Paxton *et al.* (1996) showed that if adolescent girls have a tendency to compare their bodies with others' and believe that their friends are concerned about dieting, and encouraged dieting, they would probably begin dieting.

In some cases a preoccupation with dieting leads to a severe eating disorder called **bulimia nervosa**. Adolescents with this disorder engage in uncontrollable binge eating

Principles of motor development

Paralleling the physical growth of the body is its motor development. Motor development should be seen as part of the holistic development of the individual, which includes perception, action and cognition (Thelen 1995) and continues throughout childhood and adolescence and into adulthood, following a predictable sequence.

As children mature, **motor skills** develop gradually from a set of reflex actions to a complex set of motor abilities. A lot of research has been done on the sequence of motor development and its relationship to physical development (Bayley 1956; Connolly & Dalgleish 1989; Corbin 1980; Fagard & Jacquet 1989; Gallahue 1976, 1982; Gesell 1925; Matthew & Crook 1990; Thomas 1990). Researchers have also been interested in whether motor development can be accelerated through environmental influences. While it does not appear that motor development can be accelerated, there is considerable evidence that physical and motor development can be retarded under the impact of poor environmental conditions such as sickness, accident or gross physical neglect.

Sequence of motor development

Motor development proceeds by way of the dual processes of **differentiation** and **integration**. *Differentiation* refers to the gradual progression of children's motor coordination from gross overall movement patterns to more refined and functional movements as they mature. *Integration* refers to children bringing various opposing muscle and sensory systems into coordinated interaction with one another (Gallahue 1976, 1982).

Differentiation and integration

Key principles of motor development are maturation,

followed by a combination of purging of the stomach contents through laxatives, diuretics or self-induced vomiting, strict fasting and strenuous exercise (Griffiths & Channon-Little 1996). As you can appreciate, cycles of binge eating, followed by purging and severe dieting, can cause physical and psychological health problems that can be life-threatening (Johnson & Conners 1987). Recent Australian estimates suggest that about 2 per cent of adolescent girls and 1 per cent of adolescent boys are clinically bulimic, and one teenager in 1000 is anorexic. Similar figures are obtained in New Zealand (Bushnell *et al.* 1990, 1994; Maude *et al.* 1993).

Bulimia nervosa can lead to the development of the most serious eating disorder—**anorexia nervosa**. The Eating Disorders Association of South Australia concluded that anorexia is the third most common disease in Australian females aged 15–24 years and mortality rates after 20 years are between 15 and 20 per cent (Gregor 2004). Recent statistics (www.betterhealth.vic.gov.au) reveal that approximately 17 per cent of men are dieting at any given time; one in 10 people with anorexia are male, and 4 per cent of men purge after eating. Anorexic individuals restrict their eating to such an extent that they become painfully thin, and the malnutrition that accompanies the illness leads to additional side effects such as brittle, discoloured nails, pale skin, fine dark hairs appearing all over the body, and extreme sensitivity to cold. Menstrual periods also cease (Berk 2004). Anorexia is a severe disorder for which proper medical help must be obtained. While adolescent girls seem to be most susceptible to both bulimia nervosa and anorexia nervosa, boys and adults of both sexes are also affected.

As we have suggested, there are many explanations of the causes of dieting and eating disorders such as bulimia nervosa and anorexia nervosa, including cultural, familial and psychological conditions, and a range of treatments exists which are beyond the scope of this book (see Berger 1991; Berk 1996; Fairburn & Beglin 1990; Romeo 1986). As an educator, you have an important responsibility to advise your students about healthy eating habits, particularly through the personal development program in place at your school. Where possible, stereotypes of ideal body types portrayed in the media should be discussed in the context of 'normal' adolescent development.

Where it becomes apparent that a particular student may be bulimic or anorexic, professional help and guidance should be obtained. Early identification of anorexic students is very important in order to permit treatment before the development of irreversible medical complications. Five per cent of anorexic individuals die as a result of the severity of this problem (Romeo 1986).

It is of interest here to consider whether there are cultural differences in the onset of eating disorders. In particular, are there differences between cultures for which food is a more or less central aspect of socialising within the family and community? Do children who come from ethnic backgrounds that emphasise healthy and plentiful eating become socialised into the pursuit of thinness, and defy family and cultural expectations regarding food in their quest for the 'ideal' body shape?

motivation, experience and practice (Gallahue 1976, 1982; Malina & Bouchard 1991; Schmidt 1975, 1982; Wickstrom 1983). These elements are not hierarchical but mutually independent (Thelen 1995).

Maturation

Neurological maturation

Neurological maturation is important because not all the centres of the brain are operational at birth—many brain centres that control movement develop over time. By approximately five years of age, however, the brain is capable of stimulating and coordinating the wide range of activities in which children engage. *Growth in perceptual capacities* is very important to the development of motor skills (Thelen 1995). Maturation of the physical systems develops progressively. Larger muscle systems, controlling large body movements such as walking, running and holding, develop before the striated muscle systems, which control **fine motor movements** such as the manipulation of fingers on a keyboard or the use of a pair of scissors. These striated muscles are not really fully developed until adolescence, and so there are motor movements beyond children's capacity until after puberty. Nevertheless, children are generally capable of a full range of differentiated motor movements that are later integrated into performing complex motor skills by middle childhood. For example, while children of five can hop, skip and jump, they have yet to develop the coordination skills necessary to combine these fluently into one action—hop–skip–jump, which comes later.

It is unwise, therefore, for parents and teachers to attempt to teach children motor skills before they are maturationally ready. Activities such as toilet training, feeding and dressing should be left until children give

It's not always this easy when you're little!

...and it's not that easy when you're older, either!

evidence that they are ready to be taught. Our experience is that it is relatively easy for the parent and teacher to know when a child is ready and willing to learn new motor skills—just listen to and watch the child. It is usually expressed by an imperative 'I can do it!' by the youngster. Children will leave you in no doubt as to what they think you should let them do. (Be prepared to put up with mess and chaos at this time in the knowledge that, under most circumstances, it will be short-lived.)

Motivation

In recent theories of motor development, *motivation* is considered to be the driving force behind children acquiring motor skills rather than pre-specified genetic instructions (Thelen 1995). Children appear to be innately interested in learning a wide range of motor skills. Even tasks as ordinary as undoing buttons and tying shoelaces, which signify some independence from adults, can motivate children to acquire important motor skills through practice. At particular times, motor skills become the focus of much voluntary activity and children will spend endless time learning to skip, play with a yo-yo or master elaborate string games in order to demonstrate skills comparable with their peers'.

Experience

At the point of readiness (indicated by the child's maturity and motivational level), parents and teachers must give children *appropriate experiences* to develop motor skills. It is potentially quite harmful if the experiences are inappropriate, such as play equipment being wrongly sized or if the social climate surrounding the practice of the skills is overly competitive, restrictive or demanding. In these cases, the enthusiasm of children to acquire the skills can be dampened. Limited competence in fundamental motor skills at an early age can negatively affect future performance in physical and motor activities (Gallahue 1989) with related consequences to self-concept. Past the point of readiness, motivation may dissipate and later attempts to learn particular skills may be more difficult. Youngsters can learn to rollerskate and swim much more easily than older people. Even after the optimal age, however, motor skills may still be learned, although the earlier a skill is learned the better, because children are more supple, adventurous, agreeable to repetition and have more time to practise. Children who fail to develop motor skills appropriate for their age participate less in organised sports and other physical programs. This has significant consequences for their individual well-being.

Practice

Implicated in what we have said above is the *need for practice* to facilitate the development of motor skills. Some systems mature without much practice, such as bowel and bladder control; other skills based on muscle control, such as skipping, need extensive practice. When children show a readiness to learn particular motor skills, they are also willing to put endless hours into practising the skill. You can probably recall various motor skills that you acquired after many hours of dedicated practice. An interesting aspect of this is that it doesn't appear to bore children. Whether it is learning to click one's fingers, whistle or rollerskate, the activity often appears quite compulsive to children until it is mastered. As we get older, such dedication to acquiring new motor skills begins to wane.

Cutting with scissors is a motor skill developed over time with plenty of practice.

Are there individual differences in motor development?

While motor development follows a predictable pattern, there are many individual differences. Some children never crawl and some learn to walk earlier than others. Some children never develop a skill in balance, while others rival tightrope walkers. Some children are precocious in most skills, while others may be slow.

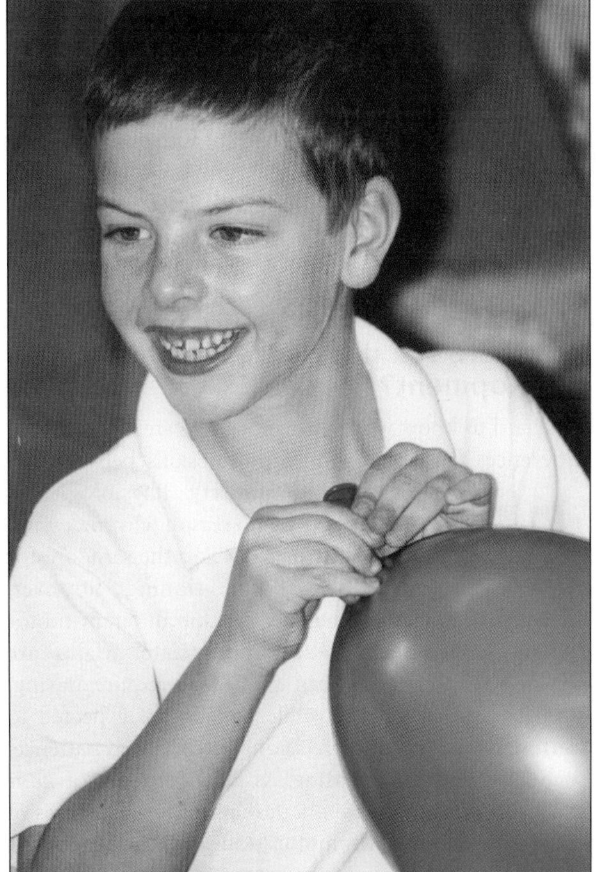

Even blowing up one's first balloon is a significant motor achievement.

As well as genetic influences, the child's experiential background affects the growth of motor skills. Some children are encouraged and stimulated in their efforts and exposed to a wide range of models demonstrating diverse motor skills. In other cases, demanding, critical or overprotective parents may inhibit the development of confidence, while limited experiences and a deprived environment may stultify growth. For all of these variations, there exist general age-related norms for the development of motor skills. If a child does not reach a given level of development within these norms, an abnormality may be present. The delayed development may be the result of a poorly maturing physiological system or the absence of relevant experiences. The early detection of motor problems and the start of appropriate intervention programs is very important to eliminate or hold to a minimum many physical and related emotional problems that may impact on the child's learning (Walkley *et al.* 1993).

Awkwardness

Children also go through stages when they may appear awkward, and when motor skills are occasionally insufficiently developed for body maturation. However, pathology should only be suspected when children's control over body movements falls well below age norms (Holt 1991). Children vary in their awkwardness, and at every age more children tend to fall below the norm in *motor coordination* than above it. The one individual may be awkward at some activities but not at others. While adolescents become less coordinated in particular tasks from time to time, Malina (1990) found no point in the adolescent growth process at which individuals become consistently less coordinated or skilful on physical tasks.

Are there sex differences in motor development?

Non-sexist educational programs

It is hard to know whether or not there are any inherent differences in the growth of motor skills between the sexes prior to puberty. Physiologically, there seems to be no reason why males and females shouldn't develop the same motor skills. Cultural conditioning, however, ensures that males and females develop different motor skills that are seen as sex-'appropriate'. Males are generally expected to learn skills that require daring, strength and endurance, while females are expected to learn skills that require precision, dexterity and patience, such as sewing and knitting. As a consequence of *non-sexist educational programs* a number of these features of sexist conditioning of motor skills are changing. For example, many schools are introducing cross-sex and mixed-sex sporting and health programs; and craft activities, such as woodwork, sewing and knitting, are being taught to both females and males. Many schools resist co-educational classes, however, because of the perceived differences in ability between females and males, the desire to allow females to participate free of the domination of males, and the restrictions imposed by single-sex sporting organisations and competitions.

Recess timing and children's playground and classroom behaviours

As we have noted earlier, childhood is a time when physical activity is very important for physical and motor development. It is also a period when social skills are developed and practised. In some ways, classrooms are quite artificial environments for children as they require students to be sedentary for relatively long periods of time doing seatwork and, in general, not interacting with their peers socially. These seatwork periods are punctuated by relatively small periods of free physical and social activity at recess and lunch breaks. Some schools have one morning recess break of about 15 minutes, followed by a longer 45-minute lunch break, and then an afternoon without a break. Other schools have more frequent short breaks. What are the effects of frequency and length of break on students' playground and classroom behaviours? Our knowledge of distributed practice (Chapter 4) would suggest that frequent breaks are probably advantageous for students, as they alleviate the potential for tiredness and boredom—in other words, students learn best when their efforts are distributed across tasks (Pelligrini & Bjorklund 1997; Pelligrini, Huberty & Jones 1995). Furthermore, the timing and length of the recess break may have implications for subsequent behaviour when the students return to the classroom. Students should return to the classroom after these breaks refreshed and motivated once more to engage in cognitive tasks. There is some evidence for this, although it might take some time for boisterous out-of-classroom behaviour to subside and for the students to settle back into seatwork. Of course, for the positive effects of playground activity to be manifest, students would need to be returning to interesting and relevant activities. If they return to boring, repetitive activities, no amount of breaks are likely to improve their attention to the task.

Theory also suggests that there will be greater levels of social and physical behaviour the longer the period of deprivation from those behaviours. This is called the deprivation-rebound hypothesis (Pelligrini *et al.* 1995). In other words, if students have long periods of deprivation from physical and social activity prior to recess, they are more likely to be very active when recess comes.

Periods of rest and relaxation alternating with periods of activity are needed for growing bodies.

As we have indicated above, in the context of physical and motor development, there may be differences in level of activity at recess depending on the sex of the students and their age, with males being more physically active than females. Research also shows that level and type of activity depends upon the climate and the venue (inside or outside). Schools should look carefully at their recess policies to ensure that they are getting best value for the time students spend in recess. Perhaps distributed recess would be more effective. What do you think?

QUESTION POINT

Havighurst (1959) defined a 'developmental task' as a task that arises at or about a certain period in the life of an individual, successful achievement of which leads to happiness and success with later tasks, while failure leads to unhappiness in the individual, disapproval by society and difficulty with later tasks.

For Havighurst, the 'teachable moment' is an optimal educational time when the body is ready, society approves and the self is prepared.

1 Discuss the notion of 'developmental task'.
2 List what you consider to be major developmental tasks for each of the developmental stages noted in this chapter.
3 Discuss the notion of 'teachable moment'. Relate this discussion to the developmental tasks you listed in 2. How would you, as an educator, ensure that these developmental tasks were accomplished successfully by your students?

Why are young children happy to expend great energy developing motor skills?

ACTION STATION

The objective of this exercise is to observe the physical skill of skipping with a rope for children of ages five, six and seven years. Select three children, one of each age. They should show average physical development for age in terms of height, weight and general coordination skills.

Ask each of the children to skip using a skipping rope and make observations during the skipping. In particular, observe the position of hands and feet, skill in jumping the rope, skill in hand and foot coordination, and any idiosyncratic mannerisms as the child is skipping.

Compare the skipping behaviour of the three children and relate your findings to the developmental sequence outlined in this chapter. You should discuss the principles of maturation, motivation, experience, practice, optimal age and individual differences in your report.

ACTION STATION

Draw a timeline of your personal biography in terms of physical and motor development. In particular, highlight the developmental tasks of most importance to you personally. How did you progress through these tasks? You might like to discuss your biography in a small group and evaluate individual differences and similarities.

Learning to write is a motor skill that takes enormous concentration and practice.

ACTION STATION

This activity is designed so that you can compare the physical and motor coordination skills of children across grades. Some activities require fine muscle coordination which develops only with time. For example, cutting out paper models may be a very difficult task for young children. What other tasks may be very difficult for young children? What coordination tasks may cause difficulty in late childhood and adolescence? Why?

Select a range of motor activities such as skipping, balancing, running, hopping, swinging, dancing, clapping, cutting paper, building matchstick houses, colouring in, writing, drawing, throwing, catching, tying laces, doing up buttons. Select a group of children from infants to middle high school and compare their performances on a selection of the tasks. Design a table to collate your results. Discuss your findings within a small group. What general principles do you see illustrated?

EXTENSION STUDY

Physical form and opportunities for development

According to Sheldon (1940, 1970; Sheldon & Stevens 1942; Sinclair 1989), body type gives a clue to personality characteristics. Sheldon developed two descriptive typologies, one dealing with temperament with three major classifications—viscerotonia, somatonia and cerebrotonia—and one dealing with physique with three major classifications—endomorphs, ectomorphs and mesomorphs. His research showed a very high level of relationship between temperament and physique. Large, round people, known as *endomorphs*, were more likely to be sociable, jolly, happy, placid and slow-moving (viscerotonia). Muscular, solid people, known as *mesomorphs*, were more likely to be forceful, aggressive, unsympathetic, loud, direct and action-oriented (somatonia). Skinny, angular people, known as *ectomorphs*, were more likely to be non-sociable, intense, shy and intellectual (cerebrotonia).

Nobody belongs exclusively to only one of these types. According to Sheldon, each of us has elements of all three in us, and in measuring a person's physique Sheldon assigned a score of 1 to 7 on each of them, which is known as the person's somatotype or body type.

A number of reasons have been suggested for the striking relationship between predominant body type, abilities and personality. For example, an individual's body type may limit the range of activities engaged in or, conversely, present particular opportunities for the individual to develop in specific ways. It is also believed that the relation between physique and temperament may be a product of stereotyping and the social expectations that individuals incorporate into their behaviour. A further explanation may be that the environmental factors that influence the development of physique may be the same ones that influence the development of personality. For example, parents who are determined to make their children great athletes may not only encourage the training and development of the body through exercise and relentless practice, but develop the mind as well to cope with the discipline such training demands. And, finally, it is thought that the genes that lead to the development of body type may also be influential in the development of personality (see Hall & Lindzey 1970; Liebert & Spiegler 1987). In any event, a large number of studies have indicated a substantial relationship between physique and temperament (although not to the level found in Sheldon's work) (Fontana 1986).

Are there educational implications of body type?

Unfortunately, little new research into Sheldon's work has been carried out in recent years, which means we are still unable to draw firm conclusions from it, although it appears to have some well-founded support (Fontana 1986; Wells 1983). Sheldon's theory has made a valuable contribution in

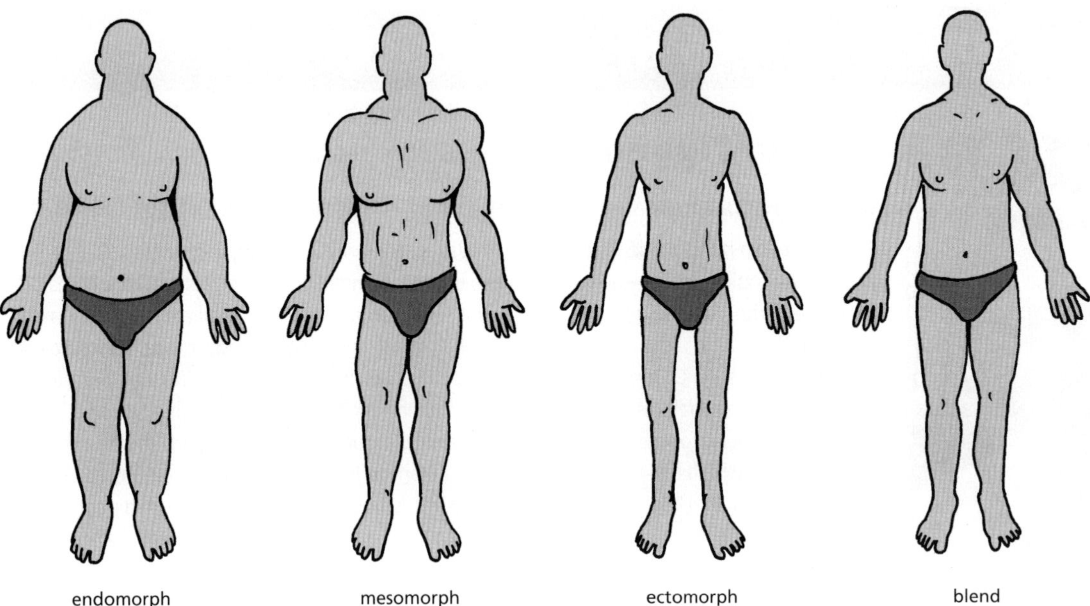

Figure 12.3 *Body types*

alerting us to the fact that our body shape may very much influence our view of self. How we and others view our body shape becomes incorporated into our self-concept. Indeed, most recent self-concept scales include a subscale for physical self-concept (see, for example, Marsh 1993; Marsh & Craven 1997). Research (Lerner 1969; Lerner & Korn 1972; Staffieri 1967) has shown that from early childhood through to adolescence the preferred body shape is mesomorphic. In children's stories the mesomorph is described as brave, attractive, strong and intelligent. Less favourable adjectives are reserved for the ectomorph and endomorph. Furthermore, mesomorphs appear to be more popular in the classroom than either of the other body types (Staffieri 1967).

Clearly, educators need to avoid stereotyping children on the basis of their physique. There are several potential dangers in doing so. We might, for example, expect muscular-looking children (mesomorphs) to be mainly, or perhaps exclusively, interested in sport and consequently supply little encouragement for their talents in music or dance. We might expect thin, angular children (ectomorphs) to be only good at, and interested in, intellectual activities, and fail to provide the opportunities and encouragement for them to become involved in physical activities. Finally, fatter children (endomorphs) may be consigned to passive activities, with no great physical challenges being made available. Furthermore, educators may inadvertently contribute to children's negative self-images by choosing the more stereotypically attractive for public roles such as presentations and demonstrations.

The fact that attitudes to body types are socially conditioned is very easily demonstrated cross-culturally. In Fiji and a number of other islander communities, body bulk is considered highly desirable and, instead of starving before their wedding (which is often the norm in Western societies), brides-to-be eat up to ensure good rounded proportions! In these cultures size is associated with fertility, fecundity and sexuality. Some Western research also suggests that men prefer rounded women to thin women (once model types are discounted!).

Related research into teachers' expectations, impressions and judgments of physically attractive students indicates that these students are usually judged more favourably by teachers in a number of dimensions including intelligence, academic potential, grades and various social skills (Ritts, Patterson & Tubbs 1992). It appears that teachers expect physically attractive students to be more intelligent and to attain a higher level of education than less physically attractive students. Furthermore, physically attractive students are rated by teachers as more friendly, more attentive, more popular and more outgoing (Ritts *et al.* 1992). When judged in terms of committing a serious misconduct, physically less attractive students are considered to be more chronically anti-social than more attractive students, for whom the behaviour is considered an aberration (Dion 1972).

The root of these expectations is not clear. However, it behoves us as teachers to take care not to hold unwarranted assumptions about students because of physical appearance.

Theory and research into practice

Marika Tiggemann — BODY IMAGE

BRIEF BIOGRAPHY

I completed an honours degree (my thesis topic was reaction time!) at the University of Adelaide in 1975, and then embarked on a Ph.D. on the topic of learned helplessness under the supervision of Professor Tony Winefield, which was completed in 1980. Thus my early training was in experimental psychology, and in learning and memory. The last study for my thesis was an attempted application of learned helplessness theory in the field, to an analysis of unemployment. This taught me survey methodology. I came to Flinders University as senior tutor in 1981, and have gradually worked my way up the academic ladder to professorial status. When I arrived as a junior academic, I didn't have available to me the equipment or facilities for conducting experiments, and so I was forced to have a long hard think about what I might really be interested in doing. I came up with the answer 'something to do with women and bodies and eating' which coalesced into 'body image', and I have been researching this in some way ever since. This was well before body image became the 'hot' topic that it is now, and of course, my thinking has evolved markedly over time. The thing that links my areas of research (learned helplessness, unemployment, body image) is an interest in issues of control and controllability.

Although I have been at Flinders University all this time, I have had opportunity to visit and collaborate with other researchers all over the world. In particular, I have spent sabbatical time at the University of Toronto (with Professors Janet Polivy and Peter Herman), at Sheffield University, at Tallinn Pedagogical University in Estonia, and at the C. Mondino Neurological Institute in Pavia in Northern Italy. Along the way I had a daughter. Highlights of my academic career include invitations to address the Inaugural South Australian Body Image Conference in September 2000 and the International Conference on Eating Disorders in Orlando, Florida, in April 2004. These days I spend a lot of my time reviewing manuscripts and grants. In particular, I am consulting editor for *Psychology of Women Quarterly*, and associate editor for the newly launched journal entitled *Body Image*.

RESEARCH AND THEORETICAL INTERESTS

My research interests lie primarily in the area of body image, very broadly defined. I also have related interests in attributional style, food cravings, and all aspects of women's health.

In most of my work on body image, I adopt a sociocultural perspective, which attributes the current high levels of body dissatisfaction and disordered eating among women (and, increasingly, among men) in Western societies to current rigid societal standards for beauty. For women, the current ideal is tall, young, smooth-skinned and extraordinarily thin. For men, the ideal is a muscular mesomorphic vee-shape, with well-developed upper body but narrow hips and flat stomach. These ideals are transmitted and reinforced in a number of ways—for example, through family, peers and the mass media. The female thin ideal is actually impossible for most women to achieve, at least by healthy means. The resulting futile pursuit of thinness has the potential negative consequences of body dissatisfaction, lowered self-esteem, excessive dieting practices, and the possible emergence of clinical eating disorders.

Within this general framework, there are several major strands to my research. I have been particularly interested in the role of the mass media as the most pervasive purveyor of sociocultural ideals and have employed several different methodologies to investigate this. Focus groups of adolescent girls have reported that looking at thin models in the fashion magazines, for example, does make them feel bad about their own bodies (Tiggemann, Gardiner & Slater 2000). My cross-sectional research has shown that reading fashion magazines and watching particular genres of television (soap operas, music videos) are related to body dissatisfaction and disordered eating (Tiggemann & Pickering 1996; Tiggemann, in press). My experimental research has demonstrated that acute exposure to thin female ideals (magazine advertisements or television commercials) leads to immediate decreases in mood and body esteem (Hargreaves & Tiggemann 2002; Tiggemann & McGill 2004). The mechanism for these negative effects seems to be social comparison, whereby individuals compare themselves with the media images (an upward social comparison) and find themselves lacking.

A second major strand investigates the effects of dieting on psychological well-being and performance. Although there are undoubted benefits of weight loss for some people, dieting carries a number of unintended negative consequences. For example, my research has shown that dieting is associated with mood swings (Tiggemann 1994) and lowered self-esteem

(Tiggemann 1997). We also have gathered increasing evidence that dieting results in impaired cognitive performance. Dieters do more poorly on complex cognitive tasks than non-dieters, and this is not attributable to differences in nutritional status, weight or personality. We (and others) believe this is a function of the preoccupying cognitions concerning weight, food and body shape known to characterise dieting, which take up valuable cognitive resources (Kemps & Tiggemann, submitted; Shaw & Tiggemann 2004).

I have also been interested in body image across the lifespan. Not surprisingly, most research has focused on the experience of adolescent girls and young adult women. However, we now have increasing evidence that the wish to be thinner emerges much earlier in girls, as young as six years old (Lowes & Tiggemann 2003; Tiggemann & Lowes 2003). At the other end of the age spectrum, the major finding is that body dissatisfaction is remarkably stable across the female lifespan, at least until women are in their sixties or seventies (Lynch & Tiggemann 2001; Tiggemann 2004). So, dissatisfaction with our bodies and a wish to be thinner is truly 'normative' for women in our society, no matter what their age.

Finally, I am interested in stereotyping and discrimination on the basis of weight. We have confirmed that both children (Tiggemann & Anesbury 2000) and adults (Tiggemann & Rothblum 1997) have very negative stereotypes of fat people. Our research has focused on the underlying reasons for this. It seems that both children and adults erroneously believe obesity to be largely under volitional control, and that the degree of controllability assigned predicts the extent of negative stereotyping.

THEORY AND RESEARCH INTO PRACTICE

The fact that in our society it is statistically normal for women and girls to be unhappy with their bodies has always struck me as a very sad facet of modern life. The very centrality and importance of physical appearance causes what I see as a great deal of unnecessary misery and is a waste of human potential. The adoption of a sociocultural model of body dissatisfaction offers a number of potential targets. At the most obvious macro-level, a number of advocacy groups, as well as girls and women themselves, are calling for a broader representation of a range of women and girls in fashion magazines, for example. Similarly, this was a major recommendation in the AMA (Australian Medical Association) Position Statement ratified in 2002 on Body Image and Health. I was part of a team, the CBA/AMA National Body Image Advisory Group (2000–02), who developed this position statement, which we hope will benefit medical practitioners and, indirectly, the wider community.

Although it is unlikely that societal practices will change in the short term, the research also proposes a number of other sites for intervention. In particular, it supports education in media literacy, whereby young people can be taught to critically examine and deconstruct the glorified images they are presented in the media. The research also points to a number of mediating and moderating variables. For example, social comparison has been identified as an important process variable. If women and girls can be persuaded not to compare themselves with media images (or other women), then many of the potential negative consequences can be avoided. Second, although almost everyone is subject to a virtual barrage of media images, not all girls become preoccupied and unhappy with their bodies, and only a small number succumb to clinical eating disorders. The research identifies a number of variables which make people more or less vulnerable to negative effects of media exposure. These include playing sport and high self-esteem, which seem to serve as protective factors making girls more resilient to media (and other) effects. Thus, programs that aim to get more girls playing sport (interestingly, adolescent girls give up playing sport at a much greater rate than adolescent boys), or to increase general global self-esteem, should also improve body image.

At a general level, the research carries the implication that discussions and interventions need to start earlier than we have previously thought, certainly before adolescence. The most useful aim would be to prevent girls from developing body dissatisfaction before it starts. Hence, it would also be useful for parents, childcare workers and the teachers of young children to be made aware of these issues. Parents and teachers who, for example, make negative comments about their own weight act as unwitting role models for young children. This is, of course, hard to avoid, as parents and teachers (like the rest of society) have also absorbed the societal values surrounding weight and physical attractiveness, which largely go unchallenged.

The unintended negative consequences of dieting mean that I take an anti-dieting stance. There is considerable debate in the literature about the efficacy of dieting for obese people, but in my view, anyone who is not obese should be dissuaded from dieting. As it stands, most of the people dieting are young adolescent girls of normal weight (and sometimes under-weight). For these girls, dieting leads to the range of negative consequences listed above, and just increases the focus on their bodies. The inevitable failures of dieting can result in a cycle of shame and feelings of loss of control and just exacerbate the problem. At a societal level, a focus on purely weight (as a single number on a scale) is not helpful. It would be far better to identify health or fitness or physical activity or lower blood pressure as the desired outcome. Certainly the current focus on obesity can only add to the stigmatisation and discrimination suffered by fat children and adults.

KEY REFERENCES

Lowes, J. & Tiggemann, M. (2003) Body dissatisfaction, dieting awareness and the impact of parental influence in young children. *British Journal of Health Psychology*, **8**, 135–47.

Tiggemann, M. (2003) Body image across the adult life span: Stability and change. *Body Image*, **1**, 29–41.

Tiggemann, M. & McGill, B. (2004) The role of social comparison in the effect of magazine advertisements on women's mood and body dissatisfaction. *Journal of Social and Clinical Psychology*, **23**, 23–44.

ACTIVITIES

1 Marika Tiggemann relates a number of her research interests—such as learned helplessness, unemployment and body image—to issues of control and controllability. What do you see as the links between these?

2 In many chapters of this book we refer to sociocultural perspectives on a whole range of learning- and motivation-related issues. Marika Tiggemann brings a sociocultural perspective to the issue of body dissatisfaction. Discuss with your fellow students what are the elements of this sociocultural perspective, and why this perspective is so important.

3 What does Marika Tiggemann see as the main influences on body dissatisfaction and disordered eating? What types of research have been conducted to examine these influences, and what have the findings indicated? What are some potential solutions to the problems associated with body dissatisfaction and disordered eating, and how is this information of use to you as an educator?

4 Dieting seems to be a preoccupation in much of the Western world. Why is there such a preoccupation with dieting, and what are some of the potential problems associated with dieting?

5 Much of Marika Tiggemann's research relates to Sheldon's body type theory. Reread the section on Sheldon and discuss with your fellow students what links there are between Sheldon's theory and Tiggemann's findings on stereotyping and discrimination on the basis of weight. You should read the recommended references to examine this issue.

QUESTION POINT

Does our body shape influence our view of self? How might teachers overcome the influence on children and adolescents of physical stereotypes that are portrayed so dynamically in the media?

General physical health and the school environment

Students spend many hours at school, and it is our responsibility as teachers to make the school's physical environment as healthy as possible for them. Good lighting, heating and ventilation are essential in every classroom. Students should sit at desks that are the proper height and in seats that support their backs. Playgrounds should have adequate shelter from the elements, as well as shade and proper seating. This is particularly important as schools introduce student welfare policies that include skin-care provisions. There should be adequate open spaces for children to run around in, and areas should be designated for particular

What purpose does sports afternoons serve in the school timetable?

Group games are a fun way of developing physical and motor skills.
Photo: Natalie Thew

physical activities. It is potentially dangerous when 12-year-old boys and girls mix with younger children when playing. Many children go home with scrapes and bruises received when run into by hurtling missiles (human, or inanimate ones such as tennis balls). Toilets should be well designed, ventilated and clean. There should always be adequate soap and toilet paper. Schools should also supply mirrors so that students can groom themselves.

Testing one's physical prowess becomes quite exhausting.

Physical activities such as dance should be available for all body types.

Because children's bodies are undergoing significant structural changes during the primary years, schools should ensure that children sit in desks and chairs that fit, wear shoes that fit, and don't carry unreasonably heavy loads of books to school.

Potential health problems

From time to time, physical problems that go unnoticed in the home become apparent in school. Difficulties with sight and hearing, for example, can impede the effective learning of students at school. Routine testing of sight and hearing when children begin school is an important means of minimising difficulties. Vigilant teachers can alert parents to seek medical attention in minor cases. At other times, students may require special school facilities (see Chapter 9).

Some children may undergo periods of temporary deafness as a result of ear infections, particularly in the infant grades. Parents and teachers should monitor these

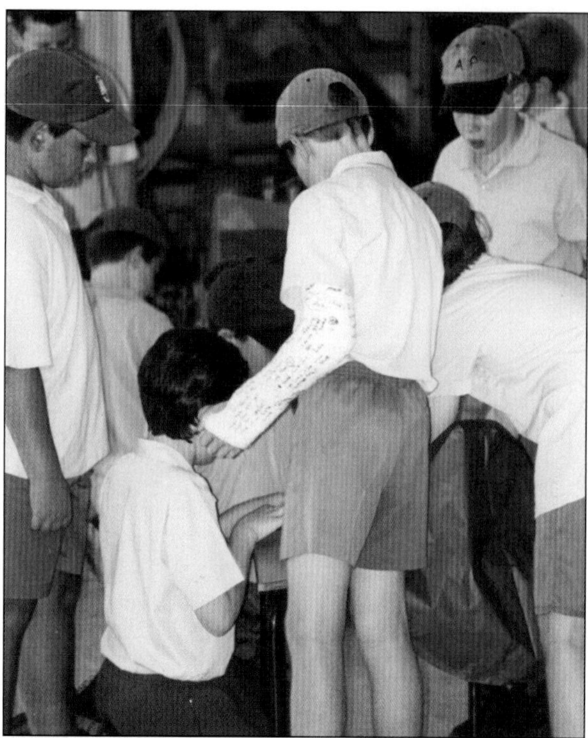

Broken bones are one of the potential health problems during late childhood. What can the school do to alleviate problems?

events to prevent long-term problems. Apart from hearing difficulties affecting learning and motivation, continued absences, as a result of ineffective treatment of the problem, will cause children to fall further and further behind in their work. This will also have repercussions in terms of self-esteem and self-confidence.

Hearing problems

Most vision problems can easily be corrected by the use of eyeglasses. Parents and teachers should be on the lookout for temporary eye disorders such as conjunctivitis, which can be caused by children rubbing their eyes with dirty hands. This is readily treated with antibiotics; however, if left untreated it can lead to serious eye problems such as scarring of the cornea (Harris 1985; Lunde & Lunde 1980; Smart & Smart 1977; Starfield & Pless 1980).

Seeing problems

As discussed earlier, dietary deficiencies are often responsible for abnormal growth patterns. In Western societies such as Australia and New Zealand, there should be no excuse for children and adolescents being *malnourished*. There are those, however, who do arrive in our schools *undernourished*. Sometimes this is a result of poor parenting and lower socio-economic status. Obviously, under circumstances where school learning and motivation suffer, the school must assume some responsibility for the adequate nourishment of the child.

Nutrition, malnourishment, undernourishment, obesity

Counterpointing undernourishment is the problem of *obesity*. Many children and adolescents are obese, which reduces their ability to exercise the physical and motor structures in their body essential for healthy development. Some obesity may be genetically linked, but many overweight children and adolescents become so through a poor diet that includes too much food and empty calories for their level of activity and laziness, with too much time spent in front of the television predisposing them to little exercise and endless snacking on the wrong kinds of food. In part, poor eating habits are set up in the home through parental feeding practices, such as rewarding children with high-calorie foods and snacks. At other times, poor eating may be associated with stress reduction or traumatic events such as divorce or death (see Berk 1996). Again, while teachers and schools are not responsible in the first instance for children's obesity, a school's health program should be designed to educate children and adolescents in good eating and exercise habits. Healthy food should be available at school.

From time to time, students miss school due to childhood illnesses and bouts of flu and colds. Irregular attendance of students due to ill health needs to be carefully monitored and some form of intervention program developed to assist the child and the family. Some children and adolescents miss substantial periods at school because of chronic and persistent illnesses such as respiratory problems, asthma and bronchitis, urinary tract infections, migraines and diabetes (Holt 1991; Starfield & Pless 1980). As a result, they may also develop behavioural and learning problems and have restricted opportunities for physical activity. Teachers need to support the individual and their family through

Childhood illnesses may lead to behavioural and learning problems

'It's called a sandwich!'

encouragement and remedial help. The policy of mainstreaming means that increasing numbers of individuals with chronic illnesses and impairments will be found in the regular classroom. This issue is dealt with in Chapter 9.

All teachers need to be familiar with the range of common illnesses that affect children during the early years of schooling. Particular infectious diseases must be reported to a doctor, and students excluded from school for the prescribed period. While there has been a decline in infectious diseases such as measles, mumps and polio since mass immunisation for these diseases became common, it is apparent that increasing numbers of parents are not having their children immunised. As a result, more and more children are coming to school having suffered debilitating bouts of these illnesses.

Physical safety and legal requirements

As described above, the early childhood and primary years of schooling coincide with periods of rapid physical growth and motor development during which children are particularly energetic and keen to test out their newly developing physical skills. Accidents such as broken arms and legs, concussion, scrapes and bruises increase sharply at this time (Heffey 1985), but such injury can be minimised by appropriate supervision by parents and teachers. The *duty of care* that teachers have as part of their role means that they must be aware of dangerous activities and possess qualifications for sports coaching. For any physical activity there should be proper physical conditioning of the students; proper supervision of the sport; well-fitted protective equipment (such as helmets, knee and elbow pads, groin protectors, mouthguards); careful grouping of students according to weight, height and ability; and opportunity for every student who wishes to participate in some sport in accordance with their skills, health and level of physical maturation to do so (Lunde & Lunde 1980).

There is a significant legal responsibility on teachers to ensure the safety of their students. In some contexts (for example, outdoor excursions such as hiking and camping and other sporting activities), teachers sometimes badly judge the capacity of students to cope with the experiences (Bransgrove 1990). Some teachers decide that, regardless of age, it is well within the individual capacity of a student to perform certain tasks, given the individual's size and strength. Such decisions may be very hazardous and overly demanding on individuals. Their natural excitement, curiosity and adventurousness may place them at risk unless the teacher is aware of this and takes steps to maximise safety. The author vividly recalls taking a group of 35 Year 5 boys to the Sydney Harbour Bridge pylon lookout as part of an excursion. It appeared that whatever level of the pylon he was on, most of the boys were on other levels, hanging over edges to get better views! He was beside himself trying to keep all of them safely behind the barriers and sighed with relief at the end of the day that no disaster had befallen the group! Our experience leads us to believe that whenever students are taken on an excursion, the teacher must plan carefully for every eventuality. Many Departments of Education require teachers supervising excursions to have earned various first aid certificates.

WHAT WOULD YOU DO?

MORE THAN HISTORY ON HIS MIND

I had occasion to talk to a 16-year-old student in one of our Year 11 history classes about his recent irregular attendance. When he came through the door I could not help noticing how tall he was, nor could I miss the very closely cut hair and the rather large earring. I sensed a possible confrontation looming so I spoke quite softly to him. I told him it was my duty to speak to him and I also reminded him that his work output, or lack of it, indicated a likelihood of failing the subject.

He clearly appreciated what I was saying, but when I went on to tell him that I should inform his parents, tears began to well up in his eyes. It was immediately clear that history was not really on this young man's mind. I asked David to sit down and we talked. From what I could gather, the past three years of David's life had been a living hell. Years of physical abuse had left a residue of guilt and fear, and he had recently become an intravenous drug user.

Case studies illustrating National Competency Framework for Beginning Teaching, National Project on the Quality of Teaching and Learning, Australian Teaching Council, 1996, p. 54. Commonwealth of Australia copyright, reproduced by permission.

What would you do to help David?

WHAT WOULD YOU DO? (cont.)

MORE THAN HISTORY ON HIS MIND

After almost an hour of listening, I explained to him that I was not equipped to help him but that there were a number of people in the school who were trained to help him overcome his burdens. I advised him to seek out one of these people. The next day Margaret, a colleague, asked to speak to me. She told me that David had told her that he had been speaking to me and he had told her a lot of his problems. He had agreed to Marg's suggestion that they would sit down with his parents to try and solve them.

David has since left our school and taken a course at a commercial college. Margaret sees David and his family regularly, and two months later tells me that things are now going really well for David.

I feel good about this story for a number of reasons. I think I was partly instrumental in helping David begin to solve his personal problems. Second, I am proud of the fact that one of my colleagues was willing and able to find the time to work closely with the family in helping David to work things out.

Case studies illustrating National Competency Framework for Beginning Teaching, National Project on the Quality of Teaching and Learning, Australian Teaching Council, 1996, p. 54. Commonwealth of Australia copyright, reproduced by permission.

What do you think took place at the discussion between David, his parents and Margaret? Why did this appear to work so successfully? What special skills would a teacher need to initiate the action that Margaret took? Relate the issues to material covered in this and the next two chapters.

KEY TERMS

Anorexia nervosa (p. 435): severe restriction of eating tending to malnutrition

Asynchrony (p. 426): differential growth spurts

Bulimia nervosa (p. 434): uncontrollable binge eating followed by purging

Canalisation (p. 421): regularity of development of some characteristics of heredity

Cephalocaudal development (p. 422): head-down development

Developmental tasks (p. 423): age appropriate physical, motor, social and cognitive tasks that are mastered by children

Differentiation (p. 434): in motor development, refers to the gradual progression of children's motor coordination from gross to refined movements

Fine motor movements (p. 435): voluntary body movements that involve the small muscles

Integration (p. 434): in motor development, refers to the coordination of various opposing muscle and sensory systems into ccordinated interaction

Interpersonal asynchrony (p. 429): physical development varies from individual to individual

Intrapersonal asynchrony (p. 429): uneven physical development within an individual

Maturation (p. 421): genetically programmed changes over time providing a point of readiness for learning

Motor skills (p. 434): physical skills using the body or limbs such as walking and holding

Physical development (p. 421): changes in body structure over time involving cephalocaudal and proximodistal development

Proximodistal development (p. 422): axis-out development

Puberty (p. 426): the point in an individual's physical development that marks the onset of full reproductive functions

Pubescence (p. 428): changes that result in sexual maturity

Secular trend (p. 430): accelerated physical and sexual development

ON-LINE LEARNING

If you go to http://www.pearsoned.com.au/mcinerney, you will have hot links directly to these sites:

Girl talk

This site provides information for female pre-teens and teens on a range of sexual issues. Consider the information in this site and discuss with others whether the site makes a positive contribution to sexual education.

http://www.gurl.com/topics/sex

Sexpedia

This is a website designed by the Discovery Channel and provides all types of sexual information.

http://health.discovery.com/centers/sex/sexpedia/sexpedia.html

Ask Alice

This is another health and sexuality information site. Review it and consider its usefulness.

http://www.goaskalice.columbia.edu/

Child development basics

These sites provide a wealth of information for following up topics covered in this chapter:

http://www.cdipage.com/development.htm;
http://www.indiaparenting.com/develop/index.shtml;
http://www.childdevelopmentinfo.com/health_safety/physical_development.shtml

Coalition for positive sexuality

A sex education site designed for teenagers.

http://www.positive.org/Home/index.html

Kids Health

This site provides lots of useful information on physical and sexual development of children, designed for children. Review the site and consider its strengths and weaknesses.

http://kidshealth.org/kid/index.jsp

Teaching teens

This site provides lesson ideas for teaching teens about sexual development. Critique the presentation in the context of Chapter 12.

http://www.teachingteens.com/tpubrty.htm

WEB DESTINATIONS

If you go to http://www.pearsoned.com.au/mcinerney, you will have hot links directly to these sites:

Australian Institute of Family Studies

This site will provide you with information on topics covered in this and subsequent chapters.

http://www.aifs.gov.au/

Teaching Teens

This site provides an index of almost every topic you want to know about in relation to the physical development of teenagers!

http://www.teachingteens.com/list.htm

Engenderhealth

A site dedicated to health issues related to sexuality and gender.

http://www.engenderhealth.org/index.html

Gender and Queer Studies

This site provides a lot of useful information on sexual development and related issues. It is particularly useful in that it provides an overview of the types of information and experiences adolescents are currently exposed to through the media.

http://www2.fmg.uva.nl/sociosite/topics/index.html

NHS Healthcare Guide

A useful site for looking up information on a range of developmental issues and problems such as eating disorders, puberty and obesity.

www.healthcareguide.nhsdirect.nhs.uk

Eating disorders

An excellent site for locating information related to a range of eating disorders such as bulimia and anorexia nervosa.

http://www.mirror-mirror.org/eatdis.htm

■ **Sheldon's body types**

This site provides further information on Sheldon's body types. Sheldon's typology of body types has provided the base for many physical education programs, as illustrated in the following website.
http://www.innerexplorations.com/psytext/3.htm

■ **Body Types**

http://www.ideodynamic.com/enneagram-monthly/EM_archiv.htm?1999/EM_9901_a1.htm~Article

RECOMMENDED READING

Corbin, C. B. (1980) *A Textbook for Motor Development*. Dubuque, IA: William C. Brown.

Gallahue, D. L. (1989) *Understanding Motor Development: Infants, Children, Adolescents*, 2nd ed. Brisbane: John Wiley.

Gregor, S. (2004) The man behind the mask: Male body image dissatisfaction. *INPSYCH*, **26**, 27–9.

Griffiths, R. A. & Channon-Little, L. (1996) Psychological treatments and bulimia nervosa: An update. *Australian Psychologist*, **31**, 79–96.

Holt, K. S. (1991) *Child Development. Diagnosis and Assessment*. London: Butterworth-Heinemann.

Malina, R. M. & Bouchard, C. (1991) *Growth, Maturation, and Physical Activity*. Champaign, Ill: Human Kinetics Books.

Maude, D., Wertheim, E. H., Paxton, S., Gibbons, K. & Szmukler, G. (1993) Body dissatisfaction, weight loss behaviours and bulimic tendencies in Australian adolescents with an estimate of female data representativeness. *Australian Psychologist*, **28**(2), 128–32.

Paxton, S., Wertheim, E., Gibbons, K., Szmukler, G. L., Hillier, L. & Petrovich, J. L. (1991) Body image satisfaction, dieting beliefs, and weight loss behaviours in adolescent girls and boys. *Journal of Youth and Adolescence*, **20**, 361–97.

Sinclair, D. (1989) *Human Growth after Birth*. Oxford: Oxford University Press.

Tanner, J. M. (1990) *Fetus into Man. Physical Growth from Conception to Maturity* (revised and enlarged). Cambridge, MA: Harvard University Press.

Thelen, E. (1995) Motor development. A new synthesis. *American Psychologist*, **50**, 79–95.

CHAPTER

13 Personal development and effective learning

Overview

Academic learning depends not only upon things such as intelligence, but also on the whole range of personal qualities that a person brings to bear on the learning task. In this chapter we consider personality development and, in particular, how individuals develop as people: how they relate to others and to themselves; how they develop personal goals and ambitions in life; how they acquire moral values; and how they react to the many problems and challenges they meet in life. The main focus in this chapter is on the work of Erikson, Freud, Rogers and Maslow. Each of these personality theorists has made a valuable contribution to our understanding of how individuals develop a sense of self.

In the description of Erikson's psychosocial theory of personality development we cover the stages of psychosocial development and the process of identity formation. We emphasise, especially, the importance of caregivers, teachers and peers in an individual's personality development, and that of parental and grandparental involvement in schools. We briefly describe elements of Freudian theory that are of interest to educators.

We also consider the humanistic theories of Rogers and Maslow. Our main focus is on the notion that parents, caregivers and teachers act as facilitators of children's personal and intellectual development by supplying them with appropriate opportunities, resources, support and non-evaluative feedback.

13

Learning objectives

After reading this chapter, you will be able to:

- outline key elements of the developing person;
- describe Erikson's psychosocial theory of personal development;
- name Erikson's eight developmental stages, and discuss environmental conditions that facilitate positive development;
- apply principles derived from Erikson's psychosocial theory of personal development in educational settings;
- explain identity formation during adolescence and critically examine the notion of 'identity crisis';
- outline and critically analyse Marcia's identity statuses;
- explain the importance of parental involvement in children's education;
- describe Freud's psychosexual theory;
- apply principles derived from Freud's psychosexual theory of personal development in educational settings;
- describe key elements of humanism, and discuss the application of these in educational settings;
- outline Maslow's hierarchy of needs, and discuss educational settings and teaching methods to meet the needs of students;
- discuss the relationship of humanism and constructivism;
- consider the sociocultural dimensions of personality development.

While reading our description of personal development, consider the Learner-centred Psychological Principle below and Teaching Competence Box 13.1. At the end of the chapter, review these and demonstrate how you would implement the principles covered in both.

LEARNER-CENTRED PSYCHOLOGICAL PRINCIPLE

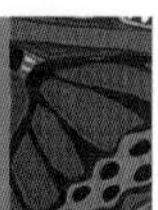

Personal beliefs, thoughts and understandings resulting from prior learning and interpretations become the individual's basis for constructing reality and interpreting life experiences.

Unique cognitive constructions form a basis for beliefs and attitudes about others. Individuals then operate out of these 'separate realities' as if they were true for everyone, often leading to misunderstandings and conflict. Awareness and understanding of these phenomena allow greater choice over the degree to which one's beliefs influence one's actions and enable one to see and take into account others' points of view. The cognitive, emotional and social development of a child, and the way that child interprets life experiences, are a product of prior schooling, home, culture and community factors.

APA Task Force on Psychology in Education (1993, January), p. 9. Reprinted with permission. http://www.apa.org/ed/lcp.html#The%2014%20Learner

TEACHING COMPETENCE Box 13.1

The teacher develops positive relationships with students

Indicators

The teacher:

- regards all students as individuals and treats them with respect;
- acts to establish a learning community in which all students are engaged;
- encourages students to take intellectual risks;
- is sensitive to students' emotional needs and provides support;
- applies skills of negotiation, mediation and conflict resolution.

Case studies illustrating National Competency Framework for Beginning Teaching, National Project on the Quality of Teaching and Learning, Australian Teaching Council, 1996, Element 2.2, p. 38. Commonwealth of Australia copyright, reproduced by permission.

The developing person

Personality is stable; that is, we do not change into fundamentally different people from day to day. Personality is also organised and integrated—that is, its attributes are interrelated. Personality is formed as a result of the interaction between innate biological mechanisms and the environment, and it is distinctive, each personality being unique (Fontana 1986). In the following sections we examine a number of theories of **personality development**. Consider each theory in terms of the points above and, especially, the implications of each for your role as an educator or parent.

The personal self

Personal identity formation becomes increasingly important to adolescents.

Erikson's stages of personal development

A personality theory with great intuitive appeal and usefulness for teachers in understanding and supporting the development of personality in students under their care is Erik Erikson's personality theory (Elkind 1977; Erikson 1963, 1968). Erikson has built upon many of the basic notions of Freudian theory which we cover briefly later in this chapter. However, while Freud's focus was on psychosexual development, Erikson focuses on psychosocial development. Furthermore, while Freud believed that the first five or so years of life set the foundations for lifelong personality characteristics, Erikson sees personality development as a lifelong journey which he has aptly named the *eight ages of man*. (Perhaps, today, we should refer to the 'eight ages of people', but it loses something in the adaptation.)

Side by side with the *psychosexual stages* of development described by Freud are Erikson's **psychosocial stages** of **identify formation**, in which the individual has to establish new basic orientations to the social world. At each stage there is the potential for positive and negative experiences. A healthy personality is, by and large, one that has successfully accomplished the tasks appropriate to each stage. Erikson allows for the fact that earlier, poorly resolved conflicts may be compensated for, in part, by later fulfilling experiences.

Table 13.1 lists these eight stages and compares them with Freud's psychosexual stages.

Infancy and early personal development

The infant requires nurturant care. Loving care leads to feelings of well-being and a sense of the world as a safe place in which to be. Inconsistent or rejecting care fosters within children a basic mistrust, fear and apprehension of the caregivers, which may be generalised to other people and to the world at large. The dichotomy between *trust* and *mistrust* arises at each successive stage of development.

With greater mobility and a growing command of language, toddlers test themselves out in the world of experience. Of course, this means that children increasingly run into controls exerted by parents and other caregivers. Depending on the amount of *autonomy*

Table 13.1 Erikson's eight stages of personality development

Period of development	Freud's psychosexual stages	Erikson's psychosocial stages
Birth to 1 year	Oral stage	Basic trust *v* mistrust
1 to 3 years	Anal stage	Autonomy *v* shame and doubt
3 to 6 years	Phallic stage	Initiative *v* guilt
6 years to puberty	Latency stage	Industry *v* inferiority
Adolescence	Genital stage	Identity *v* role confusion
Young adulthood		Intimacy *v* isolation
Middle adulthood		Generativity *v* self-absorption
Old age		Ego integrity *v* despair

allowed and support given, children develop a sense that they are able to control themselves. On the other hand, if the caregivers are overly restrictive, harshly critical or impatient, and consistently do for children what they could do for themselves, children may develop a sense of *shame and doubt* about their capacities to do things. When our daughter Alexandra was three she often pushed our hands away with an imperative 'I can do it!' Children at this age need to be given opportunities to pour drinks, feed themselves, flush toilets, dress themselves, and so on. Accidents will occur and must be handled sympathetically by the adult. Naturally, a balance must be struck between the need to allow children autonomy to explore and do new and exciting things, and the need to protect them from danger.

Early to late childhood personal development

Early to middle childhood is a time when children initiate many activities, confident and assured of their own motor and intellectual abilities. However, it is also a time when the energy and inquisitiveness of children can be exasperating for parents and teachers as they struggle to cope with children's boundless energy and the five-hundredth question of the day. Children who are given freedom and opportunity to initiate and test their newly acquired powers of communication and physical agility develop *initiative* and self-assurance. In contrast, if children are overly restricted or made to feel that they are engaging in a 'silly' or 'wrong' activity, making a mess or taking up too much time, they may develop a sense of *guilt* over self-initiated activities that will persist through later life stages. Often, different expectations are held for girls than for boys, such that differential restrictions are applied by parents (and at times by teachers) (Fontana 1986). This can lead to problems when children wish to initiate activity in supposed gender-inappropriate areas. For example, boys who want to dance and girls who want to play football sometimes come in for a hard time and are made to feel uncomfortable and guilty over their choices. Schools are implementing anti-sexism programs to address this problem, although many homes still strongly support children's initiatives in sex-stereotyped areas.

The period of *industry* versus *inferiority* coincides with late childhood and is a time of great productivity. We remember how excited both our daughters were to be involved in producing projects, inventions, craftwork and stories. Children at this time show a great interest in what makes the world tick, how things are done and why they are done in a certain way. They are capable of increasingly sophisticated thought and argument. Of course,

Parental love and care is important for all ages.

First days at school are always exciting. They indicate developing independence.

this is also a busy time for parents and teachers as they bat and field questions related to all manner of things, and have to defend their right (as adults) to make the final decision at times, against the protests of children who think they know better! This is a time to encourage children in their productivity and creativity as they make and build things. Children who are restricted, criticised, told not to make a nuisance of themselves or a mess may develop feelings of inferiority. The child's peer group becomes an increasingly important influence also, as it gives feedback to the child about their abilities which helps to reinforce feelings of industry or inferiority (see Chapter 14).

Adolescence, identity formation and personal development

The period of *identity* versus *role confusion* is a particularly important stage for the development of self-identity. This period occurs during adolescence and is a time of increasing social contacts. Adolescents integrate what they have learned about themselves and begin to test their identity out in the wider world. In particular, adolescents compare their experiences with their peers, and become interested in relationships, religions, politics and society in general. Becoming members of sporting associations, religious groups and social networks outside the family grows increasingly important and helps to define for individuals where they belong. Role confusion results when an adolescent feels lost, unattached or confused in social identity. This might be the result of inadequate opportunities to form social networks outside the family or be residual from poorly resolved conflicts in earlier stages. For example, individuals who already feel inferior and guilty may choose not to test themselves in the wider community of peers and relationships and, therefore, deny themselves further opportunities for personal growth. Conversely, individuals with a poorly developed **identity** may either go to extremes to become part of a group or engage in antisocial or anti-personal behaviour, such as delinquency and substance abuse, to reduce their sense of confusion. Essentials of adolescent identity formation are found in Table 13.2.

Some writers suggest that, unless adolescents go through some type of **identity crisis**, where they clarify and become aware of personal values that they commit themselves to, little psychological growth can occur. Research suggests that many adolescents do not undergo such a crisis and therefore fall short of mature identity achievement (Marcia 1980; see also 1966, 1967). Instead, identity foreclosure results, in which adolescents prematurely identify with the values and goals of their parents without questioning whether they are right for them. James Marcia, basing his work on that of Erikson, proposed four identity statuses that resolve the identity crisis: **identity diffusion**, **foreclosure**, **moratorium** and **identity achievement**. Each status relates to an individual's commitment to a career, personal value system, sexual attitudes and religious beliefs.

1 *Identity diffusion:* where there is no crisis and no commitment. This is exemplified in the adolescent or young adult who flits from job to job, commitment to commitment, and relationship to relationship with little personal investment. Identity diffusion may be the product of earlier unresolved conflicts, or it may result from perceived blocks in the environment, such as parental disapproval or cultural barriers. It is often characterised by self-doubt, anxiety, depression and apathy.
2 *Foreclosure:* where there is no crisis, and commitment is based on the will of the parents or other significant people, such as ministers of religion or romantic partners. This is exemplified by the young adult who becomes a teacher or chemist because 'Dad and Mum expect it' or who goes into Dad's business, without any personal valuing of the career. It might also occur as a result of an adolescent falling into a career in which they already have a perceived interest or talent (for example, sporting or artistic skills), without leaving scope to develop other areas of interest. Identity foreclosure can lead to discontent in later life.

3 *Moratorium:* where the individual is experiencing crisis and working out roles and commitments. This is exemplified by the young adult who tries out a variety of personal and social options before making a commitment. The delay in making a commitment may be the product of family events, socio-economic position, educational deprivation and other social barriers. An individual may drop out of university for a period of time to 'sort out' whether this is really the right career path. Choosing to return, or to go in a different direction, facilitates the achievement of identity. Some students delay making a choice until they have temporarily broken the ties of their families and schooling. Again, this process can facilitate the ultimate choice in which there is a personal commitment.

What elements of identity characterise this adolescent? How might these be different for adolescents from other cultural groups?

'Unfortunately, er ... it's Faith and Sky, isn't it...? Although these suggestions are splendid, school uniform design is entirely determined by the Department.'

4 *Identity achieved:* having already explored alternatives, identity-achieved individuals are committed to a clearly formulated set of self-chosen values and goals. They feel a sense of psychological well-being, of knowing who they are and where they are going. When asked about career or life changes, they might respond that they are pretty sure that what they are doing is right for them.

Identity achievement and moratorium are considered healthy alternatives, whereas adolescents who can't proceed past the identity diffusion or identity foreclosure stage have difficulties in adjustment. They need extra assistance and counselling to answer the important question, 'Who am I?'

Table 13.2

Essentials of adolescent identity formation

- Developing a philosophy of life that includes moral values and an orientation to religion.
- Integrating enduring temperamental qualities and basic dispositions into a well-rounded adult character.
- Establishing a gender-role identity.
- Developing a sense of self as a sexual being.
- Developing a sense of self in relation to politics and social issues.
- Contemplating future intimate relationships.
- Developing a vocational identity.

(Source: Based on Erikson 1968; Peterson 1996)

EXTENSION STUDY

Sociocultural influences and identity formation

A relevant question to ask about Marcia's identity statuses, particularly in countries such as Australia and New Zealand and others characterised by ethnic diversity, is whether these identity statuses are relevant in cross-cultural settings. Cross-cultural research seems to indicate that the same patterns do occur across cultures (Scarr, Weinberg & Levine 1986). However, Marcia's interpretation certainly highlights the individualistic component of identity formation in which the individual is reacting to social situations shaping identity, rather than being embedded within and part of the social milieu. As we have discussed earlier in our treatment of Vygotsky, a social contructivist view of identity formation would emphasise more emphatically the idea that a person's identity may be inseparable from the group identity in which it is situated (see, for example, Penuel & Wertsch 1995). Erikson emphasised that one of the important elements of identity formation is for it to be validated by others in the community. Hence an individual's cultural identity, nurtured by members of their own cultural community, is essential to personal identity formation. In many societies the idea of individual identity, as we understand it in Western societies, may be contradictory to identity as it is understood in those societies in which social identity takes precedence over individual identity.

The notion of identity formation and identity crisis is certainly thrown into strong relief when we consider individuals who come from ethnic minority groups in multi-ethnic societies such as Australia, New Zealand, the United States, Canada and the United Kingdom. In their case, there

Parental involvement and identity formation

Probably the most critical factor in the development of a sense of identity is the nature of the relationship that children and adolescents maintain with their parents (Conger 1977; Santrock & Yussen 1992). Establishing a strong ego identity will be facilitated if a sufficiently rewarding, interactive relationship exists between the child or adolescent and both parents (see Chapter 14). It is important that the same-sex parent serves as an adequate model for personally and socially effective and appropriate behaviour. It is also important that the opposite-sex parent is an effective individual, and approves of the model provided by the same-sex parent and the child's own identification with this model.

Adolescent identity formation and parental developmental problems

Having adolescent children can be quite trying for parents. Adolescents challenge cherished values, such as religious beliefs, moral values, political allegiances and parental authority (Montemayor & Flannery 1991; Steinberg 1991). It is also important to note that this can be a period of change and personal stress for parents. With adolescent children, many parents are entering their middle years; as well as having ambivalent attitudes towards the growing independence of their children and often lacking expertise in handling the developmental problems of this age, parents may also be experiencing their own emotional problems and conflicts that impact on parent–child interactions—problems such as marital dissatisfaction, economic burdens, career re-evaluation, and health and body concerns such as menopause (Santrock & Yussen 1992; Silverberg & Steinberg 1990). The lack of communication between parents and adolescents and the conflicts that often result can be better understood, and better advice given, if this parental perspective is taken into account. Such problems may be exacerbated for migrant parents who see, as well, cherished cultural values dissipating as their adolescent children become increasingly assimilated into the cultural norms of their new country.

At the time that adolescents are moving away from parent dependency, they often substitute peer dependency. Adolescents seek out and listen to the advice of peers on many issues, especially those involving immediate consequences, such as clothes, entertainment, fads, and so on. Peers exert a great deal of pressure on each other to conform. They also give each other the opportunity to express the frustrations and problems they have at home. However, adults often exaggerate the power of the peer group, particularly as it relates to sexual behaviour, substance abuse and delinquency. It is important to note that, as well as parents and peers, other forces within society strongly influence the adolescent, including the popular media and other adults such as teachers, coaches and part-time

Adolescent identity formation and peer dependency

may be an even stronger clash of forces orienting the development of their sense of identity (see Germain 2004). For example, while the Anglo-Australian child or Pakeha is socialised within a world in which society at large, family and peer group share many common values and traditions, children from other groups, such as Lebanese, Chinese, Aboriginal and Maori, may well find that they are influenced by conflicting forces. For example, while Anglo-Australian children are encouraged by society, family and peer group to develop individuality and autonomy, many ethnic children may be encouraged by their families and cultural groups to remain interdependent. Therefore, these children receive conflicting messages from the wider society, school, peers and their cultural community. On multiple levels such as moral values, dress, use of spare time, political views, dating, education, career choice and religion, there is potential for conflicting messages and identity conflict (Partington & McCudden 1992). This may be further exacerbated for females, who traditionally are given even less freedom to make personal decisions (on such matters as dating, education and career choice) than males in particular ethnic communities.

Australian and New Zealand initiatives in multicultural education are aimed (among other goals) at fostering and supporting some important elements of cultural continuity (such as language maintenance) so that students from minority cultural groups are supported in their developing sense of self. Indeed, it seems that some students adjust well to a situation in which they are bicultural and able to function effectively in both worlds with an integrated sense of self (Cahill & Ewen 1987; see also Germain 2004). Inevitably, however, there will be culture clashes, and your primary task as an educator will be to assist the student in resolving the conflict. We discuss these issues in detail in Chapter 10.

employers. (For a fuller discussion of this issue, read Chapter 14.)

Young adulthood and beyond

During the next period, *intimacy* versus *isolation*, young adults develop the ability to share with others and care about other people selflessly. It is through this selfless caring that we develop a sense of intimacy with others. If a sense of intimacy is not established with friends or a marriage partner, the result, according to Erikson, is a sense of isolation, of being alone without anyone to share with or care for.

In the earlier stages of personality development, people are somewhat self-absorbed in the sense that experiences are interpreted in terms of what they mean to the individual. As psychologically healthy individuals

Why are peers so important as adolescents move away from dependence on parents, and what types of behaviour may be modelled?

Even in old age, we have the potential for personal growth. This elderly man is completing a crossword puzzle.

progress through the stages, they become more other-oriented. In the seventh stage, which occurs during middle adulthood and is referred to as *generativity* versus *self-absorption*, individuals become aware of, and more involved with, things and people outside their immediate families. They become concerned for the future of the world and the younger generation. Those who fail to establish a sense of generativity stagnate in a state of self-absorption in which their personal concerns and comforts become of primary concern.

In the final period, *integrity* versus *despair*, there is still the potential for personal growth. Integrity characterises the older individual who looks upon life's journey as an adventure of self-discovery, in which positive and negative experiences have been melded into a personality with which the individual is content. On the other hand, old age may bring to the individual despair and regret for lost opportunities and direction. The task of sharing wisdom and encouraging others is accepted with enthusiasm by those who develop integrity.

As with the earlier stages, society has an important role to play here in fostering within individuals a sense of integrity. Communities and families that respect the elderly and give them opportunities to be productive facilitate the development of a sense of integrity. On the other hand, elderly people who are 'shelved' and left to finish their lives isolated from events of importance, such as sharing in the rearing and teaching of children, may feel very undervalued and experience despair. We should remember that old age means many different things in different societies. Ours, along with many other Western and rapidly changing societies, tends to undervalue the contributions that older people may make.

The role of society in personal development of the elderly

QUESTION POINT

How might Erikson's theory help you, as an educator, to understand the day-to-day behaviour of children and adolescents in an educational setting?

Parental involvement in schools contributes greatly to children's learning.

Classroom applications of Erikson's theory

Importance of teachers and peers

There are several features of Erikson's theory that make it attractive to people in the helping professions such as teaching. Freud's theory suggests that the early years of life and, in particular, parenting practices related to feeding, toilet training and the inculcation of sexual identity and values have the major role to play in personality development, with other events and interpersonal contacts being of relatively minor importance. Erikson's theory, while agreeing that there is an initial onus on parents to support positive personal growth in children, argues strongly that other people, such as teachers and peers, become increasingly important as children grow older, and that personality development is a continuous process, with growth, development and change occurring whenever children are given positive or negative experiences.

Furthermore, earlier negative experiences such as parental neglect, which leads to a sense of mistrust in children, can be alleviated by later positive experiences such as a caring school and teacher, thereby fostering a sense of trust within the children. Children who have their sense of industry derogated at home can have it revitalised at school through the actions of caring and stimulating teachers. We must add here, however, that action can occur both ways. A child who comes to school with a well-developed sense of trust

Positive psychosocial experiences compensate for negative ones

may have it undermined by an uncaring teacher or bullying peers, and a child who is always building and inventing at home may lose interest in a classroom dominated by regulation and a lock-step curriculum that demands conformity to the norm.

A key to understanding Erikson's theory is the knowledge that, at each period of development, experiences can be positive or negative and the total personality at any particular time reflects the balance struck between them. If children experience basically negative or confusing experiences, they may be unable to establish a sense of self-identity, a process that Erikson called **role confusion**. This may be reflected in delinquent behaviour, losing one's identity in the group, or extreme identification with atypical groups (such as punk gangs) or substance abuse. Younger children may simply withdraw from mainstream experiences, while older children may 'drop out'.

Parental and grandparental involvement in school

Erikson's theory gives a sound rationale for parental and grandparental involvement in schools. This involvement can be as simple as paying attention to children's play and responding to their questions, listening to children read, acting as a sounding board for ideas (when parents and teachers are too busy), modelling different attitudes and values for children to incorporate into their growing sense of self, reinforcing children for their efforts and, finally, even direct involvement in the instruction of children (see, for example, Fantuzzo, Tighe & Childs 2000; Grolnick *et al.* 1997; Mattingly *et al.* 2002). Many older people are given little opportunity to contribute to the development of society, especially to the personal and academic growth of youngsters. As grandparents, many are excluded from any significant participation in the rearing of their grandchildren or of children in general, yet they have an enormous contribution to make. Childcare settings and schools should, therefore, actively encourage parental and grandparental involvement in their programs, and develop appropriate structures to facilitate this. Of course, there are tremendous benefits for the older people as well. In a sense, they are extending their period of generativity and maximising the positive forces that will lead them to feel a sense of integrity for a life well spent.

Research indicates that parental involvement in the education of their children is a good predictor of student learning and success (Bauch & Goldring 2000; Desimone 1999; Fantuzzo, Tighe & Childs 2000; Grolnick *et al.* 1997; Hill 2001; Hill & Craft 2003; Hoover-Dempsey & Sandler 1997). For example, parents' beliefs in their children's general school competence increase their children's task-focused behaviours at school, and parents' beliefs in their children's competence in mathematics, for example, contributes directly to the children's higher mathematical performance (Aunola, Nurmi, Lerkkanen & Rasku-Puttonen 2003; Hill & Craft 2003; see Pezdeck, Berry & Renmo 2002 for a contrary view). Parent–school involvement also appears to improve children's social behaviour and interactions among peers, and may be positively associated with rule compliance and sociability at school for children. Additionally, research suggests that children with parents who are involved in school have better emotional adjustment and better communication and social skills, as well as greater achievement orientation (Hill & Craft 2003). A cautionary view on the belief that parental involvement in children's education leads to better student learning is provided by Mattingly *et al.* (2002), listed in our recommended reading section at the end of the chapter. You should find this article interesting and useful.

Many schools actively involve parents in a wide range of school activities beyond just fundraising and tuck-shop duties, while other schools appear to have a 'closed-door' policy towards parents. Even when schools have an 'open-door' policy, many teachers complain that parents are not supportive of the school's efforts and show too little interest and involvement in their children's academic progress (Bauch & Goldring 2000).

What makes some schools more attractive to parental involvement than other schools? It appears that schools that promote a caring atmosphere and require parent volunteering seem to have stronger parental involvement. Schools in higher income areas also seem to have greater parental involvement, as do schools with more limited focus (for example, selective schools). Of these factors, a caring atmosphere seems to be the most strongly related to parental involvement (Bauch & Goldring 2000). This appears to be irrespective of school size and socio-economic status (see also Hoover-Dempsey & Sandler 1997). This finding strongly supports the contention of Erikson that schools need to be caring environments in order for children—and their families, for that matter—to thrive.

Caring atmosphere

Why do parents become involved in their children's education?

There are three potential reasons for parents to become involved in their children's education: (1) the parents' construction of their role in the child's life; (2) the parents' sense of efficacy for helping their child to succeed in school; and (3) the general invitations, demands and opportunities for parental involvement

Theory and research into practice

Robert D. Strom — THE IMPORTANCE OF PARENTS AND GRANDPARENTS IN CHILDREN'S EDUCATION

BRIEF BIOGRAPHY

Teaching has been a continuing source of satisfaction. My first students were adolescents from disadvantaged families in St. Paul, Minnesota and Detroit, Michigan. Working in these environments was the basis for my initial books: *Teaching in the Slum School* (1965), *The Inner City Classroom* (1966) and *The Urban Teacher* (1971). After three years in the public school classroom and completion of the doctorate, I took a position as project research director at the National Education Association in Washington DC. The task was to design and conduct studies leading to understanding of why students drop out and to identify ways to increase graduation rates. The chance to introduce new ways of thinking about teacher and student roles was presented when the College of Education faculty at The Ohio State University invited me to join them. My responsibility was to present the required basic educational psychology course attended by 800 students training to become teachers. This experience taught me the importance of modelling optimism for beginning educators so that they could respond to difficulties and challenges.

Since 1969 I have been teaching child, adolescent and parent development courses at Arizona State University. My enthusiasm for teaching and the desire to learn from students has led to my recognition as a Danforth Foundation Scholar, North Atlantic Treaty Organization Scholar (University of Ankara, Turkey) and Fulbright Scholar at the University of the Philippines in Manila, Canberra University in Australia, and the University of Stockholm in Sweden. My publications include 20 books, 300 articles and four measurement instruments about lifespan development and evaluation. Methods to unite families and schools have been described in my books *Psychology for the Classroom* (1969), *Teachers and the Learning Process* (1971), *Values and Human Development* (1972), *Parent and Child in Fiction* (1977), *Parent and Child Development* (1978), *Educational Psychology* (1982), and *Educating Adolescents and Learning from Them* (2005).

RESEARCH AND THEORETICAL INTERESTS

My goals for research and development have been to help educators of every age group and parents at each stage of their long-term role as teachers. Studies began in the 1960s with construction of environments for observing parents and teachers interacting with young children. I found that the best way to help individual parents is to first become aware of their strengths and educational needs. This task requires tools that are psychometrically sound. Such measures were scarce for the focus of my inquiry, so I decided to pursue the arduous task of developing instruments that could also be used by other scholars concerned with parent development. There was a need to determine the expectations parents had for their children and themselves as teachers. The Parent as a Teacher Inventory (PAAT) (1983; 1995) consists of 50 Likert-type items on which parents of children aged three to nine describe their feelings about Creativity, Frustration, Control, Play, and the Teaching–Learning process. This instrument is used as a pre-test and post-test to identify the education needs of parents and to evaluate outcomes of interventions such as Head Start and Even Start.

The parent role is considered most stressful when a child is 10 to 14 years of age. To provide support, my wife Shirley and I devised the Parent Success Indicator (PSI) (1998). This two-generational measure identifies favourable qualities of parents and aspects of their behaviour where education seems warranted through parent self-reports and the perceptions of their children. The six subscales of 60 Likert-type items emphasise Çommunication, Use of Time, Teaching, Frustration, Satisfaction, and Information Needs. Common uses for the PSI are to: find out how mothers and fathers perceive their assets and limitations during this demanding period of parenting; determine how they are seen by daughters and sons; compare child and parent impressions of the parent performance; give feedback to individual parents about attitudes and behaviours they should consider changing; design curriculum for parent groups with shared characteristics; and detect how parent–child interaction changes in response to educational programming.

Parents and children are not the only ones whose efforts are required in the quest to strengthen families. Grandparents are an important resource, especially in minority families where they more commonly care for children before and after school than other surrogates. The Grandparent Strengths and Needs Inventory (GSNI) (1993) helps grandparents to learn about themselves so that they can continue to grow and offer support to their families. The GSNI, designed with my wife Shirley, consists of three separate surveys for grandparents,

parents and grandchildren. Grandparents complete a self-impression survey on Satisfaction, Success, Teaching, Difficulty, Frustration, and Information Needs. In the two other versions, children and parents make known their perceptions of a particular grandparent. The three-generational survey offers a comprehensive perspective of family interaction, and highlights attitudes and behaviours grandparents should maintain and those they should reconsider.

Learning to work in groups is essential for interdependence and promotes productivity in the classroom, workplace and family. A problem faced by teachers using cooperative learning is how to identify team skills of students in group work. The Interpersonal Intelligence Inventory (III)(2002), co-authored with my son Paris, contains 25 criteria that adolescents and adults apply in evaluating peer and self-performance. Students need practice to become self-critical, a vital ingredient for personal growth. Responses inform teachers about team interaction from the students' point of view. The goals for using this tool are to: identify team skills that each student demonstrates; provide anonymous feedback from peers; compare self-impressions with the observations of teammates; detect learning needs; credit hard workers for their initiatives; detect slackers; and produce a portfolio record of social skills for individuals and groups.

THEORY AND RESEARCH INTO PRACTICE

In 1983, Arizona State University enabled me to establish the Office of Parent Development International. The six goals of the office are research and development of: (1) curriculum and processes to prepare teachers to become partners with parents; (2) curriculum and processes to assist parents in their long-term role of raising children; (3) curriculum and processes to guide grandparents in defining their supportive role; (4) curriculum and processes to make intergenerational communication more common and mutually satisfying; (5) curriculum and processes for adult children to acquaint them with the needs of their ageing parents; and (6) a model of learning for uniting support systems that incorporate technological, cultural, ethnic and generational sources. Our office team has trained parents, grandparents, teachers, psychologists, social workers and administrators worldwide to achieve their purposes. The instruments that I have formulated with colleagues for research are widely used and commercially available. An explanation of the theoretical basis and assumptions for each of the measures are described in articles at the Office of Parent Development International website (http://www.public.asu.edu/~rdstrom).

Some of my research findings are constant across cultures. (1) The amount of time parents and children spend together is the best predictor of parent success as perceived by adolescents and parents. The way for parents to become better informed about what is happening in the lives of their children appears to be spending five or more hours a week doing things together. (2) The greatest difficulty mothers report is arranging leisure time for themselves. In a hurried society, children need mothers as models of how to deal with stress by setting aside periods for relief and renewal, and managing time so that they have a sense of personal control in their lives. Mothers believe they teach children how to cope with stress. However, adolescents assign poor ratings for maternal performance in this context. Similar cross-cultural results are recorded for fathers. (3) Differences in generational perceptions of parent and grandparent success are greater than between cultures. There is a need to recognise that cohort populations may be more alike than are different age groups within the same nation or ethnicity. Global efforts to increase appreciation for other cultures should expand to include understanding generational difference within societies.

Mentors have influenced my research agenda. Professor Gordon Allport at Harvard University provided a powerful model of interpersonal intelligence, and encouraged me to link child and parent development as a research emphasis. Professor Paul Torrance motivated me to place high priority on preservation of creativity beyond childhood and to support restoration of imagination in parents and grandparents. Dr Torrance and I wrote *Mental Health and Achievement* (1965) and *Education for Affective Achievement* (1973). I was honoured to present the annual Torrance Lecture on Creativity at the University of Georgia and acknowledge his impact on my work and family. Another mentor was Professor Sydney Pressey of the Ohio State University who wrote the first book on psychological development through the lifespan (1939). Dr Pressey urged me to make the study of middle and old age an essential part of my career and to rely on insiders as informants about ageing. Our discussions about lifelong learning contributed to my motivation for writing *Human Development and Learning* (1987), *Becoming a Better Grandparent* (1991) and *Achieving Grandparent Potential* (1992). I am fortunate to be part of a family that values creative thinking. My wife Shirley and our sons Steven and Paris help build my ideas, generate different perceptions to consider, and encourage the pursuit of dreams.

KEY REFERENCES

Strom, P. & Strom, R. (2002) *Interpersonal Intelligence Inventory*. Bensenville, IL: Scholastic Testing Service.

Strom, R. (1995) *Parent as a Teacher Inventory*. Bensenville, IL: Scholastic Testing Service.

Strom, R. & Strom, S. (1993) *Grandparent Strengths and Needs Inventory*. Bensenville, IL: Scholastic Testing Service.

Strom, R. & Strom, S. (1998) *Parent Success Indicator*. Bensenville, IL: Scholastic Testing Service.

ACTIVITIES

1 Bob Strom believes that parents have an important and long-term role as teachers of their children. Discuss with your fellow students why parents should be considered teachers, and how this role might effectively be conducted. How might schools and educators collaborate in this?

2 Bob Strom refers to a number of inventories he and others have written to facilitate the understanding of parent and grandparent roles in education, including the PAAT, the PSI and the GSNI. Using the website http://www.public.asu.edu/~rdstrom, explore these inventories. How might they be used in your educational setting? You might like to try one or other of them out.

3 Bob Strom is a great believer in the importance of grandparent involvement in the development of children. What extra assets can grandparents provide in the healthy development of their grandchildren?

4 Another of Bob Strom's research interests is cooperative group work (see Chapter 8). He and Paris Strom have written the Interpersonal Intelligence Inventory (III) which helps to identify team skills demonstrated by students, provides feedback from peers, compares self-impressions with the observations of teammates, detects learning needs, provides credit to hard workers for their initiatives, detects slackers, and produces a portfolio record of the social skills of individuals and groups. Discuss with your fellow students each of these elements and why they are important to developing effective collaborative group work. Design an inventory that you think would tap into each of these dimensions. Access a copy of the III and compare your assessment tool with that designed by the Stroms. You might like to try the III out in a classroom situation.

5 Bob Strom outlines some of the key findings from his research. Consider these in the context of material read in this and other chapters on the importance of parents to children's growth and development. What other characteristics might be important?

provided by both the child and the child's school (Grolnick *et al.* 1997; Hoover-Dempsey & Sandler 1997). The parents' role construction refers to parents' beliefs about appropriate actions they should undertake for and with their children. Many of these roles are 'defined' through social rules and expectations of what makes a good parent, and by the social supports provided parents. As you would guess, this will vary according to the social and community groups the family belongs to, the nature of the family structure (for example, single-parent or two-parent family), as well as according to the life events impacting on parents at any given time (such as divorce or job redundancy) (Grolnick *et al.* 1997). In communities that value education and believe that parents should be involved, more parents are likely to be involved. This may vary by socio-economic or cultural grouping (Hoover-Dempsey & Sandler 1997). For example, as you will see from Chapter 10, some groups believe that schooling and teaching is the prerogative of teachers, and parents should not be involved. For some other groups, a strong feeling of alienation from schooling might induce parents not to participate in their children's schooling. This could, for example, characterise parents from indigenous minority groups such as the Australian Aboriginal and Navajo, where schooling has, in the past, been associated with dislocation from cultural roots.

In some instances, parents might value education and perceive that it is appropriate to be involved but nevertheless do not participate in the schooling of their children. This might be because they lack a feeling of efficacy for helping their children at school. This notion of *efficacy* is similar to self-efficacy, which we covered in Chapter 6. Parental self-efficacy concerns parents' beliefs about their general ability to influence their child's developmental and educational outcomes, about their specific effectiveness in influencing the child's school learning, and about their own influence relative to that of peers and the child's teacher (Hoover-Dempsey & Sandler 1997). Many parents believe they cannot help, or cannot provide the materials, such as books and computers, needed to assist their children effectively. Lack of efficacy may characterise many parents who are poorly educated themselves, not well off financially, or from a cultural and language background different from the school. Conversely, parents who feel they can help their children are more likely to be involved in their children's schooling. Feelings of efficacy are related to a parent's belief that with effort children can improve and so it is worthwhile helping children to put in the extra effort.

It is likely that parents' feelings of efficacy change as their children move through schooling. Parents who feel competent to help their children at primary levels might feel less competent as children progress through high school. Indeed, there is commonly a drop-off in parental involvement at the high school level. This might be because the subject matter becomes more difficult or because schools become less inviting places for parents.

Finally, in order for parents to become involved they need to feel that both the children and the school want them to become involved. In other words, parents may value education and believe they can help, but feel excluded from the process. It is important, therefore, that schools encourage parents to feel that their involvement is welcome. When parental involvement is required by schools, achievement outcomes of students are enhanced (Bauch & Goldring 2000). It is also likely that as children become older, and begin to focus on independence and autonomy, they become less welcoming of their parents' involvement in their schooling. Indeed, a whole host of personality variables characterising individual children will impact on a decision of particular parents to become involved or not.

Despite the complexities of why some parents become involved in their children's education and why some don't, it is well established in the research literature that effective parental involvement is beneficial for students, teachers, schools and the parents themselves. In our own research, we have consistently found that students, parents and teachers rank parents as the primary influence in whether or not students achieve at school (McInerney & McInerney 2000). We need, therefore, to work out strategies at the school level to maximise the involvement of parents.

Table 13.3 indicates some supportive classroom and school practices suggested by Erikson's approach.

Freud's psychosexual theory

Freud (1856–1939) is familiar to everyone in one way or another. Our language is replete with expressions—such as ego, superego, repression and rationalisation—that have been taken from his theoretical work. Freud's theory is powerful and controversial, and the study of personality owes much to the original work of this man. Indeed, many later theories of personality can only be understood in the context of Freud's work (Fontana 1986; Liebert & Spiegler 1987). Fontana (1986, pp. 44–5) suggests that:

> For the teacher, Freud's main contribution is that he gave us a new way of looking at childhood in stark contrast to the belief that misbehaviour and other personality problems in children are the invariable result of wilfulness to be corrected by stern and rigid discipline. To Freud, the child is very much more sinned against by the adult world than sinning, very much more a victim of the mistakes of his parents than of mistakes of his own making. But Freud did more than simply focus attention upon childhood experiences. He suggested that the way in which these experiences influence later personality development can only be understood if we explore the unconscious as well as the conscious mind.

Table 13.3 **Essentials of Erikson's theory for classroom practices**

Teachers should:

- *Trust* v *mistrust*—support and encourage the child. Alleviate distress and uncertainty promptly. Be responsive and consistent.
- *Autonomy* v *doubt*—allow opportunities for self-control, self-care and responsibility. Free choice of activities should be included in the curriculum.
- *Initiative* v *guilt*—encourage children to make decisions, choose activities and have a real impact on the work of the classroom. Be tolerant of accidents, mistakes and 'mess' as children 'go it alone'. Avoid labels such as 'good' and 'bad'.
- *Industry* v *inferiority*—help children to set realistic goals of achievement, and help them to feel a sense of accountability for what they achieve. Set the classroom up so that it is mutually supportive through the operation of group goal structures. Alleviate the negative effects of competition and peer pressure. Reward and acknowledge the achievement of goals.
- *Identity* v *role confusion*—encourage the development of trust, autonomy, initiative and industry as these form the basis of the sense of identity the adolescent strives to achieve at this time. Be sensitive to the needs of the adolescent as they cope with the ambivalent and confusing messages received from parents, teachers, peers and society in general. Be consistent, warm and understanding. Be prepared to give advice when sought, and be prepared to see the advice not taken.

TEACHER'S CASE BOOK

Parent help!

On his first day in Year 2, Phillip told Miss Carter: 'I can't read and I can't write.' A literacy assessment revealed that his language skills were at a similar level to those of most children entering Transition. Concerned to provide Phillip with the extra support he needed, Miss Carter tried to set aside 15 minutes each day during the language block to work with him. But she hadn't taken into account Phillip's tenacity: whenever she sat down to write with him he would commence long-winded anecdotes about his family, show her a treasure he had brought to school, anything to avoid focusing on the writing task. Because of the limited time Miss Carter had allowed, she found herself becoming frustrated and impatient and then feeling guilty because she knew this would only serve to worsen Phillip's already negative attitude to writing.

Miss Carter spoke about her problem to a more experienced staff member, who told her of a parent, Mrs Burke, who had just completed the Parents as Tutors course and was eager to begin working with children in the school.

At first Miss Carter was reluctant to contact Mrs Burke, being worried that she would regard Miss Carter's problem as a failure. However, when she finally did enlist Mrs Burke's support she realised how much help parents can be to a classroom teacher. Once a week, Mrs Burke spends the whole language block guiding Phillip through reading and writing activities that she and Miss Carter have planned together.

Miss Carter still tries to set aside 15 minutes for Phillip each day, but she no longer gets impatient or tries to rush him because she is now confident that he is receiving adequate support with literacy from Mrs Burke.

Case studies illustrating National Competency Framework for Beginning Teaching, National Project on the Quality of Teaching and Learning, Australian Teaching Council, 1996, p. 20. Commonwealth of Australia copyright, reproduced by permission.

Case study activity

How else might parents be welcomed into the classroom as facilitators of students' learning? What advantages and potential problems might there be?

These parents are collecting their children after school. Why might even this level of involvement in school be important for some children?

Components of personal development

Freud (1962a, 1962b, 1973) likened the mind to an iceberg in which the smaller visible part represents the region of the consciousness, while the much larger mass below the water represents the region of the unconscious. In this vast domain of the unconscious is a great underworld of vital, unseen forces that exercise a strong control over the conscious thoughts and deeds of individuals. The life force of personal action is called *libido* (the creative energy in all individuals) and *thanatos* (the destructive urge in all individuals). For Freud, healthy personality growth is the product of an individual passing through a series of psychosexual experiences with an eventual balance being struck between three forces—the **id**, which may be described as the source of basic biological needs and desires; the **ego**, which might be described as the conscious, rational part of personality; and the **superego**, which might be described as the seat of conscience. While these three systems can be identified as separate hypothetical structures, behaviour for the mature person is nearly always the product of an interaction between the three. Rarely does one system operate to the exclusion of the other two, except in cases where the balance is broken.

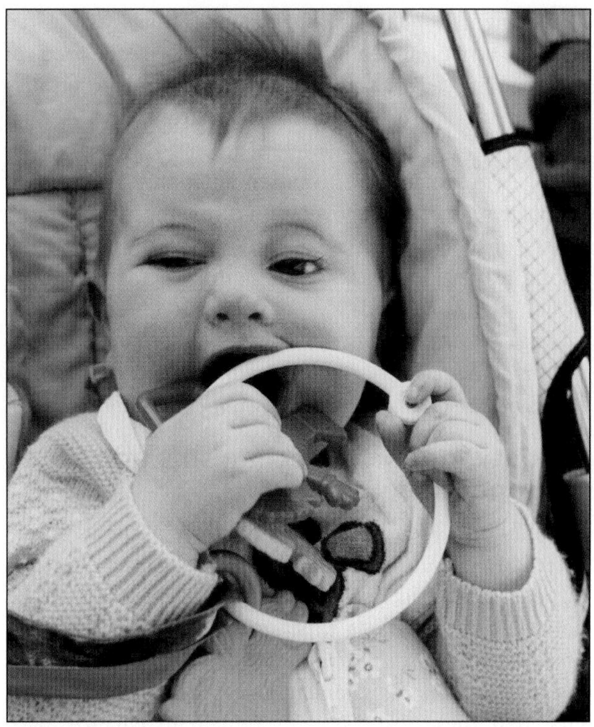

Children learn about the world by a variety of means—including chewing!

Stages of psychosexual development

Healthy personality development and psychosexual stages

As these three mental systems evolve, individuals experience five clearly distinguishable **psychosexual developmental stages.** Each of these can be defined in terms of individuals satisfying needs through three erogenous zones—the mouth, the anus and the genital organs. Actions by children involving these zones bring children into conflict with their parents. The resulting frustrations and anxieties, as well as satisfying experiences, stimulate the development of a large number of adaptations, defences, compromises and sublimations which are ultimately incorporated into the mature personality (Hall 1964; Hall & Lindzey 1970; Liebert & Spiegler 1987; Pervin 1989).

Oral stage

During the *oral* stage, breastfeeding and supplying the comfort needs of the child are the primary focus of the child's attention. The quality of nurturing that children receive during this time affects their feelings of dependence and trust in the world.

Anal stage

During the *anal* stage, toilet training and controlling the child's impulses are a major focus of attention. If the training and discipline emphasise positive independence and control, feelings of confidence in self are developed. Alternatively, if experiences during this time are overly restrictive or punitive, negative personal characteristics develop, such as destructiveness, messiness, and so on.

Toilet training can be a fun experience for children. Why is it important to make it enjoyable?

During the *phallic* stage, sexual feelings associated with the functioning of the genital organs are the focus of activity. This is the time when the individual identifies with the same-sex parent and sexual identity is developed. Finally, after a period of *latency*, children enter the *genital* stage when there is the transformation of the individual into a reality-oriented, socialised adult. During adolescence, sexual attraction, socialisation, group activities, vocational planning, and preparations for marrying and raising a family begin to come to the fore in well-stabilised behaviours. Table 13.4 presents each of these stages of personality development.

Phallic stage
Genital stage

Anxiety, defence mechanisms and personal development

Throughout Freud's personality development stages there is a dynamic interaction between the three elements of personality—id, ego and superego. Depending on the nature of the conflicts experienced and on the modes of resolving them, individuals will develop positive or negative personality characteristics. Freud considered it vital that these three systems remain in balance, with a smooth transfer of energy from id to ego to superego. When the balance is upset, the personality may break down into excessive anxiety. As any one of the three systems can dominate, this means that we can have three distinct forms of **anxiety**: neurotic, realistic or moral (Fontana 1986).

Neurotic anxiety occurs when the individual fears that the instinctive forces of the id will control their behaviour. *Realistic anxiety* exists when the individual is dominated by the ego to such an extent that id-driven behaviour (such as eating or sexual behaviour) becomes impossible to enjoy, and the individual is unable to devote energy to any superego demands such as the welfare of others. *Moral anxiety* occurs when the superego dominates and the individual becomes trapped in an over-rigid value system taken over from their parents. The individual is excessively scrupulous and compulsively on guard against anything that might arouse feelings of guilt. They reject both the pleasure principle of the id and the reality principle of the ego and inhabit, instead, an unreal world of taboos and forbidden things (Fontana 1986).

One of the goals of ego behaviour is to protect and enhance one's sense of self. At times, **defence mechanisms** activate which protect an individual's sense of self (Liebert & Spiegler 1987). All defence mechanisms have two characteristics in common:

1 They deny, falsify and/or distort reality.
2 They operate unconsciously so that the person is not aware of what is taking place.

While the use of defence mechanisms is normal (and all of us resort to them unconsciously from time to time), overuse of them impedes the development of a mature personality. The major defences are:

- repression;
- reaction formation;
- rationalisation;
- regression;
- fixation;
- projection;
- fantasy; and
- denial.

Repression is removing from consciousness painful or shameful experiences and thoughts, or the process of preventing unacceptable impulses or desires from reaching consciousness. The purpose is essentially to protect the ego from processes that are incompatible with the individual's high evaluations of self. For example, a soldier may flee the battlefield in a moment of cowardice and be found wandering dazed some time later, with absolutely no recollection of what has occurred.

Reaction formation occurs when a repressed feeling or emotion is replaced by its opposite; for example, a feeling such as hatred may be hidden from awareness by the substitution of its opposite. A wife with an invalid husband may unconsciously wish to be rid of him, but this negative wish may be expressed as unusual concern for his welfare. At this point, readers sometimes ask: 'But how does one pick out the genuine concern from one that is a reaction formation?' In general, the reaction

Table 13.4 Freud's stages of personality development

Oral	(lasts about one year) The mouth is the principal focus of dynamic activity.
Anal	(2 to 4 years) The anus is the principal focus of dynamic activity.
Phallic	(4 to 5 years) The sex organs are the principal focus of dynamic activity.
Latency	(approximately 6 years to pubescence) Period during which sexual impulses are held in a state of repression.
Genital	(puberty through to adulthood) The genitals are the principal focus of dynamic activity.

formation is characterised by excessiveness: it is showy, extravagant and compulsive.

Rationalisation is a defence mechanism we can all understand and relate to. It occurs when we unconsciously give socially acceptable reasons for our conduct in place of real reasons. We may tell ourselves that it is better that we eat the leftover chocolates so that our sister doesn't get pimples or too fat, or that we should go to the movies with our friend instead of studying because the other person really needs our company. Come on, own up—have you used rationalisation to justify your behaviour to yourself? Most people have.

Regression occurs when a child or adult engages in behaviour more characteristic of an earlier stage of development in order to reduce tension and anxiety. An older child may begin to wet the bed again when a new baby arrives in the home. The child fears being displaced and seeks attention, but can't express it consciously because the need arises out of jealousy and is therefore unacceptable. While some forms of regression are indicative of severe problems, such as the adult psychotic who plays with dolls when under stress, most forms of regression are relatively mild. Many adults chew pens during an exam, eat excessively when worried, or masturbate when stressed. In each case the individual retreats to an earlier level of coping with anxiety.

The arrival of a younger sibling can sometimes induce older children to regress to earlier forms of behaviour.

Fixation occurs when an immature form of defence mechanism is consistently used rather than a more mature defence mechanism, such as sublimation. In extreme cases, this may lead to the emergence of a personality disorder in which the further growth of character is blocked by an obsessive personality pattern (Peterson, Beck & Rowell 1992).

Projection is a defence mechanism that many of us can relate to. It occurs when we ascribe our own unconscious motivation to other people, such as when we accuse others of being angry, hateful or deceitful as a defence against our own anger, hatred or deceit.

Fantasy protects the ego by seeking imaginary satisfactions in place of real ones. In the past, children were often told that it was wrong to have 'impure thoughts', although the fantasy sexual world that is created alleviated the need for children to engage in inappropriate overt sexual behaviour. Today, there is much debate over video pornography in which violence is portrayed and its supposed effect on reducing or increasing sexual crimes. One argument goes that individuals who may otherwise engage in such activities use these videos to fantasise and sublimate their sexual drives in a relatively harmless way. What do you think?

We discuss in Chapter 6 the effect of modelled violence where no punishing consequences follow and how this can increase the likelihood of the enactment of the behaviour in the real world.

When *an individual denies the existence of painful experiences and thoughts* (such as a refusal to accept that a loved one has died), **denial** functions as a defence. Some grossly overweight or underweight people deny that they have a problem and distort their body image accordingly.

Current status of Freud's theory

While few psychologists today accept all of Freud's major theoretical concepts (and we have given only the briefest overview of some of these), the theory is still considered very important. It provides a broad insight into the development of personality, especially the importance of our unconscious in motivating behaviour, as well as the influence of early socialisation within families on subsequent personality development. In this sense, Freud's theoretical framework helps us to understand the emotional development and problems of children.

On a broader level, Freud's theory has been influential in the development of many other theoretical perspectives on personality development. Educational and psychological literature on personality development very often presumes that the reader has some basic understanding of Freudian psychology (Liebert & Spiegler 1987; Mischel 1986; Pervin 1989).

Nevertheless, Freud's theory has been criticised for two basic reasons. First, many consider that his theory overemphasises the sexual nature of personality development. In his emphasis on critical events related to the oral, anal and phallic stages, and the successful resolution of problems at these times, he appears to have neglected other important dimensions affecting the development of personality (such as community and intellectual influences). Furthermore, Freud's emphasis that the early years of development leave an indelible mark on the personality for good or ill seems to be contradicted by evidence that the personality is in a state of continual development, and that later life experiences can and do make up for inadequate experiences in early life (Liebert & Spiegler 1987). Other criticisms relate to the lack of clear definitions of some of the components of his system, and the difficulty inherent in empirically testing and measuring these components (Pervin 1989).

Criticisms of Freud's theory

Classroom implications of Freud's theory

Elements of Freud's theory are useful for teachers in understanding behaviour in the classroom. Identification, anxiety, displacement and defence mechanisms are very useful concepts.

Identification with teachers

Much personality development results from children incorporating values held by significant others through the process of *identification*, and teachers as well as parents are powerful models in this process.

Earlier we discussed three forms of anxiety: neurotic anxiety, realistic anxiety and moral anxiety. Children can develop neurotic anxiety if they are not helped by teachers and parents to recognise and come to terms with their instinctual behaviour. They need to recognise that instinctual drives are normal, but that they need to strive to strike a balance between what is an acceptable/unacceptable satisfaction of these drives. A preoccupation with these instinctual drives can develop into neuroticism. Neurotic anxiety sometimes displays itself in *acting-out behaviour*—for example, when an apparently placid and well-controlled child has a violent outburst of rage.

Anxiety

Realistic anxiety may be caused by brutal shocks or frightening experiences, but it may also be caused in children by such things as excessive demands for academic success or standards of behaviour, by a background of domestic strife, or the uncertainties of having to start a new school with a new teacher.

Moral anxiety may be produced by repressive moral training and may provoke self-punishment in children through feelings of unworthiness or inadequacy. Sometimes ritualistic gestures such as excessive handwashing (called obsessional-compulsive behaviour) develop in an attempt to remove such feelings symbolically (Fontana 1986).

Classroom and school behaviour will sometimes reflect *displacement*. For example, children will be 'out of sorts' at times, owing to a range of causes, and will displace their annoyance, aggression and anger on their peers and teachers. Children who are abused at home may act in very antisocial ways at school. It is well to remember that children's behaviour (as well as our own) is the result of a complex interplay of unconscious forces and we, as teachers and parents, must take the time to work through the possible reasons for specific behaviour, particularly when the behaviour is different from the typical or is apparently inexplicable.

Displacement as school behaviour

When under stress, children will unconsciously resort to *defence mechanisms* to protect their ego, that component of the personality that suffers the anxiety feelings. One example we remember was hearing a teacher berate a very young child for stealing money from her purse, with the child protesting her innocence. 'But you were seen doing it!' The teacher became more and more exasperated and the child more upset. Under these circumstances Freudian theory would suggest that the teacher desist, for the child's response may very well be what the child believes, with repression or denial blocking an acceptance of the reality.

Pupil use of defence mechanisms

Under stress, some children may regress and resort to thumb sucking or wetting themselves. This is not uncommon when children first start school. Of course, rather than reprimanding the child, a supportive and loving environment must be provided so that the child can feel secure and resolve the conflict in a healthy fashion. Stress such as that caused by test anxiety (see Chapter 11) may also lead to regression. In some cases this regression may be relatively harmless, such as eating excessively or masturbating at these times; on other occasions it may be more serious, such as an inability to cope with the situation and engaging in withdrawal or bizarre behaviour. For example, general graffiti, scatological toilet graffiti and school vandalism may be examples of both regression and 'acting-out' behaviour. Again, when such behaviour is severe, it is important to investigate the reasons for the behaviour and attempt to alleviate the conditions causing it.

Many accusations and counter-accusations between children at school are the result of projection; for example, John says he doesn't want to play with Bill because Bill doesn't like him, when the truth is that John is afraid that Bill doesn't want to play with him. Some children may project that their teacher is lazy and a poor teacher when the student is in fact the lazy one.

Rationalisation is commonly used by children to excuse sloppy work, cheating and a range of inappropriate behaviour within the school context, while fantasy is used to relieve boredom and inability to cope.

Finally, Freudian theory emphasises the important role that significant individuals, such as teachers, play in the early personality formation of children. Excessively restrictive practices (such as extreme discipline) lead to resentment and an attempt by children to resolve the conflict in potentially harmful ways.

ACTION STATION

Try your hand at classifying defence mechanisms. In the following story, a number of alternative endings are given. Suggest which defence mechanism (if any) is operating.

> Jack, an accountant, was ambitious and worked very hard at his job to obtain a promotion to chief accountant of his firm. Then his colleague, John, was promoted to the position desired by Jack and became Jack's superior. Jack was very unhappy about this state of affairs and in his reveries thought of all sorts of nasty events that could befall John so that he would then be able to assume his rightful place as chief accountant. After a number of months John suffered a serious heart attack and ended up in hospital. Jack was shocked.

1 Jack became very solicitous of John's welfare, spending long hours with him in hospital. Defence mechanism: ____________

2 While shocked, Jack believed that John had been unsuited to the job and had brought on the heart attack himself by his ambition and overwork. Defence mechanism: ____________

3 While shocked, Jack believed that he had only the best interests of the company at heart and that ultimately it would be better for the company if he were made chief accountant. Defence mechanism: ____________

4 When questioned regarding his future intentions for the position, Jack denied ever having wanted the job. Defence mechanism: ____________

5 Jack began to drink heavily and appeared to lose interest in his job. Defence mechanism: ____________

QUESTION POINT

Discuss the role of defence mechanisms in the personality development of children and adolescents.

Humanism and personal development

Humanistic psychologists stress the individual potential for good in all human beings. They perceive people as free and unique, self-directed, and capable of setting goals, making choices and initiating action. Humanist psychologists further believe that, in order to function most effectively and to maximise their potential, individuals must first become aware of their internal thoughts and feelings regarding themselves and the world. By consciously describing such thoughts and feelings, individuals become more aware of how these influence their behaviour and may therefore be better able to control them. The thoughts and feelings that individuals have about themselves focus around three broad areas (Weinstein & Fantini 1970):

1 *Identity:* Who am I? Where am I going?
2 *Connectedness:* How do I fit or relate with other people? Do people like me?
3 *Power:* What are my limits? What control do I have over my life?

Human development and self-knowledge, self-control and productive living

For humanist psychologists, personal development is a process of answering these questions. Humanism further holds that a critical aspect of this learning process is the ability to judge whether or not our thoughts and feelings are personally productive, and then make whatever modifications are necessary. The ultimate goals of this search for self-knowledge are greater self-control and more positive living. This process of self-knowledge depends on people's interactions with one another, as it is through these interactions that we become aware of our own identity.

Carl Rogers and 'realness'

Much of the impetus for this approach can be traced to the work of the clinical psychologist Carl Rogers (1961, 1969, 1976, 1977, 1983). Rogers' personality theory is based on two main assumptions (Liebert & Spiegler 1987):

1 Human behaviour is guided by each person's unique self-actualising tendency.
2 All humans need positive regard.

Two terms drawn from Rogers' writings illustrate well the emphasis he places upon the individual's role in the development of personality. First, **client-centred therapy** (as opposed to directive therapy) relates to Rogers' belief that individuals strive to fulfil themselves and that we all, given a supportive interpersonal environment, have the necessary resources within ourselves to achieve this. In other words, an individual's personal growth towards healthy, competent and creative functioning is largely inner-controlled and driven, rather than outer-directed (as is implied in contrasting behavioural approaches, see Chapter 6).

The second term is **phenomenology**, which denotes Rogers' belief that an individual's 'real' world is what the individual *perceives*, rather than what may actually be. In other words, reality is personal and subjective. Perceived reality is known as our *phenomenological field*. Simply speaking, if we perceive that we are ugly, untalented and unlikeable, objective evidence to the contrary may make little difference to our sense of self. Instead, our phenomenological field has to be altered so that 'reality' may be perceived in a different light.

Parents and teachers as facilitators of children's personal development

Humanists, such as Rogers, redefine the role of parents and teachers in childrearing and education. Parents and teachers must stand back and, in a sense, allow room for children to grow in a caring but non-controlling environment. Parents and teachers become facilitators of children's development by supplying appropriate opportunities, resources, support and non-evaluative feedback to promote children's growth, development, maturity and ability to cope with life. Of fundamental importance here is the need for parents and teachers to be *real* to the children in the sense of being caring, trustworthy, dependable and consistent at a deep level. In essence, parents and teachers need to be perceived by the child as part of their phenomenological world, for it is only in this circumstance that they can effectively facilitate children's personal growth. Independence, creativity, self-reliance and self-evaluation are all encouraged, and children take responsibility for their own learning and development. There is a strong emphasis in this approach on interpersonal relationships and feelings, where parents and teachers are perceived as joint voyagers with children on the way to self-discovery. Indeed, the approach suggests that, as teachers and parents, we too grow through this process and that unless we also develop as 'real' people we cannot hope to be facilitators of others' growth to realness.

Maslow's hierarchy of needs

Deficiency needs and growth needs

Another humanist psychologist, Maslow (1968, 1970, 1976), viewed personal development as a process of natural growth in which all individuals would realise their potential provided the environment was supportive. He believed that individuals seek to satisfy particular needs, the ultimate goal being that of **self-actualisation**, and conceived of human needs as arranged in a hierarchy. The lower levels of this hierarchy, basic needs, are termed **deficiency needs** while the higher levels are called **growth needs** or *meta-needs*.

Physiological needs come first, according to Maslow. Children who are hungry, thirsty or sleepy will be preoccupied with actions to alleviate this need, and there will be little motivation to be involved in other activities. A number of schools in low socio-economic areas have instigated breakfast programs for children who come from homes where they may not have been adequately fed in the morning. The purpose is, of course, to satisfy this need so that the children can concentrate more effectively on learning, a need higher up in the hierarchy. The physiological needs do not have to be as graphic as illustrated by chronically hungry children. Just being too

It is very important that schools are safe places. These students can relax and begin to enjoy learning.

cold, or too hot, or too hungry for 'little lunch' is enough to distract children (and teachers) from the task of learning.

The next level is *safety needs.* Children have a need to feel safe and secure. Preoccupation with their physical welfare will distract children from personal development and effective learning. A teacher in a school that served a refugee hostel near an aerodrome in Sydney recalls the experience of children in her class from war-torn Lebanon ducking under their desks whenever a plane flew overhead. Her first weeks of teaching were taken up with restoring the children's sense of safety. Another graphic example of this need for safety is children who come from homes where physical abuse is prevalent. These children often withdraw from involvement in classroom activities, as they are preoccupied with the events that dominate their lives at that time.

All schools have introduced pastoral care policies that attempt to identify and alleviate the problems suffered by neglected and battered children. On a less graphic level, children who are being pushed around by other students or who fear the wrath of the teacher may also be using a lot of mental energy working through these threats and protecting themselves (physically and mentally) instead of attending to their learning. The lives of these children are made miserable to varying extents and, as a result, they are often insecure and lacking in self-esteem (Smith & Ahmad 1990). Continued insecurity makes it very difficult for them to reacquire confidence in themselves and, of course, confidence is a prerequisite of effective motivation and learning.

Pastoral care programs

The third level of Maslow's hierarchy is the *need to belong.* Initially, this need is fulfilled through the family, but as children widen their social network this need must also be fulfilled through contact with others outside the family. A feeling of being one of the group and having a cohort with whom to identify within the school is important to children (Osterman 2000). Isolates and outcasts, or children scorned by others, can be distracted from their schoolwork. Children can be cruel to each other and great unhappiness often results when an individual feels isolated from the group. Teachers must be aware of this and facilitate good interpersonal relationships and a sense of belonging within the classroom, which foster good classroom motivation (Osterman 2000).

Need to belong

The fourth need, *need for self-esteem,* relates to an individual's need to feel worthwhile and important in the eyes of others. Again, the initial way in which this is fulfilled is through the family. However, we are all aware that there are times when children are denigrated within the family and come to school with very negative self-concepts. In these cases the school (and teachers) must do everything in their power to enhance the individual's feelings of self-confidence, worth, strength, capability and adequacy. School programs and procedures, as well as classroom practices, must be designed to maximise students' feelings of self-worth.

Need for self-esteem

Last, according to Maslow, is the need for *self-actualisation.* At this level, individuals strive to satisfy their need to grow intellectually and spiritually.

Maslow proposes that these needs are hierarchically ordered so that higher-level needs (or motivators) only become operational as lower-order needs are satisfied. We should consider the developmental stages of children in this context. Very young children will be dominated by physiological needs, while older children will be interested in testing themselves out in the environment, especially in relation to their physical abilities and their capacity to avoid danger. In middle childhood, as well as these needs, children will be testing themselves out in the social world, where the need for affection and belonging becomes relatively more important. Last, as children grow older they develop clearer ideas about themselves as individuals with varying capacities which they wish to test. Thus, the need to feel competent, and to receive approval and recognition from others, becomes increasingly important.

While we note that human needs appear to arrange themselves in a hierarchical order, and that success at one level of need usually requires prior satisfaction of another more prepotent need, human motivation is affected by biological, cultural and situational forces, all interacting. While acknowledging the apparent logic of Maslow's hierarchy, humans are very complex creatures and there are many situations that contradict his approach. For example, many people will persist at a task long after they become hungry or thirsty because they are intensely interested in their work. At times, people are motivated to perform behaviour that appears to contradict their basic needs for safety and belongingness because of the functioning of a higher need such as self-esteem or self-actualisation. In the activities related to this chapter, you will be asked to consider the whys and wherefores of this issue.

Other influences on personal development

Maslow's hierarchy is generally presented as a triangle with basic needs at the base and self-actualisation at the apex. We have always found the model somewhat static. It does not effectively suggest the dynamic and organic nature of motivation as perceived by humanist psychologists. We prefer our *sunflower model* instead which, we believe, more effectively illustrates the interaction between basic needs, growth needs and fulfilment. The sunflower can burst into flower even while other elements of the structure (such as leaves and stem) are withering. Furthermore, the model represents a more organic and integrated system and truly captures the spirit of the humanist ideal of self-actualisation. Given a reasonably supportive environment, the seed contains the dynamism for growth of the sunflower. Table 13.5 provides some essentials of humanism for education.

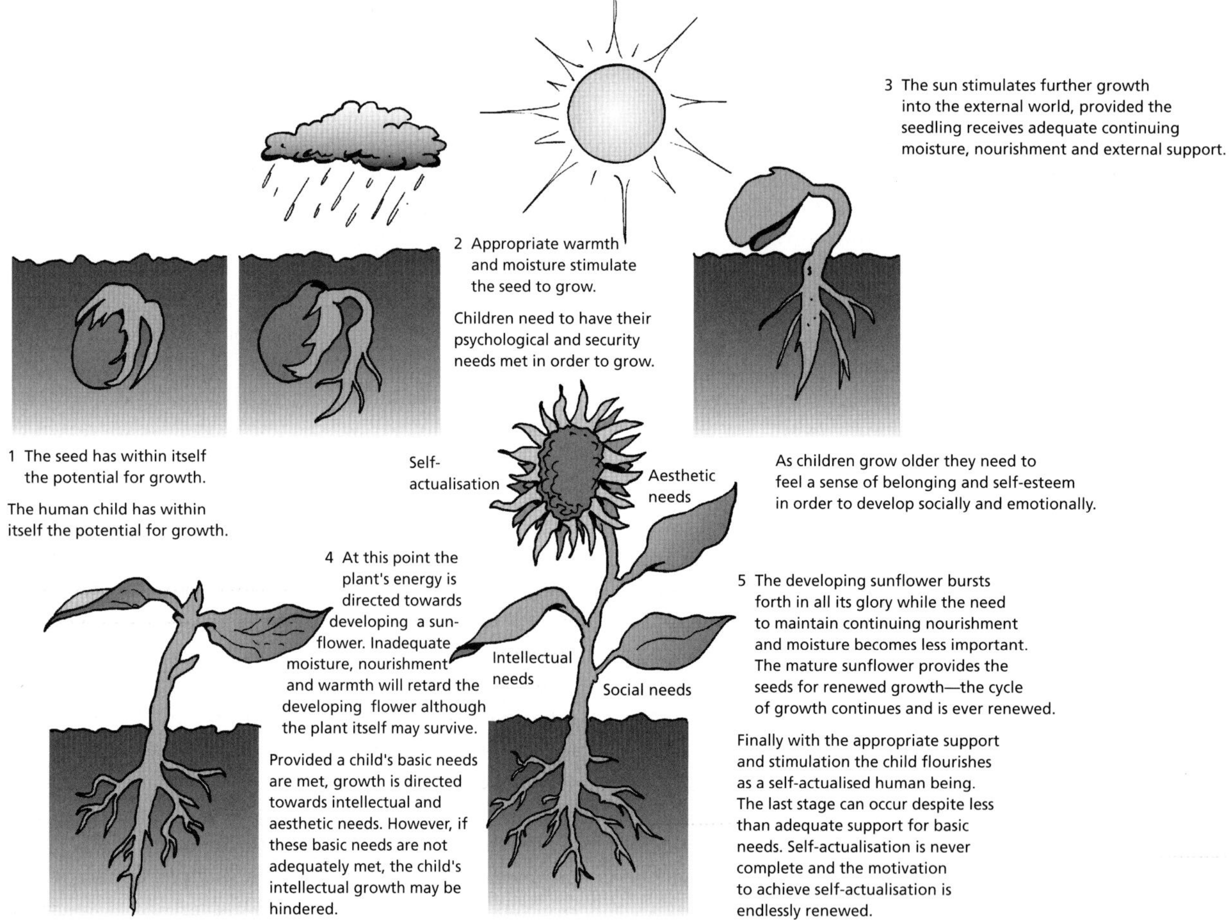

***Figure 13.1** The McInerney sunflower model of human self-actualisation*
(Source: Based on Maslow 1954)

Table 13.5

Essentials of humanism for education

Teachers should:

- be in touch with themselves and willing to disclose their feelings;
- establish the primacy of the learner;
- prize the learner as an individual having worth in their own right;
- develop realness, acceptance and empathetic understanding;
- suspend judgment and accept the prerogative of others to hold their own values;
- develop the ability to understand students' reactions from the inside;
- establish a safe and secure classroom and school environment;
- establish a non-restrictive learning environment.

TEACHER'S CASE BOOK

The water drop story

I see part of my teaching role as being a liaison between parents and children. I have a number of children in my third class whose parents are divorcing, and each child is experiencing his or her own set of problems.

One little girl in particular was having trouble coping with the problems at home and was coming to school engaging in antisocial behaviour. She was fighting, name-calling, teasing and taking other children's things. This had been going on for about eight months, since before the last Christmas holidays. The source of her problems became more evident to me in her writing. While writing a story about a drop of water, she mentioned marriage and a life without divorce. I felt it was my responsibility to make an interview with each of the parents separately to bring the situation to their attention.

Mum took the child's writing with her on a regularly scheduled visit to the child's counsellor. Dad has since remarried. Both parents appreciated the feedback and agreed on how important the contact is between both homes and school to help this little girl try to overcome her problems. One good thing is that this child has developed quite a good friendship with another girl who has had a similar experience in her family.

Case studies illustrating National Competency Framework for Beginning Teaching, National Project on the Quality of Teaching and Learning, Australian Teaching Council, 1996, p. 21.

Case study activity

How does this case study illustrate a number of the issues discussed in this chapter?

Classroom implications of humanistic perspectives

Realness, acceptance and empathy

Humanists believe that effective teaching and classroom management is largely a function of positive teacher–student and student–student relationships. In this, the teacher's role is central in building positive interpersonal relationships and promoting a positive socio-emotional climate (Sokolove *et al.* 1986). Rogers (1976) emphasises three qualities *in teachers* that he believes will have maximum effect in facilitating learning in their students: *realness*—that is, being in touch with one's self, willing to disclose one's feelings and developing along the path to self-actualisation; *acceptance*—that is, prizing the learners as individuals having worth in their own right, being able to suspend judgment and accept the prerogative of others to hold their own values; and *empathetic understanding*—that is, having the ability to understand the student's reactions from the inside, and a sensitive awareness of the way the process of education and learning appears to the student.

In essence, Rogers considers that the development of a positive self-concept and positive self-regard in an individual is derived from empathetic others helping the individual to see and develop inherent potential. This is achieved by interacting with that individual in a positive, accepting way, even if disapproval is felt at outward actions.

Safe classrooms and schools and bullying

Schools need to be safe and secure environments in which children can work energetically. According to Maslow, teachers need to work within this needs framework to make learning environments satisfying to students and to maximise their motivation. As basic needs are satisfied, the meta-needs, or the needs related to self-actualisation, become important. There is growing concern today about the level of bullying in our schools (Andreou & Metallidou 2004; Cerezo & Ato 2005; Marsh *et al.* 2001; Newman, Murray & Lustier 2001; Rigby & Bagshaw 2003; Woods & Wolke 2003), which is incompatible with a safe learning environment. Students are bullied when they are repeatedly exposed over time to negative consequences on the part of one or more other students with the intention to hurt (Olweus 1997). The NSW Department of Education and Training says:

> Students learn best in environments in which they feel safe. Bullying devalues, isolates and frightens people so that they no longer believe in the ability to achieve. It has long term effects for those doing the bullying, their targets and the onlookers. Every student has the right to expect that he or she will spend the day—both in and out of the classroom—free from bullying and intimidation . . . it is the responsibility of the whole school community to maintain the right to feel safe and valued at school. (NSW Department of Education and Training 1999, p. 1)

Bullying and victimisation in the school have been recognised universally as damaging the psychological,

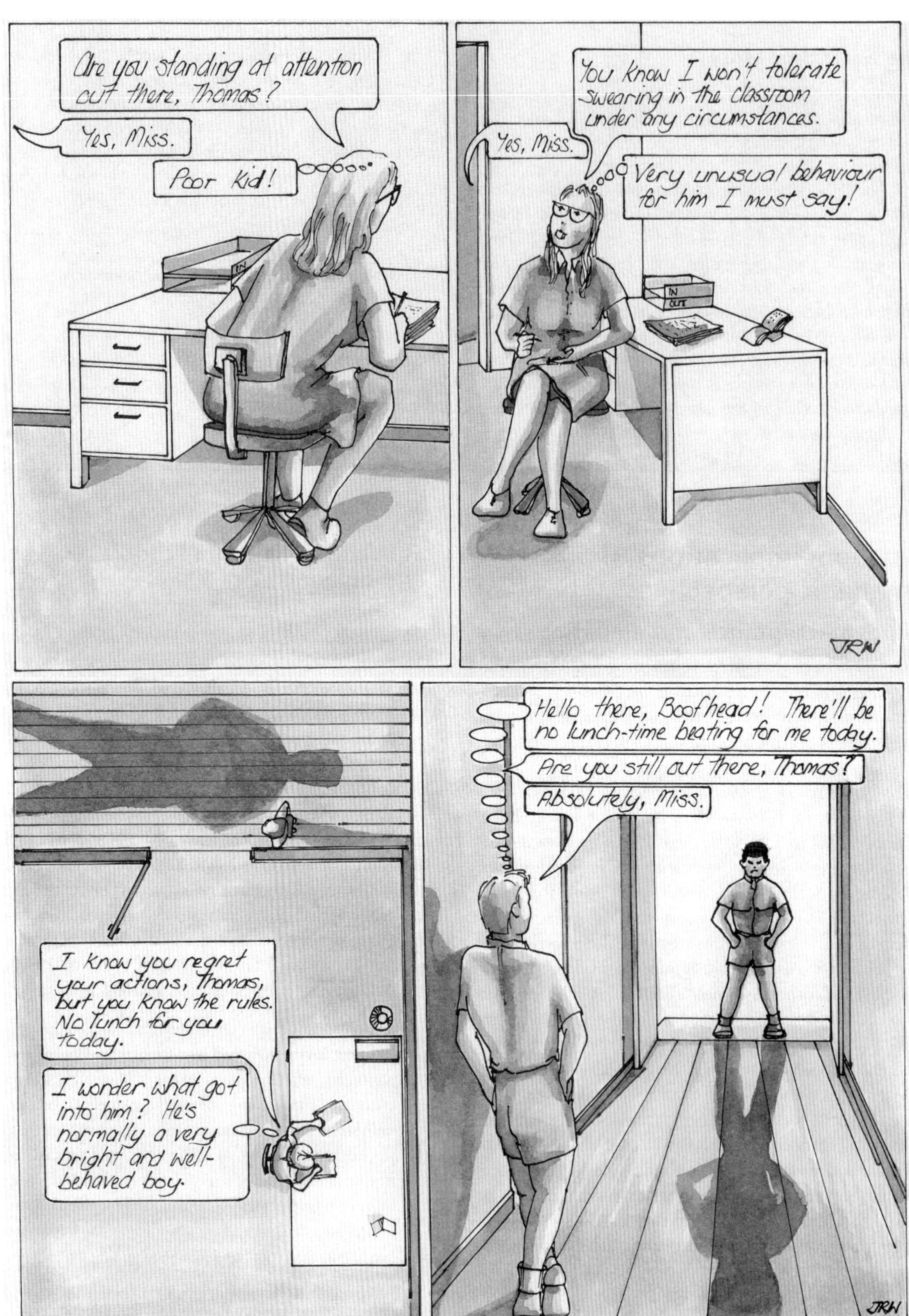
Are you standing at attention out there, Thomas?
Yes, Miss.
Poor kid!
You know I won't tolerate swearing in the classroom under any circumstances.
Yes, Miss.
Very unusual behaviour for him I must say!
JRW
I know you regret your actions, Thomas, but you know the rules. No lunch for you today.
I wonder what got into him? He's normally a very bright and well-behaved boy.
Hello there, Boofhead! There'll be no lunch-time beating for me today.
Are you still out there, Thomas?
Absolutely, Miss.
JRW

social and even physical development of children (Smith & Brain 2000; Smith & Sharp 1994; Pellegrini 1998; Slee 1995a, 1995b; Woods & Wolke 2003). The detrimental effects of bullying on mental and physical health problems include lowered self-esteem, depression, increased anxiety, greater rates of hyperactivity and behaviour problems (Woods & Wolke 2003). Those students who engage in bullying behaviour are predisposed to later antisocial, criminal, delinquent and violent behaviour (Farrington 1993). Bullying incorporates a wide range of behaviours: name calling, extortion, physical violence, slander, exclusion from the group, damage to others' property and verbal intimidation (Smith & Sharp 1994). It is differentiated from other forms of aggressive behaviour in that it involves a more powerful group/individual dominating through violence, aggression or intimidation a less powerful group/individual over an extended period of time (Olweus 1995, 1996).

Another type of bullying—relational bullying—has been described recently. Relational bullying includes actions such as social exclusion and malicious rumour spreading (Woods & Wolke 2003). The extent of bullying is surprising. Rigby and Slee (1993) reported that one in six students in Australian schools reported being bullied at least once a week; one in 10 reported being an active bully, and many students admit to—even boast about—bullying others. Similar situations were found in schools in Canada, England, Greece, Ireland, Scandinavia and Scotland (see, for example, Andreou & Metallidou 2004; Boulton & Underwood 1992; Nicolaides, Toda & Smith 2002; Olweus 1995, 1996; Warden *et al.* 2003). The causes of bullying are not clear; however, low self-esteem by the bully may be an important cause, along with school structure (small schools appear to have less bullying than large schools because students might know each other better), peer dynamics (such as individuals wanting to maintain peer status, and bullying is seen to be a way to maintain this), the size and affiliative nature of the peer groups (for example, bullying individuals with a large number of friends may result in the bully gaining disapproval and retaliation, whereas isolates may be easy targets for bullying) (Fox & Boulton 2005) in-group/out-group status (with children with fewer friends being victimised more frequently) and retaliatory aggression (when the victimised turns bully) (Marsh *et al.* 2001; Pellegrini 2002; see also Farmer *et al.* 2002). One of the paradoxical aspects of bullying in schools is that it is often tolerated by teachers and parents as part of a child's 'growing up' and that the associated experiences might be valuable life lessons. Hence, adults, perhaps inadvertently, are contributing to bullying behaviour at school (Pellegrini 2002). Indeed, bullies are often socially reinforced for bullying because of the sense of power they have satisfied in the view of onlookers. Evidence suggests, however, that bullying has detrimental effects on children and should not be a normal part of growing up. In fact, it should not be a part of any caring educational environment.

Anti-bullying programs

In order to alleviate bullying in schools (and other educational settings such as training camps and apprenticeship programs) many schools are introducing anti-bullying intervention programs to indicate clearly that bullying is an unacceptable form of behaviour no longer condoned by teachers, parents or other students. These programs have some common features. They usually adopt a whole-school-community approach which attempts to shape the ethos of the school so it is clearly anti-bullying (see, for example, Pellegrini 2002; Rigby & Bagshaw 2003). They seek to help both bullies and victims come to understand the negative effects of bullying, use strategies at the individual level, provide information and support to students, teachers and families, and integrate the program into the school curriculum (see, for example, Marsh, Parada, Yeung & Healey 2001; Nicolaides, Toda & Smith 2002; Pellegrini 2002; Woods & Wolke 2003).

While whole-school approaches are effective in minimising bullying, it is not an easy task. Pellegrini suggests that to be effective these programs must be inclusive, involving all key players (students, parents, teachers, administration). Second, success depends on having good leadership that is committed to the whole-school approach. Pellegrini also suggests that victims of bullying need to be trained in social skills so that they become less likely to be isolates, and therefore the target of bullying. As we said above, students who have strong affiliative networks at school are less likely to be bullied. Rigby and Bagshaw (2003) suggest that these whole-school programs are less effective among early adolescents because both the bully and the bullied doubt the teachers' interest in and conflict resolution skills to handle the situation, and hence are reluctant to collaborate with the teacher and school in alleviating bullying within the school context. In other words, teachers appear to have a credibility problem with students when it comes to dealing with bully/victim problems.

Rigby and Bagshaw (2003) make a number of suggestions to improve this situation. First they suggest that it is essential that teachers demonstrate that their interventions result in an improved situation for the bullied students. It must not result in making the situation worse. Second, teachers must make a more

EXTENSION STUDY

Open classrooms

Clearly, the most important aspect of humanism for teachers is the socio-emotional climate established within the classroom. Humanism does not necessitate a particular approach to teaching; indeed, approaches as diverse as behavioural and cognitive (see Chapters 3–6) can be effectively suffused with humanism. It is a frame of mind about the centrality of the student in the learning process and the importance of a supportive and non-restrictive learning environment. Nevertheless, humanistic practitioners have attempted to develop a range of teaching approaches that more clearly reflect the humanistic philosophy. These have included open education, open classrooms, open scheduling, and many forms of curricula that emphasise affective learning such as *values clarification* (see Thibadeau 1995). Open education is a form of education the goal of which is to respond to students on the basis of their individual behaviours, needs and characteristics (Thibadeau 1995). Many other practices encouraged by the humanist approach are now part of mainstream educational practice: child-centred programming, individualising instruction, encouraging independent work, pupil choice and responsibility, de-emphasising competition and emphasising cooperation (see Chapters 7 and 8). Alternative forms of assessment such as observation and portfolios, negotiated curricula and negotiated assessment, together with an emphasis on criterion-referenced evaluation rather than norm-referenced evaluation, also fit within a humanist philosophy of child-centred education. Many of these approaches are discussed in this book (see Chapter 11).

Research does not support the notion that approaches such as open classrooms are more effective than conventional schools and classroom practices (Jackson & Harvey 1991). Indeed, while there was a strong push for open classrooms and open schools in the 1970s, they have all but disappeared in the 1990s. While research demonstrates that, on average, open classrooms of the 1970s did not lead to achievement gains greater than those in standard classroom programs, most research also finds that students' academic achievement did not suffer in open classrooms; in several areas, such as creativity, self-concept and attitudes

concerted effort to work with students who are prepared to collaborate with teachers in countering bullying, and specifically they suggest working through student anti-bullying committees, which give support and credibility to the efforts of teachers and counsellors. Next, they suggest that interventions should, in general, be non-punitive, thus reducing the likelihood of retaliation by the bully. Where this is not possible, Rigby and Bagshaw suggest that increased surveillance of the victim is necessary to ensure no further damaging bullying occurs. Finally, Rigby and Bagshaw recommend that better training must be made available for teachers in how to handle bullying. What do you think of these suggestions? (See also, Nicolaides, Toda & Smith 2002.)

QUESTION POINT

Why do you think bullying is so rampant in our schools? What can be done to alleviate it?

Humanism and constructivism

We emphasise that a principal application of humanism to education is the establishing of effective classroom communication between both teachers and students, and students and students. This emphasis has survived and is flourishing in all good classrooms. The open classroom philosophy and principles derived from it are also very well suited to the types of educational programs being advocated today. Humanism encourages students to construct their own learning, facilitated by effective teachers and an appropriate learning environment that is connected to the students' experiences and concerns (Rothenberg 1989).

QUESTION POINT

Which theory of personality appeals to you most? Why? Are the theories mutually exclusive?

QUESTION POINT

Consider the implications of each of the theories covered in this chapter for children living in tribal settings (such as Australian Aboriginal and Maori children), rural Westernised settings and urbanised settings. Which different factors are likely to affect development in each case?

towards school, students in open classrooms did better than students in traditional classrooms (Giaconia & Hedges 1982; Rothenberg 1989). Unfortunately, because of the many mistakes made in the design and implementation of open classrooms their potential was never realised (Jackson & Harvey 1991; Rothenberg 1989; Thibadeau 1995). One problem, for example, was that teachers were not well prepared to teach effectively in open settings. A number of research studies at the time that claimed to demonstrate the ineffectiveness of this approach also facilitated its demise. Subsequent reanalysis of the data and methodology of several of these studies has shown them to be flawed (see Asher & Hynes 1982; Walberg 1984). Perhaps open education and free schools were more effective than was believed at the time.

Other psychologists have adopted views similar to those of Rogers, based largely on his philosophy. Noteworthy among these are Ginott, Glasser, Gordon and Dreikurs, who have developed humanistic ideas for the classroom, particularly with regard to forms of communication and discipline. As we have indicated earlier, teachers are an integral part of the interactive process in their classroom. By modelling interpersonal communication skills, teachers may help to initiate and facilitate teacher–student and student–student interaction, which in turn will guide students in learning to use these skills (see Chapter 8).

Ginott (1972) maintains that, in effective communication, the teacher should address the situation (that is, the actual behaviour) rather than the individual's personality. Consequently, a teacher would say to a student 'Not completing homework prevents effective learning' rather than 'You are a lazy so-and-so for not completing your homework'. Glasser (1969), on the other hand, stresses teacher involvement with the student in an accepting, non-judgmental manner. He focuses on the development of the student's social responsibility and feelings of self-worth. Dreikurs' (Dreikurs & Cassel 1975, 1995) viewpoint emphasises the democratic classroom in which the teacher maintains their position as leader, but encourages a sharing of responsibility and mutual trust.

We have described these approaches only briefly, and you are recommended to follow them up in other sources. A number of these approaches are considered in greater detail in the chapter on classroom management (Chapter 8).

WHAT WOULD YOU DO?

DANIEL'S PET

In order to better understand the children in my Grade 2 class during my final semester of early childhood field experience, I devised some questionnaires asking a variety of questions. One question was 'My pet's name is . . .'.

In respect of this question, Daniel had crossed out this question and wrote 'I hate the word pet'. I am ashamed to admit that when I saw this I took it quite personally and was offended. I felt it was a simple question requiring a simple answer. I felt I was a reasonable/agreeable person, and I had never forced any child to answer any question if they didn't wish to. Therefore, he didn't have any right to cross out one of *my* questions and write a silly comment such as the fact that he doesn't like the word 'pet'.

Case studies illustrating National Competency Framework for Beginning Teaching, National Project on the Quality of Teaching and Learning, Australian Teaching Council, 1996, p. 32. Commonwealth of Australia copyright, reproduced by permission.

Analyse this case study from a humanist perspective. What might have caused Daniel's reaction? Why did the teacher react in this way? What might the resolution be? Now see the resolution.

WHAT WOULD YOU DO? (cont.)

DANIEL'S PET

Daniel was away sick for a few days so I wasn't able to ask him about it until nearly a week later. I reminded him of the question on the sheet and of the comment he had written, then asked why he didn't like the word 'pet'.

At first Daniel didn't want to talk about it. I have to admit that I thought he was just trying to avoid having to confront that he had done something inappropriate. However, Henry was seated next to him and overheard the question. He said he knew what it was all about. Daniel told him not to tell, but Henry blurted out that Daniel's cat had recently died.

Daniel then reluctantly told me that it was true. He looked quite upset and said that he still felt sad. He said that when he read the question it made him want to cry. I apologised for the fact that the question on the sheet had upset him and that it had brought back sad memories for him. He seemed to accept my apology and said it was okay.

I then made a mental note never to jump to conclusions about a child's intentions without giving them the benefit of the doubt and asking them about it first.

Case studies illustrating National Competency Framework for Beginning Teaching, National Project on the Quality of Teaching and Learning, Australian Teaching Council, 1996, p. 32. Commonwealth of Australia copyright, reproduced by permission.

Show how this case study illustrates the elements of Rogers' humanism—realness, acceptance and empathetic understanding.

KEY TERMS

Anxiety (p. 468): feelings of uneasiness and tension

Client-centred therapy (p. 472): counselling that emphasises the individual's role in developing a healthy personality

Defence mechanisms (p. 468): in Freud's theory, unconscious psychological processes used to protect one's sense of self

Deficiency needs (p. 472): the four lowest levels of Maslow's needs—self-esteem, belonging, safety and survival—that must be met before higher needs can be attended to

Denial (p. 469): denying the existence of painful experience

Ego (p. 467): conscious, rational part of personality

Fantasy (p. 469): imaginary satisfactions in place of real ones

Fixation (p. 469): using immature defence mechanisms

Growth needs (p. 472): the higher self-actualisation needs in Maslow's hierarchy

Hierarchy of needs (p. 472): Maslow's model of seven levels of human needs from basic physical needs to higher-order self-actualisation needs

Humanism (p. 471): approach to personality development that emphasises personal freedom, choice, self-determination and striving for personal growth

Id (p. 467): source of basic biological needs and desires in personality

Identity (p. 456): in Erikson's theory, the defining of a personal, social, sexual and occupational self during adolescence

Identity achievement (p. 456): in Marcia's theory, a stage of identity development that occurs after an individual experiences a period of crisis and decision making

Identity crisis (p. 456): clarifying and becoming aware of personal values
Identity diffusion (p. 456): in Marcia's theory, a stage of identity development that occurs when an individual fails to make clear their choices for the future
Identity foreclosure (p. 456): in Marcia's theory, a stage of identity development that occurs when an individual prematurely adopts the ready-made positions of others, such as parents
Identity formation (p. 454): the conscious and unconscious ways in which an individual incorporates the values of others into their sense of self
Identity moratorium (p. 456): in Marcia's theory, a stage of personality development that occurs when individuals pause and reflect on what the future might hold
Personality development (p. 454): changes in personality as one matures
Phenomenology (p. 472): what the individual perceives rather than what actually may be
Projection (p. 469): ascribing our unconscious motivation to other people
Psychosexual development (p. 467): in Freud's theory, the relationship of personality development to the sexual and aggressive drives of children
Psychosocial stages (p. 454): in Erikson's theory, relationship of ego development to the social environment
Rationalisation (p. 469): giving socially acceptable reasons for our conduct
Reaction formation (p. 468): replacing repressed feeling with the opposite
Regression (p. 469): retreating to an earlier form of coping behaviour
Repression (p. 468): removing from consciousness painful thoughts
Role confusion (p. 461): inability to establish a sense of self-identity
Self-actualisation (p. 472): individuals strive to satisfy their need to grow intellectually and spiritually
Superego (p. 467): seat of conscience within personality

ON-LINE LEARNING

If you go to **http://www.pearsoned.com.au/mcinerney**, you will have hot links directly to these sites:

■ **Family involvement**
We have discussed the importance of the family throughout this chapter and others. Consider the material at this website.
http://www.awesomelibrary.org/Office/Main/Involving_Family/Involving_Family.html

■ **Personality Compass**
Using the information contained in this chapter, critique the material presented at the Personality Compass site. Discuss your views with others.
http://www.personalitycompass.com/

■ **Bullying**
This site provides ideas on how to handle bullying. It is written for children. Consider how useful this site would be and how you would use it in the school and classroom contexts.
http://www.bbc.co.uk/learning/

■ **Bullying (2)**
This site provides further ideas on how to handle bullying.
http://www.scre.ac.uk/bully/

WEB DESTINATIONS

If you go to **http://www.pearsoned.com.au/mcinerney**, you will have hot links directly to these sites:

■ **Awesome School**
We have listed the following website before. It is very useful to follow up a number of key areas of study. This is an excellent site for locating information and other relevant websites.
http://awesomelibrary.org/

■ **Learning Network**
This site provides a lot of interesting information for parents to assist with educating their children. Many key topics are covered, such as 'raising kids' and 'gifted and talented'.
http://www.familyeducation.com/home/

■ **Great ideas in personality**
This site, provided through Psychlopedia, provides snapshot views of a range of personality theories, as well as learning activities. It provides links to on-line papers for discussion and other related websites.
http://www.personalityresearch.org/

■ **Personality project**
This site also provides interesting material and activities to further your knowledge of a variety of personality theories.
http://personality-project.org/personality.html

■ **Identity and coming out**
A site devoted to gay and lesbian issues in identification formation.
http://www.youth-suicide.com/gay-bisexual/links2.htm

RECOMMENDED READING

Bauch, P. A. & Goldring, E. B. (2000) Teacher work context and parent involvement in urban high schools of choice. *Educational Research and Evaluation*, **6**, 1–23.

Desimone, L. (1999) Linking parent involvement with student achievement: Do race and income matter? *Journal of Educational Research*, **93**, 11–30.

Fontana, D. (1986) *Teaching and Personality*. Oxford: Basil Blackwell.

Germain, E. R. (2004) Culture or race? Phenotype and cultural identity development in minority Australian adolescents. *Australian Psychologist*, **39**, 134–42.

Hoover-Dempsey, K. V. & Sandler, H. M. (1997) Why do some parents become involved in their children's education? *Review of Educational Research*, **67**, 3–42.

Mattingly, D. J., Prislin, R., McKenzie, T. L., Rodriguez, J. L. & Kayzar, B. (2002) Evaluating evaluations: The case of parent involvement programs. *Review of Educational Research*, **72**, 549–76.

Nicolaides, S., Toda, Y. & Smith, P. K. (2002) Knowledge and attitudes about school bullying in trainee teachers. *British Journal of Educational Psychology*, **72**, 105–8.

Osterman, K. F. (2000) Students' need for belonging in the school community. *Review of Educational Research*, **70**, 323–67.

Penuel, W. R. & Wertsch, J. V. (1995) Vygotsky and identity formation: A sociocultural approach. *Educational Psychologist*, **30**, 83–92.

Pellegrini, A. D. (2002) Bullying, victimization, and sexual harassment during the transition to middle school. *Educational Psychologist*, **37**, 151–63.

Rigby, K. & Bagshaw, D. (2003) Prospects of adolescent students collaborating with teachers in addressing issues of bullying and conflict in schools. *Educational Psychology*, **23**, 535–46.

Thibadeau, G. (1995) Open education. In L. W. Anderson (ed.) *International Encyclopedia of Teaching and Teacher Education*, 2nd ed. Tarrytown, NY: Pergamon.

Woods, S. & Wolke, D. (2003) Does the content of anti-bullying policies inform us about the prevalence of direct and relational bullying behaviour in primary schools? *Educational Psychology*, **23**, 381–401.

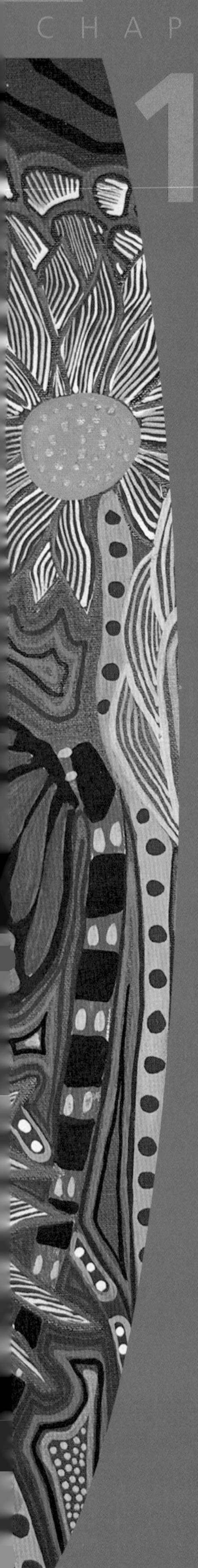

CHAPTER

14 Social, emotional and moral development

Overview

In this chapter we consider the influence of the family, school and peer group on the social, emotional and moral development of the child. In particular, we concentrate on three important aspects. The first of these is the continuing process by which our sense of personal identity is established. The second is the nature of family relationships and their effects on the child's self-reliance and independence. The third is the importance of peer group interaction for sexual development and group acceptance. In this context we look at the function of groups, gangs, cliques and friendships. We also look at adolescent alienation and the issue of adolescent suicide in particular.

We consider the nature and development of the self-concept, how it is structured and formed, whether (and how) it changes over time, whether there are group differences in self-concept, and what effect it has on motivation and behaviour.

Finally, we consider moral development in detail and examine closely the work of Piaget, Kohlberg (and neo-Kohlbergian approaches), Gilligan and Turiel.

14

Learning objectives

After reading this chapter, you will be able to:

- describe key aspects of the social and emotional development of individuals from childhood to adolescence;
- outline the importance of play to social development and describe developmental forms of play;
- outline the nature and importance of identity formation in adolescence;
- describe the importance of family and peer relationships to the development of identity;
- define self-concept and relate it to self-esteem;
- outline the relationship between positive self-concept and desirable learning outcomes;
- describe the 'big-fish-little-pond' and 'frame of reference' effects;
- describe adolescent alienation and the factors that might lead to adolescent suicide;
- describe and discuss prevention programs to alleviate adolescent suicide;
- compare and contrast the main theories of moral development;
- discuss gender differences in moral development;
- describe and discuss cross-cultural considerations of moral development theory and application;
- consider the classroom applications of moral development theory;
- describe what is meant by caring schools.

Consider the relevance of this final Learner-centred Psychological Principle as you read this chapter on social, emotional and personal development.

LEARNER-CENTRED PSYCHOLOGICAL PRINCIPLE

Social influences on learning. Learning is influenced by social interactions, interpersonal relations and communication with others.

Learning can be enhanced when the learner has an opportunity to interact and to collaborate with others on instructional tasks. [Sometimes this is referred to as peer-assisted learning (Rohrbeck, Ginsburg-Block, Fantuzzo & Miller 2003).] Learning settings that allow for social interactions, and that respect diversity, encourage flexible thinking and social competence. In interactive and collaborative instructional contexts, individuals have an opportunity for perspective taking and reflective thinking that may lead to higher levels of cognitive, social and moral development, as well as self-esteem. Quality personal relationships that provide stability, trust and caring can increase learners' sense of belonging, self-respect and self-acceptance, and provide a positive climate for learning. [In other words, when an individual's need for belonging is met, positive outcomes occur. Within schools, a perceived sense of school belonging is related to enhanced motivation, achievement, and positive attitudes towards school (Anderman 2002).]

Family influences, positive interpersonal support and instruction in self-motivation strategies can offset factors that interfere with optimal learning such as negative beliefs about competence in a particular subject, high levels of test anxiety, negative sex role expectations, and undue pressure to perform well. Positive learning climates can also help to establish the context for healthier levels of thinking, feeling and behaving. Such contexts help learners feel safe to share ideas, actively participate in the learning process, and create a learning community.

TEACHER'S CASE BOOK

It's my hole!

Consider the following episode taken from a scene at a preschool where two three-year-olds (Sarah and Zach) begin to fight because each has accidentally invaded the other's territory, in this case while they were absorbed in parallel play in a sandpit. The teacher intervenes in the following way:

'Zach, what do you want to tell Sarah?' she asks, squatting down between them. Zach is crying; Sarah has punched him hard.

'I don't like her. She's stupid,' sobs Zach.

'You're really angry at Sarah. Can you tell her what she did to make you mad?'

'Hit me,' says Zach sadly.

'You hit me first,' Sarah retorts indignantly.

'Zach, did you hit Sarah?' He nods.

'Why?'

'My hole!' he wails, the memory of the violation of his play suddenly much more painful than his sore shoulder. 'She messed up my hole!' He tries to hit Sarah again.

'What hole?' frowns Sarah, genuinely puzzled. 'I didn't mess up no hole.'

'Can you show Sarah your hole, Zach?' the teacher asks. He certainly can.

'Here,' he shouts. 'It was right here, and I digged it and digged it . . .'

'Sarah, Zach is really sad about his hole,' explains the teacher. 'Do you think maybe you could help him fix it?'

Sarah nods vigorously, grabbing her bulldozer.

'No!' says Zach. 'No 'dozer!'

'Do you want to fix the hole yourself, Zach?' the teacher asks. He nods yes. 'Then could you show Sarah where to drive her bulldozer so that she won't muck up your hole again?'

Zach gestures a wide detour with his arm. Sarah bulldozes off in the correct direction. Zach begins to dig again with his shovel, and his very important hole begins to reappear.

Adapted from Jones & Reynolds (1992), p. 27.

Case study activity

There are many ways in which different teachers might have reacted to the children in this instance, from a permissive 'Let them work it out for themselves' to a stern reprimand for hurting each other, or even the loss of the 'privilege' to play while they were sent to the naughty corner to 'think about what they had done wrong'. What do you think of the teacher's reaction? Is it what you would have done?

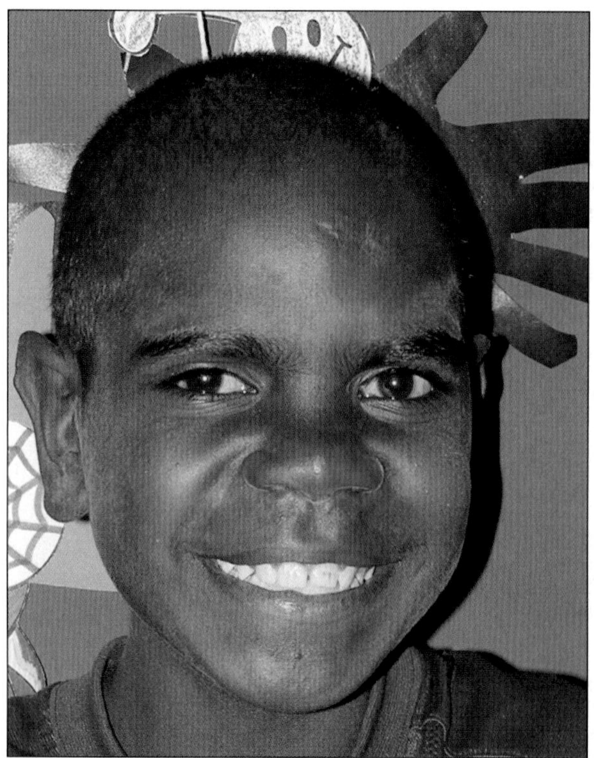

Children who are well-adjusted and happy enjoy school.

Social and emotional development in childhood

As we have indicated in Chapter 6 (see also Chapter 8 on cooperative group work), the social worlds of children play a very important role in their cognitive development. Children observe and model social and academic skills and standards for performance displayed by others, and they are rewarded for behaving in ways that are valued by teachers and peers. Children must also be socially as well as intellectually adept if they are to be successful students (Diehl *et al.* 1998; Jimerson, Egeland & Teo 1999; Wentzel & Berndt 1999). The development of a social identity becomes increasingly important to children as they grow older. What is the importance of family relationships to social and emotional development? Sociability has its roots in the interactions of the baby and its parents or other caregivers, and these early experiences will either encourage or deter the baby's tendency to approach other human beings. In the early years in the home, parents and siblings are the most important elements in the development of a child's social self. As children grow older, mothers typically spend less time with them while fathers become more important influences in their development, involving themselves

The role of siblings in socialisation

more in children's activities, such as hobbies, sports and clubs. Siblings also act as important socialising influences on each other. The most persuasive characteristics of this relationship are competition and concern about being treated equally by parents. While competitive interaction is a fact of sibling life, there are many positive and neutral interactions that benefit the child's social and emotional development. Someone close in age to the child may be able to communicate more effectively than parents can. In areas such as dealing with peers, coping with difficult teachers and discussing taboo subjects, siblings are often of more assistance and support than parents. Older siblings may model appropriate behaviour and attitudes to a range of events dealing with identity, physical appearance and sexual behaviour, areas in which the parents may be unwilling or incapable of helping the child. Of course, sometimes the reverse can occur with older siblings modelling inappropriate behaviour and attitudes.

In our Western society, parents begin to give their children increasing independence as they grow older (although this is not a universally practised custom). Many parents encourage their children to take on part-time paid work and to achieve independent goals, thereby fostering a sense of industry (refer to the section on Erikson in Chapter 13). Indeed, parenting styles reflecting involvement, autonomy and support may promote the development of a healthy sense of autonomy (see, for example, Grolnick, Kurowski & Gurland 1999).

Often personal, social and emotional problems begin to surface as children enter school, with rates of referral for primary children being considerably higher than for preschool children. Common problems are oppositional and acting-out behaviour, poor discipline, and personal characteristics such as shyness, unhappiness and withdrawal. Many of these emotional and behavioural problems are related to the home backgrounds of the children. Indeed, the changing nature of society and family structure has put new pressures on young children and brought new responsibilities to the school and teachers (see, for example, Kaslow 2001). In many households both parents work, so increasing numbers of children leave for school and arrive home after school without adult supervision. Many children in our classrooms come from single-parent homes, the result of separation, divorce or parental death. It is increasingly common for the single parent to be the father. Many children suffer trauma as a result of such effects of divorce as custodial arrangements, the nature of the custodial parent–child relationship, and the availability and reliance on support systems (Berk 2004; Santrock & Yussen 1992; see also Guttman & Rosenberg 2003). In this, and in other circumstances where children lose parents, the classroom teacher becomes an important element in the child's support structure. During middle and late childhood, peers, teachers and other adults become more important (Berk 2004; Peterson 1989; Santrock & Yussen 1992).

It is important to note here that conceptions of families these days in contemporary societies are quite diverse, including the nuclear two-generation family united by marriage and having conceived their own children, to extended three- and four-generation families living together, foster families, adoptive families that may be bi- or multiracial, single-parent families headed primarily by the mother or the father, commuter families in which one or both parents see the children infrequently, gay or lesbian couples without or with children, remarried/step-families, and several people living together with no legal ties to each other, but with strong mutual commitments (Kaslow 2001). In much of the following description of social, emotional and moral development we take a perspective based largely on the

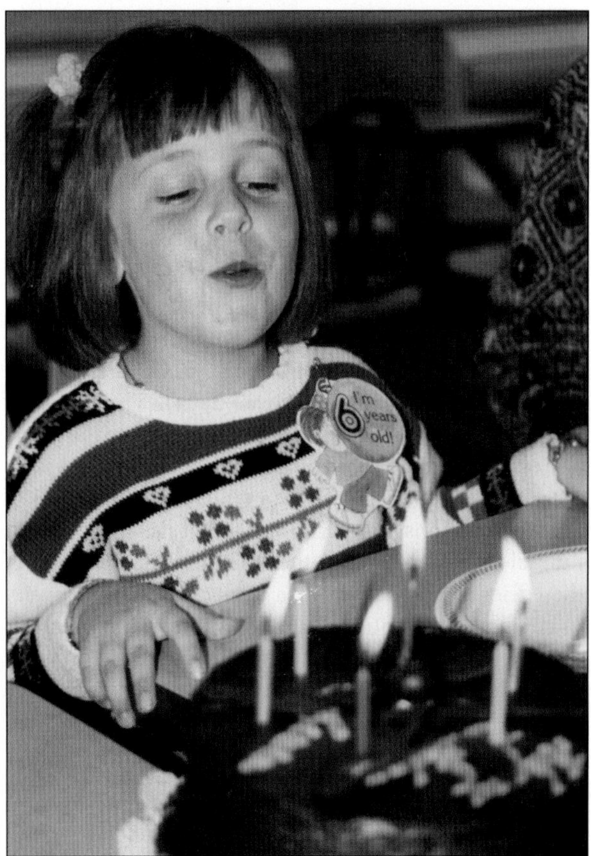

Birthdays are usually a happy social event in families, signifying growth to maturity.

typical nuclear family. How do you think these different family types potentially impact on the development of children? What family type were you brought up in, and how do you think that this influenced your social, emotional and moral development?

The importance of the peer group

Peer group importance
Cliques
Sex cleavages
Non-sexist education practices

The significance of the peer group increases as children progress through school. As this occurs, children sometimes organise themselves into more or less exclusively girl or boy cliques. Often rituals and rules are established to keep other individuals out of the group, but cliques become less rigid as children approach puberty. Most schools now implement non-sexist education practices that cut across sex-based cliques, although in out-of-school activities most children prefer to get together in single-sex groups.

Emotional development and small-group membership

Small friendship groups are very important to the identity of the child. Having friends has been associated with good grades and test scores, involvement in school-related activities, and increased pro-social behaviour. Children with friends tend to be more sociable, cooperative and self-confident when compared with their peers who don't have friends (Fredrichs, Blumenfeld & Paris 2004; Wentzel, Barry & Caldwell 2004). They are also more independent, emotionally supportive and altruistic. Friends and friendship groups are obviously very important to children and adolescents. The characteristics of students' friends and the features of their friendships may influence students' self-perceptions, attitudes and behaviours across a wide range of areas (Berndt 1999; see also Roberts & Quayle 2001; Wentzel, Barry & Caldwell 2004). Through *peer modelling* and reinforcement, children can acquire and test out their growing personal, social and physical skills in a group that is supportive (Williams & Stith 1980). Peer interactions are reciprocal—that is, they have a mutual impact on each other. An important aspect of these friendships is in the area of *emotional development*. In coping with emotional conflict, young friends express considerable emotion, sympathy and support for each other (Peterson 1989). Family and cultural backgrounds play critical roles in the development of both informal and formal peer groups. Children's perception of security in the mother–child relationship, for example, has been shown to be related to the formation of positive peer relationships in middle childhood (Kerns, Klepac & Cole 1996). Therefore, even though children and adolescents often spend greater amounts of time with their peers than with their parents, isolation from parental values does not necessarily ensue (Jarvinen & Nicholls 1996).

The relationship between siblings is a very important element in social development.

Consider the types of play listed in the Extension Study feature on pages 490–1. In what ways would the development of social, emotional and communication skills occur in each?

ACTION STATION

Schools are significant influences in the social development of children. The classroom forms a mini world for the child, with leaders and followers, responsibilities, rules and roles to be performed. Much can be learned about the social interaction in a classroom by compiling a *sociogram*.

Procedure

Ask a class of children to select three partners from their class that they would like to work with in a free activity, such as project work or craft. For very young children in infants it may be necessary to ask each child individually rather than expect them to write names down. The children should be picking partners on the basis of friendship rather than expertise and they should not discuss their choices with one another prior to their selection. Assure the children that their choice will be confidential. Collect the data and construct a matrix that illustrates the choices each child has made, using a key that indicates first, second or third choice.

From the data you will be able to gather the following insights into your class.

1 The children who are popular with each individual for a particular activity.

2 The number of times each child was chosen (referred to as the child's *sociometric status*).

3 Self-contained groups or mutual choices in the classroom (clusters, triangles, cliques, reciprocal choices).

4 Any cleavages that exist between groups in the classroom based on sex, race, ability, etc.

5 The most popular children in the class (*stars*).

6 The least popular children in the class.

7 Non-chosen children who make choices (*isolates*).

The information can be represented diagrammatically by constructing a target sociogram. On a large sheet of paper draw three concentric circles. Using triangles for males and circles for females, represent each child on the graph, with those with the highest sociometric status (those who were chosen frequently) in the innermost circle, and the least chosen in the outer circle. Draw arrows radiating from each person to the people chosen. A colour key should be used to represent first, second or third choice. Reciprocal choices may be represented by double arrowheads. Patterns of social interaction may be seen at a glance from these diagrams.

It might be necessary to experiment with the format to obtain the clearest diagram. Shifts in social interaction may be noted by drawing sociograms for a range of activities (which may lead to different choices) and by giving sociometric tests over a 12-month period, one each month.

Social and emotional development, social identity and adolescence

Few developmental periods are characterised by so many changes at so many different levels as adolescence (Eccles *et al.* 1993). We consider a number of these changes in earlier chapters. While it is not uncommon for adolescents to experience some problems during this time, most pass through puberty and adolescence without significant psychological or emotional difficulties. Most adolescents develop a positive sense of personal identity and manage to form adaptive peer relationships at the same time as maintaining close relationships with their families. A number, nevertheless, experience difficulties that cause deep emotional stress and anxiety which leads them into a downward spiral that ends in academic failure and dropping out of school. Indeed, research shows that poor socio-emotional adjustment and conduct problems are associated with past, present and future academic achievement problems (Eccles *et al.* 1993; Jimerson *et al.* 1999; Petersen 1985, Petersen *et al.* 1995; Simmons & Blyth 1987). Educators must be sensitive to the needs of all adolescents at this time in order to provide the emotional supports needed for healthy social and emotional development (Frydenberg & Lewis 1990, 1991, 1993).

Social development and identity formation during the adolescent years acquire more significance than they had at any previous time. When considering overall *social development* during adolescence, attention should be focused on four important aspects. The first of these is the continuing process by which a sense of personal identity is established. (We consider this in some detail in Chapter 13.) The second aspect is the nature of the family relationships and its effect on the adolescent's self-reliance and independence. The third, peer group interaction, focuses specifically on the development of heterosexual relationships and group acceptance, while the fourth aspect deals with the opportunities provided by social environments, including the school, for healthy personal and social development of the individual.

Identity formation and social development

Family relationships, social development and relationship to academic adjustment

Research has shown that parenting styles have a considerable impact on social development and academic adjustment. The original work of Baumrind (1967; see also Conrade & Ho 2001) highlighted three possible patterns of parenting styles—authoritative, permissive and authoritarian. Later theorists (Maccoby & Martin 1983) expanded this to four prototypic patterns of parenting which included warmth and demandingness dimensions: authoritative style (high warmth and high behavioural demandingness); authoritarian style (low warmth and high demandingness); indulgent-permissive (high warmth and low demandingness) and rejecting-neglectful (low warmth and low demandingness). Research clearly shows that the most effective parenting style for personal and school adjustment is the authoritative style (see, for example, Choo & Tan 2000; Strage & Brandt 1999). There is some evidence that, in general, mothers are more authoritative in their parenting than fathers and that fathers are more authoritarian, although in the Conrade and Ho study fathers, while being less authoritative, were not more authoritarian (Conrade & Ho 2001). There is also some evidence that there are gender differences in parenting styles—that is, mothers and fathers treat their sons and daughters differently, with boys, for example, being

EXTENSION STUDY

Play and personality development

Play is very important to the social, emotional and cognitive development of children (Cherney *et al.* 2003; Moyles 1995). The interpersonal interactions between peers during play, particularly those involving pro-social or aggressive interactions, influence social development. Exposure during play to the opinions, ideas, feelings and feedback of peers enables children to move beyond egocentric thought to consider the point of view of others (Coolahan *et al.* 2000; see also Chapter 2). It is also believed that positive play experiences at school enhance an individual's learning behaviours—for example, motivation, feelings of competence, persistence and positive attitudes—while reducing classroom behaviour problems. Children who engage in less positive play experiences are more likely to lack motivation and to engage in disruptive behaviour (Coolahan *et al.* 2000; Lillemyr 2001). Indeed, so important is play to the cognitive, social and physical development of children that many educational settings beyond the early school years include both free and structured play opportunities within the formal school program as an instructional strategy, over and above what happens spontaneously in play at recess times (Lillemyr 2001). Conversely, at many other schools the opportunity for play becomes significantly reduced as students move from kindergarten to first grade and beyond. In effect, the reduction in free and structured play limits the opportunities for students to learn through social interaction with peers. As some children are less socially competent in interactive play situations, teachers, as well as providing play opportunities, should also foster interactions between children at various levels of interactive play competence. This may help to alleviate inappropriate classroom behaviour and help develop social competence in all children (Coolahan *et al.* 2000).

To understand the role of play, it may be helpful to categorise the social elements of children's play in the following way (Parten 1932):

- *Solitary:* The child plays alone, unaware of others.
- *Onlooker:* The child looks on at the play of others but is not directly involved in it.
- *Parallel:* Children play alongside others doing similar things, but with little or no interaction.
- *Associative:* Children play as a group, using the same materials, but do not appear to share a plan of action or common purpose.
- *Cooperative:* Children play with each other, making up and taking turns in games that have a shared goal.

As children develop, so do the complexity and social nature of their play. While *solitary* and *onlooker* play is characteristic of young children, and *associative* and *cooperative* play is more typical of the older child, it is inaccurate to use the categorisation of social play as a marker of social maturity. Just as young children may take part in the interactive games or associative play when they play pretend games and chatter to each other (Howes, Unger & Seidner 1989), so older children may also engage in solitary play in which they play quietly for a period by themselves, showing that they are now able to concentrate on a task (Smith 1978). As for onlooker play, even adolescents may remain on the side until they have worked up the confidence to participate in a group 'game' to which they are newcomers. While intellectual development may be quite advanced, the young person may lack the social skills and self-esteem to engage in cooperative interaction with unfamiliar individuals or those who appear exclusive.

Symbolic re-enactment of real-life and imaginary experiences is referred to as *sociodramatic* play. Sociodramatic play in childhood provides the greatest opportunity for children to learn social skills and gain an understanding of how they respond to others (and vice versa) in a social group of peers. For instance, the choice of who is allowed to participate in dramatic play or to contribute to the rules of the game sends messages about one's self-worth. Adult and societal roles are also explored or re-enacted in dramatic play when children become television characters or members of their family, not only in manner but in vocalisation. In the following example, our daughter Laura was debating with two friends their respective roles in a dramatisation of *The Wizard of Oz*.

'You be the Wicked Witch and I'll be the Good Witch coz I've got blonde hair.'

'So you have to sound all cackley and mean, and I have to be beautiful and wear a pretty dress, and talk sweetly.'

'Who's going to be the Wizard? We don't have any boys!'

'We'll have to skip that bit.'

'What about when Dorothy gets back home? Her aunty would be really worried about her—maybe she should cry.'

'I think she would give Dorothy a smack for being gone so long.'

In addition to social skills, many language and interpersonal skills are learned through cooperative and associative play as children have to interact with one another in the business of problem solving, negotiating, resolving disputes, turn-taking and sharing resources. The teacher has an important role to play in providing the language needed to describe the conflicts that erupt in children's play and in assisting children in understanding the perspective of others who may often inadvertently thwart them.

Erikson's stages in relation to play

In the context of Erikson's stages of psychosocial development (see Chapter 13), there are three stages that are particularly relevant to children's play. Between the ages of about one and three, in the stage of autonomy that has grown out of the trust consolidated in the earlier stage of infancy, children enter a *period of exploration*. In terms of exploratory play, a sense of independence grows as the caring adult demonstrates respect for the child's growing capabilities in their beginning language and physical actions on the world, and shows warmth in the relationship with the child. Where doubt is expressed about the child's abilities by significant others, self-doubt may develop.

During the *period of play*, as the years between three and six, before children begin formal schooling, are known (Jones & Reynolds 1992), the exercise of initiative becomes paramount. In the course of play, this may be demonstrated in rough-and-tumble games, investigations into hitherto unknown places and things, and acts of physical and verbal daring. We can think of many occasions when our youngest has disappeared for a surprisingly long period of time (when it is quiet for too long, invariably something is going on), only to discover that she has taken the initiative to explore a box of glitter and fabric paints, using them to paint her legs, or to see how the tape recorder works. It takes a great deal of parental restraint not to show anger when the paint exploration ends in a stained cream carpet and the tape recorder will only work at slow speed. The danger of dampening a child's sense of initiative and turning it to guilt is very real in countless experiences of such play. According to Erikson, the ability to choose, plan and accomplish actions without anxiety during this stage is the key to healthy psychosocial development.

When children are in middle childhood and at school, they enter the *period of investigation* where industry leads them to develop a sense of personal control rather than a sense of incompetence and inferiority. Play activities through which this development can be fostered include both physical and social games such as sports or hand clapping, marbles and card or board games, as well as the investigative classroom experiences designed by teachers. Structured cooperative learning activities during this time allow children to learn and practise social skills such as turn-taking, encouraging others and negotiating, as well as language and communication skills such as asking questions, active listening, clarifying and explaining (see Chapter 8 for further discussion of cooperative learning). Once again, support from the child's social environment helps to resolve the developmental conflict at this stage and leads into the period of identity formation during adolescence.

Using play in the social and emotional development of the child

We have already described the importance of the teacher in providing an environment in which children can feel challenged and stimulated intellectually, as well as feeling safe to explore and to express themselves. Just as important is the role of the teacher in fostering the social and emotional development of the child. This can be done through a range of activities including role play, semi-structured shared conversations in which children can relate personal experiences and feelings, and the use of puppets to act out social problems for preschoolers and kindergarten children, or drawings and stories for older children.

What reasons might this older adolescent have for the jewellery and striking hairstyle?

subjected to more physical punishment than girls, and in particular, fathers being more authoritarian with their sons. There is also evidence that there are cross-cultural differences in parenting styles. Whereas authoritative or democratic parenting styles are associated with achievement for Euro-Americans, for African Americans, particularly females, authoritarian parenting styles are associated with higher levels of achievement and social competence (Hill 2001; see also Ogakaki & Frensch 1998). A study by Bempechat *et al.* (1999; see also Bempechat & Drago-Severson 1999) indicates that ethnic groups differ in academic socialisation practices such as the relative emphasis on ability and effort, guilt about parental sacrifice for the children's education, emphasis on the importance of education to get ahead in life, and valuing scholarship. All of these have an impact on identity formation.

As discussed earlier (Chapter 13), probably the most critical factor in the development of ego identity is the nature of the relationship the child continues to have with their parents. In the last decade, developmentalists have begun to explore the role of *connectedness to parents* in adolescent development. Adolescents continue to seek help from their parents for both major and minor developmental problems, including interpersonal, health and educational problems (Fallon & Bowles 1999). Findings suggest that attachment to parents may facilitate adolescents' social competence and well-being, as reflected through self-esteem, emotional adjustment and physical health (Kobak & Sceery 1988; Santrock & Yussen 1992). Adolescents who have secure relationships with their parents have higher self-esteem and better emotional well-being. Attachment to parents during adolescence may serve the adaptive function of providing a secure base from which adolescents can explore and master new environments and a widening social world in a psychologically healthy way (Santrock & Yussen 1992; see also Guttmann & Rosenberg 2003). This connectedness to parents also promotes competent peer relations and positive close relationships outside the family (Kerns *et al.* 1996).

Closely allied with the relationship of the adolescent to their parents are the issues of adolescent *autonomy* and *independence* (Peterson 2004). There is typically a temporary increase in family conflict during adolescence over autonomy and control while the dimensions of these are renegotiated (Buchanan, Eccles & Becker 1992). The degree of difficulty that the adolescent encounters in establishing independence depends on a number of factors: the consistency, rate and extent, and complexity of independence training that is sanctioned by society as a whole, and reflected in organisations such as schools, together with the childrearing practices and models of behaviour provided by the parents.

Independence training and the development of autonomy

In optimal situations parents stimulate and reinforce this process of growing autonomy, self-determination and independence. For adolescents to feel a sense of autonomy, they should perceive that they have input into family decision making. It appears that those who feel they have such an input have higher self-esteem and greater school motivation. It appears that such children also make an easier transition into high school (Eccles *et al.* 1993). In contrast, excessive parental control is linked to lower intrinsic school motivation, to more negative changes in self-esteem following high school transition, to more school misconduct associated with this transition, and to greater investment in peer social attachments and even delinquency (Eccles *et al.* 1993; Mak 1994). It is not possible to determine whether the parental control is the cause or result of these aspects of adolescent behaviour. They probably interact. It is also necessary to add that too little parental control also leads to significant negative consequences.

Continuing good relationships with parents is essential to developing a healthy sense of identity.

Conflict with parents

During adolescence children move in wider social circles and are increasingly exposed to the values and modes of behaviour of their peer group and to belief systems of different families. This circumstance may provide the basis for conflict within the home, particularly when there is a perceived clash between what peers are able to do within their families and what the individual is able to do in their own family (Pearson & Love 1999). The nature and quality of the communication processes between parents and adolescents and their use of particular problem-solving procedures may lead either to conflict escalation or to more effective management of family disputes. The adolescent's concern with fairness, freedom and autonomy may lead to neglect of well-learned problem-solving skills such as compromise, or to select less effective conflict resolution methods that are contending and hostile, thus exacerbating conflict with parents (Pearson & Love 1999). This can be related to our discussion of justice orientation and care orientation later in the chapter. Adolescents should be encouraged to take a more care-oriented perspective centred on principles of concern for others, and care for the self. Through this approach, potential conflict might be reduced as the adolescent becomes more empathetic, able to take the perspective of others and therefore more inclined to use less confrontational conflict resolution strategies, such as conceding and cooperative negotiation. Hence it would seem useful to promote care value-systems among children and teenagers through education programs.

Independence and conflict within the home

In multiracial countries such as Australia and New Zealand, the norms for autonomy and independence training vary widely from one cultural group to another and from one set of parents to another. This variation can cause considerable difficulty for some children from groups that do not encourage independence in the same way as mainstream groups. There can be a cultural clash when children are expected to behave in contradictory ways depending on social circumstances. We deal with this issue in Chapter 10 (see also Rosenthal, Ranieri & Klimidis 1996).

QUESTION POINT

We should be cautious of the common assertion that parental and peer group values are necessarily mutually incompatible and that an inevitable consequence of heightened peer group dependence during adolescence is a sharp decline in parental influence. What evidence have you seen for this assertion? What contrary evidence is there?

The importance of the peer group to adolescents

The peer group

At the time when adolescents are moving away from parent dependency, they often substitute peer dependency. Peers exert a great deal of pressure on each other to conform. Children and adolescents seek out and listen to the advice of peers on certain issues, especially those involving immediate consequences, such as clothes, entertainment and fads. Indeed, research suggests that peers play a vital role in the psychological development of most children and adolescents, and the quality of their peer interactions will have a bearing on academic performance and school behaviour (Berndt 1999; Fredrichs, Blumefeld & Paris 2004; Guay, Boivin & Hodges 1999; Wentzel, Barry & Caldwell 2004). Changes in the structure of Western society have implications for adolescence. Changes that have had an impact are a decline in the extended family, growing numbers of two-career families and the increasing institutionalisation of age segregation—for example, through exclusive retirement villages, cheaper insurance for the over-fifties, and fewer employment opportunities for those over 50. These factors, as well as expanded communication networks among the young, and delayed entrance into adult society, have increased the importance of the peer group as a developmental influence (Conger 1977). How might peers influence academic behaviour? Connell and Wellborn (1990) propose three processes thought to influence learning: (1) relatedness—that is, perceiving oneself as being related to others in the school context; (2) competence—that is, perceiving oneself as capable in school activities; and (3) autonomy—that is, experiencing choice and control in one's school activities. While feelings of autonomy are most likely to be influenced by teachers and parents, relatedness and competence, while influenced by parents and teachers, are also likely to be influenced by the quality of one's interaction with the peer group. Negative peer relationships may foster feelings of loneliness and lack of relatedness that then affect one's feeling of competence (Roberts & Quayle 2001). Competence has been shown to predict academic achievement. There is evidence in support of the negative impact of loneliness and peer rejection on students' academic performance (Diehl *et al.* 1998; Guay *et al.* 1999). However, research also indicates that parents can influence their children to a much greater extent than peers and that, even in cases where students do not have friends, the negative effects of peer rejection can be offset by being liked by the teacher (Wentzel 1999; Wentzel, Barry & Caldwell 2004). For example, parental reactions to grades and under-controlling family styles may be related to lower performance, while autonomy-supportive family styles (such as including children in decision making) may be related to higher academic performance (Guay *et al.* 1999; see also Jimerson *et al.* 1999; Kurdek & Sinclair 2000; Strage & Brandt 1999). Research has also indicated that the use of autonomy-supportive techniques by teachers and school administrators predicts school achievement through motivational processes (Guay *et al.* 1999). In our own research, students consistently report that having friends at school is nice, but not essential to being motivated or not at school. Many students report that they don't really care what other students think of them and whether or not they have friends at school. Other factors, such as supportive parents and holding personal goals to achieve, are considered more important (McInerney & McInerney 2000).

Adults often exaggerate the negative power of the peer group, particularly as it relates to sexual behaviour, drug use and delinquency (Berger 1991; see also Berndt 1999). The influence of the peer group and, in particular, special friends is just as likely to be positive as negative, depending on the friends' characteristics. For example, students whose friends have high grades are likely to improve in their own grades, while students whose friends are disruptive in school are likely to become more disruptive themselves (Berndt 1999; see also Diehl *et al.* 1998). Other groups, such as adults, teachers, coaches and part-time employers, also strongly influence adolescents' attitudes and behaviour.

Quality of adolescent friendships

One factor that appears to be important in whether or not friendships will be influential is the quality of the friendship. It appears that if students have a high-quality friendship, in which friends validate and care about each others' emotional well-being, support intimacy and self-disclosure, resolve conflicts effectively, and provide instrumental help and companionship (Guay *et al.* 1999; Wentzel 1999), they are more likely to be influenced than if the friendship is of low quality. As a result of this, it is important not to group poorly adjusted students together in groups as they may form high-

The peer group is more likely to have a positive rather than negative influence. What are some of the positive influences a peer group may have?

quality friendships that will mutually reinforce the alienation. Rather, it would appear more beneficial to help poorly adjusted students form friendships with better-adjusted students. Research suggests that individuals with positive friendships are higher in classroom involvement, perceive their conduct as better, feel they are more accepted by their peers, and have higher general self-esteem than students with less positive friendships (Berndt 1999).

Adolescent grouping

An adolescent group contains several interrelated levels of organisation. The most inclusive peer group structure is the *crowd*; next is the *clique*; and then there are individual *friendships*. The **crowd** is the least personal of these groups. The members of a crowd meet because of their mutual interest in particular activities, such as sporting activities, rather than because they are mutually attracted to each other. The **clique** is smaller in size. Members are attracted to each other on the basis of similar interests and social ideals. Cliques involve greater intimacy between members and have more group cohesion than crowds. A more intense interaction characterises these groups. Finally, adolescents develop a number of personal friendships vital to their emotional and social development (Dunphy 1969; Hill 1995; Peterson 1989; Santrock & Yussen 1992; Zigler & Stevenson 1993). Research on friendships (Berndt & Perry 1990) during adolescence has identified these distinct features:

- loyalty and faithfulness;
- avoidance of intense competition, while aiming for equality through sharing; and
- the perception of relationships as emotionally supportive.

Friendships

While popularity and peer acceptance may be stable from childhood to adolescence, sexual maturation and sexual behaviour provide new influences that affect an adolescent's behaviour within a group. Among some of these new factors and influences affecting peer group acceptance are dress, entertainment, sport, dating, drugs, dropping-out and politics. The group or clique one belongs to makes a statement about the values held by the individual in a social context. Group identity at this time often overrides individual identity (Santrock & Yussen 1992).

Same-sex friendships are important in the social and emotional development of adolescents.

Being part of a group sometimes requires the adoption of some customs. What customs may characterise this group?

QUESTION POINT

What is the importance of the peer group to adolescent development? Identify the characteristics of most importance.

Adolescent sexuality

The fact that puberty equips the adolescent for mature sexual enjoyment and for reproduction makes sexuality another special concern during this phase of life. Adolescent sexuality relates to social and personal identity formation in a dramatic way, and it also relates to parental influences and peer group associations. Sexual maturity on one level leads to a growing sense of independence and maturity in the adolescent, while on another it may lead to rebellion against the mores of both parents and society (Brooks-Gunn & Furstenberg 1989). The hormonally induced increase that takes place in sexual drive, and the unfamiliar, frequently unpredictable and mysterious feelings, fantasies and impulses that accompany this phenomenon often create tensions for the adolescent (Brooks-Gunn & Furstenberg 1989; Turner & Helms 1991). Many adolescents find sexual adjustment difficult. Integrating sexuality meaningfully with other aspects of the adolescent's developing sense of self and of relations to others, with as little conflict and disruption as possible, is a major developmental task for both girls and boys (Peterson 1989; Santrock & Yussen 1992). The development of a sexual identity is perhaps more complex in a modern society such as Australia and New Zealand where sexual mores are more flexible than in past years, and models of alternative 'sexual' lifestyles abound. For example, it is more acceptable today for youth to identify as gay, and there are various mechanisms in place through schools and health clinics to support children in their identification. However, having said this, there is still considerable concern by adolescents 'coming out' which can cause major psychological stress. Our Internet activities for this chapter cover some key issues related to this.

School environments and the development of adolescents

As suggested above, adolescence is a time of great personal change on a number of levels. The rapidity and depth of these changes often cause considerable problems for adolescents. At the time when hormonal activity is causing changes to body shape, intellectual development and personal development, and when families are reshaping expectations of appropriate roles for the maturing individual, the adolescent is set adrift, in a sense, from the security of primary school. It is an interesting phenomenon that during adolescence, along with all the other changes, profound changes also occur in the individual's educational environment. It is at this stage that many children who were doing well at and enjoying school begin to lose interest and develop patterns of behaviour inimical to successful school

TEACHER'S CASE BOOK

Happy families

Miss Osbourne's Grade 10 drama class was one of diverse interests, mixed ability and widely differing social groups. These students had never worked together in four years of high school. Miss Osbourne decided to embark on a children's theatre production in first term in order to establish positive and supportive relationships within the class. She let them know that she had high expectations of all members of the group.

The production was carefully cast to suit the personality and qualities of each individual, and each student was able to experience success, not just the more able students. All students were treated equally and each role was valued in the production, no matter how small or large it was. Miss Osbourne worked at building a good rapport and positive relationships with all of the students.

The production was a great success, and the children from associated primary schools proved to be enthusiastic audiences. The entire experience was tremendously positive for Miss Osbourne's students and their self-esteem soared.

Miss Osbourne was able to build upon the positive and supportive relationships that had been developed and secured through this successful group enterprise. Students who had never worked together in four years of high school had come together as a cohesive group. They now looked forward to working together and for the remainder of the year referred to themselves as the 'happy family'.

Case studies illustrating National Competency Framework for Beginning Teaching, National Project on the Quality of Teaching and Learning, Australian Teaching Council, 1996, p. 46.

Case study activity

At the beginning of each school year, new classes are made up of many students who don't know each other. As teachers, what activities can you devise that might ensure that each new group refers to itself as a 'happy family'? Why is this important?

completion. Many educationalists suggest that this occurs because *there is a mismatch between what the school offers in terms of a supportive social and intellectual environment for adolescents, and what they actually need* (Eccles *et al.* 1993). Eccles *et al.* (1993, p. 94) believe that:

Mismatch between school and adolescent needs

> . . . the environmental changes often associated with transition to junior high school seem especially harmful in that they emphasize competition, social comparison, and ability self-assessment at a time of heightened self-focus; they decrease decision making and choice at a time when the desire for control is growing; they emphasize lower level cognitive strategies at a time when the ability to use higher level strategies is increasing; and they disrupt social networks at a time when adolescents are especially concerned with peer relationships outside of the home.

Eccles *et al.* (1993) demonstrate that a decline in motivation for learning as adolescents enter high school is not an inevitable result of the students' adolescent development, but rather reflects non-adaptive school and

Why is socialising with the opposite sex important for adolescents?

Boyfriends and girlfriends become an increasing interest during puberty.

classroom practices which lead to these declines. With appropriate school and classroom strategies in place, adolescents can proceed through high school with enhanced motivation for learning.

In Chapter 7 we consider characteristics of school environments that might have a negative impact on students' learning and motivation, such as task structure, grouping practices, evaluation techniques, motivational strategies, locus of responsibility for learning and the

For many adolescents in high school, the best parts of the day are before and after school. How can schools motivate learning during adolescence?

Theory and research into practice

James W. Chapman — SELF-ESTEEM, SELF-CONCEPT AND READING

BRIEF BIOGRAPHY

Following an appalling academic performance at secondary school, I graduated with a B.A. (Hons) degree in Education at Victoria University of Wellington (VUW). I trained to be a secondary teacher of history, social studies and geography at Christchurch College of Education. During this training year, I conducted research on Maori and Pakeha (White) adolescent boys' identity status and field dependence/independence, and graduated with an M.A. in Education at VUW. Following two years of teaching I entered the Ph.D. program in educational psychology at the University of Alberta in Canada. During this time I worked on two major research projects relating to the measurement of academic self-concept, and the affective characteristics of children with learning disabilities. When I completed my doctorate in 1979, I returned to New Zealand to take up a lectureship at Massey University. An expected two- to three-year stint at Massey has lasted 25 years. I have undertaken two major research programs. The first was a longitudinal study of academic self-concept, achievement expectations, and causal attributions of intermediate school students with learning difficulties. The second is a longitudinal study of language-related and cognitive motivational factors in beginning reading achievement. During the last 10 years, I have also been head of the Department of Learning and Teaching, and I am currently pro vice-chancellor (dean) of the College of Education. I am an international member of the Self Research Centre based at the University of Western Sydney, and president-elect of the US-based International Academy for Research in Learning Disabilities. I enjoy my family of four (adult) children, my interest in photography, reading, rugby and running, and I share my wife's professional interests in organisational development and management.

RESEARCH AND THEORETICAL INTERESTS

My Masters supervisor, John Nicholls, who was one of the leading researchers and theorists in the motivation field, sparked my interest in self-system factors. My interest in self-concept has focused on the development of suitable instruments for assessing achievement-related self-perceptions, and on their causal interplay with school achievement. During my doctoral studies I developed with my supervisor, Fred Boersma, the *Perception of Ability Scale for Students* (PASS). This scale was one of the first dedicated measures of academic self-concept designed for use with children from ages eight to 12 years. With my current research partner, Bill Tunmer, I have developed the *Reading Self-Concept Scale*, which is for use with children who are five to eight years old. Of particular interest more recently is the question of when achievement self-perceptions, especially reading self-concept, start to interact with emerging reading achievement. This issue is important, because reading is the first formal learning task encountered by children in school, and skilled reading acquisition is a crucial foundation skill for learning in other areas. Because many studies show that academic self-concept is strongly related to academic achievement, a key question is whether achievement causes academic self-concept, or whether academic self-concept causes achievement. Most researchers consider that there is a reciprocal relationship between the two. I have been interested in identifying the point in time when academic self-concept starts to influence achievement behaviours. Studies I have co-authored suggest that reading self-concept and reading achievement start to interact early during children's schooling, and can be detected during the second year of school. For children who quickly develop either competence or difficulties in learning to read, the relationship emerges during the first few weeks of schooling. Further, we observed declines in reading self-concept in children for whom an early intervention reading program was ineffective. These studies are consistent with the view that academic self-concept tends to develop initially in response to early learning experiences, and then starts to influence subsequent learning. Ineffective reading instruction is associated with poor reading performance for many children, who in turn tend to develop poor reading self-concepts.

A further strand of research relates to self-efficacy beliefs in reading. These are the perceptions held by people about the extent to which they can successfully execute courses of action, such as being able to use a learning strategy confident that it will likely cause success on a learning task. Most measures of self-efficacy assess the confidence with which individuals *expect* to be able to complete a task. I hold that a more effective self-efficacy measure assesses the sense of personal *agency* in being able to complete a learning task or solve a learning-related problem. With this in mind, Bill Tunmer and

I developed a measure of reading self-efficacy to examine the relationship between children's efficacy beliefs and the word identification strategies they use in reading. We found that children who use word attack skills for identifying unfamiliar words in text are more likely to develop a sense of agency in reading, because word attack strategies are more reliable than guessing or using contextual cues. Those who rely on unreliable strategies do not develop the same sense of personal agency in causing successful reading outcomes. Because personal agency beliefs are associated with motivation and academic performance, instruction should include attention to the use of strategies that are reliable, and that can be seen by individuals to be causally related to specific learning outcomes.

Another strand of research has involved an examination of the nature, causes and motivational correlates of the highly controversial constructs of learning disabilities and dyslexia.

THEORY AND RESEARCH INTO PRACTICE

The applied value of my research has been threefold. The first is in regard to my development of two published measures of self-concept. The *Perception of Ability Scale for Students* and the *Reading Self-Concept Scale* have been used by researchers, teachers and school psychologists to identify children with poor self-concepts who either experience or are at risk for experiencing difficulties with learning. Identification of those with negative self-concepts can assist in designing appropriate intervention strategies that include self-concept enhancement approaches.

Identification of relationships between learning disabilities and self-concept has been of value in designing more appropriate remedial intervention strategies. Research on self-concept enhancement tends to show that attempting to improve self-concept independently of improving learning performance is of limited value. On the other hand, a more productive approach to improving academic self-concept involves attribution retraining, whereby children are taught to identify the causal links between the learning behaviours and strategies they use with specific learning outcomes. Children tend to improve their academic self-concepts when they believe that they can positively influence learning outcomes.

My research with Bill Tunmer on the link between self-efficacy and word identification strategies is of interest to classroom teachers. The results of this research highlight the importance of teachers instructing children to place a greater emphasis on the use of word-level skills than on text-based skills (sentence context, language prediction) for identifying unfamiliar words in text. From both a reading skills perspective and from a motivational viewpoint, the use of word-level skills is more generative (new words can be more easily learned when word patterns are identified) and more reliable than word identification skills that do not focus on the letter-to-sound elements of words.

My theoretical work on the nature, causes and identification of learning disabilities and dyslexia has contributed to the debate on the usefulness of these constructs. This work has provided some support for the New Zealand policy that rejects the formal identification and classification of children with learning disabilities or dyslexia. Empirical work with Bill Tunmer in New Zealand has shown that there is little to distinguish the reading-related language abilities of children who are defined as dyslexic on the basis of discrepancies between reading comprehension and listening comprehension (which is a measure of receptive language ability), and the abilities of children who are also poor readers but who do not have discrepancies between reading and listening comprehension. Based on this and similar studies, we have concluded that all children in regular classrooms who have reading problems are likely to benefit from similar remedial methods, and that distinguishing between dyslexic poor readers and general poor readers is of little value. Having said that, I have written critically of the reluctance in New Zealand to provide widespread and systematic remedial programs for children who do have learning and reading difficulties.

Finally, research with Bill Tunmer and Jane Prochnow on the Reading Recovery (RR) program has provided important information about the limitations of this widely used early intervention program. Along with other researchers, we found that children who enter RR invariably have phonological processing (identifying the sounds that make up words) difficulties. This program has very limited activities that can help children to improve their phonological processing skills, which is a serious limitation because proficiency in phonological processing is a necessary (though not sufficient on its own) requirement for developing competence in reading. Children who are most likely to benefit from RR instruction are those who have more advanced levels of phonological processing ability. Working with Sandra Iversen, we have demonstrated that the inclusion in RR of activities designed to improve phonological processing skills can significantly improve children's reading performances.

KEY REFERENCES

Chapman, J. W. & Tunmer, W. E. (2003) Reading difficulties, reading-related self-perceptions, and strategies for overcoming negative self-beliefs. *Reading and Writing Quarterly*, **19**, 5–24.

Chapman, J. W., Tunmer, W. E. & Prochnow, J. E. (2000) Early reading-related skills and performance, reading self-concept, and the development of academic self-concept: A longitudinal study. *Journal of Educational Psychology,* **92**, 703–8.

Chapman, J. W., Tunmer, W. E. & Prochnow, J. E. (2001) Does success in the Reading Recovery program depend on developing proficiency in phonological processing skills? A longitudinal study in a whole language instructional context. *Scientific Studies of Reading,* **5**, 141–76.

ACTIVITIES

1 James Chapman is particularly interested in the relationship between reading and self-concept, and when academic self-concept starts to influence achievement behaviour. Why is reading important as a foundation skill for learning in other areas? Why is reading self-concept important to the development of good learning skills generally, and what role do effective/ineffective reading programs play in this?

2 James Chapman is also interested in self-efficacy beliefs in reading. What is the difference between self-efficacy beliefs and self-concept in reading? How is knowledge of self-efficacy beliefs in reading useful for teachers?

3 James Chapman and others developed two measures of self-concept: the *Perception of Ability Scale for Students* and the *Reading Self-Concept Scale,* which have been widely used by researchers, teachers and school psychologists. Obtain copies of each of these scales and analyse their components. How would you use these instruments in your educational setting?

4 James Chapman considers attributional retraining a useful way of improving academic self-concept. Review the material in Chapter 7 on attribution theory. How could you use attributional retraining in your educational setting?

5 James Chapman and others critique the Reading Recovery program. This program is commonly used internationally as an intervention program for those experiencing reading difficulties. Consider the Reading Recovery program. What are its essential elements? What is the research evidence in support of its effectiveness? What are the essential elements of the critique that Chapman and others level at the program? What do they suggest as alternative approaches to remedial reading? You will need to do an Internet search and read the key references above in order to address this issue.

quality of student–teacher interactions. We also suggest alternative strategies that provide for a better student–school match in Chapters 7–11. Table 14.1 presents some essentials of a healthy school environment for adolescent students.

QUESTION POINT

Discuss and evaluate the role of the school in the development of social identity in adolescents.

Table 14.1 Essentials of a healthy school environment for adolescent students

Teachers and administrators should:

- provide a 'small-school' feel for students so that they can identify with the organisation;
- develop positive student–teacher and student–student relationships within what is perceived as a caring and safe environment;
- provide the optimal level of structure for students' current level of maturity while also providing a sufficiently challenging environment to encourage further cognitive and social development;
- implement assessment strategies that emphasise personal improvement and achievement rather than those based on competition and social comparison. Avoid using normative grading criteria and public forms of evaluation;
- provide opportunities for students to work in a number of social groupings—teacher/student, peer/peer, small groups and full class;
- provide opportunities for students to have a choice of learning activities and assignments;
- provide opportunities for students to have some control over classroom management (such as class rules, seating arrangement, homework) and discipline practices;
- trust students and provide opportunities for student autonomy, decision making, participation and self-regulation;
- discuss classroom processes with students so that they perceive and make use of the opportunities made available for autonomy and control;
- develop a sense of teacher efficacy—feel that as a teacher you can make a change.

(Source: Based on Eccles *et al.* 1993; Maehr 1991; Maehr & Anderman 1993; Maehr & Midgley 1991)

Older members of a community can serve as excellent role models for younger members and help to enhance their self-esteem.

Acknowledgment: Goolangullia Aboriginal Education Centre, University of Western Sydney

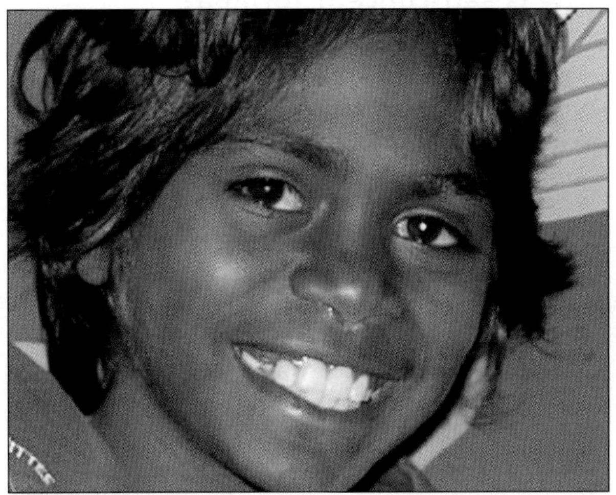

A healthy self-concept is important to everyone.

Self-concept, self-esteem and effective learning

Throughout much of what we have discussed so far are woven the notions of **self-concept** and **self-esteem**. These terms are often used interchangeably. However, some researchers argue that self-concept is descriptive—that is, it refers to descriptive information about oneself such as height, hair colour, ability in sports, and so on, whereas *self-esteem* is the evaluative component of self-concept—that is, it refers to how one feels about these objective qualities of self-description (see, for example, Valentine, DuBois & Cooper 2004). In this sense, self-esteem reflects the components of self-concept judged to be important by a particular individual. We will use the term *self-concept* in our discussion to cover both the descriptive and evaluative dimensions.

Self-concept may also be distinguished from *self-efficacy* (see, for example, Bong 1998; Bong & Clark 1999). We have discussed self-efficacy in Chapter 6 and you might want to reread this material. As you will recall, self-efficacy refers to a person's conviction about their capacity to actualise a desired outcome. In this sense, self-efficacy, compared with self-concept, deals primarily with the cognitively perceived capability of the self. It concerns people's own competence assessments in a given area among other personal attributes. Self-concept is a broader construct because it embraces a range of descriptive and evaluative inferences, with their ensuing affective reactions (Bong & Clark 1999).

Understanding self-concept is essential, as self-concept is an important educational outcome. In other words, schools and teachers work to enhance self-concept across a range of areas. An understanding of self-concept and of how it functions in the school context is important because it contributes to a number of other valued outcomes (Marsh 1993; Yeung & King Por Wong 2004). Broadly, we all have a general idea of what we mean by the term *self-concept* and often use it in our everyday speech. We talk about some people having a good self-concept, while others are thought to have a poor self-concept. In essence, we are referring to an individual's self-beliefs relating to perceived competence in a variety of areas such as academic schoolwork and sport, and to beliefs about physical attractiveness, sociability, self-worth and so on, and that the more positive these self-beliefs, particularly in the academic context, the more positive the achievement (Burnett & Howard 2002; Valentine, Dubois & Cooper 2004). Generally, we believe that a person's self-beliefs influence their behaviour. Individuals who have a positive self-concept, for example, are expected to be more motivated to perform particular activities than those who have a poor self-concept, and success in performing certain activities is believed to enhance self-concept. The relationship between self-concept and behaviour (particularly in terms of success and failure) is presumed to be reciprocal (see, for example, Marsh & Craven, 1997).

The many faces of self-concept

The notion of self-concept has a long history (Wylie 1979; see also Byrne 1996, 2002) and has been the subject of much research attempting to study its content and structure, its changes over time, group differences in its composition, and its effects on motivation and behaviour (Marsh 1990a; Marsh & Craven 1997; Purdie & McCrindle 2004; Wigfield & Karpathian 1991). Initially, self-concept was considered a unidimensional construct. In other words, individuals were thought to have a positive or negative view of themselves in a global sense. Instruments were designed which, in essence, summed up a person's self-concept with one score. Most people now reject the idea that a personality characteristic as rich as self-concept can be summarised so simply. Today, most researchers (such as Harter 1990; Marsh & Shavelson 1985; Shavelson & Bolus 1982; Shavelson & Marsh 1986) consider self-concept as *multidimensional*—that is, comprising many dimensions. Some theorists believe that these dimensions are organised in a hierarchy from differentiated lower levels to more general notions about self, while others believe that the dimensions are relatively distinct but may also be accompanied by a more general concept of self.

Constructs and self-concept

Multidimensional and hierarchical notions of self-concept

Effective classrooms can do a great deal to foster a healthy self-concept in children.

Marsh (1990a; Marsh & Craven 1997; see also Yeung *et al.* 2000), for example, believes that an individual's multidimensional self-concept is composed of lower-level self-concepts such as those for physical ability, physical appearance, peer relationships, parent relationships, reading ability, general school ability and mathematics ability. These are then clustered into higher-order self-concepts such as non-academic self-concept, academic English self-concept and academic mathematics self-concept. At a higher level still, there is the general self-concept. Relationships exist laterally and vertically between the various dimensions. As you can see, this type of model explores the richness and complexity of the self-concept construct, and makes a nonsense of generalising that a person has a single positive or negative self-concept. Of course, a difficulty with this approach is that one is never sure whether the model actually includes all the possible forms that self-concept might take or, indeed, whether the most important ones have been included. How would you describe your own self-concept generally and in relation to specific dimensions as described in the Marsh model?

How is self-concept formed?

Theorists believe that the self-concept is formed through *social interaction* and *social comparison*. Feedback from significant others such as parents, siblings, peers and teachers is influential in the growth of one's multifaceted self-concept. Social *frames of reference* indicate to us what our capacities and qualities are under particular circumstances. For example, on an objective criterion some individuals may be quite good at mathematics, yet when they use others who are superior at mathematics as a frame of reference they may develop a relatively negative mathematics self-concept (for example, see Marsh & Craven 1997; Marsh & Johnston 1993; Marsh, Walker & Debus 1991; see also Bong 1998). This is sometimes referred to as an *external frame of reference*. Furthermore, according to Marsh we tend to compare our self-perceived skills in one area (such as mathematics) with our self-perceived skills in another (such as English) and use this internal, relativistic impression as a second basis for arriving at our self-concept in particular areas (Marsh 1991; Skaalvik & Skaalvik 2002). This is sometimes referred to as an *internal frame of reference*.

External and internal frames of reference

Hence individuals who are good at both mathematics and English may, nevertheless, have a more negative self-concept in mathematics if they perceive that they are better at English and vice versa. This explains why even slow learners differentiate their self-concepts across subjects and hold high self-concepts in some areas even though their objective performance may be poor. Marsh (1990b; Marsh & Craven 1997; see also Skaalvik & Skaalvik 2002) has called this effect the *internal–external frame of reference effect*. This effect seems to be universal among students from a wide range of cultures (Marsh & Hau 2004).

Because of the operation of this internal/external frame of reference effect, all children have positive and less positive self-concepts in some areas of their learning. Teachers often make the erroneous assumption that those students who are perceived to have high ability and who are doing well academically must have uniformly high positive self-concepts in all areas, while those who are perceived as having low ability and are doing less well academically must have uniformly low self-concepts across all areas. In fact, as we have indicated, self-concept is much more differentiated than this—we all feel more positive about ourselves in some areas and less positive in other areas.

Does self-concept change as children grow older?

It appears that the foci of self-concept change as children grow older. Young children seem to focus on behavioural and physical characteristics, whereas older children focus on more abstract psychological characteristics (Wigfield & Karpathian 1991). As children's notions of what constitutes effort, ability, achievement, success and failure develop over time, so also do their beliefs about their competencies (and hence self-concept).

Developmental changes in self-concept

It also appears that in the infants and early grades, children's self-concepts across a range of areas are uniformly high and less differentiated than older children's. As children have more academic and non-academic experiences, their self-concepts become more differentiated and begin to be less positive. There appears to be a decline in some measures of self-concept, including academic self-concept and physical self-concept, as children move from primary school to junior high school (Obach 2003; Tonkin & Watt 2003). Throughout high school, individuals revise aspects of their self-concept, and some aspects become more positive relative to others. After adolescence (beginning in Year 9 or 10), multifaceted self-concept begins to rise once more in a variety of areas and becomes relatively stable, and academic self-concept becomes more strongly related to academic achievement (Eccles *et al.* 1993; Guay, Marsh & Boivin 2003; Marsh 1990a; Marsh & Craven 1997). Can you speculate on reasons why this might occur?

Is there a relationship between self-concept, average school performance and school achievement?

There is a relationship between a student's self-concept and school performance, but this is content-specific. In other words, mathematical performance is related to mathematics self-concept, English performance is related to English self-concept, and so on. Research also shows that self-concepts in specific school subjects are significantly related to subsequent coursework selection—to choices of what subjects students want to study and the choices of what they actually do pursue (Marsh & Yeung 1997). As suggested above, self-concept is formed in interaction with others, hence educational settings influence an individual's self-concept. For this reason, it is often better for a bright individual to be a big fish in a little pond—that is, doing well among a mixed-ability group—than to be a little fish—that is, performing at an average level in a high-ability group. In the former case, it is easier for students to establish and maintain positive feelings about their academic accomplishments, which serve to reinforce further academic pursuits. In selective educational environments, where the average ability of students is high, it is more difficult to establish and maintain these positive feelings. Selective high schools, and gifted and talented classes may, therefore, be disadvantageous to some students because of this 'big-fish-little-pond' effect, and this effect seems to be broadly relevant across a wide range of cultural groups (see Byrne 2002; Craven, Marsh & Print 2000; Marsh & Craven 1997; Marsh, Hau & Craven 2004; Marsh & Hau 2003). In these selective settings, high-ability students may choose less demanding coursework and have lower academic self-concepts, lower achievement scores, lower educational aspirations and lower occupational aspirations than similar students in non-selective educational environments. It appears from this that high-ability students are better off in non-streamed schools. This view is controversial—what do you think? In Table 14.2 on page 506 we suggest some strategies to enhance self-concept in educational settings.

Big-fish-little-pond effect

We have suggested that feeling good about one's abilities in an academic area fosters academic striving behaviours that can maximise and even change academic achievement. Studies indicate that it is possible to enhance self-concept, which in turn may enhance school achievement.

Can self-concept be enhanced?

Theory and research into practice

Herbert W. Marsh — SELF-CONCEPT, BIG FISH AND FRAMES OF REFERENCE

BRIEF BIOGRAPHY

I graduated from Indiana University in 1968 with Honours in psychology and then went to UCLA where I completed a Master's (1969) and a Ph.D. (1974) in psychology. Shortly before completing my Ph.D. I accepted a position as the foundation director of a program to collect students' evaluations of teaching effectiveness at UCLA and later established a similar program at the University of Southern California. In 1980 I moved to Sydney University where I spent 10 years as a lecturer, senior lecturer, and reader in the Faculty of Education. In 1990 I accepted my current position as professor of educational psychology at the University of Western Sydney. Here I served as the inaugural dean of graduate studies and pro vice chancellor of research, and was awarded the inaugural Doctorate of Science and Vice Chancellor's Award for Ph.D. supervision. In 1998 I founded the SELF (Self-concept Enhancement and Learning Facilitation) Research Centre that is home for most of my ongoing research activity.

I have published widely in a variety of educational and psychological research journals. International studies of citations in academic journals have indicated that I am among the top 10 researchers in several fields, the most widely cited Australian researcher in both education and psychology, and the 13th most widely cited psychology researcher in the world across all disciplines of psychology. In 1992 I received a Career Achievement Award from the American Educational Research Association for research in students' evaluations of university teaching.

RESEARCH AND THEORETICAL INTERESTS

My major areas of research interest include:

- Self-concept and motivational constructs: Theory, measurement, research and enhancement;
- Teaching effectiveness and its evaluation: Theory, measurement, research and enhancement;
- Higher education with a particular emphasis on students' evaluation of teaching;
- Developmental psychology;
- Quantitative analysis, particularly confirmatory factor analysis, structural equation modelling and multilevel modelling;
- Sports psychology with a particular focus on physical self-concept and motivation;
- The peer review process in relation to both journals and research grants;
- Peer support and anti-bullying interventions;
- Cross-cultural research, particularly in relation to self-concept measurement and tests of theoretical models.

My approach to new areas of research is initially as a methodologist; I first focus on methodological issues that cut across specific content areas. From this perspective I evaluate many different topical issues, such as second-language instruction and immersion programs, school bullying and peer support interventions, relations between university teaching and research productivity, effects of part-time employment during school, extracurricular activities, effects of changes in family configurations, the peer review process, and so on. Sometimes my research emphasis is on the application or development of new analytic procedures, and the specific content of the application is of secondary interest. In this way I have conducted research, often in collaboration with other researchers, in a wide variety of areas. My substantive contributions are focused in a few specific areas such as self-concept.

The improvement of self-concept is an important goal in many areas of psychology, education and the social sciences, and it is also seen as a vehicle for affecting other variables (for example, academic achievement). Despite a long history, and thousands of studies by researchers in diverse disciplines, reviews of self-concept research typically identify methodological weaknesses, a lack of theoretical models, and the poor quality of measurement instruments. I began my research with the development of appropriate instruments to measure self-concept at different ages, and focused on the measurement problems—reliability, dimensionality, structure, validity—that have plagued previous research. Hence, a major product of my self-concept research is the set of Self Description Questionnaires (SDQ) for measuring multidimensional self-concepts. These instruments are widely used and have been translated into several languages. My self-concept research has focused on:

- measurement of self-concept's multidimensional structure;
- relations between academic self-concept and educational accomplishments;

- causal ordering of academic self-concept and academic achievement;
- age and gender differences;
- the perceptions of significant others such as teachers, parents and peers;
- self-attributions for the causes of one's successes and failures;
- psychological masculinity and femininity;
- educational remedial/intervention programs;
- enrolment at academically selective high schools;
- enrolment at single-sex versus coeducational schools; and
- cross-cultural comparisons.

THEORY INTO PRACTICE

I originally coined the expression *big-fish-little-pond-effect* in relation to findings from my self-concept research showing average-ability students to have poorer academic self-concepts when they attended schools where the average ability level was high. I initially speculated that the lowered academic self-concept resulting from attending such schools would more than offset possible advantages for at least some students. A variety of studies have shown the robustness of this effect. I subsequently tested further implications with American data collected at a randomly selected 1000 high schools (the High School and Beyond data). This data allowed me to test the implications of attending high-ability high schools on outcomes as diverse as self-concept, school grades, performance on standardised tests, the amount of time spent on homework, taking advanced coursework, and going to university. Quite remarkably, the effect of attending high-ability high schools was negative for every one of the outcome variables considered. Whereas students from high-ability high schools outperform students from average-ability high schools, they typically do not do as well as would be expected on the basis of their ability upon entering such schools. In terms of a value-added model, the contribution of high-ability high schools is typically negative. The OECD recently collected achievement test scores and a psychological inventory that included some of my self-concept measures in nationally representative samples of 15-year-olds in 26 countries. The results of this study showed that the effects on self-concept of attending academically selective high schools were consistently negative across all countries, demonstrating the cross-cultural generalisability of the results.

Does academic self-concept cause achievement, or does achievement cause self-concept? In my research I developed methodologically stronger longitudinal designs to evaluate this issue. My research supports a reciprocal effects model in which academic self-concept is both a cause and an effect of design achievement. Thus, teachers wanting to enhance either of these outcomes should focus on both simultaneously, because they are mutually reinforcing. In an interesting extension of this work, I evaluated swimming self-concepts of 275 of the top swimmers in the world immediately prior to each of two international championships. Whereas prior personal best performances contributed to swimming self-concepts, self-concept contributed to championship performances beyond the substantial contribution of prior personal bests.

Further material relevant to my self-concept research in particular is available on the SELF Research Centre website: http://self.uws.edu.au/.

KEY REFERENCES

Marsh, H. W. & Craven, R. (1997) Academic self-concept: Beyond the dustbowl. In G. Phye (ed.) *Handbook of Classroom Assessment: Learning, Achievement, and Adjustment* (pp. 131–98). Orlando, FL: Academic Press.

Marsh, H. W. & Dunkin, M. J. (1997) Students' evaluations of university teaching: A multidimensional perspective. In R. P. Perry & J. C. Smart (eds) *Effective Teaching in Higher Education* (pp. 241–320). New York: Agathon.

Marsh, H. W. & Hau, K-T. (2003) Big fish little pond effect on academic self-concept: A cross-cultural (26 country) test of the negative effects of academically selective schools. *American Psychologist*, **58**, 1–13.

Marsh, H. W., Hau, K-T. & Kong, C-K. (2000) Late immersion and language of instruction (English vs. Chinese) in Hong Kong high schools: Achievement growth in language and non-language subjects. *Harvard Educational Review*, **70**, 302–46.

ACTIVITIES

1. Herb Marsh considers it essential for research to utilise good methodologies that enable a close examination of phenomena of interest. In his research he has covered a wide range of issues. Select an issue of interest and do further investigation through the SELF Research Centre website (http://self.uws.edu.au/) and through the Internet. Write a report of your investigation.
2. Discuss with your fellow students the importance of self-concept to effective learning. Relate some of your personal experiences to each other. In what areas do you think you have a strong self-concept? In what areas do you think you have a weaker self-concept? How have these feelings towards yourself influenced your school and social behaviours? Compare these with the experiences of other students. Are there common elements in your experiences?
3. Probably the most extensively used self-concept measurement scales are the Self Description

Questionnaires (SDQ). Obtain a copy of one or more versions of the SDQ and analyse its components. What aspects of self-concept are measured? How do these aspects relate to one another? In order to address this issue, you should read the key readings listed above, as well as material available through the SELF Research Centre.

4 A major contribution Herb Marsh has made to theoretical, research and applied literature is the big-fish-little-pond effect. Discuss with your fellow students what this effect is and how it might affect students in both streamed and regular classrooms, as well as in selective schools.

5 We might think that a high academic self-concept leads to better school achievement, or alternatively that high school achievement leads to high academic self-concept. Herb Marsh found that both influence each other. He therefore recommends that teachers wanting to enhance either of these outcomes should focus on both simultaneously because they are mutually reinforcing. Discuss with your fellow students how you might indeed focus on both in your classrooms. Indicate some practical programmatic measures you would adopt.

Table 14.2 Essentials of developing positive self-concept in educational settings

Teachers should:

- develop assessment tasks that encourage individual students to pursue their own projects that are of particular interest to them. To the extent that students pursue their own unique projects and feel positive about the results, they should be able to maintain a positive academic self-concept;
- reduce social comparison and competitive learning environments;
- provide students with feedback in relation to criterion reference standards and personal improvement over time, rather than comparisons based on the performance of other students;
- emphasise to each student that they are a very able student, and value the unique accomplishments of each student so that all students feel good about themselves;
- enhance students' feelings of being connected to other students in the classroom.

(Source: Based on Marsh & Craven 1997)

We hope that we provide you with many suggestions throughout this text on how to enhance the self-concept of students in your care.

An alternative view of self-concept formation

Self-guides and self-concept formation

An alternative view of self-concept is put forward by Higgins (1987; Roche & Marsh 1993). In contrast to Marsh's rather structured view of the composition of the self-concept, Higgins suggests that self-concept is phenomenologically based. For Higgins, the relationships (or discrepancies) between our perception of our actual self and five potential standards of self (or 'self-guides') influence our beliefs and feelings about self and ultimately motivate behaviour. The discrepancies between the perceived actual self and these other 'self-guides' are also related to an individual's overall feelings of self-esteem. The 'self-guides' are: the ideal person we would like to be; the person we feel obliged to be, given social and personal norms; what we believe other significant people (such as parents and teachers) consider is our actual self; what we believe other significant people consider we should ideally be like; and what we believe other significant people consider we ought to be like, given our realistic limitations. Not all these 'self-guides' are salient to particular individuals. Higgins' contribution is important to our understanding of the self-concept, as it highlights the important elements of the self-system that influence motivated behaviour and self-esteem.

Our major focus in this text is individual learning and motivation. A crucial question for us to answer, therefore, is how a child's self-concept relates to their motivation,

Are there differences between boys and girls in how they spend their leisure time? How might this influence their sense of belonging or alienation?

behaviour and school achievement. We discuss this question a number of times throughout the text.

QUESTION POINT

Consider the notion of a multidimensional self-concept. In particular, discuss how frames of reference (internal and social comparison) may influence the development of self-concept at each of the different developmental stages of early, middle and upper primary, lower secondary and upper secondary. Are the influences of frames of reference more likely to be significant at one level than another or for different areas of school activity (such as academic, clubs, sporting and so on)?

ACTION STATION

This activity is designed to sensitise you to some of the sources of information that orient the development of our self-concept. It is best performed in a small group of peers.

1. List five characteristics that would describe you as you are (perceived self).
2. List five characteristics that would describe you as you would like to be (ideal self).
3. List one characteristic of each member of the group (observed self). The observed self-ratings are distributed to the relevant group member.
4. Compare your perceived, ideal and observed self. What differences do you notice? What is the real self? Discuss your findings within the group.

Social development and alienation

In our rapidly changing world, many children and adolescents become alienated. Alienation in the school context may involve four dimensions: powerlessness, social estrangement, meaninglessness and normlessness (Mau 1992; Oerlemans & Jenkins 1998). **Powerlessness** refers to a student's feeling of lack of control over their life. **Social estrangement** refers to a student's feelings of physical or mental isolation from their situation. **Meaninglessness** refers to a student's feelings of the irrelevancy of what is happening to them at the present. **Normlessness** refers to a student's rejection of society's rules and norms (Mau 1992; Oerlemans & Jenkins 1998). While each of these constructs of alienation is conceptually distinct, they may act in concert or alone. In other words, an adolescent might feel powerless and the meaninglessness of what they are doing, yet not be socially estranged. The roots of the alienation are very complex and may include family background, personality characteristics (such as self-esteem) and school influences such as perceived relevance of curricular.

Alienation can express itself in dropping out of school, truancy, delinquency and substance use and abuse, risky sexual behaviour, violence, and mental health difficulties (Greenberg *et al.* 2003). At its most severe, alienation can also manifest itself in psychophysiological and psychological disturbances such as obesity, anorexia nervosa, migraine, gastrointestinal upsets, anxiety, phobias and depression—and, in its most extreme form, suicide (Oerlemans & Jenkins 1998; Santrock & Yussen 1992; Voelkl & Frone 2000; Zigler & Stevenson 1993). Teachers and schools must identify students at risk of alienation and implement policies and teaching programs to assist them to develop a positive identity of themselves as individuals and school learners (see, for example, Bryant & Zimmerman 2002; Greenberg *et al.* 2003). Each of the components of alienation described above indicates different strategies for intervention. Among potential intervention strategies are alternative teaching approaches, remedial programs and curricula adaptations, alternative and vocational education programs, flexible school structures—such as senior high schools and authority and power sharing through student participation in decision making, counselling, work experience programs, and parental and community involvement in schooling. Programs that appear most successful in reducing alienation are those that improve students' sense of belonging while alleviating social estrangement, that allow students to actively engage in the curriculum and empower them to make decisions, thus alleviating meaninglessness (see, for example, Anderman 2002). These programs may include practical options, such as work experience and prevocational and life skills training, which are perceived by students as increasing the meaningfulness of learning (Oerlemans & Jenkins 1998; see also Bryant & Zimmerman 2002; Greenberg *et al.* 2003). It is also very important for initiatives to have strong leadership, to be coordinated, and to be linked to the overall mission of the school (Greenberg *et al.* 2003).

Additionally, it is necessary to work with families in order to prevent and alleviate youth alienation and problem behaviours, as strong families and effective parents are critical to the prevention of these problems. Research indicates that a positive family environment (for example, positive parent–child relationships, parental supervision and consistent discipline, and communication of family values) is the main reason youth do not engage in delinquent or unhealthy behaviours. These protective family factors are even more strongly related to inhibiting problem behaviours among minority youth and females (Kumpfer & Alvarado 2003). In our book we describe many features of effective teaching that will help to reduce the occurrence of alienation (at least as far as the school and teachers are able).

Social skills, antisocial behaviour and academic achievement

Among the reasons given for students becoming alienated is their failure to develop effective social skills (see, for example, Sarris, Winefield & Cooper 2000). Social skill involves 'the ability to interact with others in a given context in specific ways that are socially acceptable or valued and at the same time personally beneficial, mutually beneficial, or beneficial primarily to others' (Combs & Slaby 1977, p. 162). Poor social skills in childhood and adolescence have been linked to poor academic achievement, low self-esteem, antisocial and aggressive behaviour, a higher incidence of contact with the police and the juvenile system, and antisocial or delinquent behaviour in adulthood (Sarris *et al.* 2000). Antisocial or delinquent behaviour early in life is also associated with major problems in adulthood, including loneliness, alcoholism, substance abuse, criminal behaviour, marital difficulties, employment problems and mental health problems (Sarris *et al.* 2000). Again the roots of antisocial and delinquent behaviour are quite complex and may include family status variables such as socio-economic status and employment history, family size and parenting characteristics such as poor supervision, lack of parental involvement, parents' rejection of the child and parental aggressiveness (Sarris *et al.* 2000). Appropriate social skills intervention programs are an important element to include in school social development programs.

Moral development

As caregivers, parents and educators, we are intimately involved in the process of communicating values to children and adolescents. It is helpful to understand, therefore, the ways in which the development of the moral self is believed to occur. Widely differing conceptions exist of how we develop a sense of morality and whether morals are universal or culturally based and acquired through socialisation. In the following sections we look at the theories put forward by Piaget, Kohlberg, neo-Kohlbergians, Turiel and Gilligan.

Piaget and moral development

Developmental theories such as those of Piaget and Kohlberg present the view that increasingly sophisticated **moral reasoning** develops through an invariant sequence of stages. Piaget contends that all morality consists of a system of rules that is handed from adults to children. Through training, practice and developing intellect, children learn to nurture respect for these standards of conduct (Hoffman 1980; Piaget 1965). In order to collect his data, Piaget used the same clinical interviewing approach used to elicit responses to cognitive tasks, and questioned scores of Swiss children aged between five and 13 years about their understanding of rules, and their interpretations of right and wrong. In particular, Piaget examined the relationship between *intention* and notions of *right* and *wrong*. Children were given two stories and asked to judge which of the two boys in the story was naughtier: the boy who was well intentioned but caused more damage, or the boy who was not well intentioned and caused less damage. Children were asked to give reasons for their answers.

Morality of constraint and morality of cooperation

> **Story A:** A little boy called John is in his room. He is called to dinner. He goes into the dining room. But behind the door there was a chair, and on the chair there was a tray with 15 cups on it. John couldn't have known that there was all this behind the door. He goes in, the door knocks against the tray, bang go the 15 cups, and they all get broken.
>
> **Story B:** Once there was a little boy whose name was Henry. One day when his mother was out he tried to get some jam out of the cupboard. He climbed up on a chair and stretched out his arm. But the jam was too high up and he couldn't reach it and have any. But while he was trying to get it he knocked over a cup. The cup fell down and broke (Piaget 1965).

In general, Piaget found two different *moral orientations*, one typical of preoperational children and one typical of children in the late concrete substage (10 to 12 years). He found that younger children tend to focus on observed consequences of actions and believe in absolute, unchanging rules handed down by outside authorities. Piaget named this stage one of **heteronomous morality**, or *moral realism*, in which children adopt the morality of constraint. ('Heteronomous' means under the authority of another.) Children in this stage tend to view behaviours as totally right or wrong, and think everyone views them in the same way. Children judge whether an act is right or wrong on the basis of the magnitude of the consequences, the extent to which it conforms to established rules and whether or not the act is punished.

With older children, the focus is on the inferred intentions behind the act with a belief that rules can be constructed and changed by social agreement. This stage is referred to as the stage of **autonomous morality**, where children adopt the *morality of cooperation* (Cowan 1978; DeVries 1997; Hersh, Paolitto & Reimer 1979; Hoffman 1980). In the context of Piaget's stories, therefore, younger children believe that John is the naughtier child because he broke more cups, despite the fact that he didn't break them on purpose. Older children judge that Henry is the naughtier child because they take into account the intention behind the act that led to the damage.

Children in the heteronomous stage show a great concern for rules and believe they can't be changed. Children at the autonomous stage no longer view rules as fixed, but rather as flexible, socially agreed upon principles of cooperation that can be changed with the agreement of others affected by the rules. A greater sense of **reciprocity** characterises the moral reasoning of older children; that is, the welfare of others and a concern for fairness is important, because it is only then that one can expect fairness in return. At this stage, the belief in a morality of reciprocity means that duty and obligation are no longer defined in terms of obedience to authority, but as a social contract reflecting the mutual needs of oneself and others, called a *morality of reciprocity*.

Reciprocity in moral reasoning

Young children also believe in **immanent justice**, and believe that if they are punished they must have done wrong. Older children can differentiate punishment from wrongdoing; in other words, they can maintain their innocence in the face of punishment. Older children also

EXTENSION STUDY

Adolescent suicide

There has been growing public concern over the level of adolescent suicide in Australia, New Zealand and the United States (Davis 1992; Garland & Zigler 1993; Graham *et al.* 2000; Kosky 1987; Pritchard 1992). Across these countries there are approximately 11 suicide deaths per 100 000 individuals in the adolescent age range each year. The situation in Australia is particularly worrying for male suicide rates. While the suicide rates in young women (15–24 years) have remained relatively stable for the past 20 years at around five deaths per 100 000, the overall frequency for males in 2002 was 19 per 100 000 (Australian Bureau of Statistics 2003). In 2002 suicide represented 25 per cent of all deaths for males aged 15–24 years and 15 per cent of all female deaths in the same age groups. In fact, Australia's young male suicide rate is the fourth highest among the Western countries. These figures are considered a low estimate, as it is difficult to ascertain whether some deaths ascribed to accidents (such as car accidents or drug overdoses) are actually suicides. There is also a reluctance to report suicides among some groups owing to religious implications, insurance problems and family concerns.

Suicide is the third most frequent cause of death among adolescents after motor accidents and murder (Garland & Zigler 1993). Of further concern is the fact that the rates for adolescent suicide have increased dramatically over the last 30 years in comparison with the general population increase. Males complete suicide approximately four times as often as females; however, females attempt suicide at least three times as often as do males. This statistical difference in attempted suicide rates might be an artifact of reporting methods and, in particular, data collected through mental health clinics, which are utilised more by females than by males. Not included in the data are attempted suicides by incarcerated males, which is quite common. If these figures were taken into account the gender difference in attempted suicide rates would diminish.

The difference in completed suicide rates between males and females may also be explained by the different methods used, with males more likely to impulsively use violent methods, such as shooting and hanging, which are successful. In contrast, females more often use less violent methods, such as overdoses of substances, which allow time for treatment. Furthermore, females may benefit from protective factors such as a greater reliance on interpersonal relationships for support and more positive help-seeking attitudes and behaviours (Garland & Zigler 1993).

There are ethnic differences in suicide rates, with Anglo males more likely to commit suicide than males from other ethnic groups. This difference appears to reflect religious and cultural values that establish *protective taboos* within particular groups, and perhaps the *extended social network* in which adolescents from particular ethnic groups receive more immediate support (Eskin 1992, 1995; Lester & Icli 1990; Scott, Ciarrochi & Deane 2004; Wasserman & Stack 1993). Suicide has also been linked to antisocial, aggressive behaviour, and as the incidence of this is greater among males this could partly explain their greater levels of completed suicide. Aboriginal and Maori youth are disproportionately represented in suicide rates, and these have increased substantially over recent years from previous very low levels (Graham *et al.* 2000; Hunter 1991). Among the reasons given for this increase in suicide rates among indigenous people are the cumulative effects of changing patterns of family life over the past two decades.

Although the number of adolescents who commit suicide is of great concern, it is still a relatively infrequent occurrence (Graham *et al.* 2000). It is difficult, therefore, to discover clearly the primary factors that cause adolescents to attempt suicide. *Primary risk factors* appear to be drug and alcohol abuse, a previous suicide attempt, affective illness such as depression, antisocial or aggressive behaviour, family history of suicidal behaviour and the availability of a firearm (Garland & Zigler 1993; Shochet & Osgarby 1999). Among other suggested risk factors are stressful life events, such as family turmoil, increased pressure on children to achieve and to be responsible at an early age, severe parent–child conflict, overly demanding or protective parenting, abusive or neglectful parenting (Nicholson, McFarland & Oldenburg 1999), and the mass media giving publicity to suicide which encourages social imitation.

However, in many cases of attempted suicide none of these factors appears to play an obvious part, while in many other cases adolescents who have exposure to some or all of these factors do not attempt suicide. In short, it is very difficult to predict suicidal behaviour.

It appears that in cases of completed suicide there has been a preceding shameful or humiliating experience, such as an arrest, a perceived failure at work or school, a rejection by a loved one such as a parent, or difficulties resulting from sexual orientation such as homosexuality (Garland & Zigler 1993).

What can we do to prevent mental health problems and suicide?

In Australia, New Zealand and the United States, up to one in three children and young adolescents suffer from diagnosable mental health problems, which include behaviour problems, anxiety, depression, drug and alcohol use, and delinquency. However, few of these receive formal help from specialist mental health services (Adelman & Taylor 1998; Nicholson *et al.* 1999; Roeser, Eccles & Strobel 1998). These social, emotional and behavioural difficulties may impact on student motivation and the ability of individuals to benefit from schooling. Because students then fall behind scholastically, the emotional, social and behavioural problems may become further exacerbated. In other words, there is a reciprocal relationship between mental health and school achievement (Roeser *et al.* 1998). It is very important, therefore, that teachers, counsellors and school personnel are well informed about student mental health problems and adolescent suicide, know how to recognise students at risk, and have in place appropriate support procedures to assist individuals and their families (see, for example, Adelman & Taylor 1998; Nicholson *et al.* 1999). Table 14.3 presents some warning signs of suicide. When an individual's behaviour becomes atypical and includes a number of these features, it might be an indication that the adolescent is thinking about suicide. At these times, effective teacher counselling, support and referral are necessary.

Programs have been initiated to help prevent adolescent suicide. Two common approaches are *telephone crisis counselling* and *curriculum-based programs*, although the latter are less common in Australia. Garland and Zigler (1993) believe that these approaches are of limited benefit and, in the case of curriculum programs, may be dangerous because they tend to 'normalise' suicide as a reaction to stress that can affect all adolescents. By de-emphasising the fact that most adolescents who commit suicide are mentally ill, these programs reduce potentially protective taboos against suicide. These programs also tend to overstate the incidence of suicide, therefore making it appear more normal. When this is added to increased media coverage of adolescent suicide, it could well be that a number of susceptible individuals become convinced that it is appropriate behaviour in times of stress.

We suggest above that many of the primary factors associated with youth suicide are common to other alienated behaviours, such as delinquency and substance abuse. As a result, some primary prevention programs have been designed to address negative behaviours such as depression, lack of social support, poor problem-solving skills, and hopelessness in students before problems arise. In addressing these, it is thought that the root source of much adolescent suicidal behaviour is also addressed. Many schools, therefore, have personal development, health and physical education programs which aim to increase the adolescent's self-esteem, social confidence, regulation of emotion, and ability to anticipate and solve problems (Adelman & Taylor 1998; Shochet & Osgarby 1999). In particular, it is felt that problem-solving skills training and self-efficacy enhancement for adolescents may be the most effective suicide prevention programs (Cole 1989). We stress the importance of these factors throughout our text as a means of enhancing effective learning and the development of a sense of self within learners.

Family support programs have also been instigated for families undergoing crises, and these appear to alleviate a range of problems, including substance abuse and delinquency. As these factors are also associated with adolescent suicide, it is thought that family support programs provide a primary preventative against suicide as well. This is particularly important, as there is considerable evidence that strong parental attachments and expressions of warmth and caring have been found to protect adolescents from depression and anxiety. Hence, it is important to support families in developing the strategies to provide a cohesive family which provides for close supportive relationships rather than ones characterised by conflict (Shochet & Osgarby 1999).

Table 14.3 **Warning signs of potential suicide**

- Putting personal affairs in order, such as giving away treasured possessions and/or making amends.
- Talking about suicide directly or indirectly ('You won't have to worry about me much longer') and/or saying goodbye to family and friends.
- Protracted periods of sadness, despondency and/or 'not caring' anymore.
- Extreme fatigue, lack of energy, boredom.
- Emotional instability—spells of crying, laughing.
- Inability to concentrate, becoming easily frustrated and/or distractible.
- Deviating from usual patterns of behaviour (for example, decline in grades, absence from school and/or discipline problems).
- Neglect of personal appearance.
- Change in body routines (for example, loss of sleep or excessive sleep, eating more or less than usual, and/or complaints of headache, stomach ache, backache).

(Source: Based on Capuzzi 1989)

recognise that others may hold different points of view, and in their judgments of right and wrong stress intentions as well as consequences. Punishment should fit the 'crime', rather than being the capricious act of a powerful 'other'.

Piaget believes that the narrow perspective of the younger child reflects the strong 'coercive' influence that adults have over children of this age. Younger children have a rigid view of discipline and punishment, while older children distinguish between punishment and guilt. The development from stage one to stage two reflects the growing ability of children to decentre—that is, to take the perspective of others. This development is facilitated by peer interaction through which one's individual perspective is challenged by the perspectives, needs and demands of other individuals. The resulting *cognitive disequilibrium* motivates children to resolve the conflict and contradictions by reorganising patterns of moral thought (refer to Chapter 2).

Peer interaction and moral development

Critique of Piaget's theory

In general, Piaget's view that children pass from a morality of constraint to a morality of cooperation, and that this is facilitated by intellectual growth, peer interaction and a diminution in adult authority, has been supported by research (Berk 2004). However, as with Piaget's theory of cognitive development, this theory has also been subjected to considerable criticism. In particular, it appears that even quite young children can distinguish between social-conventional and moral rules, with the former far less immutable. We discuss this further in our next section on Kohlberg. Furthermore, it is believed that the stories told by Piaget underestimated children's moral understanding. If you refer back to stories A and B on page 509 you will see that the good intention was coupled with more damage, while the poor intention was coupled with less damage. It is possible that this confused children in their understanding of intention versus consequences, and they focused their answers on the consequences.

Preschool and primary children appear quite able to judge the difference between well-intentioned and ill-intentioned behaviour in terms of naughtiness when changes are made to the stories' structure (Grueneich 1982; Nelson-Le Gall 1985; Yuill & Perner 1988). When stories are modified to make the intentions the focus rather than the consequences, by holding the consequences constant while varying the intentions, children distinguish between well-intentioned and ill-intentioned acts. Children also distinguish between well-intentioned and ill-intentioned acts when the character's intentions are given last in the story, or by making story events very meaningful to children by role playing the behaviour.

Finally, Piaget's conception of a two-stage developmental sequence in moral development appears too simple to explain the complexity of moral development as it occurs across the lifespan. The next section deals with the work of Lawrence Kohlberg, who brings a

How might the interaction of younger and older students enhance moral thinking?

lifespan view to moral development that he relates to the complex life events of developing individuals.

Kohlberg's stages of moral development

Kohlberg's core assumptions

Piaget did not work out his theory of moral development in any detailed fashion. However, Piaget's initial ideas were built on by Lawrence Kohlberg, who developed the most extensive theory of moral development to date. Kohlberg's developmental stage theory (Kohlberg 1976, 1977, 1978, 1981; see also Rest *et al.* 1999b) is based on four core characteristics. First, Kohlberg's theory is cognitive—that is, it emphasises thought processes involved in moral decision making rather than alternative possibilities, such as socialisation processes. Second, the theory emphasises the personal construction of knowledge about morality. In other words, the meanings of 'rights', 'duties', 'justice', 'social order' and 'reciprocity' are personally constructed through experience, albeit formed within the context of wider ideologies and practices within a particular cultural or social group. Third, the theory is developmental. Each level of moral judgment must be attained before the individual can perform at the next higher level, and the attainment of a higher level of moral judgment appears to involve the reworking of earlier thought patterns rather than an additive process of development. Kohlberg believed that moral development occurs as an invariant sequence no matter what the national or subcultural group happens to be. Finally, the theory emphasises moral development as a growth from conventional to postconventional moral thinking (Rest *et al.* 1999b).

Piaget studied the development of morality by presenting to children of various ages pairs of stories that illustrated different degrees of responsibility for particular actions.

In this activity you will evaluate Piaget's belief that two fundamental levels characterise children's moral thinking. Select three children of differing ages—say, six, nine and 12. Tell the children the following two stories:

Story 1

A little boy called Frank once noticed that his mother's sink was full of dirty dishes. While the mother was in the yard Frank began to wash the dishes so that when his mother came in the washing-up would be done. But while he was washing-up he dropped five dishes and smashed them.

Story 2

Although his mother had told him not to, a little boy called Robert thought it would be fun playing with his mother's dishes. While he was playing one dish dropped and smashed.

After telling the stories, ask the subjects to say which child is naughtier and to give the reasons for their answers. Record verbatim the responses of the children and write a brief report illustrating what the experiment shows about the moral judgments of children. To complicate the issue further, you could add to the first story the fact that the mother had told the child not to touch anything in the kitchen! You might also like to hold the consequences the same—that is, that the children break the same number of dishes.

Kohlberg's methodology

To assess the level of cognitive reasoning, Kohlberg adopted a similar methodology to Piaget—that is, a form of clinical interview. Children were presented with three moral dilemmas on which they had to make a moral judgment. Depending on the justification given for their judgment, children were categorised as belonging to a particular stage of moral development (rather like children being categorised as preoperational, concrete or formal thinkers on the basis of their answers to Piagetian problems; see Chapter 2). To understand the procedure, we ask you to complete the following exercise taken from Kohlberg's work.

Moral dilemma

In Europe, a woman is near death from a special kind of cancer. There is one drug that the doctors think might save her. It is a form of radium that a druggist in the same town has recently discovered. The drug is expensive to make, but the druggist is charging 10 times what the drug cost him to make. He paid $200 for the radium and is charging $2000 for a small dose of the drug. The sick woman's husband, Heinz, goes to everyone he knows to borrow the money, but he can get together only about $1000, which is half of what it costs. He tells the druggist that his wife is dying and asks him to sell the drug cheaper or let him pay later. The druggist says, 'No, I discovered the drug and I'm going to make money from it.' Heinz is desperate and considers breaking into the man's store to steal the drug for his wife.

1 Should Heinz steal the drug? Why or why not?
2 If Heinz doesn't love his wife, should he steal the drug for her? Why or why not?
3 Suppose the person dying is not his wife but a stranger. Should Heinz steal the drug for a stranger? Why or why not?

4 (If you favour stealing the drug for a stranger): Suppose it's a pet animal he loves. Should Heinz steal to save the pet animal? Why or why not?
5 Why should people do everything they can to save another's life, anyhow?
6 It is against the law for Heinz to steal. Does that make it morally wrong? Why or why not?
7 Why should people generally do everything they can to avoid breaking the law, anyhow?
8 How does this relate to Heinz's case?

(Source: From Hersh *et al.* 1979)

Answers to the dilemma

Typically, answers to the dilemma will range across the following beliefs (see Rest 1973, 1979; Sprinthall & Sprinthall 1990):

- Stealing the drug isn't bad, because Heinz asked to pay for it first or will pay for it in the future.
- Heinz only wants to save his wife, and after all the druggist is a bit of a crook himself.
- While stealing in itself is wrong, it can be excused if the reason is good, such as saving the life of one's wife, or because the action of the druggist is bad.
- Despite the obvious need to steal, Heinz must be prepared to accept punishment and pay back the money.
- The drug should not be stolen, as individuals should maintain the social order reflected through rules and regulations.
- While social order is important, the principle of preserving human life is more important still, which makes it morally right to steal the drug.

Kohlberg categorised responses to these dilemmas under three main levels of moral development: *pre-conventional*, which reflects a concern for avoiding punishment; *conventional*, which reflects a concern with rules and regulations; and *postconventional*, which reflects higher-level ethical principles (Kohlberg 1981). These levels are described more fully in Table 14.4.

We note here that Kohlberg was not so much interested in the actual decision as to whether Heinz should steal the drug or not, but rather the reasons given for the decision. In effect, individuals at all levels could say 'steal the drug', but for the preconventional thinker it might be because Heinz probably won't get caught, for the conventional thinker it might be because punishment can be willingly accepted for a good, but not legal act, while for the postconventional thinker it might be because the law is a bad law.

We have often set the above exercise for groups ranging from five or six years of age through to adulthood. We and our students have found that it is relatively easy to group the answers into one of three basic categories: a morality that seems to reflect a concern for *avoiding punishment* and *egocentric concerns*; a morality that seems to reflect an understanding of *rules and regulations* and their function in a society; and a morality that seems to be concerned with *ethical principles* which may take precedence over laws. Through these case studies we have found anecdotal evidence for Kohlberg's three main levels of moral development—preconventional, conventional and postconventional (Kohlberg 1981). However, when attempting to make finer distinctions within each level in accordance with Kohlberg's theory, we have tended to become confused and often disagreed over the particular stage of reasoning. Kohlberg divides each level into two stages. Table 14.4 outlines the components of each, based on the work of Kohlberg (1981) in *The Philosophy of Moral Development*.

ACTION STATION

Some time ago in Queensland, laws were promulgated against public protest marches. On one occasion, just before the Commonwealth Games, a large demonstration was organised to protest against the government's dilatory approach to granting Aboriginal citizens land rights. It is interesting to consider the various arguments of people interviewed at the time to justify or oppose marching. Some argued that laws were laws and hence, irrespective of the worthiness of the cause, should be respected; otherwise, how could we tell our children to obey laws? Others argued that it wasn't wise to march as there was a risk of fines and possible gaol sentences. Many were concerned about the negative opinion our overseas visitors would have of Australians (and Aboriginal Australians, in particular) if the marches disrupted the Commonwealth Games. Some argued that the rights of Aboriginals to land justice was a more important consideration than obeying laws, concern for personal welfare, or being seen as doing the right thing by our fellow citizens. Others weren't particularly concerned with the land rights issue, but considered the law against marching an immoral law, in itself, and believed that individuals were obligated to protest against such a law whenever possible.

Each of these arguments may be categorised according to Kohlberg's schema. Why don't you try your hand at it? By the way, the Queensland laws against public marches were repealed.

QUESTION POINT

In their explanations of moral development, both the behavioural theory and the social cognitive theory, with

Table 14.4 Aspects of moral reasoning

Level and stage	Individual's moral perspective
Level 1 Preconventional *Stage 1: Punishment and obedience*	A person at this stage doesn't consider the interests of others or recognise that they may differ from one's own. Actions are considered in terms of physical consequences such as to avoid punishment and obtain rewards. Those in authority have superior power and should be obeyed. Punishment should be avoided by staying out of trouble.
Stage 2: Individualism, instrumentality and exchange	A person at this stage is aware that everybody has interests to pursue and that these can conflict, so integrates conflicting demands through instrumental exchange of services, letting others meet their own interests and being fair. However, the needs of the individual are paramount, and it's all right to do things (such as cheating, bribing and stealing) if you get away with it and no one else is hurt in the process.
Level 2 Conventional *Stage 3: Mutual interpersonal expectations, relationships and conformity*	A person at this stage is aware of shared feelings, agreements and expectations that take primacy over individual interests. Believes in the Golden Rule, putting oneself in the other person's shoes. Does not yet consider generalised system perspective, and likes to be seen as doing the right thing by other people. Behaviour conforms strictly to the fixed conventions of society in which one lives.
Stage 4: Social system and conscience	A person at this stage takes the viewpoint of the system, which defines roles and rules. The individual 'does one's duty', shows respect for authority and believes in maintaining social order for its own sake. Individual relations are considered in terms of place in the system. In other words, the individual is willing to go against social convention and the desire to be one of the crowd and please others in order to uphold laws that are seen as important for the stability of the community.
Level 3 Postconventional or principled *Stage 5: Prior rights and social contract*	The person at this stage is aware of values and rights prior to social attachments and contracts. Norms of right and wrong are defined in terms of laws or institutionalised rules, which are seen to have a rational base such as expressing the will of the majority and maximising social utility or welfare, and are necessary for institutional or social cohesion and functioning. Duty and obligation are defined in terms of contract, not the needs of individuals. At this stage, laws can be challenged as being 'good' or 'bad', and indeed the interpretation of the law itself can be challenged. Lawyers, Supreme and High Court judges spend much of their time arguing at this level. Fundamentally, laws are viewed as human inventions and, as such, are modifiable and not sacrosanct.
Stage 6: Universal ethical principles	In stage 6, individuals consider circumstances and the situation, as well as the general principles and the reasons behind the rules. Orientation is not only to existing rules and standards, but to principles of moral choice involving appeal to logical universality and consistency. Although law is important, moral conflict is resolved in terms of broader moral principles. Indeed, at times it may be moral to disobey laws.

(Sources: Based on Damon 1983; Hersh *et al.* 1979; Hoffman 1980)

the former's emphasis on the roles of reinforcement and punishment in learning moral values, and the latter's emphasis on learning through observing models, offer significant challenges to the stage concept of moral growth. In fact, the social cognitive theorist Bandura maintains that moral judgments are quite situation-specific and that: 'Stage theorists are able to classify people into types only by applying arbitrary rules to coexisting mixtures of judgments spanning several "stages" and by categorising most people as being in transition between stages' (Bandura 1977a, p. 43). Is the stage concept really useful in explaining moral development?

Current status of Kohlberg's theory

Dynamics of moral growth

As with most theories, Kohlberg's is not set in concrete and the passing years have seen a number of challenges and changes to the theory, largely as a result of the intensive research that has been conducted. Basically, Kohlberg's framework has stood up well to the scrutiny of these researchers. Evidence has accumulated that individuals do move from very unsophisticated and egocentric forms of moral reasoning to increasingly sophisticated forms, and the stages outlined by Kohlberg, by and large, have received empirical support. The progression appears to be

ACTION STATION

The basic teaching procedure for developing moral awareness, according to Kohlberg, is group discussion on hypothetical and real-life moral conflict situations. The aim of Kohlberg's moral dilemma situations is to challenge children to raise their level of moral reasoning by confronting them with points of view that illustrate higher levels of reasoning. Structure a situation where several people discuss the story of Heinz included on pages 513–14. In this exercise you will attempt to categorise children's level of moral reasoning according to Kohlberg's framework. Observe and record their viewpoints about the story of Heinz. Is there any conflict? Any changing of positions? Naturally, if you have access to a class of children or adolescents, you might like to try it out on the class. The following grid will help you to classify the responses.

Subject	Response	Level	Reason for categorisation
Age Sex			
Age Sex			
Age Sex			

invariant—that is, an individual doesn't regress from a typically higher form of reasoning to a typically lower form, and stages are not skipped (Walker 1982).

If you look back at Table 14.4 you will see that Kohlberg's original theory consisted of six stages. In the light of subsequent research, however, there have been a number of modifications and elaborations to the theory (Kohlberg, Levine & Hewer 1983). It is now clear that principled reasoning does not emerge in any substantial way during the secondary school years, and that most children up to about Year 10 are functioning at stages 2 and 3, with stage 2 rapidly declining. In the latter years of high school and early adulthood, stage 1 thinking has virtually disappeared, stage 2 thinking is considerably reduced, and stage 3 begins to decline with the rise of stage 4 thinking. Basically, the ages at which various levels of moral reasoning decline and rise have been revised upwards in the light of new evidence and a re-evaluation of old data (Sprinthall & Sprinthall 1990). Furthermore, because postconventional thinking was so rare among the subjects interviewed, stage 6 has been dropped from the reformulation of the theory, while stage 5 has been modified to include some of the features of stage 6 (Damon 1983; Palmer 2003; Shweder, Mahapatra & Miller 1990).

Modifications to the theory

It has also become quite apparent that individuals do not reason at one stage exclusively; rather, while typically reasoning at one stage, called the *modal stage*, they also understand and value reasoning at the next level up on the scale. Part of their reasoning is also at one stage lower (Rest 1973; Turiel 1966, 1983). It is important to note here that the dynamism for moving from one stage to the next higher stage appears to be the cognitive conflict engendered when one is confronted with a level of reasoning that is higher than one's current level. For educators and parents, this gives a rationale for holding moral dilemma discussions among individuals functioning at varying (but close) stages of moral reasoning. However, research tends to indicate that the challenge should not be too great—for example, when there is a mismatch between a stage 2 and a stage 4 or 5 thinker (see Enright *et al.* 1983; Mosher 1980; Norcini & Snyder 1983; Walker 1983).

Modal stage of moral reasoning

Interviews and moral reasoning

From his research Kohlberg believed that the responses of children to moral dilemmas presented in interview situations represent underlying forms or structures of moral thought which are universal—that is, not dependent on particular socialisation practices within particular cultural communities. He also felt that moral development is an active process with children generating moral structures through interaction with other persons and through role taking in social situations. In particular, children are stimulated to move on to a higher stage of moral development when confronted with some genuine moral conflict that calls into question their typical beliefs. In order to investigate and demonstrate this, Kohlberg put a lot of faith in the interview method, which 'has been assumed to provide a clear window into the moral mind. The interview method presumes that a person both is aware of his/her own inner processes and can verbally explain them' (Rest *et al.* 1999a, 1999b, p. 295). However, others have questioned the value of interviews in uncovering the depth of moral reasoning that might characterise individuals.

For example, in questioning the belief that young children are incapable of advanced moral reasoning, Shweder *et al.* (1990; see also Rest *et al.* 1999a, 1999b) make the intriguing point that language (which is used to elicit moral judgments) is very often a quite inadequate means of explaining how individuals reason and think. Shweder *et al.* (1990, p. 143) state:

> Kohlberg's theory of moral development is about the development of moral understandings, yet his moral dilemma interview methodology is a verbal production task that places a high premium on the ability to generate arguments, verbally represent complex concepts, and talk like a moral philosopher. It is hazardous to rely on such a procedure when studying moral understandings because one of the most important findings of recent developmental research is that knowledge of concepts often precedes their self-reflective representation in speech. Young children know a great deal more about the concept of number, causation, or grammaticality than they can state.
>
> . . . Those who study moral understandings with Kohlberg's moral dilemma interview have reduced the study of moral concepts to the study of verbal justification of moral ideas. The study of moral understanding has been narrowed . . . to the study of what people can propositionalise. That is dangerous because what people can state is but a small part of what they know.

This statement gives a lot of food for thought. Obviously, children and adults may be able to reason at a higher moral level than their feeble attempts at explanation indicate. It might help to explain why so few individuals are classified as operating at the principled level. It appears that those who have been classified as such (for example, Mahatma Gandhi, Martin Luther King and Mother Teresa) were also skilled communicators of their thoughts! This gap between language skills and moral reasoning is illustrated by a response of our daughter. We asked Laura, at three years old (almost four, as she kept telling us), how she knew what was good and what was bad. 'Because I have a good brain!' she replied with glee.

Turiel's perspective on the development of morality in social settings

Some criticisms of the Piagetian and Kohlbergian approaches relate to the confusion that may exist between *conventional rules* and *moral imperatives*. Writers such as Turiel and Nucci (Nucci 1987; Turiel 1983; Wainryb & Turiel 1993) argue that an understanding of social conventions such as rules of dress, greetings and appropriate behaviour in social settings progresses through developmental levels reflecting underlying concepts of social organisation, and that this development is different from the stages of moral development relating to issues that are universal and unchangeable such as proscriptions against stealing, injury and slander. Moral transgressions are viewed as wrong, irrespective of the presence of governing rules, while conventional acts are viewed as wrong only if they violate an existing rule or standard. Children's and adults' responses to events in the moral domain focus on features intrinsic to the acts (such as harm or justice), while responses in the context of conventions focus on aspects of the social order (rules, regulations, normative expectations). Moral transgressions are viewed as more serious than violations of convention, and acts performed for a moral reason are considered more positive than ones performed because of convention (Nucci 1982; Turiel 1983; Wainryb & Turiel 1993).

Of course, some rules have both an implied moral and conventional dimension, and conformity to the rule may reflect either moral or conventional reasoning, or a combination of both forms. For example, many drivers don't exceed the prescribed alcohol level while driving because they generally feel that it is immoral to endanger the lives of other drivers on the road. Other drivers obey the law because they are afraid of random breath testing and the consequences if they are over the limit. Most people are probably influenced by both motives.

Influences on the development of moral behaviour

Three important influences on our moral behaviour are the moral values we have internalised through our socialisation, our exposure to models of moral behaviour, and the informational assumptions that provide the basis for our decision making (Wainryb & Turiel 1993). An individual's informational beliefs and assumptions about relevant aspects of reality have a bearing on the individual's interpretation of an event. For example, the belief that a foetus is (as assumed fact) a person makes abortion comparable with murder. On the other hand, if a foetus is not considered human life, then abortion is seen as a personal choice that does not involve a moral transgression. It is for these reasons that people can have so many different moral perspectives on the same act (Wainryb & Turiel 1993).

Moral actions and conventional actions

A major difference between this perspective and those of Kohlberg and Piaget is the belief that even very young children can differentiate between actions that are moral and those that are conventional. For example, children believe that they shouldn't break the classroom rule against talking (conventional rule), but that talking would be okay if the rule were removed. On the other hand, children believe it is wrong to hurt another child irrespective of the existence of a rule forbidding it. Because of this differentiation, moral and values education should reflect this distinction.

Young children are also able to distinguish just and unjust authority, and take into account the age and status of authority figures, their formal position in the social

Authority

hierarchy, their ability to sanction and punish, and the extent of their expertise and knowledge. For example, children accept parental commands regulating activities such as house chores, but reject parental commands to steal or cause harm (Wainryb & Turiel 1993).

For Turiel and others, it seems that children's moral judgments do not simply and directly reflect adults' values, teaching and commands, or the attitudes and opinions of significant groups such as religious ones. Rather, it appears that moral and social understandings and decisions result from a developmental process that stems from the child's social interactions and observations, which are then interpreted and modified according to the child's understandings and assumptions.

Moral reasoning, moral behaviour and explanations

Research examining the relationship between moral reasoning and moral action has found only a weak relationship. Nevertheless, the relationship is in the expected direction. In other words, people who have been classified as functioning at a higher level of moral reasoning will avoid behaviour such as cheating more often than those who have been classified as functioning at a lower level (Blasi 1980; Damon 1983; Palmer 2003).

Various reasons are given for the weak link between moral reasoning and moral behaviour. These include various personal and situational factors, such as other competing attitudes and motives, emotions, the presence of other people, level of information available, information about potential consequences; these can all affect what we do irrespective of our moral reasoning (Palmer 2003). We are all aware that circumstances can facilitate or inhibit what we believe to be moral behaviour irrespective of our moral beliefs. For example, a person might be pressured by peers to commit an offence that they would not have done by themselves. In other circumstances, financial exigencies might play a role in decisions. For example, for a woman with a large family of young children, the possibility of another pregnancy may persuade her to practise contraception, even though this may be proscribed by her church. All of us have had tussles of conscience when competing demands make a simple direct relationship between moral beliefs and behaviour problematic.

Gender differences in moral development: Gilligan's view

Kohlberg's stage theory has been criticised by Carol Gilligan (1977, 1982) who has highlighted the potential for gender bias in the methodology used by Kohlberg, which may lead to men being classified as functioning at higher levels of moral reasoning than females. She argues that, because all Kohlberg's original subjects were male, the 'model' reasons derived for moral decisions used to structure the stage theory reflect a male perspective rather than a universal one. For example, she believes that men speak of rights, while women speak of responsibilities; men highlight rationality, while women highlight caring and concern; men are seen as searching for general principles that can be applied to any moral dilemma and women as concentrating on particular situations, relationships and people. Gilligan maintains that Kohlberg's system of scoring the interviews, therefore, based upon male reasoning, penalises women so that more women are represented at lower levels of moral reasoning relative to men. Furthermore, she believes that, as the stages are based on a male perspective, they present a very limited view of moral reasoning. While Gilligan and her colleagues argue that traditional Kohlbergian measures are biased against females, most research shows that Kohlberg's measurement methods and scoring schemes do not yield reliable gender differences in moral judgment scores (Braebeck 1982; Damon 1983; Palmer 2003; Sprinthall & Sprinthall 1990; Walker 1984; Walker, De Vries & Trevetham 1987).

Morality of care

Despite the apparent controversy, Gilligan has nevertheless highlighted some important dimensions of moral reasoning not emphasised in Kohlberg's theory. While Kohlberg emphasises the **justice perspective**—a perspective that focuses on the rights of the individual: individuals stand alone and independently make moral decisions—Gilligan (1982) focuses on a **care perspective** that views people in terms of their connectedness with and concern for others.

In studies with girls aged from six to 18 years of age, Gilligan (1982) shows that girls consistently reveal a detailed knowledge about and interest in human relationships. Gilligan believes that this causes a dilemma for many girls, who perceive that their intense interest in intimacy and relationships is not highly regarded in a male-dominated culture. Although society values women as caring and altruistic, such characteristics may limit females' opportunities in society at large. Females who choose to adopt achievement-driven values characteristic of the male are considered selfish. If they don't, they are not regarded as the equal of males! Gilligan believes that the conflict experienced can have a serious impact on the development of the female's self-concept and lead to depression and eating disorders among adolescent girls (Santrock & Yussen 1992).

There has been considerable research support for Gilligan's claim that the moral reasoning of females and males is concerned with different issues. Some schools have taken seriously Gilligan's ideas that girls should have greater value placed on their **morality of care**, rather than being encouraged to be independent and self-sufficient. They have done so by emphasising cooperation rather than competition across the curriculum, a theme developed in Chapters 7 and 8. It is also believed that boys benefit from such teaching approaches.

Morality of care

It is important to note that there is not an absolute gender difference and the two perspectives are not incompatible (Santrock & Yussen 1992). Indeed, males can express deep concern for the welfare of others and develop intimacy and altruistic characteristics, while females can be justice-oriented. In many cases, neither perspective dominates.

Compare and contrast the perspectives of Kohlberg and Gilligan. Organise a debate on the topic 'That women are more care-oriented than men'. Does this hold true today in Western society? What about in other cultures?

QUESTION POINT

Discuss the belief implicit in Kohlberg's theory that moral values are universal.

Morality and cross-cultural considerations

Not everyone agrees with the notion that moral development is contingent upon the natural unfolding of structures as the child matures, and with the emphasis placed on the process of self-discovery of social moral rules, independent of social context or culture. Shweder, Mahapatra and Miller (1987) argue that young children acquire their social knowledge through a process of cultural transmission. From this perspective the cultural milieu of the child takes on a greater role in shaping moral responses, leading to a relative rather than a universal stance on questions of right and wrong (see also DiMartino 1989).

Cultural relevance

Naturally, Kohlberg's comprehensive theory of moral development, with its claims to universalism, has been tested in a wide range of cultural contexts. Two issues are worth noting here. First, the original stories constructed by Kohlberg reflect a Western, middle-class orientation and, as such, may not be suited for use in other cultural contexts. Attempts have been made to rewrite the stories for particular cross-cultural use (DiMartino 1989; Sprinthall & Sprinthall 1990).

Are there universal moral values?

A greater problem than culturally suitable stories really hits at the heart of the theory, and this is the conception that there are universal moral values that characterise postconventional moral thinking—values such as liberty, equality, safety, the elimination of suffering and the preservation of human life. Other writers (DiMartino 1989) suggest that, far from being universal, moral values may be culturally specific—for example, the value of free speech and human individual dignity may very well reflect a democratic perspective rather than a universal value. Even on contentious issues within the one community, such as Australia or New Zealand, we see a diversity of opinion on laws related to abortion, euthanasia and homosexuality, so that when we move to other cultures the complexity becomes even greater. For example, birth control is considered immoral in many cultures, while polygamy is considered moral. Those holding to the universalistic notion argue that, irrespective of the recognition of wrongness (in behaviour such as polygamy or abortion), certain behaviours are wrong regardless of social mores and man-made laws. In his latest formulation of the theory, Kohlberg paid greater attention to this issue (Kohlberg *et al.* 1983; Shweder *et al.* 1990). As you can see, this is a very complicated issue, and one that is far from resolution.

Neo-Kohlbergian approaches to moral development

A number of theorists are developing from Kohlberg's theory a new approach that has been termed neo-Kohlbergian (Rest *et al.* 1999a; see also Cummings, Dyas, Maddux & Kochman 2001). Essential differences between the neo-Kohlbergian approach and that of Kohlberg are the way in which theorists assess moral development and the direct links drawn between moral thinking and information processing. Instead of interviews, neo-Kohlbergians use multiple-choice recognition tasks, which ask participants to rate and rank a set of items that are designed to activate moral schemas. This 'test' is called the Defining Issues Test (DIT). Instead of referring to stages of moral development, neo-Kohlbergians refer to moral schemas. Moral schemas are more concrete conceptions of the moral basis of behaviour than Kohlberg's stages, which are relatively abstract, particularly at the higher levels. In other words, the content of an

Defining Issues Test

act (indicated through a schema) can be used as a measure of moral thinking as well as the structure of the reasoning (cognitive operations represented in stages in Kohlberg's theory, and assessed content-free through interviews on moral dilemmas). Rather than thinking of moral development as a step-like procedure as in Kohlberg's theory, neo-Kohlbergians emphasise the more fluid overlapping of ways of thinking about moral issues that characterise individuals as they move from more primitive ways of thinking to more advanced ways. Finally, neo-Kohlbergians believe that morality is a social construction that reflects the community's experiences, particular institutional arrangements, deliberations and aspirations that are supported by the community (Rest *et al.* 1999a). This has links with our description of social constructivism earlier in the text. In contrast, as we have noted earlier in this chapter, Kohlberg argued for the universality of moral reasoning and values.

Moral schemas

There are three moral schemas represented in the DIT: the Personal Interests schema, the Maintaining Norms schema and the Postconventional schema. The Personal Interests schema develops in childhood, while the other two are typically developed in adolescence and adulthood (Rest *et al.* 1999a). The Personal Interests schema includes elements of Kohlberg's stages 2 and 3 and justifies a decision by appealing to the personal stake that a person has in the consequences of an action as well as concerns for those with whom the person has a personal affectionate relationship. Society-wide norms are not apparent or relevant to decision making. The Maintaining Norms schema, drawn from Kohlberg's stage 4, implicates society-wide norms. Indicative of this level of reasoning is reference to the necessity of having and maintaining societal norms that facilitate the harmonious working of society and that are applied even with strangers. Formal law, that is publicly set and known by everyone, is used for ensuring that social norms are applied uniformly across society. Individuals, in adhering to the law, anticipate that others will also do their duty by the law. There is a partial reciprocity implied, as obeying the law might not benefit all the participants in the same way. In the Maintaining Norms schema there is a duty orientation, which emphasises the need to obey authorities out of respect for the social system. There is a strong link between law and order in this schema. In essence, maintaining the social order through adherence to laws defines morality in this schema. The Postconventional schema reflects moral obligations that are based on shared ideals that are reciprocal and open to debate, tests of logical consistency and the experience of the community (Rest *et al.* 1999a). Four elements are proposed as comprising postconventional schema. First, the person believes that laws and regulations are social conventions that can be renegotiated to address a new moral purpose, rather than being immutable. Second, laws and regulations should reflect higher ideals regarding human interaction or organisation. Many laws today have overturned earlier laws in order to address ideals such as equal opportunity, minimal rights and protection for everyone, privacy and intimacy, and so on. Third, these ideals that shape codes of behaviour should be sharable—that is, embraced by others and justifiable through rational critique. Fourth, the Postconventional schema holds that laws should be fully reciprocal—that is, they should not only apply to everyone equally but be equally just to everyone. That is, there should not be laws that favour particular groups over others. Both the Maintaining Norms and Postconventional schemas seek to establish consensus. In the first schema this is through appeals to existing practice and existing authority, while in the latter it is through appealing to ideals and logical coherence.

As with Kohlberg's theory, there is considerable debate over the merits of the neo-Kohlbergian approach and the methodology used, and considerable research effort has been directed at examining these issues, which is beyond the scope of this book (see Rest *et al.* 1999b; Thoma *et al.* 1999). If you are interested you should follow up this material by reading some of the research and associated literature and, in particular, examine the DIT.

Classroom applications of moral development theory

At the very least, our consideration of theories of moral development has highlighted a number of important issues for educators and parents. First among these is the notion that moral reasoning increases in sophistication as children get older, and that there is a relationship between moral reasoning and cognitive development. We cannot therefore expect children to hold the same moral perspective as ourselves and, indeed, children may consider it is acceptable to cheat and lie if, for example, it's for a good reason or can be concealed. Sermonising to children about their 'immoral' behaviour may well be a fruitless exercise if we are using arguments based on stages more than one in advance of the child's level.

Children and moral values

Second, our discussion has drawn attention to the importance for moral growth of the child's own direct social experience and their active efforts to draw meaning

Testing moral rules

from its contradictions. Clearly, the school and classroom supplies the first large environment in which children test out their moral rules. Cooperative grouping will provide a good environment for peer interaction that will promote cognitive and moral growth (see Chapters 2 and 8).

Can we teach moral values?

There are two basic approaches to teaching moral values. The first approach reflects a behavioural/social cognitive approach. In this approach, children learn to be good by being exposed to virtuous deeds and actions through models (such as texts and films) and being reinforced for appropriate behaviour. The values to be learned are predetermined and programmed into the curriculum (see, for example, Bennett 1993; Lickona 1991; Wynne & Ryan 1997). The second approach, cognitive developmental, reflects the theories of Kohlberg and others and emphasises the personal or social construction of moral beliefs and values (Bebeau, Rest & Narvaez 1999). Our discussion above calls into question many of the more traditional didactic methods of 'teaching' moral values. Indeed, the whole notion that moral values can be taught must be reconsidered. When we went to school it was common practice for social studies texts to present moral stories based on the lives of famous people such as Abraham Lincoln, Lewis Carroll, Helen Keller, Florence Nightingale, Mahatma Gandhi, Albert Schweitzer and the occasional (but very infrequent) Australian. It was anticipated that the reader would learn to be moral by reading about moral behaviour. However, there is little evidence that such an approach has any effect on the development of moral character (Bebeau *et al.* 1999).

At the most elementary level, such a didactic approach fails to take heed of the gap between the moral behaviour practised by great people such as Albert Schweitzer or Marie Curie and children's ability to understand, evaluate and incorporate the values so demonstrated (see, for example, Narvaez 1998, 1999; Narvaez *et al.* 1999). We can remember vividly as 10-year-olds wondering what 'on earth' we were supposed to get out of the stories. Were we to go to darkest Africa and convert the heathens, or perhaps discover radium or free slaves? (We had only a limited understanding of what slaves were.) Furthermore, the absence of contemporary models made the exercise somewhat unreal for children, and the approach predominantly reflected a Christian viewpoint of morality that is increasingly less appropriate in multicultural Australia and New Zealand. Such approaches to teaching, based on behaviourism and social learning theory, are still popular, but the question must be asked whether children are learning meaningful values which they can incorporate into their behaviour, or simply learning to listen and, perhaps, recall what was said. Narvaez (1998, pp. 20–1) makes the following comment that is important for us to consider:

> Those who use moral stories to build moral character should be aware that children may be understanding the stories in ways different from the author's intention or the perspective of the instructor. In fact, explicit educational curricula and instruction concerning moral topics such as social behavior change (e.g., drug use prevention or abuse recovery) may not be properly understood if the moral judgment capacities of the audience are not accommodated. Just as teachers attempt to match the reading level of a text with the student's level of reading skill, moral and social education programs should attempt to match the moral reasoning level of a text with the student's level of moral reasoning.
>
> In short, the development of 'moral literacy' is more complicated than often believed. Merely reading moral stories to children is unlikely to be enough for them to understand the intended message.

Four-component framework of moral education

Effective moral education should account for the complexities of social and moral reasoning (Wainryb & Turiel 1993). It should, therefore, be geared towards stimulating the development of moral concepts, fostering an understanding of the distinctions, relations and conflicts between moral and social concepts, as well as guiding children's comprehension of the ways in which access to information modifies social and moral decisions. Rest and his colleagues (Bebeau *et al.* 1999; Bebeau & Thoma 1999) propose a four-component framework that should guide the development of moral education programs. Each of these components highlights an issue to be addressed in order to encourage and develop moral behaviour.

1 *Moral sensitivity* (interpreting the situation as moral). This emphasises that moral behaviour can only occur if an individual assesses the situation as moral and is aware of how one's actions affect other people.
2 *Moral judgment* (judging which of the available actions are most moral). This emphasises the selection process, choosing one action over another.
3 *Moral motivation* (prioritising the moral over other significant concerns and personal values such as careers, affectional relationships, institutional loyalties, and so on). This emphasises the choice made to be moral over other possible behaviours that are valid and significant.

4 *Moral character* (being able to construct and implement actions that service the moral choice). This emphasises the processes by which one constructs an appropriate course of action, avoids distractions and maintains the courage to continue.

ACTION STATION

The value of the four-component framework lies in its usefulness for understanding the reasons for moral failing, thus enabling the educator to design more effective educational experiences, and the researcher to generate researchable variables (Bebeau *et al.* 1999). Consider some events in which you believe less moral behaviour was evident. Analyse the behaviour in the context of the four components above. Which components are more likely to explain the behaviour? As an example, a professional assassin might be weak on all four components. On the other hand, the assassin might only be weak on moral motivation. Now consider how you might design a moral education program that takes into account each of these four components. Discuss this within a group and then write elements of the program. You would need to indicate the developmental level at which the program was to operate (for example, young children, adolescents or adults).

ACTION STATION

Bebeau *et al.* (1999) suggest that while most moral education programs address at least one component, few address all four. Consider a range of approaches to moral education, such as the dilemma discussion approach promoted by Kohlberg, the traditional character education approach as advocated by Wynne and Ryan (1997), the sensitivity approaches as advocated by Gropper (1996), and the communitarian approach as advocated by Etzioni (1993). Consider which of the four components listed above are addressed in each of the programs. Try to locate programs that address all four components.

Today, the approach to teaching moral values is more likely to be through discussion of problems that are real and meaningful to children at their particular stages of development, rather than through the didactic approach. One popular approach is *moral dilemma presentations*. The first step in this may be the presentation of a moral problem by a teacher. Children are invited to contribute their views on appropriate solutions and, in particular, their reasons for the solution. These solutions and views may be listed on a board and discussed. Within any group there will be a range of views expressed, and these will usually represent a range of stages. In the discussion, children are challenged to consider their own point of view. For children reasoning at higher levels, lower-level solutions expressed by their peers will be understood but rejected. However, cognitive conflict will be set up for children reasoning at lower stages, and they will be challenged to move upwards. Judicious comments by the teacher, together with elaboration of views by children functioning at the higher levels, facilitate this movement (Peak 1971). Research tends to support the belief that children do progressively make more sophisticated judgments as a consequence of being exposed to such programs.

Moral dilemmas

QUESTION POINT

Consider the implications of each of the theories covered in this chapter for children living in tribal settings (such as Australian Aboriginal and Maori children), rural Westernised settings and urbanised settings. What different factors are likely to affect development in each case?

ACTION STATION

In the context of personal development education, and the threat posed by HIV/AIDS and sexually transmitted diseases, have a group of adolescents debate whether condom-vending machines should be placed in high schools. Attempt to categorise the various responses using Kohlberg's schema. Monitor the expressed views of the students. Is there any shifting of perspective because of the social interaction? Report your findings.

Caring schools

It would seem obvious that in order to encourage the development of moral values and behaviour in students, educational environments should be moral places. Today there is considerable emphasis on schools having a culture of caring in which interpersonal relationships are considered very important to the social, moral and cognitive development of students (Gilligan 1982; Goldstein 1999; Noddings 1992, 1995; Osterman 2000; see also Anderman 2002; Davis 2003). This is very much in line with humanist perspectives on education considered in Chapter 13, and links have also been drawn with Vygotsky's social constructivism and, in particular, the notion of the Zone of Proximal Development (see, for example, Goldstein 1999; Tappan 1998; and Chapter 2).

Caring refers to teachers' abilities to empathise with and invest in the protection and development of young people (Chaskin & Rauner 1995). According to Noddings, caring has three components: receptivity, engrossment and motivational displacement. *Receptivity* refers to full openness to the other person and a compelling obligation to respond. *Engrossment* refers to fully receiving and experiencing what the other person is saying or presenting as if one were that person. *Motivational displacement* refers to the willingness the carer has to give primacy to the goals and needs of the cared for. The caring relationship has to be reciprocal, with the cared for receiving the caring that is offered. This is indicated when the cared for responds in word or deed in a way that recognises that care has been given. It is through this recognition and response that the carer receives validation for the caring act, thus completing the cycle (Tappan 1998). The response of the cared for is the carer's reward and is the impetus for continued caring (Goldstein 1999).

The roles of carer and cared for are not fixed but are characterised by reciprocity and mutuality. In other words, the carer and cared for can reverse roles as opportunities arise. In the school context, students can learn to be both carers and cared for. Noddings (1992; Tappan 1998) suggests four central components of a moral education that reflects a caring perspective. These are:

1 *Modelling:* students are shown how to care by teachers, parents and other adults acting as caregivers.
2 *Dialogue:* students, the cared for and the caring are involved in open-ended dialogue which represents a joint quest for understanding, insight, appreciation or empathy. It is an opportunity for the caring to explore with the cared for what they are trying to show or model. In effect, it demonstrates engrossment in the cared for.
3 *Practice:* learning how to care takes practice, hard work and persistence. This practice should be active, engaged and experientially based.
4 *Confirmation:* students are encouraged to affirm and encourage the best in others.

Reflecting this curriculum of caring, changes have been made to many school organisations, curriculum content and emphases, and there has been a development of community service education and extensions of contact with parents and communities.

Moral development and constructivism

The process of development of moral concepts arises from children's personal cognitive growth and experiences in the social world. The appreciation of the moral component of social experiences depends upon the cognitive level at which the child is functioning. It is in making sense of these social experiences that children perceive their salient moral aspects—for example, pain or injustice—and generate ideas on how people should act towards each other. These moral rules are not based on given rules or adult teachings but, rather, children construct their own judgments through abstractions from their experiences. As children grow older they re-evaluate existing concepts and construct new ones that are qualitatively different. Moral development, therefore, presents an interplay between individual cognitive development, what we have referred to earlier as personal constructivism, and cognitive development within the social context, which we have referred to earlier as social constructivism. Cognitive theories of moral development tend to focus on one or other element. The moral development theories of Piaget and Kohlberg and the neo-Kohlbergian approaches are personal constructivist in emphasis. The approaches of Turiel, Gilligan and Noddings are more social constructivist in emphasis.

WHAT WOULD YOU DO?

MORAL OBLIGATIONS

As part of a Year 10 science options unit, students examine the bioethical issues that arise in science. One strategy involves students working in groups and role playing a hospital ethics committee where they must select four patients who will receive a liver transplant. Students are given a list of 15 potential patients to choose from. Students must negotiate until they reach a consensus on the four patients who will receive this life-saving operation. An important part of the activity is a debriefing where, as a class, they debate why they chose or rejected particular patients.

In this particular class, Jenny, an intelligent, forthright student, argued against the selection of Patient F, a four-year-old refugee who would be adopted after the operation. 'He should not be considered. Our taxes should not be used to give transplants to foreigners who have not contributed to this country,' she stated.

Case studies illustrating National Competency Framework for Beginning Teaching, National Project on the Quality of Teaching and Learning, Australian Teaching Council, 1996, p. 42. Commonwealth of Australia copyright, reproduced by permission.

How would you proceed from this point? Now consider what the teacher did.

WHAT WOULD YOU DO? (cont.)

MORAL OBLIGATIONS

I waited for comment from the students. It is important that they form their own ethical stance, rather than be told what to think. Thus, in general, I deliberately avoid stating my own opinions. In this situation, however, I felt I must speak.

'Jenny, Australia is a wealthy country and as such has a moral obligation to assist other countries, especially in the medical area. In fact, health funding is allocated specifically for compassionate medical assistance.'

Katrina raised her hand. 'Yes, Katrina,' I said.

'I agree,' she said. 'Even though he can't pay for the operation, when he is adopted he will grow up and pay taxes just like our parents.'

At the end of this lesson I reflected on my comment. I decided that, even though each student must develop their own ethical values, they also need to be informed about the values that are generally held by our society.

Case studies illustrating National Competency Framework for Beginning Teaching, National Project on the Quality of Teaching and Learning, Australian Teaching Council, 1996, p. 42. Commonwealth of Australia copyright, reproduced by permission.

What do you think? Was the teacher's response appropriate? What did you suggest? How does the case study illustrate the development of moral reasoning as proposed by Piaget and Kohlberg?

KEY TERMS

Autonomous morality (p. 509): children view moral rules as flexible, socially agreed upon principles that can be changed

Care perspective (p. 518): views people in terms of their connectedness with others and concern for others

Clique (p. 495): a small group of close friends

Crowd (p. 495): a large, loosely organised group interested in a common activity

Heteronomous morality (p. 509): children view moral rules as fixed and unchangeable

Immanent justice (p. 509): punishment means that wrong has been done

Justice perspective (p. 518): focuses on the rights of the individual: individuals stand alone and independently make moral decisions

Meaninglessness (p. 508): student's feeling of the irrelevancy of what is happening to them at the present

Moral reasoning (p. 509): the thinking processes involved in deciding right from wrong

Morality of care (p. 519): a morality based upon connectedness and concern for others

Normlessness (p. 508): student's rejection of society's rules and norms

Play (p. 490): provides tools and symbols for representing personal reconstructions of experience

Powerlessness (p. 508): student's feeling of lack of control over their life

Reciprocity (p. 509): socially agreed upon principles of cooperation that can be changed with agreement of others who are involved

Self-concept (p. 501): broadly based individual beliefs about self in physical, social and academic domains

Self-esteem (p. 501): judgments about one's worth and the feelings associated with these

Social estrangement (p. 508): student's feeling of physical or mental isolation from their situation

ON-LINE LEARNING

If you go to http://www.pearsoned.com.au/mcinerney, you will have hot links directly to these sites:

- **Classroom practices and moral development**

Consider and discuss the range of suggestions made at this website for moral instruction in classrooms. Take one of the approaches presented and implement a lesson based upon the approach in a classroom environment using the guidelines presented.
http://tigger.uic.edu/~lnucci/MoralEd/practices.html

- **Self-esteem self test**

This site, maintained by the Wellness International Network, provides a self-test for self-esteem. Complete the test and critique it by referring to theoretical perspectives on self-esteem and other methods of assessing self-esteem.
http://www.wellnessnet.com/testesarticle.htm

WEB DESTINATIONS

If you go to http://www.pearsoned.com.au/mcinerney, you will have hot links directly to these sites:

- **Studies in moral development and education**

This web page links together educators, scholars and citizens who want to share their work and learn more about research, practices, and activities in the area of moral development and education.
http://tigger.uic.edu/~lnucci/MoralEd/index.html

- **Overview of moral development theories**

This web page is sponsored by the office for studies in moral development and character formation located at the College of Education at the University of Illinois at Chicago. It provides a further overview of the theories of Piaget, Kohlberg, Turiel and Gilligan.
http://tigger.uic.edu/~lnucci/MoralEd/overview.html

- **Adolescence change and continuity**

Adolescence is a time when our bodies, our families, our schools and the larger society demand that we change. This website provides an introduction to some of the developmental changes that shape our lives between puberty and the end of university. This site provides information about basic changes, settings and issues that are particular to the teenage years, including the influence of the peer group, the importance of the family, delinquency, identity formation, sexual maturation and social transitions. This site was produced by students taking two courses at the Pennsylvania State University.
http://inside.bard.edu/academic/specialproj/darling/adolesce.htm

- **Youth suicide problems**

This website deals with gay and bisexual male suicide problems, related issues, and little-known concepts related to youth suicide.
http://www.youth-suicide.com/gay-bisexual/

RECOMMENDED READING

Anderman, E. M. & Maehr, M. L. (1994) Motivation and schooling in the middle grades. *Review of Educational Research*, **64**, 287–309.

Bebeau, M. J., Rest, J. & Narvaez, D. (1999) Beyond the promise: A perspective on research in moral education. *Educational Researcher*, **28**, 18–26.

Berndt, T. H. (1999) Friends' influence on students' adjustment to school. *Educational Psychologist*, **34**, 15–28.

Bryant, A. L. & Zimmerman, M. A. (2002) Examining the effects of academic beliefs and behaviors on changes in substance use among urban adolescents. *Journal of Educational Psychology*, **94**, 621–37.

Buchanan, C. M., Eccles, J. S. & Becker, J. B. (1992) Are adolescents the victims of raging hormones? Evidence for the activational effects of hormones on moods and behavior at adolescence. *Psychological Bulletin*, **111**, 62–107.

Conrade, G. & Ho, R. (2001) Differential parenting styles for fathers and mothers: Differential treatment for sons and daughters. *Australian Journal of Psychology*, **53**, 29–35.

Davis, A. (1992) Suicidal behaviour among adolescents: Its nature and prevention. In R. Kosky, H. S. Eshkevari & G. Kneebone (eds) *Breaking Out: Challenges in Adolescent Mental Health in Australia*. Canberra: Australian Government Publishing Service.

DeVries, R. (1997) Piaget's social theory. *Educational Researcher*, **26**, 4–17.

Eccles, J. S. *et al.* (1993) Development during adolescence. The impact of stage–environment fit on young adolescents' experiences in schools and in families. *American Psychologist*, **48**, 90–101.

Garland, A. & Zigler, E. (1993) Adolescent suicide prevention. Current research and social policy implications. *American Psychologist*, **48**, 169–82.

Goldstein, L. S. (1999) The relational zone: The role of caring relationships in the co-construction of mind. *American Educational Research Journal*, **36**, 647–73.

Graham, A., Reser, J., Scuderi, C., Zubrick, S., Smith, M. & Turley, B. (2000) Suicide: An Australian Psychological Society Discussion Paper. *Australian Psychologist*, **35**, 1–28.

Greenberg, M. T., Weissberg, R. P., O'Brien, M. U., Zins, J. E., Fredericks, L., Resnik, H. & Elias, M. J. (2003) Enhancing school-based prevention and youth development through coordinated social, emotional and academic learning. *American Psychologist*, **58**, 466–74.

Hill, J. (1995) School culture and peer groups. In L. W. Anderson (ed.) *International Encyclopedia of Teaching and Teacher Education,* 2nd ed. Tarrytown, NY: Pergamon.

Jarvinen, D. W. & Nicholls, J. G. (1996) Adolescents' social goals, beliefs about causes of social success, and satisfaction in peer relations. *Developmental Psychology*, **32**, 435–41.

Jones, E. & Reynolds, G. (1992) *The Play's the Thing*. New York: Teachers College Press.

Kohlberg, L. (1981) *The Philosophy of Moral Development*. San Francisco: Harper & Row.

Mak, A. (1994) Parental neglect and overprotection as risk factors in delinquency. *Australian Journal of Psychology*, **46**, 107–11.

Marsh, H. W. (1990) A multidimensional, hierarchical model of self-concept: Theoretical and empirical justification. *Educational Psychology Review*, **2**, 77–172.

Marsh, H. W. & Craven, R. (1997) Academic self-concept: Beyond the dustbowl. In G. Phye (ed.) *Handbook of Classroom Assessment: Learning, Adjustment and Achievement*. San Diego, CA: Academic Press.

Moyles, J. R. (ed.) (1995) *The Excellence of Play*. Buckingham, UK: Open University Press.

Nicholson, J. M., McFarland, M. L. & Oldenburg, B. (1999) Detection of child mental health problems in the school setting. *The Australian Educational and Developmental Psychologist*, **16**, 66–77.

Oerlemans, K. & Jenkins, H. (1998) There are aliens in our school. *Issues in Educational Research*, **8**, 117–29.

Palmer, E. J. (2003) An overview of the relationship between moral reasoning and offending. *Australian Psychologist*, **38**, 165–74.

Pritchard, C. (1992) Youth suicide and gender in Australia and New Zealand compared with countries of the Western world (1973–1987). *Australian and New Zealand Journal of Psychiatry*, **26**, 609–17.

Purdie, N. & McCrindle, A. (2004) Measurement of self-concept among Indigenous and non-Indigenous Australian students. *Australian Journal of Psychology*, **56**, 50–62.

Rest, J., Narvaez, D., Bebeau, M. & Thoma, S. (1999) A Neo-Kohlbergian approach: The DIT and schema theory. *Educational Psychology Review*, **11**, 291–324. (This is in a special issue on moral development in adolescents and adults. The entire issue is worth reading.)

Roeser, R. W., Eccles, J. S. & Strobel, K. R. (1998) Linking the study of schooling and mental health: Selected issues and empirical illustrations at the level of the individual. *Educational Psychologist*, **33**, 153–76.

Rogers, C. S. & Sawyers, J. K. (1988) *Play in the Lives of Young Children*. Washington DC: NAEYC.

Rosenthal, D., Ranieri, N. & Klimidis, S. (1996) Vietnamese adolescents in Australia: Relationships between perceptions of self and parental values, intergenerational conflict, and gender dissatisfaction. *International Journal of Psychology*, **31**, 81–91.

Shochet, I. & Osgarby, S. (1999) The Resourceful Adolescents Project: Building psychological resilience in adolescents and their parents. *The Australian Educational and Developmental Psychologist*, **16**, 46–65.

Simmons, R. G. & Blyth, D. A. (1987) *Moving into Adolescence: The Impact of Pubertal Change and School Context*. Hawthorne, NY: Aldine de Gruyter.

Skaalvik, E. M. & Skaalvik, S. (2002) Internal and external frames of reference for academic self-concept. *Educational Psychologist*, **37**, 233–44.

Smilansky, S. (1990) Sociodramatic play: Its relevance to behavior and achievement in school. In E. Klugman & S. Smilansky, *Children's Play and Learning*. New York: Teachers College Press.

Tappan, M. B. (1998) Sociocultural psychology and caring pedagogy: Exploring Vygotsky's 'Hidden Curriculum'. *Educational Psychologist*, **33**, 23–33.

Turiel, E. (1983) *The Development of Social Knowledge: Morality and Convention*. New York: Cambridge University Press.

Wainrub, C. & Turiel, E. (1993) Conceptual and informational features in moral decision making. *Educational Psychologist*, **28**, 205–18.

Wilson, J. C. (2001) Are today's children more able to distinguish right from wrong than their earlier counterparts? *The Australian Educational and Developmental Psychologist*, **18**, 15–24.

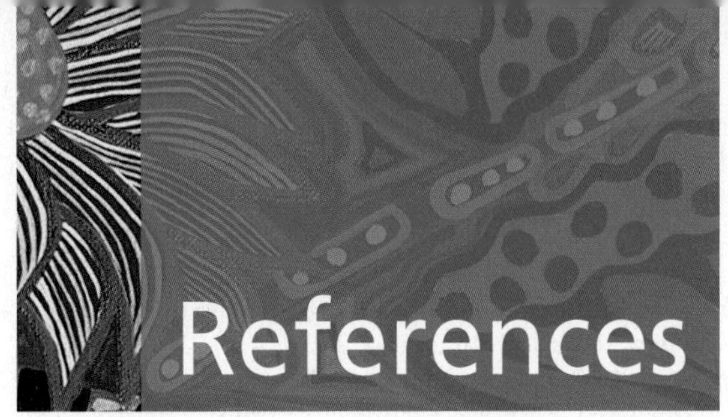

References

Abedi, J., Hofstetter, C. H. & Lord, C. (2004) Assessment accommodations for English language learners: Implications for policy-based empirical research. *Review of Educational Research*, **74**, 1–28.

Ablard, K. E. & Lipschultz, R. E. (1998) Self-regulated learning in high-achieving students: Relations to advanced reasoning, achievement goals, and gender. *Journal of Educational Psychology*, **90**, 94–101.

Abrami, P. C., Chambers, B., d'Apollonia, S., Farrell, M. & De Simone, C. (1992) Group outcome: The relationship between group learning outcome, attributional style, academic achievement, and self-concept. *Contemporary Educational Psychology*, **17**, 201–10.

Abrami, P. C., Chambers, B., Poulsen, C., De Simone, C., d'Apollonia, S. & Howden, J. (1995) *Classroom Connections: Understanding and Using Cooperative Learning*. Ontario: Harcourt Brace.

Abramson, L. Y., Seligman, M. E. P. & Teasdale, J. D. (1978) Learned helplessness in humans: Critique and reformulation. *Journal of Abnormal Psychology*, **87**, 49–74.

Abu-Rabia, S. (2003) The influence of working memory on reading and creative writing processes in a second language. *Educational Psychology*, **23**, 209–22.

Ackerman, P. L. (2003) Cognitive ability and non-ability trait determinants of expertise. *Educational Researcher*, **32**, 15–20.

Adams, P. (1991) The video vanguard opens fire. *The Weekend Australian*, 13–14 April.

Adelman, H. S. & Taylor, L. (1998) Reframing mental health in schools and expanding school reform. *Educational Psychologist*, **33**, 135–52.

Adelson, J. (ed.) (1980) *Handbook of Adolescent Psychology*. New York: John Wiley.

Aiken, L. R. (2004) *Psychological Testing and Assessment*, 11th ed. Boston: Allyn & Bacon.

Ainley, J. & Lonsdale, M. (2000) Non-attendance at school. Report to DETYA, ACER, Melbourne.

Ainley, M., Hidi, S. & Berndorff, D. (2002) Interest, learning, and the psychological processes that mediate their relationship. *Journal of Educational Psychology*, **94**, 545–61.

Ainley, M. D. (1986) What is it like if it's too big to grasp? *SET Research Information for Teachers*, number 1, item 7.

Ainley, M. D. (1993) Styles of engagement with learning: Multidimensional assessment of their relationship with strategy use and school achievement. *Journal of Educational Psychology*, **85**, 395–405.

Airasian, P. W. (1991) *Classroom Assessment*. New York: McGraw-Hill.

Airasian, P. W. (1995) Classroom assessment. In L. W. Anderson (ed.) *International Encyclopedia of Teaching and Teacher Education*, 2nd ed. Tarrytown, NY: Pergamon.

Albert, L. (1996a) *Cooperative Discipline*. Circle Pines, MN: American Guidance Service.

Albert, L. (1996b) *A Teacher's Guide to Cooperative Discipline*. Circle Pines, MN: American Guidance Service.

Albert, L. (1996c) *Cooperative Discipline Implementation Guide: Resources for Staff Development*. Circle Pines, MN: American Guidance Service.

Alberto, P. A. & Troutman, A. C. (1982) *Applied Behavior Analysis for Teachers. Influencing Student Performance*. Columbus, OH: Charles E. Merrill.

Alcorso, C. & Cope, B. (1986) *A Review of Multicultural Education Policy 1979–1986*. NACCME Commissioned Research Paper No. 6. Woden, Australia: National Advisory and Coordinating Committee on Multicultural Education.

Alexander, P. (2003) Can we get there from here? *Educational Researcher*, **32**, 3–4.

Alexander, P. A. (1995) Superimposing a situation-specific and domain-specific perspective on an account of self-regulated learning. *Educational Psychologist*, **30**, 189–93.

Alexander, P. A. (2000) Toward a model of academic development: Schooling and the acquisition of knowledge. *Educational Researcher*, **29**, 28–33.

Alexander, P. A., Kulikowich, J. M. & Jetton, T. L. (1994) The role of subject-matter knowledge and interest in the processing of linear and non-linear texts. *Review of Educational Research*, **64**, 210–52.

Alfassi, M. (1998) Reading for meaning: The efficacy of reciprocal teaching in fostering reading comprehension in high school students in remedial reading classes. *American Educational Research Journal*, **35**, 309–32.

Alleman, J. & Brophy, J. (1997) Elementary social studies: Instruments, activities, and standards. In G. Phye (ed.) *Handbook of Classroom Assessment: Learning, Achievement, and Adjustment*. San Diego, CA: Academic Press.

Allen, M. (1986) And are they intelligent? *Journal of Christian Education*, **85**, 35–43.

Alper, S. & Ryndak, D. L. (1992) Educating students with severe handicaps in regular classes. *Elementary School Journal*, **92**, 374–87.

Altermatt, E. R., Jovanovic, J. & Perry, M. (1998) Bias or responsivity? Sex and achievement-level effects on teachers' classroom questioning practices. *Journal of Educational Psychology*, **90**, 516–27.

American Psychological Association (1997) *Learner-centered Psychological Principles: Guidelines for School Redesign and Reform*. Washington, DC: American Psychological Association.

Ames, C. (1984) Competitive, cooperative, and individualistic goal structures: A cognitive-motivational analysis. In R. Ames & C. Ames (eds) *Research on Motivation in Education: Student Motivation (Volume 1)*. Orlando: Academic Press.

Ames, C. (1990) Motivation: What teachers need to know. *Teachers College Report*, **91**, 409–21.

Ames, C. (1992) Classrooms: Goals, structures, and student motivation. *Journal of Educational Psychology*, **84**, 261–71.

Ames, C. & Ames, R. (eds) (1985) *Research on Motivation*

in Education: The Classroom Milieu (Volume 2). Orlando: Academic Press.

Ames, C. & Ames, R. (eds) (1989) *Research on Motivation in Education: Goals and Cognitions (Volume 3)*. Orlando: Academic Press.

Ames, R. & Ames, C. (1991) Motivation and effective teaching. In L. Idol & B. F. Jones (eds) *Educational Values and Cognitive Instruction: Implications for Reform*. Hillsdale, NJ: Lawrence Erlbaum.

Ames, R. A. & Ames, C. (eds) (1984) *Research on Motivation in Education: Student Motivation (Volume 1)*. Orlando: Academic Press.

Anderman, E. M. (2002) School effects on psychological outcomes during adolescence. *Journal of Educational Psychology*, **94**, 795–809.

Anderman, E. M., Austin, C. C. & Johnson, D. M. (2002) The development of goal orientation. In A. Wigfield & J. S. Eccles (eds) *Development of Achievement Motivation*. San Diego, CA: Academic Press.

Anderman, E. M., Griesinger, T. & Westerfield, G. (1998) Motivation and cheating during early adolescence. *Journal of Educational Psychology*, **90**, 84–93.

Anderman, E. M. & Maehr, M. L. (1994) Motivation and schooling in the middle grades. *Review of Educational Research*, **64**, 287–309.

Anderman, E. M., Maehr, M. L. & Midgley, C. (1999) Declining motivation after the transition to middle school: Schools can make a difference. *Journal of Research and Development in Education*, **32**, 131–47.

Anderson, C. A. & Bushman, B. J. (2002) Media violence and the American public revisited. *American Psychologist*, **57**, 448–50.

Anderson, D. & Walker, R. (1990) Approaches to learning of beginning teacher education students. In M. Bezzina & J. Butcher (eds) *The Changing Face of Professional Education. Collected Papers of the AARE Annual Conference, Sydney University, 1990.* Sydney: AARE.

Anderson, J. R. (1982) Acquisition of cognitive skill. *Psychological Review*, **89**, 369–406.

Anderson, J. R. (1983) *The Architecture of Cognition*. Cambridge, MA: Harvard University Press.

Anderson, J. R. (1990) *Cognitive Psychology and its Implications*, 3rd ed. New York: W. H. Freeman.

Anderson, J. R., Greeno, J. G., Reder, L. M. & Simon, H. A. (2000) Perspectives on learning, thinking, and activity. *Educational Researcher*, **29**, 11–13.

Anderson, J. R., Reder, L. M. & Simon, H. A. (1996) Situated learning and education. *Educational Researcher*, **25**, 5–11.

Anderson, J. R., Reder, L. M. & Simon, H. A. (1997) Situative versus cognitive perspectives: Form versus substance. *Educational Researcher*, **26**, 18–21.

Anderson, L. M. & Prawat, R. S. (1983) Responsibility in the classroom: A synthesis of research on teaching self-control. *Educational Leadership*, **41**, 62–6.

Anderson, L. W. (1985) A retrospective and prospective view of Bloom's 'Learning for Mastery'. In M. C. Wang & H. J. Walberg (eds) *Adapting Instruction to Individual Differences*, Berkeley, CA: McCutchan.

Anderson, L. W. (1986) Research on teaching and educational effectiveness. *Curriculum Report*, **15**, April.

Anderson, L. W. (ed.) (1989) *The Effective Teacher. Study Guide and Readings*. New York: McGraw-Hill.

Anderson, L. W. & Burns, R. B. (1987) Values, evidence, and mastery learning. *Review of Educational Research*, **57**, 215–22.

Anderson, V. & Hidi, S. (1989) Teaching students to summarize. *Educational Leadership*, **46**, 26–8.

Andre, T. (1986) Problem solving and education. In G. D. Phye & T. Andre (eds) *Cognitive Classroom Learning: Understanding Thinking and Problem Solving*. Orlando: Harcourt Brace Jovanovich.

Andreou, E. & Metallidou, P. (2004) The relationship of academic and social cognition to behaviour in bullying situations among Greek primary school children. *Educational Psychology*, **24**, 27–41.

Andrews, G. R. & Debus, R. L. (1978) Persistence and causal perception of failure: Modifying cognitive attributions. *Journal of Educational Psychology*, **70**, 154–66.

Ansley, T. (1997) The role of standardised achievement texts in grades k–12. In G. Phye (ed.) *Handbook of Classroom Assessment: Learning, Achievement, and Adjustment*. San Diego, CA: Academic Press.

Arlin, M. (1984) Time, equality, and mastery learning. *Review of Educational Research*, **54**, 65–86.

Armstrong, D. & Savage, T. (1983) *Secondary Education: An Introduction*. New York: Macmillan.

Aronson, E., Blaney, N., Stephan, C., Sikes, J. & Snapp, M. (1978) *The Jigsaw Classroom*. Beverly Hills, CA: Sage.

Ashby, M. S. & Wittmaier, B. C. (1978) Attitude changes in children after exposure to stories about women in traditional or nontraditional occupations. *Journal of Educational Psychology*, **70**, 945–9.

Asher, W. & Hynes, K. (1982) Methodological weaknesses in an evaluation of open education. *Journal of Experimental Education*, **51**, 2–7.

Ashman, A. F. & Conway, R. N. (1993) *Using Cognitive Methods in the Classroom*. New York: Routledge.

Ashman, A. F. & Elkins, J. (eds) (2002) *Educating Children with Diverse Abilities*. Sydney: Prentice Hall.

Ashman, A. F. & Gillies, R. M. (1997) Children's cooperative behaviors and interactions in trained work groups in regular classrooms. *Journal of School Psychology*, **35**, 261–79.

Ashton, P. T. & Webb, R. B. (1986) *Making a Difference: Teachers' Sense of Efficacy and Student Achievement*. White Plains, NY: Longman.

Assor, A., Kaplan, H. & Roth, G. (2002) Choice is good, but relevance is excellent: Autonomy-enhancing and suppressing teacher behaviours predicting students' engagement in schoolwork. *British Journal of Educational Psychology*, **72**, 261–78.

Astor, R. A., Meyer, H. A. & Behre, W. J. (1999) Unowned places and times: Maps and interviews about violence in high schools. *American Educational Research Journal*, **36**, 1, 3–42.

Atkins, W. & Lewis, P. (1982) Partial integration of the severely retarded and the normal child. *ASET*, **3**, 23–7.

Atkinson, J. W. (1964) *An Introduction to Motivation*. Princeton, NJ: Van Nostrand.

Atkinson, J. W. (ed.) (1958) *Motives in Fantasy, Action and Society*. Princeton, NJ: Van Nostrand.

Atkinson, J. W. & Feather, N. T. (eds) (1966) *A Theory of Achievement Motivation*. New York: John Wiley.

Atkinson, J. W. & Raynor, J. O. (1974) *Motivation and Achievement*, Washington, DC: V. H. Winston.

Attie, I. & Brooks-Gunn, J. (1989) Development of eating problems in adolescent girls: A longitudinal study. *Developmental Psychology*, **25**, 70–9.

Aunola, K., Nurmi, J-E., Lerkkanen, M-K. & Rasku-Puttonen, H. (2003) The roles of achievement related behaviours and parental beliefs in children's mathematical performance. *Educational Psychology*, **23**, 404–21.

Australian Bureau of Statistics (2003) *Mindframe and Mental Health (MMMH) Project*. Australian Bureau of Statistics.

Australian Teaching Council (1996) *Case Studies Illustrating National Competency Framework for Beginning Teaching. National Project on the Quality of Teaching and Learning*. Canberra: AGPS.

Ausubel, D. P. (1963) *The Psychology of Meaningful Verbal Learning*. New York: Grune & Stratton.

Ausubel, D. P. (1966a) Cognitive structure and the facilitation of meaningful verbal learning. In R. C. Anderson (ed.) *Readings in the Psychology of Cognition*. New York: Holt, Rinehart & Winston.

Ausubel, D. P. (1966b) In defense of verbal learning. In R. C. Anderson (ed.) *Readings in the Psychology of Cognition*. New York: Holt, Rinehart & Winston.

Ausubel, D. P. (1968) *Educational Psychology: A Cognitive View*. New York: Holt, Rinehart & Winston.

Ausubel, D. P. (1977) The facilitation of meaningful verbal learning in the classroom. *Educational Psychologist*, **12**, 162–78.

Ausubel, D. P. (1978) In defense of advance organizers. A reply to the critics. *Review of Educational Research*, **48**, 251–7.

Bailey, J. (1992) Australian special education: Issues of the eighties. Directions for the nineties. *Australian Journal of Special Education*, **16**, 16–25.

Bailey, S. M. (1993) The current status of gender equity research in American schools. *Educational Psychologist*, **28**, 321–39.

Bain, A. (1992) Issues in the integration of regular and special education: An Australian perspective. *Australian Journal of Education*, **36**, 84–99.

Bakopanos, V. & White, R. (1990) Increasing meta-learning. Part 1: Encouraging students to ask questions. *SET Research Information for Teachers*, number 1, item 11.

Balla, D. & Zigler, E. (1975) Preinstitutional social deprivation, responsiveness to social reinforcement and IQ change in institutionalized retarded individuals. *American Journal of Mental Deficiency*, **80**, 228–30.

Balson, M. (1992) *Understanding Classroom Behaviour*, 3rd ed. Melbourne: ACER.

Bandura, A. (1962) Social learning through imitation. In N. R. Jones (ed.) *Nebraska Symposium on Motivation*. Lincoln, NE: University of Nebraska Press.

Bandura, A. (1969) *Principles of Behavior Modification*. New York: Holt, Rinehart & Winston.

Bandura, A. (1976) Self-efficacy: Toward a unifying theory of behavioral change. *Psychological Review*, **84**, 191–215.

Bandura, A. (1977a) *Social Learning Theory*. Morristown, NJ: General Learning Press.

Bandura, A. (1977b) Analysis of modeling processes. In H. F. Clarizio, R. C. Craig & W. A. Mehrens (eds) *Contemporary Issues in Educational Psychology*, 3rd ed. Boston: Allyn & Bacon.

Bandura, A. (1986) *Social Foundations of Thought and Action*. Englewood Cliffs, NJ: Prentice Hall.

Bandura, A. (1991) Self-regulation of motivation through anticipatory and self-regulatory mechanisms. In R. A. Dienstbier (ed.) *Perspectives on Motivation: Nebraska Symposium on Motivation (Volume 38)* (pp. 69–164). Lincoln, NE: University of Nebraska Press.

Bandura, A. (1993) Perceived self-efficacy in cognitive development and functioning. *Educational Psychologist*, **28**, 117–48.

Bandura, A. (1997) *Self-efficacy. The Exercise of Control.* New York: Freeman.

Bandura, A. & Walters, R. (1963) *Social Learning & Personality Development*. New York: Holt, Rinehart & Winston.

Banks, J. A. (1993) Multicultural education: Historical development, dimensions, and practice. *Review of Research in Education*, **19**, 3–49.

Barab, S. A. & Plucker, J. A. (2002) Smart people or smart contexts? Cognition, ability, and talent development in an age of situated approaches to knowing and learning. *Educational Psychologist*, **37**, 165–82.

Barker, K., Dowson, M. & McInerney, D. M. (2002) Performance approach, performance avoidance and depth of information processing: A fresh look at relations between students' academic motivation and cognition. *Educational Psychology*, **22**, 571–89.

Barnes, G. R. & McInerney, D. M. (1996) A motivational model of intention to enrol in senior secondary science courses in New South Wales schools. *Australian Journal of Psychology*, **48**, 86.

Barron, F. (1969) *Creative Person and Creative Process*. New York: Holt, Rinehart & Winston.

Barry, K. & King, L. (1993) *Beginning Teaching*, 2nd ed. Wentworth Falls, NSW: Social Science Press.

Bar-Tal, D. (1978) Attributional analysis of achievement-related behavior. *Review of Educational Research*, **48**, 259–71.

Bates, T. C., Castles, A., Coltheart, M., Gillsepie, N., Wright, M. & Martin, N. G. (2004) Behaviour genetic analyses of reading and spelling: A component processes analysis. *Australian Journal of Psychology*, **56**, 115–26.

Bauch, P. A. & Goldring, E. B. (2000) Teacher work context and parent involvement in urban high schools of choice. *Educational Research and Evaluation*, **6**, 1–23.

Baumrind, D. (1967) Child care practices anteceding three patterns of preschool behavior. *Genetic Psychology Monographs*, **75**, 43–88.

Baumrind, D. (1989) Rearing competent children. In W. Damon (ed.) *Child Development Today and Tomorrow*. San Francisco, CA: Jossey-Bass.

Bayley, N. (1956) Individual patterns of development. *Child Development*, **27**, 45–74.

Beach, K. (1999) Consequential transitions: A sociocultural expedition beyond transfer in education. *Review of Research in Education*, **24**, 101–39.

Beal, C. R. (1999) Special issue on the math-fact retrieval hypothesis. *Contemporary Educational Psychology*, **24**, 171–80.

Bebeau, M. J., Rest, J. & Narvaez, D. (1999) Beyond the promise: A perspective on research in moral education. *Educational Researcher*, **28**, 18–26.

Bebeau, M. J. & Thoma, S. J. (1999) 'Intermediate' concepts and the connection to moral education. *Educational Psychology Review*, **11**, 343–60.

Becker, J. & Varelas, M. (2001) Piaget's early theory of the role of language in intellectual development: A comment on De Vries' account of Piaget's social theory. *Educational Researcher*, **30**, 22–3.

Bee, H. (1992) *The Developing Child*, 6th ed. New York: HarperCollins.

Beilin, H. (1987) Current trends in cognitive development research: Towards a new synthesis. In B. Inhelder, D. de Caprona & A. Cornu-Wells (eds) *Piaget Today*. London: Lawrence Erlbaum.

Beishuizen, J. J. & Stoutjesdijk, E. T. (1999) Study strategies in a computer assisted study environment. *Learning and Instruction*, **9**, 281–301.

Bell, H. (1986) White teacher, black learner: The influence of the cross-cultural context on teaching practice. *Australian Journal of Adult Education*, **26**, 29–33.

Bell, H. (1988) An overview of some Aboriginal teaching and learning strategies in traditionally oriented communities. *Aboriginal Child at School*, **16**, 3–23.

Bellanca, J. & Fogarty, R. (1991) *Blueprints for Thinking in the Cooperative Classroom*, 2nd ed., revised in Australia by J. Dalton. Vic.: Hawker Brownlow Education.

Bempechat, J. & Drago-Severson, E. (1999) Cross-national differences in academic achievement: Beyond etic conceptions of children's understanding. *Review of Educational Research*, **69**, 287–314.

Bempechat, J., Graham, S. E. & Jimenez, N. V. (1999) The socialization of achievement in poor and minority students. A comparative study. *Journal of Cross-Cultural Studies*, **30**, 139–58.

Bennett, C. (2001) Genres of research in multicultural education. *Review of Educational Research*, **71**, 171–217.

Bennett, W. J. (ed.) (1993) *The Book of Virtues*. New York: Simon & Schuster.

Benton, R. (1989) Will it hurt? Teaching in Maori, or Pitjantjatjara. *SET Research Notes for Teachers*, number 1, item 13.

Berardi-Coletta, B., Dominowski, R. L., Buyer, L. S. & Rellinger, E. R. (1995) Metacognition and problem solving: A process-oriented approach. *Journal of Experimental Psychology: Learning, Memory, and Cognition*, **21**, 205–23.

Berger, K. S. (1991) *The Developing Person Through Childhood and Adolescence*, 3rd ed. New York: Worth.

Berk, L. E. (1996) *Infants, Children and Adolescents*, 2nd ed. Boston: Allyn & Bacon.

Berk, L. E. (1997) *Child Development*, 4th ed. Boston: Allyn & Bacon.

Berk, L. E. (2004) *Development Through the Lifespan*. 3rd ed. Boston, MA: Allyn & Bacon.

Berkowitz, S. J. (1986) Effects of instruction in text organization on sixth-grade students' memory for expository reading. *Reading Research Quarterly*, **21**, 161–78.

Berliner, D. C. (1986) In pursuit of the expert pedagogue. *Educational Researcher*, **15**, 5–13.

Berliner, D. C. (1988) Simple views of effective teaching and a simple theory of classroom instruction. In D. Berliner & B. Rosenshine (eds) *Talks to Teachers*. New York: Random House.

Berliner, D. C. (1989) Furthering our understanding of motivation and environments. In C. Ames & R. Ames (eds) *Research on Motivation in Education: Goals and Cognitions (Volume 3)*. Orlando: Academic Press.

Berliner, D. C. & Tikunoff, W. (1976) The California Beginning Teacher Evaluation Study: Overview of the ethnographic study. *Journal of Teacher Education*, **27**, 24–30.

Berlyne, D. E. (1960) *Conflict, Arousal and Curiosity*. New York: McGraw-Hill.

Berndt, T. H. (1999) Friends' influence on students' adjustment to school. *Educational Psychologist*, **34**, 15–28.

Berndt, T. J. (1992) *Child Development*. Orlando: Harcourt Brace Jovanovich.

Berndt, T. J. & Perry, T. B. (1990) Distinctive features and effects of early adolescent friendships. In R. Montmayor, G. Adams & T. Gullotta (eds) *From Childhood to Adolescence: A Transition Period?* New York: Sage.

Bidell, T. R. & Fischer, K. W. (1992) Beyond the stage debate: Action, structure, and variability in Piagetian theory and research. In R. J. Sternberg & C. A. Berg (eds) *Intellectual Development*. New York: Cambridge University Press.

Biehler, R. F. & Snowman, J. (1990) *Psychology Applied to Teaching*, 6th ed. Boston: Houghton Mifflin.

Bigge, J. & Sirvis, B. (1982) Physical and multiple handicaps. In N. Haring (ed.) *Exceptional Children and Youth*. Columbus, OH: Charles E. Merrill.

Bigge, M. L. (1971) *Learning Theories for Teachers*. New York: Harper & Row.

Biggs, J. (1987a) Reflective thinking and school learning. An introduction to the theory and practice of metacognition. *SET Research Information for Teachers*, number 2, item 10.

Biggs, J. (1987b) *The Learning Process Questionnaire: Manual*. Melbourne: ACER.

Biggs, J. (1987c) *Student Approaches to Learning and Studying*. Melbourne: ACER.

Biggs, J. (1988) The role of metacognition in enhancing learning. *Australian Journal of Education*, **32**, 127–38.

Biggs, J. & Collis, K. (1982) *Evaluating the Quality of Learning: The SOLO Taxonomy*. New York: Academic Press.

Biggs, J. B. (1984) Motivational patterns, learning strategies and subjectively perceived success in secondary and tertiary students. In J. R. Kirby (ed.) *Cognitive Strategies and Educational Performance*. New York: Academic Press.

Biggs, J. B. (1991a) Good learning: What is it? In J. B. Biggs (ed.) *Teaching for Learning*. Melbourne: ACER.

Biggs, J. B. (ed.) (1991b) *Teaching for Learning. The View from Cognitive Psychology*. Melbourne: ACER.

Biggs, J. B. & Moore, P. J. (1993) *The Process of Learning*, 3rd ed. Sydney: Prentice Hall.

Biggs, J. B. & Telfer, R. (1987a) *The Process of Learning*, 2nd ed. Sydney: Prentice Hall.

Biggs, J. B. & Telfer, R. (1987b) *Student Approaches to Learning and Studying*. Melbourne: ACER.

Blackburn, M. A. & Miller, R. B. (2000) Predicting academic cheating: The relationship among cheating, motivational goals, cognitive engagement, and classroom goal structures. Paper presented at the Annual Meeting of the American Educational Research Association, New Orleans, April.

Blanck, G. (1990) Vygotsky: The man and his cause. In L. C. Moll (ed.) *Vygotsky and Education*. New York: Cambridge University Press.

Blasi, A. (1980) Bridging moral cognition and moral action: A critical review of the literature. *Psychological Bulletin*, **88**, 1–45.

Bleichrodt, N. & Drenth, P. J. D. (1991) *Contemporary Issues in Cross-Cultural Psychology*. Amsterdam/Lisse: Swets & Zeitlinger.

Bloom, B. S. (ed.) (1956) *Taxonomy of Educational Objectives*. Handbook 1: *Cognitive Domain*. London: Longman.

Bloom, B. S. (1984) The 2 sigma problem: The search for methods of group instruction as effective as one-to-one tutoring. *Educational Researcher*, **13**, 4–16.

Bloom, B. S. (1987) A response to Slavin's mastery learning reconsidered. *Review of Educational Research*, **57**, 507–8.

Bloom, B. S., Hastings, J. T. & Madaus, G. F. (1971) *Handbook on Formative and Summative Evaluation of Learning*. New York: McGraw-Hill.

Bloom, B. S., Krathwohl, D. R. & Masia, B. B. (1964) *Taxonomy of Educational Objectives: The Classification of Educational Objectives*. London: Longman.

Bloom, B. S., Madaus, G. F. & Hastings, J. T. (1981) *Evaluation to Improve Learning*. New York: McGraw-Hill.

Bloom, R. W. (2002) On media violence: Whose facts? Whose misinformation? *American Psychologist*, **57**, 447–8.

Blumenfeld, P. C. (1992) Classroom learning and motivation: Clarifying and expanding goal theory. *Journal of Educational Psychology*, **84**, 272–81.

Bodine, R. J. & Crawford, D. K. (1999) *Developing Emotional Intelligence. A Guide to Behavior Management and Conflict Resolution in Schools.* Champaign, IL: Research Press.

Boekaerts, M. (1995) Self-regulated learning: Bridging the gap between metacognitive and metamotivation theories. *Educational Psychologist*, **30**, 195–200.

Boekaerts, M. (1998) Do culturally rooted self-construals affect students' conceptualization of control over learning? *Educational Psychologist*, **33**, 87–108.

Boggiano, A. K. & Barrett, M. (1992) Gender differences in depression in children as a function of motivational orientation. *Sex Roles*, **26**, 11–17.

Bong, M. (1998) Tests of the Internal/External Frames of Reference Model with subject-specific academic self-efficacy and frame-specific academic self-concepts. *Journal of Educational Psychology*, **90**, 102–10.

Bong, M. & Clark, R. E. (1999) Comparison between self-concept and self-efficacy in academic motivation research. *Educational Psychologist*, **34**, 139–53.

Bornholt, L. J. & Cooney, G. H. (1993) How good am I at school work and compared with whom? *Australian Journal of Education*, **37**, 69–76.

Bosacki, S. L. (2000) Theory of mind and self-concept in preadolescents. Links with gender and language. *Journal of Educational Psychology*, **92**, 709–17.

Boud, D. (1981) Towards student responsibility for learning. In D. Boud (ed.) *Developing Student Autonomy in Learning.* London: Kegan Paul.

Boud, D. (1985) *Studies in Self Assessment. Implications for Teachers in Higher Education. Occasional Publication No. 26.* Sydney: Tertiary Education Research Centre, University of New South Wales.

Bouffard, T. (2000) Changes in self-perception of competence and intrinsic motivation among elementary school children. Paper presented at the annual meeting of the American Educational Research Association, New Orleans, 24–28 April.

Boufoy-Bastick, B. (1997) Using language policies to highlight and contrast the values that shape multicultural societies: Examples from Singapore and Australia. *Australian Journal of Education*, **41**, 59–76.

Boulton, M. J. & Underwood, K. (1992) Bully/victim problems among middle school children. *British Journal of Educational Psychology*, **62**, 73–87.

Bower, G. H., Clark, M., Lesgold, A. M. & Winzenz, D. (1969) Hierarchical retrieval schemes in recall of categorized word lists. *Journal of Verbal Learning and Verbal Behaviour*, **8**, 323–43.

Boyd, R. (1993) Gender differences in gifts and/or talents. *International Journal of Educational Research*, **19**, 51–64.

Boylan, C., Battersby, D., Wallace, A. & Retallick, J. (1991) Understanding exemplary teaching. *SET Research Information for Teachers*, number 1, item 13.

Braaksma, M. A. H., Rijlaarsdam, G. & van den Bergh, H. (2002) Observational learning and the effects of model-observer similarity. *Journal of Educational Psychology*, **94**, 405–15.

Brady, L. (1985) *Models and Methods of Teaching.* Sydney: Prentice Hall.

Braebeck, M. (1982) Moral judgement: Theory and research on differences between males and females. *Developmental Review*, **3**, 274–91.

Braggett, E. (1987) Recent developments in provision for the gifted: Across Australia. In J. Relich & J. Ward (eds) *Academically Gifted-Educationally Disadvantaged? Providing for the Intellectually Gifted and Talented.* Sydney: NSWIER.

Brainerd, C. J. (1978) *Piaget's Theory of Intelligence.* Englewood Cliffs, NJ: Prentice Hall.

Brandt, R. (1990) Overview. *Educational Leadership*, **48**, 3.

Brandt, R. S. (1986) On creativity and thinking skills: A conversation with David Perkins. *Educational Leadership*, **43**, 12–18.

Bransford, J. D. & Schwartz, D. L. (1999) Rethinking transfer: A simple proposal with multiple implications. *Review of Research in Education*, **24**, 61–100.

Bransgrove, T. (1990) Responsibilities of Australian teachers in law: Some implications for teacher training. In M. Bezzina & J. Butcher (eds) *The Changing Face of Professional Education. Collected Papers of the AARE Annual Conference, Sydney University, 1990.* Sydney: AARE.

Brantlinger, E. (1997) Using ideology: Cases of nonrecognition of the politics of research and practice in special education. *Review of Educational Research*, **67**, 425–59.

Bråten, I., Samuelstuen, M. S. & Strømsø, H. I. (2004) Do students' self-efficacy beliefs moderate the effects of performance goals on self-regulatory strategy use? *Educational Psychology*, **24**, 231–47.

Brattesani, K. A., Weinstein, R. S. & Marshall, H. H. (1984) Student perceptions of differential teacher treatments as moderators of teacher expectations effects. *Journal of Educational Psychology*, **76**, 238–47.

Braun, C. (1976) Teacher expectations: Social psychological dynamics. *Review of Educational Research*, **46**, 185–213.

Brentnall, R. & Hodge, A. (1984) *Policies on Multicultural Education in Australia: An Overview.* Sydney: Sydney CAE.

Brim, O. G. & Kagan, J. (eds) (1980) *Constancy and Change in Human Development.* Cambridge, MA: Harvard University Press.

Brizuela, B. M. & Garcia-Sellers, M. J. (1999) School adaptation: A triangular process. *American Educational Research Journal*, **36**, 345–70.

Broadbent, C. (1989) Personality and learning. In P. Langford (ed.) *Educational Psychology. An Australian Perspective.* Sydney: Longman Cheshire.

Brooks, J. G. (1990) Teachers and students: Constructivists forging new connections. *Educational Leadership*, **48**, 69–71.

Brooks-Gunn, J. & Furstenberg, F. F. (1989) Adolescent sexual behavior. *American Psychologist*, **44**, 249–57.

Brooks-Gunn, J. & Petersen, A. C. (eds) (1983) *Girls at Puberty. Biological and Psychosocial Perspectives.* New York: Plenum Press.

Brooks-Gunn, J. & Warren, M. P. (1989) The psychological significance of secondary sex characteristics in 9- to 11-year-old girls. *Child Development*, **59**, 161–9.

Brophy, J. (1981) Teacher praise: A functional analysis. *Review of Educational Research*, **51**, 5–32.

Brophy, J. (1983) Research on the self-fulfilling prophecy and teacher expectations. *Journal of Educational Psychology*, **75**, 631–61.

Brophy, J. (1985a) Teacher–student interactions. In J. Dusek (ed.) *Teacher Expectancies.* Hillsdale, NJ: Lawrence Erlbaum.

Brophy, J. (1985b) Teachers' expectations, motives, and goals for working with problem students. In C. Ames & R. Ames (eds) *Research on Motivation in Education: The Classroom Milieu (Volume 2).* Orlando: Academic Press.

Brophy, J. (1986) Teacher influences on student achievement. *American Psychologist*, **41**, 1069–77.

Brophy, J. (1987) Synthesis of research on strategies for motivating students to learn. *Educational Leadership*, **45**, 40–8.

Brophy, J. (1988) Research linking teacher behavior to student achievement: Potential implications for instruction of Chapter 1 students. *Educational Psychologist*, **23**, 235–86.

Brophy, J. & Evertson, C. (1976) *Learning from Teaching: A Developmental Perspective*. Boston: Allyn & Bacon.

Brophy, J. & Good, T. L. (1986) Teacher behavior and student achievement. In M. C. Wittrock (ed.) *Handbook of Research on Teaching*. New York: Macmillan.

Brouwer, N. & Korthagen, F. (2005) Can teacher education make a difference? *American Educational Research Journal*, **42**, 153–224.

Brown, A. L. & Campione, J. C. (1986) Psychological theory and the study of learning disabilities. *American Psychologist*, **41**, 1059–68.

Brown, A. L. & Palincsar, A. S. (1989) Guided, cooperative learning and individual knowledge acquisition. In L. B. Resnick (ed.) *Knowing, Learning, and Instruction: Essays in Honor of Robert Glaser*. Hillsdale, NJ: Lawrence Erlbaum.

Brown, M. J. (1982) The Victorian accelerated secondary programme with particular attention to mathematics. *Unicorn*, **8**, 273–80.

Brown, S. K. (1983) The sex factor in the selection of intellectually talented youth. *Education Research and Perspectives*, **10**, 85–103.

Bruner, J. S. (1960) *The Process of Education*. Cambridge, MA: Harvard University Press.

Bruner, J. S. (1961) The act of discovery. *Harvard Educational Review*, **31**, 21–32.

Bruner, J. S. (1966) *Toward a Theory of Instruction*. London: Belnap Press.

Bruner, J. S. (1974) *Beyond the Information Given*. London: Allen & Unwin.

Bruner, J. S. (1985) Models of the learner. *Educational Researcher*, **14**, 5–8.

Bryant, A. L. & Zimmerman, M. A. (2002) Examining the effects of academic beliefs and behaviors on changes in substance use among urban adolescents. *Journal of Educational Psychology*, **94**, 621–37.

Bryk, A. S. & Hermanson, K. L. (1993) Educational indicator systems: Observations on their structure, interpretation, and use. *Review of Research in Education*, **19**, 451–84.

Buchanan, C. M., Eccles, J. S. & Becker, J. B. (1992) Are adolescents the victims of raging hormones? Evidence for the activational effects of hormones on moods and behavior at adolescence. *Psychological Bulletin*, **111**, 62–107.

Buchs, C., Butera, F. & Mugny, G. (2004) Resource interdependence, student interactions and performance in cooperative learning. *Educational Psychology*, **24**, 291–314.

Buck, R. & Green, Y. (1993) Teacher–researcher collaboration to enhance student motivation and learning. Paper presented at the annual meeting of the American Educational Research Association in Atlanta, April.

Bullivant, B. M. (1986) Are Anglo Australian students becoming the new self-deprived in comparison with ethnics? New evidence challenges conventional wisdom. In *Theory, Structure and Action in Education*, papers of the Annual Conference of the Australian Association for Research in Education, Ormond College, University of Melbourne, November 1986. Melbourne: AARE.

Bullivant, B. M. (1988a) Missing the empirical forest for the ideological trees: A commentary on Kalantzis and Cope. *Journal of Intercultural Studies*, **9**, 59–69.

Bullivant, B. M. (1988b) The ethnic success ethic challenges conventional wisdom about immigrant disadvantages in education. *Australian Journal of Education*, **32**, 223–43.

Burkam, D. T., Lee, V. E. & Smerdon, B. A. (1997) Gender and science learning early in high school: Subject matter and laboratory experiences. *American Educational Research Journal*, **34**, 297–331.

Burnett, P. C. & Howard, K. (2002) Discriminating between primary school students with high and low self-esteem using personal and classroom variables. *The Australian Educational and Developmental Psychologist*, **19**, 18–29.

Bushman, B. J. & Anderson, C. A. (2001) Media violence and the American public. *American Psychologist*, **56**, 477–89.

Bushnell, J. A., Wells, J. E., Hornblow, A. R., Oakley-Brown, M. A. *et al.* (1990) Prevalence of three bulimia syndromes in the general population. *Psychological Medicine*, **20**, 671–80.

Bushnell, J. A., Wells, J. E., McKenzie, J. M., Hornblow, A. R. *et al.* (1994) Bulimia comorbidity in the general population and in the clinic. *Psychological Medicine*, **24**, 605–11.

Butler, D. L. (1998) The strategic content learning approach to promoting self-regulated learning: A report of three studies. *Journal of Educational Psychology*, **90**, 682–97.

Butler, D. L. & Winne, P. H. (1995) Feedback and self-regulated learning: A theoretical synthesis. *Review of Educational Research*, **65**, 245–81.

Butler, K. (1986) *Learning and Teaching Style*. Australia: Hawker Brownlow.

Butler, R. (1987) Task-involving and ego-involving properties of evaluation: Effects of different feedback conditions on motivational perceptions, interest, and performance. *Journal of Educational Psychology*, **79**, 474–82.

Butler, R. (1988) Enhancing and undermining intrinsic motivation: The effects of task-involving and ego-involving evaluation on interest and performance. *British Journal of Educational Psychology*, **58**, 1–14.

Butler, S. (1990) *The Exceptional Child*. Sydney: Harcourt Brace Jovanovich.

Byrne, B. (1996). *Measuring Self-concept across the Life Span. Issues and Instrumentation.* Washington, DC: American Psychological Association.

Byrne, B. (2002) Validating the measurement and structure of self-concept: Snapshots of past, present, and future research. *American Psychologist*, **57**, 897–909.

Byrne, D. G., Byrne, A. E. & Reinhart, M. I. (1993) Psychosocial correlates of adolescent cigarette smoking: Personality or environment. *Australian Journal of Psychology*, **45**, 87–95.

Byrne, D. G. & Reinhart, M. I. (1998) Psychological determinants of adolescent smoking behaviour: A prospective study. *Australian Journal of Psychology*, **50**, 29–34.

Cahill, D. & Ewen, J. (1987) *Ethnic Youth: Their Assets and Aspirations*. Canberra: AGPS.

Cairns, L. (1995) Analysis and modification of behavior. In L. W. Anderson (ed.) *International Encyclopedia of Teaching and Teacher Education*, 2nd ed. Tarrytown, NY: Pergamon.

Cambourne, B. & Turbill, J. (1990) Assessment in whole language classrooms: Theory into practice. *Elementary School Journal*, **90**, 337–49.

Cameron, J. & Pierce, W. D. (1994) Reinforcement, reward, and intrinsic motivation: A meta-analysis. *Review of Educational Research*, **64**, 363–423.

Cameron, J. & Pierce, W. D. (1996) The debate about rewards and intrinsic motivation: Protests and accusations do not alter the results. *Review of Educational Research*, **66**, 39–51.

Campbell, L., Campbell, B. & Dickinson, D. (1999) *Teaching and Learning Through Multiple Intelligences*, 2nd ed. Boston: Allyn & Bacon.

Campbell, S. J. *et al.* (1992) *Unlocking Australia's Language Potential. Profiles of Nine Key Languages in Australia: Arabic (Volume 1).* Deakin: The National Languages and Literacy Institute of Australia.

Canfield, R. L. & Ceci, S. J. (1992) Integrating learning into a theory of intellectual development. In R. J. Sternberg & C. A. Berg (eds) *Intellectual Development*. New York: Cambridge University Press.

Canter, L. (1990) Assertive discipline: More than names on a board and marbles in a jar. In *Educational Psychology 90/91 Annual Editions*. Guilford, CT: Duskin.

Canter, L. & Canter, M. (1976) *Assertive Discipline: A Take Charge Approach for Today's Educator*. Seal Beach, CA: Canter & Associates.

Canter, L. & Canter, M. (1992) *Assertive Discipline: Positive Behavior Management for Today's Classroom*. Santa Monica, CA: Lee Canter & Associates.

Caprara, G. V., Barbaranelli, C., Borgogni, L. & Steca, P. (2003). Efficacy beliefs as determinants of teachers' job satisfaction. *Journal of Educational Psychology*, **95**, 821–32.

Capuzzi, D. (1989) *Adolescent Suicide Prevention*. Ann Arbor, MI: ERIC Counselling and Personnel Services Clearing House.

Care, E. (1996) Implications of learning style and interests for educational programs. Paper presented at the 31st Annual Conference of the Australian Psychological Society, Sydney, 25–29 September.

Carey, S. (1987) Theory change in childhood. In B. Inhelder, D. de Caprona & A. Cornu-Wells (eds) *Piaget Today*. London: Lawrence Erlbaum.

Carney, R. N. & Levin, J. R. (2000) Mnemonic instruction, with a focus on transfer. *Journal of Educational Psychology*, **92**, 783–90.

Carney, R. N., Levin, J. R. & Morrison, C. R. (1988) Mnemonic learning of artists and their paintings. *American Educational Research Journal*, **25**, 107–25.

Carr, K. & Ritchie, G. (1991) Evaluating learning in mathematics. *SET Research Information for Teachers*, number 1, item 15.

Carver, C. S., Scheier, M. F. & Weintraub, J. K. (1989) Assessing coping strategies: A theoretically based approach. *Journal of Personality and Social Psychology*, **56**, 267–83.

Case, R. (1985a) *Intellectual Development: A Systematic Reinterpretation*. New York: Academic Press.

Case, R. (1985b) *Intellectual Development. Birth to Adulthood*. Orlando: Academic Press.

Case, R. (1992) Neo-Piagetian theories of child development. In R. J. Sternberg & C. A. Berg (eds) *Intellectual Development*. New York: Cambridge University Press.

Casey, W., Jones, D., Kugler, B. & Watkins, B. (1988) Integration of Down's syndrome children in the primary school: A longitudinal study of cognitive development and academic attainments. *British Journal of Educational Psychology*, **587**, 279–86.

Cassidy, S. (2004) Learning styles: An overview of theories, models, and measures. *Educational Psychology*, **24**, 419–44.

Castles, S., Kalantzis, M., Cope, B. & Morrissey, M. (1988) *Mistaken Identity. Multiculturalism and the Demise of Nationalism in Australia*. Sydney: Pluto Press.

Catania, A. C. (1980) Operant theory: Skinner. In G. M. Gazda & R. J. Corsini (eds) *Theories of Learning*. Itasca, IL: F. E. Peacock.

Cavior, N. & Dokecki, P. (1973) Physical attractiveness, perceived attitude similarity, and academic achievement as contributors to interpersonal attraction among adolescents. *Developmental Psychology*, **9**, 44–54.

Cavior, N. & Lombardi, D. A. (1973) Developmental aspects of judgment of physical attractiveness in children. *Developmental Psychology*, **8**, 67–71.

Cazden, C. B. (1990) Differential treatment in New Zealand: Reflections on research in minority education. *Teaching and Teacher Education*, **6**, 291–303.

Cellerier, G. (1987) Structures and functions. In B. Inhelder, D. de Caprona & A. Cornu-Wells (eds) *Piaget Today*. London: Lawrence Erlbaum.

Center, Y., Ward, J., Ferguson, C., Conway, B. & Linfoot, K. (1989) *The Integration of Children with Disabilities into Regular Schools: A Naturalistic Study*. Stage 2 Report. Macquarie University: Special Education Centre.

Cerezo, F. & Ato, M. (2005) Bullying in Spanish and English pupils: A sociometric perspective using the BULL-S questionnaire. *British Journal of Educational Psychology*, **25**, 353–67.

Chambers, S. M. & Clarke, V. A. (1987) Is inequity cumulative? The relationship between disadvantaged group membership and students' computing experience, knowledge, attitudes and intentions. *Journal of Education Computing Research*, **3**, 495–518.

Chan, D. W. (2003) Multiple intelligences and perceived self-efficacy among Chinese secondary school teachers in Hong Kong. *Educational Psychology*, **23**, 522–33.

Chao, R. K. (1994) Beyond parental control and authoritarian parenting style: Understanding Chinese parenting through the cultural notion of training. *Child Development*, **65**, 1111–19.

Chapman, J. W. (1988) Learning disabled children's self-concepts. *Review of Educational Research*, **58**, 347–71.

Charles, C. M. (1999) *Building Classroom Discipline*, 6th ed. New York: Longman.

Chaskin, R. & Rauner, D. (1995) Youth and caring: An introduction. *Phi Delta Kappan*, **76**, 667–74.

Cherney, I. D., Kelly-Vance, L., Glover, K. G., Ruane, A. & Ryalls, B. O. (2003) The effects of stereotyped toys and gender on play assessment in children aged 18–47 months. *Educational Psychology*, **23**, 95–106.

Chess, S. & Gordon, S. G. (1984) Psychosocial development and human variance. In E. W. Gordon (ed.) *Review of Research in Education (Volume 11)*. Washington, DC: AERA.

Chi, M. T. H., Glaser, R. & Rees, E. (1982) Expertise in problem solving. In R. Sternberg (ed.) *Advances in the Psychology of Human Intelligence (Volume 1)*. Hillsdale, NJ: Lawrence Erlbaum.

Chinn, C. A. & Brewer, W. F. (1993) The role of anomalous data in knowledge acquisition: A theoretical framework and implications for science instruction. *Review of Educational Research*, **63**, 1–49.

Chinn, C. A. & Malhotra, B. A. (2002) Children's responses to anomalous scientific data: How is conceptual change impeded? *Journal of Educational Psychology*, **94**, 327–43.

Chiu, C., Salili, F. & Hong, Y. (2001) Multiple competencies and self-regulated learning: Implications for multicultural education. Greenwich, CT: Information Age Publishing.

Chiu, M. M. (2004) Adapting teacher interventions to student needs during cooperative learning: How to improve student problem solving and time on-task. *American Educational Research Journal*, **41**, 365–99.

Chmielewski, T. L. & Dansereau, D. F. (1998) Enhancing the recall of text: Knowledge mapping training promotes implicit transfer. *Journal of Educational Psychology*, **3**, 407–13.

Choo, O. A. & Tan, E. (2000) Fathers' role in the school success of adolescents: A Singapore study. In D. M. McInerney & S. Van Etten (eds) *Research on Sociocultural Influences on Motivation and Learning*. Greenwich, CT: Information Age Press.

Clyne, M. (1983) Bilingual education as a model for community languages in primary schools. *Journal of Intercultural Studies*, **4**, 23–35.

Clyne, M. (1988) Bilingual education. What we can learn from the past? *Australian Journal of Education*, **32**, 95–114.

Coates, B., Pusser, H. E. & Goodman, I. (1976) The influence of

'Sesame Street' and 'Mister Rogers' Neighborhood' on children's social behavior in the preschool. *Child Development*, **47**, 138–44.

Cobb, P. (1994) Where is the mind? Constructivist and sociocultural perspectives on mathematical development. *Educational Researcher*, **23**, 13–20.

Cobb, P. & Bowers, J. (1999) Cognitive and situated learning perspectives in theory and practice. *Educational Researcher*, **28**, 4–15.

Cognition and Technology Group at Vanderbilt (1993) Integrated media: Towards a theoretical framework for utilizing their potential. *Journal of Special Education Technology*, **12**, 71–85.

Cognition and Technology Group at Vanderbilt (1997) *THE JASPER PROJECT: Lessons in Curriculum, Instruction, Assessment, and Professional Development*. Mahwah, NJ: Lawrence Erlbaum.

Cohen, E. G. (1986) *Designing Group Work: Strategies for the Heterogeneous Classroom*. New York: Teachers College Press.

Cohen, E. G. (1994a) *Designing Group Work: Strategies for the Heterogeneous Classroom*, 2nd ed. New York: Teachers College Press.

Cohen, E. G. (1994b) Restructuring the classroom: Conditions for productive small groups. *Review of Educational Research*, **64**, 1–35.

Cole, D. A. (1989) Psychopathology of adolescent suicide: hopelessness, coping beliefs and depression. *Journal of Abnormal Psychology*, **98**, 248–55.

Cole, D. A., Vandercook, T. & Rynders, J. (1988) Comparison of two peer interaction programs: Children with and without severe disabilities. *American Educational Research Journal*, **25**, 415–39.

Cole, P. G. & Chan, L. K. S. (1987) *Teaching Principles and Practice*. Sydney: Prentice Hall.

Cole, P. G. & Chan, L. K. S. (1990) *Methods and Strategies for Special Education*. Sydney: Prentice Hall.

Collins, C., Kenway, J. & McCleod, J. (2000) Gender debates we still have to have. *Australian Educational Researcher*, **27**, 37–48.

Collins, J. K. & Plahn, M. R. (1988) Recognition accuracy, stereotypic preference, aversion, and subjective judgment of body appearance in adolescents and young adults. *Journal of Youth and Adolescence*, **17**, 317–34.

Collis, K. (1989) Evaluation. In P. Langford (ed.) *Educational Psychology. An Australian Perspective*. Sydney: Longman Cheshire.

Collis, K. & Biggs, J. (1986) Using the SOLO taxonomy. *SET Research Information for Teachers*, number 1, item 3.

Coloroso, B. (1994) *Kids are Worth It! Giving your Child the Gift of Inner Discipline*. New York: William Morrow.

Combs, M. L. & Slaby, D. A. (1977) Social-skills training with children. In B. Lahey & A. E. Kazdin (eds) *Advances in Clinical Child Psychology (Volume 1)*. New York: Plenum Press.

Commonwealth Schools Commission (1983) *Participation and Equity in Australian Schools: The Goal of Full Secondary Education*. Canberra: AGPS.

Conger, J. J. (1977) *Adolescence and Youth. Psychological Development in a Changing World*, 2nd ed. New York: Harper & Row.

Conklin, K. R. (1976) Wholes and parts in teaching. In M. L. Silberman, J. S. Allender & J. M. Yanoff (eds) *Real Learning. A Sourcebook for Teachers*. Boston: Little, Brown & Co.

Connell, J. P. & Wellborn, J. G. (1990) Competence, autonomy, and relatedness: A motivational analysis of self-system processes. In M. R. Gunnar & L. A. Stroufe (eds) *Minnesota Symposium on Child Psychology (Volume 22)*. Hillsdale, NJ: Lawrence Erlbaum.

Conner, K. *et al.* (1985) Using formative testing at the classroom, school, and district levels. *Educational Leadership*, **43**, 63–7.

Conners, R., Nettle, E. & Placing, K. (1990) Learning to become a teacher: An analysis of student teachers' perspectives on teaching and their developing craft knowledge. In M. Bezzina & J. Butcher (eds) *The Changing Face of Professional Education. Collected Papers of the AARE Annual Conference, Sydney University, 1990*. Sydney: AARE.

Connolly, K. & Dalgleish, M. (1989) The emergence of a tool-using skill in infancy. *Developmental Psychology*, **25**, 894–912.

Conrade, G. & Ho, R. (2001) Differential parenting styles for fathers and mothers: Differential treatment for sons and daughters. *Australian Journal of Psychology*, **53**, 29–35.

Constantini, A. F. & Hoving, K. L. (1973) The effectiveness of reward and punishment contingencies on response inhibition. *Journal of Experimental Child Psychology*, **16**, 484–94.

Coolahan, K., Fantuzzo, J., Mendez, J. & McDermott, P. (2000) Preschool peer interactions and readiness to learn: Relations between classroom peer play and learning behaviors and conduct. *Journal of Educational Psychology*, **92**, 458–65.

Cooper, M. A. (1999) Classroom choices from a cognitive perspective on peer learning. In A. M. O'Donnell & A. King (eds) *Cognitive Perspectives on Peer Learning*. Mahwah, NJ: Lawrence Erlbaum.

Copeland, A. P. & Weissbrod, C. S. (1980) Effects of modeling on behavior related to hyperactivity. *Journal of Educational Psychology*, **71**, 875–83.

Copeland, W. D. (1987) Classroom management and student teachers' cognitive abilities: A relationship. *American Educational Research Journal*, **24**, 219–36.

Corbin, C. B. (ed.) (1980) *A Textbook of Motor Development*. Dubuque, Iowa: Wm C. Brown.

Cordingley, A., Lai, Y. C., Pemberton, M., Smith, J. & Volet, S. (1998) Regulation of learning in vocational education: An exploratory study. *Issues in Educational Research*, **8**, 15–32.

Corkill, A. J. (1992) Advance organizers: Facilitators of recall. *Educational Psychology Review*, **4**, 33–67.

Corno, L. (1992) Encouraging students to take responsibility for learning and performance. *The Elementary School Journal*, **93**, 69–83.

Corno, L. & Mandinach, E. B. (2004) What we have learned about student engagement in the past twenty years. In D. M. McInerney & S. Van Etten (eds) *Research on Sociocultural Influences on Motivation and Learning (Volume 4), Big Theories Revisited*. Greenwich, CT: Information Age Publishing.

Corno, L. & Rohrkemper, M. M. (1985) The intrinsic motivation to learn in classrooms. In C. Ames & R. Ames (eds) *Research on Motivation in Education: The Classroom Milieu (Volume 2)*. Orlando: Academic Press.

Corno, L. & Snow, R. E. (1986) Adapting teaching to individual differences among learners. In M. C. Wittrock (ed.) *Handbook of Research on Teaching*, 3rd ed. New York: Macmillan.

Corson, D. (1993) Restructuring minority schooling. *Australian Journal of Education*, **37**, 46–68.

Costa, A. L. (1984) Mediating the metacognitive. *Educational Leadership*, **42**, 57–62.

Costa, A. L. & Marzano, R. (1987) Teaching the language of thinking. *Educational Leadership*, **45**, 29–33.

Cotton, J. L. & Cook, M. S. (1982) Meta-analysis and the effects of various reward systems: Some different conclusions from Johnson *et al. Psychological Bulletin*, **92**, 176–83.

Covington, M. V. (1984) The motive for self-worth. In R. Ames & C. Ames (eds) *Research on Motivation in Education: Student Motivation (Volume 1)*. Orlando: Academic Press.

Covington, M. V. (1992) *Making the Grade. A Self-Worth Perspective on Motivation and School Reform*. New York: Cambridge University Press.

Covington, M. V. (1999) Caring about learning: The nature and nurturing of subject-matter appreciation. *Educational Psychologist*, **34**, 127–36.

Covington, M. V. (2000) Goal theory, motivation, and school achievement: An integrative review. *Annual Review of Psychology*, **51**, 171–200.

Covington, M. V. (2002a) Rewards and intrinsic motivation: A needs-based developmental perspective. In T. Urdan & F. Pajares (eds) *Motivation of Adolescents*. New York: Academic Press.

Covington, M. V. (2002b) The developmental course of achievement motivation: A needs-based approach. In A. Wigfield & J. S. Eccles (eds) *Development of Achievement Motivation*. San Diego, CA: Academic Press.

Covington, M. V. (2004) Self-worth theory goes to college: Or do our motivation theories motivate? In D. M. McInerney & S. Van Etten (eds) *Research on Sociocultural Influences on Motivation and Learning (Volume 4), Big Theories Revisited*. Greenwich, CT: Information Age Publishing.

Covington, M. V. & Omelich, C. L. (1979). Effort: The double-edged sword in school achievement. *Journal of Educational Psychology*, **71**, 169–82.

Covington, M. V. & Omelich, C. L. (1984a) An empirical examination of Weiner's critique of attribution research. *Journal of Educational Psychology*, **76**, 1214–25.

Covington, M. V. & Omelich, C. L. (1984b) Task-oriented versus competitive learning structures: Motivational and performance consequences. *Journal of Educational Psychology*, **76**, 1038–50.

Covington, M. V. & Omelich, C. L. (1987) 'I knew it cold before the exam': A test of the anxiety-blockage hypothesis. *Journal of Educational Psychology*, **79**, 393–400.

Cowan, P. A. (1978) *Piaget: With Feeling. Cognitive, Social and Emotional Dimensions*. New York: Holt, Rinehart & Winston.

Cox, B. D. (1997) The rediscovery of the active learner in adaptive contexts: A developmental-historical analysis of transfer of training. *Educational Psychologist*, **32**, 41–55.

Cramer, P. (1980) The development of sexual identity. *Journal of Personality Assessment*, **44**, 601–12.

Craven, R. G., Marsh, H. W. & Print, M. (2000) Gifted, streamed and mixed ability programs for gifted students: Impact on self-concept, motivation, and achievement. *Australian Journal of Education*, **44**, 51–75.

Cravioto, J. & DeLicardie, E. R. (1975) Environmental and learning deprivation in children with learning disabilities. In W. M. Cruickshank & D. P. Hallahan (eds) *Perceptual and Learning Disabilities in Children (Volume 2)*. Syracuse, NY: Syracuse University Press.

Crooks, T. J. (1988) The impact of classroom evaluation practices on students. *Review of Educational Research*, **58**, 438–81.

Crooks, T. J. & Mahalski, P. A. (1986) Relationships among assessment practices, study methods, and grades obtained. In J. Jones & M. Horsburgh (eds) *Research and Development in Higher Education (Volume 8)*. Sydney: Higher Education Research and Development Society of Australasia.

Cropley, A. J. (1993a) Creativity as an element of giftedness. *International Journal of Educational Research*, **19**, 17–30.

Cropley, A. J. (1993b) Giftedness: Recent thinking. *International Journal of Educational Research*, **19**, 89–97.

Cruickshank, W. M., Hallahan, D. & Bice, H. V. (1976) The evaluation of intelligence. In W. M. Cruickshank (ed.) *Cerebral Palsy: A Developmental Disability*, 3rd ed. Syracuse, NY: Syracuse University Press.

Csikszentmihalyi, M. (1975) *Beyond Boredom and Anxiety*. San Francisco: Jossey-Bass.

Csikszentmihalyi, M. & Nakamura, J. (1989) The dynamics of intrinsic motivation: A study of adolescents. In C. Ames & R. Ames (eds) *Research on Motivation in Education: Goals and Cognitions (Volume 3)*. Orlando: Academic Press.

Cummings, R., Dyas, L., Maddux, C. D. & Kohman, A. (2001) Principled moral reasoning and behavior of preservice teacher education students. *American Educational Research Journal*, **38**, 143–58.

Cummins, J. (1999) Alternative paradigms in bilingual education research: Does theory have a place? *Educational Researcher*, **28**, 26–32.

Cunningham, T. H. & Graham, C. R. (2000) Increasing native English vocabulary recognition through Spanish immersion: Cognate transfer from foreign to first language. *Journal of Educational Psychology*, **92**, 37–49.

Curry, L. (1990) A critique of the research on learning styles. *Educational Leadership*, **48**, 51–5.

Cusimano, D. & Thompson, J. (1997) Body image and body shape ideals in magazines. *Sex Roles*, **37**, 701–21.

Cutler, A. B. (1993) The first year of teaching: Developing a teacher persona. Paper presented at the Annual Meeting of the American Educational Research Association, Atlanta, Georgia, April.

Cziko, G. A. (1992) The evaluation of bilingual education. From necessity and probability to possibility. *Educational Researcher*, **21**, 10–15.

Dahl, T. I., Bals, M. E. & Turi, A. L. (2005) Are students' beliefs about knowledge and learning associated with their reported use of learning strategies? *British Journal of Educational Psychology*, **75**, 257–73.

Dai, D. Y., Moon, S. M. & Feldhusen, J. F. (1998) Achievement motivation and gifted students: A social cognitive perspective. *Educational Psychologist*, **33**, 45–63.

Dall'Alba, G. (1986) Learning strategies and the learner's approach to a problem solving task. *Research in Science Education*, **16**, 11–20.

Dalton, D. W., Hannafin, M. J. & Hooper, S. (1989) The effects of individual versus cooperative computer-assisted instruction on student performance and attitudes. *Educational Technology Research and Development*, **37**, 15–24.

Dalton, J. (1985) *Adventures in Thinking*. Melbourne: Thomas Nelson.

Dalton, J. (1992) *Adventures in Thinking: Creative Thinking and Cooperative Talk in Small Groups*. Melbourne: Thomas Nelson.

Damon, W. (1980) Patterns of change in children's social reasoning: A two-year longitudinal study. *Child Development*, **51**, 1010–17.

Damon, W. (1983) *Social and Personality Development*. New York: W. W. Norton.

Damon, W. (1984) Peer education: The untapped potential. *Journal of Applied Developmental Psychology*, **5**, 331–43.

Dandy, J. & Nettelbeck, T. (2000) The model student? An investigation of Chinese Australian students' academic achievement, studying, and causal attributions for academic success and failure. *Australian Psychologist*, **35**, 208–15.

Daniel, W. A. (1983) Pubertal changes in adolescence. In J. Brooks-Gunn & A. C. Petersen (eds) *Girls at Puberty. Biological and Psychosocial Perspectives*. New York: Plenum Press.

Dansereau, D. F. (1985) Learning strategy research. In J. W. Segal,

S. F. Chipman & R. Glaser (eds) *Thinking and Learning Skills (Volume 1)*. Hillsdale, NJ: Lawrence Erlbaum.

Dansereau, D. F. (1988) Cooperative learning strategies. In C. E. Weinstein, E. T. Goetz & P. A. Alexander (eds) *Learning and Study Strategies*. San Diego, CA: Academic Press.

Dansereau, D. F., O'Donnell, A. M. & Lambiotte, J. G. (1988) Concept maps and scripted peer cooperation: Interactive tools for improving science and technical education. Paper presented at the Annual Meeting of the American Educational Research Association, New Orleans, LA.

Darley, J. & Fazio, R. (1980) Expectancy confirmation processes arising in the social interaction sequence. *American Psychologist*, **35**, 867–81.

Dart, B. C. & Clarke, J. A. (1990) Modifying the learning environment of students to enhance personal learning. In M. Bezzina & J. Butcher (eds) *The Changing Face of Professional Education. Collected Papers of the AARE Annual Conference, Sydney University, 1990*. Sydney: AARE.

Dasen, P. R. (1972a) The development of conservation in Aboriginal children: A replication study. *International Journal of Psychology*, 7, 75–85.

Dasen, P. R. (1972b) Cross-cultural Piagetian research: A summary. *Journal of Cross-Cultural Psychology*, **3**, 23–39.

Dasen, P. R. (1974) The influence of ecology, culture and European contact on cognitive development in Australian Aborigines. In J. W. Berry & P. R. Dasen (eds) *Culture and Cognition*. London: Methuen.

Dasen, P. R. (1975) Concrete operational development in three cultures. *Journal of Cross-Cultural Psychology*, **6**, 156–72.

Dasen, P. R. & Heron, A. (1981) Cross-cultural tests of Piaget's theory. In H. C. Triandis & A. Heron (eds) *Handbook of Cross-Cultural Psychology: Developmental Psychology (Volume 4)*. Boston: Allyn & Bacon.

Davey, B. & McBride, S. (1986) Effects of question-generation training on reading comprehension. *Journal of Educational Psychology*, **78**, 256–62.

Davidson, G. R. (1984) Cognitive testing of educational minorities: A search for alternatives. *Australian Educational and Developmental Psychologist*, **1**, 39–53.

Davidson, N. (1991) An overview of research on cooperative learning related to mathematics. *Journal for Research in Mathematics Education*, **22**, 362–5.

Davies, E. & Furnham, A. (1986) The dieting and body shape concerns of adolescent females. *Journal of Child Psychology and Psychiatry*, **27**, 417–28.

Davies, E. & McGlade, M. (1982) Cultural values affecting the child at school. In J. Sherwood (ed.) *Aboriginal Education. Issues and Innovations. Perspectives in Multicultural Education (Volume 2)*. Perth: Creative Research.

Davis, A. (1992) Suicidal behaviour among adolescents: Its nature and prevention. In R. Kosky, H. S. Eshkevari & G. Kneebone (eds) *Breaking Out: Challenges in Adolescent Mental Health in Australia*. Canberra: AGPS.

Davis, H. (2003) Conceptualizing the role and influence of student–teacher relationships on children's social and cognitive development. *Educational Psychologist*, **38**, 207–34.

Davis, H. L. & Pratt, C. (1995) The development of children's theory of mind: The working memory explanation. *Australian Journal of Psychology*, **47**, 25–31.

Davydov, V. (1995) The influence of L. S. Vygotsky on education theory, research, and practice (translated by S. T. Kerr). *Educational Researcher*, **24**, 12–21.

de Charms, R. (1968) *Personal Causation*. New York: Academic Press.

de Charms, R. (1972) Personal causation in the schools. *Journal of Applied Social Psychology*, **2**, 95–113.

de Charms, R. (1976) *Enhancing Motivation: Change in the Classroom*. New York: Irvington.

de Charms, R. (1984) Motivation enhancement in educational settings. In R. Ames & C. Ames (eds) *Research on Motivation in Education: Student Motivation (Volume 1)*. Orlando: Academic Press.

De Jong, T. & Van Joolingen, W. R. (1998) Scientific discovery learning with computer simulations of conceptual domains. *Review of Educational Research*, **68**, 179–201.

de Lemos, M. M. (1969) The development of conservation in Aboriginal children. *International Journal of Psychology*, **4**, 255–69.

de Lemos, M. M. (1990) School entrance age in Australia: The current debate. In M. Bezzina & J. Butcher (eds) *The Changing Face of Professional Education. Collected Papers of the AARE Annual Conference, Sydney University, 1990*. Sydney: AARE.

De Mott, R. M. (1982) Visual impairments. In N. Haring (ed.) *Exceptional Children and Youth*. Columbus, OH: Charles E. Merrill.

De Vries, R. (1997) Piaget's social theory. *Educational Researcher*, **26**, 4–17.

Deci, E. L., Koestner, R. & Ryan, R. M. (2001) Extrinsic rewards and intrinsic motivation in education: Reconsidered once again. *Review of Educational Research*, **71**, 1–27.

Deci, E. L. & Ryan, R. M. (1991) A motivational approach to self: Integration in personality. In R. A. Dienstbier (ed.) *Perspectives on Motivation. Nebraska Symposium on Motivation, 1991*. Lincoln, NB: University of Nebraska Press.

Deci, E. L., Vallerand, R. J., Pelletier, L. G. & Ryan, R. M. (1991) Motivation and education: The self-determination perspective. *Educational Psychologist*, **26**, 325–46.

Delandshere, G. & Petrosky, A. R. (1998) Assessment of complex performances: Limitations of key measurement assumptions. *Educational Researcher*, **27**, 14–24.

Demant, M. S. & Yates, G. C. R. (2003) Primary teachers' attitudes toward the direct instruction construct. *Educational Psychology*, **23**, 483–98.

Demetriou, A. (ed.) (1987) The neo-Piagetian theories of cognitive development: Toward an integration. *International Journal of Psychology*, **22**(5/6) (Special Issue).

Dempster, F. N. (1988) The spacing effect: A case study in the failure to apply the results of psychological research. *American Psychologist*, **43**, 627–34.

Dennis, W. (1973) *Children of the Creche*. New York: Appleton-Century-Crofts.

Department of Employment, Education and Training (1992) *Technology for Australian Schools. Interim Statement*. Canberra: AGPS.

Department of School Education (NSW) (1991) *Who's Going to Teach My Child? A Guide for Parents of Children with Special Needs*. Sydney: Department of School Education.

Deregowski, J. B. (1980) Perception. In H. C. Triandis & A. Heron (eds) *Handbook of Cross-Cultural Psychology: Basic Processes (Volume 3)*. Boston: Allyn & Bacon.

Derry, S. J. (1989) Putting learning strategies to work. *Educational Leadership*, **46**, 4–10.

Derry, S. J. (1996) Cognitive schema theory in the constructivist debate. *Educational Psychologist*, **31**, 163–74.

Derry, S. J. & Murphy, D. A. (1986) Designing systems that train learning ability: From theory to practice. *Review of Educational Research*, **56**, 1–39.

Desimone, L. (1999) Linking parent involvement with student achievement: Do race and income matter? *Journal of Educational Research*, **93**, 11–30.

Desmedt, E. & Valcke, M. (2004) Mapping the learning styles 'jungle': An overview of the literature based on citation analysis. *Educational Psychology*, **24**, 445–64.

Deutsch, D. (1979) The improvement of children's oral reading through the use of teacher modeling. *Journal of Learning Disabilities*, **12**, 172–5.

Deutsch, M. (1979) Education and distributive justice: Some reflections on grading systems. *American Psychologist*, **34**, 391–401.

DeVries, R. (1997) Piaget's social theory. *Educational Researcher*, **26**, 4–17.

Diaz, R. M. (1983) Thought and two languages: The impact of bilingualism on cognitive development. In E. W. Gordon (ed.) *Review of Research in Education (Volume 10)*. Washington: AERA.

Diaz, R. M., Neal, C. J. & Amaya-Williams, M. (1990) The social origins of self-regulation. In L. C. Moll (ed.) *Vygotsky and Education*. Cambridge: Cambridge University Press.

Diehl, D. S., Lemerise, S. L., Caverly, S. R., Roberts, J. & Ramsey, S. (1998) Peer relations and school adjustment in ungraded primary children. *Journal of Educational Psychology*, **90**, 506–15.

Diener, C. I. & Dweck, C. S. (1978) An analysis of learned helplessness: Continuous changes in performance, strategy, and achievement cognitions following failure. *Journal of Personality and Social Psychology*, **36**, 451–62.

DiGuilio, R. (1995) *Positive classroom management*. Thousand Oaks, CA: Corwin Press.

Dillon, J. T. (1984) Research on questioning and discussion. *Educational Leadership*, **42**, 50–6.

DiMartino, E. C. (1989) The growth of moral judgement in young children: The role of culture. *Education*, **109**, 262–7.

Dingfelder, S. F. (2005) Fuzzy math. *Monitor on Psychology*, **36**, 30–1.

Dion, K. (1972) Physical attractiveness and evaluation of children's transgressions. *Journal of Personality and Social Psychology*, **24**, 207–13.

Diseth, A. & Martinsen, Ø. (2003) Approaches to learning, cognitive style, and motives as predictors of academic achievement. *Educational Psychology*, **23**, 195–207.

Dochy, F., Segers, M. & Buehl, M. (1999) The relation between assessment practices and outcomes of studies: The case of research on prior knowledge. *Review of Educational Research*, **69**, 145–86.

Dockett, S. & Lambert, P. (1996) *The Importance of Play*. Sydney: Board of Studies, NSW.

Dockett, S. (1994) Pretend play and the young child's theory of mind. *Journal for Australian Research in Early Childhood Education*, **1**, 51–63.

Dockett, S. (1995a) Young children's play and language as clues to their developing theories of mind. *Journal for Australian Research in Early Childhood Education*, **2**, 61–72.

Dockett, S. (1995b) *'I 'tend to be Dead and You Make Me Alive': Developing Understandings through Sociodramatic Play*. Watson, ACT: Australian Early Childhood Association.

Dockett, S. (1996) Children as theorists. In M. Fleer (ed.) *DAPcentrism: Challenging Developmentally Appropriate Practice*. Watson, ACT: Australian Early Childhood Association.

Docking, R. A. (1984) Writing school reports. *Unicorn*, **10**, 332–48.

Docking, R. A. (1986) Norm-referenced measurement and criterion-referenced measurement: A descriptive comparison. *Unicorn*, **12**, 40–6.

Doherty, P. J. (1982) *Strategies and Initiatives for Special Education in New South Wales*. A report of the Working Party on a Plan for Special Education in NSW.

Dowson, M. & McInerney, D. M. (1996a) Investigating relations between students' multiple achievement goals and key aspects of their cognitive engagement and academic performance. *Australian Journal of Psychology*, **48**, 99–100.

Dowson, M. & McInerney, D. M. (1996b) Psychological parameters of students' social and academic goals: A qualitative investigation. *Australian Journal of Psychology*, **48**, 100.

Dowson, M. & McInerney, D. M. (1997) Psychological parameters of students' social and academic goals: A qualitative investigation. Paper presented at the Annual Meeting of the American Educational Research Association, Chicago, 24–28 March.

Dowson, M. & McInerney, D. M. (2001) Psychological parameters of students' social and work avoidance goals: A qualitative investigation. *Journal of Educational Psychology*, **93**, 35–42.

Dowson, M. & McInerney, D. M. (2003) What do students say about their motivational goals? Towards a more complex and dynamic perspective on student motivation. *Contemporary Educational Psychology*, **28**, 91–113.

Dowson, M. & McInerney, D. M. (2005) Motivation for school and beyond: Continuing the search for cultural differences. Paper presented at the Annual Meeting of the American Educational Research Association, Montreal, April 11–15.

Doyle, W. (1986) Classroom organization and management. In M. C. Wittrock (ed.) *Handbook of Research on Teaching*. New York: Macmillan.

Doyle, W. & Rutherford, B. (1984) Classroom research on matching learning and teaching styles. *Theory into Practice*, **23**, 20–5.

Dreikurs, R. & Cassel, P. (1975) *Discipline Without Tears*. New York: Hawthorn Books.

Dreikurs, R. & Cassel, P. (1995) *Discipline Without Tears*, 2nd ed. New York: Penguin–NAL.

Dreikurs, R. (1968) *Psychology in the Classroom: A Manual for Teachers*, 2nd ed. New York: Harper & Row.

Dreikurs, R., Grunwald, B. & Pepper, F. (1982) *Maintaining Sanity in the Classroom*, 2nd ed. New York: Harper & Row.

Driver, R., Asoko, H., Leach, J., Mortimer, E. & Scott, P. (1994) Constructing scientific knowledge in the classroom. *Educational Researcher*, **23**, 5–12.

Duff, A. (2004) A note on the problem solving style questionnaire: An alternative to Kolb's learning style inventory? *Educational Psychology*, **24**, 699–709.

Dunkin, M. J. & Precians, R. P. (1993) Award winning teachers' self-efficacy regarding teaching. *South Pacific Journal of Teacher Education*, **21**, 5–14.

Dunn, R. (1990) Bias over substance: A critical analysis of the Karvale and Forness report on modality-based instruction. *Exceptional Children*, **56**, 352–6.

Dunn, R., Beaudry, J. S. & Klavas, A. (1989) Survey of research on learning styles. *Educational Leadership*, **47**, 50–8.

Dunn, R., Bruno, J., Sklar, I. K., Zenhausen, R. & Beaudry, J. (1990) Effects of matching and mismatching minority developmental college students: Hemispheric preferences on mathematics scores. *Journal of Educational Research*, **83**, 283–8.

Dunn, R., Dunn, K. & Price, G. E. (1985) *Learning Style Inventory*. Price Systems, Box 1818, Lawrence, KS 66044–0067.

Dunn, R., Dunn, K. & Price, G. E. (1988) Diagnosing learning styles: A prescription for avoiding malpractice suits against school systems. *Phi Delta Kappan*, **58**, 418–20.

Dunn, R. S. & Dunn, K. J. (1972) *Practical Approaches to Individualizing Instruction: Contracts and Other Effective Teaching Strategies*. New York: Parker.

Dunn, R. S. & Dunn, K. J. (1979) Learning styles/teaching styles: Should they, can they, be matched? *Educational Leadership*, **36**, 238–44.

Dunphy, D. C. (1969) *Cliques, Crowds and Gangs*. Melbourne: Cheshire.

Dusek, J. B. & Joseph, G. (1983) The bases of teacher expectancies: A meta-analysis. *Journal of Educational Psychology*, **75**, 327–46.

Dweck, C. S. (1975) The role of expectations and attributions in the alleviation of learned helplessness. *Journal of Personality and Social Psychology*, **31**, 674–85.

Dweck, C. S. (1985) Intrinsic motivation, perceived control, and self-evaluation maintenance: An achievement goal analysis. In C. Ames & R. Ames (eds) *Research on Motivation in Education: The Classroom Milieu (Volume 2)*. Orlando: Academic Press.

Dweck, C. S. (1986) Motivational processes affecting learning. *American Psychologist*, **41**, 1040–8.

Dweck, C. S. (2002) The development of ability conceptions. In A. Wigfield & J. S. Eccles (eds) *Development of Achievement Motivation*. San Diego, CA: Academic Press.

Dweck, C. S. & Repucci, N. D. (1973) Learned helplessness and reinforcement responsibility in children. *Journal of Personality and Social Psychology*, **25**, 109–16.

Dyson, A. H. (1989) *Multiple Worlds of Child Writers: Friends Learning to Write*. New York: Teachers College Press.

Eccles, J. & Midgley, C. (1989) Stage–environment fit: Developmentally appropriate classrooms for young adolescents. In C. Ames & R. Ames (eds) *Research on Motivation in Education: Goals and Cognitions (Volume 3)*. New York: Academic Press.

Eccles, J., Midgley, C. & Adler, T. (1984) Grade-related changes in the school environment. In M. L. Maehr (ed.) *Advances in Motivation and Achievement*. Greenwich, CT: JAI Press.

Eccles, J., Wigfield, A., Harold, R. D. & Blumenfeld, P. (1993) Age and gender differences in children's self and task perceptions during elementary school. *Child Development*, **64**, 830–47.

Eccles, J. S. (1983) Expectancies, values, and academic behaviors. In J. T. Spence (ed.) *Achievement and Achievement Motivation*. San Francisco: Freeman.

Eccles, J. S. & Blumenfeld, P. (1985) Classroom experiences and student gender: Are there differences and do they matter? In L. C. Wilkinson & C. B. Marrett (eds) *Gender Influences in Classroom Interaction*. New York: Academic Press.

Eccles, J. S., Midgley, C., Wigfield, A., Buchanan, C. M., *et al.* (1993) Development during adolescence. The impact of stage environment fit on young adolescents' experiences in schools and in families. *American Psychologist*, **48**, 90–101.

Eckermann, A.-K. (1999) Aboriginal education in rural Australia: A case study in frustration and hope. *Australian Journal of Education*, **43**, 5–23.

Edwards, R. & Edwards, J. (1987) Corporal punishment. In A. Thomas & J. Grimes (eds) *Children's Needs: Psychological Perspectives*. Washington, DC: National Association of School Psychologists.

Edwards, S. & Woodward, H. (1989) Negotiating evaluation. In R. Parker (ed.) *Evaluation and Planning for Literacy and Learning: Proceedings of the Tenth Macarthur Reading/Language Symposium*. Sydney: University of Western Sydney, Macarthur.

Eggen, P. D. & Kauchak, D. P. (1988) *Strategies for Teachers: Information Processing Models in the Classroom*, 2nd ed. Englewood Cliffs, NJ: Prentice Hall.

Elawar, M. C. & Corno, L. (1985) A factorial experiment in teachers' written feedback on student homework: Changing teacher behavior a little rather than a lot. *Journal of Educational Psychology*, **77**, 162–73.

Elkind, D. (1974) *A Sympathetic Understanding of the Child: Birth to Sixteen*. New York: McGraw-Hill.

Elkind, D. (1977) One man in his time plays many psychosocial parts. Erik Erikson's Eight Ages of Man. In D. Elkind & D. C. Hetzel (eds) *Readings in Human Development: Contemporary Perspectives*. New York: Harper & Row.

Elliot, A. J. (1997) Integrating the 'classic' and 'contemporary' approaches to achievement motivation. A hierarchical model of approach and avoidance achievement motivation. In M. L. Maehr & P. R. Pintrich (eds) *Advances in Motivation and Achievement (Volume 10)*. Greenwich, CT: JAI.

Elliot, A. J. (1999) Approach and avoidance motivation and achievement goals. *Educational Psychologist*, **34**, 169–89.

Elliot, A. J., McGregor, H. A. & Gable, S. (1999) Achievement goals, study strategies, and exam performance: A mediational analysis. *Journal of Educational Psychology*, **91**, 549–63.

Elliott, E. S. & Dweck, C. S. (1988) Goals: An approach to motivation and achievement. *Journal of Personality and Social Psychology*, **54**, 5–12.

Embretson, S. E. & Schmidt McCollam, K. M. (2000) Psychometric approaches to understanding and measuring intelligence. In R. S. Sternberg (ed.) *Handbook of Intelligence*. New York: Cambridge University Press.

Emmer, E. T., Evertson, C. & Worsham, M. E. (2000) *Classroom Management for Secondary Teachers*. Boston: Allyn & Bacon.

Enright, R., Lapsley, D., Harris, D. & Shawyer, D. (1983) Moral development interventions in early adolescence. *Theory into Practice*, **22**, 134–44.

Entwisle, D. R., Alexander, K. L., Cadigan, D. & Pallas, A. (1986) The schooling process in first grade: Two samples a decade apart. *American Educational Research Journal*, **23**, 587–613.

Entwistle, N. J. (1991) Cognitive style and learning. In K. Marjoribanks (ed.) *The Foundations of Students' Learning*. Oxford: Pergamon Press.

Epstein, J. L. (1985) Home and school connections in schools for the future: Implications of research on parental involvement. *Peabody Journal of Education*, **78**, 373–80.

Epstein, J. L. (1989) Family structures and student motivation: A developmental perspective. In C. Ames & R. Ames (eds) *Research in Motivation in Education: Goals and Cognitions (Volume 3)*. New York: Academic Press.

Ericson, D. P. & Ellett, F. S. Jr (1990) Taking student responsibility seriously. *Educational Researcher*, **19**, 3–10.

Erikson, E. H. (1963) *Childhood and Society*, 2nd ed. New York: W. W. Norton.

Erikson, E. H. (1968) *Identity: Youth and Crisis*. New York: W. W. Norton.

Escribe, C. & Huet, N. (2005) Knowledge accessibility, achievement goals, and memory strategy maintenance. *British Journal of Educational Psychology*, **75**, 87–104.

Eshel, Y. & Kohavi, R. (2003) Perceived classroom control, self-regulated learning strategies, and academic achievement. *Educational Psychology*, **23**, 250–60.

Eskin, M. (1992) Opinions about and reactions to suicide, and the social acceptance of a suicidal classmate among Turkish high school students. *The International Journal of Social Psychiatry*, **38**, 280–6.

Eskin, M. (1995) Adolescents' attitudes toward suicide and a suicidal peer: A comparison between Swedish and Turkish high school students. *Scandinavian Journal of Psychology*, **36**, 201–7.

Etzioni, A. (1993) *The Spirit of Community*. New York: Simon & Schuster.

Evans, C. (2004) Exploring the relationship between cognitive style and teaching style. *Educational Psychology*, **24**, 509–30.

Evans, G. T. & Poole, M. E. (1987) Adolescent concerns: A classification for life skills access. *Australian Journal of Education*, **31**, 55–72.

Evers, W. J., Brouwers, A. & Tomic, W. (2002) Burnout and self-efficacy: A study on teachers' beliefs when implementing an innovative educational system in the Netherlands. *British Journal of Educational Psychology*, **72**, 227–43.

Evertson, C. M. (1995) Classroom rules and routines. In L. W. Anderson (ed.) *International Encyclopedia of Teaching and Teacher Education*, 2nd ed. Cambridge: Pergamon Press.

Evertson, C. M. & Emmer, E. T. (1982) Effective management at the beginning of the school year in junior high classes. *Journal of Educational Psychology*, **74**, 485–98.

Evertson, C. M., Emmer, E. T. & Worsham, M. E. (2000) *Classroom Management for Elementary Teachers*, 5th ed. Boston: Allyn & Bacon.

Fagard, J. & Jacquet, A. (1989) Onset of bimanual coordination and symmetry versus asymmetry of movement. *Infant Behavior and Development*, **12**, 229–35.

Fairburn, C. G. & Beglin, S. J. (1990) Studies of the epidemiology of bulimia nervosa. *American Journal of Psychiatry*, **147**, 401–8.

Falchikov, N. & Boud, D. (1989) Student self-assessment in higher education: A meta-analysis. *Review of Educational Research*, **59**, 395–430.

Falchikov, N. & Goldfinch, J. (2000) Student peer assessment in higher education: A meta-analysis comparing peer and teacher marks. *Review of Educational Research*, **70**, 287–322.

Fallon, B. J. & Bowles, T. (1999) Adolescent help-seeking for major and minor problems. *Australian Journal of Psychology*, **51**, 12–18.

Fantuzzo, J., Tighe, E. & Childs, S. (2000) Family involvement questionnaire: A multivariate assessment of family participation in early childhood education. *Journal of Educational Psychology*, **92**, 367–76.

Farivar, S. & Webb, N. (1993) Helping—an essential skill for learning to solve problems in cooperative groups. *Cooperative Learning*, **13**, 20–3.

Farmer, T. W., Leung, M-C., Pearl, R., Rodkin, P. C., Cadwaller, T. W. & Van Acker, R. (2002) Deviant or diverse peer groups? The peer affiliations of aggressive elementary students. *Journal of Educational Psychology*, **94**, 611–20.

Farrington, D. P. (1993) Understanding and preventing bullying. In M. Tonry (ed.) *Crime and Justice*. Chicago: University of Chicago Press.

Farver, J. M. & Wimbarti, S. (1995) Indonesian toddlers' social play with their mothers and older siblings. *Child Development*, **66**, 1493–503.

Faust, M. S. (1983) Alternative constructions of adolescent growth. In J. Brooks-Gunn & A. C. Petersen (eds) *Girls at Puberty. Biological and Psychosocial Perspectives*. New York: Plenum Press.

Feldhusen, J. F. (1989) Synthesis of research on gifted youth. *Educational Leadership*, **46**, 6–11.

Feldhusen, J. F. (1995) Creativity: Teaching and assessing. In L. W. Anderson (ed.) *International Encyclopedia of Teaching and Teacher Education*, 2nd ed. Tarrytown, NY: Pergamon.

Feldman, D. H., Csikszentmihalyi, M. & Gardner, H. (1994) *Changing the World: A Framework for the Study of Creativity*. Westport, CT: Praeger Publishers.

Fendler, L. (2003) Teacher reflection in a hall of mirrors: Historical influences and political reverberations. *Educational Researcher*, **32**, 16–25.

Fennema, E. & Peterson, P. (1987) Effective teaching for boys and girls. The same or different? In D. C. Berliner & B. V. Rosenshine (eds) *Talks to Teachers*. New York: Random House.

Ferguson, C. J. (2002) Media violence: Miscast causality. *American Psychologist*, **57**, 446–7.

Ferguson, D. L. & Ferguson, P. M. (1997) Debating inclusion in Synedoche, New York: A response to Gresham & Macmillan. *Review of Educational Research*, **67**, 416–20.

Ferguson, G. A. & Takane, Y. (1989) *Statistical Analysis in Psychology and Education*, 6th ed. New York: McGraw-Hill.

Fergusson, D. M., Horwood, L. J. & Shannon, F. T. (1982) Family ethnic composition, socio-economic factors and childhood disadvantage. *New Zealand Journal of Educational Studies*, **17**, 171–9.

Fergusson, D. M., Lloyd, M. & Horwood, L. J. (1991) Family ethnicity, social background and scholastic achievement—an eleven-year longitudinal study. *New Zealand Journal of Educational Studies*, **26**, 49–63.

Ferrari, M. & Mahalingam, R. (1998) Personal cognitive development and its implications for teaching and learning. *Educational Psychologist*, **33**, 35–44.

Feshbach, N. D. & Feshbach, S. (1987) Affective processes and academic achievement. *Child Development*, **58**, 1335–47.

Feshbach, S. & Singer, R. D. (1971) *Television and Aggression*. San Francisco, CA: Jossey-Bass.

Feuerstein, R. (1978) *Just a Minute . . . Let Me Think*. Baltimore, MD: University Park Press.

Feuerstein, R. (1980) *Instructional Enrichment*. Baltimore, MD: University Park Press.

Feuerstein, R. (1991) Cultural difference and cultural deprivation: Differential patterns of adaptability. In N. Bleichrodt & P. J. D. Drenth (eds) *Contemporary Issues in Cross-Cultural Psychology*. Amsterdam/Lisse: Swets & Zeitlinger.

Field, D. (1981) Can preschool children really learn to conserve? *Child Development*, **52**, 326–34.

Fisher, A., Monsen, J., Moore, D. W. & Twiss, D. (1989) Increasing the social integration of hearing-impaired children in a mainstream school setting. *New Zealand Journal of Educational Studies*, **24**, 189–204.

Fives, H. & Alexander, P. (2004) How schools shape teacher efficacy and commitment: Another piece in the achievement puzzle. In D. M. McInerney & S. Van Etten (eds) *Research on Sociocultural Influences on Motivation and Learning (Volume 4), Big Theories Revisited*. Greenwich, CT: Information Age Publishing.

Flavell, J. H. (1976) Metacognitive aspects of problem solving. In L. B. Resnick (ed.) *The Nature of Intelligence*. Hillsdale, NJ: Lawrence Erlbaum.

Flavell, J. H. (1979) Metacognition and cognitive monitoring: A new era of cognitive developmental inquiry. *American Psychologist*, **34**, 906–11.

Flavell, J. H. (1985) *Cognitive Development*, 2nd ed. Englewood Cliffs, NJ: Prentice Hall.

Flavell, J. H., Green, F. L. & Flavell, E. R. (2000) Development of children's awareness of their own thoughts. *Journal of Cognition and Development*, **1**, 97–112.

Flavell, J. H., Miller, P. H. & Miller, S. A. (1993) *Cognitive Development*, 3rd ed. Englewood Cliffs, NJ: Prentice Hall.

Floden, R. E. & Klinzing, H. G. (1990) What can research on teacher thinking contribute to teacher preparation? A second opinion. *Educational Researcher*, **19**, 15–20.

Flynn, J. R. (1996) What environmental factors affect intelligence: The relevance of IQ gains over time. In D. K. Detterman (ed.) *The Environment. Current Topics in Human Intelligence (Volume 5)*. Norwood, NJ: Ablex.

Folds, R. (1987) *Whitefella School*. Sydney: Allen & Unwin.

Fontana, D. (1986) *Teaching and Personality*. Oxford: Basil Blackwell.

Ford, S. (2004) Out of bounds. The influence of sporting heroes. *INPSYCH*, **26**, 22–4.

Forman, G. E. (1980) Constructivism: Piaget. In G. M. Gazda & R. J. Corsini (eds) *Theories of Learning*. Itasca, IL: F. E. Peacock.

Forsterling, F. (1985) Attributional retraining. *Psychological Bulletin*, **98**, 495–512.

Forsterling, F. (1986) Attributional conceptions in clinical psychology. *American Psychologist*, **41**, 275–85.

Fosnot, C. (1992) Constructing constructivism. In T. M. Duffy & D. H. Jonassen (eds) *Constructivism and the Technology of Instruction*. Hillsdale, NJ: Lawrence Erlbaum.

Fox, C. L. & Boulton, M. J. (2005) The social skills problems of victims of bullying: Self, peer and teacher perceptions. *British Journal of Educational Psychology*, **75**, 313–28.

Frasier, M. M. (1989) Poor and minority students can be gifted too. *Educational Leadership*, **46**, 16–18.

Frederiksen, N. (1984) Implications of cognitive theory for instruction in problem solving. *Review of Educational Research*, **54**, 363–407.

Frederickson, N., Osborne, L. A. & Reed, P. (2004) Judgments of successful inclusion by education service personnel. *Educational Psychology*, **24**, 263–90.

Frederickson, N. L. & Furnham, A. F. (1998) Sociometric-status-group classification of mainstreamed children who have moderate learning difficulties: An investigation of personal and environmental factors. *Journal of Educational Psychology*, **90**, 772–83.

Fredricks, J. A., Blumenfeld, P. C. & Paris, A. H. (2004) School engagement: Potential of the concept, state of the evidence. *Review of Educational Research*, **74**, 59–109.

Freiberg, K. L. (ed.) (1992) *Educating Exceptional Children. Annual Editions*, 6th ed. Guilford, CT: Duskin.

Freud, S. (1962a) *Two Short Accounts of Psychoanalysis*. Harmondsworth, Middlesex: Penguin Books.

Freud, S. (1962b) *A General Introduction to Psychoanalysis*. New York: Washington Square Press.

Freud, S. (1973) *An Outline of Psychoanalysis*. London: The Hogarth Press.

Friedrich, L. K. & Stein, A. H. (1975) Prosocial television and young children: The effects of verbal labeling and role playing on learning and behavior. *Child Development*, **46**, 27–38.

Friedrich-Cofer, L. K., Huston-Stein, A., Kipnis, D. M., Susman, E. J. & Clewett, A. S. (1979) Environmental enhancement of prosocial television content: Effects on interpersonal behavior, imaginative play, and self-regulation in a natural setting. *Developmental Psychology*, **15**, 637–46.

Frisch, R. E. (1983) Fatness, puberty, and fertility: The effects of nutrition and physical training on menarche and ovulation. In J. Brooks-Gunn & A. C. Petersen (eds) *Girls at Puberty. Biological and Psychosocial Perspectives*. New York: Plenum Press.

Frydenberg, E. & Lewis, R. (1990) How adolescents cope with different concerns: The development of the Adolescent Coping Checklist (ACC). *Psychological Test Bulletin*, **3**, 63–73.

Frydenberg, E. & Lewis, R. (1991) Adolescent coping: The different ways in which boys and girls cope. *Journal of Adolescence*, **14**, 119–33.

Frydenberg, E. & Lewis, R. (1993) Boys play sport and girls turn to others: Age, gender and ethnicity as determinants of coping. *Journal of Adolescence*, **16**, 253–66.

Fuchs, D., Fuchs, L. S. & Fernstrom, P. (1993) A conservative approach to special education reform: Mainstreaming through transenvironmental programming and curriculum-based measurement. *American Educational Research Journal*, **30**, 149–77.

Fuchs, L. S., Fuchs, D., Karns, K., Hamlett, C., Dutka, S. & Katzaroff, M. (1996) The relation between student ability and the quality and effectiveness of explanations. *American Educational Research Journal*, **33**, 631–64.

Fuchs, L. S., Fuchs, D., Karns, K., Hamlett, C., Dutka, S. & Katzaroff, M. (1997) Effects of task-focused goals on low-achieving students with and without learning disabilities. *American Educational Research Journal*, **4**, 513–43.

Fuchs, L. S., Fuchs, D., Kazdan, S. A., Karns, K., Calhoon, M., Hamlett, C. L. & Hewlitt, S. E. (2000) Effects of workgroup structure and size on student productivity during collaborative work on complex tasks. *Elementary School Journal*, **100**, 183–212.

Fuller, F. & Brown, O. H. (1975) Becoming a teacher. In K. Ryan (ed.) *Teacher Education: The Seventy-fourth Yearbook of the National Society for the Study of Education* (Part II). Chicago: University of Chicago Press.

Fuller, F. G. (1969) Concerns of teachers: A developmental conceptualization. *American Educational Research Journal*, **6**, 207–26.

Furnham, A. & Petrides, K. V. (2004) Parental estimates of five types of intelligence. *Australian Journal of Psychology*, **56**, 10–17.

Gale, F., Jordan, D., McGill, G., McNamara, N. & Scott, C. (1987) Aboriginal education. In J. P. Keeves (ed.) *Australian Education. Review of Recent Research*. Sydney: Allen & Unwin.

Gall, M. D. (1984) Synthesis of research on teachers' questioning. *Educational Leadership*, **41**, 40–7.

Gall, M. D. & Artero-Boname, M. T. (1995) Questioning. In L. W. Anderson (ed.) *International Encyclopedia of Teaching and Teacher Education*, 2nd ed. New York: Pergamon.

Gallagher, J. J. (1989) The impact of policies for handicapped children on future early education policy. *Phi Delta Kappan*, 121–3.

Gallagher, J. J. (1990) New patterns in special education. *Educational Researcher*, **19**, 34–6.

Gallagher, J. M. & Easley, J. A. Jr (eds) (1978) *Knowledge and Development: Piaget and Education (Volume 2)*. New York: Plenum Press.

Gallahue, D. L. (1976) *Motor Development and Movement Experiences for Young Children*. New York: John Wiley.

Gallahue, D. L. (1982) *Understanding Motor Development in Children*. New York: John Wiley.

Gallahue, D. L. (1989) *Understanding Motor Development: Infants, Children, Adolescents*, 2nd ed. Brisbane: John Wiley.

Gallimore, R. & Tharp, R. (1990) Teaching mind in society: Teaching, schooling and literate discourse. In L. C. Moll (ed.) *Vygotsky and Education*. New York: Cambridge University Press.

Galst, J. P. & White, M. A. (1976) The unhealthy persuader: The reinforcing value of television and children's purchase-influencing attempts at the supermarket. *Child Development*, **47**, 1089–96.

Gama, E. M. P. & de Jesus, D. M. (2001) Social representations of school failure in Brazilian public schools: A framework for understanding and change. In D. M. McInerney and S. van Etten (eds) *Research on Sociocultural Influences on Motivation and Learning (Volume 1)*. Greenwich, CT: Information Age Press.

Gamoran, A. (1992) Is ability grouping equitable? *Educational Leadership*, **50**, 11–17.

Gamoran, A., Nystrand, M., Berends, M. & LePore, P. C. (1995) An organizational analysis of the effects of ability grouping. *American Educational Research Journal*, **32**, 687–715.

Garcia, E. E. (1993) Language, culture, and education. *Review of Research in Education*, **19**, 51–98.

Gardner, H. (1983) *Frames of Mind: The Theory of Multiple Intelligences*. New York: Basic Books.

Gardner, H. (1993) *Multiple Intelligences: The Theory in Practice. A Reader*. New York: Basic Books.

Gardner, H. (1999) *Intelligence Reframed. Multiple Intelligences for the 21st Century*. New York: Basic Books.

Gardner, H. (2004) *A Multiplicity of Intelligences: In Tribute to Professor Luigi Vignolo* http://www.howardgardner.com/Papers/papers.html

Gardner, H. & Hatch, T. (1989) Multiple intelligences go to school. Educational implications. *Educational Leadership*, **18**, 4–10.

Gardner, M. K. & Clark, E. (1992) The psychometric perspective on intellectual development in childhood and adolescence. In R. J. Sternberg & C. A. Berg (eds) *Intellectual Development*. New York: Cambridge University Press.

Garland, A. & Zigler, E. (1993) Adolescent suicide prevention. Current research and social policy implications. *American Psychologist*, **48**, 169–82.

Garn, S. M. (1980) Continuities and change in maturational timing. In O. G. Brim & J. Kagan (eds) *Constancy and Change in Human Development*. Cambridge, MA: Harvard University Press.

Garner, R. (1990) When children and adults do not use learning strategies: Toward a theory of settings. *Review of Educational Research*, **60**, 517–29.

Garner, R. & Alexander, P. A. (1989) Metacognition: Answered and unanswered questions. *Educational Psychologist*, **24**, 143–58.

Gazda, G. M. & Corsini, R. J. (eds) (1980) *Theories of Learning*. Itasca, IL: F. E. Peacock.

Gelman, R. & Baillargeon, R. (1983) A review of some Piagetian concepts. In P. Mussen (series ed.), J. H. Flavell & E. M. Markman (vol. eds) *Handbook of Child Psychology: Cognitive Development (Volume 3)*. New York: John Wiley.

Genesee, F. & Cloud, N. (1998) Multilingualism is basic. *Bilingual Education*, **55**, 62–5.

Gentner, D., Loewenstein, J. & Thompson, L. (2003) Learning and transfer: A general role for analogical encoding. *Journal of Educational Psychology*, **95**, 393–408.

Gentry, M., Gable, R. K. & Rizza, M. G. (2002) Students' perceptions of classroom activities: Are there grade-level and gender differences? *Journal of Educational Psychology*, **94**, 539–44.

Germain, E. R. (2004) Culture or race? Phenotype and cultural identity development in minority Australian adolescents. *Australian Psychologist*, **39**, 134–42.

Gesell, A. L. (1925) *The Mental Growth of the Preschool Child*. New York: Macmillan.

Getzels, J. & Csikszentmihalyi, M. (1976) *The Creative Vision: A Longitudinal Study of Problem Finding in Art*. New York: John Wiley.

Getzels, J. & Jackson, P. (1962) *Creativity and Intelligence: Explorations with Gifted Students*. New York: John Wiley.

Giaconia, R. M. & Hedges, L. V. (1982) Identifying features of effective open education. *Review of Educational Research*, **52**, 579–602.

Gibbs, G. (1991) Eight myths about assessment. *The New Academic*, **1**, 2–4.

Gibson, S. & Dembo, M. H. (1984) Teacher efficacy: A construct validation. *Journal of Educational Psychology*, **76**, 569–82.

Gillam, B. (1992) The status of perceptual grouping 70 years after Wertheimer. *Australian Journal of Psychology*, **44**, 157–62.

Gilligan, C. (1977) In a different voice: Women's conceptions of self and morality. *Harvard Educational Review*, **47**, 481–517.

Gilligan, C. (1982) *In a Different Voice*. Cambridge, MA: Harvard University Press.

Gilligan, C. (1990) Teaching Shakespeare's sister. In C. Gilligan, N. Lyons & T. Hanmer (eds) *Making Connections: The Relational Worlds of Adolescent Girls at Emma Willard School*. Cambridge, MA: Harvard University Press.

Gilmore, L., Patton, W., McCrindle, A. & Callum, L. (2002) Single-sex classes in a Queensland primary school: An evaluation of outcomes. *The Australian Educational and Developmental Psychologist*, **19**, 49–58.

Gindis, B. (1995) The social/cultural implication of disability: Vygotsky's paradigm for special education. *Educational Psychologist*, **30**, 77–81.

Ginott, H. G. (1972) *Teacher and Child: A Book for Parents and Teachers*. New York: Macmillan.

Ginsburg, H. & Opper, S. (1988) *Piaget's Theory of Intellectual Development*, 3rd ed. Englewood Cliffs, NJ: Prentice Hall.

Gipps, C. (1999) Socio-cultural aspects of assessment. *Review of Research in Education*, **24**, 355–92.

Glasser, W. (1969) *Schools Without Failure*. New York: Harper & Row.

Glasser, W. (1992) *The Quality School*. New York: HarperCollins.

Glasser, W. (1993) *The Quality School Teacher*. New York: HarperPerennial.

Glassman, M. (2001) Dewey and Vygotsky: Society, experience, and inquiry in educational practice. *Educational Researcher*, **30**, 3–14.

Gloet, M. B. (1992) Cooperation, competition and individualism in the clever country. *Proceedings of the 10th Annual Computers in Education Conference*, July, 210–16.

Goddard, R. D. (2001) Collective efficacy: A neglected construct in the study of schools and student achievement. *Journal of Educational Psychology*, **93**, 467–76.

Goddard, R. D., Hoy, W. K. & Woolfolk Hoy, A. (2000) Collective teacher efficacy: Its meaning, measure, and impact on student achievement. *American Educational Research Journal*, **37**, 479–507.

Goddard, R. D., Hoy, W. K. & Woolfolk Hoy, A. (2004) Collective efficacy beliefs: Theoretical developments, empirical evidence, and future directions. *Educational Researcher*, **33**, 3–13.

Goldenberg, C. (1992) The limits of expectations: A case for case knowledge about teacher expectancy effects. *American Educational Research Journal*, **29**, 517–44.

Goldschmid, M. L., Bentler, P. M., Debus, R. L., Rawlinson, R., Kohnstamm, D., Modgil, S., Nichols, J. G., Reykowski, J., Strupczewska, B. & Warren, N. (1973) A cross-cultural investigation of conservation. *Journal of Cross-Cultural Psychology*, **4**, 75–88.

Goldstein, L. S. (1999) The relational zone: The role of caring relationships in the co-construction of mind. *American Educational Research Journal*, **36**, 647–73.

Goleman, D. (1995) *Emotional Intelligence*. New York: Bantam.

Good, T. L. (1987) Two decades of research on teacher expectations:

Findings and future directions. *Journal of Teacher Education*, **38**, 32–47.

Good, T. L. (1995) Teacher expectations. In L. W. Anderson (ed.) *International Encyclopedia of Teaching and Teacher Education*, 2nd ed. Tarrytown, NY: Pergamon.

Good, T. L. & Brophy, J. (1977) Teachers' expectations as self-fulfilling prophecies. In H. F. Clarizio, R. C. Craig & W. A. Mehrens (eds) *Contemporary Issues in Educational Psychology*, 3rd ed. Boston: Allyn & Bacon.

Good, T. L. & Brophy, J. E. (1990) *Educational Psychology. A Realistic Approach*, 4th ed. White Plains, NY: Longman.

Good, T. L. & Brophy, J. E. (1991) *Looking in Classrooms*, 5th ed. New York: HarperCollins.

Good, T. L. & Stipek, D. J. (1983) Individual differences in the classroom: A psychological perspective. In G. D. Fenstermacher (ed.) *Individual Differences and the Common Curriculum. Eighty-second Yearbook of the National Society for the Study of Education* (Part 1). Chicago: Chicago University Press.

Good, T. L. & Tom, D. Y. H. (1985) Self-regulation, efficacy, expectations, and social orientation: Teacher and classroom perspectives. In C. Ames & R. Ames (eds) *Research on Motivation in Education: The Classroom Milieu (Volume 2)*. Orlando: Academic Press.

Goodman, D., O'Hearn, D. J. & Wallace-Crabbe, C. (eds) (1991) *Multicultural Australia. The Challenges of Change*. Newham, Vic.: Scribe.

Goodnow, J. J. (1976) The nature of intelligent behavior: Questions raised by cross-cultural studies. In L. B. Resnick (ed.) *The Nature of Intelligence*. New York: Lawrence Erlbaum.

Goodnow, J. J. (1988) Issues and changes in the assessment of people from minority groups. In G. Davidson (ed.) *Ethnicity and Cognitive Assessment: Australian Perspectives*. Darwin: Darwin Institute of Technology.

Goodnow, J. J. (1990) The socialization of cognition: What's involved? In J. W. Stigler, R. Shweder & G. Herdt (eds) *Cultural Psychology. Essays on Comparative Human Development*. Cambridge: Cambridge University Press.

Gopnik, A. & Wellman, H. M. (1992) Why the child's theory of mind really is a theory. *Mind and Language*, **7**, 145–71.

Gordon, C. & Debus, R. (2002) Developing deep learning approaches and personal teaching efficacy within a preservice teacher education context. *British Journal of Educational Psychology*, **72**, 483–511.

Gordon, I. E. & Earle, D. C. (1992) Visual illusions: A short review. *Australian Journal of Psychology*, **44**, 153–6.

Gordon, T. (1974) *Teacher Effectiveness Training*. New York: Peter H. Wyden.

Gordon, T. (1989) *Discipline that Works: Promoting Self-Discipline in Children*. New York: Random House.

Gow, L. (1989) *Review of Integration in Australia: Summary Report*. Canberra: Department of Employment, Education and Training.

Gow, L. (ed.) (1992) Review of Literature on Service Provision for Students with Disabilities. Paper submitted to the Committee Reviewing SSPs in the Metropolitan South West Region, NSW Department of School Education, July.

Gow, L., McClellan, K., Balla, J. & Taylor, D. (1988) The teaching–learning staircase: A model of instruction to demystify special education. *Australian Journal of Remedial Education*, **20**, 26–31.

Gow, L., Snow, D., Balla, J. & Hall, J. (1987) *Report to the Commonwealth School Commission on Integration in Australia (Volumes 1–5)*. Canberra: CSC.

Graff, M. (2005) Differences in concept mapping, hypertext architecture, and the analyst-intuition dimension of cognitive style. *Educational Psychology*, **25**, 409–22.

Graham, A., Reser, J., Scuderi, C., Zubrick, S., Smith, M. & Turley, B. (2000) Suicide: An Australian Psychological Society Discussion Paper. *Australian Psychologist*, **35**, 1–28.

Graham, S. (1988) Can attribution theory tell us something about motivation in blacks? *Educational Psychologist*, **23**, 3–21.

Graham, S. (1997) Using attribution theory to understand social and academic motivation in African American youth. *Educational Psychologist*, **32**, 21–34.

Graham, S. & Golan, S. (1991) Motivational influences on cognition: Task involvement, ego involvement, and depth of processing. *Journal of Educational Psychology*, **83**, 187–94.

Graves, N. & Graves, T. (1990) *A Part to Play*. Melbourne: Latitude Publications.

Gray, J. & Bereford, Q. (2002) Aboriginal non-attendance at school: Revisiting the debate. *The Australian Educational Researcher*, **29**, 27–42.

Grbich, C. & Sykes, S. (1992) Access to curricula in three school settings for students with severe intellectual disability. *Australian Journal of Education*, **36**, 318–27.

Gredler, M. & Shields, C. (2004) Does no one read Vygotsky's words! Commentary on Glassman. *Educational Researcher*, **33**, 21–5.

Green, K. D., Forehand, R., Beck, S. J. & Vosk, B. (1980) An assessment of the relationships among measures of children's social competence and children's academic achievement. *Child Development*, **51**, 1149–56.

Greenberg, M. T., Weissberg, R. P., O'Brien, M. U., Zins, J. E., Fredericks, L., Resnik, H. & Elias, M. J. (2003) Enhancing school-based prevention and youth development through coordinated social, emotional and academic learning. *American Psychologist*, **58**, 466–74.

Greene, R. L. (1986) Sources of recency effects in free recall. *Psychological Bulletin*, **99**, 221–8.

Greeno, J. G. (1997) On claims that answer the wrong questions. *Educational Researcher*, **26**, 5–17.

Greenwood, C. R. *et al.* (1992) The classwide peer tutoring program: Implementation factors moderating students' achievement. *Journal of Applied Behavior Analysis*, **25**, 101–16.

Gregor, S. (2004) The man behind the mask: Male body image dissatisfaction. *Inpsych*, **26**, 27–9.

Gresham, F. M. (1981) Social skills training with handicapped children: A review. *Review of Educational Research*, **51**, 139–76.

Gresham, F. M. & MacMillan, D. L. (1997a) Social competence and affective characteristics of students with mild disabilities. *Review of Educational Research*, **67**, 377–415.

Gresham, F. M. & MacMillan, D. L. (1997b) What we have here is a failure to communicate: A rejoinder to Ferguson and Ferguson. *Review of Educational Research*, **67**, 421–3.

Griffin, P. & Nix, P. (1991) *Educational Assessment and Reporting. A New Approach*. Sydney: Harcourt Brace Jovanovich.

Griffiths, R. A. & Channon-Little, L. (1996) Psychological treatments and bulimia nervosa: An update. *Australian Psychologist*, **31**, 79–96.

Groisser, P. (1964) *How to Use the Fine Art of Questioning*. New York: Teachers College Press.

Grolnick, W. S., Benjet, C., Kurowski, C. O. & Apostoleris, N. H. (1997) Predictors of parent involvement in children's schooling. *Journal of Educational Psychology*, **89**, 538–48.

Grolnick, W. S., Gurland, S. T., Jacob, K. F. & Decourcey, W. (2002)

The development of self-determination in middle childhood and adolescence. In A. Wigfield & J. S. Eccles (eds) *Development of Achievement Motivation*. San Diego, CA: Academic Press.

Grolnick, W. S., Kurowski, C. O. & Gurland, S. T. (1999) Family processes and the development of children's self-regulation. *Educational Psychologist*, **34**, 3–14.

Grolnick, W. S. & Ryan, R. (1989) Parent style and children's self-regulation. *Journal of Educational Psychology*, **81**, 143–54.

Gronlund, N. E. (1985) *Measurement and Evaluation in Teaching*, 5th ed. New York: Macmillan.

Gronlund, N. E. (1991) *How to Write and Use Instructional Objectives*. New York: Macmillan.

Gropper, R. C. (1996) *Culture and the Clinical Encounter: An Intercultural Sensitizer for the Health Professions*. Yarmouth, ME: Intercultural Press.

Grueneich, R. (1982) Issues in the developmental study of how children use intention and consequence information to make moral evaluations. *Child Development*, **53**, 29–43.

Guay, F., Boivin, M. & Hodges, V. E. (1999) Predicting change in academic achievement: A model of peer experiences and self-system processes. *Journal of Educational Psychology*, **91**, 105–15.

Guay, F., Marsh, H. W. & Boivin, M. (2003) Academic self-concept and academic achievement: Developmental perspectives on their causal ordering. *Journal of Educational Psychology*, **95**, 124–36.

Guilford, J. P. (1967) *The Nature of Human Intelligence*. New York: McGraw-Hill.

Guilford, J. P. (1985) The structure-of-intellect model. In B. B. Wolman (ed.) *Handbook of Intelligence*. New York: John Wiley.

Gullickson, A. R. (1984) Teacher perspectives of the instructional use of tests. *Journal of Educational Research*, **77**, 244–8.

Gullickson, A. R. (1985) Student evaluation techniques and their relationship to grade and curriculum. *Journal of Educational Research*, **79**, 96–100.

Guskey, T. R. (1987) Rethinking mastery learning reconsidered. *Review of Educational Research*, **57**, 225–9.

Guskey, T. R. (1995) Mastery learning. In L. W. Anderson (ed.) *International Encyclopedia of Teaching and Teacher Education*, 2nd ed. Tarrytown, NY: Pergamon.

Guskey, T. R. & Gates, S. L. (1986) Synthesis of research on the effects of mastery learning in elementary and secondary classrooms. *Educational Leadership*, **43**, 73–80.

Guthrie, L. F. & Hall, W. S. (1983) Continuity/discontinuity in the function and use of language. In E. W. Gordon (ed.) *Review of Research in Education (Volume 10)*. Washington: AERA.

Gutiérrez, K. D. & Rogoff, B. (2003) Cultural ways of learning: Individual traits or repertoires of practice. *Educational Researcher*, **32**, 19–25.

Guttmann, J. & Rosenberg, M. (2003) Emotional intimacy and children's adjustment: A comparison between single-parent divorced and intact families. *Educational Psychology*, **23**, 457–72.

Hacker, D. J. & Tenent, A. (2002) Implementing reciprocal teaching in the classroom: Overcoming obstacles and making modifications. *Journal of Educational Psychology*, **94**, 699–718.

Hadwin, J. A., Brogan, J. & Stevenson, J. (2005) State anxiety and working memory in children: A test of processing efficiency theory. *Educational Psychology*, **25**, 379–93.

Haertel, E. (1985) Construct validity and criterion-referenced testing. *Review of Educational Research*, **55**, 23–46.

Haight, W. L. & Miller, P. J. (1993) *Pretending at Home: Early Development in a Sociocultural Context*. Albany, NY: SUNY Press.

Hales, L. W. & Tokar, E. (1975) The effects of quality of preceding responses on the grades assigned to subsequent responses to an essay question. *Journal of Educational Measurement*, **12**, 115–17.

Halford, G. S. (1982) *The Development of Thought*. Hillsdale, NJ: Lawrence Erlbaum.

Halford, G. S. (1989) Reflections on 25 years of Piagetian cognitive developmental psychology, 1963–1988. *Human Development*, **32**, 325–57.

Halford, G. S. (1993) *Children's Understanding: The Development of Mental Models*. London: Lawrence Erlbaum.

Hall, C. S. (1964) *A Primer of Freudian Psychology*. New York: Mentor Books.

Hall, C. S. & Lindzey, G. (1970) *Theories of Personality*, 2nd ed. New York: John Wiley.

Hall, J., Gow, L. & Konza, D. (1987) Are we integrating or maindumping students with special needs? *The NSW Journal of Education*, **7**, 20–4.

Hall, K. (1992) Co-assessment: The bridge between student self-assessment and teacher-assessment. A paper presented at the 12th Annual International Seminar for Teacher Education, The University of New England, Armidale, NSW, 24–30 April.

Hallahan, D. & Kauffman, J. (1988) *Exceptional Children: Introduction to Special Education*, 4th ed. Englewood Cliffs, NJ: Prentice Hall.

Halle, T. G., Kurtz-Costes, B. & Mahoney, J. L. (1997) Family influences on school achievement in low-income, African American children. *Journal of Educational Psychology*, **89**, 527–37.

Halpern, D. F. (1997) Sex differences in intelligence. *American Psychologist*, **44**, 1014–15.

Halpern, D. F. & LaMay, M. L. (2000) The smarter sex: A critical review of sex differences in intelligence. *Educational Psychology Review*, **12**, 229–46.

Hancock, D. R. (1995) What teachers may do to influence student motivation: An application of expectancy theory. *The Journal of General Education*, **44**, 171–9.

Hannan, T. (2005) Assessing children: Hits and myths. *InPsych*, **27**, 14–17.

Hanson, S. L. & Ginsburg, A. L. (1988) Gaining ground: Values and high school success. *American Educational Research Journal*, **25**, 334–65.

Harackiewicz, J. M., Barron, K. E. & Elliot, A. J. (1998) Rethinking achievement goals: When are they adaptive for college students and why? *Educational Psychologist*, **33**, 1–21.

Harackiewicz, J. M., Barron, K. E., Pintrich, P. R., Elliot, A. J. & Thrash, T. M. (2002) Revision of achievement goal theory: Necessary and illuminating. *Journal of Educational Psychology*, **94**, 638–45.

Harackiewicz, J. M., Barron, K. E., Tauer, J. M. & Elliot, A. J. (2002) Predicting success in college: A longitudinal study of achievement goals and ability measures as predictors of interest and performance from freshman year through graduation. *Journal of Educational Psychology*, **94**, 562–75.

Harari, O. & Covington, M. V. (1981) Reactions to achievement behavior from a teacher and student perspective: A developmental analysis. *American Educational Research Journal*, **18**, 15–28.

Haraway, D. J. (1991) *Simians, Cyborgs, and Women. The Reinvention of Nature*. New York: Routledge.

Hareli, S. & Weiner, B. (2002) Social emotions and personality inferences: A scaffold for a new direction in the study of achievement motivation. *Educational Psychology*, **37**, 183–93.

Harris, M. (1985) *Textbook of Child Care and Health*. Sydney: Science Press.

Harris, S. (1990) *Two-way Aboriginal Schooling: Education and Cultural Survival.* Canberra: Aboriginal Studies Press.

Hart, E. R. & Speece, D. L. (1998) Reciprocal teaching goes to college: Effects for postsecondary student at risk for academic failure. *Journal of Educational Psychology*, **90**, 670–81.

Harter, S. (1990) Issues in the assessment of the self-concept of children and adolescents. In A. LaGreca (ed.) *Through the Eyes of a Child.* Boston: Allyn & Bacon.

Harvey, D. & Green, C. (1984) Attitudes of New Zealand teachers, teachers in training and non-teachers toward mainstreaming. *New Zealand Journal of Educational Studies*, **19**, 34–44.

Hastings, R. P. & Oakford, S. (2003) Student teachers' attitudes towards the inclusion of children with special needs. *Educational Psychology*, **23**, 87–94.

Hattie, J. (1992) Measuring the effects of schooling. *Australian Journal of Education*, **36**, 5–13.

Havighurst, R. J. (1959) *Human Development and Education.* New York: Longmans, Green.

Haviland, J. M. (1979) Teachers' and students' beliefs about punishment. *Journal of Educational Psychology*, **71**, 563–70.

Hayes, S. C., Rosenfarb, I., Wuhfert, E., Munt, E. D., Korn, Z. & Zettle, R. D. (1985) Self-reinforcement effects: An artifact of social standard setting? *Journal of Applied Behavior Analysis*, **18**, 201–14.

Heckhausen, H. (1991) *Motivation and Action* (trans. by Peter K. Leppmann). Berlin: Springer-Verlag.

Heffey, P. G. (1985) The duty of schools and teachers to protect pupils from injury. *Monash Law Review*, **11**, 12.

Helson, R. (1971) Women mathematicians and the creative personality. *Journal of Consulting and Clinical Psychology*, **36**, 210–20.

Henderson. J. G. (1992) *Reflective Teaching. Becoming an Inquiring Educator.* New York: Macmillan.

Hendry, G. D. (1996) Constructivism and educational practice. *Australian Journal of Education*, **40**, 19–45.

Hendry, G. D. *et al.* (2005) Helping students understand their learning styles: Effects on study self-efficacy, preferences for group work, and group climate. *Educational Psychology*, **25**, 395–407.

Hennigan, K. M. *et al.* (1982) Impact of the introduction of television on crime in the United States: Empirical findings and theoretical implications. *Journal of Personality and Social Psychology*, **42**, 461–77.

Henson, R. K. (2002) From adolescent angst to adulthood: Substantive implications and measurement dilemmas in the development of teacher efficacy research. *Educational Psychologist*, **37**, 137–50.

Henson, R. K., Tyson Bennett, D., Sienty, S. F. & Chambers, S. M. (2000) The relationship between means-end task analysis and context specific and global self-efficacy in emergency certification teachers: Exploring a new model of teacher efficacy. Paper presented at the annual meeting of the American Educational Research Association, 28 April, New Orleans.

Heron, A. & Dowel, W. (1973) Weight conservation and matrix-solving ability in Papuan children. *Journal of Cross-Cultural Psychology*, **4**, 207–19.

Hersh, R. H., Paolitto, D. P. & Reimer, J. (1979) *Promoting Moral Growth: From Piaget to Kohlberg.* New York: Longman.

Hewitt, D. (2000) A clash of worldviews: Experiences from teaching Aboriginal students. *Theory into Practice*, **39**, 111–18.

Higgins, E. T. (1987) Self-discrepancy: A theory relating self and affect. *Psychological Review*, **94**, 319–40.

Hill, J. (1995) School culture and peer groups. In L. W. Anderson (ed.) *International Encyclopedia of Teaching and Teacher Education*, 2nd ed. Tarrytown, NY: Pergamon.

Hill, J. P. & Lynch, M. E. (1983) The intensification of gender-related role expectations during early adolescence. In J. Brooks-Gunn & A. C. Petersen (eds) *Girls at Puberty. Biological and Psychosocial Perspectives.* New York: Plenum Press.

Hill, N. E. (2001) Parenting and academic socialization as they relate to school reading: The roles of ethnicity and family income. *Journal of Educational Psychology*, **93**, 686–97.

Hill, N. E. & Craft, S. A. (2003) Parent–school involvement and school performance: Mediated pathways among socio-economically comparable African American and Euro-American families. *Journal of Educational Psychology*, **95**, 74–83.

Hill, S. & Hill, T. (1990) *The Collaborative Classroom.* Melbourne: Eleanor Curtin Publishing.

Ho, R. (1994) Cigarette advertising and cigarette health warnings: What role do adolescents' motives for smoking play in their assessment? *Australian Psychologist*, **29**, 49–56.

Ho, R. & McMurtrie, J. (1991) Attributional feedback and underachieving children. Differential effects on causal attributions, success expectations, and learning processes. *Australian Journal of Psychology*, **43**, 93–100.

Hoffman, D. M. (1996) Culture and self in multicultural education: Reflections on discourse, text, and practice. *American Educational Research Journal*, **33**, 545–69.

Hoffman, M. L. (1980) Moral development in adolescence. In J. Adelson (ed.) *Handbook of Adolescent Psychology.* New York: John Wiley.

Hogan, T., Rabinowitz, M. & Craven, J. A. (2003) Representation in teaching: Inferences from research of expert and novice teachers. *Educational Psychologist*, **38**, 235–47.

Hoge, R. D. (1988) Issues in the definition and measurement of the giftedness construct. *Educational Researcher*, **17**, 12–16.

Hoge, R. D. & Coladarci, T. (1989) Teacher-based judgments of academic achievement: A review of literature. *Review of Educational Research*, **59**, 297–313.

Hoge, R. D. & Renzulli, J. S. (1993) Exploring the link between giftedness and self-concept. *Review of Educational Research*, **63**, 449–65.

Hohepa, M., Jenkins, K. & McNaughton, S. (1992) Maori pedagogies, the role of the individual and language development. Paper presented at the AARE/NZARE conference 'Educational Research: Discipline and Diversity'. Geelong, Victoria.

Holland, C. J. & Kobasigawa, A. (1980) Observational learning: Bandura. In G. M. Gazda & R. J. Corsini (eds) *Theories of Learning.* Itasca, IL: F. E. Peacock.

Hollins, E. R. (1996) *Culture in School Learning. Revealing the Deep Meaning.* Mahway, NJ: Lawrence Erlbaum.

Holt, K. S. (1991) *Child Development. Diagnosis and Assessment.* London: Butterworth-Heinemann.

Honig, A. S. & Wittmer, D. S. (1996) Helping children become more prosocial: Ideas for classrooms, families, schools and communities. *Young Children*, January, 62–70.

Honigsfeld, A. & Schiering, M. (2004) Diverse approaches to the diversity of learning styles in teacher education. *Educational Psychology*, **24**, 487–507.

Hoong, W., Houghton, S. & Douglas, G. (2003) Objectivity of boys with Attention-Deficit/Hyperactivity Disorder (ADHD) and their mothers when responding to a caricatured portrayal of ADHD. *Educational Psychology*, **23**, 492–505.

Hoover-Dempsey, K. V. & Sandler, H. M. (1997) Why do some

parents become involved in their children's education? *Review of Educational Research*, **67**, 3–42.

Horn, J. M. (1983) The Texas adoption project: Adopted children and their intellectual resemblance to biological and adoptive parents. *Child Development*, **54**, 268–75.

Horowitz, F. D. & O'Brien, M. (1986) Gifted and talented children. State of knowledge and directions for research. *American Psychologist*, **41**, 1147–52.

Howes, C., Unger, O. & Seidner, L. B. (1989) Social pretend play in toddlers: Parallels with social play and social pretend. *Child Development*, **60**, 77–84.

Huck, S. W. & Bounds, W. G. (1972) Essay grades: An interaction between graders, handwriting clarity and the neatness of examination papers, *American Journal of Educational Research*, **9**, 279–83.

Hunter, E. M. (1991) An examination of recent suicides in remote Australia. Further information from the Kimberley. *Australia and New Zealand Journal of Psychiatry*, **25**, 197–202.

Hunter, M. (1982) *Mastery Teaching*. El Segundo, CA: TIP Publications.

Hunter, M. (1991) Hunter design helps achieve the goals of science instruction. *Educational Leadership*, **48**, 79–81.

Hutchins, E. (1990) The social organization of team navigation. In J. Galegher, R. E. Kraut & C. Egido (eds) *Intellectual Teamwork: Social and Technological Foundations of Cooperative Work*. Hillsdale, NJ: Lawrence Erlbaum.

Hyde, J. S. & Jaffee, S. (1998) Perspectives from social and feminist psychology. *Educational Researcher*, **27**, 14–16.

Idol, L., Jones, B. F. & Mayer, R. E. (1991) Classroom instruction: The teaching of thinking. In L. Idol & B. F. Jones (eds) *Educational Values and Cognitive Instruction: Implications for Reform*. Hillsdale, NJ: Lawrence Erlbaum.

Idol, L. & West, J. F. (1993) *Effective Instruction of Difficult to Teach Students. Instructors' Manual*. Austin, TX: Pro-Ed.

Individuals with Disabilities Education Act Amendments, Pub. L. No. 105-117 (1997).

Ingvarson, L. & Greenway, P. (1984) Portrayals of teacher development. *The Australian Journal of Education*, **28**, 45–65.

Inhelder, B. & de Caprona, D. (1987) Introduction. In B. Inhelder, D. de Caprona & A. Cornu-Wells (eds) *Piaget Today*. London: Lawrence Erlbaum.

Inhelder, B., de Caprona, D. & Cornu-Wells, A. (1987) *Piaget Today*. London: Lawrence Erlbaum.

Iran-Nejad, A. (1990) Active and dynamic self-regulation of learning processes. *Review of Educational Research*, **60**, 573–602.

Irvine, S. H. & Berry, J. W. (eds) (1988) *Human Abilities in Cultural Context*. Cambridge: Cambridge University Press.

Irwin, K. (1989) Multicultural education. The New Zealand response. *New Zealand Journal of Educational Studies*, **24**, 3–18.

Irwin, K. (1992) Maori education 1991: A review and discussion. In H. Manson (ed.) *New Zealand Annual Review of Education*. Wellington, NZ: Education Department, Victoria University.

Irwin, K. (1993) Maori education in 1992: A review and discussion. In H. Manson (ed.) *New Zealand Annual Review of Education*. Wellington, NZ: Education Department, Victoria University.

Irwin, K. & Davies, L. (1992) A regional study of the school based factors affecting achievement for Maori girls in bilingual immersion and mainstream classes, units and schools at primary level. Paper presented at the AARE/NZARE conference 'Educational Research: Discipline and Diversity'. Geelong, Victoria.

Iversen, I. H. (1992) Skinner's early research: From reflexology to operant conditioning. *American Psychologist*, **47**, 1318–29.

Jackson, K. & Harvey, D. (1991) Open schools or conventional: Which does the job better? *New Zealand Journal of Educational Studies*, **26**, 145–53.

Jackson, P., Reid, N. & Croft, C. (1980) *SHEIK: Study Habits Evaluation and Instruction Kit*. Melbourne: ACER.

Jarvinen, D. W. & Nicholls, J. G. (1996) Adolescents' social goals, beliefs about causes of social success, and satisfaction in peer relations. *Developmental Psychology*, **32**, 435–41.

Jenkins, J., Spelz, M., Odom, L. & Samuel, L. (1985) Integrating normal handicapped pre-schoolers: Effects on child development and social interaction. *Exceptional Children*, **52**, 7–17.

Jenkins, J. R., Odom, S. L. & Speltz, M. L. (1989) Effects of social integration on preschool children with handicaps. *Exceptional Children*, **55**, 420–8.

Jenkinson, J. & Gow, L. (1989) Integration in Australia: A research perspective. *The Australian Journal of Education*, **33**, 267–84.

Jimerson, S., Egeland, B. & Teo, A. (1999) A longitudinal study of achievement trajectories: Factors associated with change. *Journal of Educational Psychology*, **91**, 116–26.

Johnson, C. & Conners, M. E. (1987) *The Etiology and Treatment of Bulimia Nervosa: A Biopsychosocial Perspective*. New York: Basic Books.

Johnson, D. S. (1981) Naturally acquired learned helplessness: The relationship of school failure to achievement behavior, attributions, and self-concept. *Journal of Educational Psychology*, **73**, 174–80.

Johnson, D. W. & Johnson, R. T. (1975) *Learning Together and Alone: Cooperation, Competition, and Individualization*. Englewood Cliffs, NJ: Prentice Hall.

Johnson, D. W. & Johnson, R. T. (1985a) Cooperative learning and adaptive education. In M. C. Wang & H. J. Walberg (eds) *Adapting Instruction to Individual Differences*. Berkeley, CA: McCutchan.

Johnson, D. W. & Johnson, R. T. (1985b) Motivational processes in cooperative, competitive, and individualistic learning situations. In C. Ames & R. Ames (eds) *Research on Motivation in Education: The Classroom Milieu (Volume 2)*. Orlando: Academic Press.

Johnson, D. W. & Johnson, R. T. (1989–90) Social skills for successful group work. *Educational Leadership*, **47**, 30.

Johnson, D. W. & Johnson, R. T. (1989a) Toward a cooperative effort: A response to Slavin. *Educational Leadership*, **46**, 80–1.

Johnson, D. W. & Johnson, R. T. (1989c) Cooperative learning. In L. W. Anderson (ed.) *The Effective Teacher*. New York: McGraw-Hill.

Johnson, D. W. & Johnson, R. T. (1992) Encouraging thinking through constructive controversy. In N. Davidson & T. Worsham (eds) *Enhancing Thinking through Cooperative Learning*. New York: Teachers College Press.

Johnson, D. W. & Johnson, R. T. (1994) *Learning Together and Alone: Cooperative, Competitive, and Individualistic Learning*, 4th ed. Boston: Allyn & Bacon.

Johnson, D. W. & Johnson, R. T. (1995) Why violence prevention programs don't work—and what does. *Educational Leadership*, **52**, 63–8.

Johnson, D. W., Johnson, R. T. & Stanne, M. B. (2000) *Cooperative Learning Methods: A Meta-analysis*. http://www.cooplearn.org/pages/cl-methods.html

Johnson, D. W., Maruyama, G., Johnson, R. T., Nelson, D. & Skon, L. (1981) Effects of cooperative, competitive, and individualistic goal structures on achievement: A meta-analysis. *Psychological Bulletin*, **89**, 47–62.

Johnson, S. M. & Birkeland, S. E. (2003) Pursuing a 'sense of success': New teachers explain their career decisions. *American Educational Research Journal*, **40**, 581–617.

John-Steiner, V. & Mahn, H. (1996) Sociocultural approaches to learning and development: A Vygotskian framework. *Educational Psychologist*, **31**, 191–206.

Jones, E. & Reynolds, G. (1992) *The Play's the Thing*. New York: Teachers College Press.

Jones, F. (1987a) *Positive Classroom Discipline*. New York: McGraw-Hill.

Jones, F. (1987b) *Positive Classroom Instruction*. New York: McGraw-Hill.

Jones, J. (1981) Study skills: Panacea, placebo or promise? *SET Research Information for Teachers*, number 2, item 13.

Jones, M. B. (1988) Autism: The child within. In K. L. Frieberg (ed.) *Educating Exceptional Children*, 6th ed. Guilford, CT: Duskin.

Jones, S. M. & Dindia, K. (2004) A meta-analytic perspective on sex equity in the classroom. *Review of Educational Research*, **74**, 443–71.

Jones, V. F. & Jones, L. S. (1995) *Comprehensive Classroom Management: Creating Positive Learning Environments*, 4th ed. Boston: Allyn & Bacon.

Jordan, D. F. (1984) The social construction of identity: The Aboriginal problem. *The Australian Journal of Education*, **28**, 274–90.

Jordan, D. W. (1997) Social skilling through cooperative learning. *Educational Research*, **39**, 3–21.

Joyce, B., Showers, B. & Rolheiser-Bennett, C. (1987) Staff development and student learning: A synthesis of research on models of teaching. *Educational Leadership*, **45**, 11–22.

Joyce, B. & Weil, M. (1972) *Models of Teaching*. Englewood Cliffs, NJ: Prentice Hall.

Judge, C. (1987) *Civilization and Mental Retardation*. Kew, Victoria: C.J. Publishing.

Kagan, J. (1965) Reflection-impulsivity and reading ability in primary grade children. *Child Development*, **36**, 609–28.

Kagan, J. (1966) Reflection and impulsivity: The generality and dynamics of conceptual tempo. *Journal of Abnormal and Social Psychology*, **71**, 17–24.

Kagan, J. & Kogan, N. (1970) Individual variations in cognitive processes. In P. Mussen (ed.) *Carmichael's Manual of Child Psychology*. New York: John Wiley.

Kagan, S. (1985) Learning to cooperate. In R. Slavin *et al.* (eds) *Learning to Cooperate, Cooperating to Learn*. New York: Plenum Press.

Kagan, S. (1992) *Cooperative Learning*. San Juan Capistrano, CA: Kagan Cooperative Learning.

Kagan, S. (1994) *Cooperative Learning*. San Juan Capistrano, CA: Kagan Cooperative Learning.

Kahle, J. B., Parker, L. H., Rennie, L. J. & Riley, D. (1993) Gender differences in science education: Building a model. *Educational Psychologist*, **28**, 379–404.

Kail, R. & Bisanz, J. (1992) The information-processing perspective on cognitive development in childhood and adolescence. In R. J. Sternberg and C. A. Berg (eds) *Intellectual Development*. New York: Cambridge University Press.

Kalantzis, M. & Cope, B. (1987) Multicultural education in crisis? The needs of non English speaking background students. *Migration Action*, **9**, 23–9.

Kalantzis, M. & Cope, B. (1988) Why we need multicultural education: A review of the 'ethnic disadvantage' debate. *Journal of Intercultural Studies*, **9**, 39–57.

Kalantzis, M., Cope, B., Noble, G. & Poynting, S. (1990) *Cultures of Schooling: Pedagogies for Cultural Difference and Social Access*. London: Falmer.

Kalyuga, S., Ayres, P., Chandler, P. & Sweller, J. (2003) The expertise reversal effect. *Educational Psychologist*, **38**, 23–31.

Kanaya, T., Scullin, M. H. & Ceci, S. J. (2003) The Flynn Effect and U.S. policies. The impact of the rising IQ scores on American society via mental retardation diagnoses. *American Psychologist*, **58**, 778–90.

Kantowitz, B. H. & Roediger, H. L. (1980) Memory and information processing. In G. M. Gazda & R. J. Corsini (eds) *Theories of Learning*. Itasca, IL: F. E. Peacock.

Kaplan, A., Gheen, M. & Midgley, C. (2002) Classroom goal structure and student disruptive behaviour. *British Journal of Educational Psychology*, **72**, 191–211.

Kaplan, R. M. & Pascoe, G. C. (1977) Humorous lectures and humorous examples: Some effects upon comprehension and retention. *Journal of Educational Psychology*, **69**, 61–5.

Karabenick, S. A. (1998) Strategic help seeking. Implications for learning and teaching. Mahway, NJ: Lawrence Erlbaum.

Karabenick, S. A. (2004) Perceived achievement goal structure and college student help seeking. *Journal of Educational Psychology*, **96**, 569–81.

Karvale, K. A. & Forness, S. R. (1987) Substance over style: Assessing the efficacy of modality testing and teaching. *Exceptional Children*, **54**, 228–39.

Karvale, K. A. & Forness, S. R. (1990) Substance over style: A rejoinder to Dunn's animadversions. *Exceptional Children*, **56**, 357–61.

Kaslow, F. W. (2001) Families and family psychology at the millennium: Intersecting crossroads. *American Psychologist*, **56**, 37–46.

Kaufman, A. S. (2000) Tests of intelligence. In R. J. Sternberg (ed.) *Handbook of Intelligence*. New York: Cambridge University Press.

Kazdin, A. E. (1973) The effect of vicarious reinforcement on attentive behavior in the classroom. *Journal of Applied Behavior Analysis*, **6**, 71–8.

Kearins, J. (1988) Cultural elements in testing: The test, the tester and the tested. In G. Davidson (ed.) *Ethnicity and Cognitive Assessment: Australian Perspectives*. Darwin: Institute of Technology.

Keats, D. (1994) Cultural contributions to schooling in multicultural environments. In E. Thomas (ed.) *International Perspectives on Culture and Schooling: A Symposium of Proceedings*. London: Institute of Education.

Keats, D. M. & Keats, J. A. (1988) Human assessment in Australia. In S. H. Irvine & J. W. Berry (eds) *Human Abilities in Cultural Context*. Cambridge: Cambridge University Press.

Keats, D. M., Munro, D. & Mann, L. (eds) (1989) *Heterogeneity in Cross-Cultural Psychology*. Lisse: Zwets & Zeitlinger.

Keefe, J. W. & Ferrell, B. G. (1990) Developing a defensible learning style paradigm. *Educational Leadership*, **48**, 57–61.

Keenan, T., Olson, D. R. & Marini, Z. (1998) Working memory and children's developing understanding of mind. *Australian Journal of Psychology*, **50**, 76–82.

Keith, T. Z., Reimers, T. M., Fehrmann, P. G., Pottebaum, S. M. & Aubrey, L. W. (1986) Parental involvement, homework, and TV time: Direct and indirect effects on high school achievement. *Journal of Educational Psychology*, **78**, 373–80.

Kelly, E. B. (1988) Learning disabilities: A new horizon of perception. In K. L. Frieberg (ed.) *Educating Exceptional Children*, 6th ed. Guilford, CT: Duskin.

Kelly, K. (2000) New independence for special needs students. In D. T. Gordon (ed.) *The Digital Classroom*. Cambridge, MA: Harvard Education Letter.

Kerns, A., Klepac, L. & Cole, A. K. (1996) Peer relationships and preadolescents' perceptions of security in the child–mother relationship. *Developmental Psychology*, **32**, 457–66.

Kester, L., Kirschner, P. A. & Merriënboer, J. J. G. (2005) The management of cognitive load during complex cognitive skill acquisition by means of computer-simulated problem solving. *British Journal of Educational Psychology*, **75**, 71–85.

Kidd, G. J. (1996) Links between tertiary students' interests, learning styles, and academic achievement. Paper presented at the 31st Annual Conference of the Australian Psychological Society, Sydney, 25–29 September.

King, A. (1990) Enhancing peer interaction and learning in the classroom through reciprocal questioning. *American Educational Research Journal*, **27**, 664–87.

King, A. (1991) Effects of training in strategic questioning on children's problem-solving performance. *Journal of Educational Psychology*, **83**, 307–17.

King, A. (1992a) Comparison of self-questioning, summarizing, and notetaking-review as strategies for learning from lectures. *American Educational Research Journal*, **29**, 303–23.

King, A. (1992b) Facilitating elaborative learning through guided student-generated questioning. *Educational Psychologist*, **27**, 111–26.

King, A. (1993) From sage on the stage to guide on the side. *College Teaching*, **41**, 30–5.

King, A. (1994) Questioning and knowledge generation. *American Educational Research Journal*, **31**, 338–68.

King, A. (1997) ASK TO THINK—TEL WHY: A model of transactive peer tutoring for scaffolding higher level complex learning. *Educational Psychologist*, **32**, 221–35.

King, A., Staffieri, A. & Adelgais, A. (1998) Mutual peer tutoring: Effects of structuring tutorial interaction to scaffold peer learning. *Journal of Educational Psychology*, **90**, 134–52.

King, N. J., Ollendick, T. H. & Gullone, E. (1990) School-related fears of children and adolescents. *Australian Journal of Education*, **34**, 99–112.

Kingsley, H. L. & Garry, R. (1957) *The Nature and Conditions of Learning*, 2nd ed. Englewood Cliffs, NJ: Prentice Hall.

Kirk, S. & Gallagher, J. (1983) The exceptional child in modern society; individual differences and special education; children with visual impairments; children with multiple, severe and physical handicaps. In S. Kirk & J. Gallagher (eds) *Educating Exceptional Children*, 4th ed. Boston: Houghton Mifflin.

Kirschner, D. & Whitson, J. A. (1998) Obstacles to understanding cognition as situated. *Educational Researcher*, **27**, 22–8.

Klahr, D. & Wallace, J. G. (1976) *Cognitive Development: An Information Processing View*. Hillsdale, NJ: Lawrence Erlbaum.

Kleinbaum, D. G., Kupper, L. L. & Muller, K. E. (1988) *Applied Regression Analysis and Other Multivariate Methods*, 2nd ed. Boston: PWS-Kent.

Kleinfeld, J. (1975) Effective teachers of Indian and Eskimo students. *School Review*, **83**, 301–44.

Kleinfeld, J. (1998) *The Myth that Schools Shortchange Girls: Social Science in the Service of Deception*. Washington, DC: Women's Freedom Network.

Klich, L. Z. (1988) Aboriginal cognition and psychological nescience. In S. H. Irvine & J. W. Berry (eds) *Human Abilities in Cultural Context*. Cambridge: Cambridge University Press.

Kobak, R. R. & Sceery, A. (1988) Attachment in adolescence: Working models, affect regulation, and representations of self and others. *Child Development*, **59**, 135–46.

Koffka, K. (1935) *Principles of Gestalt Psychology*. New York: Harcourt Brace.

Kogan, N. (1971) Educational implications of cognitive styles. In G. S. Lesser (ed.) *Psychological and Educational Practice*. Glenview, IL: Scott, Foresman & Co.

Kohlberg, L. (1969) *Global Rating Scale: Preliminary Moral Judgment Scoring Manual*. Cambridge, MA: Center for Moral Education.

Kohlberg, L. (1976) Moral stages and moralization: The cognitive-developmental approach to socialization. In D. A. Goslin (ed.) *Handbook of Socialization Theory and Research*. Chicago: Rand McNally.

Kohlberg, L. (1977) The cognitive-developmental approach to moral education. In H. F. Clarizio, R. C. Craig & W. A. Mehrens (eds) *Contemporary Issues in Educational Psychology*, 3rd ed. Boston: Allyn & Bacon.

Kohlberg, L. (1978) Revisions in the theory and practice of moral development. In W. Damon (ed.) *Moral Development: New Directions for Child Development* (No. 2). San Francisco: Jossey-Bass.

Kohlberg, L. (1981) *The Philosophy of Moral Development*. San Francisco: Harper & Row.

Kohlberg, L., Levine, C. & Hewer, A. (1983) *Moral Stages. A Current Formulation and Response to Critics*. Basel, Switzerland: Karger.

Kohler, W. (1925) *The Mentality of Apes* (E. Winter, trans.). New York: Harcourt Brace.

Kohn, A. (1991) Group grade grubbing versus cooperative learning. *Educational Leadership*, **48**, 83–7.

Kohn, A. (1996a) By all available means: Cameron's and Pierce's defense of extrinsic motivators. *Review of Educational Research*, **66**, 1–4.

Kohn, A. (1996b) *Beyond Discipline: From Compliance to Community*. Alexandria, VA: Association for Supervision and Curriculum Development.

Kokkinos, C. M., Panayiotou, G. & Davazoglou, A. M. (2004) Perceived seriousness of pupils' undesirable behaviours: The student teachers' perspective. *Educational Psychology*, **24**, 109–20.

Kolb, D. (1976) *Learning-style Inventory. Technical Manual*. Boston: McBer.

Koop, T. & Koop, G. (1990) Reflective teaching as professional empowerment. In M. Bezzina & J. Butcher (eds) *The Changing Face of Professional Education. Collected Papers of the AARE Annual Conference, Sydney University, 1990*. Sydney: AARE.

Kornhaber, M., Krechevsky, M. & Gardner, H. (1990) Engaging intelligence. *Educational Psychologist*, **25**, 177–99.

Kosky, R. (1987) Is suicidal behaviour increasing among Australian youth? *Medical Journal of Australia*, **147**, 164–6.

Kounin, J. S. (1970) *Discipline and Group Management in Classrooms*. New York: Holt, Rinehart & Winston.

Kounin, J. S. (1977) *Discipline and Group Management in Classrooms*. 2nd ed. New York: Holt, Rinehart & Winston.

Kouzma, N. M. & Kennedy, G. A. (2000) Academic stress, self-efficacy, social support, and health behaviours in female Victorian Certificate of Education (VCE) students. *The Australian Educational and Developmental Psychologist*, **17**, 24–43.

Kozulin, A. & Presseisen, B. Z. (1995) Mediated learning experience and psychological tools: Vygotsky's and Feuerstein's perspectives in a study of student learning. *Educational Psychologist*, **30**, 67–75.

Krathwohl, D. R., Bloom, B. S. & Masia, B. B. (1956) *Taxonomy of Educational Objectives. The Classification of Educational Goals.* Handbook 11: *Affective Domain*. London: Longman.

Kuhn, D. & Pearsall, S. (2000) Developing origins of scientific thinking. *Journal of Cognition and Development*, **1**, 113–29.

Kukla, A. (1972) Attributional determinants of achievement-related behavior. *Journal of Personality and Social Psychology*, **21**, 166–74.

Kulhavy, R. W. (1977) Feedback in written instruction. *Review of Educational Research*, **47**, 211–32.

Kulik, C-L. C., Kulik, J. A. & Schwalb, B. J. (1983) College programs for high-risk and disadvantaged students: A meta-analysis of findings. *Review of Educational Research*, **53**, 397–414.

Kulik, J. A. & Kulik, C-L. C. (1984) Effects of accelerated instruction on students. *Review of Educational Research*, **54**, 409–25.

Kulik, J. A. & Kulik, C-L. C. (1988) Timing of feedback and verbal learning. *Review of Educational Research*, **58**, 79–97.

Kumar, V. K. (1971) The structure of human memory and some educational implications. *Review of Educational Research*, **41**, 379–417.

Kumpfer, K. L. & Alvarado, R. (2003) Family-strengthening approaches for the prevention of youth problem behaviors. *American Psychologist*, **58**, 457–65.

Kurdek, L. A. & Sinclair, R. J. (2000) Psychological, family, and peer predictors of academic outcomes in first- through fifth-grade children. *Journal of Educational Psychology*, **92**, 449–57.

Kutnick, P. & Jules, V. (1993) Pupils' perceptions of a good teacher: A developmental perspective from Trinidad and Tobago. *British Journal of Educational Psychology*, **63**, 400–13.

Kyriacou, C. (1986) *Effective Teaching in Schools.* Oxford: Basil Blackwell.

Kyriacou, C. (1991) *Essential Teaching Skills.* Oxford: Basil Blackwell.

Ladson-Billings, G. (1995) Toward a theory of culturally relevant pedagogy. *American Educational Research Journal*, **32**, 465–91.

Ladson-Billings, G. (1999) Preparing teachers for diverse student populations: A critical race theory perspective. *Review of Research in Education*, **24**, 211–47.

Lam, T. C. M. (1992) Review of practices and problems in the evaluation of bilingual education. *Review of Educational Research*, **62**, 181–203.

Lampert, M. & Clark, C. M. (1990) Expert knowledge and expert thinking in teaching: A response to Floden and Klinzing. *Educational Researcher*, **19**, 21–3.

Lange, D. (1988) *Tomorrow's Schools: The Reform of Education Administration in New Zealand.* Wellington, NZ: Department of Education.

Langer, J. A. (2000) Excellence in English in middle and high school: How teachers' professional lives support student achievement. *American Educational Research Journal*, **37**, 397–439.

Langlois, J. H. & Stephan, C. W. (1981) Beauty and the Beast: The role of physical attractiveness in the development of peer relations and social behaviour. In S. S. Brehm, S. M. Kassin & F. X. Gibbons (eds) *Developmental Social Psychology*. New York: Oxford University Press.

Larkins, A. G., McKinney, C. W., Oldham-Buss, S. & Gilmore, A. C. (1985) Teacher enthusiasm: A critical review. In H. S. Williams (ed.) *Educational and Psychological Research Monographs.* Hattiesburg, MS: University of Southern Mississippi.

Laskey, L. & Hallinan, P. (1990) Reflection and reality: The prospects for teacher candidates. In M. Bezzina & J. Butcher (eds) *The Changing Face of Professional Education. Collected Papers of the AARE Annual Conference, Sydney University, 1990.* Sydney: AARE.

Laszlo, J. I. (1996) Paper-pencil skills at the pre-primary age. *Australian Journal of Psychology*, **48**, 116.

Lee, C. D. (2001) Is October Brown Chinese? A cultural modelling activity system for underachieving students. *American Educational Research Journal*, **38**, 97–141.

Lee, J. (2002) Racial and ethnic achievement gap trends: Reversing the progress toward equity. *Educational Review*, **31**, 3–12.

Lee, O. & Anderson, C. W. (1993) Task engagement and conceptual change in Middle School science classrooms. *American Educational Research Journal*, **30**, 585–610.

Lee, V. E., Bryk, A. & Smith, J. B. (1993) The organization of effective secondary schools. *Review of Research in Education*, **19**, 171–267.

Lee, V. E., Marks, H. M. & Byrd, T. (1994) Sexism in single-sex and co-educational independent secondary school classrooms. *Sociology of Education*, **67**, 92–120.

Lee, V. E. & Smith, J. B. (1995) Effects of high school restructuring and size on early gains in achievement and engagement. *Sociology of Education*, **68**, 104–29.

Lee, V. E. & Smith, J. B. (1999) Social support and achievement for young adolescents in Chicago: The role of school academic press. *American Educational Research Journal*, **36**, 907–45.

LePore, P. C. & Warren, J. R. (1997) A comparison of single-sex and coeducational catholic secondary schooling: Evidence from the National Educational Longitudinal Study of 1988. *American Educational Research Journal*, **34**, 485–511.

Lepper, M. R. & Greene, D. (eds) (1978) *The Hidden Cost of Reward: New Perspectives on the Psychology of Human Motivation.* Hillsdale, NJ: Lawrence Erlbaum.

Lepper, M. R. & Hodell, M. (1989) Intrinsic motivation in the classroom. In C. Ames & R. Ames (eds) *Research on Motivation in Education: Goals and Cognitions (Volume 3).* San Diego, CA: Academic Press.

Lepper, M. R., Keavney, M. & Drake, M. (1996) Intrinsic motivation and extrinsic rewards: A commentary on Cameron and Pierce's meta-analysis. *Review of Educational Research*, **66**, 5–32.

Lerner, R. & Korn, S. (1972) The development of body build stereotypes in males. *Child Development*, **43**, 908–20.

Lerner, R. M. (1969) The development of stereotyped expectancies of body-build-behavior relations. *Child Development*, **40**, 137–41.

Lester, D. & Icli, T. (1990) Beliefs about suicide in American and Turkish students. *The Journal of Social Psychology*, **130**, 825–7.

Lester, F. K., Lambdin, D. V. & Preston, R. V. (1997) A new vision of the nature and purposes of assessment in the mathematics classroom. In G. Phye (ed.) *Handbook of Classroom Assessment: Learning, Achievement, and Adjustment.* San Diego, CA: Academic Press.

Leung, D. Y. P. & Kember, D. (2003) The relationship between approaches to learning and reflection upon practice. *Educational Psychology*, **23**, 61–71.

Levin, B. (1985) Equal educational opportunity for children with special needs: The federal role in Australia. *Law and Contemporary Problems*, **48**, 213–73.

Levin, J. R. (1985) Educational applications of mnemonic pictures: Possibilities beyond your wildest imagination. In A. A. Sheikk (ed.) *Imagery in Education: Imagery in the Educational Process.* Farmingdale, NY: Baywood.

Levin, J. R., Shriberg, L. K. & Berry, J. K. (1983) A concrete strategy for remembering abstract prose. *American Educational Research Journal*, **20**, 277–90.

Levine, M. P. & Smolak, L. (1998) The mass media and disordered eating. In W. Vandereyeken (ed.) *The Prevention of Eating Disorders*. New York: New York University Press.

Levine, M. P., Smolak, L. & Hayden, H. (1994) The relation of sociocultural factors to eating attitudes and behaviours among middle school girls. *Journal of Early Adolescence*, **14**, 471–90.

Lewandoski, L. J. & Cruickshank, W. M. (1980) Psychological development of crippled children and youth. In W. M. Cruickshank (ed.) *Psychology of Exceptional Children and Youth*, 4th ed. Englewood Cliffs, NJ: Prentice Hall.

Lewis, R. (1994) Classroom discipline: Preparing our students for democratic citizenship. Paper presented at the Annual Conference of the Australian Association for Research in Education, Newcastle, November.

Lewis, R. (1997) *The Discipline Dilemma*, 2nd ed. Melbourne: ACER.

Lewis, R. & Lovegrove, M. N. (1984) Teachers' classroom control procedures: Are students' preferences being met? *Journal of Education for Teaching*, **10**, 97–105.

Lewis, R. & Lovegrove, M. N. (1987) Teacher as disciplinarian. *Australian Journal of Education*, **31**, 187–204.

Lickona, T. (1991) *Education for Character*. New York: Bantam.

Liebert, R. M. & Spiegler, M. D. (1987) *Personality. Strategies and Issues*, 5th ed. Chicago: The Dorsey Press.

Lillemyr, O. F. (2001) Play and learning in school: A motivational approach. In D. M. McInerney & S. Van Etten (eds) *Research on Sociocultural Influences on Motivation and Learning*. Greenwich, CT: Information Age Press.

Lillemyr, O. F., McInerney, D. M., Søbstat, F. & Valås, H. (2004) Play, learning and self-concept in primary school: A multicultural perspective. In Proceedings Self-concept, motivation and identity: Where to from here? Third International Biennial SELF Research Conference, Berlin, Germany, 4–7 July.

Linn, M. C., Lewis, C., Tsuchida, I. & Songer, N. B. (2000) Beyond fourth-grade science: Why do U.S. and Japanese students diverge? *Educational Researcher*, **29**, 4–14.

Linn, M. C. & Petersen, A. C. (1985) Emergence and characterization of sex-differences in spatial ability: A meta-analysis. *Child Development*, **56**, 1479–98.

Linn, R. L., Baker, E. L. & Dunbar, S. B. (1991) Complex, performance-based assessment: Expectations and validation criteria. *Educational Researcher*, **20**, 15–21.

Linnenbrink, E. A. & Pintrich, P. R. (2002) Achievement goal theory and affect: An asymmetrical bidirectional model. *Educational Psychologist*, **37**, 69–78.

Lipsky, D. & Gartner, A. (eds) (1989) *Beyond Separate Education: Quality Education for All*. Baltimore, MD: Paul H. Brookes.

Lipson, M. Y. (1983) The influence of religious affiliation on children's memory for text information. *Reading Research Quarterly*, **18**, 448–57.

Little, E. (2005) Secondary school teachers' perceptions of students' problem behaviours. *Educational Psychology*, **25**, 369–77.

Livson, N. & Peskin, H. (1980) Perspectives on adolescence from longitudinal research. In J. Adelson (ed.) *Handbook of Adolescent Psychology*. New York: John Wiley.

Lloyd, L. (1999) Multi-age classes and high ability students. *Review of Educational Research*, **69**, 187–212.

Lo Bianco, J. (1987) *National Policy on Languages*. Canberra: AGPS.

Lo Bianco, J. (1988) Multiculturalism and the national policy on languages. *Journal of Intercultural Studies*, **9**, 25–38.

Lo Bianco, J. (1990) A hard-nosed multiculturalism: Revitalising multicultural education? *Vox*, **4**, 80–94.

Lockhart, A. S. (1980a) Motor learning and motor development during infancy and childhood. In C. B. Corbin (ed.) *A Textbook of Motor Development*, 2nd ed. Dubuque, IA: William C. Brown.

Lockhart, A. S. (1980b) Practices and principles governing motor learning of children. In C. B. Corbin (ed.) *A Textbook of Motor Development*, 2nd ed. Dubuque, IA: William C. Brown.

Logan, L. M. & Logan, V. G. (1971) *Design for Creative Teaching*. Toronto: McGraw-Hill.

Lohaus, A., Elben, C. E., Ball, J. & Klein-Hessling, J. (2004) School transition from elementary to secondary school: Changes in psychological adjustment. *Educational Psychology*, **24**, 161–73.

Lohman, D. F. (1989) Human intelligence: An introduction to advances in theory and research. *Review of Educational Research*, **59**, 333–73.

Lohman, D. F. (2000) Complex information processing. In R. J. Sternberg (ed.) *Handbook of Intelligence*. New York: Cambridge University Press.

Loo, R. (2004) Kolb's learning styles and learning preferences: Is there a linkage? *Educational Psychology*, **24**, 99–108.

Lorayne, H. & Lucas, J. (1974) *The Memory Book*. New York: Stein & Day.

Lou, Y., Abrami, P. C., Spence, J. C., Poulson, C., Chambers, B. & d'Apollonia, S. (1996) Within-class grouping: A meta-analysis. *Review of Educational Research*, **66**, 423–58.

Loughran, J., Mitchell, I., Neale, R. & Toussant, D. (2001) PEEL and the beginning teacher. *Australian Educational Researcher*, **28**, 29–32.

Loveland, K. K. & Olley, J. G. (1979) The effect of external reward on interest and quality of task performance in children of high and low intrinsic motivation. *Child Development*, **50**, 1207–10.

Lucangeli, D., Tressoldi, P. E., Bendotti, M., Bonanomi, M. & Siegel, L. S. (2003) Effective strategies for mental and written arithmetic calculation from the third to the fifth grade. *Educational Psychology*, **23**, 507–20.

Lunde, D. T. & Lunde, M. K. (1980) *The Next Generation. A Book of Parenting*. New York: Holt, Rinehart & Winston.

McAllister, G. & Irvine, J. J. (2000) Cross cultural competency and multicultural teacher education. *Review of Educational Research*, **70**, 3–24.

McCann, T. E. & Sheehan, P. W. (1985) Violent content in Australian television. *Australian Psychologist*, **20**, 33–42.

McCaslin, M. & Good, T. L. (1996) The informal curriculum. In D. C. Berliner & R. C. Calfee (eds) *Handbook of Educational Psychology*. New York: Macmillan.

McCaslin, M. & Good, T. L. (1998) Moving beyond sheer compliance: Helping students develop goal coordination strategies. *Educational Horizons*, Summer, 169–76.

McClellan, V. (1989) Young smokers: Rebellion, conformity and imitation. *SET Research Notes for Teachers*, number 1, item 5.

Maccoby, E. E. & Martin, J. A. (1983) Socialization in the context of the family: Parent–child interaction. In E. M. Hetherington (ed.) *Handbook of Child Psychology: Socialization, Personality, and Social Development (Volume 4)*, 4th ed. New York: John Wiley.

McCombs, B. L. & Marzano, R. J. (1990) Putting the self in self-regulated learning: The self as agent in integrating will and skill. *Educational Psychologist*, **25**, 51–69.

McCombs, B. L. & Pope, J. E. (1994) *Motivating Hard to Reach Students*. Washington, DC: American Psychological Association.

McCormack, S. (1989) Response to Render, Padilla, and Krank: But practitioners say it works! *Educational Leadership*, **46**, 77–9.

McCroarty, M. (1992) The societal context of bilingual education. *Educational Researcher*, **21**, 7–9.

McDaniel, T. (1983) 'Well begun is half-done': A school-wide project for better discipline. *SET Research Information for Teachers*, number 1, item 9.

McGaw, B., Banks, D. & Piper, K. (1991) *Effective Schools. Schools that Make a Difference.* Melbourne: ACER.

McGaw, B., Piper, K., Banks, D. & Evans, B. (1992) *Making Schools More Effective.* Melbourne: ACER.

McGregor, H. A. & Elliot, A. J. (2002) Achievement goals as predictors of achievement-relevant processes prior to task engagement. *Journal of Educational Psychology*, **94**, 381–95.

McInerney, D. M. (1979) *Education for a Multicultural Society Report.* Sydney: Milperra College of Advanced Education.

McInerney, D. M. (1984) *Inquiries into Creativity.* Sydney: Macarthur Institute of Higher Education.

McInerney, D. M. (1986) The determinants of motivation of Aboriginal students in school settings. Paper presented at the inaugural research conference of the Australian Institute of Multicultural Affairs entitled 'Ethnicity and Multiculturalism 1986 National Research', Melbourne, 14–16 May.

McInerney, D. M. (1987a) Teacher attitudes towards multicultural curriculum development. *Australian Journal of Education*, **31**, 129–44.

McInerney, D. M. (1987b) The need for the continuing education of teachers: A multicultural perspective. *Journal of Intercultural Studies*, **8**, 45–54.

McInerney, D. M. (1987c) The need for the continuing education of teachers in non-racist education—an Australian perspective. *Multicultural Teaching*, Special Issue: *Continuing Education*, **6**, 31–5.

McInerney, D. M. (1988a) A cross-cultural analysis of student motivation in school settings: An Australian perspective. In E. Thomas (Chair), *Educational Issues and Cross-cultural Psychology*, Symposium conducted at the 9th International IACCP Congress, Newcastle, Australia.

McInerney, D. M. (1988b) Psychological determinants of motivation of urban and rural non-traditional Aboriginal students in school settings: Summary of findings, conclusion and recommendations. Paper presented at the Annual National Conference on Aboriginal Issues, Nepean CAE.

McInerney, D. M. (1988c) The psychological determinants of motivation of urban and rural non-traditional Aboriginal students in school settings: A cross-cultural study. Unpublished doctoral dissertation presented to the University of Sydney, Australia.

McInerney, D. M. (1989a) A cross-cultural analysis of student motivation. In D. M. Keats, D. Munro & L. Mann (eds) *Heterogeneity in Cross-Cultural Psychology*. Lisse: Zwets & Zeitlinger.

McInerney, D. M. (1989b) Urban Aboriginal parents' views on education: A comparative analysis. *Journal of Intercultural Studies*, **10**, 43–65.

McInerney, D. M. (1989c) Psychological determinants of motivation of urban and rural non-traditional Aboriginal students in school settings. In P. Moir and M. Durham (eds) *Contemporary Issues in Aboriginal Studies*. Sydney: Firebird Press.

McInerney, D. M. (1990a) The determinants of motivation for urban Aboriginal students: A cross-cultural analysis. *Journal of Cross-Cultural Psychology*, **21**, 474–95.

McInerney, D. M. (1990b) Sex differences in motivation for Aboriginal students in school settings. In M. Bezzina & J. Butcher (eds) *The Changing Face of Professional Education. Collected Papers of the AARE Annual Conference, Sydney University, 1990.* Sydney: AARE.

McInerney, D. M. (1991a) The behavioural intentions questionnaire. An examination of construct and etic validity in an educational setting. *Journal of Cross-Cultural Psychology*, **22**, 293–306.

McInerney, D. M. (1991b) Key determinants of motivation of urban and rural non-traditional Aboriginal students in school settings: Recommendations for educational change. *Australian Journal of Education*, **35**, 154–74.

McInerney, D. M. (1992a) Indigenous educational research: Can it be psychometric? Paper presented at the AARE/NZARE conference 'Educational Research: Discipline and Diversity', Geelong, Victoria.

McInerney, D. M. (1992b) Cross-cultural insights into school motivation and decision making. *Journal of Intercultural Studies*, **13**, 53–74.

McInerney, D. M. (1992c) Contemporary issues in cross-cultural studies. *Journal of Intercultural Studies*, **13**, 74–6.

McInerney, D. M. (1993) Psychometric perspectives on school motivation and culture. Paper presented at the symposium entitled 'International Perspectives on Culture and Schooling', Department of International and Comparative Education. Institute of Education, London University, 11–13 May.

McInerney, D. M (1994) Psychometric perspectives on school motivation and culture. In E. Thomas (ed.) *International Perspectives on Culture and Schooling: A Symposium of Proceedings*. London: Institute of Education.

McInerney, D. M. (2003) What do Indigenous students think about school and is it any different from the Anglos? Paper presented at the combined AARE & NZARE Conference, Auckland, 29 Nov–3 Dec.

McInerney, D. M., Davidson, N., Suliman, R. & Tremayne, B. (2000) Personal development, health and physical education in context: Muslim and Catholic perspectives. *Australian Journal of Education*, **44**, 26–42.

McInerney, D. M., Dowson, M. & Hinkley, J. (1996) Relations between students' academic performance and teachers' perceptions of their conduct. *Australian Journal of Psychology*, **48**, 121.

McInerney, D. M., Hinkley, J. & Dowson, M. (1996) Children's beliefs about success in the classroom: Are there cultural differences? *Australian Journal of Psychology*, **48**, 121.

McInerney, D. M. & McInerney, V. (1990) Causes and correlates of dropping out: A cross-cultural comparison. In R. A. Peddie (ed.) *Nationhood, Internationalism and Education*, Proceedings of the Eighteenth Annual Conference of the Australian and New Zealand Comparative and International Education Society, University of Auckland, 3–5 December. Auckland: ANZCIEA.

McInerney, D. M. & McInerney, V. (1996a) Cooperative, self-regulated learning or teacher-directed instruction? Efficacy and effect on computer anxiety and achievement. An aptitude-treatment-interaction study. *Australian Journal of Psychology*, **48**, 122.

McInerney, D. M. & McInerney, V. (1996b) School socialization and the goals of schooling: What counts in classrooms and schools characterized by cultural diversity. Paper presented at the annual meeting of the American Educational Research Association, New York, 8–12 April.

McInerney, D. M. & McInerney, V. (2000) A longitudinal qualitative study of school motivation and achievement. Paper presented at the annual meeting of the American Educational Research Association, New Orleans, 24–29 April.

McInerney, D. M., McInerney, V., Ardington, A. & De Rachewiltz, C.

(1997) School success in a cultural context: Conversations at Window Rock. Paper presented at the annual meeting of the American Educational Research Association, Chicago, 24–28 March.

McInerney, D. M., McInerney, V., Bazeley, P. & Ardington, A. (1998) Parents, peers, cultural values and school processes: What has most influence on motivating indigenous minority students' school achievement? A qualitative study. Paper presented at the annual meeting of the American Educational Research Association, San Diego, 13-17 April.

McInerney, D. M., McInerney, V., Cincotta, M., Totaro, P. & Williams, D. (2001) Teacher attitudes to, and beliefs about, multicultural education: Have there been changes over the last twenty years? Paper presented at the annual meeting of the American Educational Research Association, Seattle. 10–14 April.

McInerney, D. M., McInerney, V. & Marsh, H. W. (1997). Effects of metacognitive strategy training within a cooperative group learning context on computer achievement and anxiety. *Journal of Educational Psychology*, **89**, 686–95.

McInerney, D. M., McInerney, V. & Roche, L. (1994a) Universal goals of school motivation? An application of LISREL to cross-cultural research. Paper presented at the Australian Association for Research in Education Conference, Newcastle, 27 November–1 December.

McInerney, D. M., McInerney, V. & Roche, L. (1994b) Achievement goal theory and indigenous minority school motivation: The importance of a multiple goal perspective. Paper presented at the Australian Association for Research in Education Conference, Newcastle, 27 November–1 December.

McInerney, D. M. & Sinclair, K. E. (1991) Cross-cultural model testing: Inventory of school motivation. *Educational and Psychological Measurement*, **51**, 123–33.

McInerney, D. M. & Sinclair, K. E. (1992) Dimensions of school motivation. A cross-cultural validation study. *Journal of Cross-Cultural Psychology*, **23**, 389–406.

McInerney, D. M. & Swisher, K. (1995) Exploring Navajo motivation in school settings. *Journal of American Indian Education*, **34**, 28–51.

McInerney, D. M. & Van Etten, S. (2001) *Research on Sociocultural Influences on Motivation and Learning (Volume 1)*. Greenwich, CT: Information Age Press.

McInerney, D. M. & Van Etten, S. (2004) *Research on Sociocultural Influences on Motivation and Learning (Volume 4), Big Theories Revisited*. Greenwich, CT: Information Age.

Macintosh, T. (1993) Education taps into info high-tech style. *The Australian*, 15 June.

MacIver, D. J., Young, E. M. & Washburn, B. (2002) Instructional practices and motivation during middle school (with special attention to science). In A. Wigfield & J. S. Eccles (eds) *Development of Achievement Motivation*. San Diego, CA: Academic Press.

MacKay, G. (1990) Writing and computer skills of first year teacher trainees. In M. Bezzina & J. Butcher (eds) *The Changing Face of Professional Education. Collected Papers of the AARE Annual Conference, Sydney University, 1990*. Sydney: AARE.

McKeachie, W. J., Pintrich, P. R. & Lin, Y-G. (1985) Teaching learning strategies. *Educational Psychologist*, **20**, 153–60.

McKeith, W. T. & Daniel, J. (1990) Extension for gifted and talented children—P.L.C. Sydney, Australia. *Unicorn*, **16**, 177–83.

McKenzie, W. (2001) *It's Not How Smart You Are—It's How You Are Smart. Howard Gardner's Theory of Multiple Intelligences*. http://www.surfaquarium.com/mi.htm.

McKinney, C. W., Larkins, A. G., Kazelskis, R., Ford, M. J., Allen, J. A. & Davis, J. C. (1983) Some effects of teacher enthusiasm on student achievement in fourth-grade social studies. *Journal of Educational Research*, **76**, 249–53.

MacKinnon, D. (1962) The nature and nurture of creative talent. *American Psychologist*, **17**, 484–95.

McKinnon, D., Owens, L. & Nolan, P. (1992) The learning mode preferences of primary, intermediate and secondary students in New Zealand. Paper presented at the AARE/NZARE conference 'Educational Research: Discipline and Diversity', Geelong, Victoria.

McLoughlin, C. (1999) The implications of the research literature on learning styles for the design of instructional material. *Australian Journal of Educational Technology*, **15**, 222–41.

McLoyd, V. C. (1979) The effects of extrinsic rewards of differential value on high and low intrinsic interest. *Child Development*, **50**, 1010–19.

McMillan, J. H. (1992) *Educational Research. Fundamentals for the Consumer*. New York: HarperCollins.

McMillan, J. H. & Schumacher, S. (1989) *Research in Education. A Conceptual Introduction*, 2nd ed. New York: HarperCollins.

McNally, D. W. (1977) *Piaget, Education and Teaching*. Sussex: Harvester Press.

Madden, N. A. & Slavin, R. E. (1983) Mainstreaming students with mild handicaps: Academic and social outcomes. *Review of Educational Research*, **53**, 519–69.

Maehr, M. L. (1984) Meaning and motivation: Toward a theory of personal investment. In R. Ames & C. Ames (eds) *Research on Motivation in Education: Student Motivation (Volume 1)*. Orlando: Academic Press.

Maehr, M. L. (1989) Thoughts about motivation. In C. Ames & R. Ames (eds) *Research on Motivation in Education: Goals and Cognitions (Volume 3)*. Orlando: Academic Press.

Maehr, M. L. (1991) The 'psychological environment' of the school: A focus for school leadership. In P. Thurston & P. Zodhiates (eds) *Advances in Educational Administration*. Greenwich, CT: JAI Press.

Maehr, M. L. & Anderman, E. M. (1993) Reinventing schools for early adolescents: Emphasizing task goals. *The Elementary School Journal*, **93**, 593–610.

Maehr, M. L. & Braskamp, L. A. (1986) *The Motivation Factor: A Theory of Personal Investment*. Lexington, MA: Lexington Press.

Maehr, M. L. & Buck, R. M. (1993) Transforming school culture. In M. Sashkin & H. Walberg (eds) *Educational Leadership and Culture: Current Research and Practice*. Berkeley, CA: McCutchan.

Maehr, M. L., Kan, S., Kaplan, A. & Peng, W. (1999) Culture, motivation and achievement: Towards meeting the new challenge. *Asia Pacific Journal of Education*, **19**, 15–29.

Maehr, M. L. & McInerney, D. M. (2004) Motivation as personal investment. In D. M. McInerney & S. Van Etten (eds) *Research on Sociocultural Influences on Motivation and Learning (Volume 4), Big Theories Revisited*. Greenwich, CT: Information Age Publishing.

Maehr, M. L. & Midgley, C. (1991) Enhancing student motivation: A school-wide approach. *Educational Psychologist*, **26**(3 & 4), 399–427.

Maehr, M. L., Midgley, C. & Urdan, T. (1992) Student investment in learning: A focus for school leaders. *Educational Administration Quarterly*, **18**, 412–31.

Mael, F. A. (1998) Single-sex and coeducational schooling: Relationships to socioemotional and academic development. *Review of Educational Research*, **68**, 101–29.

Mageean, B. (1991) Self-report: A note on psychology and instruction. *Australian Journal of Education*, **35**, 41–59.

Mager, R. F. (1973) *Measuring Instructional Intent or Got a Match*. Belmont, CA: Fearon.

Mager, R. F. (1990a) *Preparing Instructional Objectives*, 2nd ed. London: Kogan Page.

Mager, R. F. (1990b) *Measuring Instructional Results*, 2nd ed. London: Kogan Page.

Maggs, A., Argent, I., Clarke, R., Falls, J. & Smart, G. (1980) Australian direct instruction research across classrooms. *The A.S.E.T. Journal*, **12**, 13–23.

Mak, A. (1994) Parental neglect and overprotection as risk factors in delinquency. *Australian Journal of Psychology*, **46**, 107–11.

Maker, J. (1987) Teaching the gifted and talented. In V. R. Koehler (ed.) *Handbook for Educators*. White Plains, NY: Longman.

Malin, M. (1990) The visibility and invisibility of Aboriginal students in an urban classroom. *Australian Journal of Education*, **34**, 312–29.

Malina, R. M. (1990) Physical growth and performance during the transitional years (9–16). In R. Montemayor, G. R. Adams & T. P. Gullotta (eds) *From Childhood to Adolescence. A Transitional Period?* Newbury Park, CA: Sage.

Malina, R. M. & Bouchard, C. (1991) *Growth, Maturation, and Physical Activity*. Champaign, IL: Human Kinetics Books.

Mamlin, N. & Harris, K. R. (1998) Elementary teachers' referral to special education in light of inclusion and prereferral: 'Every child is here to learn . . . but some of these children are in real trouble'. *Journal of Educational Psychology*, **90**, 385–96.

Management Review: NSW Education Portfolio (1989) *Schools Renewal. A Strategy to Revitalize Schools Within the New South Wales Education System*. Sydney: NSW Education Portfolio.

Marchant, G. J. (1985) An information processing model: Structures and implications. Unpublished manuscript, Northwestern University, Evanston, IL.

Marcia, J. E. (1966) Development and validation of ego identity status. *Journal of Personality and Social Psychology*, **3**, 551–8.

Marcia, J. E. (1967) Ego identity status: Relationship to change in self-esteem, 'general adjustment', and authoritarianism. *Journal of Personality*, **35**, 119–33.

Marcia, J. E. (1980) Identity in adolescence. In J. Adelson (ed.) *Handbook of Adolescent Psychology*. New York: John Wiley.

Marjoribanks, K. (1980) *Ethnic Families and Children's Achievements*. Sydney: Allen & Unwin.

Marjoribanks, K. (1987) Gender/social class, family environments and adolescents' aspirations. *Australian Journal of Education*, **31**, 43–54.

Marks, G. (1992a) Integration of students with disabilities: Confusing social justice and economic imperatives. Paper presented at the AARE/NZARE conference 'Educational Research: Discipline and Diversity', Geelong, Victoria.

Marks, G. (1992b) The politicisation of the language of integration. Paper presented at the AARE/NZARE conference 'Educational Research: Discipline and Diversity', Geelong, Victoria.

Markus, H. & Kunda, Z. (1986) Stability and malleability of the self-concept. *Journal of Personality and Social Psychology*, **51**, 858–66.

Marsh, H. W. (1984) Self-concept, social comparison, and ability grouping: A reply to Kulik and Kulik. *American Educational Research Journal*, **21**, 799–806.

Marsh, H. W. (1990a) A multidimensional, hierarchical model of self-concept: Theoretical and empirical justification. *Educational Psychology Review*, **2**, 77–172.

Marsh, H. W. (1990b) Influences of internal and external frames of reference on the formation of math and English self-concepts. *Journal of Educational Psychology*, **82**, 107–16.

Marsh, H. W. (1991) Failure of high-ability high schools to deliver academic benefits commensurate with their students' ability levels. *American Educational Research Journal*, **28**, 445–80.

Marsh, H. W. (1993) Academic self-concept: Theory, measurement and research. In J. Suls (ed.) *Psychological Perspectives on the Self (Volume 4)*. Hillsdale, NJ: Erlbaum.

Marsh, H. W. (1993) Physical fitness self-concept: Relations of physical fitness to field and technical indicators for boys and girls aged 9–15. *Journal of Sport and Exercise Psychology*, **15**, 184–206.

Marsh, H. W. & Craven, R. (1997) Academic self-concept: Beyond the dustbowl. In G. Phye (ed.) *Handbook of Classroom Assessment: Learning, Achievement, and Adjustment*. San Diego, CA: Academic Press.

Marsh, H. W. & Hau, K-T. (2003) Big-fish-little-pond effect on academic self-concept: A cross-cultural (26 country) test of the negative effects of academically selective schools. *American Psychologist*, **58**, 364–76.

Marsh, H. W. & Hau, K-T. (2004) Explaining paradoxical relations between academic self-concepts and achievements: Cross-cultural generalizability of the internal/external frame of reference predictions across 26 countries. *Journal of Educational Psychology*, **90**, 56–67.

Marsh, H. W., Hau, K-T. & Craven, R. (2004) The big-fish-little-pond effect stands up to scrutiny. *American Psychologist*, **59**, 269–71.

Marsh, H. W. & Johnston, C. F. (1993) Multidimensional self-concepts and frames of reference: Relevance to the exceptional learner. In F. E. Obiakor & S. W. Stile (eds) *Self-Concept of Exceptional Learners: Current Perspective for Educators*. Dubuque, IA: Kendall/Hunt.

Marsh, H. W., Parada, R. H., Yeung, A. S. & Healey, J. (2001) Aggressive school troublemakers and victims: A longitudinal model examining the pivotal role of self-concept. *Journal of Educational Psychology*, **93**, 411–19.

Marsh, H. W. & Shavelson, R. (1985) Self-concept: Its multifaceted, hierarchical structure. *Educational Psychologist*, **20**, 107–23.

Marsh, H. W., Walker, R. & Debus, R. (1991) Subject specific components of academic self-concept and self-efficacy. *Contemporary Educational Psychology*, **16**, 331–45.

Marsh, H. W. & Yeung, A. S. (1997) Coursework selection: Relations to academic self-concept and achievement. *American Educational Research Journal*, **34**, 691–720.

Marshall, H. H. (1987) Motivational strategies of three fifth-grade teachers. *Elementary School Journal*, **88**, 135–50.

Marshall, H. H. (1996) Implications of differentiating and understanding constructivist approaches. *Educational Psychologist*, **31**, 235–40.

Martin, A. J. (2003a) Boys and motivation. *The Australian Educational Researcher*, **30**, 43–65.

Martin, A. J. (2003b) *How to Motivate Your Child for School and Beyond*. Sydney: Bantam.

Martin, J. (2004) Self-regulated learning, social cognitive theory, and agency. *Educational Psychologist*, **39**, 135–45.

Martin, N. K. (1997) Connecting instruction and management in a student-centred classroom. *Middle School Journal*, March, 3–9.

Marzano, R. J. & Arredondo, D. E. (1986a) *Tactics for Thinking*. Aurora, CO: Mid-continent Regional Educational Laboratory.

Marzano, R. J. & Arredondo, D. E. (1986b) Restructuring schools through the teaching of thinking skills. *Educational Leadership*, **43**, 20–6.

Marzano, R. J. & Costa, A. L. (1988) Question: Do standardized tests measure general cognitive skills? Answer: No. *Educational Leadership*, **45**, 66–71.

Maslow, A. H. (1968) *Toward a Psychology of Being*, 2nd ed. Princeton, NJ: Van Nostrand.

Maslow, A. H. (1970) *Motivation and Personality*, 2nd ed. New York: Harper & Row.

Maslow, A. H. (1976) Defense and growth. In M. L. Silberman, J. S. Allender & J. M. Yanoff (eds) *Real Learning. A Sourcebook for Teachers*. Boston: Little, Brown & Co.

Mason, J. & Levi, N. (1992) *The Identification of Effective Teaching Practices. A Study of Teachers in Years K–12 in the Liverpool Cluster of the Metropolitan South-West Region*. Sydney: Faculty of Education, University of Western Sydney, Macarthur.

Masselos, G. & Hinley, C. (1981) The child with special needs from a migrant family. *Australian Journal of Early Childhood*, **6**, 35–8.

Matiasz, S. (1989) Aboriginal children and early childhood education. *Early Childhood Development and Care*, **52**, 81–91.

Matthew, A. & Crook, M. (1990) The control of reaching movements by young infants. *Child Development*, **61**, 1238–57.

Mattingly, D. J., Prislin, R., McKenzie, T. L., Rodriguez, J. L. & Kayzar, B. (2002) Evaluating evaluations: The case of parent involvement programs. *Review of Educational Research*, **72**, 549–76.

Mau, R. Y. (1992) The validity and devolution of a concept: Student alienation. *Adolescence*, **27**, 731–41.

Maude, D., Wertheim, E. H., Paxton, S., Gibbons, K. & Szmukler, G. (1993) Body dissatisfaction, weight loss behaviours and bulimic tendencies in Australian adolescents with an estimate of female data representativeness. *Australian Psychologist*, **28**(2), 128–32.

Maurer, A. (1974) Corporal punishment. *American Psychologist*, **29**, 614–26.

Maxwell, T. W., Marshall, A. R. A., Walton, J. & Baker, I. (1989) Secondary school alternative structures: Semester courses and vertical grouping in non-state schools in New South Wales. *Curriculum Perspectives*, **9**, 1–15.

Mayer, J. D. & Cobb, C. D. (2000) Educational policy on emotional intelligence: Does it make sense? *Educational Psychology Review*, **12**, 163–83.

Mayer, J. D., DiPaolo, M. T. & Salovey, P. (1990) Perceiving affective content in ambiguous visual stimuli: A component of emotional intelligence. *Journal of Personality Assessment*, **54**, 772–81.

Mayer, J. D., Salovey, P. & Caruso, D. (2000) Models of emotional intelligence. In R. J. Sternberg (ed.), *Handbook of Intelligence*. New York: Cambridge University Press.

Mayer, R. E. (1989) Models for understanding. *Review of Educational Research*, **59**, 43–64.

Mayer, R. E. (1996) Learners as information processors: Legacies and limitations of educational psychology's second metaphor. *Educational Psychologist*, **31**, 151–61.

Mayer, R. E. (2004) Should there be a three-strikes rule against pure discovery learning? The case for guided methods of instruction. *American Psychologist*, **59**, 14–19.

Mayer, R. E., Bove, W., Bryman, A., Mars, R. & Tapangco, L. (1966) When less is more: Meaningful learning from visual and verbal summaries of science textbooks lessons. *Journal of Educational Psychology*, **88**, 64–73.

Mayer, R. E. & Massa, L. J. (2003) Three facets of visual and verbal learners: Cognitive ability, cognitive style, and learning preferences. *Journal of Educational Psychology*, **95**, 833–46.

Meece, J. L. & Holt, K. (1993) A pattern analysis of students' achievement goals. *Journal of Educational Psychology*, **85**, 582–90.

Meece, J. L. & Miller, S. D. (1996) Developmental changes in children's self-reports of achievement goals, competence, and strategy use during the late elementary years. Paper presented as part of an invited symposium at the Annual Meeting of the American Educational Research Association, New York, April.

Meeker, M., Meeker, R. & Roid, G. (1985) *Structure-of-Intellect Learning Abilities Test (SOI-LA)*. Los Angeles: Western Psychological Services.

Merrett, F. & Tang, W. M. (1994) The attitudes of British primary school pupils to praise, rewards, punishments and reprimands. *British Journal of Educational Psychology*, **64**, 91–103.

Merrett, F. & Wheldall, K. (1990) *Positive Teaching in the Primary School*. London: Paul Chapman.

Messer, S. B. (1976) Reflection-impulsivity: A review. *Psychological Bulletin*, **83**, 1026–52.

Messick, S. (1976) *Individuality in Learning: Implications of Cognitive Styles and Creativity for Human Development*. San Francisco: Jossey-Bass.

Messick, S. (1984) The nature of cognitive styles. Problems and promise in educational practice. *Educational Psychologist*, **19**, 59–74.

Messick, S. (1989) Meaning and values in test validation: The science and ethics of assessment. *Educational Researcher*, **18**, 5–11.

Messick, S. (1995) Cognitive style and learning. In L. W. Anderson (ed.) *International Encyclopedia of Teaching and Teacher Education*, 2nd ed. Tarrytown, NY: Pergamon.

Metherell, T. (1989) 'Technology High Schools: Meeting the Challenge', NSW Department of Education press release.

Midgley, C. & Edelin, K. C. (1998) Middle school reform and early adolescent well-being: The good news and the bad. *Educational Psychologist*, **33**, 195–206.

Midgley, C., Arunkumar, R. & Urdan, T. C. (1996) 'If I don't do well tomorrow, there's a reason': Predictors of adolescents' use of academic self-handicapping strategies. *Journal of Educational Psychology*, **88**, 423–34.

Midgley, C., Kaplan, A. & Middleton, M. (2001) Performance-approach goals: Good for what, for whom, under what circumstances, and at what cost? *Journal of Educational Psychology*, **93**, 77–86.

Miller, A., Fergusson, E. & Moore, E. (2002) Parents' and pupils' causal attributions for difficult classroom behaviour. *British Journal of Educational Psychology*, **72**, 27–40.

Miller, G. A. (1956) The magical number seven, plus or minus two: Some limits on our capacity for processing information. *Psychological Review*, **63**, 81–97.

Mischel, W. (1986) *Introduction to Personality. A New Look*, 4th ed. New York: Holt, Rinehart & Winston.

Modgil, S. & Modgil, C. (eds) (1976) *Piagetian Research*. Windsor: NFER.

Modgil, S. & Modgil, C. (eds) (1982) *Jean Piaget: Consensus and Controversy*. New York: Praeger.

Moll, L. C. (ed.) (1990) *Vygotsky and Education*. Cambridge: Cambridge University Press.

Mollick, L. B. & Etra, K. S. (1981) Poor learning ability or poor hearing? In K. L. Frieberg (ed.) *Educating Exceptional Children*, 6th ed. Guilford, CT: Duskin.

Montemayor, R. & Flannery, D. J. (1991) Parent–adolescent relations in middle and late adolescence. In R. M. Lerner, A. C. Petersen & J. Brooks-Gunn (eds) *Encyclopedia of Adolescence (Volume 2)*. New York: Garland.

Moore, P. (1991) Reciprocal teaching of study skills. In J. B. Biggs (ed.) *Teaching for Learning*. Melbourne: ACER.

Morgan, M. (1984) Reward-induced decrements and increments in intrinsic motivation. *Review of Educational Research*, **54**, 5–30.

Mosher, R. (ed.) (1980) *Moral Education: A First Generation of Research and Development*. New York: Praeger.

Moshman, D. (1982) Exogenous, endogenous, and dialectical constructivism. *Developmental Review*, **2**, 371–84.

Moss, P. A. (1992) Shifting conceptions of validity in educational measurement: Implications for performance assessment. *Review of Educational Research*, **62**, 229–58.

Moss, P. A. (1996) Enlarging the dialogue in educational measurement: Voices from interpretive research traditions. *Educational Researcher*, **25**, 20–8.

Moyles, J. R. (ed.) (1995) *The Excellence of Play*. Buckingham, UK: Open University Press.

Mulryan, C. M. (1996) Cooperative small groups in mathematics: The perceptions and involvement of intermediate students. *Set Research Information for Teachers*, 1, **12**, 1–4.

Munnings, A. (1980) A cross cultural investigation of strategies used in concept learning by Australian and Malaysian adolescents. Unpublished Honours thesis, Department of Psychology, University of Newcastle, Australia.

Munns, G. (1996) Teaching resistant Koori students. Towards non-reproductive education. Unpublished doctoral dissertation presented to the University of New England, Armidale, Australia.

Munter, S. (1993) Learning for tomorrow. *The Gen*, June, 2.

Murdock. T. B. (1999) The social context of risk: Status and motivational predictors of alienation in middle school. *Journal of Educational Psychology*, **91**, 62–75.

Murray, J. P. (1973) Television and violence: Implications of the Surgeon General's Research Program. *American Psychologist*, 472–8.

Mussen, P. H. & Jones, M. C. (1957) Self-conceptions, motivations and interpersonal attitudes of late- and early-maturing boys. *Child Development*, **28**, 243–56.

Mussen, P. H. & Jones, M. C. (1958) The behavior-inferred motivations of late- and early-maturing boys. *Child Development*, **29**, 61–7.

Nadolski, R. J., Kirschner, P. A. & Van Merriënboer, J. J. G. (2005) Optimizing the number of steps in learning tasks for complex skills. *British Journal of Educational Psychology*, **75**, 223–37.

Naglieri, J. A., Drasgow, F., Schmit, M., Handler, L., Prifitera, A., Margolis, A. & Velasquez, R. (2004) Psychological testing on the Internet. *American Psychologist*, **59**, 150–62.

Naglieri, J. A. & Rojahn, J. (2001) Gender differences in planning, attention, simultaneous, and successive (PASS) cognitive processes and achievement. *Journal of Educational Psychology*, **93**, 430–7.

Narvaez, D. (1998) The influence of moral schemas on the reconstruction of moral narratives in eighth graders and college students. *Journal of Educational Psychology*, **90**, 13–24.

Narvaez, D. (1999) Using discourse processing methods to study moral thinking. *Educational Psychology Review*, **11**, 377–93.

Narvaez, D., Gleason, T., Mitchell, C. & Bentley, J. (1999) Moral theme comprehension in children. *Journal of Educational Psychology*, **91**, 477–87.

Nathan, M. J. & Petrosino, A. (2003) Expert blind spot among preservice teachers. *American Educational Research Journal*, **40**, 905–28.

National Board of Employment, Education and Training (1990) *Teacher Education in Australia*. Canberra: AGPS.

Natriello, G. (1989) The impact of evaluation processes on students. In R. E. Slavin (ed.) *School and Classroom Organization*. Hillsdale, NJ: Lawrence Erlbaum.

Natriello, G. & Dornbusch, S. M. (1984) *Teacher Evaluative Standards and Student Effort*. New York: Longman.

Naveh-Benjamin, M. (1991) A comparison of training programs intended for different types of test-anxious students: Further support for an information-processing model. *Journal of Educational Psychology*, **83**, 134–9.

Nedd, D. M. & Gruenfeld, L. W. (1976) Field dependence-independence and social traditionalism. A comparison of ethnic subcultures of Trinidad. *International Journal of Psychology*, **11**, 23–41.

Neisser, U. *et al.* (1996) Intelligence: Knowns and unknowns. *American Psychologist*, **51**, 77–101.

Nelson, J., Lott, L. & Glenn, H. (1997) *Positive Discipline in the Classroom*. Rocklin, CA: Prima.

Nelson, R. B., Cummings, J. A. & Boltman, H. (1991) Teaching concepts to students who are educable mentally retarded. In K. L. Frieberg (ed.) *Educating Exceptional Children*, 6th ed. Guilford, CT: Duskin.

Nelson-Le Gall, S. A. (1985) Motive–outcome matching and outcome foreseeability: Effects on attribution of intentionality and moral judgments. *Developmental Psychology*, **21**, 332–7.

New South Wales Department of School Education (1990) *Multicultural Activities for Schools*. Sydney: NSW Department of School Education.

New South Wales Department of School Education (1991a) *Policy for the Education of Gifted and Talented Students*. Sydney: NSW Department of School Education.

New South Wales Department of School Education (1991b) *NSW Government Strategy for the Education of Gifted and Talented Students*. Sydney: NSW Department of School Education.

New South Wales Department of School Education (1991c) *Implementation Strategies for the Education of Gifted and Talented Students*. Sydney: NSW Department of School Education.

Newby, T. J. (1991) Classroom motivation: Strategies of first-year teachers. *Journal of Educational Psychology*, **83**, 195–200.

Newman, F. M. (1997) Authentic assessment in social students: Standards and examples. In G. Phye (ed.) *Handbook of Classroom Assessment: Learning, Achievement, and Adjustment*. San Diego, CA: Academic Press.

Newman, R. S. (2002) What do I need to do to succeed . . . when I don't understand what I'm doing!?: Developmental influences on students' adaptive help seeking. In A. Wigfield & J. S. Eccles (eds) *Development of achievement motivation*. San Diego, CA: Academic Press.

Newman, R. S., Murray, B. & Lustier, C. (2001) Confrontation with aggressive peers at school: Students' reluctance to seek help from the teacher. *Journal of Educational Psychology*, **93**, 398–410.

Nicholls, J. G. (1976) Effort is virtuous, but it's better to have ability: Evaluative responses to perceptions of effort and ability. *Journal of Research in Personality*, **10**, 306–15.

Nicholls, J. G. (1984) Conceptions of ability and achievement motivation. In R. Ames & C. Ames (eds) *Research on Motivation in Education: Student Motivation (Volume 1)*. Orlando: Academic Press.

Nicholls, J. G. (1989) *The Competitive Ethos and Democratic Education*. Cambridge, MA: Harvard University Press.

Nicholls, J. G., Cheung, P., Lauer, J. & Patashnik, M. (1989) Individual differences in academic motivation: Perceived ability, goals, beliefs, and values. *Learning and Individual Differences*, **1**, 63–84.

Nicholls, J. G., Patashnick, M. & Nolen, S. B. (1985) Adolescents' theories of education. *Journal of Educational Psychology*, **77**, 683–92.

Nicholson, J. M., McFarland, M. L. & Oldenburg, B. (1999) Detection of child mental health problems in the school setting. *The Australian Educational and Developmental Psychologist*, **16**, 66–77.

Nickerson, R., Perkins, D. N. & Smith, E. (1985) *The Teaching of Thinking Skills*. Hillsdale, NJ: Lawrence Erlbaum.

Nicolaides, S., Toda, Y. & Smith, P. K. (2002) Knowledge and attitudes about school bullying in trainee teachers. *British Journal of Educational Psychology*, **72**, 105–8.

Nixon, P. (1991) Alison has the right concepts. *Western Australian Education News*, Ministry of Education, October, 9.

Nixon, P. (1992) Telematics: High-tech communications. *Western Australian Education News*, Ministry of Education, April, 28.

Noddings, N. (1992) *The Challenge to Care in Schools: An Alternative Approach to Education*. New York: Teachers College Press.

Noddings, N. (1995) Teaching themes of care. *Phi Delta Kappan*, **76**, 675–9.

Noddings, N. (1998) Perspectives from feminist philosophy. *Educational Researcher*, **27**, 17–18.

Nolen, S. B. (1988) Reasons for studying: Motivational orientations and study strategies. *Cognition and Instruction*, **5**, 269–87.

Nolen, S. B. & Nicholls, J. G. (1993) Elementary school pupils' beliefs about practices for motivating pupils in mathematics. *British Journal of Educational Psychology*, **63**, 414–30.

Nolen, S. B. & Nicholls, J. G. (1994) A place to begin (again) in research on student motivation: Teachers' beliefs. *Teaching and Teacher Education*, **10**, 57–69.

Norcini, J. & Snyder, S. (1983) The effects of modeling and cognitive induction on the moral reasoning of adolescents. *Journal of Youth and Adolescence*, **12**, 101–15.

Novak, J. D. (1981) Effective science instruction: The achievement of shared meaning. *The Australian Science Teachers Journal*, **27**, 5–13.

Nucci, L. (1982) Conceptual development in the moral and conventional domains. Implications for values education. *Review of Educational Research*, **49**, 93–122.

Nucci, L. (1987) Synthesis of research on moral development. *Educational Leadership*, **44**, 86–92.

Nuthall, G. (1996) Commentary: Of learning and language and understanding the complexity of the classroom. *Educational Psychologist*, **31**, 207–14.

Nuthall, G. (2000) The anatomy of memory in the classroom: Understanding how students acquire memory processes from classroom activities in science and social studies units. *American Educational Research Journal*, **37**, 247–304.

Nuthall, G. & Alton-Lee, A. (1990) Research on teaching and learning: Thirty years of change. *The Elementary School Journal*, **90**, 547–70.

O'Connor, M. C. (1998) Can we trace the 'efficacy of social constructivism'? *Review of Research in Education*, **23**, 25–69.

O'Donnell, A. M. & King, A. (eds) (1999) *Cognitive Perspectives on Peer Learning*. Mahwah, NJ: Lawrence Erlbaum.

O'Leary, K. D. & O'Leary, S. G. (1977) *Classroom Management. The Successful Use of Behavior Modification*, 2nd ed. New York: Pergamon.

O'Neil, J. (1990) Making sense of style. *Educational Leadership*, **48**, 4–9.

Obach, M. S. (2003) A longitudinal-sequential study of perceived academic competence and motivational beliefs for learning among children in middle school. *Educational Psychology*, **23**, 323–38.

Oerlemans, K. & Jenkins, H. (1998) There are aliens in our school. *Issues in Educational Research*, **8**, 117–29.

Offer, D., Ostrov, E., Howard, K. L. & Atkinson, R. (1988) *The Teenage World: Adolescents' Self-image in Ten Countries*. New York: Plenum Medical.

Office of Multicultural Affairs (1990) *Multicultural Policies and Programs: An Overview*. Canberra: AGPS.

Ogbu, J. U. (1983) Minority status and schooling in plural societies. *Comparative Education Review*, **27**, 168–90.

Ogbu, J. U. (1992) Understanding cultural diversity and learning. *Educational Researcher*, **21**, 5–14.

Ogbu, J. U. (1997) Understanding the school performance of urban blacks: Some essential background knowledge. In H. Walberg, O. Reyes & R. P. Weissberg (eds) *Children and Youth: Interdisciplinary Perspectives*. Norwood, NJ: Ablex.

Ogbu, J. U. (1999) Beyond language: Ebonics, proper English, and identity in a black American speech community. *American Educational Research Journal*, **36**, 147–84.

Ogbu, J. U. & Matute-Bianchi, M. E. (1986) Understanding sociocultural factors in education: Knowledge, identity, and adjustment in schooling. In California State Department, Bilingual Education Office, *Beyond Language: Social and Cultural Factors in Schooling Language Minority Students*. Sacramento, CA: California State University, Los Angeles, Evaluation, Dissemination and Assessment Center.

Okagaki, L. & Frencsh, P. A. (1998) Parenting and children's school achievement: A multiethnic perspective. *American Educational Research Journal*, **35**, 123–44.

Olneck, M. (2000) Can multicultural education change what counts as cultural capital? *American Educational Research Journal*, **37**, 317–48.

Olweus, D. (1995) Bullying or peer abuse at school: Facts and interventions. *Current Directions in Psychological Science*, **4**, 196–200.

Olweus, D. (1996) Bullying at school: Knowledge base and an effective intervention program. *Annals of the New York Academy of Sciences*, **74**, 265–76.

Olweus, D. (1997) Bully/victim problems in school: Facts, and intervention. *European Journal of Psychology of Education*, **12**, 495–510.

Oosterheert, I. E., Vermunt, J. D. & Denessen, E. (2002) Assessing orientations to learning to teach. *British Journal of Educational Psychology*, **72**, 41–64.

Open University (1981) *Measuring Learning Outcomes*. Milton Keynes: Open University Press.

Orr, E. (1989) 'Engineers don't carry handbags?!' *SET Research Information for Teachers*, number 1, item 7.

Osborne, J. W. (2000) Testing stereotype threat: Does anxiety explain race and sex differences in achievement? Paper presented at the annual meeting of the American Educational Research Association, New Orleans, 24–28 April.

Osborne, R. (1980) *Force: LISP Working Paper Number 16*. Hamilton, NZ: SERU, University of Waikato.

Osborne, R. J. & Gilbert, J. K. (1980) A technique for exploring students' views of the world. *Physics Education*, **15**, 376–9.

Osterman, K. F. (2000) Students' need for belonging in the school community. *Review of Educational Research*, **70**, 323–67.

Owens, L., Nolan, P. & McKinnon, D. (1992) A comparison of the learning mode preferences of students in four countries—Australia, New Zealand, England, USA. Paper presented at the

AARE/NZARE conference 'Educational Research: Discipline and Diversity', Geelong, Victoria.

Paas, F., Renkl, A. & Sweller, J. (2003) Cognitive load theory and instructional design: Recent developments. *Educational Psychologist*, **38**, 1–4.

Paas, F., Tuovinen, J. H., Tabbers, H. & Van Gerven, P. W. M. (2003) Cognitive load measurement as a means to advance cognitive load theory. *Educational Psychologist*, **38**, 63–71.

Paikoff, R. L. & Brooks-Gunn, J. (1990) Physiological processes: What role do they play during the transition to adolescence? In R. Montemayor, G. R. Adams & T. P. Gullotta (eds) *From Childhood to Adolescence. A Transitional Period?* Newbury Park: Sage.

Pajares, F. & Valiante, G. (2000) Toward a positive psychology of academic motivation: Achievement goals, expectancy beliefs, value, optimism, invitations, and authenticity. Paper presented at the meeting of the American Educational Research Association, New Orleans, 24–28 April.

Pajares, R. L., Miller, M. D. & Johnson, M. J. (1999) Gender differences in writing self-beliefs of elementary school students. *Journal of Educational Psychology*, **91**, 50–61.

Palincsar, A. S. & Brown, A. L. (1984) The reciprocal teaching of comprehension-fostering and monitoring activities. *Cognition and Instruction*, **1**, 117–75.

Palmer, E. J. (2003) An overview of the relationship between moral reasoning and offending. *Australian Psychologist*, **38**, 165–74.

Papalia, D. E. & Olds, S. W. (1989) *Life Span Development. First Australian Edition* (Australian eds Lindsay Gething & Desmond Hatchard). Sydney: McGraw-Hill.

Paris, S. G. & Ayres, L. R. (1994) *Becoming Reflective Students and Teachers with Portfolios and Authentic Assessment*. Washington DC: American Psychological Association.

Paris, S. G., Lipson, M. Y. & Wixson, K. K. (1983) Becoming a strategic reader. *Contemporary Educational Psychology*, **8**, 293–316.

Paris, S. G. & Newman, R. S. (1990) Developmental aspects of self-regulated learning. *Educational Psychologist*, **25**, 87–102.

Paris, S. G. & Oka, E. R. (1986) Self-regulated learning among exceptional children. *Exceptional Children*, **53**, 103–8.

Parker, L. E. & Lepper, M. R. (1992) The effects of fantasy context on children's learning and motivation. Making play more fun. *Journal of Personality and Social Psychology*, **62**, 625–33.

Parten, M. B. (1932) Social participation among preschool children. *Journal of Abnormal and Social Psychology*, **27**, 243–69.

Partington, G. & McCudden, V. J. (1990) Classroom interaction: Some qualitative and quantitative differences in a mixed-ethnicity classroom. *Australian Journal of Teacher Education*, **15**, 43–9.

Partington, G. & McCudden, V. (1992) *Ethnicity and Education*. Wentworth Falls, NSW: Social Science Press.

Pascuale-Leone, J. (1969) Cognitive development and cognitive style. Unpublished doctoral dissertation, University of Geneva.

Paterson, J. F. (1992) Attitudes towards the integration of students with disabilities. Paper presented at the AARE/NZARE conference 'Educational Research: Discipline and Diversity', Geelong, Victoria.

Paulson, F. L., Paulson, P. R. & Meyer, C. A. (1991) What makes a portfolio a portfolio? *Educational Leadership*, **48**, 60–3.

Paxton, S. J., Schutz, H. K. & Muir, S. (1996) Friend and peer-related variables predict body image dissatisfaction, dieting, binge eating and extreme weight loss behaviours in adolescent girls. Paper presented at the 31st Annual Conference of the Australian Psychological Society, 25–29 September, Sydney.

Paxton, S., Wertheim, E., Gibbons, K., Szmukler, G. L., Hillier, L. & Petrovich, J. L. (1991) Body image satisfaction, dieting beliefs, and weight loss behaviours in adolescent girls and boys. *Journal of Youth and Adolescence*, **20**, 361–97.

Peacock, D. & Yaxley, B. (1990) Teacher as reflective practitioner: An evolving research agenda. In M. Bezzina & J. Butcher (eds) *The Changing Face of Professional Education. Collected Papers of the AARE Annual Conference, Sydney University, 1990*. Sydney: AARE.

Peak, G. J. (1971) The cognitive-developmental approach to moral education: An American viewpoint. *Inside Education*, August, 779–83.

Pearson, K. L. & Love, A. W. (1999) Adolescents' value systems, preferred resolution strategies, and conflict with parents. *Australian Journal of Psychology*, **51**, 63–70.

Pease-Alvarez, L. & Hakuta, K. (1992) Enriching our views of bilingualism and bilingual education. *Educational Researcher*, **21**, 4–6.

Pelham, W. E. & Murphy, H. A. (1986) Attention deficit and conduct disorders. In M. Hersen (ed.) *Pharmacological and Behavioral Treatment: An Integrative Approach*. New York: John Wiley.

Pellegrini, A. D. (1998) Bullies and victims in school: A review and call for research. *Journal of Applied Developmental Psychology*, **19**, 165–76.

Pellegrini, A. D. (2002) Bullying, victimization, and sexual harassment during the transition to middle school. *Educational Psychologist*, **37**, 151–63.

Pellegrini, A. D. & Bjorklund, D. F. (1997) The role of recess in children's cognitive performance. *Educational Psychologist*, **32**, 35–40.

Pellegrini, A. D. & Horvat, M. (1995) A developmental contextualist critique of attention deficit hyperactivity disorder. *Educational Researcher*, **24**, 13–19.

Pellegrini, A. D., Huberty, P. D. & Jones, I. (1995) The effects of recess timing on children's playground and classroom behaviors. *American Educational Research Journal*, **32**, 845–64.

Penney, R. K. (1967) Effect of reward and punishment on children's orientation and discrimination learning. In R. H. Walters *et al.* (eds) *Punishment*. Harmondsworth, Middlesex: Penguin Books.

Penneycook, A. (1994) *The Cultural Politics of English as an International Language*. London: Longman.

Pennypacker, H. S. (1992) Is behavior analysis undergoing selection by consequences? *American Psychologist*, **47**, 1491–8.

Penuel, W. R. & Wertsch, J. V. (1995) Vygotsky and identity formation: A sociocultural approach. *Educational Psychologist*, **30**, 83–92.

Perkins, D. G. (1980) Classical conditioning: Pavlov. In G. M. Gazda & R. J. Corsini (eds) *Theories of Learning*. Itasca, IL: F. E. Peacock.

Perkins, D. N. (1981) *The Mind's Best Work*. Cambridge, MA: Harvard University Press.

Perkins, D. N. (1988) Creativity and quest for mechanism. In R. J. Sternberg & E. E. Smith (eds) *The Psychology of Human Thought*. Cambridge: Cambridge University Press.

Perkins, D. N. (1992) What constructivism demands of the learner. In T. M. Duffy & D. H. Jonassen (eds) *Constructivism and the Technology of Instruction*. Hillsdale, NJ: Lawrence Erlbaum.

Perret-Clermont, A. N. & Schubauer-Leoni, M. L. (1989) Social factors in learning and teaching: Towards an integrative perspective. *International Journal of Educational Research*, **13**, 573–684.

Perry, C. (1996) Learning styles and learning outcomes based on Kolb's learning style inventory. *SET Research Information for Teachers*, **10**(1), 1–4.

Perry, C., Ball, I. & Stacey, E. (2004) Emotional intelligence and teaching situations: Development of a new measure. *Issues in Educational Research*, **14**, 29–43.

Perry, K. E. (1998) Young children's self-regulated learning and contexts that support it. *Journal of Educational Psychology*, **90**, 715–29.

Perry, K. E. & Weinstein, R. S. (1998) The social context of early schooling and children's school adjustment. *Educational Psychologist*, **33**, 177–94.

Perry, N. & Winne, P. (2004) Motivational messages from home and school: How do they influence young children's engagement in learning. In D. M. McInerney & S. Van Etten (eds) *Research on Sociocultural Influences on Motivation and Learning (Volume 4), Big Theories Revisited*. Greenwich, CT: Information Age Publishing.

Perry, N. E. (2002) Introduction: Using qualitative methods to enrich understandings of self-regulated learning. *Educational Psychologist*, **37**, 1–3.

Pervin, L. A. (1989) *Personality. Theory and Practice*. New York: John Wiley.

Petersen, A. C. (1985) Pubertal development as a cause of disturbance: Myths, realities, and unanswered questions. *Genetic, Social, and General Psychology Monographs*, **111**, 205–32.

Petersen, A. C. (1987) Those gangly years. *Psychology Today*, June, 28–34.

Petersen, A. C. *et al.* (1995) Adolescent development and the emergence of sexuality. *Suicide and Life-Threatening Behavior*, **25**, 4–17.

Petersen, A. C. & Taylor, B. (1980) The biological approach to adolescence. In J. Adelson (ed.) *Handbook of Adolescent Psychology*. New York: John Wiley.

Peterson, C. (2004) *Looking Forward Through the Lifespan: Developmental Psychology*, 4th ed. Sydney: Prentice Hall.

Peterson, C., Beck, K. & Rowell, G. (1992) *Psychology. An Introduction for Nurses and Allied Health Professionals*. Sydney: Prentice Hall.

Peterson, P. L. (1988) Teachers' and students' cognitional knowledge for classroom teaching and learning. *Educational Researcher*, **17**, 5–14.

Peterson, P. L. & Fennema, E. (1985) Effective teaching, student engagement in classroom activities, and sex-related differences in learning mathematics. *American Educational Research Journal*, **22**, 309–35.

Petrill, S. A. & Wilkerson, B. (2000) Intelligence and achievement: A behavioral genetic perspective. *Educational Psychology Review*, **12**, 185–99.

Pezdek, K., Berry, T. & Renmo, P. A. (2002) Children's mathematics achievement: The role of parents' perceptions and their involvement in homework. *Journal of Educational Psychology*, **94**, 771–7.

Phillip Institute of Technology (1984) *Review of the Commonwealth Multicultural Education Program (Volume 1)* (Report to the Commonwealth Schools Commission). Canberra: CSC.

Phillips, D. C. (1995) The good, the bad, and the ugly: The many faces of constructivism. *Educational Researcher*, **24**, 5–12.

Phillips, M. (1997) What makes schools effective? A comparison of the relationships of communitarian climate and academic climate to mathematics achievement and attendance during middle school. *American Educational Research Journal*, **34**, 633–62.

Phye, G. D. (ed.) (1997) *Handbook of Classroom Assessment. Learning, Adjustment, and Achievement*. San Diego, CA: Academic Press.

Phye, G. D. & Andre, T. (1986) *Cognitive Classroom Learning. Understanding Thinking and Problem Solving*. Orlando: Harcourt Brace Jovanovich.

Piaget, J. (1954) *The Construction of Reality in the Child* (trans. by M. Cook). New York: Basic Books.

Piaget, J. (1963) *Origins of Intelligence in Children* (trans. by M. Cook). New York: Norton.

Piaget, J. (1965) *The Moral Judgment of the Child*. New York: Free Press.

Piaget, J. (1970a) *The Science of Education and the Psychology of the Child*. New York: Orion Press.

Piaget, J. (1970b) Piaget's theory. In P. H. Mussen (ed.) *Carmichael's Manual for Child Psychology*. New York: John Wiley.

Piaget, J. (1971) *The Children's Conception of the World* (trans. by J. Tomlinson & A. Tomlinson). London: Routledge & Kegan Paul.

Piaget, J. (1974) *Understanding Causality* (trans. by D. Miles & M. Miles). New York: Norton.

Pick, A. D. (1980) Cognition: Psychological perspectives. In H. C. Triandis & W. Lonner (eds) *Handbook of Cross-Cultural Psychology (Volume 3). Basic Processes*. Boston: Allyn & Bacon.

Pines, A. L. & Leith, S. (1981) What is concept learning in science? Theory, recent research and some teaching suggestions. *The Australian Science Teachers Journal*, **27**, 15–20.

Pintrich, P. (1988) A process-oriented view of student motivation and cognition. In J. S. Stark & L. A. Mets (eds) *Improving Teaching and Learning Through Research. New Directions for Instructional Research (Volume 57)*. San Francisco: Jossey-Bass.

Pintrich, P. R. (2000) Multiple goals, multiple pathways: The role of goal orientation in learning and achievement. *Journal of Educational Psychology*, **92**, 544–55.

Pintrich, P. R. & De Groot, E. V. (1990) Motivational and self-regulated learning components of classroom academic performance. *Journal of Educational Psychology*, **82**, 33–40.

Pintrich, P. R. & Garcia, T. (1991) Student goal orientation and self-regulation in the college classroom. In M. L. Maehr & P. R. Pintrich (eds) *Advances in Motivation and Achievement: Goals and Self-regulatory Processes (Volume 7)*. Greenwich, CT: JAI Press.

Pintrich, P. R., Marx, R. W. & Boyle, R. (1993) Beyond 'cold' conceptual change: The role of motivational beliefs and classroom contextual factors in the process of conceptual change. *Review of Educational Research*, **63**, 167–99.

Pintrich, P. R. & Schrauben, B. (1992) Students' motivational beliefs and their cognitive engagement in classroom academic tasks. In D. Schunk & J. Meece (eds) *Student Perceptions in the Classroom*. Hillsdale, NJ: Lawrence Erlbaum.

Pintrich, P. R. & Zusho, A. (2002) The development of academic self-regulation: The role of cognitive and motivational factors. In A. Wigfield & J. S. Eccles (eds) *Development of Achievement Motivation*. San Diego, CA: Academic Press.

Pitoniak, M. J. & Royer, J. M. (2001) Testing accommodations for examinees with disabilities: A review of psychometric, legal, and social policy issues. *Review of Educational Research*, **71**, 53–104.

Pledger, C. (2003) Discourse on disability and rehabilitation issues. *American Psychologist*, **58**, 279–84.

Plucker, J. A. (1999) Is the proof in the pudding? Reanalysis of Torrance's (1958 to present) longitudinal data. *Creativity Research Journal*, **12**, 103–15.

Plucker, J. A., Beghetto, R. A. & Dow, G. T. (2004) Why isn't creativity more important to educational psychologists?

Potentials, pitfalls, and future directions in creativity research. *Educational Psychologist*, **39**, 83–96.

Pokay, D. & Blumenfeld, P. C. (1990) Predicting achievement early and late in the semester: The role of motivation and use of learning strategies. *Journal of Educational Psychology*, **82**, 41–50.

Polesel, J. (1990) ESL, ideology and multiculturalism. *Journal of Intercultural Studies*, **11**, 64–72.

Pollock, M. (2001) How the question we ask most about race in education is the very question we most suppress. *Educational Researcher*, **30**, 2–12.

Pomerantz, E. M., Altermatt, E. R. & Saxon, J. (2002) Making the grade but feeling distressed: Gender differences in academic performance and internal distress. *Journal of Educational Psychology*, **94**, 396–404.

Poole, M. E. (1987) Multiculturalism, participation and equity: Discussions on educational processes, policies and outcomes. *Australian Educational Researcher*, **15**, 21–36.

Popham, W. J. (1999) Why standardized tests don't measure educational quality. *Educational Leadership*, March, 8–15.

Popkewitz, T. S. (1998) Dewey, Vygotsky, and the social administration of the individual: Constructivist pedagogy as systems of ideas in historical spaces. *American Educational Research Journal*, **35**, 535–70.

Poplin, M. S. (1988) Holistic/constructivist principles of the teaching/learning process: Implications for the field of learning disabilities. *Journal of Learning Disabilities*, **21**, 401–16.

Porter, A. C. & Brophy, J. (1988) Synthesis of research on good teaching: Insights from the work of the Institute for Research on Teaching. *Educational Leadership*, **45**, 74–85.

Porter, R. P. (1990) *Forked Tongue: The Politics of Bilingual Education*. New York: Basic Books.

Portes, P. (1999) Social and psychological factors in the academic achievement of children of immigrants: A cultural history puzzle. *American Educational Research Journal*, **36**, 489–507.

Powell, J. P. & Anderson, L. W. (1985) Humour and teaching in higher education. *Studies in Higher Education*, **10**, 79–90.

Prawat, R. S. (1989) Promoting access to knowledge, strategy, and disposition in students: A research synthesis. *Review of Educational Research*, **59**, 1–41.

Prawat, R. S. (1998) Current self-regulation views of learning and motivation viewed through a Deweyan lens: The problems with dualism. *American Educational Research Journal*, **35**, 199–224.

Pressley, M. & Woloshyn, V. (1995) *Cognitive Strategy Instruction that Really Improves Children's Academic Performance*. Cambridge, MA: Brookline.

Pressley, M. (1995) More about the development of self-regulation. Complex, long-term, and thoroughly social. *Educational Psychologist*, **30**, 207–12.

Pressley, M., Harris, K. R. & Marks, M. B. (1992) But good strategy instructors are constructivists. *Educational Psychology Review*, **4**, 3–31.

Pressley, M., Johnson, C. J., Symons, S., McGoldrick, J. A. & Kurita, J. A. (1989) Strategies that improve children's memory and comprehension of text. *The Elementary School Journal*, **90**, 3–32.

Pressley, M., McDaniel, M., Turnure, J., Wood, E. & Ahmad, M. (1987) Generation and precision of elaboration: Effects on intentional and incidental learning. *Journal of Experimental Psychology: Learning, Memory and Cognition*, **13**, 291–300.

Price, L. (2004) Individual differences in learning: Cognitive control, cognitive style, and learning style. *Educational Psychology*, **24**, 681–98.

Prillaman, A., Eaker, D. & Kendrick, D. (eds) (1994) *The Tapestry of Caring: Education as Nurturance*. Norwood, NJ: Ablex.

Print, M. (1981) The curriculum enrichment project for primary schools. *Unicorn*, **7**, 265–71.

Pritchard, C. (1992) Youth suicide and gender in Australia and New Zealand compared with countries of the Western world (1973–1987). *Australian and New Zealand Journal of Psychiatry*, **26**, 609–17.

Puntambekar, S. & Hübscher, R. (2005) Tools for scaffolding students in a complex learning environment: What have we gained and what have we missed? *Educational Psychologist*, **40**, 1–12.

Purdie, N. & Hattie, J. (1996) Cultural differences in the use of strategies for self-regulated learning. *American Educational Research Journal*, **33**, 845–71.

Purdie, N., Hattie, J. & Carroll, A. (2002) A review of the research on interventions for attention deficit hyperactivity disorder: What works best? *Review of Educational Research*, **72**, 61–99.

Purdie, N., Hattie, J. & Douglas, G. (1996) Student conceptions of learning and their use of self-regulated learning strategies: A cross-cultural comparison. *Journal of Educational Psychology*, **88**, 87–100.

Purdie, N. & McCrindle, A. (2004) Measurement of self-concept among Indigenous and non-Indigenous Australian students. *Australian Journal of Psychology*, **56**, 50–62.

Putnam, R. T. & Borko, H. (2000) What do new views of knowledge and thinking have to say about research on teacher learning? *Educational Researcher*, **29**, 4–15.

Qin, Z., Johnson, D. W. & Johnson, R. T. (1995) Cooperative versus competitive efforts and problem solving. *Review of Educational Research*, **2**, 129–43.

Quaiser-Pohl, C. & Lehmann, W. (2002) Girls' special abilities: Charting the contributions of experiences and attitudes in different academic groups. *British Journal of Educational Psychology*, **72**, 245–60.

Quiocho, A. & Rios, F. (2000) The power of their presence: Minority group teachers and schooling. *Review of Educational Research*, **70**, 485–528.

Rasmussen, K. L. (1998) Hypermedia and learning styles: Can performance be influenced? *Journal of Multimedia and Hypermedia*, **7**, 291–308.

Rawsthorne, L. J. & Elliot, A. J. (1999) Achievement goals and intrinsic motivation: A meta-analytic review. *Personality and Social Psychology Review*, **3**, 326–44.

Reeve, J., Deci, E. L. & Ryan, R. M. (2004) Self-determination theory: A dialectical framework for understanding sociocultural influences on student motivation. In D. M. McInerney & S. Van Etten (eds) *Research on Sociocultural Influences on Motivation and Learning (Volume 4), Big Theories Revisited*. Greenwich, CT: Information Age Publishing.

Reeve, J., Nix, G. & Hamm, D. (2003) Testing models of the experience of self-determination in intrinsic motivation and the conundrum of choice. *Journal of Educational Psychology*, **95**, 375–92.

Reis, S. M. (1989) Reflections on policy affecting the education of gifted and talented students. Past and future perspectives. *American Psychologist*, **44**, 399–408.

Relich, J. & Ward, J. (eds) (1987) *Academically Gifted–Educationally Disadvantaged? Providing for the Intellectually Gifted and Talented*. Sydney: NSWIER.

Render, G. F., Padilla, J. N. & Krank, H. M. (1989) What research really shows about assertive discipline. *Educational Leadership*, **46**, 72–5.

Renner, J., Stafford, A., Lawson, J., McKinnson, J., Friot, F. & Kellogg, D. (1976) *Research, Teaching, and Learning with the Piaget Model*. Norman, OK: University of Oklahoma Press.

Renninger, K. A. & Hidi, S. (2002) Student interest and achievement: Developmental issues raised by a case study. In A. Wigfield & J. S. Eccles (eds) *Development of Achievement Motivation*. San Diego, CA: Academic Press.

Renzulli, J. S. (1986) The three-ring conception of giftedness: A developmental model for creative productivity. In R. J. Sternberg & J. E. Davidson (eds) *Conceptions of Giftedness*. New York: Cambridge University Press.

Rest, J. R. (1973) The hierarchical nature of moral judgment: A study of patterns of comprehension and preference with moral stages. *Journal of Personality*, **41**, 92–3.

Rest, J. R. (1979) *Development in Judging Moral Issues*. Minneapolis: University of Minnesota Press.

Rest, J., Narvaez, D., Bebeau, M. & Thoma, S. (1999a) A neo-Kohlbergian approach: The DIT and schema theory. *Educational Psychology Review*, **11**, 291–324.

Rest, J., Narvaez, D., Bebeau, M. & Thoma, S. (1999b) *Post-conventional Moral Thinking: A Neo-Kohlbergian Approach*. Mahwah, NJ: Lawrence Erlbaum.

Reyna, C. & Weiner, B. (2001) Justice and utility in the classroom: An attributional analysis of the goals of teachers' punishment and intervention strategies. *Journal of Educational Psychology*, **93**, 309–19.

Reynolds, A. (1992) What is competent beginning teaching? A review of the literature. *Review of Educational Research*, **62**, 1–35.

Reynolds, M. C. (1984) Classification of students with handicaps. In E. W. Gordon (ed.) *Review of Research in Education (Volume 11)*. Washington, DC: AERA.

Rhode, G., Morgan, D. P. & Young, K. R. (1983) Generalization and maintenance of treatment gains of behaviorally handicapped students from resource rooms to regular classrooms using self-evaluation procedures. *Journal of Applied Behavior Analysis*, **16**, 171–88.

Rickard, A. G. (1981) The planning of a district-based innovation for gifted children. *Unicorn*, **7**, 254–74.

Ridberg, E. H., Parke, R. D. & Hetherington, E. M. (1971) Modification of impulsive and reflective cognitive styles through observation of film-mediated models. *Child Development*, **5**, 369–77.

Riding, R. & Grimley, M. (1999) Cognitive style and learning from multimedia materials in 11-year-old children. *British Journal of Educational Technology*, **30**, 43–59.

Riehl, C. J. (2000) The principal's role in creating inclusive schools for diverse students: A review of normative, empirical, and critical literature on the practice of educational administration. *Review of Educational Research*, **70**, 55–81.

Rietveld, C. (1988) Adjusting to school. Eight children with Down's syndrome. *SET Research Information for Teachers*, number 1, item 2.

Rigby, K. & Bagshaw, D. (2003) Prospects of adolescent students collaborating with teachers in addressing issues of bullying and conflict in schools. *Educational Psychology*, **23**, 535–46.

Rigby, K. & Slee, P. T. (1993) Dimensions of interpersonal relation among Australian children and implications for psychological well-being. *Journal of Social Psychology*, **133**, 33–42.

Ringbom, H. (1987) *The Role of the First Language in Foreign Language Learning*. Avon, UK: Multilingual Matters.

Ritchie, J. (1983) Corporal punishment and attitudes to violence of secondary school students. *New Zealand Journal of Educational Studies*, **18**, 84–7.

Ritts, V., Patterson, M. L. & Tubbs, M. E. (1992) Expectations, impressions, and judgements of physically attractive students: A review. *Review of Educational Research*, **62**, 413–26.

Roberts, C. M. & Quayle, D. (2001) Loneliness in children: Behavioural, interpersonal and cognitive correlates. *The Australian Educational and Developmental Psychologist*, **18**, 9–25.

Robinson, F. P. (1970) *Effective study*, 4th ed. New York: Harper & Row.

Roche, L. A. & Marsh, H. W. (1993) The comparison of nomothetic (highly structured) and idiographic (open-ended) measures of multifaceted self-concepts. Paper presented at the AARE Annual Conference, Fremantle, Western Australia.

Roderick, M. & Camburn, E. (1999) Risk and recovery from course failure in the early years of high school. *American Educational Research Journal*, **36**, 303–43.

Roeser, R. W. (1998) On schooling and mental health: Introduction to the special issue. *Educational Psychologist*, **33**, 129–33.

Roeser, R. W., Eccles, J. S. & Strobel, K. R. (1998) Linking the study of schooling and mental health: Selected issues and empirical illustrations at the level of the individual. *Educational Psychologist*, **33**, 153–76.

Rogers, B. (1990) *You Know the Fair Rule*. Melbourne: ACER.

Rogers, B. (1994) *The Language of Discipline: A Practical Approach to Effective Classroom Management*. Plymouth, UK: Northcote House.

Rogers, B. (1995) *Behaviour Management: A Whole-school Approach*. Gosford, NSW: Ashton Scholastic.

Rogers, B. (1997) *Cracking the Hard Class: Strategies for Managing the Harder than Average Class*. Gosford, NSW: Ashton Scholastic.

Rogers, B. (1998) *You Know the Fair Rule*, 2nd ed. Melbourne: ACER.

Rogers, C. R. (1951) *Client-centered Therapy: Its Current Practice, Implications and Theory*. Boston: Houghton Mifflin.

Rogers, C. R. (1961) *On Becoming a Person*. Boston: Houghton Mifflin.

Rogers, C. R. (1969) *Freedom to Learn*. Columbus, OH: Charles E. Merrill.

Rogers, C. R. (1976) The interpersonal relationship in the facilitation of learning. In M. L. Silberman, J. S. Allender & J. M. Yanoff (eds) *Real Learning. A Sourcebook for Teachers*. Boston: Little, Brown & Co.

Rogers, C. R. (1977) Learning to be free. In H. F. Clarizio, R. C. Craig & W. A. Mehrens (eds) *Contemporary Issues in Educational Psychology*, 3rd ed. Boston: Allyn & Bacon.

Rogers, C. R. (1980) *A Way of Being*. Boston: Houghton Mifflin.

Rogers, C. R. (1983) *Freedom to Learn: For the 80s*. Columbus, OH: Charles E. Merrill.

Rogers, K. B. & Kimpston, R. D. (1992) Acceleration: What we do vs what we know. *Educational Leadership*, **50**, 58–61.

Rogers, W. A. (1989) *Making a Discipline Plan. Developing Classroom Management Skills*. Melbourne: Thomas Nelson.

Rogoff, B. (1995) Observing sociocultural activities on three planes: Participatory appropriation, guided appropriation and apprenticeship. In J. V. Wertsch, P. Del Rio & A. Alverez (eds) *Sociocultural Studies of the Mind*. Cambridge: Cambridge University Press.

Rogoff, B. & Chavajay, P. (1995) What's become of research on the cultural basis of cognitive development? *American Psychologist*, **50**, 859–77.

Rohrbeck, C. A., Ginsburg-Block, M. D., Fantuzzo, J. W. & Miller, T. R. (2003) Peer-assisted learning interventions with elementary school students: A meta-analytic review. *Journal of Educational Psychology*, **95**, 240–57.

Rohwer, W. D., Rohwer, C. P. & B-Howe, J. R. (1980) *Educational Psychology. Teaching for Student Diversity*. New York: Holt, Rinehart & Winston.

Romeo, F. F. (1986) *Understanding Anorexia Nervosa*. Springfield, IL: Thomas.

Rosenfeld, M. & Rosenfeld, S. (2004) Developing teacher sensitivity to individual learning differences. *Educational Psychology*, **24**, 465–86.

Rosenshine, B. & Meister, C. (1995) Direct instruction. In L. W. Anderson (ed.) *International Encyclopedia of Teaching and Teacher Education*, 2nd ed. Tarrytown, NY: Pergamon.

Rosenshine, B., Meister, C. & Chapman, S. (1996) Teaching students to generate questions: A review of the intervention studies. *Review of Educational Research*, **66**, 181–221.

Rosenshine, B. & Stevens, R. (1986) Teaching functions. In M. C. Wittrock (ed.) *Handbook of Research on Teaching*, 3rd ed. New York: Macmillan.

Rosenshine, B. V. (1971) *Teaching Behaviours and Student Achievement*. London: National Foundation for Educational Research.

Rosenshine, B. V. (1979) Content, time and direct instruction. In P. L. Peterson & H. J. Walberg (eds) *Research on Teaching: Concepts, Findings, and Implications*. Berkeley, CA: McCutchan.

Rosenthal, R. (1973) The Pygmalion effect lives. *Psychology Today*, September, 56–63.

Rosenthal, R. & Jacobson, L. (1968) *Pygmalion in the Classroom: Teacher Expectations and Pupils' Intellectual Development*. New York: Holt, Rinehart & Winston.

Rosenthal, D., Ranieri, N. & Klimidis, S. (1996) Vietnamese adolescents in Australia: Relationships between perceptions of self and parental values, intergenerational conflict, and gender dissatisfaction. *International Journal of Psychology*, **31**, 81–91.

Ross, J. A. (1994) The impact of an inservice to promote cooperative learning on the stability of teacher efficacy. *Teaching and Teacher Education*, **10**, 381–94.

Ross, J. A. (1998) Antecedents and consequences of teacher efficacy. In J. Brophy (ed.) *Advances in Research on Teaching (Volume 7)*. Greenwich, CT: JAI Press.

Roth, W. (2001) Gestures: Their role in teaching and learning. *Review of Educational Research*, **71**, 365–92.

Rothenberg, S. (1989) The open classroom reconsidered. *The Elementary School Journal*, **90**, 69–86.

Rothman, S. L. (1990) A critical analysis of education for children identified as gifted and talented and implications for teacher education. In M. Bezzina & J. Butcher (eds) *The Changing Face of Professional Education. Collected Papers of the AARE Annual Conference, Sydney University, 1990*. Sydney: AARE.

Rowe, H. A. H. (1984a) Problem solving strategies. *SET Research Information for Teachers*, number 2, item 13.

Rowe, H. A. H. (1984b) *Problem Solving and Intelligence*. Hillsdale, NJ: Lawrence Erlbaum.

Rowe, H. A. H. (1988a) Metacognitive skills: Promises and problems. *Australian Journal of Reading*, **2**, 227–37.

Rowe, H. A. H. (1988b) Teaching thinking and learning skills. *Curriculum Issues*, **15**. Sydney: Catholic College of Education.

Rowe, H. A. H. (1988c) *The Teaching of Critical Thinking: Assumptions, Aims, Processes and Implications*. Melbourne: ACER.

Rowe, H. A. H. (1989a) Teach learning strategies. *SET Research Information for Teachers*, number 1, item 14.

Royer, J. M. (1986) Designing instruction to produce understanding: An approach based on cognitive theory. In G. D. Phye & T. Andre (eds) *Cognitive Classroom Learning. Understanding Thinking and Problem Solving*. Orlando: Harcourt Brace Jovanovich.

Rubie, C. M., Townsend, M. A. R. & Moore, D. W. (2004) Motivational and academic effects of cultural experiences for indigenous minority students in New Zealand. *Educational Psychology*, **24**, 143–60.

Rueda, R., MacGillivray, L., Monzó, L. & Arzubiagia, A. (2001) Engaged reading: A multi-level approach to considering sociocultural factors with diverse learners. In D. M. McInerney & S. Van Etten (eds) *Research on Sociocultural Influences on Motivation and Learning*. Greenwich, CT: Information Age Press.

Ruffels, M. J. (1986) A study of critical thinking skills in grade 10 students in a Tasmanian high school. Unpublished Masters thesis submitted to the Tasmanian State Institute of Technology.

Rundus, D. & Atkinson, R. C. (1970) Rehearsal processes in free recall: A procedure for direct observation. *Journal of Verbal Learning and Verbal Behaviour*, **9**, 99–105.

Ryan, R. M., Connell, J. P. & Deci, E. L. (1985) A motivational analysis of self-determination and self-regulation in education. In C. Ames & R. Ames (eds) *Research on Motivation in Education: The Classroom Milieu (Volume 2)*. Orlando: Academic Press.

Ryan, R. M. & Deci, E. L. (1996) When paradigms clash: Comment on Cameron and Pierce's claim that rewards do not undermine intrinsic motivation. *Review of Educational Research*, **66**, 33–8.

Ryan, R. M. & Deci, E. L. (2000) Intrinsic and extrinsic motivations: Classic definitions and new directions. *Contemporary Educational Psychology*, **25**, 54–67.

Ryan, R. M., Gheen, M. H. & Midgley, C. (1998) Why do some students avoid asking for help? An examination of the interplay among students' academic efficacy, teachers' social-emotional role, and the classroom goal structure. *Journal of Educational Psychology*, **90**, 528–35.

Rysavy, S. D. M. & Sales, G. C. (1991) Cooperative learning in computer-based instruction. *Educational Technology Research and Development*, **39**, 70–9.

Sachs, J. (1989) Match or mismatch: Teachers' conceptions of culture and multicultural education policy. *Australian Journal of Education*, **33**, 19–33.

Sackett, P. R., Hardison, C. M. & Cullen, M. J. (2004a) On interpreting stereotype threat as accounting for African American-White differences on cognitive tests. *American Psychologist*, **59**, 7–13.

Sackett, P. R., Hardison, C. M. & Cullen, M. J. (2004b) On the value of correcting mischaracterizations of stereotype threat research. *American Psychologist*, **59**, 48–9.

Sackett, P. R., Schmitt, N., Ellingson, J. E. & Kabin, M. B. (2001) High-stakes testing in employment, credentialing, and higher education. Prospects in a post-affirmative-action world. *American Psychologist*, **56**, 302–18.

Salomon, G. & Perkins, D. N. (1989) Rocky roads to transfer: Rethinking mechanisms of a neglected phenomenon. *Educational Psychologist*, **24**, 113–42.

Salomon, G. & Perkins, D. N. (1998) Individual and social aspects of learning. *Review of Research in Education*, **23**, 1–24.

Salovey, P. & Mayer, J. D. (1990) Emotional intelligence. *Imagination, Cognition, Personality*, **9**, 185–211.

Sanson, A. & Di Muccio, C. (1993) The influence of aggressive and neutral cartoons and toys on the behaviour of preschool children. *Australian Psychologist*, **28**, 93–9.

Sanson, A., Prior, M., Smart, D. & Oberkaid, F. (1993) Gender differences in aggression in childhood: Implications for a peaceful world. *Australian Psychologist*, **28**, 86–92.

Santrock, J. W. & Yussen, S. R. (1992) *Child Development. An Introduction*, 5th ed. Dubuque, IA: William C. Brown.

Sarason, I. G. (1972) Experimental approaches to test anxiety: Attention and the uses of information. In C. D. Spielberger (ed.) *Anxiety: Current Trends in Theory and Research (Volume II)*. New York: Academic Press.

Sarason, I. G. (1975) Test anxiety and the self-disclosing coping model. *Journal of Consulting and Clinical Psychology*, **43**, 143–53.

Sarris, A., Winefield, H. R. & Cooper, C. (2000) Behaviour problems in adolescence: A comparison of juvenile offenders and adolescents referred to a mental health service. *Australian Journal of Psychology*, **52**, 17–22.

Sawyer, R. K. (2004) Creative teaching: Collaborative discussion as disciplined improvisation. *Educational Researcher*, **33**, 12–20.

Scarr, S. & Weinberg, R. A. (1983) The Minnesota adoption studies: Genetic difference and malleability. *Child Development*, **54**, 260–7.

Scarr, S., Weinberg, R. A. & Levine, A. (1986) *Understanding Development*. San Diego, CA: Harcourt Brace Jovanovich.

Schank, R. C. & Towle, B. (2000) Artificial intelligence. In R. J. Sternberg (ed.) *Handbook of Intelligence*. New York: Cambridge University Press.

Schloss, P. J. (1992) Mainstreaming revisited. *Elementary School Journal*, **92**, 233–44.

Schmeck, R. R. (ed.) (1988) *Learning Strategies and Learning Styles*. New York: Plenum Press.

Schmidt, R. (1975) *Motor Skills*. New York: Harper & Row.

Schmidt, R. (1982) *Motor Control and Learning: A Behavioral Emphasis*. Champaign, IL: Human Kinetics Books.

Scholl, G. T. (1987) Appropriate education for visually handicapped students. In K. L. Frieberg (ed.) *Educating Exceptional Children*, 6th ed. Guilford, CT: Duskin.

Schraw, G., Flowerday, T. & Reisetter, M. (1998) The role of choice in reader engagement. *Journal of Educational Psychology*, **90**, 705–13.

Schraw, G. M. & Moshman, D. (1995) Metacognitive theories. *Educational Psychology Review*, **7**, 351–71.

Schunk, D. H. (1982) Effects of effort attributional feedback on children's perceived self-efficacy and achievement. *Journal of Educational Psychology*, **74**, 548–56.

Schunk, D. H. (1983) Ability versus effort attributional feedback. Differential effects on self-efficacy and achievement. *Journal of Educational Psychology*, **75**, 848–56.

Schunk, D. H. (1987) Peer models and children's behavioral change. *Review of Educational Research*, **57**, 149–74.

Schunk, D. H. (1989) Self-efficacy and cognitive skill learning. In C. Ames & R. Ames (eds) *Research on Motivation in Education: Goals and Cognitions (Volume 3)*. Orlando: Academic Press.

Schunk, D. H. (1990) Goal setting and self-efficacy during self-regulated learning. *Educational Psychologist*, **25**, 71–86.

Schunk, D. H. (1991) Self-efficacy and academic motivation. *Educational Psychologist*, **26**, 207–31.

Schunk, D. H. (1996) Motivation in education: Current emphases and future trends. *Mid-Western Educational Researcher*, **9**, 5–11.

Schunk, D. H. & Pajares, F. (2004) Self-efficacy in education revisited: Empirical and applied evidence. In D. M. McInerney & S. Van Etten (eds) *Research on Sociocultural Influences on Motivation and Learning (Volume 4), Big Theories Revisited*. Greenwich, CT: Information Age Publishing.

Schutz, H. K., Paxton, S. J. & Muir, S. (1996) Friendship clique similarity on body image attitudes and dieting-related behaviours in adolescent girls. Paper presented at the 31st Annual Conference of the Australian Psychological Society, 25–29 September, Sydney.

Scott, G., Ciarrochi, J. & Deane, F. P. (2004) Disadvantages of being an individualist in an individualistic culture: Idiocentrism, emotional competence, stress, and mental health. *Australian Psychologist*, **39**, 143–53.

Scriven, M. (1967) The methodology of evaluation. In R. Tyler, R. Gagne & M. Scriven (eds) *Perspectives of Curriculum Evaluation*. Chicago, IL: Rand McNally.

Seagoe, M. V. (1972) *The Learning Process and School Practice*. Scranton, PA: Chandler.

Seegers, G., van Putten, C. M. & de Bradbander, C. J. (2002) Goal orientation, perceived task outcome and task demands in mathematics tasks: Effects on students' attitude in actual task settings. *British Journal of Educational Psychology*, **72**, 365–84.

Semb, G. B. & Ellis, J. A. (1994) Knowledge taught in school: What is remembered? *Review of Educational Research*, **64**, 253–86.

Sfard, A. (1998) On two metaphors for learning and the dangers of choosing just one. *Educational Researcher*, **27**, 4–13.

Shann, M. H. (1999) Academics and a culture of caring: The relationship between school achievement and prosocial and antisocial behaviors in four urban middle schools. *School Effectiveness and School Improvement*, **10**, 390–413.

Sharan, Y. & Sharan, S. (1992) *Expanding Cooperative Learning Through Group Investigation*. New York: Teachers College Press.

Shaughnessy, M. F. (1993) The concept of giftedness. *International Journal of Educational Research*, **19**, 5–15.

Shavelson, R. J. & Bolus, R. (1982) Self-concept: The interplay of theory and methods. *Journal of Educational Psychology*, **73**, 3–17.

Shavelson, R. J. & Marsh, H. W. (1986) On the structure of self-concept. In R. Schwarzer (ed.) *Anxiety and Cognitions*. Hillsdale, NJ: Lawrence Erlbaum.

Sheldon, W. H. (1940) *The Varieties of Human Physique: An Introduction to Constitutional Psychology*. New York: Harper.

Sheldon, W. H. (1970) *Atlas of Men. A Guide for Somatotyping the Adult Male at all Ages*. Darien, CT: Hafner.

Sheldon, W. H. & Stevens, S. H. (1942) *The Varieties of Temperament*. New York: Harper & Row.

Shepard, L. A. (1989) Why we need better assessments. *Educational Leadership*, **46**, 4–9.

Shepard, L. A. (1991) Psychometricians' beliefs about learning. *Educational Researcher*, **20**, 2–16.

Shepard, L. A. (1993) Evaluating test validity. *Review of Research in Education*, **19**, 405–50.

Shipman, S. & Shipman, V. C. (1985) Cognitive styles: Some conceptual, methodological, and applied issues. In E. W. Gordon (ed.) *Review of Research in Education (Volume 12)*. New York: AERA.

Shochet, I. & Osgarby, S. (1999) The Resourceful Adolescents Project: Building psychological resilience in adolescents and their parents. *The Australian Educational and Developmental Psychologist*, **16**, 46–65.

Shouse, R. C. (1996) Academic press and sense of community: Conflict, congruence, and implications for student achievement. *Social Psychology of Education*, **1**, 47–68.

Shuell, T. J. (1986) Cognitive conceptions of learning. *Review of Educational Research*, **56**, 411–36.

Shuell, T. J. (1988) The role of the student in learning from instruction. *Contemporary Educational Psychology*, **13**, 276–95.

Shuell, T. J. (1990) Phases of meaningful learning. *Review of Educational Research*, **60**, 531–47.

Shuker, R. (1989) 'I Want My MTV'. *SET Research Information for Teachers*, number 1, item 4.

Shweder, R. A., Mahapatra, M. & Miller, J. C. (1987) Cultural and moral development. In J. Kagan & S. Lamb (eds) *The Emergence of Morality in Young Children*. Chicago: University of Chicago Press.

Shweder, R. A., Mahapatra, M. & Miller, J. C. (1990) Culture and moral development. In J. W. Stigler, R. A. Shweder & G. Herdt (eds) *Cultural Psychology. Essays on Comparative Human Development*. Cambridge: Cambridge University Press.

Siegal, M. (1991) *Knowing Children. Experiments in Conversation and Cognition*. Hillsdale, NJ: Lawrence Erlbaum.

Siegler, R. S. (1991) *Children's Thinking*, 2nd ed. Englewood Cliffs, NJ: Prentice Hall.

Siegler, R. S. & Richards, D. D. (1982) The development of intelligence. In R. J. Sternberg (ed.) *Handbook of Human Intelligence*. Cambridge: Cambridge University Press.

Sigel, I. E. & Cocking, R. R. (1977) *Cognitive Development from Childhood to Adolescence: A Constructivist Perspective*. New York: Holt, Rinehart & Winston.

Silberman, M. L., Allender, J. S. & Yanoff, J. M. (eds) (1976) *Real Learning. A Sourcebook for Teachers*. Boston: Little, Brown & Co.

Silverberg, S. B. & Steinberg, L. (1990) Psychological well-being of parents with early adolescent children. *Developmental Psychology*, **26**, 658–66.

Simkin, K. (1991) Classroom management and ethnic diversity. In M. N. Lovegrove & R. Lewis (eds) *Classroom Discipline*. Melbourne: Longman.

Simmons, R. G. & Blyth, D. A. (1987) *Moving into Adolescence: The Impact of Pubertal Change and School Context*. Hawthorne, NY: Aldine de Gruyter.

Simpson, E. J. (1972) The classification of educational objectives in the psychomotor domain. *The Psychomotor Domain (Volume 3)*. Washington: Gryphon House.

Sinclair, D. (1989) *Human Growth after Birth*. Oxford: Oxford University Press.

Sinclair, K. E. & Nicoll, V. (1981) Sources and experience of anxiety in practice teaching. *South Pacific Journal of Teacher Education*, **9**, 1–18.

Skaalvik, E. M. & Skaalvik, S. (2002) Internal and external frames of reference for academic self-concept. *Educational Psychologist*, **37**, 233–44.

Skinner, B. F. (1948) *Walden Two*. New York: Macmillan.

Skinner, B. F. (1951) How to teach animals. *Scientific American*, **185**, 26–9.

Skinner, B. F. (1954) The science of learning and the art of teaching. *Harvard Educational Review*, **24**, 86–97.

Skinner, B. F. (1965) Why teachers fail. *Saturday Review*, 80–1, 98–102 (16 October).

Skinner, B. F. (1968) *The Technology of Teaching*. New York: Appleton-Century-Crofts.

Skinner, B. F. (1971) *Beyond Freedom and Dignity*. New York: Alfred A. Knopf.

Skinner, B. F. (1977) The free and happy student. In H. F. Clarizio, R. C. Craig & W. A. Mehrens (eds) *Contemporary Issues in Educational Psychology*, 3rd ed. Boston: Allyn & Bacon.

Skinner, B. F. (1984) The shame of American education. *American Psychologist*, **39**, 103–10.

Skinner, B. F. (1986) Programmed instruction revisited. *Phi Delta Kappan*, **68**, 103–10.

Sladeczek, I. E. & Kratochwill, T. R. (1995) Reinforcement. In L. W. Anderson (ed.) *International Encyclopedia of Teaching and Teacher Education*, 2nd ed. Tarrytown, NY: Pergamon.

Slavin, R. E. (1980) Cooperative learning. *Review of Educational Research*, **50**, 315–42.

Slavin, R. E. (1983) When does cooperative learning increase student achievement? *Psychological Bulletin*, **94**, 429–45.

Slavin, R. E. (1985a) Team-assisted individualization: A cooperative learning solution for adaptive instruction in mathematics. In M. C. Wang & H. J. Walberg (eds) *Adapting Instruction to Individual Differences*, Berkeley, CA: McCutchan.

Slavin, R. E. (1985b) An introduction to cooperative learning research. In R. Slavin, S. Sharan, S. Kagan, R. Hertz-Lazarowitz, C. Webb & R. Schmuck (eds) *Learning to Cooperate, Cooperating to Learn*. New York: Plenum Press.

Slavin, R. E. (1987a) Ability grouping and student achievement in elementary schools: A best-evidence synthesis. *Review of Educational Research*, **57**, 293–336.

Slavin, R. E. (1987b) Mastery learning reconsidered. *Review of Educational Research*, **57**, 175–214.

Slavin, R. E. (1987c) Developmental and motivational perspectives on cooperative learning: A reconciliation. *Child Development*, **58**, 1161–7.

Slavin, R. E. (ed.) (1989a) *School and Classroom Organization*. Hillsdale, NJ: Lawrence Erlbaum.

Slavin, R. E. (1989b) On mastery learning and mastery teaching. *Educational Leadership*, **46**, 77–9.

Slavin, R. E. (1990) *Cooperative Learning. Theory, Research, and Practice*. Boston: Allyn & Bacon.

Slavin, R. E. (1991a) Group rewards make groupwork work. *Educational Leadership*, **48**, 71–82.

Slavin, R. E. (1991b) *Educational Psychology. Theory into Practice*, 3rd ed. Englewood Cliffs, NJ: Prentice Hall.

Slavin, R. E. (1992) When and why does cooperative learning increase achievement? Theoretical and empirical perspectives. In R. Hertz-Lazarowitz & N. Miller (eds) *Interaction in Cooperative Groups: The Theoretical Anatomy of Group Learning*. Cambridge: Cambridge University Press.

Slavin, R. E. (1995) *Cooperative Learning*. In L. W. Anderson (ed.) *International Encyclopedia of Teaching and Teacher Education*, 2nd ed. Tarrytown, NY: Pergamon.

Slee, P. T. (1995a) Bullying: Health concerns of Australian secondary school students. *International Journal of Adolescence and Youth*, **5**, 215–24.

Slee, P. T. (1995b) Peer victimization and its relationship to depression among Australian primary school students. *Personality and Individual Differences*, **18**, 57–62.

Smagorinsky, P. (1995) The social construction of data: Methodological problems of investigating learning in the zone of proximal development. *Review of Educational Research*, **65**, 191–212.

Smagorinsky, P. (2001) If meaning is constructed, what is it made from? Toward a cultural theory of reading. *Review of Educational Research*, **71**, 133–69.

Smart, M. S. & Smart, R. C. (1977) *Children. Development and Relationships*, 3rd ed. New York: Macmillan.

Smilansky, S. (1990) Sociodramatic play. Its relevance to behavior and achievement in school. In E. Klugman & S. Smilansky (eds) *Children's Play and Learning*. New York: Teachers College Press.

Smith, I. (1987) Gifted and talented children. Are they educationally disadvantaged? *Current Affairs Bulletin*, **63**, 28–32.

Smith, I. D. & Gopinathan, S. (2000) Better, worse or different? A critique of 'Using language policies to highlight and contrast the values that shape multicultural societies: Examples from Singapore and Australia' by Beatrice Boufoy-Bastick (1997). *Australian Journal of Education*, **44**, 43–50.

Smith, J. (1979) Violence and television. New research findings. *The Primary Journal*, **4**, 2–6.

Smith, M., Duda, J., Allen, J. & Hall, H. (2002) Contemporary measures of approach and avoidance goal orientations: Similarities and differences. *British Journal of Educational Psychology*, **72**, 155–90.

Smith, N. & Smith, H. (1991) *Physical Disability and Handicap*. Melbourne: Longman Cheshire.

Smith, P. (1999) Drawing new maps: A radical cartography of developmental disabilities. *Review of Educational Research*, **69**, 117–44.

Smith, P. K. (1978) A longitudinal study of social participation in preschool children: Solitary and parallel play re-examined. *Developmental Psychology*, **12**, 517–23.

Smith, P. K. & Ahmad, Y. (1990) The playground jungle: Bullies, victims and intervention strategies. *SET Research Information for Teachers*, number 1, item 6.

Smith, P. K. & Brain, P. (2000) Bullying in schools: Lessons from two decades of research. *Aggressive Behavior*, **26**, 1–9.

Smith, P. K. & Sharp, S. (1994) The problem of school bullying. In P. K. Smith & S. Sharp (eds) *School Bullying Insights and Perspectives*. London: Routledge.

Smolicz, J. J. (1986) National policy on languages: A community language perspective. *Australian Journal of Education*, **30**, 45–65.

Smolicz, J. J. (1987) Education for a multicultural society. In J. P. Keeves (ed.) *Australian Education. Review of Recent Research*. Sydney: Allen & Unwin.

Smolicz, J. J. (1991) Language, culture and the school in a plural society: An Australian perspective for the 1990s. *Migration Monitor*, **23–24**, 3–15.

Smolucha, F. (1992) Social origins of private speech in pretend play. In R. M. Diaz & L. E. Berk (eds) *Private Speech: From Social Interaction to Self-regulation*. Hillsdale, NJ: Lawrence Erlbaum.

Smyth, E. (1999) Pupil performance, absenteeism and school drop-out: A multi-dimensional analysis. *School Effectiveness and School Improvement*, **10**, 480–502.

Snodgrass, D. M. (1991) The parent connection. *Adolescence*, **26**, 83–7.

Snow, C. E. (1992) Perspectives on second-language development: Implications for bilingual education. *Educational Researcher*, **21**, 16–19.

Snow, R. E. (1986) Individual differences and the design of educational programs. *American Psychologist*, **41**, 1029–39.

Snowman, J. (1986) Learning tactics and strategies. In G. D. Phye & T. Andre (eds) *Cognitive Classroom Learning. Understanding Thinking and Problem Solving*. Orlando: Harcourt Brace Jovanovich.

Soar, R. (1966) *An Integrative Approach to Classroom Learning*. ERIC Document Reproduction Service No. ED 033 749.

Soar, R. & Soar, R. (1979) Emotional climate and management. In P. Peterson & H. Walberg (eds) *Research on Teaching: Concepts, Findings, and Implications*. Berkeley, CA: McCutchan.

Sofo, F. (1988) Critical thinking skills and self-esteem. In *Educational Research in Australia: Indigenous or Exotic?* Unpublished papers presented at the annual conference of the Australian Association of Research in Education held at the University of New England, Armidale, NSW, 30 November–4 December. Armidale, NSW: AARE.

Sokolove, S., Garrett, J., Sadker, D. & Sadker, M (1986) Interpersonal communications skills. In J. Cooper (ed.) *Classroom Teaching Skills: A Handbook*. Lexington, MA: DC Heath.

Solano-Flores, G. & Trumbull, E. (2003) Examining language in context: The need for new research and practice paradigms in the testing of English-language learners. *Educational Researcher*, **32**, 3–13.

Solas, J. (1992) Investigating teacher and student thinking about the process of teaching and learning using autobiography and repertory grid. *Review of Educational Research*, **62**, 205–25.

Solomon, D., Watson, M., Schaps, E., Battistich, V. & Solomon, J. (1990) Cooperative learning as part of a comprehensive classroom program designed to promote prosocial development. In S. Sharan (ed.) *Recent Research on Cooperative Learning*. New York: Praeger.

Sonn, C., Bishop, B. & Humphries, R. (2000) Encounters with the dominant culture: Voices of indigenous students in mainstream higher education. *Australian Psychologist*, **35**, 128–35.

Sowder, J. T. (1998) Perspectives from mathematics education. *Educational Researcher*, **27**, 12–13.

Splitter, L. (1988) On teaching children to be better thinkers. *Unicorn*, **14**, 40–7.

Springer, C. (1991) The pleasure of the interface. *Screen*, **32**, 303–23.

Springer, L. Stanne, M. E. & Donovan, S. S. (1999) Effects of small-group learning on undergraduates in science, mathematics, engineering, and technology: A meta-analysis. *Review of Educational Research*, **69**(1), 21–51.

Sprinthall, N. A. & Sprinthall, R. C. (1990) *Educational Psychology. A Developmental Approach*, 5th ed. New York: McGraw-Hill.

Sprinthall, R. C., Schmutte, G. T. & Sirois, L. (1991) *Understanding Educational Research*. Englewood Cliffs, NJ: Prentice Hall.

Staffieri, J. R. (1967) A study of social stereotype of body image in children. *Journal of Personality and Social Psychology*, **7**, 101–4.

Staffieri, J. R. (1972) Body build and behavioral expectancies in young females. *Developmental Psychology*, **6**, 125–7.

Stallings, J. A. & Kaskowitz, D. H. (1975) A study of follow-through implementation. Paper presented at the meeting of the American Educational Research Association, Washington, DC.

Stanley, J. (1978) Radical acceleration: Recent educational innovations at Johns Hopkins University. *Gifted Child Quarterly*, **20**, 66–75.

Stanley, J. (1980) On educating the gifted. *Educational Researcher*, **9**, 8–12.

Starfield, B. & Pless, I. B. (1980) Physical health. In O. G. Brim & J. Kagan (eds) *Constancy and Change in Human Development*. Cambridge, MA: Harvard University Press.

State Services Commission (1989) *Employment for Education. A Guide for School Trustees and Principals*. Wellington, NZ: State Services Commission.

Stecher, B. M. & Herman, J. L. (1997) Using portfolios for large-scale assessment. In G. Phye (ed.) *Handbook of Classroom Assessment: Learning, Achievement, and Adjustment*. San Diego, CA: Academic Press.

Steele, C. M. & Aronson, J. (1995) Stereotype threat and the intellectual test performance of African Americans. *Journal of Personality and Social Psychology*, **69**, 797–811.

Steele, C. M. & Aronson, J. A. (2004) Stereotype threat does not live by Steele and Aronson (1995) alone. *American Psychologist*, **59**, 47–55.

Stefanou, C. R., Perencevich, K. C., DiCintio, M. & Turner, J. C. (2004) Supporting autonomy in the classroom: Ways teachers encourage student decision making and ownership. *Educational Psychologist*, **39**, 97–110.

Steffe, L. P. & Gale, J. E. (eds) (1995) *Constructivism in Education*. Hillsdale, NJ: Lawrence Erlbaum.

Steinberg, L. (1991) Parent–adolescent relations. In R. M. Lerner,

A. C. Petersen & J. Brooks-Gunn (eds) *Encyclopedia of Adolescence*. New York: Garland.
Stephens, R. & Stephens, G. (1986) Integration at the chalk face. *SET Research Information for Teachers*, number 1, item 6.
Sternberg, R. (1986) *Intelligence Applied: Understanding and Increasing Your Own Intellectual Skills*. New York: Harcourt Brace Jovanovich.
Sternberg, R. J. (1985) *Beyond IQ: A Triarchic Theory of Human Intelligence*. New York: Freeman.
Sternberg, R. J. (1998a) Principles of teaching for successful intelligence. *Educational Psychologist*, **33**, 65–72.
Sternberg, R. J. (1998b) Abilities are forms of developing expertise. *Educational Researcher*, **27**, 11–20.
Sternberg, R. J. (1998c) Teaching triarchically improves school achievement. *Journal of Educational Psychology*, **33**, 374–84.
Sternberg, R. J. (2000) *Handbook of Intelligence*. New York: Cambridge University Press.
Sternberg, R. J. (2001) What is the common thread to creativity? *American Psychologist*, **56**, 360–2.
Sternberg, R. J. (2003) What is an 'expert student'? *Educational Researcher*, **32**, 5–9.
Sternberg, R. J. & Davidson, J. E. (1985) Cognitive development in the gifted and talented. In F. D. Horowitz & M. O'Brien (eds) *The Gifted and Talented: Developmental Perspectives*. Washington, DC: American Psychological Association.
Sternberg, R. J. & Grigorenko, E. L. (eds) (1997) *Intelligence, Heredity, and Environment*. New York: Cambridge University Press.
Sternberg, R. J. & Powell, J. S. (1983) The development of intelligence. In J. H. Flavell & E. M. Markham (vol. eds) *Handbook of Child Psychology: Cognitive Development (Volume III)*, 4th ed. New York: John Wiley.
Sternberg, R. J., Torff, B. & Grigorenko, E. L. (1998) Teaching triarchically improves school achievement. *Journal of Educational Psychology*, **3**, 374–84.
Stiggins, R. J. (1985) Improving assessment where it means the most: In the classroom. *Educational Leadership*, **43**, 69–74.
Stigler, J. W., Shweder, R. A. & Herdt, G. (eds) (1990) *Cultural Psychology*. Cambridge: Cambridge University Press.
Stigler, S. M. (1978) Some forgotten work on memory. *Journal of Experimental Psychology: Human Learning and Memory*, **4**, 1–4.
Stipek, D. (2002) Good instruction is motivating. In A. Wigfield & J. S. Eccles (eds) *Development of Achievement Motivation*. San Diego, CA: Academic Press.
Stoll, C. (1995) *Silicon Snake Oil*. New York: Doubleday.
Stoneman, Z. & Brody, G. H. (1981) Peers as mediators of television food advertisements aimed at children. *Developmental Psychology*, **17**, 853–8.
Strage, A. & Brandt, T. S. (1999) Authoritative parenting and college students' academic adjustments and success. *Journal of Educational Psychology*, **91**, 146–56.
Strom, R. D. & Strom, P. S. (2002) Changing the rules: Education for creative thinking. *Journal of Creative Behavior*, **36**, 183–200.
Styczynski, L. & Langlois, J. H. (1977) The effects of familiarity on behavioral stereotypes associated with physical attractiveness in young children. *Child Development*, **48**, 1137–41.
Suliman, R. & McInerney, D. M. (2005) Academic excellence: Dream or reality for children of migrant families. Paper presented at the Annual Meeting of the American Educational Research Association, Montreal, April 11–15.
Sultana, R. (1989) What's keeping them back?! Life choices and life chances. *SET Research Notes for Teachers*, number 1, item 12.
Sulzer-Azaroff, B. (1995) Behavioristic theories of teaching. In L. W. Anderson (ed.) *International Encyclopedia of Teaching and Teacher Education*, 2nd ed. Tarrytown, NY: Pergamon.
Sund, R. B. (1976) *Piaget for Educators: A Multimedia Program*. Columbus, OH: Charles E. Merrill.
Swan, S. & White, R. (1990) Increasing meta-learning. Part 2 Thinking books. *SET Research Information for Teachers*, number 2, item 11.
Swanborn, M. S. K. & de Glopper, K. (1999) Incidental word learning while reading: A meta-analysis. *Review of Educational Research*, **69**, 261–85.
Swanson, D. B., Norman, G. R. & Linn, R. L. (1995) Performance-based assessment. Lessons from the health professions. *Educational Researcher*, **24**, 5–11.
Swanson, H. L. & Hoskyn, M. (1998) Experimental intervention research on students with learning disabilities: A meta-analysis of treatment outcomes. *Review of Educational Research*, **68**, 277–321.
Swanson, H. L. & Lussier, C. M. (2001) A selective synthesis of the experimental literature on dynamic assessment. *Review of Educational Research*, **71**, 321–63.
Swanson, H. L., O'Connor, J. E. & Cooney, J. B. (1990) An information processing analysis of expert and novice teachers' problem solving. *American Educational Research Journal*, **27**, 533–56.
Sweller, J. (1990) Cognitive processes and instructional procedures. *Australian Journal of Education*, **34**, 125–30.
Sweller, J. (1993) Some cognitive processes and their consequences for the organisation and presentation of information. *Australian Journal of Psychology*, **45**, 1–8.
Swift, J. N. & Gooding, C. T. (1983) Interaction of wait time feedback and questioning instruction on middle science teaching. *Journal of Research in Science Teaching*, **20**, 721–30.
Symonds, P. M. & Chase, D. H. (1992) Practice vs motivation. *Journal of Educational Psychology*, **84**, 282–9.
Talkington, L. W. & Altman, R. (1973) Effects of film-mediated aggressive behavior and affectual models on behavior. *American Journal of Mental Deficiency*, **77**, 420–5.
Tamir, P. (1995) Discovery learning and teaching. In L. W. Anderson (ed.) *International Encyclopedia of Teaching and Teacher Education*, 2nd ed. Tarrytown, NY: Pergamon.
Tannenbaum, A. J. (1986) Giftedness: A psychosocial approach. In R. J. Sternberg & J. E. Davidson (eds) *Conceptions of Giftedness*. New York: Cambridge University Press.
Tanner, J. M. (1961) *Education and Physical Growth. Implications of the Study of Children's Growth for Educational Theory and Practice*. London: University of London Press.
Tanner, J. M. (1990) *Fetus into Man. Physical Growth from Conception to Maturity*. Revised and enlarged. Cambridge, MA: Harvard University Press.
Tappan, M. B. (1998) Sociocultural psychology and caring pedagogy: Exploring Vygotsky's 'Hidden Curriculum'. *Educational Psychologist*, **33**, 23–33.
Tasker, R. (1981) Children's views and classroom experiences. *The Australian Science Teachers Journal*, **27**, 33–7.
Taylor, R. P. (ed.) (1980) *The Computer in the School: Tutor, Tool, Tutee*. New York: Teachers College Press.
Teasdale, G. R. & Teasdale, J. I. (1993) Culture and schooling in Aboriginal Australia. Paper presented at the symposium International Perspectives on Culture and Schooling, at the Department of International and Comparative Education, Institute of Education, London University, May.
Teasdale, G. R. & Teasdale, J. I. (1994) Culture and schooling in Aboriginal Australia. In E. Thomas (ed.) *International*

Perspectives on Culture and Schooling: A Symposium of Proceedings. London: Institute of Education.

Terwilliger, J. (1997) Semantics, psychometrics, and assessment reform: A close look at 'authentic' assessments. *Educational Researcher*, **26**, 24–7.

Terwilliger, J. S. (1998) Rejoinder: Response to Wiggins and Newmann. *Educational Researcher*, **27**, 22–3.

TESOL (1997) *ESL Standards for pre-k-12 Students*. Alexandria, VA: TESOL.

Tharp, R. G. & Gallimore, R. (1988) *Rousing Minds to Life*. New York: Cambridge University Press.

The National Languages and Literacy Institute of Australia (1993) *Languages at the Crossroads. The Report of the National Enquiry into the Employment and Supply of Teachers of Languages other than English*. Melbourne: Author.

Thelen, E. (1995) Motor development. A new synthesis. *American Psychologist*, **50**, 79–95.

Thibadeau, G. (1995) Open education. In L. W. Anderson (ed.) *International Encyclopedia of Teaching and Teacher Education*, 2nd ed. Tarrytown, NY: Pergamon.

Thies, A. P. (1985) Neuropsychological approaches to learning disorders. In E. W. Gordon (ed.) *Review of Research in Education (Volume 12)*. New York: AERA.

Thoma, S. J., Narvaez, D., Rest, J. & Derryberry, P. (1999) Does moral judgment development reduce to political attitudes or verbal ability? Evidence using the Defining Issues Test. *Educational Psychology Review*, **11**, 325–41.

Thomas, A. (1979) Learned helplessness and expectancy factors: Implications for research in learning disabilities. *Review of Education Research*, **49**, 208–21.

Thomas, E. (ed.) (1994) *International Perspectives on Culture and Schooling: A Symposium Proceedings*. University of London Institute of Education: Department of International and Comparative Education.

Thomas, E. L. & Robinson, H. A. (1972) *Improving Reading in Every Class: A Sourcebook for Teachers*. Boston: Allyn & Bacon.

Thomas, G. (1988) Room management in mainstreamed/integrated classrooms. *SET Research Information for Teachers*, number 1, item 5.

Thomas, J. R. & French, K. E. (1985) Gender differences across age in motor performance: A meta-analysis. *Psychological Bulletin*, **98**, 260–82.

Thomas, J. W. (1988) Proficiency at academic studying. *Contemporary Educational Psychology*, **13**, 265–75.

Thomas, J. W. & Rohwer, W. D. (1986) Academic studying: The role of learning strategies. *Educational Psychologist*, **21**, 19–41.

Thomas, R. M. (ed.) (1990) *The Encyclopedia of Human Development and Education. Theory, Research and Studies*. Oxford: Pergamon Press.

Thomas, T. (2004) Psychology in a culturally diverse society. *Australian Psychologist*, **39**, 103–6.

Thompson, T. (1993) Characteristics of self-worth protection in achievement behaviour. *British Journal of Educational Psychology*, **63**, 469–88.

Thorndike, E. L. (1913) *The Psychology of Learning*. New York: Macmillan.

Thorndike, E. L. (1931) *Human Learning*. New York: Appleton-Century-Crofts.

Thorndike, R., Hagen, E. & Sattler, J. (1986) The *Stanford–Binet Intelligence Scale*, 4th ed. Chicago: Riverside.

Thurstone, L. (1938) *Primary Mental Abilities*. Chicago: University of Chicago Press.

Tiedemann, J. (1989) Measures of cognitive styles. A critical review. *Educational Psychologist*, **24**, 261–75.

Tiedemann, J. (2000) Parents' gender stereotypes and teachers' beliefs as predictors of children's concept of their mathematical ability in elementary school. *Journal of Educational Psychology*, **92**, 144–51.

Tiggemann, M. & Crowley, J. R. (1993) Attributions for academic failure and subsequent performance. *Australian Journal of Psychology*, **45**, 35–9.

Tobias, S. (1985a) Test anxiety: Interference, defective skills, and cognitive capacity. *Educational Psychologist*, **20**, 135–42.

Tobias, S. (1985b) Computer-assisted instruction. In M. C. Wang & H. J. Walberg (eds) *Adapting Instruction to Individual Differences*, Berkeley, CA: McCutchan.

Tobias, S. (1994) Interest, prior knowledge, and learning. *Review of Educational Research*, **64**, 37–54.

Tobin, K. (1987) The role of wait time in higher cognitive level learning. *Review of Educational Research*, **57**, 69–95.

Tobin-Richards, M. H., Boxer, A. M. & Petersen, A. C. (1983) The psychological significance of pubertal change: Sex differences in perceptions of self during early adolescence. In J. Brooks-Gunn & A. C. Petersen (eds) *Girls at Puberty. Biological and Psychosocial Perspectives*. New York: Plenum Press.

Tonkin, S. E. & Watt, H. M. G. (2003) Self-concept over the transition from primary to secondary school: A case study on a program for girls. *Issues in Educational Research*, **13**, 27–54.

Torrance, E. P. (1962) *Guiding Creative Talent*. Englewood Cliffs, NJ: Prentice Hall.

Torrance, E. P. (1966) *Torrance Tests of Creative Thinking: Norms-technical Manual*. Princeton, NJ: Personnel Press.

Torrance, E. P. (1973) Non-test indicators of creative talent among disadvantaged children. *Gifted Child Quarterly*, **17**, 3–9.

Torrance, E. P. (1986) Teaching creative and gifted learners. In M. Wittrock (ed.) *Handbook of Research on Teaching*, 3rd ed. New York: Macmillan.

Townsend, M. A. R., Manley, M. & Tuck, B. F. (1991) Academic helpseeking in intermediate-school classrooms: Effects of achievement, ethnic group, sex and classroom organization. *New Zealand Journal of Educational Studies*, **26**, 35–47.

Treffinger, D. (1982) Gifted students, regular classrooms: Sixty ingredients for a better blend. *Elementary School Journal*, **82**, 267–83.

Trent, S. C., Artiles, A. J. & Englert, C. S. (1998) From deficit thing to social constructivism: A review of theory, research, and practice in special education. *Review of Research in Education*, **23**, 277–307.

Tricker, J. E. & McCabe, M. P. (1999) Refinement of the Eating and Me scale: Body image and eating patterns of preadolescent children. *The Australian Educational and Developmental Psychologist*, **16**, 29–40.

Tschannen-Moran, M., Woolfolk Hoy, A. & Hoy, W. (1998) Teacher efficacy: Its meaning and measure. *Review of Educational Research*, **68**, 202–48.

Tucker, C. M. & Herman, K. C. (2002) Using culturally sensitive theories and research to meet the academic needs of low-income African American children. *American Psychologist*, **57**, 762–73.

Tuckman, B. W. (1988) *Conducting Educational Research*, 3rd ed. San Diego, CA: Harcourt Brace Jovanovich.

Tudge, J. (1990) Vygotsky, the zone of proximal development and peer collaboration: Implications for classroom practice. In L. C. Moll (ed.) *Vygotsky and Education*. New York: Cambridge University Press.

Turiel, E. (1966) An experimental test of the sequentiality of developmental stages in the child's moral judgment. *Journal of Personality and Social Psychology*, **3**, 611–18.

Turiel, E. (1983) *The Development of Social Knowledge: Morality and Convention*. New York: Cambridge University Press.

Turkington, C. (1987) Special talents. In K. L. Frieberg (ed.) *Educating Exceptional Children*, 6th ed. Guilford, CT: Duskin.

Turner, J. S. & Helms, D. B. (1991) *Lifespan Development*, 4th ed. Fort Worth: Holt, Rinehart & Winston.

Turney, C. *et al.* (1985a) *Sydney Micro Skills Redeveloped, Series 1 Handbook*. Sydney: University of Sydney Press.

Turney, C. *et al.* (1985b) *Sydney Micro Skills Redeveloped, Series 2 Handbook*. Sydney: University of Sydney Press.

Unsworth, G. & Ward, T. (2001) Video games and aggressive behaviour. *Australian Psychologist*, **36**, 184–92.

Urban, K. K. (1993) Fostering giftedness. *International Journal of Educational Research*, **19**, 31–49.

Urdan, T. (2004) Predictors of academic self-handicapping and achievement: Examining achievement goals, classroom goals structures, and culture. *Journal of Educational Psychology*, **96**, 251–64.

Urdan, T. C. (1997) Achievement goal theory: Past results, future directions. In M. L. Maehr & P. R. Pintrich (eds) *Advances in Motivation and Achievement (Volume 10)*. Greenwich, CT: JAI.

Urdan, T. C. & Giancarlo, C. (2001) A comparison of motivational and critical thinking orientations across ethnic groups. In D. M. McInerney & S. Van Etten (eds), *Research on Sociocultural Influences on Motivation and Learning (Volume 1)*. Greenwich, CT: Information Age Press.

Urdan, T. C. & Maehr, M. L. (1995) Beyond a two goal theory of motivation and achievement: A case for social goals. *Review of Educational Research*, **65**, 213–43.

Urdan, T. C., Midgley, C. & Anderman, E. M. (1998) The role of classroom goal structure in students' use of self-handicapping strategies. *American Educational Research Journal*, **35**, 101–22.

US Congress (1975) *The Education for all Handicapped Children Act of 1975*. Washington, DC: US Government Printing Office.

Valdes, G. (1998) The world outside and inside schools: Language and immigrant children. *Educational Researcher*, **27**, 4–18.

Valentine, J. C., DuBois, D. L. & Cooper, H. (2004) The relation between self-beliefs and academic achievement: A meta-analytic review. *Educational Psychologist*, **39**, 111–33.

Vallance, R. & Vallance, D. (1988) Punmu wangka: A 'right way' desert school curriculum 1984–1987. *Curriculum Perspectives*, **8**, 71–6.

van den Berg, R. (2002) Teachers' meanings regarding educational practice. *Review of Educational Research*, **72**, 577–625.

Van Horn, M. L. & Ramey, S. L. (2003) The effects of developmentally appropriate practices on academic outcomes among former head start students and classmates. *American Educational Research Journal*, **40**, 961–90.

Van Merrienboer, J. J. G., Kirschner, P. A. & Kester, L. (2003) Taking the load off a learner's mind: Instructional design for complex learning. *Educational Psychologist*, **38**, 5–13.

Van Patten, J., Chao, C-I. & Reigeluth, C. M. (1986) A review of strategies for sequencing and synthesizing instruction. *Review of Educational Research*, **56**, 437–71.

Van Tassel-Baska, J. (1989) Appropriate curriculum for gifted learners. *Educational Leadership*, **46**, 13–15.

Veenman, S. (1984) Perceived problems of beginning teachers. *Review of Educational Research*, **54**, 143–78.

Vialle, W. (1991) Tuesday's children: A study of five children using multiple intelligences theory as a framework. Unpublished doctoral dissertation, University of South Florida.

Vialle, W. (1993) Identifying children's diverse strengths: A broader framework for cognitive assessment. Paper presented at the 17th national AASE conference.

Vialle, W. (1994) Profiles of intelligence. *Australian Journal of Early Childhood*, **19**, 30–4.

Virilio, P. (1987) The overexposed city. *Zone*, **1**(2), 15–31.

Virilio, P. (1991) *The Aesthetics of Disappearance*. New York: Semiotext(e).

Voelkl, K. E. & Frone, M. R. (2000) Predictors of substance use at school among high school students. *Journal of Educational Psychology*, **92**, 583–92.

von Glaserfeld, E. (1995) *Radical Constructivism: A Way of Knowing and Learning*. London: Falmer Press.

Vrugt, A., Oort, F. J. & Zeeberg, C. (2002) Goal orientations, perceived self-efficacy and study results amongst beginners and advanced students. *British Journal of Educational Psychology*, **72**, 385–97.

Vygotsky, L. S. (1962) *Thought and Language* (ed. and trans. by E. Hanfmann & G. Vakar). Cambridge, MA: MIT Press.

Vygotsky, L. S. (1978) *Mind in Society. The Development of Higher Psychological Processes* (ed. by M. Cole, V. John-Steiner, S. Scribner & E. Souberman). Cambridge, MA: Harvard University Press.

Vygotsky, L. S. (1987) *Thinking and Speech* (ed. and trans. by N. Minick). New York: Plenum Press.

Wadsworth, B. J. (1989) *Piaget's Theory of Cognitive Development*, 4th ed. New York: Longman.

Wainryb, C. & Turiel, E. (1993) Conceptual and informational features in moral decision making. *Educational Psychologist*, **28**, 205–18.

Walberg, H. J. (1984) Improving the productivity of America's schools. *Educational Leadership*, **41**, 19–27.

Walden, E. L. & Thompson, S. A. (1981) A review of some alternative approaches to drug management of hyperactive children. *Journal of Learning Disabilities*, **14**, 213–17.

Walker, D. F. (1987) Logo needs research: A response to Papert's paper. *Educational Researcher*, **16**, 9–11.

Walker, L., De Vries, B. & Trevetham, S. (1987) Moral stages and moral orientations in real-life and hypothetical dilemmas. *Child Development*, **58**, 842–58.

Walker, L. J. (1982) The sequentiality of Kohlberg's stages of moral development. *Child Development*, **53**, 1330–6.

Walker, L. J. (1983) Sources of cognitive conflict for stage transition in moral development. *Developmental Psychology*, **19**, 103–10.

Walker, L. J. (1984) Sex differences in the development of moral reasoning: A critical review. *Child Development*, **55**, 677–91.

Walker, R. A. & Barlow, K. (1990) The provision of education for gifted and talented children in private primary schools: A critical examination. In M. Bezzina & J. Butcher (eds) *The Changing Face of Professional Education. Collected Papers of the AARE Annual Conference, Sydney University, 1990*. Sydney: AARE.

Walkley, J., Holland, B., Treloar, R. & Probyn-Smith, H. (1993) Fundamental motor skill proficiency of children. *The ACHPER National Journal*, Spring, 11–14.

Wallace, A., Boylan, C., Sharman, J. & Kay, R. (1990) The all girls science class: A longitudinal study. In M. Bezzina & J. Butcher (eds) *The Changing Face of Professional Education. Collected Papers of the AARE Annual Conference, Sydney University, 1990*. Sydney: AARE.

Wallace, R. C. (1985) Adaptive education: Policy and administrative perspectives. In M. C. Wang & H. J. Walberg (eds) *Adapting Instruction to Individual Differences*. Berkeley, CA: McCutchan.

Wallach, M. & Kogan, N. (1965) *Modes of Thinking in Young Children*. New York: Holt, Rinehart & Winston.

Wallas, G. (1926) *The Art of Thought*. New York: Harcourt Brace.

Walters, G. C. & Grusec, J. E. (1977) *Punishment*. San Francisco: W. H. Freeman.

Walters, J. (1993) Computer education beacon schools. *Australian Educational Computing*, **8**, ACEC 1993 Edition, 81–4.

Walters, R. H., Cheyne, J. A. & Banks, R. K. (eds) (1972) *Punishment*. Harmondsworth, Middlesex: Penguin Books.

Wang, M. C., Gennari, P. & Waxman, H. C. (1985) The adaptive learning environments model: Design, implementation and effects. In M. C. Wang & H. J. Walberg (eds) *Adapting Instruction to Individual Differences*. Berkeley, CA: McCutchan.

Wang, M. C. & Lindvall, C. M. (1984) Individual differences and school learning environments. In E. W. Gordon (ed.) *Review of Research in Education (Volume 11)*. Washington: AERA.

Wang, M. C., Reynolds, M. C. & Walberg, H. J. (eds) (1988) *Handbook of Special Education: Research and Practice*. Oxford: Pergamon Press.

Wang, M. C. & Walberg, H. J. (eds) (1985) *Adapting Instruction to Individual Differences*. Berkeley, CA: McCutchan.

Wang, M. C., Walberg, H. & Reynolds, M. C. (1992) A scenario for better—not separate—special education. *Educational Leadership*, **50**, 35–7.

Wann, D.L., Melnick, M. J., Russell, G. W. & Pease, D. G. (2001) *Sport Fans: The Psychology and Social Impact of Spectators*. New York: Routledge.

Warden, D., Cheyne, B., Christie, D., Fitzpatrick, H. & Reid, K. (2003) Assessing children's perceptions of prosocial and antisocial peer behaviour. *Educational Psychology*, **23**, 547–67.

Ware, M. C. & Stuck, M. F. (1985) Sex-role messages *vis-à-vis* microcomputer use: A look at the pictures. *Sex Roles*, **13**, 205–14.

Warren, L. J. (2000) School-related stress and coping strategies in Victorian Year 11 students. *The Australian Educational and Developmental Psychologist*, **17**, 44–57.

Warren, M. P. (1983) Physical and biological aspects of puberty. In J. Brooks-Gunn & A. C. Petersen (eds) *Girls at Puberty. Biological and Psychosocial Perspectives*. New York: Plenum Press.

Wasserman, I. & Stack, S. (1993) The effect of religion on suicide. An analysis of cultural context. *Omega—Journal of Death and Dying*, **27**, 295–306.

Watkins, D. & Hattie, J. (1981) The learning process of Australian university students: Investigations of contextual and personological factors. *British Journal of Educational Psychology*, **51**, 384–93.

Watkins, D., McInerney, D. M., Akande, A. & Lee, C. (2003). An investigation of ethnic differences in the motivation strategies for learning of students in desegregated South African schools. *Journal of Cross-Cultural Psychology*, **34**, 189–94.

Watkins, D., McInerney, D. M., Lee, C., Akande, A. & Regmi, M. (2002) Motivation and learning strategies. A cross-cultural perspective. In D. M. McInerney & S. Van Etten (eds) *Research on Sociocultural Influences on Motivation and Learning (Volume 2)*. Greenwich, CT: Information Age.

Watson, J. B. (1913) Psychology as the behaviorists view it. *Psychological Review*, **20**, 157–8.

Watson, J. B. (1916) The place of a conditioned reflex in psychology. *Psychological Review*, **23**, 89–116.

Watson, J. B. (1930) *Behaviorism*, 2nd ed. Chicago: University of Chicago Press.

Weaver-Hightower, M. (2003) The 'boy turn' in research on gender and education. *Review of Educational Research*, **73**, 471–98.

Webb, N. M. (1980) A process-outcome analysis of learners in group and individual settings. *Educational Psychology*, **15**, 69–83.

Webb, N. M. (1982) Peer interaction and learning in cooperative small groups. *Journal of Educational Psychology*, **74**, 642–55.

Webb, N. M. (1985a) Verbal interaction and learning in peer-directed groups. *Theory into Practice*, **24**, 32–8.

Webb, N. M. (1985b) Student interaction and learning in small groups: A research summary. In R. Slavin, S. Sharan, S. Kagan, R. Hertz-Lazarowitz, C. Webb & R. Schmuck (eds) *Learning to Cooperate, Cooperating to Learn*. New York: Plenum Press.

Webb, N. M. (1987) Helping behavior to maximize learning. Paper presented at the annual meeting of the American Educational Research Association, Washington, DC, April.

Webb, N. M. (1989) Peer interaction and learning in small groups. *International Journal of Educational Research*, **13**, 21–39.

Webb, N. M. & Farivar, S. (1994) Promoting helping behavior in cooperative small groups in middle school mathematics. *American Educational Research Journal*, **32**, 369–95.

Webb, N. M. & Farivar, S. (1999) Developing productive group interaction in middle school mathematics. In A. M. O'Donnell & A. King (eds) *Cognitive Perspectives on Peer Learning*. Mahwah, NJ: Lawrence Erlbaum.

Webb, N. M. & Kenderski, C. N. (1985) Gender differences in small-group interaction and achievement in high- and low-achieving classes. In L. C. Wilkinson & C. B. Marrett (eds) *Gender Influences in Classroom Interaction*. Orlando: Academic Press.

Webb, N. M., Nemer, K. M., Chizhik, A. W. & Sugrue, B. (1998) Equity issues in collaborative group assessment: Group composition and performance. *American Educational Research Journal*, **35**(4), 607–51.

Webb, N. M., Trooper, J. D. & Fall, R. (1995) Constructive activity and learning in collaborative groups. *Journal of Educational Psychology*, **87**, 406–23.

Weill, M. P. (1987) Gifted/Learning disabled students. Their potential may be buried treasure. *The Clearing House*, **60**, 341–3.

Weiner, B. (1972) Attribution theory, achievement motivation, and the educational process. *Review of Educational Research*, **42**, 203–15.

Weiner, B. (1979) A theory of motivation for some classsroom experiences. *Journal of Educational Psychology*, **71**, 3–25.

Weiner, B. (1984) Principles for a theory of student motivation and their application within an attributional framework. In R. Ames & C. Ames (eds) *Research on Motivation in Education: Student Motivation (Volume 1)*. Orlando: Academic Press.

Weiner, B. (1990) History of motivational research in education. *Journal of Educational Psychology*, **82**, 616–22.

Weiner, B. (1994) Integrating social and personal theories of achievement striving. *Review of Educational Research*, **64**, 557–73.

Weiner, B. (2004) Attribution theory revisited: Transforming cultural plurality into theoretical unity. In D. M. McInerney & S. Van Etten (eds) *Research on Sociocultural Influences on Motivation and Learning (Volume 4), Big Theories Revisited*. Greenwich, CT: Information Age Publishing.

Weiner, B. & Kukla, A. (1970) An attributional analysis of achievement motivation. *Journal of Personality and Social Psychology*, **15**, 1–20.

Weinert, F. E. & Helmke, A. (1995) Interclassroom differences in instructional quality and interindividual differences in cognitive development. *Educational Psychologist*, **30**, 15–20.

Weinstein, C. E. & Hume, L. M. (1998) *Study Strategies for Lifelong Learning.* Washington, DC: American Psychological Association.

Weinstein, C. E. & Mayer, R. E. (1986) The teaching of learning strategies. In M. C. Wittrock (ed.) *Handbook of Research on Teaching*, 3rd ed. New York: Macmillan.

Weinstein, C. E. & Underwood, V. L. (1985) Learning strategies: The how of learning. In J. W. Segal, S. F. Chipman & R. Glaser (eds) *Thinking and Learning Skills: Relating Instruction to Research (Volume 1).* Hillsdale. NJ: Lawrence Erlbaum.

Weinstein, C. S. (1998) 'I want to be nice, but I have to be mean': Exploring prospective teachers' conceptions of caring and order. *Teaching and Teacher Education*, **14**, 153–64.

Weinstein, C. S. & Mignano, A. J. (1993) *Elementary Classroom Management.* New York: McGraw-Hill.

Weinstein, J. A. & Fantini, M. F. (1970) *Toward Humanistic Education: A Curriculum of Effect.* New York: Praeger.

Weinstein, R. S. (1989) Perceptions of classroom processes and student motivation: Children's views of self-fulfilling prophecies. In C. Ames & R. Ames (eds) *Research on Motivation in Education: Goals and Cognitions (Volume 3).* Orlando: Academic Press.

Weinstein, R. S., Marshall, H. H., Sharp, L. & Botkin, M. (1987) Pygmalion and the student: Age and classroom differences in children's awareness of teacher expectations. *Child Development*, **58**, 1079–93.

Weiser, M. (1991) The computer for the 21st century. *Scientific American*, **265**, 66–75.

Weissberg, R. P., Kumpfer, K. L. & Seligman, M. E. P. (2003) Prevention that works for children and youth. *American Psychologist*, **58**, 425–32.

Wellman, H. M. & Gelman, S. A. (1992) Cognitive development: Foundation theories of core domains. *Annual Review of Psychology*, **43**, 337–75.

Wells, B. W. P. (1983) *Body and Personality.* London: Longman.

Wenderoth, P. (1992) Perceptual illusions. *Australian Journal of Psychology*, **44**, 147–51.

Wentzel, K. R. (1991a) Social competence at school: Relation between social responsibility and academic achievement. *Review of Educational Research*, **61**, 1–24.

Wentzel, K. R. (1991b) Social and academic goals at school: Motivation and achievement in context. In M. L. Maehr & P. R. Pintrich (eds) *Advances in Motivation and Achievement: A Research Annual (Volume 7).* Greenwich, CT: JAI Press.

Wentzel, K. R. (1996) Social goals and social relationships as motivators of school adjustment. In J. Juvonen & K. R. Wentzel (eds) *Social Motivation: Understanding School Adjustment.* New York: Cambridge University Press.

Wentzel, K. R. (1997) Student motivation in middle school: The role of perceived pedagogical caring. *Journal of Educational Psychology*, **89**, 411–19.

Wentzel, K. R. (1998) Social relationships and motivation in middle school: The role of parents, teachers, and peers. *Journal of Educational Psychology*, **90**, 202–9.

Wentzel, K. R. (1999) Social-motivational processes and interpersonal relationships: Implications for understanding motivation at school. *Journal of Educational Psychology*, **91**, 76–97.

Wentzel, K. R. (2002) Are effective teachers like good parents? Interpersonal predictors of school adjustments in early adolescence. *Child Development*, **73**, 287–301.

Wentzel, K. R., Barry, C. M. & Caldwell, K. A. (2004) Friendships in middle school: Influences on motivation and school adjustment. *Journal of Educational Psychology*, **96**, 195–203.

Wentzel, K. R. & Berndt, T. J. (1999) Social influences and school achievement: Overview. *Educational Psychologist*, **34**, 1–2.

Wertheim, E. H., Mee, V. & Paxton, S. J. (1996) Body image and weight loss behaviours among adolescent girls and their parents. Paper presented at the 31st Annual Conference of the Australian Psychological Society, 25–29 September, Sydney.

Wertheimer, M. (1980) Gestalt theory of learning. In G. M. Gazda & R. J. Corsini (eds) *Theories of Learning.* Itasca, IL: F. E. Peacock.

Wessells, H. G. (1982) *Cognitive Psychology.* New York: Harper & Row.

West, P. (1999) Boys' underachievement in school: Some persistent problems and some current research. *Issues in Educational Research*, **9**, 33–54.

Westwood, P. (1995) Effective teaching. Paper presented at the North West Region inaugural special education conference, 'Priorities, Partnerships (and plum puddings)', Armidale, 25–27 June.

Wheldall, K. & Merrett, F. (1990) What is the behavioural approach to teaching? In V. Lee (ed.) *Children's Learning in School.* London: Hodder & Stoughton.

Wheldall, K. (ed.) (1987) *The Behaviourist in the Classroom.* London: Allen & Unwin.

White, R. & Baird, J. (1991) Learning to think and thinking to learn. In J. B. Biggs (ed.) *Teaching for Learning. The View from Cognitive Psychology.* Melbourne: ACER.

White, R. T. & Gunstone, R. F. (1989) Metalearning and conceptual change. *International Journal of Science Education*, **11**, 577–86.

Wickstrom, R. L. (1983) *Fundamental Motor Patterns*, 3rd ed. Philadelphia: Lea & Febiger.

Wideen, M., Mayer-Smith, J. & Moon, B. (1998) A critical analysis of the research on learning to teach: Making the case for an ecological perspective on inquiry. *Review of Educational Research*, **68**, 130–78.

Wigfield, A. (1994) Expectancy–value theory of achievement motivation: A developmental perspective. *Educational Psychology Review*, **6**, 49–78.

Wigfield, A. & Eccles, J. S. (1989) Test anxiety in elementary and secondary school students. *Educational Psychologist*, **24**, 159–83.

Wigfield, A. & Eccles, J. S. (2000) Expectancy–value theory of achievement motivation. *Contemporary Educational Psychology*, **25**, 68–81.

Wigfield, A. & Eccles, J. S. (2002a) *Development of Achievement Motivation.* San Diego: CA: Academic Press.

Wigfield, A. & Eccles, J. S. (2002b) The development of competence beliefs, expectancies for success, and achievement values from childhood through adolescence. In A. Wigfield & J. S. Eccles (eds) *Development of Achievement Motivation.* San Diego, CA: Academic Press.

Wigfield, A., Eccles, J. S. & Rodriguez, D. (1998) The development of children's motivation in school contexts. *Review of Research in Education*, **23**, 73–118.

Wigfield, A. & Karpathian, M. (1991) Who am I and what can I do? Children's self-concepts and motivation in achievement situations. *Educational Psychologist*, **26**(3 & 4), 233–61.

Wigfield, A., Tonks, S. & Eccles, J. S. (2004) Expectancy value theory in cross-cultural perspective. In D. M. McInerney & S. Van Etten (eds) *Research on Sociocultural Influences on Motivation and Learning (Volume 4), Big Theories Revisited.* Greenwich, CT: Information Age Publishing.

Wiggins, G. (1989) A true test: Toward more authentic and equitable assessment. *Phi Delta Kappan*, **20**, 703–13.

Wiggins, G. (1997) Practicing what we preach in designing

authentic assessments. *Educational Leadership*, December 1996–January 1997, 18–25.

Wiggins, G. (1998) An exchange of views on semantics, psychometrics, and assessment reform: A close look at 'authentic' assessments. *Educational Researcher*, **27**, 20–2.

Wilkins, R. (1987) A school discipline strategy. *SET Research Information for Teachers*, number 1, item 14.

Wilkinson, L. C. (1988–89) Grouping children for learning. Implications for kindergarten education. *Review of Research in Education*, **15**, 203–50.

Williams, J. & Stith, M. (1980) *Middle Childhood. Behavior and Development*, 2nd ed. New York: Macmillan.

Williamson, A. (1991) Learning 'white way': Curriculum, context, and custom in schooling Torres Strait Islanders before World War II. *Australian Journal of Education*, **35**, 314–31.

Wills, T. A. (1986) Stress and coping in early adolescence: Relationships to substance use in urban high schools. *Health Psychology*, **5**, 503–29.

Wilmore, J. H. (1989) The female athlete. *SET Research Information for Teachers*, number 2, item 5.

Windschitl, M. (2002) Framing constructivism in practice as the negotiation of dilemmas: An analysis of the conceptual, pedagogical, cultural, and political challenges facing teachers. *Review of Educational Psychology*, **72**, 131–75.

Wine, J. D. (1971) Test anxiety and study habits. *Journal of Educational Research*, **65**, 852–4.

Winitsky, N. E. (1991) Classroom organisation for social studies. In J. P. Shaver (ed.) *Handbook of Research on Social Studies Teaching and Learning*. New York: Macmillan.

Winkler, R. C. (1985) Behaviour modification and clinical psychology in Australia. In N. T. Feather (ed.) *Australian Psychology. Review of Research*. Sydney: Allen & Unwin.

Winne, P. H. (1995a) Information processing theories of learning. In L. W. Anderson (ed.) *International Encyclopedia of Teaching and Teacher Education*, 2nd ed. Tarrytown, NY: Pergamon.

Winne, P. H. (1995b) Inherent details in self-regulated learning. *Educational Psychologist*, **30**, 173–87.

Winne, P. H. (1997) Experimenting to bootstrap self-regulated learning. *Journal of Educational Psychology*, **89**, 397–410.

Withers, G. & Cornish, G. (1985) Assessment in practice: Competitive or non-competitive. In B. Hannan (ed.) *Assessment and Evaluation in Schooling*. Victoria: Deakin University.

Witkin, H. A., Moore, C. A., Goodenough, D. R. & Cox, P. W. (1977) Field-dependent and field-independent cognitive styles and their educational implications. *Review of Educational Research*, **47**, 1–64.

Witte, K. L. & Grossman, E. E. (1971) The effects of reward and punishment upon children's attention, motivation, and discrimination learning. *Child Development*, **42**, 537–42.

Wittrock, M. C. (1986a) *Handbook of Research on Teaching*, 3rd ed. New York: Macmillan.

Wittrock, M. C. (1986b) Students' thought processes. In M. C. Wittrock (ed.) *Handbook of Research on Teaching*, 3rd ed. New York: Macmillan.

Wittrock, M. C. (1992) Generative learning processes of the brain. *Educational Psychologist*, **27**, 531–42.

Wittrock, M. C. & Alesandrini, K. (1990) Generation of summaries and analogies and analytic and holistic abilities. *American Educational Research Journal*, **27**, 489–502.

Wolf, D., Bixby, J., Glenn, J. III & Gardner, H. (1991) To use their minds well: Investigating new forms of student assessment. *Review of Research in Education*, **17**, 31–74.

Wolf, D. P. (1989) Portfolio assessment: Sampling student work. *Educational Leadership*, **46**, 35–9.

Wolfgang, C. H. & Glickman, C. D. (1986) *Solving Discipline Problems. Strategies for Classroom Teachers*, 2nd ed. Boston: Allyn & Bacon.

Wollen, K. A., Weber, A. & Lowry, D. (1972) Bizarreness versus interaction of mental images as determinants of learning. *Cognitive Psychology*, **3**, 518–23.

Wolman, B. B. (1989) *Dictionary of Behavioral Science*, 2nd ed. New York: Academic Press.

Wolters, C. A. (1998) Self-regulated learning and college students' regulation of motivation. *Journal of Educational Psychology*, **90**, 224–35.

Wolters, C. A. (2003a) Regulation of motivation: Evaluating an underemphasized aspect of self-regulated learning. *Educational Psychologist*, **38**, 189–205.

Wolters, C. A. (2003b) Understanding proscrastination from a self-regulated learning perspective. *Journal of Educational Psychology*, **95**, 179–87.

Wolters, C. A. (2004) Advanced achievement goal theory: Using goal structures and goal orientations to predict students' motivation, cognition, and achievement. *Journal of Educational Psychology*, **96**, 236–50.

Wood, E., Groves, A., Bruce, S., Willoughby, T. & Desmarais, S. (2003) Can gender steroptypes facilitate memory when elaborative strategies are used? *Educational Psychology*, **23**, 169–80.

Wood, E., Motz, M. & Willoughby, T. (1998) Examining students' retrospective memories of strategy development. *Journal of Educational Psychology*, **90**, 698–704.

Woods, S. & Wolke, D. (2003) Does the content of anti-bullying policies inform us about the prevalence of direct and relational bullying behaviour in primary schools? *Educational Psychology*, **23**, 381–401.

Woodward, H. (1993) *Negotiated Evaluation*. Sydney: Primary English Teachers' Association.

Woolfolk Hoy, A. & Tschannen-Moran, M. (1999) Implications of cognitive approaches to peer learning for teacher education. In A. M. O'Donnell & A. King (eds) *Cognitive Perspectives on Peer Learning*. Mahwah, NJ: Lawrence Erlbaum.

Wortman, C. B. & Loftus, E. F. (1992) *Psychology*. New York: McGraw-Hill.

Wragg, E. C. (1995) Lesson structure. In L. W. Anderson (ed.) *International Encyclopedia of Teaching and Teacher Education*, 2nd ed. Tarrytown, NY: Pergamon.

Wright, D. & Wiese, M. J. (1988) Teacher judgment in student evaluation: A comparison of grading methods. *Journal of Educational Research*, **82**, 10–14.

Wright, J. & Jacobs, B. (2003) Teaching phonological awareness and metacognitive strategies to children with reading difficulties: A comparison of two instructional methods. *Educational Psychology*, **23**, 17–47.

Wright, M. R. (1989) Body image satisfaction in adolescent girls and boys. *Journal of Youth and Adolescence*, **18**, 71–84.

Wright, S. C., Taylor, D. M. & Macarthur, J. (2000) Subtractive bilingualism and the survival of the Inuit language: Heritage versus second language education. *Journal of Educational Psychology*, **92**, 63–84.

Wyatt, T. (1996) School effectiveness research: Dead end, damp squib or smouldering fuse? *Issues in Educational Research*, **6**, 79–112.

Wylie, R. (1979) *The Self-concept: Theory and Research on Selected Topics*. Lincoln, NE: University of Nebraska Press.

Wynne, E. & Ryan, K. (1997) *Reclaiming our Schools: A Handbook on Teaching Character, Academics and Discipline.* New York: Charles E. Merrill.

Yates, F. A. (1966) *The Art of Memory*. Chicago: University of Chicago Press.

Yates, G. C. R. & Yates, S. M. (1978) The implications of social modelling research for education. *The Australian Journal of Education*, **22**, 161–78.

Yee, A. H. (1992) Asians as stereotypes and students: Misperceptions that persist. *Educational Psychology Review*, **4**, 95–132.

Yeigh, D. A. (2002) Controllability, information processing, and learning motivation: Moderation of working memory by perceptions of control. *The Australian Educational and Developmental Psychologist*, **19**, 66–87.

Yelon, S. L. & Weinstein, G. W. (1977) *A Teacher's World. Psychology in the Classroom*. New York: McGraw-Hill.

Yeung, A. S., Chui, H., Lau, I. C., McInerney, D. M., Russell-Bowie, R. & Suliman, R. (2000) Where is the hierarchy of academic self-concept? *Journal of Educational Psychology*, **92**, 556–67.

Yeung, A. S. & King Por Wong, E. (2004) Domain specificity of trilingual teachers' verbal self-concepts. *Journal of Educational Psychology*, **96**, 360–8.

Yewchuk, C. R. (1993) The handicapped gifted. *International Journal of Educational Research*, **19**, 65–75.

Yuill, N. & Perner, J. (1988) Intentionality and knowledge in children's judgements of actors' responsibility and recipients' emotional reaction. *Developmental Psychology*, **24**, 358–65.

Zeidner, M. (1995) Adaptive coping with test situations: A review of the literature. *Educational Psychologist*, **30**, 123–33.

Zeidner, M., Roberts, R. D. & Matthews, G. (2002) Can emotional intelligence be schooled? A critical review. *Educational Psychologist*, **37**, 215–31.

Zellermayer, M., Salomon, G., Globerson, T. & Givon, H. (1991) Enhancing writing-related metacognitions through a computerised writing partner. *American Educational Research Journal*, **28**, 373–91.

Zellner, D. A., Harner, D. E. & Adler, R. L. (1989) Effects of eating abnormalities and gender perceptions of desirable body shape. *Journal of Abnormal Psychology*, **98**, 93–6.

Zelniker, T. & Jeffrey, W. (1976) Reflective and impulsive children: Strategies of information processing underlying differences in problem solving. *Monographs of the Society for Research in Child Development*, **41** (5, Serial No. 168).

Zigler, E. F. & Stevenson, M. F. (1993) *Children in a Changing World. Development and Social Issues*, 2nd ed. Pacific Grove, CA: Brooks/Cole.

Zigmond, N. (1995) An exploration of the meaning and practice of special education in the context of full inclusion of students with learning disabilities. *Journal of Special Education*, **29**, 109–15.

Zimmerman, B. J. (1990) Self-regulated learning and academic achievement: An overview. *Educational Psychologist*, **25**, 3–17.

Zimmerman, B. J. (1994) Dimensions of academic self-regulation: A conceptual framework for education. In D. H. Schunk & B. J. Zimmerman (eds) *Self-regulation of Learning and Performance: Issues and Educational Applications*. Hillsdale, NJ: Lawrence Erlbaum.

Zimmerman, B. J. (1995) Self-regulation involves more than metacognition: A social cognitive perspective. *Educational Psychologist*, **30**, 217–21.

Zimmerman, B. J. (1998) Academic studying and self-regulation. *Educational Psychologist*, **33**, 73–86.

Zimmerman, B. J. (2004) Sociocultural influence and students' development of academic self-regulation: A social-cognitive approach. In D. M. McInerney & S. Van Etten (eds) *Research on Sociocultural Influences on Motivation and Learning (Volume 4), Big Theories Revisited*. Greenwich, CT: Information Age Publishing.

Zimmerman, B. J., Bandura, A. & Martinez-Pons, M. (1992) Self-motivation for academic attainment: The role of self-efficacy beliefs and personal goal setting. *American Educational Research Journal*, **29**, 663–7.

Zimmerman, B. J. & Kitsantas, A. (2002) Acquiring writing revision and self-regulatory skill through observation and emulation. *Journal of Educational Psychology*, **94**, 660–8.

Zimmerman, B. J. & Martinez-Pons, M. (1990) Student differences in self-regulated learning: Relating grade, sex, and giftedness to self-efficacy and strategy use. *Journal of Educational Psychology*, **82**, 51–9.

Zimmerman, B. J. & Schunk, D. H. (eds) (1989) *Self-regulated Learning and Academic Achievement: Theory, Research and Practice*. New York: Springer-Verlag.

Zohar, D. (1998) An additive model of text anxiety: Role of exam-specific expectations. *Journal of Educational Psychology*, **90**, 330–40.

Zuroff, D. C. (1980) Learned helplessness in humans: An analysis of learning processes and the roles of individual and situational differences. *Journal of Personality and Social Psychology*, **39**, 130–46.

academic press (in schools) Emphasises academic climate reflected through demanding curricula, clear achievement goals, high teacher expectations and time on task.

academic self-handicapping Students create impediments to successful performance on tasks in order to provide an excuse other than lack of ability for poor performance should it occur.

accommodation (Piaget) Altering existing schemes or creating new ones in response to new experiences.

achievement motivation A desire to excel at learning tasks which is related to pride in accomplishments.

achieving orientation Students utilise whatever learning styles lead to high grades.

acrostics and acronyms Memory devices using first letters of concepts to facilitate recall.

adaptation (Piaget) Adjustment to the environment.

adaptive education Educational approaches designed to accommodate individual differences.

advance organiser (Ausubel) A statement about a new topic providing structure for relating it to what students already know.

affective domain (In learning) Related to feelings, attitudes and values.

alternative assessment Activities that attempt to situate the assessment within 'real' contexts of learning and involve construction of knowledge, disciplined enquiry and value of the achievement beyond school.

anorexia nervosa Severe restriction of eating tending to malnutrition.

anticipatory set Focuses student attention by reminding them of what they already know.

anxiety (Freud) Feelings of uneasiness and tension.

applied behaviour analysis The application of behavioural learning principles to understand and change behaviour.

assertive discipline (Canter) Protecting and restoring order in classrooms through use of reinforcement and punishment.

assimilation (Piaget) Relating new experiences to existing schemes of knowledge.

asynchrony Differential growth spurts.

attainment value The importance of doing well on the task to motivation.

attention deficit hyperactivity disorder Disruptive behaviour disorders characterised by low attention to task and high activity levels.

attention-interference theory Students find it hard to focus attention on the tasks because of self-doubts and task-irrelevant thoughts.

attribution theory Individuals' reasons for success and failure influence their future motivation.

attributional retraining Training individuals to change their patterns of attributions to enhance motivation.

authentic assessment Measurement of important abilities using procedures that simulate the application of these abilities to real life.

autism Extreme inability to relate to other people, characterised by withdrawal and bizarre behaviour.

automaticity A process that occurs when information or operations are overlearned and can be retrieved and used with little mental effort.

autonomous morality (Piaget) Children view moral rules as flexible, socially agreed-on principles that can be changed.

behaviour modification Systematic application of operant conditioning to change behaviour.

behavioural genetics The study of the relative contribution of environmental and heredity factors to differences in human thought and behaviour.

behaviourism A theory of learning that focuses on external events as the cause of changes in observable behaviours.

bilingual/bicultural education Education programs that offer instruction to non-English speakers in English and another language.

bulimia nervosa Uncontrollable binge eating followed by purging.

canalisation Regularity of development of some characteristics of heredity.

care perspective Views people in terms of their connectedness with others and concern for others.

caring school Emphasises teachers' and students' social and emotional needs as a precursor to academic learning.

centration Preoccupation with visual perception.

cephalocaudal development Head-down development.

cerebral palsy Paralysis resulting from brain injury.

chunking A mental strategy by which we break long and complex series into smaller chunks to facilitate learning and recall.

classical conditioning A process of learning based on pairing stimulus and response connections.

classification Constructing classes of objects.

classification table The grouping of objects that are alike into categories according to common characteristics.

classroom management Things a teacher does to establish an effective learning environment.

client-centred therapy (Rogers) Counselling that emphasises the individual's role in developing a healthy personality.

clique A small group of close friends.

coding frame (Cognitive) A hierarchy of ideas or concepts to organise knowledge.

co-evaluation Evaluation shared between teacher and students.

cognition The use of thinking processes such as attention and perception.

cognitive domain In Bloom's taxonomy, dealing with thinking and knowing.

cognitive learning theories Explanations of learning that focus on the internal mental processes individuals use in their effort to make sense of the world.

cognitive load theory Concerned with the design of instructional methods that efficiently use people's limited cognitive processing capacity to apply acquired knowledge and skills to new situations.

cognitive strategies Cognitive approaches that enable the learner to attack a problem more effectively.

cognitive style Stable perceptual and thinking processes.

combinatorial logic Using systematic analysis to solve problems.

community languages Non-English languages spoken in immigrant communities.

comparative organiser Makes use of similarities and differences between new material and existing cognitive structure.

competitive goal structure Students' performance is judged on the basis of relative performance with other students, and the attainment of rewards is only possible if other students don't attain them.

componential intelligence (Sternberg) Ability to acquire knowledge, think and plan, monitor cognitive processes and determine what is to be done.

concept map A two-dimensional diagram representing the conceptual structure of subject matter.

conceptual tempo The degree to which people are cognitively reflective or impulsive.

concrete operations Piaget's third stage characterised by individuals operating logically with concrete, visual materials and by classifying and ordering serially.

conditional knowledge Knowledge of when and why to apply various cognitive skills.

conditioned response (Classical conditioning) A response to a previous neutral stimulus learned through association in the process of conditioning.

conditioned stimulus (Classical conditioning) The stimulus that elicits a new response as a result of the conditioning process.

conditioning A process of behavioural learning.

conservation (Piaget) Characteristics of an object remain the same despite changes in appearance.

constructivism Piaget's view that children construct their own understanding through interaction with their environment.

constructivist views of learning Emphasise the active role of the learner in building understanding.

content validity evidence Choosing assessment items from the appropriate domain.

contextual intelligence (Sternberg) Ability to adapt to contexts to optimise opportunities.

control theory (Glasser) Based on school's responsibility to prevent misbehaviour by fulfilling student needs.

convergent thinking Narrowing thinking to a single answer.

cooperative discipline Discipline based on meeting students' needs for belonging so that they choose to cooperate with the teacher and each other.

cooperative goal structure Group members share rewards and punishments on the basis of overall cooperative group performance.

coping models Show their hesitations and errors while performing a task, but gradually improve their performance and gain self-confidence. Coping models illustrate how determined effort and positive self-reflections may overcome difficulties.

coping strategies Strategies used to guarantee success and avoid failure.

corrective discipline Stopping misbehaviour through the use of authority or punishment.

cost In expectancy-value theory, the physical and emotional resource implications.

countercondition Reduction or elimination of a classically conditioned response.

creativity Imaginative, original thinking or problem solving.

criterion-referenced measurement and evaluation Comparing an individual's achievement with criteria of performance.

criterion validity evidence Comparing results with other evidence for consistency.

crowd A large, loosely organised group interested in a common activity.

crystallised intelligence Acquired learning.

cultural-historical theory (Vygotsky) Cognitive development is the transformation of basic, biologically determined processes into higher psychological functions through socialisation and education.

culturally relevant teaching Teaching that is responsive to the cultural backgrounds and needs of students.

culture of caring Environment in which deep care for oneself and others, for the natural world and for the human-made world is modelled and taught.

culture-free test A test without apparent cultural bias.

decentering Focusing on a range of perceptual cues.

declarative knowledge Knowledge about memory, facts, definitions, generalisations and cognitive rules.

deep learning A student's active search for meaning, underlying principles and structures in knowledge.

defence mechanisms (Freud) Unconscious psychological processes used to protect one's sense of self.

defensive pessimism Unrealistically low expectations of individuals for ever succeeding or discounting the importance of the work in an effort to minimise feelings of anxiety over potential failure.

deficiency needs The four lowest levels of Maslow's needs—self-esteem, belonging, safety and survival. These must be met before higher needs can be focused on.

denial (Freud) Defence mechanism denying existence of painful experience.

development tasks Age-appropriate physical, motor, social and cognitive tasks that are mastered by children.

developmentally appropriate education Optimal match between the developmental stage of the child and logical properties of material to be learned.

dialect A variation of standard English that is distinct in vocabulary, grammar or pronunciation.

differentiation (of motor development) Refers to the gradual progression of children's motor coordination from gross to refined movements.

direct instruction A highly structured, goal-oriented approach to teaching, characterised by teacher presentations, teacher modelling and student practice with feedback.

directive I-messages Clear, non-accusative statements of how something is affecting the teacher.

discipline Methods adopted to manage student behaviour and involvement in learning.

discovery learning Material is not presented to the learner in its final form but rather the learner discovers relationships, solutions and patterns.

disequilibrium (Piaget) A state of distress when confronted by a new situation until successful adaptation occurs.

disinhibitory effect (Social cognitive theory) Outcome expectations and functional value of behaviour increases likelihood of observed behaviour being performed.

DISTAR Direct Instruction System for the Teaching of Arithmetic and Mathematics.

distributed cognition Knowledge is distributed through a group so that the group can function effectively.

distributed practice Practice spread over time with rest intervals.

divergent thinking Coming up with many possible solutions to problems.

ego (Freud) Conscious, rational part of personality.

egocentricity Assuming others experience the world as we do.

elicitation/facilitation Performing behaviour similar to but not identical to modelled behaviour.

emotional intelligence The capacity to process emotional information accurately and efficiently, including the capacity to perceive, assimilate, understand and manage emotion.

enactive (Bruner) Learning through actions on objects.

encoding The process by which we represent information mentally.

environment Genetically programmed development of individuals is influenced by external forces such as climate, food and family background, and by our internal non-genetic environment such as toxins, bacteria and viruses.

equilibration (Piaget) Search for mental balance between cognitive schemes and information from the environment.

equivalence The reliability that results when two equivalent or parallel forms of the same test are administered to a group at about the same time and the scores are related.

essay tests and assignments A form of measurement in an extended-response format testing ability to organise and express ideas, and to defend arguments.

evaluation Qualitative judgments on data.

expectancy-value theory Motivation as a result of expecting and valuing success in an activity.

experiential intelligence (Sternberg) Ability to formulate new ideas to solve problems.

expository organiser (Ausubel) Presents an overview of the relevant concepts for students to attend to.

expository teaching (Ausubel) The teacher presents information to students in a relatively finished form.

external locus of control Individuals who believe that they have little control over their own learning.

extrinsic motivation Motivation created by external factors such as rewards and punishment that may lead to surface learning.

extrinsic reinforcement The application of rewards by the teacher or parent that influences student behaviour.

face validity evidence Making the test look right.

fading (Behaviourism) The eradication of operantly conditioned behaviour through the withdrawal of reinforcement.

failure-accepting students Students who fail repeatedly and come to accept their failures as a sign of low ability.

failure-avoiding students Students who are motivated achieve in order to maintain their sense of personal value when judged by external performance.

fantasy (Freud) Imaginary satisfactions in place of real ones.

feedback Information about the accuracy of a student's response used to improve future performance.

field dependence Cognitive perceptual processing in which stimuli are perceived as parts of a whole.

field independence Cognitive perceptual processing in which stimuli are differentiated and then organised.

figurative knowledge Thinking about problems in concrete terms.

fine motor movements Voluntary body movements that involve the small muscles.

fixation (Freud) Using immature defence mechanisms.

fixed interval reinforcement Reinforcement presented after a set period of time.

fixed ratio reinforcement Reinforcement presented after a set number of responses.

fluid intelligence The capacity of a person to learn new things.

Flynn effect The systematic rise in IQ scores over time necessitating the renorming of IQ tests periodically.

focused evaluation Intensive evaluation of a student's development over a selected period of time.

formal operations Piaget's fourth stage, characterised by the ability to solve problems abstractly and to think combinatorially—processes characteristic of scientific thinking.

formative measurement and evaluation Continuous monitoring of the teaching learning process to ensure effectiveness.

formative reports Reporting progressively on student progress throughout a learning sequence.

free-rider effect In group work, the tendency for some students to be allowed to 'come along for the ride' and not contribute or learn anything, either by choice or accident.

gender stereotyping A view of sex roles that results in distorted or limited visions of what it means to be male or female.

general teaching efficacy Relates to a teacher's belief about whether teaching can impact student learning despite external constraints such as the locale in which the school is located, the cultural background of the students, and the socio-economic backgrounds of the students.

gestalt A meaningful pattern that the brain constructs from sensory information.

goal theory Students' purposes in learning influence the nature and quality of their motivation and engagement in learning.

grading on the curve Grades are distributed so that they follow a normal distribution.

group alerting (Kounin) Capturing students' attention and quickly letting them know what they need to do.

group focus (Kounin) Teacher's ability to keep students attentive and actively involved in learning tasks.

grouping structures Individual, competitive, cooperative.

growth needs (Maslow) The higher self-actualisation needs in Maslow's hierarchy.

guided peer questioning Peers are trained to ask thought-provoking questions and generate elaborated responses.

heredity Genetically programmed human development of individuals.

heteronomous morality (Piaget) Children view moral rules as fixed and unchangeable.

hierarchy of needs Maslow's model of seven levels of human needs from basic physical needs to higher-order self-actualisation needs.

high-need achievers Individuals for whom the need to achieve is greater than the fear of failure.

homeland school School that has an element of formal structure, but where there is little emphasis on learning Western knowledge or language.

humanism (Motivation) Approach to personality development that emphasises personal freedom, choice, self-determination and striving for personal growth.

hypothetical reasoning Reasoning based on assumptions.

iconic (Bruner) Learning through seeing images.

id (Freud) The source of basic biological needs and desires in personality.

identity (Erikson) The defining of a personal, social, sexual and occupational self during adolescence.

identity achievement (Marcia) A stage of identity development that occurs after individuals experience a period of crisis and decision making.

identity crisis Clarifying and becoming aware of personal values.

identity diffusion (Marcia) A stage of identity development that occurs when individuals fail to make clear choices for their future.

identity foreclosure (Marcia) A stage of identity development that occurs when individuals prematurely adopt the ready-made positions of others, such as parents.

identity formation The conscious and unconscious ways in which individuals incorporate the values of significant models into their sense of self.

identity moratorium (Marcia) A stage of identity development that occurs when individuals pause and reflect on what the future might hold.

IEP Individualised educational plan.

immanent justice Punishment means that wrong has been done.

impulsive style Cognitive style of responding quickly but often inaccurately.

inclusive education Teaching students with disabilities in regular classrooms.

individual accountability Keeping students individually responsible for their involvement in learning.

individualised goal structure Students are judged and rewarded on the basis of their own performance irrespective of the performance of other students.

information processing The human mind's activity of receiving, processing, storing and retrieving information.

information processing constructivism Focuses on the learner actively selecting, organising and integrating incoming experience with existing knowledge to create understanding.

information-processing skills theory In testing situations students' anxiety is produced through ineffective information-processing skills.

inhibitory effect (Social cognitive theory) Inhibiting behaviour to avoid negative consequences.

instructional objectives General statements of what students should be able to do as a result of instruction.

integration (of motor skills) Refers to the coordination of various opposing muscle and sensory systems into coordinated interaction.

intelligence Ability to acquire knowledge, think and plan, monitor cognitive processes and determine what is to be done.

intelligence quotient Intelligence test score comparing chronological and mental age.

interference effect The process that occurs when remembering certain information is hampered by the presence of other information.

inter-marker reliability Consistency between scores obtained from two markers.

intermittent reinforcement Presenting reinforcement after only some appropriate responses, not after every response.

internal consistency reliability Scores on comparable halves of the test are similar.

internal locus of control Individuals who think they have substantial control over their learning.

interpersonal asynchrony Physical development varies from individual to individual.

intrapersonal asynchrony Uneven physical development within an individual.

intrinsic motivation Motive that keeps individuals at tasks through its own inherent qualities.

intrinsic value The enjoyment one gets from a task.

intuitive thinking (Bruner) Making imaginative leaps to correct perceptions or workable solutions not based on formal processes of reasoning.

jigsaw A cooperative structure in which each member of a group is responsible for teaching other members one section of the material.

journals and portfolios Collections of students' work achievements.

justice perspective Focuses on the rights of the individual: individuals stand alone and independently make moral decisions.

keyword method Mnemonic associating new words or concepts with similar-sounding cue words and images.

kohanga reo All-Maori language and culture immersion environment for preschool children.

Kohlberg's assumptions Cognitive processing, personal construction, development, and progression from conventional to postconventional.

law of effect (Thorndike) Any action producing a pleasant effect will be repeated in similar circumstances.

learned helplessness The expectation of continued failure of an individual based on previous experiences.

learning Process through which experience causes permanent change in knowledge or behaviour.

learning outcomes The expected specific achievements that students are to show in observable ways at the end of instruction.

learning set Learning expectations.

learning strategies Plans for approaching learning tasks.

learning styles Cognitive, affective and physiological behaviours of individuals influencing their learning.

least restrictive environment (Special needs education) Placing each individual with a disability in as normal an educational environment as possible.

lesson review Making connections with concepts and ideas covered in earlier lessons.

locus of control Whether individuals locate the reasons for success or failure in personal or external factors.

logical consequences Positive or negative results that have a obvious (logical) connection.

low-need achievers (Expectancy-value theory) Individuals for whom the fear of failure is greater than the need to achieve.

massed practice Practice concentrated in long periods.

mastery goal Individuals are oriented towards developing new skills, trying to understand their work, improving their level of competence, or achieving a sense of mastery.

mastery learning A teaching approach where students must learn one unit and pass a test at a specified level before moving to the next unit.

mastery models Demonstrate rapid learning and make no errors while performing a particular task.

maturation Genetically programmed changes over time providing a point of readiness for learning.

meaning orientation Students adopt deep processing strategies to maximise personal understanding.

meaningfulness Connecting new ideas with ideas already stored in long-term memory.

meaninglessness Student's feelings of the irrelevancy of what is happening to them at the present.

measurement The process of collecting specific quantitative data.

mediated learning (Vygotsky) Learning through socially organised instruction.

mental age In intelligence testing, a score based on average abilities for a particular age group.

metacognition Knowing about how one thinks and the ability to regulate it.

method of loci A mnemonic device involving the association of items to be remembered with a series of places, or loci, that are already fixed in memory.

mnemonics Memory devices that aid retrieval.

modelling Learning as a result of observing a model.

momentum (Kounin) Starting activities promptly, keeping their pace energetic and closing them decisively.

moral reasoning The thinking processes involved in deciding right from wrong.

morality-based goals A motivational system based on helping others.

morality of care A morality based upon connectedness and concern for others.

motivation Internal state that instigates, directs and maintains behaviour.

motor reproduction In social cognitive theory, converting symbolic representations into motor movements.

motor skills Physical skills using the body or limbs, such as walking and holding.

movement management (Kounin) Maintaining student interest and attention by avoiding jerkiness through interruptions and managing smooth transitions between tasks.

multiple intelligences (Gardner's theory of intelligence) A person's nine separate abilities—logical-mathematical, verbal, musical, spatial, bodily-kinesthetic, interpersonal, intrapersonal, naturalist, existential.

negative reinforcement Reinforcement that strengthens a response because the response removes some painful or unpleasant stimulus or enables the individual to avoid it.

NESB Non-English-speaking background students.

no-lose approach In conflict resolution, neither teacher nor student is winner or loser.

nominal realism (Piaget) Words have a power in and of themselves.

normal distribution Measurement scores distributed evenly around the mean.

normlessness Student's rejection of society's rules and norms.

norm-referenced measurement and evaluation Comparing an individual's achievement with other students'.

object permanence The understanding that objects have a separate, permanent existence.

objective tests Multiple-choice, matching, or true or false items, reliability of marking enhanced.

observational learning (Social cognitive theory) Learning by observation and imitation of others.

operant conditioning Learning in which voluntary behaviour is strengthened or weakened by consequences or antecedents.

operants Voluntary behaviours emitted by a person or animal.

operations Thought processes.

operative knowledge Thinking about problems theoretically.

oral presentations Provide the opportunity for students to tell the examiner what they know.

origins and pawns Terms used to describe students' perceived level of control in learning situations.

overlapping responses (Kounin) A teacher attending to two or more matters at once in the classroom.

overlearning Practising past the point of mastery.

part learning Unit of learning broken down into subunits for learning.

peer evaluation Student involvement in the evaluation of the work of other students.

pegword mnemonics A mnemonic device that involves associating items to be learned with appropriate key words that are easily visualised.

perception Interpretation of sensory information.

performance-approach goal Students want to do better than their classmates so that they will be recognised as competent by their peers, teachers and parents.

performance-avoidance goal Students do their academic work primarily because they fear appearing incompetent.

personal constructivism Emphasises the intrapersonal dimensions of learning—knowledge is actively built up through child-determined exploration and discovery.

personal teaching efficacy Relates to the teacher's belief that they have personal qualities to positively impact students' learning.

personality development Changes in personality as one matures.

phenomenalistic causality Regarding things happening together as causally related.

phenomenology What the individual perceives, rather than what actually may be—'reality' is personal and subjective.

physical development Changes in body structure over time involving cephalocaudal and proximodistal development.

physiognomic perception Attributing lifelike qualities to inanimate objects.

play Provides tools and symbols for representing personal reconstructions of experience.

positive discipline (Jones) Discipline based on a belief in the capacity of students to control their own behaviour and to be responsible and cooperative.

positive interdependence (Cooperative group work) Students must demonstrably function as a group with a shared goal.

positive reinforcement A stimulus that increases the probability of an operant (behaviour) recurring as a result of its being added to a situation after the performance of the behaviour. It usually takes the form of something pleasant.

positive teaching Identifying rewards relevant to students and making these rewards contingent on appropriate social and academic behaviour.

powerlessness Student's feeling of lack of control over their life.

PQ4R A system for reading for understanding involving previewing, asking questions, reading, reflecting, reciting and reviewing.

practicals, simulated tasks and role plays Measurement tasks that approximate what is required in the 'real' world.

practice play Use of objects to explore the world.

pragnanz (Gestalt) Organising unorganised stimuli into patterns that make sense.

preoperational stage Piaget's second stage before children acquire logical operations.

preventive discipline Verbal and non-verbal strategies for preventing misbehaviour.

private speech (Vygotsky) Children's self-talk which guides their thinking and action—these verbalisations eventually become internalised as inner speech.

proactive facilitation Earlier learning assists later learning of new material.

proactive interference Earlier learning interferes with new learning.

procedural knowledge Knowledge of how to perform various cognitive activities.

productions (Cognitive) Higher-order cognitive procedures that apply knowledge to solve problems.

programmed instruction Instruction that emphasises reinforcement by providing the student with immediate feedback for every response. Information is provided sequentially in small units, and the learner does not proceed to a new unit until mastery of the present one is demonstrated.

projection (Freud) Ascribing our unconscious motivation to other people.

projects Extended practical work to encourage learning.

proportional reasoning Applying ratio to solve problems characteristic of formal thought.

propositional thinking Working logically through an argument characteristic of formal thought.

pro-social behaviour Behaving in a socially responsible way.

proximodistal development Axis-out development of the body.

psychomotor domain (Bloom) Dealing with action and physical development.

psychosexual development (Freud) Relationship of personality development to the sexual and aggressive drives of children.

psychosocial stages (Erikson) Relationship of ego development to the social environment.

puberty The point in an individual's physical development that marks the onset of full reproductive functions.

pubescence Changes that result in sexual maturity.

punishment The addition of an unpleasant stimulus to a situation as a consequence of behaviour that has occurred. The aim is to suppress behaviour rather than establish new behaviours.

quality school In Glasser's approach students are encouraged to produce their best work being provided with quality teaching, evaluation, curriculum, resources and atmosphere.

radical constructivism Theory of knowledge and learning asserting that all knowledge is individually constructed and equally valid.

radical constructivists Believe that individuals construct knowledge on the basis of their own experiences.

rationalisation (Freud) Giving socially acceptable reasons for our conduct.

reaction formation (Freud) Replacing repressed feelings with the opposite.

reality therapy (Glasser) A discipline approach based on the premise that each individual has a need for self-worth and that, in order to feel worthwhile, they must maintain a satisfactory standard of behaviour.

reception learning Material to be learned is presented to learners in a relatively complete and organised form by the teacher.

reciprocal peer questioning Small groups ask and answer each others' questions about lessons.

reciprocal teaching A method to teach reading comprehension strategies based on modelling.

reciprocity Socially agreed upon principles of cooperation that can be changed with agreement of others who are involved.

recursion (Vygotsky) Moving in and out of the zone of proximal development.

reflective style Cognitive style of responding slowly, carefully and accurately.

regression (Freud) Retreating to an earlier form of coping behaviour.

Regular Education Initiative An educational movement that advocates giving regular teachers the responsibility for teaching students with disabilities.

reinforcement Consequences used to shape behaviour.

reinforcer Any event that strengthens a response.

reliability Consistency and stability of a measure over time.

representational thinking Basis for anticipating actions mentally.

repression (Freud) Removing from consciousness painful thoughts.

reproducing style Students adopt a shallow processing approach such as rote learning.

response Observable reaction to stimulus.

response cost Removal of positive reinforcers as a punishment.

retention (Cognitive) The transfer to memory of material for later retrieval.

retrieval (Cognitive) The process of accessing information from long-term memory.

retroactive facilitation Later learning consolidates prior learning.

retroactive interference New learning impedes the retention of old learning.

reverse thinking Mentally reversing operations.

routines Behaviours that relate to specific activities or situations.

rubrics A table of instructional specifications to guide instruction and evaluation.

rules Guidelines that define general standards of behaviour.

scaffolded instruction (Vygotsky) Providing structured guidance in learning episodes that allows the learner to progress through the zone of proximal development.

schedules of reinforcement Continuous and intermittent routines for administering reinforcement.

schemata Networks of connected ideas or relationships.

schemes Cognitive structures to organise perception and experience.

secular trend Accelerated physical and sexual development.

self-actualisation (Maslow) Individuals strive to satisfy their need to grow intellectually and spiritually.

self-concept Broadly based individual beliefs about self in physical, social and academic domains.

self-efficacy (Bandura) One's perceptions of one's own ability to succeed on valued tasks.

self-esteem Judgments about one's worth and the feelings associated with these.

self-evaluation Students are challenged to set learning goals and to evaluate progress towards these goals.

self-fulfilling prophecy An erroneous teacher expectation that becomes confirmed.

self-handicapping strategies Creating some impediment to performance so that the individual has a ready excuse for potential failure.

self-regulation Responsibility for learning outcomes assumed by the learner including self-generated thoughts, feelings and actions for attaining academic goals.

self-worth protection A general strategy by which students withhold effort when risking failure.

sense of competence Beliefs about personal competence in a particular task.

sensorimotor stage Piaget's first stage when children acquire goal-directed behaviour and object permanence through the senses and motor activity.

sensory input Receiving stimuli through the senses.

serial position effect Remembering the beginnings and ends of lists while forgetting the middle.

seriation Organising elements by size classification.

shaping (Behavioural) Reinforcing progressive steps towards a desired goal or behaviour.

short-answer questions Short response format recalling information.

short-term memory Working memory, holding a limited amount of information briefly.

simulated environments Assessment programs that enable students to perform particular activities in a lifelike manner.

situated learning Learning is context bound and tied to the specific situation in which it is learned, making transfer difficult.

Skinner box Experimental box designed to isolate stimulus–response connections.

social cognitive theory A theory of learning that emphasises learning through observation of others.

social constructivism Emphasises the construction of shared knowledge in social contexts.

social estrangement Student's feelings of physical or mental isolation from their situation.

social goals A wide variety of needs and motives to be connected to others or part of a group.

sociocultural constructivism Emphasises the wider social, cultural and historical contexts of learning and the reciprocal interaction of these with the individual learning to construct shared knowledge.

socio-economic status Relative standing in society based upon education and income.

spiral curriculum (Bruner) Concepts presented at higher levels of abstraction as learning develops.

stability Similar scores obtained on separate testings.

standardised tests Tests that have been normed on large samples—an individual's score on the test is compared with the scores of the norming group.

state anxiety An anxiety experienced in certain situations such as exams.

stereotype threat Learning stereotypes (such as females are not good at mathematics) produce anxiety in individuals that they may confirm the stereotype—this anxiety then impacts on the level of performance.

stimulus Cue that activates behaviour.

stimulus generalisation (Behaviourism) The performance of a learned response in the presence of similar stimuli.

structuralism Piaget's belief that intellectual development occurs through a series of stages characterised by qualitatively discrete structures.

structure of grouping (Cognitive) Underlying logical structure of thinking.

Student Teams-Achievement Divisions (Slavin) Cooperative learning with heterogeneous groups and elements of competition and reward.

successful intelligence (Sternberg) That set of mental abilities used to achieve one's goals in life, given a sociocultural context, through adaptation to, selection of and shaping of environments.

summative measurement and evaluation Determines whether learners have achieved learning objectives.

summative reports Reporting on a student's achievement at the end of the learning sequence.

superego (Freud) Seat of conscience within personality.

supportive discipline Putting a stop to misbehaviour in its early stages to prevent it escalating.

surface learning Students learn in a superficial way often characterised by rote memorisation.

sustaining expectation effect Teachers expect students to maintain behaviour patterns and don't recognise improvements.

symbolic Learning through abstract symbols such as words.

symbolic play Using mental representation of objects to imitate the real world.

taxonomy of learning objectives A classification system for learning objectives—cognitive, affective and psychomotor.

teacher efficacy The personal belief that a teacher can influence student learning.

Teams–Games–Tournament (Slavin) Learning arrangement in which team members prepare cooperatively, then meet comparable individuals of competing teams in a tournament game to win points for their teams.

test anxiety A state of anxiety about not performing well when being evaluated in a test situation.

testing stereotype threat Involves the fear and anxiety produced when one feels one is in danger of fulfilling a negative stereotype about one's group.

theories of mind Children's ability to impute mental states to oneself and others.

'three Cs' Helping students to feel capable, connected and able to make contributions.

timeout The removal of reinforcement, in practice isolating a student from classroom activities for a brief period.

tools of learning (Vygotsky) Tools such as symbol systems (numbers and language) and technology (print and computers) that allow people in a society to communicate, think, solve problems and create knowledge.

trait anxiety A general anxiety that pervades much of what one does in life.

transfer of learning The application of knowledge learned in one context to another related context.

transformation Attending to changes in states.

triarchic theory of intelligence (Sternberg) The three intellectual capacities (componential, experiential and contextual) that lead to more or less intelligent behaviour.

two-way schools An attempt to introduce Western knowledge while at the same time taking active steps to promote culture and language maintenance.

utility value The perceived value of an activity to meeting one's goals.

validity (in measurement) Appropriateness of measure.

variable interval reinforcement Reinforcement presented variably after appropriate response.

vicarious reinforcement Observing reinforcing consequences to others.

wait-time The length of time between the teacher's question and the student's response.

whole learning Focusing on the full unit of learning and binding it together into a meaningful whole.

'withitness' and visual scanning (Kounin) Preventive management strategies in which the teacher constantly monitors the classroom and is aware of what is happening at all times.

work sample assessments Assessments based on performance at the actual tasks.

work-avoidance goals Students deliberately avoid engaging in academic tasks, and/or attempt to minimise the effort required to complete academic tasks.

working memory A store for the performance of mental operations.

zero reject model (Special needs education) Despite disabilities all individuals are educated in local schools.

zone of proximal development The stage at which a child's skills can be developed with the assistance.

Index

Page numbers in *itals* indicate figures and tables.